READER'S DIGEST

DIGEST

MANUAL

READER'S DIGEST
DIY MANUAL

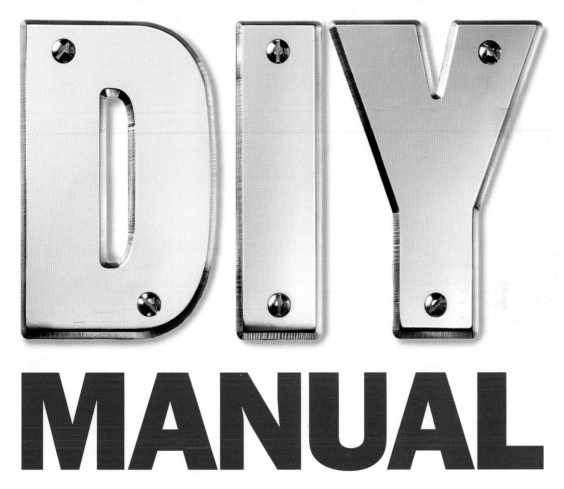

Published by the Reader's Digest Association Ltd
London • New York • Sydney • Montreal

contents

Find out how planning and building regulations will affect
you before you embark on major improvements to your home.
Find out what you need to consider when planning a loft
conversion, home extension, adding a conservatory and more.

1
Know your home

Foundations

Foundations are as old as houses – literally. They carry the weight of the building, transferring the load safely to the soil beneath so the structure stands securely.

A three-bedroom detached house typically weighs around 120 tonnes, so adequate foundations are clearly essential. Yet until the late 19th century, all that was required of them was that they should 'rest on solid ground'. Only in 1879 were statutory requirements introduced for houses to have a concrete strip foundation that we would recognise today. It had to be just 230mm thick.

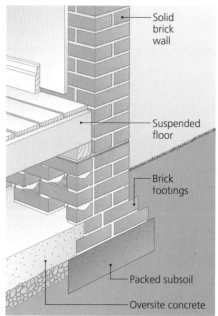

Solid brick wall

Suspended floor

Brick footings

Packed subsoil

Oversite concrete

Many older properties may have little more than rammed earth or stone foundations, with stepped brickwork built up to ground level to help to spread the load of the walls. By contrast, modern homes often have deep concrete trench foundations, especially on clay or gravel subsoils that do not carry loads well. The area within modern concrete foundations is usually covered with a reinforced concrete ground slab; older properties usually had suspended timber ground floors (see pages 10–11).

What to do when cracks appear

If your house starts to develop cracks in external or internal walls, or around the edges of solid floor slabs, seek professional help without delay. The best place to start is the building control department of your local authority. Not only will the inspectors have a thorough knowledge of local soil conditions; they will also be able to put you in contact with approved contractors if remedial work is necessary.

THE TROUBLE WITH FOUNDATIONS

Because foundations are out of sight, the only time they cause any concern is when they appear to be failing to do their job. They can suffer from several problems, in which cause and effect may be unclear. All produce similar symptoms: small cracks in the house walls to begin with, then larger ones – often linking door and window openings, and following a zig-zag path up the walls as mortar joints fail. Finally, if the problem is very severe, parts of the structure seem about to separate as cracks extend to the full height of the building. Here are some of the commonest problems affecting house foundations.

Settlement All new houses settle to some degree. Slight movement in the ground occurs as it is compacted to a uniform degree by the new load imposed on it. The result is usually a few small cracks in the structure which stop developing when settlement is complete, and which can be repaired with no risk of recurrence.

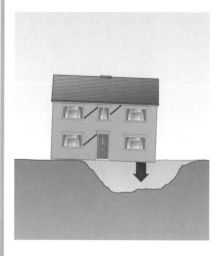

Differential settlement An extension or addition to a property may be built with different foundations to the original, and the new part may settle and start to separate from the existing building over time. The problem was common with bay windows and back additions in Victorian houses, and is seen today with home extensions built on inadequate foundations and not tied properly to the existing structure, or where changes occur in the ground.

Ground movement The moisture content of the ground beneath the house changes with the seasons. This is especially pronounced with clay soils, which contract and expand more than other soil types, especially during and after a severe drought. A similar problem is called frost heave, caused

Ground sinks as tree drains ground in dry spells

Ground swells if tree felled

by water within the soil freezing and expanding upwards, displacing the foundations; it occurs mainly in porous sandy and chalk subsoils. Ground movement can also be caused by trees too close to the house, either sucking moisture from the ground as they grow, or no longer doing so if they are felled. Lastly, cracked and leaking underground drains can saturate the subsoil or cause soil erosion, depending on the soil type.

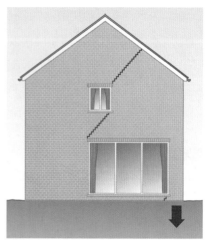

Overloading Foundations may become overloaded when structural alterations are carried out to the building. For example, removing a load-bearing internal wall and installing a rolled steel joist (RSJ) to carry the weight of upper floors transfers that load to the walls at each end of the RSJ and thence to their foundations, which may not have been designed to take that sort of load.

Subsidence True subsidence is the result of the collapse of underground chambers – either natural ones such as caves, or man-made ones such as disused mine shafts. The effects on a building can be catastrophic.

Exterior walls

Walls vary in construction and finish, which may be purely decorative or have weather-proofing properties. The way the outside walls are built reveal your house's age with some accuracy.

Solid walls Houses built before about 1920 have solid walls of brick or stone – brick walls are usually about 230mm thick; the thickness of stone walls depends on the type of stone used. Buildings taller than two storeys, such as Georgian terraced houses, often have thicker walls in the lower storeys to carry the extra load.

Cavity walls Houses built since about 1920 have cavity walls – developed as a way to prevent damp penetrating solid wall structures. Early examples have two brick walls (called leaves) about 100mm thick separated by an open cavity 50–75mm wide. The two leaves were held together by metal wall ties for extra stability.

Blockwork Newer houses have the inner leaf of the cavity wall (and the outer one too if the exterior is rendered or has tiling or weather-boarding) built of insulating blockwork rather than brick. This reduces heat losses through the walls, and their thermal efficiency can be increased still further by using insulation in the wall cavities. This may fill the cavity completely, or may be held against the inner leaf so that water penetrating the outer leaf can run down to ground level rather than across to the inner leaf. The two leaves of the wall are tied together with galvanised wire, stainless steel or plastic wall ties.

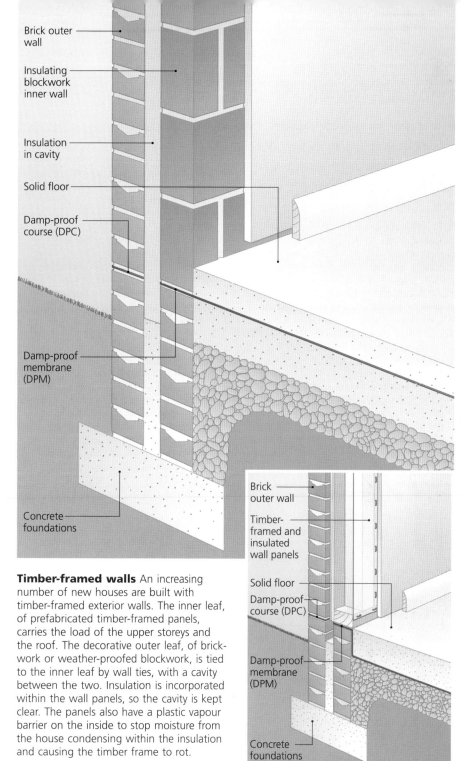

Brick outer wall

Insulating blockwork inner wall

Insulation in cavity

Solid floor

Damp-proof course (DPC)

Damp-proof membrane (DPM)

Concrete foundations

Brick outer wall

Timber-framed and insulated wall panels

Solid floor

Damp-proof course (DPC)

Damp-proof membrane (DPM)

Concrete foundations

THE TROUBLE WITH WALLS

Water and frost are the biggest enemies of exterior walls. Defective pointing (page 408), damaged rendering (page 409) and failed weatherproofing (page 204) can allow moisture to penetrate the structure, causing damp patches to appear indoors. Damp masonry can be damaged by frost, which freezes water within the wall structure and makes it expand, splitting the faces off bricks and detaching rendering from the masonry.

Settlement of the foundations (see opposite) can cause severe cracking in external walls. Failure of the wall ties can cause a cavity wall to bow outwards.

What to do
Most minor faults can be repaired by a competent do-it-yourselfer; the cross-references above will take you to the relevant pages of the book.

Timber-framed walls An increasing number of new houses are built with timber-framed exterior walls. The inner leaf, of prefabricated timber-framed panels, carries the load of the upper storeys and the roof. The decorative outer leaf, of brickwork or weather-proofed blockwork, is tied to the inner leaf by wall ties, with a cavity between the two. Insulation is incorporated within the wall panels, so the cavity is kept clear. The panels also have a plastic vapour barrier on the inside to stop moisture from the house condensing within the insulation and causing the timber frame to rot.

Wall finishes

External finishes The walls may be exposed brick or stone with mortar pointing. Solid brick walls will show headers (the ends of the bricks) alternating with stretchers (their long sides) laid in one of several regular patterns called bonds. Cavity brick walls will show only stretchers, laid with a half-brick overlap in what is known as stretcher bond.
Rendering Cement or lime mortar applied as a weatherproof coating may be smooth or textured, and there are many regional variations. A universal rendered finish is pebble-dashing, created by bedding small stones in the mortar coat. Rendering and pebble-dashing are often painted to improve their looks and weather resistance.

Other external wall finishes include clay tiles hung on timber battens, timber weather-boarding, timber shingles and plastic cladding. Timber finishes may be left to weather, or may be stained or painted for decorative effect.

Internal finishes Masonry walls are usually given an internal finish of plaster – one or two undercoats and a thin finish coat. Lime plasters are found in older houses, whereas modern houses have gypsum-based plaster which is thinner and harder. Some older houses have plaster applied over wooden laths fixed to wall battens; these walls sound hollow when tapped. A similar effect is achieved in some modern houses by dry-lining exterior walls with plasterboard on wall battens, as an alternative to wet plastering. Timber-framed houses have plasterboard cladding on the inner face of the wall panels. Both these wall finishes sound hollow when tapped, and require special care when making wall fixings.

Ground floors

Ground floors in very old buildings are simply that: the ground beneath the house, levelled and covered with flagstones or a layer of rough concrete.

Solid floors like these were notoriously damp and extremely cold. Only slate kept the dampness out. During the early 19th century, asphalt was introduced to form a damp-proof layer in the floor construction, and the use of quarry and ceramic tiles became widespread as a surface for ground floors. But the Victorians acknowledged the difficulty of damp-proofing solid floors effectively, and turned to timber ground floors as an alternative. Properly constructed, these floors were not only free from damp; they were also much warmer underfoot. However, they were prone to rot, and solid concrete ground floors are once again the norm in most modern houses.

Timber ground floors

A traditional timber ground floor is supported on joists. The ground beneath the floor is covered with a layer of concrete (the oversite concrete, usually laid level with the wall foundations). The ends of the joists are either fitted directly into holes left in the brickwork or are supported on (and nailed to) a horizontal timber wall plate resting on a ledge of masonry. The resulting underfloor void (called the crawl space for obvious reasons) is a minimum of 300mm deep, and often more. A damp-proof course (also known as a DPC) between the wall plate and the masonry protects the timber from damp. Intermediate supports

If the ventilation of the underfloor void is inadequate, the structure will often become plagued by dry rot, a ravenous form of wood-destroying fungus which can eventually cause its total collapse.

Joist ends are prone to attacks of wet rot, which are often linked to localised failures in the damp-proof course in the house walls. Another problem is that the void can be invaded by rodents and other pests, which use it as an easy access route into the house itself.

What to do

Make sure that the void is well ventilated by keeping airbricks clear of obstructions. Replace damaged airbricks to deny pests entry. If the floor appears springy at the edges, wet rot may be affecting the joist ends. It may be possible to reinforce them with new wood, but large-scale replacement of the floor structure may be necessary.

If there is a tell-tale musty smell in ground-floor rooms and you find dry rot, the entire floor structure will have to be replaced and the area sterilised before a new floor is constructed. Both these jobs are best left to specialist contractors.

Minor faults involving damage to floorboards can be repaired by a competent do-it-yourselfer (see pages 125–6).

called sleeper walls are built up off the oversite concrete at roughly 3m intervals to prevent the relatively shallow joists from sagging across large spans. These are of honeycomb construction to allow air movement through the underfloor void – essential to keep the floor timbers dry and free from rot. They also carry a wall plate (resting on a DPC) to which the joists are nailed.

The floor surface is formed of softwood boards which are nailed to the joists. These were made from square-edged boards until the 1930s, and generally tongued-and-grooved thereafter. Square-edged boards became unpopular because they usually shrank and created gaps, which caused draughts.

Modern solid ground floors

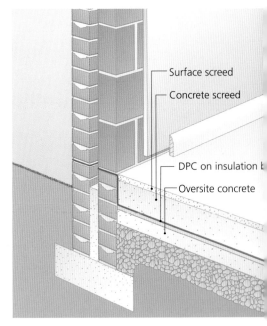

Surface screed

Concrete screed

DPC on insulation b

Oversite concrete

By the end of the 19th century, it had become obvious that timber ground floors caused more problems than they solved, and a solid floor – waterproofed initially with asphalt and later with heavy-duty plastic membranes – once again became the norm in house construction.

These floors consist of a bed of rammed hardcore, filled with sand (a process known as blinding) and topped by a layer of concrete 100–150mm thick. A damp-proof membrane (DPM) is laid over the concrete, and a further screeding layer of mortar or fine concrete up to 63mm thick is added to form the final floor surface.

The latest Building Regulations require solid floors to be insulated, and the structure now includes a thick layer of rigid polystyrene or other foam insulation. This is placed between the hardcore and the concrete.

The commonest problem with solid ground floors is a failed DPM. This can usually be remedied by sealing the floor slab with a liquid damp-proofer, covered with a new thin surface screed (see page 247).

Damp may also be caused by leaks in buried plumbing or heating pipes, which will have to be excavated and repaired. It is possible to hire a concrete breaker (with vibration damping) to do this job yourself. Wear protective clothing and goggles, and make sure you know where water and gas pipes have been laid.

An uneven concrete floor can be treated with a self-smoothing compound which will raise the floor level by about 10mm.

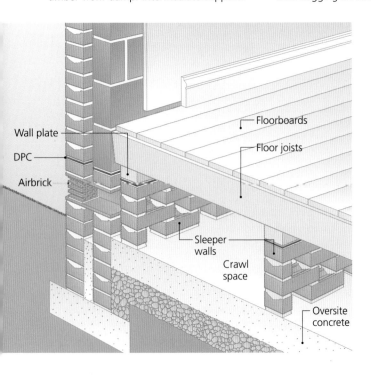

Wall plate

DPC

Airbrick

Floorboards

Floor joists

Sleeper walls

Crawl space

Oversite concrete

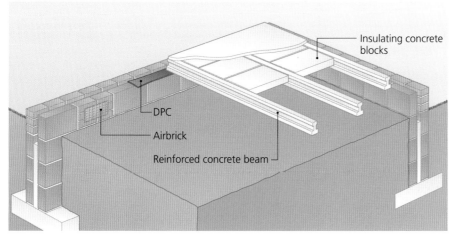

Insulating concrete blocks

DPC

Airbrick

Reinforced concrete beam

Another recent development is the use of suspended concrete ground floors, mainly on sloping sites where a solid infill would be prohibitively expensive. The floor is formed by inverted T-shaped beams of reinforced concrete that span the underfloor void, like traditional timber floor joists. Insulating concrete blocks rest on the flanges of the beams to form the floor slab, which is then topped with a fine screed as for solid floors.

Upper floors

Two and three-storey houses invariably have upper floors supported on timber joists. These span individual rooms and are supported by load-bearing walls between rooms on the ground floor.

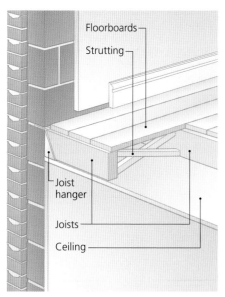

Floorboards

Strutting

Joist hanger

Joists

Ceiling

In older houses, the joist ends rest either in sockets in the outer walls, or on ledges in the masonry if the wall thickness decreases as the storeys rise.

In more modern buildings, they are supported by metal joist hangers built into the masonry. The joists are usually deeper (up to 230mm) than those in a suspended timber ground floor because they often have no intermediate supports.

The whole structure may be stiffened by the insertion of solid or herringbone strutting between the joists; this has another advantage – it also helps to prevent the joists from warping and distorting the floor surface. It will be covered with square-edged or tongued-and-grooved floorboards in older homes, or with sheets of flooring-grade chipboard in more modern ones.

Openings in the floor structure – round a stairwell, for example, or a chimney stack – are formed with doubled joists called trimming joists running parallel with the floor joists at either side of the opening. Trimmer joists are fixed at right angles to the trimming joists to form the other sides of the opening. The trimmer joists also support the cut (trimmed) ends of the floor joists adjoining the opening. The trimmer and trimmed joists are supported on joist hangers in modern homes and are fixed with cut timber joints in older buildings. The ends of upper floor joists in the modern home are tied into the masonry with special restraint joist hangers at 2m intervals to give the external walls extra support. Joists running parallel with the walls are tied to them with transverse steel strapping, which usually extends over two or three joists.

THE TROUBLE WITH UPPER FLOORS

The only major problem likely to affect upper floors is sagging of the floor structure, caused either by overloading of inadequately sized joists or by alteration work involving the removal of supporting partitions. Excessive notching of joists during plumbing or wiring installation work can also lead to joists being weakened and sagging under a load. Minor damage to floorboards is usually the result of boards having been lifted for the installation of wiring and pipework.

What to do

It may be possible to strengthen a sagging floor structure by bolting new joists alongside the existing ones, or by installing a transverse support beam in the room below to support the centres of the affected joists. Both these jobs are best left to a specialist contractor. Minor repairs to floorboards are straightforward DIY jobs (see pages 126–7).

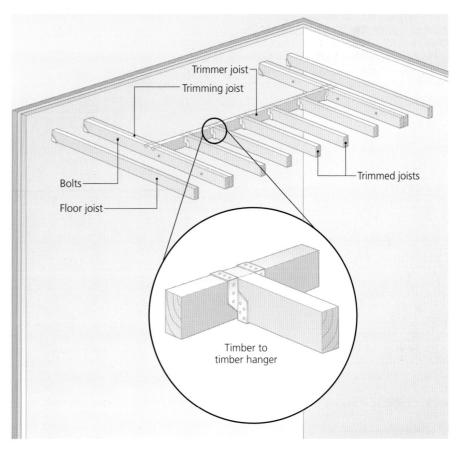

Trimmer joist

Trimming joist

Trimmed joists

Bolts

Floor joist

Timber to timber hanger

Internal walls and ceilings

Internal walls divide the space within the house into rooms of different sizes. They also contribute significantly to the stability of the building, and may support the structure of the storey above.

The way internal walls are built depends largely on the age of the house, and knowing about their structure can affect how you carry out DIY work on them.

Internal partitions

You can discover what type of partition walls you have by tapping the wall surface to see if it is solid or hollow, and then following this with test-drilling to reveal the materials used to construct it.

Brick walls In most properties built before the 1930s, internal partitions in ground-floor rooms are generally of brickwork, one brick thick, built in stretcher bond. With plaster on both faces, they are about 140mm thick overall. They support the floor joists of first floor rooms, and most of them are load-bearing. At least one of these walls will continue into the first storey (and higher storeys in multi-storey buildings), and will help to carry the load of the roof structure, so they, too, are load-bearing. Bear this in mind if you are considering removing walls to alter room layouts.

Block walls In properties built later than about 1930, 100mm thick concrete blockwork is used instead of brick for ground-floor load-bearing partitions and, again, these may be extended into upper storeys to support the roof structure. The plaster is generally thinner (and harder) than on old brick partitions, so the walls will measure about 125mm thick. You may also find non-loadbearing blockwork partitions, which are built in thinner blockwork.
    You can confirm whether you have brick or block partition walls by making some test drillings into them. Drill three holes in an equilateral triangle, each hole about 50mm from the others; this guarantees that at least

one hole will miss a mortar joint. Brick dust will be reddish or yellowish, whereas block dust will be grey or black.

Timber stud partitions Timber-framed walls, built with 100 x 50mm or 75 x 50mm sawn timber, are used as internal partitions in houses of all ages. The vertical studs are fixed at regular intervals (commonly 400mm, although spacings vary in older properties) between a timber head plate nailed to the ceiling joists and a corresponding sole plate fixed to the floor.

Horizontal noggings are fitted between the studs to stiffen the structure and prevent warping of the studs.
    Timber stud partitions may be load-bearing, although partitions in upper floor rooms are usually not, especially if their position does not coincide with a partition in the floor below. As a general rule, partitions of 75 x 50mm timber are never

---

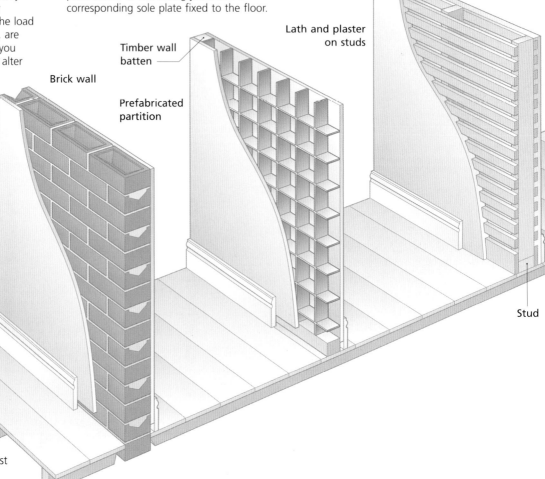

Brick wall

Timber wall batten

Prefabricated partition

Lath and plaster on studs

Stud

load-bearing. The framework will be clad in lath and plaster up to 20mm thick in older houses, and in 9.5 or 12.7mm thick plasterboard in those built since the late 1940s. A single test drilling will instantly reveal which type of cladding you have.

In houses built since the late 1960s, the roof structure is generally built using trussed rafters, which span the external walls of the house and do away with the need for load-bearing partition walls in upper floors. In houses with this type of roof structure, all upstairs partitions are timber-framed.

Prefabricated partitions In houses built in the last 20 years or so, you may encounter internal partitions built using prefabricated wall panels instead of the usual plasterboard on a timber frame. They consist of outer layers of plasterboard bonded to a cardboard core of egg-box construction, and are 1200mm wide and only 50mm thick. The panels rest on a timber sole plate and are fixed to timber battens at each end and at panel junctions.

Plasterboard on studs

Lightweight blockwork

Ceilings

There is much less variation in the construction of ceilings, compared with partition walls. The age of the house is the key to the method used.

Ceilings are probably the most neglected surface in the house. They get little more than the most perfunctory decoration compared with walls, floors and woodwork, and tend to get noticed only when they start to cause trouble. However, they are a very good indicator of when things are going wrong. Check your ceilings regularly for sagging, damp marks and stains. Cracks in a plastered ceiling should be checked and monitored, to see if they worsen.

Lath and plaster ceiling

Lath and plaster Until the use of plasterboard became commonplace after the 1940s, ceilings were formed of lath and plaster in the same way as timber stud partition walls. Split or sawn timber laths 25–40mm wide and up to 13mm thick were nailed to the undersides of the ceiling joists, spaced about 10mm apart. The first coat of plaster was then applied and forced up between the laths to provide a fixing key. You can see these plaster ridges clearly if you view the ceiling surface from above – in a loft, for example. Two further coats of plaster were then applied to give a ceiling thickness of up to about 25mm.

—Lath
—Joist
—Plaster

Timber You may come across boarded ceilings in unrestored Victorian houses, especially in cellars and basement rooms. These consist of tongued-and-grooved boards nailed directly to the ceiling joists, and were generally gloss-painted.

Plasterboard Ceilings in modern houses consist of sheets of 9.5mm plasterboard nailed to the ceiling joists, and to noggings fixed between the joists to support the board ends. The joints between the boards are taped to prevent movement cracks from developing, and the plasterboard is either skim-coated with plaster or decorated directly – often with a textured coating such as Artex.

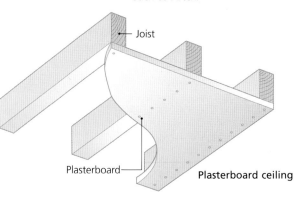

— Joist

Plasterboard—

Plasterboard ceiling

Openings in partitions

In old internal brick partitions, door openings are commonly spanned by stout timber beams. Blockwork partitions have openings spanned by short lintels, of reinforced concrete or galvanised steel. Openings in timber-framed partition walls are suitably spaced between a pair of vertical studs, with the sole plate cut away and a cross-piece fixed between the studs to create the door head.

The opening is lined with a timber frame fixed to the masonry or the wall studs. The joint between wall surface and door frame is covered by an architrave moulding.

THE TROUBLE WITH CEILINGS

Lath and plaster ceilings often fail with age because of the loss of the key between the plaster and the laths. Plasterboard ceilings may crack along the board joints, especially if these were not properly taped during installation. Both types can be holed by physical damage, and are badly affected by plumbing leaks. Minor leaks can cause staining which is difficult to conceal, and major ones can cause the ceiling to collapse.

What to do
Minor damage to any ceiling can be patched with plaster or plasterboard. Old lath and plaster ceilings in poor condition are best replaced with a new plasterboard ceiling. See pages 230–1 for details of the work involved.

Staircases

The staircase in your home acts as a major decorative feature, dominating the hall and landing it connects.

The most important feature of staircase design and construction is safety. Many deaths and injuries are caused by falls on stairs, especially among children and the elderly. The current Building Regulations have precise requirements for the steepness of a domestic staircase, the number and size of its treads and risers, the layout of landings and, most importantly, the provision of handrails and guarding on landings and alongside the flight. However, many millions of homes were built before these modern standards were introduced.

Staircase layouts

The simplest staircase layout is a straight flight of stairs, rising from the hall to the landing. It is usually flanked by a load-bearing wall on one side, and may rise between two walls in the centre of the house or against a party wall. In modern houses, a standard straight flight has 13 steps, including the landing level.

The commonest alternative to the straight flight is to split it into two shorter parts, with a small landing in between.

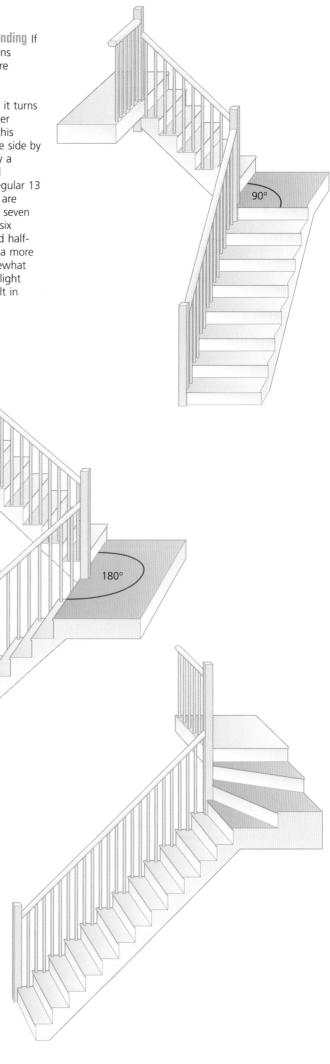

Quarter-turn with square landing If the top part of the flight turns through 90°, there is a square quarter landing at the turn.

Dog-leg with half landing If it turns through 180°, there is a wider rectangular half landing. In this layout the two parts may rise side by side, or may be separated by a space, creating an open-well staircase. In each case the regular 13 treads of a straight staircase are replaced by a lower flight of seven treads and an upper one of six treads. Both quarter-turn and half-turn staircase layouts create a more open stairwell, and are somewhat safer in use than a straight flight because a trip does not result in such a long fall.

Stair flight with winders at the top Stairs can also change direction with the use of triangular winder treads. These take up less space than a flight with a quarter landing, and are normally used in a group of three or four steps at the bottom or top of the flight to turn the stairs through 90°. A spiral staircase, seldom found in the home (at least, as a main staircase) consists solely of winders.

<hr>

THE TROUBLE WITH STAIRCASES

General wear and tear on staircases results in creaking treads and split or cracked tread nosings (the front edge that overhangs the riser below). There is obviously a potential safety risk if the balustrade is loose, or if any components are broken.

Shrinkage and settlement can result in the closed string of the staircase pulling away from the wall next to the flight. Loose or failed fixings can result in joints opening up anywhere on the flight.

Insect attack can be a problem, especially in understairs cupboards where exposed rough wood provides a perfect site for wood-boring insects such as woodworm to lay their eggs. The tell-tale exit holes left in the wood by the emerging beetles are a sure sign of an infestation.

What to do
You can carry out minor repairs to the staircase and its balustrade yourself (see pages 258–9). Call in a professional to tackle major repairs. Woodworm can be tackled with DIY treatments, since the affected area is relatively small and self-contained.

Staircase construction

The way a staircase is built has changed little over the centuries. However, mass production has led today to standardisation of sizes and dimensions, and anything out of the ordinary must still be hand-built.

Strings A typical staircase consists of two angled side timbers, called strings, fixed between the two floor levels that the stairs connect. Where the staircase has one open side, the string at that side may be cut into steps along its top edge. The outer ends of the treads rest on these steps, instead of being housed in grooves in the sides of the string. This is called an open string; the other (uncut) string is a closed string.

Treads and risers The horizontal treads and vertical risers that form each step are supported in grooves in the strings, and are held in place by glued wedges. The short riser wedges are fitted first and are trimmed off flush with the underside of the tread below. The longer tread wedge locks the riser wedge in place when it is driven into its groove.

The treads and risers are tongued-and-grooved together on a traditional staircase. In addition, pairs of triangular blocks are glued into the internal angles between each tread and the riser below it. On modern stairs the treads and risers may be butt-jointed, again with blocks in the internal angles.

The risers are absent on open-plan staircases, and the strings are often linked with steel rods beneath the treads for extra stability. Alternatively, there may be a central bearer called a carriage running the length of the staircase to support the treads.

Handrail construction A staircase rising between two walls needs no guarding but, for safety's sake, a handrail is often fixed to one or both walls – either direct to the masonry, or mounted on wall brackets. On other staircases, a stout newel post is fitted at the top and bottom of the flight. These are bolted to the floor joists at each end of the flight, or bedded in the floor screed and secured with a metal dowel if the ground floor is solid. Original newel posts will be a single component, but replacements are dowel-jointed into a stub of the original (below). The ends of the outer string are tenoned into mortises cut in the posts. Additional posts are installed wherever the staircase changes direction – at a quarter or half landing. They are often topped with decorative knobs, or finials.

Handrail A handrail is fitted between the newel posts, just below their tops, using special angled brackets to form the primary guarding on the staircase and, if required, round the landing.

Balusters The space between the handrail and the staircase string is filled with evenly spaced vertical balusters, horizontal rails, wrought iron panels, safety glass or solid panelling. This secondary guarding is there to stop someone using the stairs from falling between the handrail and the string. If balusters are used, their top ends are nailed into a channel machined in the underside of the handrail.

On a closed-string staircase, the bottom ends fit into the groove in a continuous base rail fixed to the top edge of the string. Small spacing fillets of wood are fitted between the balusters under the handrail and on the base rail. On an open-string staircase, the bottom ends of the balusters fit into notches cut in the treads, and are retained there by mouldings pinned and glued to the tread ends.

Bullnose step The lowest step (sometimes two steps) of the flight may project beyond the bottom newel post, and their open ends have a characteristic rounded shape. They are known as bullnose steps.

Closed string
Tread housing
Wedge
Tongued riser
Grooved tread
Moulding
Baluster housing

Step assembly

Riser housing
Mitred butt joint
Open string

Handrail
Metal brackets
Decorative knob
Cover buttons

Spacing fillets
Base rail

Newel centre
Newel base
Bullnose step

Turned balusters

Handrail
Fillet
Baluster

Handrail assembly

Doors

An external door has to be thoroughly weatherproof and secure. An internal door is a decorative feature of the room where it is installed. Both come in a wide range of types and styles, in a number of standard sizes.

External door frames

The timber frame for an external door is prefabricated, and consists of a sill, two side members called jambs and a door head. The components are jointed with mortise and tenon joints or held together with steel dowels. The sill is usually made from hardwood for durability, and projects from the frame like a window sill to throw rainwater clear of the wall below.

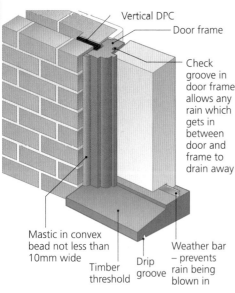

Vertical DPC
Door frame
Check groove in door frame allows any rain which gets in between door and frame to drain away
Mastic in convex bead not less than 10mm wide
Timber threshold
Drip groove
Weather bar – prevents rain being blown in

The door sill has grooves machined in its underside. The outermost is the drip groove which stops water from running back under the sill, while the inner one helps to fix the frame on its mortar bed when it is set in place in the wall just above the level of the house damp-proof course. A plastic or metal strip called a weather bar is set in a groove in the upper surface of the sill. This stops water from blowing under the door when it is closed.

The sides and head of the frame are rebated, allowing the door to close securely against the frame. This rebate also contains a drip groove or, on modern frames, integral weatherstripping.

Aluminium and steel-framed plastic (uPVC) door frames are made up in a similar way from specially-formed cross sections, and usually incorporate weatherstripping as part of the design.

The frame of an external door is set in place before the walls are built up around it, and is tied into the masonry with galvanised steel ties screwed to the frame and bedded into the mortar courses.

Internal door frames

Internal doors usually have simple three-sided timber frames, made from two jambs and a door head. The frame is commonly referred to as a door lining. In older houses it may be rebated like an external frame, but in modern houses it is usually formed from plain timber. Slim timber battens called stop beads are pinned to the door lining after installation to form a rebate against which the door closes.

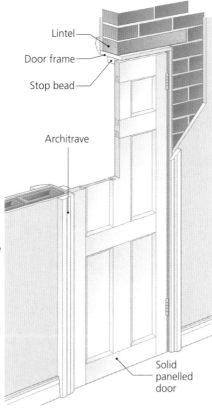

Lintel
Door frame
Stop bead
Architrave
Solid panelled door

In a masonry wall The lining is fixed direct to the masonry – probably with large cut nails in older properties, and with screws and wallplugs or nailable frame fixings in a modern house. The timber used is usually about 25mm wider than the wall thickness, creating an edge against which the wall plaster can be finished. This joint is covered with architrave mouldings pinned to the edges of the door lining once plastering is complete.

In thin (75mm) blockwork partitions, the sides of the frame may extend from floor to ceiling, with the door head fixed between them and the space above it filled with blockwork. This type of storey-height frame is stronger than one built into an opening with a lintel over it.

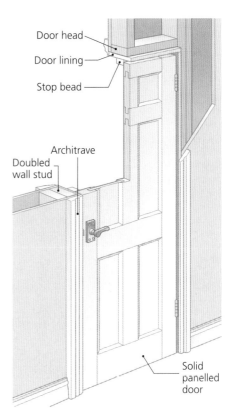

Door head
Door lining
Stop bead
Architrave
Doubled wall stud
Solid panelled door

In timber-framed partition walls Vertical studs form the sides of the opening and the door head is nailed between them. Sometimes thicker studs are used here, or double studs are fitted for extra strength and rigidity. A thin door lining is nailed within the opening, providing an edge to which the plasterboard cladding on the partition can be abutted.

Again, architrave mouldings cover the join and stop beads form a rebate against which the door closes.

Safe glazing

Part N of the Building Regulations lays down strict rules about the use of glass in and next to doors. It applies to all new and replacement work.

Briefly, glass panels in all doors and in fixed panes beside door openings should be of toughened glass marked 'Made to British Standard BS6206 Class A'. This requirement also applies to any double-glazed panels.

Ordinary 6mm glass may be used in small panes (up to 0.5m^2 in size and with one side no more than 250mm long).

THE TROUBLE WITH DOORS

Rot is the main enemy of external doors and their frames if they are not kept in good decorative order, or if the sealant between frame and masonry fails. Internal and external doors can suffer from warping or binding in their frames, and may be affected by worn or damaged hinges. Most minor faults can be repaired by a competent do-it-yourselfer (see pages 188–91).

Replacing a damaged or unfashionable door requires moderate carpentry skills (pages 192–5), and you may prefer to leave the job to a carpenter.

Choosing doors

If a door is to be fitted at an entrance, style is not the only criterion – choose it with resistance to weather (and burglars) in mind as well. For inside the house, you need an interior grade door which is cheaper and lighter. Flush interior doors are generally less expensive than panelled doors. For an older house, you may be able to find suitable secondhand doors.

External doors

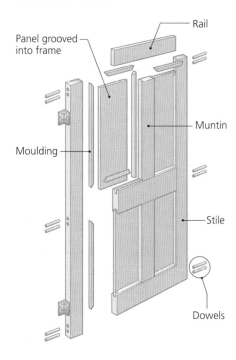

Rail

Panel grooved into frame

Moulding

Muntin

Stile

Dowels

There are several types of external door. The traditional timber front door is a solid or glazed door, usually of panelled construction. It is available in many different styles, in hardwood and softwood.

It consists of two vertical outer components called stiles, linked by top and bottom rails and sometimes also a centre rail. Central vertical components called muntins link the rails in a traditional panelled door, but may be omitted if the door is fully glazed. All these components were traditionally assembled with mortise-and-tenon joints, but nowadays dowel joints are often substituted.

The inner edges of the components are machined – either with grooves to hold solid panels of timber or plywood, or with rebates to accept panes of glass which are held in place with beading on the inner face of the door. Multi-paned doors have no centre rail or muntins. An interlocking framework of glazing bars is fixed between the stiles and the top and bottom rails, as in a multi-paned window.

Flush doors are sometimes fitted as external doors, especially where they lead to the side or rear of the house. The door may be solid or part-glazed, and usually has a softwood frame with plywood facings.

Aluminium external doors are usually simple frames containing solid and glazed panels. Steel-framed uPVC and GRP (glass-reinforced plastic) doors may be of similar design, and are also available in a variety of panelled styles in imitation of traditional timber door styles.

External timber and aluminium doors

Made in a range of standard sizes. The most widely available are 1981 x 762mm and 1981 x 838mm – the metric equivalents of traditional imperial sizes. Door thickness is a standard 44mm, to allow for the fitting of mortise locks without weakening the door structure.

Steel-framed uPVC doors are available in similar sizes for installation in timber frames, or can be supplied complete with matching frames (2085 x 920 is a typical overall size).

Patio doors The modern equivalent of French doors, consisting of two or more large glazed panels fitted into an outer frame. The doors may be of timber or uPVC, and are invariably double-glazed. In two-door units, one pane is fixed and the other slides. In multi-door units one or two panes may slide. Units are available in widths from 1530mm upwards.

French doors Double doors, usually fitted at the back of the house. The doors are side-hung within an outer frame, and have rebated meeting edges. They are usually part or fully glazed. The outer frame may incorporate fixed glazed panels at each side of the doors. Timber and uPVC types are available, in widths from 1220 to 1830mm.

Internal doors

Internal doors are usually only 35mm thick compared with the standard 44mm of an external door. This makes them lighter and easier to hang.

Internal doors may be panelled like a traditional front door, or flush-faced. Panelled doors are made in softwood and hardwood, with a choice of two, four or six panels which may be solid or glazed. Construction is similar to that of an external door.

Flush doors Have a lightweight softwood outer frame clad on each side with a layer (called a skin) of man-made board. Hardboard skins are used on the cheapest flush doors, and plywood – often with a decorative surface veneer – on more expensive ones. The doors are lipped in solid timber to protect the edges of the skins. The core of the door is usually a cardboard egg-box filling, with a solid block of wood glued to the inside of one of the frame stiles to take a lock or latch. The edge with the lock block is marked clearly, so it can be hung the correct way round.

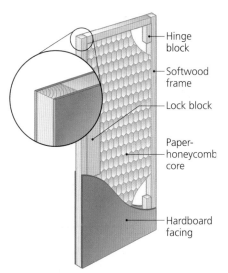

Hinge block

Softwood frame

Lock block

Paper-honeycomb core

Hardboard facing

You can also buy 'flush' doors with moulded or embossed facing panels made from medium-density fibreboard (MDF). They are a very good imitation of panelled doors, and do not suffer from shrinkage round the panels as solid wood doors do. They are sold ready-primed.

Internal doors are also made in standard sizes. The most common heights are 1981 and 2032mm, and standard widths are 686, 762, 813 and 838mm. Narrower internal doors are also available, intended to be hung in pairs from bi-fold door gear. They are often fitted as doors to alcove cupboards, or where there is no room for a standard door to open.

Windows

Windows come in more shapes, sizes and styles than almost any other component of a typical house.

They are also often more troublesome than other parts of the house because they are made from a complex mix of components. This is multiplied by the fact that even a small terraced house will have half a dozen windows, and a detached house may have twice as many.

TYPES OF LINTEL

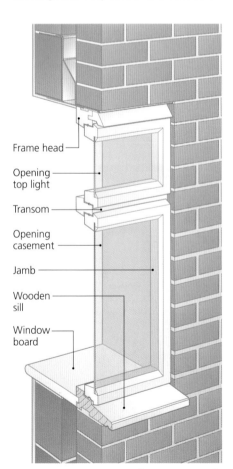

Standard pressed steel

Steel and block

Steel and wood

Steel and concrete

Through-the-wall concrete lintel

Concrete boot lintel

Window and door openings are spanned by lintels – load-bearing beams that support the masonry above them. They are made from galvanised steel or reinforced concrete, and sometimes both. Steel lintels are virtually invisible from outside, since the metal lip supports facing brickwork over the opening. Hollow types incorporate insulation material to prevent condensation inside. Plain concrete lintels have a visible outer face that can look unsightly. In a cavity wall, a damp-proof barrier, called a cavity tray, stops any rainwater that penetrates the outer leaf from crossing the cavity at the lintel.

Openings in internal masonry walls are spanned by a timber lintel in old houses, and by a slim concrete or box steel lintel in newer ones.

Window frames

Window frames are built into the house walls in much the same way as an external door (see page 16). Modern windows are positioned so that the frame is set back from the face of the masonry by only about 25mm – a fact that contributes significantly to the often short life of wooden casement windows when compared with Victorian sash windows. These were set back so that the inside of the frame was flush with the internal wall surface, and as a result the frame was much less exposed to the weather. In areas of the country rated as having severe weather exposure (mainly Scotland and Northern Ireland), Building Regulations require windows to be recessed for this very reason.

Wood is still the most popular material for making window frames. Modern high-performance hardwood windows treated with microporous paints or stains offer excellent durability, and their integral draught-stripping ensures efficient weatherproofing. Cheaper softwood windows need more regular maintenance, but they are the lowest cost choice for new or replacement work.

Steel windows were briefly popular during the 1930s and 1940s, but suffered severely from rust even when they were galvanised. Their slim, fashionable appearance was more than outweighed by the fact that the frames ran with condensation, and they could not readily be double-glazed. They are still to be found in many unmodernised properties of the period, often with the opening casements rusted (or painted) permanently shut.

Aluminium windows took their place by the 1960s, creating a trend for uncluttered picture windows. They tended to weather badly, and needed a timber sub-frame because the metal frames were not very strong. They endured for some years in patio door format, but even here other materials have now taken their place.

Plastic (uPVC) windows have a stranglehold on the replacement window market, where they offer a unique combination of comfort and warmth with a promise of being virtually maintenance-free. They are less widely used in new work, because they are more expensive to specify and their looks are not as aesthetically pleasing as a well-proportioned wooden window. Their longevity is not yet proven.

Casement windows

The casement window is the most widely used type in modern housing. In its simplest form it consists of a square or rectangular outer frame containing a single framed pane of glass called a casement. This is side-hung in the same way as a door. The frame may be divided into two or more sections by vertical mullions, and each section may contain an opening casement or a fixed pane. Further variety is introduced by fitting horizontal transoms near the top of each section, allowing the fitting of a small opening top light above

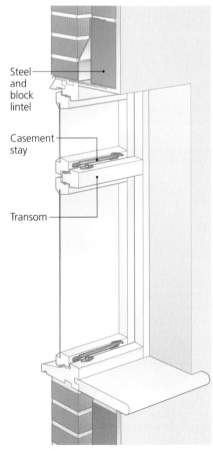

Frame head

Opening top light

Transom

Opening casement

Jamb

Wooden sill

Window board

Steel and block lintel

Casement stay

Transom

Components of a casement window

the side-hung casement – an arrangement that covers every ventilation requirement.

Individual casements may contain glazing bars and a number of smaller panes of glass, rather than a single large pane – styles known generally as cottage (four panes) or Georgian (six or eight panes). Casements are held closed by a simple handle and wedge, and held in an open position with a casement stay and peg. Top ventilators usually have just a casement stay.

A casement frame consists of a head, two side jambs and a sill. These components, and any mullions and transoms, are joined with mortise and tenon joints. To help to prevent rain penetration round the opening casements and top ventilators, drip grooves are machined round the inner faces of the frames, mullions and transoms. There are additional grooves round the edges of casements and top ventilators. On high-performance windows, integral weatherstripping is also fitted to make the opening parts of the window weatherproof.

In new buildings, casement frames are usually built into the walls as they rise, and are secured with galvanised ties screwed to the frame and anchored in the mortar courses. Replacement windows are generally secured at the sides by screws and wallplugs or nailable frame fixings.

A variation on the casement style is created by arranging the frame sections at a slight angle to each other to form a projecting bow window, or at bigger angles (up to 90°) to create a bay window.

Sash windows

The sash window was the favoured window style in homes until early in the 20th century. It is a highly complex construction, built into the inner face of the house wall in a rebate in the masonry. This contains the concealed channels for the counterweights that balance the two sliding sashes. Because the frame is set back in this way, there is usually a sub-sill of stone or quarry tiles on which the frame sill rests.

The window frame consists of a head, a sill and two jambs. Each jamb is a vertical box, consisting of an outer lining, a pulley stile, an inner lining and a back lining. A moulding called the parting bead is pinned down the centre of the visible face of the pulley stile. This forms a track between it and the projecting lip of the outer lining to form a vertical track in which the outer (top) sash slides. A second moulding called the staff bead is fixed down the inner edge of the pulley stile to create a parallel track for the inner (bottom) sash.

Near the top of each track, a pulley is fitted into a slot in each pulley stile. This allows the sash cords that connect each sash to its weights to run in and out of the weight compartments as the sashes are raised and lowered. At the bottom of each track is a removable cut-out pocket that gives access to the weight compartments if the sash cords need replacing.

The sashes are square or rectangular frames, sometimes sub-divided by glazing bars into two, four or six smaller panes. The

stiles at the top of the inner sash and the bottom of the outer sash are often extended into decorative horns. A catch mounted on the meeting rails allows the windows to be secured in the closed position.

The modern version of the sliding sash window replaces the cords and weights with clever spring-loaded spiral balances, which are mounted on the faces of the frame sides. Each sash is attached to its two spiral balances by fixing plates at its bottom corners.

THE TROUBLE WITH WINDOWS

The commonest problem with all wooden windows is rot. It can attack the frame, its casements or sashes at the joints if water is able to penetrate, and at any point where the glazing putty fails.

Casements can bind or stick in their frames, much as a door does, making them difficult to open and close. Hinges can be damaged if the casement is allowed to swing open violently or any weight is put on it.

Sashes can bind against the pulley stiles, rattle in high winds and let in draughts. However, their biggest problem is failed sash cords, which can be tricky and time-consuming to replace.

Lastly, glass in any window may be cracked or broken by an impact, or by the window slamming shut.

What to do
The most important thing you can do to give your windows the longest life is to maintain them regularly, especially as far as their decoration is concerned (see pages 414–15). It is failed paintwork that allows rot to gain an initial foothold in window woodwork.

You can carry out most of the everyday repairs a window might need yourself (see pages 203–11 and 412–13). Replacing a window is a fairly major undertaking (see pages 214–15), and is one you may prefer to leave to a carpenter or builder.

Draughtproofing of sashes can also prevent rattling and will cut down on the amount of noise that comes in. This is a task best undertaken by professionals as it involves removing sashes from their frames and lining them with strips of insulation.

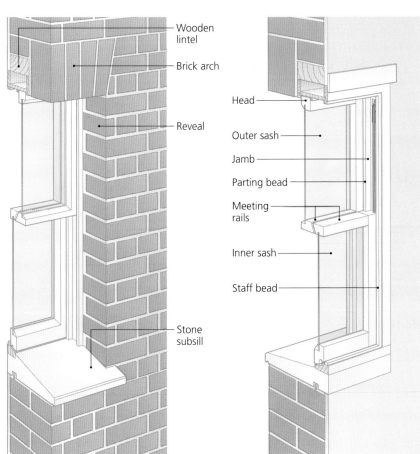

Wooden lintel

Brick arch

Reveal

Stone subsill

Head

Outer sash

Jamb

Parting bead

Meeting rails

Inner sash

Staff bead

Components of a sash window

Pitched roofs

Most houses have pitched roofs, sloping on one or more sides and clad with tiles or slates.

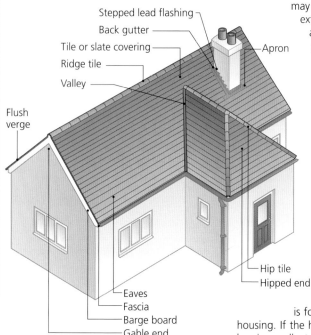

Stepped lead flashing
Back gutter
Tile or slate covering
Ridge tile
Valley
Apron
Flush verge
Hip tile
Hipped end
Eaves
Fascia
Barge board
Gable end

Until around the 1960s, pitched-roof construction was a job for skilled carpenters, who would cut and fix the individual timbers one by one to form the roof structure the house required. Modern houses are built almost exclusively using prefabricated roof trusses, which allow the roof structure to be erected much more quickly and also eliminate the need for internal load-bearing walls in all but the largest properties.

Traditional roof construction

The simplest pitched roof is called a lean-to or mono-pitch roof. It is a slope that usually abuts a wall at its higher end. The roof consists of sloping rafters, resting at each end on a horizontal timber wallplate. It may be installed on single-storey extensions, porches and attached garages and, in the past, was often used to roof the additions at the rear of Victorian terraces.

The span of a pitched roof can be increased considerably by butting two mono-pitch roofs together to form a so-called double-pitch roof. The two roof slopes meet at a ridge board, and the bottom ends of the rafters forming each slope are tied together by joists to create a rigid triangular structure. Gable walls fill in the open ends of the roof. This type of roof structure is limited in span to about 4m, and is found mainly in terraced housing. If the house has an internal load-bearing wall, struts can be added between the purlins and a wallplate resting on top of the internal wall. The addition of a collar tie between the rafters at the level of the purlins creates a roof structure that can comfortably span the width of most houses.

THE EAVES OF THE HOUSE

At the eaves, the rafters either project beyond the walls or are cut off flush with them. A vertical fascia board protects the cut ends of the rafters and carries the roof gutters.

1 Flush eaves

If the eaves project, a horizontal soffit board fills the gap between the fascia board and the house wall. In modern construction, the soffit incorporates ventilation strips to allow an air flow through the loft.

2 Closed eaves

If the roof projects beyond a gable end, angled timbers called barge boards protect the outer rafters and the end of the ridge board.

3 Open eaves

A duo-pitch roof may have sloping ends (called hips) instead of gables. Each hip is formed by two diagonal hip rafters that support the end of the ridge board, and short jack rafters are fitted between the hip rafters and the wallplates to complete the roof structure.

Where two duo-pitched roofs meet in an L-shape, they form an external hip and an internal valley, which is supported by a valley rafter and jack rafters in the same way as a hip is formed. The valley is either lined with a lead gutter or with specially shaped valley tiles (see Roof coverings, right).

Ridge board
Wall plate
Binder
Hanger

Purlin
Common rafter

Joist
Strut

Loadbearing internal wall

Purlin roof The commonest type of duo-pitch roof is the purlin roof. This has a horizontal beam called a purlin running between the gable ends along each slope of the roof, midway between the ridge board and the eaves, to provide extra support for the rafters. This increases the unsupported span of the roof to about 7m.

Prefabricated roofs

Almost all modern (post 1960s) house roofs are built using roof trusses, which are prefabricated in a variety of shapes to cater for most roof designs. Each roof truss combines rafters, joists and struts in a W-pattern to create a frame that is extremely strong and can span the external walls of the building with no need for internal load-bearing walls. The triangular structure does not deform under load, so the timbers used can be slimmer in cross-section than those in a traditional roof. This has the advantages of lower cost, lighter weight and ease of handling on site. The trusses can also be fixed by relatively unskilled workers, as little carpentry is involved in installing them.

The components of each roof truss are butt-jointed and fixed together with galvanised steel connector plates. They are positioned at 600mm centres on wallplates at each side of the span, and are nailed into place. There is no ridge board, but the row of trusses has to be braced to prevent it from collapsing sideways. Horizontal braces are fitted where the W-shaped internal supports meet the rafters and the ceiling joists, and diagonal braces are added across the underside of each section of the roof slope, running from the ridge to the eaves. The roof structure is tied to the house walls with galvanised steel straps to prevent the roof from lifting or gable walls collapsing in high winds.

Trussed rafter

Bracing

Wall plate

Roof coverings

Pitched roofs are traditionally covered with tiles or slates (see page 388). Other materials such as split stone and thatch are found in localised areas of the country, but their installation, maintenance and repair are beyond the scope of this book and are best left to specialist contractors.

In older houses, the roof covering is laid on closely spaced horizontal battens nailed across the upper edges of the rafters. In old roofs, this method allowed fine rain and snow to blow through the gaps between the tiles or slates and into the roof space. This was prevented by trowelling a mixture of mortar and animal hair into the gaps from inside the roof (a process called torching) or by boarding the roof slope – an expensive solution found only on better-quality houses. Since the 1930s it has been usual to lay underfelt (called sarking) over the rafters before the battens are fixed.

Slates and plain tiles

There are always two layers of tile or slate at any point on the roof, and three layers directly over each batten. This double-lapping prevents the water running off one tile or slate from entering the roof space through the gap between the tile or slate in

the course below. Slates are nailed to the battens at every course. Plain tiles have nibs on the back which hook over the roof battens, and are usually nailed only at every third or fourth course.

Other types of tile, such as traditional pantiles and large modern concrete tiles, overlap or interlock with their neighbours in each course. This prevents rain penetrating between their edges, so they can be laid with a single lap. This saves on both labour and materials when covering the roof. Tiles are fixed to the battens with nails or, more commonly on modern roofs, with side-fixing clips. Usually every third course is fixed, plus all perimeter tiles.

Flashings

Where a roof slope meets a wall or a chimney stack, the join must be waterproof. This is what flashings do. Lead, zinc, copper and mortar have all been used, but lead is the most common material in use today. It is cut into strips that are let into the mortar joints of the wall and shaped to overlap the roof covering.

Ridges and hips

Special half-round or L-shaped tiles are bedded on mortar or dry-fixed to the ridge board and hip rafters. Hips on plain-tiled roofs may be finished with specially-shaped bonnet hip tiles, which continue the tile coursing neatly round the hip. Valleys may also be tiled or lined with lead sheeting. At verges – where the roof slope meets a gable wall – the gaps between the tiles and the masonry may be filled with mortar, or the roof edge may be finished with special verge tiles. See pages 391–2 for more details.

THE TROUBLE WITH ROOFS

A well-built pitched roof will last for decades (or longer), but several problems are commonplace. Individual slates and tiles can slip out of position if their fixings fail, allowing water to penetrate the roof structure, and ridge and hip tiles can be dislodged by high winds if their mortar bedding fails. Slates can become brittle with age, and both tiles and slates can be damaged by careless roofing contractors or reckless householders climbing on the roof surface. Metal flashings can be torn or lifted by high winds, and mortar flashings may simply crack and fall out.

What to do

Unless you have the proper access equipment (see page 387) and are experienced in working at heights, it is safest to leave all roofing work to professional roofing contractors. You may be able to carry out minor repairs close to the eaves via a ladder. If you feel you are capable of carrying out work on the roof slope, you can replace tiles and slates (see pages 389–92) and repair flashings (page 393).

Flat roofs

Flat roofs are relatively uncommon on new homes today. In the 1960s and 1970s, every home extension had one because it was cheap and quick to erect.

Poor quality felting on these roofs led to a host of problems, and many owners of flat roofs eventually gave up the constant round of repairs and put on a pitched roof instead. Planners, too, grew disillusioned with flat roofs on domestic buildings and it is now very difficult to get consent to build anything new with a flat roof. Despite this, there are many flat roofs still in existence and giving reasonable service.

Flat roof construction

A flat roof is not truly horizontal; it needs a slight slope to drain rainwater off its surface. The basic structure consists of a series of parallel joists, usually running across the shorter dimension of the roof

and spaced at 400, 450 or 600mm centres. On spans of more than about 2.5m, solid or herringbone strutting is fixed between the joists to prevent them from warping.

Where an extension roof abuts a house wall, the ends of the joists nearest the house are supported on joist hangers or on a wall plate bolted to the wall. The other ends rest on a wall plate on top of the outer wall of the extension. This wall plate is secured to the wall with galvanised strapping to prevent strong winds from lifting the roof structure.

To create the required slope, which should be 1 in 60 for a felted roof, tapered battens called furring strips are fixed to the top edges of the joists. If the roof slope is to run at right angles to the joist direction, the strips also run at right angles to the joists.

The roof decking is then nailed in place. It may be tongued-and-grooved softwood boards, roofing-grade chipboard (which is coated with bitumen) or exterior-grade plywood. Softwood should be 19mm thick, while boards are usually 18mm thick. Boards are normally laid with their long edges across the joists, and solid struts or noggings can be positioned at 1220mm centres to provide extra support for the board edges.

Roof coverings

There are two materials commonly used on new domestic flat roofs; built-up felt and mastic asphalt. You may find lead, copper or zinc sheet roofs on older properties, especially on flat-topped window bays and porches.

Felt is usually built up in three layers, bonded together with hot or cold bitumen. Felt is available in several types, and the choice (and cost) will affect the life of the roof. The cheapest felts are based on mineral or glass fibre, and are generally used nowadays only for outbuildings. More expensive high-performance felts based on polyester fibres and fabrics are much more durable. As an alternative to bonding each felt layer to the one below with bitumen, torch-on felts have been developed. These have extra bitumen on one face that is melted with a blowtorch as the felt is unrolled into position.

The top layer of felt needs protecting against the effects of sunlight. Solar protection is usually provided by dressing the roof surface with a layer of small stone chippings, or by applying a solar reflective paint. Chippings are best bonded to the felt surface to prevent them from drifting

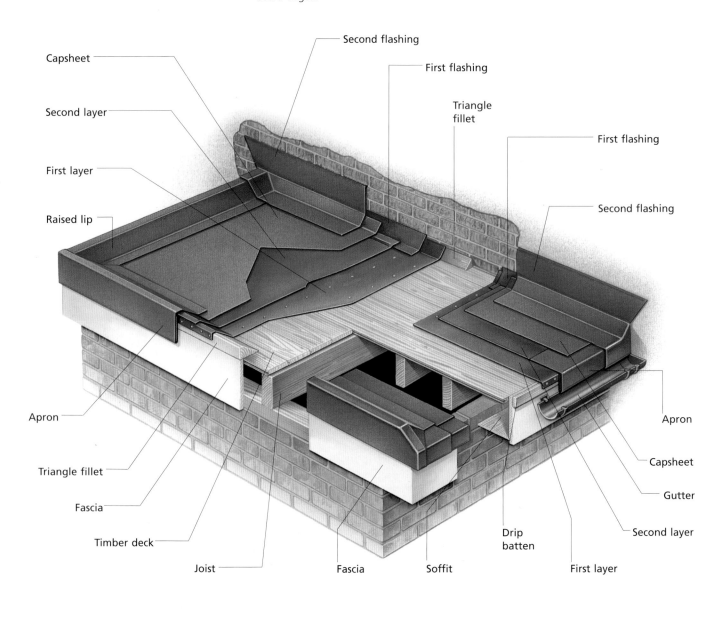

into gutters, but bonded chippings are more difficult to remove if the roof needs repairing.

Asphalt is a seamless roof covering made from natural or synthetic bitumen. It is melted in a cauldron and applied hot, over a layer of sheathing felt, in two layers to a total thickness of 18-20mm. It is used as an alternative to built-up felt on roofs that are used as balconies or roof gardens.

THE TROUBLE WITH FLAT ROOFS

Failure of the roofing felt is the commonest problem with existing flat roofs. A standard bitumen-bonded three-layer roof has a life expectancy of 10 to 15 years if well maintained, and less if it is subjected to regular foot traffic and the careless use of ladders or other access equipment, both of which can damage the felt. Weathering of the felt opens up cracks and pinholes that allow moisture to penetrate, causing blisters in the felt when the moisture is turned to vapour in hot sun. Seams and edges can be lifted in high winds, causing the felt to tear and allowing water penetration. Once water has penetrated, dampness in the roof structure can allow rot to develop. This initially causes the decking to subside between the joists, and may eventually lead to collapse of the roof structure if not remedied.

What to do

It is important to inspect flat roofs regularly – at least once a year – so that small defects can be identified and treated before they cause major trouble. You can repair blisters and splits yourself (see page 396) and carry out other minor repairs such as fixing faulty flashings (page 393). More widespread problems may need an overall waterproofing treatment (page 397). Full-scale replacement of an existing felted roof is a major project which you may prefer to leave to a professional roofing contractor.

Insulation and ventilation

A basic flat roof is a poor insulator, with just decking above the joists and a plasterboard ceiling below to keep the heat in. Old flat roofs may contain no insulation at all, or just a thin layer of glass fibre blanket laid above the ceiling. As a result, the rooms below it will be cold and expensive to heat. New or recently-built flat roofs always incorporate insulation, and this is provided in a number of different ways.

Cold roof

Insulated flat roofs are divided into two categories – cold roofs and warm roofs – according to where the insulation layer is placed.

In a cold roof, the insulation is placed above the ceiling and between the joists, so that the decking and the cavity between it and the insulation will be cold in winter. Unless the ceiling incorporates a vapour barrier, moisture rising through it will form condensation within the roof structure, rendering fibre insulation useless, saturating the ceiling and encouraging rot in the roof timbers. Since the fascia boards effectively seal the cavity, ventilation must be provided by openings equivalent to a 25mm wide strip all round the eaves of the roof. Condensation is still a potential problem, however, and because of this warm roofs are now preferred on new buildings.

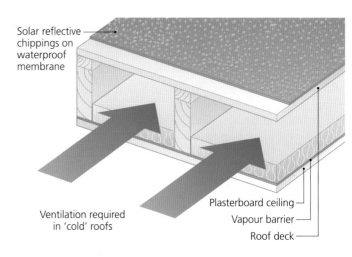

Solar reflective chippings on waterproof membrane

Ventilation required in 'cold' roofs

Plasterboard ceiling

Vapour barrier

Roof deck

Warm roof There are two main types of warm roof construction. In both, the insulation is placed above the roof deck, keeping it and the roof structure warm. This means a greatly reduced incidence of condensation, so ventilation of the roof space is no longer required, although a vapour barrier is still incorporated in the structure.

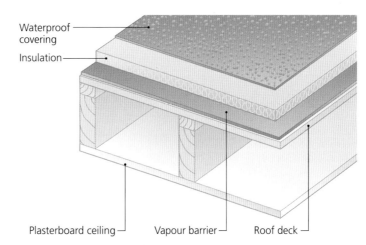

Waterproof covering

Insulation

Plasterboard ceiling

Vapour barrier

Roof deck

Sandwich roof

Insulation in the form of rigid boards is placed over a vapour barrier on top of the deck, and is protected by the final roof covering

Inverted roof

The insulation is placed above the roof covering, and is held down by ballast in the form of paving stones or a layer of pebbles. This protects the roof covering from extremes of temperature and accidental damage, and can

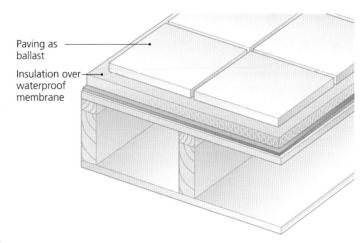

Paving as ballast

Insulation over waterproof membrane

be used to upgrade the insulation of an existing roof without any structural work. It has two drawbacks. Firstly, repairs to the roof, if needed, are more difficult to carry out because the ballast and insulation must first be removed. Secondly, the ballast may impose too great a load on an insubstantial roof structure; a surveyor should always check this aspect before an inverted roof is used on an existing roof structure.

Rainwater and drainage systems

In heavy rain, a lot of water falls on the roof of your house. 25mm of rain – a good cloudburst by British standards – means the whole of your roof area, covered to a depth of 25mm.

On a typical roof with an area of, say, 160m², that 25mm of water adds up to a total of 4m³ of water, or a volume of 4000 litres. Collecting it safely and getting rid of it is the job of the house's rainwater system.

Gutters and downpipes

Water running off a roof is collected in gutters fixed to the fascia boards. The gutters must be big enough to collect the occasional downpour without overflowing, and for most houses a gutter 100 or 112mm in width will do the job.

They discharge the water they collect into downpipes, which run down the house walls to ground level. A downpipe 68-75mm in diameter is usually big enough to carry the discharge from 100 or 112mm gutters.

Gutter outlets These are fitted at downpipe positions, discharging directly into the downpipe if the house eaves are flush with the wall. If the eaves overhang, an offset double-bend pipe called a swan's neck links the gutter to the downpipe.

Where two roof slopes meet in a valley, the rainwater is usually discharged from the valley gutter into a fitting called a hopper. A downpipe runs from the hopper down to ground level. A rainwater hopper may also collect waste water from upstairs baths and washbasins.

Cast iron downpipes Iron pipes have integral fixing lugs that are secured to the house walls with large pipe nails driven into wooden wedges in the mortar joints of the wall. Each pipe end fits loosely into the top of the length below. Bends divert the pipe where necessary, and single branch fittings allow two downpipes to be joined. At the base of the pipe, an angled fitting called a shoe discharges the water over the grate of an underground gully (see right).

uPVC rainwater systems In most modern houses, gutter systems are plastic. They are very similar to their cast iron counterparts in terms of the components used, but are much lighter. They are available in black, grey, white and brown.

Joints are made using fittings with integral rubber seals and plastic clips. The gutters may be half-round, or may have a deep oval or square trough cross-section. All are supported on brackets screwed to

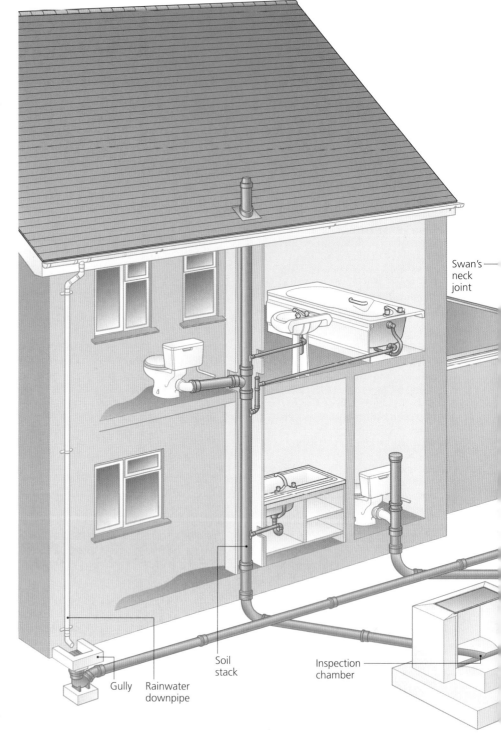

Swan's neck joint

Soil stack

Inspection chamber

Gully   Rainwater downpipe

the fascia boards. The gutters discharge into downpipes that are fixed to the wall with separate brackets.

Aluminium gutters These are seamless, and are formed on site by passing lengths of aluminium strip through a shaping machine. The lengths are joined to special outlet, angle and stop-end fittings to make up the gutter run. Matching downpipes are available to complete the system.

Check gutters and downpipes regularly – preferably during heavy rain – to see that they are working properly.

Gullies

At ground level, downpipes discharge into an underground fitting called a gully. If rainwater and waste water flow into the same drains, the gully contains a U-bend which prevents drain smells from rising up the downpipes. The bend also acts as a trap for debris washed down from the roof slope, preventing it from being washed into the drains.

• In old houses, the gullies will be made of earthenware (called vitrified clay), also used for the underground drains (below). Modern houses have plastic (uPVC) gullies and drains.

• If the house has separate rainwater and waste water drains, a trap is not needed and the downpipes can be connected directly to the underground rainwater drain by an underground elbow fitting. The gully may be a single round or square pot, with the downpipe shoe discharging over it through a grating that can be removed for cleaning if the trap becomes blocked.

• If the gully also drains water from a garden, it may have two inlets – one for the downpipe and another to take surface water. This type is a back-inlet gully.

• In modern plastic installations, the downpipe does not discharge over a grating, but passes through it, straight into the gully trap. A removable grating allows access to the trap for cleaning.

• If the house has separate rainwater drains, the downpipe is connected to the drains via an underground elbow, with a ground-level access point nearby to allow blockages to be cleared if they occur.

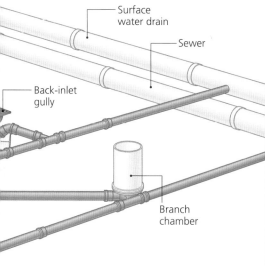

Surface
water drain
Sewer
Back-inlet
gully
Branch
chamber

Underground drains

Drains are a mysterious underworld to most homeowners, and are noticed only if they get blocked. Knowing where they run and how they work makes dealing with this occasional occurrence much less traumatic.

Soil stacks Homes built since about the 1950s have one or more uPVC soil stacks to gather all the household waste water and carry it into the drains. All appliances – including WCs – are connected directly into the stack, which is now sited inside the house to do away with all the unsightly external plumbing of the old two-pipe system.

Manholes Each stack discharges into a manhole, which may be a traditional rectangular brick chamber or a plastic moulding fitted with a round metal cover.

As with earthenware drains, extra manholes are installed to connect in other branch drains, or at any point where the drain run changes direction. Finally the drain run connects into the main sewer.

Soakaways Rainwater is collected separately from waste water, and is taken by buried pipes to a main surface water drain or into a sunken chamber called a soakaway. They are usually buried in both front and rear gardens, and allow the collected rainwater to soak away into the subsoil.

Cesspools and septic tanks

In areas where there is no mains drainage system, household waste water can be led into an underground cesspool – a large holding tank that has to be emptied regularly for disposal elsewhere.

A septic tank is a tiny sewage treatment plant, breaking down the material piped into it by a combination of filtration and bacterial action. The effluent is safe enough to be discharged into the subsoil, and residual solid material has to be cleaned out of the tank from time to time.

THE TROUBLE WITH GUTTERS AND DRAINS

By far the most common problem with both rainwater and drainage systems is a blockage, leading to an overflow from the affected part of the system. This may be caused by leaves and wind-blown debris in gutters and hoppers, or by unsuitable materials being flushed into the drainage system.

Leaks are another problem, easily solved in rainwater systems but more difficult to tackle in underground drains.

Old cast iron gutters often suffer from serious (and sometimes terminal) rust.

What to do
Clearing blockages, fixing leaks and dealing with other rainwater system problems is generally a simple matter of routine maintenance (see pages 400–5) You can tackle most drain blockages yourself with the aid of a set of drain rods, which you can buy or hire when required (see pages 406–7).

OLDER HOMES

In houses built before about 1950, a two-pipe system carried waste water from the house (and often rainwater from the roof as well) to the underground drains. One large-diameter pipe called the soil pipe took waste from WCs directly into the drains by an underground elbow; a trap to keep drain smells out was not needed because the WC pan contained one, but the pipe was extended to eaves level to ventilate the drain section.

Waste water discharged directly into a trapped gully from appliances such as a sink at ground-floor level, or into a wall-mounted hopper from basins and other appliances in upstairs rooms.

A downpipe linked the hopper to the gully below, which was connected to a separate section of the drains. All these pipes were mounted on the walls of the house, and looked extremely unsightly.

The underground section of the soil pipe and the drain run from each gully met at an underground brick chamber

Hopper
Gully

called an inspection chamber or manhole, fitted with a cast iron cover. Inside the manhole, the branch pipes run into an open channel, allowing each section of the drains to be cleared via the manhole using drain rods if it became blocked. The outlet from the chamber ran on as a single underground drain, via further manholes installed to connect in other branch drains or where the drain run changed direction. The last manhole before the main sewer was built as an interceptor manhole, and contained a trap to prevent sewer gases from entering the drainage system of individual houses. This type of manhole was prone to frequent blockages, and has not been used for many years.

Fireplaces, flues and chimneys

Central heating has made the fireplace almost redundant in modern homes, although consumer demand means that one is still often provided in the main living room.

In older homes there was a fireplace in every room, and the construction of the flues that were needed to discharge the smoke was the most complex part of the whole house structure.

In terraced houses, the flues were built into the party walls between the properties. In larger houses, there would often be two or more chimney stacks, each containing two or four flues and serving downstairs and upstairs fireplaces, plus a separate chimney for the coal-fired boiler that heated the house's hot water supply.

Fireplaces

The simplest type of fireplace, found in old and unmodernised homes, is just a brick opening at the base of the flue. A free-standing grate is set on a concrete hearth, and the fire is built within the grate. As it burns, the hot gases it creates rise into the flue and draw fresh air in from the room through the base of the grate to keep the fire burning.

This arrangement is very wasteful of heat, and often suffers from smoke blowing back into the room. Birds also have a habit of falling down the open flue.

Firebacks

Most fireplaces have a shaped fireback built into the basic brick recess. This is a shaped fireclay unit, available in several pieces that are bonded together with fire cement at assembly. The fireback helps to retain the heat of the fire, reflecting it back into the room. The void between the fireback and the brick recess is usually filled with a mixture of sand, lime and broken brick (or simply builder's rubble) in older homes, or with lightweight insulating concrete in newer ones.

Flues

The fireplace is linked to the open flue above it with a sloping connector called a throat. This was formed from mortar in older homes, but in modern chimneys a pre-cast concrete throat unit is built in as the chimney is constructed. The joints between the fireback and the throat are sealed with fireproof rope. This also seals the joint between the fireback and a decorative fire surround fitted round the fireplace opening.

The concrete hearth is often topped with a decorative 'superimposed' hearth of ceramic or quarry tiles or stone slabs.

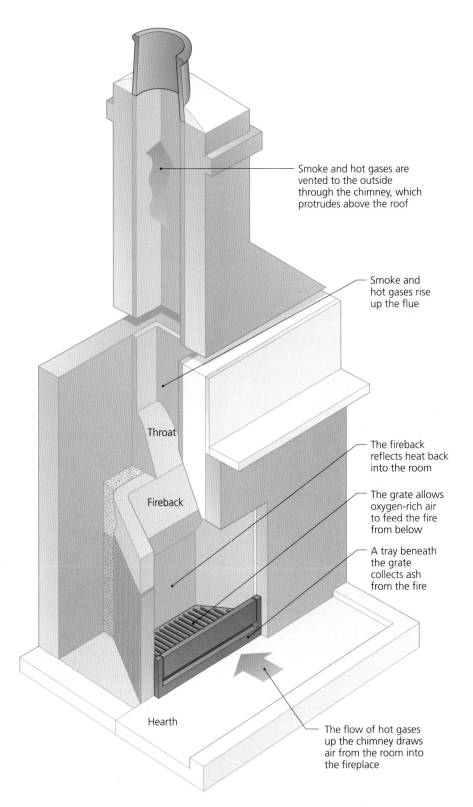

Smoke and hot gases are vented to the outside through the chimney, which protrudes above the roof

Smoke and hot gases rise up the flue

Throat

Fireback

The fireback reflects heat back into the room

The grate allows oxygen-rich air to feed the fire from below

A tray beneath the grate collects ash from the fire

Hearth

The flow of hot gases up the chimney draws air from the room into the fireplace

Chimney construction

Modern chimneys are lined with special interlocking clay flue blocks, which allow for a smooth upward flow of smoke and prevent soot and tar from collecting. Such deposits are in any case less of a problem today, thanks to the widespread use of processed fuels rather than raw coal.

The chimney stack projects above the roof line so that down-draughts do not affect the upwards draw of the flue. Each flue within the chimney is topped by a chimney pot, which is set on a mortar bed and secured by a shaped cap of mortar called flaunching round its base. If the flue

has become disused, the pots may have been removed and replaced by a cowl or a cover slab. The latter is likely to be found where the fireplaces have themselves been decommissioned and blocked up.

The traditional chimney is a hollow brick column with an open hearth or fireplace at the bottom and a chimney pot at the top. Generally speaking, the higher the chimney is, the more efficient it is at drawing smoke and fumes up and away. The chimney may be free-standing (especially in a timber-framed house), but is usually built into an external or internal wall for support. On an external wall, the flue may be built on the inside of the wall or on the outside.

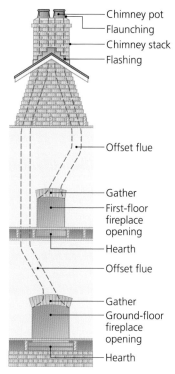

- Chimney pot
- Flaunching
- Chimney stack
- Flashing

- Offset flue

- Gather
- First-floor fireplace opening
- Hearth
- Offset flue

- Gather
- Ground-floor fireplace opening
- Hearth

An inside flue creates a projecting chimney breast flanked by two alcoves within the room, whereas an outside flue leaves the fireplace opening flush with the wall surface. The chimney is straight if it has a single flue. If it contains multiple flues, each is offset so that the downstairs flue by-passes the upstairs fireplace.

Old flues were unlined, or were rendered internally with mortar, which cracked and failed as time went by. Condensation within the flue could eventually carry tar and soot stains through the unprotected masonry to ruin room decorations. Soot would accumulate within the flue, often leading to messy soot falls and eventually to chimney fires.

THE TROUBLE WITH CHIMNEYS

Indoors, the main problem with chimneys, especially disused ones, is tar and soot staining being carried through to the inner face of the flue by condensation occurring within it. Externally, the exposed part of the chimney stack can suffer from failed pointing and flaunching, loose chimney pots, damage to the brickwork and to the flashings that weatherproof the junction between the stack and the roof slope.

What to do
Make sure that disused flues are properly capped off and have adequate ventilation at top and bottom. Inspect the chimney stack regularly so that faults can be spotted and rectified before they become serious. Unless you are experienced in working at heights, it is best to leave chimney stack repairs to a professional builder.

Insulation and ventilation

Your house would be cold in winter without insulation, and unhealthy without ventilation. These unseen but vital aspects of your home need to be understood and maintained.

Roof insulation

Roofs in new homes will be insulated to current Building Regulations standards. A house with a pitched roof and a loft used for storage will have insulation between (and possibly over) the ceiling joists, to a thickness of about 200mm. If the loft has been converted for use as habitable rooms, the underside of the roof slope and the walls forming the loft room(s) will be insulated to a similar standard. Flat roofs will incorporate insulation, probably as a warm roof structure.

If you have a pitched roof with less insulation than the current standards require, you can lay extra insulation over what is there already, or insulate the roof slope if the roof space is to be used as a loft conversion (see pages 243–5). Use wrapped glass fibre blanket insulation for convenience and ease of handling. If you have a flat roof with inadequate insulation, consider converting it to a warm roof structure by adding insulation above the existing roof covering (see page 23).

Wall insulation

Modern homes incorporate insulation within their cavity walls to meet Building Regulations requirements. Timber-framed houses have insulation within their load-bearing wall panels. Older houses with unfilled cavity walls can be insulated by pumping insulation material into the cavity through holes drilled in the outer leaf of the wall. This is a job that must be carried out by an approved installer, and requires Building Regulations approval to ensure that the walls are in suitable condition, and that the installation fills the cavity entirely.

Houses with solid walls have poor insulation performance, and improving this is a major undertaking. It can be done by insulating and dry-lining the external wall surfaces indoors – a highly disruptive job, but one which can be carried out on a DIY basis (see page 232).

External insulation is a less disruptive but more expensive option which will materially alter the appearance of the house, and which may need planning consent.

It involves fixing insulation material to the wall surfaces and waterproofing it with timber or tile cladding, or with a layer of rendering applied over expanded metal mesh. It is a job for a specialist contractor.

Floor insulation

Houses with solid ground floors built since the early 1990s have to include a layer of insulation to meet Building Regulations requirements. Older houses have no such insulation, so ground floor slabs can feel very cold. Adding insulation involves laying rigid polystyrene boards over the existing floor surface and adding a new floating floor of chipboard – a process that raises the existing floor level by at least 70mm.

Suspended timber ground floors are easier to insulate, because insulation can be placed between the floor joists. However, the job will involve lifting and re-laying floorboards unless there is an accessible crawl space below the floor. Adding 100mm thick rigid insulation will improve the floor's insulation significantly.

Window and door insulation

Recently-built and modernised houses will benefit from double-glazed windows, and efficiently draughtproofed door and window frames. In older houses, replacing existing single-glazed windows with double-glazed ones will significantly improve their insulation performance (see page 211). Replacing the glass in existing windows with double-glazed sealed units may be possible depending on the design of the frames, but may be as expensive as replacing the windows. Installing secondary glazing inside the existing windows (see pages 212–13) will be cheaper but is not as effective and tends to look intrusive.

If existing doors and windows are not draughtproofed, installing the relevant products is a simple job to tackle on a DIY basis (see pages 216–17).

Ventilation

Appropriate ventilation is essential in four main areas of the home.
- Lofts must be ventilated to prevent condensation within the roof space – achieved by eaves ventilation in new houses. In older houses, ensure that the eaves are not blocked by loft insulation.
- Voids beneath suspended timber ground floors need ventilation to prevent rot from attacking the floor timbers. This is provided by airbricks in the house walls; ensure that these are not obstructed or blocked.
- Kitchens and bathrooms need ventilation to disperse cooking odours and steam. This ventilation can be provided by openable windows, but it is useful to supplement this with extractor fans. These are essential in internal rooms with no windows.
- Efficient ventilation is a matter of life and death in rooms containing fuel-burning appliances such as boilers and gas fires. Installers of new equipment (who must be CORGI registered) will ensure that appropriate levels of ventilation are provided, and you can call in a gas safety inspector to check an existing installation.

2
Basic skills and tools

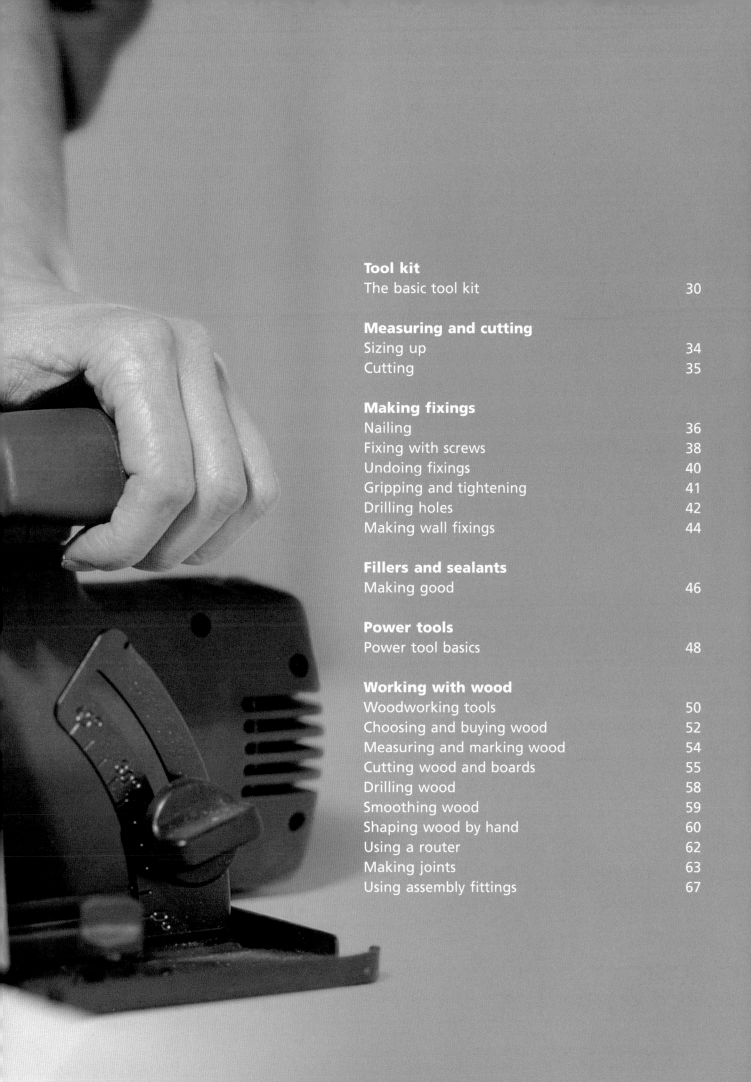

The basic tool kit

This section introduces the tools you will need to tackle all the run-of-the-mill DIY jobs you are likely to face as a householder. Some are essentials that no home should be without, while others can be bought as and when you need them. You will find tools for woodwork dealt with on pages 50 to 65.

General purpose tools

The tool box

You will need a sturdy tool box in which to store your DIY hand tools. Many sizes and styles are available; to start with, pick a light but sturdy plastic case with a lift-out tray for small tools. You can always buy a second or a bigger one as your tool kit grows. Avoid metal tool boxes; they are heavy to carry around and they rust.

Pincers

Looking more like an instrument of torture than a DIY tool, pincers are extremely useful jacks of all trades. They are designed primarily for pulling out unwanted pins, tacks and nails – from floorboards, for example – but can also be put to other tasks, such as pulling out picture hooks without damaging the plaster, or nibbling awkward shapes out of ceramic tiles. Pincers are usually about 200mm long, and are inexpensive to buy.

Pliers

A pair of combination pliers is another multi-purpose tool that is well worth having in your tool kit. Their serrated jaws are useful for gripping all sorts of things, such as the wire loop that holds the bath plug on its chain, the corroded piston on a faulty ballvalve or the shattered remains of a light bulb stuck in its lampholder. You can use them as a makeshift spanner if none is to hand. You can twist and cut wire, and straighten bent metal. Basic pliers have metal handles; if comfort in use matters, buy electrician's pliers with insulated plastic handles instead.

Knife

A trimming knife with replaceable blades is a DIY essential. A standard blade will cut paper, card and thin sheet materials such as plasterboard, and will mark clear cutting lines on all sorts of surfaces. Fitted with special blades, the knife can cut sheet flooring, plastic laminates, even wood and metal. Knives are available with fixed blades (initially covered by a slip-on blade guard, which is

Tool box

Pincers   Pliers

Nail punch

Tenon saw

Trimming knife

Claw hammer

Junior hacksaw

Filling knife

Pin hammer

often lost), or with retractable blades which are safer to use and to carry around. Most knives allow you to store spare blades (except long wood and metal-cutting ones) inside the knife handle. Make sure you have plenty of spares.

Hacksaw
Hacksaws take replaceable blades, and are designed to cut metal. You might need one to cut through a rusty nail or bolt, or an unwanted pipe. A hacksaw will also cut through plastic – a curtain rail, for example – and can even be used for cutting small pieces of wood such as timber mouldings. For all these jobs, an inexpensive junior hacksaw is ideal. It takes slim 150mm long blades, which are held in tension by the spring of the one-piece steel frame. Buy a pack of spare blades too.

Saws
If you plan to cut any wood larger than a slim moulding (which your junior hacksaw will deal with), you need a proper saw. Invest in a tenon saw, which has a rectangular blade about 250mm long stiffened along the top with a strip of brass or steel. The handle is either wood or moulded plastic. As its name implies, the tenon saw is designed primarily for cutting woodworking joints, but it will cope with all sorts of other minor woodwork jobs such as trimming wall battens or cutting a shelf to length. The thickness it will cut is limited by the depth of the blade.

Hammers
The most versatile hammer to have is a claw hammer, which will drive all but the smallest pins and can also be used to lever out old nails by fitting the grooved claw under the nail head. Choose one with a metal or glass-fibre shaft and a rubber grip, with a head weighing 16 or 20oz (hammers still come in imperial sizes).

To accompany your claw hammer, buy a nail punch (also known as a nail set). This is a small steel tool about 100mm long, with a knurled shaft and a tapered point. It is used with a hammer to drive nail heads below the wood surface, preventing the hammer head from striking and denting it.

Add a small pin hammer to your tool kit if you drive a lot of small nails and panel pins. It will have a wooden handle and a head weighing about 4oz.

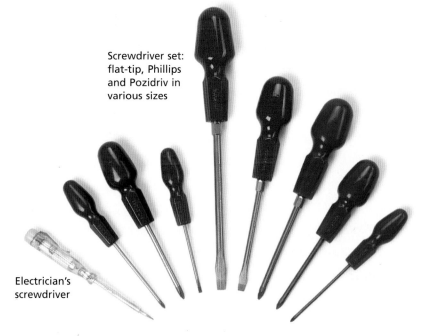

Screwdriver set: flat-tip, Phillips and Pozidriv in various sizes

Electrician's screwdriver

Screwdrivers
Within reason, you can never have too many screwdrivers. Screws come with head recesses of different types, ranging from straight slots to cross and hexagon shapes, and in different sizes.

To start with, you need a flat-tip screwdriver with a blade about 125mm long for slotted-head screws, and a No. 2 Phillips cross-tip screwdriver which will also drive other types of cross-head screws such as Pozidriv and Prodrive.

You will also need a small electrician's screwdriver for fiddly jobs. This has an insulated handle, for safety's sake.

If you need more screwdrivers, it is worth looking out for screwdriver sets sold in a storage case. These typically include two or three drivers for slotted-head screws, plus Phillips and Pozidriv drivers in two sizes for large and small cross-head screws of different types. The set may have a master handle, into which you slot the blade you need for the task. This type of set saves space but can be fiddly to use if you have a complicated project in hand.

Filling knife
This tool has a wood or plastic handle and a flexible steel blade, and is used for applying filler to holes and defects in wood or plaster. Buy a 25mm and a 50mm knife for everyday use. Do not confuse a filling knife with a stripping knife, which has a stiffer blade.

Measuring and marking

Straightedge
A long steel or aluminium straightedge is essential for many DIY jobs, from checking the flatness of surfaces (a tiled wall, for example) to guiding a trimming knife when cutting things like vinyl flooring. Buy one 1m long for maximum usefulness, with both metric and imperial markings along it.

Tape measure
You need a steel tape measure for measuring and estimating jobs. An ideal size is a 5m tape, which will cope with measuring up a room as well as taking smaller measurements. Most have metric and imperial markings, so you can use the tape as a handy conversion device. Pick one with a lock that keeps the blade extended while you use it.

Spirit level
This tool is essential if you are to get things like shelves and curtain tracks level, and for checking anything that needs to be truly vertical. It is a plastic or alloy bar with vials containing an air bubble set into the long edge and usually at each end. The level is horizontal or vertical when the bubble is exactly centred between the marks on the appropriate vial. Buy a metal one at least 300mm long. To check levels over longer distances, you can balance it on a timber straightedge.

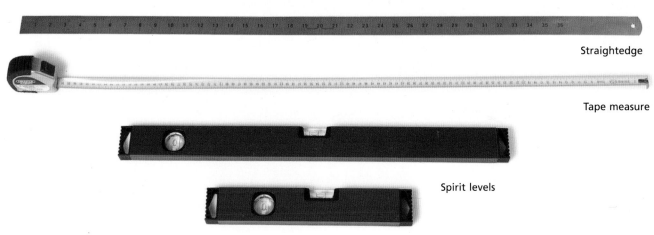

Straightedge

Tape measure

Spirit levels

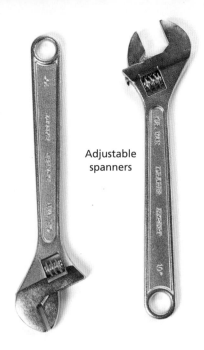

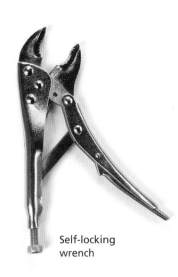

Adjustable
spanners

Self-locking
wrench

Holding and gripping

Spanners

Spanners are better at turning nuts and
bolts than pliers, and you will probably
have to undo something that's bolted
together or tighten a leaky plumbing fitting
sooner or later. What you need is an
adjustable spanner with a jaw opening up
to about 30mm – big enough to grip the
nuts on plumbing fittings, yet capable of
tackling smaller nuts too. The so-called
crescent pattern with its offset head is best
at getting into awkward positions.

Self-locking wrench

This versatile tool, commonly known as a
Mole wrench from the name of the original
maker, can be used like a pair of pliers or
as a makeshift extra spanner. Its serrated
jaws will grip round things like the knurled
nuts on waste traps, and its lockable jaws
mean you can use it as a clamp when you
need an extra pair of hands.

Power tools

Jigsaw

A jigsaw is one of the most useful of all
power tools. Even if you do not do much
woodwork, you can justify its purchase for
its all-round versatility. It has a relatively
short blade that protrudes from the
baseplate of the saw, and this cuts on the
upstroke. Because of the thinness of the
blade, you can make curved cuts with it as
well as straight ones, simply by driving the
saw blade along a marked cutting line. You
can also make cuts away from the edge of
the workpiece – to fit a letterbox in a front
door, for example, or make a cut-out in a
worktop for an inset sink or hob.

Although the jigsaw is primarily
designed for cutting wood and man-made
boards, it will also cut materials such as
metal, rigid plastic and ceramic tiles as long
as the correct type of blade is fitted.

Features to look out for when choosing
a jigsaw are adequate power (at least 500
watts), variable speed, a dust bag or
vacuum cleaner attachment to help to

collect dust, and a blade fitting
arrangement that does not need tools.
Keep a stock of standard wood-cutting
blades for general work, and buy specialist
blades only when you need them.

Cordless jigsaws are available, but they
are comparatively expensive and probably
not worth the cost unless you plan to do a
lot of cutting far from a power source.

Sander

Finishing new wood, keying the surface of
paintwork before redecorating it, and
removing surplus material such as plaster
filler are all jobs that require sanding –
using an abrasive paper to create a smooth
surface. You can do the job by hand, but
for all but the smallest areas this is one of
the most tedious and time-consuming DIY

jobs. A power sander does all the work in a
fraction of the time, and even gathers up
the dust if you buy the right type.

Power sanders come in more varieties
than any other tool, ranging from tiny
hand-sized finishing sanders to high-
powered belt sanders. There are even
sanders with interchangeable heads for
sanding awkward areas. As a first choice
for general smoothing work, an eccentric or
random-orbit sander is probably the best.
This combines the fine finish of an orbital
sander with the fast stock removal of a disc
sander, and can be fitted with a wide range
of abrasive sheets.

Most random-orbit sanders take circular
sanding discs 115 or 125mm in diameter.
You attach the discs to the baseplate with
touch-and-close (Velcro) fastenings. Holes in
the discs line up with holes in the baseplate
through which the sander's motor extracts
dust, either depositing it in a small dust bag
or delivering it via a hose connection to a
vacuum cleaner.

Drill

You will need a power drill for all sorts of
DIY jobs. The most versatile choice is a
cordless drill, which has a rechargeable
battery and can be used anywhere without
the need for a power supply. Cordless drills
are not as powerful as mains-powered
models (see page 58), and can be more
expensive. However, they double up as a
power screwdriver thanks to their low
chuck speed, and their reverse gear allows
you to undo screws as well. A model with
hammer action will drill holes in all but the
hardest walls. Battery sizes range from 9.6V
(volts) up to a massive 24V; a drill rated at
14.4 or 18V will be powerful enough to
cope with almost every job. Choose one
that is comfortable and well-balanced to
hold, and is not too heavy to handle easily.
Keep a spare battery, so that one can be
kept fully charged while the other is in use.

Jigsaw

Sander

Flat wood drill bits

Screwdriver bits for drill

Cordless drill

14.4V

Countersink drill bit

Twist drill bits

Masonry drill bits

Other useful tools

Staple gun
The DIY version of the office stapler has all sorts of uses. It will fix webbing or fabric to furniture frames, trellis to fences and low-voltage wires to skirting boards, all the time leaving one hand free to hold whatever you are fixing. You will also find it ideal for securing carpet underlay to floorboards, attaching fabric to roller blinds and even making small picture frames. The most versatile will fire staples of different sizes.

Cable and pipe detector
This small battery-powered device detects the presence of electricity cable and plumbing pipes buried in the house walls. Some will also locate ceiling joists and the timber frame inside a partition wall, by detecting the line of fixing nails that holds the plasterboard cladding in place. Use it as a precaution to check for hidden pipes or cables before driving nails or drilling holes for wall fixings.

Cartridge gun
Many ready-to-use fillers, sealants and adhesives are now sold in standard-sized cartridges. To be able to use them, you need a cartridge gun. This inexpensive tool has an open metal or plastic frame which holds the cartridge, and is fitted with a simple trigger and piston mechanism which extrudes the contents of the cartridge as the trigger is squeezed. Cartridges come in two standard sizes, and you may need two gun sizes to take them.

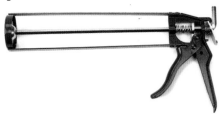

Drill bits
Your cordless drill will need a range of drill bits for the various jobs it can do.

Twist drill bits Make small holes in wood, man-made boards and metal. Buy a set of HSS (high-speed steel) drill bits containing sizes up to 10mm, stored in a metal case which will last longer than a plastic one. Carbon steel bits are cheaper than HSS ones, but become blunt more quickly.

Flat wood bits Drill larger holes in wood and boards, and come in sizes from 12mm up to 32mm. Buy them as and when you need them and store them in their packaging – usually a plastic sleeve.

Masonry drill bits Make holes in solid walls, usually to take wallplugs when making wall fixings. Do not buy a boxed set, which will contain sizes you will never use. Instead, match the sizes you buy to the wallplugs and other fixings you usually use – probably 6, 7 and 8mm. You may need longer and larger drills to make holes in walls for pipes and cables; buy them when you need them. Store them all in a tray in your tool box.

Screwdriver bits enable you to drive and remove screws using your cordless drill as a power screwdriver. One two-ended bit will probably be supplied with your drill; add a set containing bits for slotted-head, Phillips, Pozidriv and Torx screws.

Lastly, you will also need a countersink drill bit. This makes cone-shaped recesses in wood or metal to accept the heads of countersunk screws.

Work and access

Stepladders
A light but sturdy stepladder is essential for high-level work. Choose one that is versatile – some can be used in various conformations, for use in stairwells, for example – and has a grab rail and platform for resting tools or paint pots at the top. Make sure the feet have non-skid covers. Accessories such as clip-on trays, stand-offs (which keep the ladder away from the wall) and paint hooks are useful.

Workbench
The last essential for everyday DIY is a portable workbench. You can use it to support things while you cut, drill and assemble them, and its jaws will act as a large vice for gripping anything from a length of pipe to a room door. You can even stand on it at a pinch. Small basic types are surprisingly cheap; larger models cost more, but may have extra features, such as dual height settings and movable jaws.

Sizing up

Many DIY jobs involve three essential but unrelated jobs: measuring the size of things, positioning them to a true horizontal or vertical, and checking that making fixings will not cause damage to cables or pipework concealed within the house structure. Here are the tools you need for these jobs, and how to use them.

Measuring up

A retractable tape measure consists of a coil of printed steel stored on a spring-loaded drum within a plastic or metal case. The spring retracts the extended tape back into the case, which usually has a simple lock to hold the tape in the extended position if required. The strip has a slight curve in cross-section to keep it stiff when in use, and measurements are printed on the concave face, usually in metric and imperial. A 5m tape is long enough to take room measurements without being unnecessarily bulky to carry in the pocket.

1 To take an internal measurement (of an alcove, for example), hold the free end against one surface and extend the tape until the side of the case is against the opposite surface. Add the width of the case to the last measurement visible on the tape where it emerges from the case. The case width is usually printed on the case, but is typically 50 or 65mm. Always read off and mark measurements with the eye vertically above the tape if it is horizontal, or level with the tape if it is vertical. If you do not do this, a visual error called parallax occurs and the mark you make will be inaccurate. Always measure and mark twice to eliminate the risk of introducing this error.

2 The end of the tape is fitted with a small metal lug. To take an external measurement (of a piece of wood, for example), hook the lug over one end of the wood and draw the tape out until you can read off and mark the measurement.

Checking horizontals and verticals

A spirit level tells you whether surfaces are truly horizontal or vertical. It consists of a metal or plastic bar with parallel edges into which one or more clear plastic vials are set. The vial in the long edge of the level indicates a true horizontal, while vials at each end indicate a true vertical. Each vial contains an air bubble and is marked with two parallel lines. When the bubble is centred between the marks, the tool is level or vertical according to which vial is being used. Long spirit levels are more accurate than short ones; buy a spirit level at least 300mm long and ideally 1m long.

1 To check a horizontal, rest the level on the surface being checked and view the vial in the long edge from directly above or beside the level. Adjust the surface until the bubble is precisely centred between the marks on the vial.

2 To check a vertical, hold the level against the surface and view the vial at the end with the eye at the same level. Adjust the position of the surface until the bubble is centred in the vial.

3 Some spirit levels have one end vial set in a movable mounting marked with an angle scale. Rotate the mounting to the required angle and use the level to set a surface to that specific angle. However, this is less accurate than other tools for this job (see page 54).

Locating concealed hazards

A cable and pipe detector is a hand-held battery-powered electronic device that will reveal the presence of electricity cables or plumbing pipework concealed in the house structure. It is important to be aware of their presence whenever you are making fixings (with nails or with screws and wallplugs) into a wall, floor or ceiling, since piercing one could cause personal injury, physical damage or both.

In some cases it is obvious where buried services are located. For example, you can expect there to be a vertical cable run immediately above a light switch, or pipework above or below a flush-mounted thermostatic shower mixer valve. In other cases, using the detector can avoid a potential accident.

Some detectors will locate only live electrical cables; others will detect any buried metal – cable, pipework, even the line of nails fixing plasterboard to a hidden wall stud or ceiling joist.

Switch the detector on and set its sensitivity according to the manufacturer's instructions. Pass it slowly back and forth over the area you are testing. The detector will bleep and may flash a light when it senses a hazard, enabling you to mark and avoid its route when making any fixings.

Cutting

Once you have measured how big something needs to be, your next job is to cut it to size. The tools you need for this depend on what you are cutting, and on how thick it is. Whichever tool you are using, make sure that it is sharp. A blunt tool requires more effort to use, and is more likely to slip or cut off course as a result – either injuring you or damaging the workpiece.

Using a trimming knife

A sharp trimming knife will cut all sorts of thin sheet materials, from wallpaper and soft floorcoverings to plasterboard. You can use it freehand, but you will get better results if you place a steel straightedge over the cutting line and draw the knife blade along its edge. Make sure your free hand is anchoring the straightedge securely, and that your fingertips are out of the way of the knife blade.

1 When using a trimming knife on the workbench or on the floor, always place a cutting board or a piece of scrap hardboard beneath whatever you are cutting. This will allow the knife to cut cleanly through the workpiece without scoring and damaging the surface below.

2 Hold the knife securely and draw it along the straightedge in one continuous movement. If necessary, make two or three passes rather than trying to cut the material in one go; the harder you have to press, the more risk there is that the blade will slip off line. Always cut against the side of the straightedge next to the waste material.

Using a tenon saw

A tenon saw will cut wood and man-made boards. Its cutting depth is limited to about 75mm by the presence of the stiffening along the top edge of the blade. This also limits the width of the workpiece that can be cut; in practice, it is difficult to make a cut longer than about 300mm with this tool.

Whatever you are cutting must be held securely. You can clamp it in the jaws of your workbench. However, it is easier to hold small workpieces using a simple aid called a bench hook (page 51). You can buy one, or make one from scrap wood and board. To make one, glue and screw two pieces of softwood batten to opposite faces of a rectangle of plywood measuring about 250 x 150mm.

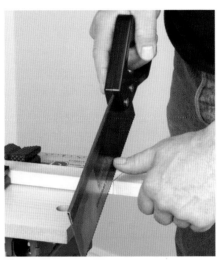

1 To cut a piece of wood to length, mark the cutting line on it (see page 54). Hold it securely on your workbench with the thumb of your free hand next to the cutting line to guide the saw blade. Position the saw blade so it will cut just on the waste side of the cutting line, and draw it towards you at about 45° to start the cut.

2 Once the saw teeth begin to bite, start to cut the wood with light but firm strokes. Remember that it cuts on the forward stroke only. Start to flatten out the angle of the saw. Complete the cut with gentle strokes, holding the saw almost level with the wood surface, to avoid splitting the underside of the wood. Support the off-cut with your free hand if the workpiece is held in the jaws of the workbench.

Using a hacksaw

A junior hacksaw will cut metal and rigid plastic – and wood with a small cross-section, such as timber mouldings. Make sure that the blade is fitted with the points of the teeth facing away from the handle, so it will cut on the forward stroke.

1 The hacksaw blade tends to snatch when cutting thin metal, so it is best to secure the workpiece in the jaws of your workbench. Most have grooves machined in the mating edges of the jaws for holding round objects such as copper pipe or a metal wardrobe rail.

2 Start the cut on the waste side of the marked line, as for cutting wood with a tenon saw. A strip of masking tape makes a good cutting guide. Draw the blade towards you two or three times to start the cut, taking care to keep the blade on line.

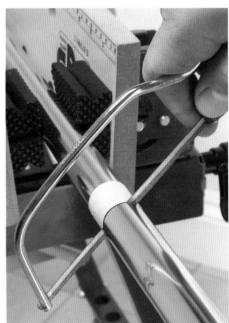

3 Saw with firm forward strokes. On metal tubing, the teeth will tend to snatch as you start the cut. Do not let the blade jump out of the cut as you proceed. Complete the cut with a few gentle strokes.

Nailing

A nail is one of the simplest fixing devices. Its point is driven through whatever you are fixing and on into the material beneath until its head is flush with the surface. Different nail types and sizes are used for different jobs, but in practice you will need only a small range to cope with everyday DIY jobs – see Choosing nails, opposite. You need a hammer to drive nails in, and a small tool called a nail punch to enable you to finish driving the nail without marking the surface with the hammer head.

Using a claw hammer

A claw hammer will drive all but the smallest nails with ease, and its claw will extract nails that are misaligned or bent while being driven in. Hold it near the end of the handle and watch the hammer head to make sure that it strikes the nail head squarely.

1 Hold the nail between your thumb and forefinger and start it with a few gentle taps of the hammer head. Check that it is at right angles to the surface.

2 Release the nail and drive it in with harder blows. For large nails, keep your wrist stiff and swing hammer and forearm from the elbow. On rough work, hammer the nail head in flush with the surface.

Using a pin hammer

A pin hammer or lightweight ball-pein hammer (shown here) is easier to handle when driving small panel pins, tacks, upholstery nails and glazing sprigs (used to hold glass panes in wooden window frames).

1 Hold the pin between your thumb and forefinger and tap it in with the flat end of the hammer head.

2 When it stands by itself, drive it in with the hammer head, flexing your wrist to control the hammer. Drive the pin fully home, or use a nail punch to recess its head in the wood, if necessary.

Removing a bent nail

If you bend a nail as you drive it, stop and remove it. Do not try to straighten a bent nail or drive it fully home at an angle. Pull it out and replace it with a new nail.

Place a piece of card or thin wood on the surface beside the nail. Hook the hammer claw under the nail head and pull the handle towards you to draw out the nail. Keep the handle vertical so you do not widen the opening of the nail hole.

Using a staple gun

A hand-operated staple gun fires metal staples, and can be used for many light fixing jobs. The staples work like two-pronged nails, relying on the crossbar between the pins to fix the material in place. The staple is ejected at high speed, so take care not to fire the gun unless its baseplate is securely pressed against the workpiece.

1 If the model accepts staples of different lengths, select the correct size for the job in hand. Load the magazine and test the gun by firing a staple into some scrap material.

2 Position the material to be fixed. Place the staple gun over the fixing position and squeeze the trigger to fire the staple. Repeat the process to make further fixings, reloading the magazine if it runs out.

Choosing nails

The two nail types you are likely to use most frequently are oval wire nails and panel pins. For everyday fixings, keep a supply of these in a compartmentalised storage box. Buy other types of nail as and when you need them.

Oval wire nails Have an oval cross-section and a stubby head. These are the most commonly used nails. Position them with the oval parallel with the wood grain to avoid splitting the wood. Punch in the nail head and fill over it for an invisible fixing. Use these nails for securing the joints in light timber frames, and for other general woodwork jobs.
Sizes From 25 to 150mm; useful sizes to keep are 50 and 75mm.

Masonry nails Specially hardened round steel nails, used to fix wood to masonry and preferred nowadays to cut clasp nails for similar jobs. They are very hard to remove without damaging the masonry, and can shatter while being driven if not struck straight.
Sizes From 25 to 100mm.

Annular (ring-shank) nails Have a ridged shank which grips wood better than a smooth wire nail. They are used in situations where the fixing has to resist being pulled apart, and are almost impossible to remove once driven. They are particularly good for making fixings into man-made boards.
Sizes From 20 to 100mm.

Clout nails Short galvanised nails with a wide flat head, used for fixing roof tiles and slates.
Felt nails are shorter versions, which are designed for fixing roofing felt.
Sizes 50 and 75mm for clout nails and 12 and 25mm for felt nails.

Cut nails Traditional nails cut from flat metal sheet. Cut clasp nails are still used to fix wood to masonry (skirting boards, for example), while cut floor nails – also known as floor brads – are used to fix floorboards to their joists.
Sizes Various sizes are available.

Panel pins Have a round cross-section and a small flat head. As the name implies, they are used chiefly for fixing thin sheet materials to an underlying timber framework. They are also ideal for fixing timber mouldings in place, although pilot holes for the pins may be needed in small mouldings to avoid splitting the wood. Hardboard panel pins have a diamond-shaped head that is driven in flush with the board surface, and often have a coppered finish.
Sizes From 15 to 50mm; useful sizes to keep are 20, 25 and 40mm.

Plasterboard nails Have a cone-shaped head (like a countersunk screw) and a jagged shank to grip the framing to which the board is being fixed. They have a galvanised finish.
Sizes 30 and 40mm, for fixing 9.5 and 12.7mm thick plasterboard respectively.

Round wire nails Have a round cross-section and a large flat head. They are used on rough woodwork, such as the framework for a partition wall or a garden pergola.
Sizes From 25 to 150mm.

Using masonry nails

Choose a nail long enough to penetrate solid masonry to a depth of at least 25mm. Fixing a 25mm batten to a plastered wall therefore requires a nail at least 65mm long to allow for the thickness of the plaster. On bare brickwork, drive nails into the bricks, not into the mortar courses.

1 Drill pilot holes in the wood at each fixing position to accept the nail shank. Insert the nails, hold the wood in position against the wall and check that it is horizontal or vertical as required.

2 Drive in one end nail, striking its head squarely and hammering it flush with the surface of the wood.

3 Drive in the other end nail next. This ensures that the wood is not forced out of position as intermediate nails are driven in.

Using picture hooks

Picture hooks are pinned to walls with hardened steel pins, usually about 25mm long. Traditional single-pin and twin-pin metal picture hooks are designed to hold the pin at an angle to the wall surface; plastic varieties hold a group of small headless masonry pins at right angles to the wall, and may be secured by a longer pin once they are fixed in position.

1 Hold the picture on the wall where you want to hang it. Place a small spirit level on top of the frame to check that it is level, then lightly mark the positions of its top corners on the wall.

2 Place the picture face down. Mark the centre of its top edge and fit the hook to the cord. Pull the hook towards the mark until the cord is taut. Measure the distance between the top of the hook and the top of the frame.

3 On the wall, mark the centre point between the two marks made in step 1. Measure down from it the distance taken in step 2, and mark the wall there. Pin the hook in place with its top level with this mark. Hang and level the picture.

Fixing with screws

A screw is a stronger fixing device than a nail. Its thread grips the material into which it is driven, and its head secures the item being fixed. Unlike a nail, a screw can be withdrawn easily to undo the fixing.

As with nails, different types and sizes of screws are used for different jobs, but for everyday DIY you will need only a small selection. You need a screwdriver to drive screws, and to work successfully the screwdriver tip must match the size and shape of the recess in the screw head. You can drive (and remove) screws by hand, or with a cordless screwdriver or drill.

Screwing wood to wood

Start by choosing a screw with a countersunk head that is long enough to pass through the piece you are fixing, and halfway through the piece you are fixing it to. The screw head will be flush with the surface once the screw has been driven in. Screws come in different diameters called gauge numbers, but for most jobs you will need only two. Gauge 8 screws up to 50mm long will be thick enough for most jobs; use a thicker gauge 10 screw up to 75mm long for heavier-duty fixings.

1 Mark where you want the screw hole in the piece of wood you are fixing. Fit a twist drill bit the same size as the screw shank in your drill, and drill a clearance hole right through the wood. Place scrap wood beneath the workpiece so you do not drill into your workbench. See page 42 for more information about using a drill.

2 Exchange the twist drill bit for a countersink bit and drill the cone-shaped recess for the screw head in the mouth of the clearance hole. It should be as wide as the screw head.

3 Hold the piece of wood you are fixing in position over the piece you are fixing it to. Push a nail (or a bradawl if you have one) through the clearance hole you drilled in step 1 to mark the screw position on the piece below. Drill a pilot hole 2mm in diameter at the mark, to half the depth of the wood.

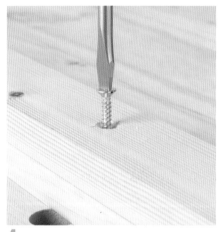

4 Reposition the two pieces of wood and insert the screw through the clearance hole in the top piece so it enters the pilot hole in the piece beneath. Tighten it fully with your screwdriver until the screw head is fully recessed in the countersunk hole.

Screwing metal to wood

Most metal fixtures – such as door handles, window catches, coat hooks and shelf supports – have countersunk holes for their fixing screws.

You can use a countersunk screw to attach them, but screws with raised countersunk heads look more attractive. They are available in brass, chrome and stainless steel, and matching screws are often supplied with the fixture.

If you have to supply your own, make sure the screw shank will pass through the clearance holes in the fixture. The screws should be long enough to pass halfway through the wood you are fixing into.

Door hinges are an exception; they are always fixed with countersunk screws.

Some metal fixtures – particularly those used out of doors, such as gate hinges – do not have countersinks, and are fixed with round-head screws. The hemispherical screw heads sit proud of the surface.

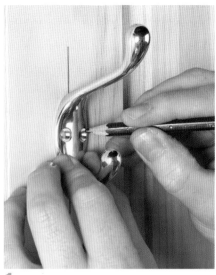

1 Decide where you are going to position the fixture. Hold the fixture in position and mark each screw position on the wood in pencil through the clearance holes.

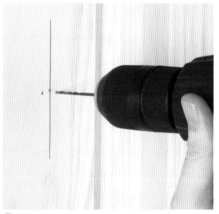

2 Drill a 2mm pilot hole at each mark, to half the thickness of the wood. If you find it difficult to gauge the depth, use a guide on the drill bit – a strip of masking tape, for example. Stop when the guide touches the wood.

3 Replace the fixture over the holes and drive in the screws. If there is more than one, only tighten them fully when you are sure the fixture is straight and level.

Screwing into metal or plastic

You may want to make a fixing into a metal or plastic surface – for example, to mount a roller blind to a uPVC window. You need a special self-tapping screw for this sort of job. The screw needs a pilot hole, and cuts its own thread as it is driven in. Self-tapping screws are made from hardened steel, and come with countersunk, raised countersunk and pan heads (the last resembles a roundhead screw, but with the head flattened).

Screwing into walls and ceilings

You cannot simply drive a screw into most walls or ceilings to make a fixing. There are two exceptions: if you have a timber-framed partition wall and the fixing position coincides with one of the vertical frame members, or if you are making a ceiling fixing directly into a joist. Otherwise you have to drill a hole and insert a special fixing device to hold the screw in place. See pages 44–45 for more details.

Using a power screwdriver

Driving screws with a power screwdriver is much quicker and easier than driving them by hand, especially when using cross-head screws. You can use a cordless drill on a slow speed setting, or buy a cordless screwdriver instead. Both tools use interchangeable screwdriver bits, which are available to fit all common screw heads. It is actually cheaper to buy a set of these bits and a cordless tool than it is to buy individual screwdrivers. You can use a power driver with slotted-head screws, but there is a greater risk of the bit slipping out of the slot and damaging the workpiece than with hand screwdriving.

1 Select the screwdriver bit to match the screw size and recess type. Fit it in the drill chuck, or use the magnetic bit holder supplied with the bits.

2 If you are using a cordless drill, set it to the screwdriving symbol and choose an intermediate torque setting (for example, 3 on a scale of 1 to 5).

3 Fit the screw into the tip of the screwdriver bit and offer it up to its pre-drilled hole.

Choosing screws

Most of the fixings you make will require countersunk screws. Traditionally, all screws had slotted heads and were driven with a flat-tip screwdriver. Today, screws are designed for driving with a power screwdriver, and their heads have a specially shaped recess to engage the screwdriver tip more positively than a flat-tip driver does in a slot. The most common recesses are cross-shaped.

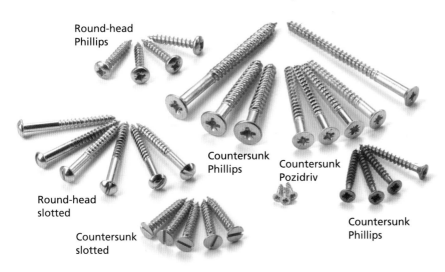

Round-head
Phillips

Round-head
slotted

Countersunk
slotted

Countersunk
Phillips

Countersunk
Pozidriv

Countersunk
Phillips

4 Start the drill or screwdriver and drive in the screw. With a cordless drill, the torque setting selected should allow the clutch to slip as the screw is tightened. If this does not happen, select a different torque setting until it does.

5 Set the screwdriver or drill to reverse to undo a screw.

Phillips These screws have a simple cross, and are found mainly in flat-pack furniture kits and on domestic appliances.

Pozidriv and Prodrive A star-shaped recess grips the screwdriver tip more securely than a slotted head. Drivers for Pozidriv and Prodrive screws are interchangeable. In each case the No 2. size will drive screws up to gauge 10.

Woodscrews Traditional woodscrews are threaded only for part of their length. Many modern countersunk screws have continuously-threaded shanks and other features such as twin threads that are designed to make them quicker and easier to drive.

For everyday use, store a small selection of Pozidriv or Prodrive countersunk woodscrews in individual containers. The most useful sizes are: 19, 25, 38 and 50mm in gauge No. 8; 50 and 75mm in gauge No. 10.

Other screw head types Raised countersunk and round-head woodscrews usually have slotted heads. Other head types you may encounter – especially in flat-pack furniture kits and on domestic appliances – include internal-hex screws with a plain hexagonal recess, driven with an Allen key; Torx screws and Uni-screws with specially shaped hexagonal recesses; Robertson screws with a square recess. Each type requires a special screwdriver.

Undoing fixings

Many DIY jobs involve undoing an existing fixing. How you go about this depends on analysing how the fixing was originally made. It also depends on whether you need to do the job with care, or whether you can take a 'wrecking' approach. Here are some of the options.

Removing old screws

In most cases, there are three things that make old screws hard to remove.
• Their heads are often over-painted, making it difficult to engage a screwdriver tip positively.
• Plain steel screws tend to corrode with time, so their screw threads grip the wood tightly and are very difficult to free.
• The screw head may have been damaged as the screw was driven in, with the result that the screwdriver tip slips out of the slot or recess as you try to undo the screw.

1 Use a pointed tool such as a bradawl or a knife to scrape paint out of the slot or recess in the screw head, so that the screwdriver tip fits it properly. Then try to undo the screw.

2 Before attempting to undo a rusty screw, place the screwdriver in the slot or recess and strike the end of the handle firmly two or three times with a hammer. This often breaks the grip of the threads in the wood and makes it easier to undo the screw. With slotted-head screws, try angling the screwdriver blade in the slot before you strike its handle. This will turn the screw slightly and should have the same effect.

3 If the screw head is damaged and the screwdriver tip will not allow any torque to be applied to it, you will have to drill it out. Fit a twist drill bit about half the diameter of the screw head in your drill. Hold it against the centre of the screw head and drill slowly into it. When you reach the screw shank, the drilled-off head will spin off on the drill shank. Continue drilling until you have completely drilled out the screw shank, and separate the components it was securing.

Alternatively You can use a screw extractor – a threaded bolt that fits the chuck of a cordless drill. It is screwed into a pilot hole drilled in the screw head, and is then reverse-driven to draw out the damaged screw.

Removing old nails

Because nails are driven flush with the surface, removing them without damaging what they are fixing is almost impossible.

1 The best approach is to try to prise away whatever the nail is securing – for example, by levering up a floorboard or pulling a skirting board away from the wall. One of two things will happen.

2 The nail head may be lifted slightly, allowing you to grip it with a claw hammer or pincers and pull it out.

3 Often the nail will not move but will tear through the material it is fixing, allowing you to remove this and then tackle the exposed nail as before. Use this approach to remove old carpet that has been tacked down, to tear hardboard off an old panelled door or to pull plasterboard away from partition walls and ceiling joists.

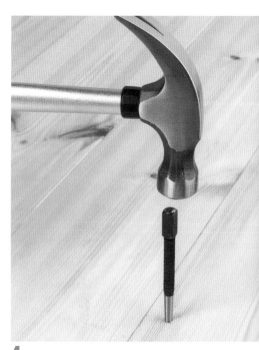

4 You can try another approach if it is not essential to remove the nail. Use a nail punch and hammer to drive the nail head through the material it is fixing so you can free it. This is the best way of lifting old floorboards that are to be saved and re-laid, as it minimises damage to the boards.

5 If large nails have been used to assemble a framework – in a partition wall that is being demolished, for example – it may be possible to free the fixings by knocking the individual joints apart. The nails are often driven in at an angle in structures of this sort, and a few carefully aimed blows with a club hammer will open up joints and make them easy to separate.

Gripping and tightening

Around the house you will have to tackle a variety of small jobs where you need to get a grip on something.

You might need to tighten up a plumbing fitting that has started to weep a little water, or to dismantle a tap to change a tap washer. If you have taken down something fixed to a wall, you may want to remove the old wallplugs and fill the holes before fixing it somewhere else. Your tool kit should contain an assortment of gripping tools to help you to improvise solutions to problems like these.

Adjustable spanners

Spanners tighten and loosen nuts and bolts, which generally have hexagonal or square heads. There are more types of spanner than almost any other tool, but you can cover yourself for most domestic jobs with a couple of adjustable spanners. These have one fixed and one movable jaw, which you adjust with a worm-drive screw.

The largest nuts you are likely to have to tackle around the house are those on plumbing fittings and connectors, which are generally between 25 and 30mm 'across the flats' – measured from opposite sides of the nut. An adjustable spanner big enough to cope with these can also be used on smaller nuts.

1 To work on a nut, open the jaws of the spanner and slip it into place.

2 Tighten the movable jaw so the spanner grips opposite flats on the nut securely.

3 Work out which way to turn the nut. A nut is screwed on in a clockwise direction, so your spanner must move in the same direction to tighten the nut, and counter-clockwise to loosen it. Use reasonable force to turn the spanner as required.

4 Some jobs need two spanners. For example, to tighten a leaking brass compression fitting joining two lengths of copper pipe, you need one spanner to grip the hexagonal ring in the middle of the fitting, and the other to tighten the leaking nut where the pipe enters it. See Chapter 10 for more information on using spanners for a variety of plumbing jobs.

Pliers

Pliers were originally designed for cutting, bending and twisting wire, and electricians use them for all those jobs when doing wiring work. However, you can use pliers for all sorts of everyday gripping jobs. Here are a few practical examples.

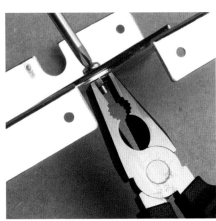

1 Use pliers to grip small nuts if you do not have a suitable spanner. For example, attaching a metal curtain track to its wall brackets may involve tightening a nut onto a small screw with a slotted head. Here pliers are ideal for holding the nut while you do up the screw with a screwdriver. Pliers will also grip a ballvalve piston while you unscrew its end cap to replace a failed washer (see page 339), and will turn off the lockshield valve on a radiator if you need to remove it (see page 376).

2 Use pliers to remove the metal base of a broken light bulb from its lampholder. Turn off the power at the mains before you do this. Then push the tip of the pliers into the base of the bulb and turn it counter-clockwise to remove the bulb base from either a bayonet or screw lampholder.

3 Use pliers to pull unwanted wallplugs out of the wall. When you have unscrewed whatever was fixed to the wall, drive the screw back into the plug for a few turns. Then grip the screw head with the pliers and pull screw and plug straight out. Fill the hole for an invisible repair.

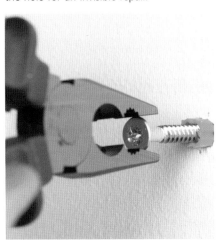

Self-locking wrench

This tool can be used as a spanner, as a wrench (for gripping round objects such as metal tubing, for example), as pliers and even as a simple clamp. The jaws can be adjusted to a range of settings, and then locked into place.

1 Close the jaws onto whatever you want to grip by squeezing the handles, and turn the adjuster screw counter-clockwise until the handles close.

2 If the workpiece is too small for the tool to lock on with the handles closed, keep squeezing the handles and turn the adjuster screw clockwise until the jaws touch the work. Operate the release lever, turn the adjuster a little more and squeeze the handles to lock the jaws onto the workpiece.

3 To release the locking action, hold the handles together and operate the release lever.

Drilling holes

There are few DIY jobs that do not involve drilling a hole at some stage. Your cordless drill is the power source for all these operations, used in conjunction with a range of drill bits and other accessories.

Get to know your drill

Cordless drills run on rechargeable batteries, and all but the cheapest come with two batteries. Make sure you know how to remove and insert the batteries, and how to operate the battery charger. Check whether the battery can be left to trickle-charge for hours, or whether it has a fixed recharge time.

Next, read the instructions. These will tell you how to select the following:
• Forward and reverse gears.
• The correct speed setting for drilling, screwdriving and, if the drill has the option, hammer action for making holes in masonry.
• The correct torque setting, which enables you to apply the optimum turning force when driving screws into different materials.
   Most cordless drills come with a carry case. Keep the drill in it when you are not using it. If you do not have a case, buy one. DIY stores stock a selection; take your drill in to test its fit before you buy.

Fitting drill bits

Select the right type of drill bit for the job you are doing (page 33).

1 Open the chuck by twisting the knurled ring and fit the end of the drill bit inside it.

2 Tighten the locking ring until you feel it start to slip. The drill bit is now secure. Select forward gear and the drilling or hammer-drilling option, and you are ready to start work.

Drilling freehand

Most people drill holes by simply pointing the drill at the surface and squeezing the trigger. With very few exceptions, drilled holes have to be at 90° to the surface.

1 If you have a good eye, check from two angles that you are holding the drill at more or less the right angle. This is good enough for many drilling jobs.

2 If you want to check the angle more accurately, hold the drill in position and set a try square against the surface you are drilling into. The drill bit should be parallel with the metal blade of the try square.

Drilling small holes in wood or metal

Fit a twist drill bit of the required diameter and select the drilling setting on the drill.

1 Secure the workpiece on your workbench, with some scrap wood underneath if you are drilling a hole right through it. This prevents you from damaging your bench jaws, and also guarantees a clean exit hole through the workpiece.

2 Hold the drill tip at the mark and check that you are holding it upright. Drill the hole through the workpiece and on into the scrap wood. In metal, withdraw the drill bit while it is still running so that it does not jam in the hole.

Drilling large holes in wood

Fit a flat wood bit of the required size and select the drilling setting on the drill.

1 Secure the workpiece on the bench with scrap wood beneath it.

2 Position the lead point of the drill bit at the mark and start drilling. As the cutting blades begin to bite and cut the hole, they will cut evenly if you are holding the drill upright. Drill on into the scrap wood, which will guarantee a clean exit hole through the workpiece.

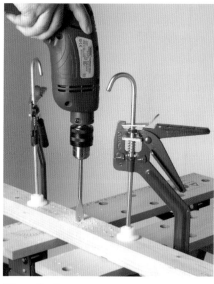

Alternatively Clamp the wood so the drill can emerge from the underside into free air. Drill the hole until the lead point just penetrates the wood. Turn it over, locate the lead point in the hole and drill out the rest of the hole. This will reduce the risk of leaving a rough exit hole. Use this technique for jobs such as fitting a cylinder lock to a front door (see page 198).

Drill bit varieties

Apart from the basic selection of drill bits outlined on page 33, you may need to buy others for specific DIY jobs.
   Long twist drills are available in lengths of up to 165mm (and 8mm in diameter). They are used for making holes in thick components such as timber-framed partition walls.
   Reduced-shank drills are available in diameters up to 20mm (most standard twist drills go up to 10 or 13mm only). They have 13mm diameter shanks to fit the maximum chuck size on most cordless drills.

Drill accessories

Apart from drilling holes, your cordless drill can do a number of other jobs if fitted with the right accessory. Here are some of the most useful.

Wire brushes
Remove rust or old paint from metal surfaces with one of these. There are two types, cups and wheels, both available in a range of sizes. Between them they will allow you to get into awkward corners as well as tackling flat surfaces. Most have a built-in spindle; some have a separate spindle called an arbor so you can fit different brushes on one spindle.

Sanding attachments
These good all-rounders allow you to carry out small-scale sanding jobs on flat surfaces if you do not have a power sander. Sanding discs fit on a stiff rubber backing disc and are held on by a washer and screw. Their only disadvantage is that they can leave swirl marks across the grain of the wood if you use too coarse a paper. Make sure you finish a job with medium or fine grades for a very smooth, unmarked surface. Paper discs are fine for sanding wood if the job is

reasonably small. For bigger jobs with wood, or with metal or masonry surfaces, choose more durable abrasive-coated metal discs instead. Coarse discs can remove material very quickly. Flap-wheel sanders have tongues of double-sided abrasive paper fixed to a centre spindle, and are good for sanding curved surfaces. Also good for curves are drum sanders. They consist of a thick disc of foam plastic, coated with abrasive paper.

Polishing pads
Take the hard work out of polishing your car's paintwork or the furniture with a lambswool pad or bonnet, which fits over the rubber backing pad of a disc sander. Foam drum polishers work in a similar way.

Paint mixers
To mix and stir paint and other mixes such as wallpaper paste and tile grout, fit one of these to your drill. They are made of plastic

or metal and will give paint or other liquids a thorough mixing. Use them only with a slow speed setting on your drill to avoid splashing.

Light-duty pump
This accessory can cope with jobs such as emptying a garden pond or mopping up after a plumbing disaster. The drill drives an impeller inside the pump casing, which has inlet and outlet spigots to take lengths of standard garden hose. Make sure you use the manufacturer's recommended setting on your drill.

Hole saws
If you have to cut a perfectly round hole in a piece of wood, the best way to do it is with a hole saw. It is a cylinder of steel with teeth at one end and a central twist drill that makes the starting hole. Hole saws can be bought singly or in sets, and can cut holes of up to 65mm in diameter. For more information, see page 50.

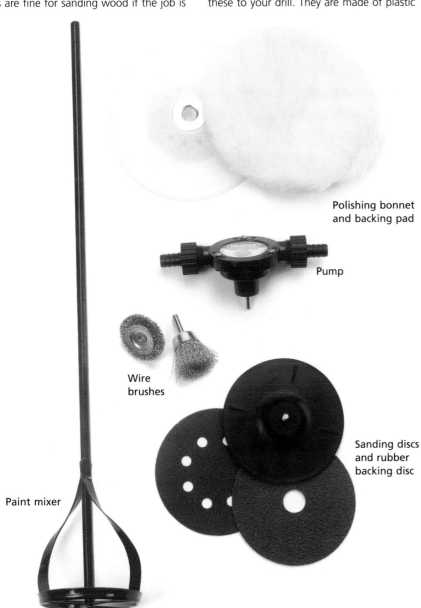

Polishing bonnet
and backing pad

Pump

Wire
brushes

Paint mixer

Sanding discs
and rubber
backing disc

AIDS TO ACCURATE DRILLING

If you do a lot of woodwork, it will be worth investing in a bench-mounted drill stand (see page 58). For everyday drilling jobs, a drill guide is a cheaper and more versatile option. It has a flat baseplate and a spring-loaded clamp to hold the drill body at 90° to the baseplate. Fit the drill in the guide and tighten the securing clamp. Press the baseplate against the surface you are drilling – wood on the workbench, or a tiled wall in the bathroom – and start drilling a perfect 90° hole. Use the centring guide to drill holes in the centre of the workpiece edge. The baseplate can also be adjusted to allow drilling at any angle between 45° and 90°, should you need this facility.

Making wall fixings

Fixing things to walls is the key part of many everyday DIY jobs, from fitting shelves and curtain tracks to putting up a mirror or hanging a display cabinet. It is an easy job as long as you use the right fixings and the correct technique. Done wrongly, the fixing will fail, with potentially serious consequences.

Assessing the job

The first step is to discover what sort of wall is involved, because this dictates how you make a fixing into it.
• Masonry walls sound solid when tapped; most exterior walls and internal ground-floor walls are of this type.
• Timber-framed internal partition walls and ceilings sound hollow, whether they are clad with plasterboard or the lath and plaster found in pre-1945 houses.
• Dry-lined masonry walls also sound hollow. This is because they have a layer of lath and plaster (in pre-1945 houses) or plasterboard on a framework of timber battens attached to the masonry, instead of solid plaster.
• Timber-framed houses have dry-lined plasterboard walls throughout.

Masonry walls

For fixings in solid masonry, you have to drill a hole in the wall and insert a hollow wallplug that will grip a screw when one is driven into it. To make a secure fixing, the plug and screw must penetrate solid masonry to a minimum depth of 25mm. On a plastered wall you must therefore make an allowance for the thickness of the plaster (about 13mm in a modern house, and up to 20mm in older houses). For heavy-duty fixings the screw must penetrate up to 40mm, so use a 50 or 63mm screw.

Choosing wallplugs

Moulded plastic wallplugs are available in a range of sizes in two main types: smooth and flanged. Smooth plugs fit entirely within the drilled hole, with the neck of the plug just below the wall surface. Flanged plugs have a surface flange that fits flush with the wall surface. Choose a plug to match the length and gauge of the screw you intend to use. The drill diameter to use will be marked on the plastic 'tree' to which the plugs are fixed, or on the packaging.

Frame plugs are moulded plastic or expanding metal wallplugs with an extended sleeve, and are designed for fixing timber door and window frames to walls.

Making the fixing

Fit a masonry drill bit of the required size in the drill chuck. Select the drilling setting (or hammer action if you have it) on the drill. If it has two speed settings, select the lower speed.

1 Measure the length of the wallplug you intend to use, and wrap a piece of visible tape round the drill bit to act as a depth mark. Position it at a distance of 5mm plus the plug length from the tip of the bit.

2 Press the tip of the bit against the wall where you plan to drill and check by eye that the drill is at right angles to the surface.

3 Start the drill and apply firm pressure to drill out the hole. On deep holes, withdraw the bit once or twice so the flutes on the drill bit can clear dust from the hole.

4 Drill until the tape reaches the wall surface. Then withdraw the bit while the drill is still running to clear drill dust from the hole.

5 Insert the wallplug to check that it will fit. Pass the screw through whatever you are fixing and drive it into the wallplug. If the plug turns in the hole as you tighten the screw you have made the hole too large and the fixing will fail. Pull the plug out and fit a larger one.

Using frame plugs

These plugs come in a range of sizes to suit different frame thicknesses. They are sold complete with long wood screws or special hammer-in screws.

1 Set the frame in position and mark the locations of the fixings. If possible, ensure that they will be made into solid masonry, not into the mortar joints between courses.

2 Choose a twist drill bit to match the diameter of the frame plug. Select drilling and high speed on your drill. Drill a clearance hole through the frame at each fixing location. Stop drilling and withdraw the still-rotating drill bit to clear the debris.

3 Switch to a masonry drill bit of the same diameter. Select hammer action (if you have it) and low speed on your drill. Measure the length of the frame plug, and wrap a piece of tape round the drill bit to act as a depth mark. Position it at a distance of 5mm plus the plug length from the tip of the bit.

4 Insert the drill bit through the clearance hole until it touches the masonry, and start drilling the hole there. Withdraw the drill bit at intervals to clear the debris. Drill until the tape depth stop reaches the surface of the frame.

5 Insert the frame plug and tap it fully home with a hammer so its flange is flush with the frame. Drive in the wood screw or the hammer-in screw to complete the fixing.

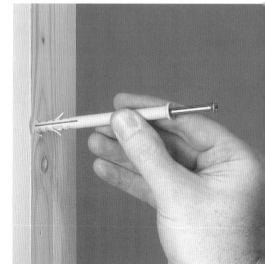

Partition walls and ceilings

You can make fixings into internal partition walls and ceilings in one of two ways.
• Locate the wall frame members (the studs) or the ceiling joists, and screw through the cladding into solid timber. To do this, you need to use an electronic joist detector, or make some test drillings through the cladding. In modern houses, wall studs and ceiling joists are at 400mm centres. In older houses the spacings may be as wide as 450mm or even 600mm.
• If the stud or joist positions do not coincide with where you want to make your fixings, drill a hole in the cladding and insert a cavity fixing device that will expand and grip the inner face of the cladding. The device must be strong enough to support the load on the fixing.

Choosing cavity fixings

A wide range of cavity fixings is available, made from moulded plastic or metal. The fixing is inserted through a hole in the wall cladding, and a wood screw (or the machine screw supplied with the fixing) is tightened into it. This draws up and compresses part of the fixing against the inner face of the wall cladding, providing a firm grip for the screw. The fixing remains in place in the wall if the screw is removed.

Spring toggles (right) have two spring-loaded wings that flip outwards once the fixing is inserted, to grip the inner face of the wall cladding. The toggle is lost in the cavity if the screw is removed.

Cavity fixings are sold as suitable for light, medium or heavy loads. As a general rule, use plastic or metal screw-in fixings (above) for light loads. Use plastic anchor fixings or spring toggles for medium loads, and metal anchor fixings for heavy loads such as a wall cabinet or radiator. The metal anchor fixing has four wings that grip against the inner face of the wall cladding as the machine screw is tightened.

Making the fixing

You can drill through plasterboard or lath-and-plaster with a twist drill bit. Match the drill size to the fixing you are using. Select the drilling setting on your drill, and high speed on a two-speed drill.

1 Press the tip of the drill bit into the surface and check by eye that the drill is at right angles to the surface. Drill until the drill bit breaks through the cladding, and withdraw it while it is still rotating to clear debris from the hole.

2 Push the fixing into the hole until its flange is flush with the surface. Remove the machine screw if one is supplied (except for spring toggles).

3 Pass the machine screw (or wood screw) through whatever you are fitting. Drive the screw into the fixing and tighten it fully.

Spring toggles

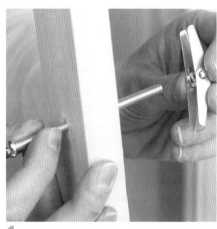

1 Do not put a spring toggle straight into its hole. Instead, remove the machine screw and pass this through whatever you are fitting.

2 Reattach the toggle to the screw, fold up its wings and push them through the hole. Check that the wings have opened by pulling on the fixing, then tighten the screw fully.

Dry-lined walls

Dry-lined walls have a cavity 25–40mm wide between the lining and the solid masonry behind. How you make a fixing depends on the load to be supported. For lightweight items you can use plastic or metal screw-in fixings, as for partition walls. Medium-weight items need a cavity anchor, but the cavity depth restricts the types of fixing you can use. Heavyweight items must be supported on fixings made into the masonry using a long screw and wallplug. The best type is a frame plug long enough to pass through wall cladding and cavity, and penetrate masonry by about 40mm.

Making the fixing

Use a twist drill to match the diameter of the frame plug to make a hole in the wall cladding at the fixing location. Then switch to a long masonry drill bit of the same size and wrap tape round it to indicate the total drilling depth (cladding plus cavity plus 40mm). Select drilling (or hammer action if your drill has it) and slow speed.

1 Insert the masonry drill bit through the hole in the wall cladding and check that it is at right angles to the surface.

2 Drill the hole to the depth indicated by your tape depth stop. Withdraw the drill bit from time to time to clear the hole of debris, which will fall into the cavity.

3 Insert the frame plug and check that its flange fits flush with the surface of the wall cladding. Pass the screw through whatever you are fixing and drive it into the plug.

Timber-framed houses

In a timber-framed house, internal walls are timber-framed partitions and you should make fixings into them as described, left. External walls are lined with plasterboard, but behind this is a vapour barrier and a layer of glass fibre insulation. Fixings should be made into the vertical timber frame members wherever possible. Otherwise use cavity fixings, as for other partition walls.

Fixings in external walls

Use a twist drill bit to match the size of the fitting. Select drilling and high speed on the drill. Press the tip of the drill bit into the wall surface and check by eye that the drill is at right angles to the surface.

Drill until the drill bit just breaks through the wall cladding. If you drill any deeper, you will penetrate the vapour barrier and the drill bit will pull tufts of insulation out of the hole. Insert the cavity fixing and screw whatever you are fitting into place.

Making good

Making good means restoring something to its original state, and it is a task that is involved in many everyday DIY jobs. Woodwork can be dented or split. Plaster can crack or come away from the surface beneath. Gaps can open up where skirting boards and architraves meet the wall. All these defects need making good, using the appropriate filler or sealant and the right tools. The basic techniques for making good minor defects are described here; for more details, see pages 78–79.

Choosing fillers

There is a daunting array of fillers available in DIY stores, ranging from traditional dry powder that you mix with water, to ready-mixed products in tubes, tubs, tins and cartridges. Powder fillers can be kept for a long time if they are stored in dry conditions, but ready-mixed fillers have a finite shelf life. Buy them only if you have a lot of filling to do in a short space of time, and are likely to use up most of the filler.

You need three basic types of filler for everyday DIY – a filler for wood, a filler for plaster and a filler for gaps. So-called 'all-purpose' fillers are available, but as with all products of this type their performance is a compromise. They will fill anything adequately, but you will get better results with a one-job filler designed specifically for its purpose.

FILLERS FOR WOODWORK

Most of the woodwork round the house will be painted or varnished, and unless it is brand new will need to have dents and scratches filled before being finished.
• If the wood is to be painted over, standard wood filler in a tub will be adequate. Some are white and others come in a neutral woody colour.
• If you are filling wood that is stained or varnished, you need a matching filler – called wood stopping. It comes in a range of colours, and you can mix in a little woodstain to get a perfect match.
• A specialist filler is linseed oil putty – used for fixing glass into wooden window frames. Soft enough to allow the glass to be bedded into it, it sets rock hard and can be painted after a fortnight.

Repairing woodwork

Existing woodwork, whether painted or varnished, can become dented or chipped from everyday wear and tear. These defects need filling before the surface is given a new finish. Use interior wood filler on woodwork that will be painted, and wood stopper in a matching wood shade for woodwork that will be varnished.

There are also two-part products for really tough filling jobs. They consist of a basic filler and a chemical hardening agent. You add a small amount of the hardening agent to activate the ingredients of the filler, to start the setting process. This type of filler is particularly good for repairing damage caused by rot.

1 Sand the damaged area with fine wet-and-dry abrasive paper. This will smooth any rough edges to the damage, and will key the surface so that the filler will bond better to it. Wipe away any dust with kitchen roll moistened with white spirit.

2 Use your filling knife to press wood filler or stopper into the damage, leaving it a little proud of the surrounding surface. Leave it to set hard.

3 Sand the filled area smooth with fine abrasive paper, then wipe away dust with kitchen roll as in step 1. The repair is now ready for redecorating.

Repairing plaster

The plaster on your walls and ceilings is a hard but fairly brittle material, so it may develop cracks or dents if it is knocked. It will also crack if the structure to which it is stuck moves, as often happens with the plaster on timber-framed walls and ceilings.

Use a ready-mixed wall filler for repairing small cracks and dents, and ready-mixed plaster for patching larger areas. To fill gaps where a hard-setting filler keeps falling out, use a non-setting mastic sealant instead (see Filling gaps, opposite).

1 To fill a surface crack in plaster, rake out loose material with the blade of your filling knife, leaving only the sound plaster.

2 Use an old paintbrush to brush out any dust remaining in the crack. It is important to make the area as clean as possible.

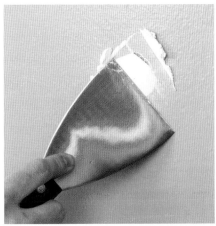

3 Load some filler onto your knife and draw the blade firmly across the crack to press the filler into it. Repeat as necessary to fill the entire length of the crack, then draw the blade along it to smooth off any excess filler.

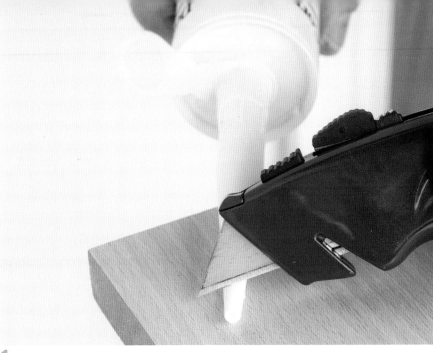

1 Once you have chosen which sealant or mastic is suitable for the job, cut the nozzle of the cartridge at an angle so it will extrude a bead of mastic a little wider than the gap you need to fill.

4 Hold the nozzle at 45° to the crack and draw the nozzle along it, squeezing the trigger to maintain a steady flow of mastic. The flow rate should match the speed of the nozzle as you move it along the gap. Do not leave any gaps. If you do, go back and fill them.

4 Allow the filler to set hard, then sand the surface by hand or with a power sander, using fine abrasive paper. Dust off any fine particles. The surface is now ready for redecoration.

Filling gaps

Houses are full of problem gaps – where walls and ceilings meet, along the join between skirting boards or architraves and walls, around window frames and along the back edges of kitchen worktops.

They are difficult to fill with conventional hard-setting fillers because the gap expands or contracts as temperature and humidity changes, and this cracks the filler.

A non-setting mastic bonds to both surfaces and stretches to accommodate the movement. Different types are available for different jobs, but an acrylic decorator's mastic or sealant is ideal for most interior filling jobs in areas that will remain dry. Apply it with a cartridge gun. It comes in white only but can be painted over.

For areas that get damp, such as a bathroom or kitchen, there is a waterproof silicone sealant that is claimed by its manufacturer to last for up to 30 years. It is white, and can be painted over if desired.

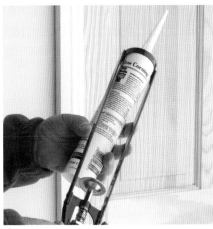

2 Most cartridges are made to fit a standard gun, so once you have the gun, all you need each time is the appropriate cartridge. Insert the cartridge in the gun and pump the trigger until the plunger touches the base of the cartridge.

3 Gently squeeze the trigger. This will push the plunger down through the cartridge and begin to force mastic out of the nozzle.

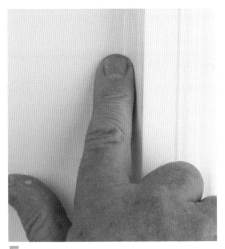

5 When you have filled the gap, press the piston release lever on the gun to stop the flow of mastic. Smooth the surface of the mastic with a clean, wetted fingertip. When the mastic has hardened sufficiently, you can paint over it.

Power tool basics

Many DIY tools need sharp blades or powerful motors to be able to do their jobs properly. This means that they can cause injury if they are not used correctly and with care. Never bypass or deactivate any safety guard fitted to the tool.

Using a jigsaw

A jigsaw with a 400-500 watt motor is adequate for most DIY tasks, though you may want extra power when you discover how useful this tool is.

A jigsaw will cut wood, man-made boards and several other materials if it is fitted with the correct type of blade. You can buy a basic model very cheaply. Key features to look out for are variable speed, an adjustable soleplate so you can make cuts at angles other than 90°, and some means of collecting or extracting sawdust – either a dust bag or an adaptor so you can connect it to a vacuum cleaner. Some jigsaws now feature blade clamps that do not need tools. If the saw is not sold with a carry and storage case, you can buy one from DIY stores to keep the tool safe when you are not using it.

Making a short cut

Select the right blade for the job and fit it in the blade clamp. Secure whatever you are sawing to the workbench with a clamp, or by holding it in the bench jaws. The saw will tend to snatch at the workpiece if you simply hold it with your free hand.

1 You can make short cuts freehand – for example, to cut a wall batten or a piece of skirting board to length. Mark the cutting line and rest the front of the saw's soleplate on the edge of the workpiece.

2 Start the saw at a slow speed and move it forwards so that the blade starts to cut just on the waste side of the cutting line. Make sure the soleplate is flat on the surface of the workpiece.

3 As the cut proceeds, increase the saw speed and check that you are keeping the blade on line. As you complete the cut, support the off-cut with your free hand. Stop the saw as soon as the blade is free.

CHOOSING JIGSAW BLADES

Blades for cutting wood and man-made boards come in fine, medium and coarse versions; the closer the teeth, the finer the cut. The maximum cutting depth is usually between 50 and 75mm, depending on the blade. Wood-cutting blades will also cut plastic sheet materials. You need extra-fine blades for cutting metal, and there are also special blades available for cutting ceramic tiles and glass-reinforced plastics (GRP). Check that any blades you buy are compatible with your make of saw; not all are interchangeable between brands.

Making a long straight cut

Because the saw blade is narrow, it can wander off-line on long, straight cuts made freehand. On thick materials, there is also a tendency for the blade to deform under load, giving a cut that is not at 90° to the surface of the workpiece. To prevent the first problem, use a saw guide. To counteract the second, let the saw cut at its own speed rather than forcing it.

1 If the jigsaw is supplied with a side fence – a tee-shaped bar projecting from the side of the soleplate – you can use it to make cuts up to about 150mm from the edge of the workpiece. Clamp the fence in the required position and make a test cut on some scrap wood to check the setting.

2 Position the saw so the blade is aligned with the cutting line and the fence lies against the edge of the wood.

3 Move the saw forwards as the cut proceeds, keeping the fence against the edge of the workpiece. Allow the blade to run out of the cut at the far end.

Using a guide batten

To make a cut further from the edge of the workpiece than the fence will allow, use a guide batten. This is a strip of wood clamped across the workpiece to guide the edge of the saw's soleplate along the cut.

1 Mark the cutting line, align the saw blade with it and place the batten next to the side of the soleplate.

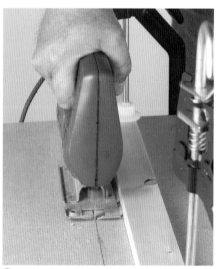

2 When you are happy with its position, clamp it to the workpiece and check that the clamps will not interfere with the travel of the saw. Make the cut by running the edge of the soleplate against the batten.

Making a curved cut

Mark the cutting line on the workpiece. Avoid starting a curved cut at the edge; the blade will skate off it as you try to start the cut. Instead, drill a hole in the waste area large enough to admit the saw blade and begin the cut there.

1 Start the cut as for a straight cut, positioning the blade on the waste side of the cutting line. Move the saw forward at its own speed – don't attempt to push it – following the cutting line by eye.

2 Cut more slowly on sharp curves, turning the saw body gradually so the blade can follow it closely. In this instance, the curve was a continuation of a straight cut, so no starter hole was required.

Making an internal cut-out

Mark the cut-out on the workpiece; if you are cutting a square or a rectangle, draw a line in from each corner at 45°. You will be placing the point of the drill bit on this line.

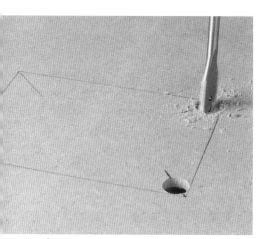

1 If you use a 16mm spade bit, place the point of the bit at least 8mm into the waste area from the corner, on the 45° line. Drill all four holes.

2 Insert the saw blade and rest the soleplate on the workpiece. Follow the cutting line to the next drill hole for straight cuts, or carry on cutting round a curve.

3 At the next corner, let the saw blade run right into the angle. Then turn the blade in the drill hole and start the next straight cut. Repeat at the third corner to run the saw back to your starting point.

4 Use abrasive paper to smooth the edges of the cut and to square up the internal corners.

Using a power sander

A random-orbit sander will cope with most everyday sanding jobs. You can buy a basic tool quite cheaply.

Key features to look for are a 125mm diameter sanding pad, a locking switch for continuous operation, and some form of dust extraction via a dust bag or vacuum cleaner attachment. Most sanders now use touch-and-close (Velcro) fastenings to attach the abrasive discs to the sanding pad. However, these are comparatively expensive.

CHOOSING ABRASIVES

The sanding discs for this type of sander use aluminium oxide grit as the abrasive, bonded to a strong backing fabric. If the sander has a through-the-pad dust extraction system, the sheets have holes in them that coincide with holes in the sanding pad, allowing the machine to draw dust up through the pad as you work. Make sure that the discs you buy are compatible with your make of sander; not all brands are interchangeable.

There is a range of disc grades, from coarse, for fast removal of material, to extra fine for finishing work. Some brands use a numbering system to indicate the coarseness of the abrasive grit; the lower the number, the coarser the grit. Typical figures are 180 (coarse), 240 (medium) and 400 (fine).

Sanding without scratches

A random-orbit sander is the simplest of all power tools to use. Its action is designed to leave no scratch marks on the surface of wood when used with a fine grade abrasive disc.

1 Select the correct grade of abrasive disc for the finish you want to achieve, and attach it to the sanding pad so the holes in disc and pad are aligned. Press the disc firmly into place on the pad.

2 Connect the sander to the hose of your vacuum cleaner using the adaptor provided, and switch the vacuum cleaner on. Alternatively, fit the dust bag if the tool has one.

3 Hold the disc against the surface you want to sand and switch on the power. Keep the sander moving backwards and forwards over the surface.

4 Be prepared to switch discs as you work to achieve the finish you want. For example, you may need to start with a coarse disc to remove an old surface finish, followed by medium and then fine discs to create a perfectly smooth surface.

Woodworking tools

These are the tools you will need if you plan to be more than an occasional weekend woodworker, cutting a wall batten to size or trimming the odd shelf to length. It complements the basic tool kit described on pages 30–33, and can be built up tool by tool as your woodworking horizons expand.

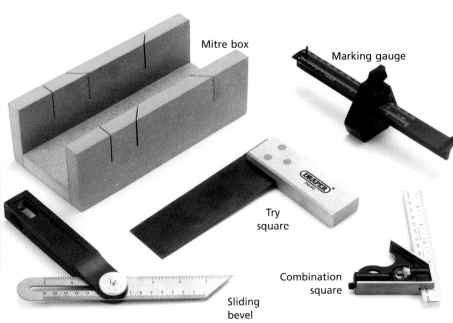

Mitre box

Marking gauge

Try square

Combination square

Sliding bevel

Tools for marking

Marking gauge
This tool consists of a wooden beam with a hardened steel pin set into it near one end, and a wooden block that slides along the beam and can be secured to it with a thumbscrew. The pin scribes a line at a fixed distance from the edge of the workpiece. It is used when marking out woodworking joints, and is also useful for jobs such as centring locks on door edges and marking the depth of hinge recesses.

Mitre box
A three-sided open-ended box with guide slots pre-cut in its opposite sides, used to guide a tenon saw blade when making 45° mitre cuts. The size of the box restricts the size of pieces that can be cut with it.

Try square and combination square
A try square has a rectangular metal blade fixed at 90° to a wooden, metal or plastic stock. It is an essential tool for marking a cutting line at right angles to the edge of a workpiece, and is also used for checking internal and external angles. A combination square is a variation on the theme, with a movable stock that can be used to mark 45° angles as well as right angles.

Sliding bevel
This tool is a sort of adjustable try square with a metal blade that can be set at any angle and locked in place with a wing nut. It is particularly useful for fitting shelves in out-of-square alcoves, and for fitting staircase balusters.

Tools for sawing

Circular saw
A circular saw is essential if you plan to cut up sheets of man-made boards, fit your own kitchen worktops or lay floorboards. A circular saw makes accurate, straight cuts, and its tilting soleplate can be set to allow cuts at any angle between 45° and 90°.

A basic circular saw takes blades 150mm in diameter and has a maximum cutting depth of about 45mm. Larger and more powerful semi-professional models take blades 190mm or 230mm in diameter, offering cutting depths of 65mm and 80mm respectively at 90° and 45 or 60mm at 45°. Some have a dust extraction facility.

Blades are available for fine cutting, cross cutting and rip cutting wood and man-made boards, and for cutting laminated chipboard kitchen worktops. Check that any blades you buy are compatible with your make of saw.

Coping saw
Designed for making curved cuts in wood and boards, it has a slim replaceable blade mounted in a U-shaped steel frame with a handle at one side. The frame holds the blade in tension, and allows the blade to be rotated to prevent the frame from fouling the edge of the workpiece.

Hole saw
This attachment for a power drill is used to cut holes in wood and boards that are larger than the maximum size of a flat wood bit (around 38mm). The blade is a short length of saw formed into a cylinder and fitted into a blade holder. This carries a pilot drill at its centre which starts the hole and guides the saw blade into the wood. Hole saws are sold in sets of several blades, up to about 75mm in diameter.

Mitre saw
This useful tool consists of a framed saw with a fine-toothed blade mounted on guide bars over a steel base. The guide bars can be rotated to position the saw at any angle between 45° and 90° to the workpiece, which is clamped in place between the blade and the base while the cut is made. It is more accurate than a mitre box, and can cut wider components.

Padsaw
The padsaw has a short tapered blade fitted into a handle, and is used mainly for cutting holes in the centre of the workpiece, such as a keyhole in a door. You need a starter hole so you can insert the blade and start the cut.

Panel saw
The panel saw has a plain steel blade about 560mm long, typically with around 10 teeth per inch (tpi), fitted to a wooden or plastic handle. As its name implies, it is used mainly for cutting up panels of man-made boards by hand, as a low-cost alternative to using a circular saw. The blade may be PTFE-coated to minimise friction, and the best saws have hard-point teeth that will stay sharp for longer than standard teeth. Fit the blade guard when storing the saw.

Circular saw

Panel saw

Coping saw

Hole saw and blade holder

Padsaw

Hole saw blades

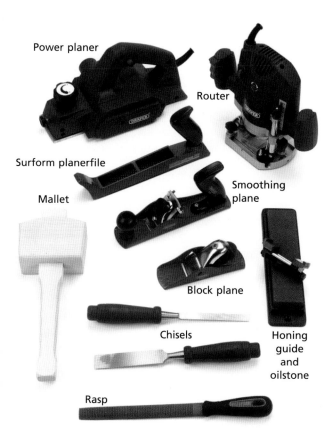

Power planer

Router

Surform planerfile

Mallet

Smoothing plane

Block plane

Chisels

Honing guide and oilstone

Rasp

Tools for shaping

Chisels

Chisels are essential for cutting many woodworking joints. They also chop out slots (mortises) for door locks, form recesses for hinges and do all sorts of general paring and shaping jobs. To start with, buy a set of bevel-edge chisels in 6, 12, 19 and 25mm sizes, ideally contained in a storage case so they do not get muddled up with other tools in your tool box. Keep the plastic blade guards on their tips when they are not in use. To keep the blades sharp, you will need an oilstone and some light machine oil. A honing guide will help you to sharpen them at the correct angle.

Mallet

This wooden hammer with a square beechwood head is used mainly for striking chisel handles when cutting woodworking joints, and for assembling joint components.

Planes and power planers

The bench plane is the traditional tool for reducing wood to the cross-sectional size you want, and for finishing it with flat, smooth edges. It consists of a steel blade held at an angle to the tool's soleplate in an adjustable mount. The small block plane and the larger smoothing plane are most widely used.

The power planer does the work of a bench plane much more quickly. It has a rotating cylinder into which a replaceable cutting blade is fitted, and can be used to remove up to 2–3mm of wood in each pass of the tool. It can also cut rebates when fitted with a detachable guide, and the groove in its soleplate allows it to chamfer edges too.

Router

The router is a power tool with a motor that drives a cutter at very high speed. Straight cutters produce slots and grooves; shaped cutters create a wide range of edge mouldings. The tool is mounted on a baseplate on springs, allowing it to be 'plunged' into the work to a pre-set depth. Edge and circle guides allow the tool to follow the shape of the workpiece or to cut circular recesses. Many routers now feature dust extraction, and come with a few router bits. Extra bits can be bought singly or in sets as required.

Rasp

This tool is a coarse file used for shaping wood, especially curved surfaces. Buy a half-round rasp with one flat and one curved surface, which will shape convex and concave curves.

Surforms

The Surform range of shaping tools all have perforated blades that work like a miniature cheese grater, removing wood in a series of fine shavings. The range includes planes and files in several styles; the planerfile with its reversible handle is the most versatile. The blades are all replaceable when blunt.

Honing guide and oilstone

This wheeled guide holds a chisel or plane blade at the correct angle while it is being sharpened on an oilstone. It also holds it square to the surface of the stone. The oilstone is made of natural or synthetic abrasive material and usually has a fine and a coarse face; it is lubricated with light machine oil.

Workbench tools

Bench hook

This simple wooden bench aid is used to hold small workpieces on the workbench, for example when cutting them to length with a tenon saw (see page 33). The hook is positioned on the workbench with the lower batten against its front edge. The workpiece is held against the upper batten.

Clamps

Clamps come in many different styles and sizes, and are used for two main jobs. The first is holding workpieces securely on the workbench while they are cut, drilled or shaped. The second is clamping components such as woodworking joints together while the adhesive sets. G-clamps and screw clamps are traditional designs, but fast-action trigger clamps and spring clamps are quicker and easier to use.

Drill stand

This bench aid clamps your power drill in an upright position on your workbench, making it easy to drill holes in workpieces at precisely 90° to the work surface – something that is difficult to judge accurately by eye. The running drill is moved up and down in the stand with a lever, and the depth of drilling can be pre-set to create stopped holes if required. Take your drill with you when buying a stand, so you can check that it will fit. You can also get a dowelling jig which allows you to drill correctly aligned holes for the three most common dowel sizes (6, 8 and 10mm).

Glue gun

This mains-powered tool dispenses blobs of hot-melt adhesive at the squeeze of a trigger, and is invaluable when assembling woodworking joints. The adhesive comes in sticks which you insert into the back of the gun. They are melted and extruded from the nozzle when you squeeze the trigger.

Vice

You can grip large workpieces in the jaws of your portable workbench. However, for smaller items it is useful to have a bench-mounted vice, which you can attach to the workbench as needed. Traditional metal workshop vices are clamped in place; you can also buy a lightweight resin vice that fits into the holes in your workbench jaws.

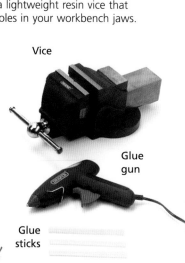

Drill stand

Bench hook

Vice

Glue gun

Clamps

Glue sticks

Choosing and buying wood

The basic raw materials for most DIY woodworking projects are softwood – cut from coniferous trees such as pine and spruce – and man-made boards. Hardwood from deciduous trees such as oak, beech, teak and mahogany is expensive and harder to work than softwood, and is used mainly for making furniture. However, hardwood mouldings are widely available, and are popular because they hold detail better than the softwood equivalent.

Softwood

Softwood is not only easy to work, but it almost invariably comes from renewable sources, so is not depleting valuable stocks of rare woods or destroying forests.

Buying softwood
You can buy softwood from DIY stores or from local timber merchants. Wood from timber merchants is generally cheaper, and they are much more welcoming to the do-it-yourselfer than they used to be. They also stock a wider range of wood types and sizes.

However, for small amounts of wood, the convenience of the DIY store probably outweighs the extra cost involved.

Softwood sizes
Softwood is available in sawn and planed finishes, in a range of cross-sections that are described in millimetres but are still commonly referred to by their imperial equivalents – 2 x 1in equals 50 x 25mm, for example.

It is important to realise that the quoted sizes are the actual dimensions of the wood when it leaves the sawmill. A piece of sawn wood described as 100 x 50mm will be that size, give or take a millimetre or so to allow for shrinkage. Planing the rough-sawn wood removes from 3mm to 6mm from each dimension, so a piece of planed wood described as 100 x 50mm (its nominal size) will actually measure about 95 x 47mm in cross-section.

To avoid mistakes when you are building things in wood, get into the habit of using the measured size of the wood you are using, rather than the nominal size, when working out dimensions.

Commonly available widths for softwood are 25, 38, 50, 75, 100, 150 and 225mm (the last usually available only in Parana pine). Common thicknesses are 12, 19, 25, 38 and 50mm.

Softwood is sold in lengths that are multiples of 300mm (known as a metric foot, and about 5mm shorter than the old imperial one). Commonly available lengths are 1.8, 2.4 and 3m.

Structural timbers such as floor joists are available in longer lengths.

Softwood faults
When buying softwood, check it for faults. The most serious is warping, where the wood is bent or twisted along its length.

This can be disguised when wood is sold in bundles, as in many DIY stores. Do not be afraid to open bundles and examine individual lengths before you buy, because warped wood is useless for most projects. Try to hold the timber at eye level, and look along its length to check for warping. It helps to have someone with you, to hold the other end.

Other faults that can spoil softwood are excessive knots – especially dead ones where the heart of the knot has fallen out – and end splits (called shakes).

Reject any wood with these faults because you will find you cannot use it when you get it home.

Hardwood

Hardwood is used in the home mainly in the form of decorative mouldings and as veneers on man-made boards. If you want a particular hardwood as an alternative to softwood – for shelves or a windowsill, for example – look for a specialist timber merchant in your local *Yellow Pages*.

Man-made boards

Man-made boards allow you to use wood wider than that available from any tree. There are two main types: boards made from real wood, glued together in thin veneers or solid strips, and boards made from ground-up wood chips or fibres bonded together into a uniform sheet. Each has its uses, its advantages and disadvantages.

Buying man-made boards
Boards of all types are available from DIY stores and timber merchants. As with softwood, timber merchants are generally cheaper and stock a wider range of types and board sizes.

The standard board size for all types is 2440 x 1220mm, a straightforward conversion from the old imperial 8 x 4ft sheet. Most board types are also available in smaller sizes, equal to one half or one quarter of a full-sized sheet (nominally 2440 x 610mm and 1220 x 610mm), and also in 1830 x 610mm panels.

So-called furniture panels – mainly plastic-faced or veneered chipboard (see opposite) intended for shelving and making kitchen cabinets – are now made in metric sizes which are fractionally smaller than their imperial-based equivalents.

Real wood boards

The oldest of the man-made boards is plywood. Blockboard is little used today, its place in the woodworker's stockroom taken by timberboard (also known as stripwood).

Plywood Sheets that consist of a number of thin wood veneers called plies, bonded together with adhesive. The grain direction

in each layer is at right angles to that of its neighbours, resulting in a board that is stable and equally strong in either direction. The grain direction of the outer plies (there is always an odd number) runs the length of the board.

The board surface is smooth, but the edges tend to splinter when cut and can be difficult to finish neatly.

Exterior-grade (WBP) plywood is made with waterproof adhesives, and is used in damp situations indoors (such as under ceramic floor tiles) as well as for outdoor structures.

Plywood with decorative hardwood outer veneers is used for making furniture and cladding flush doors.

Blockboard A board with a core of softwood strips bonded together edge to edge, and finished with one or two veneer plies on each face.

Blockboard is stronger along the length of the board than across it. It is used mainly for making decorative veneered door blanks, and is hard to find in board form. It is very expensive.

Timberboard A composite board made by gluing together parallel softwood strips to form wide boards suitable for shelving, table tops and worktops as an alternative to blockboard.

The boards are usually 18mm thick, and are intended for staining and varnishing.

Fibreboard and particle board

Hardboard and chipboard were once the most widely used board types, but medium-density fibreboard (known to everyone as MDF) has now taken its place for many DIY projects.

Hardboard Made from heavily-compressed wood fibres, with one smooth surface and one with a mesh texture. It is widely available in just one thickness: 3mm.

Hardboard has little strength, and is mainly used to form the back panels of cabinets and bookcases and the bases of

drawers (especially in its white plastic-faced form). It is also used for jobs such as boxing in pipes or lining timber floors where the strength of the board is unimportant. It is possible to get perforated hardboard, which is useful in workshops where tools are to be kept on the wall. Hooks fitted into the holes at the appropriate spots can make a place for every tool.

Also available is oil-tempered hardboard, which is stronger and denser and can be used outdoors.

Chipboard Also known as particle board. Chipboard consists of wood chips bonded together with resins. It has relatively smooth surfaces but rough, crumbly edges that are difficult to finish neatly.

Chipboard is commonly available in 12 and 18mm thicknesses. It is a heavy and dense board that blunts tools quickly, because of its high resin content. It is not as strong as plywood and has poor load-bearing strength – chipboard shelves always tend to sag unless they are well supported – and is mainly used in its plastic-faced form for kitchen units and flat-pack furniture, and in plain 22mm thick sheets for flooring.

Extra-thick 28 and 38mm chipboard forms the core of laminated kitchen worktops.

Medium-density fibreboard (MDF) Made from fine wood fibres bonded together with resin under high pressure to create a board with a fine, even texture and smooth faces and edges. MDF is easier to cut and shape than other board types, and is now widely used for all indoor panel work as well as a wide range of flat-pack furniture.

It is available in 6, 9, 12 and 18mm thicknesses. Cutting, drilling and sanding the board produces a fine dust that can be unpleasant to inhale, so it is advisable to wear a face mask when working with it.

Wood mouldings

Most of the wood used in woodworking is square or rectangular in cross section. Mouldings are made by machining wood to create a variety of other cross sections.

Many of these are used for structural jobs as diverse as making windows and doors and forming skirting boards and wall cladding. Other mouldings are purely decorative, being used to edge boards, to cover gaps or to trim and finish things like built-in furniture.

Structural mouldings are generally relatively large in section and machined from softwood, although hardwood versions are available at a price. They include skirting boards, architraves, dado and picture rails, staircase handrails and balusters, windowsills and wall cladding. You can also buy structural mouldings machined from MDF and factory-primed ready for painting. They have well-finished edges and are free from knots, warping and other defects.

Decorative mouldings are machined from hardwoods such as ramin, and include small trim mouldings in quadrant, scotia, half-round and corner profiles.

Embossed trim mouldings are created by impressing decorative designs onto the face of pre-machined mouldings.

Measuring and marking wood

The first step in making anything using wood or a man-made board is to measure and mark your workpiece so that you can cut it to size. Take as much care with this as with every other stage in the woodworking process; making a mistake at the start can spoil the entire job.

Starting square

You can generally assume that man-made boards have edges that are square to each other. The same applies to the ends of sawn and planed softwood. However, wood or board offcuts in your workshop may not have square ends or edges, and it is very important to square them up before using them.

1 To check whether an end or edge is square, hold the stock of your try square against the adjacent edge and align the blade with the edge you are checking.

2 If it is not square, move the try square away from the corner by about 5mm and mark a line across the workpiece against the try-square blade with a trimming knife or a sharp pencil.

3 On softwood, use the try square and marker to continue the squared line onto the other faces of the workpiece. The line on the fourth face should meet up with the one on the first face.

4 Cut off the waste to leave a perfectly square end or edge (see facing page).

Measuring

Use a steel ruler for measurements of less than about 300mm, and a tape measure for longer measurements. Always work in millimetres, even if you prefer to think in imperial sizes; it is only too easy to get confused with fractions of an inch, but an exact measurement in millimetres is extremely accurate.

1 Align the end of the ruler with the squared-up end of the workpiece, or hook the end of the tape over the end and extend it as required. Make sure that your eye is vertically above the figure on the ruler or tape that you want to use, and mark the workpiece at that point with a knife or pencil.

2 Hold the try square with its blade aligned with the mark, and square the cutting line across the face of the workpiece. On softwood, continue the line round the workpiece as in step 3, left.

Multiple components

Every saw cut you make removes a small amount of wood, equal to the width of the saw teeth. If you want four pieces of wood each 300mm long and you mark up four successive cutting lines 300mm apart on a length of softwood, each piece will be marginally shorter than 300mm when you cut it off. To avoid this, always mark and cut each component before marking and cutting the next.

You must also allow for the width of the saw cut when marking out man-made boards, ready for cutting into a number of smaller panels. Mark parallel guide lines 3mm apart at the edge of each panel, instead of a single line, so you can saw between the lines when you cut the panels.

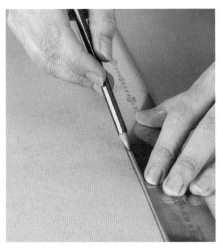

Using a combination square

You can use a combination square in the same way as a try square to mark lines at 90° to the edge of the workpiece. The design of the square also allows you to mark cutting lines at 45°.

1 Make a mark on the edge of the workpiece where you want the cutting line to begin.

2 Slide the stock to the end of the blade and hold the 45° face against the edge of the workpiece in line with the mark and with the blade extending across its width.

3 Mark the cutting line across the workpiece with a knife or sharp pencil. Alternatively, use the removable scribing pin fitted into the tool's stock.

Using a sliding bevel

A sliding bevel allows you to copy an existing cutting angle – on a replacement staircase baluster, for example – or to set a new angle using a protractor.

1 To copy an existing angle, loosen the wing nut on the tool. Hold the stock against one surface forming the angle and move the blade to touch the other surface. Tighten the wing nut to lock the blade in place.

2 To set a new angle, use a protractor to position the blade at the required angle and lock it in place.

3 Transfer the tool to the workpiece and use it like a try square to transfer the angle of the cutting line to the new wood.

Cutting wood and boards

You can use a hand or power saw to cut wood to length and board panels to size. Power saws save time and effort, but for smaller jobs you may not want the trouble of setting up a power saw. Whichever you use, it is important that the workpiece is held securely so that the saw blade cannot snatch it loose and damage it.

Using a bench hook

The best way of holding mouldings and other small workpieces – up to about 50 x 25mm in size – is to use a bench hook. You can buy one or make one from a piece of timber and two offcuts.

1 Place the lower batten against the near edge of your workbench and place the workpiece against the upper batten. If the batten is inset from the edge of the base, position the cutting line just beyond the end of the batten. If it is not, let the workpiece project beyond the edge of the base by about 25mm.

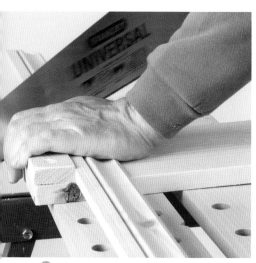

2 Position the saw blade just on the waste side of the cutting line, guiding it against the side of the thumb of your spare hand. Start the cut with a few light backward strokes of the saw.

3 Saw with the blade at 45° to begin with, then lower it to the horizontal once the cut is established. If the bench hook batten is inset, complete the cut by sawing into the base of the bench hook. This ensures a clean cut with no splinters on the underside of the workpiece.

If the batten is not inset, complete the cut with gentle strokes to minimise splitting on the underside.

Using a mitre box

You can hold and cut small workpieces in a mitre box, which is itself clamped in the jaws of your workbench. The guide slots in the box allow you to make cuts at 45° as well as at 90°.

1 Mark the cutting line on the workpiece (see opposite). Place it in the box with the cutting line aligned with the slots you want to use. If these do not extend to the base of the box, place a piece of scrap wood beneath the workpiece so that you can saw into it, to avoid leaving a ragged finish.

2 Fit the tenon saw into the slots in the mitre box and use your free hand to hold the workpiece in place. Make the cut with the saw held horizontally. Take care not to widen the slots by letting the saw wander off line.

Using a vice

If you have a woodworking vice, you can use it to hold small workpieces while you cut them. Stick slim packing pieces of scrap wood to the vice jaws with epoxy adhesive to protect the workpiece from being marked by the steel jaws. Never tighten the jaws more than necessary to hold the piece firmly. Soft wood is easily dented.

Using a panel saw

A panel saw is used to cut wood that is too thick for the tenon saw, and to cut man-made boards into smaller panels. It can be used for both cross-cutting (cutting across the grain) and ripping (cutting with the grain). Wood should not be allowed to vibrate while it is being cut, so securing it firmly is essential to a good, clean cut and a satisfactory result.

Even when you take the greatest amount of care, it is possible that the exit cut may be a little rough. To avoid this, always start with the good side of the wood facing upwards in the bench – this way, any minor defects in the cut won't affect the finished job quite as much.

1 To cut wood across the grain, clamp it in the jaws of your workbench with the cutting line clear of the bench frame. Start the cut with a few gentle backwards strokes of the saw blade, then continue cutting with the blade at an angle of about 45°. Hold the offcut with your free hand as you complete the cut to prevent the wood from splintering on the underside.

2 To cut smaller panels from a larger sheet of board, you need to support it on both sides of the cut unless you are sawing close to the board edge. You can rest the panel over the open jaws of your portable workbench and saw between them, but you need to take care not to hit the bench framework. Alternatively, rest the board on two planks supported at each end, or use an open stepladder laid on its side as a makeshift support (below).

3 Kneel over the workpiece so that your eye is above the cutting line and your arm in line with it. Start the cut on the waste side of the marked line and saw as far as is comfortable. Reposition yourself and the board to continue the cut, and complete it using short saw strokes to avoid splintering the board.

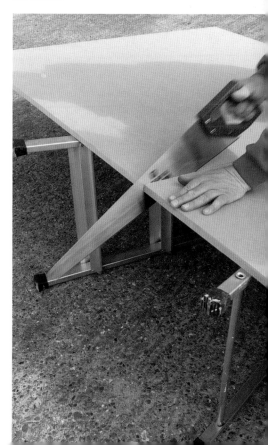

Using a coping saw

If the saw is already fitted with a blade, check the blade tension by tightening the screw-up handle on the tool. To fit a new blade, unscrew the handle fully and unhook the ends of the old blade from their holders. Hook the ends of the new blade into the holders, with the teeth facing away from the handle, and tighten it fully.

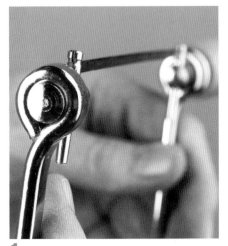

1 To make a cut starting at the edge of the workpiece, check that the pins on the blade holders are aligned with the frame. Start the cut with the blade at right angles to the edge. Follow the marked cutting line carefully.

2 As you saw along the cutting line, you may need to rotate the blade to stop the frame from fouling the edge of the workpiece. Unscrew the handle slightly, rotate both blade holder pins to the required angle and re-tighten the handle. Repeat as necessary to allow the blade to follow the curve.

3 To make an internal cut-out, mark its outline and drill a hole through the workpiece within the waste area large enough to admit the saw blade. Unhook the blade from the frame, thread it through the hole and re-attach it to the frame.

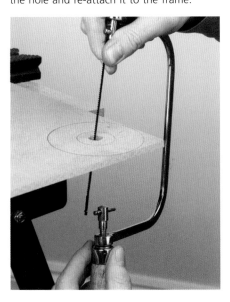

4 Cut from the hole towards the marked outline, then follow it round until you return to your starting point. To allow the blade to turn corners in straight-sided cut-outs, drill a hole within the outline at each corner. Square up the corners with abrasive paper when you have removed the cut-out.

Using a padsaw

The padsaw is ideal for making cut-outs and cutting curves where it is not possible or practicable to use a coping saw. Two typical jobs for it are making cut-outs in plasterboard walls to fit electrical wiring accessories, and cutting keyholes in doors.

Cutting a hole in a wall

1 To make an enclosed cut, mark its outline and drill a starter hole within the waste area big enough to admit the saw blade. If the cut-out is to be square or rectangular, drill a hole at each corner so that you can turn the blade to cut along the next side.

2 Insert the saw blade and start cutting along the marked line. Use short saw strokes in a plasterboard wall to avoid damaging the cladding on the opposite side of the frame.

Cutting a keyhole

To cut a keyhole, drill the starter hole at the top and mark the sides of the slot needed to admit the tongue of the key. Insert the saw blade right through the hole and cut down both sides of the slot. Use a narrow chisel (page 60) to chop out the waste wood, working from both sides of the door.

Using a hole saw

The hole saw will cut perfectly round holes in wood, man-made boards, plasterboard and sheet metal or plastic. Select the blade diameter that matches the hole you want to make and clip it into the circular arbor, or blade holder. Fit the arbor into the chuck of your power drill.

1 Locate the pilot drill bit at the centre of the cut-out and start the drill slowly. As the drill penetrates the surface, the saw teeth will start to cut into it. The cut will be even all round if you are holding the drill at a 90° angle to the surface.

2 If you are cutting a workpiece on your bench, clamp some scrap wood beneath it and saw through the workpiece into the scrap to ensure a clean exit hole.

Using a circular saw

Before you use a circular saw for the first time, read the instructions supplied with it and familiarise yourself with all the controls and safety features. Check that you have the right type of blade for the material you want to cut (see panel below).

CIRCULAR SAW BLADES

Use blades of the correct diameter for your saw. The number of teeth is a general guide to its cutting performance: many small teeth ensure a fine cut; fewer large teeth give a fast but coarse cut. Special blades are available for cutting man-made boards and laminates.

1 To remove or change a blade, make sure that the saw is unplugged. Use the Allen key provided with the saw to loosen the retaining nut. For blades with large teeth, jam a screwdriver blade between the saw teeth and the soleplate to stop it turning. For fine blades, hold the saw blade down firmly on some scrap wood. Release the old blade from its spindle, fit the replacement with the teeth pointing forwards and tighten the nut fully.

2 To set the cutting depth you require, place the saw on its side and loosen the lever that locks the saw body to the soleplate. Move the saw body until the saw teeth just project beyond the thickness of the material you are cutting. Tighten the lever again.

3 To make a cut up to about 150mm from the edge of the workpiece, fit the adjustable side fence in its clamp. Set it the required distance from the saw blade and tighten the wing nut. Clamp the workpiece to your workbench.

4 Rest the front edge of the soleplate on the edge of the workpiece and align the narrow guide notch with the marked cutting line. Hold the fence against the side edge of the workpiece.

5 Start the saw and let it run up to full speed, then move it forward until the blade begins to cut. Move the saw forward slowly, with its soleplate flat on the workpiece and the fence running against its side edge.

6 Let the saw run out at the end of the cut before releasing the trigger. Make sure that the blade has stopped before setting the saw down.

7 To make a cut beyond the reach of the fence, clamp a guide batten across the workpiece, parallel with the marked cutting line, and run the edge of the soleplate against it. Align the guide notch with the cutting line and check the position of the batten before starting the cut. Check that the clamps will not foul the saw body as you make the cut.

8 To make an angled cut, loosen the wing nuts at the front and back of the soleplate and rotate the saw body to the setting you want. Lock the nuts and test the cutting angle on some scrap wood.

9 Align the left-hand edge of the wider guide notch on the front of the soleplate with the marked cutting line. Start the saw and feed the blade into the workpiece, then move the saw forward to make the cut. Keep the notch aligned with the cutting line. Remember that cutting depths are reduced when making angled cuts.

Drilling wood

Almost every woodworking project involves drilling holes, and much of this will be done on your workbench.

You can of course use your cordless drill (see pages 42–43), but for workshop use, a corded drill is a worthwhile addition to your tool kit. Its higher drilling speeds allow you to work faster and more accurately, and the extra power means that you can drill bigger holes than a cordless drill can manage. It will also drill large or deep holes in dense masonry (page 44) that are beyond the capacity of a cordless drill.

Get to know your drill

Mains drills have power ratings in watts (W), ranging from about 500W for small single-speed drills up to 750W or more for big semi-professional models. Most have variable speed control from 0 to about 3000rpm; some have two speed ranges. The more powerful drills have the advantage of a 13mm chuck (most cordless drills have only a 10mm chuck) that will take larger-diameter twist and masonry drill bits.

Before you use the drill for the first time, read the instructions. These will tell you how to select the following:
• The correct speed setting for the material you are drilling.
• Drilling, hammer-drilling or screwdriving.
• The correct torque setting (if available) for driving screws.
• Forward or reverse gear (for removing screws and freeing jammed drill bits).

Most corded drills come with a carry case; keep the drill in it when you are not using it. If you do not have a case, buy one. DIY stores stock a selection, so take your drill in to test its fit before you buy.

Using your drill

Follow the instructions given on pages 42–43 for cordless drills. These explain how to fit drill bits into the drill chuck, and how to carry out a range of basic drilling operations in wood and metal.

The main differences between the drill types are that mains drills tend to be larger and heavier to handle than cordless drills, and they operate at much higher speeds. This last point makes it essential to clamp your workpiece to the bench before carrying out any drilling operation. The power of the drill can snatch a hand-held workpiece from your grasp.

Using a drill stand

A drill stand holds the drill in a movable clamp mounted on a vertical pillar. It can be clamped in place on your workbench, or can be bolted to it if you have a permanent bench rather than a portable one. The stand allows you to drill holes at precisely 90° to the surface of the workpiece, which is placed on the stand's base. This accuracy is particularly important for jobs such as making dowel joints or drilling the recesses in cabinet doors for spring-loaded hinges.

The stand can also be set up to allow you to drill stopped holes to a precise depth.

Take your drill with you when you shop for a drill stand, to ensure that it will fit in the clamp. Some drill stands will not accept drills with keyless chucks.

1 Mount the drill in the stand and fit the drill bit you want to use (see page 33 and panel right). Check the travel of the drill in the stand to ensure that the drill bit will penetrate the workpiece without drilling into the bench beneath the stand's base.

2 Place the workpiece beneath the drill and lower the drill bit so it just touches the surface. Adjust its position until the bit is at the drilling mark; then clamp the workpiece to the bench.

3 Set the depth of travel on the stand if you want to drill a stopped hole. Test the result on some scrap wood first.

4 Raise the drill, squeeze the trigger and lock it on. Lower it and drill the hole, then raise the drill while it is still running to clear sawdust from the hole. Release the trigger lock.

DRILL BITS YOU MAY NOT HAVE ALREADY

Dowel drill bits These resemble twist drill bits, but have a centre point and cutting spurs (like a miniature flat wood bit) that enable them to drill holes more accurately than a twist drill bit when making dowel joints (page 64). They are available in 6, 8 and 10mm diameters to match ready-cut hardwood dowel sizes.

Auger drill bits Used to drill deep holes in wood up to 25mm in diameter, for which a flat wood bit would be too inaccurate. They have a screw-threaded lead point and a cutting spur, with deep spiral flutes to clear the debris from the hole. They are available in diameters up to 25mm, in two lengths – 100 and 200mm.

End mill bits Used to drill shallow stopped holes such as those required when fitting recessed cabinet hinges and certain assembly fittings (page 67). They come in a range of sizes, but the most widely used sizes are 25, 26 and 35mm.

Smoothing wood

Whether you are working with wood or man-made boards, you will need to sand the surface smooth before you can apply a decorative finish to it. Do this by hand, or use one of the many different power sanders now available.

Sanding by hand

The traditional way of smoothing wood is to wrap a piece of abrasive paper round a cork sanding block and to rub it along the direction of the grain. Sanding across the grain can leave scratches which are difficult to remove and can mar a clear finish. Glasspaper (often incorrectly still called sandpaper) is the cheapest sheet abrasive available, but aluminium oxide abrasives cut better and last longer. Both types are sold in standard 280 x 230mm sheets.

Glasspaper Made in a series of grades: 3, 2½ and S2 are coarse; M2, F2 and 1½ are medium; 1, 0 and 00 are fine.

Aluminium oxide paper Graded by numbers, running from 40, 50 and 60 (coarse) through 80, 100 and 120 (medium) to 150, 180 and beyond (fine).

You will usually need only fine grades for finishing planed timber and board surfaces, but you may need other grades for smoothing cut ends and board edges.

Note that silicon carbide abrasive paper, also known as wet-and-dry paper, is not intended for use in sanding bare wood. Its main DIY use is for smoothing metal and keying existing painted or varnished surfaces prior to redecoration.

Power sanding

Disc sanding attachments (used with a power drill) can leave tell-tale scratches. Integral power sanders give better results. Different types do different jobs. See page 49 for how to use a random-orbit sander. All use aluminium oxide abrasive sheets, graded as for hand abrasives (see left).

Using a finishing sander

This sander scrubs the surface of the wood, moving its baseplate in small orbits to give a very fine, scratch-free surface finish. Large models take third-sheets (230 x 93mm) of abrasive paper; smaller models called palm sanders take quarter-sheets (115 x 70mm) or special own-brand shaped sheets. Those with a dust extraction facility use perforated sanding sheets, often attached with touch-and-close (Velcro) fastenings. Make sure the sheets you buy will fit your sander.

1 Select the correct grade of abrasive sheet for the finish you want to achieve, and attach it to the sanding pad so that the holes in sheet and pad are aligned. Press it firmly into place on the pad.

2 Connect the sander to the hose of your vacuum cleaner using the adaptor provided, and switch the vacuum cleaner on. Or fit the dust bag if the tool has one.

3 Hold the tool against the surface you want to sand and switch on the power. Keep the sander moving backwards and forwards over the surface until it is smooth.

Using a belt sander

A belt sander is ideal for fast removal of material – for example, smoothing rough-sawn timber in the garden – and it will also strip paint and sand other materials such as plastic or metal if fitted with the appropriate abrasive belt. Note that there are more than a dozen different belt sizes available to fit different belt sander makes and models, so make sure you buy the correct size for your machine.

1 Release the roller tension lever and fit the belt over the rollers. Check that it is aligned with the edges of the rollers and tension the belt. Also check the tracking adjustment to ensure that the belt is positioned correctly. If it is not, it will run off the rollers in use.

2 Fit the dust bag or connect the sander to your vacuum cleaner hose via the adaptor supplied.

3 Switch the sander on and drive it over the surface you are sanding, working only along the grain direction. Keep the tool moving, or you will gouge out more material than necessary and leave an uneven finish. Change to finer grades of belt to achieve the finish you want.

Using a detail sander

This small orbital sander uses triangular sanding sheets attached to a matching pad, and is used for sanding into corners where an orbital sander will not reach. It does not usually have a dust bag. Some models have a rotating head that allows you to use all three corners of the sheet before replacing it; on fixed-head machines you reposition the abrasive sheet.

Shaping wood by hand

Most of the wood you use will be in standard sizes or will be a ready-machined moulding, and the range of sizes and cross-sections available will meet most of your requirements.

Sometimes, however, you need to shape a piece of wood for a particular purpose. Chisels, rasps and Surforms will help you to do this. If you need a component that is not available as a standard size or profile, you will have to alter its cross-section or shape. For this you need a plane and a router respectively. You can cut curves with a suitable saw (see pages 48 and 56). Rounded ends or surfaces curved in more than one direction need another approach.

Paring with a chisel

The simplest way to form a rounded end or corner is to trim (pare) it with a chisel.

1 Mark the shape you want to cut on your workpiece. Clamp it securely on your workbench, with some scrap wood or board underneath it to protect the bench surface. Cut off the bulk of the area with a saw before you use the chisel.

2 Use a sharpened chisel (see opposite) to pare the remaining wood. Continue trimming off finer and finer shavings until you have cut back to the marked line.

3 Smooth the resulting curve with a fine rasp (see below) and then abrasive paper.

Shaping with a wood rasp

A rasp is often confused with a file, which is a metalworking tool and has parallel cutting edges machined across its blade. Rasp blades have individual raised teeth, which remove wood in the same manner as a very coarse abrasive paper. The tool cuts on the forward stroke. If the teeth become clogged with wood fibres as you work, clean them with a wire brush.

1 Mark the curve you want to shape on the workpiece, and clamp it securely in a vice or the jaws of your workbench.

2 Hold the handle in one hand and place the tool on the work. Steady the tip of the blade with your other hand to keep the blade flat on the surface.

3 Push the tool forwards to start shaping the wood, repeating the stroke and moving the contact point round the curve as you work to create the required shape.

4 To shape a concave curve, use a round rasp or the rounded face of a half-round rasp and work from both sides of the workpiece to prevent splintering.

Shaping with a Surform

A Surform is a rasp with a difference, having individual cutting teeth stamped out of a thin steel sheet. Different tools in the range have a blade that is flat, gently rounded, curved along its length or rolled into a cylinder, and each is used in a different way. The blades are replaceable.

1 Hold the tool parallel with the wood grain and push it along the wood in a series of steady strokes.

2 Clear shavings from the inside of the blade from time to time. As you near the shape you want, turn the tool slightly to alter the cutting angle and produce finer shavings.

HELPFUL TIP

There are different Surforms for specific jobs. Use a half-round blade to shape concave curves, as for a rasp (see step 4 above). Use a round file to shape tight curves and holes – again work from both sides of the wood to avoid splintering. The Surform shaver tool has a smaller blade, and is designed to cut on the pull stroke. Use it in tight corners where the larger tools cannot reach.

Using a plane

A bench (jack) plane about 350mm long is used to reduce the cross-section of wood from an off-the-peg size to the dimensions required. Its blade must be sharp to cut the wood cleanly (see right) and must be correctly adjusted.

1 Sight along the soleplate of the plane to check that the blade is set square to it, and that it projects by the correct distance. Use the lateral adjustment lever behind the blade to set the cutting edge squarely, and the knurled nut between blade and handle to alter the blade projection.

2 Mark the cutting line on both faces of the workpiece and clamp it securely in your workbench. Hold the plane on the near end of the workpiece and use your free hand to grasp the front handle. Press the fingers of this hand against the side of the workpiece to guide the plane along its edge.

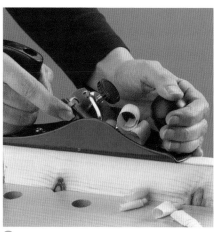

3 Plane from one end of the workpiece to the other in smooth, steady strokes. Let the plane run off the wood at each end of the stroke. Regularly check your progress towards the marked lines. Remove shavings from the jaws as you work.

Sharpening blades

Chisel and plane blades must be kept sharp if they are to cut well – and safely. You are more likely to force a blunt tool, with the increased risk of it slipping and injuring you or damaging the workpiece. To sharpen them you need an oilstone, a honing guide and some light machine oil.

Prepare a new oilstone for use by pouring a teaspoonful of oil onto it and smearing it over the stone. Leave it to soak in, then apply a second spoonful and repeat the process. Wipe off any excess oil with absorbent paper.

1 Clamp the blade in the honing guide, following the instructions. Check that the blade projects by the correct distance and tighten the clamping nuts fully.

2 Pour a little oil on the stone (use the fine side if it has two different faces). Move the guide up and down the stone in a figure of 8 pattern so you use as much of the surface as possible. You will wear a groove in the stone if you simply run the blade up and down the middle. Press down on the honing guide to keep the chisel tip flat against the stone.

3 Release the blade from the guide and rub its flat side back and forth across the stone to remove the curl of metal (the burr) formed on the cutting edge by the sharpening process.

Using a power planer

A power planer is useful for re-sizing work as well as jobs such as fitting new doors. Read the instructions and ensure you know how to fit and change the cutting blades.

For general bench work, use the planer in the same way as a bench plane. If you are working on a door, fit the guide fence to the planer and clamp the door on your portable workbench so you can plane the ends and edges as shown below.

1 Mark cutting lines on the workpiece, set the cutting depth on the planer and fit the fence.

2 Place the front of the soleplate against the end of the door with the fence resting on its face, and switch the tool on. Move it forwards, guiding it with both hands.

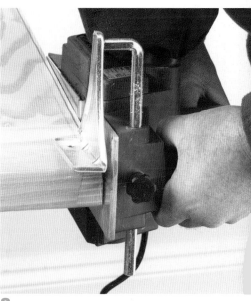

3 As you complete each pass, let the planer run off the end of the workpiece. Repeat until you reach the marked lines.

4 You can use a power planer to chamfer edges at 45° too, by letting the groove in the soleplate run along the edge of the workpiece. Mark guide lines on each face of the work and plane down to them.

Using a router

Depending on which accessories and bits you fit, you can use a router to create edge profiles, grooves and recesses in solid wood and in man-made boards – MDF takes routed effects especially well. The bit rotates at extremely high speed, so the tool needs careful handling. Read the instructions and practise on some scrap before tackling your first job.

Setting up the router

1 To fit your selected cutting bit, use the spanner and locking pin provided. Place the router on its side and lock the chuck (called the collet) with the pin. Loosen the collet with the spanner and insert the bit as far as it will go. Tighten the collet fully and remove the locking pin.

2 To set the routing depth, stand the router on the workbench and undo the winged nut securing the depth rod so it is free to move. Loosen the side handle, press the body of the router down until the bit touches the bench surface and tighten the handle again.

3 Read off the value indicated on the depth scale and add the required routing depth to it. Set the pointer on the depth rod to this combined figure and tighten the winged nut below the scale. Loosen the side handle and allow the router body to rise up on its springs. Check that the routing depth is correct by making a test cut on some scrap wood.

4 If the machine has a dust extractor facility, fit the adaptor and connect it to the hose of your vacuum cleaner.

Routing an edge profile

The router cutter rotates counter-clockwise when viewed from above the tool. Always feed the cutter into the wood from the right, so it is turning into the wood it is about to cut away. If you work in the opposite direction, the speed of the machine may wrench it from your grasp with some force, and you are likely to damage your work.

1 Select the cutter you want to use and fit it in the collet. Set the cutting depth required (see step 2, below left). Clamp the work securely to your workbench, and check that the clamps will not impede the router as you move it along the edge.

2 Rest the edge of the soleplate on top of the workpiece. Switch the router on, press the body down on its springs and guide it sideways into the edge you are shaping. Cut in until the guide pin touches the edge of the workpiece.

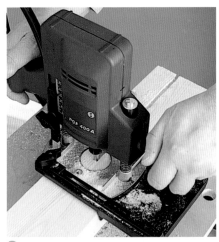

3 Move the router slowly forwards, with the baseplate flat on the surface of the workpiece. Let the cutter run off at the far end of the cut and switch off the power.

Using a guide fence

To machine a groove parallel with the edge of the workpiece, fit the guide fence to the router soleplate using the guide plates and winged screws. Mark the position of the groove on the workpiece and set the cutting depth required.

1 Place the router on the workpiece with the cutter aligned with the marked line. Move the fence in against the edge of the workpiece and tighten the securing screws.

2 Position the router soleplate on the end of the workpiece with the fence pressed against its edge. Start the motor, loosen the side handle and press the router body down to the pre-set cutting depth. Tighten the handle again.

3 Start the motor and move the router forwards slowly to cut the groove. Keep the fence pressed against the edge of the workpiece. Let the cutter run out at the end of the groove and switch off the motor.

Using a guide batten

If you want to cut grooves further in from the edge of the workpiece than the fence will allow, use a guide batten instead (see page 48). Clamp it across the workpiece and guide the flat side of the router soleplate against it as you machine the groove. Check that the clamps will not impede the movement of the router.

Choosing router bits

Bits for DIY routers usually have 6mm diameter shafts and tungsten carbide cutting tips. Grooving cutters are plain, while shaping (edge) cutters have a guide wheel that runs against the edge of the workpiece and stops the bit from cutting too deeply. You can buy bits singly, but it is better to buy a set complete with a storage case.

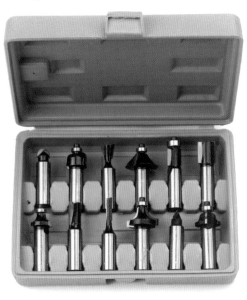

Making joints

Joining wood to wood is an essential skill to master, but you do not need the skills of a cabinet-maker to make a good job. The type of joint you choose will depend on how strong you want it to be, and on how important its appearance is. This section will help you to make those choices, and demonstrate some basic skills that will be useful for a wide range of woodworking projects.

Basic joints

Butt joints These are the easiest joints to make. They are formed by aligning the two components (such as the sides of a box) so that the edge of one overlaps the end of the other. Butt joints can also be used to join wood edge to edge – to make a table top, for example. There are several options for joining the components:
• Fix the corner joint together with nails or screws and strengthen with wood glue.
• Reinforce a corner or edge joint with hardwood dowels or oval-shaped slips of compressed wood called biscuits.
• Use one of the ingenious assembly fittings that were originally designed for use in flat-pack furniture (page 67).
• Use a metal angle bracket or a corrugated fastener (below), although these remain visible unless you take steps to hide them.

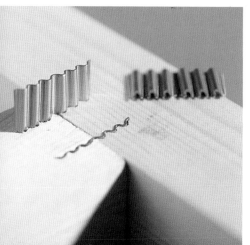

Mitre joints Butt joints that meet at a 45° angle are called mitre joints. They are used mainly in frames where the appearance of the corner joint is important – in a picture frame, for example, or where the architrave mouldings round a door opening meet. Like butt joints they can be nailed, screwed, dowel-jointed or biscuit-jointed, and are usually glued as well.

Halving joints As their name implies, halving joints are made by cutting away half of each component so they fit together neatly. The joint is stronger than a butt joint because the parts interlock. If the joint is also glued, it is even stronger because the glued contact area between the parts is bigger. The joint is usually nailed or screwed. Halving joints are used mainly in frames, and components can be joined in L, T or X shapes. The last two – called tee halving joints and cross halving joints respectively – need a slot cut in one or both components (see page 66).

Mortise-and-tenon joints These are serious woodworking joints, formed by fitting a shaped peg (the tenon) into a matching slot (the mortise). They are used mainly in fine furniture making, and are also found in framed doors, sash windows and the like. You are unlikely ever to need the complete joint, but cutting a mortise is essential for fitting a front door lock (page 198).

Using a try square to mark up joints

The most important feature of any woodworking joint is that it should be square, and the try square (page 50) is the tool to use for checking this. You also need a try square for marking cutting lines at 90°, both when cutting wood to length and when marking out halving joints.

1 Mark where you want to cut your workpiece to length. Hold the stock of the try square against its edge at the mark, with the blade across the width, and mark the line with a trimming knife or sharp pencil.

2 Turn the workpiece through 90°, align the try square with the marked line on its face and mark the line on its edge. Repeat the process to continue the marked line all the way round the workpiece. This continuous line will help you to cut the wood squarely to length.

3 To mark out a corner halving joint, clamp the two pieces together and check with the try square that they are at 90° to each other. Mark the edge of each piece on the face of the other.

4 Separate the two pieces and use the try square to continue the marked lines onto the edge of each piece.

Using a marking gauge

To mark out a halving joint, you need a marking gauge (page 50). This enables you to mark the thickness of the wood you want to cut away from each component to make the joint.

1 Loosen the thumbscrew on the block and slide it along the beam so the pin is approximately half the thickness of the workpiece away from the block. Tighten the screw.

2 Hold the block against one face of the workpiece and mark the edge with the pin. Then hold it against the opposite face and repeat the mark. If they coincide, the gauge is correctly set. If they do not, move the block slightly and repeat the process until they do. Tighten the screw fully.

3 Hold the block against the face of each component in turn, and slide it along so the pin marks the halving line on each edge of each component, extending to the end from the cutting line you marked with the try square.

4 Join the edge marks across the end grain of each component. Then cross-hatch the area to be cut away in pencil on each component, ready for the joint to be cut.

Using a mortise gauge

The mortise gauge has two pins, one of which is movable, and is designed for marking the width of a mortise on the edge of the workpiece (or a door, if you are fitting a mortise lock). You set the pin separation first to match the width of the tenon (or the lock body). You then position the block so the two pins mark the mortise in the centre of the edge, in the same way as using a marking gauge to mark a centre line when marking out a halving joint. However, most woodworkers today drill out mortises with a flat wood bit that matches the mortise width, rather than cutting them with a chisel, so there is no need to mark it in the traditional way.

Making dowel joints

The positions of the dowel holes must be carefully matched in the two components being joined. Use a drill bit that matches readily available sizes of hardwood dowel – commonly 6 or 8mm in diameter. It's a good idea to use a drill stand or a dowelling jig to ensure that the holes are drilled at precise right angles to the face of the workpiece, and to the correct depth.

1 Use a combination square to mark a centre line on the end or edge of the first component to be drilled. Mark the dowel positions on this line and corresponding marks on the second component.

2 Drill a hole at each cross in the first component, making the holes a little deeper than half the length of the dowel. Use a drill stand or clamp the dowelling jig to the workpiece and use it to guide the drill bit.

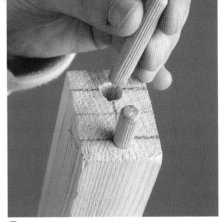

3 Squeeze some wood glue into the holes and insert the dowels. Drill the dowel holes in the second component, ready for the joint to be assembled.

4 Check the alignment of the two components before squeezing some glue into the holes and assembling the joint.

5 Use a wooden mallet to drive the dowels home. Wipe away any surplus adhesive with a damp cloth.

HELPFUL TIP

One way to ensure accurate holes is to drill dowel holes in one of the pieces to join, then put specially designed metal marker pins in the holes. Offer up the pieces in exactly the position you want and knock them together firmly. The markers will leave indentations in the other piece of wood, ready for perfectly-matched holes to be drilled in it.

2 Then complete the cut down to the shoulder marks, holding the saw blade at right-angles to the workpiece.

Making biscuit joints

You need a power tool called a biscuit jointer to cut the slots for the biscuits in the two components. Follow the instructions supplied with the tool to cut the slots. Then squirt woodworking adhesive into the slots, insert the biscuits and assemble the joint. Clamp the joint until the adhesive has set.

Making mitre joints

You can cut mitre joints freehand after marking the cutting angles with a combination square (see advice on using a try square on page 50), or by using a protractor and ruler. Alternatively, you can use a mitre box (page 50) to guide the saw. For the best results a mitre saw (page 50) is the ideal tool to use.

1 Mark the joint positions on each component. Set the cutting angle to 45° by rotating the saw's baseplate, then lock it.

2 Clamp the workpiece in place on the base of the mitre saw and lower the saw blade to check that the cut will be aligned with the mark. Then make the cut. Repeat for the other component of the joint.

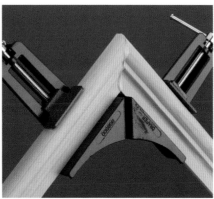

3 Apply adhesive to one mitred end and assemble the joint. Check that it is square, set it aside and leave it until the adhesive has set. You can reinforce the joint by driving a panel pin or a screw in from each side of the joint, or you can drill holes in each mitred face to take dowels. You can also reinforce mitre joints with biscuits (see above left). Special cramps are available (above) that will hold the joint accurately while the adhesive sets.

Making corner halving joints

Once you have marked out the two components (page 63), you can cut and assemble the joint. You need a tenon saw and some wood adhesive (or a glue gun).

1 Clamp each component on its edge and, starting the cut at an angle, begin to saw along the grain.

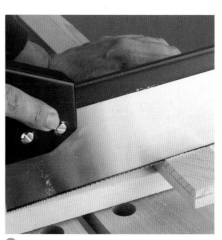

3 Using a bench hook (page 51) to steady the workpiece, cut carefully across the width to form the shoulder.

4 Squirt some adhesive onto the cut faces of one component and assemble the joint. Clamp it for maximum bond strength, with cardboard or scrap wood between the clamp jaws and the workpieces to prevent dents. Use your try square to check that the joint is a perfect right angle. Wipe away excess adhesive with a damp cloth.

Making tee halving joints

As with a corner halving joint, use the two components you wish to join to mark the outline of the joint.

1 Clamp the two components together, check that they are at right angles and mark the edges of each component on the face of the other one.

2 Use a marking gauge to mark the joint thickness on the edge of each component. Cut the piece forming the leg of the tee in the same way as for a corner halving joint (page 65).

3 Using a tenon saw, make two parallel cuts on the waste side of the marks on the piece forming the cross-bar of the tee. Saw down to the halfway line. Then make several more cuts to the same depth within the waste area (below).

4 Clamp the workpiece securely and, using a sharp chisel, begin to chisel out the waste wood between the outer saw cuts.

5 Work from opposite sides in turn so as to avoid splintering, until the base of the notch is flat and is level with the halfway lines on the edges.

6 Test the fit of the two components, and shave away any excess wood with your chisel if necessary.

7 Glue and assemble the joint as for a corner halving joint (page 65).

Making cross halving joints

Mark out the joint from the two components as before, then use your tenon saw and chisel to create two matching notches as for cutting the cross-piece of a tee halving joint. Test the fit and assemble the joint as before.

FORMING MORTISES

Mortise joints are mainly used in professional woodworking, such as the production of fine furniture. The only time you are likely to need a mortise is when installing a mortise lock in a front or back door. See pages 198–9 for more details of how to do this.

Using assembly fittings

As the use of man-made boards – especially veneered and plastic-coated chipboard – for making furniture became widespread in the 1970s, it was clear that traditional woodworking joints were not appropriate for joining this type of material. Manufacturers began to devise various mechanical means of connecting the panels, and the assembly fitting was born.

Types of assembly fitting

These fittings are now widely used throughout the furniture industry, particularly in flat-pack furniture which the consumer assembles at home.

Early fittings were surface-mounted and obtrusive, but many of the newest fittings are completely concealed once assembly is complete. They are strong and easy to use, although the wordless instructions that often accompany flat-pack furniture do not always make this clear.

Here are some of the most common types, with details of how they are fitted and assembled. Familiarise yourself with them to make assembling flat-pack furniture easier. For more information on using assembly fittings and assembling flat-pack furniture, see page 169.

Screwed fittings

The problem with making screw fixings into chipboard and MDF (medium-density fibreboard, now very widely used in panel furniture) is that the board structure does not hold screws well. One solution is to use the wallplug principle, and to set a screw-in socket in the edge of one component to receive a screw driven in through the face of the other component.

A variation on this type of fixing is the cross dowel. An internally threaded steel dowel is set in a hole drilled in the face of one component, close to the edge. This receives the threaded end of a machine screw passing through a hole in the second component and into the edge of the first one. A slot in the dowel allows its threaded hole to be aligned with the machine screw. It is used mainly to link panels to rails.

Screw and cross dowel

Cam fittings

A cam fitting is one of the neatest types of assembly fitting. Various designs are available, but all work on a similar principle. A screwed peg is inserted into one component of the joint, and its peg located in a bush (the cam) inserted in a hole drilled in the other component. The cam is rotated through 90° to lock the two components together. The dowel-and-bush fitting is a variation that works in much the same way.

The so-called Klix fitting is the type favoured by most flat-pack furniture manufacturers. The screwed peg fits into a hole drilled in the second component, and passes through a hole in the edge of the first component to enter the cam. This contains a spiral slot that draws the two components tightly together as it is turned to lock it onto the peg. It is used mainly to connect panels.

One-piece joint block with dowel pegs

One-piece joint block

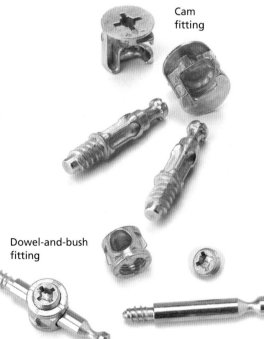

Cam fitting

Dowel-and-bush fitting

Joint blocks

The joint block was the earliest type of assembly fitting. Its simplest form is a single rectangular block which fits into the internal angle between two butt-jointed components, and is fixed to each one with wood screws. The two-part block is stronger and easier to assemble once fitted in place. One block is screwed to each panel; then a short screw connects the two blocks together.

A variation on the one-piece joint block has dowel pegs moulded on one face of the block. The pegs fit in holes drilled in one component, and a thick screw (or two) passes through the other face of the block at an angle to make it easy to drive into the second component. This fitting is widely used to attach worktops to kitchen cabinets.

3
Home decorating

Tools and preparation

There is a huge variety of tools available in DIY stores, and new ones are being introduced all the time. Choosing the right tools can make a job both faster and easier.

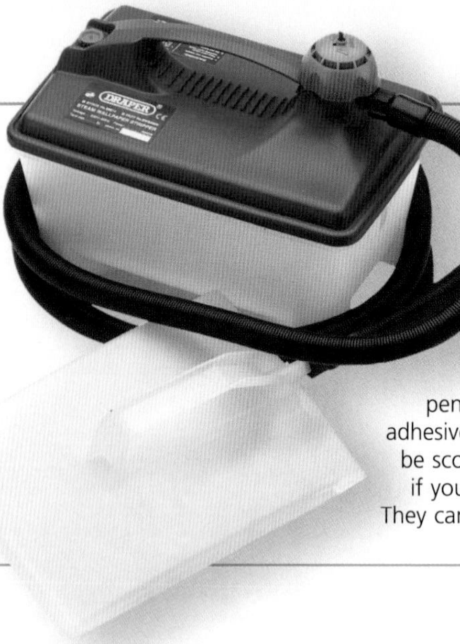

Sanding tools Have a variety of abrasive papers to hand for smoothing filler or any roughness on stripped walls or woodwork. Wet-and-dry paper can be used dry or damped with water. A flexible sanding block has an abrasive coating on four sides. Rinse and squeeze out before using to rub down a painted surface before repainting. This destroys the glaze while removing dirt. Powered sanding tools clean stripped surfaces quickly. But don't try to strip paint with a sander as the abrasive will become clogged.

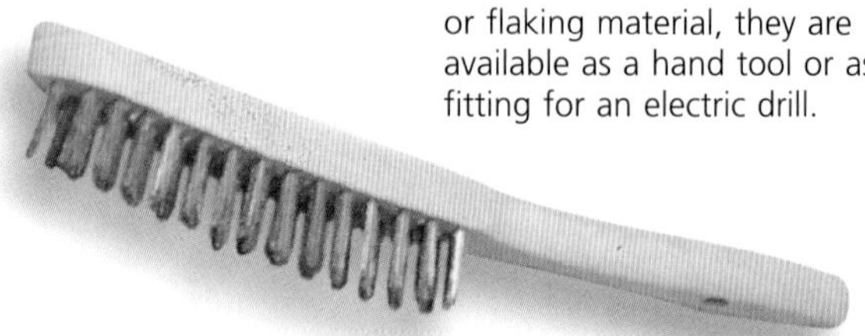

Steam stripper This is the most efficient tool for stripping wallpaper or papered surfaces that have been painted.
It consists of a water reservoir and a hose, which is connected to a steam plate. When the water heats up, steam is forced up the hose and out through the plate. This penetrates the wall covering and softens the adhesive underneath (painted paper must first be scored). It's worth buying a steam stripper if you plan to strip more than one room. They can also be hired.

Wire brush Used to remove loose or flaking material, they are available as a hand tool or as a fitting for an electric drill.

Filling knife A filling knife is like a scraper with a more flexible blade. Use it to press filler into holes and cracks and to level it flush with the surface.

Flexible sanding block

Glass scraper

Combination shave hook

Triangular shave hook

Broad blade paint scraper

Narrow blade paint scraper

Broad blade filling knife

Narrow blade filling knife

Scrapers/strippers Scrapers or stripping knives have a flat, slightly sprung blade, which may be broad or narrow. Broad scrapers are used for stripping wallpaper. Other scrapers are used to remove softened paint from flat surfaces.
Shave hooks, with triangular or curved blades set at right angles to the handle, are used to strip paint from moulded woodwork such as window or door frames and banisters. You can now buy a super-efficient scraper with a long handle for leverage and strong, sharp replaceable blades.

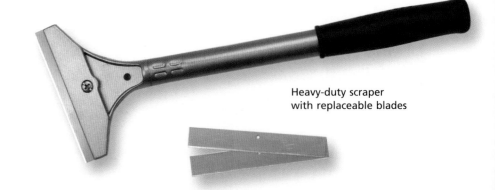

Heavy-duty scraper with replaceable blades

Hot-air guns Hot-air guns have largely superseded blowtorches to soften paint before stripping. They work like a superheated hair dryer and are much safer than blowtorches as there is no naked flame.

Hot-air gun

Protect yourself Each year thousands of injuries are caused by falls from chairs or insecure ladders, rust particles or tile chips flying into eyes or burns from paint stripping chemicals. Wear safety goggles to protect your eyes; wear a face mask if there is a lot of dust; protect your hands with suitable gloves; keep dirt out of your hair with a cap or scarf; and don ear defenders for noisy jobs.

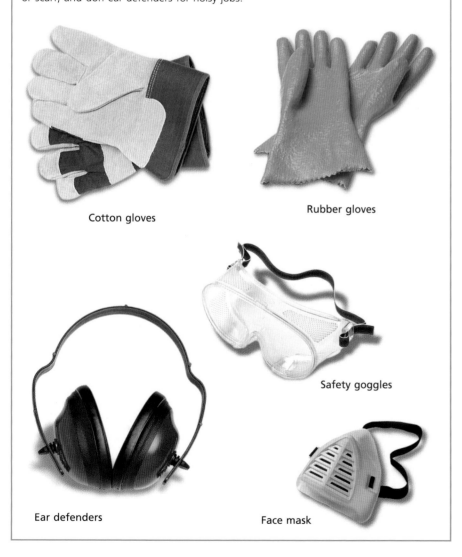

Cotton gloves

Rubber gloves

Safety goggles

Ear defenders

Face mask

Before you start to decorate

Most preparatory work creates mess and dust. Clear out everything you can and put remaining furniture in the middle of the room and cover with dustsheets. Tape plastic bags over wall and ceiling lights, sockets and switches to keep water out.

If you can, it is a good idea to lift carpets. Otherwise, protect them with dustsheets and possibly plastic sheeting as well. Take down curtains and lightshades and take off door furniture. All surfaces must be clean, dry and stable before you begin decorating. Treat damaged or problem areas and strip old paint and paper if necessary. If the surface of a stripped wall is rough in places, rub it with coarse abrasive paper on a sanding block.

Be height conscious

Use a stepladder that is high enough for you to reach the ceiling without stretching or standing on the top rung. In a stairwell, a combination ladder is useful. A stepladder can also act as a trestle for a scaffold board. Borrow another stepladder or hire a trestle for the other end of the board, which must be at least 38mm thick.

You can hire scaffold towers to use in some stairwells. The tower must be vertical, so take time to adjust the feet. Never reach forwards from a scaffold tower, or lean sideways from a ladder or stepladder.

Preparing walls and ceilings

Any professional decorator will tell you that preparation is crucial to a good finish. It's time-consuming and hard work stripping off old finishes – and even new, bare plaster needs priming – but your job will be far easier if you know what to do.

Painted or wallpapered surfaces

Gloss painted
• If repainting and existing paint is sound, wash with sugar soap and water.
• If papering, rub surface with a damp flexible sanding pad to remove the sheen and provide a key. Ideally, hang lining paper.

Emulsion painted
• If emulsion is peeling, strip back to a sound base. There may be distemper underneath.
• If the emulsion is sound, wash and roughen the surface with sugar soap and water.
• If papering, use heavy-duty paste with minimum water.

Distemper
Distemper forms a chalky barrier which prevents paint or paper adhering to the wall.
• Scrub off with a rough cloth or a nylon pan scourer and water.
• If there is a thick coating, damp the whole area, then scrape with a wide stripping knife. Never scrape bad cases of distemper without wetting it; it makes too much mess.
• Coat any remaining distemper with stabilising solution and leave to dry.

LEAD IN PAINT
Paint with a high lead content can cause lead poisoning. All household paint available in this country is now completely lead-free. However, paint in older houses – as a rough benchmark, pre-1960s – may have lead painted surfaces. Use a Lead Paint Test Kit to check. If the surface is sound, paint over it. If you need to strip the paint, take precautions: always wear a face mask conforming to BS EN149 and open the windows. Use a liquid chemical stripper, put all waste into a sealed bag and consult your local Environmental Health Department for details of safe disposal.

Standard wallpaper
• Soften ordinary wallpaper with water and a little washing-up liquid.
• Add a handful of cellulose paste to each bucket of water – it helps to hold the water on the wall.
• Use a scraper to lift off the paper.

Painted wallpaper
• Roughen the surface with coarse abrasive paper before you wet it or use a steamer.
• If the paint is thick, you may have to score the surface with a wallpaper scorer.
• Never use a wire brush – if slivers of metal become embedded in the plaster, they will rust and stain wall coverings.

Vinyls, washables and wipe-clean papers
• Buy or hire a steam wallpaper stripper especially if the wall is covered with layers of old paper. Score the surface first so that water can penetrate.
• Vinyls are easier to strip – the vinyl skin can be pulled from its backing, then the backing can be soaked and stripped.
• With some modern papers and vinyls (called easy-strip), the backing can be left on the wall as lining paper for the next wallcovering. This only works if the paper is well stuck. If there are any loose areas, strip the whole lot off.

Tiles, textures and bricks

Imitation tiling
This looks a bit like vinyl flooring on the wall. It was usually put up with a strong adhesive and can be hard to remove.
• Pull the top layer from its backing.
• Soak off the backing and old adhesive with hot water, scraping it away as it softens.
• Alternatively, try using a steam wallpaper stripper.
• If the adhesive is very stubborn, try using a hot-air gun to soften it.

Textured coatings
Thick coatings applied by brush or roller on ceilings and walls are difficult to remove.
• You could try using a steam wallpaper stripper (see right).
• Alternatively, try a proprietary textured-paint remover which works like a chemical paint stripper.
• If you simply want to repaint the textured surface, lightly scrub it with a mild solution of sugar soap and water and allow to dry.

Polystyrene tiles
Expanded polystyrene ceiling tiles can be painted with emulsion but never with gloss paint. To remove tiles, lever each one away from the surface and then scrape off the glue (see page 76).

Ceramic tiles
If tiles are to be painted, make sure they are clean and dry, then use a specialist tile paint. You cannot hang wallpaper over tiles so you may wish to remove them (page 76). This is hard work, and may necessitate replastering the wall.

Cork tiles
Cork tiles cannot be painted over, though you may be able to cover them with lining paper and wallpaper.
• Prise each tile away from the wall with a wide stripping knife or a bolster chisel.
• To remove hard lumps of glue, follow the instructions for taking down expanded polystyrene tiles (page 76).

Exposed brick
• Brush the bricks to remove dust.
• Paint interior bricks with emulsion or leave unpainted.

Steam-stripping a ceiling

You can use a steam wallpaper stripper to remove old painted or washable wallpaper from a ceiling. Because you will be using the steaming plate above head level, take precautions to protect yourself from being splashed by very hot water. Wear a baseball cap or similar headgear, safety goggles, a long-sleeved shirt and work gloves. Set up a work platform across the room, rather than trying to work from steps, so you can hold the steaming plate in front of you as you work across the ceiling strip by strip. Put down plenty of dustsheets, and let the scrapings fall to the floor.

A steam stripper will also help to remove old textured ceiling finishes such as Artex, allowing you to scrape the softened coating off area by area. Be warned, however; this is a messy and time-consuming job, and you may prefer to employ a plasterer to apply a skim coat of plaster over the old finish to create a smooth ceiling surface.

Problem surfaces

Efflorescence
Damp can cause chemicals in mortar or plaster to come to the surface and form a whitish fluff called efflorescence. Brush this off the wall, then apply an alkali-resisting primer or a stabilising solution.

Stains
Cover stains made by tar deposits in a flue or rust marks on a wall, for instance, with an aluminium primer-sealer. This stops the stain from bleeding through the new paint.

Damp
Do not isolate damp by applying an impervious coating – this will simply cause it to move elsewhere, creating fresh problems. Find and cure the cause (page 246).

Holes and cracks
Brush away any loose or crumbling plaster from small holes and cracks, and repair the area with an appropriate filler (page 78).
Larger holes, gaps and cracks require more extensive treatment (pages 222–7).

Uneven plaster
Level out slight irregularities with a skimming coat of surface plaster.

Preparing and stripping wood and metal

Whether your woodwork or pipework are brand new or old and coated with layers of paint, they will need some preparation before you decorate. Adding another layer of paint to a door, window frame or radiator will seldom hide imperfections in the layer beneath.

Woodwork

New bare wood
• Apply knotting to all visible knots to stop resin bleeding from them.
• Look for cracks and blemishes which need filling. Use fine surface filler for interior wood.
• Smooth the wood by hand, using fine abrasive paper, working with the grain. Alternatively, use an orbital or multi-purpose power sander, again working with the grain. Be gentle, because with power tools even the finer grades of abrasive paper remove wood very fast.

Old bare wood
• If there are signs of wet rot – soft patches easily penetrated by a penknife blade – then these will need dealing with: see page 247.
• Fill all cracks and gaps with filler as for new wood. When set, smooth with fine abrasive paper.
• As soon as preparatory work is complete, apply a coat of wood primer.

Painted wood
If paint is sound and in good condition, do not strip it unless the thickness causes an obstruction – making windows hard to open, for instance. Instead, clean with sugar soap and water. This removes dirt and keys the existing paint so that new paint will adhere to it.

Keying (roughening a gloss surface very finely) is essential; without it new paint is easily damaged and scratched off.

Where paintwork is slightly damaged but mainly sound, only work on the damaged areas. Rub with a damp flexible sanding pad to remove all loose material, wipe clean and allow to dry. Prime bare wood where it is exposed. Then lightly rub the whole area with very fine abrasive paper and wash with sugar soap, as for sound paintwork. Fill small chips with fine surface filler.

Varnished wood
Use a chemical paint stripper or varnish remover to get back to bare wood.

Stained wood
If the wood is to be painted and the stain is old, rub down with a flexible sanding pad. If the wood is to be sealed to give a natural finish, remove the stain with a wood bleach. Follow the instructions on the can.

Wood treated with preservative
Coat the wood with an aluminium primer-sealer. Otherwise the preservative may bleed through.

Metal

New iron and steel
Wipe off grease with lint-free rag, then use abrasive paper to remove rust and wipe clean. Apply metal primer.

Old rusted iron and steel
• Wear safety goggles and leather gloves for protection.
• Use wire brushes and abrasive paper to remove all rust.
• Fill any serious pitting with epoxy-based filler. If it is left untreated, rust can eat through thin metal, leaving holes. This quite often happens to old steel window frames.
• Epoxy-based filler is a rust inhibitor, so it can be applied to sound surfaces still showing signs of rust discoloration.
• Before painting the metal, apply a metal primer. This contains zinc to prevent further rusting. Different primers are available for different types of metal.

Aluminium alloy and anodised aluminium (such as windows and patio doors)
These materials have a very shiny surface and, in good condition, do not need painting. But if you want to match a decorating scheme, clean them first with white spirit, dry off and then apply enamel paint direct. No primer or undercoat is necessary.

Copper (such as central heating pipes)
Remove any protective grease with white spirit and rub away any discoloration with fine abrasive paper or wire wool. Wipe clean, then apply gloss paint or enamel paint direct. No primer or undercoat is necessary. Ordinary gloss can withstand the heat of water passing through the pipes.

Stainless and chromium-plated steel
This should not require painting but, if desired, apply gloss paint or enamel paint direct after removing any grease with white spirit.

Painted metal window frames
As with painted woodwork in good condition, do not interfere with sound paint on metal, unless a build-up of paint is making frames too tight. If the paint does not need stripping, clean down the frames with sugar soap and water. Key the surface with fine abrasive paper or wire wool, then apply a primer and gloss paint.

Where rust is lifting paint
This may be found in older houses where window frames were not galvanised. Wear safety goggles and brush away flaking paint with a wire brush. Scrape back the remaining paint to reveal bright metal. Do not ignore any hidden rust; it can lead to a new attack. Treat with rust inhibitor, apply a metal primer and paint with gloss.

A hot-air gun will make paint bubble up from the surface. It can then be scraped away with a stripping knife – or a shave hook for tricky shaped mouldings.

Stripping wallpaper

Stripping wallpaper cannot be rushed. If the paper is not wet enough, it will be difficult to remove. You can use a scraper and water or a steam stripper. In either case, it's a good idea to perforate the paper first using an orbital wallpaper scorer. This allows water or steam to penetrate the surface and soften the paste.

Tools *Bucket; sponge or old paintbrush; dust sheets; wide stripping knife; wallpaper scorer (serrated scraper or orbital scorer).*

Materials *Water; wallpaper paste; washing-up liquid.*

Stripping standard wallpaper

1 Cover the floor with dustsheets.

2 Go over the surface of the paper with a scoring tool.

3 Fill a bucket with warm water. Add a handful of wallpaper paste and a squirt of washing-up liquid. The paste helps to hold the water on the wall and the detergent acts as a wetting agent which speeds up the penetration of the water.

> **HELPFUL TIP**
>
> Wetting the wall with a hand-held garden spray gun is quicker than using a brush or sponge.

4 Wet a whole wall, applying water generously with a large sponge or an old paintbrush.

TEXTURED WALL COATINGS

Removing a thick textured coating is a messy job – especially if it's a ceiling. You can use a textured-paint remover or a steam wallpaper stripper (see page 72). Before you start, clear all furniture and protect the floor with newspaper, which can be thrown away as it becomes covered with stripped compound. Wear a cap, gloves and goggles.

Removing the coating
• If using paint remover, apply thickly with a large paintbrush and leave it to penetrate for the time given on the container. When the surface has softened, strip it off with a wide-bladed wallpaper scraper. Wash the surface with water and washing-up liquid before redecorating.
• If using a steam wallpaper stripper, allow the steam to break through the paint barrier and soften the material underneath. Then scrape it off with a stripping knife.

Alternatively You can cover a textured coating with a thin skim of plaster, or by attaching battens to the wall and putting up sheets of plasterboard, but these are both expensive options. For a quicker and cheaper DIY solution, a smoothing compound is now available, which can be applied to an entire wall or ceiling with a wide flexible knife.

SAFETY NOTE Never sand a textured coating – either with a power tool or by hand. Many old coatings contain asbestos which is dangerous if inhaled.

5 Leave the water to soak into the surface for at least five minutes.

6 Test to see whether the paper is ready to be stripped. Slide the edge of a wide stripping knife under the wet paper either at the bottom of the length or at a seam.

7 Hold the knife at an angle of about 30° and push it away from you, up the wall. Do not let the blade gouge the plaster. If the paper does not wrinkle and is hard to lift, it needs to soak for longer.

8 Sponge on more water if necessary and try the test again – if the paper wrinkles, pull it away from the wall upwards. It should come away in a fairly big strip.

9 Ease the stripper under the wet covering again and continue to peel away paper. If the paper won't come off the wall despite a good soaking, use a steam wallpaper stripper.

> **SAFETY TIP**
>
> If you have to get paper out from behind a light switch or socket, switch off electricity at the consumer unit (fuse box) before loosening the faceplate screws.

Stripping washable, heavy relief and painted paper

Wallpaper that has been covered with paint can be removed in the same way as standard wallpaper, but the coating must be scored vigorously to allow the water to penetrate.

Tools *Bucket; sponge or old paintbrush; wide stripping knife; water; wallpaper paste; washing-up liquid; scoring tool, serrated scraper or wallpaper scorer.*

1 Score the surface with a serrated scraper or orbital scorer so that water can soak through into the paper. Do not use a wire brush or wire wool – small pieces of metal may become embedded in the plaster underneath and cause stains on the new paper surface.

2 Apply water and strip the covering as for standard wallpaper. If the covering comes off easily, it may be that it was not put up properly. Alternatively, the walls may be damp, in which case find the cause and remedy the problems before redecorating.

Vinyls and easy-strip papers

1 With a fingernail or knife blade, lift a corner of the covering away from its backing paper.

USING A STEAM STRIPPER

If you want to strip a room in a day, your best bet is to use a steam stripper.

Tools *Steam stripper; wallpaper scorer; rubber gloves; safety goggles; wide stripping knife; dustsheets.*

Before you start Cover the area with dustsheets and put on some old work clothes and a pair of rubber gloves. Read the instruction leaflet carefully.

1 Fill the tank, switch the stripper on and wait for the light to come on, indicating that the stripper is ready. This usually takes about ten minutes, when steam begins to come out of the perforated plate. While you are waiting, score the surface of the paper with a scoring tool.

2 Strip a length at a time, working from the bottom up, loosening stubborn areas with a stripping knife. Hold the plate at the bottom of the length. Keep it in position until the paper around it shows signs of damp – usually after about a minute.

2 Peel the covering away from the backing, keeping it as close as possible to the wall. If you stand back and pull the strip of top paper towards you, it may pull the backing paper with it.

3 Holding the plate in one hand over the next area you are going to strip, use the other to start scraping the paper from the first area.

4 Top up the tank as necessary, first switching off and leaving the stripper to cool for half a minute.

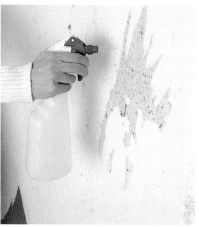

5 If you find you've missed any bits, spray them with a garden spray gun. This will soak in and allow you to scrape them off easily.

TIP Take care when using a stripper on plasterboard. The steam will soften the surface, so use a stripping knife as little as possible and do not dig it in.

3 If the backing paper is stuck securely to the wall and in good condition, use it as lining paper for the next covering. But if it is damaged or not stuck firmly, strip it off as for standard wallpaper.

SAFETY TIP

If you are stripping wallpaper around power points, wall lights or light switches, protect them with plastic bags taped on with masking tape, and switch off electricity at the consumer unit (fuse box) before using water or steam around them.

Removing tiles from walls and ceilings

Leaving tiles in place and painting or tiling over them is often the easiest option, but if you want a flat finish for painting or wallpapering the tiles will need to be removed.

Ceramic tiles

Tiles in older houses may be stuck to the wall with cement mortar – sometimes 15mm thick. If you remove them you will probably need to have the wall plastered before you can decorate. Tiles stuck with adhesive are easier to get off, but they may pull plaster with them. In this case, the surface will need to be made good.

Tools *Heavy duty gloves; safety goggles; dust mask; wide steel masonry chisel (bolster); club hammer; paint scraper. Possibly also: power sander.*

Before you start Put on protective clothing – splinters of glass from the glaze will fly in all directions as you chip away at the tiles. Close doors to prevent dust escaping from the room.

1 Prise the tiles away from the wall one at a time with a bolster chisel and a club hammer. Some will come away in one piece, others may crack and break. There is no easy technique – continue to chisel until you have removed all of the tiles.

2 Use a hot-air gun to soften old adhesive left on the wall and then scrape it off with a paint scraper.

Polystyrene tiles and cork tiles

Tools *Wide stripping knife or bolster chisel; safety goggles; possibly a hot-air gun.*

1 Lever tiles away from the surface using a wide stripping knife or bolster chisel. They are more likely to break into pieces than come off whole. Although the tiles will come away easily, adhesive – which is difficult to remove – will remain.

2 Use a hot-air gun to apply heat direct to the remaining glue and then scrape it off with a stripping knife.

Stripping poor paintwork

Paint can be stripped with the help of chemicals or heat – often it is best to use a combination of methods. If wood is to be repainted, you won't have to strip off every bit of paint, as you must if you want to varnish the wood.

Using a hot-air gun

A hot-air gun will soften paint so that scrapers can remove it more easily. Some have an attachment to shield glass from heat when stripping window frames. Because of the risk of fire, do not put any newspaper on the floor. Instead, keep a steel tray (an old baking sheet is fine) below to catch paint peelings. Wear cotton gloves (rubber gloves will make your hands too hot in the heat caused by the gun).

1 Soften the paint by moving the hot-air gun backwards and forwards. The heat is very strong so do not concentrate in one area or you may burn the surface. The paint should soften in seconds.

2 Strip the paint from flat areas with a broad-bladed scraper. Push the tool away from you or upwards. When scraping a vertical surface, make sure your hand is not immediately below the hot paint, which may drop onto it.

3 When using a shave hook on mouldings, hold it at an angle, so that hot paint cannot fall onto your hand.

4 If you accidentally scorch the surface, rub fine abrasive paper along the grain to remove charred wood.

5 Apply a wood primer and paint.

SAFETY TIP

Any pre-1960s paintwork is likely to contain lead. Wear gloves and a face mask when stripping old paint. Seal the waste in a bag and contact your local council for details of how to dispose of it – don't burn it.

Paint strippers

Chemical strippers are good at removing paint completely from wood, especially if you want to varnish it. Most are applied in liquid form or as a paste. They are useful for stripping window frames, where heat could crack the glass. However, this method can be slow and costly. Always neutralise strippers – as directed on the container – before redecorating.

Using liquid strippers Wear safety goggles and protect your hands with rubber gloves. If you spill any on your skin, wash off immediately. Open all the windows because these products give off strong fumes.

1 Use an old paintbrush to apply liquid stripper. The paint wrinkles and breaks up about 15 minutes after application. Give the stripper enough time to work – if you try to strip the paint too soon it will not come away and another application of stripper will be needed. If you leave it too long, it will dry and begin to harden again.

2 Remove the paint using a shave hook on moulded surfaces – pulling the tool towards you.

3 On flat surfaces, push a wide scraper away from you. A heavy build-up of paint will need more than one application.

Using paste or gel strippers Use this type of stripper on vertical surfaces. It will not run to the floor, is easier to control and more effective.

1 Protect the surrounding area with newspaper. Apply the stripper in a thick coat, which will slowly set on the surface while the chemicals work beneath.

2 Follow the manufacturer's instructions; it is usually best to cover the paste with cling film and occasionally spray it with water.

3 After the recommended time (hours rather than minutes), scrape away the paste – it will bring the old paint with it.

Choosing fillers

A huge range of fillers is available, with new ones being brought out all the time. Here are the main ones.

Hairline crack filler For fine cracks in plaster, plasterboard and painted surfaces.
• Liquid filler applied by brush from a tin.
• Dries white in 10 minutes.
• Not suitable on damp surfaces.
• Fully dry in 24 hours.

Paste filler For cracks up to 2mm, small blemishes indoors and gaps in wood.
• Comes in tubes and tubs.
• Surface dry in 30–60 minutes; rapid repair versions dry in 5–20 minutes.

Internal plaster repair Gives a smooth finish to damaged plaster surfaces.
• Sold in ready mixed and powder form.
• Fill deep holes (over 50mm) in layers.
• Dry in 24 hours.

Exterior filler General filling for external masonry, concrete and paving.
• Available ready mixed or as powder.
• Sets in 1 hour and is drillable.
• Dries to a grey, weatherproof finish.

All-purpose filler For cracks and holes in most materials, inside and out.
• Powder or paste; some types are mixed with a diluted adhesive for outside use.
• Dries to a tough, weather-resistant surface that should be painted.
• Do not expose to permanent damp.

Polyester-based metal filler Cracks in metal gutters and downpipes.
• Chemically bonded filler and catalyst.
• Quick setting – use within 5 minutes.
• Can be sanded after about 20 minutes.

Wood fillers Repairs cracks and small holes in wood, inside and out.
• Solvent-free paste in tubes and tubs.
• Comes in various wood colours.
• Sets in about 10 minutes; can be sanded, drilled and stained.
• Epoxy-based wood fillers are very strong. Use to any depth; they can be drilled, screwed or planed when dry. The chemically bonded filler and catalyst is quick-setting, so use within 5 minutes.

Frame sealant Fills gaps between masonry and window or door frames.
• Flexible, rubbery paste applied from container fitted into cartridge gun.
• Forms a skin after about 4 hours and can then be painted.
• Available in white and other colours.

Foam filler Largely used for holes or gaps round pipes through a wall, inside or out.
• Sticky foam applied to dampened surface from pressure spray.
• Expensive but good for awkward areas.
• Workable for about 5–7 minutes.
• Expands to 60 times its original volume and moulds to fit shape of hole. Can be cut, sanded and painted when dry.

Filling small holes and cracks

Small cracks, dents, holes or gouges in plaster walls or ceilings can be repaired with interior filler.

Tools *Old paintbrush; filling knife; abrasive paper and block, or power sander. Possibly also: trimming knife; large paintbrush; cold chisel; garden spray gun; length of wood.*

Materials *Suitable filler.*

1 Rake out the crack with a filling knife. If the crack is in plasterboard and the paper surface has been torn, cut off jagged edges with a sharp trimming knife.

2 Brush the crack with a dry brush to remove dust.

3 Load filler onto the end of the filling knife blade and draw the blade across the crack. Scrape the excess off the blade, then draw it down the crack to remove excess filler from the wall and smooth the surface.

4 For deeper holes, build up the surface in layers, working from the edges. Wait about two hours for each layer to dry before applying the next.

5 When the filler is completely dry, smooth it to the level of the surrounding surface with medium or fine abrasive paper wrapped round a wooden block, or use a power sander with fine-grade sandpaper.

HELPFUL TIP

If the filler pulls away from the wall as you smooth it with your filling knife, try wetting the blade.

Filling awkward gaps and holes

Some holes cannot be filled properly with standard interior fillers. You can buy special fillers to deal with them.

Awkward gaps include the long cracks running from the top to the bottom of a wall – especially in stairwells. These can be filled, but if they open up again, this could indicate a structural problem and you need advice from a builder or surveyor.

Cracks often occur at wall joints or wall-and-ceiling joints and between walls and woodwork. All these can be filled with a flexible mastic.

Foam filler

Deep cavities – around a pipe through a wall, for example – can be difficult to fill but the job is easier if you use foam filler. Wear the gloves supplied – the foam is very sticky until it sets.

Before you start Experiment to see how fast the foam comes out of the nozzle and how much it expands.

1 Brush any dust out of the hole and dampen the surface with water.

2 Allowing for expansion, release foam into the hole. You may only need a thin bead.

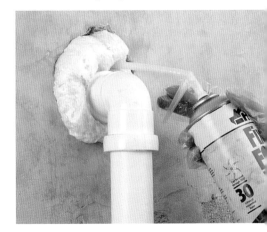

3 Leave the foam for 1 to 2 hours. When it has set, cut any excess away with a hacksaw blade or a sharp knife. Wear a mask to avoid inhaling the dust.

Flexible mastic

Gaps between walls and window frames, skirting boards, door frames and staircases, move. Therefore they should be filled with a flexible mastic that sticks well and resists cracking. The mastic is applied with a cartridge gun.

• If the cracks are deep, half-fill them with thin strips of expanded polystyrene before applying the sealant.
• Make sure the sealant reaches to both sides of the gap. Press it in and smooth the surface with a wetted fingertip.

HELPFUL TIP

Instead of licking your fingertip to run along a bead of sealant, dip it in a solution of 50:50 water and washing-up liquid. If you have sensitive skin, use the back of a wetted teaspoon instead.

Using wood filler

The type of wood filler you choose depends on whether the wood is going to be painted or simply waxed or varnished.

Wood must have a well-prepared surface before the final finish is applied. This means filling any holes before the wood is finally sanded smooth. If the wood is to be left its natural colour, buy a wood filler that matches. If it is going to be painted, fill with an interior filler.

Tools *Filling knife; abrasive paper; electric sander.*

Materials *Interior filler or wood filler.*

1 If you plan to paint the wood, use a power sander with fine abrasive paper to key existing paintwork. Then wash it with a solution of hot water and sugar soap.

2 If you are repainting the area, use interior wood filler to fill any defects such as cracks or dents. Be sure to press the filler in firmly and scrape away any excess.

3 Once the filler has set hard, sand it smooth ready for painting.

4 If you intend to apply a finish through which the wood can be seen – stain, wax or varnish – then sand it smooth and fill it with a wood filler (known as stopping) that matches the colour of the bare wood as closely as possible.

5 Press the stopping into the holes and cracks, taking care not to spread it into the surrounding grain.

6 Wait until the stopping has dried to the same colour all over – usually about 30 minutes – then sand it flat.

Filling an open woodgrain

If a wooden door has a very open grain, and you want to achieve a smooth painted finish, you will need to work in a paste of fine-surface filler. Apply the filler with a flexible filling knife, pushing it right into the grain. Then wipe away the excess with a damp rag.

Tools for painting

As with all tools, quality counts. Buy the best painting tools you can afford and take care of them.

Brushes Good quality brushes improve with use, as the tips become rounded and any loose bristles come out. Cheap brushes usually contain far less bristle for a given width, and they are often badly anchored so that the bristles tend to fall out. Use cheap brushes for applying wood preservatives to rough timber or removing dust after sanding down.

Radiator brush Bristles are at right angles to the handle for painting awkward places, such as behind radiators and pipes.

Synthetic fibre brushes
• Easy to clean.
• Bristles are locked-in.
• Especially good with water-based paints.
• Standard 50mm, 25mm and 12mm brushes are ideal for painting woodwork.
• Wide 100mm or 150mm brushes are used for walls and ceilings.

Angled cutting-in brush This brush is useful for window frames as its angled tip helps you to get close to the glass without getting paint on it.

150mm brush

50mm brush

25mm brush

12mm brush

Cutting-in brush

Radiator brush

Paint shield Use a plastic or metal shield to keep paint off glass when painting window frames. You can also use one to prevent your brush from picking up dirt from a floor when painting a skirting board.

Paint kettle Pour paint into a paint kettle as required. The kettle has a handle, unlike most small paint tins. Line the kettle with foil before pouring in the paint. This can be removed and thrown away after use.

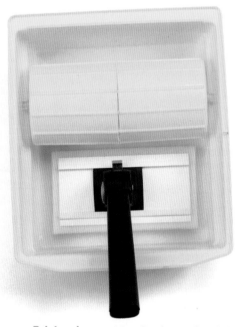

Paint pads A pad is a fine layer of mohair bonded to a foam strip, which is mounted on a handle. Pads vary in size from about 25mm square up to a width of 180mm and also come in useful shapes, such as a crevice pad for painting into corners. You need a tray for the paint.
• Pads are best for water-based paints; most solvents used for cleaning oil-based paints will attack the adhesive.
• Like rollers, some pads have hollow handles for extension poles.

50mm paint pad

150mm paint pad

100mm paint pad

Crevice pad

Rollers An easy way to spread emulsion paint quickly over large areas is with a paint roller. A metal or plastic roller tray is needed for painting with a roller.

Foam rollers These are good general-purpose rollers if a high finish is not important. They can only be used on smooth and lightly textured surfaces. Patterned foam rollers will apply textured paint in relief over a smooth surface.

Sheepskin rollers Synthetic sheepskin makes a good all-purpose roller for covering large areas with emulsion. Will cover uneven surfaces, such as woodchip.

Mohair rollers The very fine pile of mohair rollers (which are mostly synthetic) gives a high-quality finish. Suitable for paints with a sheen, such as silk emulsion and gloss.

Radiator rollers Small rollers on a longer handle are useful for painting areas difficult to reach, such as behind radiators.

Extension handles Most rollers have a hollow handle that will take a telescopic extension pole so you can reach the tops of walls or ceilings.

Sheepskin roller sleeve

Fine foam roller sleeve

Mohair roller sleeve

Roller frame

Patterned foam roller for textured coating

Telescopic extension handle for roller

Radiator roller and changeable head

Power roller A power roller makes light work of covering large areas of wall with emulsion. Paint is fed continuously along the hollow extension pole by a pump, so you never need to stop to reload the roller. Keep the roller moving to avoid drips and runs. Power rollers can be hired.

Roller tray and sheepskin roller

What goes on before the paint?

Most surfaces require a preparatory coating to make sure they are stable and sealed before you can apply any paint. Be sure to choose a coating suitable for the surface and consider whether it is indoors or out.

Take special care with any painted surface that will be exposed to the weather. The end grain of wood must be thoroughly soaked with primer to prevent the rain from penetrating. Primer by itself is not particularly weather-resistant, so do not leave a primed surface exposed to rain and wind for long. Cover it with an undercoat and a topcoat as soon as possible.

New windows, doors and other wooden fittings are usually supplied ready primed. Check for scratches and other damage and prime any areas that have become exposed. Give a second coat of primer to any areas that will become hidden by brickwork after the fitting is installed.

When using a microporous paint on bare wood, no primer or undercoat is needed. Do not apply more than two coats.

All bare or new wood needs a sealing coat of primer before it can be painted. First, coat any knots with knotting. Then apply a wood primer or an all-purpose acrylic primer. This is water-based and dries fast.

Choosing primers and other sealers

Knotting
• Paint onto resinous areas, especially knots, in wood.
• Prevents resin in wood from seeping out and discolouring paint.
• When dry, coat knotting with primer.

Primer
• Apply to new or bare wood, plaster (see below) or metal.
• Seals pores in absorbent surfaces and forms a key to which other coats grip.
• Buy primer for a specific surface or use all-purpose primer.
• Prime bare plaster with proprietary sealer or a coat of emulsion diluted to one part water and four parts paint.

Primer-sealer
• For stained walls and plaster, old bituminous coatings and areas treated with preservative.
• Contains fine scales of aluminium and forms a barrier to seal the surface.
• Apply a second coat if stain is still visible after the first has dried.

Stabilising solution
• Sometimes used to seal distemper.
• Binds together surfaces to provide a firm support for paint.
• Apply fungicide before stabilising solution on a mould-affected surface.

Fungicide
• Kills mould on any affected surface.
• When spores are dead, brush them away and apply another coat.

How much paint do you need?

Work out how much paint you need before you buy any at all. It's better to overestimate than underestimate, so as to be sure that you can complete an entire room, or the outside of your house, with paint from the same batch.

Most paint tins indicate the average area of wall or other surface they will cover, but the table below offers a rough general guide for different types of paint. Porosity, texture and the base colour of the surface will affect the amount you actually need. Highly porous surfaces, such as bare plaster, will absorb a considerable amount – especially when priming. Rough surfaces, such as woodchip or pebbledash, are also very thirsty. Two or three undercoats may be necessary to cover a very strong base colour, and always allow for at least two topcoats for good protection against the weather on external surfaces.

COVERAGE PER LITRE

Coating	Coverage
Primer	8–12m²
Undercoat	16m²
Gloss	14m²
Non-drip gloss	12m²
Emulsion	10–13m²
Masonry paint	5–10m²

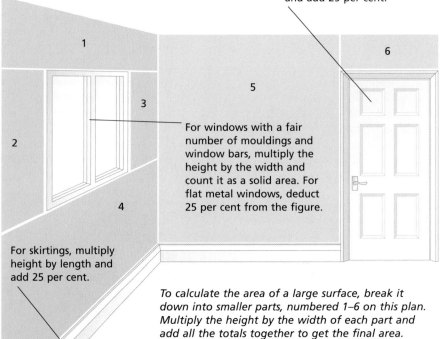

To find the area of a moulded door, multiply height by width and add 25 per cent.

For windows with a fair number of mouldings and window bars, multiply the height by the width and count it as a solid area. For flat metal windows, deduct 25 per cent from the figure.

For skirtings, multiply height by length and add 25 per cent.

To calculate the area of a large surface, break it down into smaller parts, numbered 1–6 on this plan. Multiply the height by the width of each part and add all the totals together to get the final area.

Choosing paints for every purpose

Before you buy paint, study colour charts, or buy some tester pots to try out on the wall. Paint tends to look darker once it is applied, so if you are doubtful about which shade to buy, choose the paler one.

Solvent-based paint, or gloss, is used for wood or metalwork and water-based emulsions for walls and ceilings. Solvent-based paint must be used with an undercoat, but this is not necessary for emulsion. Water-based gloss paints are also now available. They are faster to dry and easier to clean, but tend to give a less glossy finish.

Modern 'thixotropic' paints are jelly-like in consistency and ideal for less experienced decorators, as they will not drip. They may be more expensive per litre, but seldom need an undercoat or second topcoat, so may not cost more in the long run.

Solid non-drip emulsion is sold in wide shallow trays designed to take a standard decorating roller – they are ideal for painting ceilings.

The final coat of paint – the topcoat – can have a gloss, semi-gloss or matt finish. Other names for semi-gloss include eggshell, silk, satin and sheen. The glossier the paint, the tougher and more durable the surface will be. Also, look out for moisture-resistant paints developed for kitchens and bathrooms.

Common types of paint

Undercoat
• A full-bodied paint with more pigment than topcoat and good covering power.
• Used on primed surfaces, before applying topcoat, or on dark surfaces which are to be painted a paler colour.
• Apply a second coat if undercolour shows through the first coat.
• Wash brushes with white spirit.

Solvent-based (or synthetic) gloss
• Used for woodwork and metalwork. Gloss is suitable indoors and out, though some are specially designed for exterior use.
• Can also be applied to walls and ceilings.
• On wood, always use with an undercoat.
• Apply two thin coats, rather than one thick one.
• Clean brushes with white spirit.

HELPFUL TIP
Don't stir non-drip paint, even if it looks lumpy in the tin. If the paint becomes liquid because it has been accidentally stirred or shaken, leave it to re-set before using.

Water-based gloss
• Used for woodwork and furniture.
• Dries much faster than oil-based gloss.
• Gives a hardwearing finish; glossy, but not as much as the solvent-based equivalent.
• Clean brushes with water and detergent.

Non-drip or one-coat paint
• Used for interior woodwork.
• Combines undercoat and topcoat and stays on the brush well.
• Two coats may be needed when covering a dark colour.
• Clean brushes with white spirit.

Emulsion
• Water-based paint used for walls and ceilings.
• Dries quickly and does not leave brush marks.
• Can be diluted with 20 per cent water to form its own primer for bare plaster.
• Use a roller for fast coverage.
• Two or three coats may be needed.
• Clean tools with water and soap or detergent.

Anti-condensation paint
• The best paint to use in bathrooms and kitchens as it will not peel away when exposed to a lot of steam.
• A semi-porous emulsion which absorbs moisture in the air and allows it to evaporate as the air dries.
• Will not cure condensation, only reduce its effect on the painted surface by preventing droplets forming on the surface.

• Often contains fungicide to deter mould.
• Apply in the same way as emulsion.
• Clean tools with water and detergent.

Textured (plastic) coating
• Can be applied to walls and ceilings with uneven or unattractive surfaces. Exterior weatherproof versions available.
• Much thicker than paint: it forms a permanent coating which is extremely difficult to remove.
• Apply with a shaggy roller, unless the manufacturer specifies otherwise.
• Coat with emulsion once dry.
• Clean tools with white spirit.

Masonry paint
• Used for render and pebbledash.
• Two main types – textured and smooth.
• Textured paint is good for concealing minor blemishes like hairline cracks.
• Smooth paint goes a lot further.

Enamel paint
• Used for metal and wood, especially children's toys and furniture.
• Non-toxic.
• No primer or undercoat needed.
• Clean brushes with white spirit.

Other special paints
There are also special paints for floors, garage floors, tiles and melamine (for revitalising kitchen units). Matt black is used for beams and blackboards, radiator enamel stays white when hot; anti-damp paint seals in minor surface dampness.

Painting techniques

A paintbrush is a versatile tool for applying primers, undercoats and varnishes, as well as topcoats to a variety of surfaces. Use one for applying gloss to wood and metalwork and for painting where colours or surfaces meet – around windows and doors, for instance.

Using a brush

1 Stir the paint – unless it is non-drip. Make sure any liquid on the surface is thoroughly mixed into the paint by lifting the stick as you stir.

2 Choose a brush which is the right size. As a rough guide, paint window frames with a 25mm brush, door panels with a 75mm brush, and walls and other large surfaces with a 100mm brush. Grip large brushes around the handle and hold smaller brushes more like a pencil.

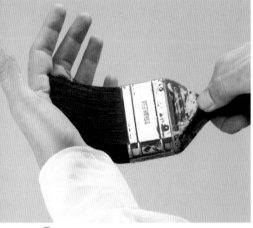

3 Flick the bristles against your hand to remove dust and any loose bristles or dried paint particles.

4 Dip the brush into a paint kettle, to about one-third of the bristle depth, to load it with paint.

5 Press the brush against the kettle wall to remove surplus paint. Do not scrape the brush over the rim of the kettle because too much paint will come off.

Painting with non-drip paint

Do not stir non-drip paint and do not remove any excess paint from the brush; it is meant to be heavily loaded. Apply the paint in horizontal bands. Don't overbrush or the paint will run.

Painting with gloss

1 Start at the top of the surface. Paint three vertical strips parallel with each other, leaving a gap just narrower than the brush width between the strips.

2 Do not reload the brush. Working from the top, brush across the painted area horizontally to fill the gaps and smooth the paint.

3 With the brush now almost dry, lightly go over the section you have just painted with vertical strokes to ensure an even coating, stopping on an upward stroke. This is called 'laying off'.

4 Using the same technique, paint a similar sized section underneath the one you have completed. Work the wet paint into the dry.

HELPFUL TIP

Line a paint kettle with aluminium foil – to make cleaning easier – and pour in paint to fill about one-third of the kettle. Do not work from the tin; you may contaminate the paint with dried paint, dirt and possibly rust from around the rim.

Painting with emulsion

1 Start at the top of the wall. Apply the paint in all directions, working horizontally across the surface and moving down when one band is complete. Do not put the paint on too thickly.

2 Lay off the paint with light brush strokes and a fairly dry brush, working in a criss-cross pattern. Lift the paint finally on upward strokes.

Painting a textured surface

When painting a surface with a heavy texture or relief, load the brush with more paint than for a smooth ceiling or wall. This cuts down the time it takes to coat the surface and fill all the little indentations. But dip to only a third of the bristle depth.

If you are painting a relief wallpaper, Anaglypta for example, use a brush as wide as you can comfortably manage without putting too much strain on your wrist. A 100mm paintbrush is ideal. With a textured coating on a wall or a ceiling, you can use a shaggy pile roller.

USING OLD PAINT

Wipe the rim before you open an old tin of paint. If a skin has formed, cut around the edge and lift it out. Stir the paint well and then strain it through an old stocking to remove any bits of hardened paint.

'Beading' where colours meet

Where walls meet the ceiling and where adjacent walls are of different colours, keep the meeting edge as straight and as neat as possible. Do not rush the job.

1 Turn the paintbrush edge on, holding it like a pen.

2 Load the brush with enough paint to cover about one-third of the bristle depth.

3 Press the brush flat against the surface so that a small amount of paint (the bead) is squeezed from the bristles. Work towards the edge gradually, rather than trying to get close immediately.

4 Draw the brush sideways or downwards along the surface, keeping your hand steady.

Cutting in

Achieve a neat finish along wall and ceiling edges by first painting the edges with a brush, before switching to a roller or pad.

1 Paint four or five overlapping strokes at right angles to the edge.

2 Cross-brush over the painted area in a long, sweeping motion, keeping parallel with the edge.

Painting with other tools

Using a roller

You can cover an area more quickly with a roller than with a brush, but you may need to apply more coats because the paint goes on quite thinly. Use a foam or mohair pile on a smooth surface and a lamb's-wool or nylon pile on a textured one.

1 Thoroughly stir the paint (unless it is a non-drip or solid roller paint).

2 Fill about one-third of the roller tray with paint. Do not overfill, or it will spill.

3 Dip the roller into the paint, then run it lightly on the ridged part of the tray. This spreads the paint evenly on the roller sleeve.

4 Push the roller backwards and forwards, alternating diagonal strokes at random.

5 Do not apply too much in one coat. And do not work too fast, or paint will be thrown off the sleeve and spatter. Try not to press the roller too hard or paint will be forced off the ends in ridges.

6 Use a small paintbrush to cut in the edges around doors, windows, corners and where walls meet the ceiling.

Using a paint pad

Paint pads are suitable for applying water-based paints. They quickly cover large areas like walls and ceilings and will cope with lightly textured surfaces.

1 Stir the paint and pour some into a flat tray or the speed tray sometimes supplied.

2 Run the pad backwards and forwards on the roller in the speed tray or hold the pad flat against the paint in the tray. Do not let it sink below the pile level. If the pad absorbs too much paint it will drip. A pad needs to be reloaded more often than a brush or roller.

3 Start painting near a corner. Move the pad in all directions with a gentle scrubbing action. Work in strips about four times the width of the pad.

4 Do not press too hard or paint may be forced off the pad in drips. With practice you should get no drips at all.

CUTTING IN WITH A PAINT PAD

As as alternative to using a brush to obtain a neat finish along wall and ceiling edges, try using an edging pad with guide wheels, which is specially designed for the job. The wheels guide the pad along the ceiling line as you push it along the wall.

Looking after brushes, rollers and pads

Always thoroughly clean paintbrushes, rollers and pads after each painting session. Use cold water to wash off water-based paint immediately and never leave any of your painting tools to soak in water.

Before you start Check on the paint tin to see what solvent is needed. Some paints require special thinners to remove them. Buy the necessary solvent at the same time as you buy the paint. Emulsion and acrylic-based paint need only plenty of clean water, plus soap or detergent. Other paints may need white spirit. You can also use a proprietary brush cleaner.

Leaving a brush loaded with paint

Pads, rollers and trays must not be left loaded with paint, but you can keep a wet brush or roller sleeve for an hour or two so long as you wrap it in tin foil or a plastic bag to keep out the air and prevent the paint from drying.

Cleaning a brush

1 Gently scrape excess paint from a brush onto paper. Use the back of a knife and work from the heel (the base of the bristles) to the tip.

2 Wash emulsion paint out of a brush under a running tap. Rub a little soap or washing-up liquid into the bristles and rinse in clean water.

3 Clean off a solvent-based paint with white spirit or proprietary brush cleaner.

4 All brushes will benefit from a final wash in soap and a rinse in clean water. Use your fingers to work out any remaining paint. Once a brush is clean, shake it vigorously outdoors to get rid of excess water.

5 When the paintbrush is dry, slip a loose rubber band over the tip of the bristles to hold them together and keep the brush in shape.

Cleaning a roller

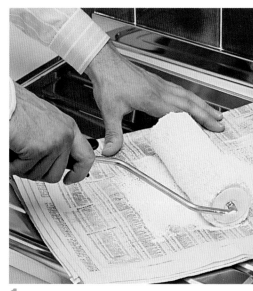

1 Run the roller over the ribbed part of the paint tray and then over sheets of newspaper to remove excess paint.

2 Remove the roller sleeve if possible. Wash under running water, working the paint out of the sleeve with your hands.

Cleaning a paint pad

1 Run the pad over paper to get rid of most of the paint.

2 Wash the pad in clean water, taking great care not to separate the mohair from the base. The process will be faster if you use a little soap, but make sure you rinse it all out in clean water.

Storing brushes, rollers and pads

Leave clean brushes and rollers to dry and then wrap them in brown paper or lint-free cloth, such as old sheeting. Store the tools flat in a warm dry place.

Paint pads are an awkward shape to wrap, so store them in sealed plastic bags to keep off dust.

How to revive a neglected brush

A brush which has not been cleaned well after use will become hard. The best way to soften a brush is to use a proprietary restorer, following the instructions on the pack. Tease out any paint particles in the base of the brush with a fine brass suede brush. Only use a restored paintbrush for rough work, like applying primer.

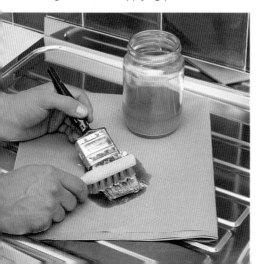

Painting walls and ceilings

To avoid spoiling newly painted surfaces with drips and spatters, paint the ceiling first, then the walls and finally the woodwork. It is a good idea to paint the ceiling (which can be a messy job) before stripping any wall coverings. But this is the only exception to the rule that all preparatory work must be done before you start painting.

Painting a ceiling

Make sure that you can safely and comfortably reach the area you are decorating. Use a scaffold board supported by trestles or stepladders. Your head should be about 75mm from the ceiling.

If you do not like working at a height, you can use an extension handle (or broomstick) fitted to the hollow handle of a roller or pad, for most of the painting. But you will need to stand on steps or a board to cut-in where the walls and ceiling meet and around the tops of doors and windows.

Paint the ceiling in strips starting near the window. If there is more than one window in the room, begin nearest the one where most light comes in. Cut in the edges as you work.

WHEN TO PAINT COVING

If you paint coving and ceiling roses after you have painted the ceiling, you will avoid getting splashes on the new paintwork. If coving is to be the same colour as the ceiling, paint it before you paint the walls, otherwise it is easier to paint coving at the end of the job.

Painting a wall

When using a roller, paint horizontal bands about 500mm wide across the wall. Work from the top to the bottom. With a brush, paint blocks about 500mm square. Start in the top right corner (or the top left one if you are left-handed). Paint the blocks from the top of the wall down and then across.

Painting different surfaces

Bare plaster Dilute emulsion to half strength with water and use it as a priming and sealing coat. Follow this with at least two coats of full strength emulsion. Use a foam or mohair roller or a paintbrush or pad as large as you can comfortably work with. Do any touching up with a small paintbrush as you go while paint is still wet.

Paper Lining paper is the ideal surface for painting, as it hides small cracks and blemishes. Apply at least two coats of paint, using whichever tool you prefer. Do not worry if small bubbles appear on the paper. They disappear as the paint dries.
• Paint high relief papers such as Anaglypta with a shaggy pile roller.
• Old wallpaper can be painted but does not give great results. Test an area first to see that the paper does not bubble or come away from the wall. If it does, you must strip the wall, but if not, apply full-strength emulsion as the first coat. The less water getting onto the wall the better. Use a roller, pad or brush.
• Do not paint over wallpapers that contain a metallic pattern – the pattern tends to show through the paint.

Painted surface New emulsion paint can be applied straight onto old provided the surface has been washed down. If there is a drastic colour change, two or three coats will be needed. Never paint over distemper – it must be removed (page 72). As a general rule, do not paint walls or ceilings with gloss; it enhances blemishes in the surface and is prone to condensation. If you want to paint an old gloss surface, first rub it down with a flexible sanding pad or fine wet-and-dry abrasive paper, damped with clean water. This destroys the glaze on the paint and helps the new paint film to grip the old. Wipe away dust before painting.

Textured coatings Use a brush or shaggy pile roller to put on the paint; you will find that emulsion gives the best result. Textured coatings are sometimes abrasive so they may rip foam rollers and can be difficult to coat thoroughly.

Ceiling tiles Paint polystyrene tiles with emulsion, as long as they are clean. Use a roller, and a small brush for the joins between the tiles. Never use a gloss paint – it creates a fire hazard when it is put on expanded polystyrene. If you plan to stick polystyrene tiles on the ceiling, it is much easier to paint them before you put them up, especially if they have chamfered edges.

Painting walls with glazes

A glaze is a thin, almost transparent film of oil-based colour. The oil slows the glaze's drying time but you still have to work fast. Glazes can be put over surfaces coated with a matt or eggshell solvent-based paint, but will not adhere to a gloss finish. The surface must be thoroughly prepared, as glazing will highlight any imperfections.

Whether or not you need to buy special tools for applying a glaze depends on which techniques you are going to use. You can sponge, rag, drag or stipple a glaze, using normal household materials – such as old cloths – or specialist products. Good stippling and dragging brushes are expensive, but cheaper versions may give poor results.

You can buy transparent oil-based glaze, called scumble glaze, which varies in shade from pale to mid-brown. As a rough guide, a 2.5 litre tin of glaze will be enough to cover all the walls in a room 3.5m x 3.5m.

Paint kettle for glaze

Flogger (for dragging)

Paint tray

Rubber gloves

Lint-free rags

Mixing jar for thinning colours

Stippling brush

100mm paintbrush

Real sponge

Artist's oil colours

Tinting the glaze

Use artist's oil colours or universal stainers to tint the glaze to the colour you want. Mixing a glaze to achieve a particular colour is a matter of trial and error which becomes easier with practice. Always mix up more glaze than you think you need – it is impossible to match a colour if you run out halfway through the job.

All the painting techniques with glazes require basic tools and materials – a paint kettle, white spirit and rags for mopping up spills, for example – as well as the particular painting tool needed to achieve the desired decorative effect.

1 Blend a small blob of colour – a little goes a long way – with white spirit.

2 Add this to the rest of the glaze in the paint kettle, stirring all the time to mix them well.

3 Test the result on the surface to be painted and repeat the process, if necessary, adding more of the same or a different colour until you are satisfied.

4 Glaze is usually diluted with some white spirit before you apply it to a surface. The consistency should be easy to work with – about the same as single cream.

5 If the glaze thickens as you work (because the white spirit has evaporated) stir in some more white spirit – but be careful with the amount because too much will weaken the colour.

Alternatively You can achieve similar painting effects with eggshell solvent-based paint, although the mixture is not strictly a glaze.
• Mix one part paint to two parts white spirit. It is best to choose white paint and then to tint it to the required colour.
• As with an ordinary glaze, blend a blob of colour with white spirit, add it to the paint mixture and try out the result. Keep blending more colour with the diluted paint until you achieve the colour you want.
• This 'glaze' dries quickly so it is more suited to sponging and ragging than to dragging or stippling.

You can produce decorative effects with emulsion paint as well – one part diluted with three or four parts water – but this dries even faster. Tint the emulsion paint with water-soluble paints – use gouache, acrylic or poster paints – and dilute the emulsion with water, not with white spirit. Always apply an emulsion 'glaze' over an emulsion base coat – not a solvent-based one.

Protecting the surface It is advisable – but not essential – to protect a decorative finish with varnish. Make sure the glazed surface is completely dry (this may take 24 hours or longer) before you do so.

Choose gloss, semi-gloss or matt varnish, depending on how shiny you want the result to be, and buy varnish with as little colour in it as possible.

Brush on a thin coat, working from the top of the wall down. If you use two coats of varnish, allow the first to dry thoroughly before applying the second. Matt varnish, which gives a good flat finish but not a tough one, will not need a second coat.

Sponging a wall

Glaze applied to the wall with a sponge produces a soft, dappled effect.

Tools *Real (not synthetic) sponge; paint kettle, flat paint tray or baking tin; rags; rubber gloves.*

Materials *Glaze tinted the desired colour; white spirit.*

Before you start Find an inconspicuous area and practise the technique until you feel confident that you are achieving an effect that you're happy with.

1 Thin the glaze with white spirit in the paint kettle, stir well and pour some into the flat tray.

2 Wear rubber gloves to protect your hands. Dip the sponge into the glaze and squeeze out the excess.

3 Dab the sponge onto the wall – do not press too hard. Work in a circular pattern to prevent the prints from becoming too regular.

4 Reload the sponge as the glaze runs out. Vary the position of the sponge on the wall so that the impressions it makes are not all the same.

5 Wash the sponge in white spirit when it becomes saturated with glaze. Squeeze it out well or you will over-dilute the glaze.

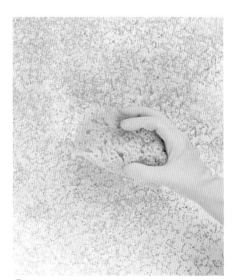

6 For a marbled effect, leave the surface to dry and then sponge on a second colour, using the same technique as before.

Ragging a wall

With ragging, the pattern is irregular, rather than even, which makes it one of the easiest and fastest decorative techniques.

Tools *A large supply of lint-free rags (all the same texture); 100mm paintbrush; paint kettle; rubber gloves.*

Materials *Glaze tinted the desired colour; white spirit.*

1 Pour the glaze into the paint kettle and thin it with white spirit.

2 Brush glaze onto the surface, beginning at the top of the wall and covering a strip about 500mm wide down to the floor.

3 Bunch up a rag into a ball and dab it over the surface to pick up glaze while it is still wet. Use one or both hands to move the rag in all directions. This is a messy job so wear rubber gloves. You may find it easier if you crumple one rag into a ball and then wrap another rag around it.

4 Change the rag whenever it becomes full and too wet to pick up more glaze. It is also a good idea to unwrap the rag and crumple it again in a different way so that the patterns you make are not all the same.

5 Continue to apply and rag off glaze until the whole wall is covered.

Dragging a wall

This technique will show up the slightest imperfection in a surface, so it is best kept for only the smoothest walls. If possible, try to get someone else to brush the glaze onto the wall, while you drag it off immediately afterwards.

Tools *Paint kettle; 100mm paintbrush; brush with extra-long bristles (called a flogger) or another wide, coarse-haired paintbrush; clean lint-free rags.*

Materials *Glaze tinted the desired colour; white spirit.*

1 Thin the glaze with white spirit in the paint kettle. It should be a thin, cream-like consistency – if it is too thick or if one of the bristles in the brush is bent, some of the dragged lines of glaze may break into droplets and spoil the effect.

2 Start in a top corner and apply a strip of glaze about 500mm wide, from the top of the wall to the bottom.

3 Again, moving from the top down, drag the dry flogger through the glaze. You may need to stand on steps to reach the top and climb down carefully as you drag the wall.

4 Keep the movement flowing and as straight as possible. However, the results will be more successful if you relax and do not concentrate too much on keeping the lines steady.

5 Do not worry if the lines are slightly crooked in places – they will not spoil the effect from a distance. Hold the flogger against the wall with light, consistent pressure.

6 If you cannot drag the whole wall in one movement, break off and then brush from the bottom up to where you stopped, overlapping slightly at the join. If you have to do this with the next strip as well, break off at a different height, so that you do not get a line running across the wall where the joins meet.

7 Wipe the flogger frequently on a lint-free rag so that the bristles remain as dry as possible and do not lose their shape.

HELPFUL TIP

You can create a similar effect to dragging by using a comb with firm teeth. Rubber or steel combs are sold by some artists' suppliers but you can also use plastic ones. You need not confine yourself to vertical lines – experiment with scallop shapes, wavy lines, ticks or criss-cross patterns.

Stippling a wall

This technique creates a uniform, soft effect. The special brush required can be bought from specialist paint shops and larger builders' merchants. Use a white or pale base coat for best results. As with dragging, speed is essential so it is easier if you have a helper.

Tools *Paint kettle; stippling brush; 100mm paintbrush; clean lint-free rags.*

Materials *Glaze tinted the desired colour; white spirit.*

1 Pour the glaze into the paint kettle and thin it with white spirit.

2 Brush the glaze onto the wall in a vertical strip about 500mm wide.

3 Go over the wet area with the stippling brush, stabbing at the surface. Keep the bristles at right angles to the wall, otherwise the brush will skid.

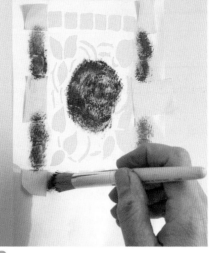

4 Wipe the brush clean on a dry lint-free rag as the picked-up glaze accumulates on the bristles, otherwise they will begin to stick.

5 Continue the process in strips across the wall.

6 Clean the brush immediately after use with white spirit, followed by a little washing-up liquid and warm water.

Stencilling

Using stencils is a quick and easy way of decorating furniture, walls and floors. Buy stencils pre-cut, or make your own.

Tools *Stencil brushes.*

Materials *Plastic stencils; paint; low-tack (easily detachable) tape or spray adhesive; masking tape; paper towel.*

1 Position the first stencil and secure it with tape or low-tack spray adhesive.

2 Use masking tape to cover any cut-outs within the stencil that you intend to paint with another colour.

3 Hold the stubby head of the brush at right angles to the stencil and dab paint onto the cut-out areas, working outwards from the centre of each cut-out.

4 Wait until paint is dry to the touch, then repeat the process for the next colour.

PAINT FOR STENCILLING

You can use any paint, so long as it is not so thin that it will run down behind the stencil. There are also stenciling paints available that are specially designed for the job. Spray paint can be used for large areas, but take care not to apply too much, or it will run. Most shop-bought stencils are made from plastic sheets, so it is easy to clean off the paint when you have finished. If you are stencilling onto woodwork, apply a finishing coat of varnish to protect the design.

Painting cornices and mouldings

Plaster or imitation plasterwork cornices and ceiling roses can be painted with emulsion to match or contrast with the ceiling and walls. Or pick out details in a second colour. Never use gloss paint on polystyrene coving – it creates a fire hazard.

Tools *25mm brush with no straggly bristles; artist's sable brush; mahl stick (see right).*

Materials *Emulsion paint(s).*

Before you start Make sure the surface is clean and smooth. Fill small cracks in plaster with interior filler, wait for it to dry and then rub down with fine abrasive paper. If a part of the cornice is broken away, repair it before you do the painting.

1 Apply the paint in thin coats, so that it does not form drips or runs. Let the paint dry between coats.

2 If you are using two colours, either paint the raised parts first or paint the whole area and fill in the recesses, when dry, with an artist's sable brush.

3 To keep your hand steady, lean on a mahl stick (a signwriter's rest). To make a mahl stick, pad the end of a piece of dowel with sponge or cotton wool wrapped in a lint-free rag.

Painting woodwork

Once the ceiling and walls are painted, move on to the woodwork, which should have been well prepared before you started work on the walls and ceiling. Whatever the surface, the order of painting remains the same.

Tools *Paintbrushes; abrasive paper; wood sanding block; thin piece of wood; dusting brush; lint-free cloth or tack rag.*

Materials *Filler for wood painted indoors; knotting; primer; undercoat; topcoat.*

FOR A PERFECT FINISH

To avoid a disappointing final appearance, sand wood smooth and fill any holes before painting.

1 Wrap a piece of abrasive paper around a wood sanding block and rub it along the grain of the wood.

2 After sanding, use a fine brush to remove all the dust, brushing in the direction of the grain to clear all crevices.

3 Press the filler into the holes, taking care not to spread it into the surrounding grain.

4 Wait until the filler has dried to the same colour all over – perhaps 15–30 minutes – then sand it flat and dust once more.

1 Brush a coat of knotting over any resinous areas or knots in the wood so they are sealed and resin cannot seep through.

2 Apply an even coat of primer to bare wood and leave it to dry.

3 Use fine grade abrasive paper wrapped around a block of wood to rub lightly over primed areas to remove any rough bits.

4 Remember to sand moulded areas as well. Use abrasive paper round a thin piece of wood, or a flexible sander.

5 Put one undercoat on light surfaces and two on dark ones. Use an undercoat appropriate to the colour of the paint.

6 When the undercoat is dry, gently rub with abrasive paper. Remove dust with a dusting brush. To pick up remaining dust, wipe with a damp lint-free cloth (a clean old handkerchief is ideal) or a tack rag impregnated with resins that remove dust.

7 Apply the topcoat with a brush that is an appropriate size for the surface.

IF THE WALLS ARE TO BE PAPERED

When a room is to be papered, take about 15mm of paint onto the wall around door and window frames, above skirting boards and below any picture rail. Then, if you leave any small gaps in the papering, the paint will show through, making the imperfection less obvious.

Varnishing woodwork

If you leave woodwork bare, it will become marked and stained over time. Varnish will protect the surface as well as bringing out the wood's natural colour and showing its grain.

Tools *Paint kettle; measuring jug; rubber gloves; paintbrushes; fine wet-and-dry sanding sponge; tack cloth; 0000-grade wire wool; duster.*

Materials *Varnish; white spirit; wax polish.*

Before you start Consider which type of varnish you want to use. The two main choices are acrylic and polyurethene. Acrylic is quick drying and odour-free; polyurethene is harder wearing but smells strongly when you apply it.

1 For best results, thin the varnish before you apply the first coat (there is no need to thin varnish for the second coat). Measure a small quantity of varnish into a measuring jug, note the volume, and pour it into the paint kettle. Next, measure about a tenth of this volume in water (if you are using acrylic varnish) or white spirit (for polyurethane) and add the water or white spirit to the varnish. Stir thoroughly. Wash out the measuring jug immediately.

2 Fold the lint-free cloth into a ball, dip it into the diluted varnish and wipe it along the grain of the wood in smooth, parallel bands. Wear rubber gloves, as this is a messy job. Discard the cloth afterwards.

CHECK THE TINT FIRST

Using a tinted varnish rather than a clear one will add colour without permanently staining the wood. There are wood shades and paintbox colours available. Before you start, test the tint of the varnish by painting patches of one, two and three coats of varnish on a piece of spare wood. If the tinted varnish is slightly too dark, add a little water to acrylic varnish or white spirit to polyurethane, and then paint more patches to see if the colour has lightened sufficiently.

3 When the first coat is dry, sand the surface lightly with a fine sanding sponge, to 'key' the surface for the next coat.

4 Wipe away all the dust with a tack cloth. If you can't find one in your DIY shop, you can make one by dipping a lint-free cloth in white spirit.

5 Brush on the second coat of varnish as soon as possible, before dust has a chance to settle back onto the surface. Apply the varnish along the grain, then brush across the grain to make sure the bands have blended. Finish off with light brush strokes along the grain.

6 It is almost impossible to achieve a perfect finish. Once the varnish has set hard, feel for any blemishes with your fingertips and rub them gently with a pad of fine wire wool dipped in wax polish.

HELPFUL TIPS

• If you need to fill wood that is to be varnished, buy a wood filler that will match the colour of the finish. Fillers are made in a limited colour range, so look at the filler colour chart in the shop and choose the nearest. If you can, take a piece of the wood with you. Do not match the wood against wet filler; it will become paler as it dries.

• To avoid creating bubbles in the varnish, don't scrape the loaded brush against the rim of the tin or across a string tied across a paint kettle; instead, just load your brush and then tap the sides of the container with the brush. The excess varnish will drip off the brush.

• If the wood looks too shiny after varnishing, you can reduce the sheen with fine wire wool. Rub gently, with the grain, to cut back the gloss so that there is hardly any reflection at all. This is particularly suitable for pale woods.

• Commercial dip-stripping in hot caustic soda is a quick and easy way to remove layers of paint from moulded doors and leave a bare wood finish suitable for varnishing. Not all doors are worth stripping, so test one before paying for a whole set; also, joints may become loose and doors may warp, so check with the company that your doors are suitable. Mark each door with a chiselled Roman numeral in the top edge to keep a note of which door belongs with which frame.

Using waxes and oil finishes

Wax and oil finishes are most often used on furniture and wood with a natural finish, where the grain of the wood is visible. Oil finishes are best suited to wood that will be subjected to moisture and frequent handling. Wax is easier to apply but the surface must be completely smooth and clean before application. Most finishes are safe to apply but always read the manufacturer's instructions first.

Applying an oil finish

Tools *Plastic cups; foam brushes; clean lint-free rags; abrasive paper; latex gloves.*
Materials *Oil finish.*

Before you start Spread out plenty of newspaper in the work area. Most oil finishes are non-toxic but wear latex gloves and dispose of used rags and brushes in an airtight container as they can spontaneously combust if left crumpled in a ball.

1 Strip off any old finish and sand the wood until smooth. Start with 80 grit paper, then 120, and finally finish with 180 grit paper, sanding in the direction of the grain to remove any scratch marks.

2 Dust off then wipe down the surface with a tack rag or a cloth, which has been sprinkled with a little linseed oil. Turn the cloth often to expose a clean surface.

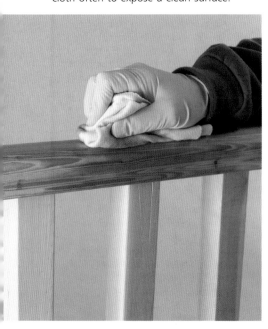

3 Use a foam brush to apply a coat of oil in the direction of the grain. Avoid over brushing and do not stop halfway through the job or a line will appear in the finish.

4 After 15 minutes use a clean rag to wipe any excess oil from the surface. When one rag becomes saturated replace it with a clean one.

5 Leave the oil to soak in for 3 hours then apply a second coat and wipe down as before.

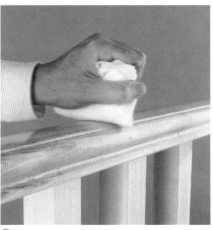

6 Leave for 24 hours and then use a soft clean cloth to buff to a smooth shine.

HELPFUL TIP

Waxes and oils will alter the colour of the wood, so test them on a scrap piece of wood or on an area which will not be visible before you start the job.

Applying a wax finish

Tools *Abrasive paper; soft cloths; latex gloves.*

Materials *Wax; acetone or denatured alcohol.*

1 Strip off any previous finishes and sand the surface smooth. Make sure that you remove any surface imperfections and scratches that will show through the finish.

2 Wipe down the surface with acetone or denatured alcohol to remove any residual surface impurities.

3 Immediately rub on the wax, as detailed in the manufacturer's instructions. Be careful not to apply too much; two thin coats are better than one thick one.

4 Use a soft lint-free cloth and buff to a smooth shine until all the wax has penetrated into the surface of the wood.

Painting doors and door frames

Doors have several faces and grain patterns going in different directions, each of which needs to be painted separately in a particular sequence for a good finish. Always open a door before you paint it. Leave the door frame until last.

Tools *Suitable brushes; perhaps cutting-in brush; paint shield.*

Materials *Masking tape; wire wool; white spirit; knotting; primer; undercoat; topcoat.*

Before you start Take off any door furniture, put down a dust sheet and hold the door open with a wedge on either side. It's a good idea to keep the door handle nearby in case the door closes.

Panelled doors

Paint the sections of the door in the sequence illustrated, for best results.

Use a brush of a suitable size to paint each part of the door – use a smaller one for the mouldings than for the panels, for instance.

Do not overload the mouldings with paint; this is a common cause of drips and runs. Keep the brush lightly loaded.

Glass panelled doors

Use a paint shield, an angled cutting-in brush or masking tape to keep paint off the glass. Whichever you use, allow paint to go onto about 2mm of the glass to seal where the glass and frames meet.

Paint the rest of the door with a broader brush – about 75mm wide. To avoid drips, do not overload the brush with paint.

If gloss paint gets on the glass, remove it with a rag damped with white spirit before it dries. If paint dries on the glass, scrape it off with a glass scraping tool.

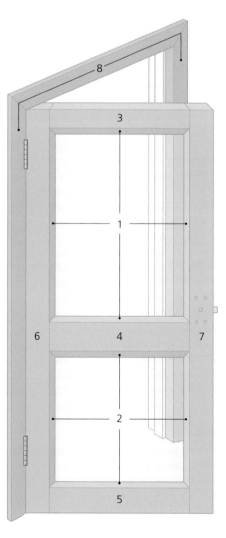

Panelled doors Paint the panels and the mouldings, then the rest of the surfaces.

Glass doors Paint the moulding around the glass before the remainder of the door.

USING TWO COLOURS

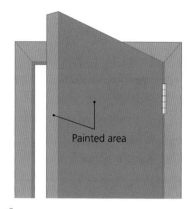

Painted area

1 If the door is painted a different colour on each side, paint the lock edge the same colour as the side of the door which opens into the room.

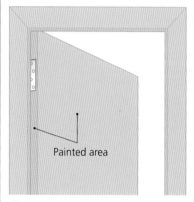

Painted area

2 Paint the hinge edge of the door so that it is the same colour as the adjacent, visible face of the door.

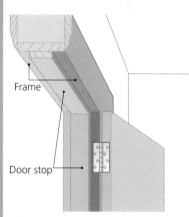

Frame

Door stop

3 If the door frame is also painted a different colour on each side, all the parts which can be seen from one side when the door is open should be painted the same colour.

In general, you don't have to paint the top and bottom edges of a door. However, if the top edge is overlooked (from a staircase, for example) paint it, so it does not stand out as bare wood.

Painting wooden mouldings

Skirting boards and picture rails are usually painted with gloss to match any other painted woodwork in the room. Balustrades are painted to match doors and other woodwork in the hall. If the walls are to be papered, paint woodwork first.

Tools *Suitable brushes; pieces of old card.*
Materials *Paint; white spirit.*

Before you start Fill damaged woodwork with fine surface filler then rub down to give a smooth finish ready for painting – gloss paint is unforgiving of imperfections and will show up every chip and dent.

Skirting boards

If you can, lift fitted carpets before painting a skirting board. When the carpet cannot be lifted, protect it with dust sheets.

1 The gap between the skirting board and the floor is likely to be full of dust. To remove the worst of it, vacuum along the skirting board before beginning. Then use a piece of card to stop the paintbrush from touching the floor.

2 Apply paint with a 50mm or 75mm paintbrush, depending on the height of the skirting board. Brush lengthways along the run of the board.

Picture rails

1 With a 25mm brush, paint two or three thin coats, not one thick one, allowing each coat ample time to dry.

2 Finish off with fine brush strokes along the run of the picture rail.

Balustrades

The wooden uprights and handrail of a staircase balustrade suffer a lot of wear and tear. It may seem like a fiddly job, but giving them a fresh coat of paint will help to keep them in good condition.

Tools *Bucket; cloths; paintbrushes; filling knife.*

Materials *Sugar soap; fine abrasive paper; white spirit; fine surface filler; wood primer.*

Before you start Make sure that all the uprights (balusters) are secure and in sound condition, and prime any areas of bare wood.

1 Wash down the woodwork with a sugar soap solution before you paint. Grease and dirt will have collected, particularly on the handrail, and will prevent the new paint from taking hold. Use fine abrasive paper to key the surface all over, then wipe it with a little white spirit.

2 Start by painting the balusters, working from the top of the staircase down, and from the top of each one in turn. Don't overload your brush with paint, or you will end up with drips and runs. If the balusters are turned in an ornate shape, let your brush follow the curves to apply paint to all the recesses.

3 You will need to move round the balustrade to paint from the staircase side as well to make sure that each baluster is completely covered.

4 Once you have painted all the balusters, move on to the handrail. Paint the underside first then give the top and sides of the handrail two coats of paint to give it a hard-wearing finish. Allow the first coat to dry thoroughly and rub it down lightly with fine abrasive paper before applying the second coat.

5 Paint the newel posts after the handrail, working from the top down and making sure that any recesses on a decorative finial at the top are well covered.

6 Finish by painting the strings – the edges of the staircase. Paint the outer string first, and any panelling that reaches down to the ground floor, then lift the carpet on the stairs and paint the inner side.

Painting interior windows

It nearly always takes more time to paint a window than you think, because of the number of surfaces and because you have to keep paint off the glass. For security reasons, you will probably want to close windows at night, so start work as early in the day as possible.

Tools *25mm or 50mm brush or an angled cutting in brush; paint shield.*

Materials *Masking tape; wire wool; white spirit; primer; undercoat; topcoat; cling film or talcum powder.*

Before you start Put down dust sheets, and protect the glass with masking tape. Fix the tape about 2mm from the frame so that a thin line of paint goes onto the glass. This will seal any gap between the glass and the frame. Or use a masking shield, moving it along as you paint and cleaning it regularly.

Casement frames

1 Open the window. Paint the frame in the order illustrated below. Do not apply too much paint in one coat or it will run and take longer to dry.

2 The painting sequence is largely determined by the fact that the brush strokes should follow the construction of the joinery; so the vertical brush strokes will 'cut off' the horizontal ones.

Order of work
Paint casement windows in this order: **1** cross-bars and rebates; **2** top and bottom cross-rails; **3** hanging stile and hinge edge; **4** meeting stile; **5** frame. The colours on the drawing indicate the extent of the numbered areas.

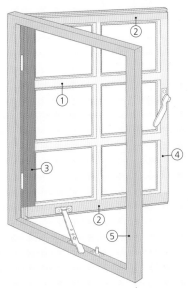

3 Keep paint off handles and stays. These look best cleaned up and left natural. Remove any dried paint splashes on metal with wire wool dipped in white spirit.

4 If you have to close casements and the paint is touch-dry but not absolutely hard, rub a little talc on the meeting surfaces. Alternatively, place a sheet of cling film between the surfaces most likely to stick.

Sash windows

1 Paint the frame following the order shown below. Almost close the window to paint the inside runners; give them a very thin coat to prevent surfaces from sticking.

2 Do not paint the sash cords or they will harden and fail earlier than they should.

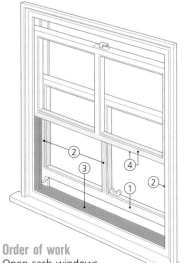

Order of work
Open sash windows and reverse their positions, then paint in the following order: **1** meeting rail; **2** vertical bars as far as possible; **3** the area that the inner sash sits on, and lower runners; **4** cross-rail and underside.

Reverse the windows, then paint: **5** cross-rail; **6** vertical bars; **7** cross-rail; **8** rest of vertical bars; **9** soffit, top runners and behind cords; **10** frame. The colours on the windows indicate the extent of the numbered areas.

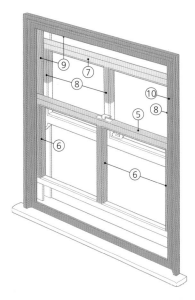

Painting metalwork

Make sure that all metalwork is clean and free from grease before painting.

Windows

Metal windows tend to be tighter fitting than wooden ones, so do not let paint layers build up on them. If the paint layers are very thick, remove the paint with a chemical stripper (page 77). In all other respects, the painting procedure remains the same as for wooden frames (see left).

Radiators

Never paint a hot radiator – always let it cool first. Wait for about an hour after you finish painting, then turn on the heating to speed up the drying process. Special radiator paint is available that will keep its whiteness despite the heat.

Before you start Check for patches of rust or bare metal that may be showing through. Rub them down with a fine wet-and-dry abrasive paper, and then touch them up with metal primer.

1 Apply gloss direct to new and already painted radiators unless there is to be a colour change, in which case apply an undercoat first.

2 Use a 50mm brush and keep the coat as thin as possible to avoid runs. You can paint a flat panel radiator with a small roller; this will not give quite as good a finish, but takes less time than painting with a brush.

3 Do not paint over control valves; they must be left free to turn.

Painting metal pipes

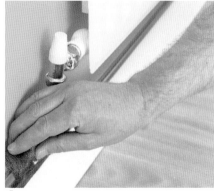

1 Make sure that steel and copper pipes are clean and free from corrosion. Use fine wire wool to clean them.

2 Apply gloss paint direct with a 25mm or 50mm brush. There is no need for a primer unless the pipe is lead. Start by brushing up and down, then smooth the paint along the length of the pipe.

3 Never paint over stop taps or controls or they will not work.

Cast-iron fire surrounds and wrought ironwork

1 Rub down and remove any rust (page 73) and prime the metal if necessary.

2 Use a suitably sized brush to coat the surface with gloss or enamel paint direct, without an undercoat.

3 If possible, remove intricate wrought ironwork and take it outside. Then spray it with an aerosol, shielding the area behind. Always use thin coats to prevent runs. Hold the can at right angles to the work and at a distance of about 300mm.

4 Keep the can parallel with the surface – moving up and down or from side to side. Never swing the can in an arc or hold it in one position for any length of time.

5 If you cannot move intricate wrought ironwork, put on two thin coats of gloss with a small paintbrush.

Dealing with paint problems

The main causes of paint breaking down are incompatible paints being applied on top of one another, poor preparation of the surface, damp or trapped moisture, grease, rot or rust.

Flaking The paint has not been keyed to the surface, which may be too smooth (as with old gloss paint) or may be chalky (as with untreated distemper). Alternatively, rotting timber may be pushing the paint off or rust may have formed underneath.
• Strip small areas by rubbing with fine abrasive paper, fill with a fine surface filler, apply a primer and repaint.
• Larger areas must be completely stripped and prepared again from scratch.

Blistering Prick a blister – if water emerges, damp is trapped under the paint or is finding its way in from behind.
• Strip the blistered paint with a hot-air gun and leave the wood until it has dried.
• Prime the surface and then repaint the whole of the repaired area.

Crazing (sometimes called orange peel) When a paint surface breaks up like mini crazy paving, incompatible paints have been used. The top layer of paint breaks up because it expands at a different rate from the one underneath.
• Usually, you must strip the paint with chemicals or a hot-air gun and start again.
• Rub down very small areas – no more than a few centimetres square – with a flexible sanding pad or with wet-and-dry paper damped with water.
• When the surface is smooth, fill the stripped area with a fine surface filler, prime and repaint.

Visible under-colour Liquid gloss does not have good covering power, so always use undercoat to hide a strong colour.
• Put on another layer of topcoat, but switch to a one-coat paint, which has more body and covering power.

Runs Too much paint applied in a thick coat results in runs that are hard to disguise.
• If the paint is still wet, brush out runs; but not if the paint has started to dry. Instead, wait until it is completely dry and then rub down with very fine abrasive paper until the surface is smooth.
• Clean with a damp rag.
• Apply a new thin topcoat.

Stains Stains occur when water in emulsion activates impurities in a wall; areas rubbed with a wire brush or wire wool develop rust stains; or deposits in an unlined flue come through the paint surface.
• Prevent stains by applying an aluminium primer-sealer before you start painting.

• If the problem occurs afterwards, brush a primer-sealer over the stain and then repaint.

Mould and discoloration Spores settling on paintwork that is damp – possibly due to condensation – often lead to mould patches.
• Treat the affected area with a fungicide as directed by the manufacturer, wash the surface clean, let it dry and then repaint.

Loss of gloss sheen Gloss paint will sink into the surface and lose its shine if the surface was not primed – or if either primer or undercoat was not left to dry completely.
• Rub down with damp wet-and-dry abrasive paper.
• Brush off the dust and wipe with a clean, damp rag, then apply a new topcoat.

Wrinkled paint Usually caused by applying a second coat of paint before the first has dried. Solvents in the wet paint underneath attack the second coat when they try to pass through it and make it wrinkle.
• Strip the paint with a chemical stripper or heat and redecorate, this time allowing each coat to dry before applying the next.

Gritty paint surface If a newly painted surface feels rough and gritty, paint has been applied with a dirty brush or has become contaminated by the surrounding areas. Or there may have been bits of skin in the paint. Always paint with clean brushes and use a paint kettle. Strain old paint through a paint strainer or a pair of tights. Use a paint shield or piece of card to guard against picking up dirt from a floor.
• When a gritty surface is dry, rub down with a damp wet-and-dry abrasive paper until it is smooth, wipe clean, then apply a new coat of paint.

Dark patches on painted wood Knots in wood which have not been sealed before you decorate may ooze resin when the sun warms them, and the resin will force its way through the paint film.
• Strip paint away with the edge of a scraper blade, then with fine abrasive paper to expose the knot.
• Brush knotting over the area to seal it, leave it to dry and repaint.

Paint will not dry The room is badly ventilated or very cold.
• Open all the windows and doors or put a heater in the room.
• If this does not solve the problem, the paint has been applied to a dirty – and probably greasy – surface.
• Strip it off with chemical stripper or heat and start again, taking great care to clean the surface thoroughly.

Insects on painted surface If you can, remove insects that get stuck to fresh paint while the paint is still wet and touch up the surface with a brush and new paint. If the paint has started to dry, wait until it has set hard and then brush away the insects – they make less of a mess that way.

Wallpapering tools

For any wallpapering job, you will need a steel measuring tape, a pencil – not a pen – to make marks and a metal straight-edge to act as a guide when you trim paper. Depending on the type of wallcovering, you will need only some of the tools listed below. Have a supply of old towels and sponges to hand for removing paste from skirting boards and for other general cleaning.

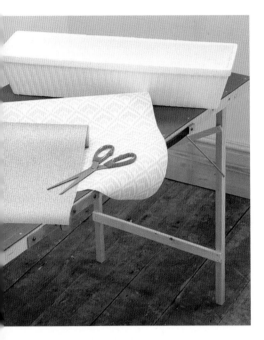

Pasting table A folding table – about 2m long and 500mm wide – is the best type because it is easily moved around. As well as being light to carry, the table must be solid enough to stand firmly on the floor.

Water trough If you are using a pre-pasted wall covering, you will need a trough for wetting each length before hanging.

Plumb line and bob Use a plumb line to mark the true vertical on a wall before hanging the first length of wallpaper – few walls are straight. Buy one or make one by tying a small weight – a metal nut or a small screwdriver– to a length of string.

Paste brush Use a 125mm or 150mm brush to apply paste. If you use an old paintbrush, make sure that it is clean. Wash the brush well in warm water after use.

Plastic bucket Any clean household bucket is fine for mixing the paste. Tie a piece of string across the rim, between the handle anchor points, and rest the brush on the string when you are not using it. Wiping the brush across the string will remove surplus paste.

Cutting guide An L-shaped piece of metal about 500mm long. Hold it against the skirting board, picture rail or coving when trimming lengths of paper on the wall with a very sharp knife. It is an alternative to creasing the paper and trimming with scissors. The correct length of the paper is achieved by tucking the paper into the crease of the guide, which is slightly shaped so that a little extra paper is left on each length.This reduces the chance of leaving gaps between the paper and the skirting board, picture rail or coving.

Scissors Paperhanger's scissors with 250mm long blades are best for the main cutting work. The longer the blades, the easier it is to cut a straight line. If possible, use stainless steel scissors because they will not rust. Wipe scissors clean after each use when cutting pasted paper, or the paste will harden on the blades and they will tear the next length. Have a pair of small scissors handy for fine trimming.

Trimming knife A knife with a razor-sharp blade is useful for trimming and cutting vinyl wall coverings. It is also sometimes easier to trim pasted paper neatly with a knife and straight-edge than with a pair of scissors – provided the paper is not too thin. Keeping the knife sharp is essential so make sure that you have plenty of spare blades; or use a knife which has a continuous blade that snaps off at intervals to give a sharp new cutting edge.

Cutting guide

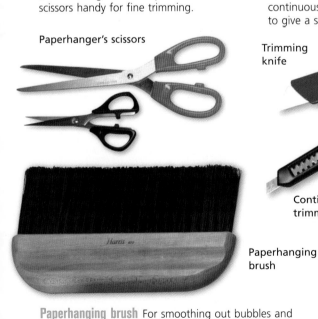

Paperhanger's scissors

Trimming knife

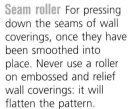

Continuous blade trimming knife

Seam roller

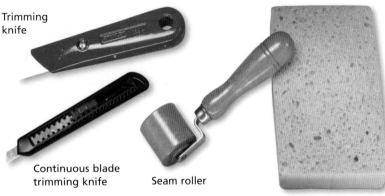

Sponge

Paperhanging brush

Paperhanging brush For smoothing out bubbles and creases in newly hung wall coverings. A large brush – between 180mm and 250mm wide – gives best results. Never use the brush for anything else and take care not to get paste on the bristles.

Seam roller For pressing down the seams of wall coverings, once they have been smoothed into place. Never use a roller on embossed and relief wall coverings: it will flatten the pattern.

Sponge Use a clean damp sponge to wipe excess paste from the surface of vinyls and washable wall coverings.

Choosing paper and paste

Lining paper Plain lining paper is designed to cover poor wall surfaces before they are papered. Sold in five thicknesses, heavier and thicker paper is less likely to tear.
Paste Use cold-water or all-purpose.

Woodchip Useful for covering uneven walls, this paper has two layers bonded together with a sprinkling of wood chippings between them. Paint with emulsion. Rough to the touch, so not suitable in children's rooms or in narrow passages.
Paste Use all-purpose, cold-water, heavy-duty or ready mixed.

Standard wallpaper Quality varies with price: cheap paper is thin and tears easily, especially when damp. It is also more difficult to hang. None of these papers is washable, so avoid using them in kitchens.
Paste Use all-purpose, cold-water or ready-mixed.

Duplex paper The top surface – often with a relief pattern – is bonded to a backing paper. It is strong, easy to hang and holds its shape. Easier to hang than other relief wallpapers.
Paste Use all-purpose, cold-water, heavy-duty or ready-mixed.

Paste-the-wall papers Available in a wide range of colours and designs. They are easy to hang (and strip off) and can be wiped clean. Paste the wall, not the paper.
Paste Use all-purpose, cold-water or ready-mixed.

Relief wall coverings Heavy papers, such as Anaglypta, embossed with a pattern during manufacture. Suitable for uneven walls and ceilings. Can be painted.
Paste Use all-purpose, cold-water or ready-mixed.

High relief wall coverings Made from material that feels like hard putty. Many designs available. Lincrusta is more durable than other relief wall coverings.
Paste Use cold-water, heavy-duty, ready-mixed or Lincrusta adhesive.

Vinyl PVC layer, with pattern or texture, bonded to paper. Durable and washable.
Paste Use all-purpose or ready-mixed (both with fungicide) or vinyl adhesive.

Hessian Available as just a roll of material, or bonded to a backing paper that keeps it from sagging. With unbacked hessian, paste the wall, not the material.
Paste Use all-purpose, cold-water, heavy-duty or ready-mixed.

Silk wall covering Silk, bonded to a fine backing paper. Expensive and delicate; joins are always visible. Best in small areas.
Paste Use all-purpose, cold-water or ready-mixed.

Japanese grasscloth Made of real grasses, bonded and stitched to a fine paper. Joins are always visible.
Paste Use all-purpose, cold-water, heavy-duty or ready-mixed.

Cork wall coverings A fine veneer of cork, stuck to a plain or painted backing paper. Colour shows through the holes. Apply paste to the wall, not the paper.
Paste Use all-purpose, cold-water, heavy-duty or ready-mixed.

Metallic wall coverings Foil bonded to a paper backing. Use only on perfect walls, as any unevenness will spoil the effect. Paste the wall, not the covering.
Paste Use all-purpose or ready-mixed (both with fungicide) or heavy-duty.

Flock wall coverings Fabric pile, bonded to backing paper. Hang as standard wallpaper but try to keep splashes of paste off the surface. Expensive, but effective.
Paste Use all-purpose, cold-water, heavy-duty or ready-mixed.

Special effects wall coverings Papers and vinyls in a wide range that give the effect of wood, stone or tiling. Used to create optical illusions. Can be overpowering, and more expensive than standard coverings.
Paste Use all-purpose, cold-water, heavy-duty or ready-mixed.

Choosing the right paste

What you need to know
• Use a paste recommended by the manufacturer of the wall covering you have chosen. In general, the heavier the wall covering, the stronger the paste will need to be.
• Many pastes can be mixed to different strengths to suit standard wallpaper or heavy vinyls by adding more or less water. Follow the instructions on the packet.
• Many wall coverings must be left to one side after they have been pasted to allow the paste to soak into the paper. The paper expands slightly when it is damp and if it is not left to soak it will continue to expand on the wall, making matching difficult and perhaps forming bubbles. In general, heavy thick coverings need to soak for longer than thin ones. Vinyls need no soaking time because vinyl does not expand when damp.

Glue size Apply to bare wall surfaces before papering. Size adds to the adhesive quality of the paste and makes surfaces slippery so the covering can be slid into place. Mix with cold water. A pack that makes 5 litres will cover enough wall for 8 rolls.

All-purpose paste For all wall coverings. Powder or flakes are mixed with varying quantities of cold water to suit the particular wall covering. Follow the instructions on the packet. Contains a fungicide. Water content varies between 4–7 litres per sachet, covering 2–10 rolls.

Cold-water paste The traditional starch-based wallpaper paste, still favoured by many professionals. For all weights of wallpaper, depending on water content. Mix with cold water, stirring well to avoid lumps. Use with glue size, to provide extra slip and adhesion. A 4.5 litre pack will do for 5–6 rolls of medium-weight paper.

Heavy-duty paste For high relief wall coverings; duplex paper; woodchip; corks; flocks; special effects wall coverings such as imitation wood panelling; imitation tiling; and imitation brick. Will hold heavy materials. Mix with cold water. A 4.5 litre pack is enough for 4–6 rolls.

Ready-mixed paste For paper and fabric-backed vinyls; paper-backed hessian; grasscloth; special wall coverings; expanded polystyrene tiles; veneers; coving. Contains a fungicide. Usually supplied in a tub. More expensive than powdered paste. A 2.5kg pack is enough for 3–4 rolls.

Vinyl adhesive For vinyl wall coverings. A powder or ready-mixed paste containing fungicide to discourage mould – essential when hanging impervious materials. 4.5 litres is enough for 4 rolls.

Lincrusta adhesive For Lincrusta relief decoration and very heavy relief wall coverings. Thick ready-mixed paste. 1 litre is enough for one roll; 2 litres for 2–3 rolls.

How many rolls do you need?

How much paper you need to buy will be affected by whether the wallpaper design has a pattern that repeats down the length of the roll and must be matched up between lengths. The larger the pattern repeat, the more paper you need and the more wastage there will be.

Most British wall coverings are sold in rolls 10.05m x 530mm, though the size may vary slightly. If your chosen paper has these dimensions, use the chart (right) to calculate how many rolls you need to buy. It is better to have too much paper than to run out and find you can't get any more. You can use any leftover paper for future repair work, or as drawer liners.

Use a steel tape to measure the height of the walls from the skirting board to the picture rail, coving or ceiling.

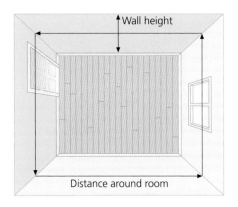

When measuring the perimeter of the room, include the width of the doors and all standard size windows – the extra paper will be needed for the trimming at the top and bottom of each length.

Only deduct the width of a window from your calculations if it is a French window, occupying a large part of a wall.

If you are papering a ceiling, measure the perimeter of the room and use the chart (above).

If you are papering a passage ceiling, measure the width of the ceiling at various places, to make sure it does not vary. Divide this measurement by the width of a roll. A narrow passage, less than a metre wide, will need only 2 widths. A wider passage may need 3 widths.

Measure the length of the passage, multiply it by the number of widths, and you will be able to work out how many rolls you will need.

HOW MANY ROLLS DO YOU NEED?

Estimate the number of rolls you will need, including the areas covered by doors and windows. Always buy a little extra to allow for experimentation and mistakes.

Walls

Wall height in metres	Measurement round room in metres										
	10	11	12	13	14	15	16	17	18	19	20
2.0 to 2.2	5	5	5	6	6	7	7	7	8	8	9
2.2 to 2.4	5	6	6	6	7	7	8	8	9	9	9
2.4 to 2.6	5	6	6	7	7	8	8	9	9	10	10
2.6 to 2.8	5	6	7	7	8	8	9	9	10	11	11
2.8 to 3.0	5	5	7	8	8	9	9	10	11	11	12

Ceilings

	Measurement round room in metres						
	9–12	13–15	17–18	20–21	22–24	26–27	29–30
Rolls needed	2	3	4	5	7	9	10

Tips on buying wallpaper

Remember the repeat

If your chosen paper has a random pattern – a sponging effect for example – or if it is plain stripes, you will need fewer rolls of paper than if there is a pattern with a drop between the repeats. Pattern repeats vary from around 75mm to 500mm or more. The pattern repeat length is generally noted on the wallpaper wrapper.

If the paper you have chosen has a large repeat, you will probably get one fewer full length out of each roll than you think, so always buy an extra roll or two. Some stores will allow you to return unused rolls if they are left unopened and you have retained your receipt.

The majority of patterned wallpapers have a straight pattern match: the same part of the design occurs along both edges, which means that each length you hang starts at the same point of the design as the length beside it.

Wallpapers with a drop pattern match have the design offset by half the pattern repeat on the two long edges of the paper. Therefore matching lengths of paper as you paste them on the wall uses up more paper. A way to reduce the amount of wallpaper wasted in this way is to cut alternate lengths from two rolls.

Special coverings

If you choose from a Continental or American pattern book – or have decided upon a special wall covering, such as hessian – check the size and use the chart provided in the pattern book to work out how many rolls you need. Rolls may be wider than standard wallpaper.

Keep to one batch

Check that all the paper comes from the same batch, to avoid colour variation between rolls. If you have to buy rolls with a different batch number, because the store does not have enough from the same batch, aim to use them in areas where any slight shading variations will not show, such as behind furniture, tucked away in a corner or in a passageway.

Lining paper

Lining paper can improve the end result of your wallpapering immensely. It comes in five thicknesses, and is often twice the length of a roll of ordinary wallpaper. So check the length on the roll and work out how many rolls you will need – you will buy too much if you assume that you need the same number of rolls as the wallpaper you choose.

Hanging standard wallpaper

Papering the walls is normally the last stage in decorating. Once you have mastered the simple techniques, the job is quick and easy.

Tools *Pasting table; bucket; brush; paperhanger's brush; steel tape measure; plumb line; pencil; wallpaper scissors and small scissors; sponge; seam roller.*

Materials *Size; wallpaper paste; wallpaper.*

Before you start Size bare walls to prevent them from absorbing paste from the wallcovering. Size also makes the surface slippery so that the covering can be slid into place. You can either buy size or use a dilute form of the paste you plan to use to hang the wall covering.

Apply size with the paste brush or a short-pile paint roller to cover the whole surface and spread the size evenly. If the size gets onto painted woodwork, wipe it off immediately with a damp cloth.

Cutting paper to length

1 Take a roll of paper and check which way the pattern goes. Decide where definite motifs should be in relation to the top of the wall.

2 With a steel tape, measure the wall height down to the top of the skirting board. Add an extra 100mm for trimming at the top and bottom.

3 Unroll the paper on the pasting table, pattern-side down, measure the length and draw a line with a pencil and straight-edge across the back.

4 Cut along the line with a pair of long-bladed scissors.

5 Turn the paper over, unroll the next length and match the pattern by placing it edge to edge with the first length. Using the cut length as a measuring guide, cut off the second length.

Continue in this way until several lengths are ready for pasting. Number them on the back so that you know the hanging order, and note which end is the top.

HELPFUL TIP

If the ceiling in a room is very uneven or sloping, do not cut lengths of paper in advance. It is much easier to hang one piece, and then match the next against it on the wall.

Pasting the paper

1 Lay the cut lengths on the pasting table, pattern side down.

2 Position the top piece of paper so that all the spare paper hangs off the table to the right. If you are left-handed, reverse all the following paper-hanging procedures.

3 Adjust the paper so that the long edge aligns with the edge of the table.

4 Load the paste brush and wipe off excess paste by dragging the brush across the string on the bucket.

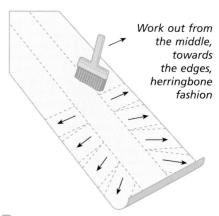

Work out from the middle, towards the edges, herringbone fashion

5 Brush the paste down the centre of the paper, then out to the edges. If any paste gets onto the table, wipe it off with a damp cloth.

6 Check that all the paper is evenly covered with paste, especially the edges. Holding the left-hand edge, loosely fold the paper over – paste side to paste side – to about the centre of the length.

7 Slide the paper to the left of the table so that the pasted part hangs off the edge.

8 Paste the right-hand end of the paper as you did the left, brushing in a herringbone pattern until the paper is all pasted.

9 Fold the paper over – without creasing it – so the top and bottom edges meet.

10 Leave the pasted paper to soak for as long as the manufacturer recommends. Thin paper and vinyl will be ready to hang almost immediately but heavier materials need to be left for 10 to 15 minutes.

LINING PAPER

If you are going to paper a room after lining it, make sure that the seams in the two papers won't fall in the same place.
• Start with a half-width of lining paper to stagger the joints.
• Do not overlap the edges: raised areas will show through.
• Do not take lining paper around corners. Trim away any excess paper so that the edges fit neatly.

Hanging the first length

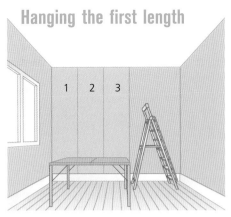

Start hanging the paper on a wall next to the window wall and work away from the light source, so that any slight overlaps will not cast shadows, which make the joins obvious. If there is more than one window in the room, treat the larger one as the main light source.

1 Pencil a mark near the top of the wall, 480mm out from the corner, so that enough paper will turn onto the window wall.

2 Hold the plumb line to the mark and let the bob hang free about 1.2m down the wall. When the bob settles, make another pencil mark directly behind the string. Check the distance to the corner all the way down the wall. If it is greater than 480mm at any point because the corner is not true, not enough paper will turn. So make the top measurement shorter, use the plumb line again and draw new pencil marks.

3 Carry the pasted length to the wall and release the top fold gently, holding it at both sides. Do not let the lower half suddenly drop – it may tear, or stretch and cause matching problems.

4 Hold the top right corner against the wall so that the right-hand edge of the paper aligns with the pencil mark. Make sure about 50mm of excess paper is left at the top of the wall for trimming.

5 Keep the left edge of the paper off the wall while you align the right-hand edge on the lower pencil mark.

6 Once the right edge is in place, smooth the paper with your hand or paperhanging brush diagonally up until the top left corner of the paper is on the wall.

7 Let go of the paper and smooth out the top half of the length with the paper-hanging brush, working from the centre outwards. Make sure the paper stays on the pencil mark.

8 Release the lower fold. Brush down the centre of the length, then out to the edges as you did when pasting, ensuring that any bubbles are brushed out. Dab down the edges with the tip of the brush or a dry, clean cloth made into a pad.

9 With the length in place, run the back of a pair of scissors along the paper where it meets the skirting board, to crease it.

10 Pull the paper gently away from the wall and cut along the crease, with the underside of the paper facing you. Brush the trimmed edge back in place. Repeat this process at the top of the length.

Alternatively A trimming guide gives a neater edge once you have learnt how to handle it properly. Slide the guide under the paper and cut off the excess with a trimming knife. The blade must be razor-sharp or it will tear the damp wallpaper. If you feel the knife pulling at the paper, change the blade immediately.

Hanging the next lengths

1 Hang the second length of paper to the right of the piece on the wall, following the same procedure but without using the plumb line. Match the top section of the left edge of the new length with the length on the wall, then run your hand diagonally up and to the right to press the top of the paper to the wall.

2 Smooth out the paper from the centre with the paperhanging brush.

3 Release the lower fold, check that the edges match and continue to brush over the paper. Trim top and bottom as before.

4 With two or three pieces hung, run the seam roller lightly down the joins of smooth papers. Do not press down the edges of textured materials, like Anaglypta, or lines will show where the pattern has been flattened.

HELPFUL TIP

Use matchsticks to mark where fittings have been taken down from a wall. Push a matchstick into each hole or wallplug, leaving it just proud of the surface. Ease the matchsticks through the paper when you smooth it over the wall. Snap the tip off each matchstick to prevent it from staining the paper.

Wallpapering around corners

All rooms have internal corners and often external ones as well – on a chimney breast for example.

Internal corners

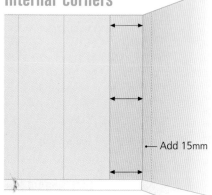

← Add 15mm

1 Measure the distance between the last length you have hung and the corner at the top, middle and bottom of the wall. Note the widest distance and add 15mm to allow for the turn onto the next wall.

2 Cut a length to this width. Keep the offcut for papering the first section of the adjoining wall.

3 Paste and hang the length. Take the overlap onto the next wall. Use the brush to smooth the paper well into the corner. If creases form, tear the paper – but cut vinyl – and overlap the torn pieces so that they lie flat.

4 Measure the offcut and hang the plumb line this distance away from the corner to find a vertical. Make pencil marks behind the line at intervals down the wall.

5 Hang the offcut with the right-hand edge aligning with the pencil marks. The length will overlap the paper turned from the previous wall. If the paper is patterned, match the two pieces as closely as possible. Use special overlap adhesive with vinyls to make the overlap stick down firmly.

External corners

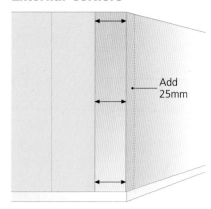

Add 25mm

Never try to turn more than 25mm around an external corner – the turned paper is likely to slant and look crooked. This technique can be applied to rounded walls as well as right-angled corners.

1 Paper the wall until there is less than one width to the corner.

2 Measure the distance between the edge of the last hung length and the corner, at the top, middle and bottom of the wall. Add 25mm to allow for the turn and cut the paper to this size.

3 Hang the length as far as the corner and take the overlap around onto the next wall. Smooth away any bubbles with the paperhanging brush.

4 Hang the offcut from the first length next to the paper on the wall, matching the pattern and butting the joins. Continue to hang lengths until you reach the internal corner. Before you paper the next wall, use the plumb line to get a vertical starting point. If the walls in the room are very out of true, it is easier to overlap rather than butt the joins – especially if the paper has a vertical pattern. Take the pasted paper around the corner. Then deduct 25mm from the width of the offcut and mark pencil lines this distance away from the corner, using the plumb line to get a true vertical. Hang the paper, overlapping the piece turned round the corner.

APPLYING BORDERS

You can buy friezes and borders to match a fabric or the colours or motif of a wallpaper. You can also buy sticky-back borders, which are a great way to brighten up a child's room.

A deep frieze at the top of a wall will make the ceiling seem lower. A 'frame' of frieze on the wall, set in about 250mm from the edge, will help to 'shrink' the long wall of a narrow hall or landing.

The frieze must go on a sound, flat surface; a heavily embossed paper is not a suitable surface.

Applying a frieze

1 For a frieze at the top of a wall, draw a straight pencil guideline; make it slightly lower than the depth of the frieze to allow for an uneven ceiling edge and apply a band of ceiling paint at the top of the wall. If the frieze is to go along the skirting and round a door, no guideline is needed.

2 Cut the frieze to length, using one piece from corner to corner.

3 Paste the frieze, fold it like a concertina and leave it for ten minutes to soak.

4 Apply it along the guideline, brushing it out well and letting out folds as you work along.

Making a frame

1 Draw guidelines that run parallel to the nearest wall edge.

2 Apply the frieze. At the corners, cut both layers with a sharp knife and remove the excess.

Peel and stick borders

Borders that are all-plastic have stronger adhesive than paper-backed vinyl. Peel off only a little of the release paper at a time, as they cannot be repositioned without damaging the paper beneath.

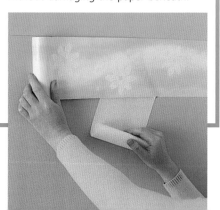

Wallpapering in awkward places

Square light switches or sockets

1 Turn off the electricity at the mains. Hang the paper from the top of the wall down as far as the switch or socket.

2 Cut the paper to the corners of the switch and pull back the flaps.

3 Partially unscrew the switch cover and pull it about 5mm away from the wall.

4 Trim away excess paper so that about 3mm of paper will sit behind the cover.

5 Gently ease the switch cover through the hole in the paper.

6 Push the paper behind the switch cover with a piece of flat wood, like a lolly stick, and then brush the paper flat against the wall, smoothing away any air bubbles.

7 Hang the remainder of the length. Tighten the switch cover screws and turn the electricity supply back on.

Circular fittings

1 Hang the length of wallpaper in the ordinary way until you reach the fixture. Pierce a hole in the paper over it with a pair of small scissors. Then make star-like cuts out to the edge of the fitting so that the paper will go to the wall.

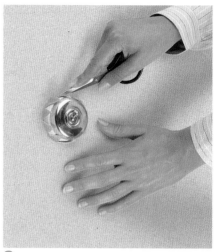

2 Crease the outline of the fitting on the paper with the back of a pair of scissors.

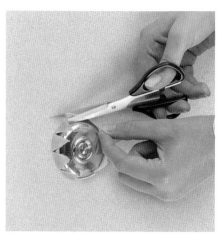

3 Cut off the surplus paper with small pointed scissors – they must be sharp or you may tear the wet paper. Follow the marked outline but allow for just a fraction of paper to turn onto the fitting so that the wall cannot show through a gap.

4 Smooth the paper flat around the fitting with a paperhanging brush. Then hang the rest of the length.

Radiators

1 Tuck the paper in behind the radiator until you reach the supporting bracket. Hang the next piece over the radiator, brushing it flat as far down as possible.

2 Use a pencil to mark the position of the wall bracket on the back of the paper and make a vertical cut in the paper from the bottom edge to the top of the bracket.

3 Feed the paper down behind the radiator and smooth down with a radiator roller. Trim it at the skirting board. Alternatively, if the radiator overhangs the skirting board, save paper by trimming it off 150mm below the top of the radiator.

4 Sponge any paste off the radiator before it dries.

HELPFUL TIP

When wallpapering a room with a radiator, turn off the radiator and allow it to cool completely before you start. Not only will it be more comfortable than working round a hot radiator, but your results will be better, because there will be no risk that the paper may dry too fast and start to curl.

Fireplaces

1 Cut the lengths of paper which are to go round the fireplace roughly to size before applying paste – so that you do not have to cope with a lot of pasted paper when trimming. Leave a margin of at least 25mm for trimming in situ.

2 Paste and hang the paper in the ordinary way as far as you can, then mark the outline of the fireplace on the paper using the back of a scissor blade.

3 Peel a little of the paper away from the wall so you can work comfortably. Cut along the marked outline. Use small, sharp scissors if there are lots of small cuts; otherwise, use paperhanging scissors. If the trimming takes some time and the paste is beginning to dry, apply a little more paste to the wall, rather than to the paper.

4 Smooth the paper in place all around the fireplace, using the points of bristles of a paperhanging brush to push the paper into awkward corners. Continue down to the skirting board.

CHIMNEY BREASTS

If you have chosen a strongly patterned wallpaper, centre it on the chimney breast and hang subsequent lengths from here towards the room corners. If there is no dominant pattern, hang the wallpaper round the chimney breast in the same way as for other corners (page 104).

Door frames

1 When you get to the door, hang a pasted full-length strip next to the last length, allowing the strip to flap over the door. Press the paper against the top corner of the architrave. Make a diagonal cut from the loose edge to the architrave top corner.

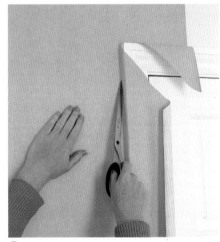

2 Brush paper into the angles between the wall and the architrave above and beside the door. Use scissors to crease the paper.

3 Trim off the excess paper along the side of the door, working from the bottom upwards. Then cut off the waste paper above the door opening.

4 Using a paperhanging brush, press the trimmed edges back into place against the edges of the architrave. Then cut the top edge of the length to fit at ceiling level, and the bottom edge at the skirting board.

5 You will probably need to hang a short length of wallpaper above the door. Use scissors to crease the paper into the angle between wall and ceiling, then into the angle between wall and architrave. Trim the paper to fit. When cutting above the architrave, leave the paper slightly over-long, so that it covers the top edge of the architrave.

6 Repeat steps 1 to 4 to hang another full-length strip at the opposite side of the door opening, again letting it overlap the door architrave so you can mark the corner and cut the waste paper away. Brush the cut edges back into place, then carry on papering the rest of the wall.

Recessed windows

1 When you reach a window recess, hang a full length drop of paper so that it overlaps the opening. If the overlap is large, you may need a helper to support the weight of the pasted paper.

2 Make a neat, horizontal scissor cut level with the top edge of the recess.

3 Make a second cut level with the top surface of the window sill.

4 If the flap of paper that you have created is enough to cover the depth of the recess, crease it into the angle with a paperhanging brush. If it is not deep enough to reach the window frame, cut and paste a strip a little wider than the gap and hang it on the side of the reveal, matching it to the pattern, if there is one.

5 Run scissors along the crease to make a defined cutting line. Peel back the paper and make a neat scissor cut to trim off the excess. Brush the paper back into place.

6 Cut a piece of wallpaper long enough to reach from the ceiling to the top of the window, into the recess and up to the frame, with extra for trimming. Hang this next to the previous full-length strip, and brush into the recess. Trim at ceiling level and where paper meets the frame. Repeat until you need another full-length piece.

7 Paper under the windowsill. Measure from the underside of the sill to the top of the skirting board, then add 50mm or so for trimming. Cut strips of paper to this length and hang them under the window, matching the pattern if necessary. Repeat to cover the rest of the wall below the window opening, stopping when the next piece needed is a full-length one.

8 Check that the last piece hung above the window is in line with the last piece below it by hanging a plumb line. If it is not, measure the discrepancy at its widest point and subtract this from the width of a piece of paper. Mark a plumb line on the wall to the right of the window at this distance from the edge of the overhanging piece of paper.

9 Hang the next whole length. Butt it up to the previous pieces if they were in line, or position its right hand edge level with the plumb line you have drawn if the paper above and below the window was misaligned.

10 There will be a gap in each top corner of the reveal. Cut a strip of paper the width of the gap at top left, but 50mm deeper than the recess. Position the paper over the gap, allowing about 25mm to turn up at the front edge onto the wall above, matching the pattern, if there is one.

11 Use a trimming knife and straight-edge to cut through both the patch and the paper above it, 15mm above the edge of the recess. Peel away the offcuts from each piece and then press the edges flat for an invisible butt join. Cover the gap in the other corner of the reveal in the same way.

Hanging special coverings

Some wallcoverings require special techniques, such as pasting the wall instead of the paper. Other papers come ready-pasted and you don't even need a pasting table to hang them successfully.

Hanging paste-the-wall paper

This type differs from standard wallpaper because you do not cut lengths from the roll before you hang it. You also paste the wall and not the wall covering.

1 Hang a plumb line and mark a true vertical on the wall as for hanging standard wallpaper (page 103).

2 Paste the area of the wall which the first length is to cover, taking the paste just beyond the width of the covering. Use an adhesive containing a fungicide and apply it with a paint roller or brush.

3 Hold the roll of paper up to the pasted area. Align the right edge with the pencil marks on the wall. Smooth the covering into place with a brush or damp sponge.

4 Gradually unroll the paper as you move down the wall, wiping away any bubbles under the surface as you work. You may find it easier if a helper holds the roll.

5 Crease the covering at the top and bottom of the length as for standard wallpaper and trim.

6 Paste an adjacent width of the wall and hang the next length as before. Make sure the pattern matches, and butt join the edges of the two pieces.

Hanging ready-pasted papers

Ready-pasted papers and vinyls are water-resistant so they do not expand in water. This reduces the chance of bubbles forming and they do not have to be left to soak.

Tools *Water trough (cheap polystyrene troughs are widely available in DIY stores); scissors; pasting brush; sponge.*

Before you start Hang a plumb line to find a true vertical and make pencil marks to act as a guide for the first length as for hanging standard wallpaper (page 103). Put down plenty of dust sheets and fill the water trough with cold water. Position it near the wall where you are going to start.

1 Measure the wall height, add 100mm for trimming and cut a length of the paper or vinyl. Check which way up it is to be hung on the wall.

2 Roll the cut length up loosely, paste side out, from bottom to top, and immerse it in the trough for the recommended time.

3 Use both hands to lift the covering out of the trough. Hold the length above the trough for a few seconds so that surplus water drains into it.

4 Hang the length, smoothing away air bubbles with a clean sponge. Work from the middle of the length out to the edges as for standard wallpaper.

5 Wipe away any excess paste at the seams with a damp rag. The paste will not stain the surface of the covering.

6 Trim the edges as you would standard wallpaper. Then cut the next length. Roll, soak and hang it following the same procedure as for the first length.

7 Keep the water trough topped up with water as you hang the lengths. Move the trough along as you work your way from one end of the wall to the other.

8 Use special overlap adhesive to get a good bond where vinyl overlaps vinyl (around corners for example) or where a seam is not lying flat.

9 Cut vinyl with scissors around awkward angles. You cannot tear it. If you have to overlap vinyl, you can make the join less noticeable by tearing off the backing paper of the top layer of vinyl, to reduce its thickness.

10 When you have hung three or four lengths, go over the seams with a seam roller to ensure that the edges are firmly stuck down.

HELPFUL TIP

Mix a small amount of paste even when you are hanging ready-pasted papers. Use it to revive areas that may have dried out while you have been trimming. Brush the paste onto the dried areas and then smooth the length into place.

Wallpapering a ceiling

Ceilings are hard to decorate – you have to work at a height and against gravity. Also, because the ceiling is usually well lit, any imperfections in your work will show up. If the ceiling is smooth, consider painting it rather than papering it. You may want to paper a ceiling for a decorative effect or line a ceiling that has hairline cracks before painting it.

Tools *Dustsheets; tacks and chalk-line; scissors; pasting brush; wallpaper hanging brush; stepladders and trestle boards; pasting table; sponge.*

Materials *Paper; wallpaper paste.*

Before you start Cover the floor with plenty of cotton dust sheets. Set up a safe working platform. Use two trestles or two stepladders and arrange a scaffold board between them so that the ceiling clears your head by about 75mm. If possible, the board should allow you to paper the length of the ceiling without rearranging the platform. Use two boards – one on top of the other – to give a firmer support if the trestles are more than 1.5m apart. Fill any holes and cracks and seal any stains.

Tips for a professional finish

1 Hang paper beginning at the main window and working away from it. If there are two windows in a room, hang the paper across the narrower width.

2 If you are hanging a decorative wallpaper, make a line parallel with the wall as a guide for the first length (this is not necessary for lining paper or woodchip – just align the paper with the wall). The wall is unlikely to be perfectly straight, so pin one end of the chalk line to the ceiling 25mm closer to the corner than the width of your paper. Take the line to the other side of the room, position it at the same measurement from the opposite corner and snap the chalk line to make a straight line to work from.

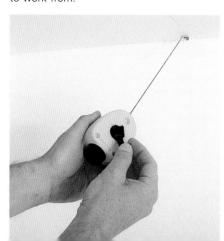

Hanging the paper

1 Brush the whole ceiling with glue size – this gives good slip and helps the adhesion.

2 Measure the ceiling, add a few centimetres for trimming at each end, and cut the first length.

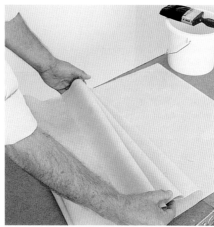

3 Paste as for paper going on a wall but, because of the length of the paper, fold it concertina fashion as you apply the paste. Keep the width of the folds to about 450mm and do not crease the folds.

4 If you are right-handed, hold the pile of folded paper in your left hand. Stand on the right hand end of the board, facing the window. If you are left-handed, hold the paper in your right hand and begin at the other end.

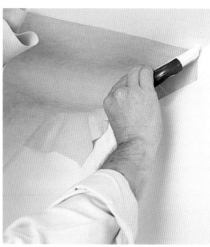

5 Release the top fold of paper. Hold it up to the ceiling and position it so that the right-hand edge aligns with the marks. Smooth the paper into the corner with your fingers. When you are satisfied that the paper is positioned correctly, gently go over it with the paperhanging brush.

6 Carefully move your left hand away to release the next fold of paper. Smooth out the paper with the brush as you move slowly to the left, checking that the paper is following the guideline. The paper will not pull away from the ceiling as long as

you keep holding the rest of the paper fairly close. If the paper pulls away easily, the paste is not strong enough, so mix up some more, adding less water. Apply the paste to the ceiling, then smooth the paper back into its position.

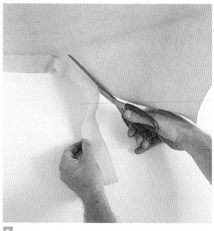

7 When the whole length is stuck to the ceiling, trim the edges against the wall and the ends. Make a crease with the back of a pair of scissors, pull the paper slightly away from the ceiling and cut away the excess.

8 Continue to hang paper in the same way, butt joining the edges.

Papering around a ceiling rose

> **SAFETY TIP**
>
> If you plan to fit paper behind a ceiling rose rather than around it, turn off the electricity at the consumer unit (fuse box) before unscrewing the rose cover.

1 Hang the first part of the length as far as the ceiling rose.

2 Make a cut in from the nearest edge of the length to the point where the fitting has to go through the paper.

3 Make a series of star-shaped cuts to go round the fitting.

4 Hang the remainder of the length. Go back to the rose and trim away the surplus paper with small sharp scissors to make a neat fit.

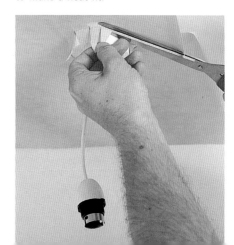

Wallpapering a stairwell

Two problems must be overcome when you paper a stairwell – how to cope with long lengths of pasted paper and how to reach the walls.

Hanging the paper

Until you are experienced, choose a good quality wall covering with a non-matching pattern. Matching long lengths is difficult because they tear easily if the paper is thin and tend to stretch. Hang the paper as on an ordinary wall, but take care when cutting lengths to size. Because stairs rise at an angle, each length of paper will need to be longer at its lower edge.

Papering a stairwell is much easier with two people. Long lengths of pasted paper are heavy to handle, so if possible get someone to stand on the stairs below where you are hanging the paper to hold the bulk of it while you hang the top.

Reaching the walls

You need to be able to reach both the head wall and the well wall from a safe working platform.

You may prefer to reach the walls from a staircase platform, especially if the ceiling is high, although it can be difficult to walk up and down the stairs while it is in place. You can hire a staircase platform designed for use on stairs, with a base only 610mm wide and adjustable feet.

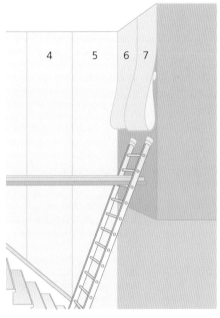

Well wall ⟶   Head wall ⟶

Wrap the ends of the ladder in rags to protect the wall

1   2   3   4   5

Use two scaffold boards if the span is more than 1.5m

Well wall
With a straight staircase, stand a stepladder on the landing – safely back from the top step – and put a straight ladder on the staircase with the top resting against the head wall and the feet against a riser halfway down the stairs. Place scaffold boards between them. Use one board on top of another for stronger support if the gap is wider than 1.5m.
• Hang the top of the paper from the board then move the platform back and smooth the bottom of the strip.

Get a second person to fix the lower half in place

Staircase with landing
On a staircase with a landing, you may have to support the platform over the balustrade. In this situation, the straight ladder must be supported at the bottom by a wooden batten screwed securely to one of the stairs.

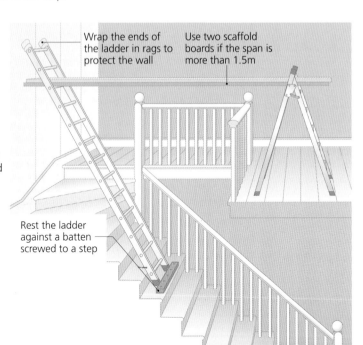

Wrap the ends of the ladder in rags to protect the wall

Use two scaffold boards if the span is more than 1.5m

Rest the ladder against a batten screwed to a step

4   5   6   7

Upper head wall
Paper the upper head wall first.
• You will probably need two or three lengths of paper. Paste and fold them before climbing onto the platform.
• Get a helper to pass them up one at a time and hang the top of each strip.
• Let them hang there.

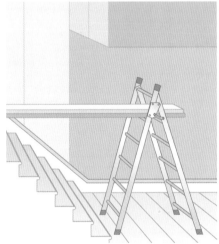

Lower head wall
• Remove the ladder and place one end of the scaffold board on a stair tread and the other on steps at the bottom of the stairs. Adjust the height of the board so that you can comfortably reach the lower half of the head wall to hang the bottom lengths.
• Hang the bottom of the paper from the new position.

Curing papering problems

Persistent bubbles
Small bubbles in wallpaper should disappear as the paper dries out. If they persist, the paper has expanded, either because it was not left to soak long enough or because new paper was applied over old.
• Cut small bubbles with a trimming knife or scalpel blade.
• Insert new paste behind the flaps with a fine artist's brush.
• Press the paper into place and wipe away excess paste with a damp rag.
• If a whole length of paper is badly affected, pull it off and hang another length, increasing the soaking time.

Paper will not slide
Water in the paste is being absorbed by the wall, or the paste is drying out too quickly. Either the wall has not been sized or the paste is too watery. Make sure you mix the paste as recommended by the maker; do not add more water to make it go farther.
• Put the problem paper back on the table.
• Mix a thicker paste and apply it to the wall, then re-hang the paper.
• If you suspect that the room's warmth is causing the paste to dry too quickly, open windows or turn off the heating.

Flattened relief pattern
Caused by too much pressure being applied when pressing the paper into position, particularly at the seams. Use very gentle pressure when applying relief papers, especially those that are heavily embossed. Do not use a seam roller on the edges; dab with a dry rag.
   Expanded vinyls will regain their shape as the foam recovers, but nothing can be done to restore the relief pattern on others.

Shiny patches on matt wallpaper
The surface has been rubbed too vigorously when being hung. Shine marks cannot usually be removed completely, but rubbing the area with a ball of white bread may lessen the shine. This method can also be used to clean non-washable wallpaper.
   Next time, smooth matt papers carefully with a clean, dry sponge or a dry nylon or lambswool paint roller. Or dab with a rag.

Staining at the seams
Old size has been reactivated by the water in the new paste. Stains cannot be totally removed, but wiping them gently with a clean, damp rag may make them less visible. To avoid this problem, wash down walls with hot water to remove any old size, and then re-size them.

Gaps at the seams
The wallpaper might have shrunk slightly as it dried out, because the paste was not strong enough to hold it in place.

Depending on the colour of the wallpaper, try painting the gap with watercolour, using a fine artist's brush, so that it is less obvious. Always use a paste suitable for the type of wallpaper being used (page 100).

Seams that lift
This often happens with vinyls and relief papers, and is caused by too little paste being applied to the edges of the paper. To re-stick the seams, lift the edge gently with the blade of a kitchen knife and apply new paste. For overlapping edges of vinyls use a special overlap adhesive.

Creases in the paper
Possibly caused by applying paper to a wall which is not perfectly flat, but more often caused by careless hanging. To avoid the problem, fill all indentations with filler or a skimming coat of plaster before papering.
   Creases can be treated in the same way as bubbles. Tear the paper, or cut the vinyl, along the crease, re-paste if necessary, and smooth down.

Damp patches on wallpaper
If wet patches remain after most of the paper has dried, damp may be striking through the wall, or the patches may be condensation forming on a cold surface.
   Do not ignore the problem: find the cause of the damp immediately and cure it. If treated immediately the damp patch will dry out without trace, but if left too long it will leave a stain.

Paper comes away from the wall
There are four possible causes: the paste is too weak to hold the weight of the paper; the surface has not been sized; the paper has been applied over old distemper or gloss paint; condensation has formed on the wall after it has been prepared.
   If only small areas of the paper are coming away from the wall, mix a new batch of paste, apply it to the wall and press the paper back into place. If whole sheets are peeling off, strip the walls and prepare the surface thoroughly.

Brown spots showing through paper
Impurities in the plaster may be the cause, left from using a wire brush or wire wool during preparation.
   Alternatively, the marks may be made by mould, formed because the surface is cold and damp.
   If the spots are excessive and obvious, strip the walls and prepare them thoroughly before redecorating. Treat them with a fungicide before repapering if damp is a problem. And if the wall is cold, line it with expanded polystyrene in roll form. Use a fungicide paste on condensation-prone walls, such as a bathroom or kitchen.

Repairing damaged wallpaper
Torn wallpaper can be patched using a piece of matching paper.

1 Tear off the paper from the damaged area, leaving only the paper which is firmly attached to the wall.

2 Hold a fresh piece of paper over the hole and adjust it so that the pattern matches the surrounding paper on the wall.

3 Tear (do not cut) a patch from the new paper and peel off a 3mm strip from the back around the edges.

4 Paste the patch and place it over the hole so that the pattern matches all round. Smooth down, working from the centre of the patch to the edges.

Patching vinyl wall covering

1 Cut a square piece of vinyl larger than the damaged area. (You cannot tear vinyl wall covering as you can paper.)

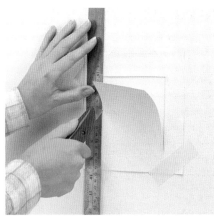

2 Tape the square over the hole and cut a square shape through both layers with a trimming knife.

3 Dry-strip the piece of old vinyl within the square.

4 Coat the patch with vinyl paste and fit it to the wall.

Tools for tiling

Many of the simple tools required for tiling – such as a pincers or pliers – may already be in your toolkit. You will also need straight battens and a plumb line to help you with positioning. The specialist tools listed here will help to make the job easier.

Platform tile cutter Modern ceramic tiles are so hard that they are more or less impossible to cut using a traditional, hand-held cutter. A platform tile cutter will cut both wall and floor tiles.

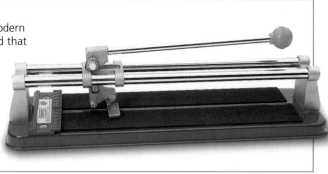

Sponge A small piece of synthetic sponge is a useful tool for pressing grout into the joins between tiles. However, most tubs of grout now come with a plastic squeegee with a flexible rubber edge (see below).

Tile file Removes rough edges from a cut tile. If a cut tile is just a little bit too big, you can also file it down to the correct size.

Spacers Small plastic crosses inserted at the corners of straight-edged tiles as they are applied to the wall ensure that there is an even gap between tiles.

Chinagraph pencil and steel rule For marking where tiles should be cut. Never use a felt-tipped pen to mark a tile – if the ink gets onto the back of the tile it may penetrate and show beneath the glazed surface.

Adhesive spreader and grouter A plastic tool with one notched edge for spreading tile adhesive, and the other edge fitted with a rubber blade for grouting. Small spreaders are usually supplied with tubs of adhesive. The notches on the spreader ensure that the adhesive is spread evenly.

Tiling gauge The gauge is a length of batten, wider than any obstruction you need to tile around. Mark the width of the tiles on the wood, plus gaps for spacers if necessary, and use the gauge to position tiles around windows or any similar breaks in the tiling.

Chinagraph pencils

Adhesive spreader and grouter

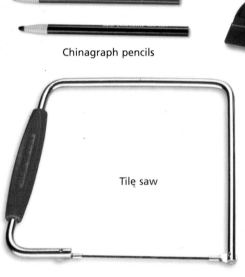

Tile saw

Tile scorer

Tile nibbler

Tile snapper with scoring blade

Steel rule

Tiling gauge

Tile saw A tungsten-carbide coated rod, mounted in a large metal frame, which acts as a cutting blade. It is the ideal tool for shaping curved tiles to fit around obstructions, such as water pipes, wash basins or baths.

Tile cutters Cutters vary in size and shape. They are used to score a clearly defined scratch across the glaze of a tile. A cutter may resemble a slim pencil with a cutting tip or have a hardened wheel set into a handle. Some cutters have two jaws to hold the tile when you break it after it has been scored. Place the scored tile between the jaws and squeeze the handles together. For the toughest tiles, use a platform tile cutter (above). This can handle tiles up to 10mm thick and both scores and breaks them.

Tile nibbler Tungsten carbide edged pincers are used for making very narrow cuts, removing waste from a curved cut or for cutting individual mosaic tiles.

Choosing ceramic wall tiles and trim

Ceramic tiles are a functional form of wall covering, particularly useful in bathrooms and kitchens. An enormous range is available in prices that vary according to size, colour and quality.

Tile sizes Wall tiles are available in sizes from 100mm square to 330 x 445 mm. Some tiles are still manufactured in notional imperial sizes, typically 4 $\frac{1}{8}$ in or 5in, giving rise to some odd metric conversions. Choosing a size that neatly fits the space you have to cover can save a lot of cutting and wastage. Remember to allow for your desired grout width when calculating how many tiles will fit your space.

Decorative tiles Many tile ranges include decorative patterned tiles, which may have a raised or printed motif that is painted by hand or machined. They can make attractive insets in a plain tiled wall.

Imported tiles Foreign ceramics are often harder, thicker and heavier than standard ceramic tiles, so experiment on a couple of tiles to see whether you can cut and shape them before you buy in bulk. Occasionally imported tiles are glazed on one or more edges. If the tiles have plain square edges you will need to use spacers.

Insert tiles In some ranges, manufacturers supply special tiles to which bathroom accessories like towel rails, soap dishes and lavatory-paper holders are attached. Even though they are heavier than ordinary tiles, they can be fixed to the wall with standard adhesive. Check that the particular insert tile you want is available in the colour you have chosen before you buy the tiles.

Mosaic tiles Small ceramic or glass tiles, known as chips, usually 20 to 25mm square. They are supplied bonded to nylon or paper mesh or faced with paper, in sheets about 300mm square or rectangles 300 x 610mm. The mesh or paper controls the spacing between the tiles.

Borders and trims

Ceramic trims You can finish off the top edge of a half-tiled wall with a row of border tiles, or use a slim pencil bead trim in a matching or contrasting colour if you prefer. Border tiles can also be used between areas of standard tiles on a fully tiled wall, for example to create the effect of a decorative dado. Border and trim tiles are made in sizes to match standard tile widths so vertical joints will align.

Plastic and metal profile trim Strips of edging trim are available in a variety of colours and finishes, from white plastic to shiny chrome and in 2.4m lengths.

A curved bead is attached at right angles to a thin perforated backing plate, which is fixed to the wall behind the last tile in each row, using tile adhesive. The tiles butt up against the edging strip, protecting their unglazed edges and creating a neat finish.

Worktop trim The neatest way of edging a tiled worktop is with a timber moulding. Paint, varnish or stain the moulding first, then screw it to the edge of the worktop to help you to position the tiles and bed them to the correct level. Use epoxy grout to fill all the joints to give the worktop a hard-wearing and hygienic finish.

EDGING A BATH OR SHOWER

When a bath or shower tray is in use, it can 'give' slightly and pull away from the bottom row of tiles around it. Flexible mastic sealant will allow for a degree of movement, but a new edging product is also available, which is designed to eliminate cracks in the sealant or grout. Bed the beaded edge into tile adhesive below the bottom row, or fix it to the face of existing tiles. Stick the adhesive sealing strip to the bath or shower tray, and it will stretch within the beaded strip as the fitting flexes.

HOW MANY TILES DO YOU NEED?

• Tiles are sold singly, or in boxes containing a specified number, or by the square metre.
• Before you buy or order tiles, measure the height and width of each part to be tiled and multiply the two figures to give the area in square metres. Add all the figures together to give the total area. Coverage is also stated on boxes. Allow 5 to 10 per cent extra for cutting and breakages.
• If you are going to use contrasting coloured or patterned tiles among plain ones, decide where they are to go and how many you need. This is easier if you make a plan of the wall on graph paper. Alternatively, cut pieces of paper into tile shapes and stick them to the wall to help you to get the height and spacing of the patterned tiles right. It will probably take a couple of hours, but it gives a better impression of how the tiles will look when the job is complete.
• There is always a slight colour variation between tiles. If you can, buy tiles in boxes with the same batch number. Then shuffle the tiles to disperse and hide any differences before you start to tile.

Preparing the surface

The glaze on tiles will highlight even tiny undulations in a wall so the surface must be as flat as possible.

Plaster

Sound, bare plaster is an ideal surface for tiling. The tile adhesive will fill minor cracks and holes; patch larger defects with a skim of ready-mixed repair plaster. Hack off any hollow areas and replaster them. Seal the surface with plaster primer. Scrape any loose paint from painted plaster. Key gloss-painted walls with coarse wet-and-dry abrasive paper.

Plasterboard

You can tile over painted plasterboard; seal bare plasterboard with two coats of emulsion paint. Use water-resistant boards such as Aquapanel instead of ordinary plasterboard for shower cubicle walls.

Papered walls

Strip all wallcoverings before tiling, and seal bare surfaces as described above.

CHOOSING TILE ADHESIVE, GROUT AND SEALANT

Tile adhesive and grout come in several forms. The most widely used is an all-in-one ready-mixed product that sticks the tiles and fills the joints, and is water and mould-resistant. It is an ideal choice for most tiling jobs. One 10 litre tub will cover an area of 10–12m².

Separate grouts and adhesives You can also buy adhesive and grout as separate products, in ready-mixed or powder form, which you mix with water. Do this only if you want to use coloured grout, or if you are tiling a kitchen worktop where a special epoxy grout is recommended for hygiene reasons. Powder products are cheaper than ready-mixed options, so may be worth considering for large tiling projects.

Sealing joints Use flexible mastic, not grout, to seal the joints between tiles and bathroom fittings or kitchen worktops (see also page 113 for a flexible beaded trim for this purpose). Use mastic also to fill internal corners and the joins between tiles and skirting boards or door architraves.

Tile spacers X-shaped plastic spacers are essential for spacing tiles evenly. They come in sizes from 2 to 5mm thick. Use 2mm spacers with 100mm square tiles, and larger sizes with bigger tiles.

Worktops

Before tiling a laminated worktop, score it with a metal abrasive disc fitted to a power drill. Coarse abrasive paper or a file will also do the job but will take longer.

Old ceramic tiles

You can tile over old tiles so long as they are securely bonded to the surface behind. Remove any loose tiles and fill the recess with repair plaster. Wash the surface with sugar soap to remove grease and soap deposits.

Man-made boards

Seal board surfaces with wood primer or diluted PVA building adhesive. Use moisture-resistant boards for bath panels and similar uses in damp areas.

Planning the tile layout

Whether you are tiling a simple splashback or an entire wall, deciding where to start is always the first step. Because an area of tiling is made up of regular units, it always looks best if the tile pattern is centred on the wall – or in the case of a splashback, on the washbasin, sink or bath that it is complementing.

Tiling around a bath

A bath is usually sited either in a corner or in an alcove. If the bath fits exactly in an alcove, the tiling should finish in line with the front edge of the bath at the head and foot; if it is in a corner, the tiling should finish flush with the front edge and the end of the bath.

1 Start each row with a whole tile at the outer edge of the bath or alcove. Centre the tiling on the back wall.

2 Once all the whole tiles are in place, finish the rows with cut tiles in each internal corner.

Tiling a splashback

A simple splashback for a washbasin or sink usually consists of two or three rows of tiles on the wall above it. Because the tiled area is self-contained, you can complete the job using only whole tiles. There are two choices for centring the tile layout. If the basin is in an alcove, centre the tiles in the alcove, positioning cut tiles of equal width at either edge.

1 Mark the centre of the basin or sink on the wall above and draw a vertical line there. Place a whole tile at either side of the line, then add more whole tiles in a row until the tiling reaches (or extends just beyond) the edge of the basin or sink (below). Add a second or third row of tiles to complete the splashback.

2 If this layout means that tiles finish just short of the edges of the basin or sink or extend too far on either side, place the first tile astride the centre line instead (bottom). This has the effect of moving the tile row along by half the width of a tile, and may create a better-looking layout. Add extra rows of tiles to reach the required height.

Positioning tiles for a splashback

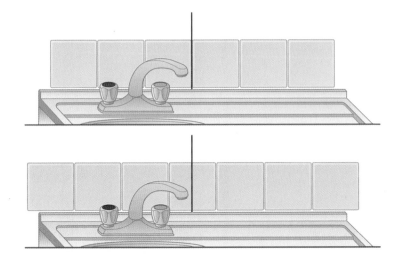

Half-tiling a wall

You can set out and centre tiles for a splashback by eye, standing tiles in a row along the back edge of the fixture to work out the best layout. On a wall, a simple aid called a tiling gauge makes the setting out much easier.

Tiling a wall to a height of about 1.2m is a popular project in a bathroom or separate WC. If the wall is unobstructed, the centring rule is simple to apply. Each row should have cut tiles of equal width at each end (except in the unlikely event that a row of whole tiles exactly fills the available space). Each column will have a whole tile at the top and a cut tile at the bottom.

You may be tempted to save work and start each column with a whole tile at floor or skirting board level, but there is a good reason why you should not do this. The floor or skirting board may not be truly level, and the effect of using it as a base-line will gradually force the tile rows and columns off square. You might get away with this on a single tiled wall, but if you are tiling all round the room the cumulative effect can be disastrous.

Using guide battens

The secret of success is to use a horizontal timber guide batten fixed to the wall beneath the bottom edge of the lowest row of whole tiles. Position it so that the gap to be filled between this row and the floor or skirting board is about three-quarters of a tile width.

You have to place all the whole tiles on the wall before you can fit any cut tiles at the ends of the rows. It is therefore a good idea to add a vertical guide batten at one side of the area, to ensure that the columns of tiles are all precisely vertical. Once all the whole tiles have been placed, both the vertical and horizontal battens are removed so the cut tiles can be measured, cut and fixed in place.

Using a tiling gauge

1 Measure the width of the wall to be tiled and mark the centre point. Hold the tile gauge horizontally, with one end less than a tile width from a corner, and align a joint mark with the centre line. If the gap at the end of the gauge is between one-third and two-thirds of a tile wide, you have a satisfactory tile layout. Mark the wall in line with the end of the gauge. This indicates where the vertical guide batten will be fixed.

2 If the gap is very narrow, or is almost a whole tile wide, it will be difficult to cut tiles to fit. You will get a better layout by moving the gauge along by half a tile width. Do this, then mark the wall in line with the end of the gauge to indicate where to fix the vertical guide batten.

3 Hold the gauge vertically to assess where the top of the tiled area will finish. Move it up so the bottom of the gauge is about three-quarters of a tile width above the floor or skirting board. Mark the wall at a joint mark to indicate the top of the tiled area. Make another mark level with the bottom of the gauge to indicate the level of the horizontal guide batten.

Fixing the battens

You now have pencil marks on the wall indicating the level of the lowest row of whole tiles, and also the edge of the column of whole tiles nearest the room corner.

1 Fix the horizontal guide batten first, using a spirit level to get it truly horizontal. If you are tiling more than one wall, fix guide battens to each wall, and check that they are precisely aligned with each other.

2 Use a spirit level to mark a true vertical line down to the horizontal guide batten from the end mark you made on the wall with your tiling gauge.

3 Fix a vertical guide batten at this point, long enough to reach up to the top of the area to be tiled. Secure the battens with masonry nails on solid walls, and with wire nails on timber-framed partitions. Leave the nail heads projecting by about 10mm so they can be pulled out easily when it is time to remove the battens.

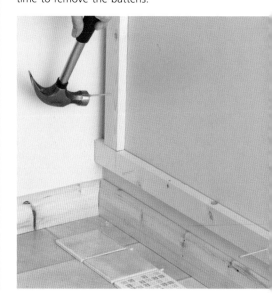

MAKING A TILING GAUGE

To make it, you need a piece of 50 × 25mm planed softwood about 2m long. Choose a piece that is straight and not warped in either direction. Place it on the floor and lay a row of tiles alongside it, with tile spacers between the tiles to create uniform gaps of the correct width. Mark a pencil line on the batten to coincide with each joint. Cut the gauge to length at the last pencil mark. You can then hold the gauge against the wall to see how whole tiles will fit in the space available. It is also invaluable for centring tiles on walls with obstacles such as windows, doors and bathroom or kitchen equipment (see page 116).

Tiling a wall

With the setting-out complete and the guide battens fixed, you can start to place the whole tiles on the wall. Put down a dust sheet to catch stray blobs of adhesive, unpack your tiles and spacers and place them nearby.

Tools *Notched spreader; stripping knife; damp cloth.*

Materials *Tiles; tile adhesive; spacers.*

1 Scoop some adhesive from the tub with your spreader and spread it on the wall in a band a little more than one tile wide. The notches form ridges in the adhesive which will be compressed to an even thickness as you place the tiles.

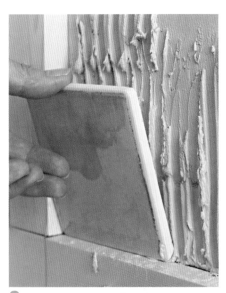

2 Place the first tile in the angle between the guide battens. Rest its lower edge on the horizontal batten, then press it into the adhesive. Check that its edge is against the vertical batten.

3 Place more tiles one by one along the row, fitting a spacer between them, until you reach the room corner. Press the spacers at the top corners into the adhesive so they will be covered when you fill the joints with grout (page 119). At the bottom corners, push one leg of each spacer into the gap between the tiles; these will be pulled out when the batten is removed.

4 Hold the edge of your tiling gauge across the faces of the tiles to check that they are flush with each other. Press in any that are proud of their neighbours.

5 Apply another band of adhesive and place the second row of tiles. Align the bottom edge of each one between the

spacers in the row below before pressing it into place. Then fit spacers between the top corners as before.

6 When you have placed the topmost row of tiles, scrape off any excess adhesive from the wall with a stripping knife and wipe off the remaining traces with a damp cloth.

7 Allow the adhesive to set for 24 hours. Then prise out the nails that are holding the guide battens in place, taking care not to dislodge the tiles. Measure and cut individual tiles, one at a time, to fit the width of the remaining gaps (page 117) and butter some adhesive onto the back with your spreader.

8 Fit spacers into the gaps between the rows of whole tiles. Then fit the cut pieces, one at a time, into the gap between the spacers. Press the cut tile into place so its face is flush with its neighbour. Repeat the process to measure, cut and fit the remaining cut tiles at both ends of each row. Then cut tiles to fill the gap between the bottom row of whole tiles and the skirting board or floor.

POSITIONING TILES AROUND A WINDOW

Tiles look best if they are centred around a window opening. Use a tiling gauge (page 115) to span the window and adjust its position until there is an equal width of tile on either side of the opening. Mark the wall to indicate the outer edge of the tiles that will need to be cut. Drop a plumb line through the first of the lines to transfer the mark to the horizontal batten at the bottom of the wall. Work from this mark towards the corner of the room, measuring full tile widths and grout joints to determine the position of the last whole tile in each row. Fix the vertical batten to the wall at this point.

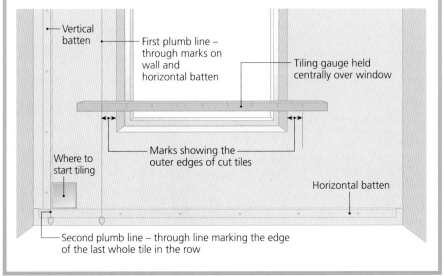

Vertical batten

First plumb line – through marks on wall and horizontal batten

Tiling gauge held centrally over window

Marks showing the outer edges of cut tiles

Where to start tiling

Horizontal batten

Second plumb line – through line marking the edge of the last whole tile in the row

Cutting tiles to fit

Tiling a splashback is easy – you probably won't even have to cut a tile. But if you are tiling a whole wall, you will encounter various obstacles.

Tools *Chinagraph pencil; steel rule; platform tile cutter; tile saw; tile nibbler; pencil; G-cramp.*

Materials *Tiles; adhesive.*

Finishing a row

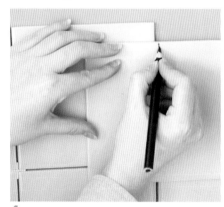

1 When you reach the end of a row, place the final tile over the previous tile and butt it up to the corner. Allow for the width of a grout joint and mark the cutting line.

2 Use a platform tile cutter to make a neat straight cut. Score the tile with the cutting wheel then use the lever to snap the tile along the line. Position the tile on the wall with the cut edge into the corner.

3 Measure the final tile in each row separately. Few walls are perfectly square, so your measurements are unlikely to be the same all the way up.

HELPFUL TIP

If you are filling gaps with cut tiles, butter the back of each tile with adhesive, then press it into place. It is much easier than trying to apply adhesive to a narrow strip of wall.

Taking a sliver off a tile

1 Platform tile cutters will not make fine cuts, less than 15mm wide. Use a hand-held tile scorer and steel straightedge. Score the tile much more deeply than you would for an ordinary cut – you need to cut right through the glaze in order to get a clean break.

2 Nibble away at the sliver of tile that is being removed, using a tile nibbler. Smooth any sharp edges with a tile file.

Cutting a curved line

1 Cut a piece of paper to the size of a tile to make a template to fit around the curved object.

2 Make a series of cuts in the edge that will butt up to the obstacle. Press the tongues against the obstacle so that the creases define its outline.

3 Use the paper as a guide to transfer the curved line with a chinagraph pencil onto the glazed tile surface.

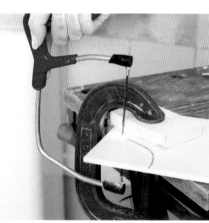

4 Clamp the tile face-up to a workbench, protecting the glaze with a board offcut sandwiched between tile and cramp. Cut along the marked line with a tile saw. Work slowly and with as little pressure as possible to avoid chipping the glaze. File away any excess if necessary to get a perfect fit.

Making holes

1 When you tile around plumbing – in a shower, for example – you may need to make holes in the tiles to allow pipes to run through. Offer up the tile from the side and from below, and mark each edge in line with the centre of the pipe. Draw straight lines to extend the marks: where they intersect is the pipe centre. Trace round an offcut of pipe – or a coin or other round object of about the same diameter – to mark a cutting line at this point.

2 Cut the tile in two along one of the lines drawn through the centre of the marked pipe hole. Score the outline of each resulting semi-circle with a pencil-type tile cutter. Use a tile nibbler to cut the hole.

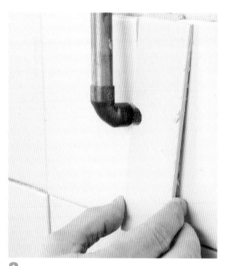

3 Fit the two cut pieces together around the pipe. Grout around the pipe or use a silicone sealant for a water-tight finish.

POWER CUTS FOR TILES

If you have a craft drill, such as a Dremel, you can use its tile-cutting attachment to make holes in tiles. Mark the cutting line as described above, but don't split the tile in two until after you have made the hole. Cut out the circle you have marked then split the tile and fit it in place.

Tiling around corners

Internal corners

Place all the whole tiles on both walls, then remove the guide battens so that you can cut and fit the tiles in the corner.

1 Measure and cut a tile to fit the width of the gap to be filled (page 117). Butter the back of the cut tile with adhesive and press it into place with the cut edge facing into the corner.

2 When the adhesive has dried, seal the angle between the two walls with a flexible waterproof mastic. This will allow for a little wall movement over time. Use masking tape to mask the joint, apply the mastic, smooth it and peel off the tape once a skin has formed.

External corners

External corners should, ideally, start with whole tiles on each wall, though this is unlikely to be possible at a window rebate. Joins can be made by butting the tiles, using plastic corner trim or sticking on a strip of timber beading.

Butt joint A simple overlapping butt joint works well if the corner is true and the tiles have glazed edges. Tile the less visible wall first, placing whole tiles flush with the corner. Then tile the other wall, overlapping these tiles to conceal the edges of those on the first wall.

Plastic corner trim Coloured plastic or chrome corner trims will protect tiles on external corners from damage and give the edge a neat finish. You can use the trim along the edges of tiled door and window recesses as well.

1 Push the perforated base of the trim into the tile adhesive on one corner so that the outer edge of the rounded trim lines up perfectly with the faces of the tiles on the adjacent wall.

2 Start tiling the second wall, easing each tile into the corner trim as you place it. Don't push it too hard – you don't want to dislodge the trim. When you have laid all the corner tiles, make sure the trim lines up with the tile faces on both walls.

A window recess

1 Tile the wall as far as the window, cutting tiles to fit. If you have to cut a tile to an L shape, cut a line from the edge to the centre of the tile using a tile saw then score a line at right angles to the cut and snap off the unwanted piece. Use lengths of plastic edging strip designed for external corners to give the edges a neat finish.

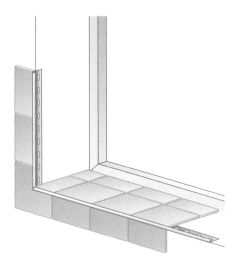

2 Lay the tiles at the bottom of the recess first. Put any cut tiles nearest the window, with cut edges against the frame.

3 Line up the first course of tiles on the side walls with the tiles on the main wall.

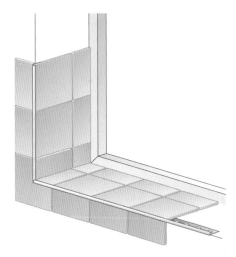

Grouting between tiles

When the tiles have been in place for at least 12 hours, fill the gaps between them with grout. This gives an attractive finished appearance and prevents dirt from collecting in the cracks.

Tools *Pieces of sponge or a squeegee; larger sponge; thin dowel or something similar for finishing; soft dry cloth.*

Materials *Grout (waterproof for kitchens or bathrooms).*

1 If the grout is not ready-mixed, prepare as recommended. With waterproof epoxy-based grout, mix only a little at a time – it sets hard quickly.

2 Press the grout firmly into the gaps between the tiles. Professionals use a rubber-edged squeegee, but if you have never grouted before you may find it easier to get the grout well into the cracks with a small piece of sponge.

3 Wipe away any grout that gets onto the surface of the tiles with a clean, damp sponge while the grout is still wet. Wipe away combined adhesive and grout or waterproof grout quickly – these are hard to clean off the tile surface once set.

4 To give the tiling a neat professional finish, run a thin piece of dowelling over each grout line. Or use the cap of a ballpoint pen, the blunt end of a pencil or a lolly stick. Wipe surplus off the surface of the tiles as you go.

5 Leave ordinary grout to dry, then polish it off using a clean, dry cloth. Another way to polish tiles effectively is to use a screwed-up ball of newspaper.

HELPFUL TIP

Revive discoloured grout by painting it with a proprietary liquid grout whitener, applied with an artist's brush. Be aware, though, that this is a slow and tedious job.

Drilling holes through tiles

Many bathroom and kitchen accessories, like soap dishes, must be screwed to the wall – in which case you may have to drill holes through ceramic tiles.

It's a good idea to make fixings in tiled walls by drilling into grout lines wherever possible, but sometimes drilling through the glaze is unavoidable. Drilling through tiles creates a lot of fine dust, which may stain nearby grouting. To catch the dust, make a simple cardboard tray and stick it to the wall with masking tape or get someone to hold a vacuum-cleaner nozzle near the drill tip as you drill the hole.

Tools *Drill; small masonry bit to make pilot hole and larger one to suit the screw, or sharp spear point bit; chinagraph pencil; screwdriver; possibly steel ruler.*

Materials *Masking tape; wall plugs; screws.*

1 Decide where you want to make the screw fixing and mark its position on the surface of the tile with a chinagraph pencil.

2 Stop the point of the masonry bit from skating over the smooth tile surface by sticking a piece of masking tape over the mark, which should show through it. Remake the mark on the surface of the tape. If you need to make more than one screw hole, use a strip of tape to cover both hole positions and mark them on the tape.

3 Make a pilot hole with the small masonry bit. Press the tip firmly against the mark on the tape. Check the drill isn't on hammer action, and start at a low speed. Drill slowly and carefully through the glazed surface of the tile. Stop drilling when the bit starts to penetrate the plaster. Using a small bit to do this minimises the risk of cracking the glaze. Repeat the process if necessary to drill a second hole through the other mark on the tape.

4 Switch to the bit that matches the screw size you intend to use. Position its tip in the hole and drill slowly and carefully through the tile and the plaster and well into the masonry.

Alternatively You can buy a special ceramic tile bit with a sharp spear point. Its shape is designed to break through the glaze immediately. This minimises the risk of skidding across or cracking the tile. The bits are available in a range of sizes.

HELPFUL TIP

If you are putting a wall plug into a tiled wall, make the hole at least 3mm deeper than the length of the plug so that it can be pushed into the wall and beyond the tile. Otherwise, when you drive in the screw, the sideways pressure may crack the tile.

Laying mosaic tiles

Mosaic tiles come in sheets with a fabric mesh backing. They are a good DIY option, being much easier to fit around obstacles than full-size ceramic tiles.

Tools *Straightedge; spirit level; tape measure; pencil; notched adhesive spreader; wood batten; trimming knife; cutting board; tile-cutting pliers; grouting tools.*

Materials *Mosaic tiles; tile adhesive; grout.*

1 Use a batten and spirit level to mark out in pencil the area you want to tile. This simple splashback is the height of a sheet of tiles above the worktop.

2 Apply tile adhesive, holding the notched spreader at an angle of 45 degrees to create ridges of an even depth.

3 Put up the first sheet of tiles, lining it up with the guideline. Press it into place with your hand, then use a wood offcut to tamp the tiles level – especially those at the edges of the sheet.

4 When you reach an obstacle, such as a socket outlet, use a sharp trimming knife to cut out sections of whole mosaic tiles. Lay the sheet of tiles on a cutting board and run the blade along the gaps.

5 Once you have cut out the section of tiles, check the fit. There will be gaps, but you can fill these later. Spread adhesive on the wall and put the cut sheet in place.

6 Lay all the whole sheets until the area is covered. Then measure the gaps left round any obstacles. You will need to cut individual mosaic tiles to fit (see box, right).

7 When all the tiles are in place, leave the adhesive to dry for 24 hours. Then grout the gaps between the tiles. Load a rubber-edged grout spreader with grout (use waterproof grout for bathrooms or kitchens), and draw it across the tiles. Clean surplus grout off the tile surfaces as you work. Before the grout sets, use a piece of slim dowel or a proprietary grout shaper to neaten the grout lines (see page 119).

SCORE AND SNAP

If you need to cut individual mosaic tiles to fill narrow gaps around obstacles, the best tool is a pair of tile cutting pliers. Trim off a strip of tiles and score a cutting line along the whole strip. Then detach individual tiles and use the v-shaped jaws of the pliers to snap the tiles one at a time.

Common tiling problems and cures

Because tiles are so hard-wearing, they are often used in areas that are damp, dirty and prone to damage. There are some common problems to look out for – treat them promptly to minimise the damage.

Mould on grout
Dark stains on grout lines may be caused by mould, which thrives in the damp and warmth of kitchens and bathrooms. Kill the mould with a proprietary fungicide, following the manufacturer's instructions. Do not use bleach. It will not destroy the roots of the mould.

Any stains left on the grout can be hidden by painting on grout whitener. When the whitener is dry, apply some more fungicide to prevent further mould.

Dirty grout
Clean grease and dirt from grout with an old toothbrush and liquid detergent in warm water, or a non-abrasive cream cleaner. When dry, paint the grout with a grout whitener.

Missing grout
If there are gaps in the grout, rake out all old grout with a proprietary grout rake (below), a small-toothed tool designed specifically for the job. Draw the rake along the grout lines, first vertically and then horizontally, to remove the old grout to a depth of about 3mm.

Use a small, stiff-bristled brush or a vacuum cleaner with a narrow nozzle attachment to remove all the debris from the joints before regrouting.

Crazed tiles
Tiles may become crazed because they are old, but new tiles may also be affected if water gets behind them. Nothing can be done to repair tiles damaged by crazing. You can paint tiles with special tile paint, though this is not as tough a finish as the original glaze. If you have spare matching tiles, you can remove the damaged ones and replace them.

Replacing a damaged tile

If you work carefully, it is a fairly straightforward task to replace a single cracked tile or remove and replace one with holes drilled in it that are no longer needed. You can also replace interspersed patterned tiles with matching plain ones to create a uniform effect.

Tools *Power drill; large masonry bit; cold chisel; hammer; safety goggles; work gloves; notched adhesive spreader; tools for applying grout.*

Materials *New tile; adhesive; grout.*

Before you start Always wear safety goggles as protection against slivers of glaze that are likely to splinter away from the tile surface as you chip away at the tile you are removing. Protect your hands with sturdy work gloves.

1 Drill holes in the centre of the tile you want to remove, using a power drill and masonry bit.

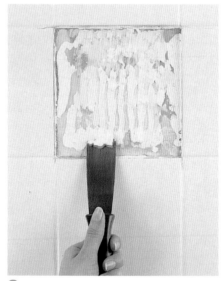

2 Insert the cold chisel, and hammer from the holes outwards towards the edges to get behind the tile. If you need to get more leverage, pack pieces of scrap wood behind the chisel as you work. Remove loose pieces of tile as they break away.

3 When you have removed the tile, carefully chisel out the old adhesive until you reveal bare wall.

CHECK THE DEPTH
If you can see an edge of a tile anywhere on the existing tiled area, check how deep the tiles are and make sure you buy a replacement to match. If you have to guess, don't buy a tile thicker than 4mm or you risk it sticking out proud of the surrounding area.

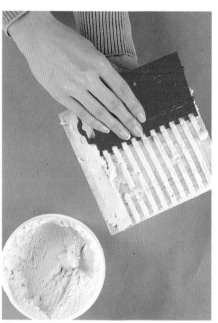

4 Butter the back of a new tile with adhesive, using the notched spreader, and fit it in place. Put spacers around the tile to ensure even spacing.

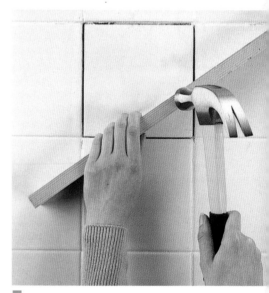

5 Lay a straightedge or offcut of timber across the repair to check that the wall is flat, adding or removing adhesive as necessary.

6 Use a damp cloth to wipe excess adhesive from the surface of the tiles. Leave the adhesive to set for about 12 hours before grouting the joins.

4

Floor coverings

Choosing floor coverings

There are many types of floor covering, with new materials being introduced all the time. Replacing an old carpet with a new laminate wood floor, or stripping old floorboards, can give a room a terrific lift. Here is a summary of what is available.

Sanded and varnished floorboards

• Suitable finish for boards in good condition and without gaps.
• The floor is sanded with a heavy-duty sanding machine that can be hired for a day or weekend. Cheap, and fairly simple to do yourself. Sanding a floor is noisy and dusty work, however.
• The finished surface is noisy underfoot. Can be draughty on a ground floor if boards are not tongued-and-grooved.
• Sweep or vacuum-clean frequently to remove grit, which can scratch the surface. Wipe up spillages with a damp cloth. Polish regularly. Lightly sand worn areas and re-varnish.

Vinyl tiles

• Huge range of colours, patterns and price. Available in imitation ceramic, wood or stone as well as cheaper smooth vinyl.
• Hygienic, easily cleaned. Resistant to spillages. Good for kitchens and bathrooms.
• Smooth vinyl is slippery when wet. Cushion-backed types are warmer, safer and quieter underfoot.
• Clean as for sheet vinyl (right), but beware of using too much water when you wash it; water could get under the joins.

Cork tiles

• Natural material, available in various finishes. Warmer material than vinyl.
• Easily cleaned when varnished or bought factory sealed. PVC-coated cork is best.
• Can become worn in heavy traffic areas unless the tiles are PVC-coated.
• Vacuum-clean or sweep regularly to remove surface dirt, and wash with solution of mild detergent. Avoid swamping with water, and do not use abrasive cleaners.

Ceramic tiles

• Range from traditional square or rectangular tiles to specialist, handmade tiles of various shapes. Some ceramic tiles are very slippery, but tiles can be obtained with an anti-slip surface.
• Long lasting, easily cleaned and highly resistant to stains and spillages. Wide choice of patterns and colours.
• Unglazed ceramic tiles tend to be porous, and are not suitable for kitchens and bathrooms.
• Expensive. Timber sub-floor needs strengthening before laying. Noisy underfoot. Cold if walked on in bare feet. Crockery breaks if dropped on it.
• Remove surface grit by sweeping or vacuum cleaning, then wash with non-abrasive detergent in water. Keep water to a minimum to prevent seepage under tiles. Scrub stubborn marks and ingrained dirt round edges of tiles.

Terracotta and quarry tiles

• Terracotta tiles and their budget-priced alternative, quarry tiles, are a more rustic alternative to ceramic tiles. Quarry tiles are less porous than terracotta tiles, but do not have the subtle shading of terracotta.
• Terracotta is warmer underfoot than other hard floor tiles. Both types are hard-wearing and can be cleaned easily. Good choice of brown and red shades.
• Noisy when walked on and not kind to dropped crockery. Their thickness makes them difficult to cut. If laid on a timber floor, these tiles require a 13mm plywood underlay.
• Terracotta tiles need a primer or treatment applied before installation (page 139), plus wax or sealant every few months to maintain their surface finish.

Sheet vinyl

• Smooth vinyl is cheaper; cushioned vinyl is softer underfoot. Wide range of patterns and colours. Linoleum is a traditional floor covering that is recently regaining popularity. It can be more difficult to lay but is very durable and more resistant to burns than vinyl. It comes in a range of colours and patterns.
• Hygienic, easily cleaned, resistant to spillages. Inexpensive flooring for kitchens and bathrooms.
• Smooth vinyl is slippery when wet. Cushion-backed varieties are warmer, safer and quieter underfoot.
• Vacuum-clean or sweep to remove grit, which can scratch. Wash with detergent. Remove scuff marks by gently rubbing with fine steel wool lubricated with white spirit, taking care not to rub through top surface.

Carpet

• Wide range of colour and price. Available as fitted carpet, carpet squares or carpet tiles. Gives feeling of warmth and comfort. Graded according to use – from heavily used stairs to low-use spare bedrooms.
• Good quality carpet is expensive. Spillages may cause permanent staining.
• Vacuum-clean frequently to remove grit which can harm fibres. Remove stains with proprietary cleaner. Rearrange carpet tiles to even out wear.

Wood

• Wood floors come as strips or mosaic panels. Some are nailed down, some are stuck down, and some simply interlock and 'float' on the floor below. Because solid timber is so expensive, most wood floors are laminate floors, consisting of a thin top veneer layer fixed to a strong bottom layer of softwood or high density fibreboard (HDF). For more about choosing laminate flooring see page 130.
• Luxurious and long-lasting in living rooms, dining rooms and halls.
• Natural wood is expensive. Laminated wood strip is cheaper, but the cheapest printed types do not wear well. Noisy underfoot.
• Remove surface dirt with vacuum cleaner to minimise scratching. Varnished floors can be wiped with a damp cloth.

Natural fibres

• Coir, jute, seagrass and sisal flooring are all made from plant fibres: coir from coconut husks; jute from the plant of the same name; seagrass from grasses grown in paddy fields; and sisal from the fleshy-leaved plant *Agave sisalana*.
• They come in a variety of weaves. A latex backing means the plant-fibre floor covering will not fray when cut to size, and can be laid with or without underlay.
• Durability differs: coir and sisal floor coverings tend to be more durable, seagrass and jute less so.
• Can stain and are vulnerable to damp – therefore they are not suitable for kitchens and bathrooms. Do not use on stairs if the finish is slippery or not hard-wearing enough.
• Vacuum-clean on a regular basis to ensure removal of grit that can harm fibres. Some types can be shampooed; others must be dry-cleaned.

FINISHES FOR STRIPPED FLOORBOARDS

• Special hardwearing floor paints are available, or you can apply emulsion and then coat it with a flooring-grade varnish. Brighten up the floor with stencils before varnishing, or paint the boards in carnival stripes.
• You can give a floor an attractive 'limewashed' finish with slightly diluted emulsion paint, and apply clear varnish over it once the paint is dry.
• Buy a wax-based liming paste, which you rub into the bare wood with a coarse cloth and then wipe off. However, you can't apply varnish over wax (it will not bond or dry properly), so you will have to finish the floor with clear wax polish. This is hard work to apply and maintain, and not very durable.

Preparing a solid floor before laying a covering

A direct-to-earth floor can suffer from three faults that make it unsuitable for a floor covering to be laid. It can be damp; a concrete floor can suffer from a condition called 'dusting'; or the floor could be uneven.

Is the floor damp?
If a floor is damp there is no point in laying a covering. The moisture will eventually destroy the covering itself and any adhesive that was used to hold it down.

Damp in a floor is not always obvious, but if a direct-to-earth floor was laid before 1940 it is unlikely to have a damp-proof membrane, and will have to be treated. Ways of dealing with damp in floors are given on page 247.

A cure for 'dusting'
A concrete floor may suffer from a condition known as dusting, in which dust continually forms on the surface, no matter how often you sweep it.

This can be cured by applying a concrete-floor sealer sold by builders' merchants. Apply it following the manufacturer's instructions. Alternatively, you can use a PVA bonding agent diluted with water.

Levelling a solid floor

For most DIY jobs, the best solution for an uneven solid floor is to choose a self-levelling compound, supplied as a powder to mix with water.

Self-levelling compound is very straightforward to use. Follow the manufacturer's instructions that come with the materials.

Be absolutely sure that you really want to use it because once the new surface is laid and has set, it's there to stay.

Tools *Bucket; scrubbing brush; steel float and/or trowel.*

Materials *Self-levelling compound; sugar soap; water.*

HELPFUL TIP

If you do not obtain a good, smooth finish after trowelling the levelling compound, sprinkle water on the surface and try again.

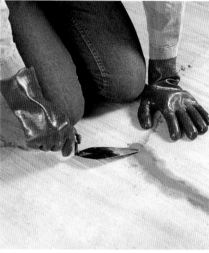

Before you start Fill any deep indentations in the floor with a sand-and-cement mix; bags of mortar to which you merely add water are ideal. To ensure a good bond, first brush a priming coat of PVA adhesive on the patch to be filled, and add a little of it to the mortar. Trowel the surface of the mortar patch as smooth as possible.

1 Clean the floor by scrubbing with a solution of sugar soap and water. Rinse and allow the floor to dry thoroughly.

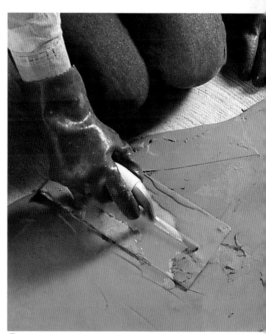

2 Pour some of the runny compound in the corner farthest from the door. Use a trowel to spread it to a depth of about 10mm – most brands include a spatula for this – and leave it to find its own level.

3 Make sure you use enough to fill in all the dips.

4 Continue working across the floor, smoothing the edges as you work.

5 It will be hard enough to walk on after an hour or so, but leave for the time specified on the packet before laying a floor covering.

Preparing a wood floor before laying a covering

Material laid on a properly prepared floor will look better and will last longer. Vinyl or cork flooring will show any ridges in the sub-floor, and will wear unevenly. Even carpet wears more quickly on the ridges.

1 Make sure that the floor is structurally sound. If it moves as you walk across it, there may be a defective joist, and you should call in a builder. If there is a feeling of sponginess, there could be an outbreak of woodworm or rot below the surface. Take up a board and check, and treat or replace as necessary.

2 Any damp in the floor must be cured.

3 Loose boards must be fixed.

4 Remove old tacks left behind from a previous covering. Prise them up with a claw hammer, pincers or tack lifter.

5 Any damaged boards will have to be replaced (page 254). If you are sanding the floor, any new boards are unlikely to match exactly the colour of the old. So replace a faulty board in a prominent place with an existing board from a less obvious spot (one that will be hidden by furniture or a rug, for example). This less conspicuous board can be replaced with a new one.

Fill knots Use car body filler to block knot holes in wooden boards before laying vinyl sheet flooring. If you don't, pressure from chair legs and similar objects could pierce and damage the floor covering.

TAKING UP OLD FLOORINGS

Old tiles and parquet that are firmly stuck can form a sound base for a new floor. But carpets and sheet vinyls – and any other flooring that is not well stuck down – must be removed before you lay a new one.

A garden spade is an excellent tool for lifting a floor covering such as vinyl tiles or lino, when the glue is not holding well. Its blade has a sharp edge that you can push under the material (file it sharper if necessary) and the long handle allows plenty or leverage for lifting. For a large area, hire a powered floor-tile stripper.

Old quarry tiles are difficult to remove, and may only reveal an unsatisfactory sub-floor underneath. It is probably best to leave them in place. If a few tiles are damaged or missing, remove damaged pieces with a bolster and club hammer – wearing safety goggles. Then replace them with new tiles (page 137), or fill the gaps with sand and cement. If a quarry-tiled floor is in a very bad state, clear out badly broken and crumbling patches, clean thoroughly, fill deeper holes with sand and cement, and then apply a self-levelling compound (page 125).

Lining a wood floor with hardboard

Lining the floor with hardboard levels off boards that are curling at the edges, covers small gaps between boards and even masks minor damage.

Hardboard also covers old stains and polishes. Lay hardboard with its mesh side up. This forms a better key for adhesives than the smooth side, and when you nail

down the sheets the nail heads will sink below the mesh and not create pimple marks in the final floor covering. After laying the boards, leave them at least overnight before laying the floor covering.

Tools *Hammer; panel saw; large paintbrush; measuring jug; bowl or paint kettle.*

Materials *Sheets of hardboard 3mm thick; water; 20mm annular nails – these have ringed shafts for extra grip – about 250g for an average sized room.*

1 The boards must be given a moisture content suitable for the room – a process known as conditioning. Otherwise they may become distorted. Brush half a litre of water into the mesh side of 1220mm square sheets, and stack them mesh side to mesh side, perfectly flat on the floor of the room they will occupy. Leave them for 48 hours before laying. The boards will adjust gradually to the humidity of the room, and dry out further when nailed down, tightening up like a drum skin to form a perfect surface for the final floor covering.

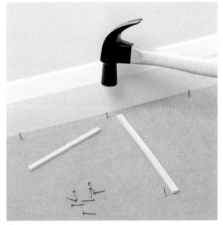

2 Begin laying the boards in a corner of the room, and start nailing along one edge of a sheet, 15mm in from the edge. Work sideways and forwards, in pyramid fashion (see below). The nails should be about 150mm apart along the edges of the board and 250mm apart in the middle of the board. It helps to use cut pieces of wood as guides for spacing the nails.

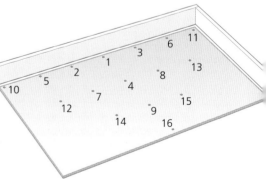

3 Butt the second board firmly against the first, and begin nailing along the meeting edge.

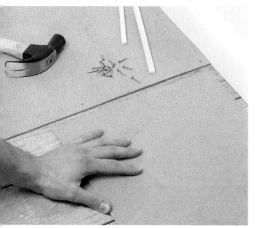

4 Continue in this way until, at the end of the row, you will have to cut a board to fit. You do not need to cut the boards to a perfect fit to the skirting board. Gaps up to 5mm do not matter. Use the offcut from the previous board to start the next row. This avoids waste, and prevents the joins from lining up across the room.

5 You will have to cut each sheet in the final row to fit the remaining space.

Restoring a wood floor

An attractive floor can be created by restoring existing floorboards. Floorboards may be stripped and varnished, or you could stain, paint or lime them before sealing with a hardwearing clear coating.

Filling holes in floorboards

Use a flexible filler to cover all nail and screw heads – nail heads should be punched below the surface, and screws may need countersinking so that their heads are below the surface. If you are painting the floor, the filler colour does not matter; if you are varnishing it, choose a filler slightly lighter in colour than the surrounding floor. Once dry, sand filler flush with the floor.

Plugging gaps between boards

There are two ways to deal with gaps between floorboards: you can fill the gaps, or you can lift and relay the entire floor.

Fill narrow gaps with flexible mastic (clear mastic will be almost invisible); wider gaps are best filled with thin lengths of square-edge moulding.

Filling gaps with moulding

1 Plane moulding strips into a slight wedge shape.

2 Apply a little woodworking adhesive before tapping a wedge into a gap, thin edge first.

3 Plane wedges down to floor level when the adhesive has set, then stain them to match the boards.

Filling small gaps

Fill gaps between floorboards with a flexible acrylic flooring filler applied with a sealant gun. If you intend to sand and varnish the boards, use a ready-mixed tub filler that can be stained to match the board colour.

RE-LAYING FLOORBOARDS

If you decide to re-lay the floorboards, you need to fit the first board tight to the wall, and using a tool called a floor cramp – which can be hired – butt each board up against the previous one.

Traditional cut brads are the best nails for fixing floorboards. The length of the brads should be two-and-a-half times the thickness of the boards.

If you are laying a floor above an old ceiling, use screws, countersinking the heads, instead of nails so as not to risk cracking the ceiling beneath as you hammer.

Restoring a woodblock floor

A woodblock (parquet or wood mosaic) floor that is not too badly damaged can be rejuvenated by sanding and sealing. The job is worth while, as such flooring is expensive and rarely fitted today. The floor may only need sanding and finishing, or you may need to replace one or more blocks.

Tools *Dust mask; nail punch and claw hammer; floor sanding machine and edging sander (a weekend's hire should be sufficient for one room); earmuffs; sanding belts (coarse, medium and fine); edging sander; old chisel; old paintbrush (for adhesive).*

Materials *Flooring varnish or other sealer; latex flooring adhesive.*

Before you start If blocks are missing, a local wood yard may be able to make replacements, or you may find them in a reclamation yard or via the Internet (try typing 'old parquet flooring' into the search engine on your computer).

1 Remove any loose blocks and scrape off the adhesive – probably black pitch – with an old chisel.

2 Spread a layer of latex adhesive into the space in the floor, about 5mm thick, using a filler knife or spatula.

3 Spread a thin layer of adhesive on the back of the block with a paintbrush and immediately put the block in place. Weigh it down by covering with a piece of plastic, a sheet of ply and several bricks, until the adhesive sets.

4 Fill any small gaps with wood filler.

5 Then use the floor sander, following directions given for sanding and varnishing a wooden floor (page 128). Because the grain lies in two directions, the floor must be sanded twice, running the second pass of the machine at right angles to the first.

6 The final sanding, with a very fine belt, will also need to be done in two directions to remove scratch marks.

7 Once the floor is clean and free of dust, apply your chosen finish.

Sanding and varnishing a wood floor

If floorboards are sound they can be sanded to reveal a beautiful natural floor.

Sanding a floor is hard, dusty, noisy work. On fairly new boards that have not been stained or become too dirty, sanding may not be necessary. Get rid of surface dirt by scrubbing with detergent and hot water. Pay particular attention to removing dirt from nail holes.

Tools *Dust mask; nail punch and claw hammer; floor sanding machine and edging sander (a weekend's hire should be enough for one room); earmuffs; sanding belts and discs (coarse, medium and fine); paint roller and wide paintbrush; fine steel wool.*

Materials *Flooring-grade varnish or other finish.*

Before you start Punch in all the nails in the floor, otherwise they will tear the sanding belts. Any tacks left from previous floor coverings should also be removed. If there are any traces of old polish, remove them with steel wool dipped in white spirit; otherwise the polish will clog up the sanding belt. Wear protective gloves.

1 Start at the edge of the room with your back against the wall. Keep the sander slightly away from the skirting board at the side otherwise you may damage it.

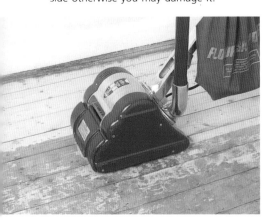

WARNING

Empty the dust bag as soon as it is about one-third full. Bulked wood dust can ignite spontaneously, especially if it is impregnated with old stain or varnish. Also empty the bag whenever you stop work for more than a few minutes.

2 It is normal to work along the length of the boards, as sanding across them causes scratches. But if the boards curl up at the edges, make the first runs diagonally across them with a coarse belt. Finish with medium and fine belts along the length of the boards.

3 On a floor where not very much stripping is needed, let the machine go forwards at a slow steady pace to the far end of the room, lifting up the drum as soon as you reach the skirting board.

4 If the boards are badly marked, wheel the sander backwards to your start point, lower the drum and make a second pass over the first one. Never pull the sander backwards when the drum is rotating, or the machine may pull sideways out of control and score the floor surface badly.

5 When the strip looks clean, move on to the next one, and continue to the end of the room. Raise the belt as you change direction, or it may damage the boards. You will have started each run about a metre out from the wall behind you. When you have covered the room, turn the machine round, and deal with that area.

Sanding the edges

Eventually, you will be left with a narrow border all round the room that the sander cannot reach. This must be stripped with an edging sander. Do not try to use a disc on an electric drill; it is not powerful enough.

HELPFUL TIP

When a floor sander is switched on, the sanding belt starts to move, but does not come into contact with the floor until you lower the drum. Never let a moving belt touch the floor while the machine is stationary, or it will gouge a hollow in the wood. The moment the belt starts to bite into the wood – and there will be enough noise to indicate this – make sure that the machine moves forwards. It will begin to do so anyway, but an inexperienced user will tend to hold it back.

1 Use the edging sander all round the edges of the room, taking care not to damage the paint on the skirting boards.

2 When the sanding is finished, vacuum-clean the floor to get rid of all the wood dust. Do not damp the floor as the water may leave marks.

3 Finally, mop the floor with a clean, dry, lint-free cloth. Be sure to shake it frequently outdoors to get rid of the last particles.

Applying varnish

The quickest way of sealing a newly stripped floor is to use a paint roller to apply the varnish. Thin the first coat as recommended on the container to aid penetration, and apply full-strength for the second and third coats. Use a power sander fitted with fine abrasive paper to sand the surface lightly between coats, and wipe it with a damp cloth to remove dust before re-coating it.

1 Apply the varnish with criss-cross passes of the roller, then finish off by running it parallel with the boards.

2 Use a paintbrush to finish the floor edges and to cut in round obstacles such as central heating pipes.

Laying a wood mosaic floor

Full-size parquet blocks are not available for DIY laying, but wood mosaic, sometimes known as finger parquet, is an easy way to achieve a similar effect.

Tools *Tape measure; chalk line; workbench; fine-toothed tenon saw; trimming knife; pencil; rag. Possibly also orbital sander or sanding block; abrasive paper (medium and fine grades); hammer; paintbrush.*

Materials *Wood mosaic panels; adhesive (with spreader); wood moulding or cork strip for the edges. Possibly also panel pins for wood moulding; varnish.*

Before you start Wood mosaic comes in square panels about 10mm thick. They are usually backed by felt, paper or netting, but some makes are wired and glued together. The pieces are flexible, and can compensate for slight unevenness in the sub-floor. If the sub-floor is very uneven, cover it with hardboard first (page 127). As wood absorbs moisture from the atmosphere, buy the mosaic panels at least two days before laying, and leave them unwrapped in the room where they are to be laid. This should prevent sudden expansion or contraction.

1 Mosaic panels are laid in the same way as vinyl and other tiles (page 133). First set them out, unglued, to ensure the widest border of cut tiles all around the room. As with most wood floors, a border of 15mm must be left between the edge of the mosaic and the skirting board to allow for expansion.

BUYING WOOD MOSAIC

If you can, check mosaics carefully before buying. Reject any with black marks on the face. This occurs if they are stacked with the felt backing of one against the face of the other, instead of face to face, and marks can be difficult to remove. Check, too, that the panels have been cut to the same size. Take one panel and hold all the others to it in turn, back to back. Rotate each panel through 90° for a further check of squareness. Inspect the surface for chips or scratches.

Prepacked panels usually have transparent wrapping, so you can see if the panels are face to face, and you should be able to see if they are all the same size.

2 Where possible, arrange the laying so that the panels can be cut between 'fingers' of wood, which only involves cutting the backing with a trimming knife.

3 When you have to cut through wood, hold the panel firmly on a workbench and use a tenon saw.

4 Use the manufacturer's recommended adhesive and spread a little at a time on the prepared floor. Lay the tiles in position, pressing them into place.

5 When you have laid the floor, cover the gap around the edges with wood moulding or fill it with strips of cork.

6 Seal the surface of the finished floor with three coats of polyurethane floor sealer, thinning the first coat with 10 per cent white spirit. Sand the floor lightly between each coat and wipe off any dust with a rag dampened with white spirit.

HOW TO REPAIR A DAMAGED MOSAIC FLOOR

If a wood mosaic floor is damaged, repair it by replacing a complete square of strips. Keep any panels left over from the original laying for repairs.

1 If possible, cut around the damaged square with a trimming knife. Cut right through the felt or paper backing.

2 Lever out the damaged square, strip by strip, using an old chisel. Be careful not to damage the adjoining piece. Scrape off the old backing and adhesive from the sub-floor.

3 Cut a new square from a spare panel, together with its backing, and glue it in place.

Choosing laminate flooring

A laminate floor forms an overlay on an existing timber or concrete floor. Most have a wood-effect finish, but you can also buy laminates that mimic ceramic, slate or terracotta tiles, or metals such as copper or brushed aluminium. Whatever the finish, all boards are coated with tough lacquer to make them resistant to staining, scratching or fading. Special laminate flooring with a water-resistant core is made for use in kitchens and bathrooms.

Laminate flooring is made from lengths of high density fibreboard (HDF). There are locking or tongue-and-groove versions. Locking planks have tongues on their sides and ends that lock together, so you don't need to glue them. It is easy to unlock them if, for example, you want to replace a damaged board or need access to the floor beneath. Tongue-and-groove boards are glued together at each join, and so cannot be lifted easily.

The flooring is generally sold in packs. The pack will state the area it covers and whether or not the product is suitable for bathrooms and kitchens. Estimate the amount you need by multiplying the width of the room by its length, and buy about 10 per cent extra to allow for wastage.

Slate-look tiles
- Pack of 5 tiles covers about 1.7m².
- Textured finish gives the impression of real slate.
- Easy to install glue-free locking system.
- Highly water resistant core , so is recommended for bathrooms, kitchens and conservatories; but not suitable for saunas or areas of very high humidity.

Copper-look laminate
- Pack of 7 planks covers about 1.9m².
- Easy to install glue-free locking system.
- Highly water resistant core, and so is recommended for bathrooms, kitchens and conservatories.

Wood laminate
Available in distressed oak, ash, rich chestnut and many other finishes.
- Pack of 9 planks covers about 2.15m².
- Easy to install glue-free locking system.
- Can be used immediately and can be re-laid up to 6 times.
- Resistant against cigarette burns, fading.
- Cannot be used in bathrooms or other humid areas.

Synthetic stripwood
- Wood-effect surface layer (above) is a photographic copy of genuine wood grain.
- Water and stain resistant, suitable for use in bathrooms and shower rooms.
- Warm and quiet underfoot.
- Easily installed by bonding direct to a plywood or solid floor.
- Unlike real wood, the floor will not need expansion room and can be fitted up to the perimeters, making it more resistant to moisture.
- Available in pack sizes of 2.5m².

Bamboo
- A new flooring material (above) available in strip and finger parquet designs.
- Dark and natural light shades.
- Tongue-and-groove boards; glue together with PVA adhesive.
- Plank size: 1.2m (length) x 120mm (width) x 15mm (thickness).
- Box of 7 boards covers about 1m².
- Warm underfoot and stronger than many woods used for timber flooring.
- Environmentally friendly: bamboo is a grass and can grow up to 15m a year.

Laying a laminate floor

A quick way to give a room a fresh, modern makeover is to lay laminate flooring. There are two main laying systems for laminate floors: locking and tongue-and-groove.

Tools *Tape measure; pencil; scissors; trimming knife; tenon saw; hand saw or jigsaw with laminate blade; hammer; tapping block or board offcut; pulling bar; power drill with flat wood bit.*

Materials *Enough underlay and laminate flooring to cover the room; adhesive tape; PVA woodworking adhesive; edging; threshold strip; panel pins; expansion strip (optional); fitting kit (which includes wedges or spacers and pulling bar).*

Putting down an underlay

An underlay must be put down before laying any type of laminate floor. This cushions the new floor and absorbs slight irregularities in the sub-floor. If you are covering a solid floor, lay a damp-proof membrane before putting down underlay. You can buy a combined underlay and damp-proof membrane, which means fitting one layer instead of two.

1 Prepare timber floors by punching in any floorboard nails with a nail punch.

2 If you have a solid concrete floor, cover it with a layer of heavy-duty polythene sheeting to protect the laminate from any dampness within the floor.

3 Lay underlay over the whole floor, trimming to fit with scissors or a trimming knife and leaving a 10mm gap round pipes.

4 Butt joins together – do not overlap them. Secure joins with tape. If using a wood fibre underlay, allow the boards to acclimatise for 24 hours in the room before laying them, and leave an expansion gap of 5mm between the boards and 10mm round the room.

Laying locking laminate

1 Start laying the first board parallel to the longest wall in the room, in a left-hand corner, putting the end with the short tongue against the wall. Insert spacers at intervals between the skirting board and the long edge and end of the board to create an expansion gap.

2 Add more boards until you reach the end of the row, where you will probably need to cut a board.

3 If the offcut is longer than 300mm, use it to start the second row. Otherwise, cut a board in half and use that. This ensures that the joints will be staggered between the rows. Fit spacers at the end.

4 Carry on placing the boards row by row. As you finish each row, enlist help to lift the row so that the long edge is at an angle of about 30° to the previous row, and lower and push down the boards to lock the rows together.

5 At the last row you will probably have to cut the final boards down in width. Lay each board in turn over the last whole board laid, and mark the width required on it by using a pencil and a board offcut held against the skirting board to scribe the wall profile on it.

6 Redraw the line 5mm nearer the exposed edge of the board to recreate the expansion gap. Cut each board to width with a jigsaw or panel saw and fit in place.

7 Remove the spacers from the edge of the flooring and conceal the expansion gap with strips of trim to match the floor. In corners, cut the moulding at 45°, using a mitre block. Use glue or nails to fix the trim to the skirting, not to the floor.

Laying tongue-and-groove laminate

The process is largely the same as for locking laminate (left). However, because gluing does not allow for mistakes, prepare and lay two or three rows without gluing to check the fit first. Always lay boards with the tongue protruding.

1 Lay the first board parallel to the longest wall in the room, with its groove facing the wall. Insert spacers to create a 10mm expansion gap.

2 Lay the next plank end-on to the first one, fitting the tongue into the groove.

3 When you have laid three whole rows, take them up and re-lay them using wood adhesive. Tap them together with the hammer and tapping block.

4 Wipe off any oozing adhesive straight away with a damp rag. Do this again once you have closed up the joints (overleaf).

5 At the end of the row, use the pulling bar to close up the joint by hooking it over the end of the board and tapping the upstand with a hammer.

6 Start the next row with the offcut from the previous row to create offset joints. Glue the grooved edge and push it into place.

7 As you work across the room, tap the boards closely together by using a proprietary tapping block and hammer to close up the joints.

8 Follow steps 5, 6 and 7 of Laying locking laminate (page 131) to fit the last row and hide the expansion gap.

Fitting boards round pipes

1 To cut round a radiator pipe, align the board with its neighbour and slide it up against the pipe.

2 Mark the pipe centre on the board edge. Then remove the board, butt it up against the skirting board and mark the pipe centre on the board's short end. Join up the marks to indicate the pipe centre.

3 Use a 16mm flat wood bit to drill a hole through the board at the mark. Cut across the board and fit the two sections round the pipe.

Alternatively Almost all laminate floors come with optional accessory kits, including radiator pipe discs. These have a hole cut for the pipe: simply align the grain and glue into place to hide ragged holes.

At door openings

Cut away a small amount of the architrave and door stop to allow the board to fit beneath it. Mark the board thickness on the frame and cut away the wood with a tenon saw. Trim the board to shape and

slot it into position. Fit a threshold bar across the door to conceal and protect the edge of the flooring. Cut the bar to the right width and glue or screw it into place.

SOLID WOOD FLOORING

Solid wood flooring can be laid over a timber sub-floor, or directly onto floor joists if the existing timber floor is being replaced. On a timber sub-floor, the boards are laid in a similar way to laminate flooring, with an expansion gap around the perimeter of the floor area. Each board is fixed to the sub-floor using a technique known as secret nailing.

1 Drive panel pins down through the tongue of each board at an angle to the floor so it passes through the body of the strip and into the sub-floor. Use 30mm pins for boards up to 20mm thick, and 50mm pins for thicker boards.

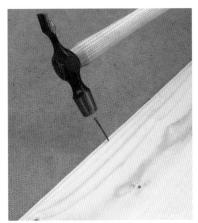

2 Start the pins with the hammer. Use a nail punch to finish driving each pin so its head finishes flush with the top edge of the tongue. You can then slot the grooved edge of the next board over the tongue and repeat the fixing to secure it to the sub-floor.

Setting out floor tiles

Lay floor tiles 'dry' from the centre of the room before you start to stick them in place, so you can achieve the best layout.

Where to start laying

Finding the centre point
Whatever type of tile you are laying, you always begin in the middle of the room, so you need to find the centre point.

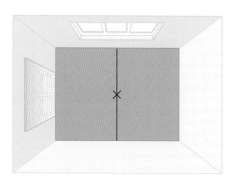

1 Measure two opposite walls and mark their centres. Snap a chalk line between these points (see box, right).

2 Measure the line and mark its centre. That is the middle of the room.

Alternatively
• If the room has a chimney breast, snap the chalk line parallel to that wall.

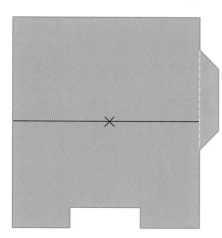

• If the room also has a bay, square it off with a line between the ends of the bay and measure along this false wall line.
• If the room is even more irregular in shape, choose one wall as the base wall. Snap a chalk line parallel to it, about 75mm away, and mark its centre point. Draw a short chalk line at right angles to this base line. To obtain the right angle, use a few tiles as a guide. Extend this line the full length of the room by snapping a chalk line. Measure this line and mark the centre.

Marking the cross-line

Once the main chalk line has been laid, a second line needs to be drawn across it at right angles. To do this, place two tiles on the floor, each with one side along the centre line and one corner on the centre point. Then snap a chalk line across the room, passing through the centre point and following the edge of the tiles.

Placing the key tile
You must now decide the position of the first (or key) tile, which will determine the position of all other tiles in the room. Ideally, all the tiles around the edge of the room should be equal in size, and at least a half tile width. Experiment by laying tiles from the centre to all edges of the room.

The key tile can be placed in any of several positions:

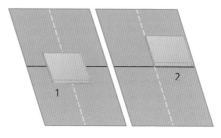

• Centrally on the middle point of the room.

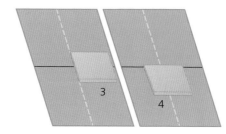

• In an angle formed by the two chalk lines.
• Centrally on the main chalk line, and on one side of the line that crosses it.
• Centrally on the crossing line, and on one side of the main one.

SNAPPING A CHALK LINE

For many jobs, you need a line across the room. Rub chalk along a length of string or buy a chalk-line reel which chalks the string for you. Tie one end to a nail in the floor and hold the other end at the far side of the room, pulling it taut. Pull the string straight up and let go. It will mark a straight line on the floor as it snaps back into place.

Centring the tiles on a feature
• Some rooms have a dominant feature such as a fireplace, or bay window. To obtain an attractive result, adjust the appropriate base line – keeping it parallel to the original line – to ensure that the tiles are centred on the feature. Once again, ensure that you get the biggest possible cut tiles at the edges.

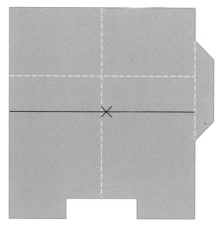

• A room may have two features. If this is the case, adjust both base lines so that the tiles can be centred on both features.
• It is not possible to centre tiles on more than two features, except by accident.

Patterns in tiles

Design your own floor patterns by combining tiles of different colours. The simplest is the 'chessboard', alternating tiles in two colours, but many other arrangements are possible.

Laying tiles diagonally

Laying tiles on the diagonal is not difficult once you have marked the floor using a homemade 'compass' or scriber.

Before you start To prevent mistakes when laying the floor, draw a scale plan of your pattern on squared paper. Then you can work out exactly how many of each colour or design you will need.

1 First improvise a compass using a thin piece of batten about 1m long with a nail in each end. Drill pilot holes, smaller than the diameter of the nails, to avoid splitting the wood.

2 Mark the cross-lines in the middle of the room in the normal way. (See Where to start laying, page 133).

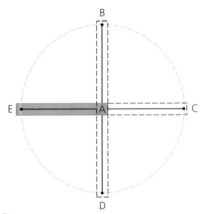

3 Put one nail of the scriber on the point where the lines cross (A), and mark four points on the cross-lines – at B,C,D and E.

4 Put one nail of your scriber on B and scribe arcs at F and G. Move the scriber to C and scribe arcs at G and H. From D make arcs at H and I, and from E at I and F.

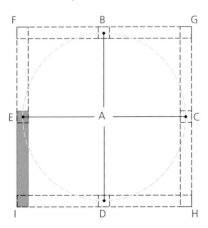

5 Snap diagonal chalk lines on the floor through the points where the arcs meet at G and I and at F and H.

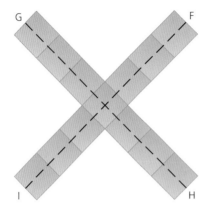

6 Lay out rows of unglued tiles along the diagonal lines, adjusting their position to get the largest cut tiles round the border, then glue down all the whole tiles.

Border tile patterns: method 1

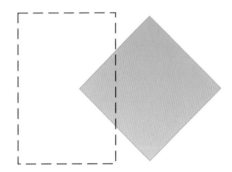

1 To cut border tiles, first make a template. Cut a piece of card with two opposite edges parallel. The distance between the edges must be the same as the distance across the tiles from corner to corner.

2 Place the tile to be cut on the whole tile nearest to the gap to be filled.

3 Place one edge of the template against the skirting board and cut along the opposite edge across the face of the tile. The piece of tile farthest from the skirting board will fit the empty space.

Border tile patterns: method 2

Diagonal tiles can be finished off with a border of part tiles laid square to the wall.

1 When you are setting out the tiles initially, place the first tile in the centre of the room to ensure that the tiles around the wall will be wider than half a tile.

2 Lay all the whole tiles.

3 Cut some tiles in half from corner to corner and lay them to square off the diagonal pattern.

4 Finally, cut the border tiles square to the wall, measuring each one individually, but sticking all of them down at the same time.

HOW MANY TILES WILL YOU NEED?

To calculate the number of tiles required, measure the room and multiply the width by the length to give the area. If the room has a bay or chimney breast, calculate it separately and add or subtract it from the main area. Each pack of tiles gives the area they will cover. (Most tile packs cover a square metre.) Divide the area of the room by the area a pack will cover to get the total number of packs you will need. Remember to buy a few extra tiles to allow for wastage.

Laying vinyl and cork tiles

Tiles take longer to lay than sheet material, but they are easier to handle and cut to fit, there is less wastage, and, if you make a mistake, ruining one tile is not nearly as serious as damaging a large sheet.

Vinyl and cork tiles are both laid in the same way. Some are self-adhesive.

Tools *Tape measure; chalk line; adhesive spreader; rag; pencil; trimming knife; scrap hardboard; metal straightedge.*

Materials *Tiles; adhesive recommended by tile manufacturer (if tiles are not self-adhesive); perhaps white spirit.*

1 Decide on the best arrangement (see Where to start laying, page 133).

2 Dust the floor and stick down the first tile, spreading adhesive on the floor.

3 Place the first tile at the start point and roll it down flat.

4 With the first tile stuck down, add adjacent tiles to form a square of four. Then work outwards from it to the walls. Where adhesive has to be spread on the floor, spread a square metre at a time.

5 If any adhesive oozes up through the joins, wipe it up immediately, using a cloth damped with water or white spirit depending on the adhesive.

Cutting border tiles to fit

The cut tiles around the edge can be dealt with in two ways. Use method 1 if adhesive is being used, and method 2 in small areas such as WCs and narrow corridors.

Method 1
Lay all the tiles except for a border of one whole tile and one part tile all the way round the room.

1 Place the tile to be cut against the last one in the row, and place another tile on top of it, pressed against the wall.

2 Draw a pencil line across the face of the tile to be cut. With some tiles you do not need to draw a line; score with a knife then snap. If the tile will not break, cut it on a piece of scrap board.

3 The two tiles now change places so the part tile lies against the wall. Put them to one side and prepare the whole row (numbering them on the back as you go), then stick them all at once.

Method 2
With this method, you lay all the whole tiles, then deal with the border of part tiles.

1 Place the tile to be cut squarely on the last tile in the row. Put a third on top, pressed against the wall.

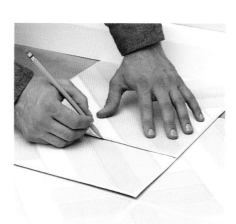

2 Draw a pencil line across the face of the tile to be cut. With some vinyl and cork tiles you do not even need to draw a line; use a knife instead of a pencil, then snap the tile in two. If the tile will not break, cut it on a piece of scrap hardboard, using a metal straightedge as a guide.

3 The part of the cut tile closer to the centre of the room will fit the empty space perfectly. Prepare the whole row, then slot them into place.

In doorways Around a doorway architrave, you will have to draw three or four lines to create the correct pattern.

Corner tiles Tiles in corners will have to be cut to length as well as width, using the same method.

Cutting round a curve

You may have to cut round an irregular shaped object such as a WC or washbasin.

1 Take a sheet of paper a bit larger than a tile. Place it over the area the cut tile will occupy, and fold it along the edges of the adjacent tiles. Tear out the corner to fit the obstacle approximately, and crease the paper firmly against its outline.

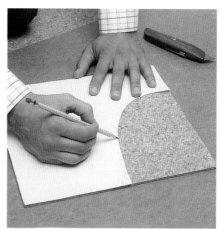

2 Cut the paper along the folds to create the template. Use it to mark the tile for cutting.

FIRE HAZARD WITH ADHESIVES

Solvent-based adhesives are highly flammable. When laying a floor with this type of adhesive, open all the windows and doors in the room and switch off any pilot lights in the room, including those in a gas cooker, gas fire or central-heating boiler. Don't smoke while you work. When you have finished, hang your working clothes outdoors to air.

Water-based adhesives are not flammable, but they take longer to dry, which slows a job down in cold weather.

Cutting round a pipe

A pipe rising from the floor will normally be at the edge of a room, so first cut a tile to fit the border.

1 Place the cut tile square on the last whole tile and push it against the pipe. Make a pencil mark where it touches.

2 Put the cut tile against the wall and push its end against the pipe. Make another mark where it touches.

HOW TO LIFT A DAMAGED VINYL TILE

To remove a damaged vinyl tile without disturbing the rest of the floor, put a piece of aluminium kitchen foil over it and press with a hot iron. Wait until the heat penetrates the tile (this will take longer on concrete than wood), then lever up a corner with a filling knife or wallpaper stripper, and pull the tile away. Lift the remaining adhesive with a filling knife heated with a hot-air gun. A larger area can be softened with a hot-air gun. The technique will not work on cork tiles, which insulate too effectively against the heat.

Lay a new tile with fresh adhesive. Do not slide it into place, or adhesive may be forced up at the edges.

3 With a try square, draw a line across the tile from the mark on the side. Then put the try square on the uncut long edge and draw a line through the other mark. (Do not put the try square on the cut edge as it may not be square.)

4 Where the lines cross is the centre of the pipe. Drill a hole the right diameter (with the tile on a piece of scrap wood), or draw round a coin of the appropriate size, and cut with a knife. Cut a slit from the hole to the edge of the vinyl or cork so you can fit it round the pipe.

Alternatively You can make a very accurate hole by punching through the vinyl with a pipe offcut the same diameter. Use a round file on the inside of the pipe to sharpen the cutting edge, then strike the other end with a hammer.

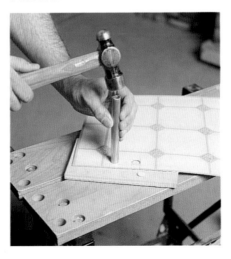

CARPET TILES

Carpet tiles are laid in much the same way as vinyl and cork (page 134). Because they are loose laid, worn or damaged tiles can be replaced. It's a good idea to buy several spare tiles and swap them regularly. That way, any colour change or wear is evened out and if a tile needs replacing, the replacement will match the existing floor.

The job will be much easier if you make yourself a carpet tile pusher.

Cut a 300mm length of 150 x 25mm timber. Drill a hole in the centre 15mm deep and glue in a piece of broom handle. Drive a nail through the wood into the handle. Drive four nails through the front, projecting by 3mm, to act as teeth.

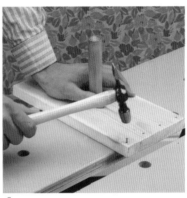

1 Set out the tiles (page 133). You can lay all the tiles with the pile running in the same direction to give the effect of a fitted carpet. Or place them chequer-board style with the pile running at right angles on alternate tiles.

2 Stick down the first tile in the centre of the room with double sided carpet tape to stop it from shifting during laying.

3 Start laying the tiles. Put the tile pusher on top of each tile you lay so that its teeth grip, then push the tile forwards into position.

4 When all the whole tiles have been laid, measure the border tiles using one of the methods on page 135. Mark the cutting line on the face of the tile by making a nick with a trimming knife on each edge. Turn the tile upside down, lay a steel rule across the two nicks, and cut with the knife. Fit a metal carpet threshold bar in the doorway.

Laying ceramic floor tiles

As with vinyl tiles, it's important to get the setting out right before you begin laying ceramic floor tiles.

Before laying ceramic tiles on a timber floor, you need to lay a base of 9mm exterior grade plywood. This provides a level, stable surface and prevents movement of the boards from cracking the tiles. Fix the plywood sheet with screws every 300mm.

You can lay ceramic tiles on top of clean concrete floors or old quarry or vinyl tiles – as long as these are stuck down firmly, and are thoroughly scrubbed with sugar soap.

Tools *String; pencil; straightedge; guide battens (50 x 25mm); claw hammer; spirit level; stripping knife; trimming knife; felt-tip pen; tile-cutting jig (can be hired); notched adhesive spreader; rubber-bladed grout spreader.*

Materials *Tiles (to work out how many you need, see page 134); tile spacers; flooring-grade tile adhesive; waterproof grout; non-setting silicone mastic.*

Where to start

1 Find the centre of the floor by pinning string lines across the room from the midpoint of each wall. Draw guidelines along the strings, then remove them. Put one tile in the angle between the lines and dry-lay a row of tiles – with spacers in between – towards one wall, to see how wide the edge gap will be.

2 Lay a second row from the centre of the room at right angles to the first row, and check the edge gap. Cutting narrow strips off ceramic tiles is difficult, so you want to avoid very narrow edge pieces, or ones that are almost a tile wide.

3 If the edge gaps will prove difficult, the answer is to shift the whole tile layout by the width of half a tile. Cross out the original guidelines and draw new ones, parallel to them but half a tile's width away. Lay out the tile rows again in order to check the fit.

4 Start work in the corner of the room farthest from the door. Nail down one timber batten at the end of one row of tiles, and the second at the end of the other. If you leave the nails proud, you can pull them out easily later on.

5 Dry-lay a square of nine tiles in the angle between the battens. If the battens don't line up perfectly against the tiles, reposition them so the tiles sit squarely.

Laying whole tiles

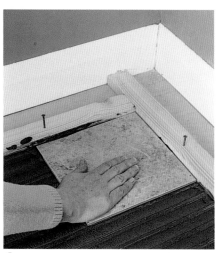

1 Spread enough adhesive for a square of nine (3 x 3) or sixteen (4 x 4) tiles. Hold the notched spreader at an angle of about 45° to the floor. Press the first tile into the right-angle created by the battens.

2 Using tile spacers to ensure even joint sizes, lay two or three more tiles in lines next to each batten. Where tiles butt up to the battens, you will need to use the spacers up-ended or snip off their lugs.

3 Complete the nine or sixteen tile square, being sure to use spacers at each corner. If you push the spacers deep into the adhesive, the grout will conceal them.

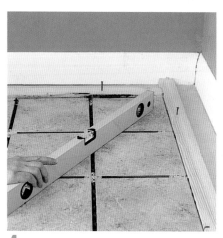

4 Now that the square is complete, use a spirit level to check each row in turn, and across the diagonals. Tamp down any tiles that are standing proud.

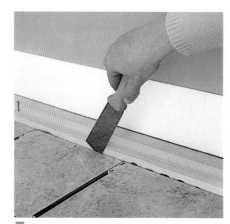

5 Continue, a square block at a time, until you cannot fit another whole tile. Run a stripping knife between the tiles and the wood battens to stop the adhesive bonding the two together. It's also a good idea to check the edges of each square block with a straightedge to make sure that the tiles are perfectly aligned.

Cutting and fitting edge tiles

Do not attempt to deal with the edges until the whole tiles have had at least 24 hours to set hard enough to walk on.

1 Use a claw hammer to remove the timber guide battens from the edges of the whole tiles.

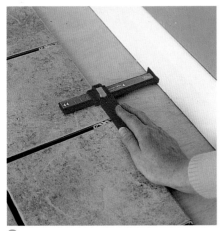

2 Measure the width of the cut pieces. Some cutting jigs come with a sliding tile gauge which makes the job easier. Otherwise use a steel rule.

3 Slot the tile gauge into the cutting jig and position the tile with one edge against the sliding arm of the gauge. Score the cutting line across the surface using the cutting wheel. Fit the tile into the cutter's jaws and press down the lever to snap it along the scored line.

HELPFUL TIP

Measure each tile to be cut individually: the room is unlikely to be perfectly square. Allow for the width of a tile spacer in each joint, and for a small expansion gap next to the skirting board. Mark the width on the tile with a felt-tip pen.

4 Apply adhesive to the back of the cut tile, not to the floor. Use the notched spreader to make uniform ridges.

5 Put spacers in each joint between the whole tiles. Leaving the corners for now, work around the perimeter of the room, laying each cut tile in place, in turn. Ensure there is a small gap between each tile and the skirting board.

6 Cut tiles for the corners of the room, and lay them in place.

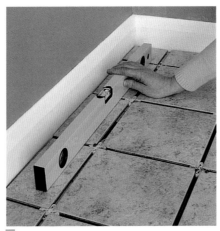

7 Use a spirit level to check that none of the edge tiles stands proud of its neighbours or the rest of the floor. Tap down tiles that are too high. Lift up a tile that is too low and add a little more adhesive.

8 Allow 24 hours for the adhesive to set hard before adding grout to the joints.

9 Fill the joints with waterproof grout, which will resist staining. Use a rubber bladed spreader to force the grout into the gaps. Clean up as you go, scraping off the excess grout with the spreader. When the grout is dry, polish off smears with an old towel.

Alternatively Seal the join between the tiles and the skirting board with flexible silicone mastic.

Laying quarry and terracotta tiles

The principles of laying quarry and terracotta tiles are no different from those of laying ceramic floor tiles. Traditionally, they are often laid on the diagonal.

If you wish to lay quarry or terracotta tiles over a timber floor, then check the depth of the joists before you buy the tiles. Joists less than 125mm will not be strong enough to support the weight of these thick, heavy tiles, and your floor will sag and crack.

A timber floor must be covered with plywood, as with ceramic tiles (page 137).

Tools *String; pencil; straightedge; guide battens (50 x 25mm); claw hammer; spirit level; felt-tip pen; notched adhesive spreader; grout spreader; tile-cutting jig or power tile-cutting saw (if tiles more than 6mm thick).*

Materials *Tiles (to work out how many you need, see page 134); tile spacers; masonry nails (for a concrete floor); flooring-grade tile adhesive and grout.*

HELPFUL TIP

Mix up tiles from different boxes before laying them. Quarry tiles have natural colour variations, and a floor looks best if the shades are randomly scattered rather than in concentrated blocks.

1 Measure one wall and mark its mid point. Mark the same distance along the adjacent wall. If you join these marks with a straightedge, you will have a guideline at exactly 45° to the walls of the room.

2 Nail the guide batten to the floor along the line, using masonry nails if the floor is concrete. Leave the nail heads proud – they will be easier to pull out later.

3 Apply a band of tile adhesive a little over one tile wide next to the batten. Press the first row of tiles into it, using spacers to ensure even gaps.

4 Once you have laid the first row, remove the batten. Spread adhesive between the row you have laid and the room corner. (If the room is very large, you may have to lay these tiles after you have completed the rest of the whole tiles in the room, and they have had 24 hours to dry.)

5 Lay all the whole tiles, working one row at a time and inserting tile spacers at each joint. In this room, whole tiles stretch from wall to wall leaving half-tile triangles next to the skirting boards. In other rooms, the gaps may be larger than half a tile.

6 As you complete each row, use a timber batten and a hammer to tamp it down. After every four or five rows, check the levels with a spirit level. If a tile is too low, prise it up, apply a blob of adhesive to its back and replace it.

Cutting and grouting

With all the whole tiles laid, you can cut and fit the border tiles, and finish the floor by filling the joints with grout.

1 Measure the space for the infill triangle, allowing room for grout (measure its short sides and transfer the marks onto the tile; then join the marks.

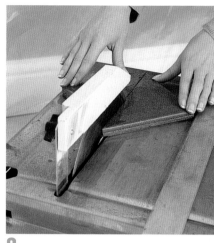

2 It is worth hiring a power tile-cutting saw for cutting quarry or terracotta tiles: its diamond cutting disc creates perfect cuts much more easily than a conventional tile-cutting jig.

3 Butter the back of each cut tile and press it into place, leaving a small gap between the tile and the skirting board.

4 After the adhesive has had 24 hours to set, you can fill the joints with grout. Use a rubber-bladed squeegee to force grout between the tiles. Clean up as you work, and after each square metre or so, finish the join by recessing it slightly with a piece of dowel or a grout shaping tool.

Quarry tiled skirting

You can buy shaped coving tiles to edge a quarry tiled floor. These are great in a kitchen or anywhere wet.

STONE FLOORING

A stone floor is one of the most expensive types of floor, but one of the most durable. Stone floors are heavy and hard to lay – especially when the slabs are of random sizes and thicknesses. They must be laid properly or the joints will crack. The job is generally best left to a professional.

A stone floor can be laid over a wooden floor, but joists will have to be strengthened to support the considerable load. Usually, stone floors are laid in kitchens and high traffic areas on the ground floor, where a concrete slab foundation makes the perfect sub-base.

A stone floor is thick – usually around 40mm. You will need to cut the bottoms off any doors that open over it. Another disadvantage is that stone feels cold underfoot. This can be solved by installing underfloor heating (right) beneath the slabs.

Granite Very hardwearing. It comes highly polished and tends to be used in minimalist kitchens and hallways.

Limestone Comes in hard and soft versions, in a range of colours. It can give a room a contemporary, minimalist feel or a traditional look.

Marble Highly polished. It comes in a range of colours and can be laid in chequerboard or other designs.

Slate Tiles are either split (riven) or cut. Riven slate has a distinctive grain and traditional look; cut slate is smooth, sleek and contemporary.

Travertine Geologically, a cross between limestone and marble. It is a low porosity stone, pale and neutral in colour. Slabs come flat and sleek, or 'pillowed' (where the profile edges of a slab are smoothed into a slight curve) for a softer look.

Tumbled stone mosaic Supplied on a mesh backing in various sizes and colours. Can be used for floors or walls, making it a popular choice for wet rooms.

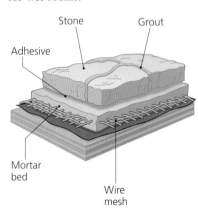

Stone   Grout

Adhesive

Mortar bed

Wire mesh

The basics of underfloor heating

Underfloor heating warms the entire surface of the floor. Even in a small room, this is a large radiant surface, which means that the heat running through the heating elements needs to be only slightly hotter than the room. By contrast, a radiator transfers heat from a very small surface, and has to be much hotter than the room it is heating.

Typically, the temperature of the water in an underfloor heating system pipe is 45–65°C compared to the 80°C surface temperature of a radiator. Most underfloor systems warm the floor to 25–28°C, which is comfortable to walk on.

There are two main underfloor heating systems – water and electric.

Underfloor heating: advantages
• Underfloor heating is unobtrusive, freeing up walls which might otherwise have radiators against them. In addition, it is quiet in use. There is even distribution of heat across each room, and individual room temperature control.
• It is safer than other systems of central heating: there is no risk of contact with surfaces that are too hot.
• The electric system is easy to install and requires no special skills.

Underfloor heating: disadvantages
• Heating systems cannot respond rapidly to quick temperature changes, and have longer heat-up and cooling-down periods than other forms of central heating.
• There is greater disruption when installing an underground heating system in an existing building than with other systems.
• The choice of floor finishing requires careful consideration, and changes of floor finish may affect performance.

SAFETY TIP

Before working on electrical systems, isolate electrical circuits and check with a tester before touching any wires or cables. If you are in any doubt about what you are doing, seek specialist advice.

Water heated systems
Water systems use warm water pumped through small diameter (usually 10mm) plastic pipes which run up and down the sub-floor. The pipes are linked into the building's central heating system. They

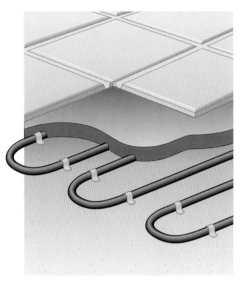

warm the floor, which in turn warms the room above. Pipes can be installed when the building is constructed or, in some cases, fitted later.

In a new construction (such as a conservatory extension) with a solid ground floor, pipes are laid within the sand-and-cement screed. Insulation beneath the pipework ensures that heat is directed into the room and energy is not wasted in heating the concrete foundations.

On upper floors and suspended wood floors (with joists and floorboards), heating pipes can be laid between the joists. An insulation layer underneath the pipework prevents the ceiling of the room below from getting warm and directs heat to where it is needed: the room above.

A water system is best installed by a qualified contractor.

Electric systems
An alternative to a wet system is an electric system. This is easier to fit, and is a more realistic DIY option. An electric mat, similar in appearance to an electric blanket, is laid on the floor, and your chosen floor covering laid on top.

Many companies supply their products to both the trade and DIY consumer, and most have technical departments that supply installation instructions and even check the completed system.

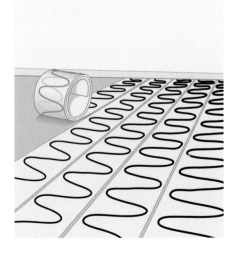

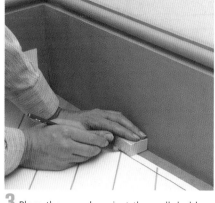

Sheet vinyl

Sheet vinyl comes in myriad designs and colours – and prices. It is faster to lay than tiles, and makes an ideal wall-to-wall floor covering for kitchens and bathrooms. Cushioned varieties are also warm and quiet underfoot.

Buying sheet vinyl

Sheet vinyl is sold in three widths – 2m, 3m or 4m – which means that in most rooms you can lay a seamless floor. If the width of the room is greater than 4m, you can lay vinyl in strips. A large sheet is heavy and unwieldy, so you may feel more confident about laying strips, even if the room is less than 4m wide. Only lengths bought from the same roll should be used on one floor: rolls may be manufactured on different machines, and therefore there may be slight differences in the colours.

You can buy backed or unbacked vinyl. Backed vinyl is cushioned by a built-in underlay which makes it softer underfoot, and is usually more expensive than the unbacked types. Some vinyls have an extra durable coating – ask the retailer which sort is best for your purposes.

Some vinyls are not stuck down – their weight holds them in place. This is useful if it is necessary to gain access to the floor underneath. Other vinyls must be glued down using adhesive recommended by the manufacturer.

HOW MUCH TO BUY

Measure the width of the room to decide how many strips you will need. Measure right into any alcoves and to the halfway point under a door. To take 2m-wide strip vinyl as an example: for every 2m or portion of 2m you will need one strip of 2m-wide vinyl. So if the room width is 3.5m, you need two strips (0.5m will be waste). Allow an extra 75mm trimming allowance on each width.

Then measure in the other direction and multiply by the number of strips. If the length is 3.3m you will need 6.6m (2 x 3.3m), plus 75mm trimming allowance on each strip – a total of 6.75m. Vinyl is usually sold by the nearest metre, so you will have to buy 7m.

If there is a pattern you will need extra for matching up – ask the retailer for advice.

Order the flooring in advance. It can then be stood upright (still tied in a roll) for at least two days in the room where it will be laid so it can reach room temperature. It will then be flexible and easier to lay; cold vinyl tends to be stiff to handle.

Laying sheet vinyl in strips

Tools *Steel tape measure; soft pencil; string longer than the room; chalk; small block of wood; a second piece of wood about 100mm long; sharp trimming knife; ruler; screwdriver; hammer.*

Materials *Vinyl to cover the floor; perhaps adhesive and notched spreader; metal cover strip and screws.*

Before you start It is best to line the floor with hardboard (page 126), but if you decide that your floor is in sufficiently good condition, lay the vinyl at right angles to the floorboards. Be aware that any gaps or ridges will make the vinyl wear unevenly. Decide how the strips of vinyl will be set out. Ideally, strips should run away from the window (or the main window if there is more than one). Joins will be less obvious than if the light strikes them at the side. Avoid having a join running into a doorway as this is an area of heavy traffic.

Marking the base line

1 Snap a chalk line (page 133) between the middle of the two walls that will be at the ends of the strips. This provides a base line to work from, as the walls will almost certainly be out of true.

2 If the first length of vinyl will cover the line, snap a second line parallel to the first where it can be seen.

3 Cut the first strip to length – the distance across the room plus 75mm for trimming.

4 Put it on the floor about 25mm away from the wall on the long side and parallel to the chalk line. Let each end ride up the wall by an equal amount.

Scribing the wall on the long side

1 At two or three points, draw a pencil line across the floor and the edge of the vinyl. These are crosschecks that will allow you to bring the vinyl back to its original position later.

2 Find out where the gap between the wall on the long side and the vinyl is greatest. Cut a small block of wood slightly longer than that measurement. This will be used for scribing the wall to make the vinyl fit exactly.

Alternatively Use a pair of compasses and set them to the same measurement.

---

3 Place the wood against the wall, hold a pencil hard against the end and move them together along the wall, tracing its contours onto the vinyl.

4 Cut the vinyl along the pencil line with a sharp knife.

5 Put the vinyl back in place – using the check marks for accurate positioning.

Scribing the end walls

1 Place the scribed edge against the side wall correctly then draw a chalk line on the floor along the opposite edge. Make a crosscheck on the edge and the floor.

2 Pull the vinyl back from the crosscheck by the length of the second piece of wood.

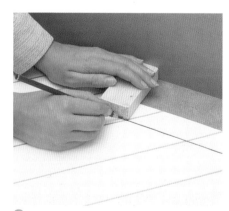

3 Keeping the outer edge of the vinyl on the chalk line, use the piece of wood and a pencil to trace the contours of the wall onto the end of the vinyl sheet.

4 Cut to this line, then use chalk line and crosscheck to position the vinyl. It should fit against the end wall. Repeat steps 2 to 4 for the opposite end of the length.

Cutting the second strip

1 The second strip will almost certainly have to be cut to width. If the excess is more than about 250mm, cut it back to that to give yourself a workable width. Make the cut on the wall side, not the side to be joined.

2 Put the cut strip on the floor with one edge touching the wall where the wall comes nearest to the first sheet. The other edge will be overlapping the first sheet; make sure that this overlap is exactly the same all the way along. Adjust it so that the pattern matches.

3 Cut the strip at each end, to leave the trimming allowance of 75mm.

4 Make a pencil mark where the second sheet rests on the first. Lift up the second sheet and measure the amount of overlap.

5 Place the vinyl flat on the floor again and use the ruler and pencil to scribe a line on the vinyl parallel to the wall, but the width of the overlap away from it.

6 Cut to this line.

7 Place the vinyl in position, and then scribe the ends as before.

Doorways

1 Scribe the vinyl around the door frame and to a line under the door. If a threshold strip has already been laid, scribe up to it.

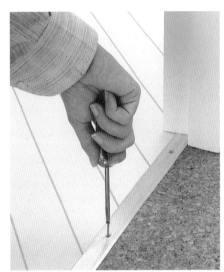

2 If no threshold strip exists, screw a metal cover strip over the vinyl and the covering beyond the door. If the floor beyond has no covering, use metal lino edging.

Chimney breast alcoves

1 Measure and cut the vinyl to fit the full depth of the alcove, plus the trimming allowance of 75mm.

2 Put it on the floor and allow it to ride up the chimney breast.

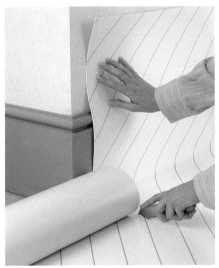

3 Make a cut parallel to the side of the alcove, leaving enough for final trimming. Allow the material to lie on the alcove floor.

4 Cut off the excess material riding up the chimney breast, leaving a trimming allowance of 75mm.

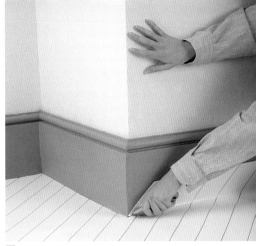

5 Trim the edges in the normal way, so that the vinyl fits the alcove, and surrounding walls. If there is a working fireplace, trim the vinyl around the hearth.

Sticking vinyl down

• Some vinyls do not need to be stuck down and will not shrink once laid.
• Other types should be glued immediately after laying. If left for any length of time – even overnight – they may shrink slightly and gaps could develop between the strips of vinyl and around the walls.
• Use the adhesive recommended by the manufacturer, and apply it to the floor with a notched spreader.
• For ordinary vinyl the floor should be glued all over.
• Cushioned vinyl needs only to be glued in a 50mm band around the room and along joins where sheets butt against each other.

Laying sheet vinyl without a seam

Most rooms can be covered with a single, seamless sheet of vinyl. This gives a neat finish, but it is hard to lay. The size of the sheet makes it cumbersome and very heavy, so you will need a helper. Trimming it to the wall also requires greater skill.

Tools *Soft broom; scissors; trimming knife; small block of wood and perhaps a metal straightedge.*

Materials *Sheet vinyl to cover the floor in one piece; adhesive and spreader (except for 'stay-flat' vinyl); cover strip for doorways.*

Before you start Work out how much vinyl you will need (page 141). To make laying as easy as possible, the sheet should be about 100mm wider than the floor on every edge – that is 200mm wider than the room in both directions. Ask your supplier to cut it to the required length and width.

Lay the sheet of vinyl flat, then re-roll it so that the shorter dimension becomes the length of the roll. This makes it easier to get into the room. Roll it with the decorative side inwards; this is the way you will need it when laying starts.

Keep the roll in the room where it will be laid for two days to reach room temperature. Have the heating on in the room in cold weather, or the vinyl will be stiff and awkward to handle.

1 Unroll the vinyl. This is hard work, and you will need help. Make sure that the longer side of the vinyl runs along the longer wall.

2 If the flooring has a pronounced pattern, adjust it so that pattern lines look to be at right angles to the wall containing the doorway by which you will most often enter the room. Sight it by eye. If it looks right, it is right.

3 For laying, the vinyl must be absolutely flat on the floor. You can ensure this by sweeping over it with a soft broom.

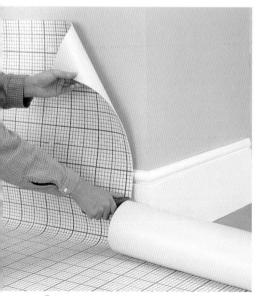

4 To fit the vinyl into an alcove, such as beside a chimney breast, get your helper to hold it while you make a cut running parallel to the side of the alcove. Take care to leave about 50mm surplus against each wall for final trimming.

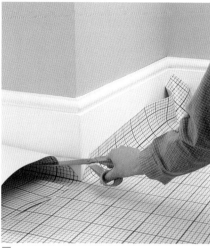

5 Lay the material on the alcove floor, lapping up against the three sides, then cut off the excess riding up the chimney breast. Again, leave about 50mm surplus against the wall for trimming.

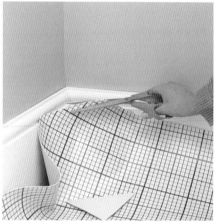

6 To fit into corners, cut off a small triangle at the corner of the vinyl, using scissors. When you push it down to the floor it will form a V, allowing it to hug the skirting. Be careful not to remove too much. First remove a triangle that is obviously too small, then take off more small strips until it is just right.

Trimming to fit

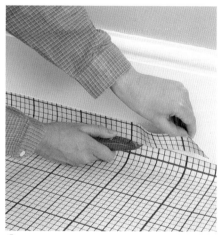

1 To trim to the wall, first run your knife along the vinyl lapping up the wall, taking off the excess so about 25mm remains.

2 Push the vinyl firmly against the skirting board with a small block of wood.

3 Place the point of the knife on the vinyl exactly where the skirting board meets the floor, and run it along the skirting with the blade at 45° to the wall. This will trim the material to fit snugly against the skirting, without leaving gaps.

4 To cut around a door frame, make a series of vertical cuts to the point where the vinyl meets the floor, then press it into the angle between door frame and floor. Trim off the excess. In the doorway itself, cut the vinyl so that it ends halfway under the door.

5 When the vinyl has been laid, stick it to the floor, unless it is the 'stay-flat' type which does not need sticking. Glue cushioned vinyls round the edges only. Non-cushioned types should be stuck down all over.

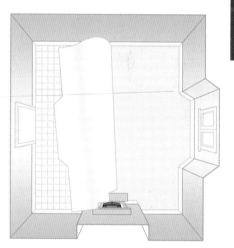

6 Roll back the sheet over half the room, and spread the adhesive on the floor.

7 Replace the sheet and press it down with the broom. Then glue the other half of the room.

8 Finish a doorway with metal cover strip.

HELPFUL TIP

Trimming vinyl that is bent up a wall is not easy and takes practice. But practising is the last thing you want to do on a large piece of expensive material. Obtain some offcuts and work on these until you get the knack. After pressing the vinyl against the wall with a block of wood, it may help to hold a metal straightedge as close to the wall as possible while you cut. Make sure the knife cuts away from the hand holding the straightedge, so if it slips you won't injure yourself.

Covering a small area with sheet vinyl

A very small room such as a lavatory can be covered by one piece of even the narrowest sheet vinyl. The best way of cutting it is to use a paper template.

Tools *Enough stiff paper (such as paper underlay) to cover the floor; perhaps adhesive tape or stapler; pencil; drawing pins or weights; scissors or knife; block of wood 40mm wide; pencil; ruler.*

Materials *Sheet vinyl; possibly adhesive and spreader.*

Make a template

1 If the paper is not big enough to cover the room, stick two pieces together.

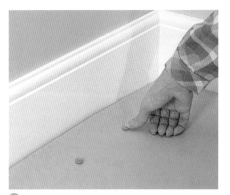

2 Put the paper on the floor with the edges folded underneath. Fix in place with drawing pins. On a solid floor use weights.

3 To fit it around obstacles such as a WC or a pipe, cut the paper from the wall inwards.

4 When the paper is laid, use scissors or a knife to trim it all the way round the room so that its edge is about 15mm from the wall or skirting board. Trim it around obstacles as well.

5 Cut a small block of wood about 40mm wide, and mark the width on it so there is no confusion later.

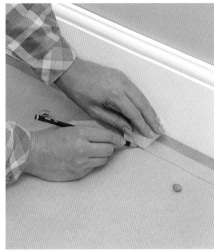

6 Put one edge against the wall and hold the pencil against the other edge. Move the block and pencil all the way around the room, tracing an outline of the room onto the paper.

7 Also trace around larger obstacles, such as the pedestal of a wash basin.

8 If a pipe comes up through the floor, put a ruler against it on four opposite faces and draw a pencil line along the outside edge of the ruler to make a square.

Cut out the vinyl

1 Lay a piece of the flooring material – right side up – on the floor of a larger room and put the template on top, fixing it in place with adhesive tape.

2 Put one edge of the wood block on the pencil line on the template. Put the pencil against the other edge and draw it along, tracing the shape of the room onto the vinyl. Do the same for large obstacles.

3 Cut the vinyl along the pencil line, using a ruler as a guide on straight lines. Put a piece of scrap vinyl or hardboard underneath to avoid damaging the floor.

4 If you have marked a square for a pipe, draw diagonal lines from the corners of the square. Where they cross is the middle.

5 Use a coin or other round object to draw a circle the diameter of the pipe. Cut out the circle with the knife. Alternatively, use a pipe offcut of the same diameter and a hammer to make a hole (page 136). Cut a slit between the hole and the nearby edge.

6 The piece of flooring will now fit the room exactly. To fit the vinyl around obstacles, make a cut from the cut-out to the nearest edge.

7 Stick down the vinyl in the normal way (page 142) unless it is a 'stay-flat' variety of cushioned vinyl which does not need to be glued.

Choosing carpet

Carpets can be soft and luxurious or practical and hardwearing. They are always the warmest choice for a floor, and modern technology means that you can buy carpet suitable for almost any area of the house.

Choosing a carpet

There are several things to consider when choosing a carpet. The first thing is the amount of wear it will get.

Durability Carpets are classified as 'light domestic' (bedrooms); 'medium domestic' (light traffic – dining room or main bedroom); 'general domestic' (living rooms); and 'heavy domestic' (hall, stairs and landings). So you need to choose a carpet hardwearing enough for its intended use.

What is it made of? The best carpets are wool, or a wool and man-made fibre blend. But many of the latest synthetics are barely distinguishable from wool, and no longer suffer from the 'static' problems that used to cause a mild static-electric shock when you touched a door handle. Synthetics are often highly stain resistant, but they will shrivel and burn quickly when exposed to intense heat.

Pile The pile determines the texture of the carpet. There are six types of pile. 'Loop' feels smooth; 'twist' is coarser; 'cord' is hard and feels ridged; 'cut' feels soft and velvety; 'velvet' is a smooth short-cut pile; 'saxony' is a long, shaggy pile.

Woven or tufted These terms are used to describe the weave of the pile. The traditional carpets like Wilton and Axminster are woven; most carpets, however, are tufted. The latter is less expensive and slightly less durable.

Integral or separate underlay
Underlay increases the life of your carpet. It stops dust from rising between the floorboards and spoiling it, and cushions the floor, making it softer to walk on. Most underlay is a rippled foam rubber, although you can still buy traditional thick felt. Foam backed carpet has built in underlay, but it is a good idea to put down a separate underlay first (page 148).

Colour and pattern A carpet is a major expense, and it is not practical to replace carpet whenever fashions change or you redecorate. Therefore, plain carpets in neutral or subdued colours are a wise choice. Small repeat patterns often work well, but bold designs can be limiting in terms of what furnishings you can put with them, and unpopular with potential house buyers. Using one carpet throughout a house makes it feel more spacious.

CARPET FIXINGS

Grippers Fitted carpets with underlay are held by gripper strips – thin lengths of wood (or sometimes metal) containing two rows of angled pins. Some grippers come with nails ready to be hammered into the floor. Wood or concrete nails are available. Or they can be stuck to solid floors – ideally with hot-melt adhesive from a glue gun.

Double threshold strips These are used to cover the edges of two carpets laid in adjoining rooms.

Angled grippers For staircases, angled grippers are fitted at the junction between tread and riser. They can be bought to fit standard-width stair carpet.

Threshold strips In doorways, threshold strips are screwed, nailed or glued to the floor. They grip the carpet with spikes and fold down over the edge to protect it.

Stair rods Stair rods are again being made, and old ones can be found in antique shops or on the Internet. Make sure you have enough for your stairs. The method of fixing is usually obvious.

CARPET LAYING TOOLS

Carpet-layer's hammer This has a narrow heavy head and is useful for fixing gripper strip to a floor or stairs, as it will drive in the nails without hitting the pins on the gripper. It will probably have to be bought from a carpet shop. Or use a hammer and nail punch.

Carpet stretcher or 'knee-kicker' This has a flat sole with teeth at one end, which grips the carpet. At the other, there is a large pad, which the layer 'kicks' with his knee. Carpet stretchers are expensive to buy, but they can be hired.

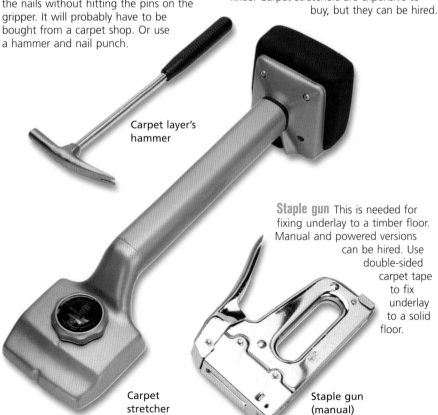

Carpet layer's hammer

Staple gun This is needed for fixing underlay to a timber floor. Manual and powered versions can be hired. Use double-sided carpet tape to fix underlay to a solid floor.

Carpet stretcher

Staple gun (manual)

Foam-backed carpet

Carpet with integral foam underlay is much easier to lay than hessian-backed carpet, which needs a separate underlay. Foam-backed carpet does not have to be stretched. It is held to the floor with double-sided carpet tape, which can be stuck to wood or concrete floors.

Tools *Trimming knife; scissors.*

Materials *Carpet, 100–150mm bigger all round than the floor; double-sided carpet tape; paper underlay.*

A one piece carpet

Many DIY superstores sell inexpensive foam backed carpets for laying in small rooms such as bathrooms or box-rooms. This is a straightforward job.

1 Put down paper underlay (see box). It must stop short of the walls by the width of the carpet tape so that the tape will stick to the floor, not to the paper.

2 Fix double-sided carpet tape all round the perimeter of the room but do not peel off the tape's backing paper.

3 Place the carpet loosely in position. If the carpet has a pile, have the pile running away from the window if possible. The surface should feel smooth when you run your hand away from the window, with the pile. If you feel resistance, you are going against the pile.

4 If the carpet has a pattern, adjust it so that it looks true when seen from the door.

5 To lay the carpet into an alcove, make a cut at a right angle to the back of the alcove. Leave 25mm excess for trimming.

6 Trim off the excess all round the room, so that the carpet is the size of the floor plus a trimming allowance of at least 25mm on each wall.

7 Trim off the excess in the corners of the room. Cut away triangles in the corners so that you can push the carpet right into the angle between the floor and the skirting. This is easily done using the back of your trimming knife (above).

PAPER UNDERLAY FOR FOAM-BACKED CARPET

On concrete floors or smooth floorboards, paper underlay can be used (an uneven floor should be lined with hardboard to level it out. See page 126). It prevents dirt from blowing up between the boards and harming the carpet. It also stops rubber or foam-backed carpets from sticking to the floor. It is sold by the roll in carpet stores and DIY superstores.

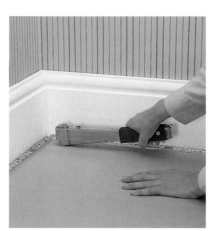

1 Beginning in a corner of the room, unroll about a metre of the paper so that it lies against the side wall and fix it in place with staple gun or double sided tape. If you plan to lay foam backed carpet, you will need to leave a border about 50mm wide right round the perimeter of the room so that the double sided carpet tape can be stuck to the floorboards.

2 Trim the end of the paper to the end wall and fix it in place.

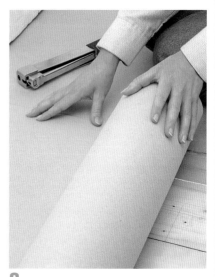

3 Roll the paper out to the far end of the room, smoothing it out as you unroll it, and fix it along both edges. Make sure the paper stays perfectly flat. Then fix and trim it at the other end.

4 Fix parallel strips of paper to cover the entire room, overlapping each length by about 25mm. The last length will probably have to be cut to width as well as to length.

8 Once the carpet is pushed well into the join between floor and skirting board, trim off the surplus with a sharp trimming knife.

9 Carefully lift up the carpet, peel off the tape's backing paper, and press the carpet firmly in place.

Foam backed carpet in two pieces

A wide room can be carpeted with two lengths of foam-backed carpet, joined together with double-sided carpet tape. The strip of floor where the two pieces of carpet will meet must be left clear of paper underlay so that the tape can be stuck directly to the floor. Make sure that the pile of both pieces lies in the same direction, or that the pattern matches.

1 Cut the first piece of carpet to length so it will run across the room with about 50mm lapping up the skirting boards at each end. Butt the machine edge of the carpet against the skirting board at one side of the room.

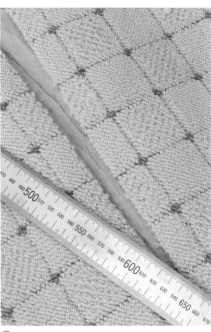

2 Cut the second piece of carpet to the same length. Cut it down in width so it is about 100mm wider than the remaining floor area of the room.

3 Position the second piece of carpet so it laps up the skirting boards by about 50mm along three sides, and overlaps the edge of the first piece by about 50mm at the meeting point. Make sure that the pattern matches – if there is one.

4 Use a sharp knife and a straightedge to cut through both layers of carpet, about 25mm from the edge of the overlapping piece.

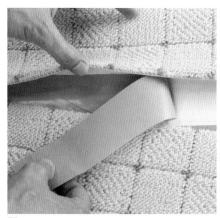

5 Turn back the edges of both pieces and stick 50mm carpet tape to the floor, centred so that both pieces of carpet will stick to it. Peel off the release paper.

6 Lay the edge of the first piece of carpet back down over the tape and press it into place.

7 Align the edge of the second piece of carpet with the first one and press it on to the tape, and against the edge of the first piece.

8 Trim the edges of the two pieces all round the room as for a one-piece carpet.

HELPFUL TIP

If your carpet frays very easily, you can reinforce the join with carpet adhesive. Once the first piece of carpet has been stuck to the carpet tape, apply a continuous bead of latex carpet adhesive along its edge. Than align the edge of the second piece of carpet with the first and press it into place. Wipe off any excess adhesive with a damp cloth.

Laying carpet with a separate underlay

It is not worth laying new carpet yourself: good-quality carpet is expensive and a fitting fee adds little to the overall cost. But used carpet is easier to lay as it has already been stretched once. So if you want to re-lay an existing fitted carpet, the job is worth trying.

Tools *Hammer and nail punch (or carpet-layer's hammer); tenon saw or hacksaw; vice or bench hook; protective gloves; trimming knife (preferably with a hooked blade) or scissors. Possibly also electric staple gun; carpet stretcher (from a hire shop); clean bolster chisel or wooden kitchen spatula.*

Materials *Gripper strip and nails or adhesive; threshold strip and screws or adhesive; underlay (felt or foam rubber); staples or tacks; carpet to cover the room in one piece.*

HELPFUL TIP

If you are laying carpet on a concrete floor, test first to make sure that central heating pipes are not lying too close to the surface. Switch the heating full on until the radiators are hot, and then walk over the floor in bare feet. If you feel heat, don't nail gripper strip; glue it instead.

Fixing grippers

1 Measure the perimeter of the room to work out how many gripper strips you will need. Gripper strips are usually sold in 1.5m lengths.

2 Put down the grippers with the pins pointing towards the wall. Leave a space slightly less than the thickness of the carpet between the gripper and the wall. This is for trimmed carpet to be tucked into later.

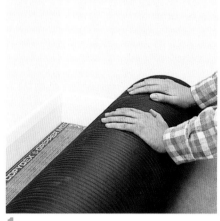

3 Nail the strips to the floor, using a small-headed carpet-layer's hammer. This will enable you to drive in the nails without hitting the pins. Alternatively, start off with a claw hammer, then use a nail punch when the nail heads get close to the pins.

4 When a radiator prevents you from getting close to the wall, fit the gripper as close as the radiator will allow.

5 When you reach a corner of the room, cut the strip to length using a tenon saw. Hold the strip in a vice or bench hook and be careful not to hurt yourself on the pins. Heavy gloves will help to protect hands. Butt-join two pieces of gripper. There is no need to cut mitre joints at the ends.

6 In a curved area, such as a bay window, cut the gripper into short pieces to follow the curve.

7 At a doorway, fit a metal threshold strip midway under the door.

Putting down underlay

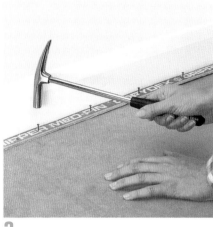

1 Unroll a short length of underlay in a corner of the room so that the end and the side lie against the gripper strip.

2 Fix the edges of the underlay to the floor with the staple gun, or with hammer and tacks. On a concrete floor, use double-sided carpet tape.

3 Roll out the underlay along the edge of the room, smoothing as you go, and fixing along both edges. Make sure it is perfectly flat on the floor. It is not necessary to stretch the underlay.

4 Where a radiator is fixed to the wall, lay the underlay up to the edge of the gripper, even if the gripper has been fitted a little way out from the wall.

5 At the end of the room trim the underlay against the gripper strip with a trimming knife or scissors.

6 When you have almost covered the room, you will have to cut the last length of underlay to width as well as to length.

Laying the carpet

1 In a larger room – or on the lawn if it is dry – cut the carpet to the size of the room to be covered. Add a trimming allowance of 150mm on all sides – even more if the carpet has a pattern. Keep the waste; it may come in handy for patching later.

2 Put the carpet in place on the floor of the room where it is to be laid. If it has a pattern, adjust it so that the pattern looks true, and does not run off line when seen from the doorway.

3 Make cuts to allow the carpet to lie flat in any alcove. Cut the carpet at a right angle to the back of the alcove and take care not to cut too far. Leave some excess for trimming around the alcove.

4 Cut off the surplus riding up the face of the chimney breast, leaving some excess for trimming.

5 Trim off the excess all round the room, leaving an allowance of about 10mm along two adjacent walls, and an allowance of about 40mm along the other two.

HELPFUL TIP

When trimming into an alcove it helps if you make vertical cuts at the corners. You can then press the carpet down on to the floor before cutting off the excess. This makes it easier to judge the appropriate allowance to be pushed down later.

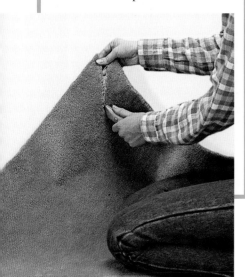

6 Start the fixing in the corner of the room with the smaller allowance. Working along one wall, run your fingers along the top of the carpet so that it engages on the gripper pins farthest from the wall. Take care not to injure fingers on the spikes.

7 Do the same along the second wall with the smaller allowance.

8 Run the head of your hammer flat along the top of the carpet, pushing it onto the other row of pins and forcing the excess carpet into the space between the gripper strip and the skirting board.

9 When the first two edges have been fixed, kneel on the carpet with your back to one of the completed walls. Push the teeth of the carpet stretcher into the carpet ahead of you and 'kick' the padded end with your knee to force the carpet forwards. Move forwards and repeat once or twice until you are close to the opposite wall.

10 Hook the carpet onto the gripper pins with your hand. It will immediately contract and be firmly fixed in place.

11 Repeat this process three or four more times across the room until the carpet is fixed all along one wall. Then turn 90° and fix it along the fourth wall.

12 When the hooking is complete, excess carpet will be left lapping up the walls. Trim this off to 10mm with a sharp trimming knife.

13 Push the remainder into the space between the gripper and skirting, using a clean bolster chisel or a wooden kitchen spatula. Take care not to scratch the paintwork if you are using a bolster.

14 Check that the excess carpet on the other two walls of the room is properly pushed down, and use the bolster or spatula where necessary.

15 Finally, tap down the cover of the threshold strip at the doorway using a piece of waste wood or carpet to protect the metal from becoming dented.

CUTTING A DOOR TO CLEAR A CARPET

After fitting a carpet, the base of the door may drag on the surface. One cure is to change the hinges for rising butts (page 192).

Alternatively, the bottom of the door can be trimmed off. You can hire a door trimming saw from tool hire shops, and trim the door without removing it from its hinges. Otherwise, with the door in place, take a thin block of wood as thick as the amount of wood to be removed. Put it on the floor with a pencil on top and run it along the door to mark the cutting line.

Take off the door and either saw or plane off the base. If you use a hand saw, work slowly to avoid splintering the face. If you use a plane, hold the door upright on its long edge in a portable work bench and plane downwards. Work inwards from each side to avoid splintering the stiles at the end. Sand the bottom of the door so that it will not damage the carpet.

Fitting a stair carpet

Laying fitted carpet on a curved staircase is usually best left to a carpet layer as this is a tricky job and the carpet must not work loose for safety reasons. But you can lay a strip of carpet, which may cover the entire width of the tread or leave painted or varnished wood visible on each side.

Tools *Tape measure; tenon saw; workbench; hammer; trimming knife and blades; straightedge; staple gun; carpet bolster chisel or clean brick bolster. Possibly also: tack lifter; spatula.*

Materials *Underlay; carpet; carpet gripper strip.*

How much carpet?

1 Measure from the front to the back of a tread (the part you walk on) and multiply the figure by the number of treads in the staircase.

2 If the stairs turn a corner on a half-landing, measure the length of half-landing and add it to the total. When you want the carpet to turn to the far end of any landing at the top of the stairs, add this measurement as well.

3 Now measure the height of a riser (the vertical part of each step) and multiply the figure by the number of risers.

4 Add this to the figure you already have. The total is the length of carpet needed to cover the stairs.

5 Measure the width of the stairs if you want full-width carpet. Carpet fixed with stair rods (see page 151) is a standard 910mm wide.

HELPFUL TIP

When measuring carpet for a curving staircase that has treads deeper at one edge than the other, take the larger measurement. Measure the depth of each tread, at its widest point, as depths may vary. In particular, the bottom tread may be deeper than the rest.

Preparing stairs for carpeting across the width of the tread

1 If an old carpet has just been removed, inspect the staircase for defects, and repair as necessary. Remove any nails or tacks left over from the old carpet with a tack lifter.

2 Cut lengths of gripper strip to the width of the stairs less 40mm. Position a strip on a tread, with a gap of about 12mm between it and the riser above it, and nail in place, with teeth on the strip pointing backwards. Repeat for all the treads. Then position and nail the strips to the risers, again leaving a 12mm gap, with teeth pointing downwards. Alternatively, use angled grippers (page 145).

3 Cut pieces of gripper strip for the sides of the treads, so they touch the strips at the back of the treads and finish 25mm in from the front edge of each tread. Nail them in place about 12mm in from the side edge, with teeth facing the side of the tread.

4 Cut underlay into separate pads for each tread. Each pad should be long enough to fit over the tread and cover the face of the riser below it, and wide enough to fit snugly between the gripper strips at the sides. Use a staple gun to fix the pads to the treads and risers. Fit a smaller underlay pad to the last riser at the top of the stairs.

SAFETY TIP

Using a staircase with only underlay pads in place is dangerous, because the pads hang loosely over the edge of the tread. Also, the pins on gripper strips are very sharp. Therefore, if the house is occupied, try not to leave the job unfinished.

Laying a full-width carpet on a straight staircase

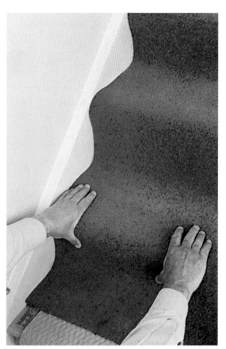

1 Measure the full width of the tread and cut one or more strips of carpet to this width, ensuring the pile direction runs down the stairs and not across them. (A carpet wears better if the pile faces down the stairs.) Working downwards from the top of the stairs, fit the first strip in place.

2 Starting at the top tread, use a carpet (or brick) bolster and hammer to drive the folds of carpet securely in between the gripper strips in each internal angle. Then pull the carpet taut over the front edge of the next tread and repeat the process.

3 If you have more than one carpet strip, cut the end of the first strip at the bottom of a riser with a trimming knife. Tuck the edge into the angle between the gripper strips, using the bolster and hammer.

4 Tuck the top edge of the next strip of carpet into the angle between the gripper strips at the rear edge of the tread and secure it with bolster and hammer. Continue fitting the strip down the stairs. Trim it to finish at the foot of the last riser, at the angle between the riser and the hall carpet.

5 When you have finished laying the carpet, use the bolster to tuck the side edges of the carpet into the gaps between the gripper strips and strings on each tread.

Fixing a carpet on a curved staircase

Choose a carpet that is woven; tufted carpets are too stiff for this job.

1 Nail gripper strips to both the riser and the tread of each stair.

2 Cut underlay to shape; the underlay for each tread will be wider at one end than the other. Staple or tack them in place, butted up against the gripper on the tread.

3 Working from the bottom of the stairs, unroll a little of the carpet. Cover the bottom tread with carpet, laid face down. Make sure to keep the carpet parallel to the sides of the tread.

4 Fix the stair gripper on the tread, trapping the carpet in place with the nails.

5 Bring the carpet over the nose of the tread and down the riser.

6 Fix it at the bottom of the riser with a strip of hardboard or plywood nailed in place through the carpet.

7 Bring the carpet back up the bottom riser to the starting point so the decorative surface is uppermost. Push the carpet onto the gripper strips with a bolster or spatula. Make sure the carpet is firmly fixed.

8 On the first curved stair bring the carpet up the riser and nail it with 25mm tacks.

9 Fold it down so that it meets the tread below and tack it in place.

10 If the curve is sharp, you may have to lay the carpet in pieces – two or three stairs for each piece.

Carpet on a curved staircase

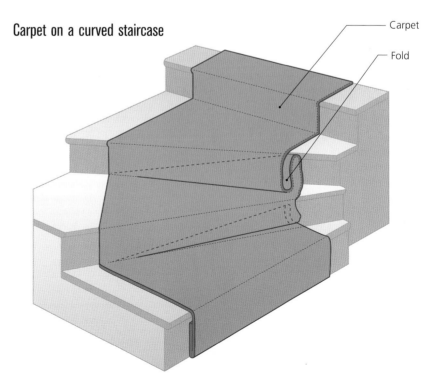

Carpet

Fold

USING STAIR RODS

When a stair carpet does not cover the full width of the tread, you can use stair rods to hold it in position.

Although the rods will keep the carpet in place on a straight staircase, they will probably not be able to hold the underlay, which must be fixed with tacks.

Put the clips for the rods at the edge of the carpet to prevent it moving sideways.

Where a staircase is curved, and perhaps also between the hall floor and the bottom riser, stair rods are used for the sake of appearance only: the carpet is actually held in place by tacks.

In the past, if you had a straight staircase and a carpet runner held by stair rods, you would have a length of overlap folded under at the bottom of the flight. You could then extend the life of the carpet by moving it up the stairs by about 75mm every year.

Landings

Full and half landings may be carpeted wall-to-wall, or may have a narrow runner laid across them.

If the landing is to have wall-to-wall carpet but the stairs are carpeted with a runner with gaps at either side, finish the stair carpet at the top of the last riser. Cut off any surplus, leaving about 25mm to fold under. Fix it with tacks along its top edge.

Lay the landing carpet in the same way as a room carpet, but take it over the top step and tack it to the top riser.

Put underlay beneath the landing carpet, overlapping the top riser of the staircase.

Half landings

Where a staircase makes a 90° turn, treat it as two flights of stairs. Cover the half-landing with one of the stair carpets. Butt the other one up to it, turn under the end and tack it down.

If the staircase makes a 180° turn, there will be a rectangular half-landing at the turn, which needs to be covered with carpet laid at right angles to the lengths on the stairs.

Carry on laying both stair carpets to the far edge of the landing, cut them off and tack them in place, without putting underlay beneath them. Lay a third strip of carpet across them to cover the landing.

There will be a gap under the landing carpet in the middle between the two strips of stair carpet. Fit a strip of underlay or some stair pads tacked in place and trimmed to size to make a level surface for the top layer of carpet. Take the landing carpet over the top step of the lower flight and tack it to the top riser. Tack down the landing carpet on all the other edges for a neat finish.

Carpet problems

Damaged or torn carpet can be a trip hazard, and should be dealt with promptly. At best, stains, rips and burns are unsightly. If you have some spare carpet from when it was first laid, fix the problem with a patch.

Patching a damaged carpet

To repair a hole or a frayed patch in a carpet, you need a piece of the same carpet slightly bigger than the damaged area. The piece may have been left over when the carpet was laid, or you can cut it from under a large piece of furniture that is never moved, where it will not show. The joins of the repair should not be visible. At first, there will be a colour difference between the new patch and the rest of the carpet, but in time this will become less obvious.

Tools *Trimming knife; hammer.*

Materials *Carpet patch; latex-based carpet adhesive; 50mm self-adhesive carpet tape (possibly double-sided); a piece of hessian larger than the patch (except for foam-backed carpet).*

Cut the new piece

1 Place the new piece over the damaged portion, ensuring that the pile runs in the same direction. (Run your hand over both carpets to find the direction in which they feel smoothest.)

2 Hold the patch firmly on the carpet and cut through both at the same time with a sharp knife. This ensures that the patch and hole are exactly the same size.

Take care not to cut through a separate underlay as well.

LOOSE CARPET

Do not rely on furniture to hold carpet in place in a room. Not only is a properly stretched and fitted carpet much neater, it is also far safer. In anything bigger than the smallest of rooms, loose-laid carpet can wrinkle and bunch over time, leading to folds or creases that will wear unevenly and can cause people to trip. If a carpet is not lying flat, deal with the problem as soon as possible, by re-laying it, and fixing it firmly in place with tacks, adhesive tape or gripper strips around the edges of the room and threshold strips in doorways.

Loose-laid carpet

1 In the case of a loose-laid carpet, roll it back and apply a carpet adhesive round the edge of the patch to about halfway up the pile. This prevents fraying.

2 Leave the adhesive to dry, then insert the patch in position.

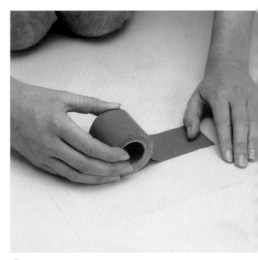

3 On a foam-backed carpet, fix the patch in place with 50mm self-adhesive carpet tape on all the edges.

With other carpets, spread carpet adhesive on a piece of hessian 50mm bigger all round than the patch. Stick it over the back of the patch and over the surrounding carpet.

4 Turn the carpet right side up and pinch the edges of the patch and the carpet between your fingers to make quite sure they stick well together.

5 Finally, tap the join all over lightly with a hammer to disguise the join as much as possible, although the colour difference will probably still be visible.

Fitted carpet

1 Apply a latex adhesive round the edges of the hole and the edge of the patch to about halfway up the pile, and leave it to dry.

2 Take four lengths of double-sided carpet tape, push them through the hole, and stick them to the floor or the underlay where the patch will join onto the main carpet. Remove the backing from the tape.

3 Place the patch in position and press it firmly down.

4 Push the edges together, and tap lightly with a hammer to bond the patch in place.

Removing stains on carpet

Try to treat stains as soon as they occur. The longer they are left, the more difficult they will be to remove.

Do not add extra liquid of any sort and do not rub the carpet. If you do so, you will only drive the stain deeper, or spread it.

If you are going to use dry-cleaning solvent or a proprietary carpet stain-removal product, test the cleaner on an unobtrusive patch of carpet first, to check its colour-fastness.

1 First scrape off any solid matter with a spoon or blunt knife. Mop up liquid by pressing on it with a dry towel or wad of tissues. Use different areas of the towel or tissues until no more moisture can be lifted.

2 If a stain still remains, treat it according to whether it is water-based or grease-based. A water based stain – a drink, for example – can be removed with a carpet shampoo; a grease-based stain, such as gravy or fat, can be removed with a dry-cleaning solvent.

3 When applying the shampoo or solvent, use just enough on a cloth to moisten the area. If you use a saturated cloth you are likely to drive the stain deeper. Turn the cloth to a dry side as soon as it becomes dirty. Work from the outside of the stain towards the middle to avoid spreading it.

4 Finally, cover the area with a thick wad of tissues weighed down with something flat and heavy, such as a phone book. The remaining moisture will be absorbed by the tissues, further reducing the risk of a permanent stain.

5 When the treated patch has dried out, it may be necessary to shampoo the entire carpet to ensure uniform colour. Carpet-cleaning firms will do the job for you, or you can hire carpet-cleaning equipment by the day (right).

GETTING PROFESSIONAL HELP

The National Carpet Cleaners' Association will provide lists of member companies in your area who will advise on stain removal and carry out cleaning work. The contact address is 62c London Road, Oadby, Leicester LE2 5DH (telephone 0116 271 9550). Check their web site for excellent advice on carpet care and stain removal, at www.ncca.co.uk

Using a hired carpet cleaner

Most DIY superstores and carpet warehouses hire out equipment for cleaning carpets. These are efficient and easy to use.

Book the carpet cleaner in advance. Most companies hire the machines by the day, so if you collect the cleaner first thing in the morning you can clean all your carpets for the price of a day's hire.

When you collect the cleaner, make sure that you buy enough of the recommended carpet shampoo. Most companies supply this on a sale-or-return basis. You will get a refund on any unopened bottles.

1 Read the instructions carefully. Before filling the unit make sure the switches are off and the hoses on the back are connected. To fill this machine, the upper tank is removed and a mixture of shampoo and water poured into the lower tank.

2 Replace the top tank and turn on the machine. On this model a trigger switch sprays the shampoo solution onto the carpet and activates a vibrating brush. Walking backwards, slowly, pull the machine towards you. As you clean, dirty water is sucked into the upper (clear) tank.

An A-Z of carpet stains

Spillages are inevitable at some time in the life of a carpet, but treated promptly a spill can often be cleaned up without leaving a stain. The advice given here will help you to remove a wide variety of spills from floorcoverings, but the same techniques can also be used to eradicate stains from soft furnishings.

Alcoholic spirits
Mop up with a dry towel or wad of tissues. Sponge with warm water. Allow to dry. Then clean with carpet shampoo. Treat any remaining stain with methylated spirit.

Animal stains
Remove loose solids with paper. Scrape the residue with a blunt knife or spoon. Blot dry with a cloth or wad of tissues. Lightly sponge with a carpet shampoo (add acetic acid for urine). If the stain is serious call a professional carpet cleaner. The most serious stains penetrate to the back of the carpet and the underlay.

Ball-point pen
Speedy action is essential. Dab with methylated spirit on a cotton wool bud. Take care not to spread the stain. On vinyl upholstery or wall coverings, immediately scrub with a nail brush and warm soapy water (the ink will cause a permanent mark if left).

Beer
Blot with kitchen towel, add a little white vinegar solution (⅓ cup white vinegar with ⅔ water), blot again then clean with carpet cleaner following the bottle's instructions.

Blood
Sponge with cold water. Blot dry. Clean with carpet shampoo if necessary. Dried stains may not clean completely.

Candlewax
Scrape off as much as possible. Cover remainder with blotting paper or brown paper. Apply the point of a warm iron. Do not allow the iron to touch nylon carpet; it may cause it to melt. Move the paper about until the wax is absorbed into it.
Clear any remaining traces with a dry-cleaning solvent.

Chewing gum
Freeze the chewing gum with blocks of ice wrapped in a plastic bag, or use a proprietary aerosol chewing gum remover.
Then break it up into pieces and brush up the bits by hand – chewing gum clogs up vacuum cleaners.

Chocolate
Scrape off the chocolate with a knife, and clean the area with carpet shampoo. Treat stubborn stains with dry-cleaning solvent when the shampoo has dried.

Cocoa
Mop up the worst and dry off with a towel or wad of tissues. Clean with carpet shampoo. Treat any remaining stain with a dry-cleaning solvent when the shampoo has dried.

Coffee
Mop up the worst of the liquid. Blot dry. Treat any remaining stain with a carpet shampoo. When dry use dry-cleaning solvent to remove grease from milk or cream.

Curry
An extremely difficult stain. Large marks should be treated professionally. With small marks, scrape off the deposit and rub lightly with borax solution (15ml borax to 500ml water). Stubborn stains can sometimes be helped with a little neat glycerine rubbed into the carpet and left for about 10 minutes. Then sponge out with warm water, and blot dry.

Dyes
Have the stain treated by a carpet-cleaning firm.

Egg
Scrape off the deposit. Treat with dry-cleaning solvent or with a proprietary carpet spot-removing kit.

Eye make-up
Moisten the area, then treat with a drop of liquid detergent on a cotton wool bud. Rinse. Treat stubborn stains with dry cleaning solvent.

Fats, grease and oil
Mop up the worst. Scrape off any deposit. Apply dry-cleaning solvent.
Heavy deposits often respond to the blotting-paper-and-iron technique (see Candlewax).

Felt-tip pen
Some felt-tip pens have spirit-base ink, some have water-based ink. Methylated spirit on a cotton wool bud will remove spirit-based ink, which has a pungent smell. But do not allow it to penetrate to a foam backing. The methylated spirit may stain a light coloured carpet. For water-based ink, use carpet shampoo.

Fruit juice
Mop up with a clean cloth or paper towels. Clean with carpet shampoo.

Gravy
Mop up with paper towels. Treat with dry-cleaning solvent. Clean with carpet shampoo.

Ice cream
Scrape up and wipe with paper towels. Treat with a dry-cleaning solvent when dry. Clean with carpet shampoo.

Ink (fountain pen)
Must be tackled immediately. Blot with absorbent paper. Sponge with warm water to remove further ink. You may need more than one application. Blot well each time.
Treat remaining small stains with a proprietary carpet spot-removing kit.

Jam/marmalade
Spoon up deposits. Wipe area with cloth wrung out in warm water. Clean with carpet shampoo. Remove any remaining stains with a proprietary carpet spot-removing kit.

Ketchup
Scoop up or wipe away excess deposits. Take care not to spread the stain. Gently rub with lather made up from carpet shampoo. Wipe with cloth wrung out in warm water. Work in direction of the pile. Treat any remaining stain with a dry-cleaning solvent.

Lipstick
Scrape off with a knife, and use a dry-cleaning solvent. Alternatively, use a proprietary carpet spot-removing kit or a little paintbrush cleaner.

Metal polish
Scrape off or blot up any deposit. Treat with carpet shampoo containing a few drops of household ammonia.

Milk
Immediate action is essential to prevent milk penetrating down into the carpet where it will give off a smell for weeks. Blot dry. Clean with carpet shampoo. If a stain remains use a dry-cleaning solvent. May need professional attention to prevent smell recurring each time room warms up.

Mud
Allow to dry. Brush, then vacuum. Clean with carpet shampoo if necessary.

Mustard
Scrape off deposits. Sponge with damp cloth. Treat with carpet shampoo.

Nail varnish
Spoon up deposit; avoid spreading the stain. Moisten a pad of cotton wool with non-oily nail varnish remover and dab on affected area. First test on a hidden corner as acetone may damage man-made fibres. Use as little as possible, as over-soaking can damage the backing. Remaining traces of colour can be removed with methylated spirit. Apply a dry-cleaning solvent if necessary.

Paint

All paint spills must be dealt with immediately. Once it has dried it is almost impossible to remove. Scrape up and wipe off as much as possible, then treat according to the type of paint.

Gloss (solvent-based) paint Sponge with white spirit or a dry-cleaning solvent. If dry, soften with paintbrush cleaner. Large areas need professional attention.

Emulsion Mop with cold water, working from the edges inwards. Large area of dried-on emulsion should be left to a professional carpet cleaner.
Acrylic Mop up with tissues. Sponge with warm water. Finish with methylated spirit or dry-cleaning solvent.

Perfume
Clean with carpet shampoo, and allow to dry. Use more shampoo if the stain persists.

Plasticine
Scrape off as much as possible, then treat the remainder with a dry-cleaning solvent.

Scorch marks
Bad scorch marks are impossible to remove as the fibres are damaged. For repairing a carpet, see page 152. For slight marks trim the pile with scissors, or lightly shave with a disposable razor. Or remove loose fibres with a stiff brush, then make circular movements with a wire brush or abrasive paper to disguise the area.

Shoe polish
Scrape off and dab with dry-cleaning solvent. Finish with methylated spirit. Clean with carpet shampoo if necessary.

Soft drinks
Mop up. Treat with carpet shampoo. Stubborn marks often respond to methylated spirit.

Soot
Vacuum the area with a suction-only type cleaner, not a brush type. Or shake a rug outside. Do not brush or the mark will spread. Use a dry-cleaning solvent to remove any small marks. Get professionals to treat large areas.

Tar
Very hard to remove. Scrape away any loose deposit. Treat with a dry-cleaning solvent. If the surface is hard, scratch it to allow the solvent to penetrate. On stubborn stains try dabbing with eucalyptus oil or paintbrush cleaner.

Tea
Mop up as much as possible. Treat with carpet shampoo. Treat any left-over stain when dry with dry-cleaning solvent which will remove the grease from milk.

Toothpaste
Scrape up any deposit and treat with carpet shampoo.

Vomit
Remove the bulk of it, sponge the area with soda water, blot with kitchen towel and then clean with carpet cleaner and blot again.

Wine
Fresh spills Sponge red wine spills with white wine then blot with kitchen towel before using carpet cleaner. Do not put salt on the carpet; it may affect the colour. Blot white wine stains with kitchen towel.
Old stains May respond to glycerine solution (equal parts of water and glycerine) left for an hour, then rinsed off. Sponging with methylated spirit may reduce very old stains.

5
Fixtures and fittings

Choosing wall fixings

Whatever you are fixing to a wall – shelving or curtain rails, for example – it is always essential to provide good, strong fittings, suitable for the load.

Fixings for solid walls

For masonry walls Use screws that will penetrate the wall by a minimum of 50mm, driven into plastic wall plugs that match the screw gauge.

On timber-framed walls Where the screws pass directly into the framing, 40mm penetration will be adequate, unless a heavy load is to be put on the shelves, when screws should go in by 50mm. Before putting up any fixing, always use a battery-powered cable detector to locate cables or pipes buried in walls.

STANDARD WALL PLUGS

Finned plastic Tapered plug with split end to allow expansion, and either fins or lugs to prevent it turning in the hole. A rim of flexible ears prevent it being pushed in too far. Each size will accept screws of several lengths and gauges.

Ribbed plastic Has no fins or lugs, but the shallow lengthways ribs prevent it from turning in the hole. Sold in colour-coded sizes.

Strip plastic Straight-sided plug with shallow lengthways ribs. Can be bought in strips and cut to length with a trimming knife. Sold in colour-coded sizes.

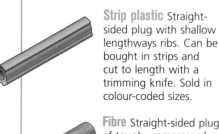

Fibre Straight-sided plug of tough, compressed fibre. Sold in various lengths, but can be cut with a trimming knife. Becoming obsolete but still available.

Masonry nail Hardened galvanised nail that will penetrate and grip when driven into bricks or blocks. Not suitable for use in concrete or hard stone. Lengths typically from 15mm to 100mm.

A fast way of fixing timber battens to brick walls. Choose a length that will penetrate beyond the fixing by about 15mm into bare masonry or about 25mm into a plastered wall. Hammer with short, positive strokes. Nails will not bend, and will shatter if not struck squarely. Wear eye protection.

Woodscrew and wall plug The fibre or plastic plug expands to fit the hole and grip the masonry wall. Plugs are in lengths from 15mm to 90mm.

For lightweight fittings, use No. 8 gauge screws and matched plugs. For heavier fittings use No. 10 or No. 12 gauge screws. The screw should be long enough to extend about 25mm into the masonry after passing through the fitting and the plaster.

Hammer-in fixing or nail plug A screw with a special thread for easy driving, ready-fitted into a nylon sleeve. It can be tapped with a hammer into a drilled hole. Lengths typically 50mm to 160mm will fix objects from about 5mm to 110mm thick.

A strong, fast method for fixing a lot of timber battens to brick or concrete. Also suitable for lightweight fixings into building blocks. The hole should extend 5–15mm beyond the screw tip. So for a screw 50mm long fixing a 10mm thick object, make wall holes at least 45mm deep.

Frame fixing A long screw ready-fitted into a nylon wall plug. Drill the hole through the frame into the wall, push or lightly tap the fixing through and tighten with a screwdriver. Lengths to secure frames from about 20mm to 110mm thick. A secure and convenient method of fixing new or replacement door or window frames to walls. Useful for repairing a door frame that has worked loose. As a guide, the depth of the masonry hole should be at least five times the diameter of the plug.

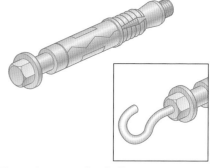

Expansion or anchor bolt A bolt with a segmented metal shield. The shield fits into a drilled hole in masonry, and expands to grip the hole sides when the bolt is tightened. Bolts range from about 5mm to 25mm in diameter, in lengths to fix objects from about 10mm to 120mm thick. The bolt head may be fixed, fitted with a nut and washer, or hook or eye shaped (inset).

A very strong, heavy-duty fixing suitable for objects such as wall cupboards, garage doors, lean-to framework, or fence and gateposts fixed to masonry. A fixed-head bolt (known as a loose bolt) is pushed through the fixture before being screwed into the shield. A nut-head (or projecting) bolt is placed in the hole with the shield and the fitting is hung on it before the nut and washer are fitted. The masonry hole needs to be wider than the hole through the fitting – generally 6mm wider than the bolt diameter.

Steel sleeve anchor or expansion bolt Steel bolts with an expanding wedge at the end for gripping against the sides of a drilled hole. Bolts have screw-on nuts and washers. Sizes are available for fixing objects ranging from about 5mm to 110mm thick.

Easy, quickly fitted heavy-duty fixing for things such as door and window frames, trunking, or hand rails. The hole can be drilled through the frame and masonry at the same time, and is the same diameter for both the fitting and the masonry. Bolt diameters are typically from 5mm to 20mm.

Plugging compound For making fixings in holes that have become enlarged because of the drill bit wandering or because a previous fixing has failed. It is supplied in a two-colour putty-like strip. Cut off the amount required with scissors. Take off the protective film and knead the strip. When the blue pigment turns white, it is ready.

Fixings for hollow walls, ceilings and lightweight blocks

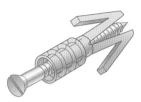

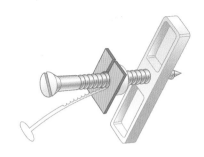

Woodscrew and plug The screw has a winged plastic plug that spreads out to grip the back of a wall or ceiling board. The plug can be re-used if the screw is withdrawn. For lightweight or medium fittings to plasterboard, hardboard or plywood (including hollow doors) up to about 25mm thick. The cavity behind the board needs to be at least 15mm deep.

Spring toggle A machine screw fitted with a spring-operated toggle bar that folds back while it is being inserted and then springs open when it is inside the cavity. The toggle is lost if the screw is withdrawn. Typical size range is for screws 50–80mm long.

A strong fixing for plasterboard or lath-and-plaster walls and ceilings. The cavity has to be at least 45mm wide – even wider for larger sizes. The toggle can be used with a hook for hanging a light-fitting from the ceiling.

Nylon toggle and collar A nylon collar that takes a wood screw and is linked by a notched nylon strip to a toggle. After insertion, the strip is used to draw the toggle towards the collar to take the screw tip and grip the back of the board. It is then cut off. Typical size is for No. 6 woodscrews. The collar closes the drilled hole and the adjustable fitting is used for fixing to plasterboard, lath-and-plaster or suspended ceilings of different thicknesses. The toggle is retained if the screw is withdrawn.

Machine screw and expanding rubber plug The screw fits into a nut in a rubber sleeve that is compressed to grip the back of the board. The plug stays in place if the screw is withdrawn. Plugs are sold with or without a screw. A strong fixing for plasterboard, plywood, hardboard, sheet metal, glass or plastic, up to about 45mm thick. The plug protects the screw from vibration and rusting. It can also be used as a wall plug in masonry where it shapes to the hole's contours.

Machine screw and metal cavity fixing
A metal plug with a nut welded in the end. It collapses to form metal wings that grip the back of the board. A strong fixing for heavyweight fixtures to hardboard, plasterboard, chipboard, plywood and fibreboard, up to about 35mm thick.

Gravity toggle A machine screw with a swinging metal bar (toggle) attached. When the screw is inserted, the toggle swings down and grips the back of the wall. It is lost if the screw is withdrawn.

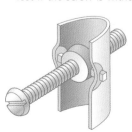

A strong fixing for plasterboard or lath-and-plaster walls. The cavity has to be at least 32mm wide, or wider for larger sizes.

SPECIAL TYPES OF WALL PLUG

Winged-arrow type
Light plastic plug that spreads out to grip the back of plasterboard. For use with No. 8 screws and lightweight fixings. The plug can be re-used.

Nylon rivet anchor
The plug is split along most of its length and is compressed into wings. For use with Nos 8–10 screws for making fixings to plasterboard, particularly partition walls. The plug can be re-used.

Expanding-wing type
The wings are forced apart to grip the back of the board. Small-sized plugs are for use with No. 6 screws in hollow doors. Longer-sized plugs are for use with No. 8 screws for medium-weight fixings to board. Cannot be re-used.

Chipboard plug
Nylon fastener with an outside thread that is hammered into a hole drilled in chipboard. It has a split end and expands to give a secure grip. For use with Nos 6, 8 and 10 screws. The plug can be re-used.

Metal self-drive
A metal device with an outside thread that is screwed into plasterboard using a No. 2 Pozidriv screwdriver. The flange on the head prevents it from accidentally pushing through the plasterboard. A nylon version is also available for lightweight fixings.

Helical wing or twist-lock type
The nylon plug has helical wings that cause it to rotate as it is tapped home with a hammer, and prevent it from coming out if the screw is ever withdrawn. For use with large diameter screws to make strong fixings into aerated blocks. Can be re-used.

Choosing shelving

Shelves can be put up just about anywhere – alcoves are a good choice, but any wall space can be used. There is a huge selection to choose from, ranging from adjustable track systems to flat-pack units or tailor made.

CHOOSING FIXED BRACKETS

Most right-angle brackets have one arm longer than the other. Fix the long arm to the wall, unless the instructions state otherwise. The width of a shelf should be only about 25mm greater than the length of the horizontal arm of the bracket. Large overhangs can lead to the shelf becoming overloaded, which may cause the brackets to fail. Always secure shelves by screwing them to the brackets.

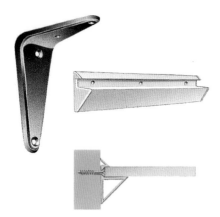

For heavy loads
• Usually made in high-strength pressed steel. One type has a continuous aluminium bracket that supports the shelf along its whole length.
• Sizes range from 75 x 50mm to 350 x 350mm. Aluminium strip comes in lengths from 600mm to 2.5m.
• Finishes include: red, black brown and white epoxy-coated; or galvanised (silvery).
• The manufacturers usually state load capacity on packaging.

For medium/light loads
Suitable for narrow shelves where other brackets are too large. Designed for reinforcing the corners of cabinets, but suitable for shelves. Radiator shelf option wedges behind radiator and needs no wall fixings.
• Sizes: 50 x 50mm; and a radiator shelf of 125mm or 150mm.
• Finishes include: cadmium-plated and galvanised (silvery).

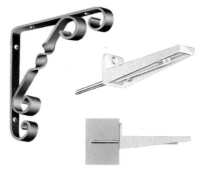

For medium/heavy loads
A range of styles for different types of medium to heavy loads. Includes wrought-iron, pressed steel, both with holes for screws, and plastic with a steel pin support (for a radiator shelf).
• Sizes range from 100 x 75mm to 240 x 240mm.
• Finishes include: red, brown, gold, yellow, green, black and silver. Radiator shelf support is in white or brown plastic.

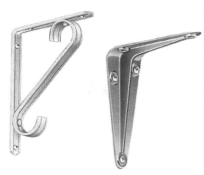

For light loads
Made in either pressed steel or aluminium, they have holes for screws.
• Sizes from 100 x 75mm to 300 x 250mm.
• Finishes include: black or grey dip painted and anodised silver, gold and white for braced bracket.

Utility shelving for sheds and garages
Medium weight, for supporting one or two shelves at a time.
• Sizes from 240 x 165mm to 310 wide by 280mm deep (double bracket).
• Finished in epoxy-coated orange only.

CHOOSING TRACK SHELVING

Consider what you will put on your shelves and choose a shelving system that is suitable – overloading is obviously very dangerous.

For heavy loads

Made of steel in lengths from 430mm to 2400mm. Uses brackets from 120mm to 610mm. Available in frost white, black, cream and gloss aluminium. Look for double hooks for extra strength. Accessories may include square book ends, spring rod book supports and universal book supports. Brands include Swish Steel-Lok.

For medium loads

Fully adjustable slot-free systems that can be used for most work around the house. Made of steel in lengths from 188mm to 2500mm. Uses brackets from 100mm to 570mm. Finishes: silver, white, brown, black, red, magnolia, gold and gloss aluminium. Accessories may include book ends, book end shelf supports, end caps, wall plates, clip on shelving supports, a fixing pack and upright connectors. Continuous shelving possible. Brands include Tebrax, Element Single Slot, Element 32 and Swish Design.

For light loads
Easily adjustable, wall-mounted steel shelving systems suitable for light domestic storage. Made of steel in lengths from 500mm to 2000mm. Uses brackets from 125mm to 320mm. Finishes: frost white, black, magnolia. Accessories may include a fixing pack. Brands include Swish Edge Slot.

CHOOSING SHELVES

White melamine-coated chipboard

Coloured melamine-coated chipboard

Heavyweight melamine-veneered chipboard

MDF clear varnished

Coated chipboard Inexpensive and needs no finishing. Choose 15mm board for light items and 18mm for heavier loads, such as books.

Medium-density fibreboard (MDF) Versatile and easy to work with but must be sealed or painted. It is relatively inexpensive. It is sold in sheets and comes in several thicknesses.

Softwood (pine) stained and polished

Wood-veneered chipboard

Plywood, coated with varnish

Hardwood (oak) polished

Timber and wood-veneered chipboard More expensive than coated chipboard and needs to be sealed, with varnish or paint, for example.

Acrylic sheet Perspex and other acrylic must be at least 12mm thick for a light-to-medium load. Bracket spacing must not be more than 400mm.

Glass shelves Must be at least 6mm thick or, ideally, toughened 9mm glass. Bracket spacing must not be more than 400mm. Get the edges of glass bevelled by the supplier, and use sturdy brackets as glass is heavy.

Floating shelves These are so-named because they have no visible means of support. They look modern, clean and attractive, and are great for display purposes. However, they are suitable only for light items. Floating shelves are available in kit form and are supported by a concealed batten or rods fixed into the wall.

BRACKET INTERVALS

Buying the cheapest shelf-and-bracket system can be a false economy if you plan to fill the shelves with heavy loads, such as books. The cheapest shelving material is the weakest, and if it is to be loaded up it will require closer support. This table is a guide to the intervals at which typical shelf materials need to be supported.

15mm chipboard (coated or plain); 15mm softwood (finished thickness)	Heavy loads 400mm Medium loads 600mm
18mm coated chipboard; 18mm MDF; 18mm softwood; 18mm hardwood	Heavy loads 500mm Medium loads 700mm
25mm MDF; 25mm softwood; 18mm plywood; 22mm hardwood	Heavy loads 700mm Medium loads 900mm
32mm veneered chipboard; 32mm softwood; 25mm plywood; 25mm hardwood	All loads 900mm

Strengthening shelves with battens and lipping

Shelves can be reinforced to improve their resistance to bending. The reinforcements can also be a decorative feature, perhaps hiding fixings or strip lights.

Apply a softwood or hardwood batten – a thick piece of wood – to the front or back edge of the shelf. It should run the full length and can be on the top or bottom. For extra strength, battens can be fixed to both front and back edges. The deeper the batten, the greater the strength. Fix the battens to the shelf with glue and screws, screwing through the shelf.

Hardwood lipping – a thin strip of wood – can be glued and pinned along the front edge. It may be the same depth as the shelf to give a decorative finish only, or it may be much deeper, which will strengthen as well as decorate.

SAFETY TIP

Use a battery-powered cable detector to check for cables in a wall on which you plan to fix shelves. It's best to avoid areas around socket outlets and wall lights altogether.

Load test Before fixing a shelf in place, check whether it will bow under the weight you intend to put on it. Rest the shelf on bricks set at the proposed bracket spacing, load it up and lay a straightedge along its surface. If the shelf bows, either move the bricks (and consequently the brackets) closer together, or increase the thickness of the shelf material.

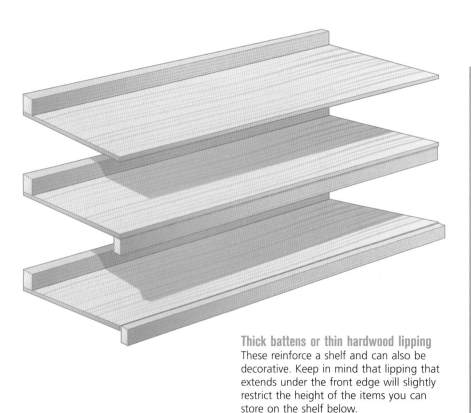

Thick battens or thin hardwood lipping These reinforce a shelf and can also be decorative. Keep in mind that lipping that extends under the front edge will slightly restrict the height of the items you can store on the shelf below.

POSITIONING THE BRACKETS

End supports Maximum bending occurs under heavy loads.

Supports set in Loads at each end balance the central load.

The bracket positions can give shelves greater resistance to bending. If the shelves extend beyond the brackets they are less likely to bend in the middle. But they must be fixed to the brackets with screws, otherwise they will tip up if a weight is placed at one end – when putting up the first pile of books, for example.

Finding your levels

When you are putting up shelves, the most important part of the job is getting the shelves horizontal and the brackets and tracks vertical.

Spirit level

Investing in a good spirit level is crucial. Levels are available in different lengths and designs, from miniature and pocket levels to long carpenter's levels and even digital levels that give a readout of a slope angle.

A spirit level has one or more clear vials filled with a liquid. When the level is truly horizontal, a bubble in the liquid floats within an area marked on the centre vial to indicate that it is exactly level (page 34).

Laser level

State-of-the-art laser levels fire a laser beam enabling horizontal or vertical guidelines to be marked quickly and accurately.

Laser levels have a wide range of uses including guaranteeing a consistent and accurate level for wall lights across a room or positioning brackets for shelves within an alcove. However, their strongest benefit is in establishing levels for setting out outdoor work, such as putting up fences or laying paving.

Using a plumb line

A plumb line is simply a weight tied to a length of string. If you hold it firmly at the top, it will hang vertically, provided that the string and weight are not touching anything. You can buy a plumb line, or make your own by tying a heavy nut to the end of a length of string.

Tools *Plumb line; a hardback book; a long screw; pencil; a long straightedge, such as a length of track from a shelving system.*

1 When fixing shelving track, mark and then drill the hole for the topmost fixing screw.

2 Plug the hole and partly drive a long screw into it.

3 Suspend the plumb line from the screw so that it hangs as close to the floor as possible.

4 Let the string become steady. Then place one edge of the book on the wall and slide it up to the string until they touch. Mark the wall where the corner of the book has come to rest.

5 Remove the book, string and screw. Using a track from the shelving system or a straight wooden batten, draw a line between the centre of the screw hole and the pencil mark. This line will be the centre line for the track or brackets to be fitted.

6 Other vertical lines on the wall can be measured from the first line, using a steel tape measure.

Putting up a fixed shelf

Whether for storage or display, fixed shelves must be sturdy, spacious and perfectly level.

Tools *Pencil; spirit level; drill; masonry or wood bit to fit wall plugs; screwdriver. Possibly a straight wooden batten.*

Materials *Brackets; screws for fixing brackets to wall; wall plugs to fit screws; shelf; small screws for fixing shelf to brackets.*

Before you start Check the walls with a battery-powered pipe and wire detector so as not to drill through any hidden pipes or cables. Use it to detect the positions of the studs on a timber-framed wall.

1 Hold a spirit level against the wall at the point where you want the shelf. Check that it is level and draw a light pencil line on the wall. For a long shelf, rest the spirit level on a straight wooden batten.

2 Hold one bracket against the wall with the top against the mark. Use the spirit level to check that it is vertical, and then mark the wall through the screw holes with the pencil.

HELPFUL TIPS

• Right-angled brackets will need screws about 45mm long to fix them to the wall. The screw must go through the plaster and at least 25mm into the brickwork, or into the wood stud if it is a stud partition wall.
• Don't use winged wall plugs to fix brackets to thin hollow walls unless the shelf is only to be used to hold a light decorative object.
• The screws should be the heaviest gauge that the holes in the bracket will take – usually No. 8 gauge on small ones and No. 10 or 12 on larger ones.

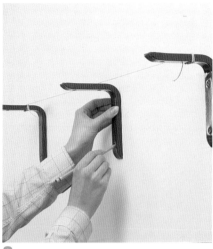

3 Repeat for the second bracket. If there are more than two brackets, it is best to fix the outside ones to the wall, and then tie a piece of string tightly between them across the tops. Then the intermediate brackets can be lined up exactly.

4 Drill holes about 45mm into the wall. Use a masonry bit (or a twist bit for wooden studs).

5 Insert plugs into masonry, and screw the brackets tightly to the wall. If the plug turns in the wall as you drive in the screw, remove it, insert a larger one and try again. Do not use plugs in wood.

6 Lay the shelf across the bracket. Using a pencil or bradawl, mark the underside of the shelf through the bracket holes.

7 Drill pilot holes for the small screws and screw the shelf into position.

Shelves in alcoves

An ideal place to fit shelves is in an alcove beside a chimney breast. This is best done using wooden battens cut and screwed to the side and rear walls of the alcove.

Positioning the battens

Tools *Tape measure; pencil; steel ruler; tenon saw; mitre box; spirit level; power drill; twist drill bits; masonry bits; countersink bit; screwdriver.*

Materials *Wood for battens 50 x 25mm; timber or MDF shelves cut to fit alcove; 63mm No. 8 screws and wall plugs; wood filler.*

Before you start Cut battens to the length of the back wall and shorter ones to the depth of each shelf. Drill and countersink screw holes no more than 300mm apart through each batten. Battens are fairly unobtrusive even if left square-ended, but to make them less noticeable the ends can be angled or curved.

1 Mark the position of each shelf, checking that the spacing between them is large enough for the items you want to store there – don't forget to allow for the thickness of the shelving material, too.

2 Hold the rear batten to the mark with a spirit level on top. Mark the wall through one end hole with the twist bit. Switch to a masonry bit and drill and plug the hole. Drive in a screw part way.

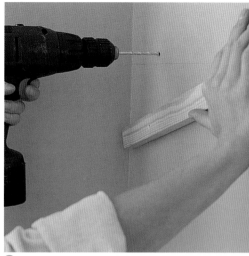

3 Hold the rear batten level and mark the other holes in the same way. Allow the batten to drop out of the way when you drill the wall, then plug the holes and drive the other screws.

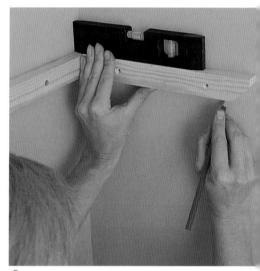

4 Position the first side batten, ensuring that it is level with the rear one. Mark the wall beneath it as a guide. Mark drill holes in the same way as for the rear batten. Repeat for the other side batten.

5 Screw the side battens into position. You will be able to hide the countersunk screw heads with wood filler.

Fitting the shelves

1 Few walls are true, and your alcove is unlikely to have perfect right angles. Hold a square of card in each internal angle, and if the alcove tapers, cut shelves to the narrower measurement and hide any gaps with beading once the shelves are in place.

2 After you have cut a shelf to fit, drill and countersink a couple of holes through each end and use woodscrews to secure the shelves to the battens.

3 You could strengthen the shelves and improve their appearance by stiffening them with beading fixed along the shelf fronts (page 162).

Adjustable track shelving systems

Track shelving systems consists of tracks which are fixed to a wall, plus brackets which fit on the tracks. Shelves can be raised or lowered by changing the positions of the brackets.

Putting up the tracks

Tools *Pencil; drill; masonry bit; screwdriver; straight wooden batten; spirit level; bradawl.*

Materials *Tracks and brackets; shelves; screws at least 50mm long to fix tracks to wall; wall plugs; screws to fix shelves to brackets.*

Before you start On a solid wall, you can drive the screws into wall plugs. In a hollow partition wall, locate the vertical studs using a cable and pipe detector (page 34) and screw directly into them.

1 Hold the first track to the wall and mark the position of the top screw with a pencil.

2 Using a spirit level or plumb line, draw a vertical line down the wall equal in length to the track.

3 Measure the position of the other tracks and draw similar vertical lines for each. Once the first vertical has been set, others can be measured off with a tape measure. Tracks are placed 700mm apart for 18mm chipboard or timber shelves, and 600mm apart for 15mm shelves.

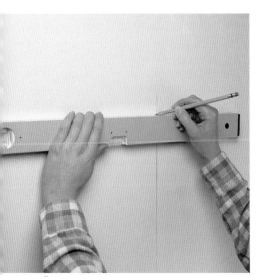

4 Use a spirit level to mark the position of the top screw hole on the other vertical lines, level with the first screw position.

Important Slotted tracks must be fixed at exactly the same height. Otherwise the shelves will not be level.

5 Drill and plug each top screw hole. Screw the tracks temporarily in position, but do not tighten. When they are all in place, check that their tops are level.

6 Use the bradawl or pencil to mark the positions of the other holes on the centre lines. Swing the tracks aside one by one, and drill and plug the holes.

7 Screw the tracks in position. As the screws tighten, watch the track to make certain it is not bending because of an uneven wall. Pack behind the track with hardboard or cardboard where hollows occur.

Putting on the shelves

1 Fit the brackets into the correct slots and put on the shelves. Shelves should be slightly wider than the brackets, but avoid wide overhangs which could tempt you to overload the system.

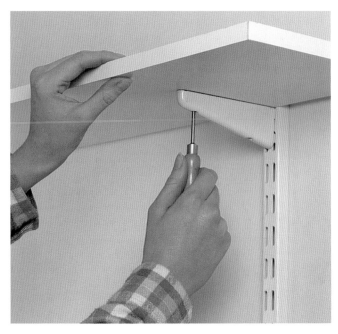

2 Line up the shelves so that their ends are above one another. Mark screw holes in the underside of the shelves by pushing the bradawl through the holes in the brackets.

3 Make pilot holes for the small screws with the bradawl, and screw the shelves in place. This improves the strength of the unit, prevents the shelves from tipping up if a heavy weight is put on one end, and stops them from sliding off if they are knocked.

THREE TRACKS FOR FLEXIBILITY

When only two tracks are used, the shelves can be adjusted for height, but each one must run the full width of the system.

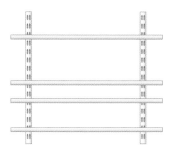

Three or more tracks enable shelves to go halfway at one height and the other half at a different height. This allows greater flexibility in storing objects of different sizes. Shelves of different depths can also be used.

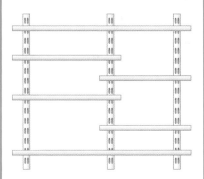

Whether two or three tracks are used, the closeness of the shelves in height is restricted by the depth of the bracket plus the thickness of the shelf.

Tailor-made shelving units

You can build shelf units to fit your own design anywhere you like. Compartments can be tailor-made for books, CDs, videos, a DVD or CD player, loudspeakers, or to display items like plates or ornaments.

Tailor-made units depend on vertical side panels to support the shelves and to hold the whole unit together. If these side panels move, the unit may collapse.

Four situations for tailor-made units

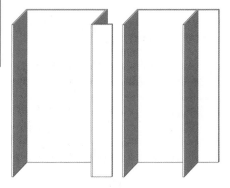

• If a unit is built within an alcove, secure the side panels to the walls (above left).

• Where one side panel is standing free, it must be secured along the whole length of its back edge to a batten screwed to the wall (above right).

• When both side panels are free, they should each be secured to the wall with battens (above left).

• For a free-standing unit, the most efficient stabiliser is a thin plywood or hardboard sheet fixed across the back (above right).

Choosing shelf supports

If you want shelves that can be moved, fit supports or support sockets to the two side panels. They can be regularly spaced at, say, 40mm intervals, or the spacing can vary. There is no point in having holes too near to the top or bottom of the unit. If the shelves are not to be moved, no extra supports are needed.

• If you are using peg-type supports, two will be needed to support each end of each shelf. Set them a short distance in from the front and back edges – for example, 20mm on shelves 200mm wide.

• Always drill holes to match exactly the diameter of peg-type supports. If the holes are too small the supports will not fit; if they are too large the supports will sag and the shelves will not be level. Keep the drill at 90° to the side panel. Wind a piece of masking tape around the bit to mark the depth of the hole.

Socket and peg (push-fit)
Plastic. The peg is pushed into a plastic socket fitted into a hole in the side panel. For an adjustable system you will need one socket for every hole in the side panels, but only four pegs per shelf.

Socket and peg (push and rotate)
Plastic. The peg is pushed (upside down) into a plastic socket in the side panel, then turned right way up to lock it in position. For an adjustable system you will need one socket for every hole in the side panels, but only four pegs per shelf.

Fixed peg (non-adjustable)
Plastic. The peg is tapped into the side panel as far as it will go. Adjust with pliers so that the flat surface is horizontal. Avoid pulling pegs out of coated or veneered board as they may tear the surface.

Dowel pegs (non-adjustable)
Natural wood (can be stained, varnished or painted). Drill holes exactly the diameter of the dowels, to about 10mm deep. Insert 25mm-long dowels. A too-tight fit can be eased with abrasive paper.

Nail-on shelf supports
Plastic, nails supplied. Position the supports on the side panels, and drive in the nail with a pin hammer.

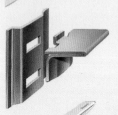

Slotted metal strip (also called bookcase strip)
Metal. Mark centre lines for two strips on each side panel, and a horizontal line to align the slots. Screw the strips in place and hook the shelf supports into the slots, allowing four for each shelf.

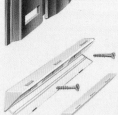

Shelf bearer
Plastic. Chipboard screws also needed – 19mm No. 6, six per pair. Use a single bearer for shelves 150–200mm wide. Use two side-by-side for shelves 300–480mm wide. Screw the bearers to the panels and close the cover strips.

Battens
Natural wood (can be stained, varnished or painted) in timber of almost any size. Cut battens as long as the shelf width or use block sections for very small shelves. Use two screws on battens up to 150mm long, three from 150–230mm and four beyond that.

Making the corners rigid

A unit with one or more free-standing side panels should be made completely rigid with plastic corner joints screwed to the top and bottom shelves and the sides. If the unit is high, one or two of the intermediate shelves should also be secured with corner joints.

Fixing side panels to the walls of an alcove

Instead of fixing battens straight to the walls of an alcove, you can fix vertical side panels and suspend the shelves from these. Side panels must be at right angles to the back wall. They must also be vertical and parallel to one another.

If, as is often the case, the walls are not flat, square or upright, the side panels will have to be mounted on spacer battens.

Gaps between the walls and the side panels can be concealed with timber strips, scribed to the shape of the wall and pinned into place.

Shelving with vertical dividers

Vertical divisions make shelves stronger, and also provide partitions to separate one area from another – books divided from hi-fi equipment, for example. As the divisions prevent long shelves from bending under heavy loads, they are particularly useful in wide shelving units.

The dividers must transfer the weight onto something solid or the shelves will still bend. There is no advantage in fitting a divider partway up a unit if you do not put more dividers below to carry the weight down to the floor or some other support.

Fixing dividers in place

• Shelf dividers can be joined to the upper and lower shelves with 38mm No. 8 chipboard screws, or oval nails or panel pins, driven down through the top shelves and up through the bottom shelves. This method is fairly simple, but requires great care to ensure that the fixings enter the centre of the dividers and do not break out to one side. Drill narrow pilot holes through the shelves to guide nails or panel pins. Shelves up to 150mm wide need two fixings into a divider at top or bottom; wider shelves need a further fixing for each extra 150mm.

• Fix the dividers to the shelves with dowel joints (page 169). The joints are invisible on the surfaces of the shelves and are structurally sounder than screws or nails. But they take longer to make.

• Join the divider to the shelves with two small corner blocks (page 168) top and bottom. The joints will obstruct the bottom corner on one side of the divider.

• Shelf dividers cut from thick timber – 50mm or more in diameter – need no fixing.

Fitting the dividers

The height of vertical dividers must be exactly the same as the distance between shelves. If they are too long or short the shelves will be out of true. They must also be cut perfectly square at the ends.

1 Plan the positions of the dividers and get them cut square and to exact size. Have all the other components cut to size and ready to assemble.

2 Number each of the shelves from top to bottom, using a soft pencil. Also mark each shelf 'top', 'bottom' and 'front', so there is no confusion as you build the unit.

3 If the gap between shelves varies from shelf to shelf, mark each divider with the numbers of the shelves it is to fit between.

4 Stand each pair of adjacent shelves on edge with the front edges uppermost, and the top face of the lower shelf against the bottom face of the upper shelf. Mark the positions of the two faces across the two edges with a pencil and try square. Mark two lines to indicate the thickness of the divider.

5 Open the boards out flat so that the inner faces are uppermost. Using a try square, mark the positions of the dividers across the faces from the marks on the edges. The fixings must be centred between the two lines.

6 Repeat the marking process with each pair of shelves.

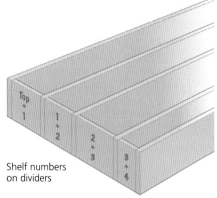

Shelf numbers on dividers

7 Before going any further, double-check that the height of the dividers and the thickness of the shelves measures up to what was expected. Stand the dividers and shelves on their back edges in numbered order. Then move the dividers to one end of the shelves so that an accurate measurement can be taken. Reduce the height of one or more dividers if the unit is over-height, or have a larger one cut.

8 If you are making a free-standing unit, mark out the joints between the top, bottom and side panels. Assemble them and then undo the fixings.

9 Assemble the shelves and dividers in their numbered order, on the floor.

10 For free-standing units, complete the construction by rejoining the side panels to the top and bottom. Line the shelves up so that they are parallel with one another and check that the front edges are flush or set back as required. Join them to the sides with corner joints.

11 For shelves and dividers which are to fit into an alcove or between sides that are already fixed; carefully lift the assembly and slide it between the uprights. Then join the shelf ends to the upright sides with shelf supports.

SUPPORTING SHELVES ON BEAMS

If you do not want to continue vertical shelf dividers down to the ground, the weight can be supported by wooden beams fixed to the bottom shelf.
• Fit the beams along the full length of the underside of the shelf close to both the front and the back edges.
• Long shelves with heavy loads require thicker beams than short shelves or shelves with light loads.

Size of beam for average loads

Shelf length	Beam cross-section
Up to 1m	50 x 25mm
1–1.5m	75 x 25mm
Over 1.5m	100 x 25mm

Building shelf compartments of different heights

When you are constructing a tailor-made shelf unit you may not want all the shelves to be the same height across their full width. You can build a unit with compartments of different sizes to suit the items you want to store there.

Adjustable shelves

The simplest and most versatile solution to flexible shelving is to divide your unit vertically with one or more upright panels extending to the full height of the unit. Use dowel joints or corner joints to fix each upright firmly in position, making sure that it is perfectly vertical.

Drill two lines of evenly spaced dowel holes in each side panel to take socket-and-peg shelf supports (page 166). You can then position shelves at any height within each section of the unit and move them easily if you need to rearrange your storage.

If the shelves on either side of a vertical support are to align, you must stagger the position of the dowel holes so that the pegs on opposite sides do not clash. Drill the line of holes in one side of the dividing panel at a slightly different distance from the front and back from the holes in the other side.

Fixed shelves

To make a truly tailor-made shelf unit, plan exactly what you intend to store and how much room it will require, then build compartments of exactly the right dimensions.

Follow the instructions for constructing the side and back panels of a shelving unit and adding vertical shelf dividers given on pages 166–7. Position the vertical dividers wherever they are needed, using them to support the ends of shelves where they extend to the height of two or more shelves or to support a very wide shelf that is liable to sag. The vertical dividers do not need to be in line with one another.

Self-assembly fixings for flat-pack furniture

When you buy an item of flat-pack furniture, it comes with fixing holes already drilled and special types of fixing to enable you to assemble it yourself easily and with the minimum number of tools. Often all you need is a special spanner or hex key supplied with the unit. Here are some of the most common fixings that you are likely to encounter.

Many of these are also available to buy separately so that you can use them when making your own units. Always use fittings in pairs and use a steel ruler, not a tape measure, when marking where to drill – it is essential for drill holes to be accurately positioned if the unit is to be square when assembled.

Two block fitting (Lok joint)

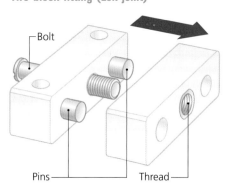

The joint consists of two plastic blocks and is normally used to join two sections of cupboard together such as a side to the base. One of the blocks is screwed to the base and the other to the side into pre-drilled holes; a bolt is then screwed in to hold the two sections firmly together. One of the advantages of this type of fixing is that it can be disassembled and reassembled whenever necessary with no loss of strength.

Plastic corner block

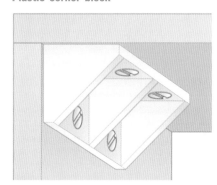

One of the simplest of the fittings that is often found in flat pack furniture. Plastic corner blocks hold two panels together at a perfect right angle. As screws are driven into the carcase material, this fitting cannot be taken apart and reused without compromising its strength.

Build a shelving unit that perfectly suits your requirements by tailor-making the shelf heights and widths according to what you want to store there. Plan your storage before you start and position fixed or adjustable shelves in appropriate places.

Dowels

Dowels are for more permanent joints and those that are not to be taken apart once assembled. Usually about 25–30mm long, they are glued in place. Like the majority of the fixings used in flat pack furniture they are tapped into factory-made pre-drilled holes. Although simple they are very effective and give a strong concealed joint.

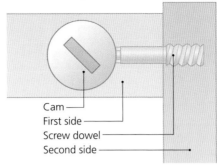

Dowel and screw fitting

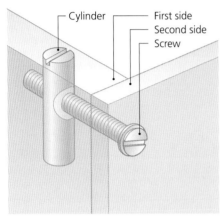

Cylinder — First side
Second side
Screw

These are one of the most popular joints used in flat pack furniture. The cylinder is inserted into a factory-made pre-drilled hole in one side of the cabinet. A machine screw is then inserted into a hole in the other side until it meets the cylinder. The two components are tightened with a screwdriver until both sides of the cabinet pull together. The slot in the head of the cylinder part of the fitting allows you to align it so that it will receive the screw (below). Although it is possible to over-tighten these fittings they do hold very securely and can be repeatedly taken apart with no loss of strength.

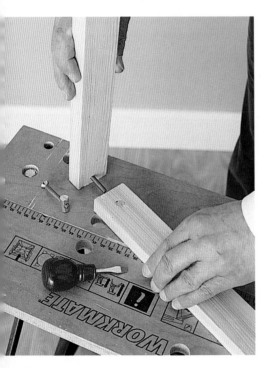

Cam lock fittings

Cam
First side
Screw dowel
Second side

Like the dowel and screw fitting, this fastening is for joining two planks or panels together. The cam is dropped into a shallow recess on the face of one part and a screw with a pronounced head or a steel screw dowel is driven into a pre-drilled hole in the other part to be joined.

The head of the screw passes through a clearance hole in the first part and into the cam. Turning the cam 90° clockwise tightens the joint.

Some cam fittings come with the peg attached to a disc the same size as the cam. Both components slot into pre-drilled holes in the panels to be joined.

Another variation on this type of fitting replaces the peg with a special moulding like a wall plug. This is pushed into a hole drilled in the edge of the second board. A pin is driven into the plug and the fitting is assembled as before.

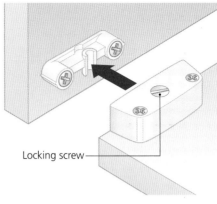

Locking screw

This cam fitting is similar to the Lok joint. The two parts of the joint are screwed into separate panels. The two panels are then brought together and the screw is turned through 90° to lock the joint.

Dowel and bush fitting

This fitting consists of a zinc alloy bush and a steel dowel. Screw the dowel into the face of one board so that when it is butt-jointed with the second board it will align with the hole drilled in the second board's edge. The dowel reaches the bush through that hole and is locked in place by turning the grub screw in the bush.

Housing and bolt fitting

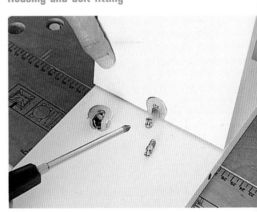

A bolt screws into the side panel of a cupboard or shelf unit and fits into the housing, which slots into a hole drilled in the underside of the shelf. These fittings are useful for strengthening shelves in an existing unit or for adding extra shelves.

Assembling flat-pack furniture

Whether you are putting together a simple bookshelf, a small bathroom cabinet or a more complex piece of flat-pack furniture, such as a computer desk with a sliding shelf, follow these steps to success.

Most flat-pack units consist of a series of panels that are fitted together to create a basic box. Extras, such as doors, shelves and internal fittings, are then added to this to complete the job. Always work in a logical order, following the instructions that came with the unit.

1 Unpack the kit and lay out all the components, including the assembly fittings and any other items of hardware such as hinges, handles and feet. Lay the panels on a carpet, other soft surface or the box they were supplied in to minimise scratches.

2 Identify all the parts, using the instructions, and check that you have the right number of fixings – there is usually a numbered checklist included with the instructions. If any appear to be missing, look inside the packaging to see if any are loose inside. If you still cannot locate the missing pieces, return the complete unit to the store and ask for a replacement.

3 Start with the base panel, adding any fixed feet first of all. Build tall units, such as bookshelves or wardrobes, on their backs to make the assembly manageable. If the unit has castors or wheels, fit these last or the unit will keep moving about as you try to assemble it.

4 Connect the first side panel to the base panel. The simplest units have pre-drilled holes through which you can drive screws supplied with the furniture (above). Many units use a combination of glued dowels and cam fixings (pages 168–9). In this case, place the dowels and screwed pegs in the base unit and then offer up the side panel. Glue and locate all the dowels in the side panel, then tighten the fixings.

5 Connect the second side panel to make a three-sided box. If the unit has a back panel, locate this in the grooves in the side panels and slide it into place. Then finish the box by fixing the top panel in position.

6 Many fixings come with cover discs that match the colour of the wood or veneer of the finished item. These make a tidy job of disguising the fixings once the furniture is complete. They can be prised out of their holes if you need access to the fixings to dismantle the furniture.

7 Follow the instructions with the unit to add any doors. They will be hung on some form of spring-loaded hinges, and the fitting and fixing holes will all be pre-drilled in the doors and cabinet sides. Fit the hinge body to the door and the mounting plate to the cabinet sides, then connect the two with the short machine screws and adjust them so they hang squarely.

8 Add any shelves, door handles and other internal or external fittings. Double-check that all the assembly fittings are tight, and that you do not have any parts left over. Finally, fit wheels or castors if these are part of the kit.

Building a computer desk

Large items of flat-pack furniture are constructed using special fixings (pages 168–9). Follow the instructions that come with the unit, using these standard techniques to guide you.

Tools *Selection of screwdrivers; perhaps a hammer; perhaps a set of hex keys.*

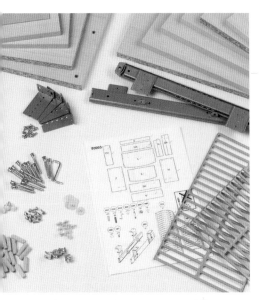

Before you start Unpack the box and lay out all the pieces and fixings. Check them against the instructions and make sure that they are all there and you know which piece is which. Often, a right and left hand piece look almost identical until you check where the fixing holes have been drilled.

1 Insert cam lock screw dowels into pre-drilled holes according to the instructions.

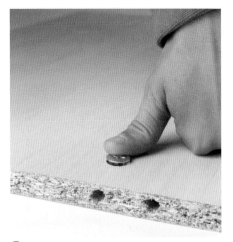

2 Use your thumb to push the cam locks into the large holes on the opposing panels, making sure that the arrow on the fitting points towards the holes on the raw outside edge of the workpiece. The cam lock pins fit into these holes, so if the locks don't face in the right direction the fixings will not work.

3 Begin to put the piece together in the order specified in the instructions. In this instance the lock pins are screwed into the cam locks using the special key supplied as part of the kit.

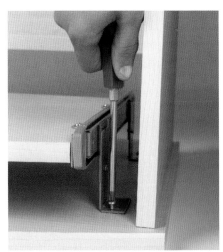

4 This workstation has a sliding keyboard table. The runners for the sliding section are fitted to the keyboard table, and then fixed to the underside of the desk. You will need to turn the desk upside down to make the fixings.

WHEN GLUING IS BEST

If you know that you will not be taking the furniture apart again at some time in the future, consider using adhesive on wood-to-wood joints for a sturdier finished piece. Ordinary white carpenters' PVA adhesive is ideal. Use a damp rag to wipe off any excess adhesive that squeezes from the joints.

5 Make up the shelf section that sits on top of the desk. This fits onto dowels that have been tapped into the desktop with a hammer. Fit the top to the base and push them together to ensure all the dowels have engaged. If you need to, hammer from above, being sure to protect the workpiece with some scrap timber.

6 Finish the item by adding any accessories. In this instance a simple plastic rack for CDs slots into the narrow stack to the left of the desk.

Choosing curtain poles and tracks

Tracks and poles come in many styles, materials and lengths. Decide on the look you wish to achieve, and then choose the components you need.

If you are not happy with the existing curtain rails or tracks in a window, or you wish to change them, there are several factors to take into account.

Privacy Is the window open to the street or overlooked by neighbours?

Light How much light comes into the room naturally, and how much more or less do you want?

Security Do you want your curtains to be open and closed automatically while you are out?

Style Is the room traditional or modern? Will old-fashioned drapes be right, or does it need minimalist blinds or sun-filters?

Once you have decided on these basic characteristics, you can set about choosing the poles and tracks to suit the window.

Bracket for wall or ceiling mounting — Endstop — Finial — Combined glider-hook

Uncorded track for mounting on brackets, and fitted with combined glider hooks

Bracketless track for top fixing — Glider — Endstop

Bracketless track for face fixing — Glider — Endstop

Bracketless track for concealed face fixing — Glider — Endstop

Brackets for ceiling fixing — Built-in cording unit — Glider — Ready-corded track for mounting on brackets — Bracket for wall fixing

Continuous track Buy all the fittings when you buy the track; the right ones could be out of stock or discontinued later. Tracks are made of steel, aluminium or plastic. Brackets to hold the track in place can be screwed into the wall or the ceiling. Some tracks fit flush to the ceiling. Bracketless tracks screw direct into a wall, ceiling or window recess. Gliders on the tracks carry the curtain hooks. Some tracks have combined glider-hooks. Endstops or finials stop the gliders running off the track ends.

Concealed track A track concealed by a pelmet or valance can be cheaper and less streamlined than one that will be on view. The brackets for holding it in place can be fixed to either wall or ceiling. The track is usually fitted in two halves with a central overlap held by a special bracket.

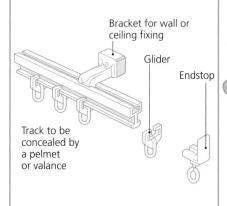

Bracket for wall or ceiling fixing — Glider — Endstop — Track to be concealed by a pelmet or valance

Poles Poles are generally used for straight runs. However, there are metal pole kits which are designed to fit right-angled bay windows. Standard poles are made in wood, metal and plastic. Some have rings encircling them, others have half-rings attached to gliders in a track inside the pole. Poles with glider tracks often have a built-in central overlap arm. Usually brackets are needed only at the ends, but a pole that is 2.4m or longer will need an extra bracket at the centre. Two-part brackets can hold the pole at different distances from the wall. There are side-fixed brackets for some poles. Finials on the ends of the pole act as endstops.

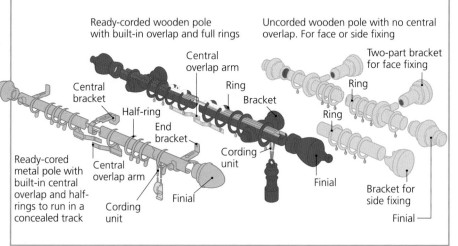

Ready-corded wooden pole with built-in overlap and full rings — Central overlap arm — Ring — Bracket — Central bracket — Half-ring — End bracket — Cording unit — Finial

Uncorded wooden pole with no central overlap. For face or side fixing — Two-part bracket for face fixing — Ring — Ring — Finial — Bracket for side fixing — Finial

Ready-cored metal pole with built-in central overlap and half-rings to run in a concealed track — Central overlap arm — Cording unit — Finial

Bay window tracks Many tracks will bend round bay windows. The maker's instructions show how much each type will bend. Some shops will bend steel track for you to the perfect shape. In a right-angled bay, you can fit three straight sections of track with connector pieces at the corners. Curtain the three sides separately.

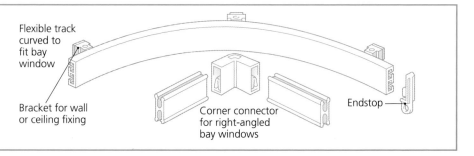

Flexible track curved to fit bay window — Bracket for wall or ceiling fixing — Corner connector for right-angled bay windows — Endstop

Wires and rods for nets Net and sheer curtains that are not opened and closed can be hung on a plastic-coated spring wire or on a plastic-coated extending metal rod. Café curtains can also be hung on wires or extending rods, or on slender poles with loops.

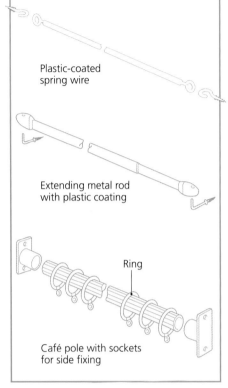

Plastic-coated spring wire

Extending metal rod with plastic coating

Ring

Café pole with sockets for side fixing

Roller blinds Blinds of various sizes and styles are available as kits which come with fitting instructions. The holding brackets are fitted to the wall or the window frame at either end of the roller, which is operated by a pulley cord. To remove a blind quickly and easily, prise it out of the snap-lock bracket with a screwdriver (below). Blinds with wooden poles and simple pins can be lifted out of their brackets.

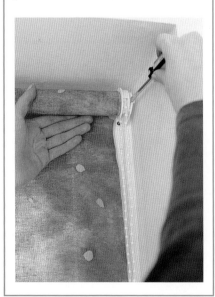

OPTIONAL FITTINGS FOR TRACKS AND POLES

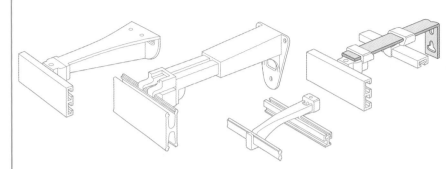

Extension bracket with fixed arm Extension brackets fitted instead of standard brackets will hold a track farther out from the wall – so that the curtains clear a projecting sill or a wooden window surround, for example.

Adjustable bracket This type of bracket has a sliding arm that you can adjust to project different amounts.

Clip-on bracket for a valance rail Secondary brackets clipped onto the main track will carry the rail for a valance.

Bracket to hold two tracks This bracket carries two tracks – one for the main curtain and another for a net curtain behind it.

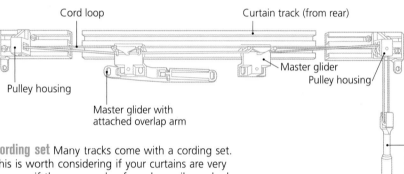

Cord loop

Curtain track (from rear)

Pulley housing

Master glider with attached overlap arm

Master glider

Pulley housing

Bracket to fix tension arm to wall or floor

Cord tension arm

Cording set Many tracks come with a cording set. This is worth considering if your curtains are very long, or if they are made of a pale, easily marked fabric. These tracks tend to be suitable for straight runs only. The cords pass through master gliders and round pulleys at the track ends. They may be pulled by two weighted knobs or may pass through a tension arm.

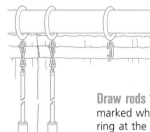

Draw rods To keep curtains made of delicate fabric from being marked when handled, fit draw rods. They clip into a glider or ring at the meeting edge of each curtain. They are available in several lengths and finishes.

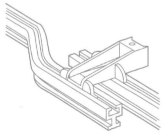

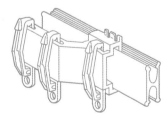

Fixed overlap arm A track behind a pelmet or valance is fitted in two halves and made to overlap by a bracket.

Sliding overlap arm For most continuous tracks there are overlap arms that slide along the track like gliders. The arm carries the leading edge of one curtain over the other.

How to put up a track or pole

It's important to let as much light as possible into a room, so let the track or pole extend far enough at the sides for even the bulkiest of curtains to draw back clear of the window.

Tools *Long wood or metal rule; pencil; bradawl; drill with wood or masonry bit; screwdriver.*

Materials *Track/pole. Perhaps a length of batten; wall plugs; plasterboard plugs; brackets or sockets, 38mm No. 6 screws; screw eyes; gliders or rings; end stops or finials.*

Before you start Most tracks or poles must be screwed into sound ceiling timbers or plugs in a wall; extra brackets on ceilings may be screwed into plasterboard plugs. The screws supplied with a track or pole are not always long enough to make secure fixings: replace them if necessary. Don't saw off any excess track or pole until you are certain there is enough overlap at either end.

Fixing brackets for a track on the wall

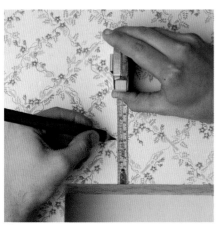

1 Mark the fixing height for the track at least 50mm above the top of the window. Brackets on which a track slots down should be at least 20mm below the ceiling to allow room for fitting the track. Brackets for clip-on tracks can be up against the ceiling.

2 Measure up from the window top every 200mm across and make pencil marks at the right height. If the track or pole is to be nearer the ceiling than the window top, measure down from the ceiling. Neither window top nor ceiling is necessarily horizontal. The track should be parallel to whichever of the two is closer or it will always look crooked.

3 Join the pencil marks with a straight line and extend it at the sides to the width of the track. Mark positions for the brackets with pencil crosses on the guide-line. Put one 50mm from each end. Space others about 300mm apart, or as specified in the manufacturer's instructions.

4 At each cross drill through the plaster into the lintel and insert a plug. On a concrete lintel, use a hammer drill. Screw a bracket into each plug.

Fixing brackets on the ceiling

1 Draw a pencil guideline on the ceiling parallel with the top of the wall where you want the track to be. Locate the joists (using a pipe and cable detector, page 34) and mark them with a pencil. If they run at right angles to the window, mark spots for drilling where the pencil guideline and the joists cross, and also 50mm from the ends of the track if the ceiling is plasterboard; do not make such hollow fixings at the ends into a lath and plaster ceiling.

On a plasterboard ceiling you can mark extra drilling places between the joists if the curtains are heavy, or if the track is going to be curved and needs a bracket to hold the curve at a point where there is no joist.

Alternatively For particularly heavy curtains, skew-nail wooden struts between the joists and drill into the struts 50mm from the ends of the track and about every 300mm between them to provide extra fixing

FIXING TO JOISTS THAT RUN PARALLEL WITH THE WINDOW

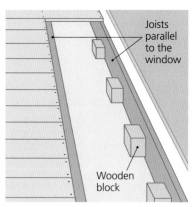

Joists parallel to the window

Wooden block

If the joists run parallel with the window and are not positioned conveniently to hold the bracket screws, you can fix wooden blocks to the side of the joist to give fixings up to 100mm away. Mark spots on the ceiling for drilling into the blocks.

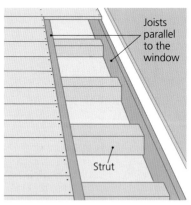

Joists parallel to the window

Strut

If the joists run parallel with the window and are more than 100mm away from the points where you need to make fixing, fit wooden struts between the joists. You can fit a strut wherever you need to fix a bracket. Mark spots for drilling into the struts.

points. This method of fixing makes sure that every bracket is screwed securely into timber above the ceiling. If you cannot gain access to the loft or the floor above the window to fix wood to the joists, a wall-fixed track is safest.

2 Drill through the ceiling at the marked spots and into the timber where possible. Where you have not drilled into timber, insert a plasterboard plug through the hole.

3 Screw the brackets into the timber or plugs (unless the track has slide-in brackets; see Fitting the track, opposite).

Fixing to a window surround

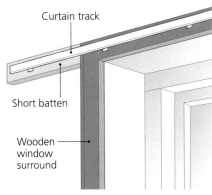

Curtain track

Short batten

Wooden window surround

Windows with wooden surrounds on the wall surface may seem to offer easy fixing points for brackets. However, the track cannot extend beyond the sides of the window. This excludes too much daylight because the curtains cannot be drawn back to clear the glass. Fix a wooden batten at each side of the window to extend the fixing width.

Fixing brackets in a recess

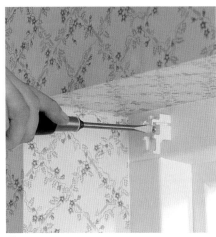

1 For tracks in a window recess, screw the brackets securely into the window frame, if it is wooden.

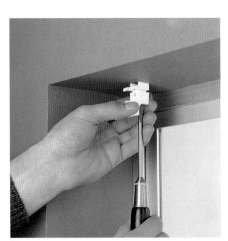

2 Where the frame is metal or PVC, screw the brackets upwards with 38mm No. 6 screws into drilled, plugged holes.

Fixing a concealed track

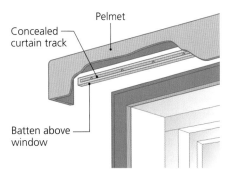

Pelmet

Concealed curtain track

Batten above window

Where a pelmet or valance is going to cover the curtain track, fix a wooden batten above the window and screw the brackets for the track into the batten.

Fitting the track
• With a wall-fixed track, clip or slot it onto the brackets.
• With a ceiling-fixed track of the clip-on type, clip the track to the brackets.
• With a ceiling-fixed track that has a channel for the brackets to slide into, position the brackets on the track before screwing them into place.
    Once the track is in position, slide on the gliders and fit the end stops or finials in place.

Fixing a pole to the wall

1 Draw a guideline on the wall as for fixing brackets for a track on the wall (opposite).

2 Measure how far above the centre of the bracket the screw hole is and make the drilling marks that distance above the line; 100mm from each end, and in the centre if needed.

Alternatively If the bracket is in two parts, make drilling marks on the guideline through the holes on the mounting plate.

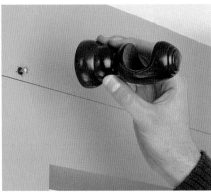

3 Drill and plug the holes. Drive in the screws, letting the heads project; or screw in place the plates for two-part brackets. Fit the brackets in place.

4 Position the pole, centring it on the brackets, and slide on the rings. Make sure that one ring is outside each end bracket

FITTING A ROLLER BLIND
If the window is in a recess, decide whether to fix the blind inside or outside the recess. If inside, measure the full width, from one side of the recess to the other. This will give you the size of the roller blind kit you require. If the blind is to go outside the recess, add 50mm.
    If the exact size of roller you need is not available, buy the next size up and cut it down by sawing the pole and trimming fabric with scissors.

Hold each bracket in its position inside the recess as near the top as possible and mark the screw holes for drilling. Make sure the brackets will be level and the same distance from the front of the recess. For a blind outside the recess, make the drilling marks 50mm above the top of the recess, and again make sure that the brackets will be level.
    Drill and plug the holes, and screw the brackets into place. Then fit the blind by clipping it into the brackets according to the manufacturer's instructions.

and the remainder between the brackets. Push the finials firmly into place at each end of the pole.

5 Drive the screw provided into the hole in the base of each bracket until it bites into the pole. This prevents the pole from being dislodged.

Fixing wires and rods

The wires and rods for net or café curtains are held by screw hooks. Screw them to the window frame if it is made of wood; if it is metal or PVC, screw them into drilled and plugged holes in the sides of the window recess.
    Some rods are held in place by sockets. One type is face-fixed; screw the sockets into wooden window frames. Another type is side-fixed for use where a window frame is not wooden; screw these into drilled and plugged holes in the sides of the recess.

Putting up plasterboard coving

Coving gives a decorative finish to the joint where the ceiling and wall meets, and also covers any unsightly gaps and cracks.

Tools *Tape measure; pencil; coving mitre box; fine-toothed saw; wide filling knife; ceiling props; hammer.*

Materials *Coving; coving adhesive; masonry nails.*

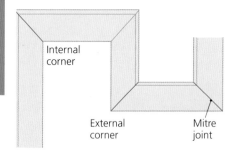

Internal corner

External corner

Mitre joint

You will need to cut mitres to join pieces of coving at internal and external corners. Use the diagram above to guide you when making your cuts.

1 Begin at an internal corner. Put a full length of coving in the mitre box with the edge that will fit against the ceiling resting on the base of the box. Cut the first mitre so it will fit into a left-hand corner.

2 Use a filling knife to butter coving adhesive along both edges of the coving. Spread an even layer about 10mm thick all the way along, but do not let too much adhesive past the flat edge sections. This will not help to stick the coving in place and will be a waste.

3 Press the coving in place against the wall and ceiling, with the mitred end in the corner. Ask a helper to hold the other end until the adhesive sticks. Alternatively, prop the coving up with a length of wood. Or drive a few masonry nails through the coving and into the wall plaster only; pull them out and fill the holes once the adhesive has set. Trim off extra adhesive.

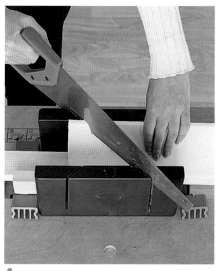

4 Cut a reverse mitre on another length of coving to join with your first cut. Position the coving so that it is facing the opposite way in the mitre box with the saw running in the other pair of guide slots.

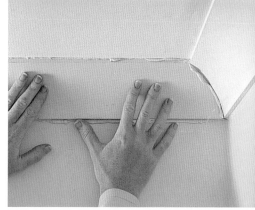

5 Spread adhesive on the coving and on the mitred end. Place it in position, pushing the mitred end against the mitred end of the length already in place. Trim off any excess adhesive along the length and from the mitre joint.

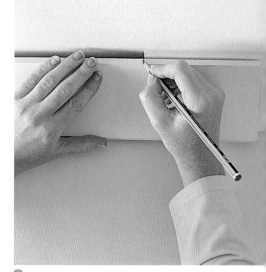

6 Repeat steps 1 to 5 for each internal corner. To make an external corner, cut coving as shown in the diagram (far left).

If a wall requires just two lengths of coving, mark and cut the second one to meet the square end of the first one partway along the wall. If the wall needs three lengths or more, fit the corner lengths at both ends, then cut one or more square-ended lengths to bridge the gap between them.

Restoring a cornice

Old cornice (ornate decorative moulding) is often clogged with paint.

1 If the cornice has been painted with a modern paint, you will have to apply paint remover. Remove accumulations of distemper by soaking a small area at a time with warm water applied with a house-plant hand sprayer. Spray repeatedly for about half an hour until the distemper has been thoroughly soaked.

2 Pick out the paint carefully with an old screwdriver, taking care not to damage the plasterwork.

3 Remove loose material with a brush so that you can see the areas that still need cleaning.

Repairing a broken cornice

If parts of the cornice have broken away, it can often be repaired with plaster of paris.

1 Mix the plaster of paris with water to a stiff paste – only a little at a time as it sets in about 3 minutes.

2 Damp the surface of the cornice, then use plaster of paris to build up the moulding in layers, using a clay modelling tool or a small knife.

Alternatively Traditional cornice lengths, ceiling roses and beadings made of fibrous plaster are available from specialist firms.

Fitting picture rails and dados

These timber mouldings will break up high walls. Fix picture rails 450–600mm below ceiling level – they are often level with the top of the door surround. Dado rails were traditionally fitted to protect the wall from chair backs and are now usually positioned at about waist height.

Tools *Pencil; straightedge; spirit level; tape measure; tenon saw; abrasive paper; power drill; coping saw; twist, countersink and masonry drill bits; screwdriver; mitre box; portable workbench; filling knife.*

Materials *Mouldings to fit walls; screws and wall plugs; wood filler.*

Before you start Buy only mouldings that are dead straight and have no large knots.

1 To fit the rail, mark a pencil line along the walls at the required height using a straight-edge and spirit level or laser level.

2 Begin at a corner. Cut the first piece of moulding to length if it runs up to an obstacle such as a door frame and sand down the sawn edge. Mark positions for screw holes at 600mm intervals on the rail. Countersink holes, or the bit may make a ragged hole. Drill the holes with a twist bit.

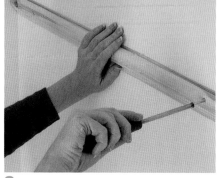

3 Line up the rail with the pencil line, and mark fixing positions on the wall through screw holes. Drill holes in the wall and plug them. Drive one end screw almost all the way in, then the other end screw. Fit the rest of the screws and tighten them all.

4 On long walls you will need more than one length of moulding. Avoid a gap opening up over time by cutting the ends that are to meet at a 45° angle. You can use a mitre box to do this (see opposite).

Tackling corners

1 A butt joint is the best choice at an internal corner, with the end of one rail scribed and cut to fit against the face of the next section. Draw the shape of the rail on the back of the next length, following the shape of a moulding offcut.

GLUING RAILS IN PLACE

You can fix rails to a wall by applying instant-grip adhesive and holding the moulding in place until the adhesive grips. This takes less time, but the rail cannot then be moved without damaging the plaster.

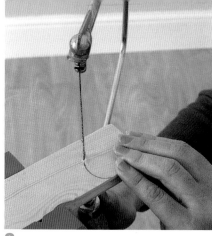

2 Use a coping saw to cut along the marked line. Sand the cut edge and make sure that it fits. Any gaps can be masked later on with wood filler.

3 Drill holes in the cut moulding, and drill and plug holes in the wall. Apply woodworking adhesive to the scribed end, place it in position and drive in the fixing screws. Remove extra adhesive with a damp cloth.

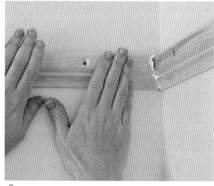

4 When taking a rail round an external corner, mitre the joint. Cut the pieces so the joint fits as closely as possible, and glue the angled pieces together as you attach the sections to the wall. If necessary, pin the joint to secure it.

5 Make sure screw heads are countersunk and nail heads are punched well below the surface. Cover the heads with wood filler.

REMOVING A RAIL

Remove an unwanted picture rail or dado by prising it away from its backing using a mallet and an old, wide wood chisel. Start at the centre of the longest length and ease it gently away, working from both edges. Wedge between the backing and the moulding with a scrap of wood or hardboard as soon as possible.

Having removed the rail, make good any holes in the plaster or any other damage. The gap left by the rail can be difficult to disguise if the plaster above and below the rail is at different levels due to the wall having been plastered after the rail was fitted.

Putting up or replacing architraves

Architraves are strips of timber moulding used to cover a joint between woodwork and a wall, such as round a door or window frame. They can be decorative or plain.

Tools *Trimming knife; chisel; pencil; mitre saw or mitre box and tenon saw; hammer; nail punch; cartridge gun.*

Materials *Architrave moulding; scrap wood; 38mm oval wire nails; woodworking adhesive; 25mm panel pins; acrylic mastic.*

Before you start Ensure new mouldings are straight, flat and as wide as any you are replacing. If they are narrower, you will need to redecorate the wall around the door, and there will be a gap between the architrave and the skirting board. If the mouldings are wider, notch the ends of the side pieces so they fit round skirting boards.

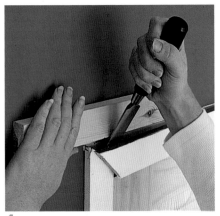

1 If you are removing an old architrave, run a knife blade between the architrave and the door frame to break the paint seal. Prise off the top section with a wide chisel while using scrap wood to protect the wall.

2 Remove the two side mouldings. Insert the blade of the chisel under a moulding from the wall edge if you can; otherwise, slide it between moulding and door frame.

3 Position a length of new moulding against the door frame, with the bottom edge of the moulding resting on the floor. Mark the position of the inside of the mitre joint on it with a pencil. Check you are sawing in the right direction, then cut the mitre, using a mitre box and tenon saw, or a precision mitre saw.

4 Hold the moulding against the door frame, line up its inner edge with the paint line on the frame and hammer nails into the moulding. Space the nails about 450mm apart. Use a nail punch to drive the heads just below the surface. Fit the other side moulding in the same way.

PIN MITRED CORNERS

For a really thorough job, pin the mitred joints of architraves together, even though they are already glued in place. Pinning will prevent the joints from gradually opening up. This is most often a problem with door frames in stud partition walls, because the walls may move slightly if the door slams, and this loosens adhesive holding the joint in place.

5 Before fixing the top section in place, place a short length of moulding upside down across the tops of the side mouldings, and mark on it the positions of the mitre joints. Then cut the two mitres at the marks and sand the edges smooth.

6 Add a little woodworking adhesive to each end of the top section, then position the section between the side mouldings. Fix it to the door frame with two nails. Use a damp cloth to remove any visible adhesive.

FILLING THE GAPS

If plaster on the wall is uneven, there will be a gap between the architrave and the wall. Fill this gap with a flexible acrylic mastic. Fit the mastic tube into a cartridge gun and pipe a 'bead' of mastic along the joint. Obtain a smooth finish by running a wet fingertip along the mastic.

Removing and replacing skirting boards

An old wooden skirting board can be levered away from the wall, but this may be difficult if it has been screwed or nailed into the masonry.

Removing a skirting board

Tools *Hammer and bolster chisel; wrecking bar; thin pieces of wood for protecting the wall and for wedging. Possibly also: trimming knife; torch; hacksaw blade; screwdriver.*

Before you start Use a sharp trimming knife to cut through any wallpaper stuck to the top of the skirting board. If the top of the board is covered with plaster, chip it away carefully first.

1 Start levering at an external corner or where skirting butts against a door frame. When removing only part of the skirting, note whether the board to be removed is overlapped by another at an internal corner. If it is, remove the overlapping board first.

2 Ease the board away from the wall with a hammer and bolster chisel, until there is enough space to insert a thin piece of wood, which will protect the wall.

3 Hold the wrecking bar near its hooked end and insert the blade behind the skirting. Prise the board away from the wall, and wedge it with a piece of wood. Move along the skirting board, wedging the board as you go, and continue until the whole board is loosened.

4 When a board is difficult to loosen, wedge a gap open to look behind and check the type of fixing used.

If the fixing is a screw, probe the front of the board to find the head (it will probably be covered with filler). Unscrew it if you can, otherwise cut through it from behind with a hammer and cold chisel or hacksaw blade.

If the fixing is a large cut nail, you can pull the board away, leaving the nail behind. If you cannot prise the nail out, break it off flush with the masonry by bending it from side to side with a series of hammer blows.

Replacing a skirting board

Plaster is rarely taken far down the wall behind skirting.
• When you are fitting new skirting, buy board of the same height as the old to avoid having to patch the plaster. Alternatively, increase the height of the new board by nailing moulding to the top.
• If new skirting board is thinner than the plaster or lining above it, pack behind with an extra piece of timber to bring it out to the required thickness.
• If the plaster does reach to the floor, fix the skirting board through it into the brickwork with screws and wall plugs.

Before you start
• Coat the back of new skirting board with wood preservative to guard against rot.
• Before fitting the new skirting board, lay it flat along the floor and mark on the front the positions of any existing fixing points (see above right) so that you can nail through the marks. Fit skirting board to existing fixing points wherever this is possible.

Types of fixing points

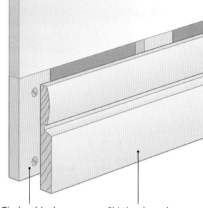

Timber block   Skirting board

The commonest type of fixing point is a timber block. Blocks are nailed or screwed to the wall at 450–600mm intervals.

Fit new blocks if necessary, using timber treated with wood preservative. Fix the blocks with masonry nails or screws and wall plugs.

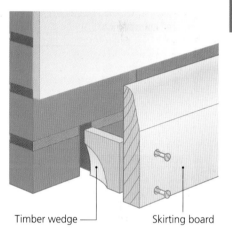

Timber wedge   Skirting board

Another type of fixing point is a timber wedge. These are inserted into the mortar joints between bricks.

If a timber wedge is damaged, remove it by partially driving in a large screw, then pulling it out, together with the wedge, using a crowbar claw or claw hammer. Make and fit a new wedge.

Gluing a skirting board

Modern instant-grip adhesives are so strong that you can secure skirting boards and other mouldings with adhesive instead of using screws or masonry nails.

Apply the adhesive evenly – a zigzag pattern works well – to the back of the moulding. Press firmly against the wall and hold in position with wood offcuts while the adhesive sets. Wipe away any excess adhesive with a damp cloth.

Forming external and internal corners

Before fitting new skirting, shape the ends of the boards where there are external or internal corners.

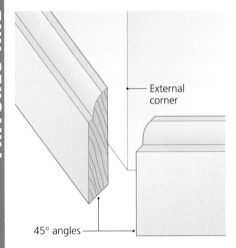

External corner

45° angles

On an external corner, mitre the two boards to meet each other at an angle of 45°. On an internal corner, shape the end of one board to overlap the other, as described below.

1 Fit one board into the internal corner and temporarily nail it in position.

2 Hold the second board butted at right angles to the first and pencil its profile onto the end of the first board.

3 Remove the first board and cut away the end along the pencilled mark with a coping saw.

4 Refit the boards with the second, uncut board pushed into the corner and the first board lapped over it.

Joining straight lengths of skirting board

When joining two straight lengths of skirting board, do not make straight butt joints, which are impossible to hide. Instead, make a scarf joint by cutting the two ends at 45° angles.

Try to position the join where it will not be seen – behind furniture, for instance.

1 Make each joint with matching 45° cuts using a jigsaw with an adjustable sole plate.

2 Fix one length of skirting board in place then position and fix the other. Apply woodworking adhesive to the cut ends and secure the joint with angled pins.

Fixing skirting to a hollow wall

Skirting board fitted to a hollow wall – a partition or a dry-lined wall – is fixed to the vertical studs and the sole plate of the framing. Locate the studs using a pipe and nail detector (page 34). Refit the board using 65mm oval nails.

Repairing moulding on a skirting board

It may be impossible to buy matching moulding to repair a damaged section of skirting board (or picture rail) in an old house. You may be able to have a similar moulding cut to order by a timber merchant. Or you can do the job yourself by cutting a matching piece with a router.

Where a small section of ornate moulding is damaged or missing, take an impression from a sound piece by pressing model-casting rubber dental-impression compound against it. Fill this mould with car-body filler. Smooth the cast and glue in place.

GAPS BELOW THE SKIRTING

A gap of about 5mm between the skirting board and the floor can be very useful if you want to push fitted carpet or vinyl flooring beneath it. But if gaps occur below newly fitted skirting because the floor is not true, the simplest remedy is to nail quadrant or scotia moulding to the bottom of the skirting against the floor.

Do not nail moulding to the floorboards, as these expand and contract more than the skirting, and another gap could open up.

Hanging pictures and mirrors

Pictures and mirrors bring life and light into a room. It's important to use fixings strong enough to bear the weight of the item.

Lightweight or medium-weight items, including small framed mirrors, can be hung from a pin-type picture hook, driven into the wall with a hammer. Make sure the plaster is sound.

A heavy or wide picture should be fixed with two hooks positioned near the ends of the cord rather than from one central hook. Alternatively, it can be hung from a round-head screw fitted into a wall plug, or hung on battens (page 181).

When you are hanging a mirror that is heavy, use mirror chain rather than picture wire or cord.

Positioning a picture

Because of the tension on a picture cord, it is difficult to judge the right spot to fix the supporting hook if you want the top of the picture to be set at a particular level and the cord to be out of sight.

1 Hold the picture against the wall exactly where you want it to hang and lightly mark on the wall the positions of the top corners. Make another pencil mark in the centre of the top edge.

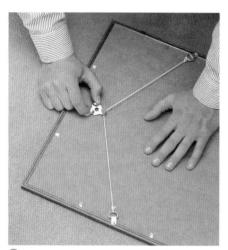

2 Lay the picture on its face, mark the top centre, and use the hook to pull the cord towards the mark until it is tight.

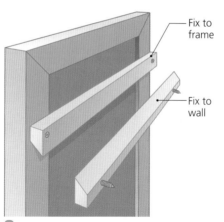

3 Measure the distance between the top of the hook and the top of the picture frame.

4 Measure down from the central pencil mark the required distance between the top of the hook and the top of the frame. Mark the spot and hammer the hook into the wall with its top against the mark.

Hanging a heavy picture on battens

Interlocking battens can be used to support a heavy picture. The battens are both cut from one piece of wood. One half is fixed to the wall, the other across the frame.

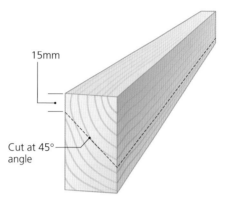

15mm

Cut at 45° angle

1 Use a piece of timber about 50mm by 20mm and slightly shorter than the picture width. Mark a line along one face, 15mm from the edge. Cut along the line with a circular saw at a 45° angle towards the batten centre.

2 Screw one piece of batten to the back of the frame about a third of its height from the top, with the point of the angle on the outside pointing downwards.

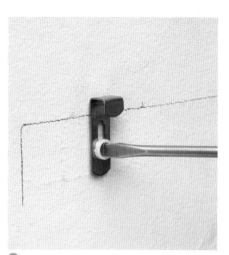

Fix to frame

Fix to wall

3 Screw the other piece of batten to the wall with the point of the angle uppermost and away from the wall.

4 Hook the frame batten over the batten on the wall.

Using sliding mirror clips

Unframed mirrors with holes ready drilled are fixed using screws. For mirrors without screw holes, use corner or sliding clips. If you are using clips, the number needed depends on the size of the mirror. You will need at least two at the bottom and two on the top and if the mirror is very large, you may need clips at the sides, too.

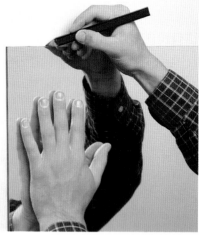

1 Use a spirit level and straight-edge to mark where you want the bottom of the mirror to lie, then hold the mirror in position and lightly mark all four corner positions and the top edge.

2 Drill holes for the bottom clips about 50mm in from the corners. Fit the clips firmly and be sure to use the plastic washers around the screw heads to cushion the back of the mirror. The top clips are also fitted about 50mm in from the top corners. Before drilling, make sure you have allowed for the distance from the top of the clip to the top of its screw slot.

3 When you secure the top clip, position the screw at the base of the slot leaving just enough play for the clip to slide when it is pushed. Then fit the mirror into the bottom clips and hold it in position while you slide the top clips down to grip the mirror.

Using mirror screws

If you are using screws, buy mirror screws with domed covers that screw into the head. Be sure to use plastic spacer washers between the back of the mirror and the wall. This allows for any slight unevenness in the wall surface, and lets air circulate behind the mirror reducing the risk of condensation.

Planning a new kitchen

The kitchen is one of the most-used rooms in the house, so if you intend to replace yours it is worth spending time planning the content and layout of your new space.

Start by drawing up a wish list of all the things you would like to incorporate and try to plan around those. Sketch out a scale plan of the room on graph paper and draw in where you would like the oven, fridge and other key appliances to go, then fit the other cabinets around this.

Don't plan your kitchen to fit exactly between two walls. It will be much easier to fit if you allow for a little tolerance at either end – walls are seldom completely flat and it is very difficult to cut down a unit by a tiny amount in order to squeeze it into a very tight space.

There must be at least 600mm directly above a hob, although it is best to avoid siting units here if you can. Try to use this space only for an extractor fan, which should be between 600 and 915mm above the hob.

Planning the work

• Solid flooring, such as stone or ceramic tiles, should be fitted before the units. This is the best way to achieve a good finish, but does mean that you pay for flooring you never see, underneath the units. Vinyl can be laid after the units and tucked under the plinths at their base.
• Consider adding halogen spots or strip lights beneath wall units to illuminate the work surface. Plan the wiring before you install the units if you want the lights to run from a single switch on the main lighting circuit.
• Run any cables or pipes to their new position before you start fitting units, when you have clear access to all the walls and the floor.
• Venting extractor fans must be fitted with ducting leading to an external wall. If the ducting is more than 5m long, the fan is unlikely to be powerful enough to expel any air. In this case, choose a recirculating model, which does not need venting to the outdoors.

• Worktops should overhang the cabinets beneath by about 20mm when the doors are in place. Most base units are 570mm deep, so a standard 600mm worktop will be a good fit, with a little tolerance for scribing it to match an uneven wall along the back edge.

Keep a minimum of 460mm between the worktop and the base of the wall units.

Allow at least 450mm on one side and 600mm on the other side of the sink to give room for stacking clean and dirty pans when washing up.

If you plan to tile the splashback between the worktop and the units, try to position the units so that you can fit a whole number of tiles, to save you cutting each tile in the top or bottom row.

Leave at least 190mm on one side and 400mm on the other side of the hob.

The working triangle

Kitchens tend to work best when they follow the 'working triangle' principle. Try to position the main food storage and preparation area, the cooker, and the sink in a triangle, spaced equally apart and with a total distance between them of no more than 7.5m. A kitchen will be frustrating to use if you have to walk a long way between the fridge and the cooker or double back time and again every time you so much as make a cup of tea.

Position the dishwasher within 1m of the sink for ease of plumbing and for rinsing dirty dishes before loading. Keep 800mm of clear standing space in front of a dishwasher for easy loading.

The minimum required space between an island unit and the surrounding units is 1.2m, so that cupboard doors on both sides can be open at once.

Next to the opening side of the fridge, try to leave at least 400m of worktop space.

Installing a fitted kitchen

A methodical approach is essential when fitting a new kitchen. Take the job one step at a time and enlist some help with lifting and positioning.

Tools *Spirit level; tape measure; power drill and drill bits; screwdrivers; jigsaw; hammer; cramps.*

Materials *Kitchen units; work surface; sink; wall plugs.*

Assembling the units

Put the cabinets together one at a time, to avoid muddling parts. All the bits might look the same, but there are often subtle differences from unit to unit. Assemble and fit the wall units before the base units; this will give you better access to the wall area.

1 Take all the components out of the box and check them against the list of contents. If anything is missing, check the box and all the packaging again.

2 Screw or hammer in the fixings to the inside of the side panels. This unit is assembled using wooden dowels and cam and screw fixings (page 169).

3 If the wall unit is to be hung from brackets, fit the cupboard section of the bracket now. Some units are assembled fully and then screwed directly to the wall.

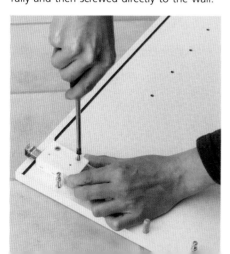

4 Slot the cam part of the cam and screw fixing into the adjacent panel and then slide it into place, tapping it down gently if necessary to get a tight fit.

5 Slide the back panel into place then complete the assembly of the other two sides.

HELPFUL TIP

Cupboard doors are easily damaged and can be a nuisance when you are trying to fit the cupboards to the wall. Mark each cupboard with a piece of masking tape on a visible surface then put a matching mark on its door, and only install the doors once all the cabinets have been fitted.

Hanging wall units

1 Measure up the wall from the floor and put a mark 1400mm up. This will be the level of the bottom of the wall units. Use a spirit level to transfer this level around the wall, where the units are to be fitted.

2 If your wall units are to be screwed directly to the wall, fix a temporary batten to the wall at this level, to help to support the units while you fix them in place.

3 If your units hang from brackets, hold the wall-mounted part of the bracket in place against the cupboard-mounted part and measure from the bottom of the cupboard to the base of the bracket. Transfer this measurement to the wall.

4 Starting with a corner unit if you have one, fix the first wall-plate in position then measure across the cupboard and then the wall to mark the position for the second.

5 Hang the cupboard on the brackets, check that it is level horizontally and vertically then tighten the brackets from inside to secure the unit in place.

6 Fix the two-part hinges to the cupboard and door; then hang the door and adjust the hinges as necessary for a good fit.

FIXING WALL UNITS TO STUD PARTITION WALLS

Wall units can be fixed to stud walls using fixings for hollow walls, but once the cupboards are fully loaded, they will be very heavy, so it is wise to reinforce the fixing area. Cut out a strip of plasterboard the length of the run of the units and 100mm wide at the position where the fixings will be made. Take care not to cut through the studs. Replace the plasterboard with a length of 100 x 25mm softwood, firmly fixed to the partition studs. Notch the bearer over the studs.

Installing base units

As with wall units, start fitting the base units in a corner and work out from there.

1 Set the first unit in position. Set the spirit level on top of the cupboard and check it is level in each direction.

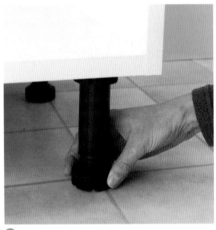

2 Adjust the leg heights until the cupboard is roughly level. Don't spend too long on it at this stage. You will need to level each complete run when all the units are in place.

3 Position the next cupboard in the run, using clamps to hold the units together while you adjust their levels.

4 Check the level of all the units around the room, adjusting their heights with the legs until they are all aligned.

SAFETY TIP

Never extend the cupboard legs to their full height, as they will lose their strength. If your floor is very uneven, pack pieces of wood beneath the legs to get the units roughly level and then use the legs for fine adjustments.

5 Screw the units back to the wall using brackets attached to the side panels or by screwing through the back panel, if this is adjacent to the wall. Then screw the units to one another, through the side panels.

6 Where two cupboards join in a corner, you will need to fit a corner post. Position this on the side panel of one of the cupboards, 2–3mm back from the front edge to avoid the door fouling on it when it opens.

7 Position the adjacent cupboard then drill through the cupboard side into the corner post and screw through the cupboard side panel to fix it.

8 Fix handles to the cupboard doors, then hang the doors on their respective cupboards, using the adjuster screw on each hinge to get a good fit. Make sure that all the doors are flush with one another when closed.

9 Glue or screw the fixing clips to the inner face of the plinth that will run beneath the cupboards. Take care to position the clips to match the position of the cupboard legs they will clip onto. Fit the plinths in place.

Fitting worktops and inset sinks

The worktops in your kitchen are one of the most prominent features, so it is important to fit them as carefully and professionally as possible.

Tools *Jigsaw; plane; try square; tape measure; pencil; pair of saw horses or workbenches; screwdriver.*

Materials *Kitchen worktop; silicone sealant; PVA adhesive; contact adhesive; inset sink.*

Before you start Always measure twice and cut once when fitting a length of worktop. Cut the surface too short and you will have made an expensive mistake. The long lengths are heavy and cumbersome, so you will need help with manoeuvring them for cutting and lifting them into place.

Fitting the worktop

1 Set the worktop on top of the base units and push it against the wall. If one end is into a corner, make sure that it is pushed up against this too.

2 Adjust the worktop until there is an even overhang at the front; this will be determined by any high spots on the wall.

3 When the overhang is even along the whole length of the run of cabinets, make a note of this measurement and deduct 40mm. This is the amount of overhang that you will be left with once you have cut the worktop to the correct depth. Scribe the profile of the wall onto the worktop surface to give you a cutting line along the back edge of the piece (see box opposite).

4 Lift the worktop onto a pair of saw horses or two workbenches – it will be too long to rest securely on just one bench – and use the jigsaw fitted with a down-cutting blade to cut to the pencil line. Lift the worktop back into position and check the fit. Remove any high spots with a sharp plane.

5 With the worktop in position, mark a line on the underside 40mm from the end of any base units and cut the worktop to this line.

6 Use a strip of matching melamine trim to cover the exposed core on the cut end. Glue it in place with contact adhesive before trimming it back with a sharp file. File towards the worktop to avoid lifting the stuck-on lipping. Some worktops come with ready-glued iron-on edging strips.

FINISHING OFF

Imperfect joins along the back of a worktop can be disguised by a strip of wood moulding, fixed in the angle between the worktop and the wall and finished with a bead of sealant. Wood mouldings look particularly effective as a finishing touch to a wooden worktop.

Alternatively Metal finishing strips give a hard-wearing edge to a worktop. They are screwed into the end of the cut worktop.

7 Drill pilot holes in the underside of the worktop, taking care not to drill too deeply and come through the surface, and drive in 18mm long screws through the top rails of the base units to fix the worktop in place.

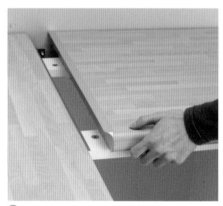

8 If worktops go around a corner use a joining strip to suit the worktop. Scribe this second section to the wall as before. Then screw the joining strip to the second length of worktop, butt it up to the first and secure it in place from below.

SCRIBING THE LINE OF AN UNEVEN WALL

Scribing is a very useful technique for achieving a neat finish when butting a worktop against a wall that is not completely flat. It can also be used to cut the bottom edge of a skirting board to fit against an uneven floor.

Press the worktop against the wall, making sure that it is square and has an even overhang all the way along the front edge. Hold a small block of wood against the wall and press a pencil up to it. Move the block of wood and pencil together along the wall, tracing the line of any lumps and bumps in the wall onto the top of the worktop.

Marking the cutting line

If you do not need to reduce the depth of the worktop, replicate this line as close to the edge as you can. A pair of compasses is a useful tool for this: set the angle of the compasses to the smallest distance between the line and the worktop edge, then run the point along the line you have drawn, drawing a matching line with the compass pencil a short distance away. Bear in mind that it is difficult to cut off a very small amount of worktop cleanly.

If you need to trim the worktop, reproduce the line at the appropriate distance from the back edge. Set the compasses to a width equal to the amount of worktop you need to remove minus the thickness of the piece of wood you used to trace the original line of the wall.

Fitting the sink

1 Place the upturned sink on the worktop. Sinks are sometimes handed if taps are to be positioned to one side or the other, in which case the sink may be supplied with a template for marking cutouts.

2 Carefully measure to ensure that the cut out will fall inside the face and end panels of the cupboard beneath, that the basin will not foul on any part of the cupboard and that the sink is parallel to the front of the worktop.

3 Use a pencil to mark the outline on the worktop.

HELPFUL TIP

Some inset sinks are supplied with a rubber gasket, which is sandwiched between the sink and the worktop to create a water-tight seal.

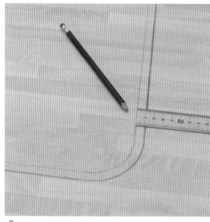

4 Copy this line 10mm in, to leave a 10mm lip for the sink to rest on. Drill a hole at each corner of the cutout, large enough for a jigsaw blade, and cut out the waste using a downward cutting blade in the saw.

5 Run a bead of silicone mastic around the underside lip of the sink (or fit the gasket) before dropping it into place.

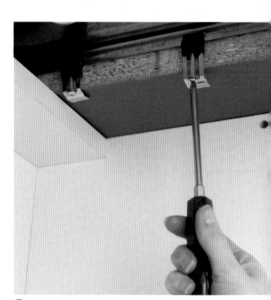

6 Use the clips supplied with the sink to secure it from inside the cupboard.

7 Wipe off any excess silicone sealant that has squeezed out and connect up the plumbing.

6
Doors and windows

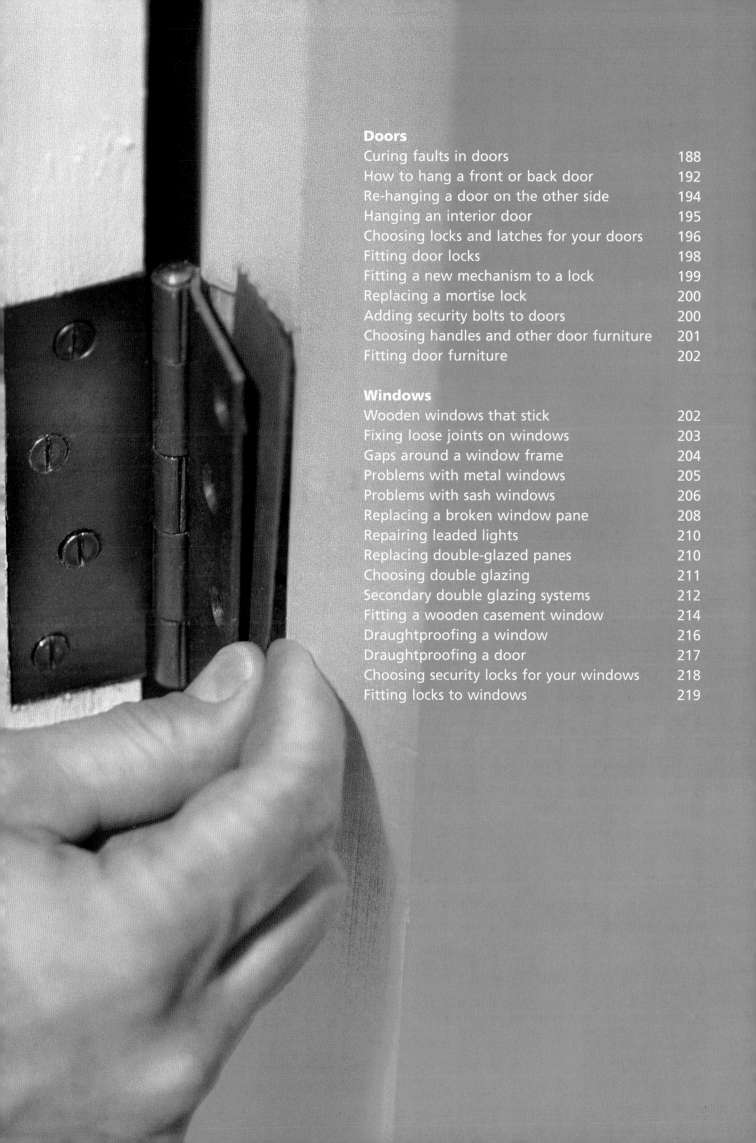

Curing faults in doors

Most faults in doors can be cured quite easily. For some jobs you may need another person to help you, or to steady the door while you work on it.

Door binding along one side

Doors often bind (stick) in their frames because regular repainting causes a build-up of paint on the edge of the door and on the frame.

1 Strip off the paint. Do this mechanically to avoid damaging the finish on the door faces. Use either a power sander or a Surform planer file.

2 Smooth the stripped surfaces with glasspaper and check that the door opens and closes easily.

3 There should be a slight gap between the edge of the door and the frame. To check for this, run a thin knife blade all round the edge of the door when it is closed. Where the gap is insufficient, strip and then plane that edge of the door. You may have to take the door off its hinges, and perhaps remove locks and latches.

4 Prime and paint the stripped edges of the door. Then let the paint dry before closing the door.

Door binding at the bottom

If an external door binds at its lower corners, the problem is often caused by moisture being absorbed through an unpainted bottom edge.

1 Take the door off its hinges and dry the bare wood thoroughly with a hot-air gun.

2 Seal the bare edge with two coats of quick-drying wood primer. Re-hang the door when the primer is touch-dry. Painting is unnecessary as the edge is out of sight.

3 If the binding is severe, hold the door on one of its long edges in a portable workbench. Mark a line to work to, then plane downwards from the edges of the door to the centre; this will avoid splintering the edge.

4 Prime the bare edge as in step 2 and re-hang the door.

Door binding at the top

You may be able to plane the top edge of a door (which is often unpainted) without taking it off its hinges. Prop it open with wedges while you work from a stepladder. Otherwise take it off its hinges and plane the whole edge as in step 3 above.

Door squeaks

Oil the hinge pins with an aerosol lubricant. Work the door backwards and forwards a few times to get the lubricant into the hinge, then wipe away any surplus with kitchen roll.

With rising butt hinges, lift the open door off the hinge pins and lightly smear them with grease or petroleum jelly. Wipe away the surplus after re-hanging the door.

Door tends to slam

The best solution for a slamming door is to fit a door closer, which slows down the speed at which the door shuts.

1 A template is always supplied with a door closer. Decide whether you want the door to open to 100° (straight into the room) or 180° (flat back to the hinge wall), and use a bradawl or a pencil to mark through the appropriate template spots.

2 Drill pilot holes and screw the door closer onto the door.

3 With the door closer fitted to the door, you can now mark the position of the pivot arm on the door architrave. Chisel out a recess and screw it in position.

4 Fix the pivot arm to the body of the closer and turn the adjusting screws so that the door shuts smoothly and slowly without slamming.

Door panels split

Sometimes splits develop in the panels of old doors. The solution depends on whether the door is painted or varnished.

Painted door
On a painted door, fill the crack with a wood filler and paint over it.

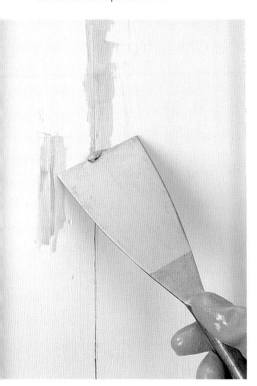

Natural wood door
On a varnished door where the filler will show, drive dowels into the edge of the door to press against the edges of the panel and close the crack.

1 First clean out old varnish or filler from the crack with a sharp knife.

2 Drill two or three 8mm diameter holes through the edge of the door to line up with the near edge of the panel. Measure the thickness of the door stile and mark the drill bit with a piece of tape to act as a depth stop.

3 Cut some 8mm dowels about 20mm longer than the width of the stiles.

4 Squirt PVA wood adhesive into the crack in the panel and into the holes in the stile. Drive the dowels into the holes so they press against the edge of the panel and close the crack.

5 Wipe off excess adhesive with a damp cloth. Leave the protruding dowel until the glue has set, then trim it off flush with the door edge. Smooth the cut end with abrasive paper.

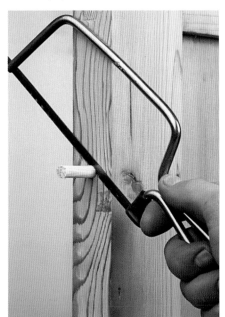

Latch will not engage

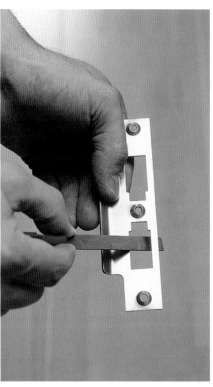

If a door sags a little, the latch bolt will be out of alignment with the striking plate. You can correct a small misalignment by unscrewing the plate and enlarging its cut-out with a small metal file.

Otherwise, remove the striking plate and re-fix it a little lower down the frame. Use a sharp chisel and a mallet to extend the recess in which it fits. If the plate has to be moved only a small distance, drill out the old screw holes and fill them with dowels. Drill new pilot holes for the fixing screws.

Lock stiff to turn

1 Spray aerosol lubricant into a surface-mounted lock using the applicator tube provided. Squirt the lubricant through the latch and bolt holes and through the keyhole.

2 If this is not sufficient, remove the lock from the door, take off one side of the case, and lightly grease the mechanism. Before starting work, note the positions of the components so they can be put back if they become displaced.

Do not use oil or aerosol lubricants in Yale-type cylinder locks; they attract grit. Instead puff graphite powder or PTFE dry powder lubricant into the keyhole.

Door frame loose

Slamming a door often leads to the frame becoming loose. Make new fixings with three frame plugs at each side of the frame. The length of the frame plugs, which come complete with hammer-in screws, should be the thickness of the frame plus at least 60mm.

1 Using a masonry bit, drill through the frame and into the wall behind it to the required depth.

2 Hammer the screw and plug into the hole until the screw head is flush with the frame.

Door hard to close

A door that is difficult to close, and tends to spring open, is said to be hinge-bound. The problem is usually caused by hinge recesses cut too deep in either the door edge or in the frame. When correctly fitted, the hinge flaps should be flush with the surface of the wood.

1 Open the door fully and then put a wedge under it.

2 Clear any paint from the slots in the hinge screws, and remove the screws.

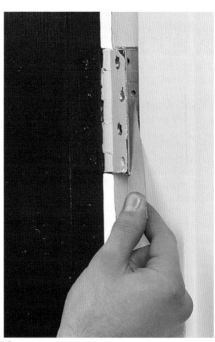

3 Get someone to steady the door while you lever the hinge flap out of its recess. Pack out the recess with one or more pieces of cardboard until the hinge is flush with the wood surface, then replace the screws. Use new screws if you damaged the slots of the old ones.

Protruding screw heads
Hinges may bind because the screws have been put in askew, or because their heads are too large to fit flush in the countersinks in the hinge flaps.

Remove the offending screws and replace them with screws with smaller heads. If they will not tighten, pack out the holes with glued-in matches.

Alternatively Deepen the countersinks in the hinge flaps so that the screw heads will be flush with the surface. Use a high-speed-steel countersink bit.

If the screws were originally set in askew, drill out and plug the old screw holes with dowels (see below) and drill new pilot holes for the screws.

Badly placed hinge flaps
Binding can also be caused by hinge flaps that are set into the frame too near to the door stop. As the door is closed, the face of the door presses against the stop.

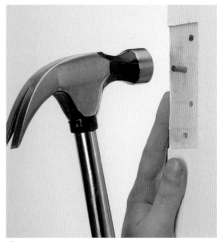

1 Remove the hinges, drill out the old screw holes and plug them with glued dowels. Chisel the dowel ends off flush with the recess.

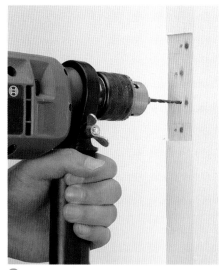

2 Drill new fixing holes so that the hinge is farther away from the door stop. The hinge pin should be just clear of the door edge. Fill the resulting gaps beside the repositioned hinges with wood filler.

Alternatively On an internal door, it may be easier to prise off and reposition the door stop, which is usually a separate piece of wood pinned to the door frame.

Door is rotting

If exterior doors have not been protected with paint or varnish, rot may set in, especially near the bottom and at joints. You can repair minor damage with wood hardener and high-performance exterior wood filler.

1 Chisel away the rotten wood and use a hot-air gun to dry the exposed bare wood.

2 Treat the area with the wood hardener. When this has soaked in and dried, fill the recess with the filler. Build it up slightly above the surface, and sand it flat when it has hardened.

3 Repaint the door to disguise the repair.

Frame is rotting

External door frames often rot near the sill. The only satisfactory repair is to insert a new piece of timber. Use an all-purpose saw; the teeth will not be blunted by accidental contact with masonry.

1 Probe the wood with a sharp knife to reveal where the soft, rotten section ends. Make a 45° downward cut into the frame about 75mm above this point.

2 Prise the rotten part away from the wall. Its bottom end was probably tenon-jointed into the hardwood sill.

3 Cut a length of new wood to fit the gap, sloping one end to align with the saw cut. Test its fit and adjust it as necessary.

The old frame may have a door stop machined into it. Make a matching section from two or more pieces of wood glued and cramped together.

4 When the new section is a good fit, treat all its surfaces with clear wood preservative. Drill and countersink holes in it, and mark the fixing positions on the wall through these holes. Drill and plug the wall and screw the section in place.

5 Where the old and new frame section join, drill 8mm holes through the joint at right angles to it. Smear glue on 8mm hardwood dowels and hammer them into the holes.

6 Trim the dowels flush with the surface when the glue has dried. Prime and paint the repair.

Door sags

When the bottom corner of the door rubs on the floor, the cause is either faulty hinges or loose joints in the door. Partly open the door and lift the handle to see if there is movement at the hinges or joints.

Faulty hinges
If the hinge screws are loose, try tightening them. If they will not hold, remove them, drill out the screw holes and plug them with glued dowels. Drill new pilot holes and refit the screws.

If the movement is in the knuckle of the hinge due to a worn hinge pin, the only cure is to fit new hinges (page 192). The hinges may not be large enough to support the weight of the door. In this case fit larger, stronger hinges, and add a third hinge midway between them if you are working on a front door.

Loose door joints
If the problem is that corner joints on a framed door are loose, glue and cramp them back into place.

1 Take the door off its hinges, and try to prise the loose joints apart.

2 Squirt woodworking adhesive into the joints and cramp them closed with sash cramps. Be sure to check that the door frame is square.

3 On the edge of the door, drive small wooden wedges into the ends of the tenons in order to prevent the joints from opening up again.

4 Drill through the face of the door and the tenon, and drive a glued dowel into the hole to lock the tenon in place.

5 Trim off the dowels flush with the surface of the door.

How to hang a front or back door

When buying a new door, measure the height and width of the frame and get a door that is either the right size or slightly too big. An exterior door is heavy, so get someone to help you if you can.

Panelled doors can have up to 20mm removed all round to fit, but most flush doors should have no more than about 10mm planed away, otherwise they may be seriously weakened.

Flush doors contain wooden blocks for fitting hinges and locks; their positions are marked on the edges of the door. When fitting the hinges and locks, note where the blocks are, as they will affect the way round that the door is placed in the frame. If you want to reverse the face of the door, most are reversible top to bottom.

You will need three butt hinges – either 75mm or 100mm long. The job will be simpler if you choose a size to fit the existing hinge recesses on the frame.

If a flush door is being fitted, buy pressed-steel cranked butt hinges (above right). A panelled door, which is heavier, requires cast butt hinges.

Tools *Pencil; tape measure; try square; marking gauge; 19mm or 25mm chisel; mallet; plane; panel or tenon saw; trimming knife; drill and twist bits; screwdriver; folding workbench.*

Materials *Exterior door; three hinges; screws to fit (check that the heads fit fully into the countersunk holes on the hinge).*

1 Remove the old door carefully, without damaging the hinge recesses on the frame. Put pieces of wood under the door to take the weight while you remove the screws, and get someone to hold it.

2 New panelled doors are sometimes protected with strips of timber or cork pads at the edges; remove these by prising them off with a broad scraper blade.

REMOVING STUBBORN SCREWS

When you remove your old door, the hinge screws may be difficult to get out. Scrape off any paint, particularly out of the slots. If a screw still will not shift, put a screwdriver in the slot and hit it with a mallet.

Choosing hinges to hang a door

Cast butt hinge Doors usually have butt hinges – two rectangular flaps (called leaves) joined by a pin running through an interlocking knuckle. Heavy exterior doors have cast leaves 75mm or 100mm long. The centre of the knuckle is fitted in line with the face of door and frame.

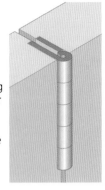

Cranked butt hinge A butt hinge that is made of folded pressed steel. It is cheaper but not as strong as other hinges, so should not be used to fix heavy exterior doors. When fitted, the whole of the large knuckle projects from the face of the door and the frame.

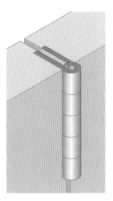

Rising butt hinge When a door opens onto a carpet, rising butt hinges are an alternative to cutting a strip off the bottom of the door. The spiral in the knuckle of the hinge lifts the door as it opens, and also tends to close it. The door can easily be lifted off the hinges. Usual sizes are 75mm and 100mm. The hinges are sold for both right-hand and left-hand hanging.

Loose-pin butt hinge The pin can be withdrawn to separate the leaves, and remove the door easily – perhaps when laying a floor covering. Decorative finials may be fitted at the top and bottom, and are unscrewed to release the pin. The hinges are usually made of brass.

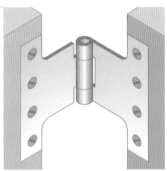

Parliament hinge These are butt hinges with projecting knuckles that enable an open door to swing clear of its surrounding frame. They are made of steel or brass, in sizes (when open) of 100mm x 100mm, 100mm x 125mm and 100mm x 150mm.

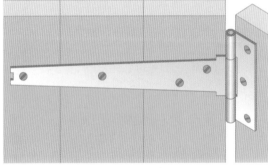

T-hinge This old-fashioned type of hinge is used mainly for garage and shed doors, but is sometimes fitted to cottage-style house doors. It is screwed to the surface of the back of the door and the frame.

Getting the fit right

1 Hold the door against the frame to mark it for trimming. A glass-panelled door is usually fitted with the putty on the outside and decorative wood beading on the inside.

2 When the door is centrally positioned, get someone to steady it, and put wedges underneath to hold it at the correct height.

3 Lightly mark the face with a soft pencil to give the correct gap round the perimeter. A panelled door should have a gap of 3mm all round to allow the wood to swell in wet weather. A flush door should have a gap of

2mm. If the frame is straight you may not have to trim all the edges of the door. However, if the frame is out of true, or if there is a fair amount of trimming to do, it will be necessary to trim all round.

4 If there is more than about 5mm of wood to remove, lay the door flat on boxes or trestles and saw it close to the trimming line, then finish off with a plane.

5 For planing, hold the door on its edge in the jaws of a folding adjustable workbench. Protect the bottom edge on scrap timber and then plane the top edge down to the pencilled trimming line.

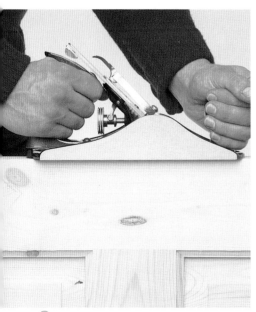

6 Plane the long edges of the door in the direction of the grain. The shavings will be removed smoothly, whereas if you plane against the grain the blade will tend to dig into the wood.

7 Plane the top and bottom edges of the door from each side towards the centre. This will avoid splitting wood at the edge of the stiles where you will be planing across the grain.

8 Stand the door in the frame on wedges and check there is the right gap all round.

9 When the fit is correct, plane a slight slope on the edges of both door stiles towards the doorstop on the frame. This will ensure that the door will close easily without binding against the frame.

Hanging the door

1 Hold the door in the frame to mark the hinge positions. If the hinge recesses in the frame are already cut to the right size, mark the top and bottom of the recesses on the edge of the door. If not, increase the size with a chisel as explained below, and then mark the top and bottom of the hinge positions on the door.

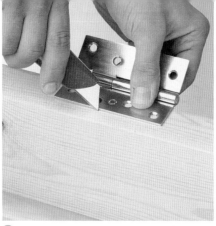

2 Hold the hinge in place on the door and mark round the edge of each hinge flap with a trimming knife. With a cranked butt hinge the whole knuckle of the hinge should project from the face of the door and from the frame. With a cast butt hinge the centre of the knuckle should be in line with the face of the door and frame.

3 Mark the thickness of the flap on the door face with a marking gauge.

4 Cut around the perimeter of the hinge recess with a sharp chisel. Then make a series of cuts about 5mm apart across the grain of the wood, and carefully pare away the waste.

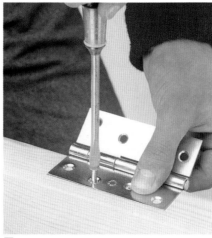

5 Screw the hinge flaps into the recesses in the door, putting only one screw in each hinge for the time being.

CUTTING A REBATE FOR A WATER BAR

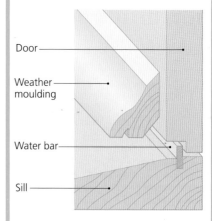

Door ——
Weather moulding ——
Water bar ——
Sill ——

A door which is directly exposed to rain, without the protection of a porch, will close against a water bar set in a groove in the sill. Some external doors are supplied with a rebate already cut in the bottom to fit over the water bar, but if your door doesn't have one, you will need to cut it yourself.
• Draw a line across the front of the door at the bottom, a little higher than the water bar.
• Set a circular saw or router to the depth of the rebate (about half the thickness of the door) and cut right along the line.
• If you have cut the door with a circular saw, finish off the rebate by holding a chisel end-on to the door and chiselling away the waste.

6 Hold the door open on wedges and screw the hinges to the frame – again using one screw each. Each screw head should lie flush with the surface of the hinge flap.

If the screw heads protrude, they will bind and prevent the door from closing. You can either deepen the countersinks in the hinge with a high-speed-steel twist bit in a power drill (page 190), or else you could buy screws one gauge size smaller.

If the screws do not tighten into the frame, glue pieces of dowel in the old screw holes and drill new ones.

7 Check that the door swings open and shut easily. If it does not close properly, the hinge positions may have to be adjusted (see Door hard to close, page 190).

8 When the door moves correctly, insert the remaining hinge screws.

Re-hanging a door on the other side of the frame

To make better use of space in a room, it is sometimes necessary to re-hang a door on the opposite side of the frame. It may then open against a wall rather than into the room.

Tools *Wedges; screwdriver; tenon saw; vice or bench hook; plane; hammer; abrasive paper; pencil; chisel; try square; mallet; trimming knife; drill and twist bits.*

Materials *Scrap softwood, or pieces of timber to match the door; wood glue; panel pins; new screws for hinges – probably 50mm No. 10 gauge.*

1 Open the door and put wooden wedges under it to take the weight.

2 Unscrew the hinges from the frame, take down the door, and remove the hinges completely.

Repositioning the hinges

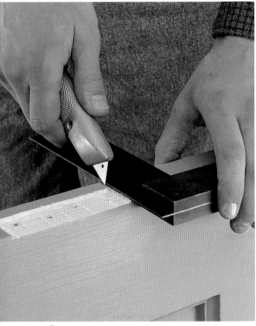

1 Use a trimming knife and try square to cut through the raised wood at the ends of the hinge recesses on the door.

SAFETY TIP

Never hang a door so that it opens onto a corridor or landing as there is a danger of walking into it.

RE-HANGING A DOOR TO OPEN OUTWARDS

Altering a door so that it opens outwards rather than inwards is very similar to re-hanging it to hinge on the other side of the frame. You will need the same tools and materials to do the job.

After removing the door, prise away the stop bead – the strip of wood on the frame that the door rests against when it is closed. To do this, use an old chisel together with a couple of wooden wedges or a bolster chisel. When you have re-hung the door in its new position, pin the stop bead back on the frame so that it fits snugly against the inside face of the door.

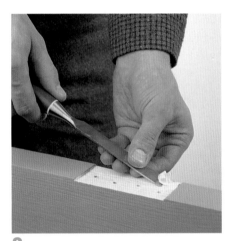

2 Remove the raised sections with a chisel, so that the recesses extend right across the door edge.

3 Hold a hinge against each recess on the opposite side from where it was originally, and cut strips of wood to fit along the other edge to fill the gaps. Use softwood if the door is painted, or matching timber if it is varnished. Cut the pieces to stand slightly raised.

4 Glue the strips in place and temporarily hold them with panel pins that are not driven right in.

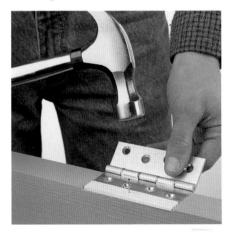

---

5 When the glue has set, remove the pins and plane the filling pieces flush with the door edge. Finish with abrasive paper.

Relocating the striking plate and lock

1 Unscrew the lock striking plate from the door frame. Cut a thin piece of wood to fill the recess, and fix it in place as described in steps 4 and 5 above.

2 When you turn the door around, the side that faced out of the room will now face inwards. The latch will be facing the wrong way to engage when the striking plate is refitted.

3 Remove the lock and reverse the latch, either by turning the lock over or by unscrewing the side of the lock and turning the latch over.

Rehanging the door

1 Hold the door in the frame with wedges under it to support it at the right height off the floor. Check that the gap between the door and the frame is equal all the way round, and that the bottom of the door will not catch on the carpet.

2 Mark the top and bottom of the hinge positions on the edge of the frame. Remove the door.

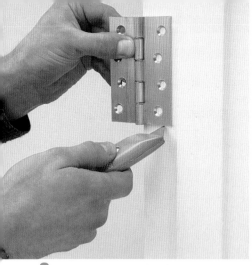

3 Hold each hinge in place on the frame and mark round its edge with a trimming knife. If it is a cast butt hinge, the centre of the knuckle should be level with the face of the frame (and the face of the door). A cranked butt hinge should have the whole knuckle projecting.

4 Mark the thickness of the hinge flap on the edge of the frame.

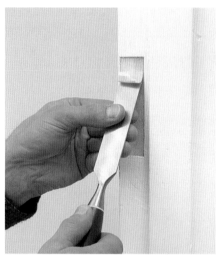

5 Cut round the scored outline with a sharp chisel. Then make a series of cuts about 5mm apart across the grain with the chisel and carefully pare away the waste.

FITTING RISING BUTT HINGES

Rising butts are available for right-hand and left-hand hanging, so make sure you buy the right type. Stand so the door will open away from you; if it is to be hinged on the left, buy left-hand hinges; if it is hinged on the right, buy right-hand hinges.

The part of the hinge with the pin is fitted (pin upwards) to the door frame, and the open spiral section is screwed to the door.

Fit them in the same way as ordinary butt hinges. It will also be necessary to plane a small slope on the inner top edge of the door on the hinge side. This prevents the door from catching on the top of the door frame as it swings open.

---

6 Repeat at the other hinge positions on the frame.

7 Drill pilot holes for one screw in each hinge on the door, and fix the hinges into the recesses, using one screw only.

8 Hold the door open on wedges, and screw the hinges to the frame – again with one screw in each hinge. Make sure that each screw head is flush with the surface of the hinge. If the screws protrude beyond the surface of the hinge the door may not close correctly.

9 Check that the door swings open and shut easily. If it does not, the hinge positions may have to be adjusted (page 190).

10 When the movement is correct, drill the remaining pilot holes and put in the screws.

11 Close the door and turn the handle and key to indent the frame where the lock striking plates will be fitted.

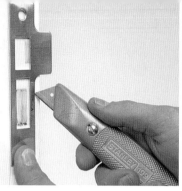

12 Mark the frame around the striking plate, and chisel out a recess. Cut out the mortises for the lock and catch. Screw the plate in place.

Hanging an interior door

Normal interior doors are hung in largely the same way as exterior doors with the following differences.

Conventional hinged doors

• As interior doors are not likely to swell because of moisture, a 2mm gap between door and frame will be enough.
• When cutting the door to fit, make sure that it will open over a carpet without rubbing. It should just brush the carpet top. Alternatively, fit rising butt hinges.
• If you need to trim more than 10mm off each edge of a standard-size door, buy an interior quality panel door. The internal support-frame of a flush door is too narrow to be substantially cut down.

Alternatively, buy a slightly undersize flush door and add timber lipping all round to make up the height and width; add no more than 10mm on each edge.
• Two hinges will be enough for hanging an interior door. Use 75mm cranked butt hinges (page 192).

Hanging bi-fold doors

Hang a bi-fold door in the same way as a conventional door, with these exceptions:

1 If the pair of doors is not already hinged together, join with three brass butt hinges.

2 Fix the door to the frame with two parliament hinges. They have projecting knuckles that let the door fold right back, clear of the architrave around the opening.

3 Where two pairs of bi-fold doors join together at the centre of the opening, glue and pin a full-height batten about 40mm x 15mm to one door to overlap the closing edge and serve as a door stop. If the meeting edges are rebated, there will be no need for the batten.

4 Fit a mortise latch and handle to the adjacent door of the other pair.

Choosing locks and latches for your doors

Choosing an appropriate lock or latch for each door in the house is crucial for safety and security. But remember that any lock is only as strong as the frame to which it is fitted and the screws you use.

Single-point locks and latches are available in two main types.
• Rim locks are screwed to the inside of the door; they are easy to install but not so secure as they are only held by screws, and could be forced off the door.
• Mortise locks are fitted (mortised) into the door edge; they are more difficult to install, but more secure because the door frame has to be smashed to get past them. A metal reinforcement, called a London bar, can be fitted to the frame beside a mortise lock, but must be ordered to size.
   Multi-point locking systems can secure a door along its full height.

BACK DOORS

A deadlock (a lock with a bolt that can be opened only with a key) is essential for side and back doors, because these doors are often glazed and in secluded positions. If there is no deadlock, a burglar can break the glass and turn a latch from the inside.

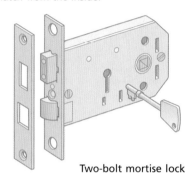

Two-bolt mortise lock

Two-bolt mortise lock The two-bolt mortise lock is also called a mortise sashlock. The latch is operated by handles on both sides of the door and the bolt can be operated only by the key. Choose one with five levers for good security (or buy an upgrader unit) and use only locks manufactured to British Standard BS3621. Narrow models are available for doors with narrow stiles. Use with rack bolts at top and bottom of the door. Take the dimensions of the old lock when buying a new one, as sizes vary according to make.

Two-bolt rim lock Screws to the inside face of the door. Simple to install but easy to tamper with. Cheaper one, two and three-lever actions are unsuitable for external doors as the only lock. Fit additional bolts at top and bottom.

FRONT DOORS

If you have glass in your front door, buy a deadlocking cylinder rimlock. This becomes unmovable if you turn the key when you leave the house, so that a burglar will not be able to reach in through a broken pane of glass to open the door.

Cylinder rim lock The lock is fitted to the inner face of the door. The latch is turned back by a key from the outside and by a handle from the inside. A 'snib' (knob) holds the latch in place – either out or in. Less secure than a deadlocking cylinder rim lock. When choosing the lock, look for one made to British Standards Institution BS3621. To keep the door locked when you are indoors, choose a model with a lockable handle, so that it can be locked from the inside as well as the outside. But ensure that a key is kept near the door in case of fire. Use with a mortise deadlock for extra security.

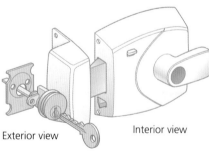

Exterior view   Interior view

Deadlocking cylinder rim lock (above) The lock is fitted to the inner face of the door. When the key is turned in the lock, the bolt cannot be forced back. On some models the main bolt automatically deadlocks when the door is closed. Bolts on standard locks are about 14mm; bolts on high-security designs are 20mm or

more. A locking handle on the inside prevents an intruder from opening the door after breaking a glass panel. Use only locks manufactured to BS3621. A BS EN 1303 Grade 5 cylinder provides anti-drill and pick resistance. Some models incorporate a lock check indicator so you can see if the door is deadlocked. Use with a mortise deadlock for added security.

Latchbolt Instead of a rim lock, a latchbolt (also called a locking latch) can be fitted. This has a bolt and a latch. The latch is operated by a handle on the inside while the bolt is key-operated from either side.

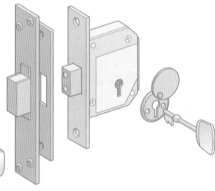

Mortise deadlock (above) The bolt cannot be turned back without using the key. The key operates levers, and the more levers there are, the harder the lock is to pick. A five or seven-lever lock with a box type striking plate gives the best security. Use with a rim lock for frequent coming and going. Cutting a mortise in a door will weaken it a little, so if you have a front door that is less than 45mm thick ask for a thin-pattern mortise lock.

PATIO DOORS AND FRENCH WINDOWS

Small security locks can be mounted on the inside of a wood or metal patio door. They operate a bolt which engages in a hole in the other door. For maximum security, fit locks at both top and bottom of the door. This is particularly advisable for old aluminium-framed patio doors which can sometimes be jemmied out of the sliding track and lifted out of the frame.

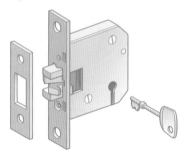

Clawbolt deadlock A pair of claws lock into the striking plate, and can only be operated by a key. The lock is mortised into the door's stile. Suitable for sliding patio doors made of wood. Metal patio doors usually come with their own lock.

Casement bolt (espagnolette bolt) The traditional way to lock French windows. A full length bolt, operated by a central handle, shoots into the frame at top and bottom. For security it should be used in conjunction with rack bolts (opposite) at the top and bottom.

INTERNAL DOORS

Internal doors are best not locked when a house is empty. Once a thief is inside he will usually not be deterred by locked doors unless they are very strong.

When the house is occupied, ground floor doors could be locked at night. A burglar trying to get from, say, the living room to the rest of the house will probably make so much noise that he will wake the occupants. For this purpose, fit a two-bolt mortise lock (left), as you would for a back or side door; handles on both sides of the door will be necessary for normal use in the daytime. There are now 'lift-and-lock' sashlocks available that allow the door to be locked and unlocked from the inside simply by lifting or depressing the handle by 45°; no key is required.

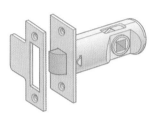

Mortise latch Only for keeping doors closed; it cannot be locked. A small model can be inserted in a circular hole. Bathroom doors normally require a latch with a 'snib', a simple locking device that can be turned from the inside for privacy. A screw slot on the outside of the door can be used to open the latch in an emergency.

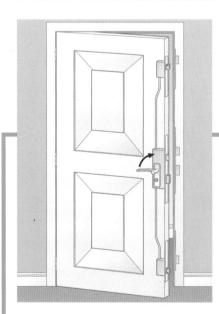

Additional devices for door security

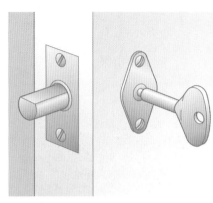

Rack bolts With every external door it is advisable to fit rack bolts to prevent forcing. The bolts are mortised into the opening edge of the door (page 200). Fit two to each door – and one at the top and bottom.

Rack bolts are an alternative method of locking a front door at night when the house is occupied.

If the glass is broken it is hard to see where the bolts are fitted. Even if the holes are found, a fluted key is needed to undo them.

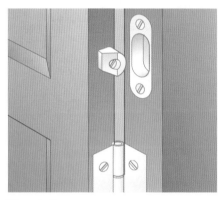

Hinge bolts It is possible to unhinge a door by using a jemmy on the hinge side. To prevent this, fit hinge bolts – two per door – about 75mm away from the hinges (page 200).

MULTI-LOCKING SYSTEMS FOR SECLUDED DOORS

External doors that are not overlooked are especially vulnerable because attempts by an intruder to gain entrance are unlikely to be spotted. To counter this, a multi-point locking system is advisable. This locking system can be used on doors 30–47mm thick, made of uPVC, composite material, timber or aluminium. Locking mechanisms can be fitted along the full length of the door. The high-security hookbolts are actuated by pulling the door handle up, and retracted by pulling the handle down. The door cannot be locked until all the bolts are thrown, and turning the key will deadlocks all locking points as well as the latch bolt.

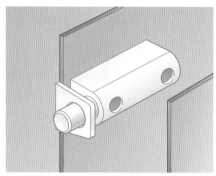

Self-locking bolts Where a door is too thin to house a rack bolt without being weakened, fit a surface mounted, self-locking bolt. It is merely screwed in place; when fitted, all screws are concealed. Pushing the bolt end slides it into the locked position, where it deadlocks and cannot be moved without the use of a key.

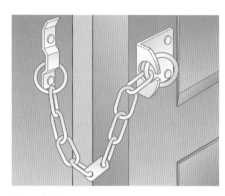

Door chains To prevent an intruder forcing his way in after ringing the doorbell, fit a chain to the front door. It allows the door to be opened just far enough to speak to a caller, but the door has to be shut again before the chain can be released to allow entry.

The strength of the device depends entirely on how well the chain is anchored to door and frame, so use the longest and heaviest-gauge screws possible.

Various patterns are available, including a simple chain, a chain combined with a sliding bolt, a chain which can be unlocked from the outside with a key, and a chain with an in-built alarm, which is triggered by an attempt to enter.

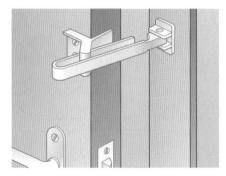

Door limiter A more substantial version of a door chain is a door limiter, with a sliding bar replacing the chain. When in place, the bar engages with the retaining part of the unit, restricting the opening of the door. The door has to be closed and the bar swung away before it can be fully opened.

Fitting door locks

Locks are vital to your security and safety, so make sure they are securely fitted and are sturdy enough to keep out intruders.

Fitting a cylinder rim lock

Tools *Pencil; tape measure; power drill and twist bits; flat wood bit (32 or 38mm); screwdriver. Perhaps chisel and mallet.*

Materials *Cylinder rim lock to British Standard BS3621.*

1 Mark the position of the key cylinder at a convenient height on the door stile, using the paper template supplied with the lock.

2 Drill the hole for the cylinder. When the point of the wood bit emerges through the door face, withdraw it and complete the hole from the other side. This will prevent the wood from splintering as the bit exits.

3 From the outside of the door, insert the cylinder throught the brass ring and into the hole. Hold the mounting plate against the inside face and fix the two together using the flat ended connecting screws supplied. The connecting bar will protrude through the mounting plate.

4 The connecting bar has grooves etched into it. Offer up the lock to the connecting bar and count how many grooves disappear into the lock. In this instance it is four. The connecting bar therefore needs to be 'four grooves' long. Mark the bar and saw off the excess with a junior hacksaw.

5 If the lock has a fore-end that screws to the door (this one doesn't), temporarily fit the lock onto the mounting plate and mark where to cut the recess. Cut it out using a sharp chisel.

6 Use the button on the lock case to latch the lock in its 'open' position. Align the arrow on the back of the case with the arrow on the rotatable slot. Fit the lock case onto the mounting plate ensuring the connecting bar engages in the lock.

7 Push the lock case downwards firmly onto the mounting plate and slide it sideways into its final position, flush with the edge of the door. Secure to the mounting plate with the two small screws supplied.

8 Close the door and mark the position of the 'staple' on the door frame, using the lock case as a guide. Then hold the staple to the frame and mark its perimeter with a pencil.

9 Chisel a recess in the door frame to hold the staple flush with the frame, and fix it in position with the screws supplied.

Fitting a mortise lock

Tools *Pencil; try square; power drill; twist drill bits; flat wood bit to match thickness of lock body; mallet; chisels; pliers; bradawl; padsaw; screwdriver.*

Materials *Mortise lock made to British Standard BS3621.*

1 Hold the lock in place against the door face. Ideally it should line up with the door's centre rail. On new flush doors, lock fixing points are often marked on the edge. Mark the dimensions of the lock casing on the door and transfer the height marks to the edge of the door using a try square.

2 Mark the centre line of the lock mortise on the edge of the door between the height marks. Then mark the depth of the lock body on the wood bit with a strip of tape, and drill an overlapping line of holes through the centre line to the depth of the lock body. Take care to keep the bit horizontal and square on to the door edge.

3 Use a mallet and a narrow chisel to square up the top and bottom of the mortise. Then use a wider chisel to trim the sides of the mortise so that the lock body will slide snugly into it.

4 Turn out the bolt of the lock with the key, then push it into the mortise and mark the shape of the fore-end (its rectangular faceplate) on the edge of the door. Grip the bolt with pliers to withdraw the lock.

5 Chisel a recess for the fore-end so the lock will fit flush with the edge of the door.

6 Hold the lock in position against the face of the door, and with a bradawl mark the centre point of the keyhole (and the handle spindle on a mortise sashlock).

7 Using a drill and twist bit, make holes through the door to take the key (and the handle spindle for a mortise sashlock), at the positions you have marked with the bradawl. Make the keyhole the correct shape by enlarging the lower part with a padsaw. Cut out the bottom of the keyhole with a narrow chisel.

8 With the bolt of the lock sticking out, push the lock into the mortise and check that the key (and handle spindle if required) will operate freely. Drill pilot holes and drive screws through the fore-end of the lock into the edge of the door.

9 For a mortise sashlock, push the handle spindle through the lock and screw the handle plates on each side of the door.

10 For a mortise lock, screw the keyhole plates on each side of the door.

11 Almost close the door and mark the positions of the deadbolt (and the latch of a sashlock) on the edge of the frame. Continue the mark onto the frame face.

12 Measure the distance from the outside face of the door to the centre of the bolt, and mark that distance on the frame, measuring from the doorstop.

13 Use the narrow chisel and mallet to cut mortises for the bolt (and latch if required). Check that the door closes properly. If not, enlarge the mortises as much as necessary.

14 Hold the lock striker plate over the two mortises and mark the outline of its faceplate on the door frame with a pencil.

15 Cut a recess for the faceplate, fit it and check that the door still closes properly. Screw the striker plate to the frame.

Fitting a new mechanism to a lock

If the keys are lost, or if you want to be sure of security when taking over a new house, it is cheaper to replace the working part of a lock than to buy a completely new unit.

Mortise lock

Buy a complete set of levers and keys for the right model of lock. If possible take the lock with you to the locksmith when you buy the new set.

Tools *Screwdriver; hammer; small piece of scrap wood.*

Materials *Lever set and keys.*

1 Remove the lock (page 200).

2 Carefully unscrew the cover plate and lift out the existing set of levers.

3 Put the new ones in place. It is vital to keep the levers in the order in which they are supplied.

4 Replace the cover plate, and fix the lock back into the door.

Cylinder rim lock

Buy a new cylinder and keys, as long as it is a straightforward lock. You cannot replace the cylinder on the type which has a locking interior handle.

Tools *Screwdriver; pliers; self-grip wrench or vice. Perhaps a mini hacksaw.*

Materials *New cylinder and keys.*

1 Unscrew the lock body from inside the door to expose the connecting screws which hold the cylinder in place.

2 Unscrew the connecting screws until the cylinder can be removed. The connecting bar will come too.

3 Hold the new connecting bar in a wrench or vice and use a junior hacksaw to cut it to the same length as the old one, so it is correctly housed in the interior handle when the cylinder is in place.

The bar is divided into breakable segments along its length.

4 Make sure that the connecting screws are also the right length. They can be cut to length with a junior hacksaw.

5 Insert the new cylinder into the hole. Tighten the screws and replace the lock body, making sure that the handle of the lock connects with the bar.

Replacing a mortise lock

When buying a new mortise lock, try to take the old one to ensure they are the same size and that the holes for the key and handle spindle match up.

Tools *Screwdriver; hammer; small piece of scrap wood.*

Materials *New five-lever mortise lock.*

1 Unscrew the handles or knobs. Unscrew the lock fore-end on the edge of the door.

2 If it is a sashlock, tap the spindle with a hammer towards the door edge to loosen the lock. Remove the spindle.

3 Lever out the lock at the top and bottom with the screwdriver, using a small piece of wood under the screwdriver to protect the door.

4 Insert the new lock in the slot, ensuring it is the right way round. Screw it in place. Replace the spindle and handles or knobs.

Adding security bolts to doors

Although most door locks are secure, you may feel the need for added safety – in which case, security bolts may be your best choice.

Fitting a rack bolt

Tools *Pencil; drill and bits (sizes according to the manufacturer's instructions); pliers; 19mm chisel; screwdriver; try square.*

Materials *Rack bolt.*

1 Mark a central point on the edge of the door where you want to fit the bolt. Use a try square and pencil to continue the mark onto the inner face of the door.

2 Drill a hole into the edge of the door to the diameter and depth of the body of the bolt.

3 Wind out the bolt and push it into the hole. Mark round the faceplate, withdraw the bolt with pliers and cut a shallow recess for the faceplate with a chisel.

4 Hold the bolt flush with the face of the door and mark the spot for the key. Drill a hole (see the manufacturer's instructions for the size) through the inside face of the door only.

5 Push the bolt back into the door and screw the faceplate to the edge of the door. Check that the bolt operates correctly. If necessary, enlarge the keyhole.

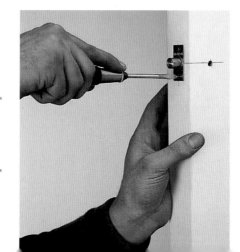

6 Screw the keyhole plate to the inside of the door.

7 Close the door and wind out the bolt to mark the door jamb. There is usually a pimple on the end of the bolt to mark the wood.

8 Open the door and drill a hole to the required depth at the mark. Check that the bolt will go smoothly into this hole.

9 Hold the cover plate over the hole, draw around it, cut out a shallow recess and screw the cover plate in place. Check the operation of the bolt and make any necessary adjustments.

Fitting hinge bolts

Tools *Pencil; drill and bits (sizes according to the manufacturer's instructions); adhesive tape; mallet; chisel; screwdriver.*

Materials *A pair of hinge bolts.*

1 Open the door fully and mark the centre of the door edge about 75mm away from the hinges at the top and the bottom.

2 Drill a hole into the door edge to the diameter and depth given on the maker's instructions.
Wrap a piece of coloured adhesive tape around the bit as a guide to the depth.

3 Push the bolt into the hole. Partially close the door so that the bolt marks the frame.

4 At this spot, drill a hole into the frame to the depth of the protruding bolt, plus a bit more for clearance. Check that the door shuts easily. If necessary, enlarge the hole.

5 Open the door and hold the cover plate over the hole. Mark the edge of the plate with a pencil and chisel out a recess so the plate lies flush with the frame.
Fix the plate in place with the screws provided.

Choosing handles, knobs and other door furniture

Door furniture is available in a multitude of designs, from ornate reproductions to simple modern styles. It may be made of cast iron, brass, aluminium, steel, ceramics, glass or plastic. Whatever the design or material, each piece of door furniture has a particular function.

HANDLES

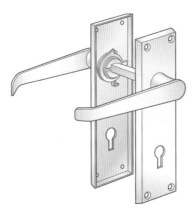

For a mortise sash lock Most commonly used for a back door. Also used with interior doors when privacy or security is a requirement. Each handle is handed left or right.

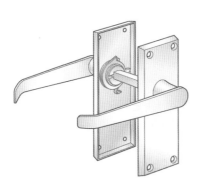

For a mortise latch The handle plate has no keyhole because a mortise latch is used on interior doors which will be left unlocked.

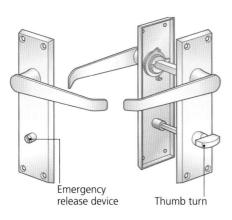

Emergency release device · Thumb turn

For a bathroom or WC A thumb-turn on the inside of the door prevents it from being opened. The outside of the door has an emergency release device. Buy either a right-hand or left-hand opening set, as the handles are not interchangeable.

DOOR KNOBS

Can be used on a mortise lock or latch, provided the spindle is far enough from the edge of the door to allow you to open the door without scraping your knuckles. Can be used for bathroom or WC doors with a privacy adaptor kit.

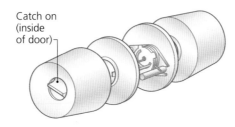

Catch on (inside of door)

For a bathroom or WC The knob has a catch that prevents the door from being opened from the outside.

DOOR FURNITURE

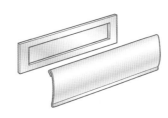

Letterplate and inner flap A standard letterplate fits on the outside of the front door. An inner flap fitted on the inside of the door gives a neat finish and helps to prevent draughts.

Door knocker
Fits to the front door instead of a bell. A wide range of designs is available.

Centre knob
For closing the front door as you leave the house. It is often fitted to the door above a central letterplate.

Pull handle
Can be fitted to either the inside or outside of a front door to provide a grip while opening or closing it.

Letterplate knockers
A horizontal letterplate (above) incorporates a handle for pulling the door closed; this can also be used as a door knocker.

A vertical option fits on the lock stile of the door. The hole allows a rim lock cylinder to be set into the knocker.

Escutcheon (open or covered) An escutcheon gives a tidy finish to the keyhole of a mortise lock. A covered escutcheon keeps out draughts.

Cylinder pull Fits under a rim lock cylinder on the outside of a front door, and is used to pull the door closed.

Bell push A bell push, which may be made of metal or plastic, is fitted to the door frame.

Fingerplate
Decorative plates to protect interior doors from becoming grubby with frequent use. Ceramic, brass and plastic are the most common types.

House numbers
The number of the house can be indicated with brass, black iron, plastic or porcelain numbers.

Fitting door furniture

The front door of a house usually needs a letterplate, a handle to close the door (which may be built into the letterplate), either a knocker or bellpush, and probably a house number.

Before you start A power jigsaw makes the job of cutting the letterplate opening much quicker than doing it by hand with a padsaw.

Letterhead

There are many different designs available for letterplates. Some incorporate a handle which can be used as a door-knocker.

Tools *Pencil; ruler; power drill and twist bits; 13mm flat wood bit; jigsaw or padsaw; chisel; abrasive paper; screwdriver; small adjustable spanner; hacksaw.*

Materials *Letterplate and fittings.*

1 Decide where you want the letterplate. On a panel door it can be fitted horizontally in the middle rail or vertically on the lock stile. On a flush door, fit it horizontally in the middle to coincide with the rail position that is marked on the edge of the door.

2 Measure the size of the flap and spring mechanism and lightly mark the outline of the required cut-out with a pencil.

3 Using the flat bit, drill a 13mm hole at each corner of the cut-out position and saw along the cut-out line. Preferably use a jigsaw with a long blade. Alternatively, you can make the cut-out with a padsaw, but it will be very slow work.

4 At each side of the cut-out, mark the positions of the holes for the fixing bolts.

5 Working from the front of the door, drill 13mm diameter holes to a depth of 13mm to accommodate the fixing lugs of the letterplate.

6 Using a twist bit the same diameter as the fixing bolts, drill from the centre of the holes right through the door.
    Smooth the edges of the holes with abrasive paper.

7 Fit the letterplate to the door and then tighten the fixing nuts with an adjustable spanner.

8 If the bolts protrude, use a hacksaw to cut them off flush with the face of the nuts.

Door knocker

1 Hold the knocker in position and press it hard against the door so that the lugs leave light marks.

2 At these positions, drill holes for the lugs and the bolts.

3 Screw the bolts into the lugs on the back of the knocker, and push them through the holes.

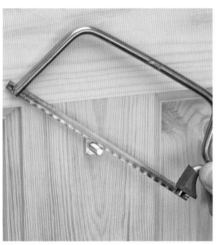

4 Tighten the fixing nuts, and if the bolts protrude cut them off flush with the face of the nuts.

LOOSE OR BROKEN HINGES

If a wooden window is sticking, the hinges may be loose or broken. Retighten them or replace them, using the same technique as for door hinges (page 192).

Wooden windows that stick

If a window will not open or close easily, examine it carefully to discover the cause.

Build-up of paint

Layers of paint that have built up over the years are a common cause of sticking windows.

1 Use a hot-air gun or chemical paint stripper to strip the edge of the window and the frame back to bare wood.

2 Check that there is a clearance gap of about 2mm between the edge of the window and the frame before repainting.

3 If necessary, plane the window edge to give enough clearance. A casement window can be removed by unscrewing the hinges from the frame. For removing a sliding sash window, see page 206.

Swollen timber

Damp that has made the timber swell is also a cause of sticking windows.

1 Strip off the paint and either let the timber dry out during fine weather, or dry it quickly with a hot-air gun.

2 When it is dry make sure there is a clearance gap of about 2mm between window and frame. If necessary, plane the edge of the window.

3 Repaint the window, ensuring that putty around the glass is well covered with paint.

Staff beads too tight

On a sliding sash window, the staff beads might have been nailed on too close to the inner sash.

1 Prise off the staff beads (see Replacing broken sash cords, page 206) and re-nail them so they lightly touch the edges of the inner sash. Before driving the nails right in, test that the sash will slide easily.

2 Rub the inside face of the staff bead with a candle to help to improve the sliding action.

3 Check that there is not a build-up of paint on the inside edge of the staff beads.

4 If necessary, loosen the old paint with a chemical paint stripper and then scrape it off. Re-coat with new paint.

Fixing loose joints on windows

The corner joints on both sash and casement windows often work loose. A painted window can be repaired with a steel corner plate. A window finished with varnish or wood stain must be repaired with glued dowels, or the repair will show.

A corner-plate repair

Flat L-shaped steel corner plates are available in various sizes. Choose one large enough to bridge the damaged area and give a secure fixing into sound wood. Before putting it on, repair any damage with epoxy filler.

Tools *Small wooden wedges; trimming knife; chisel; small paintbrush; abrasive paper.*

Materials *Steel corner plates; 25mm No. 10 countersunk zinc-plated screws; metal primer; exterior filler; paint.*

1 Drive small wooden wedges between the frame and the window to close the joint. On a sash window, first remove the staff beads (see Replacing broken sash cords, page 206).

2 Put a plate over the joint on the inside or outside of the window – or both if it is very weak – and mark around it with a knife.

Wooden wedges are useful for various DIY jobs when you want to hold something securely in position while you glue it or fix it in some other way.

1 Take a piece of softwood about 100mm long, 20mm wide and 15mm thick, and rule a pencil line across diagonally from one corner to another.

2 Hold the wood securely with cramps or in a vice while you saw along the line to produce two wedges.

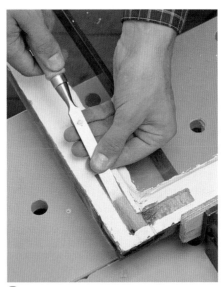

3 Cut a recess for the plate to rest slightly below the surface.

4 Fix the plate with the screws, and paint it with metal primer.

5 Cover the repair with exterior filler, smooth with abrasive paper, and paint with undercoat and two coats of gloss.

A dowelled joint

Glued dowels driven through the joint give an invisible and very strong repair.

Tools *Screwdriver; G-cramps or portable workbench, sash cramp or web cramp; drill and 6mm twist bit; chisel; hammer; panel saw; abrasive paper; paintbrush.*

Materials *6mm dowels; waterproof wood adhesive; varnish or preservative stain.*

1 Take out a casement window by unscrewing the hinges. To remove a sash window, see page 206.

2 Close the loose joints with a sash cramp or web cramp, then cramp the window to a workbench.

3 Drill holes for three 6mm dowels per joint. One goes through the face of the vertical stile to pin the tenon that protrudes from the end of the horizontal rail.

Two go through the side of the vertical stile into the end of the horizontal rail to reinforce both sides of the tenon.

4 Smear the dowels and the holes with wood glue, and drive in the dowels with a hammer.

5 When the glue has set, cut off the surplus dowel so that each one is flush with the surface of the wood.

6 Smooth the repair with abrasive paper, and coat it with varnish or preservative wood stain.

Gaps around a window frame

Gaps around the outside of the window frames will result in damp appearing on the internal walls around the window. It will also encourage rot to attack the frames.

Using frame sealant

Cracks up to about 10mm wide can be filled with frame sealant (see panel).

Tools *Trimming knife; thin screwdriver; clean rag.*

Materials *Frame sealant and applicator. Perhaps a jar of water.*

CHOOSING FRAME SEALANT

Frame sealant is commonly available from hardware shops and DIY stores in three colours – white, brown and transparent, but other colours are sometimes available.

The sealant is sold in a cartridge which may either have a screw-down applicator or has to be fitted into a trigger-operated sealant gun. The gun is not expensive to buy and will last indefinitely.

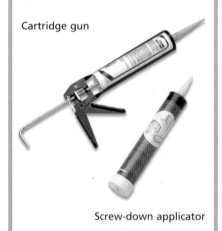

Cartridge gun

Screw-down applicator

---

1 With a trimming knife, cut the nozzle off the sealant cartridge at an angle to give the necessary width of sealant to fill the gap. Break the foil seal or cut the sealed top of the cartridge.

2 Wipe around the frame with a clean rag, and inject a bead of sealant into the crack all round. The sealant should be placed in the angle between the window frame and the wall.

For neatness, try to inject the sealant in a single run without stopping, except at corners. Release the trigger to stop the flow.

3 If it is necessary to smooth the sealant, use a wet finger.

4 Sealant can be painted once a skin has formed (one to three weeks), but it is not necessary.

EXPANDING FOAM FILLER

For large, irregular gaps that are hard to reach, use a can of expanding foam filler. This adheres to most building materials. It is injected by nozzle at any angle, after which it expands in volume, effectively sealing even hidden areas. Once hardened, the foam is heat, cold and water resistant and rot-proof. It can be cut, sanded, plastered or painted.

Sealing with mortar

If the gap is more than about 10mm wide it should be filled with mortar, which is available in small bags – ideal for jobs of this scale.

Tools *Plant sprayer; small trowel or filling knife; trimming knife; clean rag.*

Materials *Water; mortar; sealant and applicator.*

1 Dampen the crack with water. A plant sprayer is ideal.

2 Press the mortar in place with a small trowel or filling knife, so that it is level with the surface of the brickwork.

3 When the mortar has hardened, which will take two or three days, seal all round the frame with frame sealant as described above.

Problems with metal windows

Old steel windows often rust. If the putty has been dislodged or the glass cracked, first carefully chip out the putty with an old chisel or hacking knife and remove the glass. Whether or not the glass has to be removed, the renovation process is the same.

Rust in old frames

Tools *Paint scraper or small brush, for paint stripper; small cold chisel; hammer; wire brush; safety goggles; small paintbrush; gloves.*

Materials *Rust remover; zinc-based primer; undercoat; gloss paint; white spirit. Possibly paint stripper and epoxy filler.*

1 Scrape off the paint, or remove it with a chemical paint stripper.

2 Using a small cold chisel, chip off as many of the rust flakes as possible. Then wire-brush the frame by hand, or use a wire wheel or wire-cup brush in a power drill. Wear safety goggles and gloves during this part of the job.

3 Brush over the frame to remove dust and loose particles, then fill any holes with epoxy-based filler and allow it to dry.

4 Paint the prepared frame with a coat of rust remover.

5 When the rust remover is dry, apply a zinc-based metal primer, then an undercoat and two coats of gloss paint.

6 If necessary, re-glaze the window, using metal casement putty (page 209).

Warped frames

Check whether a build-up of paint or rust on the frame is distorting it. If this is so, clean it off and repaint the frame.

If the frame is warped for no apparent reason, nothing can be done to straighten it. Seal the gap between window and frame with silicone sealant. First clean both frames with soap and water and dry them thoroughly. Then put a bead of sealant on the fixed frame, making sure that it is deep enough to fill the gap.

Cover the closing frame with soapy water, shut it tight to compress the sealant, then open it at once. Leave the sealant to set, and it will form a perfect seal. Trim off excess sealant with a knife.

Paint not adhering to galvanising

On new steel frames paint will sometimes flake off the galvanised surface soon after being applied.

1 Remove existing paint with paint stripper to get right back to the galvanising.

2 Rub the frame lightly with fine wet-and-dry abrasive paper, used wet. Wipe it with a clean damp cloth.

3 When it is dry, wipe it with a clean rag soaked in white spirit, then prime with metal primer.

4 Repaint the window frame with an undercoat and gloss paint.

Condensation

Condensation is quite a common problem with metal windows, and in serious or persistent cases it can lead to the surrounding wallpaper or plaster becoming damp.

In cold weather, windows are always colder than other parts of a room, because they are thinner than the walls, so when the warm, humid air from inside the room meets the glass, condensation forms. The problem is exaggerated with metal-framed windows, because the metal of the frames gets colder than wooden or plastic frames.

The most effective solution is to fit a replacement window and frame made of timber or plastic. Even an aluminium frame will produce an improvement, as long as it is fitted with a thermal break to insulate the outside face from the inner face.

Windows that are kept permanently closed are particularly susceptible to condensation. Fitting ventilation locks to these windows and keeping them secured slightly ajar will help.

Alternatively Fit a secondary double glazing system (page 211–13) to isolate the cold metal surfaces from the warm air inside the room.

Alternatively Installing an extractor fan will also help, by extracting the moist air from the room.

Replacing broken sash cords

When a sash cord breaks, replace all four cords on the window. The other three are probably failing, too.

Tools *Old chisel; string; trimming knife; pincers; screwdriver; hammer; small weight (a screw will do); matches. Perhaps machine oil.*

Materials *Sash cords (preferably Terylene); 25mm galvanised clout (large head) nails; 25mm oval nails; filler.*

Taking out the sashes

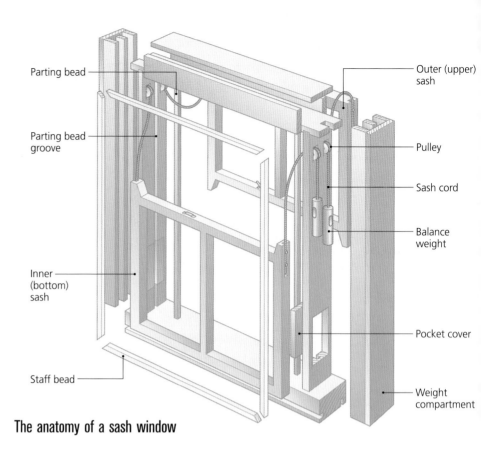

Parting bead

Parting bead groove

Inner (bottom) sash

Staff bead

Outer (upper) sash

Pulley

Sash cord

Balance weight

Pocket cover

Weight compartment

The anatomy of a sash window

1 Working from inside the room, prise off the staff beads from the front of the window frame on each side. An old chisel or a large screwdriver is a suitable tool for the job.

   Start at the centre of the staff bead to avoid damaging the mitre joints at the top and bottom. Once they have been lifted at the centre, the staff beads can be sprung out of place.

2 Lift the bottom sash out of the window as far as it will go. Rest it on a table or a portable workbench or ask someone to hold it for you.

3 Tie the end of a ball of string to the upper part of each cord (if the cords are not already broken).

4 Hold each cord in turn, and cut through it with a trimming knife. Release it gently to lower the balance weight to the bottom of the box. This will draw the string over the pulley. The string will be used to thread the new cord. Set the released sash to one side.

5 Prise the narrow parting beads out of their grooves. If they have been nailed (incorrectly) rather than merely wedged in place, remove the nails with pincers, taking care not to split the beads.

   If they are already split, buy new beads and cut them to length.

6 Lift the top sash into the room. If the cords are unbroken, tie string to the upper part and then cut the cords in the same way as before.

Fixing the cords to the weights

1 When measuring up for new cords, measure from the top of the window down to the sill, and add two-thirds again. This will allow enough spare cord for fixing at each end. Cut four pieces of cord to this length – one for each weight.

2 With the chisel, carefully prise the pocket covers from the weight channel at each side of the frame, towards the bottom. Usually they are just pushed in place, but sometimes they are screwed.

3 Reach into the pockets and lift the weights (two on each side) into the room. Leave the strings in place over the pulleys, ready to pull the new cords through.

4 Where cords have broken, tie a 'mouse' (any small weight – a screw will do) to a length of string and push it over the pulley, so that it drops down into the weight compartment and can be drawn out through the pocket.

5 Use a screwdriver to push the old pieces of cord out of the sash weights.

6 Remove the old cords from the grooves in the side of the window sashes. They are held with clout (large-head) nails which can be extracted with pincers.

HELPFUL TIP

To make a sash window slide up and down more smoothly, rub a candle over all the sliding surfaces and lightly oil the pulleys. You can do this at any time to ease running but make a point of doing it when the window is dismantled for repair.

7 Tie the end of the new cord to the string coming from one of the rear pulleys. Pull it over the pulley, into the weight compartment, and out through the pocket.

8 Untie the string, and tie the new cord to the balance weight, using a double knot. To prevent Terylene cord from fraying, heat the end with a match to melt the fibres into a solid lump.

9 Replace the weight in the pocket. Repeat the process for all four weights, then fit the pocket covers in place; they should not be nailed or glued.

Fixing the cords to the sashes

1 Rest the top (outer) sash on the inside window ledge.

2 Get a helper to pull down one of the cords so that the weight is at the top of its compartment and just touching the pulley.

3 Screw or nail the cord into the groove at the side of the sash, using galvanised screws or clout (large-head) nails. Do not fit the screws or nails close to the top of the groove; they will prevent the sash sliding all the way up. The top screw or nail must be no higher than the distance from the mid-point of the pulley to the top of the frame.

HELPFUL TIP

If you have no one to help you nail the cord to the side of the sash, pull the weight up to the top of its compartment and wind the cord around a screwdriver. It will hold the weight while you nail the other end of the cord in place.

Alternatively Jam a wedge, such as a pencil, between the cord and the top of the pulley aperture.

4 Repeat for the second cord.

5 Put the sash in place and check that it operates smoothly before you reassemble the window.

Reassembling the window

1 Refit the parting beads between the runners on each side, tapping them into the grooves so they will not move.

2 Attach the sash cords to the lower (inner) sash in the same way as the upper sash. Then fit the sash in position in the frame.

3 Refit the staff beads on each side of the frame, checking that the mitred ends match up neatly with the beads at the top and bottom. Fix them without glue, using two or three oval nails so that they will be easy to remove in the future. Do not drive the nails fully home yet.

4 Check that the lower sash operates easily. If it rattles in its runners move the beads slightly closer to the sash. If not, drive the nails home. If the staff beads are damaged, replace them with lengths of new beading mitred at each end.

5 Repair any damaged areas around the frame with wood filler. When it is dry, smooth with abrasive paper and touch up the repairs with paint.

Renewing parting beads and staff beads

Before you can renew the beads, remove the damaged ones as described under Replacing broken sash cords (page 206).

Renewing parting beads

1 Buy new parting beads the same dimensions as the old ones or slightly larger and plane them down. Cut the beads to the height of the inner frame.

2 With a plane, take a few shavings off the length of the bead on each side, towards the edge that will fit into the groove. This slight taper will ensure that the bead is a tight fit.

3 Tap the beads into the grooves; there is no need to nail them.

Renewing staff beads

Buy new staff beads the same dimensions as the old ones. Alternatively, buy new ones as close as possible in shape, and long enough to go all round the frame. You will need slightly more than the measurement of the frame to allow a little wastage for mitres to be cut at each corner.

1 Cut a 45° mitre at one end of a length of bead, using a mitre box to ensure an accurate cut.

2 Hold the bead against the frame with the mitre pressed into a corner and mark with a pencil where the other mitre is to be cut.

3 Cut a second mitre, and repeat for each length of beading all round the frame.

4 When all the lengths have been cut, wedge them in place and examine the corner joints for fit.

5 Fix each bead in place with two or three 25mm oval nails.

Fixing a sash window that rattles

Sash windows will rattle if there is too much space around each sash.

The problem occurs more often with the lower (inner) sash and is caused by the inner (staff) bead not being fixed close enough to the sash. The remedy is to remove and re-fix the two staff beads (see left). If a top sash rattles, there is no way to reduce the width of the track, but fitting draught excluders (see right) can help.

Small plastic wedges can be bought for pushing between the sashes and the beads. They stop rattles, but must be removed whenever the window is raised or lowered.

Fitting a fitch catch

Another possible cure is to change the existing window catch for a fitch catch – a cam-shaped sash fastener which draws the sashes tightly together when closed. The two parts are screwed to the upper surfaces of the meeting rails of each sash.

Fitting a draught excluder

To cure draughts and rattles in one operation, fit a nylon brush pile draught excluder to the inside face of the staff beads so that the inner face of the lower sash presses against it. Fit another strip between the outer frame and the upper sash so its outer face presses against the strip.

Alternatively Fit the draught excluder to the inner face of one of the meeting rails. This is simpler, but is only effective in reducing rattles when the window is fully closed.

Replacing a broken window pane

There is no need to call a specialist when a window pane breaks. It is quicker and much cheaper to replace it yourself.

Before you start When buying glass, tell the supplier the size of the panes. He will advise on the thickness of glass you should use and will cut them to fit.

Use 3mm glass in very small panes, such as Georgian-style windows. For windows up to about 1m square use 4mm glass. For anything larger, use 6mm glass.

When glass is to be used over a very large area such as a picture window, or where it may be mistaken for an opening, as in a patio door, or where it will be fitted within 800mm of the floor, use safety glass.

For wooden windows use linseed oil, universal or acrylic putty; for metal windows use metal casement, universal or acrylic putty. You will need about 1kg of putty for 3.5m of frame. Brown putty is available for windows that are to be finished with preservative stain. Broken glass in doors is replaced in the same way as for wooden windows, unless the door has been glazed with beads which are replaced as for square-edged double glazing units (page 210).

Tools *Leather gloves; safety goggles; glass cutter; hammer; hacking knife or old chisel; pincers; dustpan and brush; paintbrush; putty knife.*

Materials *Primer paint; putty; glazing springs; glass to fit the window.*

Removing the broken glass

1 Lay a dustsheet on the ground on both sides of the window to catch the fragments of old glass.

2 Put on leather gloves and safety goggles. Also wear thick leather shoes in case jagged pieces of glass fall to the ground.

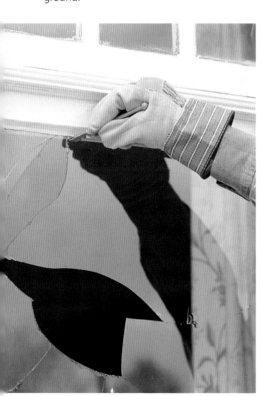

3 Using a glass cutter, score the glass all round the window, close to the putty.

4 Working from the outside, tap the glass with a hammer to break it, starting from the top. Try to keep the pieces as large as possible.

5 After breaking out as much old glass as possible, remove remaining putty and glass with a hacking knife or old chisel. Hold a hacking knife in one hand with the point against the putty and tap it on the blunt edge with a hammer. Look out for glazing sprigs embedded in the putty, or metal clips in metal frames. Pull them out with pincers. Leave the rebate in the window as clean as possible, before putting in new glass.

6 Brush all dust from the frame and paint a wooden frame with primer, which should be allowed to dry. This is not necessary on a metal window unless it is rusty (page 205). If the window has to be left overnight, cover it with a sheet of polythene or a piece of plywood (see panel, right).

Putting in the new glass

1 Mould the putty in your hands to get it soft and pliable. If it sticks to your hands, try wetting them, or take some of the oil out by rolling the putty on kitchen paper.

2 Hold the pliable putty in the palm of your hand and squeeze it out between the thumb and forefinger to form a layer about 3mm thick in the rebate all the way round the window.

3 Press the glass carefully into the rebate so it is well bedded on the putty. Press it round the edges only, taking care not to push too hard in one place – and never in the middle of the glass. It could break and cause injury.

4 Fix the glass in place with glazing sprigs inserted into the window about 250mm apart. Knock them in with the edge of the chisel or with the back of the hacking knife, sliding it along the face of the glass. The heads of the sprigs should protrude about 5mm from the frame. Trim off excess bedding putty on the inside of the pane.

5 Apply more putty to the front of the glass to fill the rebate, and smooth it off with a putty knife to form a neat triangular line of putty that covers the heads of the sprigs and lines up with the putty on the inside edge. Make neat mitres at corners.

6 Leave the putty for about two weeks to harden slightly before painting it. When you paint it, allow the paint to spread onto the glass by 3mm to keep out the rain.

Repairing leaded lights

Doors and windows may have leaded-light panels, consisting of small panes of glass held together with lead strips that are H-shaped in cross section.

Repairing cracked glass

It may not be necessary to fit new glass if the crack is only a minor one. You can try running a few drops of Glass Bond cyano-aerylate adhesive into the crack.

Replacing broken panes in a leaded-light panel is a difficult job best left to a glazier.

Curing bulges and buckles

Take the complete panel out of the frame. It may be held with putty, like an ordinary sheet of glass (page 209), or it may be held with both putty and an outer wood beading. You can remove the beading by unscrewing it or, if it is nailed, by prising it out very gently. Lay the panel on a flat surface and press the lead strips flat. Be very careful not to press too hard or you are likely to crack the glass panes.

If this does not work, it may be necessary to take the panel to a glazier to have it rebuilt. While this is being done, cover the opening in the door or window, as explained on page 209.

Dealing with leaks

Using polyurethane varnish

1 Mark the leaks with a wax crayon so repairs can be undertaken in fine weather.

2 Carefully scrape any dirt away from the edge of the lead strips.

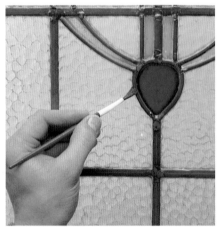

3 With a small artist's brush, paint clear, exterior grade polyurethane varnish liberally along the flanges of the strips. Take great care to seal the outside of the glass.

Alternatively Inject a bead of the clear sealant used to seal leaks around car windscreens.

4 Press the flanges down, with a helper supporting them firmly from the other side. Wipe varnish off the lead and the glass with a cloth moistened with white spirit.

Using putty

If the varnish does not work, the putty in which the glass is set must be replaced. Use soft glazier's metal casement putty. You can colour the putty grey with a little black powder paint.

1 Open up the lead strips slightly on the outside of the window by levering up the edges with a chisel. To do this it may be necessary to cut through the corner joints with a trimming knife.

2 Scrape out as much of the old putty as possible and clean out the dirt.

3 Press in the new putty.

4 Press the lead strip back in place, with a helper supporting the glass from the inside.

5 If it was necessary to cut the corner joints, glue them back together with two-part acrylic glue.

6 Wipe the excess putty off the lead and the glass.

Replacing double-glazed panes

There are three main ways of replacing broken double-glazed panes, depending on whether they are sealed stepped units, square-edge units, or are in aluminium or plastic windows.

Before you start Double glazing units must be bought ready-made to the size of your window from a glass merchant or double glazing supplier.

Sealed stepped units

Replacing sealed stepped double glazing is similar to fitting a single sheet of glass, except that spacer blocks are fitted in the rebate of the window to keep the stepped part of the double glazed unit clear of the frame.

Retain the old spacer blocks so they can be re-used, or buy new ones from your glass merchant. Window companies are unlikely to sell them.

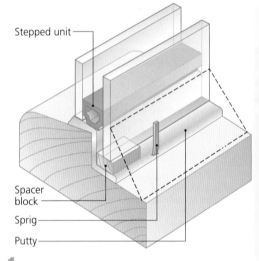

Stepped unit

Spacer block

Sprig

Putty

1 Place the spacer blocks in a bed of putty about 300mm apart along the bottom of the rebate.

2 Stand the double-glazed pane on the blocks and fix it in place with sprigs all round. Apply putty to the outside of the window in the normal way.

Square-edge units

Glazing beads are usually screwed into the outside of the window to hold square-edged double glazing units in place.

1 Unscrew the glazing beads before removing the broken glass.

2 Put a bed of non-setting putty (available from glass merchants) around the rebate. Press spacer blocks into the putty (two blocks spaced well apart on each of the four sides).

3 Lift the sealed unit into place on the spacers and press it well back into the rebate.

4 Coat the glazing beads with non-setting putty on the inside face and press them tightly in place against the glazing units.

5 Fix the beads in place with brass screws.

Aluminium or plastic windows

The glass is often in rubber gaskets, making replacement difficult. Call in a glazier, or ask the manufacturer for details on glass replacement for your particular model of window.

Choosing double glazing

Double glazing – having two layers of glass instead of one in a window – traps a layer of still air or inert gas between the panes. This acts as an insulator, but the warm inner pane also reduces cold down-draughts from the window and prevents condensation. Although double glazing will not save much on fuel bills, it will greatly increase indoor comfort. There are two main types of double-glazing – single sealed units and secondary double glazing.

How double glazing works

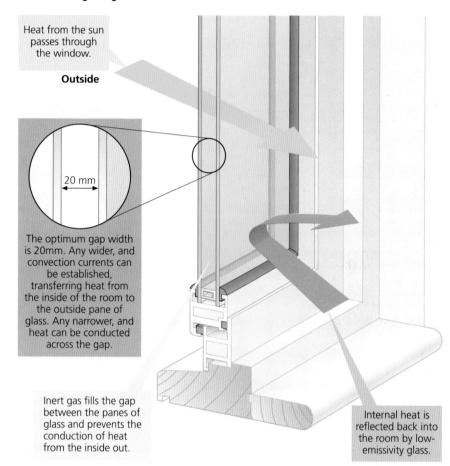

Heat from the sun passes through the window.

Outside

20 mm

The optimum gap width is 20mm. Any wider, and convection currents can be established, transferring heat from the inside of the room to the outside pane of glass. Any narrower, and heat can be conducted across the gap.

Inert gas fills the gap between the panes of glass and prevents the conduction of heat from the inside out.

Internal heat is reflected back into the room by low-emissivity glass.

Sealed units Two panes of glass separated by a spacer are bonded together and sealed at the factory before being fitted into the window frame. The panes may be separated by between 6 and 20mm; wide gaps give better insulation than narrow ones.

Secondary double glazing A pane of glass or plastic is fixed to the window frame, leaving an air gap between it and the existing glass. This is less effective than a sealed unit unless the opening part of the window is well draught-proofed. The air gaps are generally wider than in a sealed unit, allowing the air to circulate between the panes and carry heat from the warm inner pane to the colder outer one. Condensation in the gap can be a problem in cold weather.

Triple glazing A wide air gap between panes of glass (100–200mm) insulates effectively against noise, but is too wide to retain heat. Triple glazing combines a sealed twin-pane unit with a third pane, like secondary glazing, to provide excellent heat and sound insulation.

Replacement windows

Many householders acquire double glazing when having old windows replaced. All double glazing companies offer windows (usually made from uPVC – unplasticised polyvinyl chloride – with steel internal reinforcement) that are fitted with tailor-made sealed units. For maximum insulation efficiency, these should have 20mm wide air gaps.

While it is possible to buy new wooden window frames and glaze them yourself with single panes of glass, the initial cost saving far outweighs the long-term heat losses that will result. Fitting sealed units into existing wooden frames is possible, but the design of the frame often precludes the use of units with wide and efficient air gaps. If you want to investigate this possibility further, ask for advice at your local glass merchant.

Four cheap secondary double glazing systems

A house can be fitted with secondary double glazing relatively cheaply using materials that give effective results. They have to be removed in summer, and may not look very attractive. Nevertheless, the cost saving compared with having replacement windows is considerable.

Study the fitting instructions supplied with the system you choose and follow them carefully. Double-check your measurements before you order glass or rigid plastic sheet. Mistakes can be expensive.

Clean the windows, inside and out, before you start work. If you are using a system that involves adhesive tape, make sure the window frame is clean and dry. The tape will not stick to surfaces that are dirty or damp.

Existing window glass
Secondary glazing fixed to internal window frame

How secondary double glazing works
Secondary double glazing systems are fitted on the inside of an existing window. The secondary panel is usually fixed to the inside of the frame, creating a gap the depth of the frame between the exterior glass and the double glazing. Hinged or sliding systems are available from glazing companies or in kit form, allowing you to open the window without removing the double glazing.

Insulating film

A clear plastic film is stuck to the window frame and then shrunk with gentle heat from a hair dryer to remove wrinkles. Although this is not a permanent system, you could extend its life by attaching the plastic film to a frame of timber battens. The framework could be taken down when not required and kept for later use.

Tools *Scissors; hair dryer.*

Materials *Kit containing clear film and double-sided adhesive tape.*

1 Cut a sheet of film a little larger than the window, so that it overlaps all round the window frame by about 50mm.

2 Stick the double-sided adhesive tape around the frame.

3 Remove the backing from the tape and press the film against it, working from the top downwards and keeping it as taut as possible.

4 Warm the film with a hair dryer to remove wrinkles.

5 Trim off the excess film.

Plastic channelling

Strips of plastic channelling are fitted along the edges of a sheet of glass or rigid plastic. They are then fixed to the window frame with screws and fixing clips.

Some systems have hinged channelling that allows the secondary glazing to be opened. Other types are fixed to the window frame all round and cannot be opened. They have to be taken down completely in summer before any windows can be opened.

Measure the window to allow for the glass or rigid plastic to overlap onto the frame, leaving enough space for the fixing clips to be screwed to the frame.

Tools *Trimming knife or tenon saw (depending on the type of channelling); pencil; bradawl; screwdriver. Perhaps a mitre box.*

Materials *Sheet of 4mm glass or 2–4mm rigid plastic; plastic channelling; screws; fixing clips.*

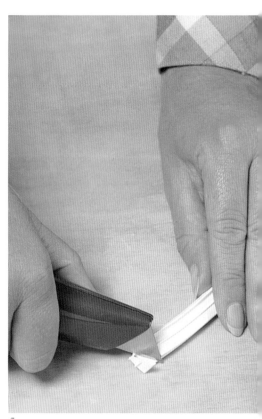

1 Cut the channelling to fit the four edges of the glass or plastic sheet. Mitre the ends to give a neat fit. If the channelling is rigid you will need a tenon saw or hacksaw and a mitre box. Push the channelling onto the glass or plastic sheet.

2 Hold the framed pane over the window while a helper marks positions for the fixing holes, following the maker's instructions for spacing.

3 Deepen the marked spots with the bradawl to provide pilot holes, and screw the fixing clips and glazing in place.

Fixing with Velcro tape

Rigid plastic sheet can be fixed with self-adhesive touch-and-close fastening tape, such as Velcro.
• When you are buying the plastic, measure it to overlap 15mm on all sides of the window frame.
• Do not use glass, because it is too heavy for the system.
• The double glazing can be removed when necessary but the loop part of the tape will have to remain in place and it may look unsightly and collect dirt.

Tools *Scissors.*

Materials *Self-adhesive touch-and-close fastening tape; 2–4mm thick clear rigid plastic; foam-strip draught excluder.*

1 Cut several pieces of tape about 40mm long. It is too expensive to use in long strips.

2 Peel the backing paper off the loop (soft) side of the tape and fix it in place at intervals around the window frame.

3 Leave the backing paper on the hook side of the tape, and press the pieces onto the loop strips.

4 Stick foam-strip draught excluder between the patches to prevent draughts.

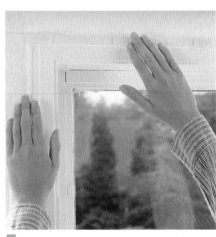

5 Peel off the remaining backing paper from the tape and press the pane in place.

Magnetic fixing tape

Rigid plastic sheets can be fitted as secondary glazing using magnetic fixing strip. The strip has two self-adhesive parts, a magnetic strip that adheres to the plastic and a metal strip to go on the frame.
• The system is designed for use with plastic up to 4mm thick. Never use it with glass because it is not strong enough to hold the weight.
• Have the plastic cut slightly larger than the window so that it overlaps onto the frame by about 25mm.

Tools *Scissors or trimming knife.*

Materials *Magnetic fixing strip; 2–4mm thick clear rigid plastic.*

1 Cut the strip to fit around the plastic, mitring the corners with sharp scissors or a trimming knife.

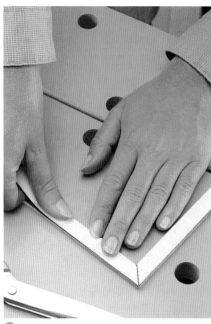

2 Stick the strip to the plastic, with the metal half upwards.

3 Press the sheet to the frame. The metal strip will stay on the frame when the plastic pane is removed.

4 The metal strip can be covered with a thin coat of paint to match the window frame. This makes it less noticeable when the sheet is removed. When redecorating, rub the surface with fine abrasive paper to prevent a build-up of paint.

Fitting a wooden casement window

Replacement wooden windows are usually needed because the existing windows have rotted beyond repair.

What to buy Buy a replacement that matches the style of the other windows in the house, but take the opportunity to upgrade it by making sure it is double-glazed and completely weather-sealed so that it is draught-free.

• Buy a standard size window and frame to fit the space. If that is not possible you can have one made to measure, but it will be much more expensive.

• Before you fit the new frame, give it an extra coat of primer or wood preservative, depending on whether it is to be painted or varnished.

Before you start Wooden casement windows are easily fitted provided they can be bought to fit the size of the existing openings.

• The most important part of the job is measuring the opening in the wall. Take measurements in several positions. Check that the diagonals are equal, which means that the opening has right-angled corners.

• With a spirit level, check that the sill and top of the frame are both level, and that the sides are vertical. If they are not, it may be best to call in a builder, or a replacement window company.

• Do not start to remove the old window until you have taken delivery of the new window.

• New windows are usually supplied without glass or double-glazed units, which are installed after the window has been fitted.

• The job is likely to last more than a day, so be prepared to cover the wall opening – or unglazed window – with polythene or hardboard overnight to keep out the weather.

Tools *Spirit level; steel tape measure; screwdriver; leather work gloves; safety goggles; claw hammer; metal container for broken glass; hacksaw blade; old wood saw; wrecking bar or lever; bolster chisel; builder's trowel; power drill; twist bits; countersink bit; masonry bit to match wall plugs; sealant gun. Possibly a plane and self-grip wrench.*

Materials *New wooden window frame; mortar (page 467); wooden wedges; 100mm No. 14 countersunk zinc-plated screws; wall plugs for screws; strip of damp-proof course the width of the window; frame sealant. Possibly also: strips of hardwood as wide as the frame's thickness; panel pins; wood mouldings to go around frame; plaster.*

Removing the existing window

1 Remove hinged windows by unscrewing the hinges. If the window is a big one, you will need a helper to support it.

2 Remove the glass from any fixed windows. Wearing the gloves and goggles, break the glass with a hammer. Remove all the pieces from the frame and put them into a metal container for safe disposal.

3 You will probably have to take the frame out in pieces. Use an old saw to cut through the vertical and horizontal timbers close to the sides, top and bottom of the frame.

4 Saw at an angle through the jamb at one side of the frame.

5 With a strong lever, such as a wrecking bar, prise the jamb that you have sawn through until it comes away from the brickwork. This will allow you to lever out the other parts of the frame – the top, the sill and finally the jamb at the other side.

If an internal window board is fitted inside the windowsill, keep it in one piece, because you will need it when you fit the new window. Try also to keep the sides of the opening intact, as you do not want to damage the wall plaster or the damp-proof strip that closes the wall cavity.

6 Clean up the sides, top and bottom of the opening with a bolster chisel to leave the bricks as smooth as possible and free from old mortar.

7 Remove any protruding screws (with a self-grip wrench) or nails (with a claw hammer). Take out any bits of timber 'horns' from the frame that may have been built into the top corners of the opening.

8 Fill any large cavities neatly with pieces of brick and mortar and wait for the repairs to dry.

TAKING OUT THE FRAME IN ONE PIECE

It might be possible to remove the old window frame in one piece.

1 Locate the screws or nails fixing the frame to the wall and clear them of mortar.

2 Cut through the screws with a hacksaw blade. Fit the blade into the handle so you can cut by pulling, not pushing.

3 Try lifting out the frame.

Begin by using an old screwdriver to clear paint from the screw slot. Then put a well fitting screwdriver blade in the slot and strike the handle with a hammer. Press hard while turning screwdriver counter clockwise. For really stubborn screws, use an impact driver – a type of screwdriver that turns automatically when struck with a hammer. Or try heating the screw head with a large soldering iron to expand the screw temporarily and break the seal between screw and frame. As a last resort, drill off the screw head.

Installing the new window frame

The new window normally comes with a new exterior sill; if a separate sill is required it should be hardwood or moulded plastic.

Normally the frame is fitted up against the existing inside window board.

1 Hold the new frame up to the opening to see if it fits. (You will probably need a helper.) There should be a clearance of about 6mm all round.

2 If the frame is slightly too big, plane a little off it. Then treat the bare wood with clear preservative followed by primer, or with water-repellent wood stain.

Alternatively If the new frame is too small, pack it out by nailing strips of hardwood up to 20mm thick to the sides. After the window has been installed, moulding can be tacked around the edges of the frame to cover the packing strips.

3 Lift the frame into place and temporarily hold it with wedges. If the window is a large one, you will need a helper at this stage. Wedge it to within 6mm of the lintel to allow space for mortar at the bottom.

The frame must be vertical, and must be pushed right back against the plaster inside the room. Use a spirit level to check that its face is vertical and that both the top and bottom of the frame are horizontal.

4 Drill holes through the jambs at suitable intervals. Position the holes where they will coincide with the mid-points of bricks, not the mortar joints. Allow the drill to penetrate far enough to mark the bricks. On most windows four fixings – at the top and bottom of each jamb – are sufficient. On windows more than 1.2m from top to bottom, put a third fixing about midway up each jamb.

5 Carefully remove the frame from the opening and check that you can see the drilling marks.

6 Using a masonry bit, drill the bricks at the marked points and insert wall plugs.

7 Countersink screw holes in the frame.

8 Lay a thin bed of mortar (page 467) on the sill brickwork.

9 Lay a strip of damp-proof course along the sill and then cover it with another layer of mortar.

10 Replace the frame and wedges at the sides and top, and check with a spirit level that it is level and the face is vertical.

11 Fix the frame by screwing into the wall plugs in the bricks.

12 Use a frame sealant to fill any gaps around the frame. Inject the sealant from a cartridge with a sealant gun. Do not use mortar; it cannot accommodate movement in the wood.

13 If needed, repair damage to rendering around the outside of the opening with mortar, and make good inside with plaster. The window is then ready for glazing and final decoration if necessary.

Choosing a draught excluder

Before you buy a draught excluder, measure the width of the gaps which need to be blocked. The packaging on most draught excluders indicates how big a gap the product is intended to fill and where it can be used.

Self-adhesive foam strip Use on casement windows and exterior doors. Quality varies a lot. Some strips perish after only one or two seasons; more expensive types will last for five years or more. Cheaper versions are made of polyurethane, which hardens with age. Sizes vary according to the manufacturer but strips are usually about 6mm thick and 10mm wide. Most strips are only supplied in white. Avoid getting paint on foam – it will harden with age, unless the strip manufacturer states otherwise.

Self-adhesive rubber strip Use on casement windows and exterior doors. Available in a limited colour range and in profiles including P and E. This type of excluder is tough and will last longer than foam. Fix to the frame as for self-adhesive foam strip (above).

Brush strips Use on exterior and patio doors, and on sash and casement windows. The strips consist of siliconised nylon pile in self-adhesive strips or in a metal plastic holder that is to be tacked to the frame, not the door or window. The strip is particularly designed for surfaces which move against each other, as on sash windows and patio doors.

Draughtproofing a window

There are many ways to improve the seal around your windows and keep out draughts. Measure the height and width of the window to gauge how much of the draughtproofing strip you will need.

Before you start Clean the window frame with water and a little washing-up liquid to remove all grease and dirt. Rinse and wait for the surface to dry.

A casement window

Most of the draughtproofing strips shown left are suitable for use on a wooden casement window. Only the strips with an adhesive backing can be used on a metal casement window.

1 Cut lengths to fit with scissors or a trimming knife.

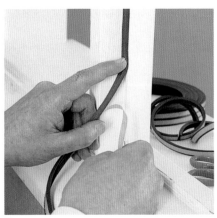

2 Peel away the protective backing as you stick down each length on the rebate. Make sure that one piece of excluder goes right into each corner.

Silicone sealant for large gaps For large or uneven gaps, a silicone sealant (also called a frame sealant) is particularly useful, but cannot be used on sash windows. It can also be used on doors. Read any advice on the container before you begin.

A sash window

Rigid brush strip is the most suitable material for sealing the sides of a sash window, as the sashes slide over it easily.

1 Measure the height of the sliding sashes and cut four pieces of brush strip – two pieces for each sash.

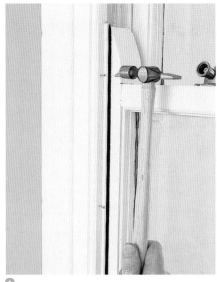

2 Fix the strip to either side of the frame: on the inside of the inner sash and on the outside of the outer sash. Use pre-holed strip, fixing it with the pins provided and a hammer. Unless the window is not opened very often, self-adhesive strip is not suitable because it is unlikely to withstand the friction from the sashes as they slide. Replace the sashes and beading (page 208).

3 Seal the gap at the top and bottom of the sashes with any of the more durable foam strips fixed to the frame or the sash.

4 If there is a draught between the top and bottom sashes of the window, fix nylon brush pile strip to the bottom sash at the meeting point.

HELPFUL TIP

To improve the adhesion of self-adhesive strips, apply a thin coating of clear all-purpose adhesive over the surface to which the excluder is to be fixed. Let the glue dry before pressing on the strips.

Draughtproofing a door

You may need to use more than one type of draught excluder on a door. Fix a foam strip around the sides and top of a door and a threshold excluder at the bottom for a snug finish.

If you are fitting one of the foam, rubber or flexible strips for the first time – or are unsure which excluder is most suitable – experiment on one door before you buy all the material you need. To calculate how much of a strip draught excluder you need to buy, measure the height and width of the door.

Some threshold excluders are designed to deflect in-blown rain as well as to stop draughts. Threshold excluders are usually sold in standard lengths for external doors and some come in two parts: one to fix to the base of the door and the other to the sill.

Adding an enclosed porch

If you put an enclosed porch around an outside door – especially if it is exposed to prevailing winds – you will greatly reduce the draughts entering the house. You will also help to reduce condensation inside if you can leave wet umbrellas and coats in a porch.

There are regulations that govern extending in front of the house building line, but porches are exempt from needing planning permission, providing the floor area is not more than 3m², and no part is higher than 3m above ground level. You must also ensure that the porch is at least 2m from the boundary between the garden and a road or public footpath. Porches are also exempt from Building Regulations control if the floor area is less than 30m².

> ## HELPFUL TIP
>
> If you cannot find the source of a draught, light a candle and hold it in front of the door or window. Move around the edge of the frame and the flame will flicker at the point where the draught is coming in. Take care not to set curtains alight.

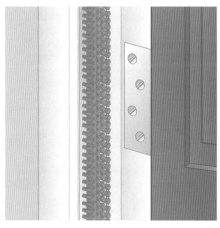

Strip excluders for the frame
Self-adhesive foam strips or nylon brush strip are cut to length and fitted to the frame. Some require pinning.

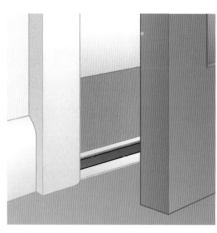

Metal or rubber seal for the sill
A plastic or metal bar fitted to the sill has a rubber insert which seals the gap under the door when it is closed.

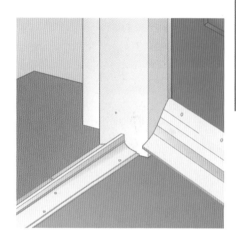

Two-piece excluders fitted to door and sill
A weatherbar is attached to the sill and a deflector is attached to the base of the door. The deflector is shaped to deflect rainwater over the weatherbar when the door is closed and the weatherbar prevents rain from being blown in beneath the door.

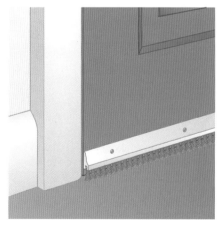

Strip excluders for the base of the door
A strip of nylon, rubber or plastic bristle mounted in aluminium. The excluder is fitted to the base of the door – on the inside – and is usually adjustable for height to give a good seal.

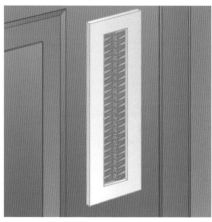

Letterbox excluder A plastic frame with two rows of nylon bristle fits over the inside of a letterbox.

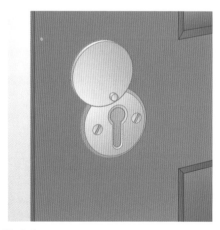

Keyhole cover A pivoted cover, or escutcheon, hangs in front of the keyhole of a mortise lock.

Choosing security locks for your windows

Windows are the main points of entry for burglars. The most common method of breaking in is to smash the glass and release the catch, but window locks will lock the frames together, make the handle immovable, or restrain the stay arm. Before buying window locks, make sure they are suitable for your windows. A lock for timber frames will come with woodscrews. Locks for metal windows will have self-tapping screws. Make sure the frames are thick enough to accommodate the device.

SASH WINDOW LOCKS

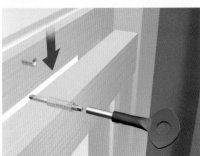

Dual screw A long, steel, key-operated screw goes through a barrel in the inner sash into a threaded sleeve in the outer sash. Fit two dual screws if the window is large.

Sash stop (left) A locking nut screws into a mounting plate on the upper sash to prevent the lower sash from sliding up. They can be positioned a little higher to allow the window to be opened a little for ventilation. Fit two to large windows.

Sash window press lock (below) A two-part surface-fitted lock secures the two meeting rails together, in place of the standard interlocking sash catch. A push bolt locks the inner and outer plate together. They are released with a key.

METAL WINDOWS

Locking clamp A key shoots a bolt from the window into a bracket mounted on the frame.

Stay bolt Fits underneath the stay arm. A bolt slides under the stay retainer, preventing the arm from being lifted.

Cockspur bolt When the cockspur handle is closed, the case of the bolt is moved up on the fixed frame and locked, preventing the cockspur from opening. Alternatively, a locking cockspur handle can be fitted.

SAFETY WARNING
- When windows are locked, keep a key in the room so a window can be opened in an emergency (but out of the reach of a burglar who may have smashed the glass).
- Do not permanently screw windows closed that may be needed as an escape route in time of fire.

CASEMENT WINDOW LOCKS

For locking frames together

Mortise rack bolt The lock is mortised into the opening frame, and the bolt slides into a hole in the fixed frame. They are suitable only for windows at least 35mm thick. More difficult to install than a surface-fitting lock, but gives excellent security. Fit close to the centre of the opening edge. On large windows, fit a mortise rack bolt at each end of the opening edge.

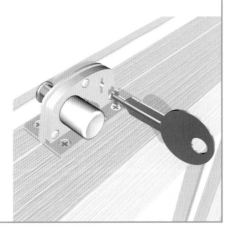

Cam lock A key turns a cam, or notched rotating shaft, into the second part of the lock, fixed to the frame, securing the two components together.

For locking the handle and stay

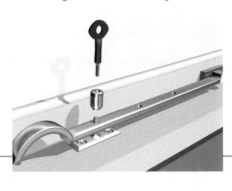

Swing-bar lock A C-shaped bar fixed to the casement swings over a locking plate on the frame to stop the window from opening. The bar can be locked with a mechanical key.

Locking handle A new handle with a lock replaces the existing cockspur handle. Once locked, it cannot be opened without the key. Make sure you buy the correct right-hand or left-hand type for your window. Some types allow the window to be locked slightly ajar for ventilation. Alternatively, a blocking bolt can be fitted to the fixed frame that prevents the cockspur handle from moving, if the cockspur is on the frame surface. The bolt is retracted with the key.

Stay lock Replaces the pegs that secure the stay when closed. The peg is threaded and is locked by screwing on a key-operated nut. Ventilation locks allow the window to be locked closed or slightly open: the peg locates in a short sliding bar fixed to the casement, so that the position can be adjusted.

Fitting locks to windows

Most locks come with their own clear fitting instructions, but these are three of the most common and effective window locks to fit yourself.

Casement window lock

Surface-mounted locks are easy to fit to casement windows, provided that the surfaces of the fixed frame and the opening casement are at right angles to each other.
• If the fixed frame is tapered, wood may have to be chiselled so the lock fits against the opening frame. Some locks are supplied with a wedge to get over this problem.
• For large windows, or for extra security, fit two locks on each frame, at top and bottom. They will withstand a jemmy attack better than a single lock.
• The technique shown below is for a swing-bar lock, but other models are installed in a similar way.

Tools *Pencil; drill and twist bits; bradawl; screwdriver. Perhaps a small chisel.*

Materials *One or two window locks, depending on size of window.*

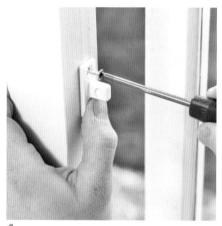

1 Open the window and position the locking plate on the frame, 1mm from the edge. Make sure it is straight, mark the position of the holes with a bradawl and screw the plate in place.

2 Close the window and position the body of the lock behind the locking plate. Fix one screw, check the operation of the lock, then drive in the second screw.

SAFETY AND SECURITY

Laminated glass
Particular windows in a house may be at risk from burglars. They may be ground-floor windows hidden from the neighbours, or they may be upstairs windows that are accessible from an extension roof, a drainpipe or a tree. Fitting laminated glass would greatly add to the security. It consists of a sandwich of glass with a clear plastic film between. Although the glass may be cracked by a blow, the plastic will resist efforts to break through. Do not use wired glass, because it has little security value.

Plastic windows
An increasing number of plastic windows are being used in houses, and they can pose a security problem. Most manufacturers of security devices do not recommend them for plastic windows because a thin plastic section offers no grip for screws. If a plastic window frame is known to have a timber inner frame, security devices suitable for a wooden frame can be used. If there are steel inserts within the plastic section, self-tapping screws could be used, as for metal frames. But locks cannot be fitted to hollow sections of windows filled with rigid foam. The ideal solution is to consult the installer of your windows at the time they are being made.

Metal-framed window lock

Locks are fitted to a steel or aluminium window frame with self-tapping screws, which should be supplied with the lock. To drill a pilot hole in the frame, use a high-speed-steel (HSS) twist bit. Most locks come with instructions giving the drill size.
    If in doubt, make the hole the same diameter as the 'core' of the screw, not the shank. Use a bit that is too small rather than too big.

Tools *Bradawl or ball-point pen; electric drill; HSS twist bits; screwdriver.*

Materials *Window lock with self-tapping screws.*

1 Hold the lock in position and mark the screw hole with a bradawl or ball-point pen.

2 Drill a pilot hole just through the metal. Provided the bit is sharp, it should not skid on the metal.

3 Screw the lock to the frame. If the screw hole is too tight, re-drill the hole one size bigger.

Dual screw sash window lock

A dual screw is a very secure locking device for a sash window, but it is not practical if the window is frequently opened.

Before you start If the window is opened often, use a surface-fitted bolt (see opposite). For large windows, fit two locks, one at each end of the centre meeting rail.
    Dual screws vary in design. Some have barrels for both inner and outer frames, other have a lockplate for the outer frame.

Tools *Drill and auger bit the width of the lock barrel; hammer and piece of wood, or a large screwdriver (depending on the model). Perhaps a small screwdriver, small twist bit and chisel (depending on model).*

Materials *One or two dual screws.*

1 Drill through the inner meeting rail and on into the outer meeting rail to a depth of 15mm. Wind some tape around the bit as a guide to the depth of the hole. Take care not to catch the edge of the glass.

2 Tap the longer barrel into the inner meeting rail, using a hammer and a piece of wood to protect it from being damaged. Squeeze it into the frame using a G-cramp if the frame is old and the glass liable to shatter.

3 Reverse the sashes. Tap the shorter barrel into the outer meeting rail. Alternatively, fit the locking plate to the outer meeting rail. If the sashes clash as they pass, recess the plate with a chisel.

4 Close the window and screw the bolt into the barrel with the key. Trim the bolt with a hacksaw if it is too long.

7

Walls, ceilings and fireplaces

Types of plaster for indoor use

Ordinary quick-setting, lightweight gypsum plaster is used by professional plasterers. For DIY users, one-coat plaster in powder or ready-mixed form is easier. Gypsum based indoor plasters are usually sold in 50kg packs, though smaller packs may be available. Choose a cement-based plaster for damp areas indoors.

Working times (the time you get to apply the plaster before it sets too solid to work) and setting times (the time the plaster takes to go hard) are given as a guide, but these are shorter in warm rooms and longer in cold.

If water is absorbed too fast from plaster, it will crack. So if you are using a standard two-coat plaster, choose the undercoat suitable for your wall – different types are made for differing wall surface absorbencies.

Browning undercoat For solid, fairly absorbent surfaces indoors, such as bricks or building blocks.
• Layers should be about 10mm thick.
• A lightweight quick-setting pink or grey undercoat, mixed with clean, cold water. Apply within 15–30 minutes of mixing.
• Sets in 1½–2 hours.
• 10kg covers about 1.5m² 10mm thick.

Bonding undercoat On dense, not very absorbent surfaces indoors – for example, concrete, engineering bricks, or surfaces treated with PVA adhesive, such as laths.
• Layers should be about 8mm thick.
• A lightweight quick-setting pink or grey undercoat, mixed with clean, cold water. Apply within 15–30 minutes of mixing.
• Sets in 1½–2 hours.
• 10kg covers about 1.5m² 8mm thick.

Finishing coat On browning or bonding undercoats.
• The layers should be about 2mm thick.
• A lightweight, quick-setting pink or grey finish plaster, mixed with clean, cold water.
• 10kg covers about 4.5m² 2mm thick.

Plasterboard finish On a plasterboard surface (ivory side).
• Layers should be about 5mm thick.
• Sets in 1–1½ hours.
• 10kg covers about 1.5m² 5mm thick.

One-coat plaster On most indoor surfaces, such as bricks, blocks or plasterboard.
• Can be applied up to about 50mm thick into cavities.
• Suitable for filling or finishing in one application.
• Mixed with clean, cold water; dries white or pink.
• Workable for 30–60 minutes.
• 8kg covers about 0.7m² 10mm thick.

Renovating plaster For use in damp conditions (but not below ground level on an unlined background), or in slow-drying places.
• Undercoat layers should be about 10mm thick, finishing layers about 2mm. Some are one-coat plasters.

• A lightweight plaster mixed with clean cold water.
• Sets in 1½–2 hours.
• Treat backgrounds with low absorbency, such as concrete or dense bricks or blocks, with a water-resisting bonding aid first.
• 10kg covers about 1.2m² 10mm thick.

Ready-mixed undercoat or one coat Used on most indoor building surfaces such as bricks, blocks, plasterboard or laths.
• Layers can be up to about 50mm thick into cavities.
• A grey paste applied straight from the container. Available in 2.5kg packs.
• Workable for about 4 hours after application.
• Slow setting – takes about 24 hours to dry.
• Can be used without a finishing coat if the surface is to be papered.
• 10kg covers about 0.75m² about 10mm thick.

Ready-mixed finishing coat On ready-mixed undercoat or other plaster surfaces.
• Layers should be about 3mm thick.
• A creamy-white paste applied straight from the container.
• Workable for about 4 hours after application.
• Sets in about 24 hours.
• 10kg covers about 2m² 3mm thick.

Accessories for use with plasterboard

Joint compound Used on plasterboard and joint tape. Sold in 10kg or 25kg packs.
• For filling and embedding joints on plasterboard by hand.
• In powder form; mixed with clean, cold water.
• Workable for up to 30 minutes.

Joint tape Used on plasterboard taper-edged joints before decorating (ivory side out).
• A 50mm wide self-adhesive tape for reinforcing plasterboard joints.

Plasterboard primer/sealer Used on ivory-coloured surface of plasterboard.
• For preparing plasterboard surface for decoration.
• Two coats will give the surface protection against moisture.
• Workable for about 30 minutes; sets in 1 hour.

Patching damaged plaster

Large cracks, holes or crumbling areas of plaster can generally be repaired quickly and cheaply with plaster.

Damage caused by damp Do not repair damage caused by damp until the cause has been remedied. If large cracks reopen after repair, get the advice of a builder or surveyor, as the cracks may be caused by structural movement of the building.

Using ready-mixed plaster

Tools *Cold chisel; club hammer; hand brush; filling knife or plasterer's trowel. Possibly also fine abrasive paper or power sander; face mask and safety goggles; large paintbrush; plastic spreader (supplied with skim-coat container).*

Materials *Ready-mixed plaster. Possibly ready-mixed skim-coat plaster.*

1 Chip away loose or crumbling plaster with a cold chisel until you reach a firm surface all round.

2 Brush away dust and debris. If bricks or building blocks are exposed, dampen the areas with water.

3 Stir the plaster and apply it to the wall with a filling knife or plasterer's trowel held at an angle.

4 Build up deep areas in layers – applied up to 50mm deep in cavities. Allow each layer to stiffen before applying the next.

5 If the surface is to be papered, fill the undercoat to the top of the damaged area. When it is thoroughly dry, smooth it with fine abrasive paper or a power sander. Wear a mask and goggles to protect you from dust.

Alternatively If the surface is to be painted, fill the top 3mm of the area with a coat of skim plaster to give smooth finish. Apply it with a large brush, in upward strokes, then spread it with light strokes. When it begins to dry, smooth it with the plastic spreader supplied.

USING ONE-COAT PLASTER

Mix the plaster according to the instructions on the packet – generally up to about 500ml cold water per 1kg of powder – until it is a smooth paste that is just stiff enough to use. Apply it in the same way as ordinary plaster (right), and finish in the same way.

Using ordinary plaster

This is the least expensive plaster, but requires skill to achieve a professional finish. It is applied in two coats and you need to work fast. It's a good idea to practise somewhere inconspicuous before beginning the job.

Tools *Cold chisel; club hammer; hand brush; large paintbrush or plant spray; clean plastic bucket; mixing stick or wooden spoon; length of wood; plasterer's trowel; carrying board (also called a hawk).*

Materials *Undercoat plaster; finishing plaster; supply of clean, cold water for mixing.*

1 Chip away loose or crumbly plaster with a cold chisel until you reach a firm surface all round.

2 Brush away dust and debris. If bricks or building blocks are exposed, dampen the areas with water.

3 Mix the undercoat plaster with cold water in a clean bucket until its consistency is between that of stiff porridge and whipped cream. Use it as quickly as possible after mixing – within 15–30 minutes.

4 Load plaster onto a carrying board. Apply it with a plasterer's trowel held at an angle of about 45° to the wall and sweep it upwards to press the plaster to the surface, flattening it slightly at the end of the stroke. Be careful not to press the trowel flat against the surface, or the plaster will pull away when you lift off the trowel.

5 If necessary, build up the damaged surface in thin layers. Wait for each successive layer to stiffen (but not to dry) before applying the next.

6 Fill the undercoat to within 3mm of the surface and while it is still wet knock off the high points by drawing a length of wood across it. Rest it on the edges of a firm surrounding surface and work upwards with a slight zigzag motion.

7 When the undercoat is dry (about 2 hours after application) mix the finishing plaster in a clean bucket to the consistency of melting ice cream.

8 Using a plasterer's trowel held at a slight angle, spread the finishing coat on top of the undercoat within about 15–30 minutes of mixing. This is a messy job, so make sure the surroundings are protected from splashes, if necessary.

9 When the finishing coat has stiffened – about 20 minutes after application – smooth the surface with a plasterer's trowel held at a slight angle, using wide backwards and forwards sweeps. While you are doing this, keep on dampening the area with water using a large paintbrush or house-plant spray.

Repairing and reinforcing corners

When filling an external corner with plaster, it can be difficult to get a level surface and a straight edge. The job is easier if it is done in two operations using a timber batten as a guide.

Tools *Cold chisel; club hammer; softwood timber batten 50 x 20mm and longer than the depth of the area to be filled; straight-edge; masonry nails; hammer; hand brush; plasterer's trowel. Possibly also carrying board; large paintbrush or plant spray; spirit level with horizontal and vertical vials; corner trowel; rubber gloves.*

Materials *Plaster. Possibly also; length of expanded metal angle beading (see panel).*

1 Cut back crumbling plaster to a firm surface and brush away debris from the damaged area.

2 Drive two masonry nails through the batten, closer to one edge than the other, and position them so that they will either be driven into the mortar between bricks, or will fit into firm plaster well beyond the edges of the damaged area, to avoid cracking more plaster.

3 Hold the wood batten vertically against the damaged edge with the nails nearer to the inner side. Use a straight-edge along the adjacent wall to align the batten with the plaster surface at the top and bottom.

4 Nail the batten gently to the wall, leaving the nail heads protruding.

5 Plaster the area with a suitable undercoat or one-coat plaster to align with the edge of the batten.

6 When the plaster has dried, remove the nails and pull away the batten to avoid crumbling the edge of the new plaster.

7 Nail the batten to the other side of the corner and then plaster the remaining damaged area in the same way.

8 If using a finishing coat, use the batten in the same way to plaster both sides of the corner.

9 Finishing the edge of the corner is easier with a corner trowel. Or you could round it off with a plasterer's trowel.

Alternatively Before the plaster hardens fully, put on a rubber glove, wet it, and run your fingers down the edge to blunt it slightly.

Repairs around sockets

1 Switch off the mains supply at the consumer unit before patching round a switch or socket.

2 Disconnect the fitting, noting the wiring connections, and remove it.

3 Whether the socket is seated in plaster or plasterboard, fill small cracks or holes with an interior filler and larger holes by one of the methods described above.

4 Wait for the plaster to dry before refitting the switch or socket.

Repairs around ceiling roses and light fittings

1 Turn off the mains supply at the consumer unit when dealing with light fittings. Repairs to the edge of a ceiling rose generally do not carry any risk of electric shock.

2 For small, difficult to reach holes and breaks in the plaster, use a small amount of expanding foam filler.

3 Squirt some filler into the space.

4 Allow it to harden and then cut away the excess with a sharp knife.

REINFORCING A DAMAGED CORNER

If an external corner is prone to damage, reinforce it with expanded metal angle beading before plastering the wall. The beading is formed from two bands of galvanised steel mesh set at right angles to a rounded centre strip. It is sold in lengths and can be cut to the required size with tinsnips and a hacksaw. Treat the cut ends and any areas of the galvanised coating accidentally damaged during installation with metal primer.

1 Fit beading against the corner with dabs of plaster about 600mm apart on each side.

2 Use a straight-edge and spirit level to make sure it is vertical.

3 Press the mesh firmly against the wall and check with a straight-edge that the centre strip, or corner bead, will not protrude above the plaster surface.

4 The bead can be used as a guide to forming a straight edge when plastering, instead of using a timber batten.

Filling gaps round waste pipes

When a new dishwasher or washing machine is fitted, it may be necessary to make a hole through the wall, to accommodate the water waste pipes.

Once the pipe is fitted, it is necessary to fill the space around the pipe in order to cut down on draughts and to prevent damp from entering the property.

Squirt expanding foam filler all round the pipe and allow it to dry thoroughly before trimming off the excess with a sharp knife. The advantage of this material is that it can be removed quite easily should you wish to move the appliance to another position.

Filling holes in lath and plaster

Fill small holes and cracks in lath and plaster in the same way as for plaster (page 222). If the hole is large enough to reveal the laths, repair depends on whether the laths are intact or broken.

If the laths are intact

1 Paint the laths with a solution of PVA building adhesive to make the surface less absorbent.

2 Fill the hole with layers of plaster in the same way as patching damaged plaster (page 223). If you are using ordinary quick-setting plaster, use a bonding undercoat plaster rather than a browning undercoat plaster.

If the laths are broken

Either patch the laths or – if the hole is not more than about 75mm across – plug the gap before you fill it with plaster.

1 To patch the laths, use a piece of expanded metal mesh, cut to the size you need with tinsnips. Wrap it round the laths to bridge the gap between broken edges.

Alternatively To plug the gap, use a ball of newspaper soaked in water and then worked round in a bowl of runny plaster.

Dealing with large areas

1 Where a large area of plaster has crumbled away from the laths, cut back the damaged area to a regular shape and patch it with a piece of plasterboard (page 226).

2 Use plasterboard that is as close to the thickness of the layer of plaster as possible. Nail the plasterboard patch, ivory side outwards, to the timber framework supporting the laths.

3 Fill the gaps round the edges with interior filler (page 78) and finish the surface of the patch with a coat of skim plaster.

Repairing holes in plasterboard

Small holes in plasterboard can be repaired in the same way as in plaster. Medium-sized holes – up to about 125mm across – need to be fitted with a backing piece to block the cavity before they are filled with plaster filler. Larger holes, or a severely damaged surface, cannot be satisfactorily repaired with a filler. The damaged section must be removed and a new piece of plasterboard patched in.

Using a backing piece

Tools *Pencil and ruler; trimming knife; drill and twist bit; padsaw or mini hacksaw; filling knife; sanding block; scissors; length of wood.*

Materials *A plasterboard offcut or a piece of MDF; piece of string 150–200mm long; a long nail or wood sliver; interior or plaster filler or coving adhesive. Possibly finishing plaster (page 222).*

1 Draw a neat square around the damaged area, and drill holes at the corners so that you can get the blade of your padsaw in. Cut along the lines to create a neat, straight-sided hole.

2 Cut a backing piece from a plasterboard offcut. It should be narrow enough to go through the hole, but long enough to overlap the hole by about 25mm at the top and bottom.

3 Bore a hole in the middle of the backing piece and thread the length of string through it.

4 Knot a nail or a sliver of wood to one end of the string to anchor it against the back of the offcut. Make sure you have the ivory side (which will be covered with plaster filler) as the front. Make a loop in the front end of the string so that it is easy to hold.

5 Apply coving adhesive or filler to the front (the ivory side) of the backing piece.

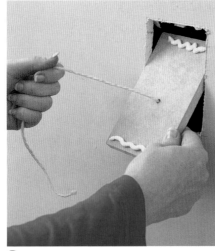

6 Guide the coated backing piece through the hole, then use the string to pull it into position against the back of the hole.

7 The patch should stick fairly quickly. Cut off the string when you are sure it has stuck firmly.

8 Use quick-setting filler to cover the patch, filling the hole to about half its depth. When it has dried, put in another layer, leaving it slightly proud of the surrounding wall.

9 With a length of wood, skim off the excess filler, leaving a smooth surface level with the surrounding area.

10 When the filler has dried completely, smooth the surface with a sanding block or a piece of fine abrasive paper wrapped round a wooden block.

Fitting a plasterboard patch

Tools *Trimming knife or padsaw; broad-bladed filling knife or plasterer's trowel; pencil; straight-edge; spirit level; try square; hammer; medium or fine abrasive paper; sponge; steel tape measure.*

Materials *Small sheet of plasterboard or offcut as thick as board on wall; two lengths of timber to fit tightly between uprights (studs) – you will need the 50 x 75mm size for a stud-partition wall or 50 x 25mm for a dry-lined wall; four 75mm oval nails; 30mm galvanised plasterboard nails; G-cramps; joint tape or scrim tape (page 222); joint compound or plasterboard finishing plaster (page 222).*

Before you start Check the thickness of the plasterboard on the wall; it will be either 9.5mm or 12.5mm thick.

1 Check that there are no pipes or cables behind the board (page 34). Use a trimming knife or padsaw to cut across the plasterboard from the middle of the damaged area outwards to each side until you reach the timber studs supporting the panel.

2 Use the straight edge of a spirit level to draw the edge line of the studs vertically on the plasterboard. Then draw horizontal parallel lines across the panel between the studs, about 50mm above and below the edge of the damaged area. Make sure the lines are at right angles to the studs.

3 Cut out the squared-off section of damaged plasterboard.

4 On each side of the opening, draw a vertical line to indicate half the width of the timber stud – usually about 25mm – and score it using a straight-edge and trimming knife.

5 Cut back the sound plasterboard down the scored lines to reveal half the width of the studs.

6 Fit the two timber pieces as cross-pieces (noggins) between the studs at the top and bottom of the opening. Position them with the 50mm thick side outwards so 25mm is under the edge of the existing plasterboard as a nailing surface for the patch.

7 Hold the noggins in position with G-cramps while you drive 75mm oval nails through the noggins and into the studs at an angle.

8 Measure the area of the hole and cut plasterboard to fit. Insert it with the ivory side facing outwards so that it can be plastered or decorated.

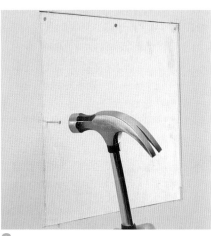

9 Nail the plasterboard to the wood surround with plasterboard nails. Set the nails at intervals of 150mm, positioned at least 12mm from the edge of the patch. Sink them into the surface of the plasterboard so they do not protrude, but take care not to damage the outer layer of paper.

10 Lightly sand edges of the joint with abrasive paper, if necessary, to remove any burring.

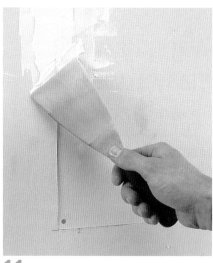

11 Using a plasterboard finishing plaster or joint compound, fill the joints and sand them smooth and flat. Then decorate the surface.

MENDING DAMAGED CORNERS

Damaged external corners of plasterboard can be repaired with battens and filler in the same way as plaster corners (pages 224–5).

Reinforce the corners with joint tape bedded in joint compound. Ideally use corner tape, which is reinforced with metal strips. Crease the tape down the centre and fit it so that the metal strips lie inwards, close against the surface of the wall. The tape gives the corner a clean, sharp edge.

HELPFUL TIP

If the surface of your plasterboard wall is dented but not broken, simply cover the dent with quick-setting filler and smooth it level with a ruler. Once it is dry, sand it smooth and redecorate.

Working with plasterboard

Plasterboard is used mainly for lining internal walls or ceilings and for building partition walls.

Plasterboard can be nailed to timber battens or joists, screwed to metal supports, or fixed directly to a masonry wall with adhesive. Use 30mm plasterboard nails with boards 9.5mm thick and 40mm nails for 12.5mm board. There are different types and thicknesses of board (see panel). Common plasterboard lengths are 1800mm and 2400mm. The widths are normally 600mm, 900mm or 1200mm. Some types are fire-resistant or moisture-resistant.

Handling plasterboard

Standard plasterboard is generally supplied bound in pairs of sheets with the grey side outwards. The binding tape identifies the type of edge and the size of the boards.

Two people are needed to carry a full-length sheet of plasterboard. Carry it on edge to avoid straining the core, and handle it with care to prevent damage to the paper-covered surface or the edges.

Store boards flat. If they warp they will be difficult to fix to walls or ceilings. Stack them in a pile not more than about 1m high, on a dry, flat surface. When removing a board from a stack, avoid dragging it, as this can scuff the surface of the board beneath.

Making a footlifter

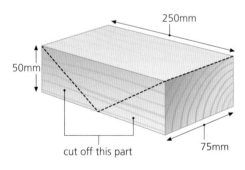

250mm

50mm

cut off this part

75mm

A footlifter, or rocking wedge, is needed to lift boards into position for nailing to a wall.
• You can make a footlifter from a piece of softwood 250 x 75 x 50mm.
• Draw lines from the top corners of the block to the centre of the base, and square them off with a try square at the ends.
• Cut away the two wedge-shaped pieces of waste to create a tool that works on the same principle as a see-saw.
• When a sheet of plasterboard is placed on one end, you lift it into place by pressing down with your foot on the other end.

CHOOSING PLASTERBOARD

Standard wallboard Has one ivory face intended for direct painting or wallpapering. Available with square or tapered edges. Use with tapered edge facing outwards for taped and filled joints or single-coat gypsum plaster finish. Use square edge out for single-coat plaster, textured coating or for painting or wallpapering. Available in 9.5mm and 12.5mm thicknesses in a variety of sheet sizes.

Thermal laminates Standard wallboard with a backing of thermal insulation. Used as an insulating lining inside an external wall or on a ceiling. 'Vapour-check' board has a water-vapour resistant membrane between the plasterboard and insulation. Many types of insulation are available, including expanded polystyrene and polyurethane foam. Thicknesses vary from 18mm up to 65mm in standard 2400 x 1200mm sheets.

Duplex plasterboard Has a foil backing to resist water vapour. The backing also acts as a reflective insulator when facing into a wall cavity. Cannot be fixed with an adhesive. Available in 9.5mm and 12.5mm thicknesses as 1800 x 900mm or 2400 x 1200mm sheets.

Baseboard Square-edged and similar to standard wallboard, but with grey-faced paper covering. Use mainly on ceilings as a substrate for gypsum-based plaster. Available in 9.5mm thickness. Sheets come in four lengths, all 915mm wide.

CUTTING PLASTERBOARD

Cut plasterboard with the ivory side upwards, using either a fine-toothed saw such as a panel saw or a trimming knife. Sawing is slower and makes more mess.

On a long length, support the sawn ends to prevent the board breaking.

To cut with a trimming knife, use it to cut the paper on the ivory side. Then lay a straight-edge along the back of the board and fold the board backwards to snap the cut open. Finally, cut the other paper backing.

Rub sawn or cut edges lightly with medium abrasive paper.

Use a padsaw (page 56) to cut holes in plasterboard to fit switches or mounting boxes.

Filling plasterboard joints

When lining a whole wall that will be plastered, painted or papered, the ivory side of the plasterboard should face into the room. In the past, the grey side was used for plastering, but the plasterboard makers now advise using the ivory side for everything.

Use tapered-edged boards to make the jointing as smooth as possible. If you have to cut ivory-faced board, you should joint the square edges in exactly the same way as you would cut the tapered edges. The steps opposite detail the methods for filling joints on both tapered-edged and square-edged boards.

Tapered edge

Square edge

Tapered-edged boards

Joint compound is workable for about 30 minutes after mixing. To begin with mix only a small amount so that you can gauge your working rate. If you mix only about a quarter of a bucketful, you can use it all up completing a number of joints up to the feathering stage. Self-adhesive mesh jointing tape is also now available and does not require jointing compound.

Tools *Clean bowl or bucket; mixing stick or wooden spoon; plasterer's trowel; broad-bladed filling knife; scissors or trimming knife; sponge; large paintbrush.*

Materials *Joint compound and joint tape or self-adhesive mesh jointing tape; clean, cold water; plasterboard primer/sealer.*

1 If you are using conventional joint tape, prepare the joint compound as indicated on the packet. Use a stiff mixture to cover nail heads and fill gaps wider than 3mm.

2 Use a broad-bladed filling knife or plasterer's trowel to press the compound into each joint, spreading it in a thin band just over 25mm wide on each side.

3 Cut a strip of tape to length and while the compound is still wet use the knife or trowel to press it on the joint. Press out any air bubbles, but make sure there is enough compound under the tape for it to stick.

Alternatively If you are using self-adhesive tape, stick it in place along the joint without first applying jointing compound.

4 Finish the joints, whichever tape you have used, with a top layer of joint compound, spread over the tape in a wide band. Smooth it flush with the surface.

5 Before the compound begins to stiffen, moisten a sponge and use it to feather out the edges into the surrounding surface and to remove excess compound without disturbing the tape.

6 When the joint has dried, apply another layer of compound in a wider band – up to 300mm – and feather the edges smooth.

7 When the surface is dry, finish the whole board for decoration by applying one or two coats of plasterboard primer/sealer.

Square-edged boards

This should only be attempted over a small area – a repair in an old plaster wall, for example – because there is a risk that it will crack at the joints. Use scrim tape and plasterboard finishing plaster, applied in the same way as ordinary plaster (page 223).

Tools *Plasterer's trowel; scissors or trimming knife; large paintbrush or plant spray; clean plastic bucket; mixing stick.*

Materials *Plasterboard finish; scrim tape or self-adhesive jointing tape; cold water.*

1 Mix the plaster in the same way as ordinary plaster. If you are using self-adhesive tape, apply the tape first.

2 If you are using scrim tape, press the plaster into the joint with a plasterer's trowel, and spread it thinly on each side to form a band about 100mm wide.

3 Cut a strip of scrim tape to length and press it into the plastered joint with the trowel. Cut self-adhesive tape to length and tape over the bare joint.

4 Apply a thin coat of plaster along the length of the tape.

5 When all the joints have been covered, apply plaster to the boarding between the joints to cover the whole area with a thin plaster coat about 5mm thick.

6 When the first coat has set, apply a second coat of the same thickness, and as it stiffens, dampen and polish it with the trowel (page 223) to make it smooth and flat.

Fitting and repairing ceilings

Modern ceilings are generally made of plasterboard, but lath-and-plaster ceilings are still found in some older houses. To reach the ceiling easily and safely, with your head about 150mm from it, use either the base section of a scaffold tower or stout scaffold boards resting on two stepladders or hired decorator's trestles.

Fitting a plasterboard ceiling

The simplest way to fit a new ceiling is to nail sheets of standard plasterboard to the ceiling joists. A new ceiling can be fitted over an existing one as long as it is only cracked, not crumbling or sagging.

If the ceiling is covered with polystyrene tiles, they can be left in place for extra insulation under the plasterboard. But you will have to locate and mark the joists in the ceiling (page 235), and use nails long enough to go through all the ceiling material and at least 25mm into the joists.

Tools *Hired panel lifter (see below) or a T-shaped floor-to-ceiling prop (known as a dead-man); hammer; saw.*

Materials *Plasterboard; nails (see Before you start, right).*

HELPFUL TIP

Plasterboard is too heavy to fix to a ceiling by yourself. Hire a panel lifter to raise the boards into place and hold them there while you drive in the fixing nails. The machine can support panels while they are fixed to walls and sloping ceilings, too.

Before you start Establish how far apart the joists are (see page 235).
• For joists up to 400mm apart, use plasterboard 9.5mm thick with 30mm galvanised plasterboard nails.
• For joists up to 600mm apart, use plasterboard 12.5mm thick with 40mm plasterboard nails.
• Make a 'dead-man' from a length of 38mm square timber the height of the room, with a piece of flat timber about 600mm long – such as a floorboard offcut – nailed to the ceiling end (see step 4).

1 Take down the old ceiling, if you can (see panel). You can then nail direct to the joists, and see any pipes and electric cables. It puts less weight on the joists and also enables you to treat the joists against woodworm if necessary.

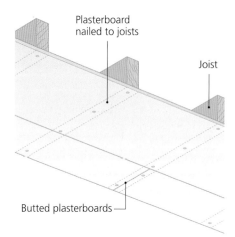

Plasterboard nailed to joists

Joist

Butted plasterboards

2 Fix boards with their long edges at right angles to the joists, with board ends butted centrally on a joist – ivory side facing downwards.

3 Stagger the rows so that adjacent boards do not butt on the same joist, cutting boards as necessary. Boards along the edge of the ceiling may need scribing if the wall is not true.

4 You will need a helper to lift each board into place at one end. To support the board at your end while you nail it, use a T-shaped floor-to-ceiling prop, known as a dead-man. Or hire a panel lifter (left).

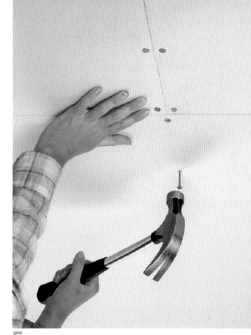

5 Nail the boards in the same way as for lining a stud partition wall (page 239).

6 When all the boards have been nailed to the joists, fill the joints between them (page 229) and finish the surface for decoration.

Gaps where wall and ceiling meet

The simplest way to cover gaps between the wall and ceiling is to fit coving – decorative moulding designed for wall and ceiling joints (page 176). A less effective alternative is to seal the gap with acrylic decorator's sealant.

Dealing with a bulge in the ceiling

On a lath-and-plaster ceiling, an area of plaster sometimes sags away from the laths to form a distinct bulge. If you can get at the ceiling from above you may be able to repair it.

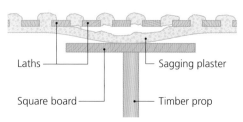

Laths

Sagging plaster

Square board

Timber prop

1 Try to push the bulge back into position using a square of chipboard or plywood nailed to a floor-to-ceiling timber prop (known as a dead-man).

2 To re-fix the plaster, you need to reach it from above – either from the loft or by lifting the floorboards in the room above.

3 Vacuum clean the area between the joists at the back of the ceiling bulge.

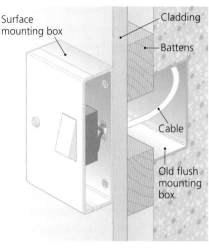

Surface mounting box

Cladding

Battens

Cable

Old flush mounting box

PULLING DOWN AN OLD CEILING

It is best to replace an old lath-and-plaster ceiling with a plasterboard one if it needs more than small localised repairs. If the plaster key has failed in one place already, it is sure to fail in others as time goes by. However, this is an extremely dusty and unpleasant job.

Prepare by clearing the room of all furniture and fittings, and lift any carpet and its underlay. Remove ceiling-mounted light fittings and insert the cable conductors into plastic terminal blocks before pushing the cable up into the ceiling void. Hire enough heavy-duty dust sheets to cover the entire floor, and invest in safety goggles, strong work gloves, a supply of disposable face masks and a cap. Wear old clothes or a disposable one-piece work suit. Set up a work platform spanning the room, using stepladders or trestles and scaffold boards. Tape up the room door to keep the dust in, and open all the windows. Put on your safety gear.

It is best to pull down the old ceiling from below, even if you have access from above via a loft, because this way you can keep the demolition under better control.

Start by making a hole in the old ceiling with a club hammer, and tear down the old plaster and the laths section by section, working parallel to the joists. A small crowbar is an ideal tool to use for this. Try to pile the debris in one corner of the room as you work.

When you have pulled down as much of the ceiling as possible, work along each joist in turn, removing any remaining pieces of lath and pulling out all the old nails. Then finish by brushing the sides and bottom of each joist with a stiff brush to remove any remaining debris.

4 Pour fairly runny bonding plaster (page 222) over the area. This should bond the ceiling plaster back to the laths, replacing the 'nibs' of holding plaster that have been broken or dislodged.

5 Leave the supporting prop in place until the plaster has dried.

If this method does not work, remove the sagging area and patch it with plasterboard. A ceiling that sags over a large area should be pulled down and replaced.

Moving switches, sockets and ceiling lights

When a wall lining such as plasterboard or timber cladding is fixed to timber battens (see overleaf), switches or sockets on the wall have to be moved forward and remounted.

Before you start Always switch off the power supply at the consumer unit before disconnecting and moving any electrical fitting.
• If you have to move a socket, it is a good time to replace a single socket with double or triple fittings, if required (page 278) – or to add an extra socket on a spur of cable (page 285).

Switches and sockets

Most light switches and socket outlets are flush mounted over a metal mounting box that is recessed into the wall. They must be brought forward before the wall lining is completed. The way you do this depends on whether you want the accessory to be flush or surface mounted in its new position. In either case, first disconnect the accessory faceplate and abandon the existing mounting box in the wall.

Flush-mounting Buy a new 35mm deep metal mounting box in single or double format to match the accessory faceplate. With cladding approximately 10mm thick fixed to 25mm thick battens, the lip of this box will be flush with the face of the cladding if it is surface-mounted on the existing wall surface.

Remove a metal knock-out disc from one side of the box and fit a rubber grommet in the hole. Screw the box to the wall beside the old box position and feed the circuit cable(s) into it through the hole, ready for reconnection to the faceplate once the wall cladding has been completed. Then you can screw the faceplate to the lugs of the new box to complete the job.

Surface mounting Buy a plastic mounting box deep enough for the accessory (usually 17mm for a switch and 25mm or 30mm for a socket outlet). Fix wall battens to the wall above and below the existing mounting box and draw the cable out of the box between them. As you fix the wall cladding, make a hole in it and pass the cable through it. Then feed it into the plastic mounting box via a knockout, and screw the box to the battens behind the cladding. Connect the cable(s) to the faceplate terminals and screw the faceplate to the box.

If the accessory was originally surface mounted and you are happy to retain this arrangement, unscrew the old mounting box from the wall and set it aside. Follow the instructions above to reposition the old box on the surface of the new cladding and reconnect the cable(s) to it.

HELPFUL TIP

If the cable is not long enough to reach the terminals of the repositioned faceplate, extend it by connecting a short length of new cable to it using a strip of terminal connector blocks.

Ceiling fittings

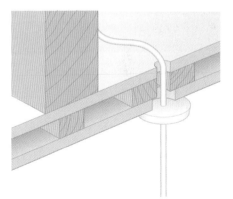

A ceiling light can be dealt with in the same way as a surface-mounted socket, with the rose back-plate remounted on top of the new panelling and screwed to battens fixed on each side of the cable outlet.

The rose position can be altered slightly as long as the cable will not be too stretched and the connections strained. If the cable will not reach the new position, fit a junction box and an extension cable as for adding a new lighting point on a spur (page 300).

Dry-lining a wall with plasterboard

Dry lining is a good way of covering poor plaster, concealing pipework, or hiding insulating material. It usually involves nailing plasterboard to a timber frame fixed to the wall.

Thermal board, which has a polystyrene backing for insulation, can be fixed direct to a plastered wall provided the wall is flat. It is held with a special adhesive and hammer-in fixings (page 158). If the wall is not flat, a timber framework is needed to provide a level surface.

How many boards do I need?

The boards do not have to fit the height of the wall exactly – a gap of up to 25mm is usually left at the bottom for expansion, and may be covered by the skirting board. Boards need not be fitted vertically. They can be fitted horizontally if this is more convenient for the wall measurements.

1 Measure the height of the wall at each end (heights may be slightly different – use the highest figure). Also measure the width at the top and bottom.

2 From these measurements work out how many boards you need. If the widths will not fit exactly, plan to place the boards so that narrow widths will fit equally at each end of the wall.

3 Allow for separate pieces of board above door frames and above and below windows.

4 If the wall height is considerably more than the board length, fit the boards in staggered long and short upper and lower panels. Or fix the boards horizontally.

Fixing battens to the walls

Remove wall fittings such as picture rails and skirting boards (page 179) for later replacement. All switches and sockets will have to be moved forward (page 231). Take down architraves (page 178) and refit them on the lining. If the wall is plastered, leave the plaster in position if it is sound; use a hammer and cold chisel to chip off slight humps. But if plaster is broken or coming away from the wall, chip it away.

Before you start Check the wall surface to see if it is true and straight. If not, find and mark the most protuberant part of the wall surface so that the timber framework can be made to accommodate it.

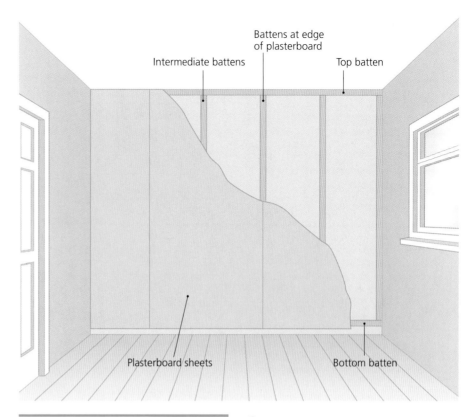

Intermediate battens · Battens at edge of plasterboard · Top batten · Plasterboard sheets · Bottom batten

Tools *Pencil or chalk; plumb line; steel tape measure; hammer or screwdriver; handsaw; padsaw; drill and twist bits; portable workbench. Possibly also; trimming knife; countersink bit; masonry bit.*

Materials *Sawn timber battens 25 x 50mm – all treated with wood preservative; masonry nails or hammer-in fixings at least 10mm longer than the combined thickness of the batten and plaster (if any); hardboard slivers for packing pieces; plasterboard; plasterboard nails. Possibly also: insulation material and tacks, drawing pins or adhesive.*

1 Lay a framing batten on its side flat against the base of the wall and mark its thickness, with pencil or chalk, along the floor for the whole length of the wall to be lined.

2 Take a batten of the same height as the wall and hold it vertical, flat against one end of the wall to be lined.

3 Using a spirit level or plumb line to keep the batten vertical, move it along the wall and mark any position where its base is outside the line marked on the floor.
On a plastered wall, any obvious plaster humps can be chipped away.

4 At the outermost floor mark, draw a second line along the floor parallel with the first.

5 Using a plumb line and timber batten, mark a line along the ceiling in line with the second floor line.

6 Use masonry nails or countersunk hammer-in fixings at about 500mm intervals to fix a horizontal batten to the base of the wall 25mm above the floor.

7 Align the outer edge of the batten with the second floor line, placing hardboard packing pieces between the batten and the wall where necessary.

8 Fit a horizontal batten to the top of the wall, against the ceiling, in the same way.

9 Use a plumb line to check that the two horizontal battens are in line. Adjust the position of the top batten if necessary.

Fixing the vertical battens

1 Measure and draw lines down the wall where the edges of boards will meet. Vertical battens will be fixed centrally on these lines.

2 Mark the positions of the intermediate vertical battens (which will lie at board centres) midway between the edge battens.

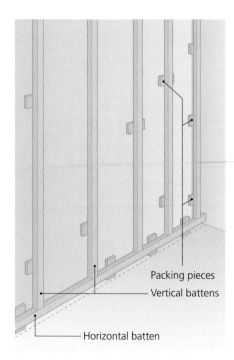

Packing pieces
Vertical battens
Horizontal batten

3 Cut vertical battens to length to fit snugly between the horizontal battens.

4 Fit the vertical battens for the plasterboard edges in the positions marked. Before driving the fixings fully home, use a plumb line to check that each batten is vertical and in line with the horizontal top and bottom battens. Pack behind the batten where necessary (see below left).

5 When you are satisfied, drive the fixings fully home.

6 Fit the intermediate vertical battens in the same way as the board-edge battens, using packing wherever necessary.

7 Fix battens all round window and door openings. Make sure they align horizontally and vertically with the other battens.

8 If necessary, put a short length of batten round electrical outlets to support board edges (see Moving switches and sockets, page 231).

9 If there are to be any fixtures such as wall cupboards, fix extra battens at anchor points in the required positions. Mark a horizontal line along the centre of the batten and the adjoining studs as a guide for fixings. Transfer it to the plasterboard when fitting.

10 If insulation materials, such as rigid polystyrene boards or glass-fibre batts, are being fitted, wedge them in place between the battens.

Fixing plasterboard to the frame

1 Cut the plasterboard to leave a gap of 13mm between the base and the floor – the board will hang 13mm below the horizontal batten.

2 Nail the board to the battens with plasterboard nails in the same way as for building a stud partition (page 238). Then fill in the joints between boards (page 228).

Creating an archway

A door that is always left open can be removed and the space turned into an eye-catching archway with an expanded metal arch-former kit.

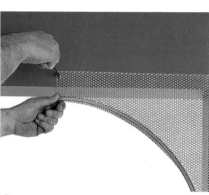

1 Fix the first section of arch-former to the opening. Use self-tapping screws on a timber-frame partition. On brick, cut back the plaster to just past where the metal reaches, and fix the arch-form to the masonry with short masonry nails.

2 Fix the other side of the arch in the same way. Then go to the other side of the opening and fix two arch-formers there.

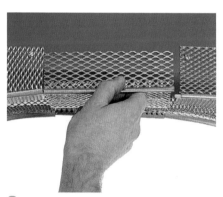

3 Cut a bridging section with tinsnips to about 6mm less than the gap. Push a corner bead connector into the open end of the corner bead at each end and slip the bridging section over them.

4 Cut a strip of mesh to form the curved underside of the arch and fix it to the curved sections with small loops of wire. Tighten the loops and snip off the excess.

5 Plaster the inside curve first, working from the bottom up. Then plaster the two wall faces, feathering the edges.

Preparing to timber-clad a wall or ceiling

Think carefully before completely cladding a small room – the effect could be overpowering. If you plan to line the ceiling and one or more walls, tackle the ceiling first.

Fitting boards along the length of a ceiling makes a room appear longer; across the width makes it look wider.

Similarly, horizontal boards on a wall make a room look longer, and vertical boards make a ceiling look higher.

Buying and preparing boards

Work out how many boards you need in the same way as for plasterboard (previous page), but remember that because the boards interlock, the width of a board is greater than the width it will cover. Buy them all at the same time and check that they are of a similar appearance – characteristics such as knots and grain pattern can vary from pack to pack. Buy boards about three weeks before you intend to put them up, and stack them flat in the room to be lined. This allows the moisture content to even out and lessens the risk of joints being pulled apart by boards shrinking.

Cover width

Fixing battens to the ceiling

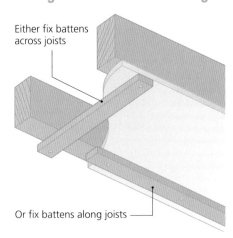

Either fix battens across joists

Or fix battens along joists

Use sawn timber battens 40mm wide and 25mm thick, treated with wood preservative (page 439). Screw them flat against the ceiling, into the ceiling joists, using countersunk screws. The fixing should be long enough to penetrate at least 25mm into the joist (see locating joists, opposite).

If, however, you want the boards to fit at right angles to the joists, position the battens along the centres of the joists.
• Fit the battens at 400–600mm intervals. Use a builder's square (page 467) to check whether the ceiling corners are true.
• If they are not, use a chalked string line to mark true lines across the ceiling as a guide to positioning the end battens.

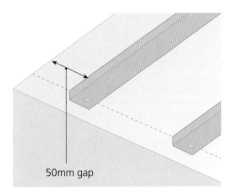

50mm gap

• Do not position the end battens right against the wall, as it makes nailing the boards to them difficult. Leave a gap of about 50mm.
• After fitting the first batten, hold a spirit level along it to check that it is horizontal. If necessary, pack hardboard pieces behind to level it.

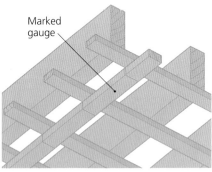

Marked gauge

• When fitting succeeding battens, use a tape measure, or make a marked gauge with another batten, to check that each batten is parallel with the adjoining one. Hold a spirit level across the two battens to check they are level, and pack out as necessary.

Fixing battens to a wall

Use sawn timber battens 40mm wide and 20mm thick, treated with wood preservative (page 439). Fix them to the wall with hammer-in fixings or countersunk screws and wall plugs. For vertical boarding, fix the battens horizontally. For horizontal boarding, fix the battens vertically. The skirting board can be left in place unless you want to remove it.
• Place battens at intervals of 400–500mm for 9mm thick boards, or at 500–600mm intervals for 12mm thick boards.
• The fixing should be long enough to penetrate at least 25mm into the wall.
• To ensure a level surface for the cladding, find the highest point of the wall (page

---

ALLOWING FOR VENTILATION

In kitchens and bathrooms, where condensation is likely, allow for airflow behind the cladding.

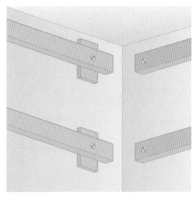

Pack behind horizontal battens with hardboard or thin plywood to lift them away from the wall. Also leave a gap at the top and bottom of the cladding. With vertical battens there is an automatic airflow if a 3mm gap is left at the top and bottom of the cladding. Use only vertical cladding on horizontal battens in kitchens and bathrooms because water can collect in the channelling of horizontal boards.

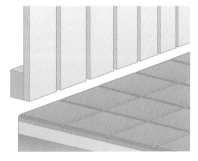

Stop the cladding slightly clear of a kitchen work surface, to prevent it getting wet, and 25mm or more clear of the top of a bath. Ceiling cladding can be stopped short to give a small gap on all edges, allowing for board expansion and ventilation. Or leave a gap at the long edges of the cladding only to give airflow between battens.

---

232), and mark a guideline on the floor or skirting board for the batten surface.
• Fit vertical battens in the same way as for dry-lining (page 233). When fitting battens horizontally, use a spirit level to ensure that each is horizontal.
• Check that the batten surfaces are all level with each other using either a spirit level or a plumb line dropped to the marked guideline. Pack behind battens with hardboard pieces where necessary to maintain a level surface.

HOW BOARDS FIT TOGETHER

Boards for timber cladding are long and narrow, and are mostly jointed together on their long edges. Solid timber cladding is usually varnished to keep it clean and prevent it from darkening.

Tongued-and-grooved with narrow V

The commonest type; generally 95–100mm wide, with a cover width of about 90mm. When the tongue is fitted into the groove of the adjoining board a narrow V-shaped channel is visible between boards.

Tongued-and-grooved with wide V

The channel formed between the boards is slightly wider than for the narrow V type, but the size and cover width of the board is generally the same.

Tongued-and-grooved with double V

The board has a wide V-joint and an extra groove cut down its centre to give the appearance of narrower panelling.
The board is wider than other tongued-and-grooved types – generally 120mm with a cover width of 110mm.

Shiplap Each board has an L-shaped edge and a curved edge. The boards fit together with the overlap over the curve, forming a channel curved along one side. When fitting boards horizontally, place the curved edge at the top. Boards may be wider than average: 120mm with a 110mm cover width.

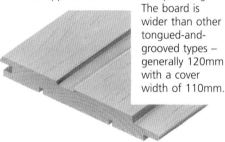

Square-edged Square-edged boards can be overlapped louvre fashion or they can be spaced with narrow channels that reveal the wall behind. Thick boards are normally used and they can be fitted without using a batten framework.

Locating joists in a floor or ceiling

Timber framework for supporting a partition wall or a ceiling lining must be fixed to solid timber joists in the floor or ceiling.

Joists are parallel timbers about 50mm thick stretched across from wall to wall to support the floorboards or ceiling. They are usually 400–600mm apart, but on a top floor, ceiling joists may be 350mm apart.

Locating floor joists

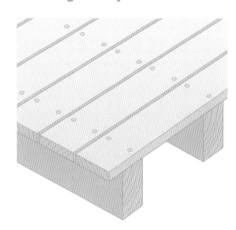

Find the position of joists by noting the lines of nails where the floorboards are fixed to them. The joists are always at right angles to the floorboards.

Locating ceiling joists from above

One way to find ceiling joists in an upstairs room is to get into the loft above and mark their positions through the ceiling.

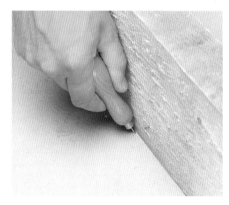

Use a bradawl to poke down through the ceiling on each side of a joist, at both ends. Measure the width of a joist and the distance between joists, and mark the position of another joist at the far side of the area through the ceiling.

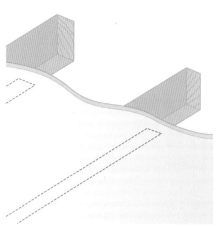

From below, you can join up the marks to show the joist positions, then measure and mark the positions of the other joists. A quick method of marking the position is with a chalked string line (page 109).

Locating ceiling joists from below

In a downstairs room you will have to find the ceiling joists from below, unless you are prepared to lift the floorboards in the room above. You can get an idea of their positions by lifting the upstairs floor covering and looking for the lines of nails.

Joists can also be located from below with a metal detector (page 34), available from DIY stores. The detector lights up when it passes over metal such as a nail head, so can be used to trace the lines of nails where sheets of plasterboard or timber laths are fixed to the joists. It will also show the paths of any metal pipes or electric cables running alongside the joists.

To find the joists without a metal detector, tap the ceiling lightly to detect a solid area, then probe with a bradawl. Use the bradawl to trace the position of one joist, and mark it with a chalked string line. From this, you can measure and mark the other joists, testing each surface with the bradawl.

Lining a wall or ceiling with timber cladding

Do not fit boards right up to wall or ceiling edges. Leave a small gap of about 3mm to allow for board expansion. If ventilation is not required, any gaps can be covered with a strip of moulding.

Stop cladding several centimetres short of a fireplace or a boiler, if you can, and use tiles or plasterboard as a surround. If you cannot stop the cladding short, protect the board edges with a metal edging strip. When fitting cladding to the wall horizontally, start at the bottom.

Tools *Spirit level; steel straightedge; steel tape measure; hammer; tongued-and-grooved board off-cut; mallet. Possibly also power saw; screwdriver; nail punch; plane; gauge made from a batten marked with the width of two or three fitted boards; try-square; push-pin magnetic nail holder.*

Materials *Cladding boards; nails, clips, screws or panel adhesive. Possibly moulding; wood filler.*

Before you start Move electrical fittings forward if necessary (page 231), or leave them in position and line round them so that they are recessed within the cladding.

Decide which of the following methods you will use to fix the boards:

Face-nailing Suitable for all types of board. Use 30mm thin lost-head or oval nails or panel pins. Position them at least 15mm in from the board edge. Drive them straight in, using a nail punch. Leave the head either flush with the surface or just below it. Nails with the head left exposed should be arranged in a uniform pattern. Where nails are punched just below the surface, fill the holes with wood filler.

Screwing Usually used only for fixing square edged boards, but advisable where any type of board may have to be removed to get at a covered-in fitting. Use 30mm roundhead or countersunk screws. Drill holes through boards before screwing.

Secret nailing A method of nailing so that nails holding the cladding cannot be seen. Suitable for tongued-and-grooved boards only. Use 30mm thin lost-head or oval nails or panel pins. Hammer the nails in at an angle through the tongue of the board. Use a thin nail punch when the head gets near to the board, and drive the nail in until the corner of the head just protrudes. If the nail is driven in too far, the tongue is likely to split. The nail head is hidden when the groove of the next board is fitted over the tongue. Nail vertical boards with the tongue on the right if you are right handed, on the left if left-handed. Nail horizontal boards with the tongue upwards. Some face-nailing is needed for boards fitted at the edge of the panelling.

HELPFUL TIPS

- When secret nailing thin dry boards such as pine, drill a pilot hole right through the board to avoid splitting the tongue.
- If a tongued-and-grooved board is difficult to slot in straight, hammer it lightly with a mallet, using a board offcut between the board and the mallet. Slot the offcut groove over the tongue of the board that you are fitting.
- Avoid fitting boards together too tightly in kitchens and bathrooms, because humidity will cause the wood to swell and expand.

Fixing boards to wall or ceiling battens

1 Position the first board at right angles to the wall or ceiling battens and about 3mm from the edge of the adjoining wall. Fit the grooved edge of a tongued-and-grooved board or the straight lip of a shiplap board to the wall.

2 Use a spirit level to check that the board is vertical or horizontal. For a board fitted to a ceiling, use a try-square to ensure that it is at right angles to the batten.

3 Fix the board to the battens using the chosen method (left).

4 Fix the second board, using a straight-edge to check the ends are aligned with the first board, and a spirit level to make sure that it is level.

5 On a ceiling, use a marked gauge (page 234) to check near each end that the first and second boards are parallel.

6 Continue fitting boards in the same way. The last board may have to be trimmed to fit the remaining space. When trimming, allow for a 3mm gap against the wall. If using secret nailing, secure the last board either with panel adhesive or by face nailing.

Fitting boards round doors and windows

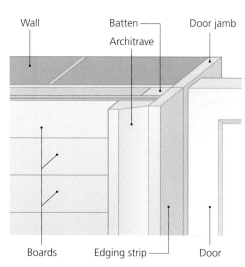

Wall — Batten — Architrave — Door jamb

Boards — Edging strip — Door

At doors and windows, remove any architraves (page 178). Fit vertical battens alongside a door jamb, leaving enough room for an edging strip to cover the batten and the edge of the end board.
• If desired, the edging strip can project in front of cladding and give an edge to which the architrave can be refitted.
• Line a deep window recess with cladding boards, with the external corners joined in one of the methods described below.
• Windowsill boards are difficult to remove. If the edges of a sill project, it is best to cut the cladding to shape to fit round them.

Joining boards at corners

How you join boards at corners will depend on whether the corner is internal or external (at a chimney breast, for example).

Internal corners

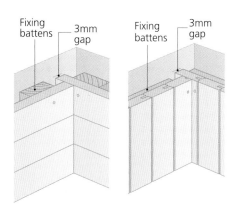

Fixing battens — 3mm gap   Fixing battens — 3mm gap

For horizontal boarding, fit one line of cladding into the corner, leaving a gap of about 3mm at the wall. Butt the cladding on the adjoining wall against it. Joints can be covered with quadrant moulding if desired.
    Vertical boarding is fitted into the corner in the same way as horizontal, with the cladding butted.

External corners

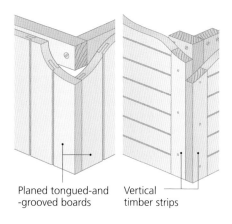

Planed tongued-and -grooved boards   Vertical timber strips

Vertical boards can be planed to remove the tongue and groove and then butted at right angles. Alternatively, you can butt the grooved edges of two boards and cover the joint with right-angled corner moulding.
    For horizontal boards, fit vertical timber strips at the corner and butt the cladding boards against them.

Cladding a wall with brick slips

Brick slips (or stone cladding) are stuck in rows in a brick-bond pattern. The joints between are filled in with mortar and pointed in the same way as for brick walls, or left open and painted later.

Soldier course

Before you start Work out how many slips will fit across the wall, and how many rows you will need to create.
    Do this by marking a wooden batten with lines 222mm apart – this allows a 10mm joint between each slip. Hold the batten horizontally against the wall and count the number of slips. Decide how to arrange any part bricks.

Now mark the other side of the batten every 75mm to see how many rows you will get. If the height fit is not exact, allow a small gap at the bottom, or insert a 'soldier course' (see below left).

Tools *Spirit level; steel tape measure; plumb line; tile cutter or saw (as recommended by the slip manufacturer); filling knife; pointing trowel.*

Materials *PVA adhesive; water; wooden spacers; mortar (page 467).*

1 Remove skirting boards (page 179) and prepare the walls as for decorating.

2 Prime the wall with one part PVA adhesive to five parts water, following the manufacturer's instructions.

3 Use a filling knife or pointing trowel for the adhesive and apply it as recommended. Keep separate tools for applying adhesive and mortar.

4 Apply the bottom row of slips, using wooden spacers to keep them apart. Fill the mortar joints afterwards. Check with the marked battens that subsequent rows are correctly spaced.

5 Point the joints as the mortar starts to stiffen and, when dry, brush away any surface mortar that is loose.

PLASTIC CLADDING

Cladding made from uPVC consists of narrow, white, hollow boards similar in appearance to timber cladding, usually with tongued-and-grooved or shiplap joints. They are particularly suitable for walls and ceilings in bathrooms or kitchens, where high moisture levels can damage wood panelling. The cellular structure of the cladding traps air inside that acts as insulation, so the wall feels warm to the touch and resists condensation. The cladding can be simply wiped clean with a damp cloth.
    Boards can be cut with a fine-toothed saw or trimmed with a sharp knife. Measure the length of cladding needed and then subtract 3mm to allow for expansion.
    The cut boards are then fitted to a framework of timber battens screwed to the wall at 600mm intervals, at 90° to the direction in which the cladding is to run. The uPVC boards are attached to the battens with concealed clips, following the manufacturer's instructions. The cladding is added length by length, each one sliding into place against the previous board. Use matching trim strips for a neat finish.

Building a stud partition

A non-load-bearing stud partition is made from plasterboards that are fixed to each side of a timber frame made from uprights (studs) fitted between top and bottom rails (head and sole plates).

These instructions are for 12.5mm thick plasterboard on a partition no more than 2.4m high. To improve sound insulation, fit a layer of glass-fibre blanket or batts (page 243) at least 75mm thick between the lining boards.

For even better insulation, build the partition with two layers of plasterboard on each side, with the joints between boards staggered. This will prevent voices at normal speaking level penetrating the partition.

Tools *Plumb line; pencil; 75 x 50mm timber offcut; bradawl; hammer; screwdriver; spirit level; power drill and twist bits; portable workbench; straight-edge; panel saw or trimming knife; footlifter (page 228); plasterboard jointing tools; medium abrasive paper. Possibly also: padsaw.*

Materials *Plasterboards 12.5mm thick and 1200mm wide; glass-fibre insulation blanket or batts at least 75mm thick; sawn timber 75 x 50mm sufficient for head and sole plates, uprights at 600mm intervals, and cross-pieces; 100mm nails; 100mm No. 10 screws; 100mm frame fixings (pages 158–9) or screws and wall plugs; 40mm plasterboard nails; plasterboard joint tape (page 222). Possibly also ceiling noggins 100 x 50mm; screws and wall plugs for fixing to a solid floor; packing such as hardboard or vinyl tile pieces; timber door casing about 100 x 25mm; skirting board; architrave moulding; 50mm panel pins or oval nails.*

Before you start Buy the interior door and casing first, because there are various door widths. Measure the height from the floor, not the sole plate. If possible, avoid positioning a door right beside an adjoining wall, against an end stud.

Finding solid fixing points

The partition must be fitted so that the head and sole plates can be securely fixed to solid floor and ceiling timbers (see Locating joists, page 235).

Position the partition in line with the floorboards, if possible, so that it can be fixed across the joists supporting the floor. If the partition has to be at right angles to the floorboards, try to position it along the line of a joist.

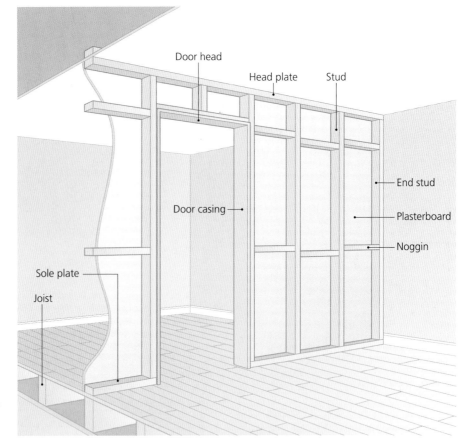

The sole plate can be fixed along a joist, as shown here, or alternatively, it can go across the joists in line with the floorboards.

Where the partition cannot be positioned along a floor joist, skew-nail 100 x 50mm cross-pieces (noggins) between the joists at intervals of 1 metre.

Position the head plate in the same way, so that it can be fixed either across the ceiling joists or parallel with one. If the plate has to be positioned between two parallel joists, fit noggins between them in the same way as for floor joists, working from the loft or from the room above.

Putting up the timber frame

1 Use a 75mm offcut to mark each end of the head-plate position on the located fixing points. Place the offcut at right angles across a joist, or centred along it.

2 Drop a plumb line from each of the marked edges and get a helper to mark each point on the floor as a guide to positioning the sole plate.

3 Temporarily fix the sole plate at about 600mm intervals, but do not drive the fixings fully home yet. Use 100mm nails for a wooden floor, driven into the joists where possible. Use 90mm No. 10 screws for fixings to a solid floor.

4 Drill through the ceiling into joists (or noggins) and screw the head plate to them temporarily, using 100mm No. 10 screws.

5 Use a plumb line to check the alignment of the two plates near each end and adjust their positioning if necessary. Then drive the fixings fully home. Mark one side of the sole plate with stud positions at 600mm centres, taking into account the width and position of any doorway.

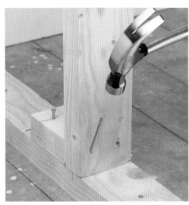

6 Mark a centre line on the 50mm thick side of the timber offcut. Place the offcut squarely across the sole plate with the two marks aligned, and pencil in the edge positions for each stud.

7 Measure and cut the studs. There should be a tight push fit between the head and sole plates. If necessary, recess the studs to fit over skirting (or coving) on the adjoining walls.

8 Push each end stud into place against the wall, using a spirit level to ensure each one is vertical. If a wall is not true, pack any gaps with hardboard or pieces of vinyl tile.

9 Fix each end stud to the wall using either 100mm frame fixings or No. 10 screws and wall plugs.

10 Get a helper to hold each of the other studs in position, while you temporarily nail an offcut to the sole plate on one side to hold the stud in place for nailing.

11 Use a spirit level to ensure that the stud is vertical on both the 75mm and 50mm sides.

MAKING A DOORWAY

1 Fit studs on each side of the doorway, far enough apart to allow 2–3mm for the hanging of the door (page 195) and for the thickness of the casing round the opening.

2 Fix a noggin across to form the door head, again allowing for the casing. The door casing should be the same width as the studs plus the thickness of the plasterboard on each side – usually 100mm overall.

3 If fitting a glass pane above the door, line this opening also.

4 To complete the doorway, saw through and remove the section of sole plate at the base of the opening.

SKEW-NAILING A JOINT

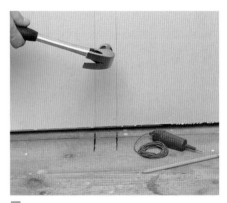

Mark the position of the join on the sole plate and temporarily nail a block of wood in place, with one edge butting up to the line. Hold the stud against the block, and drive the first nail diagonally down into the sole plate a third of the way in from one side. Remove the block and nail from the other side in the same way.

12 Nail each stud on the head and sole plates by skew-nailing (see box above). Use three 100mm nails – two one side and one on the other. Temporarily mark the stud positions on the floor as a guide when nailing the plasterboard on later.

13 Brace the studs with horizontal noggins positioned halfway between the floor and ceiling. Either skew-nail them in place, or stagger the position of adjacent noggins so you can drive the nails through the stud into the end of each noggin.

14 Fit any extra noggins needed for supporting fixtures such as wall cupboards, and mark the noggin position on the stud edges for transfer to the board.

15 Run any necessary cables through the framework (see Routing cables, page 282).

Lining the frame with plasterboard

1 Cut each board (page 228) so it is 15mm shorter than the floor-to-ceiling height.

2 Fit whole boards first, working from one side to the other. Leave narrow-width boards that need trimming to fit a side wall until last.

3 Fit each board with the ivory face outwards, holding it in position resting on the footlifter (page 228).

4 Align each edge of the board midway over a stud, using the edge of the stud as a guide to make sure it is vertical.

5 Press the board tight against the ceiling with the footlifter while you nail it to the timber framework all round the edges and into the noggins between the studs.

6 Fix plasterboard nails at least 15mm in from the edge of the board, spaced at 150mm intervals. Drive them home until the head dimples the board surface but does not burst the paper lining.

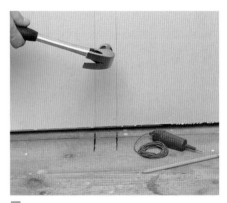

7 Use floor marks and a plumb line and straight-edge to pencil in the position of the stud at the board centre. Nail the board to it at 150mm intervals.

8 Butt end boards against the wall to cover end studs and any packing. If the wall against which the board fits is out of true, scribe the board and cut it to fit the wall contours.

9 Line the other side of the stud partition framework with plasterboard in the same way. Then fill the joints between boards (page 228).

10 Fit skirting board round the room (page 179) and an architrave (page 178) round the door frame, if necessary, to match other mouldings in adjoining rooms.

Building a metal-framed stud wall

Instead of the traditional timber-framed stud wall, a steel frame is lighter and thinner and can be positioned anywhere without danger of overloading the floor.

A metal stud partition wall will be only about 75mm thick when complete. It is ideal for dividing rooms where sound penetration is not a problem.

Tools *Portable workbench; gloves; pencil; tape measure; hacksaw; plumb line; screwdriver or power drill with screwdriver bit; masonry drill bit; spirit level; trimming knife; straightedge; filling knife.*

Materials *Metal profiles; sealing tape; 50mm wood screws; wallplugs or cavity fixings; 12.5mm plasterboard; 25mm drywall screws; joint tape; filler.*

1 Cut the head profile to size. If the new wall is to run at right angles to the ceiling joists, screw the profile to each joist. If it is to run parallel with the joists, locate a suitable joist and fix the profile to it.

2 Drop a plumbline from the head profile and mark the floor. This will be where the sole profile is placed. Cut it to length, stick self-adhesive tape to its underside and screw it to the floor.

3 Measure the distance between the head and sole profiles, and cut your first vertical stud to length, less about 5mm to allow for clearance at the top.

4 Hold the stud in place, mark the fixing holes with a pencil and drill and plug the holes.

5 Screw the stud to the wall. Repeat for the stud at the other end.

6 Cut the first intermediate stud to length and place it so that its centre is exactly 600mm from the end stud. This will ensure that the plasterboard sheets meet in the middle of each vertical stud. These studs are not screwed to the head and sole profiles – they push-fit into them.

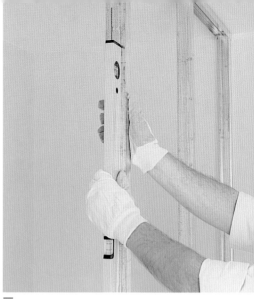

7 Fit the rest of the studs, measuring carefully and checking that they are all vertical. If there is to be a door, the kit will contain the necessary components to make a lintel and the door linings.

8 Cut the plasterboard sheets 6mm shorter than the floor-to-ceiling height, and hold them up against the ceiling. Secure them to the studs with drywall screws, about 10mm in from the edge of the board, and at 300mm centres.

9 Clad one side of the wall first, then run in any cables for wiring accessories before finishing off the other side.

HELPFUL TIPS

- If you have to cut the metal lengths, use a hacksaw.
- When cutting studs, always remove the excess from the same end, so that the internal service slots remain aligned once the wall is assembled.
- Remember to wear gloves – the profiles have very sharp edges.
- The wall relies on the plasterboard for its strength and rigidity so try to stagger the joints on the opposite side of the wall.
- If something heavy, such as a cupboard, has to be fixed to the wall, you can support it by screwing a flat steel plate to the faces of the studs. The plate is provided as part of the partition system and is fixed in place with pan-head screws.

Insulating the walls of a house

Cavity walls

Insulating cavity walls saves heat loss from a house, but it is not a DIY job. To check if the cavities have already been filled, you can drill a hole into the cavity from the outside and feel with a probe. If it is empty, call in a contractor specialising in cavity insulation.

Since it is impossible to check how well the work has been done or how long the insulation will last, you will have to rely on the contractor's integrity. You can get advice from the National Insulation Association, PO Box 12, Haslemere, Surrey GU27 3AH; www.ncia-ltd.org.uk tel: 01428 654011.

Note that walls to be insulated must show no sign of penetrating damp. The cause of any damp must be cured first and the walls allowed to dry out. The contractor should thoroughly examine the walls to make sure they are fit for filling, with no evidence of damp, or damage that may let in damp.

There are two main insulation systems to choose between, with similar installation methods.

Mineral-wool fibres or polystyrene beads

The dry system consists of mineral-wool fibres or expanded polystyrene beads being blown through holes drilled in the outer leaf of the wall until the cavity is filled.

Expanding foam

With the second system, the cavities are filled with foam. This is produced on site and pumped through holes drilled in the outer brick leaf. The foam normally dries after a few days and becomes firm. This system is not suitable for timber-framed houses.

Solid walls

Any extra width of insulation on the inside of a house wall may bring the wall out beyond skirting boards, picture rails and architraves. Often lights, wall socket, light switches and radiators will have to be repositioned.

Insulate the walls with thermal board fixed to battens (page 232). Before nailing the boards in place, pin fibre blanket to the battens.

Alternatively, fix the thermal board direct to the walls with the adhesive suggested by the board manufacturer, and a secondary fixing of hammer-in fixings or screws.

Soundproofing a room

Noise pollution is one of the distressing factors of modern life. Fortunately it is possible to cut down on the amount of sound that enters – and leaves – a room.

Depending on where you live, you may suffer from airborne noise created by nearby road, rail or air traffic, by local industry or other commercial activity, or simply by noisy neighbours with a taste for loud music and unruly dogs. If you live in a terraced or semi-detached property, or a flat, you also have the problem of sharing the building with other occupants, whose activities create noise that travels through each separating (party) wall into your home.

Cutting airborne sound

Acoustic double glazing
The single biggest improvement you can make is to have acoustic double glazing installed. This takes the form of secondary glazing, creating a gap of at least 100mm between the new glazing and the existing window glass. For the best results:
• the existing windows must be efficiently draught-proofed to prevent sound transmission through air gaps;
• the secondary glazing should use glass thicker than that in the existing windows;
• the window reveal should be lined with acoustic tiles.

It is essential that the secondary glazing is kept closed for maximum effect, but make sure that a window can be opened easily to offer an escape route in the event of a fire.

It may be necessary to provide the room with alternative means of ventilation if the window is the only source of fresh air.

External doors
To improve the sound insulation of an external door:
• replace a glazed or lightweight door with a solid one;
• ensure a door is well draught-proofed;
• fit secondary glazing to a porch or hall window.

Seal all gaps
Use non-setting mastic to seal gaps round door and window frames.

Cutting transmitted sound with an insulated lining

You can significantly reduce the sound transmitted through a party wall by building an insulated lining – similar to a timber-framed stud partition wall – parallel to but separated from the party wall. If the wall contains a chimney breast, the lining can be built in front of it if you can afford to lose the floor space. If you cannot, erect the lining in the alcoves. If the fireplace is not in use, this should be bricked up and plastered over as part of the work.

Tools *Tape measure; plumb line; hand or power saw; hammer. Possibly also power drill and drill bits; wide filling knife or plasterer's trowel; cartridge gun.*

Materials *75 x 50mm sawn softwood; 100mm round wire nails; 100mm thick loft insulation blanket; 12.5mm plasterboard; 40mm plasterboard nails; self-adhesive joint tape; joint filler; non-setting mastic.*

1 Draw a line on the ceiling parallel with the party wall and 100mm away from it. Cut the head plate to length, position its front edge on the line and nail it to the ceiling joists if it runs at right angles to them. Fix it with expanding metal cavity anchors if it is parallel to them.

2 Drop a plumb line from the head plate to the floor and make another mark. Cut the sole plate to length and nail it to the floor. Use masonry nails on a concrete floor.

3 Cut and fit studs at each side of the wall and at 600mm centres in between. Skew-nail them to the head and sole plates.

4 Cut lengths of loft insulation and hang them between the studs, tucking their ends and sides behind the framework.

5 Cut the first sheet of plasterboard to match the ceiling height. Offer it up and nail it to the framework. Fix further sheets to complete the first layer.

6 Cut and fit a second layer of plasterboard over the first layer, with the joint positions staggered. Tape and fill the joints, and seal the perimeter of the wall with non-setting mastic. Fit a new skirting board and decorate the wall.

HELPFUL TIPS

• If you live near an airport or major road, you may be able to get a local authority grant towards the costs of soundproofing your home.
• For professional advice on further means of sound insulation in the home, look up Acoustic Engineers in your local Yellow Pages directory.

Preventing condensation

Condensation occurs in a room when warm air filled with moisture meets a cold surface, such as an external wall or a pane of glass. It has become a more common problem in the home as draughtproofing has improved.

The two main ways to reduce condensation are either to reduce the amount of moisture released into the air, or to extract moist air. In extreme cases, a dehumidifier can be used to extract water from the air.

Reducing water vapour

Large amounts of water vapour are produced by cooking, laundry and bathing. Try to reduce the amount of moisture released into the air.

• In the kitchen, a hood over the cooker will reduce condensation by removing steam.

• Cover saucepans with lids when you are cooking, and use an automatic kettle that will switch itself off as soon as the water has boiled.

• If you have a tumble dryer, make sure that it is vented to the outside unless it is of the condenser type that needs no vent.

• Condensation often occurs in bathrooms, especially on cold tiled surfaces. A heated towel rail will help to raise the temperature of the room.

• Less steam will form if you run a little cold water into the bath before turning on the hot water. Keep the bathroom door shut to prevent steam from spreading to other parts of the house.

• Install an extractor fan in the bathroom and in the kitchen.

HELPFUL TIP

Use anti-condensation paint instead of standard emulsion in very steamy areas. The paint absorbs moisture during periods of high humidity and allows it to evaporate later on. The paint also contains a fungicide that reduces the risk of mould.

Installing an extractor fan

The most effective way to improve ventilation is to install an extractor fan. Position it opposite a door for best results.

Axial-flow fan

Centrifugal impeller

Axial-flow fans contain flat, propeller-like blades, and include models for mounting in a window. Centrifugal fans have a long, cylindrical impeller.

Wall-mounted fans discharge to the outside through a hole. Ceiling-mounted fans discharge along a duct above the ceiling to a hole in an external wall.

Window-mounted fans are normally cheap and easy to install, but as they tend to have smaller motors, they are more likely to be affected by strong winds than wall-mounted types. All types are driven electrically and controlled by a pull-cord switch on the fan or a separate wall switch.

A pull-cord fan is the best choice for a bathroom – a wall switch would have to be sited outside the room to comply with regulations for electrical bathroom fittings. Electricity consumption is generally low.

Fans with two or three speeds have complex electrical wiring. You may need to get the wiring done by an electrician.

Fitting a wall or window-mounted fan

1 Position the fan as high in the wall or window as possible, opposite the door or main air entry point so that air is drawn right across the room.

2 If there is a boiler or gas heater in the room, make sure it is independently ventilated. Otherwise, when doors and windows are shut the extractor fan could draw air and fumes from the boiler or heater flue into the room.

3 Make a hole in the wall or window at the chosen position. Fit the external clamp plate and grille and the inner clamp plate and fan assembly.

4 Prepare a cable route (page 282) to a spot within reach of the fan's flex. At the end of the route fit a mounting box for a flex outlet plate in a bathroom, or for a switched FCU elsewhere (pages 286–7).

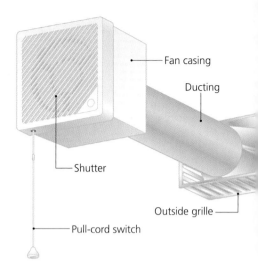

Fan casing
Ducting
Shutter
Outside grille
Pull-cord switch

Wall-mounted fan
A shutter fits onto the fan inside the room, and a grille fits on the outside wall. The two are connected by plastic ducting. This is essential in a cavity wall, but useful in a solid wall too, as it makes cleaning easier. The fan may have a pull-cord switch or a separate wall switch.

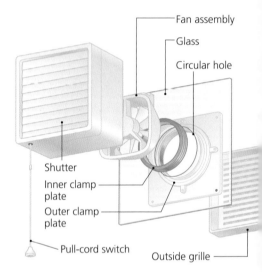

Fan assembly
Glass
Circular hole
Shutter
Inner clamp plate
Outer clamp plate
Pull-cord switch
Outside grille

Window-mounted fan
The fan is fitted around a circular hole cut in the glass and outer parts are screwed together with clamp plates on each side of the window.

5 Following the maker's instructions, make any electrical connections necessary to the fan assembly before fitting the internal grille and shutter. Some models are wired to a plug-in block. Use the flex recommended by the manufacturer.

6 Fit the grille and the shutter on the inside of the room.

7 Connect the fan into its electrical supply circuit.
• In a bathroom, follow the method described in Installing a heated towel rail (page 287).
• Elsewhere, follow the method described under Fitting an FCU for a stationary appliance (page 286).

Before buying a fan, find out how
much air it can move. Airflow
capacity is given in either cubic
metres per hour, or litres per second.

The fan extract rates required by the
Building Regulations vary from
room to room. They are:
• kitchens 60 litres per second
($215m^3$ per hour)
• utility rooms 30 litres per second
($110m^3$ per hour)
• bathrooms 15 litres per second
($55m^3$ per hour)
• separate WCs 6 litres per second
($22m^3$ per hour).

As an example, a typical 150mm
diameter wall or window fan has
an extract rate of about $280m^3$ per
hour, which is more than enough
to meet the Building Regulations
requirements for ventilating a
kitchen.

Fitting a ceiling-mounted fan

The fan is fixed into a hole in the ceiling
between joists (or into a false ceiling) in the
same way as a wall fan, except that a hole
has to be made in the ceiling.
    Fit a length of ducting from the ceiling
intake to a wall outlet. Ducting, made up
of slotted-together sections of metal or
plastic piping, should be ordered with the
fan. If it goes through a wall, it terminates
with a wall grille; if it goes through the
roof it is covered with a roof cowl.
    From an upstairs room, ducting can
pass through the loft. On the ground floor,
a false ceiling may be necessary to hide it.

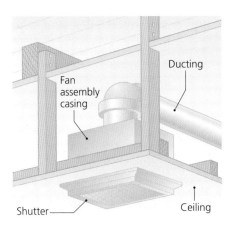

Fan
assembly
casing

Ducting

Shutter

Ceiling

A long length of ducting reduces the
airflow capacity of the fan – probably by
about 10 per cent for each metre of run.
An elbow bend will reduce it even more.
    Take this into account when working out
the size of the extractor fan required (top).

Choosing loft insulation

You can insulate a loft yourself with blanket, loose fill or sheet insulation or pay a
specialist company to blow loose-fill insulation between the joists. If you do it, lay
at least 200mm of insulation: the minimum recommended in the current Building
Regulations. A thicker layer will prevent even more heat loss. You may be eligible
for a grant – ask your local council or Citizens Advice Bureau for details.

Before you buy Find out if a supplier will
deliver the insulation. Blanket rolls and
sacks of loose-fill are very bulky for their
weight. Most cars will only hold a fraction
of the amount needed for most lofts.

How much material do I need?
Calculate the size of your loft before
buying the insulation material. Measure
the overall length and width of your
house and multiply the two figures.
Most suppliers will advise on how much
material is needed for a given area.

Blanket rolls Mineral wool or glass-fibre
blanket is supplied in rolls 100–200mm
thick. Standard rolls are 400mm wide;
combi-rolls are 1200mm wide and
have guidelines so the roll can
be cut accurately into two
600mm wide or three
400mm wide
pieces.

Plain blanket

Sleeved blanket

• Use a
panel saw to
cut through the
roll while it is still in
its wrapper, or you can
cut through single widths
with sharp scissors.
• Fibre blanket is cheap and effective,
but tends to compress as it ages.
• Insulation is not effective if water
condenses in the material. Choose
blanket sleeved in polythene which acts
as a vapour barrier. If you are using
unbacked blanket, lay a vapour barrier
before you insulate.

Mineral fibre batts Multipurpose semi-
rigid batts can be used instead of fibre
blanket in any insulation job. They are
available from 25mm to 100mm thick so
two or more batts are needed to meet
the minimum depth required for
insulating a floor. Batts are 1200mm
long and 600mm or 900mm wide,
which makes them much less
bulky and easier to handle
than blanket rolls – but
they are more
costly.

Loose fill This is supplied in sacks each
sufficient to insulate $1m^2$ and simply poured
between the joists. The depth of the joist
may need to be increased so that the
required depth of cover is achieved.

• Common loose-fill materials are
vermiculite granules, mineral fibre or
polystyrene. Granules can also be used to
top up old blanket insulation.
• Granules will blow about in a draughty
loft, so pin building paper to the joists over
the granules. Leave the tops of the joists
visible so you can walk safely.
• Allow for joists when estimating quantities
– or there will be too much left over.

Expanded polystyrene sheets Useful for
sliding into areas which have been boarded
over or which are difficult to reach – the flat
roof over an extension, for example. It can
also be used to insulate a cold water cistern,
but is too expensive for a whole loft.
• Expanded polystyrene is available
as squeeze-fit 60mm thick
slabs 610 x 402mm and
as 50mm thick general
purpose 1200 x 450mm
sheets. Specialist outlets
will also cut polystyrene
to exact requirements.
Make sure it is fire retardant.
Type A FRA will conform to
BS4735 for combustibility.

Reflective foil building paper Acts as a
vapour barrier so that moisture cannot
condense in the insulation material. Heat
also reflects off the shiny surface – either
back into the house in winter or back into
the loft in summer.
• Lay the foil between joists or
drape it over them. If using it
between joists to stop
loose granules blowing
about, pin the paper in
position. There is no need to
pin it if it is laid on the floor
beneath insulation material.
• Supplied in 25m or 50m rolls 900mm
wide by builders' merchants.

Insulating a loft

If the loft space is used only for storage then insulate the floor. But if the loft has been turned into a room – or if you plan to convert it into a room – insulate the roof slope.

If you put down flooring-grade chipboard after you have insulated between the joists, you will have a useful storage area. But remember the joists are only ceiling joists for the room below, not floor joists, so you cannot use the space as a room or store too many heavy things there.

Before you start Clear the floor space as much as possible and vacuum-clean the loft. At the same time, check for woodworm and rot, and, if necessary, call in a specialist contractor to treat it.

If the loft has no lighting, connect an inspection lamp to a socket downstairs or run a table lamp off an extension cable. A torch will not give adequate light for the job.

Fixing a vapour barrier on the floor

Tools *Scissors.*

Materials *Rolls of reflective foil building paper or sheets of polythene; masking tape.*

1 Cut the material with scissors so that it is about 50–75mm wider than the gap between the joists.

2 Lay the material in the gap. Remember that reflective foil paper must be laid foil-side down.

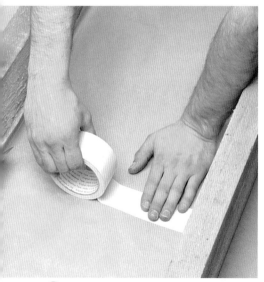

3 Seal any overlaps in the material with 50mm masking tape.

Laying insulation blanket on the floor

The spacing between joists varies but about 350mm is average. Do not cut the excess off a 400mm blanket – let it curl up on each side to make a snug fit.

Tools *Scissors; face mask; protective gloves.*

Materials *Rolls of glass fibre or mineral wool blanket.*

PROTECTING YOURSELF

Insulating products can be very irritating. Only open the packaging in the loft and keep the hatch closed while you are working. Wear protective gloves and overalls or a long-sleeved shirt, and tuck sleeves and trouser legs into gloves and socks. If fibres do get into the gloves, they will cause more irritation than if you wore no gloves at all. Wear a suitable face mask and throw it away after use. It is also a good idea to wear a safety helmet to protect your head against the rafters.

1 Start unrolling the blanket between two joists at the eaves at one end of the loft.

2 Do not take the material right into the eaves; you must leave a gap of about 50mm so that air can come in through the soffit and flow through the loft. If the air cannot circulate, condensation may form.

3 Press the blanket down lightly as you unroll it so that it lies flat but do not squash it so that it becomes compressed.

4 When you reach the other side of the loft, cut the blanket with scissors, again taking care not to block where essential ventilation comes in under the eaves.

5 Continue to lay insulation between the other joists.

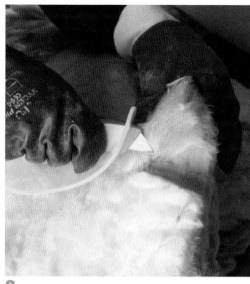

6 When joining two rolls, make a butt join, pressing the ends close to each other. Cut the insulation so that it fits tightly around pipes.

7 Try to slip insulation under loose electric cables to prevent them overheating. Where practicable, fix cables to the sides of the joists to keep them out of the way.

8 Never insulate under the cold water cistern. Leave a gap in the insulation so that warm air from below will keep the chill off the base of the cistern and help to prevent the water from freezing.

Insulating with loose-fill

It is easy to insulate with loose-fill granules – pour them between the joists and level out. Make a levelling gauge so that the granules are at an even depth. Most ceiling joists are 100–150mm deep so filling level with the top will not provide adequate insulation. The top of the joists must be raised by nailing 50mm square battens to them to increase the insulation depth. Do not spread insulation on top of the joists as you cannot see where it is safe to walk.

Cut a piece of scrap wood to a wide T-shape that will fit the gap above the loose-fill. The 'arms' should rest on top of the joists, so that when you run the gauge between two joists the granules are spread to a consistent depth.

HELPFUL TIP

If the loft does not have a boarded floor, you must keep your weight on the joists. Do not step on the plaster or plasterboard – your foot will probably go through. Find a stout board thick enough to take your weight and long enough to be laid across at least two joists. It may be easier if you have two or three boards so you don't have to keep moving the one you are on.

• Cut a piece of glass-fibre or mineral-fibre blanket or thick expanded polystyrene sheet to fit above the loft hatch.

• To fix the blanket, hammer two or three nails along each edge of the door, depending on its size. Tie string over the top of the material and loop it around the nails to hold it in place. Do not pull the string so tight that it squashes the blanket.

• Alternatively, cut a piece of polythene sheet large enough to cover the blanket. Fix the sheet over the blanket, holding the edges in place with drawing pins.

• If you are using expanded polystyrene sheet, stick it to the door with polystyrene ceiling tile adhesive.

• Make sure that the hatch door is a tight fit. Fix a foam, rubber or flexible draught excluder (see chart, page 217) to the rebate so that damp air cannot pass through into the cold loft above and possibly cause condensation problems.

HELPFUL TIP

When laying insulation blanket, use a broom to push the blanket into the areas that are hard to reach.

THE IMPORTANCE OF VENTILATION

A good flow of air across the loft is important for keeping the roof timbers dry. In old lofts without roofing felt under the tiles or slates, air blows in and out through the gaps. If the roof has a layer of felt under the battens, then this prevents air coming in. Some modern roofs have ventilation around the eaves and also often at high level. Any insulation laid under the felt on the underside of the roof slope must allow ventilation to continue in order to clear any moisture from the surface of the felt. A gap of 50mm behind the insulation is usually enough to ensure good ventilation, provided there is room at the ridge for the air to escape and room at the eaves for it to enter. If you are in any doubt about the best way of carrying out the insulation work, consult your local building control officer.

Insulating a roof

If you want to use your loft for storing items that need to be kept warm and dry it is advisable to insulate the underside of the roof. This will also keep the loft cooler in summer.

Tools *Knife or large pair of scissors; staple gun. Possibly power drill.*

Materials *Glass-fibre insulation batts; garden netting. Building paper, hardboard sheets or foil-faced plasterboard; drywall screws.*

1 Hold a length of insulation up to the underside of the roof and mark the width of the rafter gaps on the insulation.

2 Using scissors or knife, cut the insulation to fit between the rafters. Small off-cuts can be placed in the eaves first, to provide a spacing to maintain the air gap.

3 Do not hammer anything into the rafter because you could dislodge a tile or slate. Use a staple gun and nylon garden netting to hold the insulation in place. You may need a helper with this part of the task.

4 For a quick, simple finish, staple sheets of building paper to the rafters. Where two strips of building paper join, make sure they overlap by at least 100mm and tape along the join with waterproof adhesive tape. Alternatively, screw hardboard sheets to the rafters.

5 For an even better finish, you can screw foil-faced plasterboard to the rafters, as shown. The foil should face the roof. Use plasterboard drywall screws, which can be put in with a power drill.

Coping with a flat roof

Flat roofs should be insulated at the time they are built. If you are having an extension added to your house, make sure that insulation is incorporated when the roof is constructed.

Flat roofs must be ventilated above the insulation to prevent condensation on the timbers. You can do this by drilling small holes in the fascia or soffit board to take ventilator insect screens.

• If an existing roof lacks insulation, remove a fascia board so that you can see into the space between the roof lining and ceiling. The fascia board will either be nailed or screwed to the ends of the ceiling joists.

• Slide sheets of expanded polystyrene – preferably 75mm thick – into the gap. If you cannot take off a fascia board, line the ceiling below, preferably with thermal board.

• Alternatively, you can place insulation above the roof decking if access to the roof void is not possible. There are several ways of doing this, but the simplest involves laying sheets of rigid polystyrene or other exanded foam insulation on the roof decking, covering it with a permeable geotextile membrane and placing a layer of ballast on top to keep the membrane and insulation in place on the roof surface.

Diagnosing the causes of damp

Damp problems can be due to a number of causes – rain getting through the walls or roof, moisture being absorbed from the ground, condensation settling on cold surfaces, or a mixture of these. Make sure you know what the cause of dampness is before you try to cure it. Otherwise, you may be dealing only with part of the problem, or worse still adopting the wrong remedy for the sort of damp involved.

Damp can seep through gaps around windows (above) or lead to mould growth in a built-in wardrobe (right).

Spot the tell-tale semi-circles
In an old house with a slate damp-proof course (DPC) slight movement of the building can crack the slates, allowing damp from the ground to rise into the masonry above the crack. A single point of failure will cause a patch of damp that can be up to 1m across, while multiple cracks will lead to an almost continuous band across the affected wall.

Prod the paintwork
Use a bradawl to test the soundness of skirting boards if there are signs of rising damp in downstairs walls or the underfloor space. The backs of skirting boards are usually left unpainted, and as a result they readily absorb moisture from the masonry. However, severe deterioration is often not apparent because of layers of paint on their face sides.

Crossing the bridge
If you think you have rising damp, locate the DPC and make sure it isn't covered by a flowerbed, path, drive or patio. Look for rendering that has been applied over the DPC. Check whether there is a vertical DPC sandwiched between the house wall and a garden wall built up against it. Curing these common causes of rising damp will solve the problem at little or no cost.

Try the foil test
If you aren't sure of the cause of a damp patch, try the foil test. Dry the surface of the wall with a fan heater, then tape some kitchen foil tightly over the damp area. If the surface of the foil is wet after 24 hours you have condensation. If the foil is dry but the wall surface beneath it is damp, you have rising or penetrating damp. Discount rising damp if moisture is more than 1m above outside ground level.

Getting through the gaps
Patches of dampness on walls around windows and doors are usually caused by rain getting through gaps between their frames and the surrounding masonry. Where damp is below the opening, it may be because there is no drip groove to stop the water creeping under a protecting sill or threshold. If there is a drip groove, make sure rain is not passing across it because it is blocked with paint or mortar.

HELPFUL TIP

Some specialist companies offer a free survey to check for rot and insect attack. If they find a problem, they will quote for treating the infestation or curing the damp, or they can supply you with the chemicals you need if you want to do the job yourself.

Looking for a leak in the roof
Discovering exactly where a pitched roof is leaking can be difficult. Rain can trickle down the underside and along the sides of the rafters before it drips onto the loft floor. Clues such as dampness on a party wall or chimney stack in the loft may indicate that flashings are defective or missing. Getting someone to play a hose on the roof area by area while you remain inside the loft can also help to reveal where water is getting in.

Check the plumbing
Leaks in plumbing and central heating pipework can cause damp patches which could be misinterpreted as rising or penetrating damp. This is especially common where pipes run beneath a floor or are buried in wall plaster. A pinhole leak in buried pipework can release a lot of water over time. You can either expose the fault and replace the affected pipes, which will cause a lot of disruption. Or you can leave them in situ and bypass them by installing new ones.

Suspect condensation
If the roof isn't leaking but the loft timbers and insulation are damp, the culprit is probably condensation. This is caused by warm, moisture-laden air rising into the loft from the rooms below and condensing on cold surfaces within the loft space. This could cause rot in the roof timbers and staining to ceilings.

Deal with steam
The kitchen and bathroom are the main sources of condensation in the home. Bathing, cooking, washing-up and washing and drying clothes pour a lot of steam into the air. Portable gas heaters and paraffin stoves also create lots of moisture. Poor room ventilation and efficient draught-proofing stop the wet air being replaced with cooler drier air from outside. Unventilated cupboards built against outside walls can suffer badly from condensation. This can lead to unsightly mould growth that will quickly spoil clothes stored there.

How to treat rot and mould

If timber becomes damp and does not dry out – perhaps because there is a lack of ventilation – wet rot, dry rot or mould may develop. In sound, seasoned wood, up to 15 per cent of its weight will be moisture. If the moisture content rises by between 6 and 10 per cent, fungi can begin growing rapidly.

Preventing fungi from forming in the first place

• Deal with any damp as soon as you find it and ensure that the ventilation in the house is adequate.
• Check regularly that the airbricks round the outside of the house are clean and free from obstruction.
• A suspended timber floor needs to be thoroughly ventilated with approximately one airbrick for every 30m² of floor.
• If you discover a damaged airbrick or if you find that an airbrick is missing, put one in (page 410). There should also be an airbrick indoors at the base of a chimney breast if the flue has been blocked off.

Wet rot

Several different species of fungi attack very wet wood causing wet rot. It is most likely to occur outside at the bottom of a door, window frame or fence, for example, but even inside it is much more common than dry rot, and easier to eradicate since it can only spread over damp timber surfaces.
• If wood turns dark and shrinks, and sparse dark or white strands become visible on the surface, wet rot may have set in. The wood will crack along the grain. Test the wood by prodding it with a sharp screwdriver, bradawl or knife. If the wood is soft and pulpy, it needs treatment.
• Deal with the cause of the damp. When the wood has dried out, the wet rot will die. Treat damaged wood with a wood repair system (page 412) or replace with some well-seasoned wood.

Dry rot

Damp, unventilated conditions indoors are perfect for dry rot. It does not occur outside. This is a much more serious condition than wet rot, and the timber need not be wet before the fungus takes hold. Early growth forms white fluffy strands which later thicken and resemble dirty cotton wool. The fruiting body which develops resembles large, pancake-like lichen, and is rusty-coloured with a grey-white rim.

The fluffy strands will spread across masonry or metalwork seeking out timber. They can extend 12m or more. Dry rot can spread rapidly, and it is very difficult to eradicate; every strand must be traced and killed to prevent the risk of a new outbreak. If they are not killed, strands can remain dormant for several years and then start into growth again.
• Affected wood becomes dry, soft and brittle, cracking across the grain. Dry rot smells musty and is often hidden from view – behind skirting boards, under floorboards, or behind paint.
• Treating dry rot is not a DIY job. Call in a specialist company.

Mould

In damp, warm conditions, mould may affect paint and wallpaper and sometimes grout – perhaps if a waterproof grout has not been used to fix tiles in a bathroom or kitchen.
• Never use bleach to treat mould. Although this will kill the mould flowers, it will not harm the root and the problem will recur within a few weeks.
• If mould has ruined a wall covering, strip the covering off. If paintwork is affected, wash the surface with warm soap or detergent and water. Treat the wall with a proprietary fungicide. Wear gloves as protection and brush on two or three coats.
• When putting up new wallpaper, use a paste containing fungicide. Most pastes for vinyls are suitable.

Damp-proofing basements and cellars

Rooms below ground level are prone to damp, especially if the house is in a hollow. Some damp problems can be solved with DIY methods, but if the walls have been treated and they still weep, seek advice from a surveyor.

Treating slight damp

If the damp is slight, treat the walls with a bituminous waterproofing compound.

1 Prepare the surface so that it is clean and free from old paint or wallpaper.

2 Apply two coats of the treatment, following the manufacturer's instructions.

Providing a tougher barrier against damp

Use a moisture-curing polyurethane sealant. The urethane resin in this liquid sets by the action of moisture upon it and forms a water resistant film.

1 Prepare and clean the surface thoroughly. If you have soaked off old wallpaper, wait for the walls to dry and then apply three coats.

2 Wait about two or three hours between coats – the previous coat should have lost its tacky feel before you brush on the next.

Dealing with damp in a concrete floor

Damp rising through a concrete basement floor indicates that there is no damp-proof membrane in the floor, or that if there is, it has failed or been punctured at some point. It is difficult to locate such failures.

1 If the damp is not severe, remove dust and other loose material from the surface and repair any cracks or small potholes.

2 Dry the floor surface as much as possible, for example by playing warm air from a fan heater across it.

3 Brush on three coats of moisture-curing polyurethane sealant, allowing each to become touch-dry before applying the next. No more than four hours should elapse between coats.

4 If you plan to lay a self-smoothing compound over the treated floor surface to provide a new, flat surface for laying floor coverings (page 125), scatter dry sand over the final coat of sealant while it is still damp. Leave for three days, then brush off excess sand. Lay the self-smoothing compound following the manufacturer's instructions.

HELPFUL TIP

If a mortgage lender's survey reveals trouble – perhaps dry rot or woodworm – the lender will usually insist that the work is carried out by a professional who will give a guarantee. Banks and building societies will not accept DIY work.

Removing an old fireplace

An unwanted fireplace opening can be permanently bricked up, or it can be boarded up in case you want to reopen it later. Or you can keep the fireplace opening as a wall recess by sealing off the bottom of the flue. Before sealing off a fireplace, get the chimney swept and then have the stack capped by a builder.

SAFETY TIP

Removing a chimney breast is not a DIY task and can have disastrous results if carried out incorrectly. The chimney breast may be load-bearing and removing it could destabilise the floor (and fireplace) above. If you want to remove a chimney breast, have it done professionally.

A cast-iron surround

Cast-iron surrounds generally enhance the value of a property – people like to have an open fire, or to fit a gas-log burner into an existing opening. Think carefully before removing an original feature like this. If you decide to go ahead, remove the fireplace surround carefully, as you may be able to sell it.

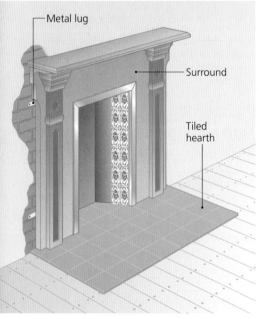

Cast-iron surround Old cast-iron surrounds can be valuable. They are usually fixed to the wall through lugs hidden underneath the plaster. Often there is an inner surround of tiles.

Labels: Metal lug, Surround, Tiled hearth

REMOVING OLD BOLTS OR SCREWS

• If you want to separate a cast-iron surround from its grate, you may have to soak bolts or screws with penetrating oil before you can undo them. Make several applications of oil over about 24 hours, if necessary.
• If they are still difficult to undo, use a nut splitter, which can be hired, to cut through the nuts. The splitter clamps round the nut or the bolt head and cuts it off as it is tightened.
• Drill out screw heads with a high-speed steel twist bit of about the same diameter as the screw shank (compare the screw head with loose screws to estimate the size). If necessary for resale, drill screw or bolt stubs from the surround and use a tap wrench to cut new threads.

1 Remove the wall covering and carefully chip away the plaster to expose the lugs at each side of the fire surround.

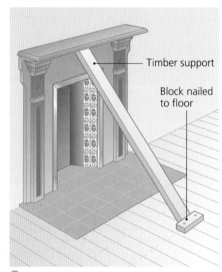

Labels: Timber support, Block nailed to floor

2 Support the surround by wedging a length of timber between the top and the floor. Cast-iron surrounds, particularly, are often top heavy. Without support the surround may fall forward when you undo the fixing screws.

3 Remove the fixing screws if possible. Otherwise, prise the lugs away from the wall, but be very careful as they are brittle and will break easily (this lowers the value of the surround).

4 The grate may be fixed to the surround with screws or bolts, and will come away with it. There is no need to separate them unless you are planning to sell the fireplace surround only.

A timber surround

A timber fireplace surround is usually screwed to battens fixed to the wall behind. There may be a tiled inner surround, which has to be removed separately.

1 Scan the timber surface to find filler covering the screw heads. If necessary, strip off the surface with paint or varnish remover to reveal the screw heads.

2 Dig out the filler to clear the screw slots, and undo the screws.

3 Lift away the surround and remove from the wall the battens used for fixing points.

4 Remove an inner tiled surround in the same way as a tiled surround (below). It is usually much lighter, however, and can be handled by one person.

A tiled surround

A tiled surround normally has a concrete backing that is screwed to the chimney breast through metal lugs, in the same way as a cast-iron surround. It is usually very heavy, and you will need a helper to hold it steady and help to lift it away. If a raised hearth is resting against the front of the surround, move the hearth first (right).

1 Remove the wall covering and plaster at the sides, near the top, to reveal the lugs. Either undo the fixings or prise the lugs away from the wall with a crowbar.

2 Get a helper to steady the surround as it comes away from the wall. If it does not come away easily, there may be another set of lugs lower down on each side.

3 Lower the surround with the aid of a helper. If possible, take it outside for breaking up. Lay the surround face downwards and cover it with sacking. Put on safety goggles and protective gloves before breaking it up with a sledgehammer.

A brick or stone surround

Before you start, check that the surround is not imitation brick or stone with facings bonded to a concrete backing. If it is, remove it in the same way as a tiled surround.

1 Begin removing bricks or stones at the top course, loosening them by chipping away the mortar with a hammer and cold chisel. Make sure you protect your eyes.

2 There may be metal ties or nails in the mortar joints, linked into the wall behind. Chip into the wall to remove them, and make good with filler afterwards.

Alternatively An expanded metal key may link the bricks to the wall.

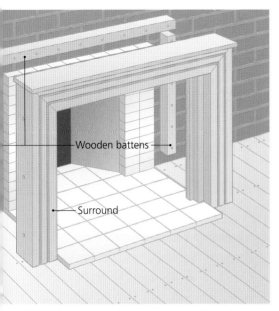

Timber surround The surround is usually screwed to wooden battens fixed to the brickwork behind.

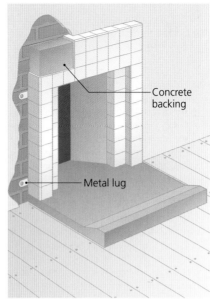

Tiled surround There is usually a concrete backing, making the surround very heavy.

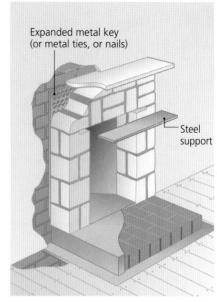

Stone surround The stones (or bricks) over the opening stand on a steel support.

Removing a raised hearth

A raised hearth may be a tiled slab of concrete or a number of stone slabs or bricks. The raised hearth is bonded to a concrete layer flush with the floor (known as the constructional hearth) with mortar.

1 Chip away the mortar with a hammer and cold chisel and prise out stones or bricks individually. Alternatively, use a crowbar to prise up a solid slab hearth.

2 Leave the constructional hearth in place. Smooth it with self-levelling compound before laying the floor covering.

Bricking up the opening

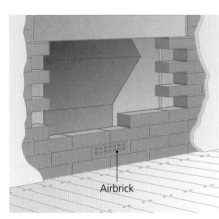

Use bricks or blocks and mortar (page 466) to block the opening, building them up in courses. The face should be level with the surrounding brickwork – that is, set back slightly from a layer of plaster.

Unless the opening is wider than about 1.2m, there is no need to tooth-in the bricks (that is, remove surrounding half bricks so that new bricks can be linked in).

1 Insert an airbrick (page 410) in the centre of the second or third course, to keep the chimney dry. If you are left with a gap about 25mm or more deep at the top of the opening, fill it in with a course of slates or part tiles.

2 Cover the brickwork with plaster to bring the surface flush with the surrounding wall.

Boarding up the opening

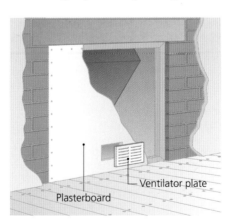

Use a piece of plasterboard or non-combustible building board cut to fit snugly into the opening.

1 Fit a frame of 50 x 50mm timber battens all round the edge of the opening, set back to allow for the thickness of the board.

2 If the opening is more than about 600mm wide, fit a central vertical batten to give extra rigidity.

3 Nail or screw the board to the battens so it lies flush with the surrounding wall.

4 Cut a hole near the bottom at the centre and fit in a ventilator plate.

5 Tape the top and side joints of the board to reinforce them (page 228).

6 Cover the board with ready-mixed skim-coat plaster, if necessary, to match the surrounding wall.

SAFETY PRECAUTION

If the opening to be blocked is linked to a common flue serving a fireplace still in use, do not fit a ventilator plate, through which hot soot may fall. When boarding up such an opening, you should use non-combustible building board.

Creating a wall recess

Screw a framework of 50 x 50mm timber battens to the inside of the opening, just above the crosspiece supporting the mouth of the flue.

1 Cut a panel of non-combustible building board to fit to the frame.

2 Make a hole in the centre, and fit through it a length of 65mm diameter rainwater pipe with a bend of about 90° at the top. Secure it in position with duct tape. The pipe keeps the flue ventilated, and the panel prevents soot and debris falling into the recess.

Opening up an old fireplace

In most cases a fireplace and grate will have been blocked off using sound building practices, but in some homes this may not be the case. It is always advisable to get expert advice from a surveyor or architect before you begin work.

Tools *Club hammer; bolster chisel; crowbar; saw; tape measure; pencil; pointing trowel. Possibly also trimming knife; wrecking bar.*

Materials *Lime mortar; new skirting board.*

Before you start Every home is different, and the way that the fireplace was blocked up will vary too. Some fireplaces will have been filled in with brick or blockwork while others may have a very simple board wedged into the opening. This is likely to be a messy job, so fold back the carpet or lay down lots of dustsheets to protect your furnishings.

1 Examine the chimney breast. If the chimney has been blocked up correctly, there will be a vent in the wall just above the skirting board. Remove this vent and use a torch to look inside the opening. This will give you some idea of the size of the fireplace opening.

2 Remove the skirting board in front of the fireplace. If this is in one long length, you will either have to remove the complete length, or make a cut on either side of the fireplace and remove a section of the skirting board.

3 Uncover the hearth. This is the solid section of floor in front of the chimney breast. It is usually a concrete slab set into the surrounding floorboards. This gives a further indication of the size of the original fireplace.

4 Tap the wall: a hollow sound indicates that the fireplace was probably blocked up with a board. If you can find the edge, which sometimes shows up as a bump under the wallpaper or paint, cut around this with a trimming knife and try to pry out the board with a wrecking bar. If this is difficult, drill a hole in the board to see whether it is plasterboard or timber. Break out a plasterboard sheet, using a club hammer, or use a padsaw or jigsaw to cut around the edge of a timber board. Unscrew or lever off any supporting battens.

Alternatively If the wall is brickwork, start from the vent and slowly knock out a few bricks at a time with a club hammer and bolster chisel. You may find it easier to remove the plaster from the area first and then go back to chip out the bricks, one by one, once you can see where the mortar joints are. Work left and right and upwards, gradually opening up the hole.

5 Cut the bricks back to the edge of the original opening before making good any joints in the brickwork at the side and back of the fireplace. Use a lime mortar specially formulated for fireplaces; you can buy this in small bags from fireplace suppliers. Regular sand and cement mortar will crack with the heat.

6 Once the fireplace is revealed you will be able to see whether the original fireback is still in place and in good condition. The fireback is a shaped section, often made from iron or fireclay, at the back of the fireplace. It is designed to reflect heat from the fire into the room, rather than allowing it to rise straight up the chimney (page 26).

7 A cracked fireback can be repaired with fire cement. Brush the area clean and spray the cracks with water to wet them, then fill them with cement. Let the cement dry for three days before using the fireplace.

8 Check the draught of the chimney by holding a lighted candle just in front of the fire opening. If the chimney is working, smoke and flame should be drawn up the chimney; if it does not happen, the chimney may well be blocked or capped off. Remove blocking within the flue. Get professional help if the flue has been capped at the top.

9 Get the chimney swept before installing a new grate and fireback (below). A professional sweep will be able to advise on the condition of the flue and will remove any build-up of soot and tar from the inside of the chimney.

Fitting a new fireplace

Installing a fireplace in an existing opening is a straightforward job but, for safety's sake, any work involving the chimney flue must be tackled by a professional.

Tools *Club hammer; bolster chisel; brick trowel.*

Materials *Fibre cement board; 75 x 25mm planed timber boards; concrete; fireback; fire-proof rope; lime mortar; corrugated cardboard; brick rubble; fire cement; fireplace surround.*

Installing a fireback

If you revealed an empty fireplace opening when you unblocked your fireplace and plan to use the fireplace for a solid fuel or coal-effect gas fire, you will need to install a fireback.

1 Measure the width of the opening. Firebacks are sold in standard widths of 400 and 450mm, but can be made in other sizes if necessary.

2 Tap along the cutting line with a club hammer and bolster chisel to split the fireback in two.

3 Lay a bed of lime mortar where the fireback will sit. Position the fireback then move it forwards slightly and sandwich lengths of fire-proof rope between it and the edges of the fireplace opening.

4 Slot two lengths of corrugated cardboard the height of the fireback behind it, mortaring them in place. When you first use the fire this cardboard will burn and leave a crucial expansion gap to allow the fireback to expand in the heat.

5 Use the broken rubble created by opening up the fireplace and mortar to fill the space behind the fireback.

6 Once you have filled to the level of the lower section of the fireback, use mortar to fix the upper section in place. Remove any excess mortar from the joint and continue filling behind the fireback.

CHECKING THE FLUE

Fires give off toxic fumes, which can kill. In a well designed and correctly working fireplace, these are exhausted up the chimney and pose no threat to occupants of the house.

Be aware of the dangers and get a professional to examine your chimney before you light a fire for the first time, whether you have opened up an old fireplace or installed a new one. Find a qualified chimney engineer in your area by contacting the National Association of Chimney Engineers (NACE).

Regular maintenance is also important. Contact the National Association of Chimney Sweeps (NACS) for a list of registered sweeps in your area.

7 Finish the fireback with a sloped line of mortar around the top edge, chamfering the join with the rear face of the flue. This will help to encourage smoke to rise up the chimney.

Installing a new fire surround and hearth

1 The hearth must be at least 200mm wider on each side than the fireplace opening, and must extend out into the room to a distance of at least 500mm from the face of the chimney breast.

2 You can make a hearth from a concrete mixture. Begin by screwing two layers of fibre cement board to the floorboards and extending these back into the fireplace opening. Screw 75 x 25mm planed timber boards together at the corners to make a formwork around the edge of the fibre cement board where it sticks out into the room. Use blocks of wood to hold it tightly in place.

3 Mix concrete from one part cement, two parts sand and three parts aggregate, and pour this into the form. Level it off with a wooden float and leave for 24 hours before removing the formwork.

Alternatively Buy a slate, granite or marble hearth at the same time as your new fire surround. Ask the fireplace supplier to cut this to size for you. It may come in two pieces: one to extend into the back of the opening and a rectangular piece to sit in front of the fireplace.

Bed the hearth on several blobs of mortar, check that it is perfectly level in all directions and wipe away any excess mortar that has seeped out at the edges from the weight of the hearth.

4 Carefully lift the fireplace surround into place. This may come as one piece, with a decorative surround and mantelpiece in one, or as separate components. Use fire cement to secure the surround to the edges of the fireback.

5 Place the new surround and mantelpiece in position and use a spirit level to check for level. Use wooden shims on either side if the surround needs to be adjusted. Then screw the surround back to the wall through the lugs provided.

6 Make good the plaster on each side of the surround. When this is dry, fit skirting boards to match those already in the room. Butt them up tightly to either side of the fireplace surround.

7 Tile or paint the hearth if it is concrete, then refit the carpet or other floor covering.

Choosing a fireplace surround and fire

A fireplace is the focus of the room but should not over-dominate. It is important to select a surround that looks right for the style of the room and house. The choice has never been wider: genuine antiques, Victorian reproductions, wood, marble, Art Deco, chrome and modern combinations of pebbles and stainless steel.

Choosing a fireplace surround

Cast-iron Victorian fireplaces were often made of cast iron, sometimes incorporating decorative tiles. Antiques and modern reproductions are available in a wide range of sizes, from slim all-in-one fireplaces, surrounds and mantelpieces to cast-iron insets that require a separate surround.

The traditional choices of cast iron grate and stone surround have a classic appeal. Many grates can be adapted to accommodate a gas fire if you prefer.

Stone The classic, clean lines of stone have an appeal that is timeless. Marble and limestone are popular choices, but many other options are also available.

Brick The warm colour and texture of a brick surround gives a room the cosy appeal of a cottage or farmhouse.

Tile Popular in the early and mid 20th century, tiled surrounds suit rooms decorated in the styles of those times and often have an Art Deco design. You can also use new tiles to change the look of an existing surround or hearth – but check first that they will withstand the heat.

Wood A wood surround can be simple or ornate, traditional or modern, stained or painted, as you wish.

Choosing a grate

Cast iron The traditional choice for an open fire. Usually has a tray beneath the grate for collecting ash and easy cleaning. Cast-iron fronts are available to disguise the workings of a coal-effect gas fire.

Concrete or stone For a more modern look, the clean lines of a stone grate can be complemented by a simple surround in a colour to match the rest of the room.

Stainless steel An ultra-modern alternative to the traditional Victorian grate is a stainless steel bowl filled with fire-resistant stones or pebbles. A gas flame provides the heat, which is retained by the stones to create a more intense warmth.

Clean lines suit a minimalist setting. Here, gas burns through heat-retaining stones.

8

Floors and staircases

Lifting and replacing a floorboard

You may need to lift a floorboard in order to access pipes or cables beneath the floor for repairs.

Tools *Thin-bladed knife; drill and twist drill bits; jigsaw; bolster chisel; hammer; screwdriver. Also for tongue-and-groove boards: circular saw (or panel saw or flooring saw).*

Materials *50 or 75mm floorboard nails; 75mm No. 8 screws; pieces of timber about 40mm square and 100mm longer than the width of the boards.*

Before you start First find out whether the boards are tongue-and-groove or square edge by poking a thin-bladed knife between them. If they are square edge, the blade will pass right through.

Removing a square-edge board

Before lifting the board, you must cut across it at each end just before it meets a joist. Lines of nails indicate joist centres.

1 Drill a 10mm starting hole near the edge of the board you want to remove, and complete the cut across it with a jigsaw.

HELPFUL TIP

Whenever you do not need access below the floor, put the board back loosely in position, even if only for a few minutes, to stop the risk of someone stepping into the hole.

2 Starting at one end, prise out fixing nails by levering up the board with a bolster chisel.

3 Once you have loosened one or two sets of nails, push the handle of a hammer under the board as far from the loose end as possible, and try to prise the board up. This sends a shock wave along the whole length, loosening nails farther along, which you can then remove.

4 Push the hammer farther forward, and repeat the process, until the board is free.

How to remove tongues

On tongue-and-groove boards, the tongues on each side of the board must be removed. If adjoining boards are to be lifted, only the tongues at the outer edges of the group need cutting.

1 Adjust the depth of cut on a circular saw so that the blade just protrudes below the underside of the tongue. Since floorboards are usually 19mm thick, the underside of the tongue will be about 13mm below the surface. This will avoid pipes and cables. If you do not have a circular saw, use a panel or flooring saw. Cut at a shallow angle.

2 Place the blade between the boards, switch on the power, and move the saw along the length of board.

3 With the tongues removed you should be able to see the joists between the boards. Remove the board in the same way as a square-edge board.

Replacing the board

Use new nails and proper floorboard brads. You will not be able to nail the board to a joist at its ends as it has been sawn off before the joists.

1 Screw a short batten to the side of each joist, its top edge jammed hard up against the underside of adjacent floorboards still in position. Nail the board to the batten.

CURING LOOSE AND SQUEAKING BOARDS

A floorboard squeaks because it is not firmly held to its joist. When someone steps on it, it springs under the weight, rubbing against a neighbouring board. A squeak can be temporarily cured by dusting talc down the side of the board.

Not all loose boards squeak – there may be too big a gap around them – but even so they should be properly secured before a floor covering is laid, otherwise you will feel (and hear) the movement under new flooring.

A board becomes loose when one or more of its fixing nails loses its grip due to vibration or the movement of the joist below. Prise out the nail if it is still there and refix the board with a screw big enough to fill the hole left by the nail. A 50mm No. 8 screw should be suitable.

The screw will hold the board securely in place, and as it goes exactly into the same hole as the nail there should be no danger of striking a cable or pipe.

Alternatively If you have old ceilings, it may be wise to screw the boards down. Vibration from heavy hammering can cause ceiling damage. Screws are also useful if access may be needed to pipes or cables beneath the floor in future.

Replacing a damaged floorboard

Follow the instructions opposite to lift the damaged board. It is then a simple job to cut and fit a replacement.

Tools *Saw; hammer; perhaps a chisel; perhaps an electric drill and 2mm twist bit.*

Materials *Floorboards exactly the same thickness and width as the old ones – you may need to have these specially cut and planed at a timber yard; 50 or 75mm floorboard nails; perhaps scraps of hardboard or plywood and panel pins.*

Laying square-edge boards

1 Cut the timber to the same length as the old boards.

2 Lay the new boards in place and nail them to each joist with floorboard nails.

Laying tongue-and-groove boards

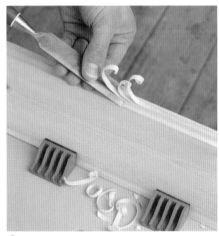

1 Cut the first board to length, and shave off its tongue with a chisel or plane.

2 Lay it in position, butting its former tongued edge to the grooved edge of an existing board.

3 If a second board is needed, cut it to length, lay it on the joists and tap it into place so that its tongue locates in the groove of the first new board. Continue with the other boards.

4 When you come to the final board, you will probably have to shave off its tongue, as you will not be able to manoeuvre it into place with the tongue attached.

Alternatively Shave off the underside of the groove of the second to last board. It may be possible to tap the last board into place with tongue intact.

5 Fix the boards to the joists with floorboard nails. You will be able to see the positions of the joists from the lines of nails in the existing floorboards.

6 If nails have to be driven in near the end of a board, first drill pilot holes smaller than the nails to avoid splitting the wood.

Replacing a floor with chipboard

If a floor is beyond repair, it can be replaced more cheaply with chipboard than with new floorboards.

Flooring-grade chipboard is sold in two thicknesses – 19 and 22mm. For joists up to 460mm apart, use 19mm board. Chipboard is heavy, so use the smallest sheets available unless you have someone to help you. You can use square-edge boards, but sheets with tongue-and-groove edges make a more stable floor, and edge joints do not need any support battens.

Lay boards flat in a pile inside the house as soon as they are delivered or they may distort. At least 24 hours before you begin work, loose-lay them so they can adjust to the moisture content of the room.

Tools *Circular saw; panel saw or flooring saw; hammer; brush for applying adhesive; rag; pencil.*

Materials *Chipboard; No. 10 gauge annular ring nails – 55mm nails for 19mm sheets, 60mm for 22mm sheets; lengths of 50mm square timber; 75mm oval nails; PVA wood adhesive.*

1 Start by taking up enough of the old floorboards to give space for the first row of chipboard sheets.

2 If there is not enough space between skirting board and joist to push in the chipboard, the skirting board will have to be removed from the wall (page 179).

3 Lay the first sheet of chipboard in one corner of the room.

4 A gap of 10mm must be left around the edge of the room to allow the chipboard to expand in damp weather. If you have removed the skirting, you can see this easily; if not, then push the sheet of chipboard hard against the wall beneath the skirting board, draw a line where it meets the skirting and then pull it out by 10mm.

HELPFUL TIPS

• If access may be needed in future to a cable or central heating pipe, fix the sheet above it with screws, which are much easier to remove than nails.
• If you are flooring an upstairs room or loft, and the ceiling below is weak, drill pilot holes in the chipboard for the nails. This reduces vibration when you hammer them in.

JOIST ALERT

The wall on one side of the room may be a hollow partition erected after the floor was installed. It is likely to cover the top of a joist. If so, you must nail a length of 50mm square timber to the side of the joist to provide a fixing point for the chipboard.

You can see the position of the joists by the rows of nails in the floorboards. If the partition wall has been built between joists, no fixing point for the chipboard will be available and a new joist must be installed. This is a job for a builder.

Square edge sheets

1 Lay square-edge sheets with the long edge parallel with the joists. They must be supported on every edge, so the long sides should rest on the centre of a joist, and the ends should rest on a nogging.

2 Make the nogging from a piece of 50mm square-section wood placed between the joists and fixed with 75mm oval nails driven down at an angle through the nogging and into the joist.

3 If the width of the sheet does not suit your joists, cut the sheet to fit. However, if this involves too much waste it may be a better idea to use tongue-and-groove sheets which are laid across the joists and so do not have to be cut to width.

4 Nail the sheets at 300mm intervals all the way round, putting the nails 10mm in from the edge. On intermediate joists put nails about 600mm apart.

Tongue-and-groove sheets

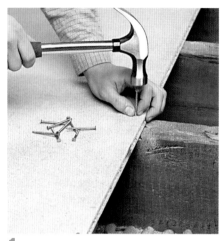

1 Position tongue-and-groove sheets with the long edge across the joists and nail them down. Drive four nails into each joist, one 10mm from each edge and the others at equal distances.

2 The sheet must be supported at the ends, so saw off any overhang close to the side of the joist.

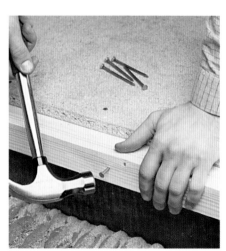

3 Nail a 20mm square-section batten to the side of the joist, flush with the top, and fix the next board to it.

If you need to hammer tongue-and-groove sheets together, use a block of wood to protect the edge from damage.

Completing the job

• Coat the meeting edges of all boards with PVA wood adhesive, then push them firmly together. The adhesive will prevent the floor from squeaking. Wipe any glue from the surface with a damp cloth.
• When you come to the end of a row, cut the sheet to fit. Use the offcut to begin the next row so that the joins do not coincide.

Draughtproofing a timber ground floor

Air can come up into the room if the boards are merely butted together, particularly in older properties.

Draughtproofing a floor depends on the size of the gaps. Fill large gaps (wider than 6mm) with wood. Smaller gaps can be filled with mastic applied via a sealant gun. The mastic colour does not matter if you are laying a new floor covering. If you intend to sand the boards, choose a sealant close to the desired colour, or one that will absorb stain when you apply it to the boards. Rot will not set in after you have sealed the gaps as long as air can move freely beneath the floor through airbricks.

Large gaps

Tools *Mallet; plane; power sander or flap-wheel attachment on a power drill.*

Materials *Thin strips of softwood planed to a wedge section; PVA wood adhesive.*

1 Apply adhesive to the two long sides of a wedged strip of wood.

2 Tap the wood into place with a mallet, aiming to make its top edge flush with the floor surface.

3 When the adhesive has set, use a power sander or a flap-wheel attachment to smooth any raised parts of the strip.

Small gaps

Tools *Sealant gun; filling knife for removing excess.*

Materials *Flooring sealant cartridges; lining paper or similar for wiping excess filler from knife (newspaper will cause black stains).*

1 Check the width of the largest gap between the boards, and cut the cartridge nozzle off at an angle to give a bead of the correct width.

2 Load the cartridge into the sealant gun and squeeze the trigger to start the flow of filler.

3 Draw the nozzle along each joint in turn, allowing the filler to sink in.

4 As you complete each joint, use the filling knife to remove excess filler and wipe the blade on some lining paper or similar material. Repeat the process to fill each joint in turn.

WHEN THE FLOOR IS TO BE COVERED

If you are laying a floor covering, you do not need to fill the gaps between the floorboards. Instead, lay sheets of hardboard over the whole floor (page 125). This will provide a flat surface for the new floor covering as well as draughtproofing the floor. If the cracks are small and the floorboards are level, lay foil-coated building paper – foil side up – under a carpet. This is cheaper than hardboard, and will stop draughts and also reflect some warmth back into the room.

SEALING THE GAP BELOW A SKIRTING BOARD

A skirting board is often fitted so there is a gap between it and the floor. If carpet has not been pushed into this gap, draughts may come up from below a timber floor. To seal a gap, use panel pins to fix quadrant beading (see picture) to the base of the skirting board, pressing it tight to the floor. Do not pin beading to the floor, or the boards will not be able to expand and contract, as they normally do when the weather varies from damp to dry.

INSULATING TIMBER FLOORS

If all the floorboards in a downstairs room have to be lifted (page 256), take the opportunity to fit underfloor insulation.

One way is to staple nylon garden netting across the joists and place lengths of loft insulation blanket between them. Draw the netting up tight so the blanket does not sag between the joists.

The other way is to cut rigid foam insulation boards into strips to match the joist spacing and support them on battens nailed to the joist sides.

How a staircase is built

Stairs consist of treads (the part you walk on) and risers (the vertical pieces in between). The treads may be nailed to the risers, or the risers may have tongues slotted into a groove in the treads.

At each side the treads are supported by a piece of timber called a string. A closed string has its top and bottom edges parallel, and the treads and risers slot into grooves. A cut string has a zigzag profile with the treads resting on the horizontal section.

A wall-side string is always closed, but the outer string may be either type. Staircases with cut strings are easier to repair than ones with closed strings.

On the open side of the staircase balusters are attached to the string at the bottom and the handrail at the top.

Many houses have a cupboard below the staircase, with the underside of the stairs left exposed. This is convenient for repairs. However, the underside may be covered with plaster, which would have to be removed before repairs could be done.

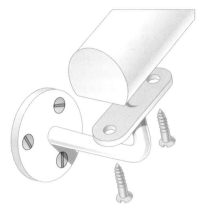

Wall handrail A handrail can be fixed to a wall on a bracket (above), or a specially shaped rail can be screwed directly to the wall (below).

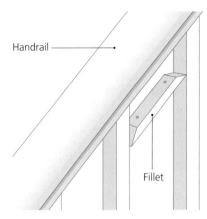

Handrail

Fillet

Handrail fillet On some staircases the balustrades are fitted to the handrail between wooden fillets. On others they are simply nailed.

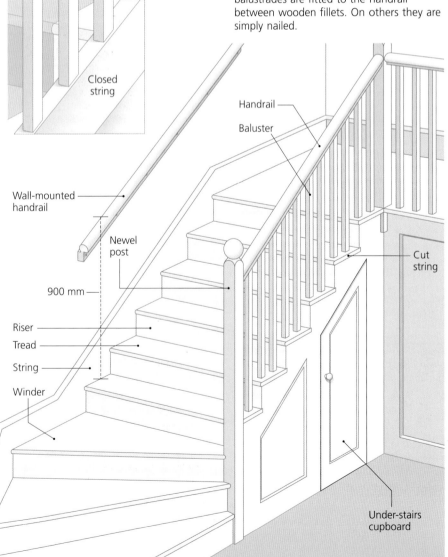

Closed string

Wall-mounted handrail

Newel post

900 mm

Riser

Tread

String

Winder

Handrail

Baluster

Cut string

Under-stairs cupboard

Fixing creaking stairs

Stairs creak when a tread or riser is not securely fixed and rubs against an adjacent piece of wood. The cure is straightforward if the underside of the staircase is accessible.

Determine which tread is creaking. If you have a cupboard under the stairs, ask someone to walk slowly up the stairs: you should be able to see which treads are flexing as well as hear the creak.

Working from underneath

The best remedy is to add extra wood angle blocks, screwed and glued to the tread and riser from underneath.

Tools *Saw; bradawl; drill and twist bits; screwdriver.*

Materials *Blocks of wood about 40mm triangular or square in section and about 75mm long; PVA adhesive; four No. 8 screws per block (choose a length that will not break through the face of the stair).*

1 Drill four clearance holes in each block – one pair at right angles to the other.

2 Apply PVA adhesive to the blocks and push them in place.

3 Secure the blocks to the tread and riser with four screws.

4 If possible, strengthen the join between the riser and the tread below by squeezing PVA adhesive into the join. Then drive three evenly spaced screws horizontally through the riser and into the tread. Position the screws 12mm up from the bottom of the riser.

Working from above

You will have to lift the stair carpet to work on the treads. Try brushing some talcum powder into the squeaking join to act as a lubricant. If the squeak continues, screw down the front of the tread onto the riser.

Tools *Old chisel; drill and twist bits; countersink bit; screwdriver; filling knife; abrasive paper.*

Materials *PVA adhesive; 38mm No. 8 countersunk screws; filler.*

1 Using a chisel, force apart the top of the riser and the tread above, and insert some glue in the space: this is only possible if the treads and risers are not jointed together.

2 Drill clearance holes every 250mm through the tread and pilot holes into the top of the riser. Countersink the clearance holes so screws will sit below surface level. Insert the screws and screw down tight.

3 Cover screw heads with filler and smooth with abrasive paper.. If the stairs are varnished, use a matching wood filler.

Repairing broken balusters

If you still have all the pieces, it may be possible to mend a damaged baluster. If the damage is severe, you will have to replace it.

Tools *Mallet; old chisel; handsaw; hammer; vice clamp.*

Materials *New baluster if needed; nails (same length as the old ones).*

Before you start Examine the broken baluster: if it has split or a piece has broken off, apply PVA adhesive to the two surfaces and bind them with insulating tape. Clamp the baluster between two blocks of wood until the adhesive has

dried. Then remove the tape and smooth off any hardened adhesive with fine abrasive paper.

Square section balusters are easy to match, but you may have to pay a wood turner to reproduce a fancy one for you.

1 Free the baluster at the bottom. If the outer string is open (see opposite) prise off the cover moulding on the side of the tread. Then gently tap the bottom end of the baluster out of its slot with a mallet.

If the outer string is 'closed' (its top and bottom edges are parallel and the tread and riser slot into grooves), a baluster on an old staircase may be held in a mortise or it may be pinned. Scrape away the paint to check. If it is mortised use a handsaw to cut through it at the bottom following the line of the string. If it is pinned, knock it out with the mallet.

Alternatively On a modern staircase it may be held at the bottom between fillets of wood. Lift out the broken baluster, and lever out the lower fillet.

2 Remove the top part of the broken baluster by tapping it with a mallet so it is freed from the rail. If there is no space between the balusters to wield the mallet, place the end of a piece of wood against the baluster and tap the other end with the mallet. Or pull out the baluster by hand.

3 Use the broken baluster as a pattern to mark the correct slope on the top of the new one. Before you cut it to length, make sure that you have got the measurement right.

4 Hold the new baluster in a vice and cut along the marked line.

5 On an open (cut) string, fit it back in place in its notch on the tread and nail the baluster to the handrail at the top.

On a closed string, use the old baluster to cut the angle at the bottom and fit the new one in place, top and bottom. If the baluster was originally mortised into the string, it will have to be nailed in place. The repair will not be as strong as the original.

If you have to replace a fillet, tack it in place. A nail punch will help you to work in an awkward space.

FIXING LOOSE BALUSTERS

Balusters are usually fixed to the handrail by nails driven through them at an angle, and into the underside of the rail. Sometimes they are fitted between fillets of wood.

Nailing the baluster If a nail works loose, try to remove it with pincers, and insert a longer, slightly thicker nail in its place. If you can't remove it, drive another one in at a different place. On slender balusters drill a fine pilot hole first. Do not use glue. The baluster may have to be removed at some time in the future.

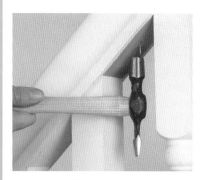

Replacing a fillet The balusters must be fitted into a groove in the underside of the rail, with the spaces between balusters filled with fillets of wood. If a fillet has dropped out, cut a new piece of wood to the right size and nail it in place. Do not use glue. A nail punch will help to drive the nail in. Baluster fillets can be bought at some DIY stores, but they may not fit your staircase.

Wall-mounted handrails

Re-fixing a handrail

A stairway with a wall on both sides usually has a wall-mounted hand-rail instead of a baluster rail. Often, the fixings come loose.

1 Take the rail down from the wall and find out why it is loose.

2 If the handrail is on a metal bracket, fill the existing screw holes with a plugging compound. Re-drill the holes, insert wall plugs and refit the handrail with screws the same size as the old ones. Make sure the fixing is secure; if not, you must reposition the brackets and make new holes.

Alternatively If the rail is screwed directly to the wall, use a longer, thicker screw than the original. You may have to drill a slightly larger hole in the rail.

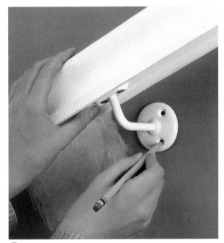

3 If the wall around the plug has become damaged, make a new fixing in a slightly different place. The brackets will also have to be repositioned on the rail. Fill any visible holes with interior filler.

Fitting a new handrail

If you are putting up a new wall-mounted handrail, it must run parallel with the string (the diagonal line of the stairs).

1 Measure 900mm up from the front of each tread and join the marks with a straightedge.

2 Fit the brackets to the rail, then get a helper to align the top of the rail with the line while you mark the fixings for the top bracket.

3 Drill and plug the wall and fix the top bracket with one screw only. Hold the bottom of the rail at the correct height and mark the positions of the other fixings.

Replacing a balustrade

Balustrade parts are available that should make fitting a new balustrade straightforward. Replacing the newel posts is often optional.

Tools *Tape measure; saw; screwdriver; wood chisel; nail punch; pin hammer; portable workbench.*

Materials *New handrail, base rail, balusters and spacer fillets; 75mm No. 10 woodscrews or angled handrail brackets; socket set to remove and fit handrail brackets; 50mm oval wire nails; panel pins.*

Before you start Measure the lengths of handrail and base rail you will need, and calculate the number of balusters. To comply with Building Regulations, balusters must be spaced no more than 100mm apart, and a handrail must be at least 900mm above the string. It may be that your old balustrade did not comply with these regulations.

1 Saw through each old baluster in turn and pull it away from the rails. Prise out the spacing fillets, and lever off the old base rail.

2 Undo any screws connecting the handrail to the newel post at each end.

Alternatively Look for a metal bracket attaching rail and newel post by prising out the handrail fillet. If you find a bracket but can't unscrew it, look for a wooden plug on the opposite side of the post and prise it out to see if there is a nut. Use a socket set to undo the nut and free the bracket.

3 Cut the new base rail to length, using the old base rail as a template. The ends are angled so they fit against both newel posts. Place it in position and secure it with 50mm wire nails about 300mm apart.

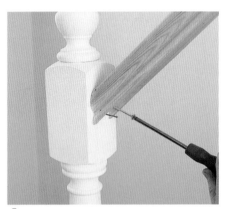

4 Use the old handrail as a template to cut the new one. Attach it to the upper and lower newels, with a helper supporting the other end in each case. Secure it to the newel with 75mm long woodscrews, or with special angled handrail brackets.

5 Use an old baluster as a pattern for cutting new ones to size. Pin fillets into the grooves in the handrail and base rail next to the top newel post, then fit the first baluster and nail it to both rails. Repeat for the other balusters.

HELPFUL TIPS

• Apply primer, paint, stain or varnish to balusters before fitting them; touch up later if necessary.
• The easiest way to fit a new newel post is to cut off the old post about 100mm above the string, and use a dowel (from a staircase parts supplier) to join on the new post.

Fitting a loft ladder

Most houses have a loft or attic which in many cases is accessed through a hatch in the upper floor ceiling. The installation of a loft ladder makes the roof space more easily accessible, for storage or as a hobbies room.

There is a wide variety of styles available in both aluminium and wood. Most if not all will fit between the width of the joists, but often the length of the existing opening is too short to accommodate a ladder. Altering the length of the hatch opening is often the trickiest part of the installation.

Tools *Hammer; screwdrivers; try square; pencil; panel saw; crowbar.*

Materials *Loft ladder; 18mm MDF; trim for opening; timber the same size as existing ceiling joists.*

Before you start Installing a loft ladder is straightforward but be sure to read the instructions that came with the ladder carefully before you start. Pull back loft insulation from between the joists while you carry out the work and replace it when

you have finished. Lofts are often dark so unless you have a light already installed you will need a portable light or head torch to illuminate the work area.

1 Remove the existing hatch, pull off the trim around the underside of the opening and remove any stops inside the hatch opening.

2 Completely remove any lining where this is fitted inside the opening. You may have to use a panel saw to cut through the centre of the wood before levering it away from the underlying joists.

3 Cut through the centre of one trimmer before knocking it out with the hammer. Be careful to avoid damaging the ceiling.

4 Refer to the manufacturer's instructions and mark the length of the opening from the existing trimmer. Square down the line on the inside faces of the joists

5 Cut a new trimmer to fit snugly between the joists. Position with reference to the pencil marks and nail in place.

6 Fix the ceiling below to the new trimmer with plasterboard screws before cutting back the ceiling flush with the edge of the new trimmer.

7 Cut and fit new trim and lining to the hatch opening as necessary and fit this into place.

8 Attach the loft ladder pivots to the top or face of the trimmer as indicated in the manufacturer's instructions.

9 Attach the ladder to the pivots and check the movement and action of the ladder.

10 Fit new architrave to cover the joint between the lining and ceiling, mitring it carefully at the corners for a neat finish.

11 Cut a new hatch cover from 18mm MDF and fit this, following the instructions that came with the ladder. In many cases the cover is attached to the underside of the ladder and will automatically close when the ladder is retracted.

MEASURING UP FOR A LADDER

• Before buying a ladder, you will need to take several measurements. It is advisable to get makers' leaflets that show the pivoting height needed by the ladder inside the loft (marked A below). This is usually 1.1m above the loft floor. If there is not enough room, collapsible ladders are available.
• The leaflets will also show the minimum length of the hatch (B) and the minimum width (C).

• For easy access to the loft, the hatch should be about 760mm long and 510mm wide. Ladders can be installed in smaller openings, but you may have difficulty carrying things into the loft.
• A standard loft ladder will fit a height of up to 2.6m, measured from the floor of the room or landing below to the top of the loft joists.

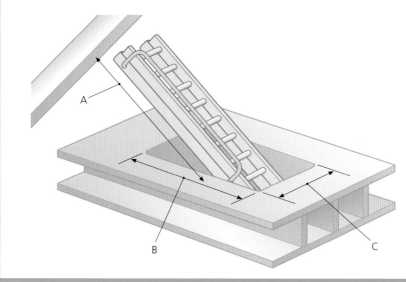

9

Wiring and lighting

Electrical emergencies

Warning: the main on-off switch on your consumer unit disconnects only the fuses or MCBs and the cables leading out from it to the household circuits. It does NOT disconnect the cables entering via the meter from the service cable. Do not tamper with these cables. They are always live at mains voltage.

Electric shock

Warning If you get a minor shock from an electrical appliance, a plug or other wiring accessory, stop using it immediately.
• Get a repair expert to check the appliance for earth safety, and replace damaged plugs and wiring accessories as soon as possible. Use PVC insulating tape to make a temporary repair.
• If someone receives a major shock, DO NOT touch bare flesh while the person is in contact with the source of the current. If you do, the current will pass through you as well, giving you an electric shock.

1 Immediately turn off the source of the current if you can.

2 If you cannot do this, grab the person's clothing and drag him or her away from the source of the current, or stand on some insulating material such as a book, and use a broom or a similar wooden object to move the person or the current source.

3 Lay a conscious but visibly shocked person flat on their back with their legs raised slightly and cover with a blanket. Do not give food, drink or cigarettes. Cool visible burns with cold water, then cover them with a dry sterile dressing. Do not apply ointments. Call an ambulance.

If someone is unconscious Place an unconscious person in the recovery position. Tilt the head back and bring the jaw forward to keep the airway clear. Cover them with a blanket and call an ambulance.

Check the person's breathing Monitor breathing and heartbeat continuously until the ambulance arrives. If either stops, give artificial ventilation or external chest compression as necessary, if you are trained to do so.

Fire in an appliance

1 If a plug-in appliance is on fire, switch the appliance off at the socket outlet and pull out the plug.

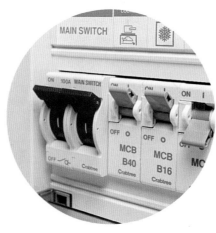

2 If a fixed appliance with no plug is on fire, turn it off at the wall switch if you can, or at the main switch on the consumer unit.

3 Do not use water on an electrical fire. Smother the fire with a rug or blanket, or use a dry-powder fire extinguisher.

4 Get the appliance checked (and repaired if possible) by an expert before you use it again.

Smell of overheating

1 If you smell burning from an appliance, turn off the switch at the socket and pull out the plug. If it is a fixed appliance with no plug, turn off its wall switch or the main switch at the consumer unit. Turn off the appliance switch. Check the flex connections and renew if necessary; if they are sound, have the appliance checked by an expert.

2 If the smell comes from a socket outlet or a plug, turn off the main switch at the consumer unit. If the plug is hot, let it cool before unplugging it. Then check its connections including the fuse contacts, and examine the flex for damage. Replace as necessary (page 274). If the socket is hot, check it for faulty connections and renew as necessary (page 278).

No electricity

1 If power throughout your house fails and neighbouring houses are also without power, there is a mains supply failure. Report it to the 24-hour emergency number under 'Electricity' in the phone book.

2 If your system is protected by a whole-house residual current device (RCD), check whether it has switched itself off. Try to switch it on again if it has.

3 If it will not switch on, the fault that tripped it off is still present on the system. Call an electrician to track it down and rectify it.

4 If you do not have an RCD and your house is the only one without power, there may be a fault in your supply cable or your main supply fuse may have blown. Do not touch it. Report the power failure as described above.

Minor emergencies

1 If one appliance fails to work, unplug it and check its plug, fuse and flex; renew them as necessary. If the appliance still fails to work, plug it in a different socket outlet to test it. If it works, the problem is with the original socket; if not, take the appliance to an expert for repair.

2 If all lights or appliances on one circuit stop working, switch off at the consumer unit and check the circuit fuse (page 270). If it is sound, there may be a fault in the circuit cable. Call in an electrician to track it down and rectify it.

Understanding the consumer unit

Modern fuse boards – called consumer units – may look different from home to home, but the basic components are the same.

Consumer unit The householder's responsibility for the system begins here. It houses the main on-off switch, the earthing terminal block for all the house circuits, and individual MCBs for each one. Some modern consumer units have blanked out spaces for additional MCBs to be installed at a later date.
• Circuits vary according to a household's needs, but always include separate lighting and power circuits.
• Label the MCBs to show which circuit each one protects. To identify the circuits, turn off the main switch and switch off one MCB at a time. Turn the main switch back on and check which lights or appliances are not working.

OLD FUSE BOXES

In older systems, each circuit is protected by a fuse, not an MCB. Each fuseholder is marked with the rating in amps of the fuse if contains. A lighting circuit is protected by a 5amp fuse, and a ring main circuit by a 30amp fuse.

If the current demanded by the circuit exceeds these ratings, the fuse melts ('blows') and the circuit is disconnected.

The fuse link inside a carrier may be a wire or a sealed cartridge.

Miniature circuit breakers (MCBs) Modern consumer units have MCBs instead of fuses. If too much current is demanded, the circuit is disconnected instantly and a switch moves to the 'off' position or a button pops out. Reset the switch to restore power to the circuit.

MCB CURRENT RATINGS

As part of a move towards European standardisation, the ratings marked on new MCBs are being changed.
 5amp becomes   6amp
15amp becomes 16amp
30amp becomes 32amp
45amp becomes 40amp

Circuit cables Individual circuits are supplied by cables running out from the consumer unit. The live conductor in each circuit cable is connected to a terminal on its MCB. The neutral conductor connects to the main neutral terminal block in the consumer unit, and the earth conductor to the main earthing terminal block.

Residual current device (RCD) An RCD monitors the balance of the live and neutral current flows. An imbalance occurs if current leaks from a circuit because of faulty insulation, or because someone has touched a live part and received an electric shock. If the RCD detects an imbalance, it switches off the supply in a fraction of a second – fast enough to prevent an electric shock from being fatal.
• When RCDs were first introduced, they often replaced the system's main on-off switch. This practice has now been discontinued because it was found unnecessary for all circuits to be RCD-protected. An RCD is now installed to protect only at-risk circuits such as those to socket outlets and some stand-alone appliances.
• An RCD in its own enclosure may have been added to an existing installation to protect new at-risk circuits.

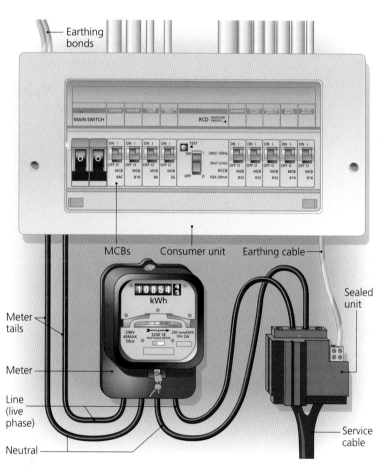

Earthing bonds

MAIN SWITCH   RCD

MCBs   Consumer unit   Earthing cable

Sealed unit

Meter tails

Meter

Line (live phase)

Neutral

Service cable

Service cable Electricity enters the home through the service (supply) cable – usually buried underground in urban areas, but often run overhead in rural areas. It carries electricity at 230 volts. The current flows along the live conductor and returns along the neutral conductor. Never interfere with the service cable, which is the property of your electricity supply company.

The term 'live' has been replaced by 'line' or 'phase' in the electrical industry. Live and neutral imply that current flows only in the live conductor, whereas both carry current at all times. The terms live and neutral are used throughout this book for clarity.

Sealed unit/service cut-out The service cable ends here. Its neutral conductor is connected to a solid terminal. Its live conductor is connected to a fuse (the service cut-out), which is usually rated at 60amps or, in modern installations, at 100amps. It is a deliberate weak link that will melt and disconnect the supply to the house if more current is demanded than the service cable can safely supply.

Do not tamper with the sealed unit.

Meter tails These two cables (live and neutral) link the sealed unit to the meter and the meter to the consumer unit.
• The live cable is covered with red insulation and the neutral cable with black.
• Each tail has an outer sheath which may match the colour of the insulation or may be grey.
• The electricity supply company must disconnect the supply before any work can be carried out on the meter tails.

Earthing cable This connects the earthing terminal block in the consumer unit (to which all the circuit cables are connected) to the earthing point provided by the electricity supply company – usually on the service cut-out or the service cable. Earth cross-bonding cables connect metal gas and water supply pipework to the earthing terminal block.

Meter A two-tariff meter with two displays may be installed to make use of night-rate electricity for storage heaters.

Understanding your electrical system

Before you do any electrical work, you need to understand some technical terms and get to grips with the different types of circuit you will find in your home.

Technical terms

Watts Electric power consumed is measured in watts (W for short). Every electrical appliance has a wattage rating marked on its rating plate. The higher the wattage rating, the more electricity the appliance consumes when it is in use.

Amps The amount of current flowing in a conductor is measured in amperes (amps or A for short). With a cable or flex, the greater the number of amps it carries, the thicker its conductors must be. Its current-carrying capacity also depends on its length and whether it is running through thermal insulation.

Volts The electrical pressure that drives current through a conductor is measured in volts (V for short). The pressure of the public supply in Britain has been standardised at 230 volts. The supply voltage may vary by plus 10 per cent (23V) or minus 6 per cent (14V) and a further drop of 6V is permitted on individual circuits.

Voltage-sensitive equipment, such as a computer or a word processor, can be protected from voltage variations by a surge suppresser.

Batteries and some portable generators and transformers supply other voltages for lighting and appliances that have been designed to operate on them.

AC and DC Mains electricity in Britain is alternating current (AC). It has an oscillating wave pattern, rather like waves of the sea, but the pattern is regular – the complete cycle from crest to crest occurs 50 times a second. This is known as the frequency of the supply and is written as 50~ or 50Hz (short for Hertz).

The electricity from batteries is direct current (DC). Its continuous flow of electrons is steady in its direction, with no oscillation.

The advantage of alternating current is that it can be transformed from one voltage to another. Because of this, a power station can supply a very high voltage to substations that reduce the voltage to feed a supply at 230V to many individual properties.

Inside the home, the voltage can be reduced again by a transformer, to supply a doorbell, low-voltage lighting or a computer printer, for instance.

Basic circuit types

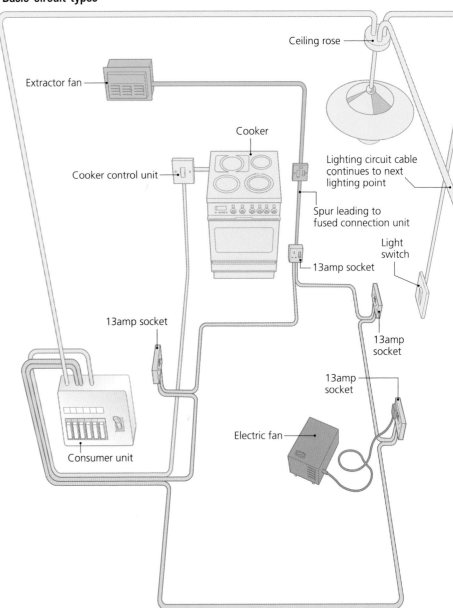

Extractor fan

Ceiling rose

Cooker

Cooker control unit

Lighting circuit cable continues to next lighting point

Spur leading to fused connection unit

Light switch

13amp socket

13amp socket

13amp socket

13amp socket

Consumer unit

Electric fan

Lighting circuit The circuit runs out from the consumer unit, linking a chain of lighting points. Cables run from each lighting point to its switch. The circuit is protected by a 5 or 6amp circuit fuse or MCB. It can safely supply up to a maximum of about 1200 watts, but in practice should not serve more than ten lighting points. The circuit would be overloaded if each of the lighting points had high-wattage bulbs.

Ring main circuit The circuit is wired as a ring that starts from the consumer unit and returns to it, allowing current to flow to socket outlets either way round the ring. It can serve a floor area of up to 100m². It is protected by a 30 or 32amp circuit fuse or MCB. It can have any number of sockets or fused connection units on it, but its maximum total load is about 7000 watts. For larger total loads and larger floor areas, additional ring circuits are needed.

Socket outlet The maximum load that can be supplied by a socket outlet taking a 13amp plug is 3000 watts. The plug is fitted with a 13amp or a 3amp fuse, according to the wattage rating of the appliance connected to it.

Spur on a ring circuit Extra socket outlets can be added to an existing ring main circuit via spurs branching off the ring at a socket outlet or junction box. In theory, each outlet on the ring could supply a spur to a single or double socket or a fused connection unit. However, the circuit including any spurs must not serve rooms with a floor area of more than 100m² – and its maximum load is still 7000 watts.

Single-appliance circuit An appliance that is a large consumer of electricity and in constant or frequent use – a cooker, a fixed water heater, or a shower heater unit, for example – has its own circuit running from the consumer unit. It would take too large a proportion of the power available on a shared circuit and would be likely to cause an overload.

A safe earthing system

The jobs described on the following pages are suitable only for modern wiring systems. Proper earthing of metal parts you can touch on electrical equipment and appliances provides vital protection from the risk of electric shock.

Earth cores in each circuit cable are connected to the earth terminal block in the consumer unit. This is connected to an earthing point provided by the electricity supply company.

Modern installations have protective multiple earthing (PME). This is earthed via the electricity supply cable's neutral connector to the 'star point' at the local electricity supply transformer, which is connected to a permanent earth at the substation.

Non-electrical metal fittings such as plumbing pipework that might come into accidental contact with the electrical system also need earthing.

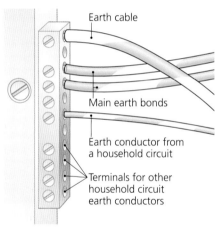

Earth cable

Main earth bonds

Earth conductor from a household circuit

Terminals for other household circuit earth conductors

The earth terminal block in the consumer unit has terminals for the earth cores in all the house circuit cables. One is for the main earth cable running to the main house earthing point. Other terminals earth metal pipes carrying water and gas.

A house in a rural area with an overhead power supply may have no earth connection via the supply cable. The house is earthed by an earth electrode (a metal spike) driven deep into the ground close to the house. This 'TT' earthing needs additional protection, provided by a residual current device (RCD).

The house wiring is connected to the earthing system via the earth cores in the circuit cables. The casing of electrical equipment is insulated or earthed by the manufacturer. Check that any metal items that you install yourself, or have installed for you, are safely earthed.

Earthing metal fittings

Non-electrical metal items – like radiators – that could come into contact with faulty electrical equipment must be bonded to the earthing system.

Main bonding

One or more green-and-yellow insulated cables called main bonding conductors should run from the earth terminal block in the consumer unit to incoming metal water, gas and oil service pipes (but not to telephone or television cables). The size of the cable should not be less than 10mm².

Main bonding

The main bonding conductors should be connected at one end to terminals on the earth block in the consumer unit and at the other to water, gas and oil pipes.

Clamps must fit tightly and be in contact with bare metal, not paint. They must be free from corrosion and should be easily accessible for inspection.

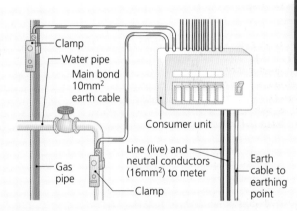

Clamp
Water pipe
Main bond 10mm² earth cable
Consumer unit
Line (live) and neutral conductors (16mm²) to meter
Gas pipe
Clamp
Earth cable to earthing point

Supplementary bonding

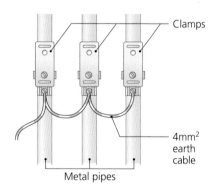

Clamps

4mm² earth cable

Metal pipes

Link airing cupboard pipes to ensure the pipework offers an unbroken metal earth route.

Link together non-electrical metal fittings in bathrooms or shower rooms with 4mm² earth cable. Such fittings might include inlet pipes to taps on the basin, bath and bidet, towel rails and the metal cradles of plastic baths. Connect the earth cable to the metal with clamps. Hide cable behind fittings and under the floor.

Supplementary bonding

Sinks, baths, taps, radiators and towel rails are among the items of non-electrical metal equipment that could be a danger if they came in to contact with a conductor carrying current or if an electrical fault occurred in the vicinity. If you can touch any of these items at the same time as earthed metalwork of electrical equipment, you should bond them to the earthing system. An electrical contractor can test whether items already in the house are correctly bonded. If the test result is not satisfactory, or if you are installing new metal items, you must also install supplementary bonding to them, using 4mm² earth cable.

In each bathroom or shower room, all metal items which you can touch must be connected together by bonding conductors and must be bonded to the house earthing system.

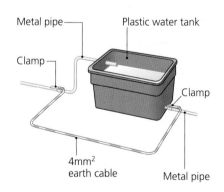

Metal pipe
Plastic water tank
Clamp
Clamp
4mm² earth cable
Metal pipe

Bridge across a plastic water tank from metal pipe to metal pipe with 4mm² earth cable.

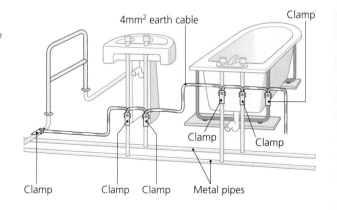

4mm² earth cable
Clamp
Clamp
Clamp
Metal pipes
Clamp
Clamp
Clamp

Installing supplementary bonding conductors

Use 4mm² green-and-yellow insulated earth cable. To connect it to metal pipes, use clamps complying with British Standard BS951.

Plan the route of the bonding cable. For a neat look, take it behind a bath panel, inside a basin pedestal, under the floor, behind a hollow wall, in plaster or in trunking.

You can lead the earth cable from the metal item either to the earth terminal in a socket outlet or to metal pipework which has been bonded.

If you are connecting it to a socket outlet, first turn off the main switch at the consumer unit and remove the fuse for the circuit the socket outlet is on. If you are going to connect it to a pipe, make sure that there is a continuous bonding cable run back to the consumer unit. Now that many water tanks and expansion tanks are made of plastic, the continuity of the bonding is interrupted. You must bridge this gap with 4mm² green-and-yellow-insulated earth cable.

The connections of supplementary bonds should be accessible for inspection and checking. Connections to the earth terminals of socket outlets are easy to inspect. Connections to pipework can be made in cupboards, behind removable panels or under the floor. If they have to be made under the floor, the section of floorboard above should be fixed with screws so that it can easily be lifted if necessary.

Metal baths and sinks are made with an earth tag. Connect the bonding cable by winding the bared end of the conductor round a bolt passed through the tag. Trap it with a metal washer secured under the nut. Make sure that the tag is clean and free of paint or enamel.

An earth clamp Use a clamp to connect the earth cable to metal pipework. Clean the pipe with wire wool first. If the pipe has been painted, strip off an area of paintwork. Screw the core of the earth cable tightly into the terminal.

Does your wiring need replacing?

You are permitted by law to rewire your home yourself. However, electricity companies have the right to test any wiring and to refuse to supply an unsafe system. Any work you carry out should comply with the Wiring Regulations drawn up for the Institution of Electrical Engineers, which are published as British Standard BS7671.

Old main switches and fuse boxes

Check the main fuse board. Look for cables from the meter going to a metal box with a main on/off switch for the installation. There may be separate switched fuse boxes for each circuit.

Inside the fuse boxes there may be circuit fuses in porcelain holders. Such a system is old and likely to be highly unsafe, and should be replaced. Replacement is especially important if each circuit has two fuses: the system could be lethal.

Old light switches
Round brass or Bakelite light switches mounted on wooden blocks are signs of a lighting system that is more than 50 years old. The lighting circuits should be rewired with new cable and fittings as soon as possible.

Old wiring – new fittings

You may have a system where the old rubber-insulated cables remain, but the switches and sockets have been replaced by modern ones. Look at the circuit cables where they emerge from the fuse box. If you find old cables, have them checked by an electrician, and plan to have the system rewired as soon as possible.

Round-pin sockets

If you have old-style round-pin sockets, your wiring system is likely to be 50 or more years old. It should be completely rewired without delay for safety reasons.

Tools for wiring work

Many of the jobs involved in wiring are non-electrical in nature – lifting floorboards, say. But for the electrical work, some special tools are essential.

Wire cutters A pair of 125mm or 150mm wire cutters will cut cable and flex, and trim cores to length.

Torch Choose one with a sturdy stand, or clip-on fitting. A powerful torch will light up work under floors and in lofts. Have a supply of spare batteries available or ideally choose a torch with a rechargeable battery.

Wire strippers
The adjustable blades will strip the insulation from cores of different sizes in cable and flex without damaging the conductors inside.

Circuit continuity tester
With a simple battery-powered tester you can check the continuity of circuits and whether a socket outlet is on a ring main circuit or on a spur.

Pliers A pair of 150mm electrician's pliers is useful for twisting cable conductor cores together prior to insertion into terminals. The cutting jaws can also be used for cutting cable and flex.

Tester screwdriver An insulated screwdriver with a 3mm blade is used for tightening terminal screws in plugs and other wiring accessories. A bulb in the handle lights up if the tip touches a live terminal or conductor.

Insulated screwdriver A larger screwdriver with an insulating sleeve on the shaft is useful for undoing and tightening plug screws and the screws fixing accessory faceplates to their mounting boxes.

Knife A sharp knife will cut through thick cable sheath and flex sheath.

Changing a fuse in a consumer unit

If you still have circuit fuses, keep spare fuses or fuse wire to hand for instant repairs if a fuse 'blows'.

Mending a rewirable fuse

1 Turn off the main on-off switch in the consumer unit. On an older system it may be in a separate enclosure near the meter. Remove or open the cover over the fuse carriers.

2 Pull out each fuse carrier in turn to find out which has blown. Scorch marks often show this, or simply a break in the wire.

3 If a power circuit is affected, switch off and unplug all the appliances on the circuit. If it is a lighting circuit, turn off all the light switches. If you do not switch everything off, the mended fuse is likely to blow again immediately you turn the main switch back on. Replace the fuse wire (below).

TYPES OF REWIRABLE FUSE CARRIER

Bridged fuse The wire runs from one terminal to the other over a plug of white arc-damping material. The carrier is ceramic.

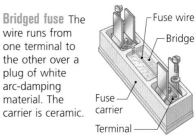

Fuse wire · Bridge · Fuse carrier · Terminal

Protected fuse
Between the terminals the wire runs through a porcelain arc-damping tube. The carrier is tough plastic.

Arc-damping tube · Fuse wire · Fuse carrier · Terminal

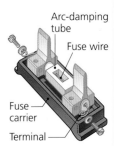

Bridge · Fuse wire · Fuse carrier · Terminal

Fuse between humps The unprotected wire passes round humps between one terminal and the other. The carrier is ceramic.

Replacing the fuse wire

1 Loosen the two terminal screws and remove any pieces of old wire. Cut a new piece of fuse wire of the correct amp rating, long enough to cross the carrier and go round both screws.

2 Wind the wire clockwise round one screw and tighten the screw.

3 Pass the wire across the bridge or thread it through the holder. If you are unsure about how the wire runs in the carrier, examine one of the intact fuses.

4 Wind the wire clockwise round the second screw. Make sure there is a little slack in the wire so that it will not snap and then tighten the screw.

5 Replace the fuse carrier in the consumer unit. Close the cover and restore the power by turning on the main switch.

Checking the circuit

Look for damage on the appliances, lights and flexes that were in use on the circuit when it failed. Make repairs if necessary, then switch on the appliances or lights one at a time. Check that you are not overloading the circuit with too many high-wattage appliances. Overloading is the likeliest cause of the blown fuse. If the fuse blows again, call an electrician.

Replacing a cartridge fuse

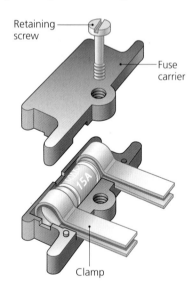

Retaining screw

Fuse carrier

15A

Clamp

Tools *Insulated screwdriver; fuse tester.*
Materials *Cartridge fuses.*

1 Turn off the main switch on the consumer unit.

2 Find out which fuse has blown: take out each fuse carrier in turn so you can test the cartridge.

3 Prise the cartridge gently from the clamps. Some carriers are in two halves and the screw holding them together has to be removed to give access to the cartridge.

4 Test the cartridge with a fuse tester (see below). Remove only one carrier at a time. Test its cartridge and replace the carrier before removing the next one for inspection and testing.

5 When you have traced the blown fuse, replace the cartridge with a new one of the amp rating shown on the carrier.

6 As with a rewirable fuse, switch off all appliances or lights on the affected circuit. Replace the fuse carrier, close the box and turn on the main switch. Check the circuit in the same way as for rewirable fuses.

Checking a miniature circuit breaker

If the consumer unit is fitted with miniature circuit breakers (MCBs) instead of circuit fuses, it is immediately clear which circuit is affected. The switch will be in the 'off' position or the button will have popped out.

1 Turn off the main switch on the consumer unit.

2 Switch off all appliances or light switches on the affected circuit. If you do not do this, the MCB may trip off again when you reset it.

3 Push the MCB switch to the 'on' position or push in the button. Then turn the main switch back on.

4 Check the circuit in the same way as for a rewirable fuse (left).

TESTING A FUSE

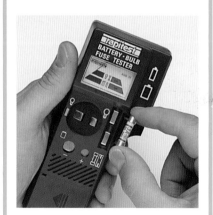

You can buy an inexpensive tester that will tell you if a cartridge fuse has blown. Some types can also check flat batteries and blown light bulbs.

Choosing the right fuse

Always use the correct fuse for the job in hand. NEVER use any other metallic object or material in place of a blown fuse in order to restore power to a circuit or appliance. Doing so would remove the protection the fuse provides, and could allow an electrical fire to start or result in someone receiving a potentially fatal electric shock.

Fuse wires

If your consumer unit has rewirable fuses, use 5amp wire for a lighting circuit, 15amp wire for an immersion heater circuit, and 30amp wire for a ring main circuit or a circuit to a cooker rated at up to 12kW.

Cartridge fuses

 **5A** Use for a lighting circuit

 **15A** Use for a storage heater or immersion heater circuit.

 **20A** Use for a 20amp radial power circuit.

 **30A** Use for a ring main circuit or a 30amp radial power circuit.

 **45A** Use for a cooker or shower circuit.

Choosing flexes

Most flex is round in cross-section and has a white PVC outer sheath that contains colour-coded insulated conductors. The live conductor is brown, the neutral blue and the earth green-and-yellow. Each conductor (called a core) is a bundle of thin wires, which is why it is so flexible. The thicker the core, the more strands it has and the more current it can carry.

Ordinary PVC-sheathed flex will withstand temperatures of up to 60°C. Heat-resistant rubber-sheathed flex will withstand temperatures of up to 85°C. Non-kink flex has a rubber sheath with an outer cover of braided fabric. Flex with an orange sheath is used out of doors to make it easy to see.

Metal light fittings and most appliances need three-core flex. Two-core flex with no earth core is used on double-insulated power tools and appliances (marked ▣), and for wiring non-metallic light fittings.

Key to flex colours
L – Live (brown)
E – Earth (green and yellow)
N – Neutral (blue)

2-core flex For non-metallic light-fittings and double-insulated appliances. Available with flat or round PVC sheath. Use 0.5mm² for up to 700W with a lampshade weight of 2kg; 0.75mm² for up to 1.4kW and 3kg; and 1mm² for up to 2.3kW and lampshade weight of 5kg.

3-core flex Used for all other appliances and for metallic light fittings and pendant lampholders requiring earthing. Has a round PVC sheath. Use 0.75mm² flex for up to 1.4kW, 1mm² for up to 2.3kW, 1.25mm² for up to 2.9kW; 1.5mm² for up to 3.6kW. Use 1.5mm² heat-resisting flex for immersion heaters.

3-core braided flex Used for portable appliances, such as irons, toasters and room heaters, with hot parts that could damage PVC-sheathed flex. Use sizes as for 3-core PVC flex.

3-core curly flex Useful for worktop appliances such as kettles, to keep flex safe and tidy. Use sizes as for 3-core flex.

Connecting flex and cable

The cores inside flex must be exposed before they can be connected to the terminals of a plug, appliance or ceiling rose.

Tools *Sharp knife; wire cutters and strippers; pliers.*

Materials *Flex. Possibly also PVC insulating tape or a rubber sleeve.*

Stripping the outer sheath

Most flex has an outer sheath of tough PVC. Remove enough to make sure that the cores can reach the terminals easily or they may be pulled out. For most connections you need to remove about 40mm of the sheath. Take care not to cut or nick the insulation on the cores as you cut the outer sheath.

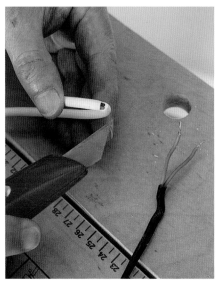

Bend the flex over and cut the sheath lightly with a sharp knife. The tension at the fold will open up a split halfway round the sheath. Fold the flex the other way and repeat. Then pull off the unwanted length of sheath.

Cutting and stripping the cores

1 Cut the individual cores to the right length to reach their terminals.

2 Set the wire strippers to match the thickness of the cores you are stripping. The core should just be able to slide out of the opening in the tool.

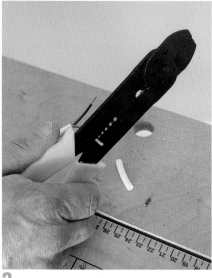

3 Press the handles together to cut the core insulation about 15mm from the tip. Rotate the strippers half a turn and pull them towards the tip of the core. The insulation will slide off.

4 Twist the strands of wire together.

Alternatively If you are preparing very thin flex for connection, strip off 30mm of insulation from each core, rather than 15mm. Twist the wire strands together, then fold the bare core over on itself in a tight U-shape. This makes it easier to insert into the terminal and provides a better electrical contact.

Fabric-covered flex

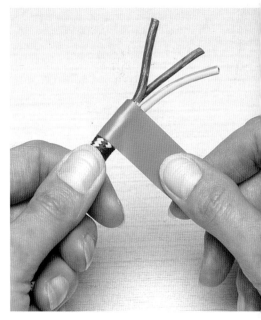

The outer cover of braided fabric on non-kink flex is likely to fray where it is cut. Wrap a strip of PVC insulating tape two or three times round the cut end of the fabric to seal down the loose threads.

Alternatively Cover the cut with a purpose–made rubber sleeve. This will be held by the cord grip of the plug. Remember to put it on before inserting the flex in the plug.

Extending a flex

Never join lengths of flex by twisting together the cores and binding the join with insulating tape. It may overheat and start a fire.

If you have to extend a flex, use a one-piece connector to make a permanent joint, or use a two-part connector if you want to be able to separate the joint. This must have three pins for connecting appliances that use three-core flex. Two-pin connectors are used mainly for connecting double-insulated garden power tools (marked with the symbol ▣) to extension leads.

Tools *Insulated screwdrivers; sharp knife; wire cutters and strippers; pliers.*

Materials *Flex connector; length of flex fitted with a plug.*

A one-piece connector

1 Unscrew the connector cover and remove it. Prepare the ends of both flexes for connection. Check that the cores (the wires) are long enough to reach the brass terminals when each flex sheath is held over its cord grip.

2 Lift out the brass barrel terminals and loosen all the terminal screws.

3 Push the cores into the terminals so that they match – brown to brown in one terminal, green-and-yellow to green-and-yellow in the second, and blue to blue in the third. Tighten all the terminal screws.

4 Loosen one screw and remove the other from each cord grip so you can swing the bar aside.

5 Fit the brass barrel terminals in their slots and position each flex sheath beneath its cord grip.

6 Replace the cord grip screws and tighten them to grip the flex sheaths securely. Fit and screw on the cover.

A two-part connector

You must fit the flex from the appliance to the part of the connector with the pins, and the flex from the mains supply to the part with the sockets.

If you fit the flexes the other way round, you will have live pins exposed if the two parts of the connector become separated while the power is switched on.

EXTENSION LEADS AND ADAPTORS

Trailing socket adaptor
This provides three or more outlets and is fitted with a fuse and neon indicator. It plugs into an existing socket and can supply a total wattage of up to 3kW. Use for low wattage appliances like computer equipment.

Plug-in adaptor Two or three plugs fit into a single outlet. Each can supply a total wattage of up to 3kW and should be fused. Do not plug one adaptor into another; the pin contacts will be poor and overheating could result.

Wire-in adaptor Makes a permanent connection for up to four low-wattage appliances and supplies total wattage of up to 3kW. Mount on the wall near the socket. Use for hi-fi or other equipment that is always kept in the same place.

1 Prepare the ends of both flexes. Separate the two halves of the connector. Remove the screw holding the terminal block inside each cover and push it out. Undo the cord grips.

2 Slide the outer covers onto the two prepared flexes.

3 Connect the cores to each terminal block with the green-and-yellow core in the middle. Make sure that the brown and blue cores in each part of the connector are opposite each other so they will connect when the parts are joined.

4 Fit each flex sheath in its cord grip and tighten the screws to hold it securely. Push each terminal block back into its cover and replace the fixing screw.

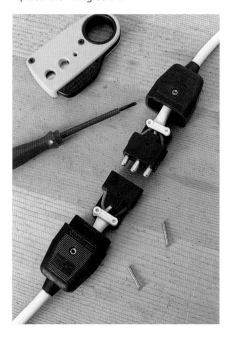

HOW TO USE AN EXTENSION FLEX SAFELY

A purpose-made extension flex with a plug at one end and a socket at the other extends the reach of a drill or other power tool. Choose a 1.5mm² flex, which is suitable for high-wattage tools. Use orange flex out of doors.

The flex can be stored on an open reel. Some flexes retract into a drum with a built-in socket. No matter how short a length you need, unwind the flex fully before use or it may overheat. Plug the flex into a residual current device (RCD) adaptor (right) at the socket outlet. This cuts off the power at once if you sever the flex and touch a live core. Or plug the flex into an RCD-protected socket outlet if one is available.

Multi-socket mains adaptor

Trailing flexes are a safety risk and look untidy. A neat alternative is to connect the appliances to a multi-socket mains adaptor.

1 Remove the mini-plugs from the connector block.

2 Screw the connector block to the wall or skirting board if required.

3 Unscrew a mini-plug cover and loosen the cord grip screws.

4 Remove the old plug from the first item to be connected and trim all the flex cores to the same length. Bare their ends.

5 Connect each core to its terminal: brown to the right, blue to the left and green-and-yellow to the centre.

6 Fit the flex sheath in the cord grip and screw down the plug cover. Insert the mini-plug into the connector block.

7 Repeat for other appliances. Plug any unused plugs into their sockets.

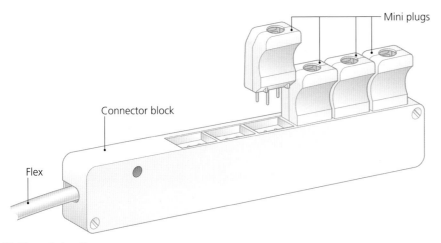

Mini plugs

Connector block

Flex

Multi-socket unit Each unit can take up to six plugs, with a maximum total load of 3kW This type of adaptor should not be used with appliances that have heating elements, such as hair dryers, irons or tumble driers, because they will overload it.

Mini-plugs Wired in the same way as standard three-pin plugs, these slot into the top of the multi-socket unit. The unit contains a 13amp fuse, and is fitted with a standard 13amp plug for connection to a socket outlet. It can be mounted on the wall nearby for neatness.

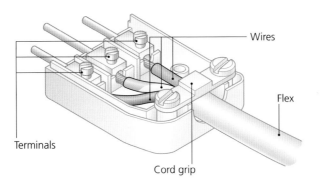

Wires

Flex

Terminals

Cord grip

CHOOSING PLUGS AND FUSES

Plastic plug Moulded plastic plugs are the commonest type. They are usually white, but other colours are available. All new plugs have plastic sleeves on the live and neutral pins, to prevent accidental finger-tip contact with live metal as you pull the plug out of its socket outlet.

Rubber plug Tough rubber plugs are intended for use on power tools. Rubber will not crack if the plug is knocked or dropped in use. You have to thread the flex through the rubber cover before connecting it to the plug terminals.

Moulded-on plug All new appliances are sold with a one-piece factory-fitted plug. These cannot be opened, so must be cut off and discarded if damaged. Hammer the pins out of line before you throw it away so it cannot be plugged into a socket outlet if found by a child. The cut end of the flex will give a shock if touched.

3amp cartridge fuse Use in plugs and fused connection units for appliances rated at up to 700 watts. Check the wattage on the rating plate of the appliance. Low wattage appliances include table or standard lamps, hi-fi equipment, home computers and ancillaries, and electric blankets.

13amp cartridge fuse Use in plugs and fused connection units for appliances between 700 and 3000 watts such as most TV sets, vacuum cleaners, large power tools, room heaters and all domestic appliances that contain a heating element.

Fitting a new plug

All electrical appliances sold in the UK must have a factory-fitted plug. This has greatly improved household electrical safety, by eliminating the need for the consumer to fit a plug to every new appliance – a task that many found difficult to carry out correctly.

However, you will need to fit a replacement plug if the factory-fitted one is damaged. Many older appliances in the home will still have hand-wired plugs, which may also need replacing over time.

Old colours	New colours
E ⏚	E ⏚
N L	N L
Black to N	Blue to N
Green to earth	Green-and-yellow
(E or ⏚)	to earth (E or ⏚)
Red to L	Brown to L

The colours of the plastic insulation on the cores in flex were changed to brown (live), blue (neutral) and green-and-yellow (earth) in 1968. Any appliance with flex cores coloured red (live) and black (neutral) should be checked for electrical safety.

All three-pin plugs are fitted with a cartridge fuse. Many contain a 13amp fuse when you buy them, but you should fit a lower-rated fuse if the appliance rating is below 700 watts (see Choosing plugs and fuses, page 273).

Tools *Insulated screwdrivers; sharp knife; wire cutters and strippers; pliers.*

Materials *Plug; flex; cartridge fuse (either 3amp or 13amp).*

1 Unscrew the cover of the new plug and remove it.

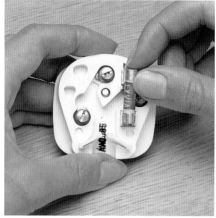

2 Prise out the cartridge fuse if necessary to reveal the terminal. Loosen the screw-down bar that secures the flex if there is one. Plastic jaws grip the flex in some plugs.

3 If you are replacing a hand-wired plug, remove its cover and loosen the terminal screws to release the flex cores from their terminals. Release the flex from the flex grip. Inspect the bare cores. If they appear damaged, cut them off and strip off some core insulation to expose undamaged wires ready for reconnection to the new plug.

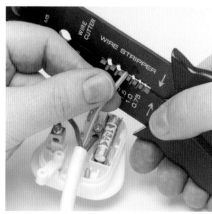

4 If you are replacing a factory-fitted plug, cut through the flex close to the plug body. Prepare the end of the cut flex (page 271). For some plugs all the cores have to be the same length, for others they have to be different lengths. Check that the prepared cores are long enough to reach their terminals with the flex sheath held in the flex grip.

5 Tough rubber plugs designed for use on power tools have a hole in the plug cover through which the flex passes before being connected to the plug terminals.

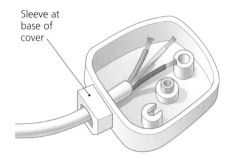

Sleeve at base of cover

6 Connect each flex core to its correct terminal. The **BR**own (live) core goes to the **B**ottom **R**ight terminal, the **BL**ue (neutral) core to the **B**ottom **L**eft terminal, and the earth core in three-core flex (green-and-yellow) to the top terminal.

7 With pillar-type terminals, loosen the terminal screw and insert the bare end of the core in the hole. Tighten the screw to trap it in place. Plugs with this type of terminal often have loose pins; remove these from the plug first if it makes connecting the cores easier.

Alternatively With screw-down stud terminals, remove the stud and wind the bare end of the core clockwise round the threaded peg. Screw the stud down to trap the wires in place.

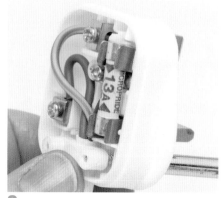

8 Arrange the cores in their channels in the plug body and place the flex sheath in the cord grip. If the plug has nylon jaws, press the flex in between them. If it has a screw-down bar, undo one screw, position the flex in the grip, swing the bar back over it and screw it down securely. Fit the fuse.

9 Replace the plug cover and make sure that it is firmly screwed together.

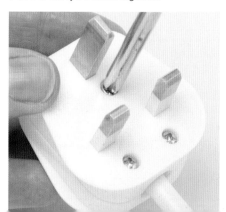

Reconnecting flex to a lampholder

The flex connections within a pendant lampholder may pull away from their terminals in time and stop the light working, but it is a simple matter to reconnect them.

• You will also need to reconnect the cores if you are shortening the flex, perhaps to fit a new lampshade that needs to be higher.
• If the lampholder is a metal one without an earth terminal, replace it with an earthed one – or with a plastic lampholder if the flex has no earth core. You must use three-core flex with a metal lampholder or metal lampshade.
• If the flex is discoloured or cracked, replace it with new flex.

Tools *Insulated screwdrivers, one with a small, fine tip; wire cutters and strippers; pliers.*

Materials *Replacement flex. Perhaps a new lampholder.*

1 Turn off the power at the consumer unit and remove the fuse or switch off the MCB protecting the circuit that you will be working on.

2 Remove the light bulb and unscrew the ring that holds the lampshade. With a very old lampholder, you may have to break the ring by crushing it with pliers; some shops sell the new rings separately. Remove the shade.

The parts of a lampholder

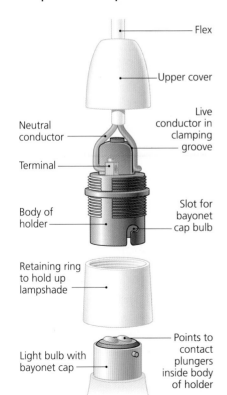

Flex
Upper cover
Live conductor in clamping groove
Neutral conductor
Terminal
Body of holder
Slot for bayonet cap bulb
Retaining ring to hold up lampshade
Light bulb with bayonet cap
Points to contact plungers inside body of holder

3 Unscrew the upper cover of the lampholder and push it up the flex to reveal the flex connections. Unhook the flex cores from the lugs on the body of the lampholder.

4 With the fine-tipped screwdriver, undo the terminal screws enough for you to draw out the flex cores.

5 The light bulb makes its connection via the two spring-loaded plungers in the base of the lampholder. Push these in to see whether they return to their original positions when released. If they do not, or if the lampholder is damaged or scorched, fit a new one.

6 Prepare the ends of the flex cores for connection (page 271).

7 If you are fitting a new lampholder, thread the new cover onto the flex.

8 Screw the brown and blue cores tightly into the lampholder terminals. It does not matter which each goes to. In a metal lampholder you must connect the green-and-yellow earth conductor to the earth terminal.

9 Hook the flex cores over the support lugs. Screw the lampholder cover on, taking care not to cross-thread it.

10 Insert the lampholder into the lampshade and screw the retaining ring in place to secure the shade. Fit the light bulb.

11 Replace the circuit fuse or switch on the MCB and restore the power at the consumer unit.

Connecting flex to a ceiling rose

If a light flex has discoloured or become brittle, it is easy to connect a new one between the ceiling rose and the lampholder.

Before you start Inside a modern ceiling rose on a loop-in wiring system (page 306) is a row of terminals in three groups. The live and neutral cores of the circuit and switch cables are connected to these. A separate terminal is marked E or ⏚ for the earth conductors.
Use the right type and size of flex for the installation (page 271). If it connects with a metal lampholder or light fitting it must have an earth core.

Tools *Insulated screwdrivers, one with a small, fine tip; sharp knife; wire cutter and strippers.*

Disconnecting the old flex

1 At the consumer unit, turn off the power and remove the fuse or switch off the MCB protecting the circuit you will be working on. It is not enough simply to turn off the light switch; the cables in the ceiling rose will still be live.

2 Remove the light bulb and shade to avoid the risk of dropping them.

3 Unscrew the cover of the ceiling rose and slide it down the flex.

4 Using the small screwdriver, loosen the terminal screws connecting the flex cores at each end of the row of terminals. Withdraw the cores.

5 If the flex has an earth core, unscrew the earth terminal enough to withdraw it. Do not dislodge the other cable earths. Next, connect the new flex (overleaf).

Connecting the new flex

1 Connect the new flex first to the lampholder (page 275).

2 Thread the new flex through the cover of the ceiling rose.

3 Prepare the new flex for connection (page 271). Take care not to strip off too much of the outer sheath. The cores have to reach the terminals without strain, but they must not show below the ceiling-rose cover; the outer sheath of the flex must enter the hole in the cover.

4 Slip the tip of the green-and-yellow-insulated earth core into the earth terminal in the ceiling rose. Make sure before you tighten the screw that the other cable earth cores from the circuit and switch cables have not been dislodged from under their terminal screws.

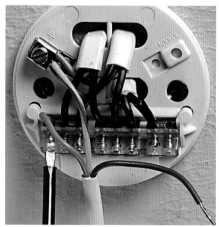

5 Connect the blue flex core to the terminal where the circuit cable neutral (black) cores are connected.

6 Connect the brown flex core to the terminal at the other end of the row where the switch cable neutral core is connected. This core is usually identified with a strip of red PVC insulating tape, to show that it is, in fact, live.

7 Hook the flex cores over the support lugs at each side of the rose baseplate.

JUNCTION BOX SYSTEM

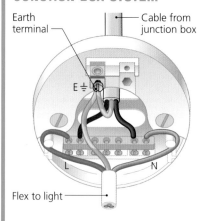

A loop-in ceiling rose might have been used on a junction box system (page 306). There will be one cable entering the base of the rose. The flex connection is the same as for a loop-in system (steps 5–7, left).

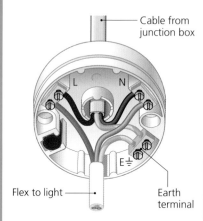

Another type of ceiling rose, used on a junction box system (above), has three or four sets of separate terminals, not in line.

1 Connect the blue flex core to the same set of terminals as the black cable core.

2 Connect the brown core from the flex to the same set of terminals as the red core from the cable.

3 Connect the green-and-yellow earth core from the flex to the same set of terminals as the earth core from the cable.

If the earth from the cable has not already been sleeved with green-and-yellow insulation, disconnect it and sleeve it before connecting it – with the flex earth – to the terminal.

8 Slide the flex cover up and screw it onto the baseplate. Replace the shade and bulb.

9 Replace the circuit fuse or switch on the MCB and restore the power.

Rewiring a table lamp or standard lamp

To fit a new flex to a table or standard lamp with no exposed metal parts, or for a double insulated lamp (marked ▣), use two-core flex without an earth core. For a lamp with metal parts, use two-core-and-earth flex.

• If the lamp has a brass lampholder without an earth terminal, you must fit a new brass lampholder with an earth terminal, or a plastic lampholder. If it is not possible to fit a new lampholder, do not use the lamp.
• The flex must be threaded up inside the lamp base. The hole to thread it through is often on the side of the lamp near the bottom.
• If the hole is underneath, the lamp base should have small feet to raise it and keep its weight off the flex.
• Some lamps have a push-through switch in the lampholder. If there is no integral switch, fit an in-line switch in the flex.

Tools *Insulated screwdrivers; sharp knife; wire cutters and strippers; pliers.*

Materials *Lamp; suitable flex. Perhaps also a flex switch.*

1 Unplug the lamp and remove the bulb.

2 With a plastic lampholder, unscrew the upper cover to release the lampshade. With a brass lampholder, unscrew the first ring.

3 With a plastic lampholder, unscrew the body from the base, then screw down the lower cover to reveal the terminals.

With a brass lampholder, unscrew and remove the second narrow ring so that you can lift out the outer lampholder section and then raise the inner section which has the flex connected beneath it.

4 Release the flex cores from the terminals. Wind the cores securely round the end of the new flex and tape the two together.

5 Gently pull out the old flex from below, using it to pull the new flex through the lamp base.

Plastic lampholder

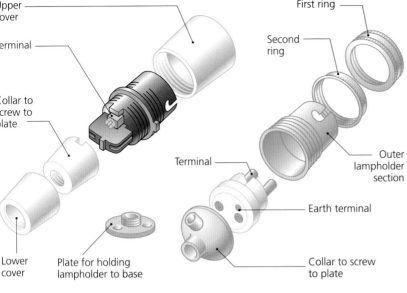

Upper cover

Terminal

Collar to screw to plate

Lower cover

Plate for holding lampholder to base

Brass lampholder

First ring

Second ring

Outer lampholder section

Terminal

Earth terminal

Collar to screw to plate

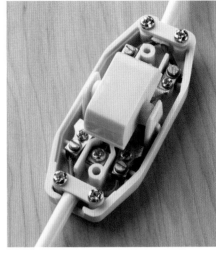

6 Prepare the flex for connection (page 271) and then finish drawing it through the lamp base until only about 40mm is protruding.

7 Screw the brown flex core into one lampholder terminal and the blue flex core into the other.
If you are using three-core flex, connect the green-and-yellow earth core to the terminal marked E (or ⏚).

8 With a plastic lampholder, screw the plastic cover over the terminals and screw the lampholder body into the lamp base. As you do so, turn the flex or it will become twisted. With a brass lampholder, lower the inner section of the lampholder back into place. Fit the outer section on top and secure it with the screw-on ring.

9 Replace the lampshade and secure it with the upper narrow ring or plastic cover. Fit the light bulb.

Fitting a switch in the flex

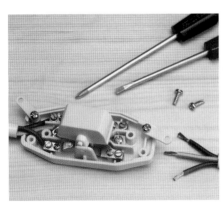

• If you are using three-core flex, use a switch with an earth terminal.
• For a two-core flex on a double-insulated lamp, no earth terminal is necessary.

1 Switch off and unplug the lamp. Cut the flex where the switch is to go and prepare the ends for connection (page 271).

2 Unscrew and remove the cover of the switch.

3 Take out a screw from each flex clamp so that you can swivel the clamps aside.

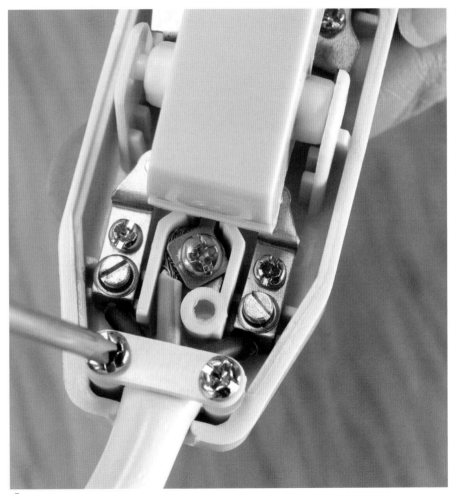

4 Release the terminal screws and connect each flex core – brown (live) to the terminals marked L, blue (neutral) to the terminals marked N, and green-and-yellow to the terminals marked E (or ⏚). Tighten the screws.

Alternatively In a switch with no earth terminal, connect the two brown cores to the terminals on the switch mechanism and the blue cores to each end of the through terminal block.

5 Screw the switch cover back into place.

Fitting a plug to the new flex

Connect the plug as described in *Fitting a new plug*, page 274.

Replacing sockets

Electric shock or fire could be caused by contact with the conductors in a damaged socket. Replace it as soon as possible.

Replacing a faceplate

If a socket outlet faceplate is cracked by an impact, do not use the socket until you have replaced the faceplate. If the socket outlet is surface-mounted, replace the mounting box as well if it is damaged. You could take the opportunity to replace a single socket with a double one at the same time.

Tools *Large and small insulated screwdriver; perhaps also a sharp knife; wire cutters and strippers; pliers.*

Materials *New socket outlet. Perhaps a new plastic mounting box, with fixing screws; green-and-yellow earth sleeving.*

1 Turn off the power at the consumer unit and switch off the MCB that protects the circuit you want to work on (or remove the appropriate fuse if you have an old-style fuse box). Plug in and switch on a lamp you know to be working to check that the socket outlet is dead.

2 Undo the screws that hold the faceplate in place and pull it away from the wall. Keep the screws; you may find that the ones supplied with your new socket outlet will not fit the lugs in the existing mounting box. In that case, use the old screws.

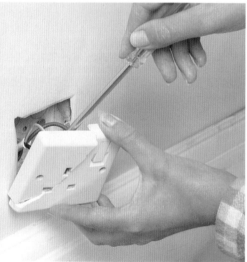

3 Loosen the three terminal screws on the back of the faceplate to release the conductors. Note how many conductors are connected to each terminal; there may be one, two or three depending on whether the outlet is on a spur, is on the ring circuit or is supplying power to an extra outlet on a spur. The new outlet must be connected in the same way as the damaged one.

4 If there is damage to the plastic mounting box of a surface-mounted socket, undo the screws holding it to the wall and remove it. Pass the cable or cables through the entry hole of a new mounting box and screw the box in place.

5 Check that the cable cores will reach the terminals on the new faceplate. If necessary, cut back the cable sheath with a sharp knife to expose longer cores, taking care not to nick the core insulation. If the earth cores are bare, cover them with green-and-yellow plastic sleeving, leaving only the metal tips exposed.

6 Insert the cores into their terminals and tighten the terminal screws firmly. Connect the red core(s) to the terminal marked L, the black core(s) to the terminal marked N, and the earth cores to the terminal marked E or ⏚. Tug each core to check that it is securely held by its terminal screw.

7 Place the faceplate over the mounting box, folding the cables carefully into it.

8 Screw the faceplate to the box. Do not over-tighten the screws or the plastic may crack.

9 Turn on the MCB for the circuit you have been working on, or replace the fuse you removed. Restore the power and check that the new socket outlet works – by plugging in a lamp, for example. If it does not, switch off again at the mains and check and tighten the connections.

Replacing a single socket outlet with a double

If the single socket outlet is surface-mounted, use a surface-mounted replacement. If it is flush-mounted (or recessed), you can fit a plastic surface-mounted box called a pattress over it. Alternatively, you can remove the existing metal mounting box, enlarge the recess and fit a larger box. Flush-mounted fittings are neater, and safer because they are less likely to be damaged by knocks from furniture. You will have to cut into the wall to fit a new double or triple flush mounting box.

Tools *Suitable tools for enlarging the recess (page 282); insulated screwdriver; sharp knife; wire cutters and strippers; pliers.*

Materials *Double or triple mounting box (or pattress, see opposite); new socket outlet; rubber grommet; screws and wall plugs. Perhaps earth sleeving.*

Removing the single outlet

1 Turn off the main switch on the consumer unit and switch off the MCB that protects the circuit you will be working on. Remove the appropriate fuse if you have an old-style fuse box. Check that the socket outlet is dead by plugging in a lamp you know to be working.

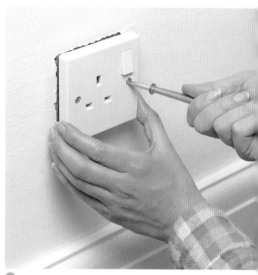

2 Unscrew the faceplate and ease it away from the mounting box. Then disconnect the cable cores from their terminals and set the old faceplate aside.

Fitting the mounting box

Flush-mounted boxes

1 Take out the screw or screws holding the old box in place and ease the box out of its recess.

2 Prepare the hole for the new mounting box (page 282).

3 Remove a knock-out (a pre-cut entry disc) from the new box. Fit a grommet in the hole to prevent the cable sheath from chafing on its edges, then feed the cable into the box and fix the box in place.

Surface-mounted boxes

1 If you are replacing a surface-mounted box, take out its fixing screws and remove it. If you are fitting a pattress, leave the old metal mounting box in place.

2 Hold the mounting box or pattress in place, check with a spirit level that it is horizontal, and use a bradawl to pierce the wall through the fixing holes.

3 Drill holes at the marked spots and insert wallplugs in them.

4 Feed the cable through a hole in the back of the box or pattress. Screw the box or pattress to the wall.

Connecting the socket outlet

1 Use pliers to straighten the tips of the cable cores. Cover the earth cores with green-and-yellow sleeving if they are bare.

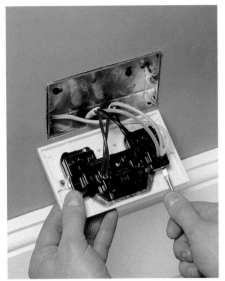

2 Screw the live (red) cores into the terminal marked L. Screw the neutral (black) cores into the terminal marked N. Screw the earth conductors into the terminal marked E or ⏚.

3 If the mounting box is metal, fit a short length of earth core (taken from a cable offcut and covered with sleeving) between the faceplate earth terminal and the earth terminal in the box. This so-called flying earth ensures that the box is safely connected to earth.

4 Fold the cables neatly into the mounting box and push the faceplate back into position over the box.

5 Screw the faceplate to the box or pattress. Do not overtighten the screws if fixing to a plastic box, or it may crack.

6 At the consumer unit, replace the fuse or switch on the MCB to restore power to the circuit you have been working on.

Choosing socket outlets and mounting boxes

There is a wide variety of socket outlets and mounting boxes to choose from. When increasing the number of outlets you have, or replacing old outlets, try to ensure that what you choose will supply enough power and sockets for any future use of electric appliances.

Plastic socket outlets
Socket outlets are available in single, double and triple configurations, with or without switches. Holes for the plug pins have spring-loaded shutters to prevent children from poking anything into them. Most sockets fit into a 32mm-deep white plastic surface box or a 25mm steel flush-mounted box; deeper (35mm) flush boxes allow more space for the wiring.

Metal socket outlets
Single and double brass, chrome and stainless-steel sockets are available in a variety of styles. There are plastic inserts round the shuttered pin holes and switches. Metal sockets fit on a flush steel box or a matching metal surface box.

Socket outlets with indicators
Both plastic and metal sockets are available with a neon indicator above each outlet. The indicator lights up to show when the socket outlet is switched on. Take care not to dislodge the small neon bulb clipped behind the coloured window when handling the faceplate.

Fused connection units

Fixed appliances, such as wall-mounted heaters and fans, should be connected to a ring circuit by a fused connection unit (FCU) with a direct flex connection, rather than by a plug. The flex from the appliance can enter the FCU through the edge or a hole in the front. The FCU may have a switch and a neon indicator, and is fitted with a fuse to match the appliance wattage.

Flex-outlet plates
In bathrooms, where socket outlets are not permitted, a fixed appliance such as a towel rail is wired into a flex-outlet plate. The cable (from a fused connection unit) goes into the back of the mounting box and the flex enters through the front on the plate and is connected to terminals on the back of it. There is no switch.

Boxes for flush mounting

Metal boxes for single, double and triple socket outlets have pre-cut discs to allow cables to enter. Knock out a disc and fit a grommet in the hole to protect the cable. The earth terminal in the box must be linked to the earth terminal on the accessory faceplate with sleeved earth core.
   Single and double plastic boxes are available for use in plasterboard walls. They also have knock-out cable entry points, but do not need grommets.

Boxes for surface mounting
Single, double and triple surface boxes are made in plastic. They have knock-out cable entry points, and do not need grommets. Metal surface boxes are also available; they are used mainly in outbuildings.

Pattress for converting a socket outlet
A mounting frame called a pattress allows a surface-mounted double or triple socket outlet to be fitted over a single flush-mounted metal box.

Working on electrical circuits

Many electrical jobs and projects involve working on the house's electrical circuits – either extending an existing circuit in some way, or adding an entirely new one. Whatever the task, the most important skill required for safety and success is the ability to plan the job carefully and carry out the work methodically.

A typical project will involve running cable from one point to another, either from the main consumer unit or a point on an existing circuit. This new cable is used for installing new wiring accessories or light fittings, and making connections to them and to the existing circuit wiring.

To minimise disruption, do all the new installation work as far as possible while leaving the power supply on. You can bury new cables in walls, run them beneath floorboards or through lengths of plastic trunking and create recesses for new mounting boxes for sockets all with the power live – in fact you may need power for some of the jobs. Leave the new cables sticking out where they terminate at a new socket outlet or light fitting and where they link to the existing circuit and turn off the power supply only when you are ready to make the final connections.

WIRING REGULATIONS

From 1 January 2005, electrical installation work must meet the requirements of a new section of the Building Regulations called Part P. It will become a legal requirement for homeowners to be able to prove that all new fixed installation and alteration work has been carried out and certified by a competent electrician.

• All work that involves adding a new circuit must either be notified to your local Building Control department, who will then inspect the work, or must be carried out by a competent person, registered with a Part P Self-Certification Scheme.

• Minor jobs, such as adding new lights or socket outlets to existing circuits and replacing existing wiring accessories are exempt from control. However, they should still be checked by a competent electrician, particularly in a kitchen, bathroom or shower room.

• If you are in any doubt as to whether a job you intend to carry out is exempt, ask your local Building Control department.

Extending circuits

Jobs such as adding extra socket outlets in a room, installing a cooker hood or shaver socket or providing new lighting points all involve adding branch lines (called spurs) to existing circuits. A spur from a ring main circuit can supply one single, double or triple socket outlet or a single fused connection unit providing a sub-circuit to a cooker hood, extractor fan, waste disposal unit, wall heater or central heating control. Before you add a spur to a lighting circuit, check that adding the extra lighting point will not overload the circuit, which can supply lights with a maximum total of 1200 watts. The first thing you have to decide is where and how to connect the spur to the wiring that is already in place.

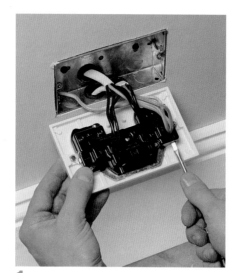

1 You can extend a ring main circuit in two ways. The spur cable can be connected into the terminals of any socket outlet or fused connection unit (FCU) that is on the main circuit. This is often the most practical solution. Note that only one spur can be connected to each outlet or FCU.

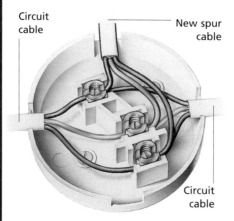

Circuit cable — New spur cable

Circuit cable

Alternatively Make a connection via a three-terminal junction box inserted in the main circuit cable. This means locating cable below floorboards but may offer a more convenient connection point if boards have to be lifted anyway to route the spur cable to its destination.

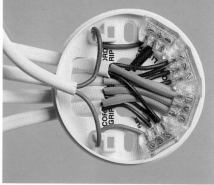

2 You can extend a lighting circuit in three ways. All three connection options require access to ceiling voids or the loft space. The spur cable can be connected directly into the terminals of an existing loop-in ceiling rose (above), or into a four-terminal junction box that is already supplying an existing lighting point (below).

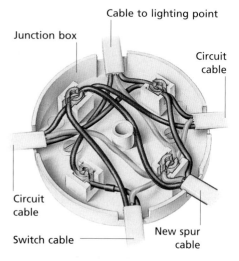

Cable to lighting point

Junction box

Circuit cable

Circuit cable

Switch cable

New spur cable

Alternatively You can make the connection via a four-terminal junction box inserted in the main lighting circuit cable. This box will supply the new light fitting and its switch. Care must be taken with this method to identify the circuit cable correctly.

Adding circuits

Jobs such as installing an electric shower or cooker require an entirely new circuit, run from the consumer unit. The circuit cable runs first to a double-pole (DP) isolating switch, then on to the appliance. For an electric shower, the double-pole isolating switch is usually ceiling-mounted and must be cord-operated for safety. The circuit then runs from here on to the shower unit, where it is connected to the appliance's terminal block.

In most situations there will not be a spare fuseway available for the new circuit cable, so one will have to be provided. There are several options.

1 If your existing fusebox has rewirable fuses, fit a separate switch-fuse unit containing two (or more) new fuseways and a double-pole isolating switch next to the existing fusebox.

2 If you have a modern consumer unit with circuit breakers (MCBs), fit a two-way or four-way enclosure that can accept MCBs (and an RCD if required).

In either case, you can install the new unit alongside the existing fusebox or consumer unit and connect the new circuit cable to it. Call in your electricity supply company or a qualified electrician to connect the new unit to the main incoming power supply; you are not allowed to do this yourself.

3 Replace the existing fusebox or consumer unit with a new, larger consumer unit to which existing and new circuit cables can be connected. This has several advantages. The new unit will provide a single main on-off switch, MCB protection for every circuit plus RCD protection for some, and can include some spare capacity for future extensions to the wiring system.

Replacing a consumer unit is a job for a qualified electrician, who will specify its contents correctly for your requirements and reconnect the unit to the incoming supply.

Choosing cable for indoor circuits

Cable is used to wire up the circuits to ceiling roses, light switches, socket outlets and fixed appliances. It has a grey or white oval PVC outer sheath to protect the conductors inside.
• The most commonly used type has two insulated conductors and a bare earth conductor, and is known as two-core-and-earth or twin-and-earth cable. The conductor with red insulation is used as the live conductor and the one with black insulation as the neutral conductor.
• Cable is made in several sizes, each identified by the cross-sectional area of the conductors in square millimetres. Each circuit is wired in cable sized to match its current demand.

Key Live (red), Earth (bare wire), Neutral (black)

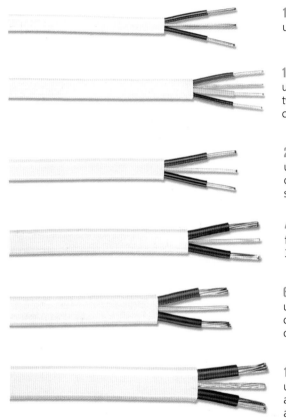

$1.0mm^2$ Two-core-and-earth, used for lighting circuits.

$1.0mm^2$ Three-core-and-earth, used for wiring between two-way switches. Cores are colour-coded for identification.

$2.5mm^2$ Two-core-and-earth, used for ring main circuits, or circuit for immersion heater, or storage heaters up to 20amp.

$4mm^2$ Two-core-and-earth, for radial power circuit with 30amp fuse.

$6mm^2$ Two-core-and-earth, used for 30amp circuit for cooker up to 12kW, or 45amp circuit for shower up to 8kW.

$10mm^2$ Two-core-and-earth, used for circuit for cooker above 12kW or shower rated above 8kW.

Sleeving for earth conductors

When you strip off the outer sheath of a cable and prepare its conductors for connection to a wiring accessory, you must always cover the bare earth conductor with a length of green-and-yellow PVC sleeving.

CABLE CORE COLOUR CHANGE

The colours used to identify the conductors (cores) in cable are going to be changed, following an amendment to British Standard BS7671 – Requirements for Electrical Installations. Cables with the new core colours are available now, and may be used for new wiring work. From 31 March 2006, use of the new cables becomes compulsory for all new wiring work in the home. There is no requirement for existing wiring to be changed.
• In two-core-and-earth cable, the red core will change to brown, and the black core to blue. The earth core will remain a bare conductor, to be covered with green-and-yellow sleeving whenever it is exposed. The cable core colours will therefore be identical to the colours used on flex cores, which were changed from red and black in 1968.
• In three-core-and-earth cable, used for two-way switching arrangements, the three cores will be brown, black and grey instead of the present red, yellow and blue. The earth core remains a bare conductor.

Preparing the circuit route

New cable can be run under floorboards and up and down walls – either buried in a channel (or 'chase') cut into the plaster, or hidden in surface-mounted trunking.

• You will have to lift floorboards to run cables in floor or ceiling voids. If the floor is solid, you will have to run it in trunking. Do not attempt to cut chases in a concrete floor; you are likely to damage the damp-proof membrane in the structure.

• Cable buried in plaster must be enclosed in oval PVC conduit. This gives the cable some protection from nails or screws driven into the wall. It is sold in a range of sizes, in 3m lengths.

Tools *Cable detector; power drill; masonry drill bits; flat wood bits; twist drill bits; club hammer; brick bolster; cold chisel; claw hammer; pencil; sharp knife; saw; chisel; spirit level; bradawl; filling knife; wire cutters and strippers; pliers; screwdrivers.*

Materials *Cable; cable clips; oval PVC conduit; galvanised nails for fixing conduit; mounting boxes with screws; wallplugs and grommets; ceiling roses; plaster or interior filler; timber offcuts; nails.*

Fitting a mounting box

1 Hold the mounting box in position. For a socket outlet it should be at least 150mm above floor or worktop level. For a light switch, it should be at about shoulder height. Check with a spirit level that the box is horizontal and draw a line round it as a guide for drilling.

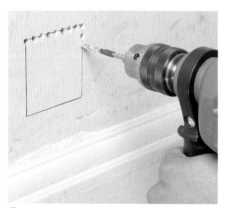

2 Using a masonry bit, drill holes all round the marked outline to the depth of the box. If the drill has no depth gauge, mark the bit with adhesive tape at the required depth and drill until the tape reaches the wall. Drill more holes within the marked area.

Alternatively Use a proprietary plastic drilling jig to drill a series of closely spaced holes in the wall. This creates a honeycomb effect which makes the masonry easy to chop out.

3 Cut out the recess to the required depth with a brick bolster and club hammer.

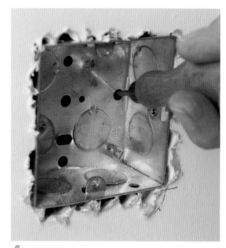

4 Brush out the recess, fit the mounting box and make marks with a pencil or bradawl through the fixing holes at the back of the box.

5 Take out the box, drill holes at the marks and insert wallplugs.

6 Knock out one of the discs stamped in the back or sides of the box for the cable to enter. Fit a grommet in the hole. However, do not screw the mounting box in place until any chases to it through the plaster have been made.

Laying cable under a floor

The cable can run alongside one joist or it can cross several.

1 Where the cable is to be at right angles to the joists, lift one or two boards to get access to the joists. Drill holes through the joists at least 50mm down from the top edge and big enough for the cable to pass through easily. Use a right-angle adaptor for this if you have one; otherwise drill the holes at a shallow angle.

2 Thread the cable through the drilled holes. Leave a little slack between the joists.

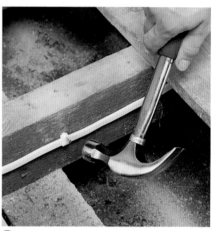

3 Where the cable runs along a joist, lift a floorboard (or a section of one) about every 500mm along the joist. Feed the cable beneath the boards and secure it with clips to the side of the joist. Run it 50mm below the top edge of the joist and hammer in a clip where the cable is exposed.

Burying a cable in plaster

1 Plan the route for the cable. It should run vertically above or below a socket outlet or switch. A horizontal run should be close to the ceiling or the skirting board. Never run it diagonally.

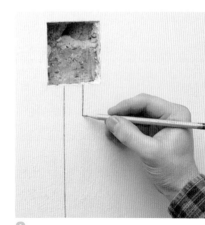

2 Mark the route with two lines 25mm apart. Avoid making sharp bends, wherever possible.

3 Check with a cable detector along the route to make sure that you are not going to interfere with any cables or pipes buried in the wall. If you are at all uncertain whether there is live wiring near the spot where you are working, switch off at the mains until you have made sure.

4 When you know that the route is safe, use a sharp knife to score along both edges of the chase.

5 Use a cold chisel and club hammer to cut out the plaster. Protect your eyes with safety goggles.

Alternatively Hire an electric chasing machine to cut out the chase. This creates a great deal of dust which spreads everywhere, so shut all doors.

6 Chisel out the plaster behind a skirting board where you are running a cable down the wall to run under the floor. You can do this without removing the skirting board.

Alternatively Use a long drill bit to make a hole behind the skirting board. Enlarge it with a cold chisel if necessary. This may be the easiest method if the skirting board is a deep one.

7 Check that the length of the chase is deep enough for the oval PVC conduit to fit easily. If it is too near the surface, only a skim of plaster or filler will cover it when you make good and it will probably crack. A covering of 5mm of plaster or filler over the conduit should be thick enough to stay sound and prevent cracking.

8 Feed the cable into the conduit and secure it in the chase with galvanised nails on each side. When the cable comes up behind a skirting, feed it into the conduit so that the end of the conduit is below the top of the skirting.

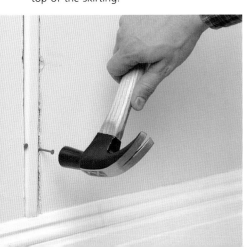

9 Leave enough spare cable at each end of the run to reach the mounting boxes easily. Ease the end of the cable or cables through the grommet into the mounting box. Slide the box into the recess and screw it into the wall behind.

Routes in stud partition walls

Cutting the route
With walls of plasterboard fixed to both sides of a timber frame, the cable can be run in the cavity behind the plasterboard. You will have to cut notches in the frame.

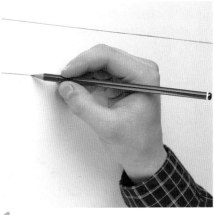

1 Use a bradawl to locate the frame, or a wiring detector to locate the rows of nails holding the plasterboard to the frame. Draw pencil lines to show where the timbers are.

2 With a sharp knife, cut away a section of plasterboard about 120mm square wherever your planned route crosses a frame member.

3 Chisel a groove in the exposed frame to hold the cable easily.

CABLE IN TRUNKING
Where it is not possible to lead cable under a floor or bury it in plaster, or if you want to reduce the labour, run the cable in surface-mounted mini-trunking. This protects the cable from damage as well as concealing it. The trunking is screwed or glued in place; the plastic cover clips on once the cables have been placed.

Mini-trunking is usually fitted along the top edge of skirting boards or alongside architraves. It is made in several sizes, some with two separate compartments.

Feeding in cable from above

1 Cut out a square of the plasterboard to reveal the top of the timber frame and drill a hole through it large enough to take the cable. You can use a long drill bit and drill at a slight angle, or fit a right-angle adaptor and drill vertically.

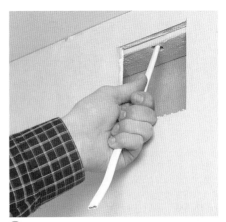

2 Thread the cable down through the drilled hole. Feed it down, ease it over each crosspiece of the frame and position it in the groove, allowing plenty of slack.

Feeding in cable from below

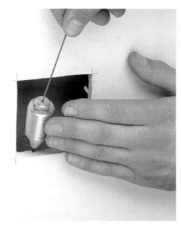

1 Cut out a square of plasterboard near floor level to reveal the base of the frame. Drill a hole through it for the cable, using a long bit and drilling at an angle or fitting a right-angle adaptor and drilling vertically. Feed a weighted cord down from the highest point the cable is to reach.

2 Tie the cord to the cable and draw it up carefully, easing it over each crosspiece of the frame, and position it in the prepared grooves. Leave plenty of slack in the cable.

Feeding in cable sideways

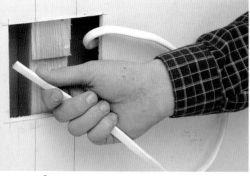

1 Push the cable along between the plasterboard panels. At each upright, draw out a loop of cable long enough to reach the next upright. Feed it along and set it in the prepared groove. When the cable is in the required position, fix it to the timbers with clips or cover the groove with a metal plate, pinned to the wood above and below, to prevent accidental damage from a nail or picture hook.

2 Cut new squares of plasterboard to replace the sections cut away. Tack them securely to the timbers at top and bottom, keeping the tacks well clear of the cable. Fill in round the edges of the squares with interior filler.

Fitting a plastic mounting box

Knock out the most convenient holes for the cable or cables to enter the mounting box. Hold the box in position, check with a spirit level that it is horizontal and draw a line round it. Cut away the marked section of plasterboard with a sharp knife. Feed the cable or cables into the box. Push the mounting box into the hole. Some boxes have spring-loaded fixing clips which simply snap into place as you push the box in; others have retractable lugs which you push out to hold the box. Prepare the conductors (page 271) and connect them to the terminals on the accessory faceplate. Screw the faceplate to the box.

Fitting a ceiling rose

A ceiling rose has to be screwed securely into wood above the plasterboard of the ceiling. It is not sufficient to screw it through plasterboard into a cavity fixing device. Plasterboard (or lath and plaster) is not strong enough to bear the weight of the light fitting and lampshade. The rose must be screwed to a joist or to a batten between joists.

1 Mark the spot on the ceiling where you want the light fitting to hang.

2 Drill up through the ceiling at the marked spot. If the drill strikes a joist, probe with a bradawl about 50mm round the hole until you find space above the plasterboard. Insert a piece of spare cable through the hole to stick up above the ceiling as a marker.

3 Examine the ceiling from above, lifting a floorboard if necessary, and locate the hole with its piece of spare cable identifying it.

4 If the hole for the cables is between joists, cut a batten to length to fit between the joists.

5 Lay the batten between the joists with its edge touching the hole for the cables and mark the edge just beside the hole.

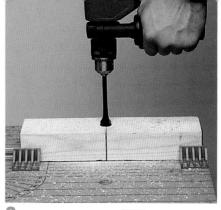

6 Drill through the centre of the batten, aligning the drill bit with the mark at the edge. The hole must be large enough to admit up to three or four cables.

Alternatively If the hole for the cables is immediately below a joist, chisel out a groove in the bottom of the joist to fit the cables. You may need to nail a block of wood to the side of the joist to widen it so you can screw the ceiling rose exactly where you wish. Chisel a groove down the side of the block that will fit against the joist. The groove must be large enough to hold three or four cables easily.

7 Thread the cables through the hole in the batten and then through the hole in the plasterboard.

8 Secure the batten to the joists with a nail hammered in at an angle at each end.

Alternatively Thread the cables through the prepared groove at the bottom of the joist and down through the hole in the ceiling. Fit the cables into the groove in the side of the prepared block of wood. Hold the block beside the joist and nail it in place, keeping the nails well clear of the cables.

9 Knock out the entry hole for the cables in the ceiling rose baseplate and thread the cables through the hole.

10 Hold the baseplate in place and insert a bradawl through the screw holes to penetrate through the plasterboard and pierce the timber above (see opposite).

11 Screw the baseplate into place.

Making good

Do not connect any sockets or switches until the walls or ceilings are made good or the connections are likely to be dislodged as you make the necessary repairs.

1 Fill all the chases cut in the plaster with new plaster or interior filler and leave it to dry completely. For the best finish, fill them in two stages and sand the repair smooth when the filler has set hard.

2 Replace any floorboards you have lifted. If any board is likely to pinch a cable where it starts to run up a wall from below the floor, cut a notch in the end of the board before you replace it. Boards, or sections of boards, that you may need to lift again in the future – to add a junction box in a lighting circuit, for example – should be screwed down, not nailed. They can then be lifted without being damaged.

Adding a spur to a ring main circuit

The easiest way of adding a socket outlet to your wiring system is to run a spur from an existing outlet on the circuit.

• The spur is wired from the back of the outlet and can supply one new single or double socket outlet, or one fused connection unit (FCU).
• Care is needed to find a suitable socket outlet for the spur connection. You must not use one that is already supplying a spur or is itself supplied as a spur.
• Make sure that the spur will not increase the floor area of the rooms served by the circuit to more than 100m².

Tools *Suitable tools for preparing the route (page 282): insulated screwdrivers; circuit tester; sharp knife; wire cutters and strippers; pliers.*

Materials *2.5mm² three-core cable; cable clips; green-and-yellow earth sleeving; mounting box with grommets and fixing screws; socket with switch.*

Finding a supply socket

1 Turn off the power at the consumer unit and take out the fuse or switch off the MCB protecting the circuit you want to work on. Check that the socket outlet is dead – for example, by plugging in a lamp that you know to be working.

2 Unscrew the faceplate of the socket outlet you plan to use for the spur. Ease it away from its mounting box until you can see the cables. If there is only one, the outlet is on a spur. If there are three, it is supplying a spur. Neither can be used to supply another spur.

3 A socket outlet with two cables may be suitable, but check with a circuit tester (see right) before you go ahead. It could be the first outlet on a two-outlet spur installed earlier (but not now permitted).

Preparation

When you have found a suitable socket outlet, ease its faceplate out and undo the terminal screws. Release the cores so that you can remove the faceplate. Remove the screws that hold the mounting box in place and carefully draw it out of its recess.

Prepare the route (page 282) for the cable from the supply socket to the new socket. Feed the cable ends into the mounting boxes for the new and the supply sockets after fitting grommets in the knock-out cable entry holes.

Fix the cable and the boxes in place (page 282) and prepare the new cable ends for connection (page 271). Put green-and-yellow sleeving on the bare earth cores.

Connecting at the supply socket

1 Match the cores on the new spur cable with those on the existing circuit cables – red to red, black to black, and green-and-yellow to green-and-yellow. Use pliers to straighten the original core tips if necessary.

2 Screw the cores tightly into the terminals on the faceplate.

The red cores go to the terminal marked L, the black cores to the one marked N, and the green-and-yellow-sleeved earth cores to the one marked E or ⏚.

3 Fold the cables carefully into the mounting box and position the faceplate over the box.

4 Screw the faceplate to the mounting box. Do not overtighten the screws or you may crack the faceplate.

Connecting at the new socket

1 Screw the cable cores into the terminals – red at L, black at N and green-and-yellow at E (or ⏚).

2 Fold the cables carefully into the mounting box and position the faceplate over the box. Screw it in place.

3 At the consumer unit, replace the circuit fuse or switch on the MCB and restore the power supply.

USING A CONTINUITY TESTER TO CHECK A SPUR

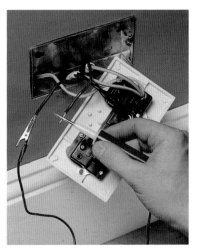

Use a continuity tester to check whether a socket outlet with two cables connected to it is on a ring main circuit.

1 Turn off the power at the consumer unit, remove the fuse or switch off the MCB protecting the circuit you will be working on, and unplug all appliances on the circuit.

2 At the socket outlet, disconnect the two red cores.

3 Attach the tester's clip to one end of each core and touch the probe to the other. If the socket is part of a ring circuit, the bulb on the tester will light up because you have completed the circuit; this is a suitable supply outlet for a spur.

If the tester does not light up, the outlet is itself on a spur and cannot be used to supply one.

Connecting a heated towel rail or electric radiator

The flex for an electrical appliance in a bathroom must be wired into a flex outlet plate that does not have a switch.

1 Run a cable from a fused connection unit (FCU) outside the bathroom (page 287) to the position of the flex outlet plate. Fit a recessed mounting box into the wall and feed the cable into it then connect the new cable at the FCU and the flex outlet plate.

2 Connect the flex cores to one set of terminals – brown to L, blue to N, and green-and-yellow to E or ⏚.

3 Connect the cable cores in the same way to the other set of terminals – red to L, black to N and green-and-yellow to E or ⏚.

4 Add a flying earth link between the earth terminals on the faceplate and in the mounting box (see page 279).

5 Screw the faceplate to the mounting box.

Wiring inside the bathroom

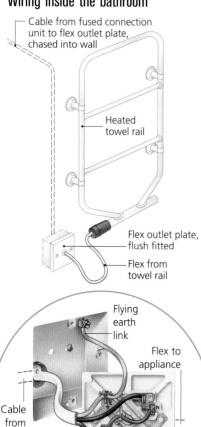

Cable from fused connection unit to flex outlet plate, chased into wall

Heated towel rail

Flex outlet plate, flush fitted

Flex from towel rail

Flying earth link

Flex to appliance

Cable from FCU

Connecting at the flex-outlet plate

Fitting a shaver point

The only electric socket outlet permitted in a bathroom is a shaver point. Connect it to the main power supply via an FCU outside the bathroom (page 287).

• There are purpose-made mounting boxes for shaver supply units. Surface-mounted boxes are available but it is safer to fit a flush-mounted metal box into the wall.
• You can install the unit on a spur led from a suitable existing socket outlet on a ring main circuit.
• The preparation and general principles of installing a shaver supply unit on a spur from a ring-main circuit are the same as those described for connecting heated towel rails or radiators at the supply socket or FCU (page 287). In the bathroom, connect the cable run from the FCU to the shaver socket (below).

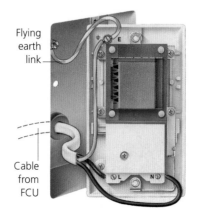

Flying earth link

Cable from FCU

Connecting at the shaver point

Installing a shaver point on a lighting spur

It is also common to install a shaver socket on a spur led from a junction box inserted in the lighting circuit above the bathroom.

1 Lead the spur cable from the lighting circuit to the shaver supply unit position, using 1mm² twin-core-and-earth cable.

2 Fit the mounting box for the shaver supply unit at about shoulder height on the wall. Feed in the cable through a grommet.

3 Prepare the end of the cable and connect the cores into the terminals on the shaver supply unit faceplate – red to L, black to N, and green-and-yellow to E or ⏚.

4 Fold the cable neatly into the mounting box and screw on the faceplate. Restore the power supply to the lighting circuit.

Installing an electric shower

An electric shower uses a lot of power in short bursts. It must have its own circuit leading from the consumer unit.

• Fit a 45amp rewirable fuse if the shower is rated at up to 8kW, and a 45amp cartridge fuse or MCB if it is rated at up to 10kW.
• The size of cable you need depends on the distance between the consumer unit and the shower heater, and on the shower wattage. Use 6mm² cable for a shower rated at up to 8kW and a circuit under 13m long. Use 10mm² cable if the circuit length is 13–20m long or if the shower is rated at more than 8kW. Use 16mm² cable if the circuit is over 20m long.
• The circuit cable runs first to a pull-cord switch with a neon indicator light.
• From the switch, the cable runs to the back or base of the shower heater unit, where it is connected to a terminal block inside the unit.
• Follow the maker's instructions on fitting the unit to the wall and plumbing it in.

Tools *Suitable tools for preparing the route (page 282); insulated screwdrivers; sharp knife; wire strippers and cutters; pliers.*

Materials *Two-core-and-earth cable of appropriate size; green-and-yellow plastic sleeving for earth conductors; cable clips; 45amp double-pole pull-cord switch with mechanical on/off indicator; shower heater unit; available 45amp fuseway or MCB at the consumer unit.*

Preparation

1 Plumb the unit over the bath or in a shower cubicle.

2 Take off the front cover of the shower heater and hold the back plate against the wall. Mark the wall through the cable entry point so that you know where to lead the cable, and also through the screw fixing points. Drill and plug the screw fixing points.

3 Check the earthing and bonding (page 267).

4 Prepare the route for the cable (page 282). There is no need to switch off the electricity until you are ready to make the final connection at the consumer unit. Make the route from the consumer unit to the pull-cord switch position on the ceiling of the bathroom or shower room. The switch must not be within the shower cubicle or directly above the bath. Continue the route from the switch to a point on the ceiling above the shower and then vertically down the wall to the position of the shower heater unit.

Wiring for an electric shower

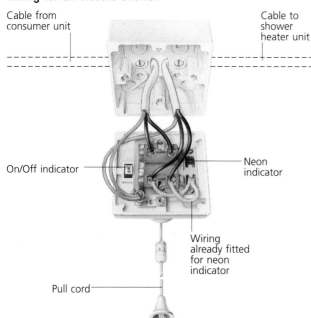

Cable from consumer unit

On/Off indicator

Neon indicator

Wiring already fitted for neon indicator

Pull cord

Cable to shower heater unit

Cable from switch

Connecting at the ceiling switch

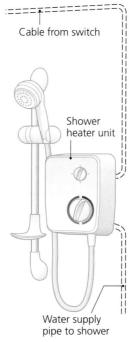

Cable from switch

Shower heater unit

Water supply pipe to shower

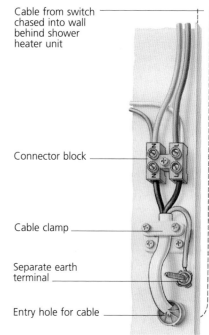

Cable from switch chased into wall behind shower heater unit

Connector block

Cable clamp

Separate earth terminal

Entry hole for cable

Connecting at the shower heater unit

---

5 Fit the baseplate for the switch to the ceiling (page 284), making sure that the fixing is secure enough to withstand the switch cord being pulled. Before you screw it in place, knock out two of the stamped circles for the cables to enter.

6 Lay the cable along the route, from the consumer unit to the double-pole switch and from the switch to the cable entry point on the shower heater unit. Allow sufficient cable at each end to reach all the terminals comfortably.

7 Feed the cable ends into the switch. Then feed the cable through the entry hole of the shower heater unit and screw the unit to the wall.

8 Prepare all the cable ends for connection (page 271). Fit green-and-yellow sleeving on all the bare earth conductors.

9 Complete the plumbing connections.

EARTH SAFETY

Cross-bond the shower supply pipework to earth by fitting an earth clamp to the pipe and connecting 4mm² single-core earth cable to it. Run the cable back to the consumer unit and connect it to the main earth terminal there.

For additional safety, the circuit should be protected by a residual current device (RCD). This may already be fitted in the consumer unit. Otherwise the circuit cable can be run via a separate RCD in its own enclosure.

Connecting the ceiling switch

1 Insert the two green-and-yellow sleeved earth cores into the terminal marked E or ⊥ and screw them tightly in place.

2 Connect the red and black cores of the cable from the ceiling switch to the shower unit. The red core goes to the terminal marked L and Load (or Out) and the black core to the terminal marked N and Load (or Out). Connect the neon indicator cores at the same time, one (it does not matter which) to the same terminal as the red cable core and the other to the same as the black core. Take care not to dislodge the bulb.

3 Connect the red and black cores of the cable from the consumer unit to the other terminals (marked Supply, Feed or In). Screw the red core to the terminal marked L and the black core to the terminal marked N. Fit the switch cover over the baseplate and screw the cover in place.

Connecting at the heater unit

Do not disturb the internal wiring already fitted in the shower unit.

1 Release the screws of the cable clamp, lead the cable under the clamp and screw the clamp back in place.

2 Connect the cores of the cable to the terminal block incorporated in the shower heater unit. Conductors will already be connected at one side of the block. Connect the red cable core to the terminal opposite the brown (or red) flex core, and the black cable core to the terminal opposite the blue (or black) flex core.

3 Instead of a pair of earth terminals on the connector block, there may be a single separate earth terminal marked E or ⊥. Connect the green-and-yellow sleeved cable earth core to this terminal.

Alternatively If the connector block has a third terminal for the earth core, connect the sleeved core to it opposite the green-and-yellow flex core already connected there.

Connecting the circuit at the consumer unit

If you do not have a spare fuseway or MCB, call a qualified electrical contractor.

1 Turn off the power at the consumer unit and remove the fuse or switch off the MCB you will be using for the new circuit.

2 Unscrew the cover of the consumer unit. If the unit has a wooden frame, drill a hole through it and feed in the new cable.

Alternatively On a metal unit, knock out the entry hole immediately above the MCB you will be using. Fit a rubber grommet into the hole and feed in the cable.

3 Check that you have stripped off enough outer sheath from the cable for the cores to reach their terminals easily.

4 Screw the cores tightly into their terminals: red to the terminal at the top of the fuseway or MCB; black to a free terminal on the neutral terminal block; sleeved green-and-yellow earth core to a free terminal on the earth terminal block.

5 Fit the 45amp fuse or 45amp MCB and replace the cover of the consumer unit.

Understanding an electric cooker circuit

An electric cooker uses so much electricity that it must have its own circuit. If it shared a circuit with other appliances the circuit would frequently be overloaded.

At the consumer unit The cooker circuit is protected by a 30amp fuse or MCB for a cooker rated at up to 12kW.
• A 45amp fuse or 50amp MCB is needed for a cooker rated at above 12kW.
• A separate oven and hob operating on the same circuit may have a higher rating than 12kW.

The cable runs from the consumer unit to a cooker control unit This is mounted above worktop height on the kitchen wall – beside the cooker, not above it.

From the control unit to the cooker The cable enters the appliance and is wired into its terminal block.
• The size of two-core-and-earth cable needed depends on both the wattage of the cooker and the length of the cable run. For a circuit with a 30-amp fuse or MCB, use 6mm² cable if the total length of the cable run is up to 20m, and use 10mm² cable if the total length of the cable runs is between 20m and 30m.
• For a circuit with a 45-amp fuse or 50-amp MCB, use 10mm² cable for a run of up to 10m, and 16mm² cable for a run of between 11m and 22m.

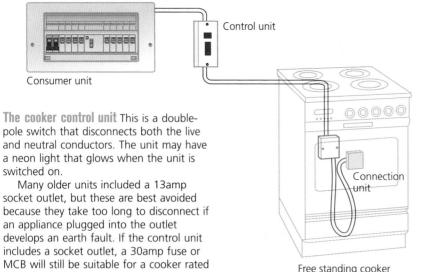

Consumer unit

Control unit

Connection unit

Free standing cooker

The cooker control unit This is a double-pole switch that disconnects both the live and neutral conductors. The unit may have a neon light that glows when the unit is switched on.

Many older units included a 13amp socket outlet, but these are best avoided because they take too long to disconnect if an appliance plugged into the outlet develops an earth fault. If the control unit includes a socket outlet, a 30amp fuse or MCB will still be suitable for a cooker rated at up to 10kW.

For a free-standing cooker A second length of cable runs from the control unit to a cooker connection unit fitted on the wall about 600mm above floor level behind the cooker. A 2m length of cable runs from the connection unit to the cooker, so that the cooker can be drawn away from the wall when necessary. Use the same size of cable for this as for the rest of the circuit.

For a separate oven and hob These can be connected to one cooker control unit provided that neither the hob nor the oven is more than 2m away from the control unit.
• You can make the connection by running two cables from the control unit, one to the oven and the other to the hob.
• Alternatively, you can run one length of cable from the control unit to one part of the cooker and a second length of cable from there to the second part of the cooker.
• No connection units are needed on the wall behind a separate oven and hob because they are permanently built in.

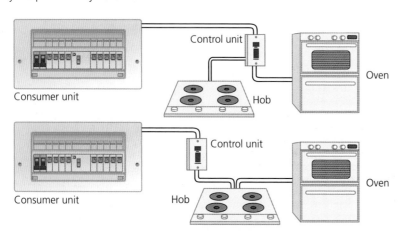

Consumer unit — Control unit — Hob — Oven

Consumer unit — Control unit — Hob — Oven

Wiring the circuit

Plan the cable route (page 282) from the cooker control unit back to the consumer unit. It can be run beneath floorboards and chased into plaster before approaching the control unit vertically; or the cable can be run in surface-mounted white plastic trunking at worktop or floor level.

Tools *Suitable tools for preparing the route (page 282); sharp knife; insulated screwdrivers; wire cutters and strippers; pliers.*

Materials *Cooker control unit with mounting box; cooker connection unit with mounting box (for a free-standing cooker); grommets; fixing screws and wallplugs; two-core-and-earth cable of the correct size; green-and-yellow plastic sleeving; cable clips; free-standing cooker or separate oven and hob; available fuse or MCB of the correct rating.*

Putting in the cables

There is no need to switch off at the mains until you are ready to connect the new circuit cable to the consumer unit.

1 Check the earthing and bonding (pages 267–8) and remedy any defects.

2 Prepare the route (page 282), leading it from near the consumer unit to the cooker control unit. From there lead it to the cooker connection unit behind a free-standing cooker, or to positions behind a separate oven and hob.

3 Fit the mounting box for the cooker control unit and, if you are installing a free-standing cooker, fit the mounting box for the connection unit. Remember to remove knock-outs from the mounting boxes for the cables to enter, and to fit grommets in the holes.

4 Fit lengths of cable along the route from the consumer unit to the control unit, and from the control unit to the connection unit or to positions behind the oven and hob. Do not feed the cable into the consumer unit but feed the other cable ends into the mounting boxes. Allow enough spare cable at the ends to reach all the terminals easily. Prepare the cable ends for connection (page 271), remembering to sleeve the earth conductors.

5 Repair the plaster and wait for it to dry. Replace any floorboards you have lifted.

Connecting at the control unit

1 Connect the cable from the consumer unit to the terminals of the control unit. Take the red core to the terminal marked L and In. Screw the black core into that marked N and In.

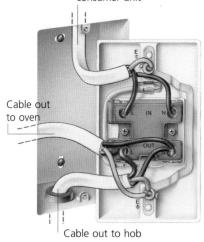

Cable in from the consumer unit

Cable out to oven

Cable out to hob

Connecting at the control unit
Two cables lead to a separate oven and hob. Only one goes to a free-standing cooker or to the oven and hob if they are to one side of the control unit.

Screw the green-and-yellow-sleeved earth core into the nearer of the terminals marked E or ⏚.

2 Connect the cable leading out to the connection unit or oven and hob into the terminals behind the control unit plate. Take the red core to the terminal marked L and Out, and the black core to the terminal marked N and Out. Connect the green-and-yellow-sleeved earth core to the nearer of the terminals marked E or ⏚.
   If you are leading separate cables to an oven and hob, there will be two outgoing sets of cores. Match the cores in pairs – red with red, black with black and green-and-yellow with green-and-yellow. Insert the pairs of cores into the correct terminals and screw them in place.

Connecting a free-standing cooker at the connection unit

1 Remove the screws holding the cover to the metal frame. Then unscrew and remove the cable clamp at the bottom of the frame.

Wiring at the connection unit

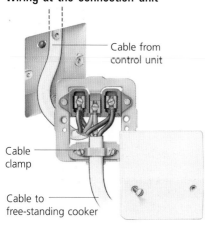

Cable from control unit

Cable clamp

Cable to free-standing cooker

2 Pair the cable cores from the control unit and to the cooker – red with red, black with black, and green-and-yellow with green-and-yellow. Screw the pairs into the terminal block on the frame – red to L, black to N and green-and-yellow to E or ⏚.

3 Screw the frame to the mounting box and screw on the cable clamp.

4 Screw the cover of the connection unit in place.

Connecting to a free-standing cooker

1 Remove the metal plate covering the terminals on the back of the cooker. Release the cable clamp.

2 Connect the supply cable cores to their terminals – red to L and black to N. Usually the cores have to be bent round a pillar and held down with brass washers and nuts. Make sure enough insulation has been removed for the bare wire to wind round the pillars. Connect the green-and-yellow sleeved earth core to E or ⏚.

3 Screw the clamp over the cable. Screw the plate back over the terminals.

Connecting to the consumer unit

1 Turn off the main switch at the consumer unit and take out the fuse carrier or switch off the MCB for the cooker circuit. Make sure the control unit and all cooker controls are off.

2 Remove the screws of the consumer unit cover and take it off.

3 Drill through the frame of the consumer unit if it is wooden, or knock out an entry hole and fit a grommet if it is a metal or plastic one. Feed in the cable. Make sure that you have removed enough outer sheath for the cores to reach the terminals.

4 Screw the black core into a spare terminal at the neutral terminal block and screw the red core into the terminal on the spare fuseway or MCB.

5 Screw the green-and-yellow sleeved earth core into a spare terminal at the earth terminal block.

6 Replace the circuit fuse or switch on the MCB.

7 Screw on the cover of the consumer unit and turn the main switch back on.

CONNECTING A SEPARATE OVEN AND HOB

If you have led two cables from the control unit, one each for the oven and hob, connect each cable in the same way as a free-standing cooker (left) and secure under the clamp.

Alternatively, if you have led one cable from the cooker control unit to the first component, you will have two cables to connect and clamp there – one from the control unit and one to the second component.

Match the cores – red with red, black with black, and green-and-yellow with green-and-yellow. Connect them to the terminals – red to L, black to N, and green-and-yellow to E or ⏚.

Connect the ongoing cable to the second component as for a free-standing cooker.

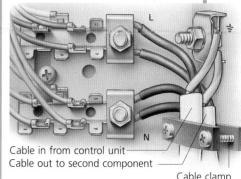

Cable in from control unit

Cable out to second component

Cable clamp

Installing a new ring main circuit

A ring main circuit to supply socket outlets starts at the consumer unit. A 2.5mm² two-core-and-earth cable runs round the rooms supplied by the circuit, looping into and out of each socket outlet before returning to the consumer unit to complete the ring.

If you have a modern consumer unit and are installing a new ring circuit – perhaps to serve an extension – you can connect the new circuit to the consumer unit. If you do not have a modern consumer unit, install the new circuit wiring then arrange with your local electricity supply company to fit a new consumer unit, connect it to their meter and wire in the new and existing circuit cables to it.

• Any number of single, double or triple socket outlets can be installed on the new ring main circuit, but the floor area of the rooms served by the circuit must not exceed 100m².

• If a socket outlet is needed in a position that is not on the most convenient route for the ring circuit, you can run a non-fused spur to it from one of the socket outlets on the ring, but you should avoid this as much as possible because it reduces the possibility of adding spurs later.

• The number of non-fused spurs must not exceed the number of outlets on the ring.

Tools *Suitable tools for preparing the route (page 282); sharp knife; insulated screwdrivers; wire strippers and cutters; pliers.*

Materials *Mounting boxes; screws and wallplugs; grommets; socket outlets (and perhaps FCUs); 2.5mm² two-core-and-earth cable; green-and-yellow plastic sleeving for bare earth cores; cable clips; fuses for FCUs; available 30amp fuse or MCB for the consumer unit.*

Preparation

1 Check the earthing and bonding (page 267) and remedy any defects.

2 Prepare the route (page 282), leading it from the consumer unit to the nearest socket outlet position on the new ring main circuit, and on from there to each socket outlet position in turn. Prepare the route for any spurs branching off the ring main circuit. Lead the route back from the final socket outlet position to the consumer unit.

3 Prepare recesses for the mounting boxes of the new socket outlets.

Planning a ring circuit

1 Draw a plan of the rooms that the ring circuit will supply. The length of cable must not exceed 60m. The new circuit might serve the kitchen only, all the other ground floor rooms, or all the upper floor rooms.

2 Mark on the plan where socket outlets are needed – and where they might be needed in the future. Most rooms will need sockets on at least two sides. Large rooms may need them on three sides and at two places along the sides. A choice of socket positions does away with flexes trailing across rooms.

4 Fit the mounting boxes in position, remembering to knock out the most convenient cable entry holes, and fit grommets in metal boxes.

5 Lay the cable along the route (page 283). Start above the consumer unit, leaving plenty of spare cable for the cores to reach the terminals in the unit easily. Do not interfere with the consumer unit at this stage. Continue along the route, taking the cable in and out of the most convenient entry holes at each mounting box. Cut the cable at each box, leaving 100mm spare at each cut. Fit branch cables along the route to any spurs. Again leave 100mm spare at each end of the cable. Lead the cable back from the last socket outlet on the circuit to the consumer unit.

6 Prepare all the cable ends for connection (page 271).

7 Repair the plaster and wait for it to dry completely. Replace any floorboards you have lifted. Do not fix them down if you will be removing old wiring from under them later.

Connecting the socket outlets

1 At each socket outlet, pair the two sets of cable cores – red with red, black with black, and green-and-yellow with green-and-yellow.

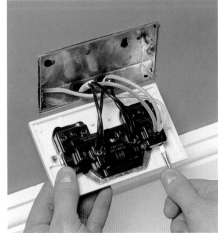

2 Screw the cores into the terminals on the rear of the faceplate – reds to L, blacks to N, and green-and-yellows to E or ⊕. Add a flying earth core (see step 3 on page 279) between the earth terminals on the faceplate and mounting box if the latter is metal.

3 Fold the two cables neatly back into the mounting box and press the faceplate into position over the box. Screw it in place until there is no gap between the faceplate and the mounting box. Do not overtighten the screws or the plastic may crack.

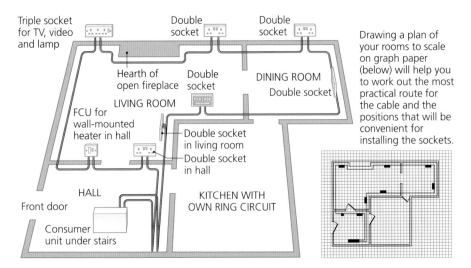

Triple socket for TV, video and lamp

Double socket

Double socket

Hearth of open fireplace

Double socket

LIVING ROOM

DINING ROOM

Double socket

FCU for wall-mounted heater in hall

Double socket in living room
Double socket in hall

HALL

Front door

Consumer unit under stairs

KITCHEN WITH OWN RING CIRCUIT

Drawing a plan of your rooms to scale on graph paper (below) will help you to work out the most practical route for the cable and the positions that will be convenient for installing the sockets.

3 Install a double socket at each new outlet. In a kitchen or living room, triple sockets may be wiser. At some positions you may want to fit a fused connection unit (FCU) rather than a socket for a stationary appliance, such as an extractor fan or freezer (page 286).

4 Very large consumers of electricity, such as cookers and instantaneous electric shower units, must have their own circuits.

Connecting spur socket outlets

1 At socket outlets supplying spurs, there will be three sets of cable cores – one from the previous outlet on the circuit, one going to the next outlet, and one for the spur. Match the cores in threes, then follow steps 2 and 3 from the previous section.

2 The socket outlet at the end of a spur has only one set of cores to connect. Follow steps 2 and 3 from the previous section.

Connecting FCUs

The appliance should be fitted in place, complete with its flex.

1 Feed the flex through the entry hole to the back of the fused connection unit (FCU) and prepare the end of the flex for connection (page 271).

2 Connect the flex cores – brown to L and Load (or Out), blue to N and Load (or Out), and green-and-yellow to the nearer of the two terminals marked E or ⏚.

3 Pair the cores from the two cables, red with red, black with black, and green-and-yellow with green-and-yellow. (If the FCU has been fitted at the end of a spur there will be only one cable.)

4 Connect the cable cores to their terminals – red cores to the one marked L and Mains (or Supply or Feed or In), black cores to the one marked N and Mains (or Supply or Feed or In) and green-and-yellow cores to the nearer of the two terminals marked E or ⏚. Add a flying earth core to a metal box (page 279).

5 Fit a 3amp or 13amp cartridge fuse in the fuseholder to suit the wattage rating of the appliance (page 270).

6 Fold the cable(s) and flex neatly into the mounting box and press the FCU faceplate into position. Screw it to the mounting box.

Having a consumer unit installed

If you do not have a modern consumer unit, arrange with your electricity supply company (or another approved electrical contractor) to install one. The installer will connect it to the meter and reconnect the new and existing circuit cables to it.

Testing the new circuit

Test the continuity of each conductor in the circuit (see panel, below right). Check and tighten all connections, if necessary.

Connecting at the consumer unit

1 Turn off the main switch on the consumer unit. Remove the retaining screws and the cover of the consumer unit.

SAFETY WARNING

The main switch disconnects only the MCBs or fuses and the cables leading out from the consumer unit to the household circuits. It does not disconnect the cables entering via the meter from the service cable. Do not interfere with these cables. They are always live at mains voltage.

---

2 Drill though the top of the consumer unit or knock out an entry hole and fit a grommet. Feed in the cables and make sure that enough sheath has been removed for the cores to reach the terminals easily.

3 Match the cores of the new circuit cables – red with red, black with black, and green-and-yellow with green-and-yellow.

4 Connect the cores to their terminals – red cores to the terminal on the spare fuseway or MCB, black cores to the neutral terminal block, and green-and-yellow sleeved earth cores to the earth terminal.

5 Switch on the MCB or fit the 30amp fuse and insert the fuseholder. Replace the cover of the consumer unit.

6 Turn on the main switch and test the circuit by connecting an appliance to each socket outlet in turn.

Disconnecting the old wiring

1 At the fuse board, turn off the main switch or switches that controlled the superseded circuits and remove any fuses. You can arrange for the electricity board to disconnect the old system from their meter.

2 Trace the cables leading from the switch to the old socket outlets down to the floor or up to the ceiling. Cut them off there.

3 At each of the old socket outlets, unscrew the faceplate and release the cable cores from the terminals. Unscrew and prise out the mounting box.

4 To remove all the old wiring you may have to lift several floorboards. Remove as much as you can and wherever possible any junction boxes, but leave any conduits in the wall. Repair the walls as necessary, and replace any floorboards you lifted.

5 Remove the old main switch and old fuse box once they have been disconnected by the supply company. Remove the cables that lead from them. If the old system has not been disconnected, do not remove the switch or fuse box. Keep the switch off and the fuse out.

TESTING A RING CIRCUIT

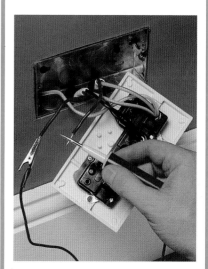

When you install a ring circuit, use a circuit tester to check that all the connections are sound before you connect it at the consumer unit. Where the two cable ends approach the consumer unit, clip the tester to the tip of one red core and put the probe on the other. If the tester fails to light, tighten the connections all round the circuit. Carry out the same checking procedure with the black and earth cores.

If the tester lights when it is linking two different cores there is a serious wiring fault and you should call in a qualified electrician.

Choosing light switches

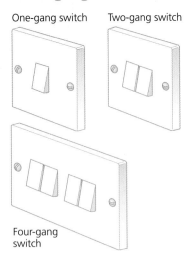

One-gang switch   Two-gang switch

Four-gang
switch

Plastic switches The most common are white plastic, designed to blend with light-coloured paintwork. There is no earth terminal for the cable behind plastic light switches; it is in the mounting box.

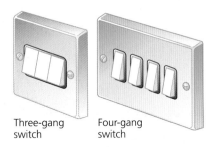

Three-gang
switch

Four-gang
switch

Metal switches Metal switches are made in satin finish or shiny brass, chrome or stainless steel; some have decorative scrolling at the edge. All metal switches must have an earth terminal on the rear of the faceplate. The switch rockers are fixed in plastic inserts.

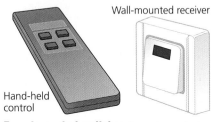

Wall-mounted receiver

Hand-held
control

Remote control switches Remote control switches are operated by an infra-red signal from a control unit; this triggers a wall-mounted receiver which acts as the switch. The receiver must be in sight of the control unit but can be up to 15m away. The switch can also be operated by hand.

Pull-cord switches
If a pull-cord switch is fitted in a bathroom the mechanism must be well out of reach of anyone who is using the bath or shower. Pull-cord switches are useful in bedrooms, too.

MOUNTING BOXES

Boxes for surface mounting can be metal or plastic, but flush-fitting boxes are only of metal. A single mounting box will take a faceplate with one, two or three switches (gangs); a double box is needed for a faceplate with four or six switches. All metal boxes must have an earth terminal for the earth core of the switch cable; many plastic boxes also have one.

Earth terminal

25mm metal box

Earth terminal

16mm metal box

Flush-mounting metal boxes A standard mounting box for a flush-fitted switch is made of metal and is 25mm deep. It is set in a recess in the wall and is screwed in place at the back. A plaster-depth box 16mm deep is also made and is used where space for the conductors is limited. Deeper (35mm) flush-mounting boxes may be needed for some dimmer switches.

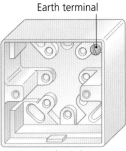

Earth terminal

16 mm plastic box

Surface-mounting boxes Surface-mounting boxes for light switches are normally plastic, but metal boxes are available to match metal light switches. Depths range from 16mm to 41mm; no hole is needed in the wall.

Boxes for architraves
Metal boxes for flush-mounted architrave switches are 27mm deep; plastic boxes for surface mounting are 16–18mm deep. Both types are available for mounting one-gang and two-gang switches.

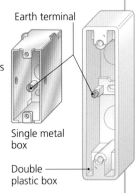

Earth terminal

Single metal
box

Double
plastic box

Boxes for stud partition walls Plastic boxes in several different styles are made for flush-fitting switches in plasterboard walls. They fit in a hole cut in the board, and have spring-loaded or rotating lugs at each side which grip the inner face of the board when the box is fully inserted. Single and double boxes are available.

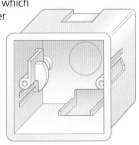

Plastic box with sprung lugs

Two-gang
dimmer

Dimmer switches Dimmer switches control the amount of light the bulb gives out. Dimmer switches can have push, sliding or rotary control; others have a touchplate. Ordinary dimmers cannot be used with fluorescent lights, but some can be used with low-voltage halogen lights.

One-
gang
switch

Two-gang
switch

One-
gang
switch

Architrave switches Architrave switches can be fitted to a door architrave or in limited wall space – for example, where two door frames are so close together that there is not enough space between them for a standard switch. Mounting boxes are made to suit them.

Standard light fittings

A ceiling rose is the connection point for the flex of a pendant light and the cables of the lighting circuit. The terminals on the rose baseplate are hidden by the screw-on cover.

The body of a lampholder is concealed inside a two-part heat-resistant cover. The top part conceals the terminals to which the pendant flex is connected. The lampshade ring secures the lamp-shade. You can buy pendant sets with the ceiling rose and lampholder pre-wired.

A batten lampholder is a ceiling rose and lampholder combined. Some batten lampholders have a deep shield over the metal bulb holder; they are for use in bathrooms to prevent accidental contact with the metal. Angled batten lampholders carry the lampholder at an angle to the base, and are intended for wall mounting – in an under-stairs cupboard, for example.

Ceiling rose

Lampholder

Batten holder

Low-voltage fittings

For essential information about low voltage lighting, see page 302.

see page 302.

WALL LIGHT FITTINGS

Small conduit box (BESA box) to use with internal wall light

The alternative is to use a fitting known as an LSC (luminaire supporting coupler) which comes in two parts: the 'socket' is attached to a conduit box in the wall; the 'plug' is on the light fitting.

Most wall lights have a circular backing plate which can be secured direct to a small conduit box (known to electricians as a BESA box), recessed into the wall. The wiring is then done inside the box, using a terminal connector cut from a strip of terminal connectors.

Terminal connector block

Uplighters are secured direct to the wall; again, the wiring can be done in a conduit box recessed into the wall.

Track lighting Mains-voltage track lighting can be wall or ceiling mounted and lengths of straight or curved track can be joined. Several types of small, neat light fittings are made to clip into the track. You can mount track over an existing lighting point, or lead flex to it from a lighting point a short distance away. Make sure that you will not overload the circuit if you fit a multi-spot track. If low-voltage halogen bulbs are used, the transformer can be built into the track, so no extra wiring is needed.

DECORATIVE LIGHT FITTINGS

There is a wide range of decorative light fittings available that are designed to be fitted flush to the ceiling surface or recessed into it.

• Light fittings with hollow baseplates may have a terminal block to which the circuit cables are connected.

• Alternatively they may have a flex tail which is connected to the lighting circuit cables using a separate strip of terminal blocks that is concealed within the baseplate.

• Light fittings with a flush baseplate must be installed over an enclosure recessed into the ceiling to contain the strip of terminal blocks that connect the fitting to the lighting circuit cables.

• Recessed light fittings are set in a hole cut in the ceiling surface. The connections to the lighting circuit cables are made within the ceiling void.

• Spotlights may be surface-fixed or recessed, and direct light in one direction only. 'Eyeball' lights are recessed and swivel to beam light at any angle. They vary in diameter but all need about 125mm of clear space above the ceiling.

• Spotlights and recessed lights can use reflector and halogen bulbs (page 296).

• Downlighters are fully or partly recessed, and cast light downwards only.

• The most economical but least attractive ceiling fitting is a fluorescent tube, covered with a diffuser.

• Heavier lights, such as chandeliers, must be supported by a chain secured to a ceiling joist.

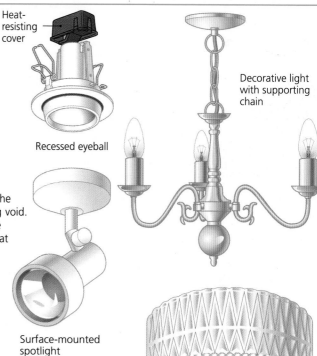

Heat-resisting cover

Recessed eyeball

Decorative light with supporting chain

Surface-mounted spotlight

Backplate and baffle for fluorescent tube

Flush ceiling light

Choosing light bulbs

The most usual source of lighting for the home, commonly called a light bulb, is properly called a tungsten filament lamp. In addition to standard light bulbs, there are low-energy and low-voltage bulbs available.

• Most light bulbs have a bayonet cap (BC) fitting to push into a BC lampholder. Some have Edison screws (ES) that fit into an ES lampholder.
• Filament light bulbs are made in a range of wattages, and last about 1000 hours.
• Long-life bulbs give a little less light and cost more, but last at least twice as long.
• Halogen lamps give a brighter, whiter light than tungsten filament lamps and also come in low-voltage types, that last twice as long.
• See page 304 for details of fluorescent tubes.

Pearl (BC)

Clear (BC)   White (BC)

Reflector bulbs
Used in spotlights and recessed lights, reflector bulbs direct light in a wide cone. They come in three main sizes: R50, R63 and R80, usually with an ES fitting.

Standard light bulbs The most common light bulbs are General Lighting Service (GLS) bulbs. They are used in pendant lights and table and standard lamps. Clear bulbs give extra sparkle to glass lampshades, and pearl bulbs diffuse the light more. Various festive bulbs are available and you can get bulbs in gentle, glare-free pastel shades, plus non-glare white for working at computers. Blue craft lights are ideal for close-up hobby work; low-wattage night-lights give soft, unobtrusive bedroom or passage lighting at night.

Halogen spots
Some mains voltage halogen spots can replace normal reflector bulbs; others need their own fitting with a 'twist-and-lock' action. For more information on low-voltage lighting, see page 302.

Halogen lamps These bulbs can directly replace standard bulbs, and give a clean, crisp white light. They are more expensive, but last twice as long. They are also available as candle bulbs for use in reflectors and uplighters.

Shaped bulbs
Used in wall and ceiling fittings, and available in a wide range of shapes, these lamps may have small bayonet caps (SBC) or small Edison screws (SES).

Low-energy bulbs Compact fluorescent lamps, designed to look like conventional light bulbs. They fit into standard bayonet or screw-in fittings, can use just one fifth of the energy of a normal filament bulb and last up to 12 times as long. They are expensive to buy, but will save you money over time. They are not suitable for use with dimmer switches.

Striplights Tungsten filament striplights are ideal for use under shelves, inside cupboards and above mirrors. To avoid glare they can be used with a baffle.

Replacing a one-way switch or fitting a new dimmer switch

If a switch faceplate is cracked, you must replace it at once to prevent the risk of users touching live parts.

Before you start If you want to fit a metal switch, the switch cable must have an earth core connected to an earth terminal in the switch mounting box.
• Most light switches control just one light, and are one-way switches with two terminals on the back. Switches with three terminals are needed only for two-way switching arrangements (page 297).
• You may want to replace an existing switch with a dimmer switch. Choose one that will fit the depth of the existing mounting box, and match its wattage range to that of the light(s) it will control.

Tools *Insulated screwdrivers (one with a small, fine tip).*

Materials *Light switch or dimmer switch.*

1 Turn off the main switch at the consumer unit and remove the fuse or switch off the MCB for the circuit you are working on.

2 Remove the screws securing the switch faceplate and ease it away from the mounting box. Keep the screws; the ones provided with the new switch may be metric and will not fit the lugs in an old pre-metric mounting box.

3 Use the fine-tipped screwdriver to release the switch cable cores from their terminals (see step 2, right). Connect the red and black cable cores to the new faceplate. If there is an earth core in the cable, it will be connected to an earth terminal in the mounting box and there is no need to disturb it.

4 If you are fitting a metal faceplate to a metal mounting box, add a flying earth link (page 279) between the earth terminal on the faceplate and the one in the box. On a plastic mounting box, disconnect the switch cable earth core from the terminal in the mounting box and connect it to the faceplate earth terminals.

5 Fold the switch cable back into the mounting box and screw the faceplate to it. Use the old screws again if necessary.

6 At the consumer unit, replace the circuit fuse or switch on the MCB and restore the power.

Replacing a one-way with a two-way switch

Two-way switches allow you to turn a light on and off from two switch positions. This is necessary for stairs and rooms with two doorways.

Before you start A length of three-core-and-earth cable has to be run between the two switches. A two-way switch has three terminals, usually marked L1 and L2 (or just 1 and 2) and COM (or COMMON). All two-gang switches are two-way types, but you can use them on a one-way system (using the common terminal and either of the other two terminals).

• In three-core-and-earth cable, the cores are colour-coded red, yellow and blue, and the earth core is bare as in other cables. There are no regulations about which terminals the three coloured cores should go to as long as the connections are the same in both switches. Usually the red core is connected to the common terminals of each switch, the yellow cores to L1 and the blue cores to the L2 terminals.

• It is also essential to tag the yellow and blue cores with red sleeving or red PVC insulating tape to show that they are live.

Tools *Suitable tools for preparing the route (page 282); insulated screwdrivers (one with a fine tip); sharp knife; wire cutters and strippers; pliers; cable detector.*

Materials *Two two-way switches; one new mounting box; screws and wallplugs; grommet; 1mm² three-core-and-earth cable; green-and-yellow plastic sleeving; red plastic sleeving or red PVC insulating tape; oval conduit; galvanised nails.*

1 Turn off the main switch at the consumer unit and remove the fuse or switch off the MCB protecting the circuit you are working on.

2 Undo the retaining screws that hold the existing one-way switch in place. Ease the faceplate away from the mounting box. Disconnect the two switch cable cores from their terminals and the earth core from its terminal in the mounting box. If the switch cable has no earth core, you must use only plastic switches and plastic mounting boxes.

3 Prepare the route (page 282) from the new switch position, up the wall, through the ceiling void and down the wall to the original switch position. Cut a chase for the new cable and a recess for the new switch mounting box. Cut a length of oval conduit to fit in the new chase, and feed one end of the three-core-and-earth cable into it. Run the cable through the ceiling void to a point above the existing switch.

4 Use a cable detector to locate the position of the cable running down to the original switch. Enlarge the chase between switch and ceiling level without damaging the cable. Cut a length of oval conduit to fit in the chase.

5 Pull the existing switch cable away from the mounting box and out of the newly-widened chase. Feed it and the new three-core-and-earth cable into the conduit and on into the existing mounting box. Fix the conduit in the chase with galvanised nails.

6 Feed the three-core-and-earth cable into the new switch mounting box and fix the box in its recess.

7 Prepare the cable for connection (page 271); remember to sleeve the bare earth cores. Use pliers to straighten the original cores.

8 At the original switch position, connect the red core from the original cable and the new yellow core to the terminal marked L1 on the new switch faceplate. Connect the red-tagged black core from the original cable and the new blue core to the terminal marked L2. Connect the new red core to the terminal marked COM.

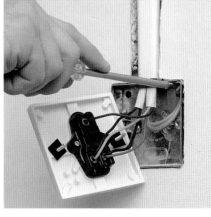

Screw the two green-and-yellow-sleeved earth cores into the terminal at the back of the mounting box.

9 If the new faceplate is metal, add a flying earth core (page 279) between the earth terminal in the mounting box and the earth terminal on the switch faceplate.

10 Fold the cables neatly into the mounting box and screw on the faceplate.

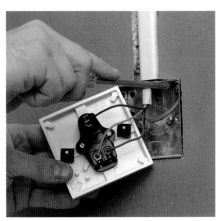

11 At the new switch position, connect the red core to the terminal marked COM, the yellow core to L1, the blue core to L2, and the green-and-yellow-sleeved earth core to the terminal in the mounting box. Again add a flying earth core if the new switch is metal.

12 Screw the new switch faceplate to its mounting box.

13 Make good round the new switch mounting box, and plaster over the two chases.

14 At the consumer unit, replace the circuit fuse or switch on the MCB, then restore the power and test the switches.

SWITCHES AND MOUNTING BOXES ON TRUNKING

Mini-trunking systems for carrying cable are connected to special surface mounting boxes with adaptors.

Replacing a pendant lampholder

Over time, lampholders and the flex they hang from get discoloured by the heat of the light bulb. Replacing them is a simple job, and gives the whole fitting a clean, fresh look.

Tools *Small electrical screwdriver; side cutters; wire strippers; trimming knife.*

Materials *Lampholder; 0.5mm² two-core flex, or 0.75mm² two-core flex for a heavy lampshade, or three-core flex if lampholder is metallic.*

1 Turn off the power to the lighting circuit at the consumer unit. Remove the lampshade, unscrew the ceiling rose cover and let it drop down the flex.

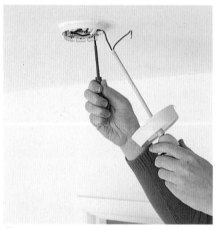

2 Note which flex core goes with which terminal on the baseplate of the rose. Loosen the terminal screws with your screwdriver and release the two cores. Take down the flex and lampholder, unscrew the lampholder cover and release the other end of the flex from its terminals.

3 Cut the new flex to length and remove the right amount of outer sheath from each end of the flex, using the old flex as a guide. Strip about 15mm of coloured insulation from each core and twist the wire strands together.

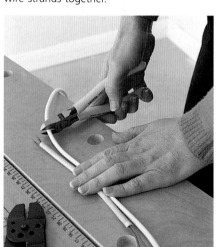

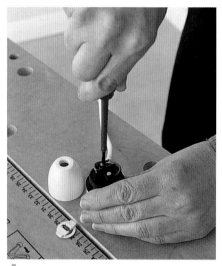

4 Connect the shorter pair of flex cores to the terminals in the new lampholder. Do the terminal screws up tightly, then hook each flex core over the plastic support lugs next to each terminal. Thread on the lampholder cover and screw in place.

5 Thread the cover of the ceiling rose on to the flex, then, with the new lampholder wired up, copy the original connections to screw the new flex to the terminals in the ceiling rose. Hook each core over its support lug and screw the rose cover on. Put back the lampshade and bulb, turn the power back on and test the light.

HELPFUL TIPS

• If you find the ceiling rose cover is stuck to the ceiling, run the tip of a knife round it to cut through any paint build-up that is locking it to the baseplate. If this doesn't work, there's no alternative but to crack the cover with a hammer, and then fit a new ceiling rose and cover.
• Release an old lampshade ring that is hard to undo by using a pair of pliers to crack the ring.

Repairing a pull-cord

A pull-cord may break at the point where it emerges from the switch. You don't need to replace the whole fitting – just buy a new cord.

Tools *Screwdriver; electrician's insulated screwdriver; scissors.*

Materials *Replacement cord. Possibly green-and-yellow earth sleeving.*

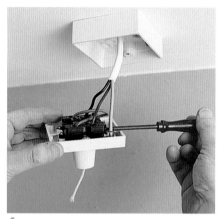

1 Turn off the power to the lighting circuit at the consumer unit. Loosen the screws securing the switch to its mounting box and pull it away. Note which cable core goes to which terminal on the switch baseplate, and then disconnect the cable cores from their terminals.

2 Remove the four screws securing the body of the switch to the back of the faceplate. Hold the two together as you do this to prevent the spring inside sending bits everywhere as you release the screws.

3 Lift off the body and examine how the switch works. In the example here, each pull of the cord turns the shaft with on/off markings 90° and makes or breaks the contacts within the switch.

4 Lift off the shaft with on/off markings so you can remove the nylon peg to which the pull-cord is attached. Leave the spring where it is. Make a note of the position of any small washers on the cord.

5 Make a knot at one end of the new cord, then thread the other end through the washer and the slot in the nylon peg. Feed the cord down through the spring and put the nylon peg back in. The wings on the side of the peg engage in the grooves beside the spring. Put the shaft with the on/off markings back in place.

6 Put the two parts of the switch together and replace the screws. Thread the cord through the fitting that connects it to the rest of the pull-cord, and knot it. Reconnect the circuit cable. If the earth core is bare, fit green-and-yellow PVC earth sleeving over it beforehand. Fit the switch back on its box.

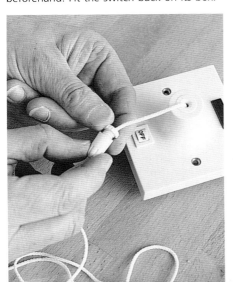

Installing a new ceiling light fitting

Replacing a ceiling rose and pendant lampholder with a new light fitting gives your room an instant update.

Tools *Screwdriver; electrician's insulated screwdriver; bradawl.*

Materials *New light fitting; 5amp connector strip. Possibly green-and-yellow earth sleeving.*

1 Turn off the power to the lighting circuit at the consumer unit. Take down the bulb and lampshade, then undo the ceiling rose cover and unscrew the rose baseplate. Note which cable cores go where before disconnecting them from their terminals.

2 Hold the baseplate in position and mark the positions of fixing holes on the ceiling, using a bradawl. If the new light fitting has room within its baseplate for the wiring connections, connect the existing cable to the fitting's terminal block.

3 Remove the terminal block from the baseplate. The fitting shown here is double-insulated and needs no earth connection, so the circuit cable earth core should be terminated in a 5amp strip connector. Wire the circuit cable live and neutral cores into the terminal block.

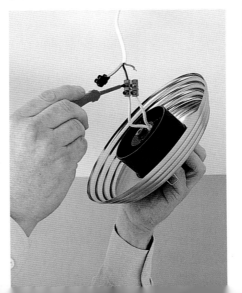

4 Put the main terminal block and the strip connector containing the earth terminal back into the baseplate. Push the excess circuit cable up into the ceiling void.

5 While holding the baseplate and surround in their final position, locate the fixing screws in the holes you have already marked, and fix screws in place to secure the fitting to the ceiling. Add a light bulb and diffuser. Switch on the power supply.

WHEN THE EARTH CORE IS MISSING OR BARE

• If there is no earth core in the light circuit cable to the old light fitting, only replace it with a double-insulated fitting marked with this symbol: ▣.
• If the earth core is a bare wire, cover it with green-and-yellow PVC earth sleeving before making the connections to the new fitting.

LOOP-IN WIRING

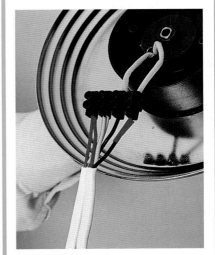

Two or three cables present at the existing ceiling rose indicates loop-in wiring, when the switch cable is wired into the ceiling rose. If this is the case, use four strip connectors wired up as above, with the circuit neutral core and the switch return core linked to the light's flex tails.

Adding an extra light

You can run a spur cable from a lighting circuit to supply an extra lighting point.

There are three places where the spur can start: at any ceiling rose on a loop-in system (page 306); at any box on a junction-box system (page 306); or at a new junction box inserted into the lighting circuit, whether it is a loop-in or a junction-box system.

Tools *Insulated screwdriver, tools for preparing the route (page 282); wire cutters and strippers; pliers.*

Materials *1mm² two-core-and-earth cable; green-and-yellow plastic sleeving; cable clips. Perhaps a three-terminal junction box to connect the spur cable.*

Preparation Turn off the main switch at the consumer unit and remove the fuse or switch off the MCB protecting the circuit you are working on. Prepare the route (page 282) and lay the new cable.

Adding to the last loop-in ceiling rose on the circuit

1 Unscrew the loop-in ceiling-rose cover and slide it down the flex. Then loosen the screws holding the rose baseplate to the ceiling. This will make it possible to work the new spur cable carefully through the ceiling in the same hole as the existing circuit and switch cables and through the entry hole in the ceiling rose.

2 Prepare the new cable for connection (page 271). Screw the rose baseplate back to the ceiling.

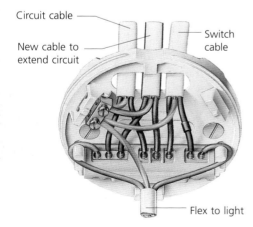

Circuit cable

New cable to extend circuit

Switch cable

Flex to light

3 Connect the red core of the spur cable to the spare terminal in the central terminal block, which already holds two red cores. Next, connect the black core to a spare

terminal in the outer terminal block to which the existing circuit cable black core is connected. Finally, connect the green-and-yellow-sleeved earth core to the separate earth terminal.

4 Screw the ceiling rose cover back in place.

Adding a spur to a junction box wiring system

1 Remove the cover of the junction box where the spur will start. You can knock out an entry hole in it for the spur, or let the spur share the same entry hole as an existing cable.

2 Prepare the spur cable for connection (page 271) and feed it into the box.

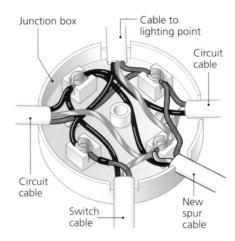

Junction box

Cable to lighting point

Circuit cable

Circuit cable

Switch cable

New spur cable

3 Connect the red core of the spur cable to the terminal where two or three red cores are already connected. Connect the black core to the terminal where two or three black cores are already connected. Connect the green-and-yellow-sleeved earth core to the terminal where the other earth conductors are already connected.

4 Screw the cover on the junction box.

Leading a spur from a new junction box in the circuit

1 Trace the cable to which you plan to connect the spur, to make sure that it is not a switch cable but the circuit cable running from one loop-in rose or junction box to the next.

2 Screw the baseplate of the new junction box to the side of a joist so that the circuit cable runs across it.

3 Cut the cable over the centre of the box, then strip back enough of the outer sheath to allow the cores to reach their terminals with the sheath still within the box. Then strip about 15mm of the core insulation from the live and neutral cores.

4 Sleeve the bare earth core with green-and-yellow sleeving.

5 Prepare the ends of the spur cable for connection.

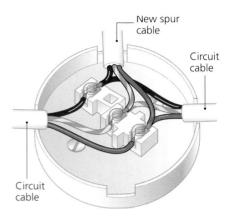

New spur cable

Circuit cable

Circuit cable

6 Connect the spur cable red, black and earth cores into the same terminals as the circuit cable cores. Then screw the cover back onto the junction box.

At the new lighting point

At the new loop-in ceiling rose, connect in the spur cable cores – the red core to the central terminal, the black core to one of the outer terminals and the sleeved earth core to the earth terminal. Connect the flex cores to the outer terminals. Run the switch cable to the new switch position and connect it to the switch terminals.

Next, connect the switch cable at the rose. The red core goes to the centre terminal, the black core to the outer terminal where the brown flex core is connected and the earth core to the earth terminal. Identify the black core as live by wrapping some red PVC tape around it.

Adding a point for a wall light

You can add a wall light by leading a spur from an existing lighting circuit.

Before you start The wall light may incorporate its own switch; if it does not, you can take the spur in and out of a junction box in the ceiling void and connect the new switch cable there.
• The wall light connections must be in a heat-resisting enclosure, so you may need to fit a metal mounting box in the wall.
• If the base of the light fitting is too small to conceal a square box, use a slim architrave mounting box. Use a round dry-lining box in a timber-framed partition wall.
• Choose a light that has been wired with an earth conductor or is double-insulated (marked ⧈).

Wiring to a wall light

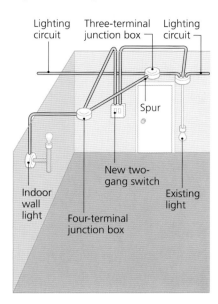

Lighting circuit | Three-terminal junction box | Lighting circuit

Spur

New two-gang switch

Indoor wall light | Four-terminal junction box | Existing light

Tools *Suitable tools for preparing the route (page 282); insulated screwdrivers; sharp knife; wire cutters and strippers; pliers. Perhaps a circuit tester.*

Materials *Wall light; 1mm² two-core-and-earth cable; green-and-yellow earth sleeving; metal mounting box, slim architrave box or round dry-lining box; short length of green-and-yellow-insulated earth conductor; connector block with three pairs of terminals (cut from a strip). Perhaps a three-terminal junction box for connecting the spur. For a separate switch, four-terminal junction box; red plastic sleeving; two-gang light switch.*

Preparation Turn off the power at the main switch in the consumer unit, and remove the fuse or switch off the MCB protecting the circuit you will be working on. Prepare the route for the spur cable. You will need to lead it above the ceiling from a convenient spot on the lighting circuit to a point immediately above the wall light position, and then down the wall.

The wall light should be about 1.8m above floor level. Make a recess there for the mounting box or slim architrave box, or cut a round hole in a plasterboard wall for a dry-lining box.

If the wall light incorporates a switch, lead the spur cable route above the ceiling to a spot halfway between the wall light position and the switch position and fit the four-way junction box there. Continue the cable run from there to the wall light position and run another cable from the junction box to a point directly above the switch. You will probably be able to complete the route by enlarging the recess in the plaster leading down the wall to the existing switch. Take great care not to damage the existing switch cable. Unscrew and disconnect the switch. You can use the single mounting box already fitted and fit a two-gang switch over it when you are ready to make the connections.

1 Lay the spur cable along the route from the circuit either to the wall light position or to the junction box position, and from there to the wall light position and also to the switch position if necessary. Secure the cable along the route.

2 At the wall light, feed the cable into its mounting box. If you are fitting a switch, feed the switch cable into its mounting box.

3 Prepare the new cable ends for connection. If you are fitting a switch, slide a piece of red sleeving on the switch cable's black core at each end.

4 Connect the spur to the lighting circuit (opposite).

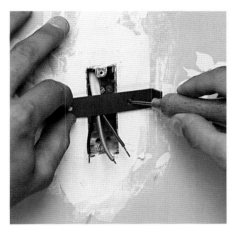

5 Hold the wall light or its bracket in place and push the bradawl through its fixing holes to check that they match up with the lugs of the mounting box. If they do not align with the box lugs – or if you are using an architrave box – make drilling marks with the bradawl. Drill at the marks and plug the holes.

6 Make good any plaster damage.

Connections at the wall light

1 Connect the red and black spur cable cores to the two outer terminals on one side of the connector block.

2 At the central terminal on the same side, connect the spur cable earth core. If you are using a metal mounting box, connect a flying earth core (page 279) to the central terminal. Connect the other end of this earth core to the earth terminal in the box.

3 Connect the flex cores from the wall light to the connector block with brown, blue and green-and-yellow cores opposite the red, black, and green-and-yellow cable cores respectively.

4 Screw the wall light over the mounting box.

For a separate switch

1 Make the connections behind the new two-gang switch. All two-gang switches are designed to operate as two-way switches. When you use one as part of a one-way system, you must use the Common terminal and one of the other two terminals. Connect the new red and red-sleeved black cores to the first switch gang using the terminals marked Common and either L1 or L2.

Connect the cores from the original cable to the second switch gang in the same way.

Screw both the green-and-yellow-sleeved cores into the earth terminal at the back of the box.

2 Screw the switch faceplate to the mounting box.

3 At the junction box, connect the red cores from the spur and switch cables to one terminal.

4 Connect the black cores from the spur cable and the cable leading to the wall light to another terminal.

5 Connect the red core from the wall light cable and the red sleeved black core from the switch cable to a third terminal.

6 Finally, connect all the green-and-yellow-sleeved earth cores to the fourth terminal.

7 At the consumer unit, replace the circuit fuse or switch on the MCB and restore the power.

Choosing low voltage lighting

Low voltage lighting uses a transformer to step down mains electricity to just 12 volts. A transformer can be attached to each individual light, or one transformer can supply several lights. A transformer can be large and heavy, so mounting it away from the lights often makes sense. One major advantage of low voltage lighting is that the risk of electric shock is minimal – it is quite safe to touch the terminals on the low voltage side of the transformer.

Separate transformers Having a separate transformer makes the light fitting compact and easily fitted into a confined space. A single transformer can run several lights, or each light may have its own box. The transformer can be mounted near the mains power supply, allowing unobtrusive cables to run to the light fitting or it can be slotted into the ceiling void alongside the light. Compact and maintenance free, transformers are a fit-and-forget item that can be hidden away on top of a kitchen cupboard or in a ceiling or wall space.

Integral transformers The outward appearance of these lights is similar to those that have a separate transformer, but these have a transformer built in to each lamp. They are generally more expensive than those with a remote transformer as not only are you paying for the cost of the lamp but also the cost of a transformer for each light source. Also, while each light fixture may be small, its transformer may be fairly bulky and this must be taken into account when siting lights.

individually or in groups or clusters where more light is required. One spotlight lamp is made up of 15 LEDs and has a life of 50,000 hours.

LEDs have several advantages: they are virtually everlasting; they don't emit heat; and they consume very little electricity. You can really indulge your fantasies with this type of lighting. For example, one LED lets you change its colour according to your mood. This lights comes with a controller that lets you alter the speed of colour change through a rainbow spectrum or choose a specific colour.

You can also fit walk-over LEDs into floors, both indoors and out. Because these lights remain cool to the touch, they are safe for use in playrooms.

Dimming If low voltage lights are to be dimmed then the dimming control must be mounted on the primary or 230 volt side of the circuit (not the transformer side). Dimming increases lamp life for low-voltage lighting, as it does for regular light bulbs.

Colour All light has what is known as a colour temperature. The higher the number, the whiter the light appears. Many low voltage lights used in shops for display purposes use halogen bulbs, which appear too white and stark for domestic use. For room lighting, low voltage incandescent bulbs give a warmer more relaxing light.

LEDs A relatively new innovation is the use of LEDs (light emitting diodes) as a light source. Until now, LEDs have been limited to indicator lights and panel lights in cars and other electronic equipment, but with the advent of ultra-bright versions, they are being used increasingly as light sources in their own right. They can be used

Choosing fluorescent lamps

A fluorescent lamp uses electronic discharge to illuminate the coating of a tube rather than relying on the glowing of a tungsten filament. It gives roughly five times as much light per watt as a tungsten light bulb and lasts at least ten times as long.

Fluorescent tubes Long white tubes, for use in fluorescent light fittings with a starter, are a fixture of many homes. However, they now come in a range of sizes and colours, including warmer tones than the traditional clinical white. The most common sizes are 26mm in diameter (labelled T8) and 16mm (T5). Less efficient 38mm (T12) tubes are still sold for older fittings. Power output depends on length: 600mm is 18W, 1200mm is 36W and 1500mm is 58W. Long-life fluorescent tubes are also available. The most energy efficient is the tri-phosphor tube which shows true colours without flickering.

Compact fluorescent lamps Also known as energy-saving lamps. These work in the same way as fluorescent strip lights, but the tube is bent back on itself and the control gear is built in, so they can be used to replace normal light bulbs with a screw or bayonet fitting.
• An 11W CFL replaces a 60W light bulb
• A 20W CFL replaces a 100W light bulb

Other options Fluorescent tubes are available in a range of shapes, including pencil shapes, bent tube shapes and glass covered lamps, which look similar to the standard light bulbs they are meant to replace. Circular fluorescent tubes are still available but are mainly restricted to use in magnifying glasses. Square (2-D) lamps have their own range of special fittings including porch lights, bulkhead lights and ceiling lights.

Fitting worktop striplights

Fitting striplights under wall-hung kitchen cupboards will throw much needed light onto a work surface beneath. A narrow trim (baffle) along the front will conceal the lights.

This is an easy job that doesn't involve mains wiring work. Once the lights are in position, you simply plug the master light (the first in the run) into a nearby mains socket, which powers all the lights. Each light has its own rocker switch. Make sure the plug has a 3amp (red) fuse, not a 13amp (brown) one.

The striplights are sold in kit form – together with fixing screws, cable clips and two-core connecting flexes that simply plug in to link the run of lights together.

This type of fitting is unsuitable for bathrooms, as the tubes are not protected from splashes.

1 Allow one fitting for every 500mm of worktop. Lay the kit out along the worktop to plan exactly where you will fit the lights, making sure that there is a socket within reach of the master light (the one with a flex and plug).

2 Mark a guideline under the units at least 50mm from the back wall. The rear of the baseplate of each light will lie against this line. If the lights are fixed too near to the wall they may overheat.

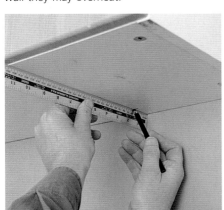

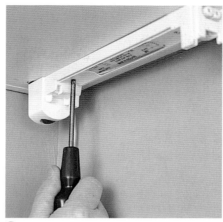

3 Remove the tubes and their holding covers and hold the first baseplate in position. Mark the positions for the fixing screws with a bradawl; you may wish to drill pilot holes. Then fix the baseplate to the underside of the cupboard using the screws provided in the kit.

4 Repeat the process for the second and any further lights, holding each baseplate against your guideline as you make the marks for the screw holes. Fix all the baseplates in position.

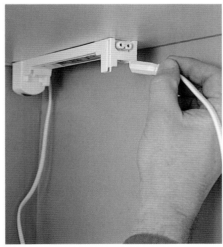

5 Once all the lights are in position, use the connecting cables to link them all together. Each linking cable has a plug at one end and a socket at the other, so it will be obvious how to fit them.

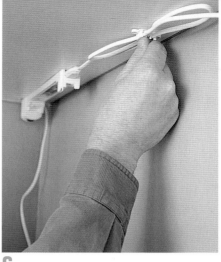

6 Neaten any excess cable using the plastic clips provided. This involves looping any surplus cable through the slots in the clip, and then fixing the clip to the underside of the cupboard with its adhesive pad.

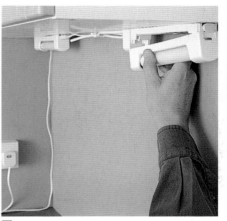

7 Put the covers and tubes on each light, plug in and switch on at the mains socket, and test each light using its rocker switch.

HELPFUL TIP

This type of lighting is not particularly attractive, but you can hide it with a strip of wood known as a baffle, without sacrificing any light. Buy a length of wood moulding (this can be painted to match your colour scheme) and fix it to the underside of the cupboards using an instant-grip adhesive.

Wiring in fluorescent lights

It is not always feasible or desirable to fit a lighting kit that runs from a mains socket. You may need to wire a fluorescent lamp fitting into the mains lighting circuit. If you are in any doubt about tackling this type of work, then hire a qualified electrician.

Fluorescent lights make good task lighting: a lamp above a desk or a dressing table, for example. They are also used as accent lights, to illuminate a picture or another feature in a room. In these instances, you will want to hide the wiring. The light itself can be operated with a pull-cord or rocker switch, or a wall-mounted light switch, usually sited near the door.

Tools *Bradawl; tools for preparing the route (page 282); sharp knife; wire cutters and strippers; insulated screwdrivers; pliers.*

Materials *Light fitting; two-core-and-earth cable; green-and-yellow earth sleeving; cable clips. Perhaps also four-way junction box; one-way light switch with mounting box, fixing screws; grommet; red plastic sleeving; insulating tape.*

Before you start To connect the fitting to the electricity supply, you will need to lead a spur to it from the lighting circuit (page 300). Remove any baffle and end covers from the fitting. Hold the base plate against the wall (or shelf) and mark the fixing points and, if necessary, the cable entry hole. Drill holes at the marks and screw the base plate of the light fitting firmly in place.

Fitting a light with a built-in switch

1 Turn off the main switch at the consumer unit and remove the fuse or switch off the MCB protecting the circuit you are working on. Thread the spur cable into the light fitting through the entry hole.

2 Connect the cable cores to the terminals of the connector block in the light fitting. Connect the red core opposite the brown flex core, the black core opposite the blue flex core, and the green-and-yellow core to the terminal marked E or ⏚. If the fitting is double-insulated (marked ▣) and has no earth terminal, cut the earth conductor of the cable and seal it with insulating tape.

3 Screw the end covers in place and fit the baffle or shade.

Fitting a light with a separate switch

1 Turn off the main switch at the consumer unit and remove the fuse or switch off the MCB protecting the circuit you are working on.

2 Lead a spur from the lighting circuit (page 300) to a junction box in the ceiling space or loft above the position for the light.

3 Prepare the cable routes. You will need one cable run from the junction box to the lighting point and another from the junction box to the switch position. Fit a mounting box for the switch.

4 Lay cable from the junction box to the light. Feed it into the light fitting through the entry hole.

5 Then lay cable from the junction box to the light switch position and feed it into the mounting box.

6 Prepare all the cable ends for connection. Remember to put a piece of red plastic sleeving over the black core of the switch cable at both ends to show that it is live.

8 Attach the light fitting and connect the cable to the terminal block (left, step 2).

9 At the light switch, connect the red core to one of the terminals and the red-sleeved black core to the other terminal. Connect the green-and-yellow earth core to the earth terminal in the mounting box. Screw the switch faceplate to its mounting box.

10 At one terminal in the junction box, connect the red cores of the spur cable and the switch cable. At another terminal connect the black cores of the spur cable and the cable from the light. At a third terminal connect the red core of the cable from the light and the red-sleeved core of the switch cable. At the fourth terminal, connect all the earth cores.

HELPFUL TIP

Tungsten filament lights are becoming more popular than fluorescent strips, because they give a better, cleaner light. However, tungsten lamps also give off heat, so old-fashioned fluorescent strips are a better choice for lights mounted beneath kitchen wall cupboards.

Fitting low-voltage spotlights

Brilliant, low voltage lights are ideal for kitchens. Because they are small, it is possible to site lights directly above where they are needed, thus avoiding the shadows and dark areas that can arise with more traditional centrally mounted lighting.

These instructions that follow relate to a typical installation of ceiling mounted recessed lights. Not all lights are identical, so be sure to read and understand the installation instructions that come with your particular lights, as there may be differences from those described here. The manufacturer's instructions will outline any restrictions on siting the lights and transformer.

Tools *Pencil; padsaw, or power drill with holesaw attachment, probably 57mm in diameter; compasses; insulated screwdriver; wire cutters and strippers.*

Materials *Low voltage light set; existing light fitting; two-core-and-earth cable; transformer; 5amp plastic strip connectors; green-and-yellow earth sleeving.*

Before you start Although low voltage lighting is very safe, the transformers connect to the 230-volt mains circuit and must be treated with the utmost respect.

1 Decide on where you want to site the lights and draw circles on the ceiling the same diameter as the light fittings. Then use a holesaw of this diameter – usually 57mm – fitted to a power drill, to cut perfect holes fast and accurately.

3 Insert the transformer through the hole you cut for the light fitting – it will be small enough to fit. Then you will need to access the ceiling void in order to position the transformer at least 100mm from the first light position. This will necessitate either lifting the floorboards of the room above or gaining access from the loft if you are working in an upstairs room.

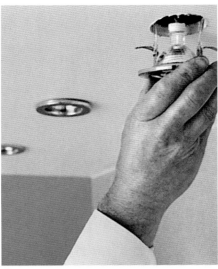

6 Fit two spring clips to each light fitting and insert the light fittings into the holes until you hear them click: as you push the light up, the shorter arms on the clips force the longer arms to flatten against the upper surface of the ceiling.

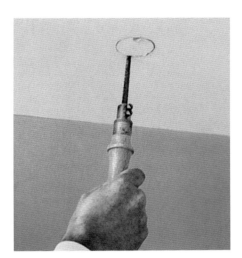

Alternatively Drill a hole inside each circle large enough to admit a padsaw blade and cut the holes by hand.

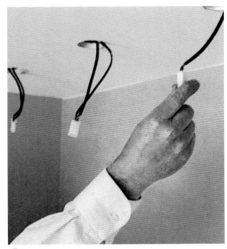

4 Still working from above, connect the wiring harness to the transformer output socket. Then take the pre-wired leads above the ceiling to the light holes. Use a power drill with a 12mm wood bit if you have to make cable holes through any joists. Feed a lead down through each hole. Then return to the room and pull each lead to its full length through the hole.

5 Connect each light to the harness by plugging it in and engaging the holding clip. Then give each cable a little tug to make sure the clip has engaged properly.

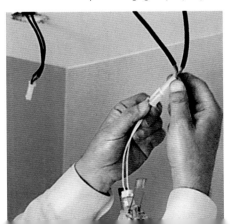

7 Fit a halogen bulb into each light fitting and snap on the metal ring clip to hold in place. Turn on the power at the main switch to check the operation of the lights. If you need to change a bulb at a later date, gently squeeze the ends of the metal ring clip together, using pliers, so you can remove it and take out the bulb. Be sure to replace it with one of the same wattage.

2 Switch off the power at the mains and remove the fuse or switch off the MCB protecting the circuit you are working on. Connect a length of 1mm² two-core-and-earth cable to a nearby ceiling rose and run it to the position of the first light. Join it to the transformer supply lead with plastic strip connectors. (See page 299 for more detail on ceiling rose connections.)

Wiring a new lighting circuit

Lighting circuits are wired with 1mm² two-core-and-earth cable. A house usually has two lighting circuits, one serving the downstairs and the other upstairs. You may need an extra circuit if you want to install a lot of extra lighting, or if you build an extension.

A lighting circuit is protected by a 5amp fuse or a 5 or 6amp MCB at the consumer unit. The maximum load that one circuit can supply is 1200 watts – that is twelve 100 watt light bulbs, or any combination of wattages adding up to 1200. In practice not more than ten lighting points are connected to one circuit.
• Bear this in mind especially when you are considering fitting a multi-spotlight track; it could overload the circuit and may require an extra circuit of its own.

For each lighting point on the circuit, the cable passes through either a loop-in ceiling rose or a junction box and is connected to terminals there. From the rose or junction box, wiring leads off to the light and to the light switch. In many houses, a light circuit will include both loop-in ceiling roses and junction boxes.

Loop-in system

A loop-in ceiling rose has a row of terminals to connect in three cables – the two circuit cables, and the switch cable – and the flex that goes to the lampholder. If the rose is the last one on the circuit, there will be only one main circuit cable.

All the connections, except the earths, are made to the same row of terminals. All can be reached simply by unscrewing the rose cover. There is no need to lift floorboards in the room above to reach them, as with junction boxes.

Junction box system

The circuit cable is not led to the lighting point but to a junction box between the lighting point and the switch position. The junction box has four terminals for connecting four cables – two circuit cables, the switch cable and the cable to the lighting point.
• This system is seldom used for a whole lighting circuit because of the extra work involved in installing a junction box for each lighting point, and the fact that once the wiring is completed the connections are not accessible without lifting a floorboard. But there are some situations where it is needed for individual lighting points. For example, strip lights, spotlight tracks, recessed lights and some other special fittings are not designed for loop-in wiring; instead they incorporate a connection block or a flex for connection to a cable from a junction box.

Planning the circuit

Consider whether each lighting point will be better suited to loop-in or junction box wiring. Position any junction boxes in a ceiling space or loft where you can screw them to joists.
• Cables to light switches must run from the rose or junction box to a spot directly above the switch and then be chased in plaster, or led inside a stud partition wall, or in trunking vertically down the wall. Never run cables diagonally across walls; there is a danger of piercing them later with fixings for pictures or built-in furniture.

Installing the circuit

Tools *Suitable tools for preparing the route (page 282); sharp knife; wire cutters and strippers; insulated screwdrivers; pliers.*

Materials *1mm² two-core-and-earth cable; green-and-yellow sleeving; red sleeving; ceiling roses; flex; lampholders; light switches with mounting boxes, screws and grommets; available 5amp fuseway or MCB in consumer unit. Perhaps 1mm² three-core-and-earth cable for two-way switches; special light fittings.*

1 Prepare the route for the circuit cable. Lead one end into the consumer unit for connection later, and run it up to ceiling level. If it is to go above the ceiling, you will have to lift floorboards to run it along and through joists.

2 Prepare the routes for the switch cables which will run from every loop-in-ceiling rose or junction box to the switch positions. If a light is to be controlled by two-way switches (page 297), prepare a route to the second switch position.

3 For lighting points that will be wired on the junction box system, prepare routes from the junction boxes to the position for the lights.

4 Fit ceiling roses where there are to be pendant lights.

5 Fit junction boxes where necessary for special light fittings, screwing the bases of each to the side of a joist.

6 Fit mounting boxes for all the switches.

7 Lay lengths of cable from above the consumer unit to the first ceiling rose or junction box, from there to the next rose or box, and so on. Leave enough cable at the ends of each length for the cores to reach all the terminals easily. Secure the cable by threading it through joists or by driving in clips to hold it to the sides of joists.

8 Lay and secure switch cables from each loop-in ceiling rose or junction box to each switch. For any two-way switches, lay three-core-and-earth cable to connect the two switches. Allow enough cable to reach all the terminals easily.

9 Feed the cable ends into ceiling roses or junction boxes and into the light switches.

10 Prepare the cable ends for connection. Sleeve the earth conductors and on all switch cables put red sleeving over the black conductor at both ends.

11 For each ceiling rose, cut a length of flex that will allow the lampholder to hang at the desired height. Connect the flex to the lampholder first, then slide the cover of the ceiling rose onto the flex and connect it to the rose.

Loop-in wiring system

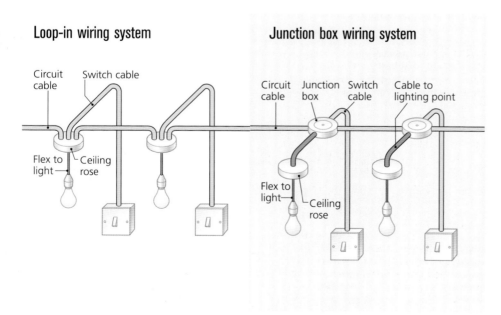

Circuit cable · Switch cable · Flex to light · Ceiling rose

Junction box wiring system

Circuit cable · Junction box · Switch cable · Cable to lighting point · Flex to light · Ceiling rose

Connecting at switches

Connect one-way switches as described on page 296 and connect two-way switches as described on page 297.

Loop-in connections at a ceiling rose

At each ceiling rose except the last one on the circuit, two circuit cables have to be connected; at the last there is only one circuit cable. There is also a switch cable and a light flex to connect at each rose.

1 In the central group of three terminals, connect the red cores from the two circuit cables and switch cable. Connect the black cores from the circuit cables to one of the outer terminals. Leave the outermost one clear for connecting the blue flex core.

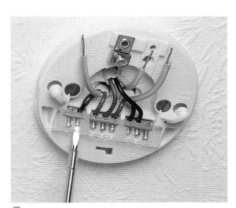

2 At the other outer terminal, connect the red-sleeved black switch core. Connect the brown and blue flex cores to the outer terminals and pass the flex cores over the hooks to take the lampshade's weight.

3 Finally, connect all the green-and-yellow-sleeved earth cores to the terminal marked E or ⏚. Fit the ceiling-rose cover.

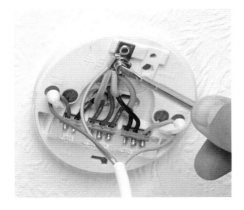

Connections at a junction box

At each junction box except the last on the circuit there will be two circuit cables, a switch cable and a cable to the lighting point. At the last box there will be one circuit cable instead of two.

1 At one of the terminals, connect the red cores from the two circuit cables and the switch cable. At another terminal, connect the black cores from the two circuit cables and from the cable to the lighting point.

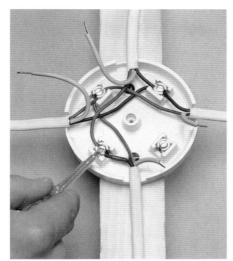

2 At a third terminal, connect the red core from the cable to the lighting point and the red-sleeved black switch core.

3 At the fourth terminal, connect all the earth cores.

4 Screw on the junction box cover.

Connecting light fittings to a junction box system

Single spotlights, multi-spotlight tracks, recessed lights and strip lights are among the special light fittings that are connected to a junction box system.

1 Fix the light fitting to the ceiling. The mounting plates to hold tracks and strips should be screwed through the plasterboard or plaster into joists or into struts nailed between the joists to give a secure fixing.

2 The light fitting may have a terminal block already holding the flex cores and ready to receive the cores from the light cable. Connect the red cable core to the terminal opposite the brown flex core. Connect the black core to the terminal opposite the blue flex core. Connect the green-and-yellow-sleeved earth core to the third terminal. If the light fitting is double-insulated (marked 回) there will be no earth terminal; cut short the cable earth core and seal it with insulating tape to make sure that it cannot touch any terminals.

Alternatively The light fitting may not have a terminal block. Instead, insulated flex cores trail from it. Feed the flex directly into the junction box. Connect the flex to the terminals as described for the cable to the lighting point in Connections at a junction box (left).

Connecting at the consumer unit

1 Turn off the main switch on the consumer unit, if you have not already.

> ### WARNING
> The main switch disconnects only the fuses or MCBs and the cables leading out from the consumer unit to the household circuits. It does NOT disconnect the cables entering via the meter from the service cable. Do not interfere with these cables. They are always live at mains voltage.

2 Remove the screws from the consumer unit cover and open it. Feed the circuit cable into the top of the consumer unit. Use an existing hole if there is room.

3 Check that you have stripped off enough outer sheath for the cores to reach the terminals easily, but make sure that the sheath enters the consumer unit.

4 Connect the new cable's red core to the terminal at the top of the spare fuseway or MCB you are using.

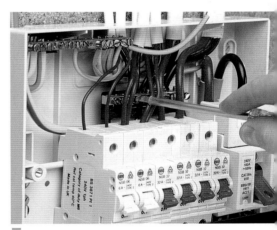

5 Connect the new cable's black core to the neutral terminal block. Then screw the green-and-yellow-sleeved earth core to the earth terminal block. If you are using a spare fuseway, fit a 5amp fuse. If you are connecting to an MCB, switch it on.

6 Fix the cover of the consumer unit back in place, refit the cover over the fuse carriers and turn the main switch back on.

Testing and making good

Fit bulbs or fluorescent lamps into the lampholders and fittings and turn on each light in turn to make sure that it is working. If not, check and tighten the connections, remembering to turn off the electricity at the consumer unit before you do so.

Adding an aerial socket outlet for a second TV set

You can connect more than one TV set to your aerial by leading the aerial cable into a splitter unit, which has one input and two outputs.

Run coaxial cable from each output on the splitter to a coaxial socket outlet near each TV set. Link each set to a socket with coaxial cable fitted with a coaxial plug at each end. Plugs vary in design but have the same basic features. There are male and female plugs to suit different socket outlets.

The aerial cable may be run outside the house and brought inside through a hole drilled in a wall or window frame. Position the splitter where the cable enters the house. The cables between splitter and socket outlets can be laid in the same way as other fixed cables.

You can use flush-fitting socket outlets over standard single mounting boxes recessed into the wall, or use surface-mounted socket outlets and boxes screwed to the wall.

Tools *Suitable tools for preparing the route (page 282); sharp knife; wire cutters and strippers; insulated screwdrivers; pliers.*

Materials *Coaxial TV cable; cable clips or trunking; splitter unit; two flush-fitting coaxial socket outlets with mounting boxes and grommets, or two surface-mounting coaxial sockets; coaxial plugs.*

1 Prepare cable routes from the position for the splitter to the position for the socket outlets and, if necessary, from where the cable enters the house to the splitter.

2 If you are using flush-fitting socket outlets, fit mounting boxes for them. Knock out a convenient entry hole in each box, fit a grommet and screw the boxes in place. Feed the aerial cable to the chosen position for the splitter.

3 Lay cable along each route from the splitter position to the socket outlet positions. Use cable clips or trunking to secure it. Avoid bending it sharply.

4 If you are fitting flush socket outlets, feed the cable end for each outlet through the grommet into the mounting box. Make good the plaster and wait for it to dry.

Alternatively For surface-mounted sockets, feed the cable end up through the floor at the base of the skirting. You will have to cut a notch or drill a hole in the floorboard to prevent it from chafing the cable. If the cable is not under the floor, feed it from the trunking to the spot where the base of the socket will be.

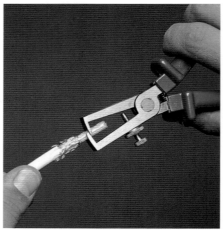

5 Prepare all the cables ends for connection. Make a 30mm slit with a sharp knife lengthwise at the end of the outer sheath. Fold back the sheath and trim it off. Loosen the wire mesh and press or fold it back to leave 20mm of inner insulation. Use wire strippers to remove 15mm of the inner insulation.

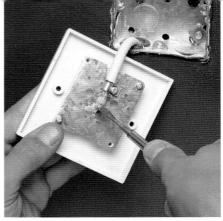

6 To connect at a flush socket outlet, screw the inner wire tightly in place at the terminal. Loosen the adjoining clamp, secure the wire mesh and cable under it and screw the clamp tight. The strands of the mesh must not touch the inner wire. Screw the socket outlet over the mounting box.

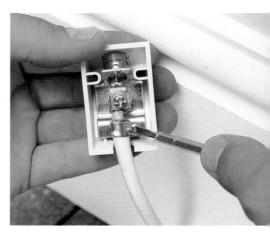

Alternatively With a surface-mounted socket outlet, loop the inner wire clockwise round the central screw and under any retaining plate. Screw it down and secure the clamp. Screw the socket outlet to the skirting board.

7 Secure the splitter to a joist or to the skirting and push the aerial cable plug into the right socket on the splitter.

8 Plug the cables that run to the sockets into the splitter outlets, and the other two cables into the socket outlet at one end and the TV set at the other end.

Choosing connectors for aerials

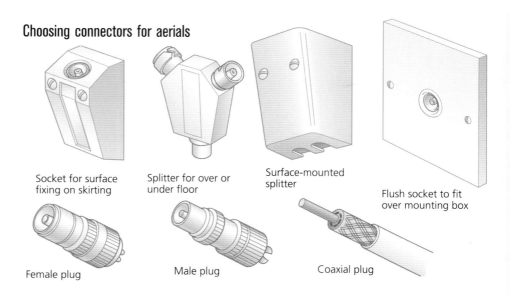

Socket for surface fixing on skirting

Splitter for over or under floor

Surface-mounted splitter

Flush socket to fit over mounting box

Female plug

Male plug

Coaxial plug

Wiring a coaxial plug

Aerial connectors can work loose over time, or you may need to extend the length of the cable to reach from the socket to your television. You can wire a new plug to a coaxial cable or repair a broken connection.

Tools *Trimming knife; pliers.*

Materials *Required length of coaxial cable; pair of coaxial plugs.*

COMPONENTS OF A COAXIAL PLUG

Coaxial plugs come in several parts, which must be separated for fitting. The wire at the centre of the cable carries the signal and connects with the pin in the male plug.

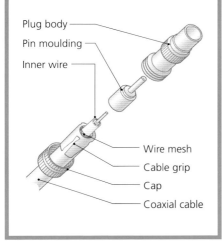

Plug body —
Pin moulding —
Inner wire —
— Wire mesh
— Cable grip
— Cap
— Coaxial cable

1 Strip away a 30mm length of the outer sheath to expose the wire mesh beneath. Fold back 20mm of the wire mesh to expose the inner insulation.

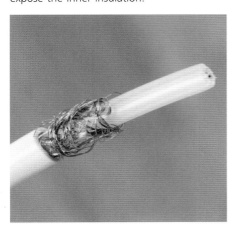

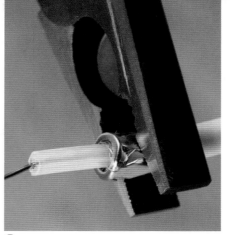

2 Use wire strippers to remove 15mm of the inner insulation (see opposite), leaving the central wire exposed. Slide the cap down the cable and fit the cable grip over the exposed mesh and cable. The strands of the mesh must not touch the inner wire. You will have to open the jaws of the grip to cover the mesh and then squeeze them together with a pair of pliers.

3 Feed the inner wire into the pin moulding and fit the moulding in the plug body. Slide the cap over the cable grip and screw it to the plug body.

4 Connect all the plugs in the same way, fitting a male or female plug as necessary to suit the connection on the socket outlet or splitter and the television set.

Splitting and combining signals for TV and audio

If you have a standard television aerial, a satellite dish and maybe an FM aerial aswell, you can combine the signals to run just one cable from the roof to the living room and then split them again to route to individual television and audio components.

1 Fit a TV/FM diplexer, or triplexer if you have three signals to combine, in the loft or wherever your television and FM aerials are mounted. This simple socket allows two or three cables to be fed in and one single cable to run out, carrying multiple signals at slightly different frequencies.

2 Run this cable to the point where you need the signals to diverge once more and fit a TV/FM diplexed twin socket (or a triple, if required) in the room.

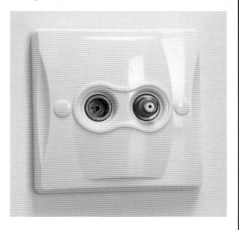

BOOSTING THE SIGNAL

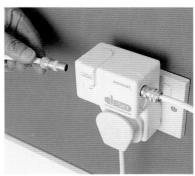

If the television signal where you live is weak, a simple plug in booster box can make a big difference to your picture quality. Plug the booster into the socket that powers your television then connect the lead from the aerial and the lead going out to the television.

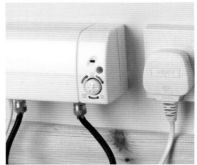

Every time you split a signal to supply an additional television set, the signal to all the sets is weakened. Using a combined splitter and booster unit solves this problem, by boosting the signal where it first enters the house. Plug in the main 'in' cable from the aerial and take out separate feeds for each set in the house.

Installing your own telephone extensions

You can install telephone extensions easily by using kits sold in electrical shops, DIY centres and phone shops.

The law requires a master socket to be fitted by the company that provides the service. You may already have one; it is a square white socket. An old-style box will not accept the new plugs.

• Once you have a new master socket you can install extensions throughout the house, provided there is no more than 100m of cable between the master socket, and the farthest extension socket, and no more than 50m between the master socket and the first extension socket.

• Extensions should not be fitted in damp areas such as bathrooms or toilets, or close to swimming pools.

• For safety reasons, telephone wiring must be kept at least 50mm from mains electric cables. The wiring works on a safe voltage, but it is advisable not to plug it into the master socket while doing the installation. If you need to join lengths of cable, use a joint box (see below).

These instructions use British Telecom fittings; others may vary slightly.

Tools *Electrical screwdriver; trimming knife; bradawl or pencil; drill and masonry bit to fit wallplug provided with kit; screwdriver; small hammer; insertion tool (provided with kit).*

Materials *Telephone socket for each extension; socket converter attached to cable; cleats; two or more telephone sets fitted with plugs. Possibly extra cable (without converter) and cleats, depending on the number of extensions.*

Main telephone and extensions

The square white master socket must be installed by the company that provides the telephone service. This socket is the starting point for all extensions, which can be fitted anywhere in the house. A converter plugs into the master socket, and its cable runs to the first extension socket where the other end is wired in. Another cable runs to the next extension. Telephones are plugged into the converter and the sockets.

HELPFUL TIP

You will probably find it easier to wire the socket before fixing it to the wall (as described).

Wiring one extension

1 Decide where the extension socket is to be placed, and plan a route for the cable. It can be fitted along walls or skirting boards, or can run above ceilings and under floors.

2 Run the cable from the master socket to the point where the extension socket will be fitted. The converter on the cable goes at the master socket end, but do not connect it yet.

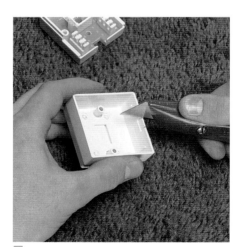

3 Fix the cable by hammering in the cleats every 300mm, but leave the last few cleats at the extension end until later.

4 Cut the cable where it reaches the extension-socket position, leaving about 75mm to spare.

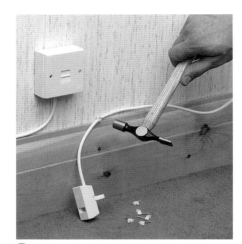

5 Unscrew the front plate from the extension socket and use a sharp knife to cut away the entrance hole which is marked on the inside of the plate at the bottom.

6 Using the trimming knife, strip about 30mm from the cable's outer sheath.

7 When there are six conductors, use the insertion tool to connect them to the socket, pushing them firmly into the grooves. Hold the tools as shown top right and push the green conductor with white

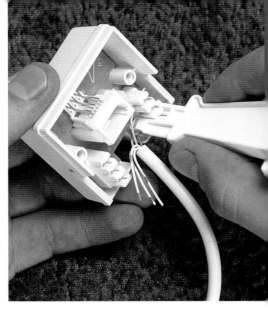

rings into the connection marked 1; blue with white rings into connection 2; orange with white rings into connection 3.

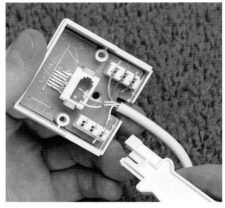

Now reverse the tool to push in the others, but be careful; the numbers 4, 5 and 6 run from bottom to top. Push the white conductor with orange rings into connection 4, white with blue rings into connection 5, and white with green rings into connection 6.

8 Hold the back plate on the wall in the chosen position and mark the wall through the middle hole with a bradawl or pencil. Drill a hole in the wall to the depth of the wallplug. Insert the wallplug and screw the box to the wall.

9 Fit the front plate onto the back plate with the two screws.

10 Plug the converter into the master socket.

11 Fit the plug from the master telephone into the socket on the face of the converter.

12 Plug the extension telephone into its own socket.

Fewer than six conductors

If there are fewer than six conductors, leave two connectors empty or choose a four-connector extension socket.

Wiring extra extensions

You can install a second extension socket by running another cable from the first extension socket. No converter is needed. A third extension socket can be installed by running cable from the second, and so on.

1 Unplug the converter from the master socket and unscrew the front plate from the first extension socket.

2 Connect the conductors of the new cable in the same order as previously, on top of the existing ones. This can be done with the socket on the wall or, if you prefer, the socket can be temporarily removed.

3 Wire the other end of the cable to the second extension socket. Continue in this way for any further extensions. Fit the new conductors on top of those already there.

4 Screw the front plates on the sockets and plug in the converter and the telephones.

What if it fails to work?

If a newly installed telephone fails to work, carry out this fault-finding procedure:
• Unplug the converter from the master socket, plug in the telephone and make a call. Test each extension telephone by plugging it into the master socket as well.
• If none of them works, the fault is in the wiring installed by the telephone company.
• If one of the phones fails to work, it is probably faulty. Return it to the supplier.
• If they all work, the fault lies in your new wiring, so check each socket to make sure that you have wired the coloured conductors to the correct numbers and pushed them right in. If the conductors are wrongly connected, pull them out one at a time with long-nosed pliers, cut off the used core and re-make the connection.
• If the sockets are properly connected, check that the cable is not kinked, cut or squashed. If it is, replace it.
• If the phones still do not work, return the sockets, joint box converter and cable to the suppliers.

More than one extension from a single point

There are some situations where you may want to run more than one extension from a single point. In this case, run cable from the converter at the master socket to a telephone joint box which will take that cable plus as many as three extensions.

1 Fit cable between the master socket and the position for the joint box. Do not plug in the converter yet.

2 Unscrew the front plate from the joint box and cut out the plastic for the cable at the top of both plates.

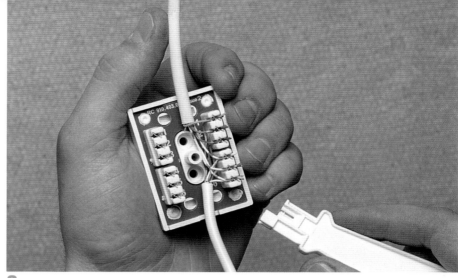

3 Fit the conductors into the joint box in the same way and the same order as in an ordinary socket. The one difference is that the six connectors are in line down the sides rather than to the left and right, so strip off about 40mm of the cable sheath to fix them. Fit one of the extension cables.

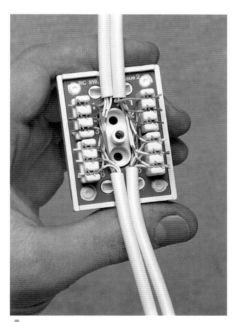

4 Fit the remaining extension cables in the same way, feeding them in from the top or the bottom.

5 Push the cable straps under the pairs of cables and through the holes at the top and bottom of the back plate, and pull them tight. Then cut off the tails.

6 Fix the backplate to the wall with the two wallplugs and screws provided.

7 Fit the extension cables to their sockets in the normal way.

8 Screw the front plates on all the sockets, then plug in the converter and all the new telephones.

COMPONENTS FOR DIY TELEPHONE WIRING

Extension sockets look like the modern master socket that is installed by the telephone company. They are wired up with a plastic insertion tool supplied with the extension kit. A converter is supplied already attached to a long length of cable that is fixed in place with cleats. A telephone joint box can be used to take up to three extensions from one point, as well as the cable. It can also be used to join two lengths of cable together if necessary.

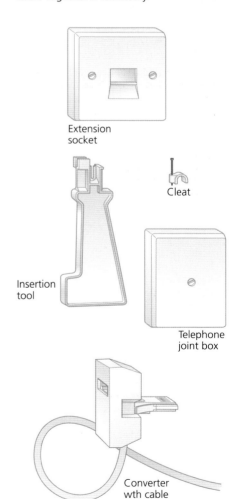

Extension socket

Cleat

Insertion tool

Telephone joint box

Converter wth cable

Wiring options for home computers

Many homes now routinely have more than one computer. Linking these together as a network allows the individual workstations to share a printer or internet connection or to transfer files from one to another automatically.

Benefits of a home network

Linking all the computers in the house on a single network makes it easy to transfer files from one to another. If you have one computer with a significantly larger hard drive than the others, you can also use that computer as a file server for the additional machines or as a back-up for the information stored on the individual PCs.

Another major benefit of a home network is the ability to share peripherals, such as printers, scanners or Webcams and to access the internet from any of the computers on the network via a single connection. Having just one computer 'live' online is a more secure option than having several computers simultaneously connected to the internet. With a high-speed broadband connection, more than one computer can be connected and online at any one time – or permanently.

Home network options

A home network system or LAN (Local Area Network) brings together all the systems that transmit electronic information around the house. This means that it is possible to integrate other services and systems into the network such as cable television, home entertainment systems, security systems and phone lines. The older traditional method is the peer-to-peer wiring method, where various jack sockets or connectors are installed along a single loop running throughout the house – in much the same way as telephone extensions are wired. Although simple to install, this kind of primitive network cannot handle voice and data signals at the same time. In addition, the more devices such as computers that are placed on the line, the more the network signal is weakened.

Wired or wireless?

A hard-wired network of Ethernet cables linking computer to computer is the cheapest and most reliable option, whichever network design you choose to use (below). Transfer of information is often faster than with a wireless signal, but the initial set-up will cause greater disruption to the house and you will have to find ways of concealing cables or making them safe. A wireless network does away with trailing cables and fixed workstations. It offers flexibility that a wired network cannot match and is particularly well-suited to lap-top computer users. However, the hardware is more expensive than that required for a wired system and the connection will be less reliable, and often also slower.

Peer-to-peer networks

The very simplest and oldest type of network is a loop-in system (above) where computers are linked in a string, known as a peer-to-peer system. In a home with only two computers, the workstations can be fitted with a network card and wired together with a single Ethernet cable. This system can also be used for more computers, but the quality of the signal is likely to be poor and if a problem develops with just one of the outlets in the string, the entire network will be affected.

Star networks

Newer network systems resolve these problems by using what is called star topology in which all the cables are distributed from a central point. With this arrangement, if one connection fails it is unlikely to affect all the rest of the computers or other devices on the system. The ideal is to install all the cables when a house is built or replastered, burying them beneath floorboards or within the wall and terminating in sockets around the house. However, it is also possible to install these in existing properties, running cables beneath floorboards and above ceilings.

The central distribution point of the network may be a hub, wired Ethernet switch or wireless router (below), depending on your requirements. A hub will connect upto four computers in an average home network reliably and cost-effectively. If you have more than four computers to link, or if you often transfer very large files, such as music or video files or want the facility for high-speed online gaming, then a wired switch may be a faster and more reliable option.

CAT5 wiring

If you are building a new house or completely renovating an existing property, it is worth considering installing CAT5 data cabling throughout. This is a more powerful Ethernet cable than the standard linking cable used in most wired networks, and is capable of carrying more data, much faster.

Even if you currently only use your home network for computer file-sharing, fitting a CAT5 network will give you the options of running telephone, computer, music or audiovisual signals throughout the house at a later date. The network also has the potential for upgrading to more sophisticated household electronics, such as room-to-room intercoms or door entry systems, touch-sensitive heating and lighting controls in each room, internet access from terminals other than home computers and much more.

Connecting computers in a star network

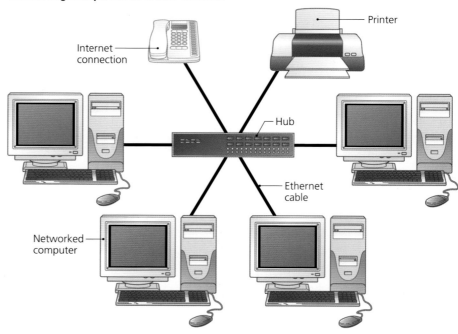

Internet connection · Printer · Hub · Ethernet cable · Networked computer

Wireless networks A wireless, or 'WiFi' network works from a hub called a router, which is wired into the internet connection, if you have one, and communicates with the computers on the network via a radio signal. Each computer is fitted with a Network Interface card: a credit card sized transmitter, and receiver that communicates with the base station, although most wireless routers allow for a combination of wired and wireless connections with computers on the network. Either the router or one of the terminals on the network may be connected to peripheral devices, such as a scanner, that each of the network computers can access.

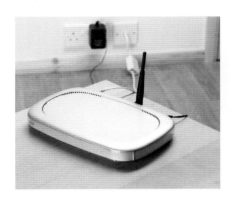

Most wireless routers have a range of upto 30m, but this is reduced if the signal has to pass through walls, particularly solid brick walls. To get the best connection to all the computers on the network, position the router high up in the house and as central as possible. A badly placed base station will lead to the signal dropping off and one or more of the computers becoming disconnected. Follow the instructions that come with the router for more specific advice on positioning.

Wireless routers are prone to interference from other household devices, such as microwave ovens, cordless telephones and automatic garage door openers. Consider this when deciding where to position your base station – putting it too close to the main cordless telephone in the house may affect the reliability of the network signal.

SHARING AN INTERNET CONNECTION

For several networked computers to access the internet through a single dial-up connection, the PC fitted with the modem must have enabled Internet Connection Sharing. Broadband routers make it the connection themselves, eliminating the need for a designated internet 'host' computer. They also have the added benefit that they often come with built-in firewall support.

Installing a home computer network

Installing a home network allows you to link several computers together to access a single Internet connection, transfer or back up files, or share peripheral devices, such as a printer or scanner.

Tools *Drill; screwdriver; possibly also wire strippers and trimming knife.*

Materials *Network router; required lengths of Ethernet cable; required length of telephone or modem cable; broadband filter, if appropriate; possibly also lengths of plastic trunking to conceal cables.*

1 Mount the network router on the wall in a convenient location close to the incoming Internet cable and to a mains power supply. Follow the manufacturer's instructions: you may need to fit a wall bracket, or simply fix two screws protruding from the wall, on which the router will hang.

2 Decide on the route the network cables will have to take to reach the computers the router is to feed. Either prepare the route for burying the cables in the wall (page 282) or cut and fit lengths of plastic trunking along the skirting boards and door architraves. Connect the modem cable from the telephone socket to the router (above), running via a broadband filter if you use an ADSL Internet connection (see opposite).

3 Run Ethernet cables out from the router to the computers it will serve. Tack the cables to the skirting board, bury them in the wall, or conceal them in plastic trunking to keep them out of the way.

4 Plug in the router to the power supply and follow the manufacturer's set-up instructions to establish the connection for each computer on the network.

Choosing a burglar alarm

Most thieves are likely to be deterred by locks on windows and doors, but you may decide to install an alarm system as an extra defence against a burglar who tries to force his way in. A noisy alarm may deter him from entering the house, or greatly reduce the time he stays there.

Before buying a system, check that the alarm is loud enough. Anything below 95 decibels has little effect and cannot be heard over any distance. Most alarms sound for about 20 minutes and then reset to avoid nuisance to neighbours. Notify your local police and your neighbours that an alarm has been fitted, and give a trusted neighbour a spare key to the system or the code number. A valuable addition to a system is a panic button, which can be used to trigger the alarm at any time. Some burglar-alarm systems are designed for DIY installation; others need to be professionally fitted.

WHOLE-HOUSE SYSTEMS THAT WARN OF A BREAK-IN

The most common alarm systems are designed to set off a bell or siren if a burglar tries to break in. Before buying one, ensure that the alarm has a 'closed' electrical circuit. This means that when the system is turned on the circuit is completed. If there is any interference – such as the wires being cut – the alarm will go off. Each system has three main components – the switches; the control; and the alarm.

Control unit The 'brain' of the system is the control unit, which receives signals from the switches and sends an electric current to activate the alarm. The system is turned on or off with a key or a push-button panel to which a code number is first keyed in.

Connected with the control unit will be some form of power supply, either mains or battery. In some models mains power will feed the system under normal conditions, but if the power is cut off for any reason, a battery will take over. The battery is automatically recharged when power is restored.

Passive infra-red (PIR) motion detectors These are small units, fitted at ceiling height, which sense movement through changes of temperature within their field of detection.

External alarm The alarm has a bell or siren that should be loud enough to frighten off potential intruders and alert neighbours. Some external sirens also incorporate a bright, flashing strobe light; others feature flashing LEDs to indicate that the system is active and to add to the visual deterrent. The external alarm box should be tamper-proof and should contain its own battery, so that it will still sound if the cable to it is cut.

Magnetic door and window contacts A magnetic switch can be fitted to a door or window that opens. One part is secured to the frame, the other to the door or casement. If the magnet is moved (by opening the door or window) the circuit is broken and the alarm is triggered.

Panic button A manually operated switch can be fitted as a panic button – at the bedside or by the front door. It is usually wired so that it will trigger the alarm whether or not the rest of the system is switched on. Panic buttons can be very sensitive; the slightest pressure will set off the alarm.

Door alarm This unit can be fitted to an external door and will set off an alarm if the door is opened. It is battery operated, so no wiring is needed. The alarm is turned off with a push-button code that you set yourself, or with a key. A delay switch allows several seconds for you to enter or leave the house without triggering the alarm.

Shed alarm This type of self-contained battery-powered alarm can be fixed in a shed, garage, caravan or greenhouse. It will pick up movement within its field of detection and activate its own alarm.

Wireless alarm systems Passive infra-red sensors and magnetic door contacts are independently battery powered and transmit a radio signal to the control unit when they sense movement; this in turn triggers the alarm. These 'wirefree' systems can be set using a remote key fob switch which doubles as a mobile panic alarm. Because the kits remove the need to run cables, they are much quicker to install. Some systems offer a repeater unit which increases the transmission range so that outbuildings may also be protected.

Closed-circuit television (CCTV) systems CCTV systems are now within the budget of most ordinary householders. Cameras are compact and systems that you can install yourself are widely available. You can choose whether to have the camera tied to its own dedicated monitor, or to utilise your own TV and video set-up. Some cameras incorporate passive infra-red (PIR) detectors to start recording only when movement is detected. When used to see who is at the front door, the sensor will automatically switch from the channel you are watching, to the surveillance camera.

Building Regulations require mains-powered smoke alarms to be fitted in new properties and existing homes that are extended or where the loft has been converted. The Home Office recommends that at least two alarms approved to British Standard BS5446 Part 1 are fitted in an average two-storey house – one downstairs in the hall and the other on the landing.

Smoke alarms should be fitted within 7.5m of the door to every habitable room – living rooms, kitchens and bedrooms. An alarm fitted to the ceiling should be at least 300mm away from a wall or ceiling light fitting. If fitted to the wall, it must be between 150mm and 300mm below the ceiling.

Smoke alarms for existing homes can be battery-operated, wired to the mains with a back-up battery or plugged into a ceiling light fitting (below).

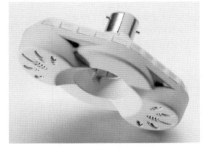

There are two basic types, ionisation and photoelectric. For good, all round protection use one of each.
• The ionisation alarm works by detecting invisible smoke particles in the air and responds quickly to fast, flaming fires, so it is a good choice for a bedroom, hall or landing. It is not suitable in or near a kitchen because it will be set off by cooking fumes.
• The photoelectric alarm 'sees' smoke and is more sensitive to smouldering fires which usually occur in furniture.

Some battery-powered alarms have indicators to show that the battery is still working; others give an audible warning when the battery is low. Plug-in alarms recharge when the light is switched on. Accumulated dust impairs performance, so clean alarms regularly using a vacuum cleaner nozzle.

Choosing time controls for security

A dark, silent house can arouse the interest of burglars. If you make the house appear occupied, by day or night, a prowler is likely to move on to an easier target.

Voices, music and lights after dark can suggest you are in – but only if used with discretion; a single light in the hall left on all evening, or a radio playing all day are more likely to betray that you are out. The illusion that you are there is given by a change in the house – music stopping, or a light going off in one room and on in another. Sockets and switches operated by timers help to create the illusion. Some sophisticated controls will memorise your schedule of switching lights on and off and reproduce it.

Light-switch timers

Time-controlled light switches are connected to the lighting circuit in place of normal switches and are wired in the same way (page 296). Some will switch on and off many times. Others switch on only once – at dusk – so there is no danger of the light shining in the daytime because a power cut has interfered with the setting.

Sensor lamp and light sensor switch

Sensors automatically switch a low-energy bulb on and off at sunrise and sunset; the lamp has a 15,000 hour life. Alternatively, a light sensor switch can be used with tungsten lighting, or fluorescent or low-energy fittings. The switch is controlled by a light-sensitive photocell that activates it when daylight fades. The switch-off time is set at 1–8 hours after the light comes on.

Programmable switch Digitally controlled, these switches offer a sophisticated combination of on/off switching and are programmable to come on at different times during the week. Features may include light sensor settings and an over-ride. Most can only be used with tungsten lighting, but others are adapted to use low-voltage or fluorescent.

Automatic outdoor light An infra-red sensor activates the light when anyone – visitor or burglar – comes within its field of vision. The sensor can be incorporated in either the light or a separate unit operating a number of lights. Once on, the light shines for a period chosen by the user.

Plug-in timers

A plug-in timer will control any appliance that plugs into a 13amp socket outlet – a radio or a lamp, to give the impression that the house is occupied, or a heater or electric blanket for convenience.

Set the required programme on the timer, plug it into a switched-on outlet, plug the appliance into the timer and switch on the appliance. It will not actually come on until the programmed time. You can override the set programme manually. There are 24-hour and seven-day timers. They vary in the number of times they will switch on and off, and in the shortest possible 'on' period.

24-hour timer Some plug-in timers allow you to design a pattern of switching on and off over a 24 hour period. Some models allow up to 48 changes in a day. Markers on a dial trigger the timer to switch on or off as the dial turns. The shortest 'on' period is usually 15–30 minutes. The pattern will be repeated every day until it is switched off or the markers are changed.

Seven-day timer These work in the same way as 24-hour timers, but switching patterns can be varied from day to day over a period of seven days; some will allow up to 84 switchings per week. The on/off pattern will then be repeated each week until altered. The minimum period for which it can be switched on is two hours.

Electronic digital timer These timers offer a number of setting programmes and may allow up to 84 switchings a week. A random setting will switch lights or a radio on or off during the power-on period, to give the impression that a house is occupied. It can be used as a daily or weekly timer and will automatically repeat programmes.

Wiring to an outbuilding

An electricity supply to a detached garage, greenhouse, garden shed or other outbuilding should be run as a permanently fixed cable from the fuse board in the house. A long flex run to the outbuilding from a socket inside the house is not acceptable, and contravenes wiring regulations.

• It is best to bury the cable despite the work involved. Cable underground does not mar the view, and with careful planning the length of the underground section can be kept to a minimum. Run the cable through the house to reach the point nearest the outbuilding to save work. If this is difficult, run the cable along the outside wall of the house to reach the point nearest the outbuilding. You can also run it along a boundary wall, but not along a fence.

• You can take the cable overhead, but it is unsightly to have it hanging immediately outside the house. It should be fixed at least 3.5m above the ground, which frequently entails fitting a timber post securely to the outbuilding to achieve the clearance. If it is more than 3m long, the cable span must be supported along its length by another wire (called a catenary) and must have a drip loop at each end.

• For underground cable, make the route of the trench as short as possible, well clear of obstacles such as rockeries, inspection chambers or trees. Allow some extra cable when you calculate the length needed in case you meet unexpected obstacles.

A professional electrician is likely to install MICC or armoured cable (see Cables and fittings for outdoor wiring, above), but these are difficult for the amateur to connect correctly without the use of specialist tools, and the various components are relatively expensive. It is easier to use ordinary two-core-and-earth cable for the entire sub-circuit between house and outbuilding, but the outdoor section of the circuit cable must be run in protective PVC conduit fixed to the walls of the buildings and laid in the trench. The run is made up using lengths of conduit linked with solvent-welded straight and elbow connectors.

• Start the new sub-circuit with an enclosure containing a 30milliamp RCD and one or two 30 or 32amp MCBs, fitted on or near the house fuse board. This serves as the isolating switch for the sub-circuit.

• Call in your electricity supply company to connect this to the meter once you have installed the new circuit wiring. You are not allowed to do this yourself.

• Inside the outbuilding, the cable should run to a socket outlet. A switched fused

Cables and fittings for outdoor wiring

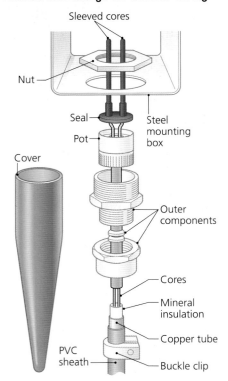

Sleeved cores

Nut

Seal

Pot

Cover

Outer components

Cores

Mineral insulation

Copper tube

PVC sheath

Buckle clip

Steel mounting box

MICC cable

Mineral-insulated copper-clad (MICC) cable has two conductors set in mineral filling inside a copper tube that acts as the earth conductor. There is an orange PVC sheath. Special tools are needed to strip off the copper tube and fit the water-tight seals. As soon as you buy the cable, seal its ends with tape. Leave the tape on until you are ready to connect it, or the filling will absorb moisture.

A waterproof gland seals the cable into a steel mounting box 44mm or more deep – deeper than boxes normally used indoors – to give room to fit the gland. A blank plate covers the front. Use copper clips to hold MICC cable.

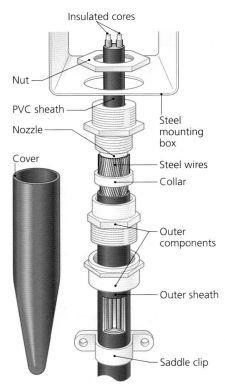

Insulated cores

Nut

PVC sheath

Nozzle

Cover

Steel mounting box

Steel wires

Collar

Outer components

Outer sheath

Saddle clip

Armoured cable

Two insulated conductors are in a PVC sheath inside steel wires that serve as the earth conductor. There is a PVC outer sheath. Three-core armoured cable has a third core, in yellow plastic, for the earth. Cover its exposed ends with green-and-yellow sleeving. This cable is the most suitable for an open position on a patio and for a supply to a garden pond. Armoured cables do not need special tools.

Use the right size and type of gland to seal the cable into a deep steel mounting box. On the two-core cable, be sure to tighten the gland nut hard to complete the earth continuity. Use galvanised, copper or plastic clips to hold the cable.

connection unit (FCU) can be run from this to provide a starting point for a fused lighting sub-circuit.

Tools *Tape measure; side cutters; wire strippers; power drill; 10mm flat wood bit; long 20mm masonry bit; hammer; spade; hacksaw; screwdrivers.*

Materials *2.5mm² two-core-and-earth cable; cable clips; green-and-yellow PVC earth sleeving; red PVC insulating tape; 20mm PVC conduit; wall clips; straight connectors and elbows; solvent-weld adhesive; sand; bricks; paving slabs; warning tape; enclosure with 30milliamp RCD and one/two 30 or 32amp MCBs; metal-clad double socket outlet and mounting box; metal-clad FCU and mounting box; 1mm² two-core-and-earth cable; batten lampholder; metal-clad light switch and mounting box; grommets; wood-screws; wallplugs.*

Work inside the house

1 Plan and prepare the cable route from the fuse board to the point where it will leave the house. With suspended timber floors, run it beneath the floorboards. Or surface-mount it in plastic mini-trunking.

2 Where the circuit cable will leave the house, locate a mortar course in the wall at least 150mm above the level of the damp-proof course. Use a long 20mm diameter masonry drill bit to drill from the outside, sloping the hole slightly upwards to discourage rainwater from entering.

3 Mount the new RCD unit on the fuse board or on the wall nearby. Remove knockouts from the base of the unit to admit the incoming meter tails and circuit cable. Clip the RCD and the MCBs onto the metal busbar, ready for connection when the new circuit wiring is complete.

Outside work

1 Plan the cable route between the house and the outbuilding, and excavate the trench along the marked route. Avoid cultivated ground if possible; a route running close to a path or boundary wall is often the ideal choice.

2 Check the depth of the trench. It should be at least 500mm deep.

3 Remove any sharp stones from the trench and put in a layer of dry sand about 50mm deep to protect the conduit.

4 Measure the conduit run and work out how many lengths of conduit you will need. Conduit is available in 2m and 3m lengths.

5 At the house end of the run, feed the end of the circuit cable into the first length of conduit. Pull enough cable through the conduit to make up the run inside the house from the entry point in the wall to the fuse board position.

6 Start to assemble the conduit run by solvent-welding lengths of conduit together with straight joints. Brush a little of the special adhesive onto the pipe end, taking care not to get any on the cable sheath. Push the fitting onto the pipe and rotate it slightly to ensure a waterproof joint. Feed the cable through the next length of conduit before joining it to the previous one. Continue adding lengths of conduit one by one in the same way.

7 Use a hacksaw to cut the last section of conduit to length as necessary. Smooth off any roughness with fine abrasive paper before joining it to the previous length.

8 As you join lengths of conduit together, lower the completed run into the base of the trench. Use large-radius elbow fittings and short lengths of conduit to take the run up to the point where it leaves the house and where it enters the outbuilding. Secure these sections of conduit to the house and outbuilding walls with clips.

9 Fit a standard elbow to each end of the conduit run and insert one into the hole in the house wall and one into the outbuilding wall. Feed enough cable into the outbuilding to allow it to be connected to the wiring accessories that will complete the sub-circuit.

WEATHERPROOF SOCKETS

Sockets and light switches that are fitted out of doors must be weatherproof. Socket outlets on the house wall can be wired as spurs from an indoor power circuit (page 285), but must include a high sensitivity (30milliamp) RCD for user protection.

10 When you have completed the conduit run and laid it in the trench, place a line of bricks on the sand bed at each side of the conduit and lay narrow paving slabs over the bricks. This ensures that any future digging cannot damage the conduit or the cable inside it. Lay lengths of special yellow-and-black plastic warning tape over the slabs.

11 Back-fill the trench with the soil you excavated earlier, and tamp it down firmly.

Work in the outbuilding

1 Decide where in the outbuilding you want to position the various wiring accessories. Because the sub-circuit is controlled and protected by the RCD and MCBs at the house end of the circuit, the simplest way of wiring up the accessories is to create a radial circuit. Run the incoming cable to the first socket, then on to any other sockets you want to install. At a convenient point in this radial circuit, include a fused connection unit (FCU) fitted with a 3amp fuse. From here a length of 1mm² cable is run to supply one or more light fittings and a separate light switch.

2 Screw the metal mounting boxes for the various wall-mounted accessories to the wall of the outbuilding. Use woodscrews driven direct into timber walls or frame members, and into wallplugs in drilled holes in masonry walls.

3 Remove metal knockout discs from the mounting boxes to admit the cables, and fit a rubber grommet into each entry or exit hole to prevent the cable from chafing.

4 Feed the incoming cable into the first mounting box and cut it to leave about 150mm of cable within the box. Then run cable from this box to the next one, cutting it to length as before. Carry on adding lengths of cable one by one to connect all the wiring accessories.

5 Prepare all the cable ends for connection by stripping about 75mm of insulation from each conductor. Cover the bare earth cores with a length of green-and-yellow PVC sleeving. Fold the ends of the earth cores over the sleeving to stop it from slipping off until you are ready to connect these conductors to the earth terminals.

6 There will be two sets of conductors to connect to the socket faceplate at each socket (except at the last one on the circuit, which will have just one set). Connect the two red conductors to the terminal marked L and the two black conductors to the terminal marked N. Connect the sleeved earth conductors to the earth terminal on the faceplate. Add a short length of sleeved earth core (taken from a cable offcut)

between this terminal and the earth terminal in the mounting box to earth the mounting box.

7 Check that all the connections are secure. Fold the conductors back into the mounting box and screw the faceplate to it. Repeat this process to connect up the other sockets on the sub-circuit.

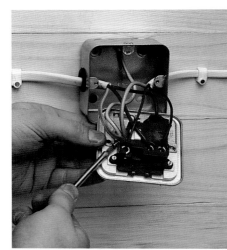

8 At the fused connection unit (FCU), connect the conductors of the incoming cable to the terminals marked FEED or IN. The red conductor goes to the terminal marked L, the black conductor to the terminal marked N and the sleeved earth conductor to E or ⏚. Add an earth link between the earth terminals on the faceplate and the mounting box as before. Connect the 1mm² cable that will supply the light fitting in the same way, but to the terminals marked LOAD or OUT. Run this cable up to the position of the batten holder or light fitting you are installing. Fit a 3amp fuse in the fuseholder and screw the faceplate to the mounting box.

9 At the batten holder or light fitting, connect in the 1mm² cable from the FCU and another 1mm² cable to run onto the light switch. The two red conductors go to the centre bank of terminals, and the black conductors to the end terminals; it does not matter which way round these two are connected. Connect the two earth conductors to the earth terminal. Screw the cover on to the batten holder.

Connecting at the RCD unit

At the new MCB/RCD unit in the house, connect the red conductor of the circuit cable to the top terminal of one of the MCBs. Connect the neutral and earth cores to their respective terminal blocks. The second MCB shown here is already wired to supply another sub-circuit. Your electricity supply company will fit the meter tails to the RCD and add the main earth cable shown.

Fitting an outdoor socket

Using power tools in the garden doesn't have to mean trailing extension leads out of a window. Run a spur from an indoor power circuit and install a weatherproof outdoor socket with a high-sensitivity RCD (residual current device) that will cut out if an electrical problem occurs.

1 A neat way to fit an outdoor socket is to drill through the back of an existing indoor outlet and locate the new one on the other side of the wall.

Alternatively, run a cable along the inside wall and drill through to the outside where you want the new socket.

2 Turn off the mains power and remove the faceplate and mounting box of the socket you will be working from. Drill a pilot hole then switch to a 10mm masonry bit at least 300mm long to drill through the wall. With the power switched off, you will need a cordless drill with a hammer action, to get through the wall.

Fitting an outdoor wall light

To install a light on an outside wall—under a porch or on a patio, follow the same method as for an inside wall light. Choose a weatherproof light fitting designed for an outside wall.

If the light is on a bracket, not a flush-fitting baseplate, you will need waterproof sealant or a rubber gasket to fit the bracket's base.

It is safest to have the switch indoors. You can take the cables for the light and the switch along the same route over the ceiling and down the indoor surface of the external wall on which you are going to install the light.

At the right height for the wall fitting – about 1.8m above ground level – drill from the back of the chase through the inner and outer leaves of the external wall to make a hole to lead the cable outside. Feed the light cable out through the hole.

Install and connect the junction box and the switch in the same way as for an indoor wall light (see page 300).

3 Screw back the mounting box and feed the new cable through the wall. Connect the old and new cores to the faceplate. There will be three cores in each terminal: the ring main cores coming in and going out, and the new spur. Reconnect the 'flying earth' cable to the box and replace the faceplate.

4 For safety, use an outside socket with an entry point through the back. Any exposed cable on an outdoor wall should be armoured or protected in a conduit (see page 317). Use the grommet supplied to make the cable hole watertight, drill out any drainage holes indicated and screw the box to the wall.

3 Connect the red and black cores to the terminals of the lampholder; it does not matter which core goes to which terminal. Connect the green-and-yellow sleeved earth core to the terminal marked E or ⊥.

Light on a bracket

1 If your light is on a bracket, not a baseplate, you cannot reach the lampholder. Flex will have been connected to it already and the flex end will stick out from the bracket. Prepare the flex cores and connect them to a terminal block.

At the terminals on the opposite side of the block, connect the cores of the light cable. Link red to brown, black to blue and earth to earth.

Coat the rim of the bracket's baseplate with sealant, or fit a rubber gasket.

5 Cover the bare earth core with PVC sleeving and connect the cores to the terminals on the faceplate. There is no need to earth a plastic mounting box. Screw the faceplate to the box. Restore the power and test both sockets before use.

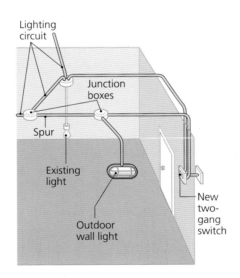

Wiring for an outdoor wall light

2 Screw the light fitting into the drilled and plugged holes. Make sure that any sealant or gasket is squeezed tight against the wall to make a weatherproof seal.

SAFETY TIP

Test the RCD before you start work every time you use your outdoor outlet. Plug in the tool, switch on and press the TEST button. If the RCD trips off, press RESET: the outlet is ready to use. If it does not, there is a fault, and you should call an electrician.

Light on a base plate

1 Hold the baseplate of the light fitting against the wall and probe with a bradawl through the fixing holes to mark drilling spots on the wall. Drill holes at the marks and insert wallplugs in them.

2 Feed the cable through the baseplate and screw the plate to the wall. Prepare the cable for connection (see page 271).

Fitting an outside switch

If you want a switch out of doors as well as inside for the new light, use a two-way sealed splashproof design. Put it on the outside wall back to back with a two-way indoor switch. You will need a short length of three-core-and-earth lighting cable for the connection between the two switches. Drill a hole between the switches and feed the three-core-and–earth cable through it. Connect the cable as described in Replacing a one-way with a two-way switch, page 297.

10

Plumbing and heating

Plumbing emergencies – what to do if:

Water pours from the loft

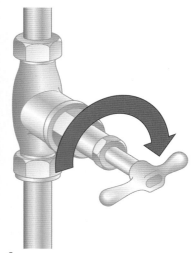

1 Turn the main stoptap off (clockwise). It is usually close to the kitchen sink (if you can't, see right). Put buckets under the leaks, then turn on all the cold taps in the house and flush all the WCs to drain the cold water storage cistern.

2 Find the cause of the trouble. It may be a burst pipe in the loft or a cistern overflow caused by a blocked overflow pipe.

No water comes from a tap

1 If no water flows from the kitchen sink cold tap, check that the main stoptap is open. If it is, call your water supply company. You will find the number under 'Water' in the phone book.

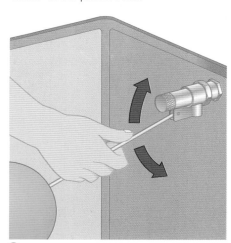

2 If no water flows from other taps, check the cold water cistern. It may have emptied because of a jammed ballvalve.

If it is empty, move the float arm sharply up and down to free the valve, then clean the valve (page 339).

Alternatively In frosty weather there may be an ice plug blocking a supply pipe. If the kitchen cold tap is working, check the flow into the cold water cistern by pressing down the ballvalve. If there is no inflow, the rising main is frozen, probably between the ceiling and the cistern inlet.

3 If the cistern is filling, check the bathroom taps. If there is no flow from one tap, its supply pipe from the cistern is frozen.

4 To thaw a pipe, strip off any lagging from the affected part and apply hot water bottles. If a pipe is difficult to get at, blow warm air onto it with a hair dryer.

WARNING Do not use a blowtorch to defrost a frozen pipe. It may cause a fire, or melt the solder in a pipe joint and cause another leak.

Hot water cylinder leaks

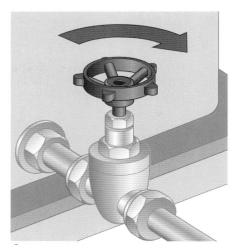

1 Turn off the gatevalve (clockwise) on the supply pipe from the cold water cistern to the hot water cylinder.

If there is no gatevalve, turn off the main stoptap and turn on all the taps to empty the cistern. (This will not empty the hot water cylinder, but will stop water from flowing into it.)

2 Switch off the immersion heater, if there is one.

3 Switch off the boiler, or put out the boiler fire.

4 Connect a hose to the cylinder drain valve, which is located near the base of the cylinder where the supply pipe from the cold water cistern enters. Put the other end of the hose into an outside drain.

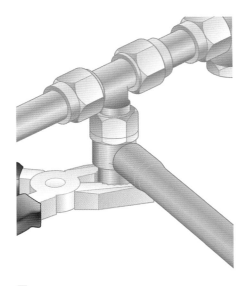

5 Open up the drain valve with a drain valve key or pliers.

6 Get the hot water cylinder repaired or replaced by a plumber.

You cannot turn off the water

If you cannot turn off the water at the main stoptap, tie up the float arm in the cold water cistern to stop it filling, turn on all the taps (except the kitchen cold tap) and flush the WCs. You can then work on the problem pipe.

To work on the rising main, locate the outdoor stoptap (page 323). Use a stoptap key (available from plumbers' merchants) to turn off the tap and cut off the mains supply to the house.

Other plumbing problems

Central heating radiator leaking page 374

Cistern water level high or low page 339

Drain or gully blocked page 407

Gutter overflowing page 400

Overflow pipe dripping page 339

Pipe has burst page 330

Sink blocked or slow to empty page 331

Tap dripping page 332

Tap flow poor page 330 (Airlocks)

Waste downpipe blocked page 402

WC cistern not flushing page 336

WC pan will not empty page 342

How water is supplied to the home

Whether for home improvements, or for tackling emergencies, it is important to know what type of water system you have, and where to find all the relevant system controls.

The cold water supply

There are two types of cold water supply in British homes: direct and indirect.

In a direct cold water supply, branch pipes from the rising main lead directly to all the cold taps and WC cisterns in the house. This means that you can drink cold water from any tap. A pipe from the rising main will usually feed a storage cistern in the loft – the reservoir that feeds the hot water cylinder.

A direct cold water system is simpler and cheaper to install than an indirect system.

BE PREPARED
Make sure that you and others in the house know where the indoor and outdoor stoptaps are, as well as the gatevalves on the supply pipes to the hot water cylinder and cold taps, and label them.

Most British homes have an indirect system. The rising main feeds the cold tap at the kitchen sink (and possibly pipes to a washing machine and an outside tap). This water is clean drinking water. It then continues up to a cold water storage tank in the roof, which supplies all other taps, the WCs and the hot water cylinder.

There are advantages to an indirect system: water from a cold water storage cistern gives even water pressure, which produces quieter plumbing and less wear and tear on washers and valves. Leaks are also less likely, and any leak that does occur will be less damaging than one from a pipe under mains pressure.

Water from a cistern is warmer than mains water, so less hot water is needed for washing and bathing. It also reduces condensation on WC cisterns. And if the house supply is temporarily cut off – for work on the mains, for example – there is a supply of stored water available for use.

SAFETY NOTE
If your house has an indirect system, do not drink water from any tap other than the kitchen one. Water from a tank may not be clean.

5 **Rising main** The service pipe enters the house, usually close to the kitchen sink (but sometimes under the stairs or in a garage), and from there is known as the rising main. Another stoptap for cutting off the house water supply should be fitted where the pipe enters the house. The rising main is usually a 15mm diameter pipe, but in areas where mains pressure is low, a 22mm diameter pipe is used.

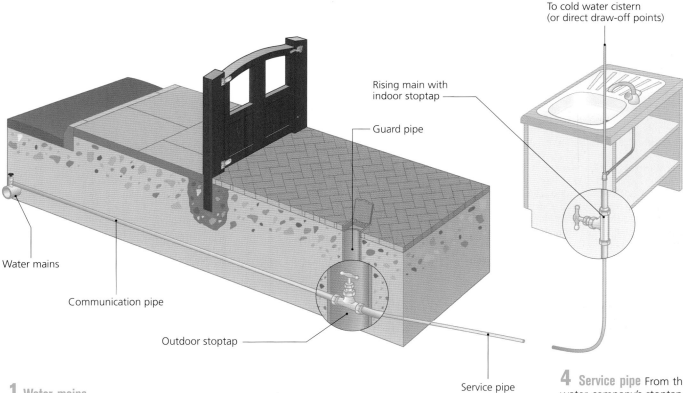

1 **Water mains** The water supply to most British homes is provided by the local water supply company, through iron or heavy plastic water mains.

2 **Communication pipe** From the mains, a pipe known as a communication pipe takes the water to the water company's stoptap – a control valve about 1m below the ground at or near the boundary of each property.

3 **Outdoor stoptap** The stoptap, which is turned with a long key, is at the bottom of an earthenware guard pipe under a small metal cover, set into the surface of the garden or the public footpath outside. In older properties, this may be the only place where the water can be turned off.

4 **Service pipe** From the water company's stoptap, a service pipe carries water into the house. The pipe should meander slightly in the trench to allow for ground movement, which would otherwise pull on the fittings at each end. To avoid frost damage, it should be at least 750mm and not more than 1.35m below ground.

Hot water supply

There are two basic hot water systems: either indirect, with all hot taps supplied from a hot water storage cylinder, or direct, where cold water is heated on demand. The latter is usual when all the cold water supplies come direct from the rising main.

Back boilers and separate kitchen boilers have largely been replaced by modern boilers that supply both hot water and central heating.

Instantaneous hot water systems
Single point water heaters may be heated by gas or electricity and are usually sited next to the point they serve. In the case of electric heaters, such as an electric shower, they must be wired to the mains via an isolating switch. Many homes are now being fitted with multipoint water heaters – most commonly combination (combi) boilers. A combi boiler combines the functions of a central heating boiler and an instantaneous multipoint water heater.

Indirect systems

You can identify an indirect system by the two water tanks in the loft. The second, smaller one, has a vent pipe over the top. This is called a header tank, or feed and expansion tank; it keeps the primary circuit topped up. The level of water in the header tank is low enough to allow the water to rise as it expands when it gets hot without overflowing.

The primary circuit With an indirect water system, the hot water cylinder contains a coil of pipe, which forms part of a run of pipework attached to the boiler. This is heated directly by the boiler. Indirectly, it heats the water in the cylinder. The coil, or heat exchanger, is actually part of the central heating circuit: its water heating function arises out of its main job, which is to heat the radiators. This heating pipework is known as the 'primary' circuit and the pipes that run to and from the boiler are known as the primary flow and return.

Primary circuit water constantly circulates while the boiler is on. The hot water tank itself works in the same way as one in a direct system.

The secondary circuit Water in the hot water cylinder is supplied from the cold water cistern, which keeps the cylinder constantly topped up as hot water is used. A vent pipe from the top of the hot water cylinder hangs over the cold water cistern, allowing air to escape. Pipes to the hot taps lead from the vent pipe. Because these branch pipes leave above the cylinder top, the cylinder cannot be drained through the hot taps. This means you don't need to turn off the boiler if the household water supply is temporarily cut off.

This system is known as a vented system. It is open to atmospheric pressure and operates under low pressure. A pump can be fitted to boost flow to showers or taps.

Unvented (sealed) hot water systems
This system is the same as an indirect system, except that it is connected to the mains. This gives mains water pressure to hot taps and showers. Many safety features are built into this type of system to allow for the greater pressure and expansion of the water. No cold water storage cistern or header tank is needed, so there is no pipework in the loft.

Direct systems

In older houses with a direct system (often back boilers or solid-fuel boilers), the water is heated directly by circulation through the boiler. Water is fed from the cold water cistern into the bottom of the cylinder and then to the boiler. The flow pipe from the top of the boiler discharges hot water directly into the top of the cylinder, forcing colder, denser water at the bottom through the return pipe back to the boiler. The hottest water, being the lightest, is always at the top ready to be drawn off.

Immersion heater This is another form of direct heating. The hot water cylinder can be heated by one or two electric immersion heaters. About 1kW of heat is needed for every 45 litres of water, so a 140-litre hot water cylinder needs a 3kW heater. Today, an immersion heater is rarely the sole form of water heating in the home. Rather, it is used to supplement a boiler system or as a way to heat water in summer when the central heating boiler is switched off.

An immersion heater has a thermostat to control the water temperature. For most homes, 55–60°C is ideal.

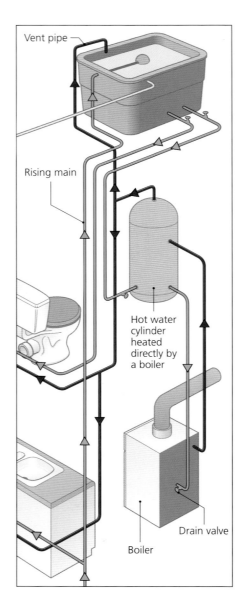

Vent pipe

Rising main

Hot water cylinder heated directly by a boiler

Drain valve

Boiler

Direct heat Hot water in the cylinder is heated by circulation through the boiler. The system cannot be used to supply central heating radiators.

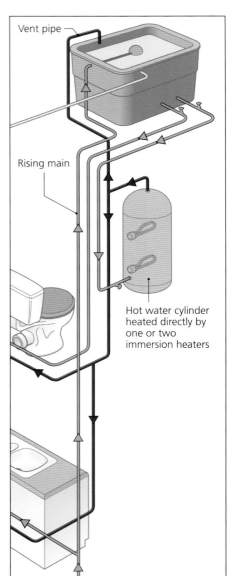

Vent pipe

Rising main

Hot water cylinder heated directly by one or two immersion heaters

Immersion heater Hot water stored in the cylinder is heated directly by electric immersion heater. The system cannot be used to supply central heating radiators.

A typical indirect (two circuit) system

1 The rising main feeds the kitchen cold tap and kitchen appliances before it rises to the cold water storage cistern.

2 The cold water cistern is filled from the rising main, and the inflow of water is controlled by a float-operated ballvalve. The capacity of the average household cistern is 230 litres, and it has an overflow pipe to carry water out to the eaves if the cistern overfills through a failure of the ballvalve.

3 Water regulations require new cold water storage cisterns and header tanks (feed and expansion tanks) to have dust-proof and insect-proof (but not airtight) covers and to be insulated against frost. The storage cistern must supply drinkable water.

4 Water from the cistern is distributed by at least two 22mm (or 28mm) diameter pipes fitted about 75mm from the bottom. One supplies WCs and cold taps – except for the kitchen cold tap. Normally the 22mm pipe goes direct to the bath cold tap, and 15mm branches feed washbasins and WC cisterns.

5 The other distribution pipe feeds cold water to the bottom of the hot water cylinder – usually a copper cylinder of about 140 litres capacity. In a typical modern house with a central heating boiler, there are two water circuits through the hot water cylinder – the primary circuit that heats the water, and the secondary circuit that distributes it (see facing page).

6 Hot water stored in the cylinder is heated indirectly by the primary water circuit through the boiler, and sometimes by an immersion heater as well. This system can also heat radiators.

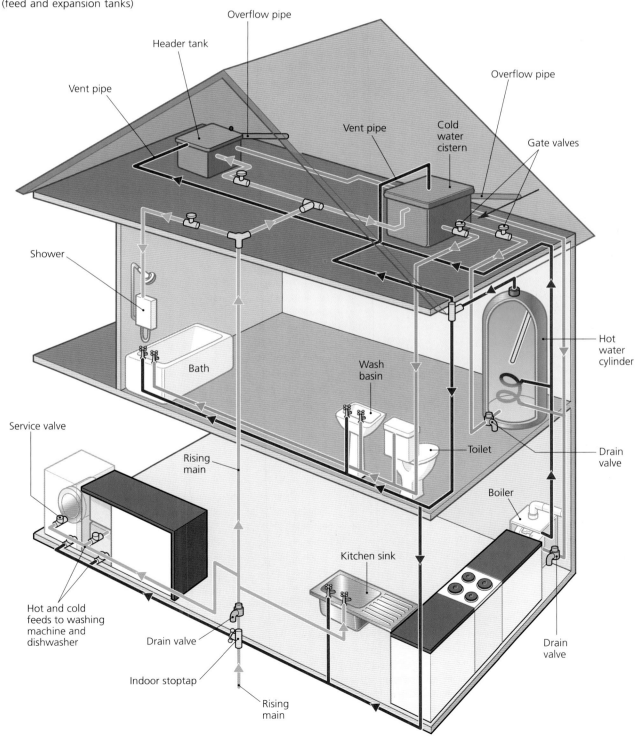

Where the waste water goes

All waste water is channelled out of the house into the main underground drain system. If you live in a house built before the mid-1960s, you probably have a two pipe drainage system; newer houses have one drain pipe – a single stack system.

Whatever the drainage system, every bath, basin or sink in the house is fitted with a trap – a bend in the outlet pipe below the plughole. This holds sufficient water to stop gases from the drains entering the house and causing an unpleasant smell. The trap has some means of access for clearing blockages. All WC pans have built-in traps.

Below ground, the household waste pipes or drains are channelled through an inspection chamber near the house to form the main drain, which runs into the water company's sewer.

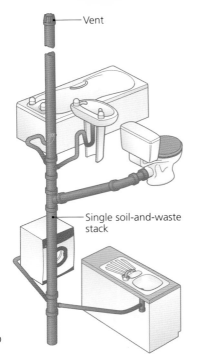

Vent

Single soil-and-waste stack

Single stack system
Modern houses have a single stack drainage system. Waste from all sinks and WCs is carried underground by a single vertical pipe known as a soil stack. This pipe may be installed inside the house and its vented top extends above the roof.

Two pipe system
Most houses built before the mid-1960s have what is known as a two pipe drainage system for waste water disposal.

1 A vertical soil stack fixed to an outside wall carries waste from upstairs WCs to an underground drain.

2 The open top of the soil stack – the vent – extends above the eaves and allows the escape of sewer gases. It is protected from birds with a metal or wire mesh guard.

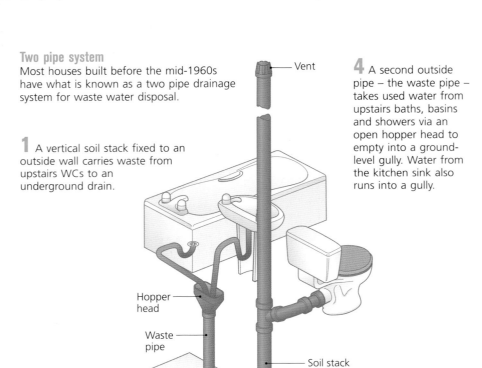

Vent

Hopper head

Waste pipe

Soil stack

Gully

3 Ground floor WCs have an outlet direct into the underground drain.

4 A second outside pipe – the waste pipe – takes used water from upstairs baths, basins and showers via an open hopper head to empty into a ground-level gully. Water from the kitchen sink also runs into a gully.

The tools for the job

You will probably have most of the basic tools needed for plumbing – such as spanners and pliers – in your toolkit. For more specialist jobs, tools and equipment can be bought or hired.

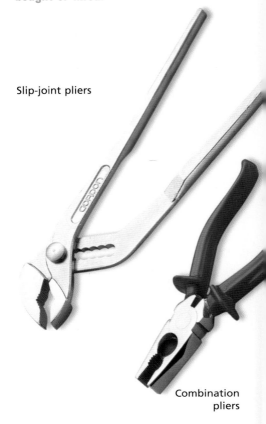

Slip-joint pliers

Combination pliers

Pliers A pair of 180mm standard combination pliers is useful for jobs such as removing split pins from cisterns, and long-nose pliers will grip a sink or washbasin outlet grid. Slip-joint pliers have adjustable jaws and are useful for a wide range of gripping jobs.

PTFE tape Makes threaded fittings watertight. Wrap the tape around the thread before screwing the joint together.

Radiator key An essential tool for bleeding air from the central heating system.

Pipe wrenches For gripping pipes, circular fittings or hexagonal nuts that have been rounded off at the edges. Two wrenches are needed for some jobs. Some pipe wrenches, such as Footprint wrenches, are operated by squeezing the handles together, but the Stillson type has an adjuster nut for altering the jaw size. Useful Stillson wrench sizes are 250mm and 360mm, with jaw openings up to 25mm and 38mm. For a cistern-retaining nut you may need a wrench or adjustable spanner that will open to about 60mm.

When using a wrench, always push or pull in the direction of the jaw opening. Pad the jaws with cloth if they are likely to damage the fitting – if it is plastic, for example.

Plunger Inexpensive tool used to clear blockages from a sink, basin or bath. Pump it up and down over the plughole.

Pipe or Stillson wrench

Footprint wrench

Plunger

Spanners

Adjustable spanner

Sink or WC auger

OTHER USEFUL TOOLS

Screwdrivers A cross-head screwdriver and two flat-bladed screwdrivers – one large, one small – are sufficient for most plumbing jobs.

Vice and workbench Not essential, but useful for some jobs, such as dismantling a ballvalve. Use a grooved jaw lining in a vice. Some portable workbenches incorporate grooves for holding a pipe.

Ladder Plumbing emergencies usually occur in the loft. A retractable loft ladder is the safest means of access. Alternatively, use a stepladder that reaches right into the loft.

Torch Plumbing is often in dark places. Keep a powerful torch (and spare batteries) handy – preferably one in a square casing so that it will stand up, or one designed to strap to your head.

Pipe repair clamp For an instant, though temporary, repair to a leaking pipe. The clamp is a two-part collar lined in rubber that you screw together around the pipe.

Plumbing putty An epoxy putty useful for patching slow leaks.

Blowtorch A torch flame is necessary for joining copper pipes with soldered capillary fittings.

Sink or WC auger Used to dislodge blockages from waste pipework. Some augers have a rotating handle to drive the wire into the blockage and break it up; others work just by pushing the wire manually into the blocked pipe.

TOOLS FOR ADVANCED WORK

Pipe-bending machine A lightweight machine is useful if you have a number of bends to make in a 15mm, 22mm or 28mm diameter pipe, and can be hired. It incorporates a curved former for shaping the bend, and separate guide blocks for each pipe size.

Hacksaw Use a large or small (junior) hacksaw to cut metal or plastic pipes.

Half-round metal file Use for smoothing the burred edge of a cut pipe.

Pipe-bending springs Steel bending springs support the inside of copper pipe while bending it by hand. Springs are sold in 15mm and 22mm sizes.

Basin wrench This wrench (also known as a crowsfoot spanner) is used for tightening or loosening the backnuts of taps.

Wire wool Use to clean inside pipe ends before making joints, and to remove rust.

Pipe cutter Quicker and more accurate than a hacksaw for cutting copper pipe. It may have an adjustable slide for cutting tubes of different diameters, and a fixed cutting wheel. Some have a tapered reamer on the front for removing the burr from the inside of the pipe. A small circular cutter known as a pipe slice is useful for cutting pipes in situ. It is fitted round the pipe and rotated to make the cut.

Immersion heater spanner This large spanner is specially designed for removing and fitting the electrical element of an immersion heater. Hire one if you need it.

Cutting off the water supply

In many homes, only the kitchen tap is fed from the rising main; others are fed from the cold water cistern. It depends whether the plumbing system is direct or indirect (page 324).

Taps fed from the cistern

1 To isolate a hot or cold tap supplied from the cistern, turn off the gatevalve on the supply pipe from the cistern. If a service valve (see right) is fitted in the pipe to the tap, turn it off with a screwdriver.

2 Turn on the tap until the water has stopped flowing.

Alternatively If there is no gatevalve or service valve on the pipe, you will have to drain the cistern.

Draining the cistern

1 Tie the ballvalve arm to a piece of wood laid across the cistern (see opposite). This stops the flow from the mains.

2 Turn on the bathroom cold taps until the water stops flowing, then turn on the hot taps – very little water will flow from them. (You need not turn off the boiler, as the hot water cylinder will not be drained.)

HELPFUL TIP

A stoptap that has been open for a long time may be jammed. To guard against this, close and open the stoptap fully twice a year. After opening it, give the handle a quarter turn towards closure. This prevents jamming without affecting water flow. If a stoptap is difficult to turn, apply a few drops of penetrating oil round the spindle base and leave for ten minutes before turning the handle again. Repeat as necessary.

TYPES OF STOPTAP AND ISOLATING VALVE

Stoptap A tap with a valve and washer that is inserted into a mains-pressure supply pipe to control the water flow through it. A stoptap is usually kept turned on, being turned off only when necessary to cut off the supply. It must be fitted the right way round (an arrow mark shows the flow direction). Most stoptaps have a crutch handle.

Drain valve A tap without a handle, opened by turning the spindle with a drain valve key. It is normally kept closed, but has a ribbed outlet for attaching a hose when draining is necessary. A drain valve is fitted in those parts of the plumbing system that cannot be drained through household taps – for instance, in the boiler or central-heating systems and on the rising main.

Gatevalve An isolating valve with a wheel handle, through which the water flow is controlled by raising or lowering a metal plate (or gate). It can be fitted either way round and is normally used in low-pressure pipes such as supply pipes from a storage cistern. With the gate open, the flow is completely unrestricted. When it is closed, the seal is not as watertight as a stoptap.

Service valve A small isolating valve operated with a screwdriver. This turns a pierced plug inside the valve to stop or restore the water flow. Normally used in a low-pressure supply pipe to a tap or ballvalve to cut off the water for repairs. A similar valve with a small lever handle and a threaded outlet is used to control the flow to the flexible supply hoses of a washing machine or dishwasher.

Taps fed from the rising main

Turn off the main indoor stoptap, then turn on the mains-fed tap until the water stops.

Draining the rising main

You may want to drain the rising main to take a branch pipe from it or to repair the main stoptap. If there is a drain valve above the stoptap, fit a short piece of hose to its outlet and open it with a drain valve key or pliers. Catch the water, usually only a litre or two, in a bucket.

Turning off the outdoor stoptap

You may need to turn off the outdoor stoptap if the indoor one is broken, jammed or has a leak from the spindle.

Stoptap keys can be bought from plumbers' merchants, but first check the type needed – the tap may have a crutch handle or a square spindle.

Alternatively If you have no stoptap key, make your own. Take a piece of strong wood about 1m long and in one end cut a V-shaped slot about 25mm wide at the opening and 75mm deep. Securely fix a piece of wood as a cross-bar handle at the other end. Slip the slot over the stoptap handle to turn it. This tool will not turn a stoptap with a square spindle.

1 Locate the stoptap, which is under a cover, about 100mm across, just inside or just outside the boundary of your property. If you cannot find the outdoor stoptap, call your water supply company.

2 Raise the cover. This may be difficult if it has not been raised for some time.

3 Insert the stoptap key into the guard pipe and engage the stoptap handle at the bottom. Turn it clockwise.

Draining down the system

Central heating systems sometimes have to be drained down – to repair a leak, for example. The following method is for an open-vented system, the most common type.

1 Switch off the boiler at the programmer or time switch.

2 Turn off the gas, either at the isolating gas cock near the boiler or by the gas meter. Make sure that the fire in a solid-fuel boiler is out and that the boiler is cold. There is no need to turn off the oil supply in an oil-fired system.

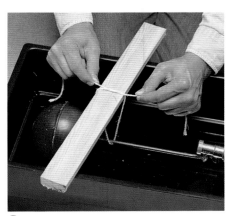

3 Shut off the water supply to the feed-and-expansion cistern. There should be a separate stoptap for this on the branch pipe from the rising main connected to the cistern's ballvalve.

  If there is no separate stoptap, or it is jammed and cannot be turned, stop the water flow into the cistern by tying up the ballvalve to a piece of wood laid across the top of the cistern.

4 Locate the drain valve, which may be near the bottom of the boiler. There may be more than one drainage point on the system. Clip a garden hose onto the outlet and run the hose to a drain outside.

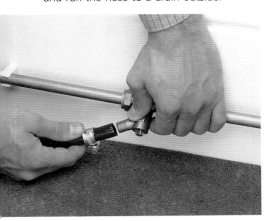

5 Locate all the points at which air is vented from the central heating system. There will be radiator vents, a vent on the primary flow near the hot water cylinder in fully pumped systems, and manual or automatic vents in the loft if circulating pipes run there. There could be additional vents at other points as well.

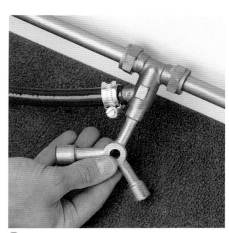

6 Open the drain valve with a spanner or pliers, turning counter-clockwise. Water will then start to flow out of the hose at a fairly slow rate.

7 Start opening the venting points at the top of the system. This will greatly speed up the flow from the drain valve. As the water level drops further, open the lower venting points until they are all open.

Refilling the system

1 Close all the drain valves and all the air vents in the system. Then check that all work on the system is finished.

2 Turn on the stoptap to the header tank, or untie the ballvalve, in order to let water back into the system.

3 Open one of the lowest air vents until water starts to flow out, then close it. Repeat with the lower air vents until the bottom of the central heating system is full of water. Then do the upper vents, and close them when the system is full.

4 Make sure that the ballvalve to the header tank has closed. The water level in the cistern should be just high enough to float the ball. The rest of the cistern space is to take up the expansion of the water in the system as it heats up.

5 If the water level is too high, close off the mains water supply to the cistern and open the drain valve to let some out. Adjust the arm on the ballvalve so that it closes the valve at the correct water level. Check that the cistern's lid and insulating jacket are in place.

6 Switch on the electricity and turn on the gas. Re-light the pilot light in a gas boiler. Turn on the system at the programmer or timeswitch. Turn up the room thermostat.

7 Re-light the boiler, following the manufacturer's instructions.

8 As the system heats up, more venting will be necessary in order to release air driven off from the water. Minor venting will be required for a few days.

9 Check for leaks again.

10 Remove the hose from the drain valve, and make sure the valve is water-tight. If it is leaking, drain the system again, and remove the spindle. The washer is on the end of the spindle. Remove it and replace it with a new one. Use a fibre type in preference to a rubber one because rubber washers tend to bake on and disintegrate.

A GOOD TIME TO ADD SERVICE VALVES

Draining down the system for repairs presents an excellent opportunity to fit service valves on the pipes supplying every tap and WC cistern ballvalve. Having done this, you will be able to repair or replace any tap or ballvalve without having to drain the system beforehand.

Repairing a burst pipe

Metal pipes are more likely to suffer frost damage than plastic pipes. Copper and stainless steel pipes are less vulnerable than softer lead pipes.

As an ice plug forms, it expands and may split the pipe or force open a joint. When the ice melts, the pipe or fitting leaks. A split copper or plastic pipe can be temporarily repaired with a proprietary burst-pipe repair clamp. In an emergency, a pipe not under mains pressure can be patched with a length of garden hose.

Make a permanent repair as soon as possible. Cut off the water supply (page 328), drain the pipe and replace the damaged length. For a split less than 90mm long in a copper pipe, you can make a permanent repair with a slip coupling.

For lead piping, use a tape-repair kit for a strong repair that will allow you to restore the water supply until a plumber can make a permanent repair (working on lead pipework is best left to a professional).

Using a slip coupling

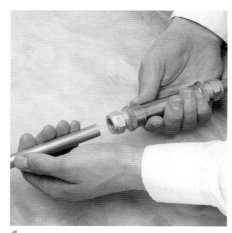

1 Cut out the damaged part and slide the slip end of the coupling (with no pipe stop) onto a pipe end. Then push it onto the other end. If it will not go in, unscrew the backnuts and slide the nuts and olives at each end along the pipe first.

2 Refit the nuts and olives and screw them up hand-tight. Then tighten the nuts for one and a quarter turns with a spanner.

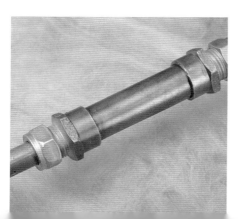

Patching a split branch pipe

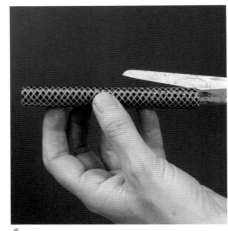

1 Cut a piece of garden hose that is long enough to cover the pipe for at least 50mm beyond the area of damage. Split the hose along its length.

2 Wrap the hose round the pipe to cover the damage and secure it with three loops of strong wire. Twist the loops closed tightly with pliers.

3 Alternatively Fit an emergency pipe repair clamp and tighten the screws fully with a screwdriver.

Dealing with an airlock

If the water flow from a tap (usually a hot tap) is poor when fully turned on, then hisses and bubbles and stops altogether, there is an airlock in the supply pipe.

Tools *Length of hose with a push-fit tap adaptor at each end. Possibly also dishcloth; screwdriver.*

1 Connect one end of the hose to the tap giving the trouble. If it is a bath tap and the hose is difficult to fit, connect to the nearby washbasin hot tap instead.

2 Connect the other end of the hose to the kitchen cold tap or to another mains-fed tap. Turn on the faulty tap first, then the mains-fed tap. The pressure of the mains water should blow the air bubble out of the pipe.

Important When applying mains pressure to a pipe in a stored-water circuit, there is a very slight risk of water from the system contaminating the mains water supply. Therefore you should do the job quickly and disconnect the hose immediately afterwards.

Airlock in a kitchen mixer

If the hot tap will not work, remove the swivel spout (page 335) and hold a cloth firmly over the spout hole while you turn on first the hot tap then the cold tap.

If airlocks keep occurring

There are many ways that air can be drawn into the water system and cause airlocks. Check these possibilities:
• Is the cold water cistern too small for the household's needs? If it is smaller than the standard 230 litres, replace it with one of standard size.
• Is the ballvalve in the cold water cistern sluggish? Watch the cistern emptying while the bath fills. If the valve does not open wide enough as water is drawn off, there will be a slow inflow and the cistern will empty before the bath is filled, allowing air to be drawn into the supply pipe. Dismantle and clean the ballvalve (page 340).
• Is the supply pipe from the cold water cistern to the hot water cylinder obstructed or too narrow? Check that any gatevalve is fully open, and replace the pipe if it is narrower than 22mm in diameter. If hot water drawn for a bath is not replaced quickly enough, the water level in the vent pipe will fall below the level of the hot water supply pipe, and air will enter.

HELPFUL TIP

When additions are made to the plumbing, make sure that all horizontal lengths of supply pipe are laid so that they fall away slightly from the main vent pipe. Any air bubbles entering the system will then be able to escape via the vent pipe.

Dealing with a blocked sink

Grease may have built up in the trap and waste pipe, trapping food particles and other debris. Alternatively, an object may be obstructing the waste pipe.

Tools *Possibly a length of wire; sink-waste plunger; sink auger or a length of expanding curtain wire; bucket.*

Materials *Possibly caustic soda or proprietary chemical or enzyme cleaner; petroleum jelly.*

Sink slow to empty

• If a sink is slow to empty, smear petroleum jelly on the rim of the plug hole to protect it, and then apply proprietary chemical or enzyme cleaner according to the manufacturer's instructions.

Sink completely blocked

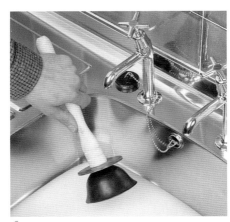

1 If the water will not run away at all, place the sink plunger cup squarely over the plug hole.

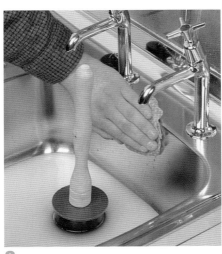

2 Stuff a damp cloth firmly into the overflow opening and hold it there. This stops air escaping through the hole and dissipating the force you build up by plunging.

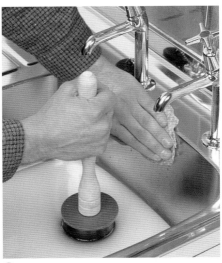

3 Pump the plunger sharply up and down. If the blockage does not clear, repeat the operation.

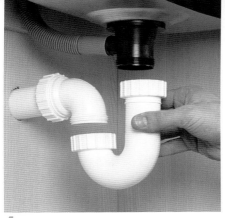

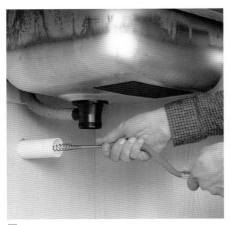

4 If plunging fails, replace the sink plug. Put a bucket under the sink and disconnect the trap. Wash it out thoroughly if it is blocked with debris.

5 If the obstruction is not in the trap, try using a plumber's snake. It is a spiral device that can be hired or bought. Disconnect the blocked pipe from its trap and feed the wire into it. Then turn the handle to rotate the spiral. This drives its cutting head into the blockage and breaks it up.

Alternatively If you have a vacuum cleaner that is designed to cope with liquids, you can use it to try to dislodge a blockage in a sink trap. Press a cloth over the overflow in the sink. Then place the suction tube of the vacuum over the plughole and switch on. This will probably loosen the blockage sufficiently to allow it to be carried away by the water flow through the trap.

Alternatively If you have poured fat into the sink and it has hardened, try warming the pipe with a hair dryer, to melt the grease. Flush plenty of hot water after it.

Other pipe blockages

Washing machines and dishwashers are often plumbed in to feed the under-sink waste trap. Alternatively, they may join the main waste pipe at a T-junction away from the sink. If all your appliances feed into the one trap, you may need to disconnect all the pipes in turn and then clean each one to solve a blockage.

Repairing a dripping tap

A dripping tap usually means that the tap washer needs renewing, but can also be caused by a damaged valve seating. If the drip is from a mixer spout, renew both tap washers.

Tools *One large open-ended spanner, normally 20mm for a 12mm tap or 24mm for a 19mm tap (or use an adjustable spanner); old screwdriver (for prising). Possibly also one small spanner (normally 8mm); one or two pipe wrenches; cloth for padding jaws; one 5mm, one 10mm screwdriver.*

Materials *Replacement washer or a washer-and-jumper valve unit; alternatively, a washer-and-seating set; petroleum jelly. Possibly also penetrating oil.*

Removing the headgear

1 Cut off the water supply (page 328). Make sure the tap is turned fully on, and put the plug into the plughole to stop any small parts falling down the waste pipe.

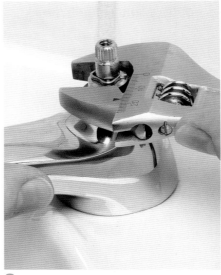

2 Unscrew or lever off the cover of a non-rising spindle tap to expose the retaining screw. Remove the screw and put it in a safe place. Remove the head.

Alternatively With a rising spindle tap, prise off the index disc and remove the retaining screw to release the capstan from the spindle. Use a wrench wrapped in cloth to unscrew the metal shroud and lift it away from the headgear nut.

3 Undo the headgear nut with a spanner. Do not force the nut, if it is stiff. Brace the tap body by hand or with a pipe wrench wrapped in a cloth, to prevent the tap from turning and fracturing the pipework attached to it.

4 If the nut is still difficult to turn, apply penetrating oil round the joint, wait about ten minutes to give it time to soak in, then try again. You may have to make several applications.

Fitting the washer

1 Prise off the washer with a screwdriver. If there is a small nut holding it in place, unscrew it with a spanner (normally 8mm). If it is difficult to undo, put penetrating oil round it and try again when it has soaked in. Then prise off the washer.

Alternatively If the nut is impossible to remove, you can replace both the jumper valve and washer in one unit.

2 After fitting a new washer or washer and jumper, grease the threads on the base of the tap before reassembling.

Rising spindle The jumper valve is in the shape of a rod and plate, and the washer is attached to the base of the plate. When changing a washer, the handle is lifted off with the headgear. When adjusting the gland nut, the handle has to be removed so that the bell-shaped cover can be pulled off out of the way.

Non-rising spindle The jumper valve and washer are the same as in a traditional rising spindle tap, but the spindle is sealed by an O-ring nut rather than a gland nut. The tap handle and headgear have to be removed to change a washer or to renew an O-ring.

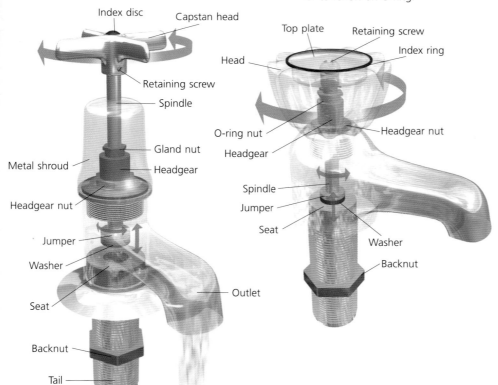

Index disc
Capstan head
Retaining screw
Spindle
Gland nut
Metal shroud
Headgear
Headgear nut
Jumper
Washer
Seat
Backnut
Tail
Outlet

Top plate
Head
Retaining screw
Index ring
O-ring nut
Headgear nut
Headgear
Spindle
Jumper
Seat
Washer
Backnut

Repairing the valve seating

- Washer-and-jumper valve unit
- Plastic seating
- Valve seat

When renewing a washer, inspect the valve seat inside the tap body. If it is scaled or scored by grit, the seal between washer and seat will not be effective even with a new washer.

The simplest repair is with a washer-and-seating set. This has a plastic seat to fit into the valve seat, and a washer-and-jumper valve unit to fit into the headgear.

When the tap is turned off, the plastic seating is forced firmly into place. It may take a few days for the new seating to give a completely watertight fit.

An alternative repair is to buy or hire a tap reseating tool and grind the seat smooth yourself.

Tap conversion kit

You may be able to get a tap conversion kits to change the style of taps and replace worn or broken mechanisms. Newer heads can be changed back to Victorian brass heads, or a tap with a crutch or capstan handle can be given a newer look. The spout and body of the tap remain in place.

Some kits have bushes to fit different tap sizes. The kits are available from most DIY stores and fitting instructions are included.

AVOIDING HARD-WATER DAMAGE TO TAPS

If you live in a hard-water area, you should check your taps for damage, once a year.

Turn off the mains water supply. One at a time check that the headgear on each tap unscrews easily. Use penetrating oil to release stiff nuts and use a spanner and a wrench wrapped in a cloth to hold the body of the tap as you turn.

If limescale has built up, remove and soak small parts in vinegar or limescale remover. Smear the thread with lubricant before reassembling.

Cleaning or replacing ceramic discs

Ceramic disc taps operate on a different principle from conventional taps that have washers and spindles. Positioned in the body of the tap is a cartridge containing a pair of ceramic discs, each with two holes in it.

One disc is fixed in position; the other rotates when the handle is turned. As the movable disc rotates, the holes in it line up with the holes in the fixed one and water flows through them. When the tap is turned off the movable disc rotates so that the holes no longer align.

Dealing with a dripping tap

If a scratched ceramic disc is causing the leak, the entire cartridge must be replaced: left-handed for a hot tap or right-handed for a cold tap. Remove the old cartridge and take it with you when buying a replacement to make sure it is the correct size and 'hand'. Ceramic taps can also drip at the base of the cartridge if the seal has perished. Replace it if necessary.

Checking discs in a ceramic disc mixer tap

1 Turn off the water supply. Pull off the tap handles (it may be necessary to unscrew a small retaining screw on each) and use a spanner to unscrew the headgear section.

2 Carefully remove the ceramic cartridges, keeping hot and cold separate. Check both cartridges for dirt and wear and tear.

Ceramic disc tap In this type of tap, one ceramic disc is rotated against another until openings in the discs line up and water can flow through.

3 If the cartridges are worn, replace with identical parts for the tap unit. Make sure the hot and cold cartridges are fitted into the correct taps.

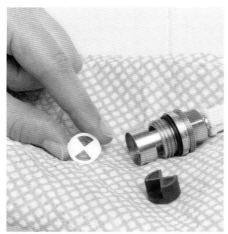

4 If the cartridges are dirty, clean them with a damp cloth. Replace the rubber seal, if it is worn. Replace the cartridge in the tap unit, fitting the hot and cold cartridges into the appropriate taps.

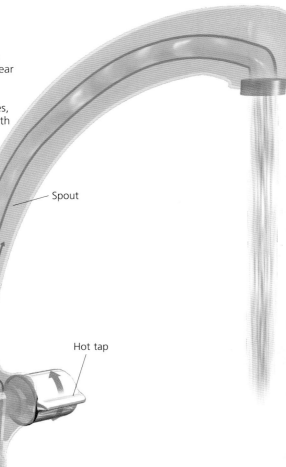

- Spout
- O-ring seals
- Index ring
- Ceramic discs
- Cold tap
- Cartridge
- Hot tap

Curing a leak from a spindle or spout

Leakage from the body of the tap – from round the spindle, the base of a swivel spout, or the diverter knob on a shower mixer tap – may indicate a faulty gland or O-ring seal.

Possible causes This sort of leak is most likely to occur on a kitchen cold tap with a bell-shaped cover and visible spindle. Soapy water from wet hands may have run down the spindle and washed the grease out of the gland that makes a watertight joint round the spindle. If the tap is used with a hose for watering the garden, back pressure from the hose connection will also weaken the gland.

On a modern tap, especially one with a shrouded head, there is an O-ring seal instead of a gland, and it rarely needs replacing. However, an O-ring seal may occasionally become worn.

Tools *Small spanner (normally 12mm) or adjustable spanner. Possibly also one 5mm and one 10mm screwdriver; penknife or screwdriver for prising; two small wooden blocks about 10mm deep (such as spring clothes pegs).*

Materials *Packing materials (gland-packing string or PTFE tape). Possibly also silicone grease; O-rings (and possibly washers) of the correct size – take the old ones with you when buying, or give the make of tap.*

Adjusting the gland

There is no need to cut off the water supply to the tap.

1 With the tap turned off, undo the small screw that secures the capstan handle and put it in a safe place (it is very easily lost), then remove the handle. If there is no screw, the handle should pull off.

2 Remove the bell-shaped cover to reveal the gland nut – the highest nut on the spindle. Tighten the nut about half a turn with a spanner.

3 Turn the tap on by temporarily slipping the handle back on, then check whether there is still a leak from the spindle. If there is not, turn the gland nut another quarter turn and reassemble the tap. Do not overtighten the gland nut, or the tap will be hard to turn off.

4 If there is still a leak, give another half turn and check again.

5 If the gland continues leaking after you have adjusted it as far as possible, repack the gland.

Replacing the packing

1 With the tap turned off and the handle and cover removed, use a spanner to remove the gland nut and lift it out.

2 Pick out the old packing with a small screwdriver. Replace it with packing string from a plumbers' merchant or with PTFE tape pulled into a thin string. Pack it in with a screwdriver, then replace the gland nut and reassemble the tap.

Renewing the O-ring on a shrouded-head tap

1 Cut off the water supply to the tap (page 328) and remove the tap handle and headgear in the same way as for renewing a washer.

2 Hold the headgear between your fingers and turn the spindle clockwise to unscrew and remove the washer unit.

3 Prise out the O-ring at the top of the washer unit with a screwdriver or penknife.

4 Smear the new O-ring with silicone grease, fit it in position, and reassemble the tap.

RELEASING THE SPINDLE

A non-rising spindle tap may have a circlip keeping the spindle in place. When you have removed the headgear, lever out the circlip so that you can gain access to the worn O-rings.

Renewing O-rings on a kitchen mixer tap

1 With both taps turned off, remove any retaining screw found behind the spout. If there is no screw, turn the spout to line up with the tap body and pull upwards sharply.

2 Note the position of the O-rings (probably two) and remove them.

3 Coat new O-rings of the correct size with silicone grease and fit them in position.

4 Smear the inside of the spout end with petroleum jelly, then refit it to the tap body.

Replacing shower-diverter O-rings

Diverters vary in design, but most have a sprung rod and plate attached to the diverter knob. When the knob is lifted, the plate opens the shower outlet and seals the tap outlet for as long as the shower is on.

1 With the bath taps turned off, lift the shower-diverter knob and undo the headgear nut with a spanner (probably 12mm size or use an adjustable spanner).

2 Lift out the diverter body and note the position of the washers and O-rings.

3 Remove the knob from the diverter body by turning it anticlockwise. You may need to grip it with a wrench.

4 Withdraw the rod and plate from the diverter body and remove the small O-ring at the top of the rod.

5 Grease a new O-ring of the correct size with silicone grease and fit it in place.

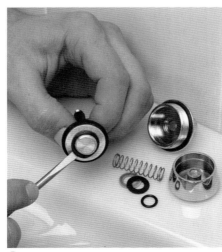

6 Replace all other rubber washers and O-rings on the base of the rod and plate. Old ones may have to be prised out.

REPACKING A STOPTAP WITH FIBRE STRING

The gland on a capstan-handle stoptap is the type most likely to need repacking. Use fibre string (from a plumbers' merchant) or PTFE tape.

1 Turn off the stoptap. Undo the gland nut, slide it up the spindle and remove it.

2 Rake out the gland packing with a penknife or similar tool.

3 To repack the gland with fibre string, steep a length in petroleum jelly and wind and stuff it into the gland with a screwdriver blade. Wind and push the string in until it is caulked down hard, then reassemble the tap.

Repairing a faulty WC cistern

An overflow or a failure of a WC to flush properly are often caused by a faulty ballvalve, which governs the water level in the cistern.

Before you start Failure to flush properly is caused by either a low water level, or a worn or damaged flap valve. To determine the cause, first check the water level.

The plastic lever arm linking the spindle of the flush control to the siphon lift rod may eventually wear out and break. Replacement lever arms can be bought and are easily fitted.

Checking the water level

1 Remove the cistern lid (it may lift off or be held by one or more screws). When the cistern is full, the water level should be about 25mm below the overflow outlet. Or there may be a water level marked on the inside wall of the cistern.

FLUSHING PROBLEMS

The most common problems with WCs are that the WC will not flush, that water runs continuously into the pan or that water runs continuously into the cistern and out through the overflow pipe. Most of these problems are easily fixed.

WC will not flush Check that the flushing lever is still attached to the internal workings of the cistern. Reattach the link or improvise a replacement from a length of thick wire. If the link is still in place, the flap valve may need replacing – this is often the cause if you need to operate the lever several times before the WC will flush.

Continuous flushing When water keeps running into the pan, the siphon may have split or the sealing washer at the base of the siphon may have perished. Both can be replaced. Alternatively, the cistern may be filling too fast, so that the siphoning action of the flush mechanism cannot be interrupted. Fit a restrictor in the float valve to reduce the water flow.

Overflowing cistern Continuous filling may be caused by a faulty float valve or a badly adjusted float arm. Try adjusting the float arm before you replace the valve.

2 If the level is low, repair or adjust the ballvalve (page 339).

If the level is too high and the cistern is overflowing or in danger of doing so, flush it, then repair or adjust the ballvalve.

If the level is correct, the problem is probably with the flap valve and you will need to renew it.

Renewing the flap valve in a standard siphon

A standard low-level suite has a full-sized cistern separate from the pan. The flap valve may be sold under the names siphon washer or cistern diaphragm. If you do not know the size you want, buy the largest available and cut it down.

A slimline cistern is repaired in the same way as a standard cistern, but some types are linked to the flush pipe with a locking ring-seal joint rather than with two nuts.

Tools *Screwdriver; wooden batten slightly longer than the cistern width; string; pipe wrench with a jaw opening of about 65mm; bowl or bucket. Possibly also sharp coloured pencil; scissors; container for bailing, or tube for siphoning.*

Materials *Plastic flap valve. Possibly also O-ring for ring-seal joint.*

1 With the cistern lid removed, lay a batten across the cistern and tie the float arm to it to stop the inflow of water.

2 Empty the cistern. If it cannot be flushed at all, bail or siphon the water out.

---

3 Use a large pipe wrench to undo the lower of the two large nuts underneath the cistern, then disconnect the flush pipe and push it to one side.

4 Put a bowl or bucket underneath the cistern and undo the large nut immediately under the cistern (this is the siphon-retaining nut). A pint or two of water will flow out as you loosen the nut.

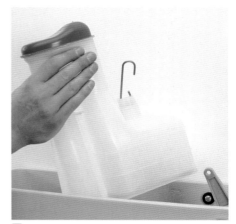

5 Unhook the lift rod from the flushing lever, lift the inverted U-pipe (the siphon) out from the cistern and lay it on its side.

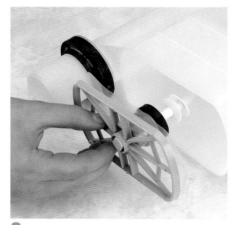

6 Pull out the lift rod and plate and remove the worn flap valve. If the new valve is too big, cut it down with scissors using the old valve as a pattern. It should touch, but not drag on, the dome sides.

7 Fit the new valve over the lift rod and onto the plate, then reassemble the flushing mechanism and reconnect the cistern.

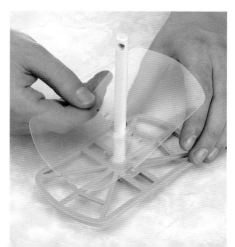

Renewing the flap valve on a close-coupled suite

On some close-coupled suites, the siphon is held by two or more bolts inside the cistern rather than by a large nut underneath. Except for this difference, the flap valve is renewed in the same way as on a standard suite.

On others, the cistern must be lifted off in order to disconnect the siphon. The flap valve can then be renewed in the same way as on a standard suite. Lift off the cistern as follows:

1 Cut off the water supply to the cistern in the same way as for a tap. Empty the cistern by flushing, bailing or siphoning out the water.

2 Disconnect the overflow pipe and water supply pipe from the cistern. They generally have screw fittings with a back nut.

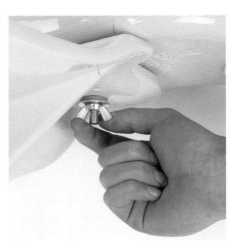

3 Undo the screws holding the cistern to the wall, and the wing nuts securing it to the rear platform of the pan.

4 Lift off the cistern from the pan and unhook the lift rod. Turn the cistern over, unscrew the retaining nut, remove the siphon and plate and renew the valve as above.

Renewing the flap valve on a two-part siphon

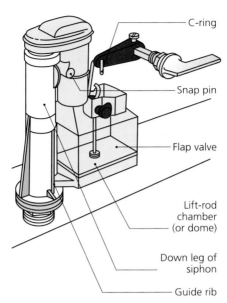

- C-ring
- Snap pin
- Flap valve
- Lift-rod chamber (or dome)
- Down leg of siphon
- Guide rib

If a cistern is fitted with a two-part plastic siphon, there is no need to stop the inflow or, with a close-coupled suite, to remove the cistern.

A two-part siphon can be fitted to most types of WC cistern. The initial fitting does involve cutting off the water supply and, if necessary, lifting off the cistern (see left). After that, maintenance is as below.

Tools *Screwdriver.*

Materials *Spares pack for size of siphon (containing flap valve); washers. Possibly also O-ring-seal.*

1 With the cistern lid removed, unhook the flush lever from the lift-rod C-ring. Remove a lever-type flush handle, as it may be in the way later.

2 Withdraw the snap pin about 30mm to disconnect the lift-rod chamber from the down leg of the siphon.

3 Slide the chamber upwards to disengage it from the guide rib on the down leg.

4 Remove the C-ring and washer from the top of the lift rod and slide the lift rod from the bottom of the chamber.

5 Take off the lift-rod washers and weight so that you can remove the old flap valve and fit a new one.

6 Before reassembling, check if the O-ring seal at the top of the chamber section is worn. Renew it if necessary.

HOW A PUSH-BUTTON FLUSH WORKS

Many modern slimline WC cisterns are too small to accommodate a traditional ball float-operated inlet valve and siphon flush mechanism, operated by a lever and float arm.

Instead, the inlet valve is either a modified diaphragm type with a very short float arm and miniature float, or an ingenious vertical valve with a float cup that fits round the central column of the valve body. Both are very quiet in operation, although the float-cup valve can be slow to refill the cistern if it is supplied with water from a storage tank, rather than being plumbed in directly to the mains.

In these slimline mechanisms, the traditional siphon flushing method (page 354) is replaced by a plastic valve-operated flush mechanism that is activated by a top-mounted push button in the cistern lid. The mechanism also incorporates an integral overflow. The push button is in two parts: you depress one part for a low-volume flush, and both sections of the button for a full-volume flush. The push button is linked to a plunger to operate the flush, rather than the conventional wire link and float arm of a traditional flushing mechanism.

Installing a float-cup inlet valve
The float-cup inlet valve and the valve-operated flush mechanism are both very ingenious in design, but can be tricky to adjust during installation. The valve should be adjusted so that the critical level mark indicated on the body of the valve should be at least 25mm above the top of the overflow pipe. There is a threaded shank at the base of the valve unit which can be screwed in and out of the valve body to adjust the overall length of the valve until you get the positioning correct.

Repair and maintenance
The float-cup inlet valve contains a rubber ring seal at the base of the cistern, which may need replacing in time, and these are not yet widely available. Be sure to keep the installation instructions after you have installed the valve so that you have a record of where to obtain any spare parts in the future.

How a ballvalve works

In a cold water storage cistern or WC cistern, the water level is regulated by a ballvalve that is opened and closed by a lever arm attached to a float.

Understanding the system

A cold water storage cistern, or a WC cistern where the supply is direct from the mains, needs a high-pressure valve. A WC cistern supplied from the cold water storage cistern needs a low-pressure valve. If the pressure is very low because the WC cistern is only slightly lower than the storage cistern, a full-way valve is needed.

Low-pressure valves have wider inlet nozzles than high-pressure valves. If a high-pressure valve is fitted where a low-pressure valve is needed, the cistern will fill much too slowly. If a low-pressure valve is fitted in a cistern supplied from the mains, water will leak past the valve.

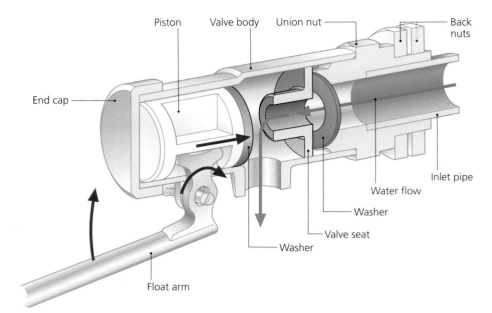

Piston | Valve body | Union nut | Back nuts
End cap | Inlet pipe | Water flow | Washer | Valve seat | Washer | Float arm

Most modern valves can be changed from high-pressure to low-pressure operation either by inserting a different fitting into the inlet nozzle or by changing a detachable inlet nozzle. Some types are suitable for high or low water pressure without any alteration.

1 When the cistern is at normal level, the float holds the arm horizontal and the valve is closed.

2 When the water level drops, the float lowers the arm and the valve opens to let more water in.

BALLVALVES IN COMMON USE

The name ballvalve is from the early type of copper ball float. Modern floats are not always balls, and ballvalves are often called float valves. Ballvalves may be made from brass, gunmetal or plastic, or may be metal with some plastic parts. The size is measured by the inlet shank diameter; 15mm or 22mm sizes are usually needed for domestic cisterns.

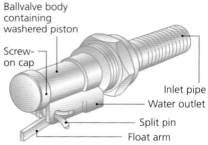

Ballvalve body containing washered piston
Screw-on cap
Inlet pipe
Water outlet
Split pin
Float arm

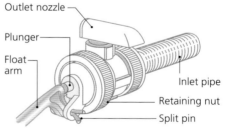

Outlet nozzle
Plunger
Float arm
Inlet pipe
Retaining nut
Split pin

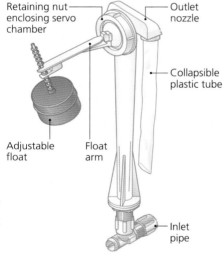

Retaining nut enclosing servo chamber
Outlet nozzle
Collapsible plastic tube
Adjustable float
Float arm
Inlet pipe

Portsmouth valve The most common type in British homes, although no longer allowed on WC cisterns, Portsmouth valves are sturdy and long-lasting. However, they can be noisy and require regular maintenance. Water hammer – vibration of the rising main – can result from the valve bouncing in its seating. The bouncing is caused by ripples on the water surface when the cistern is almost full, making the float arm shake; sometimes also by the pressure of incoming water against the valve. Scale or corrosion can prevent the valve from operating properly. Only high-pressure types are now available (for use on mains-fed cold water cisterns). There must be a method of water adjustment other than bending the float arm.

Diaphragm valve (also known as BRE, BRS or Garston) The water inlet is closed by a large rubber or synthetic diaphragm pushed against it by a plunger attached to the float arm. A detachable nylon overhead outlet nozzle discharges water in a gentle shower. Available with either a metal body (Part 2 valve) or a plastic body (Part 3 valve) and in high-pressure or low-pressure versions. The discharge spray cuts down filling noise and rippling, and the diaphragm keeps the plunger and float arm from contact with water, so they are not affected by scale and corrosion. The diaphragm can become worn, and grit can block the inlet chamber. The valve can be dismantled by hand for cleaning or replacement by undoing a large knurled retaining nut.

Servo-diaphragm valve (also diaphragm/equilibrium or Torbeck valve) A plastic valve with small float and short float arm for use only in a WC cistern. Behind a diaphragm covering the inlet is a water (or servo) chamber fed via a metering pin. Equal water pressure on each side of the diaphragm keeps it closed. When the float arm drops it opens a pilot hole in the back of the chamber, covered by a sealing washer. This reduces pressure in the servo chamber, and the diaphragm opens the inlet. The outlet is overhead and via a collapsible plastic tube. Can cope with a range of water pressures: available in bottom and side entry versions. Delivery is rapid and silent. The valve can be fitted with a filter, which collects grit that might otherwise obstruct the metering pin and pilot hole. Flow restrictors in the inlet pipe adapt it for high or low-pressures.

Adjusting the cistern water level

The normal level of a full cistern is about 25mm below the overflow outlet. The level can be raised by raising the float, or lowered by lowering the float.

Adjusting a ballvalve

Before you start If the cistern overflows, the water level is too high because the float either needs adjusting or is leaking and failing to rise to close the valve (or the valve itself may be faulty, right).

Tools *Possibly small spanner; vice.*

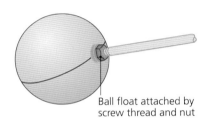

Ball float attached by screw thread and nut

On a Portsmouth-pattern valve with a ball float, unscrew and remove the float from the arm. To lower the level, hold the arm firmly in both hands and bend it slightly downwards. Then refit the float. If the arm is too stiff to bend in position, remove it from the cistern and grip it in a vice.

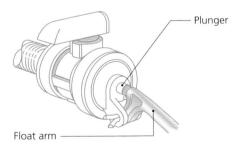

Plunger

Float arm

On a diaphragm valve with an adjuster at the top of the float arm, adjust the level by loosening the locking nut and screwing the adjuster forward, nearer to the plunger.

Alternatively Use an adjuster nut or clip near the float to move the float farther away from the valve along a horizontal arm, or to a lower position if it is linked to the arm by a vertical rod.

Repairing a faulty ballvalve

When a ballvalve does not open or close fully, it can cause airlocks and supply problems.

Portsmouth valves

Before you start If a ballvalve does not open fully, the cistern (WC or cold water storage) will be slow to fill and airlocks will occur. If the ballvalve does not close fully, the water level in the cistern becomes too high and causes a constant flow from the overflow pipe.

The water inlet of a Portsmouth valve is opened and closed by a washered piston that moves horizontally. The piston is slotted onto a float arm and secured with a split pin. Some types have a screw-on cap at the end of the piston. The water outlet is on the bottom of the valve in front of the float arm. The detachable inlet nozzle can be changed to suit the water pressure.

The valve will not work efficiently if the washer is worn or moving parts are clogged by limescale or corrosion.

Tools *Combination pliers; small screwdriver; fine abrasive paper; pencil. Possibly also penknife.*

Materials *Split pin (cotter pin); washer; petroleum jelly. Possibly also penetrating oil.*

1 Turn off the main stoptap if you are working on the cold water cistern, or close the gate valve or service valve to the WC cistern.

2 Use a pipe wrench to loosen the ballvalve end cap, if there is one, then unscrew and remove it.

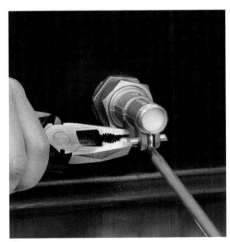

3 Use pliers to close the end of the split pin securing the float arm, then withdraw the pin. Remove the float arm and put it to one side.

4 Insert a small screwdriver blade into the slot where the float arm was seated. Use it to push the piston from the end of the casing. Catch the piston with your other hand as it comes out.

5 Clean the outside of a metal piston (but not a plastic one) with fine abrasive paper. Wrap fine abrasive paper round a pencil shaft and clean the inside of the metal valve casing.

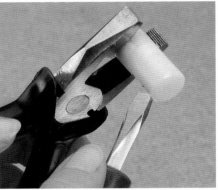

6 To renew the washer, hold the piston with a screwdriver thrust into the slot and use pliers to unscrew its washer-retaining cap. Do not force it or you may damage the piston. If a metal cap is difficult to undo, smear penetrating oil round the cap edge and try again after about ten minutes.

7 With the cap removed, use a screwdriver to prise out the washer from the inside. (If you were unable to remove the cap, try to pick out the old washer with a penknife through the cap's open centre.)

8 Fit the new washer and screw the cap back on. Tighten with pliers. (If the cap is still on, try to force the new washer through the centre hole and push it flat with your finger.) Before refitting the piston, turn on the water supply briefly to flush out dirt from the valve casing still attached to the cistern. Lightly smear the piston with petroleum jelly before reassembling the valve and float arm. Use a new split pin to secure the arm. Restore the water supply.

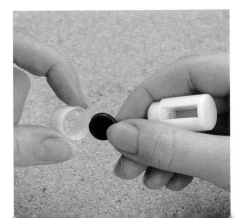

Diaphragm-type valves

The water inlet of a diaphragm-type valve is closed by a large rubber or synthetic diaphragm pushed against it by a plunger attached to the float arm. The cistern will be slow to refill if the inlet gets clogged or the diaphragm gets jammed against it.

Tools *Screwdriver. Possibly also pipe wrench; cloth for padding wrench jaws.*

Materials *Lint free rag; warm soapy water in container; clear water for rinsing. Possibly also replacement diaphragm.*

1 Turn off the main stoptap if you are working on the cold water cistern, or the gate valve or service valve on the pipe to the WC cistern (page 328).

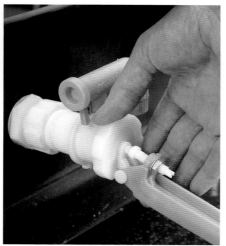

2 Unscrew the large knurled retaining nut by hand. If it is stiff, use a padded pipe wrench.

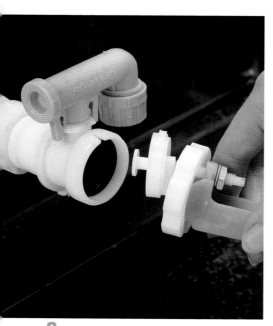

3 With the nut removed, the end of the float arm and plunger will come away. Put them to one side.

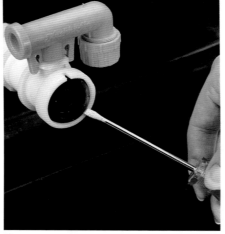

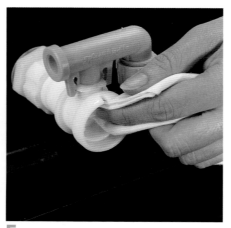

4 Use a screwdriver blade to free the diaphragm from the inlet pipe, taking care not to damage it. Note which way round it is fitted.

5 Use a piece of clean, lint-free rag to clean out any dirt and debris from the inlet pipe.

6 Wash the diaphragm in warm soapy water, then rinse it. If it is pitted or damaged, replace it. Fit with the rim inwards.

Alternatively If the valve is a servo type with a filter fitted, remove the filter and wash it in warm soapy water, then rinse it. If the servo valve has no filter, flush the part attached to the float arm under the tap.

GETTING RID OF WATER HAMMER

Banging or humming from the rising main is due to the pipe vibrating when the cistern ballvalve bounces on its seating. This occurs when the float is shaken by ripples on the water as the cistern fills. Cut down the bouncing by fitting the float with a stabiliser made from a plastic pot. Hang the pot on a loop of galvanised wire from the float arm. It should trail underwater just below the float.

Ensure that the rising main is securely clipped to the roof timbers near its entry to the cistern. Also, check that a metal bracing plate is fitted on a plastic cistern to reduce distortion of the cistern wall.

The surest way to reduce water hammer is to replace a Portsmouth valve with an equilibrium valve – a type less affected by water pressure.

7 Before reassembling the valve, turn on the water supply briefly to flush dirt or debris out of the casing. Then refit the parts and restore the water supply.

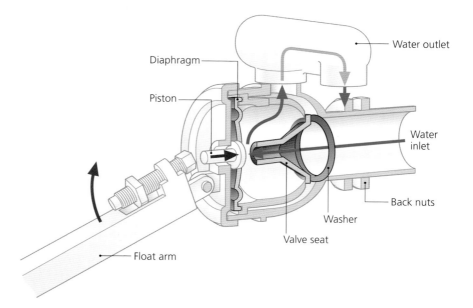

Diaphragm · Water outlet · Piston · Water inlet · Back nuts · Washer · Valve seat · Float arm

Fitting a new ballvalve

Fit a new ballvalve if the old one gets damaged or broken, or if you decide to change the type of valve to get rid of noise and vibration.

Tools *Two adjustable spanners.*

Materials *Ballvalve with float (of same size as existing valve); two flat plastic washers to fit valve inlet shank; service valve (page 328) with compression fitting inlet and tap connector outlet.*

1 Turn off the main stoptap to cut off the cistern water supply.

2 Use a spanner to undo the tap connector securing the supply pipe to the valve tail. You may need to hold the valve body or any securing nut inside the cistern steady with a second spanner.

3 Disconnect the supply pipe.

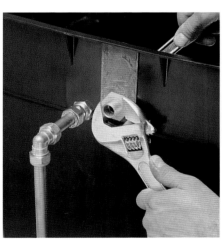

4 Undo the backnut securing the ballvalve to the cistern. Remove the valve.

5 Take off the backnut from the new ballvalve and put it aside.

6 Slip a flat plastic washer (and inner securing nut, if supplied) over the new valve tail and push the tail through the cistern and the bracing plate from the inside.

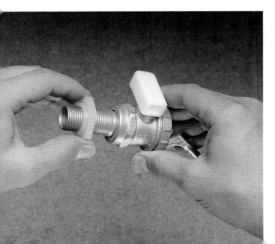

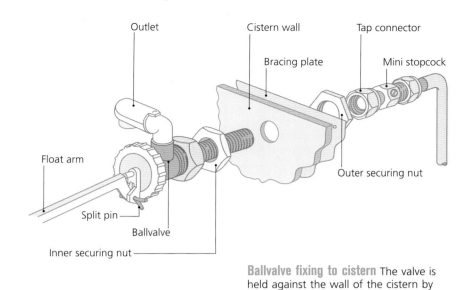

Outlet   Cistern wall   Tap connector

Bracing plate   Mini stopcock

Float arm

Outer securing nut

Split pin

Ballvalve

Inner securing nut

Ballvalve fixing to cistern The valve is held against the wall of the cistern by two backnuts on its threaded inlet tail.

7 Slip another plastic washer over the protruding tail and screw on the backnut by hand. Tighten it by half a turn with a spanner.

8 Remove the existing tap connector and fit the service valve. Screw the connector nut to the new valve tail.

9 Restore the water supply, making sure the service valve is fully open. Adjust the cistern water level (page 339).

REPAIRING A LEAKING FLOAT

For a permanent repair, a new ball float must be fitted. But to get the valve back in action again until a new float is obtained, the old one can be temporarily repaired.

Tools *Small spanner; sharp knife or old-fashioned bladed tin opener; piece of wood to go across cistern.*

Materials *Plastic bag; string.*

1 Raise the float arm to close the valve and cut off the flow of the water. Then tie the arm to a length of wood laid across the top of the cistern.

2 Unscrew and remove the ball float from the float arm.

3 Find the hole through which the water is leaking and enlarge it with either a sharp knife or tin opener.

4 Drain the water from the float, then screw it back in position on the float arm.

5 Slip the plastic bag over the float and tie it securely to the float arm with string.

6 Release the arm and lower it into position to refill the cistern.

Dealing with a faulty WC pan

The usual faults with a WC pan are blockages or leaks. A leak from the pan outlet is not difficult to repair, but a cracked pan will have to be replaced.

Clearing a washdown pan

When a washdown bowl is flushed, the two streams of water, one from each side of the rim, should flow equally to meet at the front. The water should leave the pan smoothly, not eddying like a whirlpool. If the cistern is working properly but the bowl fails to clear, something is obstructing either the flush inlet or the pan outlet.

If the flush water rises almost to the pan rim, then ebbs away very slowly, there is probably a blockage in the pan outlet (or possibly in the soil stack or drain into which it discharges.

Tools *WC plunger. Possibly also flexible drain auger; bucket; mirror; a pair of rubber gloves.*

1 To clear the pan, take the plunger and push it sharply onto the bottom of the pan to cover the outlet. Then pump the handle up and down two or three times.

2 If this does not clear the pan, use a flexible drain auger to probe the outlet and trap.

3 If the blockage persists, check and clear the underground drain (page 407).

4 Flush the cistern to check that water is entering the pan properly, with streams from each side of the rim flowing equally to meet at the front.

5 If the flow into the pan is poor or uneven, use a mirror to examine the flushing rim. Probe the rim with your fingers for flakes of limescale or debris from the cistern that may be obstructing the flush water.

Alternatively If you have no WC plunger, you may be able to use a mop. Or stand on a stool and tip in a bucket of water in all one go.

Clearing a siphonic pan

Blockages are more common in siphonic pans because of the double trap and the delicate pressure reducing pipe seal (also known as the atomiser seal). Do not use a plunger on a blocked siphonic pan because this can dislodge the seal.

A blockage can usually be cleared with an auger or by pouring several buckets of warm water into the pan. But if, after clearing the blockage, the water still rises in the pan as it is flushed, renew the seal.

Tools *Screwdriver; adjustable spanner; container for bailing or a tube for siphoning; silicone grease.*

Materials *Pressure reducing pipe seal.*

1 Remove the cistern (page 336) and locate the pipe protruding from the bottom of the siphon.

2 Remove the rubber mushroom-shaped seal and fit a replacement. Lubricate the new seal with silicone grease so that it will slide down the pipe.

3 Refit the cistern and test the flush. The water should be removed from the bowl with a sucking noise before the clean water comes in from the rim of the bowl.

Repairing a leaking pan outlet

A putty joint may leak when the putty gets old and cracked.

To replace a putty joint with a push-fit connector (page 355), the pan must be moved forward then refitted. Alternatively, you can repair the joint using waterproof building tape or non-setting mastic filler.

Chip and rake out the old putty with an old chisel and bind two or three turns of tape round the pan outlet. Then poke more tape firmly into the rim of the soil-pipe inlet. Fill the space between the rim and pan outlet with mastic. Bind two more turns of tape round the joint.

Choosing pipes and fittings

Copper and plastic are the two most common materials used in household pipework. Stainless steel piping can be used in the same way as copper. Although it is more expensive and harder to work with, it can be used safely with galvanised steel radiators, without the corrosive reaction that copper produces. Lead and iron pipes are no longer used, although they may still be found in older buildings.

Pipe sizes Domestic water supply pipes are made in metric sizes. Copper pipe is measured by the outside diameter. Standard sizes are 15mm, 22mm and 28mm. Older supply pipes were made in imperial sizes and were measured by the inside diameter. Imperial and metric piping can be joined, but an adaptor is needed for some sizes, depending on the type of joint and connector used.

Plastic supply pipes are made in the same nominal sizes as copper pipes, but have thicker walls. Medium-density polyethylene (MDPE) pipe is now widely used for underground supply pipes, and is coloured blue. Semi-flexible grey or black polybutylene (PB) and white cross-linked polyethylene (PEX) pipes are both used for indoor hot and cold supply pipes. Rigid chlorinated polyvinyl chloride (cPVC) supply pipe has also been used for some years, but is now obsolete.

PLUMBING AND EARTHING

All metal pipework must be joined to the house's main earth bonding system so that it is impossible for someone touching exposed metalwork to be electrocuted if it becomes live. See page 267 for more details.

Plastic pipe and fittings are non-conducting so if either has been used in a run of metal pipe, a 'bridging' earth wire must be fitted between the metal sections. When installing a metal bath or sink, follow the instructions on page 361.

If your house earthing system relies upon a connection to the rising main for an earthing point, this must be changed to a common earthing point near the meter. Contact a qualified electrician for advice.

Types of pipe

Copper
For hot and cold supply pipework indoors. Sold in three sizes (15, 22 and 28mm) in 2m and 3m lengths. Join with compression joints, with soldered capillary joints or with push-fit joints. Cut with a hacksaw or pipe cutter.

Advantages Withstands high temperatures. Bends easily round corners, so neat and economical to use. Can be painted. Widely available. Rigid, so needs few supports: 15mm pipe every 1m horizontally, 2m vertically; 22mm and 28mm pipe every 2m horizontally, 2.5m vertically.

Disadvantages Pipes hot to touch. May split or burst if water freezes. Brings about the corrosion of galvanised (zinc-coated) steel if joined directly to it.

Polybutylene (also known as Hep_2O pipe).
For hot and cold pipework indoors. Sold in straight lengths or in long coils. Join with Hep_2O push-fit joints or with compression joints (always with a metal support sleeve). Cut with a sharp knife or pipe cutters.

Advantages Easy to shape round bends. Pipe can be rotated in joint. Insulates well – pipes not too hot to touch. Not easily damaged by extreme cold, but cannot withstand high temperatures – must not be used within 350mm of boilers.

Disadvantages Pipework needs support to avoid sagging: 15mm pipe every 500mm horizontally, 1m vertically; 22mm pipe every 800mm horizontally, 1.2m vertically.

Cross-linked polyethylene (PEX)
For hot and cold pipework indoors. Sold in straight lengths and coils. Join with Speedfit push-fit joints or with compression joints (always with a metal pipe insert). Cut with a sharp knife or pipe secateurs.

Advantages Easy to shape round bends by hand or with a former. Can be painted. Insulates well – pipes not too hot to touch. Not easily damaged by cold but cannot withstand high temperatures – must not be used within 350mm of a boiler.

Disadvantages Needs support: 15mm pipe every 500mm horizontally, 1m vertically; 22mm pipe every 600mm horizontally, 1.2m vertically; shorter runs for hot water pipes.

BRASS IN ACID WATER

In areas where the water supply is particularly acid, check with the regional water company before using brass joints – especially if you are using copper piping. Brass is an alloy of zinc and copper, and in highly acid water a reaction between the two metals can cause the zinc to dissolve and the joint to fail. This process is known as dezincification. Use joints made of gunmetal or DR (dezincification-resistant) metal instead.

CHOOSING THE TYPE OF JOINT

There are several different joint types available. Some can be used for more than one pipe type. All the joints are available as straight couplers, elbows and tees for joining pipework, and as threaded joints for connecting pipes to taps, ballvalves, storage cisterns and hot water cylinders.

Compression joint

A brass joint with screw-on capnuts at each end. A soft metal compression ring (known as an olive) fits over each pipe. When the capnuts are tightened with a spanner, the olives are pressed against the pipe and the joint to form a watertight seal. When used with plastic pipes, a metal insert is fitted inside the pipe ends to support the pipe walls.

Advantages Widely available. Can be re-used if dismantled (with a new olive).

Disadvantages More expensive than a capillary joint. Looks clumsy. Tightening can be difficult in awkward places.

Capillary joint
A copper joint with internal pipe stops, inside which copper pipe ends are sealed with solder heated by a blowtorch. There are two types:

Soldered integral-ring type

Solder-ring joint Has a built-in ring of solid solder near each end. This is melted and flows round the pipe by capillary action as the joint is heated. Also known as a integral-ring, pre-soldered or Yorkshire joint.

End-feed joint

End-feed joint Contains no solder. Wire solder is fed into each end of the fitting as the joint is heated, and is drawn in by capillary action. Cheaper than solder-ring joints.

Advantages Widely available. Cheaper than all the other joints. Neat appearance.

Disadvantages Only for copper pipe. Cannot be re-used if dismantled. Tricky to use successfully. Special joints needed to link new metric and old imperial pipe sizes.

Speedfit joint

Speedfit type

A plastic joint with a toothed ring (called a collet) to grip the pipe and an O-ring seal. The pipe end is pushed into the joint, and can be released by holding the ring against the joint as the pipe is withdrawn. Suitable for copper and poly-butylene pipe.

Advantages Neat and unobtrusive, and very easy to use. Can be dismantled easily and re-used.

Disadvantage Relatively expensive.

Hep_2O joint

Hep_2O joint

A plastic joint with an internal grab ring and O-ring seal. The pipe end is pushed into the joint, and can be released by undoing the capnuts and prising open the grab ring with a special tool. Suitable for use with copper and cross-linked polyethylene piping (with a metal pipe insert).

Advantages Very easy to use. Designed for polybutylene pipes, but also suitable for 15mm and 22mm copper pipes. Can be undone and re-used if new grab ring is fitted. Pipe can be rotated in joint for branch alignment.

Disadvantages More expensive than metal fittings. Looks obtrusive.

Copper push-fit joint

A sleek metal joint with an internal seal that grips the pipe as it is pushed in.

Advantages No tools needed; can be undone by pushing release sleeve. Maintains earth continuity when used in copper pipe.

Disadvantage Expensive.

Threaded joints
Joints for connecting pipes to taps, cylinders and cisterns have a screw thread at one end which may be internal (female) or external (male). Threaded joints must be matched male to female. Made watertight by binding PTFE thread-sealing tape round the male thread.

Ways of joining pipes

Preparing the pipe ends

Before two pipe lengths of any material can be joined, the ends must be cut square and left smooth. Copper pipe needs careful cutting and finishing to ensure watertight joints. You can cut plastic pipes with special shears or with a sharp craft knife.

Tools *Pipe cutter or hacksaw; half-round file. Possibly also vice or portable workbench.*

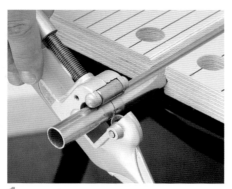

1 Cut the pipe ends square using a pipe cutter or hacksaw. Holding the pipe in a vice while sawing helps to ensure a square cut.

2 Smooth away burrs inside the cut ends with the reamer on the pipe cutter. Use a file to smooth the end and the outside of the pipe.

Making a compression joint

This is a strong and easy method of joining copper and plastic pipes. Tightening the nuts correctly is critical – the joint will leak if they are not tight enough or if they are over-tightened.

Tools *Two adjustable spanners (with jaw openings up to 38mm wide for fittings on 28mm piping); or, if you have any that fit, two open-ended spanners – capnut sizes on different makes of fittings vary.*

Materials *Compression fitting.*

1 Unscrew and remove one capnut from the fitting. If the olive has two sloping faces rather than a convex one, note which way round it is fitted, then remove it as well.

2 Take one pipe and slide the capnut over it, then the olive. Make sure the olive is the same way round as it was in the fitting if it has two sloping faces.

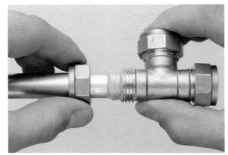

3 Push the pipe into one end of the fitting up to the internal pipe stop. Then slide the olive and nut up to the fitting and hand-tighten the capnut.

4 Hold the body of the fitting securely with one spanner while you give the capnut one and a quarter turns with the other. Do not overtighten it further. Fit pipes into other openings of the fitting in the same way.

HELPFUL TIPS

Until you have had some practice in making compression joints, take care not to over-tighten the capnuts. One way to do this is to make a scratch on the fitting and the capnut before dismantling it. When you refit and tighten the nut, you will have made a complete turn when the marks meet.

When connecting a fitting into a vertical pipe, use spring-clip clothes pegs to stop the olives and capnuts slipping down the pipe while you insert the fitting.

Making a soldered joint

This is a more difficult joint for the amateur plumber to make successfully. Too little heat will fail to make a complete solder seal inside the fitting, while too much heat will make all the solder run out.

Tools *Wire wool or fine emery paper; blowtorch; clean rag.*

Materials *Tin of flux; soft lead-free solder wire for end feed joints only. Possibly also sheet of glass fibre or other fire-proof material for placing between the joint and any nearby flammable material.*

1 Clean the ends of the pipes and the inside of the fitting thoroughly with wire wool or fine emery paper. They must show clean, bright metal to make a successful joint.

2 Smear the cleaned surfaces with flux, which will ensure a clean bond with the solder. Push the pipe into the fitting as far as the pipe stop. For an integral-ring fitting, push pipes into all the openings because all the solder rings will melt once heat is applied to the fitting. Wipe off excess flux with a clean rag, otherwise the solder will spread along the pipe surface.

3 Fix the pipe run securely in position with pipe clips.

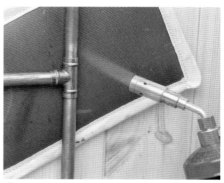

4 For an integral-ring fitting, heat the joint with a blowtorch until a silver ring of solder appears all round the mouths of the joints. Solder all the joints on the fitting in the same operation.

Alternatively For an end feed fitting, heat the joint until you see flux vapour escaping. Then remove the heat (otherwise the solder will melt too fast and drip) and apply soft solder wire round the mouth of the fitting and heat again until a silver ring of solder appears all round. If you have to leave some joints of the fitting until later, wrap a damp cloth round those already made to stop the solder re-melting.

5 Leave the joint undisturbed for about five minutes while it cools.

Making a Speedfit joint

This is a simple method that can be used to join both copper and plastic pipes. The only tools needed are those used to cut and smooth the pipe ends.

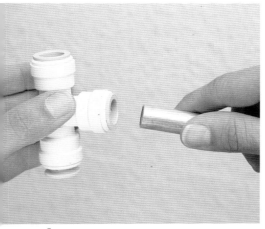

1 Take one of the pipe ends and push it into the fitting until it clicks into the toothed ring.

2 Fit piping into the other end(s) of the fitting in the same way.

Making a Hep₂O joint

This is a quick and simple method of joining polybutylene or copper pipes. To connect to old imperial-size pipework, you have to remove the capnut and O-ring seal and replace the seal with an adapter ring. Consult the manufacturer's fitting instructions.

Tools *Pencil; measuring tape.*
Materials *Silicone lubricant.*

1 Check that the cut pipe end is smooth, otherwise sharp edges could damage the O-ring seal in the fitting and cause the joint to leak.

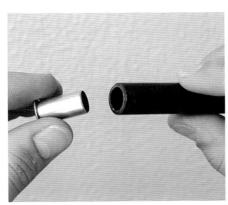

2 For plastic piping, push the metal support sleeve into the pipe end.

3 Make a pencil mark on the pipe 25mm from the end. This marks the insertion depth of the pipe into the fitting.

4 Smear the end of the pipe with silicone lubricant as far as the pencil mark.

5 Push the pipe into the fitting up to the insertion mark. If it is not pushed fully home the pipe will blow out under pressure.

Bending copper piping

Never try to bend rigid copper piping by hand without a spring to support the pipe walls – the pipe will kink at the bend if it is not supported.

Tools *Bending springs of the required diameter (15mm or 22mm); or pipe-bending machine with pipe formers and guide blocks; screwdriver; length of string.*
Materials *Petroleum jelly.*

Bending with a spring

1 If the pipe is longer than the spring, tie string to the spring end.

2 Grease the spring well with petroleum jelly and push it into the pipe.

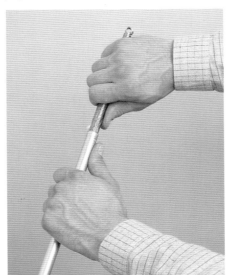

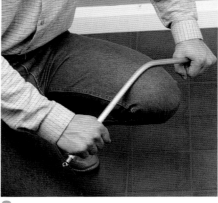

3 Bend the pipe across your knee with gentle hand pressure to the required angle.

4 Overbend the pipe a little more, then ease it gently back again. This action helps to free the spring and makes it easier to withdraw.

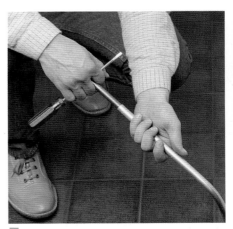

5 Insert a screwdriver blade through the spring loop. Twist the spring to reduce its diameter, then pull it out.

Bending with a machine

1 Clamp the pipe against the correct-sized semicircular former.

2 Place the guide block of the correct diameter between the pipe and the movable handle.

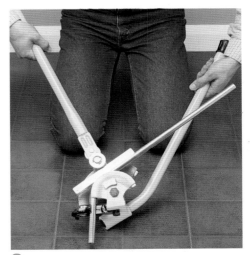

3 Squeeze the handles together until the pipe is curved to the required angle round the semicircular former.

Choosing waste pipes and traps

All waste water outlets are fitted with a trap – a bend in the piping that retains water and stops gas from the drain getting back into the room.

Plastic waste pipes are made in 40mm and 50mm diameter for sinks, baths and shower trays, 32mm for washbasins and 22mm for overflow pipes from cisterns. Pipes and fittings from different makers are not always interchangeable.

uPVC (or PVC) For cold water overflow pipes from WC and storage cisterns. Joined by push-fit or ring-seal joints or by solvent welding. White, grey, brown, sometimes black. Sold in 3m and 4m lengths.

MuPVC (modified un-plasticised polyvinyl chloride) For hot waste from sinks, baths, washbasins and washing machines. Joined by push-fit or ring-seal joints, or by solvent welding (see opposite). Ring-seals for connection to main stack. Grey, white, sometimes black. Sold in 4m lengths.

Polypropylene For cold-water overflow pipes and hot waste from sinks, baths, washbasins and washing machines. Joined by push-fit or ring-seal joints only. White and black. Has slightly waxy surface. Sold in 3m and 4m lengths.

SPECIAL JOINTS FOR WASTE PIPES

Locking push-fit (ring-seal) joint
Polypropylene joint with screw-down retaining capnuts. The sealing ring is usually ready-fitted.

Push-fit (ring-seal) joint
Rigid polypropylene sleeve with a push-fit connection. Cannot be connected to any existing copper, steel or plastic system unless a locking ring fitting is interposed.

Solvent-weld joint
A plastic sleeve with a built-in pipe stop at each end. Used with PVC piping, which is secured in the sleeve by means of a strong adhesive, recommended by the joint manufacturer.

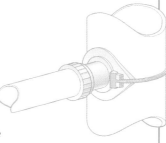

Expansion coupling
MuPVC joint designed for a solvent-weld joint at one end and a ring-seal joint at the other. Because solvent-weld joints do not allow for heat expansion, the coupling should be inserted every 1.8m in a long run of solvent-welded waste pipe.

Pipe strap
Straps or clips for supporting waste pipes are available in compatible sizes. For sloping pipes they should be fixed about every 500mm. The slope must be at least 20mm per 1m run (page 351). For vertical pipes, fix clips every 1.2m.

Stack connector
A clip-on polypropylene boss for fitting a new waste pipe into the stack, in which a hole has to be cut.

CHOOSING A TRAP

There are different types of trap for different situations. There may also be different outlet types (vertical or horizontal) and different seal depths. The seal – the depth of water maintained in the trap – is normally 38mm, but a trap with a deep seal of 75mm must, by law, be fitted to any appliance connected to a single-stack drainage pipe. This guards against the seal being destroyed by an outflow of water, allowing foul gas from the stack to enter the house.

Overflow assembly

Bath trap with cleaning eye and overflow pipe
A cleaning eye can be unscrewed to clear a blockage and is useful where access is difficult. A flexible overflow pipe can be connected to a side or rear inlet on some bath traps. The overflow is a safeguard in case a tap is left running while the bath plug is in.

Cleaning eye

Washing-machine trap
A tubular trap with a tall stand-pipe for the washing-machine waste hose, and an outlet to link to the waste pipe.

Tubular traps
A two-piece trap for a sink or basin, with an S (down-pointing) outlet (above left). Traps are also available with a P (horizontal) outlet (above right) and an adjustable inlet to allow an existing pipe to be linked to a new sink at a different height. Tubular traps are cleaned by unscrewing the part connected to the sink waste outlet.

Standard bottle trap
Use only for washbasins, which usually have a small outflow. Most have a P outlet, but an S converter may be available. Some have a telescopic tube to adjust to different heights.

Anti-siphon bottle trap
Designed to allow air to enter the trap and prevent the seal being lost. Use where there is an occasional heavy flow, or long, steep pipe run.

Fitting a waste pipe and trap

Before 1939, waste and overflow pipes for sinks, washbasins, baths and cisterns were made of lead or galvanised steel. After that, copper was used until about 1960. Since then plastic has been in general use.

Joints for joining waste pipes come in broadly the same configurations as those for joining supply pipes; some additional joints are shown opposite.

If you plan to fit a new pipe that has to be connected into a soil stack (page 326), get the approval of your local authority Building Control Officer.

Making a push-fit joint

Push-fit or ring-seal joints must be used to connect polypropylene waste pipes, which cannot be solvent-welded. Joints can be re-used with a new seal.

Tools *Hacksaw; sharp knife; clean rag; newspaper; adhesive tape; pencil.*

Materials *Push-fit joint; silicone grease.*

1 Wrap a sheet of newspaper round the pipe as a saw guide. Cut the pipe square with a hacksaw.

2 Use a sharp knife to remove fine shavings of polypropylene and any rough edges from the pipe.

3 Wipe dust from inside the fitting and the outside of the pipe.

4 On a locking-ring connector, loosen the locking ring.

Sealing ring
Locking ring

5 Make sure that the sealing ring is properly in place, with any taper pointing inwards. If necessary, remove the nut to check.

6 Lubricate the end of the pipe with silicone grease.

7 Push the pipe into the socket as far as the stop – a slight inner ridge about 25mm from the end. This allows a gap of about 10mm at the pipe end for heat expansion.

Alternatively If there is no stop, push the pipe in as far as it will go, mark the insertion depth with a pencil, then withdraw the pipe 10mm to leave an expansion gap.

8 Tighten the locking ring.

Making a solvent-welded joint

Because solvent-welded joints are neat they are suitable for exposed MuPVC pipework. However, they are permanent and should only be used where they will not need to be disturbed. Push-fit connections are used at traps, where the joint may need to be undone occasionally.

Tools *Hacksaw; half-round file; cloth.*

Materials *Solvent-weld cement; appropriate connector (see page 346); appropriate pipe.*

1 Cut the pipes to the required length with a hacksaw, remove the burrs inside and out with a half-round file, and wipe thoroughly with a clean cloth.

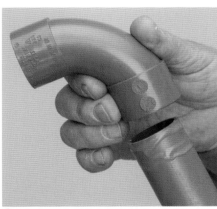

2 Apply solvent-weld cement around the end of the pipe and push it into the joint.

3 Wipe off excess cement with the cloth and allow the joint to dry before moving on to the next joint.

HELPFUL TIP

When running waste pipes along a wall, hold them in place with waste pipe clips.

Use wallplugs and screws to attach them to a masonry wall, or hollow-wall fixings on plasterboard.

Remember to check for pipes and cables before you drill.

Fitting a trap

Traps are either tubular or bottle-shaped (see Choosing a trap, left), and are made in suitable sizes to fit between a sink, bath or washbasin waste outlet and its waste pipe.

1 Check that the locking nut on the trap inlet is unscrewed and the rubber washer in position.

2 Push the trap inlet into the waste outlet and screw the nut onto the waste outlet thread.

3 Connect the trap outlet to the waste pipe with a push-fit joint.

Choosing a tap

Most taps work in the same way – turning the handle opens or closes a valve that fits into a valve seat. The valve – a rod and plate known as a jumper valve – is fitted with a washer that is replaced when it is worn and the tap drips.

Mixed measurements

New plumbing fittings come in metric sizes, but if the plumbing in your house dates from before the mid 1970s, your pipework is in imperial sizes (½in, ¾in and 1in inner diameter). Modern copper pipe comes in outer diameters of 10mm, 15mm, 22mm and 28mm. Choose 15mm pipe to join to existing ½in pipework and 28mm for 1in pipework. You will need special connectors for joining 22mm pipe to ¾in pipework.

High-neck taps

The spout on an ordinary tap is about 22mm above its base, whereas the spout on a high-neck tap will be at least 95mm above its base. With a shallow sink this allows a bucket to be filled or large pans to be rinsed with ease. High neck taps are available with capstan, handwheel and lever handles.

CERAMIC WASHERS

The latest tap designs incorporate hardwearing ceramic discs – one fixed, one moving – instead of washers, and when the tap is turned on, openings in the discs line up so that water flows through. They open or close with only a quarter turn (through 90°) of the handle.

The discs become smoother and more watertight with wear, so should never need replacing but, in hard water areas, performance may eventually be affected by limescale.

Pillar tap

The type still often used in bathrooms, with a vertical inlet that fits through a hole in the sanitaryware. The conventional tap has a bell-shaped cover – generally known as an easy-clean cover – and a capstan (cross-top) handle.

Lever handle

Another type of shrouded head has a lever handle, which is easy for elderly or disabled people to use as it can be pushed rather than gripped. Most lever-handle taps have ceramic discs so require only a quarter turn of the handle.

Handwheel handle

On modern taps, the cover and handle are replaced by a shrouded head that forms a handwheel. Shrouded heads not only give a neater appearance but also prevent water from wet hands going down the spindle and allowing detergent to wash the grease out of the tap mechanism.

Hose union bib cock

A tap with a horizontal inlet now used mainly outdoors or in the garage. Some bib taps have an angled head and threaded nozzle, suitable for use with a garden hose.

MIXER TAPS

Two taps with a common spout are known as a mixer. The taps are linked either by a deck block (flat against the surface) or a pillar block (raised). Most mixers are two-hole types that fit into a standard two-hole-sink: one for the hot tap and one for the cold. Some mixers, however, need three holes (a centre hole for the spout) and some (monobloc types) only one.

Bath or basin mixer

Hot and cold water merge within the mixer body, as both taps are usually fed from a cistern. It is illegal to fit this type of mixer on a fitting where cold water is supplied from the rising main and hot water comes from a cylinder. This is because, if mains pressure alters, differences in pressure might result in stored water being sucked back into the mains, and create the possible risk of contaminating drinking water supplies.

Monobloc mixer

A single-hole monobloc mixer tap has a compact body with the handles and spout close together. Some designs have very narrow inlet pipes. There are monobloc designs for kitchens and bathrooms. Some kitchen monobloc mixers include a hot-rinse spray and brush fed from the hot water pipe by a flexible hose, so that the spray can be lifted from its socket for use.

Kitchen mixer

The spout has separate channels for hot and cold water. This is because the kitchen cold tap is fed direct from the mains, and it is illegal to mix cold water from the mains and hot water from a storage cistern in one filling. The spout usually swivels and should be able to reach both of the bowls in a double sink. Kitchen mixers are available with capstan, handwheel and lever handles.

Bath/shower mixer

Bath/shower mixer taps have a control knob that diverts the water flow from the spout to the shower handset. It will not provide a forceful spray but is a convenient addition to a bath.

Choosing a washbasin and bidet

There is a huge choice of washbasins available, from a traditional ceramic pedestal to an ultra-modern polished limestone bowl. Pedestals hide pipework and give some support to the weight of the bowl. Wall mounted sanitaryware can look sleek, but needs a solid wall and strong fixings.

There is no standard size for basins – most are around 550 x 400mm and 125mm deep. Order taps when you order the basin or bidet to ensure that your chosen unit has the right type of holes for the fittings.

Countertop basin These are often made in acrylic or enamelled pressed steel. They usually rest on the edge of a cutout or recessed ledge in the worktop and may have a rubber sealing ring and securing clips or be secured with mastic or sealant. Undermounted basins are screwfixed to a solid worktop from beneath.

Washstand basin
Wall mounted washstand basins are usually of generous proportions and come with a surround supported on two legs so they appear freestanding. They are usually made of vitreous china or glass, with stands made of wood or chrome. The plumbing is not concealed.

Pedestal basin Usually made of vitreous china but glass versions with stainless steel pedestals are also available. Luxury models can be much bigger. The pedestal hides the plumbing and helps to support the basin, but it is not the basin's sole support: the back of the basin must be screwed or bracketed to the wall. The basin may be joined to its pedestal with fixing clips or mastic. The pedestal is screwed to floor through holes at the back. The basin's height – usually 800mm – is not adjustable.

Standalone basin These are designed to look like old-fashioned washbowls. They can be made of vitreous china, glass, stainless steel, wood and limestone. Plumbing for the basin is concealed in the unit on which it stands. Taps are fixed to the bowl or to the wall behind the basin.

Semi-pedestal basin
Usually made of vitreous china but glass versions with stainless steel pedestals are also available. The semi pedestal hides the plumbing but leaves the floor free and makes cleaning easier. The bowl is fixed in the same way as a pedestal basin.

Wall hung basin Usually made of vitreous china, glass and stainless steel, wall hung basins are available as small as 400 x 350mm or as compact corner basins and space-saving short projection designs. They can be fixed at any height (low in a nursery, for example). Plumbing is visible unless boxed in.

Over-rim bidet Usually vitreous china and typically 560–600mm deep and 350–395mm wide. The rim height of floorstanding models is about 400mm. Wall hung designs are also available and are especially suitable for wet rooms. Screwed to the floor inside the rear of pedestal. Wall-hung types (for concealed plumbing) are bolted at the rear through wall to metal support brackets.

TYPICAL WALL HUNG BASIN FIXINGS

The brackets for wall hung basins bear a heavy load and should only be fixed to a solid wall. If you have a stud wall, spread the weight with a countertop, washstand or pedestal type instead. Specialist fixings are usually supplied with the basin.

Wall plate and waste bracket The waste outlet of the wall-hung basin fits through the bracket, with its back nut below the bracket.

Concealed wall hangers A pair of hangers for a wall-hung basin is screwed to the wall. They fit into slots in the back of the basin to support it.

Rim-supply bidet Water enters under rim, so warm water warms the rim; a control diverts water to an ascending spray. This is more expensive than an over-rim bidet, and must be installed in accordance with Water Authority requirements. It is not suitable for DIY installation.

Replacing a bidet or washbasin

The operations involved in replacing a washbasin or bidet are very similar. You may need to make slight adaptations to the existing plumbing to accommodate the new appliance.

Before you start You need to turn off the water supplies to the taps, and disconnect (or cut through) the supply and waste pipes. Then you can remove the fixings holding the basin (and its pedestal, if one is fitted) or bidet in place. Fit taps, wastes and overflows to the new basin or bidet before installing it.

Tools *Basin wrench; spanner; long-nose pliers; steel tape measure; spirit level; damp cloth; screwdriver; bucket. Possibly also hacksaw.*

Materials *Basin or bidet; taps or mixer with washers; deep seal or anti-siphon bottle trap (page 346); waste outlet with two flat plastic washers, plug and chain; silicone sealant; fixing screws for wall (and floor if required); rubber washers to fit between screws and appliance. Possibly also flexible pipe with tap connectors.*

1 Fit the new taps or mixer. Place the sealing washer on the tap tail first, position the tap and screw on the backnut to secure the tap in place. Tighten it with a spanner. Check that single taps are correctly aligned.

2 If you severed the supply pipes, attach a corrugated copper or braided hose connector to each new tap tail, ready for connection to the cut supply pipes later.

3 Attach the new waste outlet. Fit one sealing washer between the outlet and the appliance, then insert the outlet in its hole. Fit the second sealing washer from below and tighten the backnut. Use pliers to hold the outlet grid and stop the waste outlet from rotating as you do this. Ensure that the slots in the outlet tail line up with the outlet of the built-in overflow duct.

4 Fit the bottle trap to the tail of the waste outlet.

5 Set the new appliance in position and mark where new wall and floor fixings will be needed. Drill and plug the wall (and drill pilot holes in the floor too if necessary) and fix it in position.

6 Connect the taps or mixer to the supply pipes. If you disconnected the old tap connectors, there may be enough play in the pipes for you to reattach them directly to the new tap tails. If there is just a small gap, fit a tap tail adaptor to each tap and attach the old tap connectors to the adapters. If you severed the supply pipes, link the flexible connectors you attached to the taps in step 2 to the supply pipes using compression fittings.

7 Connect the outlet at the base of the bottle trap to the waste pipe.

8 Restore the water supply and check all joints for leaks. If necessary, tighten them.

9 Run a bead of silicone sealant around the appliance where it touches the wall.

Connecting a washbasin If it is difficult to disconnect the water supplies to the taps on the old basin, cut through the pipes lower down and use flexible connectors to connect the new taps to the supply pipes. Fit a service valve between the connectors and the pipes at the same time so that you can isolate the taps easily for future maintenance.

An over-rim supply bidet is connected to the supply pipes in the same way as a basin. You will need adapters to connect the narrow tails of a monobloc mixer to 15mm diameter water supply pipes.

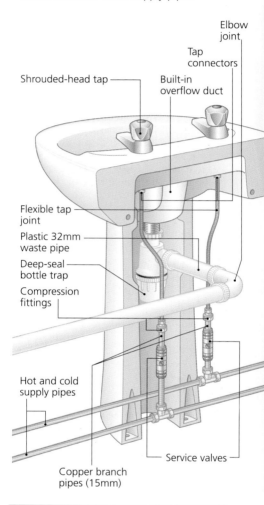

Elbow joint

Tap connectors

Shrouded-head tap

Built-in overflow duct

Flexible tap joint

Plastic 32mm waste pipe

Deep-seal bottle trap

Compression fittings

Hot and cold supply pipes

Service valves

Copper branch pipes (15mm)

HELPFUL TIP

If you want to renew the taps on an existing basin, it is often easier to cut through the supply and waste pipes and remove the basin from its supports. Even with a basin wrench, the back nuts can be extremely difficult to undo. With the basin upside down on the floor, it is easier to apply penetrating oil, and also to exert enough force without damaging the basin.

If removing the basin is not practical, the tap handles and headgear can be replaced with a tap conversion kit, sold in packs with fitting instructions.

Installing a countertop basin

Washbasins, particularly countertop basins on a vanity unit, are very often installed in a bedroom to ease the demand on a family bathroom.

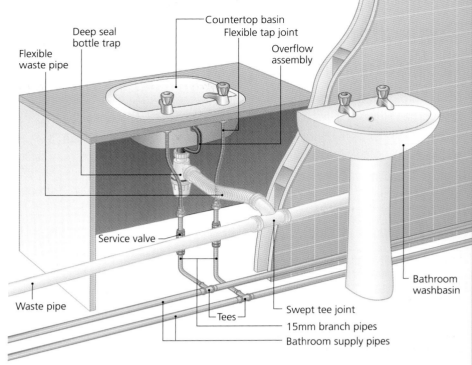

Flexible waste pipe
Deep seal bottle trap
Countertop basin
Flexible tap joint
Overflow assembly
Service valve
Waste pipe
Tees
15mm branch pipes
Bathroom supply pipes
Swept tee joint
Bathroom washbasin

Before you start Give the local authority Building Control Officer details of your proposed arrangements for the new waste pipe connections.

1 Choose a site for the basin as near as possible to the bathroom waste pipe and supply pipes – ideally against a wall adjoining the bathroom.

2 Work out how to route the waste water from the basin to an existing waste pipe or direct to an outside drain (see below right). Trace the routes of existing hot and cold supply pipes and work out the shortest route possible for the new pipe.

3 Check that the basin position will allow sufficient space for a person to use it. Generally, allow at least 640mm bending room in front of the basin, and at least 300mm elbow room at either side.

4 Check that the installation of the basin will not interfere with any electric cables, gas pipes or other fittings, especially where you need to make a hole in a wall.

5 Fit the taps, waste outlet and trap to the new washbasin as described in Replacing a bidet or washbasin (left). Use a deep-seal trap (or an anti-siphon trap, if required).

6 Cut off the water supply and use tee connectors to run hot and cold-water pipes to the basin site as 15mm branch pipes from the supply pipes to the bathroom. Do not tee into the pipes supplying a shower, unless it has a thermostatic mixer (page 359). If you find you have to tee into a 22mm distribution pipe, you will need an unequal tee with two 22mm ends and a 15mm branch.

7 Fit the waste pipe in position. If you have to make a hole through the wall, do it as for Installing an outside tap (page 363). If you plan to connect the new waste pipe into an existing one, insert a swept tee joint and link the new pipe to it.

8 Fit the basin or basin unit to the wall and connect it to the supply pipes and waste pipe (see left).

Routeing the waste pipe

The waste pipe run should be no more than 1.75m long. It must slope enough for the water to run away – not less than 20mm for each 1m of run – but the depth of fall to the pipe outlet should be no greater than about 50mm for a pipe under 1m long, or about 25mm for a longer pipe. If you cannot avoid a pipe run longer than 1.75m, prevent self-siphonage by fitting an anti-siphon bottle trap (page 346), or a Hep$_2$O waste pipe valve.

Alternatively Use a waste pipe of larger diameter – 38mm instead of 32mm. This pipe run should be no longer than 2.3m, and you will need a reducer fitting to connect 38mm pipe to the 32mm trap outlet. If you need a run longer than 2.3m, ask the advice of your local authority Building Control Officer.

Linking to an outside drain

How the waste pipe is linked to a drain depends on the household drainage system. If you are unable to link into the waste pipe from the bathroom basin, fit a separate waste pipe through an outside wall to link with a household drain.

If the bedroom is on the ground floor, direct the waste pipe to an outside gully, if possible, such as the kitchen drain. The pipe must go below the grid.

Where the bedroom is on an upper floor, the method of connecting the waste pipe depends on whether you have a two-pipe or single-stack system (page 326).

With a two-pipe system, you may be able to direct the waste pipe into an existing hopper. Alternatively, you can connect the waste pipe to the waste downpipe (not the soil-pipe) using a stack connector.

In a house with a single stack system, the waste pipe will have to be connected to the stack. For this you need the approval of the local authority Building Control Officer. There are regulations concerning the position of the connection in relation to WC inlets, and the length and slope of the pipe is particularly critical. The connection is made by fitting a new boss, which is a job best left to a plumber.

HELPFUL TIPS

If you tee into an old distribution pipe, it is likely to be an imperial size of $3/4$in internal diameter. There is no way of recognising an imperial size, except by measuring the internal diameter of the pipe once you have cut into it.

On $3/4$in copper pipe, you can fit 22mm compression joints straight onto it provided that you substitute the olives for $3/4$in olives, available at a plumbers' merchant. Similarly, the Hep$_2$O type of joint can be used if fitted with imperial O-rings.

On soldered capillary joints, use adapters, which are available from a plumbers' merchant, that convert $3/4$in piping to 22mm, before inserting the tee.

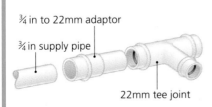

$3/4$ in to 22mm adaptor
$3/4$ in supply pipe
22mm tee joint

Flexible plastic push-fit joints are useful for fitting between the trap and waste pipe where alignment is difficult – for example, round a timber stud in a partition wall.

Renovating and repairing a bath

Major bath renovation is best done by professional firms. They take a day or two and will repair cracks or chips and apply a new coating, available in a range of colours. You can do smaller repair jobs yourself, using a DIY kit.

Repairing bath enamel

Before you start Remove every trace of grease or flaky enamel from the surface of the bath. Once clean, do not touch the surface again with your fingers.

1 Fill small surface chips with an epoxy resin filler (such as car-body filler) or use one of the proprietary bath repair kits available on the market.

2 Rub the surface smooth with fine abrasive paper, then coat the repaired area with two coats of matching bath enamel, following the instructions on the pack. Touch-up sticks are available in a variety of colours to cover small repairs.

Changing the colour

Changing an entire bathroom suite because you hate the colour can be expensive. A short-term solution is to resurface the suite using a proprietary colour-changing pack. These are available in DIY stores, and they offer a wide range of soft colours. Follow the instructions carefully (they vary) and bear in mind it will be about 5 days before you can use the bathroom again.

Repairing a plastic bath

Burns on an acrylic surface cannot be repaired. However, chips can be filled with a special acrylic repair paste available as a kit. You can polish out scratches with metal-polish wadding because the colour goes right through the material.

However, glass-reinforced plastic (GRP) can be damaged by abrasive cleaners and only the top layer of material is coloured.

Changing bath taps

Because of the cramped space at the end of a bath, fitting new taps to an existing bath can be difficult. It is often easier to disconnect and pull out the bath (see right) so that you have room to apply enough force to undo the backnuts of the old taps.

The alternative to disrupting the bathroom is to fit new tap headgear only, using a tap conversion kit.

Removing an old cast-iron bath

A cast-iron bath may weigh around 100kg, so you will need helpers to move it. A pressed-steel bath is lighter. It can usually be moved intact.

Before you start Unless you want to keep a cast-iron bath intact, it is easier to break it up after disconnecting it than to remove it whole. Be careful when you break it up, as the pieces are often jagged and very sharp.

Tools *Torch; adjustable spanner; safety goggles; ear defenders; club hammer; blanket; protective gloves. Possibly also padded pipe wrench; screwdriver; hacksaw.*

1 Cut off the water supply (page 328).

2 Remove any bath panelling. It is often secured with dome-head screws, which have caps that cover the screw slot.

3 With a torch, look into the space at the end of the bath to locate the supply pipes connected to the tap tails, and the overflow pipe. In older baths, the overflow pipe is rigid and leads straight out through the wall. In more modern types the overflow is flexible and connected to the waste trap.

4 Check the position of the hot supply pipe: it is normally on the left as you face the taps. Use an adjustable spanner to unscrew the tap connectors from the supply pipes and pull the pipes to one side. If unscrewing is difficult, saw through the pipes near the ends of the tap tails.

5 Saw through a rigid overflow pipe flush with the wall.

6 Disconnect the waste trap from the waste outlet. For an old-style U-bend, use an adjustable spanner. A plastic trap can normally be unscrewed by hand, but use a padded pipe wrench if it proves difficult. Pull the trap to one side. Disconnect a flexible overflow pipe from the overflow outlet.

7 If the bath has adjustable legs – normally brackets with adjustable screws and locking nuts – lower it to lessen the risk of damaging wall tiles when you pull it out. But if the adjusters on the far side are difficult to reach, lowering may not be worth the effort.

8 Pull the bath into the middle of the room ready for removal or break-up.

9 To break up the bath, drape a blanket over it to stop fragments flying out, and hit the sides with a club hammer to crack the material into pieces.

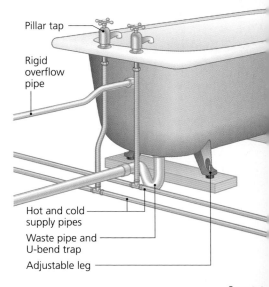

Pillar tap
Rigid overflow pipe
Hot and cold supply pipes
Waste pipe and U-bend trap
Adjustable leg

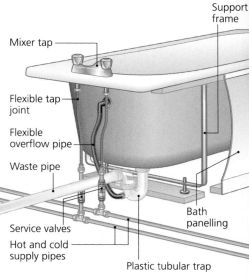

Support frame
Mixer tap
Flexible tap joint
Flexible overflow pipe
Waste pipe
Service valves
Hot and cold supply pipes
Plastic tubular trap
Bath panelling

Connections to an old and new bath
As when replacing a washbasin or bidet (page 350), add a service valve on each of the supply pipes before connecting them to the new taps. This allows them to be isolated easily for future maintenance.

Installing a new bath

This is a good time to re-think your bathroom: you can fit the new bath in a different position and take advantage of the latest designs.

Before you start Assemble as many fittings as possible onto the new bath before you remove the old one. Not only will fitting be easier before the bath is in position, but the water will not be cut off for as long.

Use flexible tap joints and a flexible waste joint. If you want to put the bath in a different position, you will have to work out how to re-route the waste pipe, as well as adapting the supply pipes.

Tools *Two adjustable spanners; spirit level; damp cloth. Possibly also long nosed pliers; small spanner; hacksaw; screwdriver.*

Materials *Bath; two 25mm thick boards to support its feet; two new taps or a mixer tap (with washers); two 22mm flexible tap joints; 40mm waste outlet (unslotted) with plug and two flat plastic washers; bath trap (deep-seal if the waste pipe links to a single stack) with flexible overflow assembly; silicone sealant; PTFE tape.*

1 Fit the supporting frame following the maker's instructions. It is usually done with the bath placed upside down.

2 Fit the taps or mixer and the tap joints in the same way as for a washbasin. Some deck mixers come with a plastic gasket to fit between the deck and the bath. On a plastic bath, fit a reinforcing plate under the taps to prevent strain on the bath deck.

3 Fit the waste outlet. This may be a tailed grid fitted in the same way as for a sink. Or it may be a flanged grid only, fitted over the outlet hole (with washers on each side of the bath surface) and fixed with a screw to a tail formed at one end of the flexible overflow pipe.

4 Fit the top end of the overflow pipe into the back of the overflow hole and screw the overflow outlet, backed by a washer, in position.

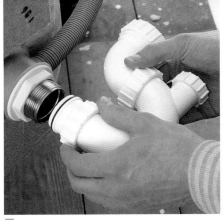

5 Slot the banjo overflow, if supplied, onto the threaded waste outlet and fit the bottom washer and back nut. Attach the trap, then fit the bath into position with a flat board under each pair of feet in order to spread the load.

6 Place a spirit level on each of the four sides of the bath to check that it is horizontal. If necessary, adjust the legs until the bath is perfectly level. Then tighten the locking nuts on the adjustable legs.

7 Fit the flexible connector on the farthest tap to its supply pipe, making a compression joint. If the supply pipe is too high, cut it back to a convenient length, leaving it too long rather than too short, as the connector can be bent slightly to fit.

8 Connect the second tap tail in the same way as the first. Then connect the trap outlet to the waste pipe (normally a push-fit joint). Restore the water supply and check the joints for leaks. Tighten if necessary, but not too much.

9 Fix the bath panels according to the maker's instructions. They may screw or clip to a wooden frame, or be fixed to a batten screwed to the floor. Fill the bath with water before sealing the joints between the bath sides and walls with silicone sealant. This ensures that the bath will not settle in use and pull the sealant away.

HELPFUL TIPS

If, on a mixer, the hot and cold indicators are on different sides from the appropriate supply pipes, reverse the discs on the tops of the taps, if possible. Alternatively, cross the flexible tap connectors to join the taps to the correct pipes.

Choosing a new bath

The style and shape of the bath you choose is based on personal preference. But it helps to have a clear idea of what you are looking for when you go to choose one.

Type Many people are happy with a standard, traditional bath, but there are exciting new types of bath available that are worth considering.
• Whirlpool systems have water jets in the side of the bath, which give the bather an invigorating massage.
• Spa baths have air nozzles in the base of the bath, forcing bubbles upwards and creating a stimulating wave action.
• Hydro baths combine whirlpool side jets with spa nozzles in the base. In addition they may offer jets to stimulate the neck and shoulders and the feet.
Material Most modern baths are made from acrylic or glass-reinforced plastic (GRP) in various colours, and are light and quite easy to install. They are usually cradled in a support frame to avoid distortion when filled.
• Vitreous-enamelled pressed-steel baths are lighter and cheaper than old-style, porcelain-enamelled cast-iron baths.
Quality Cheaper baths are thinner and tend to need more support to prevent sagging and creaking when occupied. A good-quality plastic bath should be at least 6mm thick.
• Pressed-steel and cast-iron baths are strong and firm, but can feel cold, often initially lowering the temperature of the water until they warm up. Enamel is easily chipped, and often requires special cleaning materials.
Shape Bath shapes may also include two-person, corner-fitting and circular. They can be free-standing, with ornate legs, or fitted into a panelled framework. Sunken baths are glamorous but can be rather difficult to clean.

Types of WC suite

A WC suite consists of a cistern and a pan. The cistern can be low or high level, joined by a flush pipe to the pan, or close-coupled with a direct connection. Modern suites are designed to use less water than old ones – 7 litres rather than 9 litres. When siting a WC suite, allow for at least 530mm of space in front of the pan, and for about 760mm overall space from side to side.

Types of cistern

Cisterns are made of plastic or vitreous china (ceramic), and screwed to the wall from inside, through the back. The flushing control is a central push button or a side lever (fitted to right or left of the cistern).

For the flushing action to be correct, the cistern must be at the height given by the manufacturer – usually with the base about 600mm above the floor. Water flow into the cistern is controlled by a ballvalve. A cistern fed from a cold water storage cistern is quieter than one fed from the mains.

Most cisterns still have a 9 litre flush: the dual-flush type provides 4.5 or 9 litres. Water regulations now restrict the capacity of newly installed cisterns.

The standard cistern A direct-action cistern installed at a low level is the standard option. It can also be used at high level, and is quieter than the chain-pull type. If a suite is converted from high to low-level, the standard size cistern – about 200mm from front to back – is too deep to go behind the pan, so a slimline type is needed.

A slimline cistern Measures the same as a standard cistern from side to side but as little as 115mm from front to back. However, it still provides a full flush. It may be concealed behind panelling.

Dual-flush type A variation on the direct-action cistern is the dual-flush type, which provides either a water-saving small flush, or a double-sized flush for solid waste.

Low-level suite designs
In a low-level suite, the cistern is either linked to the pan by a short flush pipe or is close-coupled, with the cistern and pan joined together in one unit.

HOW A CISTERN WORKS

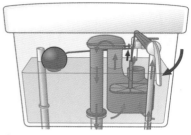

1 An inverted U-pipe in the cistern is linked to the flush pipe into the pan, and at the other end opens out into a dome (siphon). When the flush is operated, a lift rod raises a plate in the dome and throws water into the crown of the U-bend.

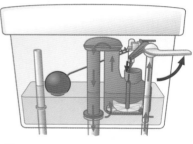

2 Openings in the plate are covered by a plastic flap valve held flat by the weight of the water. As water falls down the flush pipe, it creates a partial vacuum, causing water to be sucked up through the plate openings and to raise the flap valve.

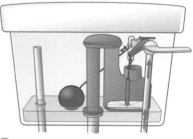

3 The base of the dome is about 10mm above the cistern bottom. When the cistern water level falls below the dome base, air drawn in breaks the siphonic action and stops the flush.

On a dual-flush cistern there is a hole in the side of the dome, and if the flush control is released immediately the hole lets in air to break the siphonic action after a gallon of water has been siphoned. When the control is held down for a few seconds, it operates a device that temporarily plugs the air hole, allowing a double flush.

Standard cistern

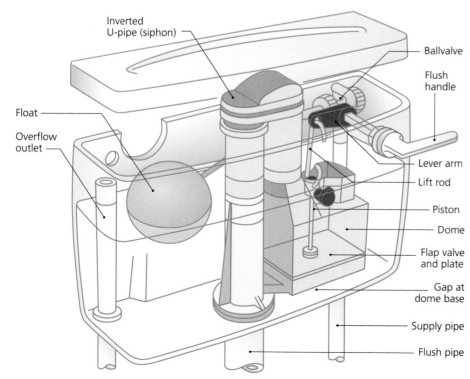

- Inverted U-pipe (siphon)
- Ballvalve
- Flush handle
- Float
- Overflow outlet
- Lever arm
- Lift rod
- Piston
- Dome
- Flap valve and plate
- Gap at dome base
- Supply pipe
- Flush pipe

Types of WC pan

Pans are normally made from vitreous china and are screwed to the floor through holes in the base of the pedestal. Some are designed to fit flush to the wall with their plumbing concealed, and some can be wall-hung.

Unless connected directly to an internal soil sack, the outlet pipe of the pan needs to be connected to a soil pipe that passes out more or less horizontally through the wall (usual for upstairs WCs) or passes vertically through the floor (common for downstairs WCs).

There are two types of pan: wash-down pans and double-trap siphonic pans.

Wash-down pan

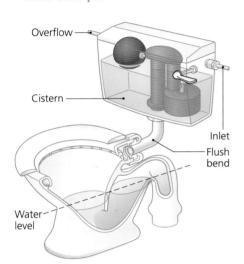

Overflow

Cistern

Inlet

Flush bend

Water level

All new pans sold today are of the wash-down pan type, where the pan is cleared by water from the cistern splashing on the sides of the pan and forcing the contents of the pan through the trap, leaving clean water in the bottom of the pan.

Three designs of pan are made: horizontal outlet; P-trap (just below the horizontal) and S-trap (vertical). The vast majority of pans now being sold have a horizontal outlet, but this can be connected to a soil pipe formerly fitted to a vertical outlet using an angled connector (below).

Double-trap siphonic pan

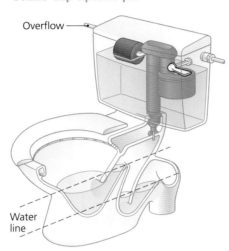

Overflow

Water line

Some existing pans are the double-trap siphonic type; these are no longer made, though spares should still be available. When the cistern is flushed, the pan starts to empty by suction before the flush water reaches it, making it very silent and efficient in operation.

MACERATOR UNITS

A macerator unit allows you to put a WC in a room distant from the main soil stack. It takes waste from the WC pan and passes it through a shredder so that it can be carried away through a small-bore (22mm or 32mm) plastic pipe. The WC pan can be 20–50m from the soil stack if the pipe is horizontal, but pumping distance and height are interlinked, so pumping vertically would restrict the horizontal distance.

The installation of a macerator unit needs to meet the Building Regulations requirements, so you should inform your local Building Control Officer if you intend to install one.

You will also need an electrical connection to drive the shredding motor and this must be via a fused connection unit (unswitched or via a flex outlet if within reach of anyone using the bath or shower).

There are a wide variety of macerator units available: the simplest is for use only with a WC; the most complex will take a whole bathroom suite (WC, wash basin, bidet and bath or shower). High-capacity units are available to take the output from a power shower. There are also macerator units designed for kitchen waste (sink, washing machine and dishwasher).

Macerator units can be bulky, but there are slimline units available that fit neatly behind a conventional WC pan, below the cistern.

TYPES OF WC PAN JOINTS

Plastic push-fit joints are now universally used and come in a variety of shapes to allow connection of virtually any pan to any soil pipe. Most joints are either straight or 90° (for horizontal or vertical soil pipes), but offset joints, extension joints and even fully flexible joints are also available.

Angled push-fit pan joint A 90° joint for converting a horizontal (P-trap) pan outlet to a down-pointing (S-trap) outlet for a floor-exit pipe. It can also be used to link a horizontal outlet to a wall-exit pipe situated at right angles to the pan.

Straight push-fit pan joint For a straight link between the pan outlet and the inlet branch to the soil pipe. The cupped end fits over the pan outlet, and the narrow (spigot) end inside the soil-pipe inlet. Different diameters and lengths are made. Before buying, check the outside diameter of the pan outlet, the inside diameter of the soil-pipe inlet, and the distance to be bridged. Joints have watertight seals at each end. Offset types can be used where the alignment is not exact.

Rubber cone joint For linking the flush pipe from the WC cistern to the flush horn of the pan.

Flush pipe Angled plastic pipe linking a separate cistern to the WC pan. Pipes for high-level suites are normally 32mm in diameter, and pipes for low-level suites have 38mm diameters.

Replacing a WC pan

At one time WC pans were always cemented to a solid floor, but the setting of the mortar often put a strain on the pan and caused the china to crack. Now they are usually screwed down to a wooden or a solid floor.

Before you start An old or cracked WC pan with a down-pointing outlet cemented to a floor-exit metal soil pipe is the most difficult type to remove. Examine yours carefully before attempting to remove it.

Tools *Screwdriver; spirit level. Possibly drill and wood or masonry bits; safety goggles; club hammer; cold chisel; rags; old chisel; thin pen, pencil or nail; trimming knife.*

Materials *WC pan and seat; pan fixing kit; rubber cone connector; suitable push-fit pan connector. Possibly also wall plugs (for a solid floor); packing (to steady the pan) such as wood slivers, vinyl tile strips or silicone sealant.*

Removing a pan with a horizontal outlet

1 Disconnect the flush pipe by peeling back the cone connector. Alternatively, chip away a rag-and-putty joint with an old chisel. Protect your eyes.

2 Undo any screws used to secure the pan to the floor.

3 Pull the pan forward slowly, moving it from side to side, to free it from the soil-pipe inlet. It should come away easily. If you have any difficulty, break the pan outlet in the same way as for a down-pointing outlet (right).

4 If the outlet joint was cemented with putty or mastic filler, chip it off the metal soil pipe inlet.

Removing a pan with a down-pointing outlet

1 Disconnect the flush pipe in the same way as for a horizontal-outlet pan.

2 Undo the floor screws, or break cement with a hammer and cold chisel.

3 To free the pan outlet, put on safety goggles and use a club hammer to break the outlet pipe just above its joint with the drain socket in the floor. Then pull the pan forward, away from the jagged remains protruding from the soil pipe socket.

4 Stuff rags into the socket to stop debris falling in, then chip away the rest of the pan outlet with a hammer and cold chisel. Work with the chisel blade pointing inwards, and break the china right down to the socket at one point. The rest of the china should then come out easily.

5 Chip away any mortar from round the collar of the socket with a hammer and cold chisel. Take care not to break the collar.

6 Clear away any mortar left where the pan was cemented to the floor, leaving a flat base for the new WC pan.

Fitting a separate pan

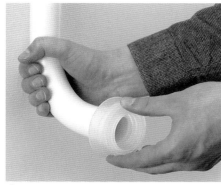

1 Fit a rubber cone connector to the flush-pipe outlet, unless one has already been fitted.

2 Fit a plastic push-on connector to the pan outlet. If the soil pipe socket for the pan is in the floor, use an angled 90° connector to link a horizontal pan outlet to the vertical inlet to the soil pipe.

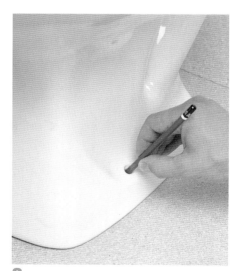

3 Mark the position of the holes in the pan on the floor, using a slim marker such as a ballpoint pen or a pencil.

4 With the pan still in position, draw a line round its base so that it can be put back in place accurately. Then remove it.

5 Cut the plastic threads on the pan-fixing brackets to length. Drill and fix the brackets so that the plastic thread lines up with the marks on the floor.

On a solid floor, such as concrete, use a masonry bit and insert wall plugs for the screws.

6 If the soil pipe inlet is a floor socket, remove the rags, taking care not to spill any of the debris in the inlet.

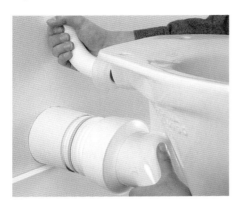

7 Carefully lift the pan into position over the plastic threads, using the previously marked outline to guide you, and at the same time positioning it so that you can push the flexible connector into the soil pipe inlet. Fold back the rubber cone connector and slip it over the flushing horn of the pan.

8 Screw on the plastic nuts to hold the pan firmly in position. However, do not tighten them fully yet.

9 Use a spirit level placed across the top of the pan to check that it is level from side to side and from front to back.

10 To level the pan, loosen the plastic nuts and pack under the pedestal with strips of vinyl tile, or use a bead of silicone sealant to steady the pan and provide an even bed. Once you are sure that the pan is level, screw it down firmly.

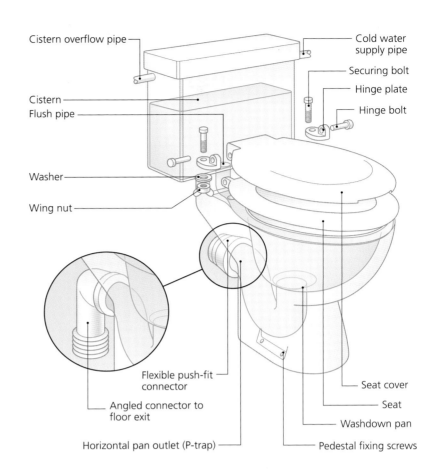

Labels: Cistern overflow pipe; Cistern; Flush pipe; Washer; Wing nut; Cold water supply pipe; Securing bolt; Hinge plate; Hinge bolt; Flexible push-fit connector; Angled connector to floor exit; Horizontal pan outlet (P-trap); Seat cover; Seat; Washdown pan; Pedestal fixing screws

Fittings for a separate low-level suite Most modern WC pans have a horizontal outlet. If the replacement pan has to be fitted to a soil pipe on a ground floor, connect the P-trap outlet of the pan to the soil-pipe inlet using an angled push-fit joint (page 355). After fitting a WC suite, you may find that condensation – particularly apparent on a ceramic cistern – is a nuisance and leads to damp walls and floors. Make sure the WC or bathroom is properly ventilated (page 242). In a bathroom, avoid drip-drying washing over the bath, as this contributes to condensation.

Checking the fitting

When fitting a new WC pan, make sure that it is level and that the connections to the flush pipe and soil pipe are true. Otherwise slow pan clearance or a blockage could result.

On an existing WC pan with old-style joints rather than flexible connectors, blockages can occur because the openings are out of true or partially obstructed by the jointing material. Putty from an old rag-and-putty joint between the flush pipe and horn may have squeezed into the flush inlet and be impeding the inflow of water.

Putty or other jointing material could be obstructing the joint between the pan outlet and the soil-pipe inlet. This is evident if the water rises slowly in the pan before it flows away.

Make sure the pan is firmly fixed and that the fixing screws have not worked loose. Check that the pan is horizontal when fixing it in place.

FITTING A NEW WC SEAT

A WC pan seat and cover are usually fixed onto hinge bolts or a rod at the back. These fit into hinge plates or covers at each side of the pan.

Hinge plates or covers are each held in place by a securing bolt that fits through a fixing hole in the back of the pan and is secured by a wing nut.

Make sure that you insert washers to shield the pan from the head of the securing bolt and the wing nut. Washers shaped to the pattern of hinge covers are often supplied. Screw the wing nuts firmly finger-tight.

A WC seat breaks easily if misused – such as if you stand on it to close a window. If you simply have to stand on something, lift the seat and balance yourself on the rim of the pan.

Planning a shower

Water pressure at the shower head is important. If it is too low, the flow of water from the rose will be weak.

For a mixer supplied from the household's stored hot and cold supplies, the bottom of the cold-water cistern needs to be at least 900mm – and preferably 1.5m – above the showerhead for pressure to be adequate.

For an instantaneous shower supplied direct from the mains, the pressure requirement varies according to the model, but in most homes it is unlikely to be too low, unless, perhaps, you live on the top floor of a block of flats, or in an old house converted into flats. Contact your local water company if in doubt.

Water supply and drainage

Little or no pipework is involved in installing a shower over a bath, but supply and drainage routes must be worked out for a shower in a separate cubicle. The drainage is often more difficult to arrange than the water supply to the shower, and you may need to get approval from your local authority Building Control Officer.

Use 15mm diameter supply pipes. To minimise loss of pressure, pipe runs to the shower should be as short and straight as possible. Avoid using elbow joints at corners – instead, bend pipes if possible to minimise resistance to flow. When routeing a pipe, ensure that fixings will not interfere with electric cables or gas pipes.

Showers that do mean extra pipework over a bath are instantaneous electric showers and mixer types. For an instantaneous shower you need a cold supply pipe taken direct from the rising main; for a mixer shower, you need hot and cold supply pipes.

Shower mixers If you are installing a manual mixer over a bath or in a cubicle, you must take the cold supply direct from the storage cistern. Taking the supply from a branch pipe supplying other taps or cisterns is unsafe because when the other fitting is in use, the cold supply to the shower could be reduced so much that the shower becomes scalding hot.

Hot water for the mixer can be taken from a branch pipe, because there is no danger if the hot supply to the shower is reduced – though it can give you a nasty chilly spray. If you take the hot supply from the cylinder distribution pipe, make the connection at a point above the height of the cylinder top.

With a thermostatic shower mixer, however, both hot and cold water can be taken from the branch pipes, as the water temperature is automatically controlled.

Achieving adequate pressure

If you do not have sufficient water pressure to supply a shower at the required position, there are two ways to increase it: you can either raise the height of the cistern or have a booster pump installed.

Raising the cistern The cold water cistern can be raised by fitting a strong wooden platform beneath it, constructed from timber struts and blockboard. You will also have to lengthen the rising main to reach the cistern, as well as the distribution pipes from the cistern.

Booster pumps These incorporate an electric motor and must be wired into the power supply. There are two main types. A single pump is fitted between the mixer control and the spray and boosts the mixed supply to the spray. A dual pump is fitted to the supply pipes and boosts the hot and cold supplies separately before they reach the mixer. Depending on the model, a booster pump will provide sufficient pressure with as little as 150mm height difference between the water level in the cistern and the spray head.

Most dual pumps need to be at least 300mm below the cold tank, but some will provide sufficient pressure to a showerhead sited higher than the cold water storage cistern, which allows a shower to be installed in an attic.

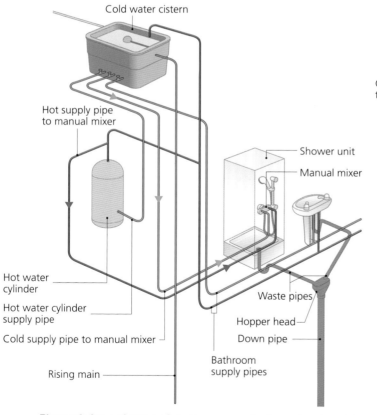

Cold water cistern

Hot supply pipe to manual mixer

Shower unit

Manual mixer

Hot water cylinder

Waste pipes

Hot water cylinder supply pipe

Hopper head

Cold supply pipe to manual mixer

Down pipe

Rising main

Bathroom supply pipes

Pipework for a shower mixer For a manual mixer, take the cold supply pipe direct from the cold water cistern to avoid risk of scalding when other cold taps are turned on. Take the hot supply from the hot water cylinder distribution pipe – tee in above cylinder height. For a thermostatic mixer, which has a temperature stabiliser, you can tee in to bathroom supply pipes.

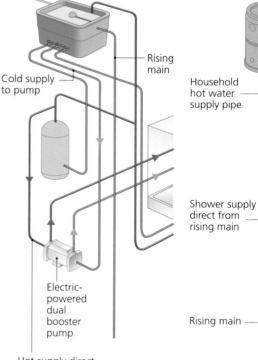

Rising main

Cold supply to pump

Electric-powered dual booster pump

Hot supply direct from cylinder

Boosting water pressure with a dual pump This boosts hot and cold water supplies separately. Some types of pump have a hot supply pipe direct from the cylinder casing, some from the vent pipe. A dual booster pump should be fitted by a plumber.

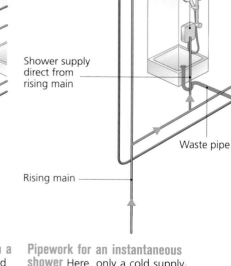

Cistern-type electric heater

Household hot water supply pipe

Instantaneous shower unit

Shower supply direct from rising main

Rising main

Waste pipe

Pipework for an instantaneous shower Here, only a cold supply, direct from the rising main, is needed. This is useful where there is no cold water storage cistern, as mains cold water and stored hot water cannot, by law, be mixed in one fitting.

Choosing a shower

The type of shower that can be installed depends in part on your household water system. Where hot and cold water are both supplied from storage tanks at equal pressure (see Indirect system, page 325), a mixer shower is the most economical option. Many showers are designed to cope with differing water pressures, such as stored hot water and cold mains water. If you connect mains water to a shower, you must fit a double seal check valve on the mains supply pipe to prevent back siphonage. Some showers come with built-in check valves. Specially designed systems are required when hot water is to be supplied from the mains via a multipoint heater or combination boiler: check the installation requirements with the shower manufacturer.

Bath/shower mixer A shower spray combined with a bath mixer tap provides a shower for little more than the cost of the bath taps, and no extra plumbing is involved. The temperature is controlled through the bath taps, which may not be convenient, and will be affected by water being drawn off elsewhere in the home.

Power shower An all-in-one shower which incorporates a powerful electric pump that boosts the rate that hot and cold water are supplied to the shower head from the storage cistern and the hot water cylinder. A power shower is unsuitable where water is supplied from a combination boiler under mains pressure. Removing waste water from a power shower fast enough can be a problem. The shower tray must cope with around 27 litres a minute, so it is probably worth fitting a 50mm waste pipe.

Shower tower A wall unit that incorporates a thermostatic mixer shower with a number of adjustable body jets. Tower units also have a fixed showerhead and a hand-held spray, and may be designed to fit into a corner or on a flat wall. Some can be installed over a bath while others are made for cubicles or wet rooms. Most require a minimum ceiling height of 2.2m. A pump is usually needed to boost water pressure.

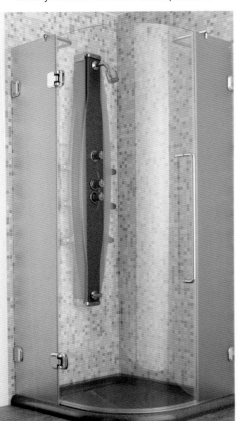

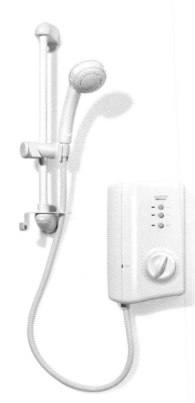

Instantaneous electric shower A wall unit plumbed in to a mains cold water supply, and heated by an electric element. The controls allow either less water at a higher temperature or more at a lower temperature, so the spray is weaker in winter when mains water is colder. Some models have a winter/summer setting. Designs fitted with a temperature stabiliser cannot run too hot or be affected by other taps in use. The unit must be wired to an electric power supply meeting Wiring Regulations requirements (page 288). This type of shower can be installed where a mixer would be illegal. Where mains water pressure is too low, a tank-fed pumped electric shower is available.

SAFETY WARNING

A showerhead on a hose must be fed through a retaining ring on the wall of the shower. This prevents the showerhead hanging in standing water in the bath or shower tray beneath and avoids potential contamination of the mains supply.

SHOWER FITTINGS

Spray roses Showerheads may be fixed or part of a handset on a flexible hose. The simplest have a single spray; multi-spray showerheads offer a choice of spray patterns selected by rotating the outer ring on the rose. Large diameter single spray showerheads offering a rain-style shower are also available.

Shower trays GRP-reinforced acrylic trays are light to handle and not easily damaged. A reconstituted stone or resin shower tray is heavy, stable and durable, but the floor must be level before it is installed. Shower trays come in sizes from 700mm^2 and are usually 110–185mm high; low level 35mm trays are available for 'walk-in' showers. Quarter circle and pentangle trays help to save space.

WETROOMS

A wetroom consists of a WC, basin and shower area. No shower tray or enclosure is fitted and water drains through a central drain set in a sloping floor, so the whole room must be waterproofed. This is not a DIY job. Wetrooms may have a powerful thermostatic mixer shower and body jets or a shower tower.

Manual and thermostatic mixers These are wall units with hot and cold water supplies linked to a single valve. In a manual mixer, temperature and volume are controlled by one dial or separately. Thermostatic mixers are more expensive. Their temperature control has a built-in stabiliser so water cannot run too hot or too cold. Computerised models have a control panel to programme temperature and flow rates and can store the data for each user. Provided water is not supplied from a combination boiler under mains pressure, this type of shower can be linked to a pump to give power shower performance.

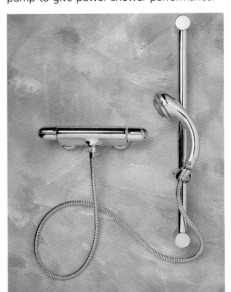

Installing a shower

Most types of shower can be fitted either over a bath or in a cubicle. The fixings and pipe routes vary according to the shower type, the bathroom layout and the shower location, but the method of installation is basically the same.

Before you start Decide on the type of shower you want, bearing in mind that the shower head must either be fitted so as to prevent it coming into contact with water in the bath or shower tray, or it must have a check valve (non-return valve) where the hose is attached to the shower control.

1 Mark the required positions of the spray head and shower control.

2 Plan the pipework to the shower control and how the waste water will be routed to the drainage system.

3 If you are fitting an instantaneous electric shower, work out the positions of the cable route and the switch (page 288).

4 Fit the shower control. Most units are available as either surface-mounted or recessed fittings, and come with fixings and instructions.

When fitting a recessed mixer, if possible mount it on a removable panel flush with the wall so that you have easy access to the controls.

5 Cut off the water supply and fit the water supply pipes. You can recess the pipes into the wall and then replaster or tile over them. However, they must be protected with a waterproof covering and have service valves fitted.

6 Fit the shower head and spray. For a separate cubicle, fit the base tray and waste fittings.

7 Connect the supply pipes to the shower control. An adaptor with a female screw thread (copper to iron) may be needed.

8 Restore the water supply and check the piping for leaks. Tighten any joints as necessary.

9 For an electric shower, turn off the electric supply at the consumer unit (fuse box). Make the necessary electrical connections (page 288), following the shower manufacturer's instructions. Restore the power supply.

10 Fit screening panels and seal the joints between the wall and screening and the tray.

Replacing a sink

You may want to replace a modern sink that has pillar taps with an old fashioned deep fireclay sink that has bib taps, or vice versa.

Some sinks have two tap holes, or holes for a two-hole mixer. Others have only one hole for a monobloc mixer. All have an outlet hole – either a 38mm hole for fitting a standard waste outlet, or a 90mm hole for fitting a waste disposal unit.

There are two basic sink designs: lay-on and inset. Lay-on sinks rest on a base unit of the same size as the sink rim. They are being replaced by inset types, which fit into a cut-out in the worktop and may be one unit or a separate bowl and drainer.

Sinks are available in a range of sizes and patterns. They are typically about 500mm wide and vary in length from about 780mm to 1.5m. Patterns vary from one bowl and a drainer in one unit, to combinations of one-and-a-half, two and two-and-a-half bowls with a drainer, two drainers, or no drainer at all. Drainers can be to the right or left side of the unit. Think about which will suit you best.

Stainless steel is the most common sink material. Enamelled pressed steel and more expensive polycarbonate are available in a range of colours. Easy-to-clean ceramic sinks are the toughest and most expensive, but china banged against them may chip.

Changing the sink height

Before choosing a sink, check the height of the waste outlet of the existing sink. The new sink may be higher or lower depending on bowl depth or the height of a new support unit. A typical waste-outlet height from a bowl 180mm deep in a unit 870mm high would be 690mm.

If the new outlet will be higher than the old one, use a telescopic trap. If the new outlet will be lower, reposition the waste pipe.

If the pipe runs into an outside drain, you may need a new exit hole in the wall. If the pipe links to a drainage or single stack, make a new connection. The downward slope should be about 20mm for every 1m of run. Connecting the waste pipe to a single stack should be left to a plumber.

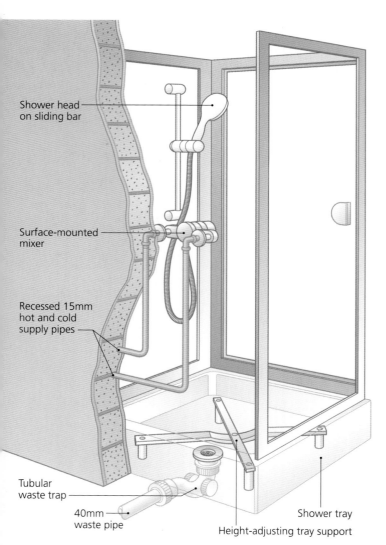

Shower head on sliding bar

Surface-mounted mixer

Recessed 15mm hot and cold supply pipes

Tubular waste trap

40mm waste pipe

Shower tray

Height-adjusting tray support

A typical cubicle installation
Screens are usually about 1.8m high. Panel widths can usually be adjusted by 25–50mm to allow for walls that are out of true. Doors may be hinged, folded (with panels shaped to keep water in), sliding with corner entry, or pivoted to give a wide entry without taking a lot of opening space. Some shower trays have an adjustable support by which the height can be altered so that the waste pipe and trap can be positioned either above or below the floorboards.

Fitting an inset sink

Most new sinks are inset into a cut-out in the worktop, and are designed for use with a monobloc mixer tap rather than two separate pillar taps, as was the case with many old-fashioned lay-on sinks. The sink may have one or two bowls and, probably, an integral draining board.

The rim of the sink is sealed in its cut-out to stop water seeping beneath it, and is held in place by locking clips underneath. The monobloc mixer tap fits into a 35mm diameter hole in the sink unit, and has two flexible 10mm pipe tails projecting from its backnut. These are linked to the existing hot and cold water supplies with reducing joints. Fit an in-line service valve to each pipe before connecting it to the tap, to make maintenance easier in the future.

Tools *Two adjustable spanners for compression joints; long-nose pliers; screwdriver; jigsaw; power drill and twist drill bits; pencil. Possibly also pipe cutter.*

Materials *Inset sink (the correct fixings are usually provided); monobloc kitchen mixer with top and bottom washers; two compression joints (probably reducers); two in-line service valves; silicone sealant; PTFE tape.*

1 Mark the shape to be cut out on the worktop according to the sink manufacturer's instructions. Check that the saw cut will not interfere with any structural parts of the base unit. Cut out the hole with a jigsaw.

2 With the sink on its face, seal round the rim and fit any earthing tag needed (page 267) into the slot marked E on the rim.

3 Fit the securing clips to the sink, following the instructions. They are commonly hinged clips that are screwed to the sink rim and can be adjusted to fit worktops 27–43mm thick.

4 Fit the mixer tap, the waste outlet and any overflow pipes to the sink. Take care to position all sealing washers correctly.

5 Fit the sink into the worktop, tightening the clips gradually in sequence. Connect the earth lead to the earthing tag if the new sink is metallic.

6 Connect the trap to the waste outlet and add any overflow pipework as instructed. Then modify and connect the supply pipework.

CONNECTING A MONOBLOC MIXER TAP

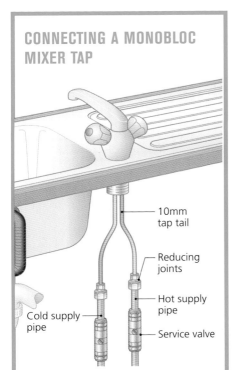

10mm tap tail

Reducing joints

Hot supply pipe

Service valve

Cold supply pipe

1 Check that the supply pipes are the right height for connecting to the tap tails. Cut the pipes if they are too high, and save the offcuts to link the new service valves to the tap tails. Label the pipes 'hot' and 'cold' so that you connect them correctly.

2 Fit a service valve to each supply pipe and turn it off with a screwdriver. Then add a short length of 15mm copper pipe to the outlet of each valve.

3 Connect the 15mm end of a reducing joint to each pipe tail.

4 Connect the narrower end of each reducing joint to its tap tail. You can bend the tap tails slightly to line up the connections, but take care not to kink them.

5 Screw up each capnut until it is finger-tight at both ends of each fitting. Hold each fitting steady with one spanner while you give each nut 1¼ turns with the other spanner.

6 Open each service valve and check each fitting for leaks. Tighten any weeping capnuts by another quarter turn.

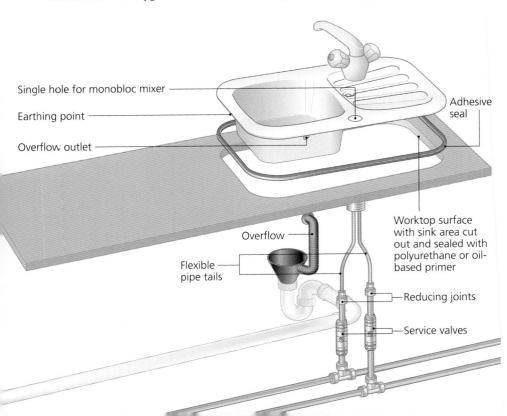

Single hole for monobloc mixer

Earthing point

Overflow outlet

Adhesive seal

Overflow

Flexible pipe tails

Worktop surface with sink area cut out and sealed with polyurethane or oil-based primer

Reducing joints

Service valves

Plumbing in a washing machine or dishwasher

A washing machine or dishwasher is easy to install beside a kitchen sink, as the existing supply and waste pipes are conveniently positioned for fitting a drain kit and branch pipes for the machine.

Before you start When a washing machine or dishwasher is newly plumbed in, a single check valve (non-return valve) must be fitted to the hot and cold pipes supplying the hoses.

Drain kits will not fit every type of washing machine, so check in the manual or with the manufacturer before choosing one.

Tools *Hacksaw or pipe slice; half-round file; two adjustable spanners; medium-sized screwdriver; measuring tape; soft pencil; two spring-clip clothes pegs; spirit level. Possibly also shallow pan.*

Materials *About 600mm of 15mm copper piping; two washing machine stoptaps; two 15mm single check valves; two 15mm equal tee compression joints; one drain kit; one hose clip of the diameter of the drain hose.*

Connecting up the water

1 Turn off the water supply to the kitchen sink cold tap at the main stoptap.

2 Mark the cold supply pipe at a point convenient for connection to the machine. Make a second mark 20mm higher.

3 Cut through the pipe squarely with a hacksaw or pipe slice at the lowest point marked. A small amount of water will run out as you cut the pipe. Cut at the second mark on the pipe and remove the section of pipe. File the pipe ends smooth.

4 Use spring-clip clothes pegs to stop the caps and olives slipping down the pipe. Fit a tee joint to the pipe with the branch outlet pointing towards the machine.

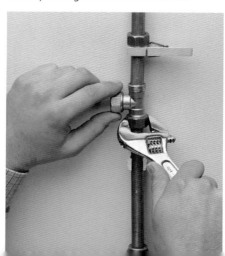

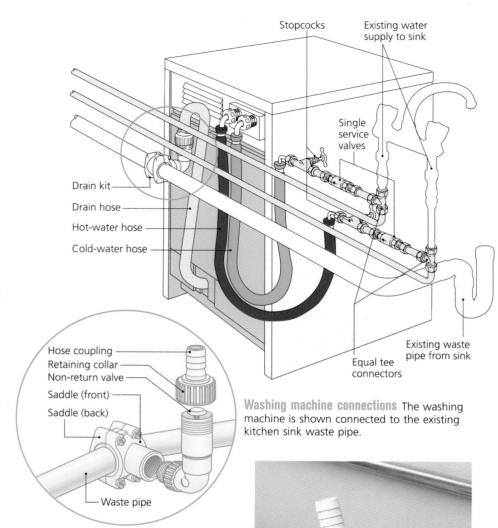

Stopcocks

Existing water supply to sink

Single service valves

Drain kit

Drain hose

Hot-water hose

Cold-water hose

Equal tee connectors

Existing waste pipe from sink

Hose coupling

Retaining collar

Non-return valve

Saddle (front)

Saddle (back)

Waste pipe

Washing machine connections The washing machine is shown connected to the existing kitchen sink waste pipe.

5 Cut a short length of pipe, fit it into the tee outlet and connect to the check valve, making sure that the valve's arrow mark points towards the machine.

6 Cut another length of pipe and fit it to the check valve outlet. It should be long enough to reach to the washing machine position.

7 Fit the other end of the pipe to the compression joint end of the machine stoptap. Connect the machine's cold-water hose to the stoptap.

8 Turn off the water supply to the hot tap over the kitchen sink (page 328). Cut the pipe and fit a tee joint, new pipe, check valve and stoptap as above. Connect the machine's hot-water hose to the stoptap and restore the hot and cold water supplies.

Fitting the waste pipe

1 Unscrew the saddle from the rest of the drain kit.

2 Fit the saddle round the waste pipe. Choose a convenient place away from joints, and well beyond the trap.

3 Screw the cutting tool into the saddle until a hole has been cut in the waste pipe.

4 Remove the cutting tool and screw on the rest of the drain kit. It includes a non-return valve to prevent water from the sink flowing into the machine.

5 Slip a hose clip over the drain hose, push it into the spigot and tighten the clip. Now the machine is ready to use. Every two or three months, unscrew the plastic retaining collar and remove any fluff that may be clogging up the non-return valve. Be sure to tighten it fully afterwards.

Installing an outside tap

Some bib taps have a threaded nozzle which is suitable for fitting a garden hose. A tap installed against an outside wall should have an angled head; otherwise you will graze your knuckles when you turn the handle.

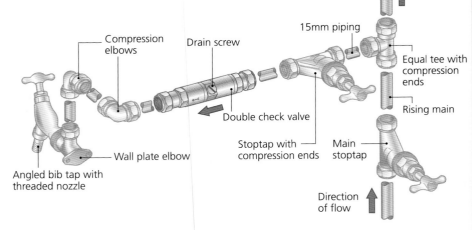

Compression elbows · **Drain screw** · **15mm piping** · **Equal tee with compression ends** · **Rising main** · **Double check valve** · **Stoptap with compression ends** · **Main stoptap** · **Wall plate elbow** · **Angled bib tap with threaded nozzle** · **Direction of flow**

What you must do Tell your water supply company before making the installation: there will be an extra charge on your water rates for the tap.
• To prevent the risk of contamination by back-siphonage, you must insert a double check valve as close to the new tap as practicable.
• Taps incorporating check valves, and check valves to screw onto the nozzles of existing taps, are also available.

About the installation This job involves running a branch pipe from the rising main through the wall to the tap position.
The instructions given here are for fitting copper pipe run from a 15mm rising main with compression fittings; other pipe materials or fittings could be used.
• You should fit a stoptap into the branch pipe, as it allows you to do the job in two stages, and in winter you can cut off the water supply to the tap and drain it to prevent frost damage.
• As an alternative to making up the pipe run yourself, outside tap kits containing all the necessary parts are available from most DIY stores.
• The best way to make a hole through the brick wall of a house is with a heavy-duty power drill and masonry bit, both of which can be hired. Choose a bit at least 325mm long and 20mm in diameter to allow the pipe to be passed through the wall easily.

Tools *Two adjustable spanners; hacksaw or pipe slice; half-round file; power drill with masonry bits; screwdriver; two spring-clip clothes pegs; soft pencil; measuring tape; spirit level.*

Materials *Angled bib tap with threaded nozzle; 15mm stoptap; 15mm double check valve; 15mm copper pipe; plastic pipe clips; 15mm equal tee; two 15mm elbows; wall-plate elbow; PTFE tape; wall filler.*

Positioning the tap

1 Mark the required position on the outside wall of the kitchen, as near as possible to the rising main.

2 Check that the mark is high enough for a bucket to be placed underneath the tap quite easily, and is at least 250mm above the damp-proof course in the house wall.

3 Make another mark for the hole through the wall about 150mm above the tap mark.

4 Take measurements from the hole mark to a point such as a window, so that you can locate and check the corresponding hole position inside.

5 Mark the position of the hole on the inside of the wall. Check that it will not interfere with any inside fitting and will be above the position of the main stoptap on the rising main.

Fitting the branch pipe inside

1 Turn off the main stoptap, then turn on the kitchen cold tap to drain the pipe.

2 If there is a drain valve above the stoptap, turn it on to drain the rising main, and prepare to collect the water that runs out in a container.

3 Mark the rising main at a point level with the hole mark on the inside wall. Make a second mark 20mm higher.

4 Cut through the rising main squarely with a hacksaw or pipe slice at the lower point marked. If there was not a drain valve above the main stoptap, be prepared for a small amount of water to run out as you cut through the pipe.

Pipework and fittings An outside tap is supplied by a branch pipe, commonly run from a tee joint fitted into the rising main. Instead of a tee joint, you can use a self-boring tap, which can be fitted to the pipe without turning off the water. No separate stoptap is then needed in the branch pipe.

5 Cut the pipe at the second mark and remove the section of pipe. Use a file to smooth the pipe ends and remove burrs, and to square the ends if necessary.

6 Fit a capnut and olive over each cut pipe end. Use spring-clip clothes pegs to stop the nuts and olives slipping down the pipes. Fit the tee into the rising main with the branch outlet pointing towards the hole mark.

7 Cut a short length of pipe and connect it to the branch of the tee.

8 Connect the stoptap to the pipe, with its arrow mark pointing away from the rising main. Angle the stoptap so its handle leans away from the wall.

9 Close the new stoptap by turning its handle clockwise. You can now turn on the main stoptap and restore the water supply to the rest of the house.

10 Cut another short length of pipe and connect it to the outlet of the stoptap.

11 Connect the check valve to the pipe, making sure that its arrow mark points in the same direction as the stoptap arrow. Then complete the pipe run (see overleaf).

Connecting the outside tap

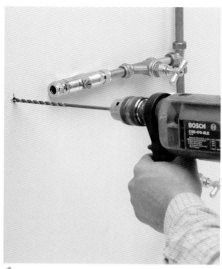

1 Use a long, slim masonry drill bit to drill through the wall from the inside first, making sure to keep the drill at right angles to the wall. Withdraw the bit at intervals to cool it and to pull out dust. Then use a 20mm masonry bit, working from both sides of the wall, to make a hole wide enough for the pipe to fit through easily.

2 Measure the distance from the hole to the newly fitted check valve.

3 Cut a length of pipe to reach between them, allowing extra for fitting into the check valve and an elbow fitting. Cut a second length to go through the wall.

4 Join the two lengths with an elbow fitting and push the pipe through the hole.

5 Connect the free end to the check valve. If this is difficult, undo the pipe at the wall elbow and connect the check valve first.

6 Outside the house, cut the projecting pipe to leave only 25mm sticking out from the wall.

7 Fit another elbow to the projecting pipe, making sure that the free end of the elbow points towards the tap position mark.

8 Measure from the elbow to the tap mark and cut another length of pipe to fit the distance.

9 Fit the pipe to the inlet of the wall-plate elbow.

10 Fit the other end of the pipe temporarily into the elbow above, then hold the wall plate against the wall and mark the position of the screw holes.

11 Put aside the wall-plate elbow and pipe end, and drill and plug the wall.

12 Join the pipe to the projecting elbow and fix the wall-plate elbow to the wall.

Fitting the tap

1 Bind PTFE tape round the tail thread.

2 Screw the tap fully into the outlet of the wall-plate elbow.

3 If the tap is not upright when screwed home, take if off again, put one or two thin fibre washers over the inlet and refit. Keep on adjusting in this way until it is tight and upright.

4 Open up the new stoptap inside, and check all the pipe joints for leaks. Tighten if necessary.

5 Turn on the newly fitted outside tap and check that it is working properly.

6 Use wall filler, sealant or polyurethane foam filler to seal round the pipe hole in the wall.

Ways of saving heat

Money is wasted if water is heated and then not used. Inefficiencies in the plumbing system, or inefficient use of heaters, can also waste heat.

Insulate the hot water cylinder A 75mm thick lagging jacket on a hot water cylinder cuts down heat loss by about 70 per cent. A 140 litre cylinder without a jacket, maintained at a temperature of 60°C, loses enough heat every week to heat about 20 baths. Many modern cylinders are foam-lagged by the manufacturer.

Keep hot water pipes short The length of pipe between the hot water cylinder and a hot tap is known as a dead leg, because hot water left in the pipe after each use of the tap cools and is wasted. The longer the pipe, the more the waste.

Water at 60°C travelling through a 15mm copper pipe loses heat equivalent to more than 1 unit of electricity for roughly each 300mm of run per week – enough to heat about 45 litres of water.

Where a hot water supply pipe to a basin or shower would involve a dead leg of piping of more than 6m long, it is wiser to use an instantaneous heater instead.

If you have an electric storage heater installed, position it as near as possible to the hot tap most often used – usually the one over the kitchen sink.

Avoid secondary hot-water circulation At one time, if a shower or tap was some distance from the hot water cylinder, there was a constant circulation of hot water to it by means of a return pipe back to the cylinder. This ensured that there was no delay in the arrival of hot water to the tap. Because of the heat lost, avoid such secondary circulation, particularly with electric heating.

Install a shower Use a shower for daily cleansing and keep the bath for relaxed soaking. A bath takes about six times as much water as a shower.

Heat water only as needed Although a thermostat gives economical heating by controlling temperature, even a well-lagged cylinder will lose heat (generally the equivalent of about 6 units of electricity a week). This can add considerably to costs if the heater is left on all the time.

Savings can be made by switching on an immersion heater or boiler only about an hour before hot water is needed, and switching it off when it is not wanted.

The most convenient way to do this is to have the heater fitted with a time switch (page 315) that is set to turn it on for times of peak household use. Time switches have a manual override to allow use of the heater at other than the set times.

Take advantage also of cheaper night rates for electricity. Details of off-peak meters and tariffs are available from your electricity supplier.

Prevent scale formation in water pipes and appliances About 65 per cent of British homes – chiefly those in the south-east and Midlands – have hard or moderately hard water. The hardness is caused by a high concentration of dissolved calcium and magnesium salts, and is evident when, for example, soap does not dissolve properly and scale forms inside the kettle and round a tap nozzle.

Hard water drying on any surface leaves a crust of the salts behind, and at high temperatures the salts solidify into scale. When scale forms inside a domestic boiler or hot water cylinder, it insulates the water from the heat and wastes fuel, and pipes gradually become blocked.

Scale can be prevented or limited by a number of methods:

1 Controlling the hot water temperature – scale starts to form above 60°C.

2 Suspending scale-inhibiting chemicals in crystal form in the cold water cistern. They need changing every six months.

3 More expensively, by plumbing a water softener into the rising main – beyond the kitchen tap and a branch to an outside tap. This leaves hard water, which most people prefer, for drinking. It is not worth softening the water for garden use.

4 By plumbing a magnetic water conditioner into the rising main directly above the main stopcock. In this, water passes through a magnetic field so that the structure of the scale-forming salts is altered; they change into fine particles that flush through the pipes instead of clustering to form scale. The conditioner has a filter that needs cleaning about twice a year.

Alternative ways of heating water

The average household uses 220–320 litres of hot water a day. Finding the best way of heating water for your home deserves some thought.

The commonest type of water-heating system is a hot water storage cylinder heated by a boiler (pages 382–3), probably combined with the central heating system. Various kinds of gas or electric heater can also be used to supplement the system, or as a complete system in themselves. They may be fed either by a low-pressure supply from the cold water cistern, or by a high-pressure supply direct from the mains.

Immersion heater
Electric element fitted into a standard storage cylinder to heat water. May be 1kW, 2kW or 3kW.
• There are three types: top-entry with one element extending almost to the cylinder bottom; top-entry with two elements – a long one for cheap night electricity and a short one for heating a small amount of water as needed; side-entry – usually a pair, one at the bottom to heat the entire cylinder and one at the top for heating small amounts.
• All types have thermostats. Can be fitted into a copper hot water cylinder as the sole means of heating, or as a supplement to a boiler. Can be renewed if the element burns out. Modern cylinders usually have 32mm or 57mm bosses in the dome or low in a side wall (or both) for heater fitting. Only water above the level of the element is heated. Expensive to use unless the storage cylinder is well insulated.

Electric storage heater (low-pressure type)
Large-capacity, heavily insulated storage cylinder supplied from the cold water storage cistern and heated by one or two immersion heaters fitted horizontally.
• When two heaters are used, the upper one can be kept on for a permanent hot water supply, and the lower one turned on for extra heat when a large volume is needed, such as for a bath. Can be installed at any convenient point to supply a number of hot taps, but must have a vent pipe to the cold water cistern.
• There are types of heater for fitting under a sink, and floor-standing types. Floor-standing types are very well insulated and are designed for use with off-peak supplies.

Electric storage heater (cistern type)
Medium or large capacity, heavily insulated storage cylinder supplied from the rising main through its own built-in cold water cistern. The cylinder is heated by one or two immersion heaters, in the same way as a low-pressure type (above). Useful for supplying a number of hot taps where the water supply is direct from the mains. The built-in cistern feeds the heater only – no other cold taps.
• There are wall-mounted types or floor-standing types. Large well-insulated floor-standing types are designed for use with off-peak supplies.

Instantaneous gas heater
The water is heated by gas as it flows through small-bore copper tubing. When the hot tap is turned on, the gas jets are ignited by a pilot light that burns continuously. The jets go out when the tap is turned off.
• Large multipoint heaters can supply all household hot taps; smaller single-point types supply one tap only. The water supply is normally direct from the rising main. The heater can be fed from a cold water cistern if it is high enough – usually at least 2m above the highest tap – to give enough pressure.
• Useful where there is no cold water storage cistern. Only the water used is heated – there is no slow cooling of unused water. But the delivery rate is slower than from a cylinder, and the flow from one hot tap is interrupted if another is turned on. It is designed to raise water temperature by about 26°C, so in cold weather – when mains water can be near freezing – the heated water is either cool or slow running. In summer it may be too hot. Some have a winter/summer setting to vary the heat.
• The heater has a flue and must be fitted against an outside wall.

Instantaneous open-outlet electric heater
Small heater, supplied direct from the rising main, in which the water is heated as it passes through. Heaters with a 7kW element are designed for showers (page 359), those with a 3kW element for washing hands.
• The water emerges through a spray nozzle. Useful for providing a shower where there is no suitable storage cistern supply or for hot water for washing hands in a cloakroom that has no hot water supply pipes.
• As with instantaneous gas heaters, these electric heaters usually raise the temperature by about 26°C, so water heat varies according to mains water temperature, but some types have a winter/summer setting. Also, the flow may be interrupted when other taps are used, unless a compensating valve is fitted.

Renewing an immersion heater

An immersion heater element can burn out after long use or if it becomes coated with limescale. Water that takes longer than usual to heat up may indicate scaling. Some immersion heaters are designed for use in hard water.

Before you start Although modern heaters have a thermostat and can be prevented from heating above 60°C – the temperature at which scale starts to form – they may be used as a supplement to a boiler that does not have the same degree of heat control.

To fit a replacement immersion heater to a low-pressure or cistern-type electric storage heater (previous page), follow the heater maker's instructions. The heater may be on a plate assembly that can be withdrawn without draining the water chamber.

Tools *Immersion heater spanner – box-type for deep lagging; electrical screwdriver; adjustable spanner; hose clip.*

Materials *Immersion heater; PTFE tape. Possibly also 1.5mm² three-core heat-resisting flex (page 271); penetrating oil.*

1 If the cylinder is heated by a boiler, switch the boiler off. Then switch off the electricity supply at the consumer unit (fuse box).

2 Stop the water supply to the cylinder. Turn off the gatevalve on the supply pipe, if there is one, or drain the cold water cistern (page 329).

3 Turn on the bathroom taps to draw off any water in the supply pipe.

4 Locate the cylinder drain valve. For an indirect cylinder (or a direct cylinder heated solely by an immersion heater) it is on the supply pipe where it runs into the base of the cistern. For a direct cylinder heated by a boiler, use the boiler drainvalve (page 329).

5 Drain water from the cylinder (page 329) as necessary – about 4.5 litres for a top-entry or high side-entry heater, or the whole cylinder for a low side-entry heater. Close the drain valve.

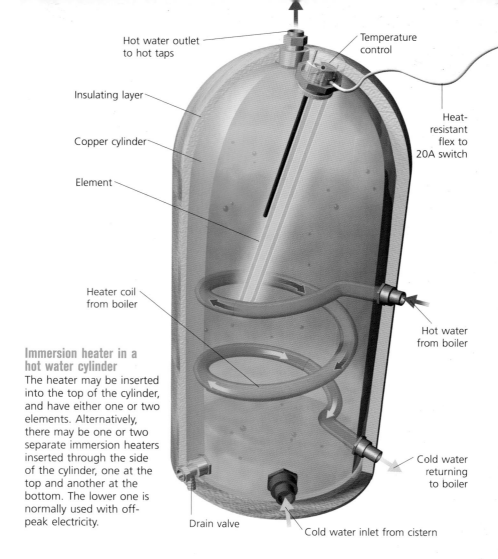

Hot water outlet to hot taps

Temperature control

Insulating layer

Copper cylinder

Element

Heat-resistant flex to 20A switch

Heater coil from boiler

Hot water from boiler

Immersion heater in a hot water cylinder

The heater may be inserted into the top of the cylinder, and have either one or two elements. Alternatively, there may be one or two separate immersion heaters inserted through the side of the cylinder, one at the top and another at the bottom. The lower one is normally used with off-peak electricity.

Cold water returning to boiler

Drain valve

Cold water inlet from cistern

6 Unscrew and remove the immersion heater cover. Note which of the three conductors is connected to which terminal, then disconnect them using an electrical screwdriver.

HELPFUL TIP

If the heater is difficult to remove, do not force it. Apply penetrating oil round the joint and leave it overnight. Alternatively, warm the joint with a hair dryer, then try loosening it again with the spanner. Do not give one strong pull. Instead, loosen the thread by giving the spanner two or three sharp taps with a hammer in the opening direction (counter-clockwise).

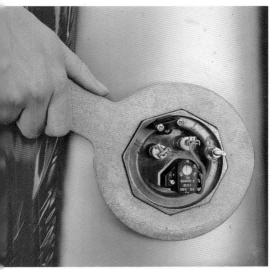

7 Use an immersion heater spanner to unscrew the old immersion heater and withdraw it from its boss. A flat spanner is suitable if there is no deep lagging.

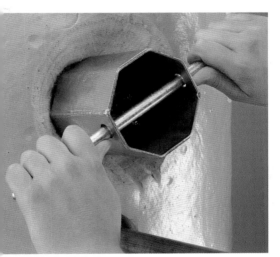

Alternatively For a deep-lagged cylinder, you will need a box-type immersion heater spanner, turned with a tommy bar.

8 If there is no fibre sealing washer supplied with the new heater, bind the thread on the tail of the new immersion heater with PTFE tape.

9 Insert the heater into the cylinder boss. In an indirect cylinder, make sure the element does not foul the heat exchanger.

10 Use the immersion heater spanner to screw the heater firmly home.

11 Restore the water supply and check for leaks round the heater boss. If there are any, tighten the heater slightly.

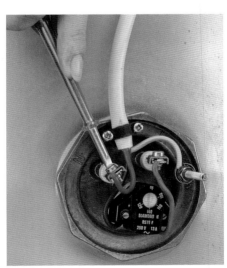

12 Remove the retaining cap of the new heater and reconnect the three electric conductors to their correct terminals. Use new flex if necessary (page 271).

13 Set the heater thermostat (see right). Set a single thermostat (or the cheap-rate thermostat on an off-peak system) no higher than 60°C in a hard-water area (to prevent scale forming), or up to 65–70°C in a soft-water area. Where two thermostats are fitted, set the one for day-time operation to 50–55°C.

14 Refit the cap on the immersion heater, then restore the electricity supply at the consumer unit (fuse box).

SETTING THE THERMOSTAT

The temperature control can normally be adjusted with a screwdriver – the settings are marked round the screw. Some two-element heaters have one thermostat, some have two.

Dual (two-element) immersion heaters sometimes have a thermostatic switch unit that can be switched to either 'bath' or 'sink'. Their thermostats cannot normally be adjusted.

Choosing pipe insulation material

Insulating pipes is critical to prevent them from freezing and bursting in very cold weather, and to minimise heat lost as hot water travels around the system.

Self-adhesive foam wrap Thin foam insulating wrap, 50mm wide, is supplied in rolls usually 5m or 10m long. Some types have a metallic finish.

There is no formula for estimating how much wrap to buy – it depends on the size of the pipes and how large you make the overlaps. Buy and use one or two packs, then work out how much more you will need to complete the job.

Before you fix the lagging, make sure that the pipes are clean and dry. Peel off the backing paper and wind the material round the pipes. Overlap the tape as you wind, especially at bends.

This flexible lagging is also useful for insulating awkward fittings, such as multiple joints and stoptaps.

Plastic foam tubes Easy-to-fit plastic foam tubes are split down one side and have to be eased open to fit them round the pipe. They are secured with adhesive tape wrapped round at intervals, or with purpose-made clips. Tubes are available to fit 15mm, 22mm and 28mm pipes. Plastic foam tube is slightly more expensive than self-adhesive foam wrap, but is much easier to fit.

Foam tubes are available in two wall thicknesses. In most cases the standard grade is sufficient, but if you live in an area that often experiences severe frosts or if your pipes are particularly exposed, it is worth investing in the thicker material.

Glass fibre blanket Pipes that are boxed in can be insulated by stuffing glass fibre blanket around the pipes.

COLD-WEATHER CHECKS

• Make sure no tap is left dripping. If that is not possible, put a plug in the bath or basin overnight. Drips cause ice to block waste pipes.
• Never allow cisterns to overfill. Water in overflow pipes can freeze, causing the cistern to overspill.
• In a long cold spell, open the loft hatch occasionally, to let in warmth from the house.
• If you leave the house for short periods, keep the central heating switched on, but turned down to the minimum setting.
• For long periods, drain the plumbing system by closing the main stoptap and opening all the taps. When the water stops running, open the drain valve near the stoptap. For central heating, see page 379.

Insulating hot and cold water pipes

Hot and cold water pipes that are exposed to the cold should be lagged to prevent winter freeze-ups.

Before you start Concentrate first on pipes that run across a loft, above an insulated floor, and those that run along outside walls in unheated rooms. Overflow and vent pipes that are exposed to the cold should also be lagged. Some pipes are boxed in. To lag them, unscrew the box and stuff pieces of glass fibre insulation all round the pipes. Make sure all pipes are clean and dry before you start.

Lagging pipes with self-adhesive foam wrap

Tools *Scissors.*

Materials *Rolls of self-adhesive foam wrap.*

Self-adhesive foam wrap is useful where there are many bends in the pipes and it would be difficult to use flexible foam tubes.

1 For pipes in the loft, begin work at the cistern. Cut pieces of foam wrap to a workable length with scissors.

2 Wrap foam round the pipe, making generous overlaps of about one-third of the width of the wrap. Take care to cover the pipe well at bends – these are the vulnerable areas most likely to freeze.

3 Take the wrap around any valves or stoptaps as you meet them, leaving only the handle exposed.

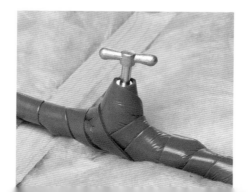

Lagging pipes with flexible foam tube

Tools *Scissors; serrated knife.*

Materials *Foam tube to match pipe size; adhesive tape; plastic clips.*

1 Lag the pipes leading from the cistern first, if you are insulating pipes in the loft. Wrap plastic adhesive tape around the first tube to hold it in place, even if the tube is one of the self-locking types. Push it up tight against the cistern so that the tank connector joint is covered.

2 Butt-join the tubes where they meet and wrap around the join to hold them tight. Cut the tube at 45° to fit it round elbows and tee fittings, and tape the joints. Alternatively secure joints with plastic clips.

3 Cut the tube to fit around the body of a gatevalve as closely as possible.

Lagging a cold-water system

Never lay lagging under a cold water cistern. Heat rising through the ceiling will help to prevent a freeze-up.

Before you start Purpose-made jackets are available to insulate most cisterns. Measure the cistern's diameter and height, if it is round, and its height, length and width if it is rectangular.

It does not matter if the jacket you buy is too large, since the sections can be over-lapped. If the cistern is an odd size or shape, or you want to provide extra insulation, use plastic-sleeved glass fibre loft insulation blanket. This is easier to handle than unsleeved blanket and will not release fibres into the air as you handle it.

Using glass fibre blanket

Tools *Steel tape measure; scissors.*

Materials *150mm thick wrapped glass fibre blanket; string.*

1 Wrap the cistern in a continuous length of blanket, which you have cut with scissors so that the edges will meet. Tie a length of string round the blanket.

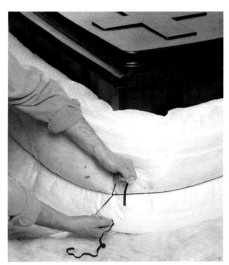

2 If necessary, wrap a second length of blanket round the tank. Cut it to length and tie it on the same way as the first layer.

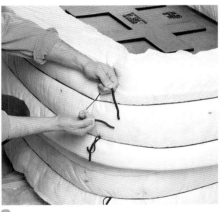

3 Extend the top layer beyond the top of the tank, to create a small rim to hold the tank's lid in place.

4 Measure the size of the tank lid. Cut a length of blanket to match and staple the ends closed. If the blanket is too wide, squeeze it up tightly to fit. Do not cut the blanket along its length.

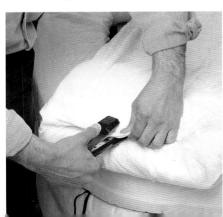

Insulating a high-level cistern

High-level tanks in roof spaces are more at risk from freezing than tanks sitting on the loft floor. This is because the heat rising from the house is not trapped under the tank.

For the same reason, the pipes leading up to the tanks are also at risk. If these pipes freeze, then there is a chance that the central heating boiler could explode. The most vulnerable pipe to freezing and bursting is the cold mains supply to the central heating tank, because the water in this pipe rarely moves so it has plenty of time to freeze.

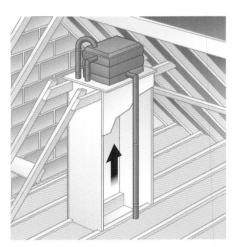

The best way to solve this problem is to build an enclosure directly under the tank in order to funnel heat upwards from the house and give added protection to the pipes. You can do this from any insulation material but the easiest to work with is fire-retardant polystyrene. It is lightweight, easy to cut and self-supporting. You can buy sheets of it very cheaply from builders' merchants. You may find even cheaper sheets with corners broken off.

Tools *Fine-toothed saw, hacksaw blade or serrated bread knife; tape measure; plumbline or spirit level.*

Materials *Sheets of polystyrene; polystyrene tile adhesive; 100mm wire nails or wooden meat skewers; adhesive tape.*

1 Use a plumbline to drop a vertical position from the edges of the high level tank down to the ceiling below. Cut and peel back the loft insulation at this point so that you have a clear area of ceiling corresponding to the shape of the cylinder.

2 Lay a piece of polythene over the ceiling at this point, cut to the same size as the base of the enclosure. This is to stop

vapour from the house, which evaporates through the ceiling, from entering the new enclosure and condensing on the underside of the tank.

3 Using the saw blade or knife, cut the polystyrene sheet to form walls from the ceiling to the tank sides. Stick the edges together with a small amount of tile adhesive and push the nails or skewers through the corners to hold the sheets in place while the adhesive dries.

4 Use a little adhesive on the ceiling around the polystyrene to seal any gaps and hold the sheets in place. Remember that lofts can be quite draughty in high winds and polystyrene can be blown around if it is not fixed.

5 Bring the polystyrene right up to the underside of the tank. The tank must be supported on an independent structure. Tape the top of the polystyrene to the sides of the tank support.

6 The tank or tanks must be very well insulated. A thin jacket is not sufficient if the tank is near the slope of the roof. Use glass fibre blanket over the top of existing insulation to increase protection.

7 Make sure that the vent pipe, which goes over the tank, has an open passage to the tank to discharge any water. The vent pipe outlet must be above the water line.

How central heating works

The type of central heating system you have may depend on the age of your house. It is important to understand how it works.

A typical pumped system

Most central heating systems warm the rooms of a house by passing hot water through radiators. There are many ways of heating the water, but it is usually through a boiler, which switches on automatically at certain times of day.

1 A room thermostat turns on the pump (or opens a motorised valve) and the boiler. The pump drives water around the system. The motorised valve opens and closes the circuits to the radiators and hot water cylinder as required by the thermostats. The water in the central heating system is separate from that supplied to the hot taps.

2 A programmer switches on the boiler and the pump at pre-set times of the day. A room thermostat controls the room temperature and turns the heating on and off as the air temperature falls and rises. The thermostat either switches on the pump or opens a motorised valve. The electrical controls start up the boiler. Water is then heated by the boiler and flows through either small bore or microbore pipes to the radiators. When the air temperature reaches the required level, the valve is closed or the pump is switched off.

3 The same water is constantly circulated around the system. In an open system, in case of leakage or evaporation, the water is topped up from a feed-and-expansion cistern. This cistern also takes up the expansion that occurs when the water heats up from cold.

4 An open-ended pipe, called the open safety-vent pipe, provides an escape route for steam and excess pressure if the boiler overheats.

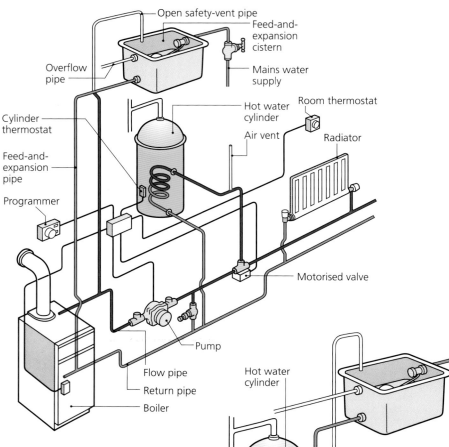

Open safety-vent pipe
Feed-and-expansion cistern
Overflow pipe
Mains water supply
Cylinder thermostat
Hot water cylinder
Room thermostat
Air vent
Radiator
Feed-and-expansion pipe
Programmer
Motorised valve
Pump
Flow pipe
Return pipe
Boiler

Gravity circulation

In some older central heating systems and in solid fuel systems, water is circulated by gravity. When water is heated it expands and hot water weighs less than cold water.

1 Hot water rises up a large pipe from the boiler to the hot water cylinder. Cooled water descends down the return pipe, pushing the lighter hot water up the flow pipe.

2 A pump, controlled by a programmer and room thermostat, drives water around the radiators. Gravity circulation is reliable as it needs no mechanical assistance, but it requires larger 28mm pipes. The system is most efficient if the cylinder is directly above the boiler.

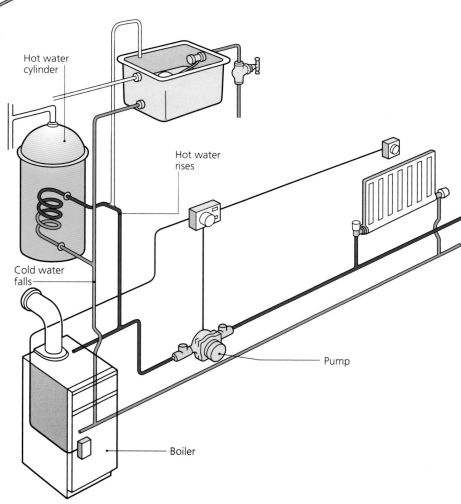

Hot water cylinder
Hot water rises
Cold water falls
Pump
Boiler

A sealed system

A sealed central heating system has an expansion vessel instead of an expansion cistern, and a pressure relief valve instead of a safety-vent pipe. The valve should be set permanently to 3 bar. Any water lost over time through minor leaks is topped up from the mains supply. Sealed systems are ideal for flats where it is difficult to find space for tanks.

1 A thermostat opens the motorised valve, which controls the circuits to the radiators.

2 The valve turns on the pump to drive water around the system, and starts up the boiler.

3 The boiler has an over-heat cut-out to prevent the system boiling should the standard thermostat fail, and on no account must a boiler without over-heat protection be fitted to a sealed system. It is now more common to use a combination boiler rather than to build up a sealed system from individual components.

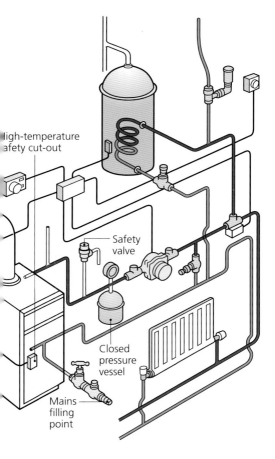

High-temperature safety cut-out

Safety valve

Closed pressure vessel

Mains filling point

Modern boilers The essential components of a sealed system are now usually housed inside the boiler. As well as saving space because of the lack of a feed-and-expansion cistern, a combination boiler also has the advantage that no hot water cylinder is needed as the boiler heats mains water and delivers hot water directly to the taps.

Controlling your central heating

Efficient temperature and time controls can save a great deal of money on fuel bills.

Room thermostat This temperature-sensitive switch is set to a pre-selected room temperature. It sends an electrical signal to switch the heating on when the air temperature falls below the pre-set level, and off when it rises above the level.

On fully pumped systems the room and hot water cylinder thermostats operate motorised valves. When these are opened they in turn switch on the boiler and pump.

On gravity hot water systems the room thermostat operates the pump and the boiler is switched on and off by the programmer.

A room thermostat is best placed in a draught-free spot on an inside wall away from direct sunlight, about 1.5m above floor level, and away from any heat sources.

Thermostatic radiator valve
The best means of controlling the temperature in each room is to fit a thermostatic radiator valve (TRV) to each radiator. The valve opens and closes according to the temperature in the room. If the room is cold, a full flow is allowed through to the radiator. Then as the room warms up, the valve closes to reduce the hot water flow through the radiator.

Rooms facing south and rooms with open fires or other heat producing appliances, such as an oven, benefit most from TRVs.

Most systems are suitable for use with thermostatic radiator valves. Seek expert advice on which ones to buy.

Leave one or two radiators without TRVs to act as a bypass, in order to maintain open circulation in the system. Alternatively, a bypass pipe can be installed just after the pump. The best type of bypass is a pressure-operated valve which opens progressively as the TRVs close the radiators down. It also helps to cut surging noises.

TRVs do not control the central heating pump and boiler, so they must be combined with a room thermostat or a boiler energy manager.

Programmers Time controls range from simple switches to complex electronic programmers.

The most useful can time space heating and domestic hot water separately, so water heating can be turned on and off at the same times of day all year round, while space heating times can vary with the season.

Electronic types can give you three control periods a day and different settings for every day of the week. Some even have a 'holiday' setting.

Water heating control
The hot water temperature is often controlled only by the boiler thermostat. So hot water to the taps is at the same temperature as the water supplied to the radiators. This is probably hotter than necessary.

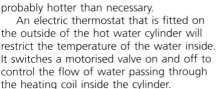

An electric thermostat that is fitted on the outside of the hot water cylinder will restrict the temperature of the water inside. It switches a motorised valve on and off to control the flow of water passing through the heating coil inside the cylinder.

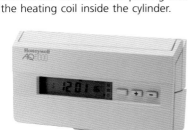

Boiler energy management Sophisticated devices make sure that the boiler works only when needed.

A boiler energy manager will reduce wasteful short cycling on a boiler – that is, when 'hot water only' is selected on a conventional central heating programmer, the boiler will continually switch on and off to keep the water in the boiler at the selected temperature. It will do this even though the hot water cylinder is already full of hot water. This 'short cycling' can add as much as 30 per cent to fuel bills.

The boiler energy manager will also take account of outside temperatures, and will regulate the central heating system accordingly. For example it will override the setting and delay the start time of the central heating on warmer days.

Updating your central heating programmer

An old-style programmer can be replaced quite easily with a more modern one.

Before you start If the old programmer has an industry-standard backplate, the programmer faceplate can be changed without complete rewiring. If the new programmer is incompatible with the old backplate, you will have to do some rewiring. Full instructions will be supplied with the new programmer.

Tools *Electric screwdriver.*

Materials *New programmer. Possibly also pencil; paper; masking tape.*

1 Turn off the power supply to the system's wiring centre and remove the fuse.

2 Undo the screw securing the faceplate of the programmer. You will usually find it on the underside.

3 Lift the bottom of the faceplate outwards. The programmer will then lift clear of the backplate that is attached to the wall.

4 Set the switch on the back of the new programmer to suit the type of system you have, as described in the instructions.

5 If the new faceplate does not fit the old backplate, study the wiring carefully and label each wire clearly. Sketch the old connections, then disconnect the cable cores from their terminals.

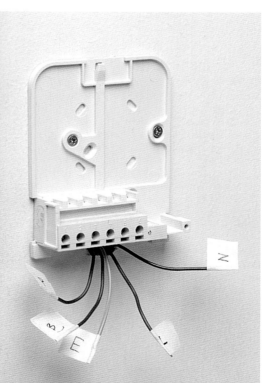

6 Remove the old backplate and attach the new one, using the manufacturer's instructions and your sketch of the old programmer to wire it up.

7 Push the new faceplate into position and restore the power supply to the wiring centre.

Central heating problems: what to do

If the hot water or heating stop working, there are some simple but useful checks that could save you a call-out fee, or help you to give an engineer helpful information about the nature of the problem.

No central heating or hot water

• Check that the programmer is set to 'on'. It may have been turned off in error.

• Check that the thermostats are turned up to the correct level.

• Check that the electricity supply is switched on and that the fuse has not blown. If the power is on and the fuse is working, but the programmer is not receiving power, there may be a loose wiring connection. Call an electrician to check the wiring and trace the fault.

• If a motorised valve is fitted, check that it is working properly. Slide the manual lever to open the valve. If there is resistance, the valve is not opening. This could indicate a burnt-out motor. Call a central heating engineer.

• If the pump is not working, you can try to start it manually. Turn off the central heating system and wait until the pump is cold. Remove the screw in the middle of the pump and turn the impeller (the pump's manual starter). On some models this is a small screw that is turned with a screwdriver, on others there is a small handle attached.

• If this does not work, try tapping the pump casing sharply, but gently, with a mallet two or three times.

• If this does not work, remove the pump (page 378), and flush clean water through it with a hosepipe. Do not submerge it in water.

• If this does not work, replace the pump (page 378).

• If the pump is running, but the boiler does not light, check that the pilot light is on and that the gas supply is turned on at the meter. If you have an oil boiler, check that the fuel is turned on and that there is oil in the tank. Check that the filter is clear.

• If the pilot light is not lit, follow the procedure in the handbook or on the boiler casing to relight it. If the flame will not stay lit, the flame failure device probably needs renewing. Call a central heating engineer.

• If a combination boiler will not light, check on the pressure gauge that the water pressure is at least 0.5 bar. If it is above this, call a central heating engineer. If it is below, top it up via the mains filling point.

• If the mains pressure to the house as a whole has dropped (check by running the taps), call your water supply company for advice.

The central heating is working but there is no hot water

• Make sure that the thermostat on the hot water cylinder is set to 60°C.

• Check that the motorised valve (if fitted) to the cylinder is open (see No central heating or hot water, left).

• Bleed the air-release valve beside the hot water cylinder (if there is one). The valve is usually located on the pipe which enters the heating coil.

Upstairs radiators are hot but downstairs radiators are cold

This is probably due to a jammed pump (see No central heating or hot water, left).

Downstairs radiators are hot but upstairs ones are cold

• Check that there is water in the feed-and-expansion cistern. If it is empty, the ballvalve has probably jammed (page 339).

• Bleed the air from the system (see Sound of rushing water in the pipes, opposite).

Noise in a central heating system

Unusual noises in a central heating system should not be ignored. The cause may be something quite easy to rectify.

Creaking in the floors and walls

Pipes expand as they heat up and contract as they cool. If the pipe is gripped tight by timber or a wall, or if it is in contact with another pipe, a creaking noise will occur when it gets hot or cold.

1 Pack some felt or pipe lagging around the pipes where they come up through the floorboards.

2 If that does not work, take up the floorboards around the source of the noise.

3 If one or two pipes are lying in a notch in a joist, and there is no room for movement, make the notch slightly wider by cutting down with a tenon saw and chiselling away the waste. Do not make the notch deeper; you may weaken the joist. Ease a piece of felt or pipe lagging under and between the pipes.

4 With the floorboards up, use a rasp to enlarge the holes through which the pipes rise to the radiator, if they are tight. Cover the pipes with pipe lagging where they pass through the boards.

5 Where pipes run the same way as the joists, make sure they do not sag or touch. Hold up sagging pipes with pipe clips fitted on struts between the joists. Put lagging between any pipes that touch.

6 If the pipes go through a wall, sleeve them with fire-resistant material, such as glass fibre matting, or pack it in around them, tamping it fairly hard with a screwdriver.

Boiler noise

• Noises from the boiler like a kettle boiling indicate a build-up of scale, caused by hard water inside the boiler's heat exchanger. Remove this by adding a chemical descaler to the system at the feed-and-expansion tank. Turn on the heating to pump the descaler around for a while, then flush the system with clean water. Empty it once more, then refill it and add a corrosion inhibitor.

• Noise may occur if the water flow through the boiler is insufficient. With modern light-weight gas boilers, water flow rate is particularly important.

• Boiler noise is often caused by air in the system, which may be the result of the open safety-vent pipe having being installed incorrectly. In this case, get expert advice on repositioning it.

Banging in the pipes

• Banging noises in the pipes may be due to overheating. To find the cause of the fault, start by checking that the boiler thermostat is working properly. Turn the boiler off but leave the pump running to help to cool the system down. Then turn the boiler on and turn up the thermostat. If you do not hear a click, turn everything off again and call a central heating engineer.

• You can cut down on the amount of noise transmitted along copper pipework by cutting out a section and inserting one or two plastic push-fit fittings into the run. If the noise persists, replacing troublesome sections of copper pipework with semi-flexible plastic pipe may be the answer.

Sound of rushing water in the pipes

Air that has entered the system, or gas that has formed as a result of internal corrosion, can cause a noise in central heating pipes like the sound of rushing water.

Try releasing the air from the air vents on the radiators, and any other venting points in the system. If the noise continues, it may be a symptom of serious faults that could eventually damage the whole system. Poor positioning of the open safety-vent pipe (page 370–1) could be the cause. Get expert help.

Humming in the pipes

An annoying humming sound usually comes from the pump. Call in an expert to find the cause.

• Anti-vibration pump brackets can be fitted that may help to reduce the problem.

• Pipes may vibrate if they are too small for the amount of water they have to carry.

• The pump speed may be set too high. Try turning down the speed control knob on the pump body by one setting. If this fails to cut the noise and also makes the radiators take longer to heat up, call in a central heating engineer. He may suggest relocating the pump.

Balancing a radiator circuit

Hot water is carried from the boiler to the radiators by a flow pipe, which branches off to supply each radiator. Cool water leaves each radiator at the opposite end and joins a return pipe carrying it back to the boiler.

Water flows most readily round the radiators nearest to the pump, so the water flow through the circuit is balanced out by adjusting the lockshield valve on each radiator. The valves are set so as to make it harder for the water to travel through the radiators nearest the boiler. If the circuit is not properly balanced, some radiators will get too hot, and others will be cool.

Tools *Two clip-on radiator thermometers; spanner; small screwdriver.*

Materials *Sticky labels; pencil.*

1 Two or three hours before you intend to start work on the radiators, turn off the central heating system to allow the water in the radiators to cool down.

A typical radiator circuit

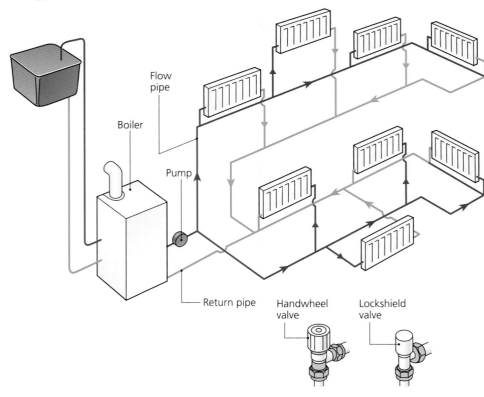

Flow pipe

Boiler

Pump

Return pipe

Handwheel valve

Lockshield valve

2 Open all lockshield valves and handwheel valves fully.

3 Turn on the central heating system. Work out the order in which the radiators heat up, and label them accordingly.

4 Clip a radiator thermometer onto the flow pipe bringing water into the first radiator, and one onto the return pipe.

5 Turn down the lockshield valve until it is closed, then open it slightly. Adjust the flow until the temperature of the flow pipe is roughly 11°C higher than that of the return pipe.

6 Repeat for all radiators in the circuit, working in the order as labelled. The lockshield valve on the last radiator will probably need to be fully open.

Leaks in a central heating system

Never ignore leaks in a central heating system. Fresh water that is drawn in to replace the lost water contains free oxygen which can cause radiators and cast iron boilers to rust.

Before you start Internal leak sealants similar to the radiator 'weld' used in cars can be used to seal very minor leaks. Pour the sealant in through the feed-and-expansion tank. Do not use leak sealant in a sealed system.

A leaking pipe joint

Most leaking pipe joints are compression fittings, which can be tightened with a spanner. Tighten the joint slightly, no more than a quarter turn. If this does not stop the leak, do not tighten any further as this will damage the joint.

1 Drain the system to below the level of the leak. Undo the nut on the leaking joint and pull the pipe out slightly.

2 Wrap two or three turns of PTFE tape around the face of the olive where it meets the joint. Tighten the nut.

3 If the leaking joint is soldered, drain the system. Heat the joint with a blowtorch and take it apart, then replace it (see page 344).

A leaking radiator valve

If the leak is from the compression joint below the valve, drain down the system to below the joint. Then call a plumber or repair the joint yourself. Use PTFE tape to cure a leak from the union nut connecting the valve to the radiator.

1 Turn off the valves at both ends of the radiator, counting the number of turns on the lockshield valve. Write the number down.

2 Put a towel and a bowl under the valve to catch water, and have a bucket and a second bowl ready.

3 Use an adjustable spanner to turn the union nut counter-clockwise (when looking from the radiator to the valve). Some water may run out.

4 Open the air vent to allow the rest of the water to flow out. Collect it in containers.

5 Wind PTFE tape tightly around the male thread on the valve tail. Start at the end and make a 50 per cent overlap on each turn.

6 Screw the nut back on, and open the valves and air vent. Open the lockshield valve by the number of turns that were necessary to close it. Check for leaks and close the air vent when water flows from it.

A leaking valve tail

The leak may be from the valve tail screwed into the radiator. Use a radiator spanner to remove it. Cover the male thread on the valve tail with PTFE tape and replace the tail.

A leaking radiator vent

If the radiator air vent leaks, drain the system to below the vent. Remove the air-vent fitting using a radiator spanner. Bind the screw joint with PTFE tape, and replace the fitting.

A leaking radiator

A small jet of water from the body of the radiator is called a pinhole leak. It is caused by internal corrosion and can happen within a few weeks of the system being fitted if the debris that collects during installation has not been removed, or if air is being drawn in.

Turn off the valves at each end to relieve the pressure. Then remove the radiator and leave the rest of the system running. Before fitting a new radiator, flush out and clean the system using a non-acidic cleaner.

Repacking a radiator gland

If a radiator valve weeps water from under the cap, the packing gland is worn. You can replace the packing with PTFE tape or thread-sealing fibre, sold by plumbers' merchants. 'Belmont' radiator valves cannot be repacked; instead they have renewable O-rings which can be replaced with a kit.

Tools *Small adjustable spanner; small screwdriver; PTFE tape; silicone grease.*

1 Turn off the valve. If it continues to leak, close the lockshield valve at the other end of the radiator.

2 Remove the cap from the leaking valve and undo the small gland nut. Slide it up out of the way.

3 Pull a length of PTFE tape into a string and wrap this around the spindle four or five times.

4 Use a small screwdriver to push the tape down into the valve body. Smear on silicone grease and re-tighten the gland nut. Replace the head and turn the valve back on.

Replacing a radiator valve

Although radiator valves normally last for years, the time will come when it is necessary to replace one.

Before you start Drain the heating system (page 329). As the system drains, open the vents on the upstairs radiators and then those downstairs.

Tools *Two adjustable spanners. Perhaps hexagonal radiator spanner; new adaptor.*

Materials *New radiator valve; wire wool; PTFE tape.*

1 Undo the nut that connects the valve to the radiator by turning it counter-clockwise. To stop the valve rotating, hold the body of the valve upright with a second spanner.

2 Undo the capnut that connects the pipework to the body of the valve, by turning it clockwise (as seen from above). Lift the valve away and let the capnut slip down the pipe.

3 If the new valve is not compatible with the old adaptor, undo it with a hexagonal radiator spanner. Clean the threads inside the end of the radiator with wire wool.

4 Screw the new adaptor into the radiator. It may need a few turns of PTFE tape around the threaded end of the adaptor first to make a watertight seal. Check that the capnut on the pipe can be threaded onto it.

5 Thread the capnut on the adaptor onto the end of the new valve and do it up, finger-tight. Then tighten with a spanner. Brace the valve body with the second spanner as you do this.

6 Slide the capnut up and connect it to the valve.

7 Refill the system and bleed each radiator to get rid of trapped air.

8 Close the radiator vents one by one as the water level rises. Check for leaks and tighten capnuts a little more if necessary.

Removing and replacing a radiator

It may be necessary to remove a radiator in order to flush out sludge that has built up inside, replace it or decorate behind it. This can be done without draining the whole system.

Tools *Polythene sheets; old towels; rags; two bowls; pliers; two large adjustable spanners; absorbent paper; hammer; hexagonal radiator spanner.*

Materials *PTFE tape. For replacement: new radiator the same size as the old one; new radiator air vent; radiator plug.*

1 Lay a polythene sheet and old towels on the floor around the radiator. This could be messy.

2 Shut the control valve by hand. Then remove the cover from the lockshield valve and use pliers or a small spanner to shut it too. Count the number of turns that this takes and write it down.

3 Put a bowl under the control valve and disconnect the union nut. Take care not to distort the pipe. Water will flow out (there may be a lot, so have bowls ready).

4 Open the air vent to increase the flow of water.

5 When it has stopped, undo the union nut on the lockshield valve. Some more water may come out.

6 Block the open ends of the radiator with twists of absorbent paper.

7 Lift the radiator off its brackets and carry it outside. You may need help.

Replacing the radiator

1 If you are replacing a radiator, but keeping the valves, remove the valve tail pieces from the old radiator. Turn the valve tail counter-clockwise (when looking at the end of the radiator).

2 Hold the new radiator in position to check if the wall brackets need repositioning.

3 Wind PTFE tape round the thread of the valve tail pieces. Screw the tail pieces in place.

4 Fit a new air vent at the same end of the radiator as before, using PTFE tape as for the valve tail. Use the radiator spanner to tighten it in. Fit a new plug if there is an open tapping in the other top end.

5 Lift the radiator onto the wall brackets and reconnect the valve union nuts.

6 Open the valves to fill the radiator with water. Let air out through the air vent, and check for leaks. Reset the lockshield valve to its original position.

WARNING

If there is a thermostatic radiator valve on a radiator, turn it down to zero before disconnecting the tail pieces and removing the radiator. Otherwise there is a risk that the valve will open, flooding the room, if the temperature drops.

Alternatively, fit the special screw-down cap, supplied with the valves, in place of the sensor to shut off the valve while the radiator is out of use.

Relocating a radiator

Changing the position of a radiator can free up valuable wall space when you change the layout of a room.

Tools *Tape measure; pencil; power drill; masonry drill bit; screwdriver; spirit level; hacksaw or pipe cutter; spanners.*

Materials *Radiator; wall mounting brackets; two radiator valves; 50mm No. 12 screws; wall plugs; 15mm copper pipe; compression plumbing fittings; PTFE tape.*

1 Lay the radiator face down and fit the wall brackets into the straps at the back, making sure they are both the same distance from the outer edge of the radiator, and from the base.

2 Measure the height of the brackets, and add 50mm to allow clearance of the skirting board. Measure the distance between them. Then transfer these measurements to the wall.

3 Hold the first bracket at the correct height on the wall. Mark the positions of the fixing holes and check that they are vertical. Drill and plug the holes, then screw the bracket to the wall with two 50mm No. 12 screws.

4 Position the second bracket at the correct distance from the first and the right height above the skirting board. Fix it with one screw through the long slot, and then check its position with your spirit level before driving in the second screw.

5 Offer up the radiator, slipping the straps on the back over the hooks on the brackets. If the radiator is level, lift it off again and fit the valves. Then replace it and connect it to the re-routed pipework.

Boxing in pipes

Exposed pipework can be concealed in boxes – but remember to insulate hot water and heating pipes before covering them.

Tools *Bradawl; screwdriver; pencil; drill bit with twist, masonry and countersink bits; panel pins; hammer; nail punch; spirit level; plane; cartridge gun.*

Materials *Timber battens; one-piece joint blocks (often used to assemble flat-pack furniture); screws and wall plugs; hardboard or 3mm thick MDF; foam pipe insulation; decorator's mastic.*

1 To box in a group of pipes in a corner, fix a batten a little wider than the depth of the pipes to the wall, using one-piece plastic joint blocks at 1m intervals.

Fix a second batten on the other side of the pipes if they are not in a corner.

2 Cut a strip of hardboard or MDF wide enough to cover the batten and the pipes and pin it to the batten with panel pins or screw it home.

3 Where pipes run along a skirting board, fit a horizontal batten above the pipes, then fit a slimmer one at floor level, and finish off with a cover strip, ready for painting or papering.

Radiators that do not heat up correctly

If your radiators are not giving out enough heat, check them all and make note of which are cool and which (if any) are hot. Some may be cooler at the top or bottom.

Radiator cool at the top

Air is trapped at the top of the radiator. Turn off the central heating. Then use a radiator bleed key to open the air vent at one end of the radiator. Air should start to hiss out. When water appears, close the vent. Hold a rag under the vent to catch the water escaping from it. Turn the heating on again.

If radiators need bleeding more than once a year, air is entering the system and this can cause corrosion. There may be a serious fault that needs expert attention. Some systems have one or more extra bleed points on the pipes either upstairs or in the loft. Manual bleed points are opened with a screwdriver.

On an automatic air valve the small, red plastic cap must be loose in order for air to escape. If it is tight, unscrew it.

Radiator cool at the bottom and hot at the top

Sludge (black iron oxide) produced by internal corrosion can build up at the bottom of a radiator and stop the circulation. Remove the radiator, take it outside and flush it through with a hose. Alternatively, add sludge removal liquid to the feed-and-expansion cistern. Two days later, drain and refill the system (page 329).

Top-floor radiators cold

Cold radiators upstairs only, often indicate that the feed-and-expansion cistern is empty. The ballvalve may be faulty (page 339).

Refill the feed-and-expansion cistern so that there is just enough water to float the ball when the water in the system is cold. The extra space accommodates expansion of the water in the system as it heats up.

Top-floor radiators hot, lower radiators cold

This is almost certainly due to pump failure (see Changing a central heating pump, page 378).

Cold radiators throughout the house

Deposits of sludge caused by internal corrosion can result in poor water circulation and radiators being cooler than they should be. The system needs to be chemically cleaned out (page 379).

Radiators farthest from the boiler are cool

The system is not properly balanced (page 374).

Top radiators heat up when hot water only is selected on programmer

Hot water naturally rises above cooler water. On a gravity driven system, hot water for the hot water cylinder is prevented from creeping into upstairs radiators when the heating is switched off by a mechanical valve, called the gravity-check valve. It is situated on the flow pipe to the upstairs radiators.

If the gravity-check valve is stuck in the open position, the pipe on either side of the valve will be warm. Call a central heating engineer to replace it.

Changing a central heating pump

You can change a central heating pump without first draining down the whole central heating system, provided that there are service valves fitted on each side of the pump.

Before you start Domestic pumps are now a standard size, but if the old pump was longer than the new one, you may need adapters to fill the gaps.

When you go to buy a replacement from a plumbers' merchant take all the details of the old pump with you. Measure the length of the old pump, and the diameter and type of the connections. Most domestic pumps have 1½in BSP threaded connections.

Also make a note of the type of pump and the setting of its output regulator (domestic pumps are available with different ratings).

Tools *Electrician's screwdriver; bowl; towels; pipe wrench or adjustable spanner; pencil and paper.*

Materials *New pump.*

1 Switch off the electricity supply to the central heating system controls at the consumer unit.

2 Make a note and sketch of how the electrical wiring on the old pump is connected. It may be helpful to label each wire. Then disconnect the wires with a screwdriver.

3 Close down the service valves on each side of the pump using the valve handle or an adjustable spanner. If there are no isolating valves, drain down the system.

HELPFUL TIPS

The central heating pump is designed to run full of clean water. Any air or sludge that gets into the water can damage the pump, so keeping the system full of water and limiting corrosion are essential. Never run the pump unless it is full of water.

If your pump is out of use in summer, as is usually the case with a combined gravity and pump-driven system, run it for a minute once a month to keep its impeller free.

4 Put a bowl and towels under the pump ready to catch any water that escapes when you remove it.

5 Unscrew the union nuts holding the pump in place. Turn them counter-clockwise (facing along the pipe towards the pump). Remove the old pump.

6 Fit the new pump in position with the new sealing washers in the unions to prevent leaks.

7 Open the isolating valves (or refill the system) and check that the unions are watertight.

8 Dry the pump carefully to remove any traces of moisture; reconnect the wiring.

9 Test the newly installed pump by switching on the electricity supply and turning on the central heating system at the programmer or time switch. You may also need to turn up the room thermostat to get the system going.

10 Once the central heating system has started up, check that the open safety-vent pipe over the feed-and-expansion cistern does not discharge water when the pump starts or stops. If it does discharge water, seek expert advice.

11 If you have had to add much fresh water to the cistern, bleed any air out of the system in order to guard against future corrosion and to protect the new pump.

Repairing a motorised valve

If a motorised valve ceases to open, its electric motor may have failed.

Before you start Use a mains tester to check whether the valve is receiving power. If it is, you will need a new motor. You should be able to buy one from a plumbers' merchant. There is no need to drain the system, but you must switch off the electricity supply to the central heating system. Just turning off the programmer is not enough, because a motorised valve has a permanent live feed.

1 Take off the valve cover and undo the retaining screw that holds the motor in place. Push the lever to open the valve, and lift out the motor. Cut off the connectors to disconnect the two motor wires.

2 Insert the new motor, then let the manual lever spring back to a closed position. Fit the retaining screw and tighten. Strip the ends and connect the wires, using the two connectors supplied with the new motor. Put back the cover.

3 Check the new motor by turning on the power and running the system.

Preventing a freeze-up

If you turn off your central heating while you go on a winter holiday, there is a danger that the system will freeze and a pipe will burst.

Lagging only reduces the speed of heat loss, so eventually the temperature of an unused system will drop to the level of the surrounding air. With a gas-fired or oil-fired system, leave the heating on and turn the room thermostat down to its minimum setting if you will only be away a few days.

Using a frost thermostat

For a long holiday, you could have a frost thermostat installed (it is also called a low-limit thermostat). It overrides the controls and turns on the system when the temperature approaches freezing point. Rising air temperature makes it turn the system off again.

Adding antifreeze

You can also add antifreeze to the water in the central heating system. Tie up the ballvalve arm in the feed-and-expansion cistern and pour in antifreeze according to the maker's instructions. Then drain off enough water via a drain valve for the antifreeze to be drawn into the system. After restoring the water level in the cistern to the correct level, turn the central heating on for a few minutes in order to thoroughly mix the antifreeze with the water.

Protecting a system against corrosion

The life and efficiency of a central heating system can be increased by adding a corrosion and scale inhibitor.

Before you start Test the water in the system every year or so for signs of internal corrosion. To do this, drain a sample of the heating system water into a jar and place two bright (not galvanised) wire nails in the jar. Screw the lid on. Wait for a week.

If the nails rust and the water turns a rusty orange, this indicates serious corrosion and you must eliminate the problem as soon as possible. If the water remains fairly clear and the nails do not rust, then no further action is necessary, since the water in the system has lost its free oxygen. A few black deposits are acceptable.

Finding out where air is entering the system

The most common cause of corrosion is air in the system. If the radiators need bleeding more than once or twice a year then too much air is being drawn into the system and this must be eliminated.

The most common areas where air gets into the system are a leaking joint on the suction side of the pump, or through the feed-and-expansion cistern.

Leaks around pumps can be repaired in the same way as other leaking joints. But if air is entering through the feed-and-expansion cistern you will need expert help.

You can find out if the feed-and-expansion cistern is the source of the problem by running the programmer through its functions and checking for any swirling movement of water in the cistern.

To find out whether the vent pipe is sucking in air, submerge the end of the pipe in a cup of water. If the pipe draws up water from the cup, then air is entering the system through the pipe and causing corrosion. You will need to call a central heating engineer to rectify the problem.

Adding a corrosion inhibitor

Corrosion inhibitors are available in liquid form. In an open-vented system the liquid is added to the system through the feed-and-expansion cistern in the loft.

In a sealed system, you can inject the corrosion inhibitor into a radiator through the air vent.

Replacing a hot water cylinder

Hot water cylinders are mostly trouble-free, but do sometimes develop leaks or become so clogged with limescale in hard water areas that they have to be replaced.

Most domestic hot water cylinders hold around 140 litres of water, so a leak should be dealt with swiftly, before it destroys the ceiling below.

Tools *Pipe grips; open-ended spanners; screwdrivers; hose; pipe clips; immersion heater spanner.*

Materials *New pre-lagged copper cylinder; PTFE tape; immersion heater fibre washer.*

Before you start Older cylinders were often lagged with a jacket, which you will need to remove. New cylinders usually come prelagged. You may have to alter the plumbing if the existing connections do not line up with those on the new cylinder.

1 Turn off the power to the immersion heater, remove the round top cover and disconnect the flex from the terminals.

2 Shut down the boiler and shut off the cold water feed to the cylinder. This pipe enters the cylinder at the bottom. If there is no gatevalve, tie the ballvalve up in the cold water tank to stop the cylinder from refilling.

3 Open the hot and cold bath taps to drain the supply pipes, but note that this does not drain the water from the cylinder.

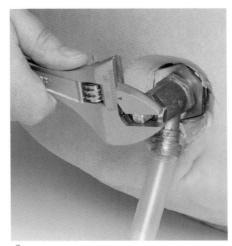

4 Attach a length of hose to the drain valve on the bottom of the cylinder. Put the other end into a drain, open the small square nut on the drain valve two turns and let the water drain from the cylinder.

5 Remove the immersion heater from the top of the cylinder by unscrewing it with a special immersion heater spanner then withdrawing it (pages 366–7).

6 Disconnect the pipes from the cylinder. Use two spanners: one to hold the securing nut on the cylinder and the other to undo the outer union nut. If you have a Conex style nut use a pipe wrench instead. You will need to disconnect the cold water inlet, the hot water outlet at the top of the cylinder and the connections to and from the heater coil if the water in the cylinder is indirectly heated (see artwork below).

7 Lift out the old cylinder, being careful not to damage the ends of the disconnected pipework.

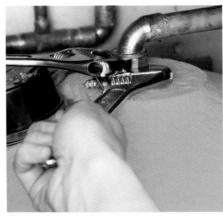

8 Wrap three layers of PTFE tape around the connection spigots on the new cylinder. Lift it back into place and reconnect the pipes, using two spanners to tighten the joint as you did when undoing the old connection.

9 Refit the immersion heater (pages 366–7). If it was fitted with a fibre washer then replace the washer or wrap PTFE tape around the threads before you refit it. Tighten with the immersion heater spanner but do not over tighten, cylinders are thin and can crease easily.

10 Reconnect the flex to the immersion heater terminals and install the cover.

11 Close the drain valve, then turn on the water supply to the cylinder. Check for leaks as the cylinder fills. If all is well, relight the boiler.

Connections to the hot water cylinder

Hot water outlet to hot taps

Immersion heater temperature control

Heat-resistant flex to 20A switch for immersion heater

Immersion heater element

Hot water inlet from boiler

Cold water returning to boiler

Drain valve

Cold water inlet from cistern

Having central heating installed: a checklist

If you are planning to have central heating installed in your house, first read as much about heating as you can so that you can discuss it with the heating contractors.

Boilers, heat emitters and controls

Read pages 382–3 first, and then gather further information on boilers and heat emitters. You can get additional information from the advisory bodies and trade associations listed here. It is also worth paying a visit to your local plumbers' merchant and picking up brochures on the latest boilers and heat emitters.

Getting quotations

Find three CORGI registered contractors in your area and ask them to quote. Give them all the same outline brief, including where you would like radiators positioned, and what temperatures you wish to achieve in the rooms. A living room temperature of 21°C when the temperature outside is −1°C is normal. If you need a margin built in for extra cold weather you should say so. Make a list of any other requirements you feel are important.

1 Be wary of paying a deposit. The first payment should be when materials are delivered. Retain a small amount of the balance (2 per cent) for faults that need fixing after completion.

2 Ask the contractor to give start and completion dates.

3 Before the job starts, decide where pipes are to run and in what order they will be laid so that you can clear the room. If you want pipes to be concealed, state this before the work starts. It will cost more than surface-mounting, but is well worth the expense.

4 If several rooms will be affected, ask the contractor to finish in one room before starting in the next one.

5 Your home should be left clean and tidy at the end of each day and should be respected – for example, there should be no loud music or smoking.

6 Work should comply with statutory requirements such as water supply regulations, the Building Regulations and all relevant codes of practice. Materials must meet the requirements of CEN (European) or British Standards where applicable.

7 'Making good' means filling in holes and replacing panels. Floorboards should be screwed back down to prevent creaking. Damaged boards should be replaced. Normally, however, making good does not include decoration.

8 Establish what other contractors will be required to help to complete the work – electricians, for example.

Where to install radiators

Naturally you want to get the maximum heat from the minimum number of radiators, so siting them correctly is essential. Consider the following points when deciding where to position radiators.

1 Radiators should be fitted in the coldest part of the room, preferably under the windows. The heat rising from the radiator will counteract the cold air falling from the glass. This produces a flow of air across the room.

2 Radiators placed on inside walls opposite a window can accentuate the flow of cold air down a window and can produce a cool draught across the floor.

3 Make sure that there is at least 100mm of space between the bottom of a radiator and the floor to allow a good circulation of air and so that the floor can be cleaned.

4 At least 40mm should be left between the wall – or the skirting board – and the back of the radiator to allow air to circulate.

5 A shelf should not be placed any closer than 50mm to the top of a radiator for the same reason.

6 A radiator installed inside a decorative casing can lose a quarter or more of its output unless the casing permits a full flow of air over all of the radiator's surfaces.

When the work is finished

The contractor must flush out the new central heating system in order to remove debris which could corrode and clog it in the future. He should then run the system to full heat and check that all the radiators heat up.

The contractor must leave you all instructions and technical leaflets, and fill out guarantee cards.

Trade associations and industry bodies

Association of Plumbing and Heating Contractors
14 Ensign House, Ensign Business Centre, Westwood Way, Coventry CV4 8JA
tel: 0800 5426060
www.licensedplumber.co.uk

The Building Centre
26 Store St, London WC1E 7BT
tel: 020 7692 4000
www.buildingcentre.co.uk

The Central Heating Information Council
36, Holly Walk, Leamington Spa, Warwickshire CV32 4LY
tel: 0845 600 22 00
www.chic-info.org.uk

CORGI
1 Elmwood, Chineham Business Park, Crockford Lane, Basingstoke, Hants RG24 8WG
tel: 01256 372200
www.corgi-gas.com

Heating and Ventilating Contractors Association
ESCA House, 34 Palace Court, London W2 4JG
tel: 020 7313 4900
www.hvca.org.uk

Institute of Plumbing
64 Station Lane, Hornchurch, Essex RM12 6NB
tel: 01708 472791
www.registeredplumber.com

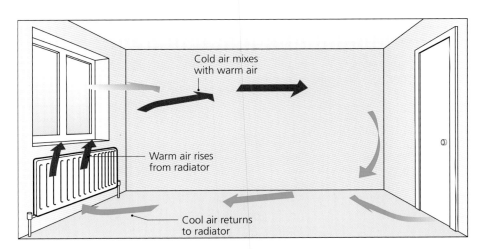

Cold air mixes with warm air

Warm air rises from radiator

Cool air returns to radiator

Choosing a boiler

Choosing an appropriate boiler for your household needs is crucial. Consider whether you need it to supply heating and hot water, the size of your household and how many bathrooms you need to service.

When choosing a boiler

• Its proposed position affects whether you need a wall-hung or floor-standing model. The boiler's distance from an outside wall or the roof will affect the type of flue you have.
• Boilers are available for all types of fuel (oil, gas, LPG, solid fuel and even electricity). Gas is the most common, followed by oil and LPG for homes with no gas supply. Oil and gas have similar running costs and are cheaper than LPG. Oil and LPG require storage tanks.
• Consider the space available – not just for the boiler, but also for a hot water cylinder and cold water tanks, and what the demands on the system are likely to be.
• Look for energy rating labels to compare running costs. Remember that some boilers need more maintenance than others.
• All boilers most be serviced regularly and faults dealt with by an expert. A new or replacement boiler must now meet Building Regulation requirements. This demands a minimum efficiency (of 78 per cent for gas boilers, 80 per cent for LPG and 85 per cent for oil) and should be installed by a CORGI or OFTEC engineer. Programmers and thermostats must be installed, too.

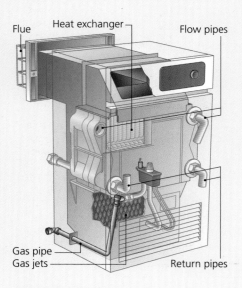

Flue · Heat exchanger · Flow pipes · Gas pipe · Gas jets · Return pipes

Conventional boiler The gas or oil-burner heats water in a heat exchanger, rather like a gas-ring under an old-fashioned kettle. Traditionally, heat exchangers have been made from cast-iron, but lighter aluminium and stainless steel are more commonly used now. Most modern, conventional boilers are wall-hung with balanced flues, but floor-standing models with conventional flues are still available. Most conventional boilers are designed for used on fully-pumped open-vented systems; a few will work with existing gravity hot-water systems.

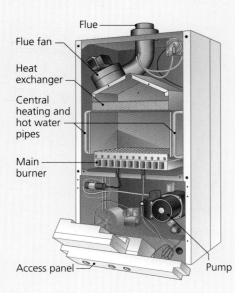

Flue · Flue fan · Heat exchanger · Central heating and hot water pipes · Main burner · Access panel · Pump

Combination boiler Also known as a 'combi' boiler, this is a central-heating boiler and multi-point water heater all in one. Hot water for the radiators is heated in its own circuit (usually sealed) in the normal way, but the boiler also heats cold water from the mains, delivering it on demand to the hot water taps around the house. The main advantages are the savings in space – no hot water cylinder or tanks – a constant supply of hot water and better water-pressure in showers. By altering the cold-water plumbing, there can also be drinking water at all cold taps. The disadvantages are the cost of the boiler and low flow-rates if more than one hot tap is being used. Some combi boilers store a little hot water so that it is immediately ready for use. Most can be used with gas or LPG, though oil-fired options are also available.

Back boiler A back boiler is a heat exchanger located behind a gas fire. Although many still exist in older houses, they are no longer an option for a new fitting for most people.

A back boiler works in much the same way as a conventional boiler, sending hot water to radiators on a central heating circuit and to a hot water cylinder, but it needs a conventional open flue, suitably lined for the fuel being used. A back boiler can be used with a fully-pumped system, or with gravity hot water circulation. The firefront may be inset into a fireplace or may protrude into the room.

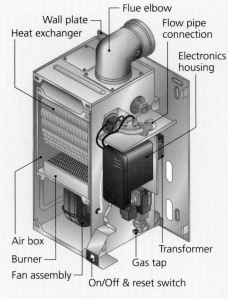

Wall plate · Heat exchanger · Flue elbow · Flow pipe connection · Electronics housing · Air box · Burner · Fan assembly · Transformer · Gas tap · On/Off & reset switch

Condensing boiler With a larger heat-exchanger than a conventional boiler, a condensing boiler is designed so that the water returning from the heating system is used to cool the flue gases, extracting extra heat that is normally lost through the flue. Often known as 'high efficiency' boilers, they are meant to be used with a fan-assisted balance flue and in a fully-pumped system. When the flue gases are cooled, water vapour will condense and so a pipe has to be installed to drain this water away.

Condensing boilers work best with lower system water temperatures, but even with normal radiator temperatures, the efficiency will be significantly greater than with a conventional system; this means the extra cost of the boiler is soon recovered in the saving in fuel costs, after which you continue to save money and reduce carbon dioxide emissions. Condensing boilers are available for use with either gas, LPG or oil. Combination condensing boilers are available, too.

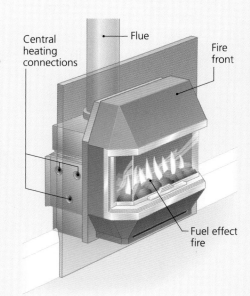

Central heating connections · Flue · Fire front · Fuel effect fire

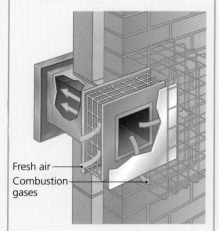

Fresh air
Combustion gases

Balanced flue In order to work properly, this two-part duct allows the combustion gases to escape and fresh air to enter. The flue is sealed so that no combustion gases can enter the room where it is installed – its other name is a 'room-sealed flue'. With a natural-draught balanced flue (as above) the boiler must be installed on an outside wall, so that the flue passes directly through the wall. With a fan-assisted balanced flue, the boiler (which contains an electric fan) can be mounted on any wall, and is connected by a duct to a flue that can be on an outside wall or pass through the roof. Fan-assisted balanced flues are more efficient, but noisier, than natural-draught flues.

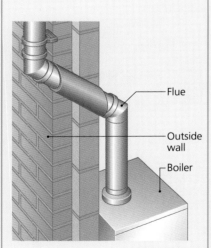

Flue

Outside wall

Boiler

Open flue This can be either a lined existing chimney or a new circular duct installed in an outside wall. The flue will take only the combustion gases, so the fresh air supply for the burner must come from the room. Consequently, special ventilators or grilles will need to be installed on outside walls.

Choosing radiators and other heat emitters

Though most people's first choice is a radiator, there are many other heat emitters that can be connected to central-heating pipes.

These include fan convectors, trench-duct heaters, skirting heaters and under-floor heaters. When mixing different types of heat emitter on the same system, fit thermostatic valves to each in order to allow full, individual control.

Radiators Despite the name, only a tiny proportion of heat given off by a radiator is emitted from the front through radiation. If you put your hand just a few inches from the front the heat is negligible. Most of the heat is given out from the top by convection.

To work properly a radiator must have a good flow of air passing from the bottom on the front and back surfaces. There must be at least 100mm clearance from the floor for air to enter and 40mm at the top.

Old style plain panel radiators have now been almost completely superseded by convector radiators, which have metal boxed fins welded to the hidden faces of the panels. They act as chimneys for hot air, almost doubling the heat output and making it possible to fit smaller radiators. There are many different styles of tubular radiator available, from modern interpretations of a traditional Victorian style (above left) to quirky wall-mounted spirals (above right).

Trench-duct heaters If windows go down to the floor, trench heaters can be installed. A pipe fitted with fins runs along one side of a trench in the floor. A dividing plate

along the centre of the trench separates the hot air rising from the pipe from the cooler air returning to be reheated.

Underfloor heaters Burying pipes under concrete floors has gained in popularity. Plastic pipe is laid in a continuous loop and carries hot water under the floor. The pipes must be fitted on top of under-floor insulation and are normally covered with a sand-and-cement screed which helps to spread the heat evenly. This is an ideal system for use with a condensing boiler, because it works well at low temperatures.

Skirting heaters

Small metal convectors run round the room just above or in place of a skirting board. This system is good for background heating and it gives an even spread of heat, which can help to prevent condensation on walls. However, it is not usually powerful enough to heat a room in very cold weather.

Fan convectors Use a fan convector where there is not enough wall space for a radiator. Special kick-space models are made to go under kitchen base units (below). Low voltage versions are available for bathrooms. Air curtain models can be installed above doors and wall units, and some models sink into the floor.

An electrical fan blows air across copper fins, which are heated by hot water from the central-heating circuit. A filter in the air intake traps dirt. This should be regularly cleaned to maintain maximum performance and to prevent noise.

11

Outdoor maintenance

What can go wrong on the roof

You may discover that the roof needs to be repaired only when stains appear on the ceiling from rain seeping into the loft.

Making regular checks in the loft for damp timber and checking the roof from the outside for signs of damage could help you to discover the problem earlier. Repair damage as soon as possible after its discovery.

To examine the roof thoroughly, set up a ladder which is at least three rungs above the gutter. If you move onto the roof, use a proper roof ladder which hooks over the ridge (see opposite).

Flat roofs

The main problem with a flat roof is that instead of draining off, water may collect on the surface and seep through even very small cracks. This can lead to rot in timbers as well as damp patches appearing on ceilings.

Felt is generally built up in layers on larger roofs, and often the top layer will blister. To repair the damage, see page 396. Bitumen felt roofs on sheds are usually only a single sheet of felt. If this starts to break up, strip it off and replace it (page 396).

Corrugated plastic sheeting may leak at overlaps or where screws or nails pass through the sheets. Seal gaps with silicone sealant or replace the sheet (see page 398).

Glass roofing may leak if the seal fails along glazing bars and rain may be driven up overlaps by strong winds. Use adhesive tape – preferably the foil type, rather than the black – to seal a glazing bar. If a poor overlap cannot be increased, seal the outer gap with silicone sealant.

WHEN SHOULD A WHOLE ROOF BE REPLACED?

It is hard to judge whether a roof should be completely re-surfaced. If a large number of the tiles or slates are broken, this is obviously needed. Faults in the structure are harder to diagnose. Bumps and hollows may have been caused by movement in the roof timbers years earlier, but it may have stabilised and be perfectly sound and weatherproof. If movement is recent, however, it may need professional attention.

If you have doubts about the soundness of your roof, pay an architect or surveyor to give an unbiased report on it; a builder's report may not be so impartial.

Ridge tiles The mortar holding these tiles in place may fail with age or if it is soaked with rain that freezes; high winds may then dislodge tiles. To replace a ridge tile, see page 391.

Roof tiles Tiles are usually nailed in place or held by the nibs that project behind each tile and hook over roofing battens. If the nibs are damaged or if the nails rust away, tiles will slide down the roof. Tiles may also be blown off by strong winds or pushed out of place by the weight of a build-up of snow that turns to ice. To replace a roof tile, see page 389.

Slates There are no nibs on slates, so they need nails to hold them. They may slip out of position if the nails rust. To replace a slate, see page 390.

Flashings When a roof surface meets a wall or chimney stack, the gap between them is sealed with flashing. Lead flashing is the most durable type; felt and mortar flashings do not last quite as long.

Flashings can become displaced when mortar joints fail (the flashing strip is pushed into the joint between bricks or pieces of masonry and sealed with

mortar). Cracked mortar flashing is usually caused by slight movement in the building or between neighbouring buildings. This movement is common and depends on the water content in the soil.

For how to repair flashings, see page 394. Check all the flashings – around chimney stacks, dormer windows and adjoining flat roofs – when making a repair.

Chimney stacks Because of its position and the potential danger, few DIY jobs can be done on a chimney stack –

special scaffolding must be erected around the stack so work can be done in safety. However, you can keep an eye on the condition of the chimney stack and have any repairs carried out quickly to prevent damp.

If a flue is not in use, rain which gets onto the flue lining can cause damp problems. Have the chimney capped with a half-round tile or a cowl to keep rain out. You can only see the edge of the flaunching (the mortar which holds the pots in place) but have it checked if any deterioration is visible. If you notice faults in the brickwork, get expert advice.

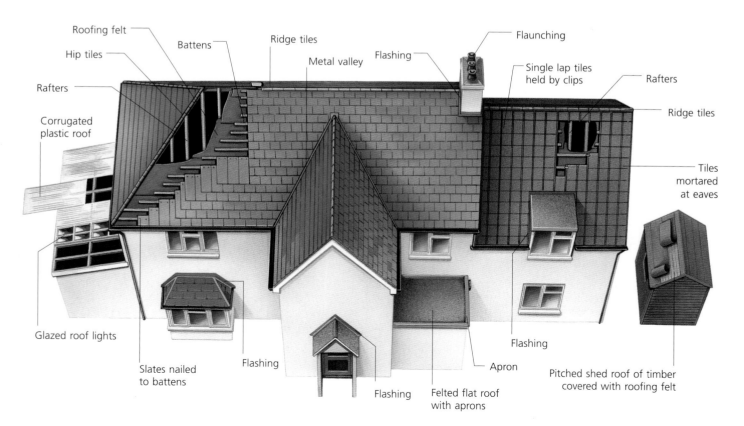

Roofing felt

Hip tiles

Rafters

Corrugated plastic roof

Battens

Ridge tiles

Metal valley

Flashing

Flaunching

Single lap tiles held by clips

Rafters

Ridge tiles

Tiles mortared at eaves

Glazed roof lights

Slates nailed to battens

Flashing

Flashing

Felted flat roof with aprons

Apron

Flashing

Pitched shed roof of timber covered with roofing felt

Roof repairs: tools for the job

It is possible to make minor repairs to your roof, but you should always have a helper and be safety-conscious when working at height.

HOW TO WORK SAFELY AT ROOF LEVEL

• Always have a helper to hand when you are working at a height. Ask them to steady the weight at the bottom of the ladder when you are carrying up heavy items.
• Have a safe place to put your tools. Fix a tray to a ladder or hold tools in a bag or pouch slung across your chest, or a tool belt.
• Wear a purpose-made safety harness with a tape attached to a firm point – such as a properly secured roof ladder.
• Lower debris to the ground in a stout sack or bucket attached to a rope. Take care not to drop anything; it could cause serious injury to someone below.

Roof ladder Never venture onto a roof without a purpose-made roof ladder fitted at one end with rubber wheels and a large hook. Using the wheels, you can push the ladder up the roof without dislodging slates or tiles. When the top of the ladder reaches the roof ridge, turn it over so that the hook lodges on the ridge securely. The ladder must reach all the way from the roof ridge to the gutter to allow you to transfer easily from the ordinary ladder on which you have climbed to gutter level. Extension pieces can be added to a roof ladder if necessary. Hire a roof ladder rather than buy one; or buy the wheels-and-hook section for fitting onto a conventional ladder.

Plugging chisel The plugging chisel, also called a seam chisel, is designed to remove mortar from between bricks or pieces of masonry. It can be used when replacing flashing. The fluted face of the blade allows debris to be cleared quickly.

Slate cutter When the handles are squeezed together, the steel blades meet and shear off the edge of the slate. Useful for cutting an oversized slate to the right size.

Slate ripper The steel blade is about 280–380mm long. It is slipped under the tile or slate to be removed until one of the barbs of its arrow-shaped tip can be hooked round a nail that is driven into the roof batten. A sharp tug, or a hammer blow on the curve of the handle, jerks the barb down, and it cuts through the nail. The ripper is then moved to the other edge of the tile or slate to cut the second nail. Slate rippers can be hired.

Tinsnips The scissor-action will cut through lead, zinc or other sheet metals used for roof valleys. Snips are made in several sizes – from 200–360mm long.

Soft-faced mallet A mallet with a head made of rubber, plastic or rawhide is used to tap sheet metal into shape – when renewing a valley, for example.

Scaffold towers If you have to work all along the gutter, hire a scaffold tower with locking wheels, guard rail and a firm platform.

Ladders Always make sure that the ladder is set up at the correct angle: 1m away from the wall for every 4m up the wall.

The ladder or scaffold tower should be long enough or high enough to reach at least 600mm beyond the working point to avoid the need to stretch.

Fit a stand-off bracket to the top of a ladder to make sure it presses against the wall, not against an insecure gutter.

For extra security, you can screw an eye bolt into the fascia board and tie the ladder to it. Always move the ladder or scaffold tower along the wall to take you within easy reach of the working point. Never lean sideways to reach the work.

Choosing roof tiles

There are four important considerations when choosing roof tiles: the type of tile used on neighbouring or adjoining houses; the cost in relation to the appearance; the weight of new tiles on existing timbers; and the slope of the roof.

Tiles or slates? Roof tiles are made of concrete, or occasionally clay, in a range of red, brown, grey and greenish shades. Shapes are available to cover different parts of the roof (see below). Because slates are comparatively expensive, a deteriorating slate roof is often replaced with cheaper tiles. However, consider whether tiles will spoil the appearance of your house. In a terrace, for instance, it looks better if all the roofs are in the same material.

Simulated slates are much less expensive than real slates and may be a better option. Or you may be able to cut costs by finding secondhand slates from roofing companies or builders' merchants. Check that they are the right size, thickness and colour.

Tiles and many simulated slates are heavier than real slates, so the roof timbers may need strengthening. Ask a surveyor or builder for advice.

Roof pitch The pitch (slope) a tile needs varies with its profile and finish. Rainwater runs freely off a smooth finish, so smooth tiles need not be as sloped as grainy ones. Makers recommend a minimum angle of pitch for each style of tile that they make.

SINGLE LAP TILES

These are also known as interlocking tiles. Usually the tile surface undulates from side to side so that one or more channels run down the tile. Courses are overlapped, with the tiles in one course aligned exactly with the tiles in the courses above and below so that the channels run all down the roof slope. Each tile in a course interlocks with the tiles on both sides. A few styles have no channels.

Some styles of single lap tiles hang from the roofing battens on nibs with alternate courses nailed to the battens through holes at the top of the tiles. Others are fixed at the sides with aluminium-alloy tile clips which are nailed to the roofing battens.

There are no single lap bonnet hip tiles but some firms make trough valley tiles (rectangular valley tiles that are set below the level of the main foot tiles).

Full-size tiles are used for the top course and there is no underlayer at the eaves. Gaps left under the undulating profile at the ridge or hip of the roof are sealed with mortar or by purpose-made profile fillers.

Single lap tiles Most are 380–430mm long and 330mm wide. They are used with standard ridge and hip tiles.

Pantiles S-shaped tiles 381mm long and 227mm wide resemble the original clay tiles characteristic of some areas of the country. They are usually made of concrete now.

PLAIN TILES

The tile surface is slightly convex and there are two nibs behind the top edge to hook over the roofing battens. Nail holes allow every third or fourth course of tiles to be nailed in place for extra stability. Courses of plain tiles are staggered so each tile overlaps the gap between two tiles in the course below.

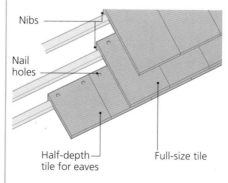

Nibs

Nail holes

Half-depth tile for eaves

Full-size tile

Half-depth tiles are made for the top course and for the under layer at the eaves. Half-width and one-and-a-half width tiles are made for starting and finishing courses at the gable ends.

Standard plain tiles These tiles are normally 265mm long and 165mm wide.

Ridge tiles These cover the gap where two slopes meet at the top. Several types are available, including versions with built-in ventilation (roof vents).

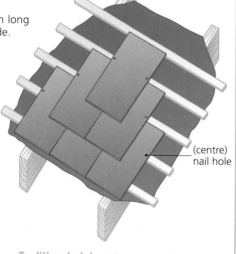

(centre) nail hole

Bonnet hip tiles Bonnets continue the line of a course of tiles round the hip where two roof slopes meet.

Valley tiles Arrow-shaped tiles bridge the gap where two roof slopes meet at an internal angle (called a valley).

Traditional slates There are still some older houses roofed with traditional natural slates. These are nailed in place on the roof battens through holes cut in the slate on site, either in the centre or in the head of the slate. Buying new slates is expensive, but second-hand ones are available for replacements and there are many simulated or reconstituted slates available in the form of single lap tiles (also called interlocking tiles), and with 'deckled' edges so that the tiles look like slate.

Roof repairs

Missing or broken slates or tiles can quickly become a problem, allowing water to penetrate the roof space and wind to lift more of the neighbouring tiles. Act promptly to fix the problem.

Making a temporary repair to a cracked tile or slate

If rainwater is coming in through a cracked tile or slate and it is not possible to get a replacement immediately, you can use flashing strip to make a temporary repair to minimise the damage done by damp. Alternatively, bituminous sealant in an applicator gun seals a fine crack with very little work: prop up the surrounding tiles and brush the crack as for flashing strip, and then inject the sealant.

Tools *Ladder with a stand-off bracket; roof ladder; wooden wedges (see box, right); wire brush; paintbrush; sharp knife; old wallpaper seam roller.*

Materials *Flashing strip primer; self-adhesive flashing strip.*

1 Raise the one or two tiles or slates that overlap the cracked one, to give you better access. Prop them up with small wooden wedges (see right). Use the wire brush to clean the surface round the crack.

2 Brush a coat of flashing strip primer into and round the crack, making a strip as wide as the flashing strip. The primer ensures a good bond between tile or slate and flashing strip.

3 Cut a piece of flashing strip from the roll with a sharp knife. Make it long enough to cover the whole crack.

4 Press the strip into place and bed it down well. Run a small wallpaper seam roller to and fro over it to firm it down.

Replacing a broken plain tile

If you don't have a spare tile of the same size and style as the broken one, a builders' yard or salvage merchant may have one or be able to obtain one for you.

Before you start Beware of matching the replacement tile to the colour your tiles were when new. The tiles may have changed colour considerably, so try to match the replacement to the colour they are now. If you can't find a good match, 'steal' a tile from an unobtrusive place on the roof – such as a side porch. A tile near the end of the bottom course will be easy to reach. Put the poor match in its place.

Tools *Ladder with stand-off bracket; roof ladder; wooden wedges; large builder's trowel. Perhaps a slate ripper.*

Materials *Replacement tile.*

WEDGES TO PROP TILES UP

To prop up tiles you need to prepare two or more wedges from 20mm thick wood. Cut them 200mm long and make them taper from 30mm at one end to a point at the other.

---

1 Lift the two tiles that overlap the broken tile from the course above. Tap a wooden wedge under each to hold it up.

2 Slip the large builder's trowel under the broken tile. Lift up the whole tile until its nibs are clear of the batten and you can draw it out towards you.

Alternatively If the broken tile is one that has been nailed to the batten, try to free it by wiggling it from side to side until the nail breaks or comes away.

If this does not free it, you will have to use a slate ripper (page 387) to cut through the nails. Slate rippers can be hired.

3 Lay the replacement tile on the trowel and slide it up under the two wedged tiles until the nibs hook over the batten. There is no need to nail it, even if the original was nailed. Take out the wedges.

Replacing a group of plain tiles

If you need to replace a group of tiles and have no spares, buy replacements of the same size and style. See advice for a single tile, left.

Tools *Ladder with stand-off bracket; roof ladder; wooden wedges (above); large builder's trowel; claw hammer; bucket on a long rope. Perhaps a slate ripper.*

Materials *Replacement tiles; 40mm aluminium-alloy roofing nails.*

1 Lift the tiles in the course immediately above the highest ones to be replaced. Lift them two at a time and slide the wooden wedges under their outer edges to hold them up. This will allow you access to the tile they overlap in the course below.

2 As each tile is exposed, slide the trowel under it and lift it until its nibs clear the batten. Then draw it out. Lower it to the ground in the bucket.

If a tile is nailed to the batten, see-saw it from side to side to try to dislodge the nails. If you cannot, use a slate ripper (page 387) to cut through the nails.

3 Work along the top course of tiles to be removed and then along the course below that, and so on until all the tiles have been removed. Once the highest course of tiles has been removed, you can lift the others without using the wedges or the trowel.

4 Fit the replacement tiles onto the battens along the bottom course first. Hook each tile over the batten by its nibs and make sure that it is centred over the gap between the two tiles below it. Then work along the courses above.

5 Nail each tile in every third or fourth course to the batten with two nails.

6 To fit the top course, hold up the tiles in the course above in pairs with wedges. Work along the row, lifting each new tile on the trowel and sliding it into place.

Replacing broken single lap tiles

Tools *Ladder with a stand-off bracket; roof ladder; wooden wedges (page 389). Perhaps a slate ripper; hammer; bucket on a rope.*

Materials *Replacement tiles. Perhaps tile clips and 40mm roofing aluminium-alloy roofing nails.*

1 Slide up the tiles that overlap onto the broken tile. Alternatively, use wedges to raise the tiles to the left and right of the broken one, but in the course above.

2 To remove the broken tile, tilt it sideways to separate it from the tiles which are interlocked with it. You will be able to free it without disturbing them. Lever the tile upwards to release it from any clip that holds it to the batten. If the clip stays in place, the new tile may slip into it. If the clip is dislodged, there is no need to replace it; a few unclipped tiles will not matter. Sometimes alternate courses are nailed in place. If your repair is to a nailed tile, use a slate ripper to cut the nails before you remove the tile.

3 Lower the broken tile in a bucket on a rope to a helper on the ground.

4 To fit the replacement tile, slide it up into place. You will not be able to nail it or clip it. Pull back into place any tiles that you pushed out of place. Remove any wedges.

Replacing a group of tiles

Remove the highest tiles as for a single tile. Lower tiles simply need tilting to free them. Remove the clips wherever you can.

When replacing the tiles, fit the lowest course first and work from right to left.

Fit a clip for each tile wherever you are able to nail it to the batten.

Lodge the hook of the clip over the ridge at the side of the tile and hammer the nail through the hole in the clip into the top edge of the batten near the bottom edge of the tile you are fitting.

You can also nail alternate courses to the battens. The highest course cannot be nailed and the last tile of all cannot be fitted with a clip because the batten will be covered.

Making repairs to slate roofs

Slates will last a century or more, but the nails holding them to battens can corrode and break, allowing the slates to slip out of position.

Before you start The two problems most likely to affect a slate roof are nail-sickness and delamination. Corrosion, or nail-sickness, can affect a large area of a roof within a few years as the nails are the same age and corrode at the same rate. The slates can be re-nailed provided that they are sound.

A more serious problem is delamination, when the surface of the slate becomes flaky or powdery and you can see many cracks and splits. Replacement is the usual solution.

Fixing slates For fixing a group of replacement slates in several courses you can use 40mm aluminium-alloy or copper roofing nails.

If these are hard to find and you only have a small group of slates to nail into place, 40mm large-head galvanised clout nails will do.

When you are replacing single slates, you will not be able to nail them because the batten will be covered by the course of slates above. You can secure each slate with a strip of metal cut from lead, zinc, or aluminium that is thin enough to bend. It is fixed between the slates (see opposite).

Slates can also be fixed with adhesive expanding foam, which can be applied under a loose slate from outside, or (if the slate is visible) from inside the loft.

How to make holes New slates will not have fixing holes in them; you will have to make the holes.

A secondhand slate may have its holes in the wrong place and need drilling. Use the old slate as a pattern to mark drilling spots. The holes are usually about half-way down the sides.

Drill the holes with an electric drill fitted with a No. 6 masonry bit; or make the hole by tapping a nail through the slate with steady, not-too-hard hammer blows.

Work from the underside, that is the side without the bevelled edges.

Replacing a broken slate

Slates may become cracked with age, or by someone clambering on the roof without using proper access equipment.

Before you start You may not be able to obtain a matching replacement slate immediately. If so, make a temporary repair to prevent water from penetrating. You can make it as for a tile (page 389).

Alternatively, you can coat the slate with mastic. Cover this with a piece of roofing felt or cooking foil cut to fit and spread another layer of mastic on top.

Replace the slate when you can obtain one that is a good match.

Tools *Ladder with a stand-off bracket; roof ladder; slate ripper; a bucket on a long rope; hammer or screwdriver. Perhaps a power drill fitted with No. 6 masonry bit, or nail and hammer.*

Materials *Replacement slate; strip of lead, zinc, aluminium or copper 25mm wide, and long enough to reach from the hole in the slate to the bottom plus 100mm; 40mm large-head galvanised clout nails.*

1 Cut through the nails that are holding the slate, using the slate ripper.

CUTTING A SLATE TO SIZE

Place the slate on a flat board and use a ceramic tile cutter and a metal rule to score a deep cutting line. To complete the cut, use a wide bolster chisel. Tap it along the scored line with gentle hammer blows. Or you can place the slate on a table with the scored line over the table edge and press down to break the slate cleanly.

If you have many slates to cut, hire a slate cutter. Cut with the top surface of the slate downwards. On a second-hand slate in particular this ensures that weathering and cutting marks match the other slates.

Alternatively, you can hire an electric tile cutter.

2 Draw the slate towards you, wiggling it from side to side to ease it from under the slates overlapping it. Take care not to let any broken pieces slide off the roof. They are sharp and can cause damage or injury. Put the pieces in a bucket and take it to the ground or lower it down to a helper.

3 Nail the metal strip to the batten, which will just be visible in the gap between the two slates the replacement is going to lap onto. Put the nail in a ready-made hole about 25mm down from the top of the strip.

4 Carry the new slate up to the roof in a bucket or put it into a bucket and haul it up with a rope.

5 Slip the new slate, with bevelled edges upwards, under the two slates in the course above. Wiggle it a little to right and left to work it upwards until its lower edge aligns with the slates on each side. Its top edge will fit tightly over the batten to which the course above is nailed.

6 Turn up the end of the metal strip over the lower edge of the slate, then bend it double and press it down flat against the slate. The double thickness prevents snow and ice from forcing the clip open.

Replacing a group of slates

You will be able to nail the lower courses of slates in place, but the top course and the course below that will have to be fixed with metal strips because the battens to which they should be nailed will be covered by slates (see Replacing a broken slate, facing page). If necessary, cut the slates to size and drill holes in them.

Tools *Ladder with a stand-off bracket; roof ladder; slate ripper; hammer; a bucket on a long rope; screwdriver.*

Materials *Replacement slates; 40mm aluminium-alloy or copper roofing nails; strips of lead, zinc, aluminium or copper 25mm wide and long enough to reach from the hole in the slate to the bottom plus 100mm.*

1 Cut through the nails securing the damaged slates, using a slate ripper. Deal first with the highest course to be removed. Ease each slate out in turn from the overlapping slates and lower it in a bucket to a helper or take it to the ground. Do not let a slate slide from the roof; it is sharp and can cause damage or injury.

Work down course by course, removing the slates. The lower ones will not be overlapped and are easier to remove.

2 Fix the bottom course of replacement slates first. Butt neighbouring slates closely and fit them with the bevelled edges upwards. Nail the slates through the holes to the batten.

3 Work upwards, course by course, nailing the slates in place. When you can no longer see the battens to nail the slates to, cut metal strips to secure the slates and fit them as described in Replacing a broken slate (opposite).

Replacing ridge, hip and bonnet tiles

Both tiled and slate roofs have the gaps at the ridge and hips covered by specially designed tiles. The tiles are most often curved, but may be angled.

Replacing a bonnet hip tile
Some tiled roofs have bonnet hip tiles to cover the gap at the hip (page 388).

Bonnet hip tiles are nailed to the hip timber as well as being bedded in mortar.

1 Remove a bonnet hip tile by chipping away the mortar above and below it with a cold chisel and club hammer and then sliding a slate ripper under the tile and giving a sharp hammer blow on the handle to cut through the nail. You can then draw out the tile towards you.

If you are removing several tiles down the hip, start at the highest one and work downwards. Clean the tiles of old mortar.

2 Brush away all dust from around the repair, then brush the area with water and with PVA adhesive.

3 If you are replacing a single tile, spread mortar to bed it on. Spread mortar also under the bonnet in the course above. Set the bonnet in place and tap it into alignment with the other tiles in the course before you smooth the mortar and clean away any excess.

4 If you are replacing several bonnets, work from the bottom upwards. Nail each, except the top one, to the timber with an aluminium nail after you have set it on the mortar. Then smooth the mortar and clean away any excess.

Replacing ridge or hip tiles

The most common problem at the roof ridge or hip is that the mortar between tiles cracks and crumbles away. Sometimes a tile may then be pushed out of place by a build-up of ice, or occasionally by strong winds. If you spot cracks early, while they are narrow, you can fill them with roof-and-gutter sealant. There are coloured sealants which make the repair scarcely noticeable.

If the mortar is crumbling or the tile itself has cracked, you will have to remove the tile and re-fix it or put a new one in its place. If it is the end ridge tile that needs a repair, you must seal up the opening left at the end. Use small pieces of slate or tile bedded in mortar. If the main roof tiles are S-shaped there will be a hollow to seal where the ridge or hip tile meets them.

Tools *Ladder with a stand-off bracket; roof ladder; cold chisel; club hammer; brush; paintbrush; small builder's trowel.*

Materials *Dry mortar mix, or cement and sharp sand; PVA adhesive; bucket of water. Perhaps replacement tiles, narrow pieces of tile or slate.*

1 With the chisel and hammer, carefully chip away all cracked or crumbling mortar until the ridge or hip tile is freed and you can lift it off. Make sure that any surrounding mortar you leave in place is sound. Clean the tile.

2 Prepare the mortar (page 466) from a bag of dry mixed material or make your own from one part cement to four parts sharp sand. To improve adhesion, add some PVA adhesive to the water, following the manufacturer's instructions. Do not make the mortar too wet; a firmer mix is easier to work with. Mix enough to half-fill a bucket.

3 Brush all dust away from the area round the repair.

4 Use the paintbrush and water to wet the roof and the existing mortar round the repair. This is especially necessary on a hot day when the mortar would lose its moisture too quickly and crack.

5 Brush PVA adhesive liberally all round the area of the repair to ensure good adhesion between the roof tiles at the ridge or hip and the ridge or hip tile itself.

6 Use the trowel to spread mortar on the roof on both sides of the ridge or hip. Cover the areas where the bottom edges of the tile to be fixed will lie.

Do not use too much mortar; there must be a gap under the ridge or hip tiles so that air can circulate to keep the timber below dry. If you lay too much mortar on the tiles, it could squeeze into the gap and fill it in when you are setting the ridge or hip tile into place.

7 The butt joints where two of the ridge or hip tiles meet can either be pointed with mortar or given a solid bedding of mortar. It is probably best to follow the method already used on the roof.

If you make a solid bedding, place a piece of slate or tile across the gap between the two sides of the ridge or hip to prevent mortar falling through.

8 Ridge or hip tiles must be dipped in water before they are set in place. Do this before you go up on the roof. Settle the tile on the mortar carefully so that it makes a smooth line with the neighbouring tiles.

Alternatively If the roof tiles have a curved profile, fill the gap between the down-curve and the ridge or hip tiles with pieces of tile or slate embedded in mortar.

Specially designed 'dentil slips' can be bought for this purpose.

9 Smooth the mortar between tiles and along the bottom edges. There must be no hollows in the mortar between the tiles because they could retain small pockets of rainwater.

10 If the re-fixed tile is at an end of the roof ridge, seal the open end with thin slips of tile or slate bedded in mortar. Smooth the end so that rainwater will flow off readily.

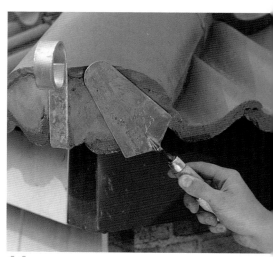

11 If you have been replacing the lowest tile on the hip, make sure the protecting hip iron has not been dislodged; remake its fixings if necessary. Then fill the end of the tile with mortar.

Repairs to verges

A roof with only two main slopes is usually sealed with mortar where the slopes meet the gable ends of the house – these are the verges.

Before you start You can seal any minor cracks in the mortar with roof-and-gutter sealant injected with an applicator gun (page 400).

If you choose a sealant to match the mortar, the repair will not be noticeable. For larger cracks you will have to make the repair with mortar.

Tools *Ladder with a stand-off bracket; cold chisel; club hammer; brush; paintbrush; small trowel.*

Materials *Dry mortar mix, or cement and sharp sand; PVA adhesive; bucket of water. Perhaps narrow slips of tile.*

1 With the chisel and hammer, chip away all cracked and crumbling mortar, leaving only sound mortar in place.

2 Prepare the mortar (page 466) from a bag of dry mixed material or from one part cement to four parts sharp sand. To improve adhesion, add PVA adhesive to the water, following the manufacturer's instructions. Avoid making the mixture too wet. Make enough mortar to half-fill a bucket.

3 Brush all dust away, then dampen the area with some water using a paintbrush before brushing on a covering of PVA adhesive.

4 Use the trowel to press the mortar firmly into the areas that have been prepared. Knock it in with the side of the trowel to make sure that there are no pockets of air in it.

5 Smooth the surface of the mortar and clean away any excess. Do not leave any ledges or hollows in the mortar that could retain rainwater.

Repairs to metal valleys

Where two roof slopes meet at the bottom, the long narrow gap between them is sealed – frequently by a tray of aluminium alloy, lead or zinc. This metal valley is overlapped by the tiles or slates, which drain rainwater into it to be carried down to the gutters at the eaves.

Since valleys are likely to carry a gushing stream of water in heavy rain, they must be kept waterproof and clear of obstructions. If moss, leaves or other debris accumulates, rainwater will build up at the obstruction and spill over the edges of the valley onto the timbers and into the roof space.

If a metal valley has developed a fine crack or is showing the first signs of corrosion, it can be repaired with a liquid bitumen compound. Liquid bitumen can also be used to make a temporary repair if you are waiting for a convenient time to replace the valley.

Holes or splits in a metal valley can be covered with a self-adhesive metal-backed flashing strip. If slight corrosion has set in over a large area, flashing strip can be used to cover the entire valley.

Repairing with liquid bitumen

Stir the waterproofing compound before you apply it. You can use it on a damp, but not wet, surface. Do not use it, however, if rain or frost are expected within about 24 hours.

Tools *Ladder with a stand-off bracket; roof ladder; wire brush; a spreader for the roof-and-gutter sealant; sharp knife or scissors; soft brush or broom.*

Materials *Roof-and-gutter sealant; roofing felt or cooking foil; liquid bitumen waterproofing compound; bucket of water.*

1 Use the wire brush to clean away dirt and loose metal fragments from the area of the valley that is going to be repaired.

2 Spread roof-and-gutter sealant over the damaged area and at least 50mm beyond it.

3 Cut out a piece of roofing felt or cooking foil to cover the damage and extend at least 50mm beyond it. Press the felt or foil down over the sealant.

4 Spread another layer of sealant on top of the felt or foil.

5 Brush the liquid bitumen waterproofing compound over the repair. As a precaution against leaks, you can brush it over the

whole valley. Apply it with a soft brush or broom, dipping the brush in water and shaking it each time before you load it with the waterproofer. Brush the compound on with even strokes, working in the same direction all the time. Throw the brush away when you have finished.

Making repairs with flashing strip

Tools *Ladder with a stand-off bracket; roof ladder; wire brush; damp cloth; paintbrush; sharp knife or strong scissors; old wallpaper seam roller.*

Materials *Medium-coarse abrasive paper; flashing-strip primer; self-adhesive metal-backed flashing strip.*

1 Use the wire brush to clean away dirt and loose metal fragments from round the crack or hole.

2 Rub over the area with the abrasive paper.

3 Wipe the surface clean with the damp cloth and allow it to dry completely.

4 Use the paintbrush to apply a coat of flashing-strip primer to the area of the repair, extending it at least 50mm beyond the damage. Leave it to dry for the time recommended by the manufacturer – usually about 30 minutes.

5 Cut out a piece of flashing strip to extend at least 50mm beyond the crack or hole all round. Cut it with a knife or pair of scissors, then peel off the backing.

6 Press the flashing strip firmly into position, using the wallpaper seam roller to bed it down smoothly.

Repairs to flashings

Where a tile or slate roof meets a wall, there is a flashing to seal the join – for example at the meeting of a roof with a chimney stack and the meeting of a bay window or porch roof with the house wall.

Flashings fitted when the house is built are usually strips of lead which can deteriorate with age. Depending on the extent of the deterioration, it may not be necessary to replace the flashing. Small repairs are quite easily achieved.

Fine cracks To repair a fine crack, inject some bituminous sealant or other roof-and-gutter sealant into it with an applicator gun and cartridge. Some sealants are available in different colours so you can choose one that will make the repair less noticeable.

Small holes or slight corrosion A patch of self-adhesive flashing strip will make a sound repair over a small hole or where there are the first signs of corrosion.
   Use the method described for a roof valley under Making repairs with flashing strip (page 393).

Renewing flashing mortar The top edge of a flashing is sandwiched into the mortar between two courses of bricks. Sometimes it works loose and lets in water.
   Repoint the joint (page 408), but first push the edge of the flashing back into the gap between courses of bricks.
   If the flashing springs out, wedge it with blocks of wood until the pointing has hardened. Then withdraw the blocks and fill the holes with mortar.

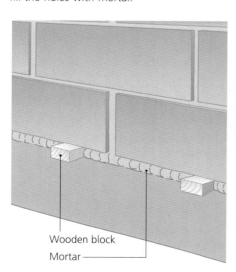

Wooden block
Mortar

Replacing a flashing

If a flashing is badly cracked or corroded, replace it with a self-adhesive metal-backed flashing strip. Unlike lead flashing, adhesive flashing is not tucked into the mortar joints.

Tools *Ladder with a stand-off bracket; roof ladder; plugging chisel and club hammer; pointing trowel; wire brush; paintbrush; sharp craft knife; old wallpaper seam roller.*

Materials *Mortar for repointing (page 466); flashing-strip primer; self-adhesive metal-backed flashing-strip.*

1 Chip out any mortar that is still holding the flashing in the joints between bricks or masonry. Use the plugging chisel and hammer. Protect your hands and eyes.

2 Strip away the old flashing.

3 Use the wire brush to clean away loose mortar and dirt from the area to be repaired.

4 Repoint the joints between the courses of bricks or masonry (page 408). Let the new pointing dry out overnight.

5 Paint a coat of flashing primer on the wall (or chimney) and roof where the strip is to go. Let it dry for 30 minutes to an hour, according to the manufacturer's instructions.

6 Cut two lengths of flashing strip, each the full length of the area to be sealed.

7 Peel off the backing of the first strip and put the strip in position, letting the width lie equally on the roof and the wall (or chimney stack). Roll the strip with the wallpaper seam roller to smooth it out and ensure that it is well stuck.

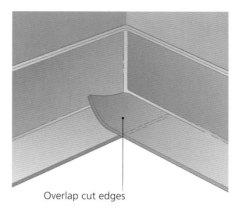

Overlap cut edges

8 At internal corners, make a snip in the lower edge of the strip and overlap the cut edges.

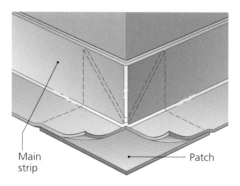

Main strip   Patch

9 At external corners, fit a square patch before the main strip; make a cut from one corner of the patch to the middle. Set the patch with the centre at the point where the wall angle meets the roof and the cut running upwards. Let the cut edges splay out round the angle. In the main strip make a cut in the bottom edge and let the cut edges splay apart over the patch. Trim off any excess at the points.

10 Peel the backing off the second strip and apply it so that its top edge is 50mm above the top edge of the first layer. Treat any corners as in the first strip. Again smooth the strip out and bed it down well with the wallpaper seam roller.

HOW A FLAT ROOF WITH APRONS IS MADE

1 **Timber deck** Flat roofs on house extensions or garages are usually made by nailing planks of tongued-and-grooved softwood or sheets of exterior grade plywood, chipboard or strawboard to the roof joists and covering them with three layers of roofing felt.

2 **Drip batten** Along the top edge of the fascia at the gutter end there is a drip batten that holds the apron away from the board, so that any drips of water fall into the gutter.

3 **Aprons** Edges of the roof that do not meet a house wall are sealed with strips of felt taken over the fascia board. These strips are called aprons and are designed to keep the fascia dry.

4 **Gutter edge** The roof has a slight fall to drain water into a gutter along one edge. The other edges should have a fillet sloping up to a raised lip so that water cannot spill off.

5 **Flashing** If the roof meets the house walls, there is a flashing at the join.

6 **Chippings** In a sunny place, the felt may be spread with chippings of limestone, granite, gravel or flint over a chipping compound. The chippings are to keep direct sun off the felt, and are not necessary in shade.

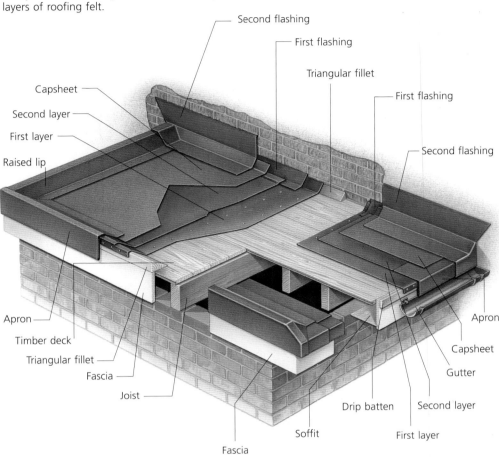

Choosing materials for a flat roof or shed

Garages and home extensions often have felted flat roofs. Felted roofs, also found on many timber garages and garden sheds, need repairing or replacing from time to time. Roofing felt is generally sold in rolls 1m wide and 10m long. Modern polyester and glass fibre felts last longer than traditional fibre-based bituminous felts. Repair products range from simple patch repair mastics to whole roof treatments that can last 20 years or more.

Roofing felt

Fibre-based roofing felt For roofs of timber garages and garden sheds; use alone or with underlay; secure with roofing nails and roofing-felt adhesive.

Polyester/glass fibre roofing felt For roofs of extensions and garages, or on sheds for longer life; combine with underlay for two-layer or three-layer system; use cold adhesive or hot bitumen.

Torch-on roofing felt For roofs of extensions and garages; use as single remedial layer or two-layer with underlay; applied by professionals with a gas torch.

Roof treatments

Aluminium paint Apply to any felted roof to reduce degradation by sunlight.

Chippings of limestone, granite, gravel or flint For flat roofs in sunny positions; sprinkle over roof surface.

Liquid rubber/elastomeric waterproofing emulsion For flat roofs covered with asphalt, asbestos or corrugated iron; use alone or with primer, according to manufacturer's instructions; brush on.

Roof repair

Bitumen waterproofing solution For repairs to felted roofs; use alone or with reinforcing mesh; brush on.

Acrylic coating For isolated repairs or whole roof cover; use brush or roller.

Repair bitumen mastic For localised repair on felted or flat roofs; trowel on wet or dry roof (aerosol also available).

Roof-and-gutter sealant Repairs cracks in flashing, felt, asphalt or guttering; applied from cartridge gun or with a filling knife.

Roof-and-gutter repair tape Repairs cracks in flashing, felt, asphalt or guttering; self-adhesive – press on.

Self-adhesive flashing Repairs cracks in flashing, felt, asphalt or guttering; use alone or with special primer; self-adhesive – press on.

Minor repairs to flat roofs

Small blisters or cracks are the most common minor defects in felt-covered flat roofs.

Before you start Scrape off any chippings carefully with an old wallpaper scraper. You can repair small blisters or cracks with a roof-and-gutter sealant (below), with self-adhesive flashing strip (see Making a temporary repair to a cracked tile or slate, page 389), or with brush-on liquid rubber (right). Repair damaged flashings as described on page 394.

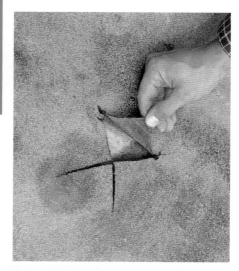

Curing bubbles A bubble may form in the felt where moisture has seeped under it and swollen in the heat of the sun. Cut a cross in the blister with a sharp knife and fold back the four flaps of felt.

Let them dry, then stick them down with a cold felt adhesive before patching the damaged area with a piece of self-adhesive flashing strip or a bitumen mastic repair compound.

Replace any roof chippings when the repairs are complete.

Bituminous sealant Apply sealant from an applicator gun to mend small cracks in roofing felt and roof tiles.

Repairing a cracked flashing

Changes in temperature and normal house movement put the flashings under stress and may cause cracks where water can seep in. The resulting wet patch indoors, however, can be several feet away from the crack because the water may run along the roof beams before dripping onto the ceiling. The crack may be difficult to spot. When you have located it, repair it with self-adhesive flashing strip (see Making repairs with flashing strip, page 393).

Repairing a hole or crack with liquid rubber

If cracks develop on a flat roof that is covered with felt or asphalt, treat the whole area with brush-on liquid rubber.

Calculate the area of the roof in square metres and buy the amount of liquid rubber recommended by the manufacturer. Liquid rubber is sold in containers ranging from 1kg to 20kg.

Tools *Ladder; stiff brush and shovel; an old 100mm paintbrush or a small broom for the liquid rubber. Perhaps a paintbrush for primer.*

Materials *Liquid rubber. Perhaps primer for liquid rubber.*

1 Use the stiff brush and shovel to clear the area of loose chippings and dirt.

2 If the area has previously been treated with a tar-bitumen coating – which gives a black, slightly rough covering – brush on a coat of primer for liquid rubber. Leave it to dry overnight.

3 Brush on a coat of liquid rubber, using all the recommended amount for the area. Leave it to dry thoroughly for 48 hours. After an hour it will be sufficiently dry not to be affected by rain.

4 Brush on a second coat of rubber, using the same amount as before.

A replacement flashing

If the flashing has cracked or corroded so much that an adhesive patch may not be able to make firm contact all over the damaged area, strip away all the flashing and plan to replace it with self-adhesive flashing strip as described in Replacing a flashing (page 394).

Seal the joint between roof and parapet (or house wall) with roof-and-gutter sealant before you apply the primer.

If your parapet is only one course of brickwork or masonry high, let the second layer of flashing overlap onto the top.

HIGH-LEVEL SAFETY

No matter how small the task, any DIY work done on a roof carries an element of danger.
• If you are working on a roof, make sure the ladder you use is securely supported. If possible have a helper with you to keep the ladder steady; if this is impossible, secure the ladder to the roof or to the building (page 387).
• Never lean over to reach a patch of roof – move the ladder instead.

Re-covering a parapet roof with reinforced bitumen

A reinforced bitumen covering consists of a layer of open-meshed reinforcing fabric between layers of a liquid-bitumen waterproofing solution. Both are sold by builders' merchants.

Before you start When estimating how much you will need, remember that there is no need to overlap the strips. Wear old shoes which you can throw away when you have finished, or Wellington boots which can remain dirty. When leaving the roof, change into clean shoes at the parapet, before stepping onto the ladder.

Tools *Ladder; stiff brush and shovel; filling knife; paintbrush; sharp knife; wallpaper seam roller; soft broom or large cheap paintbrush for the liquid bitumen.*

Materials *Roof-and-gutter sealant; flashing strip primer; self adhesive flashing strip; bitumen solution; reinforcing fabric, such as Aquaseal glass-fibre membrane.*

1 Brush the surface clean of any loose dirt and debris.

2 Press roof-and-gutter sealant into any cracks or holes, using a filling knife to force it well in.

3 Apply a coat of flashing-strip primer to a 150mm strip at the roof edge and a similar strip of the parapet or house wall adjoining. Let it dry for 30 minutes to an hour.

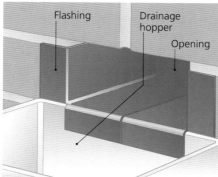

Flashing   Drainage hopper   Opening

4 Cut and fit lengths of flashing strip as described in Replacing a flashing (page 394). Continue the flashing round the sides of the opening for the drainage hopper and let it lap onto the surface of the brick or stonework. Fit a patch under the external angles as shown on page 394.

5 Cut strips of reinforcing fabric to length, allowing for them to extend 150mm up the wall at each edge. Do not lay them yet.

6 Apply a coat of liquid-bitumen waterproofing solution to the roof using a soft broom or paintbrush. The coat should be applied about 150mm up any walls that enclose the roof as well and should cover the whole flat surface and the opening to the hopper.

7 Leave for a few minutes, until the surface is tacky. Then lay the fabric strips side by side over the whole flat area and to the top of the tacky rim round all the walls. At the corners of the parapet fold the excess fabric into a neat pleat and press it flat.

8 Brush a second coat of the liquid bitumen waterproofing solution over the whole area. Apply the solution generously, especially at the parapet corners, so that you avoid dislodging the reinforcing fabric as much as possible. Then leave the surface to dry. After about two hours the roof should be dry enough not to be harmed by rain.

9 Brush a final coat of the liquid bitumen waterproofing solution all over the flat area and 150mm up the enclosing walls.

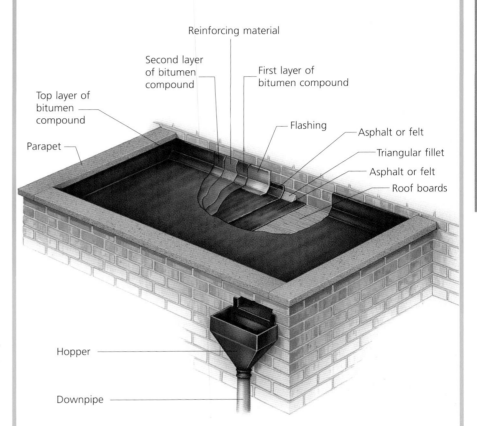

HOW A PARAPET FLAT ROOF IS MADE

Where a flat roof is the main house roof, it is usually of the parapet type. A parapet roof may also be given to a one or two-storey extension or to a detached garage, as an alternative to the more usual flat roof with aprons (page 395).

Repairs Eventually, cracks may develop in the asphalt or felt covering. You can repair minor damage as described on the facing page. If the roof lets in water in several spots, it is wisest to re-cover the whole area to prevent further damage to the roof timbers or to the rooms below. Layers of rubberised liquid bitumen reinforced with a mesh fabric will make a strong new cover over both the unsound surface and the flashings (see Re-covering a flat roof with reinforced bitumen, opposite).

Reinforcing material
Second layer of bitumen compound
First layer of bitumen compound
Top layer of bitumen compound
Flashing
Asphalt or felt
Triangular fillet
Asphalt or felt
Parapet
Roof boards
Hopper
Downpipe

Raised edges
In a parapet flat roof, the walls continue above the roof level. The parapet may be only one course of brickwork or masonry or it may be several courses.

Wooden deck
The flat area consists of softwood planks or sheets of outdoor-grade plywood or chipboard nailed to roof beams and covered with asphalt or roofing felt.

Drainage
The roof usually has a slight fall towards an opening in one side with a drainage hopper outside it connected to a downpipe that carries away rainwater. The drainage hole to the hopper must be kept clear of leaves or rubbish that could block it.

Flashing
Where the roof meets the house wall or parapet there is a triangular wooden fillet and a flashing of lead, zinc, aluminium or felt. A cracked or displaced flashing is a frequent source of trouble.

Mending a corrugated plastic roof

A corrugated plastic roof is ideal where extra light is required, but it can become brittle and need repairing.

Before you start Measure the profile of the existing plastic on the roof before you go to buy new sheeting. The sheets may have a round or a box profile and the difference between the lowest and highest points of the profile can vary from 38 to 150mm.

If the new plastic does not exactly match the old in profile, it will not make snug overlaps. The length of the screws you use must be the difference between the low and high points of the profile plus at least 25mm to penetrate the wood.

To reduce the cost of the repair, you can fit a patch. However, the patch will have to be the width of a full sheet and extend over a roof timber at top and bottom to be screwed in place.

Temporary repairs to a corrugated plastic roof can be made using clear waterproof tape. Ensure surfaces are clean and dry before pressing the tape into place.

Tools *Sharp knife; tack lifter; screwdriver; fine-toothed saw; hand drill with blunt twist bit, or electric soldering iron with 5mm bit; steel measuring tape.*

Materials *Enough corrugated plastic sheeting to make the repair with adequate overlaps; No. 8 galvanised screws of appropriate length; protective screw caps; transparent waterproof glazing tape.*

Fitting a patch

1 Use a felt pen to mark cutting lines on the damaged panel showing the area for removal. Make the top line just below a timber support and the bottom line just above a timber support.

2 Prise off the screw caps with the tack lifter and take out all the screws that were securing the panel. Carefully remove the whole panel.

3 Cut the patch to overlap the guidelines on the old panel by 75mm at top and bottom. Then cut along the guidelines on the old panel to remove the damaged part. Hold the saw at a shallow angle and support the sheet on both sides of the cut. If you have to cut to the sheet to width, cut along the valleys of the sheeting.

4 Lay the plastic for the bottom of the slope in place first. Make screw holes through the peaks that are over timbers.

Make the holes at intervals of about 450mm across the panel immediately above the cross timbers. You can melt the holes with a fine soldering iron, start them with a bradawl, or use a blunt bit in a drill. Drive in the screws across the bottom edge. Do not overtighten.

5 Lay the next piece of plastic up the slope; let its bottom edge overlap 75mm onto the piece below.

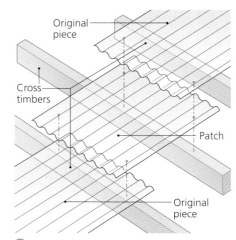

Original piece

Cross timbers

Patch

Original piece

6 Drill screw holes through peaks on the overlap at 450mm intervals. Drive screws through into the timbers but do not overtighten them.

7 Lay the top piece of plastic sheet in place overlapping the previous piece by 75mm.

8 Drill and screw the bottom edge as for the previous piece.

9 Drill holes if necessary at the top edge and screw it in place.

10 Push caps on all the screws.

11 Fit new flashing strip (page 394) where the plastic sheet meets the wall. Press it down well into the valleys.

12 Seal the edges where the layers of plastic sheeting overlap at the sides with strips of the glazing tape.

HELPFUL TIPS

Overlaps at the sides should finish in a 'valley' of the corrugation, not a 'peak'. This prevents water from entering at an overlap. If you are renewing a complete panel on the roof, allow the same overlaps as on the rest of the roof.

Cut sheets to size indoors in cold weather. Plastic becomes brittle in low temperatures and could crack.

Do not walk on the roof. Kneel on scaffold boards secured with sandbags so that they will not slide.

Fitting a whole panel

1 Cut away any flashing at the top of the damaged panel.

2 Prise off the screw caps with the tack lifter and take out all the screws that were securing the panel, then remove the panel.

3 Cut the new panel if necessary to match the length of the old one. Keep the saw at a shallow angle and take care to support the sheet on both sides of the cut. If you have to cut to the sheet to width, cut along valleys.

4 Place the new panel in position on the roof, overlapping onto the old ones at either side. If there is another panel above or below the new one, make sure that the bottom edge of the panel higher up the slope laps onto the panel below.

5 Make screw holes across the bottom if necessary. Make the holes at intervals of about 450mm across the panel immediately above the cross timbers. Melt the holes with a fine soldering iron, start them with a bradawl, or use a blunt bit in a drill.

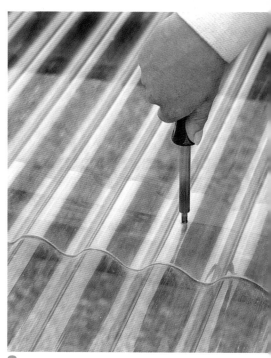

6 Drive in the screws; do not over tighten them or the plastic may split.

7 When the screws are fixed, push on screw caps. They will click into place.

8 Fit a new flashing strip (page 394) and press it down well into the valleys.

9 Seal the edges where the layers overlap with transparent waterproof glazing tape.

What can go wrong with the house exterior

Cladding Timber cladding, which forms part of an exterior wall, must be protected by preservative or paint if it is not to be affected by damp, otherwise wet rot may set in (page 246–7). Plastic cladding is not affected by damp but gaps surrounding the cladding must be tightly sealed. Follow the same procedure as for sealing gaps round window frames (page 204).

Brick walls Facing brick naturally absorbs a certain amount of rainwater, which penetrates partly into the wall. When the weather dries up, the moisture evaporates and no harm is done. In older houses, some bricks may have become over porous so that they do not dry completely. This could lead to damp penetrating indoors.

External walls Rain beating upon an external wall will be partially absorbed. Water from a dripping overflow pipe (page 339) may splash onto a wall.

Faults in a damp-proof course may allow water to rise from the ground and soak the wall. To install a damp-proof course, see page 411. Soil heaped over a damp-proof course can also cause damp.

Defective pointing will allow water to penetrate the outer leaf (the outer skin of bricks). For repointing, see page 408.

Excessive damp in an external wall should be dealt with as soon as possible before it can damage the interior. You can usually see the damp patch because the wet brickwork or masonry is a different colour from the dry parts.

Window and door frames Make sure there are no gaps around window and door frames (page 204). If rain soaks between the masonry and the frame, rot may set into the timber and must be removed (pages 412–13). Maintain the paintwork also (page 414–15) to prevent rot.

Renderings Cracks and gaps in a rendered surface may allow damp to penetrate and be held in the wall. In extreme cases, this can lead to blisters which must be cut away before the rendering is repaired. For repairing cracks, and patching rendering, see pages 408–9.

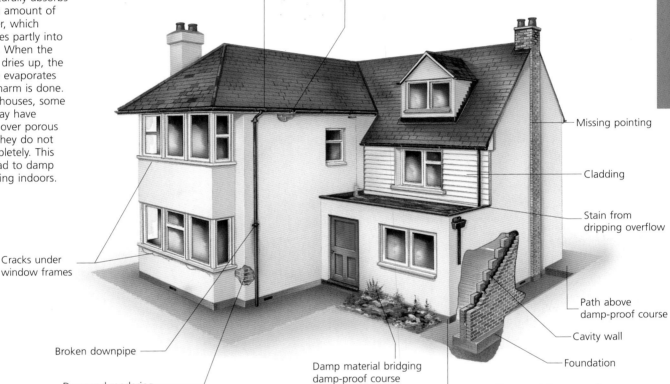

Leaves blocking gutter · Dripping from sagging gutter

Missing pointing

Cladding

Stain from dripping overflow

Path above damp-proof course

Cavity wall

Foundation

Damaged damp-proof course

Cracks under window frames

Broken downpipe

Damaged rendering

Damp material bridging damp-proof course

Gutters A gutter may leak at the joints between sections; it may become blocked and overflow; or it may sag so that water does not run away properly. In each case water may soak into the wall and penetrate to the inside, causing damp and damage to the decoration. Even on a cavity wall, water may find a way from the outer to the inner leaf of brickwork.

Cast-iron gutter sections are usually sealed with putty at joints and bolted together. The putty may disintegrate in time and, in extreme cases, bolts may rust and drop out. A plastic gutter may leak because the clip which seals two sections together has become loose, or because the neoprene gasket has perished, or because the gutter has an incorrect fall, and water spills over.

Sometimes screws holding gutter brackets to the fascia board rust away or the fascia board itself might rot, causing the brackets to move and the gutter sections to sag. For cleaning, aligning and repairing roof gutters, see pages 400–401.

Downpipes The most common problem with downpipes is that they become blocked – and if they (or the gutters leading to them) overflow or leak, damp may start in the walls.

Most downpipes first get blocked at the top and then are often obstructed farther down as the blockage sinks down the pipe under pressure of rain. For clearing blockages, see page 402.

Cast-iron pipes may crack if damp material stuck inside freezes. When they thaw the pipes will leak and the leaks may cause damage. For repairing cracked downpipes, see page 401.

Cavity walls Problems arise with cavity walls when the wall ties which link the outer and inner leaves are bridged by a mortar dropped during construction of the house. It acts as a wick, carrying moisture across the cavity to the interior wall. Cavity walls should be free of all damp before you have the cavity insulated.

Treating the external face of the wall with a silicone water repellent will cure the damp.

Mortar between bricks may become highly porous and carry water into the wall. This fault often becomes apparent after a freeze – as the water expands, it breaks up the mortar, which will crumble and fall out of joints. For how to repair the damage, see page 408.

Re-aligning a gutter

If water forms a pool, even in a cleaned gutter, instead of running away to the downpipe, the fixing screw holding the support bracket or the gutter itself at that point may be loose.

Remove the screw, tap a wall plug into the screw hole and re-screw the bracket or gutter with a new zinc-plated screw. If, when you check, you find that no screws are loose, or conversely that several are loose, the fall of the gutter may need correcting. You may have to remove a section of gutter to reach the screws.

Tools *Ladder with a stand-off bracket; hammer; screwdriver; drill with wood bit or high-speed-steel bit, or both.*

Materials *Wall plugs; zinc-plated No. 8 or No. 10 screws; two or more 150mm nails; string and nails.*

1 Drive a long, strong nail into the fascia board near each end of the loose section of gutter, immediately below it, to support it. If the loose section is longer than 2m or the gutter is iron, drive in more nails to give it sufficient support.

2 Remove the screws that hold the gutter or its supporting brackets.

3 Fix a string line along the length of the fascia board as described in Replacing cast-iron guttering with plastic (page 404–5), but put it immediately under the guttering. Give it a fall towards the downpipe of 15–20mm in every 3m.

4 If the gutter is on brackets, as most gutters are, unscrew those that are letting the gutter sag and move them left or right slightly to new positions so that you can screw into solid wood; make sure the new screw positions align with the string line to give the correct fall.

Alternatively If the gutter is screwed direct to the fascia, raise it to align correctly with the string line and drill new holes through the gutter and into the fascia, about 50mm to the side of the original holes. Refit the gutter using new zinc-plated screws.

Alternatively If the screws through the gutter have been driven into the ends of the roof rafters, not into a fascia board, fix a string line and adjust the position of the screws to bring the gutter to the correct fall. You may have to remove a tile or slate temporarily so that you can reach the screws (pages 390 and 391).

Treating rusted gutters

Treat rust as soon as you are aware of its presence. The longer it is left, the more damage will be done and the greater the size of the repair job.

Before you start Make sure you have safety goggles to protect your eyes from flying particles when removing rust. Do not rub the metal too vigorously – it does not have to shine – just remove the rust. If the inside of the gutter cannot be seen from any upstairs window, you can use up left-over gloss paint of any colour instead of buying bitumen paint.

Tools *Ladder with a stand-off bracket; safety goggles; strong work gloves; wire brush or electric drill fitted with wire cup brush or wheel; emery cloth; paintbrush. Perhaps filling knife.*

Materials *Rust-neutralising primer; black bitumen paint or left-over gloss paint. Perhaps roof-and-gutter sealant or glass-fibre filler.*

1 Rub off smaller rust spots with the emery cloth.

2 Remove larger patches of rust with the wire brush or brush wheel fitted in the drill.

3 Apply a coat of rust-neutralising primer to the cleaned parts; and to the rest of the inside of the gutter as well, if you wish.

4 Seal any small cracks in the gutter with roof-and-gutter sealant.

5 If there is a larger crack or hole, fill it with a glass-fibre filler of the kind used for car body repairs. Be sure to smooth the filling thoroughly so there is no roughness to hold water or silt.

6 Apply a coat of black bitumen or gloss paint. Allow it to dry and apply a second.

Cleaning an overflowing gutter

Gutters should be cleaned out and checked for damage each year. The job is best done in late autumn after all the leaves have fallen.

Before you start Wear sturdy work gloves to avoid scraping your hands on rough or rusty edges or on tiles or slates.

Tools *Ladder with a stand-off bracket; protective gloves; small trowel; bucket; piece of hardboard or a large rag. Possibly a hosepipe.*

1 Put the piece of hardboard at the bottom of the downpipe to prevent debris from getting into the gully or the drain, where it could cause a blockage.

Alternatively If the downpipe goes direct into the ground, stuff the rag in the top of it.

2 Scoop out any silt, grit or other debris with the trowel and put it into the bucket. Take care not to let anything drop into the downpipe. Take care not to let any debris fall down the walls because it may cause stains that are hard to remove.

3 Unblock the downpipe and pour three or four buckets of water slowly into the gutter at the end farthest from the pipe.

Alternatively Use a hosepipe to lead water there. The water should flow quickly and smoothly to the downpipe, leaving the gutter empty.
• If a pool of water remains, the gutter needs realigning (see left).
• If the water leaks through cracks or bad joints, repair the gutter (facing page).
• If the water starts to overflow at the downpipe, the pipe needs cleaning out (page 402).

Repairing leaking gutter joints

Sometimes you can spot a dripping gutter from indoors, but occasionally walk round the house during heavy rain to check on all your gutters.

Rainwater dripping through gutters and splashing the house walls will cause a water stain on the outside wall and, after a time, moss and algae will grow, disfiguring the wall. If the leak is not cured, damp will penetrate the walls, causing damage indoors. Damp quickly ruins decorations and eventually causes rot in timbers.

Leaking metal gutters

A metal gutter is difficult to take apart if the nuts and bolts have corroded, so try to seal the leak by injecting roof-and-gutter sealant into the joint with an applicator gun. First scrape the joint clean and dry it with a hot-air gun. If the leak persists, you will have to dismantle and reseal the joint. Wear strong gloves to protect your hands from rough metal.

Tools *Ladder with a stand-off bracket; gloves; safety goggles; spanner; hammer; wire brush; old chisel; small trowel; paintbrush; narrow-bladed filing knife. Perhaps a junior hacksaw and nail punch.*

Materials *Metal primer; roof-and-gutter sealant; nut and bolt of correct size.*

1 Undo the nut securing the bolt in the joint piece.

Alternatively If the nut will not move, cut through the bolt with a hacksaw and take out the shank with nail punch and hammer.

2 Gently hammer the joint piece to separate it from the gutter sections.

3 With the joint dismantled, chisel away the putty and clean rust from the whole joint area with the wire brush. Scoop away the debris with the trowel.

4 Apply a coat of metal primer to the gutter ends and the joint piece and leave it to dry.

5 Spread roof-and-gutter sealant onto the joint piece and reposition the gutter sections on it.

6 Secure the joint with the new nut and bolt.

Leaking plastic gutters

Where pieces of gutter join, or connect with a downpipe, they are clipped to a connector or union piece which has gaskets in it to make the union watertight.

Leakages caused by dirt forcing the seal slightly apart can be cured by cleaning. Squeeze the sides of the gutter inwards to release it from the union piece. If there is no dirt, the gaskets may need renewing.

Tools *Ladder with a stand-off bracket; filling knife.*

Materials *New gaskets or roof-and-gutter sealant.*

1 Squeeze the sides of the gutter sections in order to release them from the clips of the union piece.

2 Gently raise the end of each section of gutter in turn until you can see the gasket in the union piece. Peel the gasket away.

3 Fit the new gaskets, pressing them well into place.

Alternatively Fill the grooves for the gaskets with sealant.

4 Gently squeeze each gutter section in at sides to ease it back into the union piece clips.

Plastic guttering parts

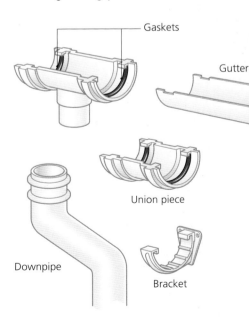

Gaskets

Gutter

Union piece

Downpipe

Bracket

Securing loose downpipes

A downpipe is held to the wall by retaining clips which are screwed into the mortar joints at intervals of about a metre.

If the pipe is not firmly held, it vibrates in strong winds, and this can loosen its joints. The sections of downpipe slot loosely one into another; do not seal them together.

Cast-iron pipes

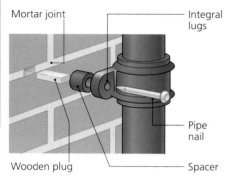

Mortar joint
Integral lugs
Screw
Pipe nail
Wooden plug
Spacer

The lugs that hold cast-iron pipes are an integral part of the pipe and are fixed with large nails called pipe nails to wooden plugs inserted in the mortar joints. If only the nails are loose, take them out and fill the hole with wood filler or insert a wall plug into it. Drive the pipe nails back in, or drive in 38mm No. 10 galvanised screws instead.

If the wooden plugs in the wall have come loose or rotted; you will have to remove them and fix new ones.

Tools *Ladder with stand-off bracket; pliers; saw; hammer. Perhaps a screwdriver.*

Materials *Softwood plugs slightly larger than the old ones; wood preservative. Perhaps 38mm No. 10 galvanised screws.*

1 Pull out the old pipe nails with pliers. You can use the nails again if they come out undamaged.

2 Remove the spacers that hold the downpipe away from the wall and keep them on one side.

3 Remove one or more sections of pipe to give access to the plugs. Sections are slotted together. Raise one as high as it will go on the section above to free the lower end from the section below.

4 Take out and discard the plugs.

5 Cut new plugs, sawing and planing or chiselling them until they almost fit the holes. Treat plugs with wood preservative and tap them into place with a hammer.

6 Put back the piece or pieces of downpipe that you have removed.

7 Set the spacers in position behind each pair of lugs and drive the pipe nails through the holes to hold the downpipe securely.

Alternatively Set the spacers in position and secure the lugs by driving galvanised screws through the holes.

Plastic downpipes

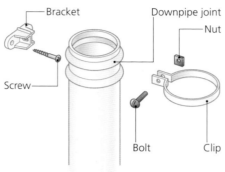

Bracket
Downpipe joint
Nut
Screw
Bolt
Clip

If a plastic downpipe comes loose from the wall, check the screws and the plastic or fibre wall plugs to see if they need renewing to give a better fixing. Use 38mm No. 10 galvanised screws.

It might be easier to move the clip up or down a little to a different mortar joint, and drill and plug new holes to get a firm fixing. Repair the old holes with mortar or exterior filler. Match the colour of the rest of the mortar to make the repair discreet.

Do not move a clip fixed at a joint in the downpipe system because it strengthens the joint. You could exchange a one-piece clip for a two-piece clip, or vice-versa, to give different fixing positions for screws.

Unblocking a downpipe

Overflow from a gutter may be caused by a blocked downpipe.

Before you start Check what is causing the blockage. It could be a ball, a bird's nest or some other object that you can simply lift out. But the most likely obstruction is a collection of wind-blown leaves lodged in the mouth of the downpipe.

A pipe with a swan-necked section at the top is more likely to become blocked than a straight downpipe.

Another indication of a blocked down-pipe is water seeping out during heavy rain from a joint where sections of downpipe connect. Because the joints are loose, not sealed, you can tell straight away where the blockage is; it is in the section immediately below the leaking joint.

Obstructions near the top

If the downpipe is blocked near the top, you can usually clear it by probing with a length of wire. Cover the drain at the bottom of the pipe to prevent any debris from falling into it. Hook out debris if you can; if you cannot, probe until it becomes loose. Flush away remaining loose debris by pouring buckets of water down the pipe or playing a strong jet of water down it from a hose. If the pipe is straight, not swan-necked, tie rags firmly to the end of a stick (such as a bamboo garden cane) to form a ball and push the obstruction loose with it.

Obstructions out of reach

Hire a flexible drain rod to clear an obstruction lower down a pipe or in a swan-necked pipe. Or, as a last resort, dismantle the lower part of the downpipe.

Tools *Ladder with a stand-off bracket; screwdriver or pliers or box spanner; long stick. Perhaps a cold chisel and claw hammer.*

1 On a plastic downpipe, remove the screws that hold the pipe clips to the wall. Work from the bottom and remove the screws and clips up to the point it leaks. If the pipe is held by two-part brackets, undo the bolts holding the rings to the back plates; leave the back plates in place.

If the pipe is cast-iron, use pliers to pull out the large pipe nails that hold the lugs to the wall. If they are rusted, use a cold chisel and claw hammer to prise the lugs from the wall; keep the nails for re-use.

2 As you free the clips or lugs that hold it, free each section of pipe from the section below and lift it away from the wall.

3 Use a long stick to push out any obstructions inside the sections.

4 Replace the pipe section by section, working from the top down, and screw or bolt back in place the clips (or nail the lugs) that hold the section to the wall.

Preventing blockages

Wire or plastic covers are sold in different sizes for fitting in mouths of downpipes.
• If there is a hopper at the top of the downpipe, fit fine-mesh wire netting over the top, securing it with fine galvanised wire.
• If there are large deciduous trees nearby, it is worth covering gutters. Lay a strip of plastic netting over a gutter to overlap the top by about 50mm at each side. About every 1m along it, thread a length of twine through the overlaps from the underside of the gutter and tie it firmly to hold the mesh taut. Check the netting surface regularly during autumn; if leaves coat it, rain cannot enter the gutter and will spill over it.

Planning a plastic gutter system

Several similar systems of black, white, brown or grey plastic guttering are made; they differ mainly in the way the lengths of gutter are joined.

Before you start Decide what system you want: in some systems, lengths of gutter overlap and clip into support brackets; in others, a union piece connects lengths of gutter and may or may not have a bracket.

Gutters are rounded or square in cross-section. Most types are clipped onto brackets which support them from below, but some square styles have brackets fixed above them. Five widths of gutter are made to give different carrying capacities to suit the area of roof draining into it.

An undersized gutter will not cope with heavy rain. If you are replacing an old gutter system, use the same size as before, or a size that is slightly larger.

Measure the total length round the fascia to estimate how much guttering to buy. Measure the height from the gutter down to the gully to estimate how much pipe to buy for each downpipe.

You will need a variety of fittings to connect the parts and hold them in place – for example, union pieces, angled pieces for corners, support brackets, downpipe brackets and downpipe shoes.

Deep gutter Guttering with a deep curve serves large roofs better than the standard half-round type.

Adaptors Adaptors will link plastic guttering to cast-iron, larger plastic guttering to smaller sizes, and rounded to square section guttering. However, it is not always possible to link one manufacturer's guttering to another's.

COLLECTING RAINWATER

Position water butts beneath downpipes from the gutters on your house, outbuildings and greenhouse to collect the run-off of rainwater from your roofs for use in the garden in times of drought. Easy-to-install DIY water butts and pipes connect to the guttering system. Alternatively, complete ready-made systems are available which can be plumbed in immediately.

Water butts should be covered to prevent the growth of algae. They should also have an overflow pipe at the top, feeding into the mains drainage system or soak-away, otherwise you will have to drain off water from time to time.

If space permits, you can link a few butts together to ensure you waste as little rainfall as possible.

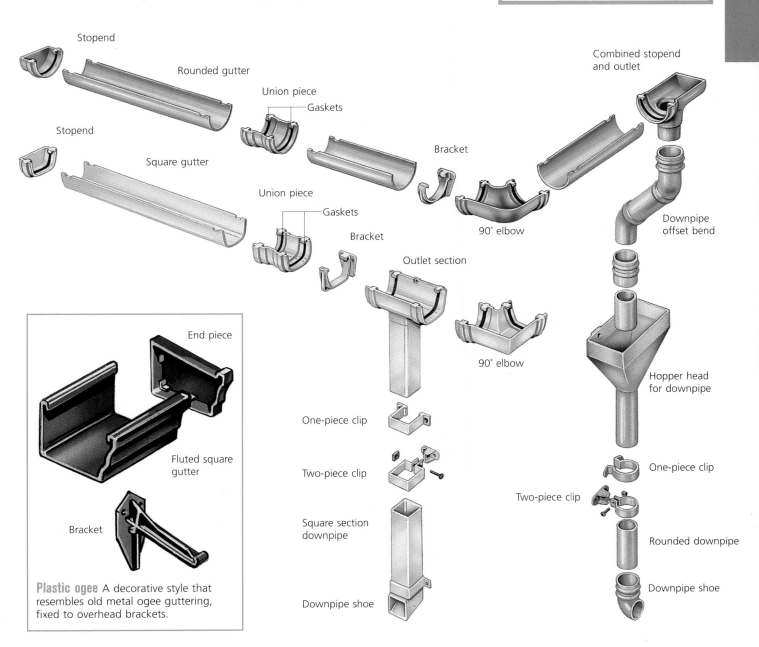

Stopend

Rounded gutter

Union piece

Gaskets

Stopend

Square gutter

Union piece

Gaskets

Bracket

Bracket

Combined stopend and outlet

Downpipe offset bend

90° elbow

Outlet section

90° elbow

One-piece clip

Two-piece clip

Square section downpipe

Downpipe shoe

Hopper head for downpipe

One-piece clip

Two-piece clip

Rounded downpipe

Downpipe shoe

End piece

Fluted square gutter

Bracket

Plastic ogee A decorative style that resembles old metal ogee guttering, fixed to overhead brackets.

Replacing cast-iron guttering with plastic

When a cast-iron guttering and downpipe system becomes too rusty to repair, you will have to replace it.

Before you start Plastic guttering is easier and cheaper to fit and needs no painting. Wear strong work gloves to handle the cast-iron; rusty edges can cause nasty cuts.

Tools *Ladder with a stand-off bracket; gloves; spanner; hacksaw; nail punch; claw hammer; rope; large screwdriver; small blowtorch; slim masonry chisel; string line and nails; plumb line; steel measuring tape; file drill with masonry bit; pointing trowel; filling knife; paintbrush; chalk. Perhaps a gutter notching tool and a wrecking bar.*

Materials *Plastic gutter; union pieces; brackets with 25mm No. 8 galvanised screws; stopends; gutter outlet section; downpipe; offset bends; solvent cement; pipe clips with 38mm No. 10 galvanised screws; wall plugs; mortar for pointing; filler and paint for fascia board. Perhaps gutter angle; downpipe shoe.*

Removing old pipes and gutters

Cast-iron sections, which may be 2–3m long, are very heavy and difficult to handle when standing on a ladder. If possible, have a helper to support each section and help you to lower it to the ground by rope.

1 Use a spanner to undo the bolts holding the gutter sections together. If you cannot, cut through each bolt with the hacksaw, then tap its shank upwards with a nail punch and hammer to free it.

2 Give sharp hammer taps at the joints where the sections meet. They will be sealed together with old putty or mastic.

3 Tie a rope round the middle of each gutter section as you free it. Lift it off the brackets and lower it to a helper who can steer it clear of windows and walls below.

4 Try with a screwdriver to undo the screws holding the brackets to the fascia board. If they are rusted in, heat the heads with a narrow blowtorch flame to expand the metal and break the grip of the rust. If the screws still will not turn, prise the brackets away from the board and pull the screws out with them. Use a slim masonry chisel and claw hammer to prise them off.

5 Take out the pipe nails holding the downpipe lugs to the wall. Use pliers or, if the nails are rusted, a wrecking bar to prise the lugs away from the wall. Work down the wall and, as you free each pair

TAKING DOWN OGEE GUTTERING

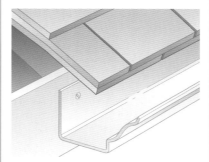

Ogee guttering does not rest on brackets but is screwed direct to the fascia board through its straight back. It is unwise to take it down without a helper. Once you take out the screws from one end, the gutter is unsupported and its weight will unbalance you. Even with a helper to support the gutter section, it is best to work from a scaffold tower, which you can hire. Anchor the tower firmly before tackling each section of gutter. Separate the gutter joints and remove the screws as for other types of cast-iron guttering.

of lugs, lift out the section of downpipe from the section below. Use the masonry chisel and hammer to take out the wooden blocks from the wall.

6 If the downpipe goes straight into the ground to connect with a gully, break up the concrete or other surround to free it.

Repairs and preparations

1 Repair the fascia board with exterior filler if necessary, before repainting it (pages 414–15). Repair damaged pointing where necessary (page 408).

2 Nail a plumb line to drop from the fascia to the gully where the downpipe will discharge. Mark its position with chalk on the fascia and wall, then remove it.

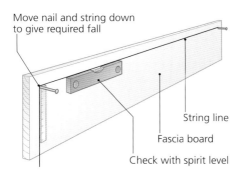

Move nail and string down to give required fall

String line

Fascia board

Check with spirit level

3 Fix a taut string line as a guide for positioning the brackets. Fit it as close up to the tiles or slates as you can. Run it from the downpipe position to the farthest point of the guttering that will drain into it. This may be at the end of the fascia board or at an angle in the guttering.

Check with a spirit level that the string is horizontal, and mark its level at the downpipe position with chalk.

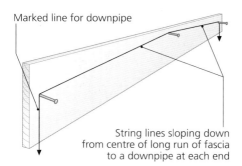

Marked line for downpipe

String lines sloping down from centre of long run of fascia to a downpipe at each end

4 Then lower the string at the chalk-mark end by the amount needed to give the correct fall and fix it taut with a nail. The fall should be 15–20mm for every 3m.

5 A long stretch of gutter may have a downpipe at each end. Fix the string line with its highest point in the centre and a fall towards each downpipe. If the outlet is in the middle of a run of gutter, fix string lines at both sides of it.

Fitting the new guttering

1 Screw a bracket in place on the fascia 200mm from the mark at the downpipe position. Align its top with the string line.

2 Screw another bracket in place 150mm from the other end of the run of guttering, aligning it with the string line at the top.

3 Space out brackets equally between these two at intervals of about 500mm.

Alternatively Assemble the gutter on the ground and measure the distance from the centre of the downpipe outlet to the centre of the union piece joining the gutter sections – and from this point to the centre of the next union piece. Mark these distances on the fascia and screw brackets there, aligning their tops with the string. Each join will be supported by a bracket and you can then space out the brackets between at intervals of up to 1m.

4 Clip the gutter, section by section, into the brackets, fitting union pieces where necessary to join the sections. Make sure that the sections are well pressed into place. Lodge the back edge of the gutter under the bracket clip first, then press the front edge down under the other clip.

5 The final section of gutter will have to be cut. Cut it on the ground after measuring off a piece of the right length.

If it runs to the end of the fascia, let it extend 50mm beyond the end of the fascia board. Cut it with a hacksaw and smooth the cut with a file.

6 Use either a gutter notching tool or a file to cut notches in the gutter rims for the stopend clips to engage in. Fit the stopend, and clip the gutter onto its bracket and into the union piece holding it to the adjoining section.

7 If there is guttering at both sides of the outlet, fit the second run in the same way as the first.

Fitting the new downpipe

1 Measure the length of pipe needed to slope inwards from the gutter outlet to the wall. Cut pipe to this length.

2 Push the offset bends onto the pipe ends and hold this zigzag unit in position at the gutter outlet to test the fit. The lower offset bend should have its outlet the right distance from the wall to accommodate the pipe clip. Saw off more pipe if necessary to achieve the right fit.

3 Clean and wash the pipe ends and the sockets of the bends.

4 With the zigzag section held together again, make a chalk mark along the pipe and onto each offset section to show the correct alignment. Take the unit apart.

5 Apply solvent cement outside the pipe ends and inside the sockets of the bends. Assemble the parts again, lining up the chalk marks.

6 Push the zigzag unit onto the bottom of the gutter outlet.

7 Hold a downpipe section in position over the bottom of the zigzag unit. See whether the top of the downpipe section is in line with a mortar joint. If not, measure how much it needs to be raised.
 Saw off this amount plus 10mm from the bottom of the zigzag unit. The extra 10mm leaves a gap to allow for expansion of the pipe in hot weather.

8 Mark, drill and plug holes in the mortar joint to screw the pipe clip into. The distance between the screw holes depends on the type of clip you are using. Hold the clip against the wall to make marks through the holes as guides for drilling.

9 Measure down the chalk mark on the wall to mark the position for drilling holes for the next pipe clip. You may have to cut the bottom end of the section of downpipe to align the clip with a mortar joint. Remember to cut off the extra 10mm again to create an expansion gap inside the socket.

10 At the bottom, cut the pipe so that the shoe will be about 50mm clear of the gully. You may need to lift out the drain grid while you fit the shoe. If the pipe goes direct into the ground, allow enough pipe to do this.

11 Drill and plug holes for brackets between the joints of downpipe sections, spacing them equally not more than 1m apart and aligning them with mortar joints.

12 When all the holes are drilled and plugged screw the pipe clips in place.

13 If the downpipe goes direct into a gully underground, repair the concrete or other surround.

Cleaning and maintaining gullies

A gully is an underground U-trap that prevents bulky waste from flowing into the drains. It is prone to blockage.

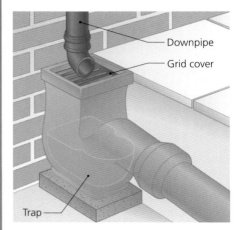

- Downpipe
- Grid cover
- Trap

A gully is fitted at the point where a downpipe or waste pipe discharges at ground level, and is then connected to the underground drains. A yard gully is similar, but is sited away from the house and collects surface water via an open grating. The trap in the gully is there to collect solid waste material, preventing it from entering the drains and causing a blockage that would be difficult to remove.

In older properties, the water discharges into a gully above a grid fitted over the trap. This grid can become blocked with leaves and other debris, resulting in waste water splashing over the surrounding area instead of passing into the trap.

In newer properties, waste pipes discharge into soil stacks, and downpipes discharge into back-inlet gullies. Here the downpipe passes directly through the grating and into the trap, so avoiding overflow problems. If the gully does not have to act as a yard gully, a screw-down cover provides access to the trap.

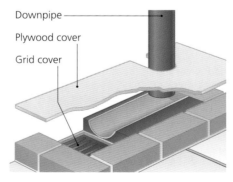

- Downpipe
- Plywood cover
- Grid cover

Channel gullies taking waste water via a half-round channel are especially prone to grid blockages. Prevent these by putting a cover on the gully. Cut it from outdoor-grade plywood 13–19mm thick. Make a hole for the waste pipe to pass through.

Clearing a blockage

1 Clear all debris from the gully grating. If necessary, prise out the grating and scrub it in hot soapy water.

2 If the blockage is deeper, remove the grating. Wear long rubber gloves or put your arm in a plastic bag. Reach into the trap, which may be up to 600mm deep, and scoop out as much debris as you can.

3 If the obstruction is too solid to scoop out, break it down with a garden trowel.

4 When the gully is cleared, scrub the sides with a nylon pot scourer and hose them down with a fierce jet of water. Disinfect all gloves and tools afterwards.

5 If you cannot find an obstruction in the gully, the blockage may be farther down the drain; see Clearing blocked drains, opposite.

Repairing a channel gully

A channel sometimes runs parallel with the house wall to lead water into a gully entrance or to hold water that comes too fast for the gully to take. The channel can crack or become loose. The rendering around it can also crack or develop hollows where water lodges and stagnates.

Repair damaged rendering with a mix of one part cement to four parts soft sand, with PVA building adhesive added for a better bond. Alternatively, buy a small bag of dry-mix sand-cement mortar to use instead, but add PVA adhesive to improve adhesion. Give the repair a smooth finish so that water does not collect.

Renewing a damaged gully

You will have to chip out the old one and the surrounding brick and rendering. You can buy ready-made vitrified clay channels from builders' merchants. Use the same mortar mix as for rendering repairs.

Tools *Chalk; cold chisel; club hammer; offcut of hardboard or thick card; trowel.*

Materials *Bricks; length of channel; mortar.*

1 To cut the channel to length, first measure and mark the length at several

> **HELPFUL TIP**
>
> If there is no brick surround to the gully entry, it is worth making one (see Laying bricks or walling blocks, page 468). It will retain small amounts of water if there is a minor blockage, and will prevent splashing or flooding of the surrounding area.

points round the pipe and join the marks with a chalk line. Lay the channel on a heap of sand and use the chisel and hammer to chip round the marked line until the channel breaks along it. Alternatively, use an angle grinder if you have one to cut the channel. Wear goggles to protect your eyes from flying dust and chippings.

2 Put a piece of hardboard over the gully inlet to prevent debris from getting in.

3 Chip out the damaged channel and the mortar and any bricks round it. If the bricks round the gully entrance are damaged, chip these out as well. Brush up the debris.

4 Mix the mortar and spread a thick layer where the channel will lie. Bed down the channel on it, setting it so that it slopes slightly towards the gully.

5 Lay a course of bricks (page 468) on edge to make a low retaining wall round the channel and gully. Set them on a bed of mortar and leave a gap of at least 25mm between the channel and the bricks alongside it. Nearer the gully the gap may need to be wider.

6 Fill the gap between the channel and the bricks with mortar.

7 Slope the mortar smoothly up to the brick surround and make sure there are no hollows to trap water.

Clearing blocked drains

Below ground, pipes carry water and waste from the house to the main drain outside the boundary of the property, or to a cesspool or septic tank. Rainwater may be led separately into the drain or into a soakaway.

Before you start Remember that the pipes below ground are laid in straight lines for as much of their route as possible. Where a change of direction is needed, the bend should be less than a right angle and there should be an inspection chamber there. A manhole cover identifies the chambers. An older property may have an interceptor chamber near the boundary before the house drain joins the main drain (see right).

The first sign of a blocked drain may be the failure of WCs and baths to drain quickly and efficiently, or an overflowing inspection chamber or gully. A gully may be cleared by cleaning (facing page). Otherwise you will have to clear the drain with rods. You can hire rods and various heads. Wear rubber gloves for the work.

Tools *Drain rods fitted with a 100mm diameter rubber plunger; pair of long rubber gloves; strong garden spade; hose; disinfectant; watering can.*

1 Locate the blockage. You will have to lift the manhole covers; a strong garden spade will raise the edge enough for you to grasp the cover. Inspect the chamber that is nearer to the main drain, septic tank or cesspool than the overflowing chamber or gully. If it is empty, the blockage is in the drain between this chamber and the higher one or the gully. If the chamber is full, inspect the chamber next nearest to the main drain or septic tank. If the chamber nearest the main drain is full, the blockage is between it and the main drain. If the drain leads to a septic tank and the last chamber is full, have the tank emptied.

2 To clear the blockage in a main drain system, insert the rod fitted with the plunger into a chamber at one end of the

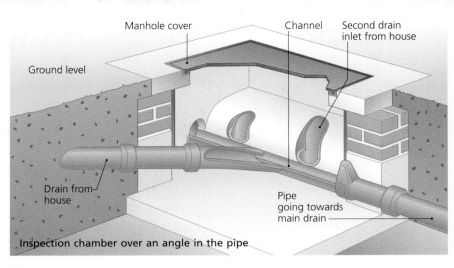

Inspection chamber over an angle in the pipe

Labels: Manhole cover, Channel, Second drain inlet from house, Ground level, Drain from house, Pipe going towards main drain

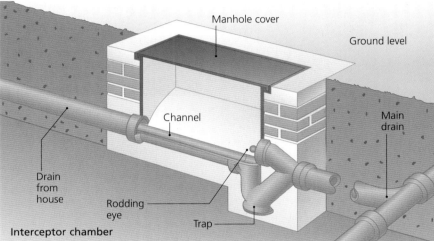

Interceptor chamber

Labels: Manhole cover, Ground level, Channel, Main drain, Drain from house, Rodding eye, Trap

Interceptor chambers If you have to clear a blockage between an interceptor chamber on your property and the main drain, you will have to insert the rods through the rodding eye. At this chamber, the drain drops through a U-trap similar to the one in a gully. The trap is there to prevent waste from the main drain entering your house drains, but it also prevents you from pushing rods through. Above the mouth of the trap there is a short projection of pipe with a plug in it. When you locate and pull out the plug, you can insert the drain rods through the hole, or rodding eye.

The trap, however, may still be blocked and you will have to scoop out the blockage with an old garden trowel bent to a right angle. When the chamber and trap are clear, hose them down thoroughly to make sure waste can flow out easily. You can either replace the plug or you can mortar a piece of tile over the eye. If you need to open the rodding eye again, the tile will knock off easily with a crowbar and hammer.

blocked section; it does not matter which of the two. If it is the empty chamber, you can see where the mouth of the pipe is, but if you work from the full chamber, you will have to probe with the plunger until you find the mouth.

3 Add more rods as necessary to work the plunger along the pipe to the blockage. Always turn the rods clockwise as you work; if you turn them counter-clockwise, they may unscrew and be left in the drain to cause a greater problem. Keep pushing against the obstruction and then withdrawing the plunger a little way.

If this will not shift the blockage, withdraw the rods and exchange the plunger for a corkscrew attachment, which will break up a tightly packed obstruction.

4 Complete the clearance by directing a strong jet of water down the drain from a hosepipe, or by filling the bath and sink and releasing the water in one gush.

5 Hose down the rods and gloves thoroughly and drench them with diluted disinfectant poured from a watering can.

Testing drains

If the drains are not blocked, but a persistent foul smell or unexpectedly wet ground make you suspect that there is a leak somewhere, arrange for the environmental health department to test the drains. You can get in touch with the department at your local authority offices.

Minor repairs to walls

Cracks, deteriorating mortar, damp and damaged brickwork are all easily repaired when the problem is small.

Repointing a wall

Where mortar joints in a wall are cracked or crumbling, use a raking out tool or a club hammer and plugging chisel to take out the old mortar to a depth of about 15mm, ready for repointing.

Before you start One problem when you are patching a number of joints, is to match the colour of the mortar with that of the surrounding joints. The only way to do this is to experiment with a few different mortar mixes (page 467), using varying amounts of sand and lime. Take a note of each mix and repoint a few joints at a time. Wait a week or two for the mortar to dry thoroughly and show its final colour before you decide on the best mix to complete the job.

Carry out repointing as in pointing (page 470), matching the shape with the surrounding joints. Before you apply new mortar, clean any dust from the joints then brush water into them. If you do not wet them, the joints will soak up moisture from the mortar and it will dry out too fast.

Dealing with a crack

Mortar is meant to be weaker than bricks or masonry so that it offers less resistance if movement beneath the foundations causes any strain on the wall. The mortar will crack before the bricks or masonry.

A single crack confined to a mortar joint, even through several courses, usually indicates limited amount of soil settlement. A repair can be made by repointing.

A brick may be cracked by minor settlement. You can replace it yourself. If a crack runs through more than the odd brick, there is a more serious strain on the foundations. Get a professional builder to deal with it as soon as possible.

Replacing a damaged brick

Remove a damaged brick by chipping away the surrounding mortar with a club hammer and cold chisel.

You can speed up the process by drilling a series of holes into the mortar first. Drill to a depth of about 100mm, then cut into the mortar all round to release the damaged brick. Chop as much mortar out of the resulting cavity as you can, ready for the new brick to be fitted. Dampen the cavity very well. Spread mortar on the base of the cavity and on the top and sides of the new brick. Tap the brick into the cavity with the trowel handle. When it is properly seated, trim away the excess mortar. Point the joints to match the others on the wall.

Dealing with efflorescence

The white powdery deposit called efflorescence is caused by dampness, which draws chemical salts from the bricks or mortar to the surface. It is harmless, and will disappear from a newly built wall once it has dried out.

You can discourage efflorescence by coating a wall with a silicone-based water repellent (below). If efflorescence does form, brush it off or treat it with a chemical masonry cleaner available from a builders' merchant. Do not wash off efflorescence; the damp aggravates the problem.

Keeping out damp with silicone water repellent

Silicone water repellent will normally cure damp problems on external walls. It stops rain from getting into the brick but it lets the wall 'breathe' so that moisture already in the material can evaporate.

If damp patches persist, you should get professional advice.

Tools *Bucket of water; wire brush; a clean old paintbrush, 100–150mm wide; paint kettle. Perhaps a ladder.*

Materials *Silicone water repellent such as Aquaseal 66; white spirit for cleaning brush.*

1 Clean the surface with water and the wire brush. Wait until the surface has dried.

2 Tape paper over the window glass, frame and ledges. You will not be able to remove splashes of silicone from them. Cover any part of a drive or path adjoining the wall you are treating. The silicone could otherwise cause blotches.

3 Pour the repellent into the paint kettle and apply a generous amount of the liquid with an old paintbrush, so that you can see it flowing down the wall.

4 If the surface soaks up all the liquid – because it is very porous – apply a second coat before the first coat dries.

5 Use white spirit to clean the paintbrush and the paint kettle when the job is finished.

Repairing cracks on a rendered wall

Before you start Hairline crazing on the surface of rendering does not need filling. Cracks that go deeper than the surface do need filling to keep the wall weatherproof. Fill the cracks with exterior filler or with rendering. Filler is convenient but uneconomical for more than one or two cracks. You can buy dry-mixed rendering in small quantities or you can make your own. The repair will show until the wall is repainted; an invisible repair is impossible to achieve.

Tools *Filling knife; brush; wet sponge or cloth; old paintbrush. Perhaps a bolster chisel and club hammer and a ladder.*

Materials *PVA adhesive; rendering or exterior filler.*

1 Draw the edge of a filling knife through the crack to form it into a V with the point of the V at the surface of the rendering and the wider part against the wall.

You can use a bolster chisel and club hammer instead of the filling knife if you find it easier.

The shape will anchor the filler below the surface and the crack is unlikely to open again.

2 Brush out the fragments and dust from the cavity to leave it as clean as possible.

3 Wet the cavity with a sponge or cloth dipped in water.

4 Paint all the inside of the cavity with PVA adhesive to improve adhesion of the filler.

5 Press the filler or rendering into the crack with the filling knife. Prod the knife into the cavity to make sure there are no air pockets in it. Smooth the filling level with the wall surface. Redecorate the wall when the filler has dried.

Patching large holes

Before you start When large slabs of rendering fall away from the wall, it is usually because a weak rendering mix has been used and become porous, or because damp has penetrated behind the layer of rendering, perhaps through a crack.

Sometimes the rendering may appear intact, when in fact it has separated from the wall behind. Check the rendering from time to time, tapping it lightly with a hammer; undamaged areas will make dead sound while defective areas give a hollow sound or fall away.

Carry out rendering work in mild weather. Frost can freeze the water in the rendering, which may cause premature cracking.

Preparing the rendering Mix the rendering from six parts plastering sand, one part cement and one part hydrated lime. Do not use builders' sand or the rendering will crack when it dries out. Use enough water to make the mixture easy to work with – not too stiff, not too sloppy.

Mix up small batches at a time. The rendering will become too stiff to spread after about 20 minutes. It is applied in two coats – a thick undercoat called the floating coat, and a thinner finishing coat.

Tools *Bolster chisel; club hammer; brush; wet sponge or cloth; steel plastering trowel; old pointed trowel or square of wood with nails driven through to project at about 38mm intervals; straight edged length of wood longer than the width of the patch; damp sponge or clean wooden float. Perhaps a ladder and a plugging chisel.*

Materials *Rendering.*

1 Use the bolster chisel and hammer to cut away any loose rendering to leave a sound edge round the patch.

2 Clean out any crumbling joints in the brickwork or masonry. Clean them out to a depth of 15mm with the plugging chisel and club hammer. Brush out all debris.

3 Thoroughly wet the area to be repaired with a sponge or cloth soaked in water. This prevents rendering from losing moisture into the wall and drying too quickly, which could cause crumbling later.

4 Apply the first coat of rendering. Take some of the mixture on the steel trowel with the handle downwards. Spread it onto the wall, starting from the bottom of the

patch and pressing the lower edge of the trowel hard against the wall as you sweep it smoothly upwards. Continue until the rendering is smooth and about 5mm below the level of the wall surface.

5 As the rendering begins to stiffen after about 20 minutes – scratch a criss-cross of lines in it with the old trowel or spiked wood to make a key for the top coat.

6 Leave the first coat to dry for at least 14 hours, then apply the finishing coat. Use the same rendering mixture as for the floating coat. This time, start at the top left of the patch. Sweep the trowel lightly across from left to right to spread the rendering over the area, leaving it standing slightly proud of the surface.

7 Continue applying trowel loads from top to bottom down the patch spreading them from left to right. Mix more small batches of rendering as necessary, but work quickly.

8 Just before the rendering begins to set – about 15 minutes after it has been applied – draw the straight-edged piece of wood upwards over the rendering to level it with the wall. Hold the wood horizontally and make sure that you are pressing its ends firmly against the wall on either side of the patch. If any hollows are showing after levelling off, fill them quickly with more rendering and level them with the straight-edged piece of wood. As the rendering starts to set, smooth its surface gently with damp sponge or a damp wooden float.

Repairing pebbledash

It is simple enough to repair damaged pebbledash, but the repair will be visible unless the wall is to be painted because the new chippings and the rendering beneath will not match the original colour. You will need about 5kg of chippings to cover a square metre.

Tools *Cold chisel; club hammer; brush; wet sponge or cloth; steel trowel; sheet of polythene; small scoop; wooden float. Perhaps a ladder.*

Materials *Soft sand and cement or dry ready-mix rendering mortar; PVA building adhesive; water; chippings.*

1 Prepare the area for repair as for Patching large holes (left) and mix and lay on a first coat of rendering in the same way, but leave it about 15mm below the level of the wall surface.

2 Wash the chippings and drain them in a garden sieve.

3 Mix the rendering for the top coat, known as the butter coat. Use five parts of sand to one cement and add some PVA building adhesive.

Mix it to a slightly softer consistency than the first coat to make sure that it is still soft when you apply the chippings.

Apply the top coat; if you have a large area to repair, work on a section which you can complete within 20 minutes before the coat starts to set.

4 Spread a sheet of polythene on the ground below the repair. Throw small scoops of pebbles hard at the rendering until it is evenly covered. Gather up and re-use the chippings that fall to the ground.

Alternatively Lift batches of pebbles up to the wall on a hawk and use a float to push them off the hawk and into the wet mortar.

5 When you have pebbledashed the patched area, press the wooden float lightly all over it to bed the chippings into the surface. Continue in the same way until the repair is complete.

Making a hole in an external wall

When fitting a fan or an airbrick in a cavity wall, you will have to bridge the cavity with ducting or a sleeve liner. You may also have to cut through insulation material in the cavity.

Drill a guide hole right through the wall. You may need to hire extra-long masonry drill bits for this – a bit 260mm long for a solid wall, or 300mm long for a cavity wall.

Tools *Heavy-duty hammer-action power drill; long and standard length masonry drill bits; club hammer; sharp cold chisel and bolster chisel; pencil or chalk; work gloves; safety goggles; pointing trowel.*

Materials *Bag of dry ready-mixed bricklaying mortar. For a cavity wall: ducting or sleeve liner.*

1 Mark the outline of the hole on the inside wall at the required position.

2 Make sure there are no pipes or cables in the way. If the inner leaf of a cavity wall is timber-framed, make sure you will not cut through a stud (see Internal walls, pages 12–13). Adjust the position of the outline if necessary.

3 Transpose the outline to the outside wall. Drill the guide hole through the wall from inside, and mark the outside wall from where the drill tip emerges. For a circular hole, drill through the centre of the marked area. For a square or rectangular hole, drill through at each corner of the marked area. Withdraw the drill bit from time to time to cool it and remove dust.

4 Wear safety goggles to protect your eyes from flying dust and debris. Cut away the plaster at the marked area inside, using a club hammer and bolster chisel. Then switch to a cold chisel and chip away the mortar between the bricks so you can dislodge them whole if possible. Work from both sides of the wall.

5 In an uninsulated cavity wall, plug the lower section of the cavity with rags to stop debris falling into it as you cut through. If the cavity is filled with foam insulation material, cut through it with a knife.

6 When the hole is complete, fit the ducting. If it is a cavity wall, fit a liner across the wall cavity. Make good round it with mortar.

Installing an airbrick

An airbrick ventilates a room or under-floor space, and is either up near a ceiling or low down under the floorboards. Underfloor airbricks are usually sited at least 150mm above ground level, and if possible below the level of the damp-proof course.

Some airbricks are made of clay, others are made of galvanised steel or plastic. All are either one, two or three bricks deep.

The amount of air a brick lets through depends on the type of holes that it has. A single brick with a square grid has roughly 1500mm² of opening compared with the 5500mm² of a steel vent with vertical slots.

A damaged airbrick provides a way for vermin to get into the house under the floorboards. Replace it as soon as you can; do not block it temporarily as this decreases ventilation under the floor, and can lead to rot in the joists and floorboards.

> ### HELPFUL TIP
>
> If the hole is square, check that it coincides with as many whole bricks as possible to make their removal easier – adjust the outline to do so if necessary. If the hole is circular, position it round a whole brick that can be removed from the centre of the area. If you need to make a round hole for an extractor fan or a new soil pipe, you can make a hole up to 150mm in diameter with a hired combi-hammer and a core drill. This will cut a neat round hole ready for the fan duct or soil pipe to be fitted.

1 To fit a new airbrick for extra ventilation, make a hole of the required size through the wall. If the brick is to be sited below the floorboards, you will be able to work only from the outside.

2 To replace a damaged airbrick, remove the old one by chipping out the mortar round it with a hammer and cold chisel (see page 408).

3 Check the liner behind the airbrick in a cavity wall, and replace if in poor condition.

4 Before fitting the airbrick, dampen the edges of the hole with water. Spread mortar in the base of the hole and on the top and sides of the new airbrick.

5 Push the airbrick into place, or tap it in with the brick trowel handle. Trim off excess mortar from the joint and point it to match the surrounding mortar joints.

6 Poke a stick or a piece of wire through the openings in the new airbrick to make sure no mortar is caught inside them that might obstruct the flow of air.

7 If the hole goes into a room, make good the inside of the hole with a filler if necessary. Then fit a plastic grille over the opening, using either a contact adhesive or screws and wall plugs.

Choosing a cavity-wall liner

In a cavity wall, a liner behind the airbrick stops the airflow being lost in the cavity. Special terracotta liners are available from builders' merchants. Straight liners are used for an airbrick fitted below a damp-proof course. For an airbrick above the course, use an inclined liner, which raises the inside hole and stops rain blowing through. Fitting an inclined liner is a job for a builder.

> ### HOW TO DIAGNOSE DAMP
>
> If damp patches appear in mild, wet weather, water is getting in from outside. If patches appear in cold, dry spells, condensation is more likely.
>
> To get a more accurate diagnosis, stick a ring of Blu-tack on the suspect surface. Press a piece of glass onto the ring so that the glass is within 5mm of the surface. Alternatively, put a piece of aluminium foil directly on the surface and seal down its edges with adhesive tape.
>
> After about 24 hours, lift the glass or foil. If moisture has formed on the underside, damp is coming from outside. If the top side is moist, the problem is condensation.

Recognising and treating damp

Damp patches at skirting-board level on an interior wall, or a tidemark as high as a metre above floor level, are two signs of damp rising from the ground.

Damp prevention

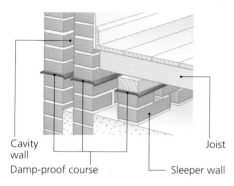

Cavity wall

Damp-proof course

Joist

Sleeper wall

To prevent damp from rising, houses are built with a damp-proof course (DPC). This is an impermeable plastic strip in modern houses, or a layer of slates or hard engineering bricks in older properties.

In most houses (except very old ones built without a DPC), you will see a thicker than usual horizontal line of pointing about 150mm above ground level, running right round the external walls. This line indicates the position of the DPC.

Defects in the damp-proofing

If the DPC deteriorates or becomes damaged, or if there is no DPC, damp is able to rise through the house walls. Rising damp will also occur if the DPC is bridged by damp material reaching above it against the outside wall – a rockery, for example, a flowerbed or even a temporary pile of building sand.

Rising damp may occur because a path or drive is too close to, or is higher than, the level of the DPC. Paths and drives must be at least 150mm below the DPC so that rainwater cannot splash above it. Where necessary, lower the path or drive surface if at all possible.

Alternatively, dig a 300mm wide channel alongside the outside wall of the house and fill it with gravel to stop rainwater splashing the wall above the DPC.

If such alterations are not practical, build a concrete skirting against the foot of the outside wall. Use a waterproofing agent in the concrete to make it impervious to water. Make the skirting reach at least 150mm higher than the path or drive and ensure there is no gap between the wall and skirting, into which water could run. Make the top of the skirting slope down from the wall so that water will run off it readily.

Installing a chemical damp-proof course

Inserting a new membrane between courses of brickwork or masonry is really a job for a professional. The best DIY solution is to install a chemical DPC. This consists of a silicone-based water-repellent fluid that is injected into the masonry until it is saturated. It then becomes impervious to water and acts as a damp-proof barrier.

DPC injection machines can be hired from most tool hire shops (to find your nearest, look in Yellow Pages under Hire Services – Tools and Equipment). The shop will supply the injection fluid, power drill and masonry drill bits of the right length and diameter. Ask for an instruction leaflet when you hire the machine, and get advice on the amount of fluid. You will need roughly 3 litres per metre of wall.

To minimise disruption to the house, the injection process is carried out entirely from the outside of the building. It is done in two stages.

Tools *Heavy-duty hammer-action power drill; masonry drill bits with depth stop; extension lead and plug-in RCD; safety goggles; work gloves; face mask; damp-proof injection machine.*

Materials *injection fluid; paraffin for cleaning machine; mortar (page 467).*

1 Drill a horizontal row of holes 75mm deep into the course of bricks or stones immediately above the existing DPC. Use a depth stop or mark the bit with tape to ensure that you drill to the correct depth. Space the holes about 120mm apart – two into each stretcher (side-on brick) and one into every header (end-on brick, only found in solid walls). If the bricks are extremely difficult to drill through – or if the walls are made of stone – make the holes in the mortar joints.

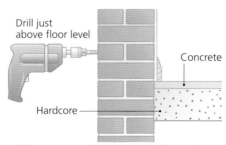

Drill just above floor level

Concrete

Hardcore

With a concrete floor, drill just above it (see above). With a suspended timber floor, drill just below it. For cavity walls, just drill into the outer leaf for the first stage of the process.

2 When all the holes have been drilled, inject the damp-proofing fluid into them. Follow the instructions supplied with the machine.

Most damp-proof injection machines consist of a pump, a suction nozzle and six injecting nozzles.

3 Insert all but one of the short injection nozzles into the prepared holes and tighten the wing nuts to hold them in place.

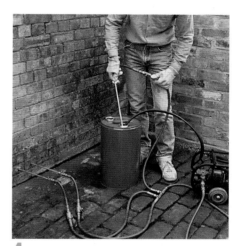

4 Hold the free nozzle over the container and turn on the pump. When fluid begins to ooze from the nozzle, turn off the pump.

5 Insert the free nozzle into a hole and tighten its wing nut. Turn on the pump. When the bricks or stones joints are saturated, fluid will 'sweat' from the surface. As soon as this happens, turn off the pump and close the nozzles.

6 Undo the wing nuts, move the nozzles to the next set of holes and repeat the procedure. Continue until you have treated every affected wall.

7 On solid walls, drill through the original holes to a new depth of 150mm. Repeat the treatment cycle, this time using the longer nozzles supplied with the machine.

8 On cavity walls, drill through the original holes into the inner leaf to a total depth of 200mm. Repeat the injection process.

9 When you have finished injecting all the holes, empty the machine and clean it with paraffin.

10 Wait for the fluid to dry; it may take two days or more. When the injected course is the same colour as the rest of the wall, fill the holes with mortar.

Repairing rot with wood-repair products

The easiest way to repair rot in a wooden window is to use a combination of wood repairing products, such as a liquid wood hardener, high-performance wood filler and wood preservative pellets.

Before you start Make sure the item you are repairing is made of painted wood – because the repair will show up on stained or varnished wood.

Tools *Old chisel, about 13mm wide; paint scraper; hot-air gun; paintbrush for applying wood hardener; filling knife; power drill; 10mm twist drill bit; hand or power sander; paintbrush for applying finishing coats to the window.*

Materials *Wood repair products (as listed above); clear wood preservative; primer, undercoat and gloss paint.*

1 Use a hot-air gun or chemical paint stripper to soften old paint, then scrape it off to reveal the extent of the rotten wood.

2 Dig away the worst of the rot with an old chisel. There is no need to cut back right into sound timber.

HELPFUL TIP

If the rot is close to a joint in the window, strengthen it with a flat steel L-shaped corner plate. Recess the corner plate to lie flush with the surface of the wood so that it is not noticeable after it is painted. See Fixing loose joints on windows, page 203.

---

3 If the timber is wet it must be dried out. Saturated wood can be covered with a flap of plastic, taped along the top, so that it dries out naturally over a couple of weeks. If it is only damp, dry it rapidly with a hot-air gun. Take care to keep the air flow away from the glass, or you might crack it.

4 When the wood is thoroughly dry, flood the rotten area with brush-loads of wood hardener. The liquid penetrates the wood, and hardens it as it dries, to give a firm base for the filler. Pay particular attention to exposed end grain. Keep flooding on the hardener until it stops soaking readily into the wood and begins to stay on the surface. Let it harden overnight.

5 Mix a small amount of the high-performance wood filler according to the instructions on the container and apply it as quickly as you can to the hole. The filler will start to harden in about five minutes – even quicker in hot weather.

6 Fill in deep cavities with a succession of layers. Because the filler hardens so quickly, even deep holes can be filled in a very short time.

7 Leave the surface of the filled hole as level as you can. After about 30 minutes it can be smoothed level with the surrounding wood with a hand or power sander. This will show up any areas where the filler is still too low.

8 Wipe away the dust and apply more filler, sanding down again afterwards so that the surface is level and smooth.

9 Drill 10mm holes about 20mm deep and 50mm apart in the wood around the repair.

10 Push one of the wood preservative pellets into each hole and then seal it with the wood filler. While the wood is dry, the pellets will remain inactive, but as soon as it becomes wet the pellets will release a fungicide which will prevent wood rot.

11 Coat any bare wood with clear wood preservative.

12 Paint the bare wood with primer and undercoat. Then give the whole window at least two coats of exterior gloss paint.

Repairing rot with new wood

The traditional way of repairing rot in a window is to cut back the rotten part to sound wood and to insert a new piece.

Before you start Wood used for the repair should match original wood in the window if it has a stained or varnished finish.

Replacing a section of sill or frame

Tools *Pencil; combination square; tenon saw or general purpose saw; chisel, about 20mm wide; mallet; vice; power drill and twist drill bits; paintbrush; plane.*

Materials *Wood to suit size of rotten section; clear wood preservative; zinc-plated No. 10 screws about 50mm long; wood dowels (same diameter as screw heads); waterproof wood adhesive; paint, varnish or preservative wood stain.*

1 Mark cutting lines on the frame about 50mm beyond signs of rot. Draw two right-angled lines on the face of the frame and then mark two more lines at about 45° to the face to form a wedge shape.

2 Using the tenon saw or general purpose saw, cut along the lines as far as possible. Brickwork may prevent you from sawing too far into a sill.

3 Complete the cut with a sharp chisel. Try to leave straight flat sides that will form a tight joint with the new wood.

4 Hold a piece of new wood against the cut-out and mark the edges of the cut-out on it with a pencil to give a cutting line.

5 Cut out the new piece with a saw and trim it with the saw or a plane until it is a good fit in the cut-out. It is better if its faces stand slightly proud of the surrounding surface.

6 Treat the cut surfaces of the frame and the new wood with clear wood preservative and allow it to dry.

PREVENTING WET ROT

Outdoor woodwork is prone to wet rot. The wood darkens and starts to crumble as the fungus that causes the condition attacks damp wood.

The best prevention is to ensure that any new timber is treated with wood preservative (page 439), and to apply regular fresh coats of wood preservative, varnish or paint. Seal round frames with a frame sealant (page 78) to prevent moisture from penetrating.

7 Glue the new wood in place, holding it with G-cramps until the glue is dry.

8 Drill pilot and clearance holes for fixing screws, about 125mm apart.

9 Drill out the holes about 15mm deep to the same diameter as the screw heads so that the heads will be sunk well below the wood surface.

10 Insert the screws and plug the holes with pieces of glued wood dowel. Drive them firmly home with the mallet.

11 Plane the faces of the insert so they are flush with the surrounding surface. Smooth with abrasive paper, and fill any gaps with exterior grade filler.

12 Finish the repair by applying paint, varnish or a preservative wood stain.

HELPFUL TIP

If the frame is to be finished with paint, it is a good idea to drill holes in the repaired area at 50mm intervals so that wood-preservative pellets can be inserted. See Repairing rot with wood-repair products, opposite.

Repairing a rotten window edge

Tools *Screwdriver; panel saw; portable workbench; plane; power drill and 6mm twist drill bit; depth stop; paintbrush.*

Materials *Piece of wood to suit the size of the rotten section; clear wood preservative; waterproof wood glue; sash cramps; 6mm dowels; paint, varnish or preservative wood stain.*

1 If the rot is on the edge of an opening casement or sash, remove it so you can work on it on your workbench. A casement window is taken off by unscrewing the hinges from the frame. For removing a sliding sash window, see page 206.

2 Saw off the rotten part by cutting right along the edge. Cut a replacement length of wood that is slightly oversize.

3 Treat the new wood and the cut surface of the window with clear wood preservative and allow it to dry. Put newspaper on the bench, and ventilate the room.

4 Apply glue to the new wood and fix it in position. Hold the repair together with a pair of sash cramps until the glue has set. Wipe away any excess adhesive.

5 Reinforce the repair by drilling through the new and old wood, and driving in glued dowels. Use a 6mm twist drill bit and dowels of the same size. Before drilling, mark the correct depth of the hole on the drill bit with a depth stop, or wrap a piece of coloured adhesive tape round it.

6 When the glue has set, cut off the protruding lengths of dowel and plane the timber to the exact width and thickness of the existing wood.

7 Fill any minor gaps with exterior wood filler. Finish bare wood with paint, varnish or preservative wood stain, depending on how the rest of the window is treated.

Decorating the outside of a house

Exterior paintwork needs repainting every five years or so. Paint deteriorates at different rates, depending on how much it is exposed to wind and rain and the direct heat of the sun and how thoroughly the surface was prepared. Check the whole house from time to time for the first signs of deterioration – usually when gloss paint loses its shine, or when emulsion becomes over-powdery to the touch.

Before you start Surfaces should be clean, stable, and stripped if the paintwork is not sound (page 72). Repair damaged areas of a rendered wall and fix gutters if they are not firmly attached to the fascia board. Some weeks before you intend to start painting, check that putty around windows is sound and, if not, replace it (page 209).

When to paint The best time to decorate is after a dry spell because paint will not take to a damp surface. Never paint in frosty conditions or rain, and do not paint on a

very windy day – or dust and dirt will be blown onto the new paint. If it starts raining, stop painting at once and wait until the surface has completely dried out.

Before you buy the paint If you are going to change your colour scheme, make sure that the new colours will fit in with the surrounding and neighbouring buildings, especially if the house is semidetached or in a terrace.

Calculate how much paint you need in the same way as for interior decorating (page 82). Rendered surfaces require more paint than smooth ones. If all the walls are to be painted, estimate the total outside area of the house by multiplying the length of the walls by the height.

The easiest way to measure the height is to climb a ladder against the wall of the house, drop a ball of string from the eaves to the ground, and then measure the length of the string. Work out the combined area of the doors and windows and deduct this figure from the total.

If you are going to paint the pipes and the outside of gutters, multiply their circumference in centimetres by their length. Divide this figure by 10,000 to give an area in square metres.

Which paint to use In general, use exterior grade gloss paint on wood and metal – gutters, downpipes, windows and doors – and use exterior grade emulsion or masonry paint on walls.

Alternatively, on bare wood you can use microporous paint, which needs no primer or undercoat. This paint allows trapped air or moisture to evaporate, reducing the risk of flaking associated with hardwoods.

You do not have to use a paint similar to the one previously used, but never put gloss paint over surfaces (mainly pipes and guttering) that are coated with bituminous paint. This tends to be less shiny than gloss and often looks thicker and softer than other paint. If you are doubtful about whether old paint contains bitumen, rub a rag soaked with petrol over the surface. If the rag picks up a brownish stain, the paint is bituminous. Either continue to use bituminous paint or, providing the surface is sound, coat it with aluminium primer-sealer, then paint with undercoat and gloss.

Safe access is most important: your ladder or scaffold tower must be secure and in good condition. Use the components of a slot-together platform tower to make a low-level, mobile work platform.

DEALING WITH PLANTS

Protect climbing plants growing up a wall from any drips or splashes of paint by untying them and covering them with paper or dust sheets. Take care not to weigh down delicate plants with heavy sheets. It is easier to paint exterior walls covered by a well-established climber or creeper after you have pruned the plant, so that you do not have to cope with masses of foliage. Ideally, fix plants to trellis, not direct to the walls.

Paint the house in this order

Complete all the preparatory work before you do any painting – but never leave a surface exposed. Protect it with at least a primer and, if possible, an undercoat before you stop work at the end of a session.

Always decorate from the top of the house downwards so that the newly painted surfaces cannot be spoilt. Paint doors and windows last. Most professional decorators work in the following order, but if you are working from a scaffold tower you may wish to paint all the surfaces you can reach before moving the tower to another site. Try to keep on painting a wall until you reach a natural break.

1 Bargeboards, fascias and soffits

All these surfaces are painted in the same way, but not necessarily at the same time. Gutters are usually painted the same colour as fascias so it is easiest to paint them immediately afterwards – before soffits, which are often painted to match the walls or windows.
- Apply knotting, if necessary, and primer to bare wood. Put on an undercoat and leave to dry. Use two undercoats if there is to be a colour change.
- Lightly sand with fine abrasive paper to remove any rough bits.
- Apply a coat of gloss with a 75mm paintbrush, finishing with the grain. Leave it to dry for at least 12 hours.
- Apply a second coat of gloss.
As an alternative to new gloss over old, a stain finish designed to be applied over gloss paint gives a finish resembling natural wood. No base coat or primer is necessary.

2 Gutters and downpipes

Whether you paint gutters and pipes together or at different times, follow the same painting procedure for both.
- Clean out debris and wash with water and detergent.
- Remove rust from the insides of metal gutters with a wire brush. Wipe the surface with a dry cloth and apply rust inhibitor or metal primer. Paint the inside of gutters with any left-over gloss paint.
- Paint gutters and pipes with exterior gloss using a 50mm brush. If there is to be a colour change, apply one or more undercoats first. If the surface is coated with bituminous paint see Choosing paints for every purpose (page 83).
- Hold a piece of cardboard behind pipes as you paint them, to protect the wall.
- Apply a second coat of paint when the first is completely dry.

Plastic gutters and pipes do not have to be painted, but if you want them to match a colour scheme, apply two coats of exterior grade gloss. Do not use a primer or undercoat. Manufacturers usually advise against painting new plastic because the paint will not adhere perfectly to it. After about a year it is safe to do so.

If you are leaving plastic gutters unpainted, unclip and remove them while you are painting the fascia boards.

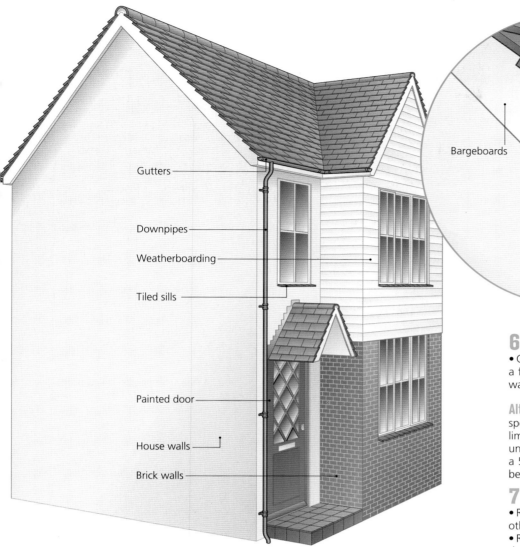

Gutters

Downpipes

Weatherboarding

Tiled sills

Painted door

House walls

Brick walls

Bargeboards

Soffit

Fascia

3 House walls
• Treat new rendering which has not been painted before with a stabilising solution or a primer recommended for such a surface by the manufacturer.
• On painted rendering – such as pebbledash, spar dash or a textured surface – no undercoat is necessary. Apply two coats of exterior grade emulsion or masonry paint with a 100mm or 150mm paintbrush or an exterior grade shaggy pile roller.
If you use a brush, work the paint into the surface with the tip of the bristles.
• Paint the area close to door and window frames with a 50 or 75mm brush.
• Do not try to paint the whole width of a wall along a house in one go. Instead, divide each wall into sections and paint one section at a time. If you cannot finish painting a wall in one session, stop at a corner of a feature – a window, for instance – so that joins will be less noticeable. Never stop in the middle of a wall. It will leave a noticeable mark.
• Wrap a collar of paper as protection around a newly painted pipe if you are painting the wall behind it. Move the paper down the pipe as you paint.
• Remember to work safely at high levels, ideally with a helper to steady ladders and pass tools.

4 Brick walls
• Avoid painting good facing brickwork – it is difficult to achieve a satisfactory finish, it cannot be successfully cleaned off later and rarely looks attractive.
• If you really want to paint it, use exterior grade emulsion and a rough surface paintbrush. Apply at least two coats.
• To clean dirty bricks, scrub them with a hard bristle brush and plenty of water. Never use soap or detergent because they create permanent white stains.

5 Windows
If a concrete sill is damaged, repair it before painting the window frame.
• Strip paint off wooden sills and make them good, filling holes and uneven areas with exterior grade wood stopping or epoxy-based filler.
• Prepare wood and metal frames as for an equivalent inside frame (page 73).
• Apply knotting to knots and resinous patches in bare wood. Then apply primer, undercoat and exterior grade gloss with a 25mm, 50mm or angled cutting-in brush.
• Paint each type of frame following the sequence on page 97.
• Take special care to seal the joint between putty and glass with new paint. This will prevent rain seeping through the window.

6 Tiled sills
• Clean window sills made of clay tiles with a fine wire brush; wash away the dirt with water and dry with a cloth.

Alternatively Clay tiles can be painted with special tile paint which is available in a limited colour range. No primer or undercoat is needed. Apply two coats with a 50mm paintbrush. The mortar joints may be painted or left natural.

7 Painted doors
• Remove metal handles, knockers and other furniture before painting.
• Replace damaged putty in a glass panelled door (page 209).
• Prepare the surface as for interior doors (page 73).
Use exterior grade gloss to finish; again follow the same sequence and method as for painting a door inside (page 95).

8 Varnished weatherboarding
• If the varnish is in good condition, rub over the surface with a flexible sanding pad damped with water to remove the glaze. Wash down with clean water, allow the surface to dry and then apply new varnish.
• If the varnish is in poor condition, strip it off (page 76). Brush on a wood preservative – stained if you want to change the colour of the wood – and then varnish as for doors above.

9 Painted weatherboarding
• Prepare as for interior painted wood (page 73). Apply knotting, if needed, then wood primer, undercoat and two coats of exterior gloss paint. Alternatively, use microporous paint suitable for exterior woodwork.
• Work from the top down, and from left to right if you are right-handed and from right to left if you are left handed.
• Paint sections about 1m long at a time, using a brush just narrower than the width of one board.
• Paint the edge of the timber first, then paint the face, finishing with strokes that go with the grain.

12

DIY in the garden

Planning an area of decking

Decking has become very popular as a surface for garden terraces. Fairly easy to lay, it is a light job compared to alternatives such as paving and concrete patios. Specialised tools are not required but the work will go faster if you can arrange a helper, especially when setting posts and handling the joists.

Decking materials

If a deck is to last for a substantial period of time, it is essential that any timber used in the construction be treated to stave off fungal attack and general deterioration caused by repeated wetting and drying. Timber can often be bought pressure-treated: in other words, preservative has been forced into the grain using specialised equipment at the sawmill. This type of treatment gives the most protection, especially for timber that is in contact with, or close to, the ground. Alternatively, brush or spray on preservative during or after installation.

MASONRY BOLTS

A secure way to attach decking to a house wall or similar structure is to use masonry bolts. Each bolt has an expanding sleeve that grips the brickwork when the bolt is tightened.

It is possible to order certain types of wood from timber merchants and decking specialists. Here are some of the types of wood available:

Softwood

Western red cedar Straight grained with an attractive smell; but has a tendency to split and dent; can be used without any treatment; very durable but soft.
Spruce Straight grained with few knots; use for out-of-ground components only.
European redwood Clearly visible grain; avoid the lower grades because they have lots of knots.
North American Douglas fir Yellow in colour with prominent grain; heavy and durable especially when treated.
British/European larch Avoid boards with lots of knots; can be expensive.
Southern yellow pine Visible grain with few knots.

Hardwood

Hardwoods are generally more expensive but will often be durable without the benefit of pressure treatment.
Teak Very durable with high strength; mid-brown colour; the king of woods for decking but very expensive.
Iroko Coarse grain, but not very visible; similar in appearance to teak but not quite so durable; brown to beige colour.
European oak Broad, straight to wavy grains; durable but expensive.
Opepe A popular choice for decking; an insignificant grain with a light brown colour; very durable.
Jarrah Straight grain and not strongly marked; dark brown.

Decking boards and tiles

Decking boards should be at least 50mm thick to combat the twisting and warping caused by fluctuating temperatures and changing moisture levels brought about by the wood being rained on and drying out.

Ready-made wooden 'tiles' are a good alternative. Up to 1m square, they can be laid on a supporting framework to form a surface deck.

Planning consent

Generally you do not need planning consent for a deck in your garden but there are exceptions. You may need permission if your house is in a conservation area, listed, or in an area of outstanding natural beauty. If you are at all unsure, a phone call to the local authority planning officer could save you having to demolish your deck because you have contravened planning codes.

Points to consider

Decking boards come in widths ranging from 75mm to 150mm. The wider boards are faster to lay because fewer are needed. They often have a grooved surface that provides grip underfoot in wet weather and helps surface water drain away.

Building a deck is generally straightforward, providing a methodical approach is adopted and you plan properly before starting work. Construction techniques vary little, whether a deck is free standing or attached to some other element in the garden. Often decks are attached to the back of the house.

Look at the planned site for your deck in relation to the rest of the landscaping in the garden and take into account any other elements that may influence the design. Look at magazines, web sites and other gardens for ideas. Consider the neighbours: will the deck be so high that you overlook your neighbour's garden? Will you have privacy when you use your deck?

MEASURING UP

To work out the amount of timber required for the job, begin by measuring the width and length of the area to be decked. Then plan the layout of the supporting framework on paper.

You need to form a straight-sided frame around the perimeter and fix transverse joints across it – every 400mm if using 25mm wide thick decking boards, or every 600mm for thicker boards. For joists over 3m long, fix transverse braces every 2m to prevent warping. Work out the number of joists you need to cover the area, and calculate the amount of timber you will need for the whole framework.

For the decking boards, find out the width and length of the boards available, then calculate the number of boards you require.

Building a deck over paving

The simplest type of deck is built directly on top of an existing area of paving – concrete, paving slabs or pavers. This must be flat and mainly level, with a very slight drainage slope away from the house.

Tools *Measuring tape; pencil; panel or circular saw; paintbrush; cordless drill with twist drill bits and screwdriver bits; spirit level; string line; mitre saw.*

Materials *75 x 50mm timber joists; clear wood preservative; 75mm and 63mm zinc-plated countersunk screws (decking screws can be bought); 100mm masonry bolts; packing materials such as pieces of wood or slate; decking boards; decking sealer or stain.*

2 If you need to secure the frame to the house wall, use 100mm masonry bolts.

3 Fix the transverse joists in position (see Measuring up, left, for how to space them). Wedge packing material under any part of the frame that is unsupported due to unevenness in the existing paving.

4 Cut the first decking board to length and lay it in place across the supporting framework and transverse joists, aligning it with one long edge. To improve drainage and ensure even spacing between the boards, use nails, pieces of card or wood spacers to leave a 5mm gap between boards, removing and re-using the spacers as you fix each board in place.

5 Using a power drill, screw two 63mm screws through the board over each joist and into every section of the outer framework. Use a string line to help you to align the screws across the deck's width. Cut the remaining boards, varying the lengths if you wish to stagger the ends, and fix in place in the same way.

1 Cut the timber into lengths to create the supporting framework. Brush cut ends with preservative and butt together in position. Drill pilot holes, then secure each butt joint using two 75mm screws. Fix joists and any transverse bracing timbers in place. Check that the framework is square and level, with a slight fall for drainage.

6 You may have to cut the final board down in width to fit it in position. Set a circular saw to match the width required. If sawing by hand, clamp the board to your workbench and tackle a metre at a time. Get a helper to support the end of the board as you work your way along it. Fix the board to the frame in the usual way. Seal or stain the deck if needed or desired.

Building a raised deck

Over bare earth, support decking with vertical posts set into the ground and secured either with in-ground concrete collars (as below) or using metal fence post spikes.

Before you start Nothing spoils the sight of a new deck more than weeds growing up through the cracks between its boards. Therefore, before constructing the deck all vegetation, including turf, must be cleared. Compact and level the ground, leaving a gentle slope towards the outer edge of the deck to allow for drainage. Then lay a weed-suppressing membrane over the surface and cover with gravel.

Tools *Drill; saw; screwdriver; try square; spade; spirit level; tape measure. Power tools such as screwdrivers and saws will reduce the workload with some of the repetitive tasks.*

Materials *Concrete blocks for posts to rest on; cement, sand and aggregate; decking boards (plain or grooved), 100 x 25mm; joist hangers and galvanised nails; stainless steel screws, countersunk; 12 x 175mm galvanised nuts, bolts and washers; wooden joists, 150 x 50mm, length depending on size of deck; wooden posts, 100 x 100mm, length depending on height of deck; decking boards.*

1 Use string lines pulled tightly between wooden pegs driven into the ground to mark out the edge of the site that will be covered by the deck. If the deck is to be oblong or square, measure the diagonals. When both diagonals are identical, the deck is a true square or oblong.

2 If the deck is going to be attached to the house, screw or bolt the wall plate to the building, ensuring that the top surface is at least 150mm below the level of the damp-proof course.

3 Mark out the centres of the joists at 300mm intervals from each end on the wall plate and nail on the joist hangers. You may need to alter the spacing slightly if the length is not divisible by 300.

4 Dig out holes 300mm deep and 300mm wide where the posts are going to go. There should be a post at each corner and one no more than every 2m across the deck. Place a concrete building block in the bottom of each hole and rest the base of a 100 x 100mm post on it.

5 Use a spirit level to ensure the posts are upright, nail temporary braces to the posts as support, then fill the holes with concrete, packing it tightly around the base of the posts.

The concrete should be a mix of one part cement, two parts sand and three parts aggregate. Double check that the posts are vertical and in line with your setting-out string, then leave them for 48 hours for the concrete to harden before continuing with the job.

6 Nail the two outside joists to the end of the wall plate, or ledger, reinforcing the corners with wooden blocks. Check that the joists are level, then drill and bolt the other end of the joists to the supporting deck posts.

You may find it easier to leave the joists a little too long and then cut them flush with the outside of the deck posts when you have fixed them in place.

7 Fix the front joist – the header joist – in place. Securely bolt it to the deck posts before trimming it flush with the outside faces of the outer side joists.

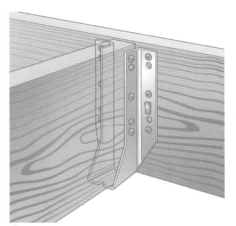

8 Nail joist hangers (above) to the inside of the header joist at identical spacing to those that you used on the wall plate, or ledger joist.

9 Cut all the joists to length, then drop them into the joist hangers and nail them in place.

10 Cut and fit the decking boards at right angles to the joists, using two screws where each board passes over a joist. Using a power screwdriver or a variable speed cordless drill, screw the boards down, 25mm in from each edge. Use a try square to make sure that each piece of decking is accurately positioned at right angles to the joists.

11 Start adjacent to the house leaving a 5mm gap between each board. Use nails, card or wood as spacers between the boards, removing and reusing the spacers as you fix each board in space.

12 If the deck is high enough to require a handrail, attach a rail to the inside of the posts 1m above the deck surface. Cut the top of the posts level with the handrail.

Anatomy of a raised deck

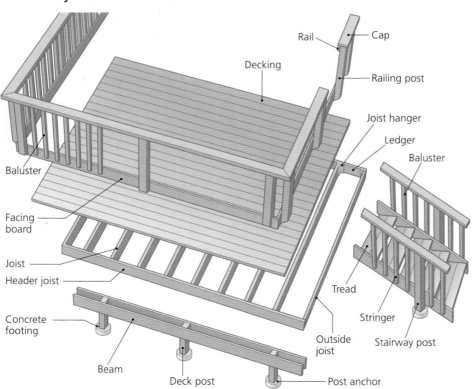

Rail — Cap
Decking
Railing post
Joist hanger
Ledger
Baluster
Baluster
Facing board
Joist
Header joist
Tread
Stringer
Concrete footing
Beam
Deck post
Post anchor
Outside joist
Stairway post

Choosing a pergola, arch or arbour

Pergolas and related garden structures may be large or small, simple or elaborate, sturdy or delicate. Often positioned against a wall or used to cover a path or link two areas of the garden, they tend to become a visual focus and therefore must be sited with care as well as soundly built.

Types of structures

Pergola A general term for a series of arches spaced at regular intervals and joined at the top by beams. It may stand alone or be a lean-to structure against a wall. It is usually intended as a support for climbing plants.

Arcade A type of pergola, either free-standing or attached to a wall, which is open to the elements.

Colonnade An arcade that covers a path linking one building to another.

Loggia A type of pergola, built against the side of a house and usually glazed or roofed overhead. It sometimes has glazed sides as well.

Arbour A structure enclosing a seat but open at the front. It is basically a pergola or arch that is closed in on three sides and typically decked with plants.

Arch A structure consisting of a pair of upright posts or pillars joined at the top by an overhead cross-beam; it is generally used to frame a path or gateway.

Site and situation

• A pergola that covers a path may entice you to explore or lead you to another area within the garden.
• Straight pergolas extend vistas and frame views, whereas a curving structure is intriguing, its end hidden from sight.
• When sited as a lean-to structure against a wall, a pergola can make an elegant transition from indoors to outdoors, especially if designed to harmonise with the style of house.
• A pergola can simply cover a patio to make an intimate outdoor sitting and eating area.

Design tips

• If lavishly decked with plants, a pergola can become an airy, colourful tunnel. Keep the design simple if the emphasis is to be on the plants.
• Left bare, a pergola or arch can have the ornamental quality of sculpture.
• For a balanced appearance, plan the length of a pergola so that the distance between each arch is the same as the span across the entrance.
• Slope the top of a lean-to pergola downwards, in case you decide later on to glaze or roof it in as a loggia.
• For a more decorative finish, pitch the roof beams upwards to produce a pointed central apex, or you can tilt, curve or shape the ends to give an oriental look.

• A height of 2.2–2.5m under the roof beams, and an entrance width of 1.5m between posts, is the minimum for comfortable passage, especially if the pergola is covered with plants.
• Err on the side of strength when choosing materials and dimensions, so the structure can withstand the force of strong winds and the heavy weight of wet foliage.

Materials

Timber The most popular material is finished timber, planed and treated with preservative. Pressure-treated wood is preferred because it resists rotting and requires no additional treatment to preserve it. However, pressure-treated wood does not take stain and paint well; therefore, it's best to use regular untreated wood if you intend to apply your own finish.

Rustic poles are an attractive alternative to prepared timber. Use natural poles complete with their bark for a truly rustic appearance, or choose stripped, treated poles for longer life.

Plastic A long-lasting composite material made from recycled plastic is available. It looks and behaves like timber but is synthetic. Garden centres supply kits made almost entirely from plastic, with parts that clip together. This could be a good option if you do not feel up to making your own pergola from scratch.

Brick or stone For large, substantial, free-standing pergolas use square pillars of brick or stone to support heavy overhead timber cross beams.

Metal Tubular metal arches, with a flat, rounded or pointed profile are modern and unobtrusive; galvanised or plastic-sheathed arches last longer than wood.

Structural hints

• Use a spirit level and plumb line for accurate positioning of posts and beams.
• Make sure right angles on squares and rectangles are true by checking that both diagonals measure exactly the same.
• The greater the distance between posts, the thicker they and the bearers must be.
• For increased strength reinforce all joints with T-shaped brackets or angle brackets.
• Diagonal reinforcing poles or corner braces also add strength, especially on rustic pole structures.
• With lean-to structures, support one end of the cross beams on a 100 x 50mm wall plate screwed or bolted to the wall. Either half-joint the ends or rest them in metal joist hangers.
• Strengthen the joints on planed timber with waterproof adhesive.
• One option for joining sections together is to use halving joints (right). Timber joined in this way makes a strong and sturdy joint with the top of both pieces flush with one another. Mark out the joint, make a saw cut down each side, then chisel out the waste.

• Hurricane clips make strong joints where the beams attach to the cross members and avoid the need for complicated joinery.

Building a pergola

A simple wooden pergola with a flat top sturdy enough to carry the weight of climbing plants can be easily assembled, though the task is made easier if two people are working together.

Tools *Sledgehammer; spirit level; chisel; mallet; spanner; drill.*

Materials *For a pergola 4m long, 2m wide and 2.2m high, 100 x 100mm timber treated with preservative, as follows: 6 upright posts 2.7m long; 2 bearers (main beams) 4m long; 5 cross beams 2.2m long; 80mm screws; 200mm screws or carriage bolts; 6 metal post spikes.*

1 Mark out the area where the pergola is to be sited. Using short lengths of timber, mark positions for the posts, three on each side, and spaced 1.5m apart each way.

2 Drive metal post spikes into the ground to support the squared timber uprights. Use a sledgehammer and protect the top of the spike with a wooden 'dolly' (which can be bought) or a suitably sized offcut of timber.

3 Wedge the posts in the metal spikes and tighten the two bolts on either side to secure each one; check they are vertical.

4 Position a bearer along the top of the posts on one side of the pergola with an equal amount overhanging at each end. Using a spirit level check that it is horizontal. Mark the position of three posts on the bearer and the two midway points between the posts.

5 Using a chisel and mallet, cut out five halving joints (page 63) at these marks, 100mm wide and 50mm deep, to house the cross beams. Do the same for the other bearer. Mark and cut corresponding halving joints in the cross beams, again allowing for an equal overhang of about 150mm at each end.

6 Set the bearers in position, together with the three cross beams that join them, over the tops of the posts. Drill through the joints and use 200mm screws or carriage bolts to fix them to the posts. Join the intervening two cross beams to the bearers with 80mm screws.

7 Finally paint or stain the completed pergola with your choice of finish, making certain that it is not poisonous to plants and animals. You may also want to add some screw-in vine eyes and plastic covered wire to encourage plants to grow over the completed structure.

ANCHORING POSTS WITH CONCRETE

If you are building a heavy structure, or erecting a pergola on a light soil, where it might be loosened in high winds, it will need a firm foundation. Bed the upright posts in concrete footings rather than using metal spikes.

1 Dig a hole for each post with a narrow spade. Make the holes about 300mm square and 600mm deep.

2 Place a layer of gravel 100mm deep in the bottom of each hole to aid drainage and prevent the bottom of each post from rotting.

3 Mix up concrete using one part cement, two parts sand and three parts aggregate, in a wheelbarrow or electric mixer. Aim for a slightly dry mix that will support the posts better than very wet concrete until the concrete hardens.

4 Set the posts in the holes and get a helper to shovel in the concrete while you check with a spirit level that the posts are vertical. Work the wet concrete around the posts with a wooden stake to compact the wet concrete and work out any air bubbles.

5 If the posts will not stay upright on their own or if it is windy add temporary braces to hold the posts vertical until the concrete hardens.

6 After 2 to 3 days remove the temporary braces. Ensure the concrete has set hard before continuing with the construction of the pergola.

Building an arbour

If you have room to build one, creating an arbour can provide a shady seat with a completely different view of the garden. Traditionally, the sides are covered with latticework to support climbing plants.

Tools *Tape measure; hand or power saw; power drill plus twist drill bits; try square; screwdriver; hammer; nail punch; trimming knife; sanding block and abrasive paper; pencil and string; paintbrush.*

Materials *For an arbour about 1.5m wide, 600mm deep and 2.4m high, preservative-treated softwood as listed, right. Also countersunk wood screws; panel pins; roofing felt and clout nails; exterior PVA woodworking adhesive; preservative wood stain.*

Making the frame

1 Cut the 75 x 25mm front and back seat rails and the three 75 x 38mm linking seat rails to length. Glue and screw them together to make the seat frame.

2 Screw the seat frame to the posts so the top of the frame is about 450mm above ground level. Attach two posts first, then get a helper to support the frame while you attach the other two posts. Check that the frame is square to the posts.

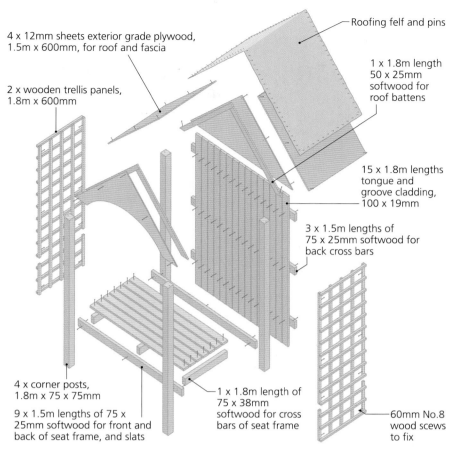

Roofing felt and pins

4 x 12mm sheets exterior grade plywood, 1.5m x 600mm, for roof and fascia

2 x wooden trellis panels, 1.8m x 600mm

1 x 1.8m length 50 x 25mm softwood for roof battens

15 x 1.8m lengths tongue and groove cladding, 100 x 19mm

3 x 1.5m lengths of 75 x 25mm softwood for back cross bars

4 x corner posts, 1.8m x 75 x 75mm

9 x 1.5m lengths of 75 x 25mm softwood for front and back of seat frame, and slats

1 x 1.8m length of 75 x 38mm softwood for cross bars of seat frame

60mm No.8 wood scews to fix

What you will need This diagram shows all the components you will need to build an arbour 1.5m wide, 600mm deep and 2.4m high – large enough for two people to sit comfortably side by side.

3 Stand the assembly upright and nail offcuts to the tops of the posts to keep it square. Screw the three cladding support rails to the rear faces of the back posts – one at the top, one about 300mm above ground level and the third in between.

USING POST BASES

If you are erecting your arbour on a paved surface or a concrete base, you can use bolt-down post bases to support it. Once you have completed the basic framework (step 3), set each post in the shoe of its base and get the whole assembly perfectly square. Drill and plug the fixing holes, insert metal sleeve anchors and bolt each base down. Then replace the frame and secure each post in its shoe.

Cladding the frame

1 Fix the cladding to the support rails plank by plank. Slide the grooved edge of each one over its neighbour's tongue and tamp it down from the top to get it level.

2 Pin the first plank to the rails through its face and punch in the pin heads. Pin subsequent planks through their tongues so the fixings are concealed when the next plank is fitted.

3 Cut and fit the six seat slats. Fit the front and rear slats against the corner posts, then space the others out evenly using a slat offcut as a spacer. Fix the slats to each rail with two countersunk screws.

4 Complete the arbour frame by adding a 1800 x 600mm lattice trellis panel at each end of the structure. Set each panel between its posts, drill clearance holes through its sides and screw it to the posts.

Adding the roof

1 Cut two gable ends from a 1500 x 600mm rectangle of 12mm plywood and sand the cut edges. Draw a curve on the front panel (below) and cut it out.

DRAWING A CURVE

To draw a curve 1200mm wide and 280mm high, mark the apex of the curve (A) 280mm above the baseline. Measure 600mm from A to the baseline to find the two foci of the ellipse (B). Drive in a small screw at each focus and tie a loop of string round them so a pencil held in the loop rests at A when the string is taut. Move the pencil round the loop to draw the outline of the ellipse.

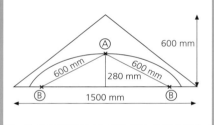

2 Glue and screw 50 x 25mm bearers to the top edges of the inner face of each gable. Glue and screw two plywood roof slopes to the top edges of the gables to complete the roof structure. Sit the roof assembly on top of the posts and drive a long screw vertically down through the roof into the top of each upright.

3 Cut a piece of roofing felt to cover the roof and fix it in place with clout nails. Add bargeboards to conceal the felt edges on the gables if you wish.

Children's play areas

Creating a safe play space in your back garden is a good idea if you have children. Take a look at the garden and see which parts you could incorporate into play areas – trees for tree houses or a sturdy branch from which to hang a swing.

You do not have to spend a fortune for your child to have a play area in the garden. If your child is old enough, involve him or her in the planning of the play area.

A secure space
One of the most versatile play areas is also one of the cheapest – a flat open area where children can run, ride bikes and generally let off steam. If there are trees, so much the better: these provide shade and encourage inventive and imaginative play.

To keep your children in one place, it is wise to have a fence or wall around the play area. Although many gardens already have walls and fences, consider a supplementary fence if your garden is large. You must also fence in pools and ponds.

Play equipment
You can buy a wide range of garden toys in wood, metal and plastic. Don't buy anything too large for your garden, and follow any assembly instructions carefully. Check all fastenings from time to time to make sure that everything is secure.

Young children love playhouses. You can spend a lot on elaborate playhouses, but a child will get just as much fun from a simple plywood box with windows cut into it. Or turn a small tool shed into a temporary den: it can revert to its former use when the children grow out of it.

Laying a safe play surface

You can minimise the risk of bumps and bruises by creating a soft surface underneath a swing, or on which to stand a climbing frame. The simplest surface is a thick layer of forest bark chips.

Tools *Scissors or sharp trimming knife; mallet; perhaps a saw; screwdriver.*

Materials *Weed membrane large enough to cover play area; edging material (such as fixed log edging, available in DIY stores); stainless steel screws; bark chips (the number of bags needed depends on area).*

1 Determine the shape and size of the area you wish to create and lay out your chosen edging. Make sure that it extends far enough around the climbing frame to break the fall of a child falling off.

2 Once you are happy with the layout, fix the edging in place. Hammer posts straight into the lawn then join the sections of edging using stainless steel screws. Lay out the weed membrane within the play area. It does not need pegging as the bark will keep it in place.

3 Rake bark chips in a thick layer (at least 50mm) over the membrane. This surface is low maintenance – all it needs is raking occasionally, and topping up with bark.

Making a sandpit

All children love sand. Here is an alternative to the bright plastic versions sold in toy shops. It has a lid to keep out rain and animals when not in use. Be sure to use playpit sand – builders' sand will stain clothes and is usually too coarse for play.

Tools *Hammer; drill with wood bits; saw; string and pegs; border edging tool; spade; screwdriver; tape measure; pencil; staple gun (or hammer and clout nails); abrasive paper.*

Materials *Eight decking boards; four 50 x 50mm sawn timber posts (about 350mm long with pointed ends) for corners; decking screws; sheet of weatherproof 12mm ply for lid and corner seats; three lengths of 50 x 25mm timber for lid lip; 2 x 2m sheet of butyl pond liner; six or more bags of playpit sand.*

The sandpit made here is 1200mm square and the depth of two decking boards

1 Decide on the position of the sandpit. Try to site it out of direct sunlight as the sand will reflect UV light, increasing the risk of sunburn. Push in a peg at each corner and stretch string all the way round. Then use an edging tool to cut through the turf along the lines to a depth of about 50mm.

2 Use a sharp spade to cut away the turf and remove the soil to a depth of about 50mm. Make the bottom as level as possible, digging out roots and stones.

3 Hammer the corner posts into the ground to the depth of two decking boards from the bottom of the excavation.

4 Measure the exact distance between the posts before sawing the decking boards to length; the boards will form butt joins at the corners. Drill pilot holes in the decking boards and, using decking screws, fix the boards to the posts.

5 Tip half a bag of sand into the hole and level it to make a smooth surface for the pond liner. Lay the pond liner in the sandpit and fill it with sand *before* trimming it to size – the weight of the sand will pull the liner further into the hole.

6 Trim the liner allowing an overhang of about 50mm all round. Then fold this under to make a neat hem and staple it to the exterior of the decking boards. Don't worry about all the creases in the corners – these will be hidden by the corner seats.

7 Cut four right-angled triangles from 12mm ply with the short sides about 350mm long. Sand the cut edges to get rid of splinters; drill pilot holes and screw them onto the corners of the sandpit.

8 To make a lid, measure the exterior dimensions of the sandpit and cut a square of plywood 50mm larger all round. Fix 50 x 25mm lipping to three sides of the lid and attach two handles to the side opposite the one with no lip. This will allow you to slide the lid on and off rather than lifting it – it will be heavy.

Choosing outbuildings

An outbuilding is any structure that is not attached to the main house but still forms part of the property. Outbuildings include functional sheds and workshops, decorative summerhouses and gazebos, and greenhouses and potting sheds. Factors to be taken into account when deciding between them include usage, style, permanence, size and budget.

Usage

Often you may simply require a garden shed which serves as a store for garden tools. Look at how many tools you have and wish to store – not just now but also in the future. Make a list of the things that you want to put into the shed and try to visualise how much space they will take up. Consider, too, the other things you may have that could be kept in a shed, such as bicycles and children's garden toys. A shed or outbuilding that is too small will lead to frustration and will probably not be used as it should. If you are thinking of keeping plants in an outbuilding – in a potting shed or greenhouse, for instance – consider whether you intend to keep them in the building during winter; also, whether you will need to use the building for general storage too.

Style

Garden outbuildings vary widely in style. Try to choose one which is sympathetic to its surroundings, both in style and size. For example, a good choice of greenhouse for a small garden is probably a lean-to style that can be placed against a sunny wall. A bigger garden, however, may well be able to accommodate a much larger and grander structure.

Permanence

Sheds and other outbuildings that are small in size can often be taken apart if you move, whereas more substantial buildings become permanent structures. Although this may make your house easier to sell or increase the value, you will have to start again at your new house if that does not have the sort of outbuilding you need.

Size and budget

• Garden sheds in kit form, with either feather-edged or shiplap treated wood panels, start at about 1.8 x 1.2m, rising to 3 x 1.8m.
• Summerhouses with double doors and a choice of roof shapes range from 2 x 1.8m up to 3.2 x 3m.
• A good minimum size for a greenhouse or potting shed is about 2.5 x 1.8m. Aluminium greenhouses with windows and/or louvres on galvanised bases are available up to 4.4 x 2.5m. Lean-tos range from 1.9 x 0.6m to 3.8 x 2.6m.
   As well as size, design and construction methods also affect price, so it is wise to shop around and look at the various options. Remember, there will also be maintenance costs to take into account.

Materials to choose from

Sheds and workshops need to be lockable and secure, and of sturdy construction; greenhouses and potting sheds must let in as much light as possible but should be strong enough to withstand the worst weather – even so, try to avoid windy sites.

Brick and block A good choice for permanent outbuildings and those that will be used as workshops and hobbies rooms where you will be spending more time than just storing things. Cavity wall construction means that the building can be properly insulated to the same standard or even higher than the main house and the installation of internal fixtures and fittings is easier. These are slower to build and more expensive than a kit-built timber framed building but will last for many years.

Wooden framed This group encompasses many types of building from the simple kit-built shed or greenhouse to the complex and expensive post-and-beam barn type construction. Kit-built structures are easy to erect and can be put up by a couple of people in a few hours. Post-and-beam construction is at the other end of the scale and may require specialised tools, techniques and labour. Wooden-framed greenhouses can be glazed right down to the ground or set on low brick walls for increased strength and plant protection.

Aluminium and other metals Metal buildings and greenhouses (see opposite) are lightweight so require attachment to a secure base, usually concrete, pavers or posts sunk into concrete in the ground. Other styles have their own galvanised base onto which the frame fits. They require little in the way of maintenance and, because they simply bolt together, make a good choice if you wish to move at some time in the future.

Glazing Glass is the traditional glazing material for windows in greenhouses. Horticultural glass is 3mm thick and is rather fragile. Toughened glass is available, but is more expensive. When choosing glass, look at it edge-on: the greener it looks, the poorer its light transmission.
   Rigid plastics are an alternative. They can be curved, are less likely to break and offer about 90 per cent light transmission. However, they are more expensive than glass and attract dirt because of the build-up of static electricity.
   The windows in most timber kit sheds are made from perspex.

Services

The versatility of many outbuildings can be extended by the supply of electricity and possibly water. This makes it possible to see when it is dark, to heat the building, and to provide water for gardening or washing the car.

Planning permission

Most outbuildings are classed as temporary structures and do not require any form of planning consent or building regulations approval. However, it is wise to check with your local Building Control officer (page 486).

Metal is a durable and low-maintenance option for a garden shed. It does not require regular treatment against rot, like wood does and is also very secure. Panels usually bolt together, so the shed can be dismantled if you need to move it.

Installing a greenhouse

Position your greenhouse away from overhanging branches and where it will get the greatest amount of sunlight, particularly during winter.

Mark out where the greenhouse will stand, making sure you have a firm foundation of the correct size and type. It is important that the foundation will be able to support the structure you have chosen, and is dry and level. You may need to lay a brick or concrete foundation (page 460). Some greenhouse kits come with their own base, which must be anchored to the ground through pins set in concrete. Have the holes dug and concrete ready.

Tools *Spirit level; ratchet or spanner.*

Materials *Greenhouse kit; ready-mixed concrete. Possibly washing-up liquid.*

1 Lay out the base frame and bolt it together on the firm, level area where the greenhouse will stand. Make sure the frame is square and sink the metal anchors into the concrete-filled holes.

2 Identify and lay out on the ground the two ends of the greenhouse framework, before bolting them together.

HELPFUL TIP

When assembling a structure such as a greenhouse framework, it is wise to bolt the sections loosely to start with, and tighten them only when the glass has been fitted. As most glass is cut to right angles, it will help you to make sure the structure will fit squarely round it.

3 Next, lay out and assemble the sides of the greenhouse framework, bolting them together loosely. With a helper, lift the back and one side of the greenhouse onto the base and hold them in position while you bolt them together, making sure the corner is square.

4 Bolt the second side and the front of the greenhouse onto the first two sections, with a helper holding them steady. Then fasten the sides and ends onto the base.

5 Fix the ridge bar of the roof into place and slot in all the roof bars.

6 Now that the structure has been erected, slide the rubber glazing strips into position along the glazing bars to cushion the glass. A small amount of washing-up liquid applied to the glazing bars helps the strips to slip into place.

7 Start glazing the structure with the glass or plastic sheets supplied. It is easier and safer to work on the roof first, before doing the sides. Fasten the glass to the glazing bars using the W-shaped glazing clips supplied.

8 Finally, assemble and glaze the door, checking that it will open and close smoothly. Once this is done, tighten the bolts of the entire structure.

Putting up a shed

A garden shed can have a variety of uses, from simply being a place to store garden tools to acting as a backyard hobbies room or workshop. Sizes vary so choose one that is large enough to cover future as well as present needs. Consider the siting of the shed carefully, particularly if you plan to run electricity to it.

Putting up a kit shed

Putting up a shed is often achievable in a few hours, but all but the smallest tool stores come in large sections, so you may need to enlist some help putting it together. Even the most basic of sheds can be greatly improved by adding some additional felt to the roof to ensure the interior stays dry.

If the shed is to be used as a workshop or hobbies room consider installing insulation within the interior timber framework and cladding the inside with plywood or hardboard for a smooth finish. Some sheds come prefinished but most arrive as bare wood in which case you will need to paint on some sort of protective finish or wood preservative.

Tools *Tape measure; power screwdriver; power drill with twist and countersink bits; pencil; spirit level; try square; trimming knife; straightedge; hammer.*

Materials *Shed kit. Possibly also additional roofing felt.*

1 Unless you are erecting your shed on a level hardstanding, you will need to create a firm and level base for the structure before you start. The sturdiest option is to lay an area of concrete (page 460), slightly smaller all round than the footprint of the shed, so that rainwater running off the shed will drain away into the ground.

Alternatively A dry base can be created by laying several paving slabs on the site of the shed and spanning them with timber fence posts, running at right angles to the bearers on the shed's floor and spaced no more than 750mm apart. Make sure that all the slabs are level with one another, so that the shed will sit square on its base.

2 Start by lifting the gable end into position and propping it upright with a post. The bottom batten of each panel should sit on the shed base, so that the panel boarding extends beyond the base.

3 Lift a side panel into place and screw it to the gable end where the frames meet.

Put three fixings at each joint, at the top, middle and bottom of the panel.

4 Complete the walls by fitting the two remaining sides. The shed should balance on the base, with the panels lipping over the floor and the battens resting on it. Do not screw the walls down to the floor yet.

5 If the shed kit includes a beam to support the roof, fix it across the shed from gable end to gable end. This will also help to brace the structure.

6 Fit the door into its opening and check that it opens and closes easily. If it doesn't, the shed may not be quite square. Loosen the roof beam and check each corner with a try square. Hammer the corners to square them up if necessary, using an offcut of timber to protect the panels of the shed.

7 Lift the roof panels into place and secure them to the roof beam, if there is one. Screw through the roof into the sides and gable ends, too, to hold the roof firmly in position.

8 Nail the completed structure to the floor of the shed.

9 Cut the roofing felt supplied with the shed into three equal pieces: one for each slope of the roof and a third to lay over the apex, overlapping each side panel by at least 75mm. Allow for an overhang of 50mm at either end.

10 Use felting nails to tack the felt in place, starting with the side panels. Space the tacks 300mm apart along the top edge of the felt and 100mm apart along the gable ends and the eaves. Lay the middle length of felt over the apex and nail it in position all round.

11 Make neat folds at the corners (see Re-felting a pitched shed roof, right) then hammer the fascia boards into place. Nail decorative fillets, if supplied, to the apex of each gable end.

12 Nail strips of corner trim onto each corner of the shed to finish the structure, then fix a sliding bolt or hasp and staple to make the door secure.

WINDOWS IN SHEDS

Most kit sheds are supplied with perspex windows, which are easy to fit into the frames that are also part of the kit. Working from the outside, fix the plastic or metal sills provided into place and secure them by nailing wooden strips (or cloaks) to the frames between windows. Move inside the shed and slide the windows into their frames. Nail beading round the frames on the inside to hold the windows in position and make them secure.

Re-felting a pitched shed roof

If there is visible damage at several spots on a shed roof, or if water leaks through in places even though you can see no damage, the bituminous felt covering needs replacing.

Before you start Bituminous felt is sold in green, black and red, and in various grades; the heavier the felt, the longer it lasts.

You will usually be able to reach the top of the roof working from a stepladder and moving it along as necessary. If you cannot reach from a stepladder and are not sure that the roof will bear your weight, get someone to help you.

Tools *Stepladder; claw hammer; sharp knife; wooden batten about 1m long; old paintbrush. Possibly also a chisel, plane and screwdriver.*

Materials *Wood preservative; bituminous roofing felt; 13mm galvanised clout nails; chalk; cold felt adhesive. Possibly some new softwood boarding or some outdoor grade plywood or chipboard; fascia boards, ridge board or eaves battens with galvanised nails or screws for fixing.*

Preparation

1 Tear off all the old felt. Prise out any old nails with the claw hammer. If any heads break off, hammer the shanks down flush so that there are no sharp projections to damage the new felt.

2 Check the timber covering of the roof for damage or rot, and replace it where necessary. Saturate any replacement wood with preservative and let it dry before use.

If a plywood or chipboard sheet needs replacing, unscrew it and screw a new one in its place with galvanised screws.

If a tongued-and-grooved board needs replacing, cut through the tongue with hammer and chisel so you can ease the board out. You will not be able to fit a tongued and grooved replacement, unless you remove the tongue. Alternatively, you can plane down a piece of softwood to fit the gap exactly. Nail it in place with galvanised nails.

3 Where a fascia board, ridge board or eaves batten is damaged or missing, fit a new one. Treat it first with preservative and fix it with galvanised screws or nails.

4 Treat the remaining roof timber with preservative and let it dry.

5 Cut the felt into strips of the right length with a sharp knife. The strips should run parallel to the ridge and overlap the roof by 25mm at each end.

Fixing the felt in place

1 Position the first strip with its lower edge overlapping the eaves by 25mm and its ends overlapping the fascia boards by 25mm at each end. Run the wooden batten along it – from the centre towards the ends – to smooth out wrinkles. Using the 13mm galvanised nails, nail the top edge of the felt to the roof timber at 150mm intervals and the bottom edge to the outside face of the eaves batten at 50mm intervals. Nail the ends of the felt strip to the outside of the fascia boards at 50mm intervals.

2 At the corners where the eaves and the fascia boards meet, fold the surplus felt into a neat triangle, bend it flat and drive a nail through it.

3 Chalk a line along the length of the felt strip 75mm below its top edge.

4 Brush a strip of adhesive onto the top edge of the felt, taking it down to the chalk line. Take care not to let it spread below the line or a black smear will show on the felt. Leave the adhesive for about 30 minutes to become tacky.

5 Position the next strip of felt carefully over the adhesive. Run the batten over the felt from the middle to the ends to smooth it out. Press down the overlap firmly.

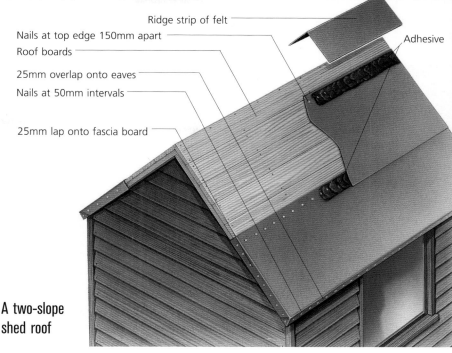

Ridge strip of felt

Nails at top edge 150mm apart

Roof boards

25mm overlap onto eaves

Nails at 50mm intervals

25mm lap onto fascia board

Adhesive

A two-slope shed roof

6 Nail the top edge at 150mm intervals and the ends at 50mm intervals.

7 If the slope is big enough to need another strip of felt, lay the next one in the same way. Leave up to 380mm unfelted at the top.

8 Repeat steps 1–7 to felt the other slope of the roof.

9 Measure the gap from the top of the felt on one side over the ridge to the top of the felt on the other side. Measure in several places. Take the highest figure, add on 150mm and cut a strip of felt this width and the length of the ridge plus 50mm.

10 Lay the felt in place, centred over the ridge, and make a chalk line along each edge to show where to put adhesive. Put the felt to one side.

11 Brush strips of adhesive about 75mm wide along each slope. Do not let adhesive spread below the chalk lines. Leave the adhesive to become tacky.

12 Lay the felt in place on the adhesive on one slope. Press it down firmly, then smooth it over the ridge and press the other edge in place. Run the batten over the felt on both slopes from the centre outwards to drive out air.

13 Nail the ends to the fascia boards at 50mm intervals. At the top angle, fold the surplus felt over neatly and drive a nail through the fold.

One-slope roofs

Pent-style sheds – in which the roof consists of a single slope – can be felted by the same method. At the top of the slope, trim the felt to overlap 25mm onto the outside face of the eaves batten and nail it there at 50mm intervals.

PATCHING DAMAGED FELT

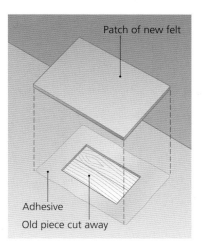

Patch of new felt

Adhesive

Old piece cut away

If a small area of felt is damaged, you can patch it with a felt off-cut and cold felt adhesive.

1 Cut out a rectangle of felt that will cover the damage and extend beyond it by at least 75mm all round.

2 Position the patch over the damage and run a piece of chalk around the edge to mark the area for the adhesive.

3 Brush the adhesive over the marked area with an old paintbrush. Do not let it spread outside the chalked area or smears will show on the roof. Leave the adhesive for 30 minutes to become tacky.

4 Lay the felt patch in position and press it down firmly from the centre to the edges to make sure no air bubbles are trapped under it.

Planning a fence

- In a windy spot, an open fence such as post and rails would offer little wind resistance. However, a solid fence would need to be very sturdy. Any solid fence higher than 1.2m is at risk of being blown down, no matter how well it is constructed, so it would be best to use open trellis to add any extra height.
- If the level of the neighbouring garden is higher and so the outside of a fence would be in contact with earth (which rots timber), consider building a fence on a low brick or block retaining wall, with gaps for concrete spurs to support timber fence posts.

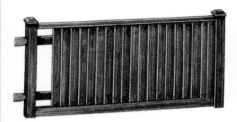

Closeboarded vertical Upright, overlapping feather-edged boards (tapered on one side) nailed to horizontal arris rails. Boards are about 150mm shorter than the post height above ground, to allow for a horizontal gravel board. Posts are usually 2.4m apart. Excellent for screening or security, but expensive. Wood needs regular preservative treatment (page 439) to prevent shrinking or rotting. Fence has to be buillt up from separate timber components.

Closeboarded horizontal Horizontal boards nailed between posts. The boards are either feather-edged overlapping, or shiplap (with a step-shaped overlap). No arris rails or gravel boards are used. Posts are usually about 1.2m apart, with 2.4m boards butt-jointed on alternate posts. More posts are needed to give the fence strength than with vertical closeboard, making the fence very solid but a more expensive choice.

Panel Ready-made panels fixed between posts. Panels may be thin interwoven slats, overlapped horizontal boards, or vertical closeboard. Panels are normally 1.8m wide; narrower sizes are made to order. Height range: 600mm–1.8m. Easy to put up, and good for screening or security. The timber needs regular preservative treatment to prevent shrinkage or rotting. Quality varies – poorly made panels are likely to distort.

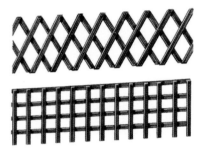

Post-and-rail (or ranch-style or railboard) Spaced horizontal rails secured to posts. Rails may be square sawn, half round, or rustic (poles, often with the bark intact). Rails (usually three) can be nailed or slotted into posts, which are usually about 1.8m apart. Height range from 300mm to 1.8m, but normally about 900mm – three rails. Suitable for a boundary or for decoration. Not as expensive as closeboard or panel fencing, and not much affected by wind. The timber needs regular painting or preservative treatment (page 439).

Square or diamond trellis Square trellis is usually made from hardwood battens forming squares of about 150mm, and can be bought in ready-made sections about 2m wide and 300mm–2m high, or as panel fencing. Diamond trellis is often expanding, and sold in 1.8m lengths with a height range of 300mm–1.2m. Sections can be fixed above each other. Rustic diamond trellis (not expanding) is also available.

WIRE FENCES

Chain link A mesh of thick, interlinked galvanised wire – plain (silver finish) or plastic coated – stretched between concrete or timber end posts by means of metal stretcher bars. The mesh is tied to two or three horizontal wires and also tied or stapled to intermediate posts. Standard height is 1m, but available up to 3m high. Sold in rolls, mesh size is normally 50mm. Good for security (especially keeping animals in or out) or boundary fencing. Fairly easy to put up, but will sag unless properly tensioned. Little maintenance is needed, except for painting timber posts, or treating them with wood preservative (page 439).

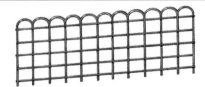

Decorative wire Straight or crimped plastic-coated wire welded or interwoven in squares or patterns. The top is usually hooped and the base spiked for sticking into the ground. Taller fencing can be stapled to timber posts. Sold either in rolls or rigid sections, with a height range of about 300–900mm, it is used mainly as decorative edging to flower borders. Easy to put up, cheap and needs no maintenance. Rolls are cheaper than rigid sections, and can be curved, but rigid sections are stronger.

Wire or plastic netting A mesh of galvanised wire or plastic stretched between posts. It is either stapled or wired to posts, or – for greater strength – stretched on horizontal wires. Height range normally 300mm to 1.2m, with mesh 13–75mm wide. Suitable for boundary or security fencing, and cheaper than chain link, but not as strong or durable. Plastic is longer lasting than wire.

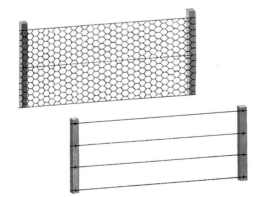

Post and wire Plain or stranded galvanised wire stretched between posts. Wire is usually sold in coils by weight – from 5 to 25kg. Coil length depends on gauge. A 5kg coil of 10g (3.15mm) plain wire is 82m long, a 10kg coil twice as long. Suitable for temporary boundary fencing, it is ideal for enclosing a large area.

Palisade or picket Spaced, upright stakes nailed to horizontal rails slotted into posts. Posts are usually about 2.4m apart, and the height range is about 900mm–1.2m. Fencing can be bought in ready-made sections about 1.8m long, with brackets supplied for fitting sections to posts. Suitable for a boundary fence. Comparatively cheap. Can be painted or treated with wood preservative (page 439).

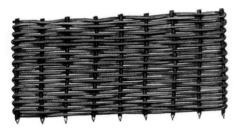

Hurdle or wattle Thin or half-round interwoven rods formed into 1.8m wide panels that can be supported on stakes or between posts. Osier (willow) rods form hurdles, hazel rods form wattles. Height range is about 600mm–2.1m. Not very long-lasting, but useful as a temporary screen for protecting growing plants. Hurdles are more expensive than wattles.

Cleft chestnut paling Stakes wired together and stretched between posts. End and corner posts are usually braced with stays. Posts are usually about 2.7m apart, and the height range is 750mm–1.8m. Suitable for a temporary boundary – while a hedge is growing, for example. Easy to put up and take down. Needs no maintenance but wires must be tensioned if the fence is to stay taut.

FENCE POSTS AND ACCESSORIES

Concrete post Heavier and more expensive than a timber post, but longer lasting and will not rot in the ground. A post 1.4m long weighs about 26kg. Posts are available with ready-made bolt holes, mortises or slots. They are generally 100mm square.

Concrete spur Short concrete post with ready-drilled bolt holes – usually 13mm across – used to support a damaged timber post. Spurs may be 75 or 100mm square. Lengths range from about 1.1 to 1.5m.

Post spike A spiked steel support (below right) driven into the ground as a base for a timber post. The post rests in a square cup above the ground. In some types the post is clamped into the cup. Concreting post spikes (right) are not pointed, but have a steel support, for anchoring into concrete. A post spike driven into soil is an unsuitable method of erecting fencing in areas subject to high winds.

Bolt-down post base A square metal cup for supporting a timber post. It has a projecting rim containing holes for bolting the base to a solid surface. It is suitable for fixing to concrete or paving slabs fully and firmly bedded in mortar, but not slabs bedded in sand.

Dolly or driving tool Metal-capped timber or resin block for fitting into a post-spike cup while hammering it in. Side handles allow the cup to be twisted for alignment.

Gravel-board clip A clip that can be nailed to a timber post to support a gravel board, particularly where a post is supported by a post spike. It is driven partly into the ground and nailed at the top.

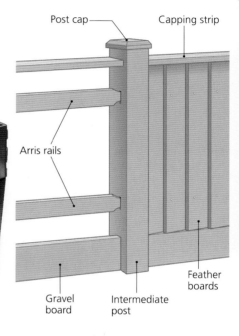

Post cap — Capping strip

Arris rails

Gravel board — Intermediate post

Feather boards

Timber post Usually softwood such as larch or pine. Buy posts ready-treated with preservative, preferably by vacuum/pressure impregnation although this is more expensive. Posts are available with ready-cut mortises for arris rails. Post sizes are normally 75 or 100mm square.

Timber post cap Flat or bevelled timber cap that is necessary for shedding rainwater and preventing rot.

Capping strip Wooden strip nailed across the top of vertical closeboard fencing to protect the vulnerable end-grain from rot.

Gravel board Board, usually made of wood or concrete, that is fitted across the base of a fence to protect the rest of the fence from rot caused by contact with damp ground.

Putting up fence posts

If the distance between fence posts is critical – for example, when fitting ready-made panels – erect posts in pairs and fit the fencing as you go. If the distance between posts is not critical, such as with post-and-wire fences, put up the posts first.

• It is advisable to buy new posts that have been pre-treated with preservative.
• Timber posts can either be concreted in or bedded in a mixture of well-compacted hardcore and soil. Concreting ensures a more solid and durable fixing, especially on soft ground, but may slightly increase the risk of rotting.
• Concrete posts must be concreted in.

Preparation

• For fences over 1.2m high, sink the bottom of the post at least 610mm below ground – or 760mm for tall concrete posts.
• For lower fences, sink timber posts 460mm, and concrete posts 610mm.
• Timber posts should have about 150mm of hardcore below them to provide drainage and lessen the risk of rotting.

The distance between posts depends on the type of fence (see pages 430–1). If the new fence replaces an old one and you want to put the posts in the same positions, you will have to dig out the stumps of the old posts, and possibly the concrete surrounding them. Alternatively, you can install a half panel or short section of fencing at each end of the fence so that the new posts fall midway between the old positions.

Tools *Post-hole borer or narrow spade – unless using spikes; string and pegs; spirit level; one timber length longer than the distance between posts; one timber length as long as the distance between posts; timber lengths for temporary post supports; mallet; hammer; timber length or earth rammer (page 451). Possibly also demolition hammer or pickaxe; sledgehammer; chalk.*

Materials *Posts of treated timber or concrete; hardcore (page 450); 50mm or 75mm fence nails. Possibly also fast-set bagged dry mix (page 458) or concrete foundation mix (page 459) – about one bucketful per hole; bolt-down post base.*

1 Mark the inside line of the fence by stretching the pegged string along its length.

2 Use the timber length to measure the distance between each hole, and cut out the area of each hole with a spade. Make a chalk mark instead if the fence crosses a solid surface.

3 Fix the first post to the wall, if necessary (see opposite).

4 If a hole has to be made in a patio, either take up a slab or the bricks, or break a concrete surface with a demolition hammer, and dig below.

Alternatively For a solid surface use a bolt-down fence base (page 431).

5 Using a post-hole borer or narrow spade, dig each hole to the required depth; remember to include an extra 150mm for hardcore beneath a timber post. Keep the hole as narrow as possible for the size of the post.

6 For a timber post, fill the base of the hole to a depth of 150mm with hardcore, well rammed down.

7 Insert a post so that one side is against the string guideline, and pack some hardcore round the base to keep it upright.

CONCRETE SHORT CUTS

To fix a fence post quickly, you can use Supamix Post Fix, which sets in about 10–20 minutes, instead of using rubble and cement. It is sold in 25kg Maxi-Packs, each sufficient for erecting one fence post.

8 Lay a length of timber across the top of each pair of consecutive posts and use a spirit level to check that the tops are level.

9 Use a spirit level to check that the post is vertical, then pack in more hardcore to support it.

10 To give a stronger temporary support, drive a nail into the post and wedge a length of timber under the nail as a brace.

11 Fill in the hole as soon as the fence has been erected. Either fill it with layers of hardcore and a mixture of soil and gravel, ramming the surface well down, or fill the hole with alternate layers of hardcore and concrete rammed well down. Slope the top layer of concrete round a timber post so that rainwater runs off away from the post.

Fixing a support stay

A post support stay – chiefly used on wire and chain-link fences fixed to timber posts – can be fitted against the post either in line with the fence or at right angles to it. Use either a spare fence post or a length of timber 75 x 50mm that has been treated with wood preservative.

The stay should be about three quarters of the length of the post it supports. Cut it so that it is at an angle of 35–40° to the vertical post. Bury the stay to about the same depth as the post, but you will have to dig a wider hole to allow for the angle of the stay. Place a brick or large piece of stone under the angled bottom of the stay to support it. Secure the stay to the post with 60 or 75mm galvanised nails.

Using post spikes

Make sure the cup of the spike is the right size for the post. You can trim the bottom of a post to fit into a smaller-sized cup, but this is not advisable as it weakens the post. The post length should be about 50mm longer than the height of the fence boards or panelling – none of it will be buried below ground.

Fit the driving tool, or dolly, into the cup, press the spike into the earth at the marked spot beside the pegged line, and drive it down using a sledgehammer.

Stop at regular intervals and check with a spirit level that the post is vertical, otherwise the post will be out of true when fitted. Use the handles of the driving tool to twist or level the spike as necessary to straighten or align it.

The spike will break through small stones, but if you hit a rock, stop and dig it out, or the spike will be pushed out of true. Take care if you are driving a spike where you know there are service pipes. Pipes are normally more than 610mm below ground, so should not be in your way.

Continue driving the spike until the bottom of the cup is level with the ground surface. Then fit a post in the cup. Secure the post in the cup either by driving nails into it through the pre-drilled holes, or by tightening the collar with a spanner.

Fixing posts on a slope

On a pronounced slope, use vertical close-boarded or post-and-rail fencing which can follow the slope and are more easily stepped in sections than panel fencing.

To make even steps, you may have to shape the ground by digging out or building up areas so that there is not too small or too large a gap under each section.

To set each pair of posts, use a wooden block on the lower post to raise the levelling timber to the height of the higher post. How long the block should be depends on the slope – the steeper the slope, the longer it will need to be.

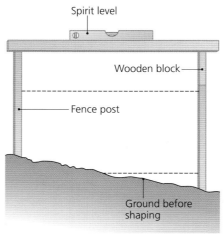

By using the same block on each post, you will ensure that all the post tops are uniformly stepped.

Fixing a timber post to a wall

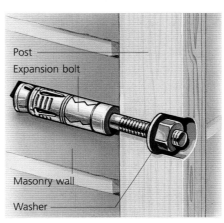

A post fixed against a wall usually rests on the surface of a path or patio, so should be cut shorter than the other fence posts by the amount they are to be buried below ground. Soak the sawn end with wood preservative overnight (page 431).

Secure a post over 1.2m high to the wall with three equally spaced expansion or anchor bolts at the top, middle and bottom. For shorter posts use two bolts. Each bolt should be twice as long as the width of the post, as half will be sunk into the brickwork. For panel fencing, the bolt heads must be recessed to lie flush with the edge of the post. On any type of fence, it is neater and safer if they are recessed.

Tools *Steel tape measure; chalk; power drill and two auger bits – one of the bolt-hole diameter, one wide enough for the nut recess, allowing for use of a spanner (or use a flat bit for the recess); masonry bit of the recommended diameter for the expansion bolt shield; spirit level; 100mm nail; hammer; box or socket spanner to fit bolt nut.*

Materials *Sawn post; two or three projecting-type expansion bolts – for fixing about 60mm thickness.*

1 Use a steel tape measure and chalk to mark the hole positions on the post.

2 Drill holes of suitable diameter through the post at each marked point, then make a hole for the nut recess about 15mm deep.

3 Hold the post in position against the wall and use the spirit level to check that it is vertical. Then insert a 100mm nail through each hole and tap it with a hammer in order to mark the hole position on the wall. Avoid mortar joints if possible.

4 Remove the post and drill holes in the wall of the correct diameter for the bolt shield, and to the depth the bolt will be sunk into the masonry. Remove debris from the hole.

5 Insert the sleeves and bolts (with nuts and washers removed) into the wall holes. Hang the post on the bolts and replace the washers and nuts. Tighten the heads with a box or socket spanner.

AN ALTERNATIVE WAY OF DIGGING POST HOLES

If you have a lot of post holes to dig, consider hiring a post-hole borer. Borers come in different sizes and styles but are, in essence, like a large corkscrew on a long handle. They save the hard work of digging, but are less effective where the ground is very stony.

To use a manual borer, twist it in and out of the ground and keep depositing the soil that gathers on the blades on the ground nearby.

Motorised borers are available to hire in one-man and two-man models, and make quick work of digging many holes.

Even faster, and more efficient, is the one-man, lightweight hydraulic auger. It is on wheels, and can be positioned easily. Use a hydraulic auger if you have more than ten post holes to dig.

Other means of digging post holes include a post-driver – a closed cylinder that fits over the post and is hammered to ram the post into the ground. This is useful where the ground is reasonably easy to work.

The one-man shovel holer is like a large pair of tongs with two sharp-edged shovels, face to face, at the end of its arms. It 'bites' out a shovel-load of soil at a time.

All these post hole borers, augers and holers can be hired from contractors listed in *Yellow Pages* under Hire Services – Tools and Equipment. To hire the borer for the shortest possible period, plan to dig all the holes in one go, even if the posts are to be put up in pairs.

Fixing panel fencing to posts

Put up posts in pairs as described on page 432. You will need a helper to lift and support large panels.

Before you start Fix each panel to its first post before positioning the second post. The fixing method depends on whether you are using nails or fence clips on timber posts, or fitting panels into slotted concrete posts. Fit a gravel board in the same way as for a closeboard fence (see opposite). If you are not using gravel boards, each panel must be fixed about 75mm off the ground, or it will quickly rot.

Tools *Power drill; wood bits; hammer. Possibly also screwdriver; two or three bricks; timber lengths for supporting panels; G-cramp.*

Materials *Posts – one more than the number of panels; panels; either nails (twelve 50mm or 75mm galvanised or alloy nails per panel) or fence clips (four per panel, with sufficient screws or nails for each clip). Annular (ring-shank) nails give the best grip. Possibly also one 1.8m gravel board for each panel; post caps (page 431).*

Nailing panels direct to posts

1 Drill pilot holes for the nails in each panel. Make six holes each end – three on each side through the inner face of the panel frame at the top, middle and bottom. Drill the holes right through.

2 Hold the panel in position against the first post (use a G-cramp if working alone). Allow enough space at the bottom of the post for fitting a 150mm gravel board, or rest the frame on bricks to leave a gap of 75mm.

3 Nail the panel to the first post, driving the nails in at a slightly upward or downward angle so that they will not pull straight out if the fence comes under pressure at a later date.

4 Position the second post with the other end of the panel butted to it. Ensure the post tops are level (page 432). Nail the end of the panel in place and concrete the post.

Using fence clips

Drill starting-holes for nails or screws that are to be driven into the panel frame, otherwise the wood could split.

Some clips are two sided with a post-fixing screw welded to one side. Screw the clips to each post before fitting the panel against it. Place a clip at the top and bottom of each post, facing opposite ways so that each side of the panel is supported. Nail each clip to the panel after fitting it.

Some clips are three sided, with no built-in screws. Screw them to the post before fitting the panel.

Some clips wrap round one side of the panel frame. Fit them to the top and bottom of the panel on opposite sides of the frame before fitting the panel and nailing the clip to the post.

(page 432)

USING CONCRETE POSTS

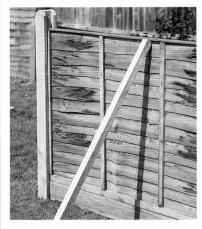

Slot the gravel board into the first post, then the panel. Support the panel with a prop while you position the second post so that it slots onto the other end of the panel.

Fixing closeboard vertical fencing to posts

This type of fencing is excellent for both screening and security, but the timber needs regular treatment to prevent shrinking or rotting.

Before you start Posts can be timber or concrete, and are available with ready-made slots (mortises) for arris rails. Some concrete posts have recesses to which the rails can be bolted. Posts for corners are usually wider than intermediate posts, and are mortised on two adjacent sides.
• Put up posts (page 432) in pairs, fitting arris rails between them. Make sure the posts are the right way round. Some posts are recessed on the bottom front edge to accommodate the gravel board, which fits directly below the overlapping feather-edged boards. The back of the fence is the side on which the arris rails are visible. Rails are normally 2.4m long, and after they have been slotted into the posts, the length to which boards can be fitted is about 2.3m.
• Use upper and lower arris rails for fencing up to 1.2m high, and an extra central rail for a higher fence. Rails may be supplied square sawn and need shaping.

Tools *Spirit level; hammer; block of wood about 90mm wide as a width gauge. Possibly also panel saw; wood plane or shaping tool; power drill with wood bits.*

Materials *Posts – one for each 2.4m section and one extra; two or three arris rails for each section; four 50mm galvanised or alloy nails for each rail; feather-edged boards treated with preservative (probably 27–29 between posts); two 50mm galvanised or alloy nails per board; one 2.4m gravel board for each section. Possibly also capping strip and nails (page 431); clips for fixing gravel boards.*

SHAPING AN ARRIS RAIL

Use a panel saw to roughly shape the two short sides of the triangular rail so they slope down to a flat stub of the same width as the fence slot. The third, widest side of the rail – to which the boards are nailed – should remain flat. Plane the surfaces smooth until the stub fits neatly into the slot to the required depth.

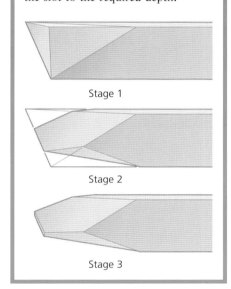

Stage 1

Stage 2

Stage 3

Fitting arris rails

1 With the end post in position (page 432), insert one shaped end of each rail into the post to the full depth of the slot.

2 Hold the second post in position while you fit the other ends of the rails into the post slots to half the depth of the slot (for intermediate posts, there will be a rail fitted in from each side).

3 Support the post temporarily with timber braces while you level it with the first post and check also that the arris rails are horizontal.

4 Adjust the post as necessary before concreting it in.

5 Nail the arris rails to the posts, driving one nail at an angle through the top of each rail and the other at an angle through the bottom of the rail.

6 Continue fitting posts and rails in the same way until the skeleton of the fence is complete.

Fitting feather-edged boards

1 Fit the first board with its thicker end butted against the post. Nail it to the centre of the top arris rail, driving the nail at a slight sideways angle.

2 Use a spirit level to check that the board is vertical before driving in the bottom nail – and the central nail, if there is one.

3 Place the width gauge on the first board, aligned with the thick edge, and fit the second board against it. The thick end of the second board should then overlap the thin end of the first board by 15mm.

4 Nail the second board to the rails, driving each nail through both boards at a slight sideways angle.

HELPFUL TIP

If the feather-edged boards need treatment with wood preservative (page 439), treat them before fitting them to the fencing. Do not apply the preservative to the fence after fitting all the boards in position, or the parts that have been overlapped will remain untreated.

5 Continue fixing boards in the same way, checking continually that they are vertical.

6 Before fitting the last three or four boards, measure the gap still remaining to see whether you need to decrease or increase the overlap to fill the rail.

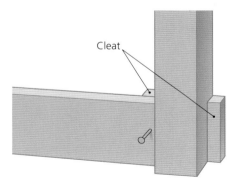

Alternatively Maintain the 15mm overlap and fill the last gap with a board fitted backwards – that is, with its thick end butted to the end post.

Fitting a gravel board

Cleat

• One way of fixing a gravel board between timber posts is to nail small wooden cleats to the foot of each post, then nail the gravel board to the cleats. Alternatively, boards can be trimmed to fit between the posts and fixed with gravel-board clips (page 431).
• For concrete posts, you may be able to use concrete gravel boards with special fixings.

Fitting a capping strip

A wooden capping strip is nailed across the top of vertical closeboard fencing to keep it straight and prevent it from rotting or snagging.

1 Saw off the fence posts level with the top of the fence boards. If the capping strip is not wide enough to completely cover the post tops, either fit a cap to each post (page 431), or slope the uncovered part.

2 Treat the exposed parts with wood preservative (page 439).

3 Place each capping strip to stretch from the centre of one section, across a post to the centre of the next section, with strip ends butted.

4 Nail the strip to the top of a post with 50mm galvanised or alloy nails.

5 Use 25mm nails to nail the strip to board tops at each end, and at one or two places in between. Take care not to split the boards. If you find that the nails are splitting the wood, drill a pilot hole for each nail.

Fixing other types of fencing

Timber posts and rails

For rails slotted into posts, put up posts in pairs (page 432) and fit the rails between. Nail the rails in the same way as arris rails (page 435), using 50mm galvanised or alloy nails.

For rails nailed to posts, put up a line of posts before fixing the rails. Allow two posts for each stretch of rails, and one for

the end of the run. Butt the rail ends on alternate posts, and stagger the centre rails so they butt on to the posts that the other two rails run across. Use 75mm galvanised or alloy nails.

Palisade or picket fencing

1 Put up posts and arris rails in the manner described for a closeboard fencing (pages 434–5).

2 Treat the exposed parts with wood preservative (page 439).

3 Use 50mm galvanised or alloy nails to fix the pales – preferably cut with pointed or rounded tops to shed the rain – to the arris rails.

4 With 75mm spaces between 75mm pales, you should need 15 pales to fill a 2.3m run of rail between posts.

5 If you are unsure that the pales will fit evenly into your run of rail, mark out their prospective positions against the rail, adjusting the space between pales so that they appear evenly spaced when seen from a few paces away.

Chain-link fencing

Concrete straining posts with ready-made holes (usually 15mm diameter) for eyebolts are normally used for chain-link fencing. Narrower intermediate posts have holes of about 9mm for fixing line wires.

Put up straining posts (page 432) at ends and corners, with intermediate posts between them at 3m intervals. End posts should each have a support stay (page 432), and corner posts two support stays. Fences of up to about 1.2m have a line wire at the top and bottom, higher fences an extra wire in the centre.

With timber posts, you can either fit the mesh with stretcher bars as described here, or use eyebolts for line wires only and staple the mesh to the posts. You may have

to drill holes for the eyebolts. Corner posts need two sets of bolt holes at right angles to each other, one set slightly higher than the other.

Tools *Spanner; pliers. Possibly also drill with 13mm wood bit.*

Materials *Straining posts and intermediate posts; chain-link mesh together with galvanised line and tie wires; stretcher-bars (one for each end post and two for a corner post), together with eyebolts and angle cleats.*

1 With the posts in place, thread a stretcher bar through one end of the chain-link roll. Bolt angle cleats to the stretcher bar, and fix each to the first post with an eyebolt (loop end inwards). Leave the roll of mesh standing on end.

2 Thread a line wire through each of the eyebolt loops, securing the wire by twisting it with pliers.

3 Run the line wires to the next straining post, and secure them to the post with eyebolts. Do not make the wires taut yet.

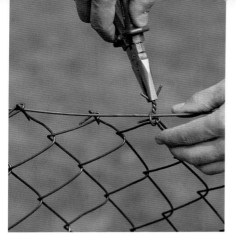

4 Unroll the chain-link mesh along the line wires, keeping it as taut as possible. Secure the mesh to the line wire with tie wires as you go along. Use tie wires at 150mm intervals on the top wire and at 450mm intervals on the bottom (and middle) wire.

5 When you reach the straining post, untwist two linked wires at the top and bottom of the mesh and unthread them to separate the secured fencing from the roll.

6 Thread a stretcher bar through the last row of meshes. Undo the eyebolts holding the line wires to the post, fit the bolts through the angle cleats of the stretcher bar, and fasten the bar to the post with the eyebolts.

7 Tauten the line wires by tightening the eyebolt nuts with a spanner as necessary. Do not overtighten, or the line wires may snap and whiplash dangerously.

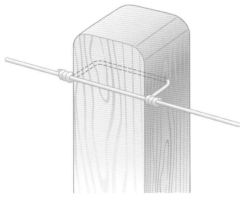

8 Use lengths of wire threaded through the intermediate post holes to secure the line wire stirrup fashion to the post.

Wire netting

Put up posts at about 1.8m or 2.4m intervals (page 432).

Use eyebolts through the posts to stretch line wires between end and corner posts in the same way as for chain-link fencing (above). The netting can be stapled to timber posts, or tied to concrete posts stirrup fashion. Use tie wires to tie the mesh to the line wires.

To keep out rabbits, bury wire mesh 150–300mm below ground. Mesh of 38 or 32mm is suitable.

Post-and-wire fencing

Put up straining and intermediate posts (page 432) in the same way as for chain-link fencing, and use eyebolts to stretch line wired between the straining posts.

The line wires can either be threaded through or tied to the bolt holes on intermediate concrete posts, or stapled to intermediate timber posts.

Fence repair and maintenance

All wood is susceptible to rot and attack by wood-boring insects, so treat fences and other garden woodwork with wood preservative regularly to prolong their life.

Timber rots in contact with earth, so whenever possible keep it from direct contact with the ground. Never pile soil against a wooden fence. Timber fence posts are most likely to rot at the bottom below ground, and will eventually collapse and bring down part of the fence unless reinforced in good time. To prevent a post rotting from the top downwards, slope the top or fit a post cap (page 431).

Featheredged boards often get brittle and start to crack if they are not kept well protected with wood preservative. So do arris rails, which take a lot of strain in supporting featheredged boards or palings, and will quickly get worse unless repaired.

Reinforcing a fence post

If the main part of a rotting post is still sound, it can be supported with a concrete spur (page 431). Alternatively, it can be cut short and refitted with its base in a metal post spike (page 431). If the rot extends higher than the top of the gravel board, you will have to free the fencing from the post on either side before you can cut the rot out. It may be simpler to replace the post.

Tools *Handsaw; old paintbrush; timber lengths for fence supports; timber length for compacting concrete; spade; hammer; drill and 13mm auger bit; spirit level with horizontal and vertical vials; spanner; hacksaw.*

Materials *Wood preservative (page 439); concrete spur; two 10mm diameter coach bolts about 200mm long; nut and washer for each bolt; concrete foundation mix (page 459).*

1 Temporarily support the fence on each side of the post with pieces of timber.

2 Remove the gravel board and cut off the rotting part of the post back to sound wood.

3 Coat the whole post, especially the bottom and end grain, with wood preservative.

4 Dig out a hole alongside the damaged post to a depth of about 450–600mm. Make the hole at least 300mm square.

5 Put the spur in the hole, fitted snugly against the post.

6 Slip coach bolts through the holes in the spur and strike them firmly with a hammer to mark their positions on the post.

7 Remove the spur and bore holes through the post at the marked spot.

8 Push the bolts through the post and spur so that the tails are on the spur side. Slip on the washers and nuts and tighten the nuts with a spanner.

9 Use a spirit level to check that the post is vertical, pushing it upright as necessary. Then brace it firmly with lengths of timber.

10 Ram hardcore into the bottom of the spur hole, then pour in the mixed concrete, pressing it well down with the end of a piece of timber.

11 Wait 24 hours before moving the timber supports, to give the concrete time to set. Use a hacksaw to cut off protruding bolt threads slightly proud of the nuts.

Replacing a timber fence post

Tools *Pincers or claw hammer; narrow spade; spirit level; length of timber longer than distance between posts; timber lengths for supporting post; earth rammer (page 451). Possibly also timber length; nails; strong rope; pile of about five or six bricks.*

Materials *Treated fence post the same size as the old one; hardcore (page 450) – probably 3–6 bucketfuls; two or three arris-rail brackets (see right); 50mm galvanised nails.*

1 Support the fence on each side of the post with lengths of timber, wedged under the panel top or upper arris rail.

HELPFUL TIP

If a post is difficult to remove, or if it breaks off and leaves a stump, lever it out using a length of timber and a large stone or a pile of bricks about 300mm high. Lash one end of the timber length to the post or stump, and lay the timber across the stone or brick pile as a fulcrum (balancing point).

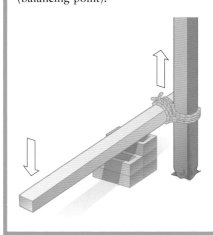

2 Free the post from the fencing. Undo panels by removing the nails or clips on each side. For vertical closeboard fencing, remove the first board on one side and saw through the arris rails. Remove nails holding the rails to the other side of the post so that they can be pulled out when the post is moved.

3 Dig down beside the post to free it at the bottom. Then remove the post and clear the hole.

4 Fit the replacement post in the same way as putting up a new post (page 432), but on a closeboard fence, fit the shaped arris rails on one side into the slots as you put the post in. Before you fill in and firm the hole, make sure the fencing will fit flush on both sides.

5 Refit sawn off arris rails to the post using metal arris-rail brackets, but nail shaped arris rails (page 435). Refit panels with nails or clips (page 434).

6 If the post top is square cut, either cut it to a slope or fit a post cap (see below). Treat sawn areas with wood preservative.

Repairing a post top

Before repairing the post, probe the top with a sharp knife to find out the extent of the rot. Saw off the rotten area back to sound wood.

Timber or metal post caps are sold ready made. Soak a home-made wooden cap in wood preservative for 24 hours before fitting. The cap should be about 15mm wider than the post top all round. Nail it to the post with two ring nails driven in on the skew – at an angle from each side. Check wooden caps periodically, and replace any with signs of rot.

A metal post cap can be home-made from a sheet of zinc or aluminium cut about 25mm wider than the post top and turned down round the edges.

Mending a cracked arris rail

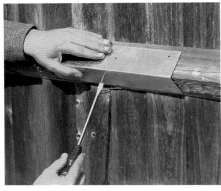

Strengthen a rail cracked in the middle with a straight arris-rail bracket – a metal bracket about 300mm long, shaped to fit the rail, with ready-made holes for screws or nails. Fasten it with galvanised or alloy 25mm screws or 50mm nails.

If the crack is near a post, use a flanged arris-rail bracket. The two flanges – projecting lugs at right angles to the bracket – are fastened to the post. If the post is concrete, use screws and wall plugs to fasten the flange to the post.

Tighten a loose arris rail by pinning it with a 10mm grooved hardwood dowel about 50mm long. Drill a hole for the dowel through the front of the post about 20mm from the edge where the loose rail fits.

Before inserting the dowel, coat it all over with waterproof adhesive. The grooves release excess glue and trapped air.

Replacing a broken arris rail

If the fence posts are concrete, the rails may be bolted to recesses in them, and are easy to replace. Or they may be fitted into mortises in the same way as timber posts, and can be repaired as described here.

Tools *Panel saw; hammer; plane or shaping tool; pencil.*

Materials *Arris rail, normally 2.4m long, treated with wood preservative; flanged arris-rail bracket (see above); 50mm galvanised or alloy nails.*

1 Hammer the boards or palings away from the damaged rail.

2 Withdraw the nails if possible and pull the damaged rail from the slots at each end. Otherwise, saw through the rail flush with the post at one end.

3 Shape one end of the new rail to fit into the post slot (page 435). Fit the new rail into the slot, mark where it will fit flush against the post at the other end, then saw it to length.

4 Refit the rail into the slot, and fix the other end to the post using the flanged bracket. Refit the boards or pales to the rail, making sure they are vertical.

Replacing a gravel board

If for any reason a rotting gravel board cannot be replaced without dismantling the fence – if it slots into concrete posts, for example – nail the new board to timber battens fitted beside the posts.

Remove the damaged board by drilling and sawing through flush with the posts at each end.

For a closeboard fence, remove a fence board at each end to make room for sawing. Support a panel on bricks.

Treat the new gravel board and the timber battens with wood preservative at least 24 hours before fitting them.

For timber posts, use 150mm battens, which can be nailed to the posts.

For concrete posts use battens 600mm long, drive about 450mm into the ground beside the posts, as near as any concrete bedding will allow.

Dig a shallow groove under the fence to make way for the new board. Fix the battens so that the board can be fitted flush with the front of a closeboard fence, or centrally under a panel fence. Support the battens from behind while you nail the gravel boards to them. Keep soil away from the board as much as possible.

Replacing a panel

Fence panels are made in standard sizes, so removing a damaged panel and fitting a new one in the same way (page 434) is not usually difficult.

If the new panel is slightly too wide, plane off a small amount of the frame on each side. If, however, it is not wide enough, close the gap with a narrow fillet of wood inserted between the post and the panel frame. Remember to treat the wood fillet with preservative before fixing it.

Repairing feather-edged boarding

Replace damaged or rotten boards with new boards that have been treated with wood preservative (see right).

One nail secures two overlapped boards, so to remove a board you will have to loosen the overlapping boards as well and pull out the common nail. Fit the new boards as on page 435.

Undamaged boards sometimes become loose because their nails have rusted. Refit the boards using 50mm galvanised or alloy nails that will not rust.

If feather-edged boards are rotting at the bottom where there is no gravel board, saw them off along the base to leave a gap of at least 150mm. Then cut and fit a gravel board (page 435).

APPLYING WOOD PRESERVATIVE

Coat existing timber fences with wood preservative regularly, particularly any joints or end grain.

Choices

A wide range of wood preservatives is available. One of the best known is creosote, which is made from tar oil. It is cheap but needs yearly application, and its fumes are unpleasant. When wet it is harmful to plants (though it is harmless when dry), and wood treated with it cannot be painted.

Most modern preservatives are either solvent-based or water-based, and contain chemicals or salts that destroy fungi and insects. Solvent-based types give off flammable fumes, and naked flames should be kept away until the preservative is quite dry – until at least 12 hours after application. Look for a warning on the container. Water-based types have no smell. Neither type is harmful to plants once dry, but guard against splashing any on plants while you are painting.

Application

The period between treatments depends on the type of wood preservative used and how exposed the fence is. Most modern preservatives will last 2 or 3 years.

Even if timber for a new fence has been pre-treated with preservative by the manufacturer, ideally by a vacuum/pressure process, coat it with more preservative before you fix it in place and thoroughly soak cut ends.

The best time to apply preservative is when the wood is thoroughly dry but the sun not too hot – probably in late summer after a dry spell, with no rain expected for a day or two. Damp wood will not absorb the preservative well.

Apply preservative with an old paintbrush or a garden pressure spray. Or there are kits on the market which pump the liquid from the container to a brush.

Always follow any safety precautions given on the container. With some preservatives you should protect your skin and eyes while you are applying them.

Coverage is generally around 4–10m² per litre, but varies with the type of preservative and the porosity of the wood.

Treated wood can then be painted the colour of your choice, but many brands contain colouring.

Choosing gates, hinges and fasteners

There are many different designs of gate available, including matching designs for most types of fencing. Some typical styles are shown below. Most of the types shown are also available as double gates. Before choosing a gate, consider from which side of the opening you want it to hang, and whether it opens over flat or rising ground.

Close boarded (feather-edged) Gates are usually ledged (with cross rails) and braced (with a diagonal bar). The top may be square or rounded.

Panel In various designs to match panel fencing. Generally 910mm wide and 50mm shorter than the fence height.

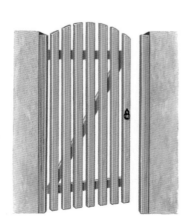

Open-boarded (palisade) With spaced vertical palings that project above the upper cross rail. Gates may be tall or short.

Open-boarded (palisade) Paling tops may be square, rounded, pointed or some other shape.

Open-boarded (framed) With spaced vertical paling that do not protrude above the top bar.

Frame and panel A timber frame with plywood panels.

Wrought iron (single) Decorative tall or small gates. Hinge and latch fittings are usually built in, or are on separate metal struts for fitting to gate supports.

Barred (field or country gate) Usually with five or seven bars and one or more diagonal braces. Available as narrow garden gates or wide single gates suitable for driveways. Some types have a swinging stile with a curved heel at the top. A narrow hunting gate is often partnered with a wide driveway gate.

Tubular steel Usually barred gates, with adjustable built-in forged eye hooks for hinge pins, and a spring-loaded bolt fastening.

BUYING GATES AND GATEPOSTS

Do not buy a gate until you are sure how wide you want it and how you are going to hang it. The width and fitting method are interdependent. Check also that the gate is designed to hang on whichever side you require – either right or left. If it is to hang across a sloping driveway, it will need to accommodate rising hinges – some types are self-closing.

Gates are made in both metric and imperial sizes. Be sure you know the exact width, because conversions are inaccurate. The width range for both systems is generally similar.

Single gates range in width from about 900mm to about 3.7m, increasing by increments of 300mm or 600mm. Double gates may range from about 4m to 6m wide. The height range is typically from about 1 to 1.75m, but gates as high as 2m and 2.5m are available.

If you are buying gateposts as well, make sure timber posts are treated with preservative (page 439). They are generally 1.8–2.4m long, and range from 100mm square to 200mm square for wide, heavy gates.

Concrete posts may be available with ready-drilled holes for centred gate fittings, or may have top and bottom holes to which a strip of timber can be bolted as a fixing point for fitting. Do not use post spikes for putting up gateposts; they do not give enough support.

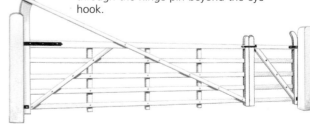

Wrought iron (double) Hinge pins may be down-pointing on the gate or upright on the support. To deter thieves, fit a split pin through the hinge pin beyond the eye hook.

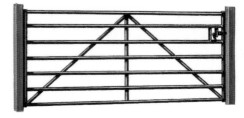

CHOOSING GATE HINGES

Tee Commonly used for hanging light or medium-weight gates flush between posts. Usually painted black.

Hook and band For hanging light or medium-weight timber gates. The band goes on the gate and the hook on the post. From 300 to 914mm long.

Heavy reversible Strong hinge for heavy gates flush between posts. Can be used either way up. Hook held to pin by cups at each end. Galvanised or black.

Cranked A cranked strap hinge for smaller gates hung flush between posts. Hinge pin (see below) fits on the post and the strap is screwed or bolted to the back of the gate. Usually galvanised.

Standard hanging set For wooden gates. A double strap is bolted to the top of the gate and its eye hooks over an adjustable hinge pin. The eye of the bottom bracket fits over the eye of a fixed, drive-in pin. The whole gate can be lifted off its hinges, if required. For pairs of gates, an adjustable bottom bracket is recommended, so that the gates can be aligned where they meet. For sloping ground, rising hinges with offset pins can be used.

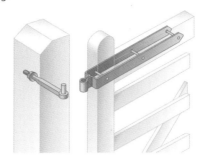

HINGE PINS FOR GATES

Drive-in With pointed single prong for fitting into drill hole in post. Usually bottom fitting.

Bolt-fixed Pin and coach bolt combined for fixing through a post. Usually top fitting.

Build-in Double-pronged fitting for building into the mortar layer of a brick wall or pier.

Adjustable Allows pin to be moved in and out while staying upright.

Flat plate With broad or narrow fixing plates for screwing onto gateposts or brick piers.

For gates centred on posts

Chelsea catch A bracket-held hook on the swinging stile fits into a catch on the inside of the gatepost.

Slim catch Fits on the inside of the gatepost to catch a striker bolt on a centred or flush-fitting gate.

Double-handed catch With a prong for fixing into the mortar of a brick pier. Suitable for built-in latch on wrought-iron gate. Has a stop to prevent the gate swinging outwards.

CHOOSING GATE FASTENERS

Super loop Loop-over fastener for double gates. Made for 50 or 75mm thick gates.

Pad bolt Can be padlocked. 200–250mm long, usually galvanised.

Oval pad bolt 100mm long bolt plate.

Locking bar with hasp and staple For padlock fastening. 100–305mm.

Ring latch set Traditional style for courtyard gates. Can be operated from either side. Usually black. About 150mm wide.

Automatic catch Fits onto a gatepost to receive a cranked bar fitted to the swinging stile of the gate.

Tower bolt 150–200mm long.

For gates hung behind posts

Automatic catch Fits onto the back of the gatepost to receive a striker bolt on the swinging stile of the gate.

Spring fastener set A flexible bar on the swinging stile that catches in a hook on the back of the gatepost. The fastener may have a knob handle for pedestrian use (as shown), or a longer, hooked handle for horse riders.

Methods of hanging a gate

There are three main ways in which a gate can be hung from timber gateposts. The method depends on the types of fitting used.

Flush between posts

The gate is hung between the posts, with the back of the gate flush with the back of the posts.

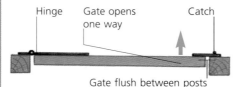

Hinge Gate opens one way Catch

Gate flush between posts

This is the usual method of hanging a timber garden gate with flush-fitting hinges. The gate opens one way only. The clearance for fittings on each side of the gate needs to be about 5mm.

Centred on posts

The gate is hung between posts, with the gate width centred on the gatepost width.

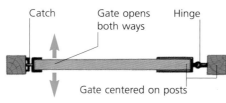

Catch Gate opens both ways Hinge

Gate centered on posts

This method is common with wrought-iron gates, which usually hook onto a pin, and with double-strap hinges on timber gates. The gate will swing both ways unless there is a stop on the fastener. Depending on the type of catch, the clearance on the hinge side may need to be as much as 100mm, and on the catch side about 55mm.

Hung behind posts

The gate is hung on the back of the posts with an overlap of 15–25mm on each side. This method can be used for a pair of gates, or a wide single gate, hung with a standard hanging set.

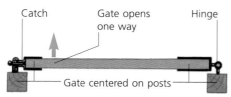

Catch Gate opens one way Hinge

Gate centered on posts

The gates can swing inwards only, and slam shut against a post. The types of fastener that can be used are limited (page 441).

Checking the design

Hanging stile Slam or swinging stile

Although some gates look the same from both sides, many have a supporting framework at the back. These types of gate should always be hung with their back on the inside.

Gates are often also designed for either right or left hanging. The hanging stile may be wider than the slam or swinging stile, to give a strong fixing for the hinges.

Wooden gates should be braced – by fixing a diagonal strut between the top and bottom rails of the frame – or they will sag over time. Where there is only one diagonal brace, the gate must be hung with the top of the brace on the closing side and the bottom of the brace on the hanging side. You can follow this convention when working out whether a gate is designed to be hung on the right or left.

Double gates must be a matched pair, designed for left and right hanging.

Fitting a gate between existing supports

1 If you can, buy a gate that is exactly the same width as the old one. Fix the hinges to the back of the new gate before you fit it. Wedge the replacement gate between the existing posts, raising it off the ground with a couple of offcuts of wood to ensure adequate ground clearance.

2 Check that the clearances are equal on both sides of the gate then mark the position of the hinges on the post. Screw the hinges to the post.

3 Hold the latch bar horizontal and screw the latch hook to the gate post and the latch

4 Remove the wedges that are holding the gate in position and check that it swings freely and that the latch works smoothly. Adjust the positioning if necessary.

If you cannot buy a gate to fit

If you are not able to find a new gate in the exact size you need, you will need to adjust the size of the gate or the gap between the posts.

If the distance between the existing timber posts or brick piers is too wide for the gate and fittings, narrow the gap by fitting timber battens on one or both sides. The gate fixings (page 441) can then be fitted to the timber battens. Make sure that the battens allow sufficient clearance for the fittings. The gate can then be hung in the way described above. Fixings are also available for fitting gates directly to a masonry pier (page 444).

If you cannot find a gate narrow enough to fit the gap between existing supports, you may be able to trim a little off both stiles of a timber gate to reduce its width. Otherwise you will either have to have a gate specially made or remove the existing gate supports and put up new ones, spaced farther apart.

Fitting a gate and posts from scratch

For a gate to hang snugly between the posts with its base at least 50mm above the ground, the width between posts must be measured accurately.

Before you start Make sure that the bottom of a diagonal brace is on the hinge side, for strength (see left).

For small, light gates, gateposts should be about 100mm square and about 600mm longer than the gate height. For bigger, heavier gates – more than 1.2m high or wide – posts should be up to 200mm square and at least 750mm longer than the gate height. Post tops should be sloped or fitted with caps to prevent rotting. Buy fittings that are either japanned (black painted) or galvanised to resist rust.

Tools *Length of timber longer than the width of gate and posts; pencil; spade or post-hole borer; spirit level; builders' square; six timber pieces for temporary post-support stays; pegs to hold stays; timber length for ramming hardcore; about six timber wedges to allow for width of gate fittings; drill and twist bits.*

Materials *Gate; two gateposts treated with timber preservative; two hinges; gate fastener; galvanised or alloy screws for hinges and fastener; two bricks or blocks; rubble or hardcore; concrete – foundation mix or 25kg bag of coarse dry concrete mix to make about one bucket per hole.*

Positioning the posts

1 Lay the gateposts parallel on flat ground with the gate face down between them. For flush fitting, raise it as necessary to line up with the back of the posts.

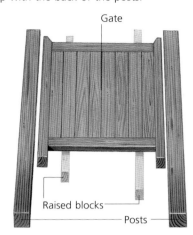

Gate

Raised blocks

Posts

2 Position the gate about 50mm below the tops of the posts.

3 Use a long piece of timber and a builder's square to make sure the posts are aligned at the top and bottom and are a uniform distance apart.

4 Place the hinges and catches in position. Adjust the posts as necessary to give clearance for the fastenings to operate.

5 Lay a length of timber across the posts about 50–75mm below the bottom of the gate, and use it as a straight-edge to mark a line across each post. This is the depth to which the posts should be sunk.

6 Check that the marked lines are at right angles and the same distance from the top of each post.

7 Mark the timber length with the position of each side of each post.

8 Use the timber length as a gauge to mark the post positions on the ground. Dig holes about 300mm square and 75mm deeper than the depth marked on the post. Drop removed soil onto a plastic sheet for easy removal.

9 Place a brick flat in the bottom of each hole.

10 Lay the timber gauge across the holes as a guide to positioning the posts. Place each post in the hole on top of the brick and get a helper to hold it upright while you temporarily support it with timber stays wedged with pegs. Check with a spirit level that each post is vertical.

11 Use a flat piece of timber and a spirit level across the top of the gateposts to check that they are level.

12 Anchor each post by ramming in rubble or hardcore. Leave the top 100mm for concrete. Add the concrete and leave it to set for 48 hours, then remove the post supports and hang the gate (overleaf). If your ground is soft, anchor the posts more securely (overleaf).

Setting posts in soft ground

On soft ground, gateposts may be pulled inwards by the movement of the gate. To prevent this, dig a trench about 300mm wide and 200mm deep between the posts and fill it with concrete.

Hanging the gate

1 Place two blocks or bricks between the gateposts and stand the gate on them. For flush hinges, line up the back of the gate with the backs of the posts. For pin fittings, centre the gate on the posts.

2 Use timber wedges to hold the sides of the gate in position with the correct clearance gaps for the fittings. Check with a spirit level that the top rail is horizontal.

3 Hold each hinge in place with the strap along the gate rail while you mark the position of the fixing holes on the post (see below). Drill pilot holes for two screws on each part of each hinge and partially fix each hinge. Then open and close the gate and check that it is level and swinging properly before you finish fitting the hinges. Partially fix the fastener on the gate and post. Then check that it closes properly before you secure the fittings.

4 Fit a post cap to each gatepost unless the post top is sloped or rounded to shed rain. If you cut a square top to a slope, make sure it is protected with wood preservative.

Hanging a gate on masonry piers

Masonry piers are usually made of large blocks of cut or ashlar stone, or bricks. Although rough stone may be used this makes hanging a gate much harder. Drilling for the hinges will be easier if you start with a pilot hole.

Tools *Hammer; drill; masonry drill bits; spirit level.*

Materials *Eyebolt hinges; gate latch; gate.*

Before you start Check the piers to make sure that they are in good order before hanging your gate and make any necessary repairs to the masonry. Special hinges are needed for hanging a gate on masonry, so don't use hinges meant for wooden posts.

1 Place the gate between the two piers. When viewed from above the gate should bisect the centre line of each pier. Sit the gate on temporary packing so that it is about 50 to 60mm above ground level.

2 Place wedges on either side of the gate so that the gate is held firmly. Use the spirit level to make sure that the top rail is level.

3 Measure down 175mm from the top rail and 250mm up from the bottom of the gate on the hanging side and put a pencil mark at these points. Transfer these pencil marks to the masonry piers then remove the gate.

4 Drill a pilot hole, then a larger hole, for the hinge: the size is dependent on the hinges that you are using. Hammer in the plug and screw in the hinge.

5 Attach the other half of the hinge to the gate, check to make sure that it swings properly and that the gap is even. If it is not, screw the hinges in or out of the piers a little to adjust their position.

6 Finally attach the latch to the other side of the gate and the striker to the pier.

Alternatively If you are building a pier to take a gate, set the gate hangers into the masonry as you work.

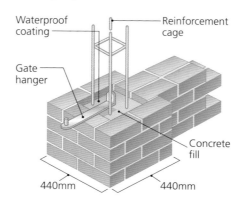

Waterproof coating — Reinforcement cage

Gate hanger

Concrete fill

440mm   440mm

Choosing gate accessories

Apart from hinges and catches a gate may need other fittings. Double gates usually need a central ground socket of some sort to fit against, and a hook to hold the gate open is also generally necessary.

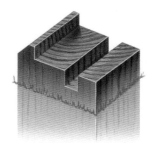

Centre stop block
Sunk into the ground at the meeting point of a pair of gates to stop them from swinging outwards, and to provide a locking point.

Drop bolts
For use with a centre stop block or a receiver socket or staple. A monkey-tail bolt (left) is easy to grasp. A heavy-duty bolt (right) is best for double gates.

Hook-type holdback Has to be fastened and unfastened by hand.

Counter-weighted hook Stops a gate from swinging too far when it is opened, and also holds it open.

You can buy fixing brackets for securing a gate post to a wall or a masonry pier. They comprise right-angled brackets with bolts that are anchored in the wall and plugs that are anchored in the post. A post secured in this way will support the hanging or closing side of the gate.

Hanging a pair of gates

Cramp double gates together and hang them in the same way as a single gate, but with a clearance gap between them. Use a strip of wood 15mm wide down the centre, and pack it out at the top to be 20mm wide, so that the gap is wider at the top. This allows for initial wear on the hinges, which would otherwise cause the gates to drop at the centre. Use two or three large G-cramps to hold the stiles together, making sure the two gates are level with each other.

If the gates are cross-braced, make sure that the bottom of each diagonal is on the hinge side, so that the tops of the two diagonals meet in the middle.

Looking after a gate

Keep gates well treated with timber preservative or paint to prevent rotting or rusting. Hinges can be smeared with oil or grease to guard against rust, but for latches, which are constantly handled, paint is preferable, unless they are galvanised or japanned metal.

Repairing rotten timber

Cut out small areas of rot on the gate back to sound wood and fill the cavity with a two-part wood-repair filler of the epoxy-resin type. This sets after about 15 minutes and can be sanded down with medium-grade abrasive paper or a power sander to a smooth finish. The repair will not be visible after repainting.

Rotting timber parts such as pales or braces can be replaced. Treat new timber with a wood preservative (page 439), using a clear coating if it is to be painted later, or buy pre-treated timber, which will last longer. A rotting or damaged gatepost should be replaced or repaired in the same way as a fence post (page 438); but do not use a post spike. Repair a rotting post top in the same way as you would a fence post top (page 438).

Dealing with rust

Keep a lookout for rust spots appearing on fittings or metal gates, and remove them with abrasive paper. Repaint the area you have rubbed down immediately – rust can recur overnight. Remove severe rusting by scrubbing with a wire brush (wear safety goggles). Do not use a proprietary remover if you are going to repaint with a rust-inhibiting paint. Once the rust is removed, you can either repaint the area with a rust-neutralising primer followed by an undercoat and gloss coat, or use a one-coat paint such as Hammerite, which is both a rust-inhibitor and a finishing paint.

Repairing a sagging gate

The most common cause of a sagging gate is hinges that have worked loose through years of use, so check the condition of the hinges first. Replace loose hinge screws with longer, galvanised screws if possible. If not, tap wooden dowels (or fibre wall plugs) into the holes and use screws of the same size.

Alternatively, if possible, refit the hinges slightly higher or lower so that the screws will be biting into firm wood. Replace worn or broken hinges.

If the hinges are in good condition, the timber joints of the gate may be loose. An isolated loose joint can be repaired by fixing a metal plate – tee, corner or straight – or an angle bracket to the joint. Try to force a waterproof adhesive up into the loose joint, then hold it together while you screw the bracket in place.

A very rickety gate should be either replaced or taken apart and remade. Clean away all old adhesive from the joints and reassemble using a waterproof adhesive. Reinforce mortise-and-tenon joints by drilling into the post and through the tongue of the tenon, then insert a glued dowel. After reassembling the gate, clamp it together while the adhesive dries.

A gate may sag because it has no diagonal brace, or because the brace is not strong enough (or the gate may have been hung on the wrong side). The brace should be firmly fitted between the cross rails on the back of the gate, with the top towards the latch.

Lift and wedge the gate into its proper position and make sure that it is a good fit before fixing the brace with waterproof adhesive and galvanised screws.

Choosing garage doors

In addition to closing off the garage, providing security and keeping the weather out of your garage, the doors are often one of the first things that most visitors to your house notice. Until 20 years ago nearly all garage doors were made of wood that had to be painted on a regular basis. Modern doors are made from a wide range of durable and low-maintenance materials, including metal, plastic and glass fibre. These are often stronger and lighter, making it possible to fit larger one-piece doors, with differing opening arrangements, such as up-and-over doors and roller doors.

Side hung doors on hinges

This is the traditional method for hanging wooden garage doors (above). The doors are hung on large hinges attached to a wooden frame screwed or bolted to the brickwork of the garage. Normally the doors are made as a pair and meet in the middle. They should be hung in the same way as hanging a pair of gates (page 442), but be sure to buy hinges that are suitable for the weight of the large doors. The doors are commonly secured using a combination of internal and external bolts and padlocks.

Wooden garage doors require regular maintenance, such as repainting, to prevent them from rotting.

Side-hung, hinged doors must open outwards for access, which prevents you from parking too close to the doors. Of all the garage door options, this one demands most clearance in front of the garage.

Up-and-over doors

(page 442)

Retractable door

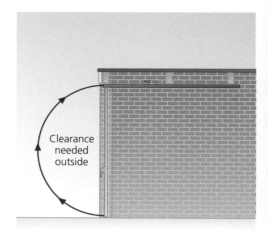

Clearance needed outside

The door is swung on pivots and runs on rails fixed to the inside of the garage roof when opened. This style of door requires a large clearance in front of it for opening. Can be made in almost any material and hangs on a 75 x 75mm wooden frame attached to the inside of the opening.

Canopy door

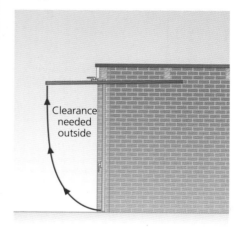

Clearance needed outside

So called because, when open, a section of the door protrudes beyond the front face of the garage. The mechanism is slightly different from the retractable door and takes up less room inside the garage. The door also requires less clearance in front of the garage for opening.

Sectional door One of the easiest to automate with electric openers (opposite). The door is made up of horizontal panels, wider than those in a roller door (right), which allow it to retract into the roof without protruding in front of the garage. It does not roll up. Does not require a wooden frame, as the door runs in rollers in a metal channel fitted inside the garage. The door closes against a lip seal to prevent draughts.

Roller door Made from slim sections that roll around a metal pole attached to the inside top of the door opening. Provides a very secure door, which takes up less space than any of the other types, does not need the roof inside the garage to be kept clear and requires no opening clearance in front of the garage. The door fits behind the opening in the brickwork, so this is a good choice if the opening is an unusual shape or not quite square. Designs are limited as the door has to be made in small sections to enable it to roll up, but doors are available in a wide range of colours. Suitable for use with automatic door openers (right).

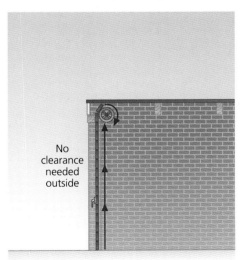

No clearance needed outside

Installing an up-and-over garage door

Garage doors can be made in almost any size to fit the opening of an existing garage. If you are buying a made-to-measure door, take very careful and accurate measurements from your garage door opening before placing the order.

Before you start Despite their size, installing an up-and-over door is an easy job, provided the wooden sub-frame that you are attaching it to is in good order and square. If you are replacing an existing door, it makes good sense to replace the frame at the same time, as it is prone to rot at the bottom of the uprights.

Tools *Hammer; screwdriver; socket spanners; power drill; tape measure; spirit level.*

Materials *Garage door; wooden shims; 75 x 75mm prepared timber door frame.*

1 Install the wooden frame into the door opening. Place shims under each leg to keep the bottoms 10mm above the level of the ground.

2 Use a spirit level to make sure that both sides of the wooden frame are plumb and the head is level. Drill through the legs 250mm up from the bottom into the brickwork of the garage wall and insert a wallplug followed by a 100mm screw.

3 Check again that the frame is plumb and level and put in two more screws each side 250mm down from the top and one in the centre of each upright.

4 Attach the fixing lugs on the metal frame of the door into the predrilled and tapped holes using the screws provided. Tighten them just enough to hold them in place but do not over-tighten them.

5 From inside the garage, lift the door into place with a helper so that the metal lugs rest against the inside of the wooden sub-frame.

6 Place 10mm spacer blocks of wood under the bottom of the door and screw the metal angle brackets to the wooden frame. Check that the door is level.

7 Attach the spring clamps to the bottom of the wooden door frame, taking the measurements from the instructions that came with the door.

8 Clip the springs onto the brackets on the door frame, then pass a long screwdriver through the top loop of the spring before pulling it up and hooking it onto the metal pegs on either side of the door.

9 Attach the top rails at one end to the inside of the wooden frame and at the other end to the ceiling rafters, using the angle brackets that are supplied with the kit. If your ceiling is unusually high, you may have to extend these brackets with slotted steel or wooden extenders.

10 Attach the lock mechanism if this is not already fitted.

11 Lightly grease the rollers and latches, then check that the door opens and closes smoothly. Make any adjustments necessary and make sure that all the fixing bolts are firmly tightened.

Installing an automatic garage door opener

It is often seen as a luxury, but a simple remote-controlled motor allows you to open your garage from inside the car. Not only does this mean that you do not have to get wet in the rain, it is seen by many people as a safety feature, as they do not have to leave the car to open or close the door.

Automatic door openers are suitable for sectional or roller garage doors (left). For roller doors, a motor turns a drum, which rolls the door up into a compact box fitted above the door opening.

The door and mechanism are easy to fit and simply require a power supply to be run to the motor. Connect the motor to a flex outlet plate run from a fused connection unit on a spur from the main garage circuit (see Fitting a fused connection unit, page 286 and Wiring electrical appliances into a bathroom, page 287). Follow the manufacturer's fitting instructions that are supplied with the kit.

Most automatic doors come with a manual override, in the form of a pole-operated winding device, for use in the event of a power failure.

Choosing a path, drive or patio

When choosing material for a path or drive, take into account the amount of wear it is likely to get, as well as the appearance – whether it will blend in with the house exterior and garden surroundings. Consider also the amount of work that will be involved in laying the material.

The cheapest materials are often those that are quickest and easiest to lay. It may be cost-effective to mix materials, such as paving slabs and bricks or gravel.

In estimating the cost, do not forget to include materials such as mortar, hardcore or sand, as well as the surface material. Also allow for the cost of any equipment you may need to hire, such as a plate vibrator.

Paving slabs

Large, flat, pre-cast concrete slabs laid on mortar. Hydraulically pressed types are strongest and should be used for a drive, which has to take the weight of one or more vehicles. Surfaces may be smooth (non-slip), polished or patterned to appear like cobbles, bricks or tiles in straight or curved designs. Reasonably quick and easy to lay on a straight site, but difficult to form into curves. Careful planning is needed on a slope or an awkwardly shaped site. Can look monotonous in large areas unless colours, shapes or textures are used to enliven the surface. Colours include grey, buff and red. Square, rectangular, hexagonal or circular shapes available.

Coverage
450 x 450mm – 4.9 slabs per m²
600 x 450mm – 3.7 slabs per m²
600 x 600mm – 2.8 slabs per m².

Sub-base For a drive: 100mm of compacted hardcore topped by 125mm of concrete. For a path or patio: 100mm of hardcore, or firm, well-rolled ground.

A patio laid with slabs of different sizes has an informal appearance and the appeal of traditional stone paving.

Paving blocks

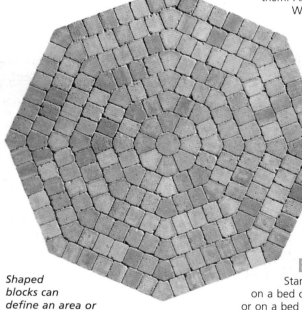

Shaped blocks can define an area or add interest to a patio.

Brick-like concrete blocks laid on a bed of thick sand, and held in place between existing walls, edging blocks or kerbing. Commonly rectangular, but interlocking decorative shapes are also available. Colours include grey, red, charcoal, brown, buff, marigold and red-grey mixtures. Blocks can be laid like brick in various bond patterns (page 465), or patterns such as basket-weave or herringbone. A herringbone pattern is best for drives because it gives blocks the stability to withstand tyre movements when vehicles are manoeuvring. Blocks take longer to lay than slabs, but look good and are easier to fit into awkwardly shaped areas. They can easily be lifted to get at underground pipes. You will need to hire a plate vibrator (pages 451, 456) to lay blocks over a large area such as a drive or patio, and a block splitter (page 456) for cutting to size where necessary.

Coverage Rectangular blocks, 200 x 100 x 65mm – 50 blocks cover 1m².

Sub-base For a drive: 100mm compacted hardcore topped with 75mm of sand compacted to 50mm when the blocks are laid. For a path or patio: firm, well-compacted ground and sand bed.

Crazy paving

Slabs of irregular shape fitted together on a bed of mortar. Broken stone or concrete slabs can be bought by the tonne or square metre. Collect your own if you can, so that you can choose your own mixture of colours, shapes and sizes, preferably mostly large and medium pieces because small pieces involve more work. Ideal for making a lively looking drive. More difficult to lay than regular slabs because the shapes have to be fitted to a pattern. Also, they may not be all the same thickness, and so may need different amounts of mortar to level them. Allow plenty of time for the job. When filling in the joints, a good way of bringing out the shapes is to draw a well-defined groove in the mortar round each slab using the tip of a brick trowel.

Coverage 1 tonne covers about 9–10m².

Sub-base For a drive: 100mm of compacted hardcore topped by 125mm of concrete. For a path or patio: 100mm of hardcore, or firm, well-rolled ground.

Bricks

Standard bricks or brick pavers laid on a bed of sand between fixed edging, or on a bed of mortar. Use special-quality F grade bricks that withstand hard weather, especially frost. Brick pavers are normally thinner than bricks and are available in square or interlocking shapes. The colour range is very wide, in browns, reds, brindles and yellows. Bricks can be laid in walling bond patterns (page 465) or others – typically herringbone and basket weave – and used flat or on edge. Paving is also available resembling old hand-made bricks in traditional basket-weave style. They are a little more difficult to lay than blocks, if bedded on mortar, but similarly flexible and suitable for almost any setting. Bricks bedded in sand have to be tapped down by hand, as they are likely to crack under a plate vibrator.

Coverage
Standard bricks, 215 x 103 x 50mm: laid flat, 40 bricks per m²; laid on edge, 50 bricks per m².
Brick-effect paving, 450 x 450 x 38mm: 4.9 pavers per m².

Sub-base As for paving blocks, but with the sand layer 55mm deep.

Concrete

Sand and coarse aggregate (crushed gravel or stone) bound together with cement and water in certain proportions (pages 458, 460) and laid, while soft, between temporary edgings. Hardens to a tough, stone-like surface. Can be mixed as you go along, or delivered in loads for large areas. The surface layer should be 100–150mm thick for a drive or 50–75mm thick for a path. Very strong, cheaper than paving slabs or blocks, and straightforward to lay. Edging formwork has to be set up in preparation. Mixing to the right consistency is critical, and mixing can be hard work. Hire a small mixer (page 460) if laying about 0.5m³ or more. Concrete hardens in about 2 hours – faster in hot weather. The surface can be given various patterned finishes.

Colouring pigments can be stirred into the mixture – the shade varies with the amount applied, and it is difficult to get a uniform colour.

Coverage Available as separate ingredients or in ready-mixed loads. Quantities per m³ are given on page 459.

Sub-base For a drive: 100mm of well-compacted hardcore and 25–50mm of ballast to fill the gaps. For a path: firm, well-rolled soil, with hardcore in soft patches or hollows.

Cold asphalt

A mixture of bitumen and finely crushed gravel or stone (macadam) spread on top of a thin coat of bitumen emulsion to 'tack' it in place, then compacted between temporary or permanent edging to form a tough, waterproof surface. Normally used to re-surface an existing drive, or for covering worn and pitted concrete or paving slabs. It is not suitable for making a new drive, but can be used for a new path provided that the hardcore base can be firmly compacted, generally by using a plate vibrator (page 451). Cheaper than paving and simple to lay, but sticky to work with. Wear protective shoes and clothing, and protect floor coverings if any is likely to be tramped into the house. The ground needs to be treated with weedkiller two weeks before the surface is laid. Supplied in bags and available in red and black. Decorative stone chippings may be provided with each bag. It tends to look monotonous in large areas, and the surface can be dented by the weight of a car on a pillar jack.

Coverage One 25kg bag covers about 0.9m² laid 20mm deep and rolled to 15mm deep. A 5kg can of emulsion covers about 7m² on a firm surface.

Sub-base For a drive: an existing surface such as concrete, paving slabs or old asphalt. For a path: well-compacted hardcore as for stone chippings (right).

Stone chippings

Can be scattered on cold asphalt as a decorative dressing, or used alone as a surface dressing, bound together with a thick coat of bitumen emulsion, to give a firm, waterproof surface, suitable for light traffic, but loose chippings may be thrown up by tyres. Normally used to re-surface an existing drive, but may be suitable for a new drive provided the hardcore base can be well compacted, generally by a plate vibrator (pages 451, 456). Colours include greyish-white, pink and grey-green. Cheap and easy to lay. The ground needs to be treated with weedkiller two weeks before the chippings are laid.

Coverage One 25kg bag covers about 2.5m². A 25kg can of bitumen emulsion covers 35m² on a hard surface, 13.5m² on a firm, dense surface or 6.5m² on a loose, open surface.

Sub-base For a drive: existing surface or 100–150mm compacted ballast. For a path: 75–100mm hardcore topped with ballast.

Gravel

A mixture of small stones laid loose on a firm surface, usually between anchored edgings. The stones are normally well-rounded pea gravel of a single size, either 10mm or 20mm. Available in white or various shades of brown. Cheap, easy and quick to lay, but can be a difficult surface for walking on or pushing a pram or bicycle across. Stones may be carried into the house on shoes. Needs regular raking or rolling. Not suitable for a drive with a pronounced slope.

Coverage A tonne covers about 15m² if laid about 25mm deep.

Sub-base For a drive or path: 100mm of well-compacted hardcore topped with 25mm of sand.

> ### ALTERNATIVE GROUND COVER
>
> A new and ecologically sound form of ground cover for drives and paths is a honeycombed grid made from recycled plastic. The grid is laid in square tiles measuring 330mm across. Each hole in the grid is 50mm deep and 60 x 60mm square, and can be filled with sand or gravel. Alternatively, you can fill the grid with a soil and fertiliser mixture that can be then sown with grass seed to create a very hard-wearing grass surface.
>
> **Sub-base** For a drive: 200–300mm compressed gravel or ballast mixture, or the same depth of ballast and sand mixture.

Edging and kerbing

For providing fixed edging to an area of paving blocks laid on a sand bed, or to confine loose or soft surfaces such as gravel or asphalt. Paving blocks can be edged with a header course of the same blocks used for the paving (page 457). Path edging is usually available in straight lengths only; standard kerbing, which is thicker and deeper, is also sold in curved lengths. Tops may be flat, chamfered, rounded, bullnosed or scalloped. Kerbing can be laid to finish above the paved surface (to check surface water or stop cars going onto the garden), flush with the paved surface, or just below the paved surface so that it is covered by grass or soil and only the paving shows. Has to be carefully set up in position on its concrete bed to finish at the correct height in relation to the surface, and with the correct crossfall and alignment if laid above or flush with the paving.

Coverage Edging: available in a wide range of sizes and shapes. Standard kerb: 600–900mm long, 100–150mm wide and 250mm or 300mm deep.

Sub-base Hardcore from base topped by a 70mm layer of concrete wide enough for the kerb thickness and a generous haunching of bedding mortar (for edging) or concrete (for standard kerbing).

Kerbstones and edging can be chosen to match a path or driveway (above) or may be used to separate a planted border from an area of gravel (top).

Preparing the sub-base for a drive, path or patio

How well a surface will support heavy loads depends to a great extent on the strength of the sub-base. A drive that has to take the weight of one or more cars needs a stronger sub-base than a path.

Before you start Some paving materials need a sub-base of hardcore only, others need hardcore topped with a layer of concrete (pages 448–9). On soft ground or where heavy traffic is likely, the sub-base may need to be even deeper.
• A drive needs to be at least 3m wide for car doors to be opened or for people to walk past a parked car.
• All drives need to be sloped from side to side (a cross-fall) so that rainwater will not lie on the surface. A cross-fall of about 1 in 40 is suitable for a drive.
• A drive should also slope away from the house, so may need a lengthways slope of 1 in 100. It can be steeper, if necessary, to follow the natural slope of the ground.
• Consult your local authority if a new driveway needs access onto a main road.

Tools *Pegs and string lines; builder's square; mallet; spade; shovel; steel tape measure; timber pegs 25mm square and 460mm long; chalk or paint; wheelbarrow; spirit level; wooden shims; earth rammer, garden roller or plate vibrator. Possibly also sledgehammer; concreting tools.*

Materials *Hardcore (see below); ballast (page 458). Possibly concrete (page 460).*

THE SUB-BASE MATERIAL

Hardcore is made up of well-broken bricks, blocks or stone and can be bought from builders' merchants. A tonne of hardcore covers roughly 5m² if it is laid 100mm deep.

Some hardcore may contain demolition rubble, which includes unsuitable material such as wood and plaster. Such hardcore will not bed down well.

Gaps in the hardcore surface are filled with a thin layer of ballast (sand and shingle) – a process known as blinding.

Hoggin is a more expensive form of hardcore, made up of gravel and sandy clay, and will bed down well.

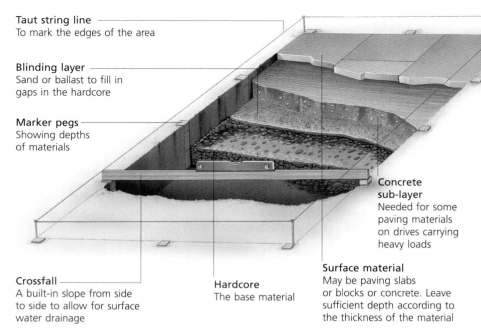

Taut string line
To mark the edges of the area

Blinding layer
Sand or ballast to fill in gaps in the hardcore

Marker pegs
Showing depths of materials

Crossfall
A built-in slope from side to side to allow for surface water drainage

Hardcore
The base material

Concrete sub-layer
Needed for some paving materials on drives carrying heavy loads

Surface material
May be paving slabs or blocks or concrete. Leave sufficient depth according to the thickness of the material

Four layers of a drive The depth of the sub-base material depends on the surface it is supporting, the weight that will have to be carried, and the nature of the ground (pages 448–9). This illustration shows a drive in cross-section.

1 Use taut pegged string lines to mark the edges of the drive area, allowing for permanent edging such as a kerb. Check with a steel tape measure that the width of the site is uniform, and use a builder's square to ensure that right angles are true. For making a curve, see opposite.

2 Decide on the direction of the crossfall. The drive should slope away from the house or garage wall. If the ground slopes naturally towards the house, build up the hardcore base to reverse the slope, if possible. Otherwise build a drainage channel and soakaway (page 452).

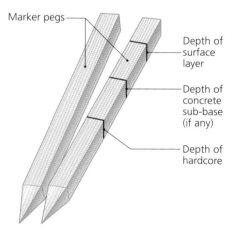

Marker pegs

Depth of surface layer

Depth of concrete sub-base (if any)

Depth of hardcore

3 Mark the timber pegs from the top to show the depths of the various layers, allowing for any bedding sand or mortar.

4 Drive a marked peg into the ground in the top corner (nearest to the house) of the area to be excavated. Set it with its top at the right level for the drive surface.

5 Drive in a row of pegs at about 1.5m intervals across the top of the site, using a spirit level between pairs of pegs to ensure a crossfall of 1 in 40 (see panel, far right).

6 Drive in a second row of pegs 1.5m farther down the drive. Set the top of each to allow for any lengthways slope necessary from the first rows – for a fall of 1 in 100 use a 16mm shim.

7 Continue with rows of pegs down the drive in this way at similar intervals, adjusting the distances of the last rows as necessary so that the final row is at the bottom edge of the site.

8 Dig out the area within the string lines to the lowest peg mark (the base of the hardcore layer). Spread the topsoil on other parts of the garden. Leave any clayey subsoil in a heap for later disposal.

9 Spread hardcore in the excavated area. Ram it down well – using an earth rammer or, for larger areas, a garden roller or plate vibrator – until it is at the marked level for the hardcore surface. If laying concrete paving blocks (page 456), break up the hardcore as small as possible with a sledgehammer before compacting it with a vibrator.

10 Add a thin layer of ballast to fill in the gaps. Ram it down well.

11 If the base material includes a layer of concrete, spread the concrete over the hardcore and blinding layer and tamp it down to the marked level.

12 Remove the pegs and fill in the holes with hardcore or hardcore and concrete before laying the paving material.

Preparing the sub-base for a path

A path that will be subject to heavy loads or that is on soft ground will need a well-compacted hardcore sub-base. Prepare it in the same way as for the sub-base for a drive, except that fewer surface marker pegs will be needed.

The path need not slope along its length, but it should have a crossfall of about 1 in 80 away from the wall if it is alongside a house (see Making a sloped surface, right).

If a hardcore sub-base is necessary, set up string lines and marker pegs and dig out the site only to the depth of the surface material and any bedding needed, such as a mortar or sand layer (pages 448–9). Slope the bottom of the excavation to one side and use a spirit level and shim across the bottom to get the required slope. Fill in any depression in the surface with well-broken hardcore. Use a garden roller to compact the surface until it is firm and even.

Marking out a curved path

Use a garden hosepipe or lengths of rope to mark the outline of the curve on each side by eye.

It is usually necessary to allow extra width between the curving sides. If they are the same width apart as the straight sides, an optical illusion will occur, making the path appear to be narrow at the curve when viewed from a short distance away.

Set up a peg and string line to follow the shape of the marked curve. The pegs will need to be closer together than when using straight string lines.

Preparing the sub-base for a patio

Do this in the same way as for a drive, but with hardcore only below the surface material. A slope of 1 in 60 away from the house or towards a drain is normally enough for drainage, but not so steep as to affect the levels of chairs and tables.

KEEPING CLEAR OF THE DAMP-PROOF COURSE

If the drive is against a house wall, make sure the base is dug deep enough for the drive surface to be at least 150mm below the damp-proof course, commonly visible as a thick line of mortar usually two or three brick courses up the wall.

Where it is not possible for the drive surface to be low enough, one alternative is to slope the drive towards the house and build a gully and soakaway. Alternatively, you may be able to build concrete skirting (see Defects in the damp-proofing, page 411) between the drive edge and wall.

MAKING A SLOPED SURFACE

Place a spirit level – on a length of timber, if necessary – across the pegs marking the surface level. Use a thin piece of wood (known as a shim) under the spirit level, or its support, on the lower-side pegs. Tap down the lower-side peg until the spirit level is set level with the shim in position.

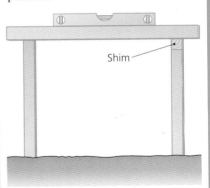

Shim

The thickness of the shim depends on the slope required and the width between pegs. For example, on a path 1m wide, you need a 13mm shim for a crossfall of 1 in 80, 16mm for 1 in 60, or 25mm for 1 in 40. For a crossfall of 1 in 40 on a drive with marker pegs spaced at 1.5m intervals, you need a 40mm shim. The calculation of the shim size need not be precise.

TOOLS FOR A SUB-BASE

Many compacting or demolition tools can be hired. Hire firms are listed in *Yellow Pages* under Hire Services – Tools and Equipment.

Earth rammer A steel handle with a heavy club end for ramming down hardcore.

Garden roller A sand or water-filled roller 100kg or heavier to be used instead of an earth rammer for compacting large areas of hardcore (or for rolling cold asphalt surfaces).

Plate vibrator Instead of a roller, you can hire a petrol-driven plate vibrator (also known as a power compactor) for ramming down large areas of hardcore. It is also used for bedding down concrete paving blocks.

Demolition or breaker hammer The easiest way to break up a concrete surface before laying a new path or drive is with an electric-powered hammer. It is fitted like a drill with a chisel or point for cutting, and can also be used with a masonry bit for drilling fixing holes into or through concrete. Hire a lightweight tool for concrete up to 100mm thick, or a heavyweight one for thicker concrete. Wear safety goggles and, if possible, steel-tipped boots when using the hammer.

Other useful tools Pegs and a string line are needed for marking the outline of an area to be excavated. The stretched string line, held taut between the pegs, is also a guide for keeping straight edges.

A garden spade is necessary for digging out soil from the sub-base area. A sledgehammer may be useful for breaking up hardcore, and a pickaxe for breaking hard ground or small areas of old concrete. Both can be hired.

You will also need concreting tools (page 457) if the sub-base needed includes a layer of concrete above the hardcore.

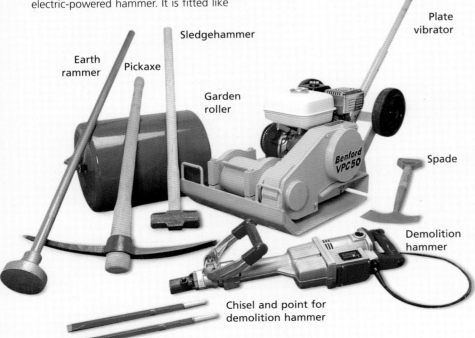

Earth rammer

Pickaxe

Sledgehammer

Garden roller

Plate vibrator

Spade

Demolition hammer

Chisel and point for demolition hammer

Masking or raising a manhole cover

When you build a drive or patio, the ground level is often slightly raised, which means that a manhole cover on an inspection chamber within the paving must be either masked with slabs or raised to fit in at the same level.

The manhole can be masked with a double seal cover, which is available from some builders' merchants. Covers are made of pressed steel and they are commonly 610 x 460mm in size.

Skeleton-type double seal cover

There are two types: the skeleton type has steel mesh within the edging frame and can be filled in with concrete (apart from the key holes); the recess type has an open tray that can be filled with loose-laid material. Plan the depth of the sub-base so that the masking cover will be flush with the surrounding paving.

To raise the height of a manhole cover, first remove the lid and lay a sheet of polythene in the base of the chamber to prevent debris falling into the drains.

Then chip away the mortar surrounding the cast-iron frame with a club hammer and cold chisel. Take care not to strike the frame, which shatters easily.

When you have released the frame, clean away the mortar covering the top surface of the brick walls of the chamber.

The material you use to add height to the chamber walls depends on the increase in height required. If the amount is less than the height of a brick – 75mm including the mortar – use brick slips or strips cut from 13mm thick concrete roofing tiles, laid in courses in the same way as bricks.

Reset the frame on a bed of sand-cement mortar – three parts sand to one part cement. Tap it gently into position using a block of wood and a club hammer. Use a spirit level to check that it is level across its width and length.

Slope the mortar round the outside downwards away from the frame to carry away rainwater.

Dealing with an airbrick

The drive or patio surface must not cover an airbrick low down in the house wall. If, however, there is no way of keeping the paved surface below the airbrick, one solution is to stop the edge of the paving short, leaving a pit at least 300mm wide in front of it. Keep the pit clear of leaves and debris.

An alternative solution is to run a duct under the surface from the airbrick to an open edge such as a retaining wall.

To fit a duct, remove the airbrick (page 408) and cement a length of 100mm diameter plastic piping for underground drainage into the hole. Use bagged sand-and-cement mortar (page 458) or a 1:4 cement-sand mix. Run the piping through the hardcore base and then cement it to a new airbrick at the other end.

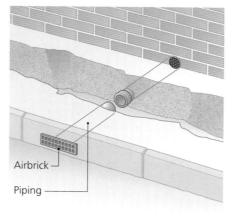

Airbrick

Piping

Building a drainage channel

If you build a drive that follows a natural slope of the ground towards the house, you will have to build a channel at the lowest edge of the drive to carry away rainwater.

Before you start Design the channel so that it runs into either an existing drain or a soakaway – a drainage pit sited at least 3m from the house.

The channel should be lined with concrete and should have a fall of about 1 in 40 towards the soakaway. Make the channel using a concrete paving mix (page 459) and shape it about 25mm deep using a length of drainpipe. Make sure there are no ridges.

Alternatively Use ready-made concrete channelling, mortared into the hardcore base. It is available from builders' merchants in about 900mm lengths. Enclosed types (as above) are about 250mm deep and 300mm wide with a narrow slot or metal grid in the top. Or you can buy dish channel with a 25mm deep dish.

Making a soakaway

Any type of soakaway is for dispersing rainwater or surface water only. It must not be used for household drainage water. Get advice from your local authority in case they have specific regulations.

A home-made soakaway

1 To make a home-made soakaway, dig a pit about 1.2m across and at least the same depth. If you hit a pan of clay that is so hard you cannot dig through it, make the soakaway longer than 1.2m to compensate for the lack of depth.

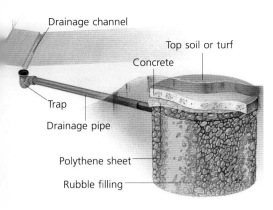

Drainage channel
Top soil or turf
Concrete
Trap
Drainage pipe
Polythene sheet
Rubble filling

2 Break up the bottom of the pit with a fork before you fill it to within about 100mm of the top with rubble, coarser at the bottom. A pit 1.2m across and 1.2m deep needs about 1.8m³ of rubble, which is roughly 25–30 wheelbarrow loads.

3 Direct the drainpipe from the channel into the rubble at a gentle slope. Fit a gully trap at the top end.

4 Cover the rubble with a sheet of heavy-gauge polythene, then add a layer of concrete (page 460) 75mm thick. Finally, cover with a layer of soil or turf.

A ready-made soakaway

You can buy a ready-made soakaway with instructions for installation. It consists of pierced concrete segments which build up into rings (see below). They are laid on a strip foundation. Water entering the soakaway seeps out through the rings and through a wrap-round separation membrane into the surrounding soil; there is no rubble filling. Rings are 300 or 420mm high and 1.5 or 2.1m across.

Ready-made soakaway

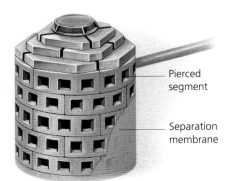

Pierced segment

Separation membrane

Laying slabs for a drive or patio

Covering your drive or patio with slabs is quick and easy, but careful planning beforehand is necessary.

Before you start Plan the size of the site so that it can be divided exactly by the dimensions of the slabs to be used, if possible. It will save you having to cut too many slabs. Allow for a gap of 10mm between slabs for mortar joints.

Make a scale plan of the site on graph paper, showing the positions and numbers of the slabs – especially if you are mixing different sizes, colours and textures. Where necessary, take up odd dimensions either by using 25mm wide mortar joints, or fill in with a small-sized unit such as a brick. Use mortar to fill small irregular areas.

Some slab manufacturers supply leaflets showing patterns that can be made using their slabs, and give an estimate of the numbers needed for different patterns.

For a drive, lay slabs on a full bed of mortar. For a path or patio where use is not heavy, lay each slab on five generous dabs of mortar (at the corners and centre).

Tools *Brick trowel; straightedge about 1.8m long; steel tape measure; marker pegs; builder's square (page 467); spirit level; wooden shim (page 451); club hammer; length of timber 100 x 50mm; brick bolster or angle grinder/masonry cutter; pencil; try square; wooden spacers 10mm thick (probably three or four per slab); piece of wood 10mm thick; two shovels; bucket; fine-rose watering can; mixing platform (page 457); damp sponge.*

Materials *Paving slabs – use hydraulically pressed 50mm thick slabs for a drive; bedding mortar mix (page 459) or bagged dry sand-and-cement mortar (page 458) for small areas.*

> **HELPFUL TIP**
>
> Store paving slabs upright, leaning against a wall. Raise them off the ground on two lengths of wood to keep the bottom edges clean.

Preparing the base

1 For a drive, prepare a hardcore and concrete base (page 450), and wait until the concrete is hard (about three days).

Alternatively For a patio, prepare a hardcore base only, with a blinding layer of sand.

2 Adjust the pegged string lines at the edge of the site as a guide to slab alignment. Drive in marker pegs as a guide to the height of the slab surface, taking into account the 25mm depth of bedding mortar, the crossfall, and any lengthways slope. Site the pegs at suitable intervals to be bridged with a spirit level, placed on a straightedge if necessary.

3 Check the marker peg levels with a spirit level and wooden shims (see Making a sloped surface, page 451). Check that the corner lines are true with a builder's square.

4 Mix the bedding mortar on a firm surface in the same way as mixing concrete (page 460), but using sharp sand and cement only. Keep one shovel solely for dry cement. Make the mortar to a fairly dry consistency to support the weight of the slab.

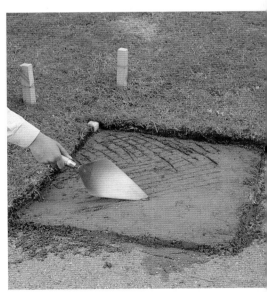

5 Use a brick trowel to spread mortar about 35–50mm thick for the first slab at one corner of the site. Roughen the mortar surface with the point of the trowel.

Laying the slabs

1 Lay the slab carefully on the mortar bed so that its outer edges are in line with the string lines.

2 Place a short length of 100 x 50mm thick timber on the slab to cushion it while you tap it down gently with a club hammer until the surface is level with the height pegs. The slab must be bedded down solidly, with no rocking movement. Ensure the compacted mortar bed is about 25mm thick – adjust the amount if necessary.

3 Use a spirit level and wooden shim to check that the crossfall and lengthways slope of the slab are correct.

4 Lay a row of edge slabs from the corner slab in the same way, in line with the guidelines and pegs. Place wooden spacers at the edge of each slab (unless it has sloped sides) to leave a uniform gap for filling in the joints later.

5 Use a straightedge to check that the surface of each slab in the row is in line with the one before. If a slab is too high, tap it down if possible, or lift it and re-lay it with less mortar. If a slab is too low, lift it, add more mortar, and re-lay it.

6 Lay edge rows out from each corner slab in the same way to form three sides of the area.

7 Fill in between the three edge rows according to your layout pattern. Use a straightedge to check the surface alignment of each slab with its adjoining slabs.

8 Wait for at least two days before removing wooden spacers and filling in the joints. Mix mortar to a dry stiff mix, using 1 part cement to 2 parts sharp sand. Force the mortar well into the joints with a piece of wood 10mm thick. For a crisp appearance and to aid drainage, tap the mortar down so that it lies a few millimetres below the slab surface.

9 Use a damp sponge to clean off excess mortar from the slabs.

Cutting a slab

1 Lay the slab on soft sand and draw a pencil line all round at the cutting point, using a straightedge and try square.

2 Score the pencil line all round, using either a brick bolster or an angle grinder with a masonry cutting disc – which makes a deep groove. Using an angle grinder is less strenuous and more accurate, but handle it carefully to avoid accidents. Wear heavy gloves and protect your eyes from flying particles with safety goggles.

3 To cut the slab, lay it flat (surface upwards). Use the bolster and hammer or the cutting disc to gradually deepen the scored line until the slab breaks cleanly when you tap it.

4 With any cutting method, it is difficult to get a smooth edge. Use cut slabs where the edges will be hidden or not obvious – such as against a lawn edge or mortar joint.

HIRE A BLOCK-CUTTER

If you have a lot of blocks to cut, lay all the whole blocks first, then hire a hydraulic block-cutter (sometimes called a block-splitter) for half a day, and use it to prepare all the cut-to-size pieces you need.

THE FIVE-POINT METHOD

Laying slabs with this method is quick and easy. Start with mortar made from four parts sharp sand to one part cement, prepare the ground and set up guide lines as described on page 453.
- Starting in one corner, place five blobs of mortar on the ground for the first slab (four corners and one in the middle).
- Wet the back of the slab with a brush, to aid adhesion and make the slab easier to slide into place.

- Lift the first slab into place on top of the blobs. You may need a helper.
- Use a piece of timber and a club hammer to tap the slab into position (see step 2, Laying the slabs, left).
- Check that it is level, then fill in any gaps at the exposed sides with mortar, cutting it flush, as you go.
- Continue in the same way with the other slabs, constantly checking levels, until all the slabs are laid.

LAYING CRAZY PAVING

Because crazy paving comes in many shapes and sizes, it is impossible to make a layout plan before you start. Instead, arrange slabs in piles of different colours and sizes, and select from the whole range as you go along. Pick out slabs with a straight edge for the borders.

You will need the same tools as for laying standard paving slabs, except for wooden spacers. It is not practicable to maintain uniform joints between slabs, but they should be no wider than 25mm, for mortar economy and good appearance.

Lay the slabs on a suitable base for a drive or patio and on a full bed of mortar, in the same way as standard slabs.

Not all pieces of crazy paving will be of the same thickness – more mortar will be needed under thinner slabs to maintain a level surface. Check with a straightedge in all directions to make sure that no pieces are tilted.

Constructing a patio

A patio makes a useful sitting or dining area in a garden. Draw a scale plan on graph paper before you begin any work, so that you can work out positions of retaining walls or steps. Make sure your patio will not block any airbricks in the house walls.

Tools *String; wooden pegs; spade; rammer or wooden post; spirit level; heavy post or vibrating plate compacter; straightedge board or timber; spacers; brush; hammer or board and mallet; trowel.*

Materials *Suitable paving materials (pages 448-449); hardcore or crushed stone (page 450); dry sand; mortar (page 467).*

1 Roughly mark out the patio area and clear it. Dig out the soil to a depth of about 150mm, then compact the base with a post or rammer. Measure and mark again, more accurately, using a string line and wooden pegs. Use a spirit level and pegs to establish the final level of the patio surface, ensuring it has a drainage slope (page 451).

2 Cover the excavated area with 100mm of hardcore or crushed stone, spreading it evenly until the surface is level.

3 Compact the hardcore with a vibrating plate compacter (which can be hired). For awkward corners, or a small area, use a heavy post to ram down the hardcore. Once this layer has been well firmed, cover it with about 80mm of dry sand. Use a board or plank with a straightedge to level and compact it.

4 Starting at a corner, set out the edging bricks in a stacking or soldier bond using a straight-edged plank to use as a guide. Insert spacers to keep the gaps even.

5 Bed the bricks onto a damp mortar mix (or a bed of sand) and use a spirit level to check them. Tamp the bricks into the mortar or sand, using a board and mallet or a hammer, until they are all level.

6 Bed the paving slabs. Spread more sand topped with dry mortar mix so that the slabs will be level with the surface of the bricks. Keep on checking the levels.

7 Sprinkle a dry mortar mix or sand over the bricks and slabs and brush it into the spaces between them. It will give a firmer finish and discourage weeds in the gaps. Make sure you fill the gaps completely.

8 When you have completed the whole area, brush off the excess sand or mortar. Allow the surface to settle for a day or two before walking on it.

Creating an optical illusion

Brick or paver patterns can be used to make the patio's dimensions look different. If bricks run lengthways they will give the impression of extra length; bricks running across a patio will make it look broader. Always keep patterns clear and simple, and avoid mixing them, for the best effects.

Granite setts, laid along the edges, finish off the paved area and provide a hard-wearing surface, unaffected by frost.

Laying paving block using a plate vibrator

Block paving needs to be well bedded to give a stable surface for a drive and carefully planned to create a pleasing finish.

Before you start The only way to lay a large area is with a plate vibrator, a light compacting machine powered by a petrol-driven motor. This compacts an area of blocks laid on sand to a level, rigid surface, compressing the sand bed from about 65mm to 50mm deep.

You can hire a plate vibrator. Be sure to ask for one suitable for compacting paving blocks; some types are too heavy. Pass it over the area as evenly as possible. Do not use it within at least 1m of an unsupported edge, where blocks are still being laid.

Paving to be compacted must be laid between firm edges, otherwise the joints will open and the blocks spread. Where there is no adjoining wall or hard edge, lay edging blocks (right) or a kerb (page 449).

Tools *Straightedge; levelling strips of 65mm wide timber as long as the width of the area to be paved; shovel; rake; kneeling board; either block splitter (see below) or brick bolster and club hammer; plate vibrator; soft broom. Possibly also brick trowel; string line and pegs; builder's square (page 467).*

Materials *Paving blocks, sharp sand – 1m³ covers about 15m² at 65mm deep. Possibly also edging blocks; foundation mix concrete (page 459); water.*

1 Prepare a hardcore base for a drive or patio (page 450), wide enough to accommodate a concrete bedding strip for any edging needed (see right). Allow space above the base for the block depth and for a 50mm layer of sand (the depth after compaction).

2 Lay edging blocks if necessary (see right), allowing for the correct crossfall and any lengthways slope (page 451).
Wait three days for the bedding mortar to harden before laying the paving.

3 Place piles of bedding sand, kept as dry as possible, along the site at about 3m intervals so that you can spread it in sections without having to walk over it.

4 Lay 65mm levelling strips on edge across the site – one where you intend to start laying and one 1–2m farther down the site. Check their crossfall with a spirit level.

5 Spread the sand evenly between the strips, using a shovel and rake. Then lay the straightedge across the strips and use it to rake off excess sand until the surface is level with the tops of the strips.

6 Prepare two or three sections to give a 3–4m² run for laying. Remove the levelling strips as you go along, carefully filling the depressions with sand.

7 Start laying blocks at one corner of the prepared sand bed, but keep off the bed. As you work forwards, lay a kneeling board across the blocks already laid but not yet compacted.

8 Lay the blocks snugly against each other according to the chosen pattern (page 448), leaving no joint gaps. Lay whole blocks first, and cut and fit part blocks later. Check corners with a builder's square. Blocks laid at the edges should stand about 10mm higher than the edging – they should bed down when compacted.

LAYING BRICKS OR BLOCKS WITHOUT A PLATE VIBRATOR

A small area of brick or block paving for a footpath or patio can be laid without using a vibrator, although the surface will not be as stable. Edging can be either paving blocks or timber formwork (page 460) thoroughly coated with wood preservative. The sand layer needs to be about 55mm deep only, as it will not be compressed as much as with a vibrator.

Before levelling the sand bed, dampen it with a fine-rose watering can until it is moist enough to hold together when you squeeze it.

9 After laying a run of about 3–4m², use the plate vibrator over the area two or three times, but keep it at least 1m back from the last row of newly laid blocks. You can then see how much the blocks are bedding down. The actual amount depends on the moisture content of the sand. If the compacted surface is conspicuously too high or too low, lift the blocks and adjust the level of the sand bed.

10 Continue in this way until all the whole blocks have been laid. Then fill in the part blocks and compact the area again with the plate vibrator as before.

11 When all the blocks have been laid and compacted, make sure that the surface is dry, then spread a layer of dry, fine sharp sand on it. Use the plate vibrator to work the sand into the crevices between the blocks to lock them in position. Get a helper to brush sand towards the vibrator, as it will be forced away by the vibrations.

Cutting paving blocks

The easiest and quickest way to cut paving blocks is with a block splitter, a hand-operated hydraulic cutter that can be hired. The alternative is to cut them with a hammer and bolster in the same way as bricks (page 470) – a lengthy job when you are paving a large area.

Laying edging blocks

A common and reliable edging is a row of paving blocks on edge, bedded in stiff sand-and-cement mortar on a layer of concrete (page 467). Use the foundation mix. Allow 200mm space for each line of edging blocks at the edges of the area to be paved.

• Make the concrete layer 75mm thick and 300mm wide, to allow 75mm on the outside and 25mm on the inside of the line of edging blocks. Make the concrete surface at the correct depth to allow the top of the edging to coincide with the finished level of the compacted paving. Generally the depth is about 80mm to accommodate the 65mm deep block and a 20mm layer of bedding mortar.

• Wait 24 hours for the concrete to harden before laying the edging on a bed of 3:1 sand-cement mortar. Use a taut string line to set the surface level, taking into account the crossfall and any lengthways fall. Slope the bedding mortar a little way up the outside of the edging to make a small haunch. Leave no joints between blocks, unless the edging is curved.

For curved edging, use a stiff sand-and-cement mortar (2:1 mix). Make the joints 10–25mm wide and pack them with mortar one day after bedding the blocks. Use a little mortar at a time, packed in with a strip of plywood. Fill to the bottom of the chamfered edge of the block, and sponge off any that smears the surface of the edging.

After completing the edging, wait three days before laying the paving blocks. Check that none of the bedding mortar used for the edging will impede the levelling of the paving blocks. If necessary cut mortar away down to the 25mm ledge of the concrete bed.

LEVELLING THE SAND WITH A NOTCHED BOARD

Where the site has fixed edging on both sides – a footpath, for example – the sand can be levelled with a notched board rested across the edging. Use a length of 100 x 50mm board with a 150mm long notch at each end. To allow for the sand compaction, the depth of the board below the notches should be about 5mm less than the depth of the paving blocks, unless you are using a plate vibrator, in which case it should be about 15mm less.

Tools for concreting

Mixing platform If you have no clean, firm surface on which to mix concrete, make one using either boards nailed to cross battens, or a sheet of 12mm thick plywood. Add a 25mm lip all round to stop concrete spilling off. For small batches, use a wheelbarrow. Wash the platform or barrow within two hours of use.

Concrete mixer You can hire a small concrete mixer. Most types will mix a load of concrete in about three minutes. The capacity of the drum is usually stated for both the volume of dry materials and the approximate volume of mixed concrete.

A mixer may be electric or petrol driven. An electric type is usually more convenient if you have a long enough extension lead. Make sure you hire a mixer that runs at 240 volts.

A small mixer is likely to be about 750mm wide. It may be a barrow type (with wheels) or be supplied with a mounting frame so that you can stand a wheelbarrow below it. A barrow type should have a safety bar at the front to stop it tipping out of control.

Wheelbarrow A heavy-duty contractor's wheelbarrow – usually 0.08m³ capacity – can be hired. If it has to be pushed over soft ground or down steps, make a barrow-run – a line of strong planks anchored with pegs or battens. Scaffolding planks about 2.5m long can be hired.

Shovels, buckets and rake Use two shovels and two strong, heavy-duty polythene buckets of identical size. Keep one shovel and one bucket for loading and measuring the cement only so that they stay dry and do not get clogged. Use a garden rake to spread the concrete. Wipe the head clean regularly, before the concrete on it sets.

Tamping beam A length of straight-edged timber 50mm thick used on edge to flatten the concrete and expel air before it sets. Use a beam about 300mm longer than the width of the concrete so that it can rest on the formwork. Tamp a narrow stretch such as a path with a beam about 100mm deep. For broad sections 2–3m across, use a 150mm deep beam with a strong handle at each end. Two people are needed to use a long tamping beam.

Surface-finishing tools For some types of surface finish you will need either a steel plasterer's finishing trowel or a wood or plastic float – tools that you may be able to hire. You can make a suitable wood float with a piece of flat wood 300 x 125mm x 19mm. Screw a D-shaped wooden handle on one side, using two short blocks and one long one with smoothed-off edges.

Arrissing tool A tool resembling a steel float, but with a rounded-over edge. Used to round off the edges of the concrete before it hardens.

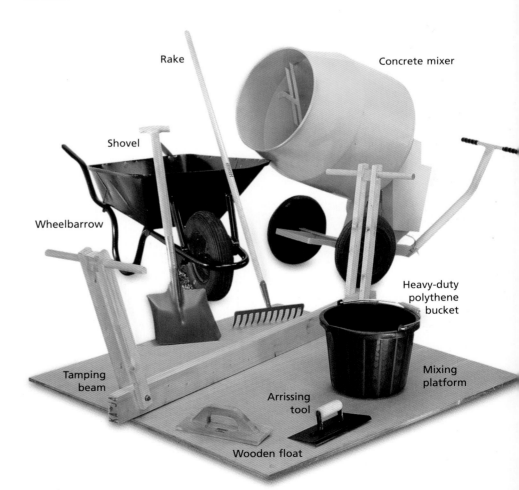

Rake

Concrete mixer

Shovel

Wheelbarrow

Tamping beam

Heavy-duty polythene bucket

Mixing platform

Arrissing tool

Wooden float

CHOOSING MATERIALS FOR MAKING CONCRETE

Concrete is made by mixing sharp sand and small stones (coarse aggregate) with cement and water. You can make concrete yourself, mixing either by hand or with a concrete mixer. Or you can have it delivered ready-mixed for immediate laying.

Mixing it yourself allows you to work at your own pace and lay sections at different times. If you buy ready-mixed concrete, it must be laid all in one go, and you usually need several helpers. But for a large area requiring a full load – likely to be about 60m² at 100mm depth – buying ready-mixed concrete can be considerably cheaper and quicker than mixing your own.

Before you decide on whether to mix your own or buy it ready-mixed, it is important to understand the options and make your choice based on various factors – cost, ease of use, the speed with which the mixture must be used and any complications which might occur in the storing of components.

Cement

Mixed lime and clay processed to a powder that sets hard when mixed with water. Grey ordinary Portland cement (OPC) is used for most concrete. White Portland cement for making decorative white concrete or mortar costs twice as much. Sulphate-resisting cement is for concrete that will be exposed to seawater or soils high in sulphates – most likely on reclaimed land or some types of clay (the local Building Control Officer will advise); it is dearer than OPC and not widely available. Do not use masonry cement, which has additives to increase water-holding and plasticity. Rapid-setting cement is for small repairs under water or in wet conditions.

How it is sold Mainly in 50kg bags, but smaller bags – down to about 2.5kg – are available for small jobs or repairs. Always check the condition of bags when buying – do not buy damp bags or bags in which you can feel lumps, which means that the cement has started to harden. To avoid waste because of hardening during storage, buy only as much as you will use in a week.

Storage Keep bags under cover, off the ground on a dry, hard surface, stacked flat and close together so that air cannot circulate round them. Moisture in the air can penetrate the paper of the bag and cause the cement to harden (this is known as air-hardening or air-setting). Once cement has hardened, it is useless, even though it can be crumbled in the hand. If you have to store an opened bag for several days, keep it dry and airtight inside a tightly tied plastic bag. Cement can irritate the skin. If any goes in the eyes, bathe them at once in cold water and get medical advice.

Sand

Use sharp sand for concreting. It is coarser than builder's (or soft) sand, which is used for making mortar (page 467). Silver sand can be used with white Portland cement for making white concrete or mortar. It is finer than sharp sand, so use slightly more cement in the mix to give it sufficient strength.

How it is sold Loose, for large amounts, either by the tonne (about 1000kg) or the cubic metre (between 1250 and 1750kg, depending on how dry it is. Available from builders' merchants, sand and gravel suppliers or quarries. Sand is cleaned by washing or dry screening. If you buy it from a quarry, make sure this has been done. Small amounts are sold in 50kg and 25kg bags at DIY and garden centres and most builders' merchants.

Storage Store it as clean and dry as possible, on a hard surface or polythene sheeting and with waterproof covering. Sand retains moisture, which increases its bulk. Fully saturated sand has a similar volume to dry sand but weighs a lot more.

Coarse aggregate

Small stones, too big to pass through a 5mm mesh, used to form the bulk of concrete. Well-graded aggregate has a balanced mixture of stone sizes, but is available graded. A 20mm maximum is used for most DIY concreting. Fine concrete is made with 10mm maximum stones.

How it is sold Either by the tonne (about 1000kg) or cubic metre (1500–1800kg). Available from builders' merchants, sand and gravel suppliers and quarries. Some suppliers sell small amounts such as 50kg in bags; these are easier to keep clean and useful for small jobs, but relatively more expensive than buying in bulk.

Storage Keep on a hard surface or tarpaulin with a covering sheet to keep it clean. If it contains a lot of dirt or debris, the concrete will be weakened. Protect your aggregate from frost – if you use it frozen, ice may form within the concrete.

All-in (combined) aggregate and ballast

A mixture of sizes of aggregate, including sand. Mixed ballast is similar but the term usually refers to gravel types of aggregate. It is often used on top of a layer of hardcore to fill in gaps when making a sub-base (page 450). Avoid unwashed ballast.

How it is sold As for coarse aggregate. Tell the supplier you want it for concrete making, as the quality varies. Well-graded material includes 60 per cent of stones bigger than 5mm. One test of the quality is to squeeze the material in your hand – if it leaves a stain because of the high silt content, avoid it.

Storage As for coarse aggregate.

Bagged dry mixes

Mixtures of cement and aggregates (usually in the proportions of 1:2:4) to which only water need be added. The different mixes include: Coarse mix (5 minute-setting) – for jobs such as putting up fence posts. Fine mix – for jobs needing a smooth surface. Sand-and-cement mix (usually 1:3 cement–sharp sand) – for patching or as a bedding mortar for slabs or edging.

How it is sold In 50kg, 40kg and 25kg bags by builders' merchants, hardware shops and DIY and garden centres. Convenient for small jobs and repairs, but expensive.

Storage As for cement. When using, tip all the material from the bag and mix the dry ingredients together thoroughly. Keep the amount you need for mixing with water

---

HELPFUL TIP

Delay laying concrete if there is any danger of freezing weather ahead. Do not lay concrete on a frozen base or using frozen aggregate.

If, after you have laid fresh concrete, a light frost is likely, cover it with a polythene sheet (page 462) topped with a layer of earth or sand.

CONCRETE COLOURING AND ADDITIVES

• You can colour concrete by adding powdered pigment during mixing, or by staining it after laying. However, the finished effect is often disappointing – colours can look patchy, and fade with weathering. This is because most pigments have a maximum percentage (usually 10 per cent) that can be used before the pigment begin to affect the strength of the concrete.

• Additives for waterproofing and frost protection can also be used, following the manufacturer's instructions.

• Waterproofers will make the concrete less easy for water to pass through.

• Frost protectors speed up the reaction between water and cement, and may reduce the risk of frost damage soon after laying, but the concrete should still be protected with sheeting.

to one side and return the remainder to the bag (keep it dry). This ensures that the mix is correctly balanced before you start adding water.

Ready-mixed concrete

For large concreting projects, such as laying a patio or drive, it may be worth getting someone else to do the mixing. You can arrange this in one of two ways.

The first involves the supplier driving to your premises with a lorry carrying the raw materials, a concrete mixer and some builder's barrows which you and your helpers use to transfer the concrete to the site. The operator will mix as much concrete as you need to any mix specification, and will charge you for the number of batches supplied. This method is ideal for jobs where the exact volume needed is hard to calculate – for example, when filling trench foundations for a garden wall.

The second involves ordering a load of ready-mixed concrete from a local supplier. A standard load is about 6m³, and some companies charge more per m³ for smaller deliveries. Tell the supplier what you need the concrete for and how much you need, and he will supply the correct mix.

The concrete can be discharged directly into place if the lorry's delivery chute can reach it – when laying a drive, for example. Otherwise you will have to barrow it to the site – a job for a fleet of helpers, since moving a cubic metre of concrete will take about 30 large wheelbarrow loads.

Note that the concrete must be placed and finished in about two hours; if this is likely to be difficult to achieve, ask for the mix to be made with a retarding agent added to slow down the setting process.

GUIDE TO BATCH MIXING

Always measure the dry materials for each batch of the concrete mix by volume, following the ratios for the three standard mixes given, right. Use a large (15-litre) polythene builder's bucket, filled to the brim.

Hand-mixing concrete is hard work. It is worth hiring a concrete mixer for the duration of the job unless you are mixing only small quantities of it at a time – for example, to set fence posts in place.

A small electric mixer will cope with one batch of any of the three mixes – for example, the six buckets (one of cement, five of aggregate) needed to make the foundation mix.

MEASURING AND MIXING CONCRETE

The ratio of cement to sand and aggregate determines how strong a concrete mix is. If you are mixing concrete yourself, order sand and aggregate combined (known as all-in aggregate). This makes ordering materials simpler, and means that you have to find storage space for only one pile instead of two.

Most builders' merchants deliver all-in aggregate in a giant reinforced sack, which helps to contain the material on site until you are ready to use it. When the sack is empty, you simply return it to the supplier. These sacks usually contain one cubic metre of aggregate, but you can order as little as half a cubic metre if that is all you need.

The volume of concrete you make depends entirely on the volume of aggregate you use. The cement does not add to the final volume because the particles fill the voids between the stones and bond them together into a solid mass as the concrete sets. This means that to make one cubic metre (1m³) of concrete you need 1m³ of all-in aggregate, plus an amount of cement that is determined by the strength of mix you are intending to make.

Three standard mixes

Foundation mix
This consists of 1 part cement to 5 parts all-in aggregate, equivalent to 6 bags of cement per m³ of all-in aggregate.

Use this relatively weak mix for any concrete that will be buried underground and not exposed to the weather. Typical jobs include laying a strip foundation for a wall (above), a base for a path or drive that will be surfaced with another paving material, or an anchor for a fence post or rotary clothes line.

General-purpose mix
Make this with 1 part cement to 4 parts all-in aggregate, equivalent to 7 bags of cement per m³ of aggregate.

Use this mix for most jobs other than foundations. Uses include a slab base for an outbuilding or garage, or a new concrete floor indoors.

Paving mix
You will need 1 part cement to 3.5 parts all-in aggregate, equivalent to 8 bags of cement per m³ of aggregate. Use this mix for concrete paths, steps, patios and drives, which will be left exposed to the weather.

Estimating quantities

To find the volume of concrete you need, measure the area and multiply this by the thickness needed. Always work in metric measurements, and add 10 per cent to the total volume to allow for wastage and the filling of uneven sub-bases.

Laying the concrete
The depth of the concrete you lay depends on its purpose:
- 75mm thick for paths and bases for garden sheds
- 100mm thick for patios
- 125mm thick for drives and garage floors
- 150mm thick for drives that will be used by commercial vehicles.

For example, a drive 10m long, 4m wide and 100mm (0.1m) thick will require 10 x 4 x 0.1 = 4m³ of concrete. Adding 10 per cent gives a final volume figure (rounded up) of 4.5m³.
If the surface is to be left exposed, paving mix is needed and the material quantities required are 8 x 4.5 = 36 bags of cement, plus 4.5m³ of all-in aggregate.

GUIDE TO CONCRETE COVERAGE

Thickness of layer (mm)	Approximate area covered by 1m³
50	18m²
75	13m²
100	10m²
125	8m²
150	6m²

Mixing concrete

Mixing by hand is hard work, suitable only for small jobs or those that can be done in easy stages – a long path laid in sections, for example. The alternative is to hire a concrete mixer.

Mixing by hand

To produce good concrete by hand you need to work carefully and methodically at a steady pace – a rushed job is likely to give disappointing results.

Tools *Mixing platform; two shovels; two heavy-duty polythene buckets of identical size – about 15 litres capacity (keep one for cement only); bucket or watering can.*

Materials *Sharp sand and coarse aggregate (or all-in aggregate); ordinary Portland cement; water (7–10 litres per 15-litre bucket of cement) – use mains water, if possible, as water from a butt or pond will contain organic substances that could affect the concrete.*

1 Set up a mixing platform as near as possible to the laying area.

2 Measure buckets of sand and coarse aggregate in the required proportions and tip them into a pile on the platform.

3 Use the cement shovel to fill the cement bucket to the top. To make sure the bucket is properly packed, knock it two or three times as you fill it, because the cement fluffs up as it is shovelled.

4 Make a crater in the top of the pile of aggregate and tip in the bucket of cement.

5 Use the aggregate shovel to mix the pile thoroughly, turning it over until it looks the same colour throughout.

6 Make a crater in the top of the mixed pile and gradually pour in about half the water. Turn the pile again, moving dry material from the edge to the middle, until the water is well mixed in. Aim for an even colour and a dryish, crumbly consistency.

7 Continue adding and mixing in water a little at a time until the pile is smooth and moist – neither crumbly nor sloppy.

8 Test the consistency by slapping along the top of the pile with the back of the shovel. If water runs out readily it is too wet. Add a small amount of cement and aggregate (in the correct proportions) and mix again until you get it right.

Using a concrete mixer

Order the cement and aggregate in time for them to be ready for use when the mixer arrives, to save on hiring time. A machine cuts down the amount of heavy work and speeds up mixing. To avoid long breaks between mixing loads, get some helpers. Except for a mixing platform, the tools and materials needed are the same as for hand mixing.

1 Switch on the revolving drum, put in half the sand and coarse aggregate, then add half the water. Allow the drum to spin for half a minute, then put in all the cement and the rest of the sand, coarse aggregate and water.

2 After two or three minutes more mixing, the concrete is ready for use. Tip it straight onto the site or use a wheelbarrow.

3 When you have finished mixing for the day, wash out the drum by mixing coarse gravel and plenty of water. Discharge the washings, then pull out the electric plug and scrub down the outside of the machine, using plenty of water.

Laying an area of concrete

Freshly mixed concrete sets and starts to harden within about two hours – faster in very hot weather – so it must be laid, levelled and given a surface finish in sections (or bays) so that it can be completed while the concrete is still workable.

Setting up formwork

Timber edging, known as formwork, is needed to contain the concrete when making a path or drive. It can be removed once the concrete has hardened. You can use old timber such as fence boards or floorboards.

Timber can also be used as a permanent edging for other types of path such as gravel, asphalt or paving blocks. If timber edging is to be permanent, it should be well soaked with wood preservative – preferably use wood pre-treated with vacuum-pressure impregnation before purchase.

Tools *Spirit level; mallet; hammer; builder's square (page 467); wooden shim (page 451). Possibly also string and pegs.*

Materials *Timber lengths as wide as the depth of the surface layer; wooden pegs 25mm square and about 300mm long – allow one peg for every 1m of edging; 50mm galvanised nails.*

1 Dig a strip about 150mm wide along each side of the sub-base surface. The strip should be as deep as the surface layer.

2 Stand a timber length on its side along one side of the sub-base, in line with the string marking line, and drive wooden pegs into the soil to support it from outside the base area. The peg tops should be at the right height above ground for the finished path or drive surface, and flush with the top of the timber edging.

3 Use a spirit level to check that the edging strip is laid to the correct lengthways fall, if there is one. Then nail it to the pegs.

4 Butt other timber lengths in the same way to form one side of the edging.

5 To allow a slope for drainage, set the timber edging on one side of the path (the side farthest from the house wall, if it is adjoining it) slightly lower than the other, according to the crossfall required (see Making a sloped surface, page 451).

6 To make a tight corner joint, butt the timbers at right angles, using a builder's square as a check. Nail them together as well as to pegs. There is no need to cut off an overlapping piece of timber on the outside of the corner.

7 On long concrete paths, fit contraction joints across the path at suitable intervals (see right).

Making a curve in formwork

1 Mark out the shape of the curve on the ground and set up pegs and a string line to follow the curve (see Marking out a curved path, page 451).

2 Use a saw to make cuts in the timber edging for about half its depth on the edge that will form the inside of the curve. Make cuts at about 125mm intervals, or closer for a sharp curve.

3 Shape the timber by nailing it to the pegs.

4 Check that the timber along each side is at the right height and the correct slope (see Making a sloped surface, page 451). Adjust as necessary by tapping it down or levering it up slightly.

Laying a base for a light building or shed

Set out the formwork in the same way as for a drive, although there is no need to make a drainage slope. Use a spirit level and builder's square to ensure that the formwork is level and that the corners are true right angles.

The size of a workable section

This depends on the rate at which you mix and place the concrete, but is likely to be about 3–4 barrowloads with hand mixing, or 6–8 with machine mixing.

With ready-mixed concrete, two people can generally spread and tamp down an area of roughly 8.5m² of concrete poured directly into the laying area before it sets.

Concrete will crack if it is allowed to dry too fast, so has to be 'cured' – that is, kept moist for three days after laying. It takes about a month to set to its full strength, but you can walk or build on it after three days (wait seven days in winter).

There is a maximum size at which any slab of concrete can be laid in one piece without danger of cracking. A surface larger than this is laid in separate sections (or bays) with control joints between to allow for contraction and expansion of the concrete.
• The maximum intervals between control joints varies according to the thickness of the concrete and the site width (see panel, right).
• In general, joints should be closer as the width gets narrower. So a path, for example, usually needs shorter bays between joints than a drive. Make the bays of equal size and as square as possible. The length can be about one and a half times the width, but no more than twice the width.
• Control joints can be placed at closer intervals to give smaller bays, if this is convenient for laying workable sections when mixing your own concrete.

Making a control joint

Tools *Mallet or club hammer, piece of softwood 25mm thick, as deep as the formwork and long enough to fit across the inside of the formwork; wooden pegs; arrissing tool.*

Materials *Hardboard filler strip as long and as deep as the softwood.*

1 Position a hardboard filler strip between the two sides of the formwork and at right angles to them. If one side of the formwork is curved, bend the filler strip to meet the side at right angles.

CONTROL JOINT INTERVALS			
Width of site	Depth of concrete		
	75mm	100mm	150mm
3m	3m	4m	5m
1–2m	2.5m	2–3m	3–4m
Under 1m	1.8m	–	–

2 Support the filler strip on the outside of the first bay to be concreted, using the piece of softwood held in position by pegs.

3 Concrete the bay (see page 462) right up to the hardboard filler, then concrete about 300mm into the second bay.

4 Lift out the softwood support and pegs but leave the filler strip in position.

5 Push the concrete against the filler strip where you have removed the softwood support, then continue laying the second bay.

6 When finishing the concrete surface (page 462), use an arrissing tool on each side of the hardboard filler strip.

Making a concrete path or drive

Prepare the sub-base and formwork allowing for a suitable drainage slope (page 450). Make the concrete surface layer 75mm thick for a path, or 100mm thick for a drive. If the drive is on soft soil such as peat, make the surface layer 150mm thick.

Tools *Rake; shovel; wheelbarrow; tamping beam; arrissing trowel; surface-finishing tools; polythene sheeting; bricks. Possibly also watering can; sharp sand.*

Materials *Freshly made concrete of a suitable mix for the job (pages 458, 460).*

1 Pour batches of concrete into the first bay to be laid.

2 Use the back of a rake to draw the batches together so that the concrete is roughly level and about 13mm higher than the top of the timber formwork.

3 Press the concrete into all corners and against all edges of the bay with a shovel or your boot. Make sure all cavities are filled, because air pockets will weaken the concrete.

4 Compact the filled bay with a tamping beam laid across the formwork. Use it with a chopping action, moving it along about half its thickness with each chop. This leaves an undulating surface.

5 Go over the high spots again, using the tamper steadily backwards and forwards with a sawing action to remove excess concrete.

6 If any depressions appear in the surface, scoop fresh concrete into them with a shovel.

7 Give a final tamp over the bay – this can be the final finish or you can apply a different finish (see right). To get a near-smooth tamped finish, pass the tamper slowly backwards and forwards with steady strokes.

For a textured finish, use the tamper with a lift and drop action. Depending on the spacing between drops, the appearance can vary from close rippled to wide rippled, like a washboard.

8 Before the concrete hardens, round off the edges by running an arrissing tool along the slight gap between the formwork and the concrete edge.

9 As soon as the concrete is hard enough not to be marked, cover it with polythene sheeting to stop it drying out too quickly. Weight the edges of the sheeting with bricks to stop it blowing away, and sprinkle some sand over the top, if necessary, to prevent ballooning.

10 Remove the covering after not less than three days, and the formwork a day or so later.

Finishing the surface

A textured finish helps to give the concrete a non-skid surface. If you leave the surface as tamped (see step 7, above), it will have a rippled appearance. Other ways of finishing the surface are shown on the right.

For a narrow path, you can apply the finish from the ground alongside. For a wide area such as a drive, work from a bridge across the formwork – lay the tamping beam across on its side, for example.

For a pathway beside a building, where you cannot stand on either side of the concrete, see Making a path or drive alongside a wall, opposite.

Ways of finishing concrete

Brush finish For a pronounced brush finish, drag a hard-bristled broom over the surface after tamping near-smooth. Hold the broom at a shallow angle so that the surface is indented but not torn up, and make all strokes in the same direction. Rinse the brush bristles if they get clogged, then shake well.

For a smoother brush finish use a soft broom and apply it with gentle strokes.

Float finish Use a wood float in overlapping circles to produce a fish-scale finish. For a plain finish, draw the float across the surface as soon as you have tamped it. If you want to coarsen the texture, let some of the concrete build up on the float face.

For a smooth, unmarked finish, skim the surface with steel plasterer's trowel. For a tight, hard-wearing finish, let the surface stiffen first.

Piped finish/shovel finish A fairly heavy pipe, such as a scaffolding tube, can be rolled over the surface like a rolling pin to give a somewhat stippled appearance. Or it can be rolled, lifted and dropped to give a ridged finish.

For a shovel finish use the back of a shovel to lightly pat the newly tamped surface using a circular movement. This gives an overlapping, fish-scale finish, as with a wood float.

Exposed stone finish Scatter a thin layer of single-sized stones after tamping. Tamp again, making sure the stones are well bedded. Let the concrete harden until the stones are well gripped, then spray the surface lightly with a fine-rose can. Use a soft broom to brush away loose material, leaving the stones partly exposed. Next day clean the surface with a stiff broom and water. Cure for about three days.

Making a path or drive alongside a wall

Instead of fixing formwork along the wall-side of the path, fit a strip of 13mm thick bitumen-impregnated fibreboard against it. It is available in 100mm, 150mm and 200mm strips. This will form a joint between the concrete and the brickwork. Remove it once the concrete has dried.

Lay the concrete in alternate bays so that you and your helper can stand on each side of the bay you are concreting and use the tamping beam parallel with the wall.

After three days, when the concrete has hardened enough to stand on, lay concrete in the empty bays. Remove the stop-ends of the formwork from the laid bays and lay the new concrete up to the hardened edge of the set concrete.

As it dries out, the concrete will shrink and pull away enough to leave a gap sufficient to serve as a contraction joint.

Laying gravel

Prepare a hardcore sub-base 100mm deep, allowing a depth of about 25mm for the gravel surface. Top the hardcore with a 25mm blinding layer of sharp sand – to fill any gaps and make a close, smooth base for the gravel. Use 10mm or 20mm pea gravel.

Unless there are walls or turf edging to contain the gravel, lay permanent edging such as kerbing (page 449) or timber formwork (page 460).

Spread the gravel with a rake over the whole area to a depth of about 15mm, then roll it with a garden roller. Spread a second layer of about 15mm, then roll again.

The surface will need regular raking or rolling as it becomes disturbed, and will probably need to be treated with weedkiller about once a year.

Alternatively Lay down a semi-permeable membrane before you put down the gravel. This allows rainwater to permeate down into the hardcore and drain away, but prevents the growth of weeds. Known as landscape fabric, it is available in rolls 1m wide and about 20m long from most DIY centres and nurseries.

Repairing paths, drives and steps

Small cracks that develop in the surface of a path or drive often result from errors in construction – weaknesses in the sub-base, for example, or faulty concrete mixing or misjudging curing times.

Before you start It is a waste of time to repair small cracks as soon as they appear. Wait to see if they increase in size and number. They may be caused by a small amount of movement in the ground below. If, after a year or so, there has been little or no increase, it is fair to assume that the ground has settled and repairs can be carried out.

If the surface develops extensive cracking or sunken areas, take it up and lay it again on a new, firm sub-base.

Refitting a loose or damaged paving slab

1 Use a spade to chop through any mortar at edge joints. Push the spade under the slab to lift it and slip a broomstick or pipe under it to roll it out. A sunken or see-sawing slab can be re-laid, but renew a cracked or chipped slab.

2 If the slab was bedded on sand, loosen up the old sand with a trowel, add more sharp sand, and lightly level the surface with a length of wood.

Alternatively If the slab was bedded on mortar, remove the old mortar with a hammer and chisel. Mix new bedding mortar in a dryish mix of one part cement to four parts sharp sand (or use a bagged sand-cement mix) and spread it over the surface with a brick trowel to a thickness of 30–50mm. Roughen the surface with the trowel point.

3 Slab edge joints may be flush or with gaps. If there are gaps, place 10mm thick wooden spacers along one long and one short edge before rolling the slab into position on a broomstick or pipe. Then space other side gaps.

4 Lay a 50mm thick piece of flat wood on the slab as a cushion while you use a club hammer to tap it down flush with the surrounding slabs. Check that it is flush using a length of straight-edged timber.

5 If you cannot tap the slab down flush, lift it again and skim off some of the bedding material. Or, if it sinks down too far, add more of the bedding material.

6 Wait at least two days before filling in the joints in the same way as for laying slabs (page 453).

Cleaning up stains

Oil, grease and rust stains, or moss, often occur on paths and drives. Most can be removed with one of the wide range of proprietary removers available from DIY, gardening or motoring stores. Cat litter is a good absorbent for spreading on fresh oil spillages.

Renewing damaged kerbing

1 Use a club hammer to loosen the damaged length of kerbing, then prise it out with a spade.

2 Dig out about 50mm of the sub-base below the removed kerbstone, then ram the surface well down with a thick piece of timber.

3 Mix bedding mortar using a bagged sand-cement mortar mix to a dryish consistency. Spread it about 75mm deep in the gap.

4 Dampen the new kerbstone and lower it into position. Cushion it with a 50mm piece of flat timber and tap it down with a club hammer until it is flush with the adjoining kerbstone.

5 Use a spirit level to check that the sides align with the adjoining kerbstone, and a straightedge to check that the surface is also aligned.

Repairing cracks or holes in concrete

Hairline cracks in concrete can be ignored. They often follow the lines of the contraction joints between sections.
• A hole can be filled if it is at least 15mm deep. If the hole is shallower, deepen it first, or the new layer will be too thin to hold firm.
• Repair concrete with a filler containing PVA adhesive (see panel, page 463) to make a good bond.
• For potholes, proprietary ready-mixed concrete filler can be used instead.

1 Widen the crack or hole below the surface by undercutting the edges with a cold chisel and club hammer. This ensures that the filler will be well anchored.

2 Remove all debris from the hole or crack and brush it with a priming coat of PVA adhesive as instructed on the container – usually one part adhesive to five parts water.

3 When the priming coat is tacky, fill the crack or hole using concrete filler (see panel, page 463). Pack it well down so that there are no air pockets, which will weaken the concrete.

4 Level off the area flush with the surrounding surface using a brick trowel or plasterer's steel finishing trowel.

5 Keep the repair covered with polythene for at least three days.

Repairing crumbling edges on a concrete path

Concrete may crumble at the edges if the edging formwork was removed too soon, or if the wet concrete was not packed well down against the formwork during laying. Air pockets below an apparently solid surface cause the concrete to break up when the edges come under pressure during use.

1 Chip away the damaged concrete back to solid material, using a cold chisel and club hammer.

2 Remove the debris, and if the sub-base is exposed, ram the hardcore well down with a ramming tool or thick length of timber. Add fresh hardcore to any soft spots and ram it well down.

3 Set up timber edging 25mm thick alongside the damaged area so that the top edge is level with the concrete surface. Support it with pegs driven into the ground.

4 Brush the exposed edge of the concrete with a priming coat of PVA adhesive mixed according to the instructions on the container – usually one part adhesive to five parts water.

5 Prepare concrete filler (page 463) and use a brick trowel to press into the exposed area, well down against the edging.

6 Level the surface with the trowel, or use a float (page 462), to give a non-slip finish.

7 Cover the repaired area with polythene to stop it drying too fast. Remove the sheeting after three days. Leave the edging longer if the path is used a lot.

Repairing a concrete step

1 Cut back a crumbling edge using a cold chisel and club hammer. If the surface is worn down, score it with a brick bolster and hammer to provide a good grip (key) for a new layer of concrete.

2 Fix timber edging round the step using pegs and bricks to keep it firmly in place. If renewing a worn surface, set the edging about 15mm higher than the surface, with the side pieces allowing a forward slope of about 10mm for water to run off.

3 Brush away dust and debris.

4 Prime the area with a mixture of PVA adhesive and water according to the container instructions – usually one part adhesive to five parts water.

5 Repair crumbling edges with concrete filler (page 463). Press it will down against the edging.

Alternatively To re-surface the step, use bagged sand-cement mix (page 458) prepared in the normal way, but first coat the surface with a solution of three parts PVA adhesive to one part water. Before it dries, apply the concrete to lie level with top of the edging.

6 Level the area. Cover for three days, as for path repairs.

Buying bricks

Bricks are mostly made from baked clay to a standard size, but some are made from lime mixed with sand or crushed stone or both (these are known as calcium silicate, sandlime or flintlime bricks). There are also concrete bricks made from cement and aggregates. They resemble clay bricks and are about the same price. Blocks are less popular and are usually concrete or stone made in various sizes.

Bricks are usually sold by numbers. Small quantities such as 100, 350 or 500 may be available from DIY stores, but builders' merchants normally sell them by the thousand. If transporting bricks, remember that 350 weigh nearly a tonne.

Grades
Bricks are graded according to their quality, which takes into account their frost resistance. F indicates frost-resistant, M moderately frost-resistant. Grades are not marked on bricks, but may be on packs. Check when buying.
Internal quality (OL, ON) For indoor use.
Ordinary quality (FN, ML, MN) For outdoor use where conditions are not severe.
Special quality (FL) For severe conditions.

Types
Different types are available in each grade, in both standard and special shapes.
Commons Bricks for use where their appearance does not matter. They may be any grade, and vary widely in quality.
Facings Bricks with an attractive surface finish on one or more sides, and of either ordinary or special grades. They are more expensive than commons, and those faced on more than one side are dearer than one-faced types.
Flettons Widely used common or facing bricks made of clay from the Peterborough, Bedfordshire and Buckinghamshire regions.

Colour and texture
There is a wide range of colours depending on the type of clay used and the manufacturing process; clay varies from area to area. Multi-coloured types are also available. Check the colours stocked by your local brick merchant, and ask to see a catalogue of other colours.

Textures are either imposed or achieved by the choice of material. They include wirecut bricks, sandfaced bricks and rustic bricks, with a mechanically imposed texture.

Using secondhand bricks
Secondhand bricks are generally expensive because they are difficult to clean. Bricks are mixed up during demolition, so it is mostly impossible to know their previous use. Don't use them for paving unless you know they are old paving bricks and are therefore likely to be frost-resistant.

Some manufacturers now produce simulated secondhand bricks. These have a weathered appearance and are safer to use.

The best way to remove the old mortar from bricks is with a bolster chisel and club hammer. Wear heavy gloves and safety goggles. Proprietary brick cleaners are not suitable for removing mortar, except for stubborn stains from brick faces. Wet the brick before applying the cleaner – this reduces surface absorption and prevents acid penetration.

Brick sizes and shapes
The standard size for bricks is 215mm long, 103mm wide and 65mm deep – fractionally smaller than the old imperial standard size. The nominal size, which allows for a mortar joint of about 10mm all round, makes it easier to calculate the number of bricks needed. It is 225 x 113 x 75mm.

A brick laid with its long face exposed is called a stretcher. A brick laid with its short face exposed is called a header. Part bricks are cut as required. A brick cut across its width is called a bat, and a brick cut lengthways is called a closer. Some bricks are indented or perforated with holes or slits to help to reduce weight.

Types of bond for brick walls

Stretcher

All bricks are laid lengthways, with a half brick at the end of every other course so that each vertical joint (perpend) centres on the bricks above and below. The wall is about 100mm thick and is known as a half-brick wall. It needs to be stiffened with piers (page 471) at each end and at 2m intervals. Insert movement joints as for a Flemish bond. Requires 60 bricks per m², not including piers and capping (top layer).

Flemish

Pairs of parallel stretchers alternated with one header in each course, making a wall 215mm thick. Closers are used on alternate courses to stagger the joints. This is known as a one-brick wall. It is more difficult to build than a half-brick wall, but stronger. Insert movement joints (page 471) every 8m for clay bricks, or every 4m for blocks or calcium-silicate bricks. Requires 120 bricks per m².

Corner and end bricks
Shaped corner bricks are known as internal or external returns. Some bricks are designed to lie on edge and others flat. Bricks shaped for special uses – known as specials – are more expensive than bricks of standard shape, and often more difficult to get. They usually have to be ordered.

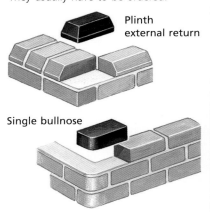

Plinth external return

Single bullnose

English garden wall

Closer

Three courses of parallel stretchers alternated with one header course. Closers are needed on header courses to stagger the joints. It is not quite as strong as a Flemish bond. Insert movement joints as for Flemish bond. Quantity as with Flemish, but cheaper because more of the bricks need be one faced only.

Random
With courses made up of blocks of varying heights fitted together. Can be used with walling blocks only. Insert movement joints (page 471) at 4m intervals. Quantity depends on block sizes and patterns.

Open (or honeycomb)
A decorative stretcher bond with spaces between bricks. The simplest and most solid pattern is with quarter-brick spaces between bricks. Variations are half-brick spaces, or half-brick spaces between header bricks that project about 60mm each side of the wall. Piers are needed as for a stretcher bond. Insert movement joints as for a Flemish bond below. Requires 50 bricks per m² for the simplest pattern, not including the piers and capping.

Ways of building a wall

A wall is built up of single layers of bricks or blocks, known as courses, cemented together with mortar. The pattern in which the courses are laid is known as a bond.

The arrangement of bricks in a bond is designed to stabilise and strengthen the wall by avoiding vertical mortar joints that run through two or more adjoining courses.

Walls built from suitable bricks (page 465) are more expensive than fencing, but last longer, provided that they are built on solid foundations and are given adequate protection from frost.

Even a low wall can be dangerous if it falls down, and frost damage can cause bricks to disintegrate. Use strong mortar and special quality frost-resistant bricks (F grade), at least for the first two courses.

If you use mainly ordinary bricks that are only moderately frost-resistant (M grade), protect the top course with a damp-proof membrane, sandwiched under coping stones. Use special shaped bricks (page 465) as a capping for frost-resistant bricks only, and fit a damp-proof membrane at least two courses below the wall top, to throw off any water that seeps down through shrunken mortar joints.

Do not use a damp-proof membrane in the lower part of a free-standing wall, as it affects stability.

You will need to get planning permission from the local authority to build a wall higher than 1m beside a public highway, or for any free-standing wall that is over 2m high.

HOW TO STORE BRICKS SAFELY

Keep bricks dry. Bricks that are damp right through do not stick well to mortar. Dampness also leads to efflorescence – a white, powdery deposit (page 408).

Stack bricks on planks laid on a hard surface. Cover the planks with plastic sheeting. Build the stack so that the outer walls lean slightly inwards and will not collapse. Cover the stack with more plastic sheeting.

Building tools you will need

Line pins and building line The flat-bladed steel pins are pushed into the mortar joints at the end of the wall once the ends or corners have been built up. The line stretched between them is raised for each course as a levelling guide while laying bricks or blocks.

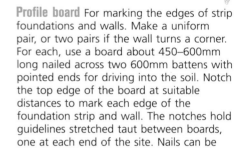

Line pins and building line

Plumb line Useful for checking that the wall is vertical. The line can be tied round and notched into a piece of board placed on the top course, so that it hangs down the wall as a guide while you work.

plumb line

Gauge rod Used to check that each course of bricks is the correct height. Make one from a length of 75 x 25mm timber. For brick courses, mark the gauge every 75mm. For screen block walling, mark the gauge every 200mm for pier pilasters, and every 300mm for blocks. If using other types of walling block, mark it to match the course heights (including mortar) required.

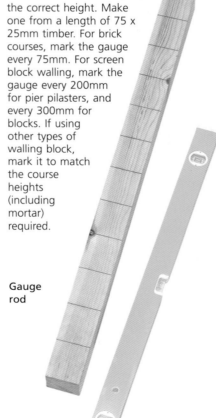

Gauge rod

Spirit level

Spirit level Used for checking the alignment of walls. It should have both horizontal and vertical vials, and preferably be about 1m long.

Profile boards

Profile board For marking the edges of strip foundations and walls. Make a uniform pair, or two pairs if the wall turns a corner. For each, use a board about 450–600mm long nailed across two 600mm battens with pointed ends for driving into the soil. Notch the top edge of the board at suitable distances to mark each edge of the foundation strip and wall. The notches hold guidelines stretched taut between boards, one at each end of the site. Nails can be used instead of notches.

Mortar board (hawk) Useful for holding mortar while working. The wooden, plastic or aluminium surface is about 300mm square, with a central handle underneath. Make one using plywood and a broom handle. It can also be used when plastering.

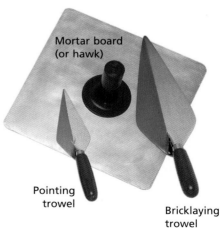

Mortar board (or hawk)

Pointing trowel

Bricklaying trowel

Pointing trowel A small trowel with a blade 75–200mm long, used for shaping mortar joints.

Bricklaying trowel A large trowel with a blade 250–330mm long, for spreading mortar when laying bricks.

Brick bolster and club hammer

Club hammer

For cutting bricks. The spade-shaped bolster chisel has a 100mm wide blade, and is used with a 1.2kg hammer. Choose one with a hand guard.

Brick bolster

Pointing tools For some types of pointing (page 470) you need extra tools for shaping joints. A piece of sacking can be used to smooth flush joints. For concave joints you need either a piece of bent 15mm copper tubing, a piece of garden hosepipe, or something similar. Alternatively, use a roller pointing and raking tool that has different blades for either shaping various joints or for raking out old mortar.

MAKING A BUILDER'S SQUARE

Use three pieces of wood about 50mm wide and 19mm thick, each accurately marked with one of the following lengths: 450mm (A); 600mm (B); 750mm (C).

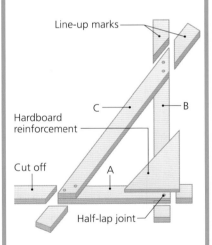

Line-up marks

C — B

Hardboard reinforcement

Cut off

A

Half-lap joint

Line up all marks carefully before nailing lengths to each other. Use a half-lap joint for A and B, then overlap C. Check the right angle with a set square, saw off any overlap, then reinforce the corner with a piece of hardboard. (Any three lengths of wood joined in the ratio 3:4:5 must form a right angle.)

How to handle mortar

Cement, sand and hydrated lime mixed with water make up the mortar used to stick bricks together.

The lime acts as a plasticiser, making the mortar smooth and workable and preventing the sand and cement from shrinking and cracking when the mortar dries. Instead of lime, you can use proprietary liquid plasticiser – usually sold in 2 litre containers.

You can buy ready-mixed bags of dry bricklaying mortar to which only water has to be added. This is more expensive, but convenient for small jobs.

Use strong mortar for a garden wall, to withstand winds and rain. The standard mix is suitable for more sheltered areas.

Preparing a mortar mix

Mortar becomes unusable within two hours of mixing (sooner if the weather is hot). It cannot be enlivened by mixing in a little more water, as this would make it too soft to support a brick. Mix it in small batches to avoid waste. After a time you will be able to gauge how much to make up at a time, according to the rate at which you can lay the bricks.

Tools *Clean mixing surface such as concrete or a mixing board; two clean shovels, one solely for cement; two same-size heavy-duty polythene buckets; watering can with fine spray rose.*

Materials *Ordinary Portland cement; hydrated lime or plasticiser; soft (builder's) sand; water.*

1 Measure out the number of buckets of sand you require on the mixing surface.

2 Use a separate bucket and shovel to measure out the cement and add it to the sand. Do not use the bucket and shovel for other ingredients or mixing, or the cement in the bag could get damp and be spoiled.

3 Mix the sand and cement together thoroughly with the other shovel until they are a consistent greyish colour.

4 Mix in the hydrated lime. Or use a proprietary plasticiser instead, following the instructions on the container for the amount.

5 Make a crater at the top of the pile and pour in a little water from a watering can. Shovel from the outside of the pile into the middle to mix in the water in the crater.

6 Continue adding small amounts of water and turning the pile over with the shovel until the mortar is a stiff mix that falls off the spade cleanly. The mortar is then ready for use.

HELPFUL TIP

Speed up the mixing process by mixing a batch of sand and lime – known as 'coarse stuff' – beforehand and add cement to it as required. Soak the amount of hydrated lime you are likely to need in cold water the night before use. Next morning, pour off the water and mix the lime with the required proportion of sand. Coarse stuff will last a day. It might stiffen up, but can be made workable by adding a little water.

PROPORTIONS FOR MIXING

Ingredient	Strong mix	Standard mix for garden wall	Approximate quantities for strong mix
Ordinary Portland cement (usually grey; white also available)	1 part	1 part	One 50kg bag for 400–500 bricks
Hydrated lime *or* Mortar plasticiser	½ part	1 part	One 25kg bag for 400–500 bricks
	As instructed on container		About 0.07 litre for each 50kg bag of cement
Clean builder's sand	4 parts	6 parts (bricks) 5 parts (blocks)	0.15m³ for every 50kg bag of cement
Bagged bricklaying mortar mix	–	–	One 40kg bag for roughly 150 bricks

Laying strip foundations

Every wall must be built on a firm, level foundation or it will soon crack and fall down.

Before you start The usual foundation is a solid layer of concrete on a bed of hardcore; though you need not use hardcore if you are satisfied that the ground beneath is firm. A low wall can be built on a flat, firm surface such as a patio, as long as it has an adequate sub-base and the slabs are set on a full bed of mortar. Set it back from the edge of the surface by the same distance as its thickness (and by a minimum of 150mm).

Tools *Spade; profile boards (page 466); string; heavy hammer; earth rammer (page 450) or stout length of timber; pencil or chalk; steel tape measure; spirit level; rake; straight-edged board; mixing platform (page 457); brick trowel.*

Materials *Hardcore (page 450); marker pegs 460mm long; concrete (page 458); sharp sand.*

1 Mark the edge of each side of the foundation strip using string lines and profile boards (see below).

2 Remove 50–75mm of topsoil and spread it elsewhere on the ground.

3 Measure from the top of each marker peg and mark lines showing the bottom of the concrete layer (page 450). Drive in marker pegs on each side of the strip at

about 1m intervals, with their tops at the required height for the surface of the concrete. Generally, the concrete is level with a hard surrounding surface, or 25–50mm below a lawn edge.

4 Level adjacent and opposite pegs using a spirit level, set on a length of board.

5 Dig a trench as wide as the marked lines and to the required overall depth, using the bottom line on the marker pegs as a guide. If the soil is still soft, dig a little deeper.

6 Fill the bottom of the trench with hardcore to the height of the guideline on the marker pegs. Ram the hardcore down well using an earth rammer or a stout length of timber. Cover with a blinding layer of sharp sand, to fill any gaps.

7 Mix the concrete (page 460) on a clean surface and shovel it into the trench. Spread it with a rake, making sure it reaches well into the corners and is level with the tops of the marker pegs. Use the edge of a straight-edged board to tamp across the concrete to expel air.

8 Remove the marker pegs and fill the gaps with concrete, smoothing the surface with the board. Leave the profile boards in position and fit string lines to mark wall edges for bricklaying.

9 Mark the positions of the string guidelines for the walls on the concrete strip. Do this either before the concrete sets (a few hours after laying) using a spirit level, or when the concrete is hard, using a chalked string line.

10 Cover the concrete (page 462) and let it cure and harden for at least three days before building on top of it.

Laying bricks or walling blocks

Take particular care in positioning and laying the first course - it is the most crucial part of the job.

Before you start Work out the bond pattern (page 465) using dry bricks, especially if the wall has any corners or piers (page 470), before laying any bricks or walling blocks on the strip foundation. Make a note of how many part bricks you will need to cut (page 470). Use special-quality frost-resistant bricks either for the whole wall or at least for the first two courses. For an ordinary (M grade) brick wall, use a damp-proof membrane under the coping.

It takes experience to achieve a 10mm thickness of mortar under a brick every time. If you have never done any bricklaying before, practise laying a few bricks with a pseudo mortar of one part lime and three parts sand. Clean the bricks within two hours so that they can be used again in building the wall. Discard the mortar.

Tools *Brick trowel; spirit level; flat, even length of timber; builder's square; gauge rod with 75mm markings; pointing trowel; line pins and building line; mortar board; jointing tools; straightedge.*

Materials *Bricks or walling blocks; coping or capping bricks; strong mortar (page 467); damp-proof membrane about 20mm narrower than the wall thickness.*

1 Leave the profile boards and string lines in position as a guide until you have completed the first course.

2 Shape the mortar with the trowel so that it looks like a fat sausage pointed at both ends.

3 Slide the trowel underneath the mortar to lift it up.

Foundation measurements

As a general guide, use a strip 150mm thick and 300mm wide for a half-brick wall up to a maximum of 1m high. Increase this to 225mm thick and 450mm wide for a one-brick wall up to 1m high, and to 300mm thick for a one-brick wall over 1m high (up to a maximum of 2m).

Profile boards Notches or nails accurately mark the outer edges of the wall and foundation strip

Taut string line Used to mark the edges of the strip

Concrete surface Provides a firm, level footing for the wall. Set 25–50mm below a lawn surface

Levelling pegs Opposite and adjacent marker pegs are levelled to ensure a flat surface

Marker pegs Indicate the surface level of the concrete while laying, and are removed on completion

Corner boards Profile boards and string lines set at right angles help to ensure accurate corners

Hardcore layer Rammed down to form a firm bed for the concrete. The top is also given a blinding layer of sharp sand to fill gaps

4 Tip the mortar onto the building surface between the marked lines (facing page) in position for laying the first brick.

5 Tap the flat of the trowel blade backwards along the mortar to flatten it to a thickness of about 20mm. The mortar will be pressed down to 10mm thick by the weight of the brick.

6 Lay the first brick in position on the mortar in line with the marked guidelines. If the brick has a frog (indentation on one side) lay it with the frog facing upwards.

7 Lay another brick in the same way a few feet farther along the line. Do not worry about its position in the bond, it is for levelling only and can be removed later.

8 Place a flat board across the tops of the two bricks and use a spirit level to check that it is horizontal. Use the trowel handle to tap down the higher of the two bricks as necessary until both bricks are level.

9 Prepare a mortar bed for the second brick of the course. Before laying the brick, hold it upright and spread mortar for the vertical joint on the end to be butted. Squash the mortar down against all four edges, or it will easily slip off. Lift the levelling brick out of the way.

HELPFUL TIPS

• When levelling bricks, you may have to remove some – either to add more mortar to a low brick, or to scrape some off a high brick that will not tap down to the right level. The replaced brick may not stick well because the mortar has lost some of its adhesion. This does not matter as long as it occurs with only an occasional brick. But if the mortar gives no grip at all, scrape it off and start again.

• On a hot day, dip each brick in water to wet the surface before laying it. This helps to prevent the mortar from drying out too quickly.

10 Lay the next four or five bricks of the course in the same way, then place a spirit level along them to check that they are horizontal. Tap bricks down with a trowel handle as necessary. If a brick is too low, remove it and add more mortar.

11 If the course turns a right-angled corner, use a builder's square to make sure it is true.

12 After completing the first course, build up at each end and corner with three or four stepped courses. Use the gauge rod to check that each course is at the correct height.

13 Insert line pins into the mortar at each built-up end. Use the line between them as a guide to levelling the top of the second course. Move it up progressively to check the levels of following courses as you lay the bricks between the stepped ends.

14 Point the joints after laying three or four courses (page 470).

15 From time to time check that the wall is both upright and straight by using a spirit level against it vertically and horizontally.

16 If using a top course of shaped bricks, sandwich the damp-proof membrane into the mortar two courses from the top. If using coping stones, sandwich it into the mortar bed for the coping.

Building a freestanding wall

Strip foundation Concrete thickness as required (see opposite)

Builder's square for checking that right-angled corners are true

Profile board Used to stretch string lines for marking edges of strip foundation and position marks for wall edges

Gauge rod For checking that each course is the correct height

Position marks Lines marked to show the wall edges, as a guide to laying the first brick course

Spirit level Use the vertical vial to make sure the wall is upright. Use horizontally to make sure the wall surface is straight

Line pins and building line A line stretched between line pins stuck in the mortar at each end, as a guide for levelling each course

Weather protection Two bottom courses or special quality bricks such as Class B engineering bricks or frost-resistant (F grade) bricks

Stepped end End bricks of the first three or four courses built up in steps before each complete course is laid

Building garden steps

There are two types of garden step: those built into an existing slope and those that are freestanding – built up from the flat between two different levels of the garden.

Before you start Whatever the type you decide to build, for comfort and safety steps should be evenly spaced and not less than 600mm wide. For two people to walk comfortably abreast, the width must be at least 1.5m.

• Steps are easiest to climb comfortably when long treads (the flat parts) are combined with low risers (the upright parts), or when short treads are used with high risers. The best relationships between the two are shown below.

• Choose building materials that blend with their surroundings, and make sure that the treads have a rough, non-slip surface.

• If the steps lead down to a house, make a narrow drainage channel as close as possible to the bottom step (see Building a drainage channel, page 452).

Working out step dimensions

To decide on the number of treads and risers for a flight of steps, measure the following:
• The height difference between the two levels.
• The length of the slope for built-in steps, or the length of ground space available for a freestanding flight to stretch.

For each measurement, calculate the number of steps needed for various combinations of treads and risers until you get more or less the same number for both measurements.

Steps in a slope

For a slope 1.8m long with a 600mm difference in height.

1 Choose a suitable riser height and divide it into the height difference. As the slope is gentle, choose a low riser: Height difference 600mm divided by 100mm riser = 6 steps.

2 The best tread for a 100mm riser is 460mm. Divide this into the slope length: Slope length 1.8m ÷ 460mm tread = 4 steps.

3 To adjust the difference, try again with a higher riser and a shorter tread: Height 600mm ÷ 120mm = 5 Length 1.8m ÷ 400mm = 4.5 So 5 steps will fit comfortably.

Freestanding steps

For a flight of freestanding steps with an overall height difference of 950mm and ground space of 1.5m.

1 In a 1.5m stretch of ground, the number of 300mm treads would be 5. But the final tread could be the top of the higher level, so the actual stretch would be 1.2m.

2 Tread 300mm deep from front to back are best with risers of 180mm. Height 950mm ÷ 180mm = 5.3 steps. This can be rounded down to 5 steps – even if the figures divide exactly, minor inaccuracies are bound to occur in the construction, so the finished measurements are seldom precise.

Building steps into a slope

Roughly shape the slope before you start building the steps. If it is steep, remove some of the soil. On an irregular slope, build up where necessary with soil from other parts of the garden.

The layout of the slope may suggest two flights of steps at right angles, with a landing in between. On a long flight, make a landing after about every ten steps to provide a resting place. On flights with high, loose soil at the sides, you will need to build low brick retaining walls (page 471).

The instructions given here are for steps built with brick risers and concrete paving slab treads, but the method is similar whatever material you use.

Tools *String and pegs; 5m steel tape measure; long length of timber; spirit level; builder's square; spade; club hammer; brick trowel; mortar mixing board; two heavy-duty polythene buckets and two shovels (for mixing concrete); short tamping beam; pointing trowel or joining tool; earth rammer; 10mm thick wooden batten. Possibly also a brick bolster.*

Materials *Hardcore – one barrowload fills about 0.5m² at 150mm deep; concrete foundation mix (page 459); bricks; bricklaying mortar (page 467); paving slabs; bedding mortar; water. Possibly also sharp sand.*

1 Fix two parallel string lines from top to bottom of the slope, as far apart as the required step width.

2 Measure a line to find the length of the slope.

TREAD AND RISER COMBINATIONS

Treads should never be less than 300mm long. Risers should be no lower than 100mm and no higher than 180mm. Their dimensions are governed to some extent by the gradient of the slope and the building material. Long treads are needed for steps up a gentle slope and short treads for a steep slope.

Brick risers, for example, are limited to multiples of 75mm – a brick laid flat – or 113mm – a brick laid on edge. The height can be adjusted with tiles or brick slips, but this may spoil the look. When using paving slabs as treads, take into account the slab thickness when calculating the riser height.

Depth of tread	Height of riser	Possible riser material
460mm	100mm	One course of bricks laid flat, topped with 25mm thick slab tread.
430mm	113mm	One course of bricks laid on edge. Or one course of bricks laid flat, topped with 38mm thick slab tread.
400mm	125mm	One course of bricks laid flat, topped with 50mm thick slab tread.
380mm	140mm	One course of 100mm walling blocks topped with 38mm thick slab tread.
360mm	150mm	Two courses of bricks laid flat.
330mm	165mm	One course of bricks laid on edge, topped with 50mm thick slab tread.
300mm	180mm	Two courses of bricks laid flat, topped with 25mm thick slab tread.

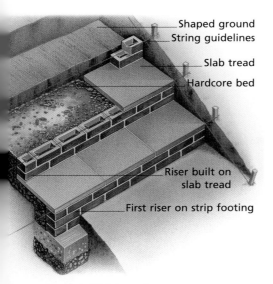

Shaped ground
String guidelines
Slab tread
Hardcore bed
Riser built on slab tread
First riser on strip footing

Steps built into a slope The ground is roughly shaped for the treads and risers. The first riser is built on a footing strip, and each following riser on the back of the previous tread. Treads are bedded on hardcore with a built-in drainage slope.

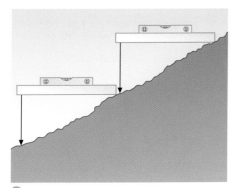

3 To measure the height difference between the levels, rest one end of a length of timber on the top of the slope and place a spirit level on it. Get a helper to hold the timber level while you measure the height of the timber above the lower ground level.

If the timber will not reach the whole way, measure to a point halfway down the slope, then measure from the same point to the lowest level. Add the two heights together for the total fall.

4 Use the height and length measurements to calculate a suitable dimension for treads and risers (see panel).

5 Fix string lines to mark the front edge of each step. Make sure they are evenly spaced, and use a builder's square to check that they are at right angles to the length lines.

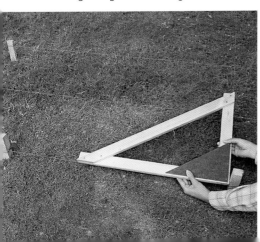

6 Use a spade to shape the ground for each step. Begin at the bottom so you always have a flat area to work from.

7 Dig a trench 125mm deep at the base of the flight to make a footing strip for the first riser.

8 Tip about 25mm of hardcore into the base of the trench and ram it well down.

9 Fill the trench with concrete, tamp level with the ground and cover it with polythene sheet.

10 Wait three days before building the first riser on the footing strip (see Laying bricks, page 468).

11 Wait at least two hours for the mortar to dry before ramming down a layer of hardcore for the first tread behind the riser. Take care not to disturb the bricks and fresh mortar. Slope the hardcore surface to the front for drainage (see right).

12 Lay paving slabs (page 453) to make the surface of the first tread. Use a full bed of mortar and project the slab about 25mm in front of the riser.

13 Build the next riser on the back edge of the first tread. Make sure the riser is vertical – use the mortar layer to adjust for the slight drainage slope on the tread.

14 Make sure the top tread is level with the surrounding ground. If necessary, slope the ground towards the tread, or raise the tread slightly – no more than 15mm.

15 Fill in between the tread slabs with mortar or sharp sand. If you use mortar, wait about 24 hours before using the steps, to allow the mortar to set.

Sloping a tread for drainage

1 Build up the hardcore surface a little higher at the back of the step. Slope the surface to level with the top of the riser at the front.

2 To check the slope, lay a spirit level from the back to the front with a 10mm thick wooden batten under the front edge, on the riser. Build up the back of the slope until the spirit level is horizontal with the wooden batten in place.

3 Check that the hardcore area is level from side to side.

Building freestanding steps

The treads of freestanding steps are supported on side walls, with the area between filled in with hardcore as a base. For a flight of up to about five steps, build the side walls centred on a concrete footing strip. For a higher flight, lay a concrete sub-base for the whole structure.

The risers can be constructed in two ways – either built across the hardcore base or built up from the ground. If they are built across the hardcore base, the hardcore has to be filled in successive layers as a riser and its corresponding side walls are built step by step. This means waiting for the brick mortar to dry out each time, but on a high flight it saves considerably on bricks.

On a low flight, it is generally easier to build up the risers from the ground and fill in all the hardcore at once. Few extra bricks are needed. The method given below is for a small flight with risers built up from the ground.

Steps can be built either at right angles to the higher level, or parallel with it. Or the flight can change direction at a landing about halfway down. A parallel flight often saves space when a lot of steps are needed.

Tools *String and pegs; profile boards (page 466); steel tape measure; spirit level; builder's square (page 467); brick trowel; two heavy-duty polythene buckets and two shovels (for mixing concrete); club hammer; tamping beam; mortar mixing board; earth rammer; pointing trowel; gauge rod; plumb line; line pins and building line; 10mm thick wooden batten. Possibly also: brick bolster.*

Materials *Hardcore – 1 barrowload fills about 0.5m² 150mm deep; concrete foundation mix (page 459); paving slabs; bricks; bedding mortar; bricklaying mortar (page 467); water. Possibly sharp sand.*

1 Measure the height difference and the ground space available, then work out the dimensions of treads and risers (page 472).

2 Prepare a concrete sub-base (page 468) either in strips or for the full area. Use a 50mm layer of hardcore topped with 75mm of concrete. Strip footings should be twice as wide as the thickness of the supporting wall.

3 Wait for three days for the concrete to harden before building the supporting walls.

4 Build supporting walls course by course according to the depths of the risers. The front wall is the riser for the first step. Mark the position of the second and subsequent risers with string and pegs. Anchor courses to an existing wall or terrace as necessary (see below). Check continually that corners are right angles and that walls are vertical, with courses at the right depth.

5 Wait until the brick mortar has set, then fill the areas between the walls and risers with hardcore well rammed down and with a drainage slope from front to back (page 473). Take care not to disturb the newly laid bricks and fresh mortar.

6 Lay the paving slabs for each tread (page 453) on a full mortar bed, ensuring they project 25mm in front of each riser.

7 Fill the gaps between the top of the side wall and the back edge of the sloped slab with mortar.

Anchoring steps to a wall

The supporting walls of freestanding steps must be anchored – or toothed in – to the wall they are built against. Half of the last brick in every other course of the step's side walls (beginning with the bottom course) is linked into the existing wall. Remove the appropriate bricks (page 408) before you start the steps.

If the flight runs parallel with the existing wall, link in a brick at the end of each riser, and in alternate courses of the back wall.

Steps built up from the ground
Steps can be built alongside an existing wall, or outwards from it. The supporting walls of the steps and the risers are built up with bricks, like an open box, and the area between them is filled in with hardcore. The treads rest on the walls and the hardcore bed.

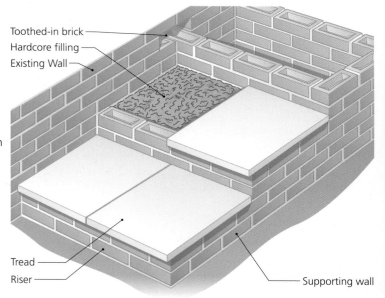

Toothed-in brick
Hardcore filling
Existing Wall

Tread
Riser
Supporting wall

Building a barbecue

A built-in barbecue gives you a custom-made cooking area designed to fit your garden. Think long and hard about the right size, the best site and the most suitable design.

The dimensions of a barbecue are dictated by the size of the grill and the charcoal pan. So purchase these first, or buy a built-in barbecue kit to use as a template.

Try to site a barbecue on or near the patio. For convenience it should also be fairly close to the kitchen. Pick a spot that is out of direct view of the house windows, if possible, unless you want to look at the barbecue all the year round, and avoid having any potential fire hazards nearby, such as fences, trellis or pergolas.

Tools *Spirit level; builder's square; stick of chalk; brick trowel; plumb line.*

Materials *Bricks sufficient for ten courses; dry-mix mortar; grill and charcoal pan, or a built-in barbecue kit.*

Before you start A firm, level base is essential. If a suitable area of concrete, slabs or brick is not available, lay a concrete foundation before you begin to build.

1 Use the spirit level to check the ground is level. Without mortar, lay out the first course of bricks in a double L shape. With the builder's square, check the corners are exact right angles and ensure that the charcoal pan will fit correctly. Draw around the bricks with chalk, then move them out of the way.

2 Mix the mortar and, using a brick trowel, put a layer of mortar on the ground. Place the first course of bricks on top. Use the builder's square to check the corners are still at right angles, and ensure the bricks are level.

3 Place a layer of mortar on top of the bricks and lay the second course of bricks so that the joints are staggered. Continue to lay courses of bricks in this way, frequently checking for level. Check that the walls are level using a plumb line.

4 Once you reach the height convenient for the charcoal pan (about six courses), lay three bricks so they stick out at right angles on each side. These bricks will support the charcoal pan. Lay a further one or two courses of bricks, then repeat the right-angled bricks to provide support for the grill. If you wish to vary the grill height, set short metal bars in the mortar between two or more courses of bricks.

5 Add a further one or two courses of bricks above the highest grill setting. If the barbecue is in an exposed position, you could raise the top by two or three more courses to create a partial windbreak.

Types of barbecue

There is a wide choice of barbecues available, ranging from basic to sophisticated models complete with tools and gadgets. The main differences are in the price and the fuel they use: charcoal or gas.

Charcoal barbecues

These are cheaper to buy than gas barbecues, but less convenient. They use solid fuel in the form of charcoal or briquettes. Check the construction is sturdy and that it has a removable lid to cover the barbecue while it cools, or to quench flames. The main drawback is that charcoal barbecues take time to get going: the coals must be lit about an hour before you want to start cooking. Also, the only way to regulate heat is by raising or lowering the grill. A charcoal barbecue can get smoky: site it where smoke will not billow into neighbours' windows.

Gas barbecues

Fuelled by bottled propane gas, these are essentially outdoor cookers. They are quick and easy to use and have adjustable controls. Gas barbecues are more substantial pieces of equipment than charcoal models and, with the weight of the gas bottle, are heavy to move around. When buying check the size in relation to what you want to cook (larger models will roast a turkey) and how easy it is to clean.

Chimeneas

These Mexican clay ovens make handsome outdoor fireplaces that can be used for cooking. They are fuelled by wood. Buy from a retailer who supplies grills and other cooking accessories to fit.

BARBECUE SAFETY

- For lighting charcoal use only products tailor-made for barbecues.
- Do not pour lighter fluid onto hot coals and never use petrol.
- Keep matches and any combustible materials well away from a barbecue.
- Keep a garden hose and/or a bucket of sand close by, in case the fire gets out of control.
- Buy a barbecue with a hood or lid to quench flames if food catches fire.
- Use long-handled tools and wear oven mitts to protect skin from burns.
- Never leave a lit barbecue unattended.

Installing a flexible pond liner

Making a pond with a flexible liner simply involves digging a hole and placing the liner inside, so that the size and shape of the pond can be to your own design.

Tools *Garden hosepipe; spade; spirit level; straight-edged plank; scissors; sand for marking out the area; bricks to use as temporary weights.*

Materials *Flexible liner; protective underlay of the same size as the liner; edging materials such as rocks, pebbles, coarse gravel, paving slabs; turf.*

Calculating the size of the liner

To find the area of liner required, multiply the length by the width as follows:
Length = maximum overall length + (2 x maximum depth) + 300mm
Width = maximum overall width + (2 x maximum depth) + 300mm
This formula works for all ponds regardless of shape and size. The extra 300mm is to allow for adequate overlap around the edges of the pond.

CHOOSING A LINER

Flexible liners are available in a range of materials from PVC to butyl rubber. Buy the best you can afford, because cheaper materials have a shorter life. The length of guarantee is a guide to a good liner; the best quality materials will be guaranteed for at least 20 years. Liners come in rolls of varying width – take this into account when planning the dimensions of the pond.

1 Mark out the shape of the pond using a hosepipe. View it from every angle including from an upstairs window. When you are completely happy with the shape and the overall position of the pond, trickle sand onto the ground to mark the outline, then remove the hosepipe.

2 Dig out the pond cavity just inside the sand mark. Make the sides slope outwards by at least 20° to stop the soil crumbling into the hole. Shape underwater shelves around the edge 300mm deep and 250–300mm wide. Outside the sand mark, remove a 450mm strip of soil or turf to a depth of 50mm to accommodate the overlap around the pond edges.

3 Use a spirit level placed on a plank to check that the rim of the pool is level all the way round, as any discrepancies will show up dramatically when the pond is full of water. If you plan to have a bog garden next to the pond, make the adjoining edge 50mm lower than the rest of the rim. Check that the underwater shelves are level, too.

4 Once digging is complete, check over the entire cavity and remove any debris and protruding stones that could damage the liner. Firm the sides with your hands to remove any soft spots that could subside later on. Line the cavity with protective underlay.

5 Cut the pond liner to size, if necessary. Lay it loosely over the cavity and weigh down the edges temporarily with bricks. When handling the liner, take care that it does not catch on any sharp objects. This part of the job is best done by two people with plenty of time to get things right.

6 Start running in water from a hose once the liner is centred over the hole. The increasing weight of the water will mould the liner to the shape of the cavity. As the liner sinks, move the weights and fold the liner neatly around shelves and corners. Continue filling the pond until the water is just below the rim.

7 Trim the liner to leave an overlap of 150mm all round. Bury the outside edge of the liner in the soil, leaving a rim of exposed liner 50–100mm wide.

8 Edge the pond with materials to conceal the liner rim. Let paving stones project over the water by 50mm to conceal the liner; turf should butt up to the edge.

Installing a rigid pond liner

Rigid liners are made of reinforced plastic. The hole you dig needs to be an accurate match for the shape of the pond: the simpler the shape, the easier this is to achieve.

Symmetrical, geometrically shaped liners are relatively easy to install (see below). A rigid liner or mould of an asymmetric shape, however, must be stood upright in position to mark out its form, or you will get a mirror image. Prop the liner upright, sticking canes in the ground to hold it in place and indicate its outline, before excavating the soil.

Tools *Spade; spirit level; straight-edged plank.*

Materials *Rigid liner; sand for marking out; hardcore or crushed stone; materials for edging, such as paving slabs. Possibly also coarse sand.*

1 Mark out the shape of the pond. Lay the liner upside down on the site and, using sand, trace the outline of the liner onto the ground. Remove the liner.

2 Cut the outline of the pond into the soil using a sharp spade to ensure straight lines.

3 Dig out the pond cavity just inside the cut lines, but only as deep as the shallow marginal shelf. Check across the edges using a spirit level and straight-edged plank to ensure that they are level.

4 Place the liner in the hole the right way up and mark around the base of the deepest part of the pond with sand. Remove the liner.

5 Cut the outline for the deep part of the pond in the soil, then dig out the hole to the correct depth. Clear away all loose stones and roots. On stony soil, make the hole a bit deeper, and place a 50mm layer of coarse sand on which the liner can rest.

6 Check that the liner fits in the hole, and dig out more soil if necessary. Ensure the liner is level in each direction by placing the spirit level along each edge. Make any necessary adjustments and back-fill with soil or sand.

7 Slowly fill the liner with water, allowing the mould to settle under its increasing weight. Check for level as it fills and adjust the liner as necessary, otherwise one edge will stand above the water line and be unsightly.

8 As the liner is filling up, back-fill the gaps with soil or sand. When it is level, prepare the ground for paving around the liner, if you are having paved edges. Place a 100mm layer of hardcore or crushed stone and ram down with a post to compact it.

9 Bed each paving slab onto the hardcore, overhanging the edge of the liner slightly. Tap each one into position and check for level before mortaring the gaps.

Installing a wall-mounted water fountain

An electric pump is the basis for all moving water features. The simple installation techniques shown here can be used for pebble fountains, rills, water chutes and many more effects.

Tools *Spirit level; power drill and masonry bit; masonry paintbrush.*

Materials *20–23 litre plastic water tank (available from builders' or plumbers' merchants); length of rigid tubing; flexible piping; pump; low-voltage transformer; wall-mounted spout; wall plug and screw; bricks or slabs to disguise tank; external waterproof paint.*

1 Lift a paving slab next to a wall and dig down to create a hole big enough for the water tank, so that it sits proud of the surrounding surface by an equal amount all the way round. Make sure that the tank sits level in the hole.

2 Surround the tank with a row of bricks or walling blocks to disguise its edge. Butt the bricks tightly together, mortaring them in place if you prefer.

3 Drill a hole in the wall and insert a wall plug and screw to hold the water spout. Hang the spout in place and check with a spirit level that it is level.

4 Attach the flexible piping to the base of the spout and feed the other end into the water tank. Connect it to the pump in the base of the tank.

5 Fill the tank with water and connect the pump to the power supply via a low-voltage transformer inside the house. Switch on the fountain to check that it is working. If it is, cut the flexible piping to length so that it runs vertically into the water tank.

6 Paint the rigid tubing, which will enclose the flexible piping, to match the wall behind it. Feed the flexible pipe through the rigid tube and attach it to the pump and water spout at either end.

SAFETY TIP

Mixing electricity with water and the outdoors can be dangerous. If you are installing a water feature that requires a mains power supply, follow the instructions for wiring outdoor electrics on pages 316–19 and always connect the water pump to an RCD.

7 Tuck the electric cable running from the pump to the electricity supply along the back of the patio paving, or protect it in a length of metal conduit.

8 Fill the water tank with enough water to cover the pump, connect the power supply and switch on the pump. Add a water-loving plant, such as a fern, with its pot raised above the level of the water to complete the display.

IDEAS FOR WATER FEATURES

• You can hide the workings of a wall-mounted water feature by chasing the pipework into an existing wall or by burying the pipes in a new wall.

• Self-contained pebble fountain kits are easy to install and can be finished in a variety of different ways. They consist of a plastic bucket with a wide lip that catches water sprayed up by the fountain and channels it back into the bucket. A pump sits in the reservoir and is covered by a plastic lid or a metal grille. The surface can be covered with cobbles or a mill-wheel, or the water can be fed from the pump through a flexible pipe to emerge from an urn or ceramic ball.

• A pump can also be used to move water along a shallow rill or garden stream. Dig a gently sloping trench for the rill and bury a water reservoir and pump at one end. Run a length of piping from the far end of the feature back to the reservoir to recycle the water.

Ten ways to keep your property safe

Most break-ins are carried out by casual thieves looking for easy pickings. A thief is unlikely to persist if he encounters locked doors and windows. Rapid entry and exit are vital for him, and he will not climb in and out of the house through broken glass. The tips on this page will all help to keep your home secure.

1 Deliveries Cancel milk and newspapers when you go away. Arrange for a neighbour to push in unexpected items like leaflets and free newspapers. If you have a glazed porch, ask your neighbour to gather up the post each morning so that it is not visible from outside.

2 Garage Add extra security to a back door inside a garage where an intruder could work totally hidden. Ensure that the garage itself is fitted with secure locks. An electronically operated, metal up-and-over door will provide the most security.

3 Ladders Keep ladders locked away. If they must be stored outside, padlock them to a wall with special brackets.

4 Sheds Make sure sheds are securely padlocked. Tools stored there could be used for a break-in. A garden spade, for example, makes a powerful lever for opening windows.

5 Security lights Outside lights that switch on automatically when a sensor picks up movement outside the house can be a real deterrent to crime. Site them in areas of the house where a burglar may try to gain access, for example high above French windows at the back or over a garage door. One fitted above a front door will also help you to see who is calling at night. Site the sensor well out of reach of intruders. Bear in mind that most domestic situations do not require high power floodlights, which can be a real nuisance to neighbours.

GETTING HELP FROM THE POLICE

If you want specific advice on how to protect your home, telephone the Crime Prevention Officer at your local police station. He will visit the house if necessary, point out weak spots in your defences and suggest the most appropriate security devices for your circumstances.

If you see anyone loitering in your street or acting suspiciously, do not disturb them. Call the police, then continue to watch unseen until they arrive.

Neighbourhood Watch groups, run in collaboration with the local police, are intended to encourage neighbours to work together by watching for anything suspicious in the area. They also stress the importance of protecting property, and marking valuables. If you are interested in getting involved in a group, contact your local Crime Prevention Officer.

10 Hedges and shrubs Avoid having high hedges and shrubs that will screen a thief from the road or from neighbours.

9 Keys Never have a name-and-address tag on your keys. At most, use your surname, with a company address or the address of a relative for them to be returned to if you lose them. Be wary of leaving home to go and collect keys from someone who says they have found them. It may be a ruse to get you out of the house while the keys are used for entry. Never leave keys in locks, under the doormat, or hanging inside the letterbox.

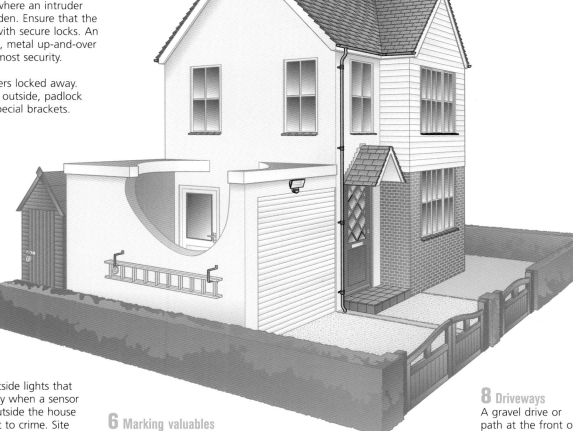

6 Marking valuables Print your house number and post code on valuable possessions with an ultra-violet marking pen. This will help police to prove they were stolen, and assist in returning them. Metal items can be marked with hammer-and-letter punches. Photograph valuable items together, showing on the photograph where they are marked.

7 Accessible windows Never leave windows open when you go out. Fitting security shutters will increase the safety of your property, obscuring the view inside and preventing access even if the window is broken. Fit locks to all windows, especially those with easy access – near flat roofs, drainpipes and trees.

8 Driveways A gravel drive or path at the front of the house is a noisy surface that will alert you to the approach of visitors or intruders. Gates at the garden boundary, particularly locked ones, are a very effective deterrent to burglars.

13
Rules and regulations

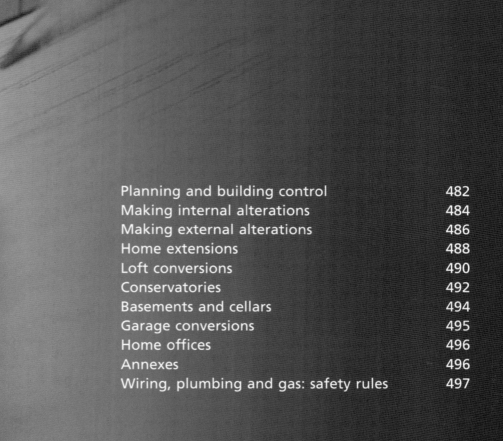

Planning and building control

If you are planning to carry out major improvements to your home, such as building an extension, adding a conservatory or knocking down a load-bearing wall, you need to know whether you require official approval for the work.

The two most important pieces of legislation that apply to projects of this sort are the Town & Country Planning Acts and the Building Regulations. Before you start work, it is your duty as the householder to find out which rules and regulations apply to the job, to seek prior permission if this is needed, and to make sure that the work complies with the rules when it has been completed. There are financial and other penalties if you do not obtain the required permission, or if you carry out work that does not comply with the rules, and you may be unable to sell a house that has been altered or extended without consent or approval.

The following information gives a general overview of the planning and building rules that apply to home improvements. It explains how to find out if consent or approval is needed, and how to go about applying for it. Specific requirements for individual improvement projects are explained on pages 484–97.

Planning permission

The Town & Country Planning Acts govern what your house looks like from the outside, the impact it has on the street where it is located, and the uses to which the house and the land it occupies are put. The way the Acts are interpreted vary from one local authority to another, but most publish guidelines that are intended to help homeowners to ensure that the work they propose to carry out will be approved. Get hold of a copy from the local planning office before you start putting pen to paper.

What you can and cannot do in planning terms is governed by so-called 'permitted development'. This allows certain improvement projects such as home extensions to go ahead if they meet specific requirements, whatever the local authority may think, and is intended to prevent planning departments from being inundated by many similar and minor planning applications. You will find the permitted development rules for individual projects outlined on the following pages.

To apply for planning permission, contact your local authority planning department and ask for the relevant forms, plus any guidance notes they publish. You will be told what the current fee is for an application. If you want clarification about whether a particular project needs permission, you can make an appointment with a planning officer to talk over your proposals.

You usually need to fill in four copies of the forms and send them in to the

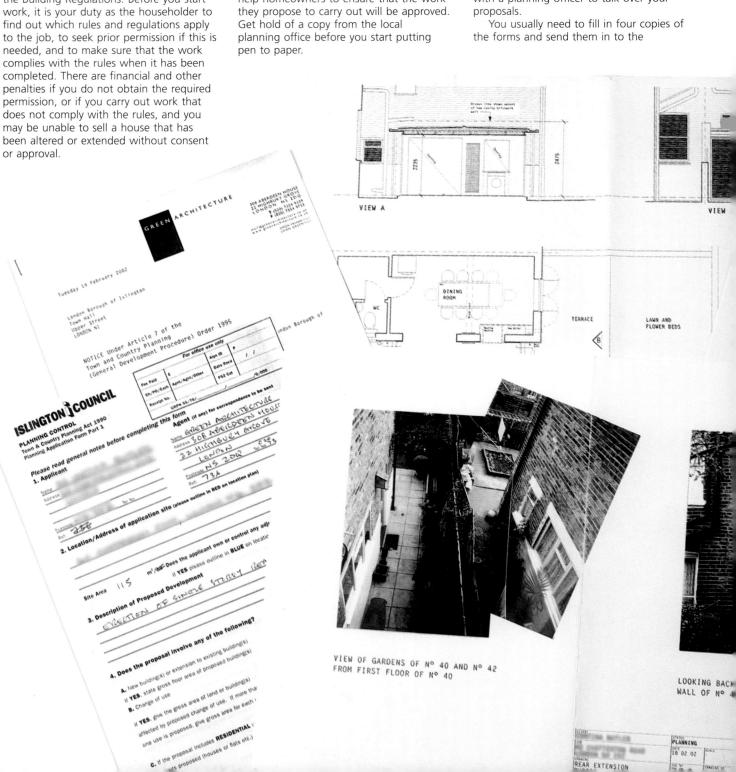

VIEW OF GARDENS OF Nº 40 AND Nº 42
FROM FIRST FLOOR OF Nº 40

department, along with four copies of the relevant plans and the appropriate fee. Your application will be considered at a planning meeting, and you should receive a decision within eight weeks. Do not start work without permission if your project needs it.

If permission is granted, it remains valid for five years. If it is refused, or you do not receive a decision within the time limit, you can appeal to the Planning Inspectorate (part of the Office of the Deputy Prime Minister) within six months. Details of how to appeal are included in the planning application paperwork.

If you carry out work without planning permission and your local authority becomes aware of this, action is likely to be taken against you. You may be allowed to make a retrospective application for permission, but you are more likely to receive an enforcement notice requiring you to restore the property to its former condition or use. You may also be prosecuted. An enforcement notice must be issued within four years of the unauthorised work being carried out. After that time, no official action can be taken. However, you may still be found out if you try to sell the house, when enquiries before the exchange of contracts are likely to uncover your actions.

Building Regulations approval

The Building Regulations exist to ensure that buildings are structurally sound and are safe and healthy to live in. Unlike planning rules, the Regulations are applied uniformly by every local authority in England and Wales; Scotland and Northern Ireland have their own Regulations, but they are all broadly similar in terms of the requirements they contain. The subject areas covered include building structure, fire safety, thermal and sound insulation, ventilation and hygiene, drainage and waste disposal, the use of fuel-burning appliances, the installation of glazing and the provision of facilities for disabled people.

To apply for Building Regulations approval for an improvement project, you can take one of two routes. The first is to deliver two copies of the relevant forms and two full sets of all plans and drawings, plus the appropriate fee, to the local authority Building Control Officer. The second is to give the department what is called a Building Notice, and to provide rather less detailed information about the work to be carried out (the application forms will set out what is required).

With either route, you can start work 48 hours after delivering the documents; you no longer have to wait for approval to be granted, although you can do so if you wish. The onus is on you to ensure that the work complies with the requirements of the Regulations, which will be subject to regular inspections as it is carried out.

The advantage of waiting for formal approval to be granted is that you will receive this in writing as firm evidence that the work satisfies the Regulations. The local authority must give a decision within five weeks,

unless you agree to an extension. With the building notice route, you only receive oral confirmation of compliance as each stage is inspected.

If you carry out work that does not meet the regulatory requirements and this is uncovered, you will be sent an enforcement notice giving you 28 days to amend the work. Failure to do this may result in the local authority appointing contractors to do the work and charging you for this. Alternatively, you may be fined a lump sum plus an extra charge for every day until you comply. An enforcement order must be issued within 12 months of the non-complying work being carried out; after that period, no official action will be taken. However, as with work done without planning permission, non-compliance may be discovered when you try to sell the property in the future.

Other restrictions on development

Your home improvement project may have to comply with other legal requirements apart from planning and building controls. These include local authority bye-laws, restrictive covenants on your property (often inherited from times past, or imposed on new developments by the local authority), and the rules applying to listed buildings or to buildings in a conservation area or an Area of Outstanding Natural Beauty (AONB) such as a National Park. (The Scottish equivalent is a National Scenic Area.) You must find out from your local authority about their requirements before you plan your project. You will need the help of a solicitor to examine the impact of restrictive covenants.

Finally, note that work involving your plumbing, wiring and gas supply may also have to meet individual rules and regulations. See pages 496–7 for more details.

Making internal alterations

The most significant internal alterations you are likely to undertake are those that involve changing the layout or use of existing rooms. You may also plan to create new door or window openings, refurbish a kitchen or bathroom, or install new heating appliances. The rules and regulations that apply to each of these projects are summarised here.

Removing an internal wall

One of the most dramatic changes you can make to the interior layout of your home is to remove one or more of the internal walls to create a new room layout. The most popular choices are removing the wall between the sitting room and dining room to create a large through living room, or the wall between the dining room and kitchen to form a large open-plan cooking and eating area. Other possibilities are removing the wall between the hall and sitting room (advisable only if you have an enclosed porch to maintain an airlock to the outside world), and the wall between adjacent bedrooms to create a large master

bedroom suite, perhaps allied with the provision of an en-suite bathroom.

These alterations do not need planning permission. However, Building Regulations approval is essential if the wall to be removed is load-bearing. Ground-floor walls usually support walls and floors in the storey above (or the roof structure in bungalows), and the load must instead be carried on suitable beams – usually rolled steel joists (RSJs) – set on adequate supports at each end. Upstairs walls may be load-bearing, but are more likely to be simple partitions, especially in modern houses with trussed-rafter roofs.

A load-bearing wall does more than carry a superimposed load. It also acts as a transverse brace between the walls at each end of it, and removing it may affect the stability of these walls. Furthermore, transferring the load carried by a solid wall via an RSJ to two small piers or other supports at each end may affect the existing wall foundations, which may need strengthening.

For this reason it is essential to seek professional advice from an architect, surveyor or qualified builder. He or she will ensure that a beam of the correct type, size and cross-section for the job is specified, that it is installed correctly and that it is adequately fire-proofed.

The new through room must also be adequately ventilated, with windows having an openable area equal to at least 5 per cent of the new room's floor area. This is unlikely to be a problem if each original room has a window.

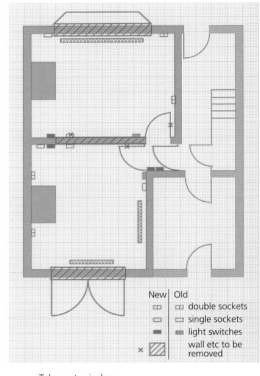

New	Old	
▭▭	▭▭	double sockets
▭	▭	single sockets
▬	▬	light switches
✕	▨	wall etc to be removed

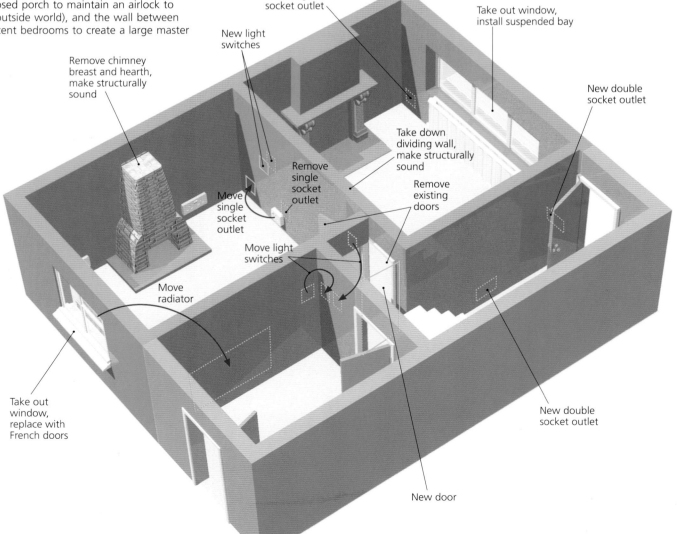

New single socket outlet

New light switches

Remove chimney breast and hearth, make structurally sound

Move single socket outlet

Remove single socket outlet

Move light switches

Move radiator

Take out window, replace with French doors

Take out window, install suspended bay

New double socket outlet

Take down dividing wall, make structurally sound

Remove existing doors

New double socket outlet

New door

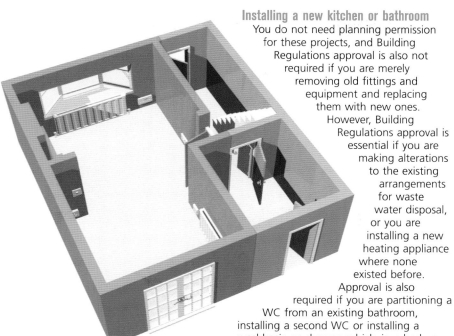

Creating new rooms

If your house has large rooms, you may be able to make better use of the space by building a partition wall across one or more of them. A downstairs room could be partitioned to create a second sitting room or a home office, while an upstairs room could be divided to create an extra bedroom for a child or a second bathroom.

Again, planning permission is not needed, but some requirements of the Building Regulations will have to be met – in particular as far as ventilation of the two new rooms and the provision of sound insulation between them is concerned. Each new room must have a window with an openable area equal to 5 per cent of its floor area. The new rooms are not allowed to share an existing window. If one of the rooms does not need a window (a bathroom, for example), it must be provided with mechanical ventilation via an extractor fan. You will also need Building Regulations approval for the waste water disposal from new bathroom facilities.

Providing access to the new rooms may involve the creation of a corridor in one of them, with some loss of usable floor space. This is essential for bedrooms, which should always have individual access, but may not matter for a home office or similar use.

Changing room layouts
You may be able to make better use of your available floor space by a combination of removing and repositioning walls. If this involves any load-bearing walls, follow the advice given above and consult a professional for advice on finding the best solution. You will need Building Regulations approval for any structural work involved, but planning permission is not required.

Installing a new kitchen or bathroom
You do not need planning permission for these projects, and Building Regulations approval is also not required if you are merely removing old fittings and equipment and replacing them with new ones. However, Building Regulations approval is essential if you are making alterations to the existing arrangements for waste water disposal, or you are installing a new heating appliance where none existed before. Approval is also required if you are partitioning a WC from an existing bathroom, installing a second WC or installing a washbasin or shower cubicle in a bedroom, again because you will have to install new waste water pipes. If the siting of a new WC makes connection to existing soil pipes difficult, the Regulations allow the use of a pumped macerator unit and small-bore pipework to carry the waste water away. Finally, you must also comply with the ventilation requirements of the Regulations for new WC cubicles.

Creating a new door or window opening

You may need planning permission for a new door or window opening that will project beyond a wall facing the road. Planning permission will almost certainly be needed if the house is in a conservation area. If the new opening is in a load-bearing wall, you will need Building Regulations approval. This will ensure that the lintel used to span the new opening is the correct type and size. It will also make sure that door and window openings in external walls are correctly damp-proofed, especially if they are of cavity construction.

Fitting new heating appliances

Building Regulations approval is needed for the installation of a new fuel-burning appliance such as a boiler or room heater, but not if it is a direct replacement for an existing appliance. Approval is also needed if its installation requires the building of a new flue. The replacement of an existing vented heating system by an unvented (sealed) system requires approval, and the work must be carried out only by an approved installer; it is definitely not a DIY job. Planning permission may be needed for the construction of a new external chimney or flue, and for the installation of a gas or oil storage tank on the property.

WORK INVOLVING A PARTY WALL

The oddly-named Party Wall etc. Act 1996 covers any construction or repair work carried out on a party wall (one shared with another property, as in a semi-detached or terraced house). It requires you to give your neighbour notice of your intentions, and gives him or her the right to agree or disagree with your proposals. It is best to engage the services of a chartered surveyor, who will take a schedule, or assessment, of the condition of the party wall before work starts, so that any disputes can be resolved over the way the work is carried out and the repair of any damage it causes.

Failure to observe the provisions of the Act can result in an injunction being served on you by your neighbour, preventing work from proceeding until agreement is reached.

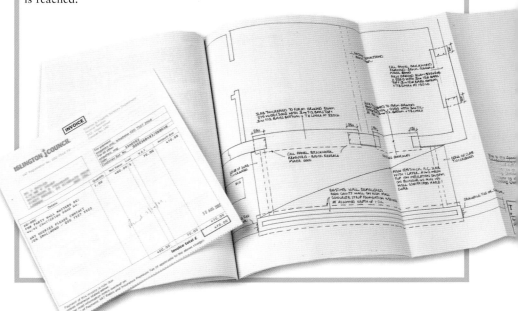

Making external alterations

Changes that affect the outside of your house tend to be rather more dramatic than anything you are likely to undertake indoors, and the rules and regulations affecting what you can and cannot do are much more specific. Here are the things you need to consider for small scale projects and alterations. Larger projects are dealt with on the following pages.

Very old or unusual trees may be protected by a tree preservation order. This prevents you from lopping or cutting down the tree and may restrict your plans for a home extension or conservatory. Your solicitor should tell you about any tree preservation orders on your property when you purchase the house, or you can check with the local planning authority.

Outbuildings

You can put up all sorts of outbuildings such as sheds, summerhouses and greenhouses on your property without the need for planning permission, so long as they meet the following conditions:
• they are not for residential use;
• they are not in front of the building line (any wall of the house facing a highway);
• they are not more than 4m high if they have a pitched roof, or 3m if the roof is flat;
• their construction does not result in more than 50 per cent of the total site being occupied by buildings (including the house). Planning permission will be needed to erect any outbuilding within 5m of the house if it exceeds 10m³ in volume, or if the house is in a conservation area or an area of outstanding natural beauty.

Outbuildings are exempt from Building Regulations control so long as their floor area does not exceed 30m². Like garages, they should be built of incombustible materials if sited within 1m of a boundary, although, in practice, many timber garden sheds are clearly in breach of this requirement.

Aerials and satellite TV dishes

TV and radio aerials attached to the house are exempt from all planning and building control. A satellite TV dish needs planning permission if it is:
• fixed higher than the top of a chimney stack or roof;
• more than 450mm in diameter and sited on a chimney;
• over 900mm in diameter if sited elsewhere;
• a second or subsequent dish on a property that already has one.

Permission is always needed to install a satellite dish on a listed building or on a house in a conservation area or area of outstanding natural beauty.

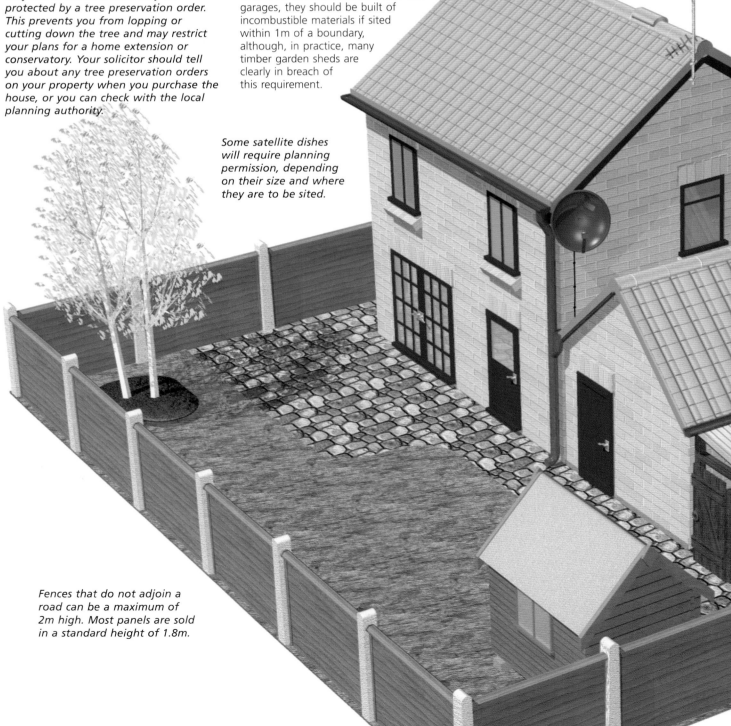

Some satellite dishes will require planning permission, depending on their size and where they are to be sited.

Fences that do not adjoin a road can be a maximum of 2m high. Most panels are sold in a standard height of 1.8m.

Garages

A garage built next to the house or within 5m of it is also classed as a home extension for planning permission purposes. You can build one without applying for permission if the permitted development volume allowances (page 489) have not already been used up for the property, and its total volume does not exceed 10m³.

A garage sited more than 5m from the house is classed as an outbuilding (see below), except in conservation areas or areas of outstanding natural beauty, where they are always classified as home extensions.

Garages are exempt from Building Regulations control so long as their floor area does not exceed 30m². They must also be built of non-combustible materials if they are within 1m of any boundary of the property.

Many houses have a garage that is either within the structure of the house or is attached to it. Such a garage is a prime target for conversion into additional living space, especially if it already has access to it direct from the house (see page 495 for more details). You generally do not need planning permission for the conversion, but you may need Building Regulations approval to ensure that it meets the thermal insulation requirements for habitable rooms. The existing building may not have cavity walls, and will certainly have no floor insulation (or roof insulation if it is attached rather than integral). Check with your local authority before proceeding.

Porches

Porches count as home extensions for planning permission purposes. A porch can be built without the need for planning permission if:
• the permitted development volume allowances (page 489) have not already been used up for the property;
• it has a floor area of 3m² or less;
• its roof is no more than 3m high;
• its outermost wall is at least 2m from any boundary between your property and a road or public footpath.
Check with your local authority if you live in a listed building, in a conservation area or in an area of outstanding natural beauty.

Porches are subject to the safety glazing requirements of Part N of the Building Regulations (page 492), but are otherwise exempt from building control.

Off-road parking

You do not need planning permission or Building Regulations approval to create a parking area for your car within the boundaries of your property, so long as the space is not used to park commercial vehicles. However, planning permission may be needed if you have to create a new access route to the parking area from the road. You will need to apply to your local authority's highways department for approval if the access route will cross a footpath or verge, unless the road is unclassified. The department will carry out the work needed to create a crossover to the road, with lowered kerbstones and a crossing surface, and will charge you for doing so.

A wall at the front of your property or one that adjoins a highway along any other boundary must be no more than 1m high.

Fuel storage tanks

Fuel storage tanks are exempt from all control so long as they do not exceed 3500 litres in capacity, are less than 3m high and are sited behind the foremost part of the house facing a highway.

Both oil and gas storage tanks are usually installed as part of a complete central heating system, and the work must be carried out by qualified fitters who can ensure that the required safety features are included.

Gas storage tanks must meet the requirements of the Gas Safety Regulations (page 497). Coal bunkers are classified as outbuildings.

Swimming pools

A swimming pool enclosure counts as an outbuilding for the purposes of planning permission, but its position and volume may mean that permission will be needed to erect it; always check with your local authority before considering building one.

If you intend to contruct an outhouse to serve as a changing room, ensure that it meets the requirements of an outbuilding (see far left)

The pool itself is exempt from planning and building control, but its excavation must take account of the presence of any buried underground services in the vicinity. It is wise to consult the building control department for advice before work starts. Lastly, you will need approval from your local water supply company to install and fill a pool. This is likely to result in a substantial increase in your water bill.

Walls and fences

You need planning permission to erect a wall or fence more than 1m high along a boundary adjoining a highway, or more than 2m high along any other boundary. Permission is also needed for any walls or fences round the boundary of a listed building. However, walls and fences are exempt from Building Regulations control. Hedges are exempt from all control, but the local authority has the right to cut back any that obscure the view of traffic or overhang the pavement.

Carports

Carports are treated as outbuildings for planning permission purposes, wherever they are sited. They are exempt from Building Regulations control so long as they do not exceed 30m² in floor area and are open on at least two sides.

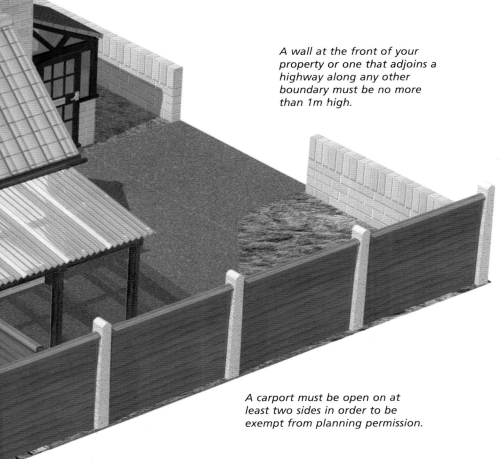

A carport must be open on at least two sides in order to be exempt from planning permission.

Home extensions

A home extension is the most popular solution to the problem of a house with insufficient living space. It can provide extra living rooms, extra bedrooms or any other type of space you need such as a bigger kitchen or a home office. The only requirement is that your property has enough free land on which to build it.

Rules and regulations

An extension is probably the biggest home improvement project anyone is likely to consider, and it is more likely to be placed in the hands of a firm of builders than to be tackled as a DIY project. Whoever does the work must ensure that it complies with all the relevant sections of the Building Regulations (see page 483 for details of how to apply for approval).

As far as planning permission is concerned, a home extension is covered by the rules of permitted development in most circumstances. This means that it can be built without the need to apply for planning permission, so long as the following restrictions are met.

Permitted volume allowance
The extension must not increase the volume of the original house by more than the permitted volume allowance (see box, facing page). The term 'original house' means the house as it was when it was first built, or as it stood on 1 July 1948 if it was built before that date.

Additional requirements
Provided the proposed extension meets the permitted volume allowances, it will not need planning permission if it meets the following extra requirements:
• the extension must not be higher than the original roof of the house;
• it must not project in front of any house wall facing a highway;
• it must not be more than 4m high if it is to be built within 2m of a boundary;
• it must not result in buildings covering more than 50 per cent of the site.

Even if the extension meets the permitted development allowances, planning permission may be needed if the extension will create a home office or a self-contained granny flat, because of the change of use of the property.

Lastly, it is possible that your permitted development rights have been removed. This may occur as a condition of a previous planning consent – for example, when a house was first built as part of a new development. Check this out with your local authority at an early stage. It does not mean that you cannot extend your house, just that you will need to apply for permission to do so.

Planning points

A successful home extension requires a lot of careful planning. The first stage is to work out what type of extra space you need. The top priority might be more bedroom accommodation, to cope with a new baby or to separate children too old to share a room. You might need more living space so family members can pursue different leisure interests in peace. A bigger kitchen, a separate utility room, an extra bathroom or a second WC could all be welcome additions.

Where to build
The site and size of an extension depends on your requirements. An extra living room or a bigger kitchen is best provided by a single-storey extension, added to the side or rear of the property according to where there is the most available space. If you need extra bedrooms, consider a two-storey extension to the side or rear. This could provide extra living space or a garage with a bedroom above, or a second extra bedroom could be created on the ground floor of the extension.

If you cannot build outwards because of the constraints of the site, your only alternative is to build upwards. A loft conversion (pages 490–1) is the obvious solution, but you may also be able to add a second storey to an existing single-storey

extension if its foundations and structure are strong enough. In both cases you will lose some existing floor space in providing access to the new rooms.

Gaining access

The next important consideration is how to gain access to the extension from the house. In the case of a single-storey extension this is unlikely to be a problem. Existing door or window openings can often be used, or new ones created if this suits the room layouts better. In a two-storey extension, access upstairs can be more difficult to plan successfully. Some loss of floor space is inevitable, since access through existing bedrooms is not practicable and may not be allowed. The use of lightweight timber partition walls makes dividing up the existing and new spaces easier, and imposes no restrictions on where the walls are sited.

Professional advice

At this point in the process you may feel that you are not getting the best possible result out of the space available. Now is the time to hand over your preliminary ideas to a professional. An architect or surveyor will be used to finding solutions to apparently intractable problems of space management. He or she will also be adept at making your extension blend in with the structure of the existing house – by matching walling and roofing materials, doors and windows and so on. You can employ a professional just to draw up the plans you will need to submit to your local authority, and leave the building work to your builder. Alternatively, your architect or surveyor can oversee the entire project from start to finish. This is a more expensive option, but relieves you of the responsibilty of finding and managing competent contractors to carry out the work.

PERMITTED VOLUME ALLOWANCES

For a terraced house or for any house in a conservation area or an area of outstanding natural beauty, the maximum volume of a permitted extension is 50m³ or 10 per cent of the volume of the original house, whichever is the greater, up to a maximum volume of 115m³.

For any other house the maximum permitted volume is 70m³ or 15 per cent of the volume of the original house, whichever is the greater, again up to a maximum volume of 115m³.

In Scotland the permitted maximum floor area is 24m² or 20 per cent of the floor area of the original house, whichever is the greater.

All the volume figures given include the volume contained within a pitched roof.

These are once-for-all allowances. If the house has been extended since 1948, that work may have used up part or all of the permitted allowance. If this is so, planning permission must be sought for the new work.

When you are adding a major home extension, paying for the services of an architect can be money well spent. Taking professional advice may help to smooth the process of obtaining planning permission and pre-empt potential problems throughout the course of the project. The Royal Institute of British Architects (RIBA) will be able to offer you advice on choosing, briefing and managing an architect and put you in touch with architects in your area.

A new extension should blend in with the existing house, mirroring construction methods and using the same materials. Sympathetic designs will be much more likely to win planning approval than proposals that are out of character with the surrounding properties.

Loft conversions

Most homes have a loft, but it is usually used only as storage space. Converting it to habitable rooms could add up to 30 per cent of usable floor area in a two-storey building, and twice as much in a bungalow. A loft conversion will cost less than a home extension of the same floor area, because the shell of the extension – the roof and the loft floor – is already in place.

Rules and regulations

Planning permission to create a loft conversion is not needed in England and Wales unless dormer windows are proposed in a roof slope facing a road, or unless any part of the conversion will project above the original roof line. In Scotland, the installation of dormer windows anywhere in the roof needs planning permission.

You will always need to apply for planning permission for a loft conversion if you live in a listed building, or if your home is in a conservation area or an area of outstanding natural beauty.

Loft conversions need Building Regulations approval to ensure that the work complies with the requirements for structural stability, safe access, ventilation, insulation, fireproofing, waste disposal (if the new loft space will contain a bathroom or WC) and means of escape in the event of fire. Because of this, you must submit full plans for a loft conversion in a two-storey building; you cannot use the Building Notice scheme (although you can for a loft conversion in a bungalow).

Planning points

If you think that a loft conversion is the solution to your space shortage, the first thing you need to do is to assess its feasibility, and this depends on how the roof was constructed.

The importance of roof construction

In houses built before the 1960s, the roof was built up on site from a framework of rafters to support the roof covering, purlins to tie the rafters together, and struts to brace the purlins against the loft floor joists and any internal load-bearing walls. The existing loft area may look awkward and cluttered, but the structure can generally be adapted to make space for a new room. This is done by relocating struts and other supports to create a clear floor area, and by inserting dormer windows if there is not enough full-height headroom over this floor area. You must employ an architect, surveyor or structural engineer to plan this work, so that the alterations do not weaken the roof structure.

Houses built since about 1960 usually have roofs constructed using prefabricated roof trusses. These are triangular frames that span the outer walls of the house, eliminating the need for internal load-bearing walls. Because of the way the roof trusses are assembled and erected, you cannot remove any of their components without seriously weakening the roof structure. Altering the structure to accommodate a loft room is therefore likely to be difficult and expensive, if not impossible. However, you may be fortunate in having a modern house built with loft conversion in mind, using so-called attic trusses instead of conventional ones with their W-shaped bracing. Attic trusses are made from thicker, wider timber components so they can carry floor loads as well as the weight of the roof covering, and they can be adapted readily to allow for the insertion of roof or dormer windows.

Non-habitable or habitable?

The end use to which you want to put a loft conversion will dictate what is involved in creating it. A simple playroom in the loft is deemed to be a 'non-habitable room', and the conversion will involve little more than creating access using a loft ladder or a space-saver staircase, framing and boarding out the roof space and perhaps adding a roof window or two.

Fitting velux windows is an easy way to allow light into a converted loft and, in most cases, does not need planning permission. This kind of conversion leaves you with limited head height towards the edges of the room, but this is useful space for storage or a low seat.

FIRE SAFETY

When you are planning a loft conversion, particularly in a two-storey building, there are fire safety requirements that must be satisfied. The loft windows must provide a means of escape in the event of fire. The Building Regulations require an opening window that is at least 850mm high and 500mm wide, with a sill at between 600 and 1100mm above the loft floor and no more than 1.7m from the roof's eaves. This will allow the use of ladders for rescue purposes. In addition, the stairwell leading to the new top storey must be fireproofed, with self-closing devices fitted to any doors opening onto the stairwell and a fire door leading to the new loft rooms. Finally, the loft floor must have 30-minute fire resistance, and interlinked mains-powered smoke detectors must be fitted on each floor of the house.

A dormer window juts out of the existing roof line (above) and cannot be installed without planning permission. Whatever your window choice, you will need Building Regulations approval for the conversion work, which includes removing supporting struts in the roof (left) and installing a staircase for access (below).

Conversion to habitable rooms – an extra bedroom and bathroom, a teenager's bedsitter or a home office, for example – is a much more complex project. The conversion will have to comply with all relevant aspects of the Building Regulations. Providing suitable staircase access may involve creating a dormer window over the new staircase to give adequate headroom, or else sacrificing existing floor space in a room below for it. The existing loft floor will almost certainly have to be strengthened to support the load that the new loft rooms will impose, either by installing deeper joists between the existing ones or by the use of rolled steel joists (RSJs) to support the new floor. The new rooms will require natural light and ventilation (and possibly mechanical ventilation in bathrooms and WCs), thermal, sound and fire insulation and a full range of wiring, plumbing and heating services.

Professional advice

Because of the potential complexity of the job, it is essential to enlist professional help in the design of the conversion at the planning stage. You could employ an architect or surveyor, either just to produce plans for your builder to execute, or to oversee the whole project. Alternatively, you could rely on a builder experienced in loft conversion work, or hand the whole project over to one of the many specialist loft conversion companies now operating nationwide.

Depending on the construction of your roof, you will need to add new supports (above) to take its weight. Always employ an architect or structural engineer to help you and to make sure that the finished result (right) is in keeping with the rest of the property.

Conservatories

A conservatory has become one of the most popular home improvement projects. It can provide extra living space for much less than the cost of a conventional extension – space that can be used as a sitting or dining area, a play area and, of course, somewhere to grow plants that would not thrive in a British garden.

Rules and regulations

A conservatory is defined as having a transparent or translucent roof. It is classed as a home extension for planning purposes, and the criteria for permitted development apply (page 488). The structure of a conservatory is exempt from Building Regulations control so long as its floor area does not exceed 30 m². However, some sections of the Regulations apply to its installation, covering the following aspects.

• Safety glazing must be used in doors, glazed panels flanking door openings and all low-level glazed panels up to 800mm above floor level, to comply with Part N of the Regulations.

• The conservatory must include ventilation openings (doors and windows) with a total area of at least 5 per cent of the combined floor area of the conservatory and the room through which it is accessed, to comply with Part F.

• There must be an opening, such as French windows or sliding patio doors, of the same size as above between the conservatory and the adjacent room.

• There must be background ventilation (trickle ventilators) in the conservatory and in the opening between it and the rest of the house with an area of at least 8000mm².

• Any structural alterations required to create access to the conservatory from the house must meet the relevant sections of the Regulations.

Planning points

A conservatory is usually sited at the back of the house. However, the layout of your property, the arrangement of your rooms and the way the house faces may make a site at the side a better choice. The amount of space you have available will dictate how big a conservatory you can build. Size costs, since conservatories are designed on a modular basis, but it is better to err on the large size than to rue the lack of space once you have fitted out and furnished your new room.

Windows

Modern conservatories have developed chiefly from the replacement window business. This means that conservatory style – at the mass-market end of the range, at least – is based on the design of the multiple window frames that make up the walls of the building. These may be made from hardwood or uPVC, and styles range from the plain and unadorned to the elaborate mock-Victorian. There is a wide choice of door and window designs, with a variety of opening mechanisms to allow for ventilation. When choosing them, pay particular attention to the level of security they offer.

Shading

Conservatories can become very hot in summer, and roof and window blinds are essential to keep out the strongest sunlight and reduce glare. They also create privacy if you use your conservatory after dark.

The conservatory walls may be full or part-glazed. Part-glazed walls may have solid uPVC infill panels down to ground level, or may be designed to sit on a dwarf brick cavity wall forming the perimeter of the building. The latter is the only viable option on a sloping site. It also allows for the creating of internal window sills, and provides a convenient mounting surface for radiators or other heaters.

A specialist conservatory company will help you to plan and visualise your project and may also carry out the installation.

A concrete slab raises the floor level of the conservatory and provides a firm foundation for the structure (above left and left). A cavity tray is inserted into the existing house wall (above) to make a watertight seal where the conservatory will butt up to the house.

The roof

The conservatory roof can be transparent or translucent. Glass roofs must be made of safety glass, and sealed unit double glazing is essential if the building is to be used in winter. Translucent polycarbonate roofs use twin or triple-walled sheeting for insulation. Both types can incorporate openable roof lights for ventilation. If possible, the roof should be designed with a slope of at least 25°; shallower slopes than this do not clean themselves very efficiently, and tend to collect algae and wind-blown debris which you will need to remove regularly.

Internal access

Access to the conservatory is likely to be via existing doors leading off a living room. If the siting of the conservatory requires a new opening to be created, it may be possible to turn an existing window into a door opening with a minimum of structural work. If a new opening is needed, you must ensure that its construction meets the requirements of the Building Regulations.

Low cavity brick-and-block walls (below) support the framework for the glazing (below right) and will also provide a fixing for wall-mounted heaters or radiators if required. When it is complete, this conservatory (far right) will connect the house and garage and provide valuable extra living space.

Site and situation

There are several potential site problems with conservatories that will need to be addressed at the planning stage.

A sloping site

If the garden slopes up from the house, a level base will have to be excavated, with retaining walls built to keep the garden at bay. If it slopes down, you could consider building the conservatory floor at a lower level and providing steps down into it from the house. A better solution is to give it a suspended floor (timber, or a concrete post-and-beam floor). This avoids having to back-fill a substantial area of ground to create a traditional solid concrete slab floor.

Obstructions

There may be obstructions, such as a soil pipe or rainwater downpipes, on the house wall against which the conservatory is to be built. Installers can generally get round these by adapting the structure or, in the case of downpipes, by relocating them. Another possible obstruction is a flue from a

boiler. Old-style round flue pipes can be accommodated with suitable heat-proofing, but balanced flue boilers will have to be repositioned so their flues do not discharge into the conservatory. Lastly, any manholes within the proposed base area will have to be built up to the new floor level and then fitted with special double-seal covers so they can be accessed if necessary.

Access for maintenance

Think about the question of future access for maintenance to walls, windows and gutters above the site of the conservatory. It is worth considering replacing windows above the new structure with a type that can be cleaned from inside the house. Some conservatory glazing bars are strong enough to support crawl boards; if they are not, removable roof panels will have to be incorporated in the design to allow the use of ladders for high-level maintenance work.

Basements and cellars

If your house has a basement or cellar that is at present used solely for storage, it may be possible to convert the space and create some useful extra living room.

A basement space is ideal for recreational uses – as a home workshop, a music room, a gym or a children's playroom – and can also be used to provide valuable storage space or extra facilities such as a utility room or an extra bath or shower room. It could even form an underground garage if providing access to it from the road is feasible.

Rules and regulations

Converting a basement or cellar will not need planning permission unless a change of use is involved – creating a self-contained flat, a home office or a garage, for example. Any structural work required will need Building Regulations approval, and if the rooms are to be habitable you will have to meet the Regulation's requirements concerning ventilation, insulation, safe access and escape in the event of fire. If the basement is to be converted for use as a garage, suitable fire barriers will have to be provided between the garage and the house above.

Planning points

Basements were built mainly in town houses to act as service areas – kitchens, sculleries and store areas – for live-in staff. They generally have full-height ceilings and extend beneath the whole ground floor of the building. They receive some natural light and ventilation via an excavated well next to the house walls, and often have an external staircase within the well to allow entry to the below-stairs area for tradesmen's deliveries, as well as an internal one for access to the house. This makes them particularly suitable for conversion to single-storey flats.

Cellars are often built only under part of the house, and have access from within it either via a steep staircase beneath the

Basements often have an existing light well and window (top) and full-height ceilings and may already have internal access from the main house, making them easy to convert into habitable rooms. By echoing the window style of the rest of the house (centre) the space within can be made light and airy, and become a comfortable space for a television room or playroom (right).

main flight of stairs, or through a trap door with steps or a wall ladder below it. In Victorian houses, the cellar often extends beneath the pavement, where a circular coal hole covered by a steel plate allowed coal deliveries to be made directly into the cellar below.

Cellars generally have no natural light or ventilation, low ceilings and often a serious damp problem.

Certificate of Treatment
by
London & Home Counties
TIMBER PRESERVATION

This is to Certify that

Address and Location of Property

Exact Description of Area Treated — Ground Floor: Kitchen/Diner

As per Survey Report & Specification dated — 23 September 1999 - T5167
has been properly treated in accordance with the schedule submitted, using high grade materials, against rising damp (injection of new DPC only).

and is guaranteed against further attack from this type of
RISING DAMPNESS /
(subject to the provisions detailed on the back of this document) for a period of

30 YEARS from — 11 October 1999.

Signed on behalf of the Company by

D.P. LONDON & HOME COUNTIES TIMBER PRESERVATION

THIS CERTIFICATE IS TRANSFERABLE.

Dealing with damp
Damp is likely to be the biggest problem in converting a basement or cellar. It is worth having a professional damp survey done to discover the extent of the problem, and to call in expert contractors to tackle it. They will lay a new floor surface over a damp-proof membrane, and will either strip and re-plaster the walls with a damp-resistant three-coat plaster system or (if the damp problem is serious) use a full-scale tanking procedure to waterproof the structure.

Access by stairs
Other parts of a basement that will need attention may include restoring external stairs and stairwells, replacing an internal staircase to comply with the Building Regulations, and replacing old timber windows, door frames and doors. A cellar will almost certainly need a new staircase and a ceiling – cellars rarely had one.

Adding services
As far as services are concerned, a basement may already have wiring and plumbing facilities, but they will probably need updating, and it is unlikely to have central heating. It may be easier to install individual room heaters than to extend the existing heating system. A cellar will probably have just electric lighting, so new circuits will have to be installed. The area will also need heating and some form of mechanical ventilation. In both basements and cellars, pumped macerator units can be used to take waste water from new plumbing appliances to the existing soil pipe or stack.

Garage conversions

If you have an integral or attached garage, there is obvious potential to convert it into additional living space. This is even more attractive if there is already access directly into the garage from the house.

Unless you have space on site to build an additional detached garage or plenty of room for off-street parking, converting your garage may leave you with a parking problem. It is also worth considering that the conversion may deter some buyers when you come to sell your house – most home-buyers say they want a garage. However, this kind of conversion is relatively easy for a buyer to reverse.

Rules and regulations

You do not need planning permission to convert a garage to living accommodation. Nor is Building Regulations approval required if all you intend to create is a non-habitable room – for use as a workshop, as a home for kitchen appliances, or as a playroom for your children.

However, if you intend to create a habitable room, you will need to satisfy the Building Regulations requirements concerning damp-proofing (the floor of an attached garage will probably not incorporate a damp-proof membrane, although an integral garage should have one) and insulation (an attached garage will have external walls just 100mm thick). You will also need approval for new waste water disposal arrangements from a washing machine or other water-using appliance. This can be done by giving your local authority a Building Notice (page 483) 48 hours before you intend to start work on the conversion.

Planning points

Non-habitable use
If the garage is to be put to non-habitable purposes, the only major job you will need to carry out is to damp-proof the floor and lay some sort of finished surface over the existing concrete slab. The best method is to apply two coats of a liquid damp-proofing compound, and to apply a fine surface screed over it to create a smooth, hard and dry floor surface. Once this has dried out, you can lay any type of floorcovering over it. The garage walls can be given a couple of coats of exterior-quality emulsion paint or masonry paint. You will also need to put up a new plasterboard ceiling in an attached garage, which will not have one.

Habitable use
In order to satisfy the Building Regulations requirements for habitable use, the floor must be damp-proofed in the same way, and must also incorporate some floor insulation. This can be done by applying a liquid damp-proofing treatment as described above, and then placing rigid polystyrene insulation boards 50 or 75mm thick on top of the floor slab. A floating chipboard floor can then be laid over the insulation, ready to receive the new floorcovering.

Integral garages will have cavity walls, so will just need dry-lining with plasterboard to create a suitable surface for decorating. An attached garage will need its walls insulating as well, and this can be done by incorporating insulation batts between the dry-lining boards and the garage walls. A vapour barrier must be included behind the plasterboard to prevent condensation from forming in the insulation.

Changing the garage door
The garage door opening will be ideal for conversion into a large front window. You may also wish to add other windows to the side or rear walls of the garage, especially if you want to partition the space within the garage. If there is no access directly into the garage, you will have to create an opening at a convenient point in the house wall. Remember that any new openings need Building Regulations approval to ensure that the lintels used are suitable.

Adding services
Finally, you will need to extend your house wiring to provide better lighting and a range of socket outlets in the conversion. You will also need to consider how to heat the new room – ideally by extending the house's downstairs heating circuit, or by using individual room heaters. If plumbing facilities are to be included, supply pipework will have to be extended from the house and provision made for getting rid of waste water. This last point will need to meet Building Regulations requirements.

Home offices

Working from home is becoming increasingly common and more and more people are looking at ways of providing a self-contained office space within their homes. Some of the possible options are outlined below.

Rules and regulations

In principle you need to apply for planning permission to work from home, since this counts as a change from purely residential to part-business use. However, many local authorities are prepared to allow home working without official permission so long as there are no outward signs of a business being run from the premises. Formal permission will be needed only if you have regular deliveries or visitors, if you store or sell goods or materially alter the character of the house or street. It is best to contact your local authority planning department for their views if you plan to start working from home.

Whether any Building Regulations approval is needed depends on the scale of the work proposed. See the options below for cross-references to specific conversions.

Conversion options

These are the most popular choices for creating a home office.

Converting a spare room This is most likely to be a bedroom, but could be another under-used room such as the dining room if there is space elsewhere in the house for meals to be taken. Partitioning a large living room is another option, but may involve creating a new window opening to give light and ventilation to the new work space. See pages 484–5 for more details.

Converting the loft This is an ideal solution if the roof structure is suitable for conversion, since the office will be separate from the rest of the house and no loss of existing living space will be involved (apart from that required for access to the loft). The conversion will need Building Regulations approval. See pages 490–1.

Converting a garage This is a viable option if you are prepared to relegate the car to the driveway or the road. An integral or attached garage is ideal, especially if it has direct access to the house. A detached garage is less suitable, especially as far as extending power and telecommunications facilities to the building is concerned. See page 495.

Building a garden office You could simply move to the garden shed, but a more satisfactory solution is to choose one of the growing number of purpose-designed garden office buildings now available (above). The building may need planning permission (check with your local authority) but will be exempt from Building Regulations control. See page 486.

Annexes

You may need to provide a 'granny flat' within your home for an elderly or disabled family member. The need is for self-contained living quarters for someone who is semi-independent but needs family support from time to time. The type of accommodation will depend on the type, size and layout of your house; some of the possible options are outlined below.

Rules and regulations

You will almost certainly need planning permission to create a granny flat, because of the change of use involved, although this may be waived if the conversion is wholly internal and has no separate means of external access. Check with your local authority before proceeding.

Building Regulations approval may also be needed, depending on what is involved in the conversion work. See below for cross-references to other relevant sections of this chapter.

Conversion options

These are the options most likely to be available to you for creating a granny flat.

Using existing rooms Choose adjacent rooms on the ground or first floor, using one as a living room with a kitchenette partitioned off it, and the other as a bedroom with en-suite bath or shower room partitioned off. See pages 484–5 for more details.

Converting the loft If the roof space is suitable for conversion, this is an ideal way of creating self-contained living accommodation. If climbing stairs poses a problem to the intended occupant, consider using the loft conversion yourself and allocating rooms on the floor below to create the granny flat. See pages 490–1.

Converting a basement Originally built to contain servant's quarters, a basement is often ideal for conversion to a granny flat because it will probably have its own entrance and rooms of a reasonable size. A cellar is less likely to be suitable. See page 494.

Converting a garage An integral or attached garage could form the basis for a granny flat, perhaps with an extension to the side or rear to increase the available floor space. An integral garage will be easier to convert than an attached one. See page 495.

Building an extension So long as you have the space and the money, this is the best option because the extension can be tailored to suit the requirements of the occupant. See pages 488–9. Note that if you have a mortgage you should notify the lender of your plans to create a granny flat. You should also inform your household insurance company.

Wiring, plumbing and gas: Safety rules

There are three more sets of rules and regulations that you need to be aware of when planning any home alterations. They deal with your wiring installation, your plumbing system and the gas supply.

Britain is one of the few countries where householders are allowed to carry out their own electrical and plumbing work, but this does not mean you have a free hand to do what you want; you still have to follow some rules. As far as work on your gas supply is concerned, any DIY work is completely out of the question; all work must always be carried out by a qualified gas fitter, and no one else.

Wiring Regulations

The Wiring Regulations are published by the Institution of Electrical Engineers (IEE) and their requirements are followed by all professional electricians. They were made into a British Standard (BS7671) in 1992, and are an extremely complex document for the lay reader to understand. At present they do not have the force of law, except in Scotland where they form part of the Scottish Building Regulations. There are plans to include them in 2005 or 2006 as a new Part P of the Building Regulations in England and Wales. When this happens, the Wiring Regulations will have the force of law throughout the UK.

An architect will draw up detailed plans showing the proposed position of any services, such as plumbing or wiring, in a new room or extension. A clear wiring scheme for a network of recessed spotlights in a new kitchen ceiling (right) will enable the electricians and builders to work together on the installation.

Whenever you employ a professional electrician, choose one who is a member of the Electrical Contractors Association (ECA) or who is on the roll of the National Inspection Council for Electrical Installation Contracting (NICEIC). Look out for the relevant logos (right) on the electrician's advertising or headed paper.

Representing the best in electrical engineering and building services

If you carry out any electrical work yourself, note that your local electricity supply company has the right to inspect and test any electrical work that it thinks may be unsafe. It can also refuse to connect a supply of electricity to an unsafe installation, or one that does not meet the requirements of the Wiring Regulations.

Water supply bye-laws

Each water supply company in Britain is responsible for producing its own water supply bye-laws. However, apart from some local variations these are based on the Model Water Supply Bye-laws, so there is a degree of consistency right across the country. You can get a copy of the bye-laws (or an explanatory leaflet about them) from your water supplier.

The aim of the bye-laws is to 'prevent waste, undue consumption, misuse or contamination of the water supply'. They

apply to any new work you carry out on your plumbing system, and also your heating system if this uses hot water to heat the radiators. A particular concern of the bye-laws is the need to prevent the contamination of the supply by used or stored water being drawn back into the mains – a problem known as back-siphonage. Many of the bye-laws are designed to prevent this from happening.

The bye-laws require you to give your water supplier at least five working days' notice if you intend to install or alter (as opposed to repairing or replacing) a bidet, a flushing cistern, a tap to which a hose may be connected, or any other fitting through which back-siphonage could occur (such as a bath fitted with shower mixer taps, for example). In Scotland you must give notice if you propose to install or alter any water fitting.

Note that these bye-laws apply only to water supply. Rules for the disposal of waste water are included in the Building Regulations (page 483).

Gas safety regulations

The Gas Safety (Installation and Use) Regulations make it illegal for anyone to carry out work relating to gas supply and fittings who is not 'competent'. In practice, this means leaving all work on your gas supply system to a qualified gas fitter who is registered with CORGI (The Council for Registered Gas Installers).

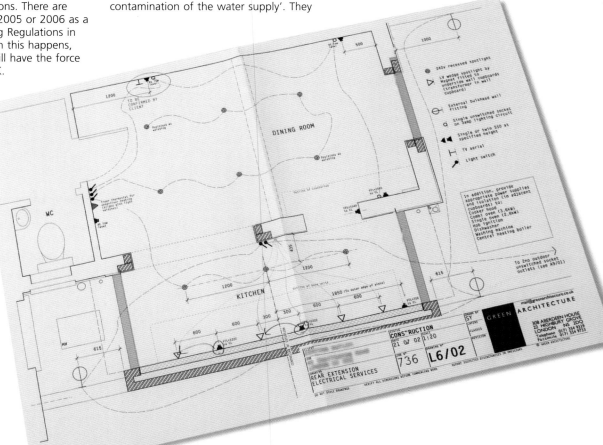

Glossary

Acrylic Water-based paint or glaze used for walls and ceilings.

Aggregate Small pieces of stone, gravel or similar material, mixed with cement to make concrete.

Airbrick Ventilated brick that allows air into a room or under a floor.

Airlock Blockage in a pipe caused by trapped air.

Alkyd paint Most solvent-based paints are now based on alkyd resin.

Ampere (amp) The measure of the rate at which electricity flows through a circuit.

Anchor bolt A sturdy bolt that is set in concrete to form an attachment for supporting members.

Angle bead A moulding made from expanded metal mesh and galvanised steel. Used as a reinforcement for plaster on external plaster corners.

Apron A flashing of sheet material (such as zinc) with its top edge set into a brickwork joint and its lower edge overlapping the roof below.

Architrave Decorative wooden moulding fitted round a window or door frame, to cover the join between frame and wall.

Armoured cable Electrical cable usually used underground. It is wrapped in a layer of steel wire to protect it from damage.

Arris The sharp edge formed where two surfaces meet at an angle.

Auger Flexible steel spring wire that can be fed along wastepipes to clear blockages. Also a drilling tool, rather like a corkscrew.

Back-siphonage Water being drawn back into the mains supply from the house plumbing system, caused by a drop in mains pressure.

Balanced flue A ducting system that allows a boiler, for example, to draw fresh air from outside the house, and also to discharge gases to the outside.

Ballvalve (ballcock) Float valve that controls the supply and level of water in a WC cistern or cold water storage cistern.

Baluster A turned piece of wood used as a support for the handrail on a staircase.

Balustrade Collective term for the parts of a staircase handrail; it includes balusters and newel posts.

Bargeboard Strip of wood covering the overhanging edge of a pitched roof at a gable.

Basecoat A flat coat of paint over which a decorative coat is applied.

Batten A narrow strip of wood used as a support for plasterboard, to box in an area or to support shelving. Useful as a straightedge, too.

Bending spring Metal coil slipped over or slid into copper pipe, to enable it to be bent without kinking.

Bibcock Wall-mounted tap, usually with a threaded outlet for use with a hosepipe.

Blinding The layer of sand spread over a hardcore base for a floor, to prevent perforation of the damp-proof membrane above it.

Blown When a surface layer such as plaster or cement render comes away from the wall behind. Also used to describe a fuse wire that has melted and broken an electrical circuit, as a result of overloading.

Bond The manner in which bricks are used in a wall; bond patterns are chosen to suit particular types of wall.

Bore The hollow part of a pipe or tube.

Bridging debris Earth or building material that covers a damp-proof course and allows water to permeate the wall above the DPC.

Burr Rough edge left after sawing through a copper pipe or a piece of wood.

Buttercoat The top layer of cement render.

Came The grooved strip of lead that holds a piece of coloured glass in a leaded light or stained glass window.

Capnut The nut used to tighten a compression joint onto pipework.

Capillary joint Soldered copper connector for joining copper pipes.

Carcass The basic structure of a bathroom or kitchen unit before doors or drawers are added.

Casement Part of a window, or an entire window. Casement windows contain both fixed and opening sections.

Caulk Water-based or acrylic flexible filler, supplied in a tube and applied with a sealant gun, to seal gaps between surfaces.

Cavity wall A house wall made of two separate 'skins', with a gap between them. They are held together with plastic or metal wall ties and the cavity is insulated.

Cement A powdery binder that bonds sand and aggregate together to form mortar or concrete.

Chalk line A piece of string, saturated with coloured chalk, used to mark out a straight line on walls, floors and ceilings.

Chamfer A narrow, flat surface along the edge of a piece of wood, normally at 45°.

Chase A groove cut into masonry or plaster, to accept a run of flex or piping.

Check valve A valve that lets water flow in one direction only.

Chipboard Man-made board made of compressed wood fibres, supplied in sheets.

Circuit The path through which an electric current can flow.

Circuit breaker (or miniature circuit-breaker – MCB) The trip switch in a consumer unit that acts automatically to break the circuit in the event of a fault. Once the fault is fixed, the MCB can be reset to restore the power.

Cladding Material used to cover a surface – usually a wall.

Cleat A small, short length of timber designed to support another piece.

Compression joint Brass connector for copper pipe, tightened and undone with spanners.

Conductor Length of wire through which an electric current can pass.

Cornice Decorative plaster or wood moulding joining the walls and ceiling of a room.

Countersink To drill a tapered hole that allows the head of a screw to lie flush with the surface.

Coving A prefabricated moulding made of plaster or polystyrene, to cover the join between the walls and ceiling.

Cross cutting Sawing across the grain of the wood, not along it.

Cross-head Type of screw with cross-shaped recess in the head, rather than a single slot. The best type to use with a power screwdriver, because it grips the screwdriver blade.

Cutting in Careful painting at corners or at junctions on a wall surface, or beside door frames and window sills.

Dado The lower part of an interior wall, often defined by a dado rail. Because it is more liable to damage it may be covered with wallpaper or wood panelling. The dado rail is sometimes called a chair rail.

Damp-proof course (DPC) A continuous layer of impervious material (formerly slate, but usually plastic) which prevents damp rising from the ground into walls.

Damp-proof fluid Used where a DPC has failed or never existed. A proprietary liquid is injected at regular points into an exterior wall, to form an impermeable layer. Also known as chemical damp-proofing.

Deadman A temporary brace used to hold up one end of a sheet of ceiling board or a length or timber, while the other end is worked on.

Dedicated circuit A circuit which runs from the consumer unit to one appliance only, such as a cooker.

Distemper A traditional water-based paint which feels powdery and wipes off with a wet cloth. To redecorate, old distemper must first be washed off entirely.

Distressing A paint effect used to give an aged appearance to wood.

Diverter valve A valve that diverts water flow from bath taps to a shower head. Also a valve controlled by a hot water cylinder and room thermostat to direct heating water as required.

Dowel A cylindrical wooden peg used to secure butt joints in woodworking.

Dragging A paint effect achieved by dragging a paintbrush in straight lines through wet glaze.

Dry lining A wall lining formed by fixing sheets of tapered-edge plasterboard to a framework of timber battens. Joints are covered with tape and plastered over.

Dry rot Fungal attack on wood and other materials. First signs are small, silky threads, which spread outwards from a concealed fruiting body.

Earth The connection between an electrical circuit and the ground. Also a terminal to which an earth connection is made.

Eaves The lower edge of the roof and rafters, that projects beyond the walls, to protect them from the weather.

Efflorescence White, powdery deposit of soluble salts, left on a wall as it dries out. Must be brushed off, not washed.

Eggshell Hard-wearing paint with a dull, matt finish. Can be acrylic or solvent-based.

Elbow Plumbing joint that forms a 90° bend in pipework.

Emulsion Water-based paint used for walls or ceilings.

Enamel A hard-wearing coating used on bathroom fittings such as old baths.

End-grain The surface of wood exposed after cutting across the grain.

Escutcheon Small plate used to finish off a keyhole. May have a cover for insulation and privacy.

Expanded metal mesh Perforated metal sheet or strip used to support plaster when patching holes in plasterboard.

Expansion joint Narrow gap in a slab of concrete that is filled with treated fibreboard to limit cracking and relieve pressure. Also the gap between a concrete slab and a house wall.

External corner A corner that juts out into a room, for example on a chimney breast.

Face edge In woodworking, the perfect, planed surface.

Face nailing Method of driving in nails perpendicular to the surface of the wood.

Factory cut edge Produced by the manufacturing process and therefore cut with precision. Exposed edges should be factory cut, rather than hand cut.

Fascia A strip of wood covering the ends of rafters, to which guttering may be attached.

Feathering Technique used in painting and plastering to smooth away the edges, so that they are undetectable.

Finial Decorative piece of wood used to finish the top of a post, usually on a staircase newel. Also the decorative end of a curtain pole.

Flashing Material used to create a weatherproof junction between a wall or chimney and a roof; or where two roofs meet.

Flaunching Sloping mortar cap holding a chimney pot on top of its stack.

Footing A narrow concrete foundation for a wall.

Formwork Timber boards fixed to pegs in the ground to form a mould when concrete is cast. Also called shuttering.

Foundation Strip of concrete cast in a trench as a base for a masonry wall or other construction.

Framed wall Horizontal and vertical timbers sheathed with plasterboard or plywood.

Frog The angled depression in one face of some house bricks.

Gable The triangular end of a pitched roof.

Galvanised Covered with a protective coating of zinc.

Gatevalve On-off control fitted on low-pressure pipework.

Gauge rod A timber batten marked at regular intervals used to check the height of tile or brick courses.

Glaze Usually colourless liquid to which paint or pigments can be added. Once applied to the surface of a wall, for example, it is worked in various ways with brushes, sponges and cloths to create paint effects.

Gloss Highly decorative, shiny paint finish.

Grommet A ring of rubber or plastic, used to line a hole to prevent cable, for instance, from chafing against a sharp edge. Blind grommets have a thin membrane that is cut when the cable is ready to be fed through.

Grout Filling compound used in the gaps between ceramic tiles.

Gusset plate Triangular brace used to reinforce the corners of wooden frames.

Halving joint Joint formed by cutting away half the depth on two pieces of same-size wood, so that when fitted together the surfaces are flush.

Hardboard Man-made board made of compressed wood pulp and sawdust, supplied in sheets.

Hardcore Crushed or broken bricks, blocks or stone, used as a filler in the construction of foundations and sub-bases.

Hawk Metal or plywood square with a handle underneath; used to hold plaster or mortar while working.

Header Brick laid in a wall with its end visible.

Head plate Timber beam that forms the top frame component in a timber-framed wall.

Helical Spiral-shaped.

Hoggin Fine ballast used to form a sub-base for concrete paving.

Housing A long, narrow channel, cut across the grain of wood to receive the edge of another board, when forming a joint.

Instantaneous heater A heater that heats water on demand, as it flows through the supply pipe. Often gas-fired.

Insulation Materials used to reduce the transmission of heat or sound. Also non-conductive material surrounding electrical wires or connections to prevent the passage of electricity.

Jamb The vertical side member of a window or door frame.

Jointer Tool used for shaping repointed mortar joints.

Jointing compound Filler used to seal gaps between sheets of plasterboard.

Jointing tape Self-adhesive tape used for covering joins between sheets of plasterboard.

Joist Wooden or steel beam used for supporting floors and ceilings.

Joist detector Electronic tool for detecting rows of nails fixing timbers in place, thus revealing joist positions. Some can be used to detect hidden electric cables and conduits.

Junction box Electrical fitting used for making connections between cables on a power or lighting circuit. Usually plastic, with a screw-on lid.

Kerf The groove cut by a saw.

Keying Technique used to roughen a surface in order to provide a better grip when plastering, painting or using adhesive.

Knotting Sealer used to cover knots in wood and prevent resin from oozing through decorative finishes.

Lagging Insulating material usually fitted over hot water cylinders, as well as pipes and tanks in unheated areas, to prevent freezing.

Laminated wood Strips of wood, glued together, to provide extra strength and thickness See also Plywood.

Latex paint Generic term for water-based paints, or those that can be thinned with water.

Laths Narrow strips of wood to which plaster is stuck, in traditional lath-and-plaster walls.

Leading edge Vertical edge of door or window farthest from the hinges.

Lighting rails Lighting system where a number of lights are positioned along a rail.

Line (also known as phase or live) The part of an electrical circuit that carries the flow of current to an appliance.

Lintel Supporting horizontal beam over an opening in masonry, such as a door, window or fireplace.

Locking-lever latch Latch mechanism with a separate locking system built in to the overall latch casing. Also called a sashlock.

Louvre vent Vent with downward-pointing slats, used to cover the end of ducting run through a wall.

Mastic Sealing compound (also called caulk sealant) that cures without fully hardening. Used for filling gaps between different materials in buildings.

MDF (medium density fibreboard) Fine wood-particle board that is easily shaped to a smooth finish. Exterior grades are water-resistant.

Melamine Tough, synthetic resin used to coat man-made boards such as chipboard.

Microporous (or moisture-vapour permeable) Describes a finish such as paint or woodstain that permits moisture to escape from wood, allowing it to dry out, at the same time protecting it from rainwater or damp.

Mitre A corner joint, made by cutting two pieces of material at a 45° angle.

Mortar Mixture of cement, sand and sometimes other additives, used in bricklaying and rendering.

Mortise A rectangular recess cut into wood to allow it to receive a matching tongue or tenon.

Moulding Wood or plaster feature used as a decorative finish on doors, walls and ceilings.

Mouse A small weight used to pass a string-line through a narrow vertical space.

Mullion The vertical dividing piece of a window frame.

Muntin Central vertical frame of a door, fixed to the top and bottom rails.

Nail guard Steel plate attached to joists or studs, to prevent accidentally nailing through joists or cables recessed into them.

Nail punch Simple tool used with a hammer, to drive nail heads below the surface of the wood.

Newel post Main post fitted at top or bottom of stairs, to support the strings (staircase sides) and the handrail.

Nogging (or noggin) Short horizontal piece of timber fixed between wall studs or ceiling joists, to stiffen the structure.

Nosing The front edge of a stair tread.

Oilstone Flat, abrasive stone, lubricated with water or oil, used for sharpening tools.

Olive Sealing ring in a brass compression joint.

Oxidise To form a layer of metal oxide, as happens in rusting.

Parting bead The strip of wood separating the two sliding sashes in a sash window.

Party wall Shared wall that divides two properties.

Penetrating oil Thin lubricant that seeps between corroded surfaces, allowing them to be eased apart.

Phase (also known as live or line) The part of an electrical circuit that carries the flow of current to an appliance.

Pier Thick column of masonry bonded into a wall to increase the wall's stability.

Pilot hole Small hole drilled to allow a piece of wood to receive a larger screw without splitting.

Plasterboard Rigid wall-covering material made of gypsum plaster, sandwiched between sheets of paper.

Plinth Detachable panel that covers the feet and base of self-assembly units such as kitchen cabinets.

Plumb Exactly vertical. A plumb line is used to establish vertical drops.

Plywood Building board made by bonding together thin layers of wood with the grain of alternate veneers running at right angles to one another.

Pointing Filling the joints between bricks with mortar and shaping them with a pointing tool.

Pressure-treated timber Wood that has been impregnated with preservative under extreme pressure.

Primer The first coat of paint applied to protect wood and metal. It reduces the absorption of subsequent layers of paint; a metal primer prevents corrosion.

Profile board Board set on edge and nailed to stakes to describe the outer limits of a building; part of the formwork.

PTFE (polytetrafluoroethylene) Material used to make tape for sealing threaded plumbing fittings.

Purlin A horizontal beam that provides intermediate support for rafters or sheet roofing.

PVA (polyvinyl acetate) General purpose adhesive. Often used as wood glue and as a bonding agent for plaster and mortar. Known as 'white glue'.

PVC (polyvinyl chloride) A plastic used for cable insulation and corrugated roofing. The unplasticised form, uPVC, is used for plumbing pipes, exterior cladding and window frames.

Quarry tiles Hard tiles that have been fired in a kiln. Used as a floor covering.

Radial circuit An electrical circuit that starts at the consumer unit and runs from one outlet to another and terminates at the last one.

RCD (residual current device) Fast-acting trip-switch that cuts off the power in the event of an earth fault.

Rebate A step-shaped recess along the edge of a piece of wood.

Reducer Plumbing joint that forms a joint between pipes of different diameter.

Render A thin layer of cement-based mortar. It can be used as a base for plastering on an inside wall, or simply painted over when on an exterior wall.

Reveal Vertical sides of a recessed door or window opening.

Ring circuit An electrical circuit that runs from the consumer unit to each outlet in turn before returning to the consumer unit.

Rip sawing Sawing along the grain of the wood, not across it.

Riser The vertical part of a step.

Rising damp Moisture entering a house from outside and below as a result of the failure of the damp-proof course in a wall or the damp-proof membrane in a concrete floor.

Rock wool Generic term used for insulating material made from mineral fibres.

RSJ (rolled steel joist) Used mainly over an opening when a load-bearing wall is removed and two rooms are turned into one.

Rubber A pad of cotton wool wrapped in a lint-free cloth and used to apply a stain or polish.

Sash A type of window with two sliding sections.

Scratchcoat The first layer of plaster or render.

Screed A thin layer of mortar applied to give a smooth surface to concrete.

Screed batten A thin strip of wood used to determine the level and evenness of a screed.

Scribe To score a line with a sharp or pointed instrument.

Sealant A caulk or mastic used for sealing along joints; usually bought in a tube and applied with a cartridge gun.

Self-levelling compound Applied to concrete floors in order to provide a level surface for further floor covering.

Secret nailing Method of nailing boards through their edges, to conceal the nails.

Sheath The outer layer of insulation covering an electrical cable or flex.

Shim A thin wooden strip used as a measure to establish a fall across a surface.

Shoe Curved outlet at the base of a rainwater downpipe that directs water away from the house.

Short circuit The accidental rerouteing of electricity between conductors, which increases the flow of current and blows a fuse or trips a miniature circuit breaker (MCB).

Shuttering Wooden framework used to enclose and contain concrete as it is poured.

Side light Narrow, non-opening window next to a door.

Size Sealer used to coat plastered or papered surfaces in preparation for wallpapering. It prevents the surface from absorbing the paste, which makes the paper easier to hang.

Skew Nailing or screwing at an angle through wood in order to provide a fixing.

Skim To apply a top coat of plaster to a wall surface.

Snake Common name for a plumber's auger.

Soakaway A pit filled with rubble or gravel into which rainwater is drained.

Soffit The underside of an archway or the eaves of a building.

Soil stack Large-diameter vertical waste pipe, vented at the top, that carries waste to the main drainage system.

Sole plate The lowest horizontal frame component of a stud partition wall.

Solvent-weld cement Adhesive used for joining some types of plastic waste pipe.

Spacers Small dividers used between ceramic tiles to keep a consistent distance between them when applying them to the wall.

Spalling Flaking of the outer face of masonry, caused by moisture expanding in freezing conditions.

Spigot The end of a pipe that fits inside a socket to form a joint with another length of pipe.

Spur Branch cable that extends an existing electrical circuit.

Staff bead The innermost strip of wood holding a sliding sash in a sash window frame.

Steam stripper Machine (usually hired) which aids the stripping of wallpaper by applying steam to the paper.

Stile The vertical side member of a door or window sash.

Stoptap On-off control fitted on mains-pressure pipework.

Stretcher Brick laid in a wall with its long sides visible.

Striker plate Metal plate set in a door frame, containing a cut-out into which the latch fits when the door is shut.

String The sides of a staircase supporting the treads.

Strutting X-shaped metal or timber braces between floor joists that give extra support.

Stud Vertical timber support in a wood-framed partition wall.

Sub-base A layer of compacted hardcore that provides a stable base for a drive, path or patio.

Sugar soap Chemical compound used to degrease paintwork prior to redecorating.

Supplementary bonding The connecting to earth of exposed metal pipework in bathrooms and kitchens.

Swan neck Arrangement of curved joints in a rainwater downpipe that brings the pipe back from the gutter to the house wall.

Tack rag Sticky cloth used for removing dust from a rubbed-down surface, prior to finishing.

Tail Connection between a tap and its supply pipe. Usually threaded, but plain on monobloc mixers.

Tamp To compact soil or concrete with repeated blows from a heavy piece of timber.

Tamping beam Length of timber with a handle at each end, used with a chopping action across shuttering to compact and level concrete.

Tee Plumbing joint that connects a branch pipe to the main pipe run.

Template Cut-out pattern made from metal, wood or paper, to provide a guide to shaping something accurately.

Tenon A projecting tongue on a piece of wood that fits into a corresponding mortise.

Terminals Connections to which the bared conductors of a cable or flex are attached.

Tie Piece of wood or metal that links opposing members and prevents outward movement, such as tie-beams found at the feet of rafters.

Tongue-and-groove Type of joint between boards in which a tongue from one board fits into the groove in another.

Transformer Electrical device that changes the voltage in a circuit.

Transom A horizontal dividing piece of a window frame.

Trap A U-shaped section of pipe below a bath, basin or sink. It is filled with standing water, to prevent smells from coming back up the pipe.

Tread The horizontal part of a step.

Trowels Tools used for bricklaying and plastering; they come in various shapes to suit their purpose.

Trunking Rectangular section plastic or metal duct for cables and pipes that protects them as they run along wall surfaces.

Undercoat Layer of paint used to obliterate the colour of the primer and build up a protective layer before applying the top coat.

Underlay Layer of plywood or particle board applied over a rough floor to provide a smooth surface suitable for tiles or other floor coverings. Also a resilient layer of foam under a carpet.

Valley Rainwater channel, usually of zinc or lead, between two sections of roof.

Vapour barrier Impervious layer that prevents the passage of moisture-laden air.

Veneer Thin layers of hardwood applied over cheaper base wood, for a decorative effect.

Vinyl Plastic material used for easy-to-clean floor coverings. Also protective covering on some wallpapers or an additive used in paint, to increase their hard-wearing and wipeable properties.

Vinyl emulsion Water-based paint ideal for bathrooms as it is easy to wipe down and keep clean.

Volt The measure of pressure that causes electric current to flow round a circuit.

Wall plate A horizontal timber beam placed along the top of a wall to support and provide attachment for joists and rafters, and to spread their load.

Wallplug Plastic or metal sheath inserted into a pre-drilled hole in a wall to house a screw.

Wall ties Metal connectors used to bind different sections of a masonry wall together.

Washer A rubber ring that prevents taps from leaking.

Watt The measure of power consumed by an electrical appliance. 1000 watts = 1 kiloWatt (kW).

Weatherboard A length of wooden moulding fixed at the base of an external door to lead rainwater away from the door.

Weephole A small hole at the base of a cavity wall that allows moisture to drain to the outside.

Wet rot Fungus that attacks wood with too high a moisture content. Not as serious as dry rot, but leads to the eventual destruction of timber.

Trade organisations and specialists

Architects

Royal Institute of British Architects (RIBA)
66 Portland Place
London W1B 1AD
Tel: 020 7580 5533
Fax: 020 7255 1541
Email: info@inst.riba.org
www.architecture.com/go/Architecture/Home.html

Architects Accredited in Building
Conservation Register
11 Oakfield Road
Poynton
Cheshire SK12 1AR
Tel: 01625 871458
Fax: 01625 871468
Email: info@aabc-register.co.uk
www.aabc-register.co.uk

Building

Building Research Establishment (BRE)
Bucknall Lane
Garston
Watford WD25 9XX
Tel: 01923 664 000
Email: enquiries@bre.co.uk
www.bre.co.uk

British Standards Institute (BSI)
389 Chiswick High Road
London W4 4AL
Tel: 020 8996 9000
Fax: 020 8996 7400
Email: cservices@bsi-global.com
www.bsi-global.com

National Federation of Builders
Construction House
56–64 Leonard Street
London EC2A 4JX
Tel: 020 7608 5150
Fax: 020 7608 5151
www.builders.org.uk

Federation of Plasterers and Drywall
Contractors
Construction House
56–64 Leonard Street
London EC2A 4JX
Tel: 020 7608 5092
Fax: 020 7608 5081
Email: enquiries@fpdc.org

Housebuilders Federation
56–64 Leonard Street
London EC2A 4JX
Tel: 020 7608 5100
Fax: 020 7608 5101
Email: hbf@hbf.co.uk
www.hbf.co.uk

Federation of Master Builders
Gordon Fisher House
14–15 Great James Street
London WC1N 3DP
Tel: 020 7242 7583
Fax: 020 7404 0296
Email: central@fmb.org.uk
www.fmb.org.uk

Institution of Structural Engineers
11 Upper Belgrave Street
London SW1X 8BH
Tel: 020 7235 4535
Fax: 020 7235 4294
Email: mail@istructe.org.uk
www.istructe.org.uk

National Association of Scaffolding
Constructors (NASC)
Carthusian Court
12 Carthusian Street
London EC1M 6EZ
Tel: 020 7397 8120
Fax: 020 7397 8121
Email: enquiries@nasc.org.uk
www.nasc.org.uk

Damp, rot and infestation

British Wood Preserving and Damp-proofing
Association
1 Gleneagles House
Vernongate
South Street
Derby DE1 1UP
Tel: 01332 225100
Fax: 01332 225101
Email: info@bwpda.co.uk
www.bwpda.co.uk

British Pest Control Association
Gleneagles House
Vernongate
South Street
Derby DE1 1UP
Tel: 01332 294288
Fax: 01332 295904
Email: enquiry@bpca.org.uk
www.bpca.org.uk

Decorating

Painting and Decorating Association
32 Coton Road
Nuneaton
Warwickshire CV11 5TW
Tel: 024 7635 3776
Fax: 024 7635 4513
Email:
info@paintingdecoratingassociation.co.uk
www.paintingdecoratingassociation.co.uk

Electricity

Electrical Contractors Association
ESCA House, 34 Palace Court,
London W2 4HY
Tel: 020 7313 4800
Fax: 020 7221 7344
Email: electricalcontractors@eca.co.uk
www.eca.co.uk

National Inspection Council for Electrical
Installation Inspecting (NICEIC)
Vintage House
37 Albert Embankment
London SE1 7UJ
Tel: 020 7564 2323
Fax: 020 7564 2370
Email: enquiries@niceic.org.uk
www.niceic.org.uk

Institution of Electrical Engineers (IEE)
Savoy Place
London WC2R 0BL
Tel: 020 7240 1871
Fax: 020 7344 5711
Email: postmaster@iee.org.uk
www.iee.org.uk

ADVICE ON THE INTERNET

There are many sites offering DIY advice on the Internet, but quite a few are linked to specific products or outlets. Make sure a web site is based on UK products and building standards. Many American sites give advice – particularly on plumbing and electrics – that does not conform with British safety standards. For impartial UK-based advice, these are some of the best.

www.bbc.co.uk/homes/diy
Very informative, with advice on most DIY jobs plus a calculations facility that helps you to work out how much paint, wallpaper, etc you will need for your specific project.

www.diydoctor.org.uk/home. htm Tips and tricks of the trade, information on products, and details of local tradespeople and specialists.

www.diyfixit.co.uk Information on general building, plumbing, electrics, woodworking, decorating, insulation and central heating.

www.easy-diy.co.uk
A comprehensive site that offers advice on products and services.

www.finddiy.co.uk A very good starting point as it offers links to other sites as well as information on tools, equipment and tradespeople.

www.homepro.com Unusual style ideas as well as down-to-earth DIY, legal and financial advice, and a guide to contractors.

Gas

CORGI (Council for Registered Gas
Installers)
1 Elmwood
Chineham Park
Crockford Lane
Basingstoke RG24 8WG
Tel: 0870 401 2200
Fax: 0870 401 2600
Email: enquiries@corgi-gas.com
www.corgi-gas-safety.com

Glass and glazing

Glass and Glazing Federation
44–48 Borough High Street
London SE1 1XB
Tel: 0870 042 4255
Fax: 0870 042 4266
Email: info@ggf.org.uk
www.ggf.org.uk

Heating and ventilation

Heating and Ventilation Contractors'
Association
Esca House
34 Palace Court
London W2 4JG
Tel: 020 7313 4900
Fax: 020 7727 9268
Email: contact@hvca.org.uk
www.hvca.org.uk

Insulation
National Insulation Association (NIA)
PO Box 12
Haslemere
Surrey GU27 3AH
Email: insulationassoc@aol.com
Tel: 01428 654011
Fax: 01428 651401
www.insulationassociation.org.uk

Energy Saving Trust (EST)
21 Dartmouth Street
London SW1H 9BP
Tel: 020 7222 0101
Fax: 020 7654 2444
www.est.org.uk

Plumbing and heating
Association of Plumbing and Heating
Contractors
Ensign House
Ensign Business Centre
Westwood Way
Coventry CV4 8JA
Tel: 0800 542 6060
Fax: 024 7647 0626
Email: enquiries@aphc.co.uk
www.aphc.co.uk

Institute of Plumbing
64 Station Lane
Hornchurch
Essex RM12 6NB
Tel: 01708 472791
Fax: 01708 448987
Email: info@plumbers.org.uk
www.plumbers.org.uk

Product information
The Building Centre
26 Store Street
London WC1E 7BT
Tel: 09065 161136*
*Calls are charged at £1.50 per minute to
cover postage and research costs.
www.buildingcentre.co.uk

Security
British Security Industry Association
Security House
Barbourne Road
Worcester WR1 1RS
Tel: 01905 21464
Fax: 01905 613625
Email: info@bsia.co.uk
www.bsia.co.uk

Master Locksmiths Association
Unit 5D
Great Central Way
Woodford Halse
Daventry NN11 3PZ
Tel: 01327 262255
Fax: 01327 262539
Email: enquiries@locksmiths.co.uk
www.locksmiths.co.uk

Woodworking
British Woodworking Association
Tel: 0870 458 6939
Fax: 0870 458 6949
Email: bwf@bwf.org.uk
www.bwf.org.uk

CONVERSION FOR LINEAR MEASUREMENTS

Metric	Imperial	Metric	Imperial
1mm	¹⁄₃₂in	320mm	12½in
2mm	¹⁄₁₆in	330mm	13in
3mm	⅛in	340mm	13½in
6mm	¼in	360mm	14in
10mm	⅜in	370mm	14½in
13mm	½in	380mm	15in
15mm	⅝in	390mm	15½in
20mm	¾in	400mm	16in
25mm	1in	420mm	16½in
30mm	1¼in	430mm	17in
40mm	1½in	440cm	17½in
50mm	2in	460mm	18in
55mm	2¼in	480mm	19in
60mm	2½in	500mm	19½in
70mm	2¾in	510mm	20in
75mm	3in	530mm	21in
80mm	3¼in	560mm	22in
90mm	3½in	580mm	23in
100mm	4in	600mm	23½in
110mm	4¼in	610mm	24in
115mm	4½in	660mm	26in
130mm	5in	700mm	27½in
140mm	5½in	710mm	28in
150mm	6in	750mm	29½in
160mm	6¼in	760mm	30in
170mm	6½in	800mm	31½in
180mm	7in	810mm	32in
190mm	7½in	850mm	33½in
200mm	8in	860mm	34in
215mm	8½in	900mm	35½in
230mm	9in	910mm	36in
240mm	9½in	960mm	38in
250mm	10in	990mm	36in
260mm	10½in	1000mm (1m)	39in
270mm	10¾in	1.2m	4ft
280mm	11in	1.5m	5ft
290mm	11½in	2m	6ft 6in
300mm	12in	5m	16ft 6in

TEMPERATURE CONVERSIONS

Rough guide

°C	°F
0	32
+5	41
10	50
15	59
20	68
25	77
30	86
35	95
40	104
45	113
50	122
55	131
60	140
65	149
70	158
75	167
80	176
85	185
90	194
95	203
100	212

For exact
temperature
conversions:
$°F = (°C \times 1.8) + 32$
$°C = (°F - 32) \div 1.8$

HOW TO CONVERT UNITS OF MEASUREMENT

Metric to Imperial

	To convert	into	multiply by
Length	millimetres	inches	0.0394
	metres	feet	3.2808
	metres	yards	1.0936
Area	square metres	square feet	10.764
	square metres	square yards	1.196
Volume	cubic metres	cubic feet	35.315
	cubic metres	cubic yards	1308
	litres	pints	1.76
	litres	gallons	0.22
Weight	kilograms	pounds	2.2046

Imperial to metric

	To convert	into	multiply by
Length	inches	millimetres	25.4
	feet	metres	0.3048
	yards	metres	0.9144
Area	square feet	square metres	0.0929
	square yards	square metres	0.836
Volume	cubic feet	cubic metres	0.0283
	cubic yards	cubic metres	0.7646
	pints	litres	0.568
	gallons	litres	4.55
Weight	pounds	kilograms	0.45359

Index

Acknowledgments

All images in this book are copyright of the Reader's Digest Association Limited, with the exception of those in the following list.

The position of photographs and illustrations on each page is indicated by letters after the page number:
T = Top; **B** = Bottom; **L** = Left;
R = Right; **C** = Centre

6–7 The Skyscan Photolibrary
17 TC, TR, B www.magnettrade.co.uk
43 BR GE Fabbri Limited
73 GE Fabbri Limited
75 TR, C, CR GE Fabbri Limited
79 C, BC, BR GE Fabbri Limited
82 GE Fabbri Limited
85 C, BR GE Fabbri Limited
93 TC, TR, BL, BC GE Fabbri Limited
96 TR, CR, BR GE Fabbri Limited
97 BR GE Fabbri Limited
98 T, B GE Fabbri Limited
104 CR, BR GE Fabbri Limited
106 TR, BR GE Fabbri Limited
107 TL, CL GE Fabbri Limited
109 TC, TR, BL, BC, BR GE Fabbri Limited
118 TL, TC, TR. BL, BC GE Fabbri Limited
120 T, TL, TR, C, BL, BC, BR GE Fabbri Limited
121 TR, BC, BR GE Fabbri Limited
124 T, B Fired Earth
125 TL Elizabeth Whiting & Associates/David Giles
130 L Witex/Floorbrand Ltd
  TR Elizabeth Whiting & Associates/David Giles
  BR Elizabeth Whiting & Associates/
  Mark Luscombe-Whyte
131 TR, BL, BC, BR GE Fabbri Limited
132 CL, BL GE Fabbri Limited
137 TC, TR, C, CR, BL, BC, BR GE Fabbri Limited
138 TL, TR, CL, C, BL, BC GE Fabbri Limited
139 TL, TC, TR, C, CR, BL, BR GE Fabbri Limited
150 L, TR, BR GE Fabbri Limited
151 TL, CL, BL GE Fabbri Limited
161 TR www.CotswoldCo.com
164 TR, BC, BR GE Fabbri Limited
168 BL Elizabeth Whiting & Associates/
  Dennis Stone
173 GE Fabbri Limited
176 TC, TR, C, CR, BL, BR GE Fabbri Limited
177 TC, TR, C, BL, BC, BR GE Fabbri Limited
178 TL, TC, TR, CR, BL, BC GE Fabbri Limited
198 TR, BR GE Fabbri Limited
199 TL, BL GE Fabbri Limited
216 TR, C, BR GE Fabbri Limited
226 L, TC, TR, C, BC GE Fabbri Limited
233 TR, CR, BR GE Fabbri Limited
240 TL, TC, TR, BL, BC, BR GE Fabbri Limited
251 T Elizabeth Whiting & Associates/David Giles
  B Red Cover/Jake Fitzjones
260 TC, TR, CR, BC, BR GE Fabbri Limited
271 L, TR GE Fabbri Limited
272 C, BL, BR GE Fabbri Limited
298 T, TL, TR, C, BL, BR GE Fabbri Limited
299 TL, TR, CL, C, BL, BC, BR GE Fabbri Limited
302 TL www.screwfix.com
  TR, BR www.ring.ltd.uk
  BL Electric Light Company
303 TL, TC, TR, C, CR, BL, BC, BR
  GE Fabbri Limited
304 GE Fabbri Limited
305 TL, TC, TR, C, BL, BC, BR GE Fabbri Limited
309 CR GE Fabbri Limited

314 BR www.screwfix.com
315 TL Cooper Security Ltd
  TC, TR, CR, BC, BR www.screwfix.com
  BL www.Fireangel.co.uk
348 T www.bathstore.com/'XT' wash basin mixer
  TL 'Cliveden' pillar taps by Armitage Shanks
  TR 'Tratto' by Ideal Standard
  CR 'Palladian' by Ideal Standard
  BL 'Hathaway' by Armitage Shanks
  BC 'Academy' by Ideal Standard
  BR 'Millenia QT' by Armitage Shanks
349 T 'Academy & Kyomi' by Ideal Standard
  TC 'Plaza' by Ideal Standard
  CR www.bathstore.com/'Square' designer basin
  CL 'Kyomi' by Ideal Standard
  C 'Meadow' handrinse basin by Ideal Standard
  BR 'The Space Studio Bidet' by Ideal Standard
353 BR www.bathstore.com/'Delta Corner'
354 C 'Plaza' close coupled WC by Ideal Standard
359 BL 'Calista' Trevi showeres by Ideal Standard
361 TC, C GE Fabbri Limited
376 BR GE Fabbri Limited
377 TL, BL GE Fabbri Limited
383 TL, TC, TR www.bisque.co.uk
  B Myson Radiators
418 TL Clive Nichols/Joe Swift/Thamasin Marsh
421 TC Clive Nichols/Designer:Jill Billington
  BL Clive Nichols/Designer:Olivia Clarke
  BC Clive Nichols/Wollerton Old Hall, Shropshire
446 TL, B www.magnettrade.co.uk
447 T www.magnettrade.co.uk
448 TR, BL www.marshalls.co.uk
449 T, B www.marshalls.co.uk
490 www.econoloft.co.uk
491 www.econoloft.co.uk
492 TL, BL, BC, BR Images courtesy of
  www.nuglas.co.uk
493 TR, BL, BC, BR Images
  courtesy of www.nuglas.co.uk
494 T, C, B The London Basement Company Ltd
496 www.thegardenescape.co.uk
497 T ECA(Electrical Contractors Association)
  C www.niceic.org.uk
  CR Corgi

Reader's Digest DIY Manual is published by The Reader's Digest Association Limited, London
Some material previously published in *Reader's Digest New D-I-Y Manual* (1987)
and *Reader's Digest Complete DIY Manual* (1994)
First Edition Copyright © 2004
The Reader's Digest Association Limited, 11 Westferry Circus, Canary Wharf, London E14 4HE
www.readersdigest.co.uk

Reprinted with amendments 2004

Editor Alison Candlin

Art Editor Julie Bennett

Assistant Editors Caroline Boucher, Judy Fovargue, Helen Spence, Jill Steed

Design Kate Harris, Jane McKenna

Editorial Consultant Mike Lawrence

New editorial material Mark Corke, Mike Lawrence

New photography Roddy Paine and Benno White of Roddy Paine Photographic Studios

Checkers Diane Carr, David Holloway, Barbara Legge, John McGowan

Proofreaders Ron Pankhurst, Barry Gage

Indexer Marie Lorimer

Reader's Digest General Books
Editorial Director Cortina Butler
Art Director Nick Clark
Executive Editor Julian Browne
Managing Editor Alastair Holmes
Picture Resource Manager Martin Smith
Pre-press Account Manager Penny Grose

The Reader's Digest Association Limited would like to thank the following
people for their help in producing the book:
Ian Atkinson, Martin Bennett, Tony Eastwood, John Lister, Pete Simmons,
Alan Smytherman, Jill Tucker, Kelly Woodgate

The Reader's Digest Association Limited would like to thank the following
organisations for the loan of tools, props and other materials
for photographic shoots:
Draper tools (www.drapertools.com), Rogers Ceramics

Typesetting, page layout, illustration, origination and production
Hardlines Limited, 17 Fenlock Court, Blenheim Office Park, Long Hanborough, OX29 8LN

Printing and binding Arnoldo Mondadori, Verona

We are committed to both the quality of our products and the service we provide to our customers.
We value your comments, so please feel free to contact us on **08705 113366**, or via our Web site at
www.readersdigest.co.uk
If you have any comments about the content of our books, email us at
gbeditorial@readersdigest.co.uk

ISBN 0 276 42933 8
BOOK CODE 400-212-02
ORACLE CODE 250008863H.00.24